The New
VEGETARIAN COOKING
for EVERYONE

Deborah Madison

TEN SPEED PRESS

Berkeley

This version of Vegetarian Cooking for Everyone

is dedicated to all my readers in the past who have cooked from the book,

shared it with others, and occasionally sent that note that makes the years spent

writing and cooking unquestionably worthwhile.

Contents

Acknowledgments

MY ORIGINAL ACKNOWLEDGMENTS REMAIN IN MY HEART, for it is still true that my knowledge of food has been shaped by friends, family, and farmers; teachers and students; writers and chefs; and those with whom I've shared time in the kitchen and at the table, both here and abroad. When it comes to cooking, inspiration and instruction spring from many sources, for food touches all of life. I am forever indebted to many individuals, both intimates and strangers, who have, in their own unique ways, been a part of the creation of this book. In looking back I see that many—editors, publishers, proofreaders, friends, and cooks—are working elsewhere, in other fields, or have even passed from this world. But my gratitude to them remains for their having made *Vegetarian Cooking for Everyone* a reality. I heartily thank the many readers who have sent me emails and letters over the years, who have spoken to me at events and offered their thoughts and opinions on the book or its recipes. Hearing from you has brought my office and kitchen, sometimes-lonely places, into the world where people cook and eat and share their lives, for which I am ever grateful.

My mother provided me with culinary curiosity in the kitchen, and my father gave me a sense of Midwestern American cooking and the importance of the garden. I am grateful to them both. Others I wish to thank are the farmers in farmers' markets everywhere, whose produce and products ensure my love of cooking season after season. I am also especially fortunate to know botanists and plant people who can answer my questions that arise about the plant world. I especially wish to thank all those who have invited me to teach in their schools throughout the years. After all, it was through teaching that I've been able to meet my readers, and their questions and curiosity inspired me to write this book. To those who have shared their recipes with me, my deepfelt appreciation for your work and generosity.

Ten Speed Press has been the parent to this revised and expanded edition of *Vegetarian Cooking for Everyone* and it is a lucky book for that reason. Those I've worked with have been so extraordinarily open and helpful. Thank you Aaron Wehner, Michele Crim, Hannah Rahill, Toni Tajima, Jenny Wapner, and all who have worked on this project—from the bottom of my heart. I am especially grateful to Kaitlin Ketchum, who had the most challenging task of wading through countless changes and additions in the making of this new edition, which she did with grace, smarts, and apparent ease.

Doe Coover, who has been my agent for some 20 years now, as always deserves a special hug of gratitude. And finally, it's the one who endures projects such as this day after day that deserves special thanks, and that would be my husband, Patrick McFarlin. He has been the patient one, willing to give tempeh a try when he'd much rather eat something else, then washing up afterward.

Introduction

PLANT LIFE CAN BE VERY ENTICING. It is visual, tactile, aromatic, and mysterious. Plant foods range from jewel-like beans with their stripes and patterns, to subtle grains, strangely beautiful seaweeds, the aromas of herbs and spices, and of course fruits and vegetables, with their many forms and colors. No less amazing is the ingenuity of man-made foods: coils of pasta, cheeses of all manner, the lustrous hues and fragrances of oils. It was this edible circus that started me cooking, and it's still there to suggest a recipe, a meal, a menu, or an excuse for a gathering.

But the idea for *Vegetarian Cooking for Everyone* came to me after teaching a weeklong cooking class at Esalen Institute in California many years ago. When it ended, I realized that it would be so helpful to have a big book, like the *Joy of Cooking*, that included all kinds of plant foods between its covers, a real soup-to-nuts kind of book. At that time, vegetarian cooking was something from the fringe, and some foods, like soy milk, for example, were downright obscure and could be purchased only at tiny health food stores. I wondered why some foods had to be hidden—couldn't they be brought forward and included as ingredients, along with other foods, in one place? As it turned out, they could. For some time now, once-obscure foods have filled our supermarkets' shelves—they're even found at gas stations and convenience stores. Today, in terms of food, the world looks very different than it did when I began writing *Vegetarian Cooking for Everyone*.

More than 17 years have passed since *Vegetarian Cooking for Everyone* first came out, and those foods that were once scarcely known are now everyday items, and new ones have appeared. In addition, our knowledge about what makes up the foods we eat has deepened, and some foods that were once viewed in such a positive way are now regarded more dubiously. Soy, for example, is not quite the star we once thought it was, and today the emphasis has shifted to fermented soy, not the more common forms, as important.

More people today feel that organically grown foods are better for one's health, and indeed, many foods we never thought would be grown and produced without pesticides,

like sugar, are available as organics. Butter isn't always bad. Olive oil is mostly good but still not really regulated; canola oil not so much. Genetically modified organisms (GMOs) are a bigger problem for us today, as they have proliferated and are still unlabeled. We were not eating kale salads at all during the seven years when I was writing *Vegetarian Cooking for Everyone*; now they're everywhere. Coconut oil was still considered a harmful saturated fat. Now it's considered a good fat, and a very delicious one, too. Plus we are now cooking with coconut water, curry leaves, and kefir lime leaves. Multiple types of seasoning salts were not on our radar; now they're part of our pantries. The pressure cooker was more feared then than appreciated; today pressure cookers are safe, popular, and used with ease. Changes in the culture of food have indeed taken place and many new ingredients are ours for the using. In this edition of *Vegetarian Cooking for Everyone*, you will find nearly all of the recipes you have come to love. But you will also find over 200 new ones and information on new ingredients we have come to know.

Another inspiration for writing *Vegetarian Cooking for Everyone* came from the questions my students asked, questions that revealed when they were at a loss in the kitchen. They helped me understand that acquiring food sense and knowledge of how food works is what allows a person to move about the kitchen free of anxiety and full of happy anticipation. The recipes are there to articulate that know-how, give confidence, and provide a structure for intuitive cooking. Today hundreds of emails from readers tell me that this has proven to be a friendly, useable guide for those learning to cook as well as those who already know their way around the kitchen, whether or not the user is vegetarian. (Many readers have begun letters and emails to me by saying, "I'm not vegetarian, but . . .") Copies of *Vegetarian Cooking for Everyone* have been given as wedding and graduation gifts and hauled off to foreign lands by people on extended trips. I have seen utterly destroyed copies in restaurants and monasteries, books with stained, swollen, and warped pages. Young people have learned to cook from it, and so have their parents who have found themselves at a loss as to how to cook for a child who suddenly will not eat meat. To thousands, it has introduced new flavors, techniques, and the pleasure of being able to cook one's own food with good results. I still use it myself.

As its title suggests, *Vegetarian Cooking for Everyone* was not intended only for vegetarians, although they would be happy to know that all of these recipes require no adjustments. I've always seen this as a book for anyone who wants to include more vegetables and other plant-based foods in their meals (isn't that everyone?), as a resource for those who wish to have meatless meals as a change from their usual diet—"meatless Mondays" have since become popular—and I wanted it to serve as a guide for those cooking for another who, for whatever reason, has needed to assume a more plant-based diet. In this edition of *Vegetarian Cooking for Everyone*, I have also flagged the many vegan recipes so that they would stand out clearly for vegan cooks.

Most vegetarians include eggs and dairy among the foods they eat. Vegans do not. There are Jewish vegetarians who apply Talmudic questioning to eating meat in regard to the inhumane treatment of most livestock animals, a question raised by many others as well, and more so today than ever. There are also those who call themselves vegetarians but eat fish and chicken, which is something I've never quite understood. There are full-time and part-time vegetarians, occasional vegetarians (sometimes called "flexitarians"), and lapsed vegetarians. And there are honest omnivores who happen to like a lot of vegetables and other plant foods in their lives, including plenty of vegetarian meals. And there are "locavores." I place myself in the last two groups. Most of the time, I happily make a meal from what others place on the side of their plate without even thinking of it as vegetarian. The reason I place myself among the omnivore/locavores is because my food concerns are based on such issues as the variety of the plant or animal I'm eating, how it is raised, where it comes from, if it's a GMO product, did it live in a concentrated animal feeding operation (CAFO), or was it free to range. I live in the American West. My neighbors are ranchers; I grow vegetables. We trade with one another, thereby mostly eating foods that come from within a few miles of our homes.

Local and organic-driven cooking and eating speak to a world where food and politics collide on a daily basis and where political action, such as voicing protest when the standards for organics are threatened, or fighting for the labeling of GMOs, is as necessary as breathing if we want to make sound, informed choices about the foods we eat. Regardless of what we cook, nothing is more important than starting with ingredients that are of the best quality we can manage, both for the way they nourish us and our environment, and because our results in the kitchen will never be better than the ingredients we start with. The advantage of using good ingredients is that they allow us to cook simply and eat well. And because our efforts in the kitchen today are so hard won, we want to be sure that the meals we make will add enjoyment to our lives and nourish us well.

Vegetarians have often used the phrase "I don't eat anything with a face" to describe their food choices as plant based. But there is another interpretation of that phrase "food with a face." The Japanese have a word for it, *teikkai*, which refers to the provenance of a food—where it comes from, how it was raised, who grew it. It is the opposite of "general foods," those faceless foods that come to us anonymously from a vague somewhere: foods without soul. During the past 17 years, we have continued to reconnect with our foods through shopping at farmers' markets, participating in CSAs, and cultivating our own gardens. Connecting to our foods directly enriches our lives by linking us to the place where we live and to those with whom we share a landscape, a culture, and a history, often over dinner, regardless of what's in the center of the plate. All good foodstuffs have their own stories and histories, which are the stories of our human history. They continue to grow and change as the patterns of culture shift. Even in the mere 17 years that *Vegetarian Cooking for Everyone* has been in print, big changes have occurred. Today it's not so necessary for one to defend his or her choice to be a vegetarian or a vegan; it doesn't raise eyebrows among friends if a carnivore decides to have the vegetarian dish in a restaurant—it's just another choice on the menu—nor is it strange if someone announces that their family eats vegetarian one (or more) days a week. There's much more openness and enthusiasm about plant-based foods than there was a decade ago. Originally, I thought that maybe this book should be called "Plant Foods for Everyone" since vegetables are only one of several kinds of plant foods, but it really didn't have the right ring. It still doesn't, but if the book were called that, it wouldn't seem so strange today. We know that plant foods are the ideal ones to eat.

Regardless of your own proclivities when it comes to what you eat—choices that may well change during the course of your life—it is my hope that *Vegetarian Cooking for Everyone* inspires you, nourishes you, and fills your table with pleasure.

CHAPTER 1

Becoming a Cook

Those who love to cook often wait for the weekends to indulge their passion, but putting a good meal on the table on weekday evenings is a struggle for many of us, no matter how simple the meal.

We have so many other options for sustenance that cooking and eating together, the most basic of human activities, has become an occasional or special event. For the first time in history, we can ask, "Why cook?" Well, here are a few reasons why we might cook.

1. If you're concerned about the quality of the food you eat, shopping for and cooking your own meals are the only way you can really know what you're eating, and even then it can be a challenge, for not all foods are clearly labeled with regard to their provenance or the presence of such things as GMOs.

2. Your home-cooked food will cost less than eating out or buying packaged food, and the quality will be higher.

3. There's the satisfaction that comes from taking responsibility for what we eat instead of turning it over to others.

4. Cooking a meal produces immediate results, unlike many of our jobs. After a long day of routine work, many people find the creative act of cooking a relaxing change of pace that renews their energy. It's a gift to be able to cook for others—and it's wonderful to be cooked for.

5. There is also the fundamental joy in cooking, born of the pleasure of using our senses—moving our fingers through a bunch of herbs, listening to the sizzle of onions, watching the colors brighten while vegetables cook, inhaling the fragrance of aromatic oils. This sensual involvement draws us into the process of cooking and teaches us about it. That sizzling sound tells us our heat is high enough; the scent of the herbs tells us whether we need to use a lot or a little; the fragrance of the oil assures us of its quality. Because these small but stellar moments occur even when cooking the simplest foods, they're present for the beginning cook as well as the expert.

In short, a home-cooked meal is more than just food. Placing a meal on the weekday table, no matter how simple, adds to the quality of our lives. It's natural to talk over a dinner, and that's where family members and friends are most likely to find out what's going on in each other's lives. Something always happens at the table.

To make cooking accessible and enjoyable, here are a few notes on kitchen savvy, so fundamental that even today they remain largely as they were 17 years ago.

Developing Your Kitchen Savvy

The Intuitive Process: All cooks should know from the start that cooking is an inexact business. Foods differ from one part of the country to another, from one part of the season to the next; stoves are different; pans conduct heat in different ways; your taste is different from mine. Directions like "season to taste" acknowledge that nothing is the same twice. Is your salt sea salt or mild kosher salt? Do you love salt or find you don't need much? Are your herbs fresh or dried? Old or new? You're the only one who can answer these questions, so you have to jump into cooking—smell, touch, and taste, then adjust as needed—regardless of how thoroughly a recipe tries to give the reader exact measurements and cooking times. As in learning a language, you stumble at first, but all of a sudden your ear—or tongue—opens up and you find yourself discerning sounds or tastes you hadn't noticed before.

Shopping: Choose what looks appealing and fresh rather than shopping strictly from a list, unless you're bent on making a particular dish. Pay attention when you shop. Produce is not handled well in this country and it's frustrating to find, once you're home, that your pepper has a spoiled spot. At the same time, produce doesn't have to be picture-perfect. Size, uniformity, and absence of flaws result from arbitrary standards imposed by the food industry. Beyond the uniformly perfect produce we see displayed, there's a wild and raunchy bunch of vegetables and fruits that are undersized or too big, twisted instead of straight, marred by hail or pecked by a bird—and all perfectly good to eat.

If you have a garden, you probably won't hesitate to use such produce.

Timing: Ultimately, experience will be the best teacher here, but timing the parts of your meal is an important skill, especially when you're entertaining. In lieu of experience, these tips can help you serve a meal without jumping up a hundred times from the table or ending up dismayed and discouraged.

Consider Your Menu: First sit down and review your menu to anticipate glitches. (This is probably not something you need to do for an everyday meal.) Make sure you don't have those unconscious repetitions of ingredients or styles (I'm always guilty of this), that you haven't chosen dishes that all need to be cooked in the oven at different temperatures, or serving four dishes that need essential last-minute attention.

Review each recipe and note things like these: Does the dish have a part that *has to be* or *can be* made ahead of time? How long does each dish take to cook?

Unless you're a very intuitive or experienced cook, or until you are, it helps to visualize what your cooking afternoon or hour is going to be like and make a list of what has to be done and when. This really will make everything go more smoothly.

Try not to have more than one or two things to do at the last minute, such as dress the salad or time that soufflé, so that you can enjoy the meal with everyone else. At least this is true of a dinner party. A weeknight meal may well be far simpler.

Setting the Table. Setting a table complements your efforts in the kitchen and is part of eating well. Try to have everything you need on the table when you sit down. Jumping up for salt and pepper breaks the flow of conversation. Cloth napkins feel good and don't waste paper, and having a napkin ring for each person means napkins can be used for several meals. Taking a moment to put butter in its dish and condiments in bowls provides a considerate feeling. Having heated plates, especially for pasta and soup, helps keep food warm throughout the meal. And you might consider turning off the phone and TV during dinner if you don't already.

Don't Apologize! When it comes to cooking for others, I have learned—am *still* learning, in truth—that it's best to keep your doubts and disappointments to yourself. When you cook, you're surrounding yourself with tastes and smells, so your finished dish doesn't always deliver the vivid impression to you that it does to others. Apologizing only makes others uneasy, whereas with nothing said, they might be completely content. I once had a restaurant customer raving about my "smoked" mushroom soup. Smoked mushrooms? I checked the pot and found, to my dismay, that the soup had scorched. I wanted to say, "You liked *that*?" But he and his friends were happy, so, with great difficulty, I swallowed my embarrassment, and said thank you. Then I threw the rest out.

Making It Possible

To be honest, many vegetarian dishes require more time to prepare than meat dishes. For starters, the vegetables themselves need to be washed, pared, and trimmed, but not all vegetables demand a lot of time to prepare or cook. A scrubbed sweet potato takes 20 minutes in the pressure cooker and asparagus cooks within minutes. Generally, the most time-consuming dishes are those with many parts or those that involve a lot of handwork like rolling or stuffing, or dishes that involve unfamiliar techniques. The following are ten tips for making cooking, especially vegetarian cooking, manageable, possible, and even efficient.

1. **Learn to Use a Knife.** Basic knife skills are essential to making cooking pleasant and quick. Use the right knife, keep it sharp, and give yourself plenty of room to work (see page 10).

2. **Learn to Work in a Nonlinear Fashion.** Cooking doesn't progress in a straight line but meanders from here to there. For example, you always put the pasta water on to boil first, even though cooking the pasta is the last step. If the onions for a soup are going to cook for 15 minutes, use that time to prepare the rest of the ingredients or another dish. This is one reason it's important to read your recipe through before starting. If you can see the whole picture, you have an enormous advantage because several things always are going on simultaneously when you cook. Like tying a shoe, it's one of those things that is hopelessly complicated to describe but is crucial to know and something repeated experience will teach.

3. **Learn to Make a Few Things Well.** Learning too many new dishes at once makes cooking trying. It's better to build your cooking vocabulary and skill dish by dish, since the foods that are easiest to make are invariably the ones you already know how to cook. So decide what you like to eat, then practice cooking that type of dish—stir-fries or sautés, for example—until you feel confident. Once you understand the basics, you'll be able to cook creatively and easily, for most types of dishes follow the same pattern. Then go on to something new. Or do as a friend of mine does: cook the same three meals for as long as your friends and family will let you.

4. **Simplify the Menu.** Consider making one- or two-dish meals standard. Or if you have a family, put out three or four dishes so that all eaters can find something they like. Having fewer dishes can be less taxing (and there are fewer plates to wash). The popularity of the stir-fry speaks to exactly this. Other simple meals might be a baked potato and a salad; soup and toast; an omelet, or a salad that's filled with vegetables, cheeses, nuts, and seeds. Fruit for dessert isn't just a healthful choice; it's easy. In winter, try putting out dried fruits and nuts along with a piece of chocolate.

5. **Develop a Routine.** In spite of the overwhelming choices we have in the kitchen, having something of a routine can save time spent thinking about what to make for dinner. Besides, as eaters we enjoy repetition, both in restaurants and at home. It's reassuring—"Oh, it was better last week" or "We're having my favorite dish!"

6. **Have Do-Aheads.** Working days in advance of a meal can become confusing, but doing a few easy things ahead does pay off later. For example, having prewashed salad greens often makes the difference between eating a salad and not. Or having some steamed beets, boiled potatoes, or cooked beans on hand and a few chopped onions ready to go makes getting a meal started much easier.

7. **Plan on Leftovers.** Certain foods can return to the table in another form, and often it takes little extra time to double a recipe. Leftover polenta can be fixed in all kinds of ways; beans, lentils, and chickpeas can go into salads, soups, stews, purees; whole grains can be frozen and later added to soups. Leftover rice, quinoa, and couscous can be shaped into croquettes or made into salads. Soups usually taste better on the second or third day.

8. **Use a Few Machines.** These can helpfully speed things up or usefully slow things down. A pressure cooker makes short work of long-cooking foods, cooking them in about one-third the time. Slow cookers slow everything down enough that food can cook while you're at work or asleep.

9. **Use a Few Good-Quality Convenience Foods.** Maybe your region has a specialty food, like tamales, that can be bought frozen and set aside for those nights when you just can't cook. Good organic canned tomatoes make a fast sauce, or you can improve a commercial sauce by adding such extras as fennel seed, rosemary, mushrooms, and olives. Canned chickpeas and black beans are resources, as are a few frozen vegetables, such as lima beans, black-eyed peas, okra, and peas. Condiments like capers, olives, Thai curry pastes, coconut milk, and roasted peppers can accomplish a lot in the kitchen. Tofu couldn't be easier to cook. A spoonful of your best olive oil adds a splendid finish to plain foods of good quality, such as a plate of asparagus or simmered green beans.

10. **Enlist Help.** About the time you think your children are able, get them started on some simple kitchen tasks. Eventually, a child can be put in charge of the whole dinner once a week, from planning the menu to cooking it. Having kids work in the kitchen is undoubtedly a struggle at first, but later it can be a great gift for the parent, while the child can take pride in making a meaningful contribution—and will leave home with a truly practical skill. The young adults who learned to cook as kids whom I interviewed for my book *What We Eat When We Eat Alone*, had a kind of cheerful self-reliance about cooking that was a great pleasure to see.

Composing a Vegetarian Menu

Replacing meat with something that's like it is one way of approaching vegetarian food, and long before the adventurous times of the 1960s, the Seventh-day Adventists were producing meat analogues—"nutlets" instead of cutlets. Since then, Americans have opened up to new ways of eating that have considerably relaxed the vegetarian approach to menu planning. When I first started cooking vegetarian food, there was a deep striving to find that "main dish," the center on which the diner focused. There has always been some dread of the meatless plate imagined as the blank space in the middle surrounded by vegetables, although with time this becomes less of an issue for vegetarians. Over the years, I've tried many menu approaches. Here are the ones that work for me and why they do.

Have Something Impressive in the Center of the Plate. When I was the chef at Greens in San Francisco, I felt that my job was to provide our many nonvegetarian customers with food that not only tasted especially good but that was visually striking as well. Their eyes would be drawn to these centerpieces, which other dishes would flatter and complement, just the way side dishes complement meat, and my hope was that the customer would feel relaxed about the meal because its form would at least be familiar. After all, when it comes to food, we're at least as conservative as we are adventurous, if not more so.

The kinds of foods that best fill this center role are generally layered, rolled, stuffed, stacked, or wrapped—food that has had something done to it. For example, you could have chard and you could have a spicy couscous dish, or you could roll the couscous in the chard leaves, present them with a sauce, and that would make all the difference between supper at home and dinner out. But many of the dishes that work well in this capacity are time-consuming to make. Getting the couscous inside the chard is indeed an extra step—*then* it needs a sauce. But it's precisely this effort that produces a dish that has focus, clarity, and enough interest that the diner's eye isn't restlessly seeking for something to be "it." I think this was a much more important consideration in the 1970s and '80s than it is today, but it still works.

A Simpler Approach. Today expectations about what's at the center of the plate are much less stressful than they used to be. A simple gratin can take the place of an impressive eight-layered crepe cake providing you don't just plop it on the plate but rather make a conscious presentation. My notion of what can be in the center includes gratins, vegetable ragouts, sautés, stir-fries, and even a roasted sweet potato. By nature, some of these dishes are formless—stir-fries and stews, for example. But you can give such dishes focus by setting your stir-fry on a noodle cake or serving a stew with a popover or over polenta. The simple act of nestling spaghetti in a wide-rimmed pasta plate gives it visual tidiness as well as helping to keep it warm.

Serial Eating: No Main Dish. Following the example of the *mezze* table and *dim sum*, many people like a meal that consists of many of small dishes. There is neither focus nor climax, but it manages to work. This approach is simply a structured grazing, or the tendency to order several appetizers from the restaurant menu instead of a main course, or offering enough choices for a picky family to dine together. At its most informal extreme, you just put all your interesting leftovers on the table. If I have people over for a glass of wine but don't have time to make a meal, then this is the approach I take. It gives us something to eat while we drink and often is as filling as if I had called it "dinner."

Dishes for Lighter Eating. Simply put, we've become happier with less. Soup, salad, a baked potato, a vegetable sauté, a quesadilla, an omelet—all make perfectly fine, light weekday entrées that are eminently doable. Taking care with setting the table and presenting the food can often balance its simplicity so that a simple menu is as satisfying for a company meal as something more elaborate.

The Role of Accompaniments. Accompaniments accomplish several things: they round out the main dish by complementing its taste or texture (the stir-fry *needs* noodles or rice), they extend time at the table so that you're dining instead of just fueling, and they offer a progression of textures and flavors. Often the accompaniment is obvious because it provides contrast and balance, like a starchy food with a vegetable main dish or a salad with gratin. The foods that fill this role are frequently vegetables, beans, and grains.

Avoiding Repetition. Is everything you're serving white or based on onions? Does it all involve last-minute timing? It's amazingly easy to repeat ingredients and techniques without even noticing until a meal is nearly on the table. When you're sketching out your menu, be sure to look at the entire meal before starting, especially if it's rather a big-deal dinner. Notice if you've chosen an onion salad, onion soup, onion gratin, and plan to make a few changes if you have. (If it's too late, you can always call such a meal an onion festival.)

Composition: Changing Levels of Intensity. First courses and appetizers are small but rich or intense so that a few small bites both ease our hunger and stimulate our interest. The next course needs to drop a little in intensity and be a little larger. A simple soup is often this ideal next step; it provides some spacing, like a comma or a dash. Then we need to go on to something heartier but not so rich that you can't comfortably eat a portion. A salad might follow, providing a lull before the final sweet note of dessert.

This progression is for a classic meal. If you're eating a succession of small dishes, these considerations aren't so important. Maybe everything is at the appetizer level of intensity, but the portions are small and varied. For everyday meals with children, you might keep these pointers somewhere in the back of your mind—they're undoubtedly not nearly as crucial as simply getting dinner on the table. For that, we need strategies, leftovers, some fast foods, and some things we know how to do well that everyone likes.

Menus for Holidays and Special Occasions

Regardless of your religious or cultural heritage, most holidays have traditional foods that don't involve meat, so vegetarians are not entirely excluded from what everyone else is eating. In fact, one way to approach the traditional holiday meal is just to make all those side dishes—they're usually more than ample and wonderfully varied—and ignore the traditional turkey, ham, lamb, or brisket. Generally, it's the candied yams, cranberries, and stuffing that people love best at Thanksgiving. Gone, hopefully, are the days when vegetarians attempted to make "turkey" out of tofu.

Another approach is to regard holidays and other special occasions as times of celebration and honor by making those foods that are special to you. These might include complicated dishes, such as ravioli or lasagne from scratch; foods that are richer than those we usually eat; or foods that are costly, such as truffles, or a galette made with lots of wild mushrooms.

Yet another approach, especially for Thanksgiving (which I am so often asked about) is to celebrate your garden, farmers' market, or region by challenging yourself and your friends to come up with a menu consisting of truly local foods.

Of course, the other things that make holidays special are the solemnity, sentimentality, or joy of the occasion, the people we're with, the care with which we prepare our homes and tables, and what's in our hearts. In my experience, the food ends up being important, but often not quite as important as we imagined it would be.

Wine with Vegetables

Wine has largely been consumed in meat-eating cultures, and pairing wines with foods usually links them directly to particular animal foods, their fats and flavors (and their sauces), while vegetables have listed somewhat to the side. So thinking about wine with vegetable involves making a shift to the other center of the plate. And while many think of this as limiting, plant foods offer a challenging but expansive platform from which to think about—and drink—wine. There are plenty of wines that are great to drink with vegetables, so you needn't restrict yourself to Sauvignon Blanc, the wine so often designated for vegetarian dishes. A good Burgundy, for example, can be enjoyed with a mushroom risotto or ragout where earthiness is present in both.

Not only meat's robust flavor but its fats and salts support bigger wines, which is one reason that cream, cheese butter, oils, and nuts—all fats—can align themselves so beautifully with those fuller-bodied reds or oaked whites that can be harder to place in the vegetarian menu. Even adding a shaving of aged parmesan or Gouda cheese to a vegetable dish can bring it into focus for wine. Fat in some form is what makes vegetables with wine work. Celery with a glass of white wine is not the same as celery stuffed with goat cheese laced with thyme. Then you might want to go right to the Loire valley for a Sancerre.

Many vegetables are naturally sweet, but not all are. Eggplant and mushroom, for example, are not sweet and both tend to be more easily allied with red wines than, say, winter squash. But as tempting as it is to try to match a vegetable with a wine and have that be useful information, what ultimately matters is how that vegetable is prepared and what it is partnered with and seasoned with, factors that can change the balance of sweetness and acidity in vegetables. Beets with ginger and chile are different than beets with butter; raw tomatoes are not the same as tomatoes cooked with garlic, olives, and mushrooms, or tomatoes simmered with cream. Asparagus is grassy when simmered, but grill or roast it and those grassy notes become something else. Add a sauce of cream and black pepper or with a soft cows' milk cheese and it's fine with a fruity red wine, an unoaked Chardonnay or a Chablis. Artichokes are more difficult, as they tend to make wine taste sweet, but grilling helps change that and so does searing, and mixing them with other vegetables and perhaps a goat cheese helps make them more flexible. If you're not already drinking wine and the artichoke comes along, consider an acidic white, such as an Arneis or Greek whites, or try a Verdicchio with an artichoke risotto. On the other hand, if you ask a dozen people to advise on artichokes and wine, you'll probably get as many different suggestions.

Herbs can influence a dish, too. Rosemary, thyme, bay, and sometimes sage set a flavor tone that is much more hospitable to fuller-bodied, softer red wines than, say, cilantro, chervil, parsley, and dill, which are happier with sharper whites or even sparkling wines.

When it comes to serving wine with salads, you'll want to consider making dressings with low-acid vinegars, citrus juices, or a greater proportion of oil to acid than usual so that the salad doesn't fight with the wine. A little crème fraîche or cream whisked into the dressing can replace some of the vinegar, too. Or consider making a vinaigrette with some avocado in it to lessen its acidity. A good way to make a wine choice is to consider using the salad ingredients themselves as ways to build a connection to a particular wine. Nuts (and nut oils) cheeses, olives, mushrooms (especially when seared or grilled), vegetables, either grilled or fresh, herbs, spices, and even fruits can suggest a linkage to particular wines, though in general, a white wine is what you'll want for a salad.

If you're cooking food from a particular part of the world, it makes sense to turn to the wines of that area. Tuscany's Chianti is a natural choice to serve with the foods and flavors of Tuscany. When it comes to Greek wines, look at some of the varietals we don't have here. Some wines I've had in Greece are neither familiar nor pronounceable, but they are absolutely right with the flavors of Greek vegetable-based dishes.

Harmonizing wines with food creates a union of tastes that's larger and more exciting than either single element, which is why we strive to make matches and pairings. But wine preferences, like any other, end up being a rather personal matter, for we all experience taste in our own ways. What tastes good or right to you may differ from my own inclinations and that really doesn't matter as long as we enjoy what we drink. Plus, not everyone is scurrying around to find the perfect wine for a particular dish. Many of us just drink what we're drinking and if there really is an argument with the wine and food, we back off the wine. Still, it's good to find out what we like and what works and one way to do that is to experiment.

To build a wine and food vocabulary, it helps to jot down what wine and food combinations really worked—and those that didn't, too! Or update your wine information by drinking new vintages as they come in and reading articles on current wines. If you can, talk with someone who knows about wines. There are many knowledgeable people, often those who run wine bars or good wine stores. I'm fortunate to have a wine guru in my friend and neighbor Greg O'Byrne, who has been the executive director of Santa Fe's Wine and Chile Fiesta for the past 20 years. I turn to him often for advice, and here is what he has to say about wines for the twenty-first century:

"It's no coincidence that the food movement over the last couple of decades toward eating lighter and healthier—more vegetables and less meat—has paralleled a change in America's wine-drinking habits. Where oak, tannin, power, and weight once ruled the day, the landscape has changed to include more and more wines of finesse, liveliness, and higher acids, all of which translates to more food friendliness.

"The welcome surge of wines with less oak, less alcohol, less weight is concomitant with wines of more acid, more palate-refreshing zippiness, and simple downright fun! Where once white wine with fish and red wine with meat meant big Chardonnay with a butter sauce and hefty Cabernet with a grilled steak, the variety and style of wines available (along with our food choices) has exploded. Wine choices for all types of dining have never been so varied. It's an exciting time.

"Unoaked higher-acid wines from Riesling, Gruner Veltliner, Albarino, Soave, Fiano di Avellino, and even Chardonnay, to name just a few, have taken over the white wine category. Reds with heft, tannin, and higher alcohols have been pushed aside for lighter-style and lower-alcohol reds from Pinot Noir, Beaujolais, Barbera, and Chianti, all of which are incredibly food-friendly because of their mouth-pleasing higher acids.

"Rosé as a category has moved out of the age-old misnomer of a sweet wine to the forefront of our dry wine-drinking habits. Every wine region and more and more wineries offer their version of a rosé wine and these blush wines made from any number of different red grapes in the style of a white wine have an unparalleled broad range of food-friendliness.

"And where once it was mostly consumed as a beverage for celebration or holidays, champagne and sparkling wine have become more and more a weekday beverage for wine consumers. And for good reason—the scrubbing bubbles and liveliness of sparkling wines have a lip-smacking appeal at our modern dining table.

"Today's wines of higher acid and less weight are lighter and livelier wines with an incomparable flexibility that happily parallels the change in our eating habits, changes that include more vegetables and spice and less fat and protein. Vegetarians (and meat eaters alike) have never had it so good."

All that said, don't forget to raise your glasses, no matter what's in them, in the name of friendship and pleasure.

Your Hands: Your Most Important Tool

Actually, our hands are most essential in cooking, not just for holding a knife but for feeling the amount of dressing on a salad, for ascertaining the readiness of bread dough in its rise, finding the soft spot in a winter squash, scraping out the seeds and veins of a roasted chile, and countless other small tasks we don't even think about. Your hands, unimpeded by gloves, can read situations sometimes even better than our eyes do. Don't hesitate to use them. Just wash them first, then afterward.

The Knife: Your Other Most Important Tool

The importance of knowing how to use a knife applies to anyone who cooks, but especially to those who are cooking lots of vegetables, because they require paring, trimming, chopping, slicing—all knife work.

While food processors have become as common as knives, and they're undoubtedly useful machines, they tend to mangle vegetables like parsley and onions. Often you can chop something more quickly by hand than you can in the machine (and the cleanup is easier), and you can cut more interesting shapes, such as a roll cut. Also, food processed in a machine never reveals the hand of the cook. I always find it much more interesting to see the person in the way he or she cuts vegetables; it's one of the things that makes hands-on cooking so vital.

When I watch people cook in their homes, I understand why they don't enjoy it: they're usually using a dull knife that's wrong for the job and trying to work on a tiny board that was probably intended for cheese. Their work is laborious, slow, and frustrating, but with the right sharp knife and plenty of room to work, they could be sailing through the prep work without strain.

WHAT YOU NEED: Of the vast selection of cutlery sold, you need only three or four knives: a few inexpensive paring knives for peeling, a 6-inch knife that's small enough to use for paring jobs but large enough for limited slicing, and a 10-inch chef's knife for chopping and slicing. A heavy cleaver is helpful for cutting into dense winter vegetables; an inexpensive small serrated knife is useful for slicing tomatoes; a larger serrated one is used for bread.

CHOOSING THE RIGHT KNIFE: Most people like stainless steel knives because they don't react chemically with foods and the blades don't rust. Carbon-steel knives slice beautifully and sharpen easily, but they stain many foods. They also need to be washed and wiped dry immediately after each use. Ceramic knives are very thin and ever sharp, ideal for fine work but expensive and brittle.

When it comes to shape, chef's knives have a triangular blade that's pointed at the tip and wide at the base so that your knuckles don't scrape the counter. This shape ensures contact with a large surface area, so they're very efficient for chopping. The Japanese vegetable knife, which is squared off rather than pointed, is similarly well designed for slicing, cutting, and chopping. Curved blades are terribly inefficient

since only a fraction of the curve comes into contact with the board at any one time. Paring knives, however, can have straight or curved blades. The curved blades are good for going around surfaces such as on potatoes or pears. I don't like to pay a lot for a paring knife—they're too easy to lose, and the cheap ones work fine.

KEEPING KNIVES SHARP: A dull knife makes work difficult and can be dangerous since you need to use a lot of pressure. A sharp knife slices through foods as if they're warm butter. Many home cooks have a hard time keeping their knives sharp, but with the electric and manual knife sharpeners now available, it isn't hard to keep a good edge on a blade. Magnets hold the blade at the correct angle for sharpening so that you don't end up with a knife that's crooked or out of whack. Don't wait until your knives are impossibly dull before sharpening them. Frequent fine tunings, as often as each time you use your main knife or once a week with a steel or magnetic knife sharpener, help keep those blades honed.

More traditionally, you can use a whetstone to sharpen a knife. Whetstones are used with running water or oil. A diamond steel is used to hone the sharpened edge of a knife and keep it sharp through hours of prep.

An alternative to sharpening your own knives is to find someone who sharpens them professionally. Often a cutlery shop does this, or there may be a knife-sharpener at your farmers' market. It will wear them down a little faster over time, but you will have well-honed blades that are sharpened evenly. If you've let your knives get seriously dull, go to the professionals. Regardless of how you sharpen your knives, store them carefully in a slotted container or knife rack so that they aren't all jumbled together, a damaging arrangement.

HOW TO HOLD A KNIFE: Grasp the handle of the knife in whatever hand you're most comfortable with. Hold it firmly enough that you have some control, but not so that your hand feels tight or tense. With your other hand, hold whatever is to be sliced, curving your fingers under your knuckles. This way you actually use your fingers as a guide for the blade rather than relying entirely on sight. Don't worry about cutting yourself; you'd have to tilt the knife at an extremely unlikely angle. Try it—you'll see! Once you get the hang of letting your curved fingers guide your cutting hand, you can hold your head upright, giving an occasional glance at your hands, instead of bending your head forward. This prevents strain from building in the shoulders and neck.

PRACTICE: Beginners often feel timid and work very slowly. One of the things you'll gain from becoming proficient is speed, and to help build proficiency you need to loosen up your arm and wrist. So take something of little consequence —the outer leaves of a lettuce or something that will be pureed—give yourself plenty of room, and just cut like crazy. Don't worry about how it comes out; just get your arm in motion. As you practice, you'll soon begin to gain control over what you're doing. Remember to keep your fingers tucked under your knuckles.

CUTTING BOARDS: Giving yourself plenty of room to work is absolutely essential. A small cutting board hampers your action, constantly confining you to an area that won't hold what you're doing. Wood is much kinder to your knife, but plastic is lighter. (Secure a lightweight board by placing it on top of a damp dish towel.) Plan to have at least two roomy boards. Use one board for garlic, onions, and vegetables and the other for fruits. The smell of garlic really does linger on a board if it's not washed well between uses. There's nothing more disappointing than eating a fruit salad that tastes like garlic.

The Rest of Your Kitchen Equipment

Once you have your knives and something to chop on, you need bowls to put things in (especially plenty of small ones), a strainer, a variety of spoons, a few pots and pans, and a vegetable peeler to make a very bare-bones working kitchen. Sometimes such kitchens are the most fun to work in, but as you discover your own cooking inclinations, you will begin to outfit your kitchen to suit your cooking style and your budget. Both undoubtedly will change many times during your life.

In general, choose the best-quality pots and pans you can afford; they last a long time if treated well, and good tools are a pleasure to use. As a rule, heavier pots and pans cook food most evenly since they're less likely to have hot spots. Still, some of my favorite pans have been cheap, lightweight skillets from the supermarket, which are good for many foods and inexpensive to replace. Always read the instructions when you buy a pan so you'll know how to season, use, and maintain its surface. Discard nonstick pans as they become scratched.

As for the materials your equipment is made from, plain aluminum discolors foods and imparts an off taste. Cast-iron pans can also discolor foods like eggs and artichokes,

but they're heavy and sturdy, and many today are lined with a nonreactive surface. Stainless steel is always a good choice, as is anodized aluminum, neither of which reacts with food. Tin-lined copper, especially if it's heavy, is the Cadillac of pots and pans, but it's expensive and requires special care to avoid scratching the surface, not to mention retinning. Some high-quality cookware sandwich layers of copper, stainless steel, and aluminum, taking advantage of the best each metal has to offer.

WHERE TO FIND IT: If you don't have much money to spend, see what you can find at garage sales and flea markets. You'll be amazed at what people discard. I keep my eyes open for well-seasoned cast-iron pans. Restaurant supply stores often have a selection of tools many stores don't have and at a lower prices. Supermarkets also carry a decent selection of basic equipment, some of which is inexpensive and works perfectly fine. Thrift stores and antiques stores are good sources for equipment that's made in the good old-fashioned way— heavy-gauge bread pans, good cast iron, crockery bowls, and Dutch ovens are some of my favorite finds.

The Equipment I Use Most in My Kitchen

Infinite pieces of equipment can find their way into a kitchen, depending on your culinary needs or fondness for acquiring things. Some especially functional pieces are described in chapters of the book where they are most likely to be used, but here are some pieces, both large and small, that I feel are essential for making your efforts productive and worthwhile.

BLENDER: Still good after all these years, my inexpensive blender gets plenty of use pureeing soups, making crepe batters and smoothies, pulverizing bread into crumbs, and many other things. An immersion blender—a handheld blender on a stick—is wonderfully efficient since you use it directly in the pot.

CITRUS ZESTER: Makes fine shreds of citrus zest in a moment and can be used to score a cucumber. Microplanes are even more efficient and make a finer zest.

DOUBLE BOILER: Once a standard item in every kitchen, a double boiler is still enormously practical since it allows you to cook foods such as polenta and flour-based sauces without constant stirring. You also can improvise by setting a bowl over a pot of boiling water. The boiling water should never touch the bottom of the bowl or pot.

FOOD MILL: This inexpensive, old-fashioned device is ideal for pureeing soups, sauces, and vegetables. Using a food mill means you don't have to seed and peel apples and tomatoes before making a sauce since it separates them out for you.

HEAVY-DUTY ELECTRIC MIXER: A heavy-duty mixer that comes with a dough hook, paddle, and wire whip is an investment but well worth it. It's terrific for making batters, pasta, and bread, for beating and whipping foods, and has attachments available for other kitchen functions.

MEASURING CUPS AND SPOONS: Especially for beginners, measuring is important. After a while, you'll find that you can eyeball amounts quite accurately. Get sturdy spoons and cups. Measuring spoons come in sets, from 1/4 teaspoon to 1 tablespoon. When measuring dry ingredients like baking soda, level off the spoon with a knife.

There are two kinds of measuring cups, one for dry ingredients and one for wet. Dry measuring cups are calibrated to the rim so that when measuring flour, for example, you can dip it into the flour sack and sweep the excess off the top. Measuring cups for liquids have a pouring lip and extra uncalibrated space at the top so that you can carry wet ingredients without spilling them. For accuracy, they should be read at eye level. You'll want at least one set of dry measuring cups and one wet measuring cup of 2- to 4-cup capacity.

MORTAR AND PESTLE: Crushing and hand-grinding foods in a mortar opens up their flavors impressively. Pestles are very efficient in spite of being hand tools. Choose a small one if you think you'll use it just for garlic or pounding spices; you can always get a larger one. Wooden mortars and pestles retain the odors of whatever you grind in them, whereas metal, ceramic, and marble ones don't. If you choose wood, dedicate it to either garlic and savory herbs and spices or to sweet spices alone.

If you don't have a mortar and pestle, you can, to some degree, approximate its effect by chopping garlic mixed with salt, then turning the knife over and using the dull side to break down the fibers.

NUT AND CHEESE GRATERS: A small handheld cheese grater is good for passing at the table along with a hunk of cheese so that everyone can grate his or her own. A handheld rotary grater makes feather-light shreds of cheese and nuts—essential for fine baking. An upright box grater is a standard piece of equipment for every kitchen. It can be used for coarse or fine grating, whether cheese or vegetables.

PEPPER AND SPICE MILLS: Essential for freshly milled pepper, which is how pepper should be. If possible, have one each for white and black pepper and also one for coarse sea salt. An electric spice mill (or coffee grinder) is great for powdering toasted whole spices, which really brings out their flavors. Use it just for spice only, though; coffee easily picks up the lingering aromas of cumin or coriander.

PRESSURE COOKER: This underutilized timesaver makes short work of beans, soups, and hefty vegetables. The new pressure cookers are fail-safe and easy to use. They don't have jigglers, and they won't blow up. They make it possible to have real food in minutes and are especially useful at high altitudes, where everything takes longer to cook. Be sure to read the instructions that come with the model you buy. Choose one that's stainless steel rather than aluminum. You needn't spend a fortune, although there are some very pricey ones available.

Becoming a Cook

SLOW COOKER: The ultimate in unattended cooking, beans and soups cook while you work or sleep. You can make a surprisingly fine soup without sautéing onions first or adding extra steps, and I believe that's how slow cookers should work: helping you out when you need help. I haven't included recipes for slow cooker dishes that involve more than one step and a long, unattended time. (You can make polenta in the slow cooker, but it's more complicated than just doing it on the stove where the results tend to be better.) Be sure you get to know the limits and possibilities of your own slow cooker. Every one is different and yours will have its own quirks. I've used a small Crock-pot, for example, and have found that it works faster than Crock-pots that belong to friends.

SALAD SPINNER: If you want dry salad greens, parsley, or shredded potatoes, you need a salad spinner, although you can get by without one if you have a mesh bag and can go outdoors to swing it or are patient with towels. There are different kinds of spinners, and some drain right into the sink—be sure that's what you want when you choose one.

SCALE: Americans are not as geared to weight as they are to volume, but a scale tells you in an instant how much you have of a vegetable, a chunk of chocolate, an odd piece of butter, a piece of cheese (important for dieters), or the weight of a piece of dough that's to be divided into rolls. It's especially helpful in making No-Knead Bread (page 595). Although most ingredients are given in volume with occasional equivalent weight measurements, weight is really more accurate. Scales also can convert to and from metric weights. I use a scale almost every day. If you decide to buy one, make sure it's easy for you to read.

SHEET PANS AND COOKIE SHEETS: Those with $1/2$-inch sides (called sheet or jelly roll pans) are essential in the kitchen for baking croutons, roulades, biscuits, breads, and so forth. Have at least two. You can also use them for cookies, even though proper cookie sheets don't have sides. Restaurant supply stores sell good, sturdy pans called half-sheets that fit into home ovens.

SPATULAS AND SPOONS: You'll want at least one big wide flat metal spatula for turning pancakes and lifting cookies off a pan and an offset spatula—one with a crook in it—for smoothing icings and batters without dragging your knuckles through them. Be sure to have a nylon spatula that won't scratch the surface of your nonstick pans. Wooden spoons stay cool in your hand and don't clang when they come into contact with metal pots, bowls, and pans. They're inexpensive, so you can have a lot of them in different sizes. Be sure to have one with a flat bottom for stirring sauces. Large metal spoons, especially one that's slotted, are also useful.

STEAMING BASKET: This inexpensive gadget fits into virtually any size pot and is essential if you like to steam vegetables and other foods. There are fancier steaming units and Chinese bamboo steamers, but the basket is efficient and basic.

SPRING-LOADED TONGS: Tongs are a must. They work as an extension of your hand and are used for grilling, turning things in a pan, picking up items that won't balance on a spatula, and reaching over hot surfaces. They're also a handy household tool—great for reaching into hard-to-get-to corners. You can find tongs at restaurant supply stores; they range in size from 8 to 18 inches. A shorter pair is most useful in the kitchen; longer ones allow you to stand back from the smoke and heat of a grill.

SAUTÉ PANS AND FRYING PANS: You can cook virtually everything in these, and many meals for four to six can be cooked in a single 12-inch pan. American sauté pans have sloping sides and are popular with restaurant cooks. Frying pans and French sauté pans have straight sides and are heavier, not meant to be picked up. Having a skillet with a cover is helpful for slow cooking, where it's important to retain moisture. A 6- or 7-inch skillet is useful for tasks like toasting pine nuts, melting butter, or frying an egg.

TIMER: Even though you'll end up judging doneness by eye and touch, a timer helps free your mind so that you can turn to other tasks until its ring summons you back.

Basic Cooking Methods

Following are descriptions for the basic cooking methods you'll be using in all recipes throughout the book.

BLANCHING OR PARBOILING: To soften a vegetable before going on to another step, to leach out bitterness, or to make skins easy to remove, vegetables are plunged into a pot of boiling water for a brief time. This is referred to as blanching or parboiling. Once they're blanched, the vegetables may be transferred to a towel, rinsed under cold running water, or plunged into a bowl of ice water, a technique called shocking, to stop the cooking.

BOILING: Boiling is a fast, efficient way to cook many things. You need a lot of water so that foods cook quickly without great loss of nutrients. A good boil means that large bubbles burble and break on the surface. Add salt just before you add your food, about 1 teaspoon to 4 cups, then add vegetables gradually enough to maintain the boil but not too slowly, or the first to enter will be overcooked. Keep the pot uncovered so that sulfurous odors of the cabbage family can escape and the colors of green vegetables can stay bright. Taste the vegetables as they cook and drain them before they're fully done since they'll continue cooking in their own heat. Remember that at higher altitudes foods take longer to cook because water boils at a lower temperature.

BRAISING: Braising is the slow cooking of vegetables in a small amount of water or vegetable stock. Aromatics may be added, and wine, vinegar, or lemon is sometimes included for the edge they provide and for their ability to keep tender vegetables firm. Often a vegetable base, such as diced carrots, onions, and celery, is cooked alongside the larger vegetables. Traditionally, it's discarded at the end, but I always find it a nice addition to a dish, either as a garnish or pureed and used to thicken a sauce.

Braises can be made on top of the stove or in the oven. If a lot of juice remains, remove the lid and simmer until it's reduced to a thick sauce or a glaze. Toward the end you can add flavor by stirring in butter and fresh herbs.

BROILING: Cooking food under direct heat browns it. Quickly cooked foods, like sliced eggplant, tofu, or croutons, can be cooked through under the broiler, while longer-cooking foods are only finished there. Keep food between 4 and 6 inches from the heat source.

COOKING WITH ACIDULATED WATER: Water made acidic with lemon juice or vinegar prevents artichokes, celery root, Jerusalem artichokes, and salsify from discoloring. For acidulated water, add 1/4 cup lemon juice or vinegar to 8 cups water. To make a blanc, which mellows the taste of the lemon, add 1 tablespoon each flour and olive oil to the mixture.

GRILLING: Grilling seems to make all foods—especially vegetables—taste particularly good.

PUREEING: Whether making a soup, a puree of vegetables or cooked beans, or baby food, there are various tools for the job.

Immersion Blender: This blender on a stick is easy to use: simply immerse it in a pot of soup or vegetables and puree. A regular blender is also good for soups.

Food Mill: This handy tool breaks up soft vegetables and forces them through the holes in the disk set in the bottom of the mill while strings, peels, seeds, and other hard-textured bits are left behind. It keeps purees light and doesn't overwork them.

Potato Masher: Another old-fashioned tool—essentially a perforated disk or wire coil on a handle—that breaks down potatoes into a smooth puree without turning them gluey.

Food Processor: Its fierce action turns potatoes to glue, but it works fine with other vegetables, such as carrots and broccoli, quickly producing silken purees. You'll need to stop and scrape down the sides.

ROASTING AND BAKING: Roasting vegetables at high heat in an open pan glazes the surfaces, sears the bottoms, and gives them a rich, concentrated flavor. Baking is gentler than roasting, frequently using lower temperatures and a covered or uncovered dish. Always preheat the oven for at least 10 minutes, or until it comes to temperature.

SAUTÉING: Sauté refers to a method (cooking vegetables in small amounts of hot oil over high heat), a pan, and a kind of dish.

To sauté, use a large skillet with sloping sides that's light enough to pick up in one hand. Vegetables need plenty of room to move around so that they can brown and sear. Piled on top of each other, they'll merely steam. If using garlic, add it toward the end of the process so it doesn't burn.

First heat the pan, then add the oil. When it's hot, add the vegetables. Grasp the handle of the pan with one or both hands, then slide it back and forth, adding a jerk as you draw it toward you. This motion makes the vegetables jump in the pan so that they turn and new surfaces are exposed to the heat. When people watch line cooks working in a restaurant, they see a lot of this sliding/jerking action. It's not that hard to learn—though you'll undoubtedly lose a few onions in the process. If you can't master the pan action, use a wooden spoon or tongs to move the vegetables around in the pan. The motion needn't be continuous; there has to be some sustained contact with the pan for vegetables to brown.

Many low-fat cookbooks suggest sautéing in water instead of in oil, but water doesn't heat to the temperature fat does and it can't sear and add flavor. If any browning does occur, it's because the natural sugars have been drawn out and caramelized.

SIMMERING: When foods are simmered, it means that they're cooked at a very gentle boil, one that barely disturbs the surface.

STEAMING: Vegetables cooked over a small amount of water retain more nutrients, and the small amount of vitamin-rich water isn't difficult to incorporate into soups and sauces. Unlike boiling, steaming is always done with a lid. It is not the best method for green beans and peas, which lose their sparkle when steam condenses and drips back over them, but most other vegetables are good candidates for steaming, whether small and tender or large and dense.

Use a collapsible stainless steel steaming basket that sits over boiling water. Sprigs of herbs, crushed seeds, and spices added to the water bathe the vegetables in a subtly perfumed steam—especially good with vegetables that absorb flavors well, like potatoes.

STIR-FRYING: Another type of sautéing that takes place at high temperature in a wok.

Cutting and Chopping Techniques

Slicing, *dicing*, *chopping*, and *mincing* are words that describe how we transform raw materials with a knife. Even though the shapes are very basic, how you cut them affects the whole feeling of a dish. Some people, including me, tend to cut things into small, precise pieces, while others use big, bold strokes. One way isn't better than the other. I'm always delighted when people make my recipes according to their own cutting inclinations. I often don't recognize the dish by its look, although I do recognize its taste, and sometimes I think it looks much better. You, too, will have your own approach, but in the meantime, here are explanations of cutting terms:

SLICED ONIONS, HALF-MOONS: Cut an onion in half through the root end, remove the skin, then lay it flat side down. With your knife aligned from the root end to the stem end, slice the onion into half-moons, following its curve. Thin slices are $1/8$ to $1/4$ inch thick, thick ones about $1/2$ inch thick.

DICED ONIONS: Lay the halved, peeled onion on a cutting board and slice into it horizontally, making parallel cuts. For a fine dice, make your cuts about $1/4$ inch apart; for a large dice, about $1/2$ inch apart. Make similar cuts going from the top down, then slice the onion crosswise. The squares of onion will fall away, completely diced.

COINS, MEDALLIONS, OR ROUNDS: For carrots, zucchini, and other long vegetables, slice them straight across in even parallel slices to produce coin-shaped pieces.

DIAGONAL SLICES: Slice long vegetables at an angle so that you'll end up with oblong pieces. The steeper the angle, the longer the slice. This technique is often used with Asian eggplants, carrots, asparagus, and zucchini.

ROLL CUT: This cutting technique, which yields substantial and interesting shapes, is used with long, thin vegetables: carrots, asparagus, skinny zucchini, and so on. First make a diagonal cut, then roll your vegetable between one-quarter and one-third around and make another cut. Repeat this rolling and cutting motion for the length of the vegetable.

JULIENNE STRIPS: These are long skinny shapes, like old-fashioned wooden matchsticks. Slice your vegetable, if it's a long one like a carrot, into long diagonals, then stack them up and slice them lengthwise into strips. Or cut your vegetable into lengths as long as you want your final piece to be, then cut the lengths into slabs as thick as you want them, then cut the slabs into strips. Batons are cut the same way, but into larger pieces that can be picked up and used for dipping or in stir-fries.

DICE: Cut vegetables into cubes between $1/3$ and $1/2$ inch across. You can do this as described for onions or make julienne strips or batons, then slice crosswise.

LARGE DICE: Squares $1/2$ to 1 inch across.

FINE DICE: Squares about $1/4$ inch across.

MINCE: Usually used for garlic and ginger. Cut into very small, indistinct pieces by quickly moving your knife back and forth over the food.

CHOP: Basically the same as dice but without the implied precision of squares. A certain irregularity of shape and size is okay.

COARSE CHOP: Larger, more imprecise pieces usually applies to vegetables that are going to be pureed.

SHREDDED: Usually applied to cabbage to be used in coleslaw or salad. Cut a cored wedge crosswise into thin slices with a knife to resemble shredded paper.

CHIFFONADE: Another term for fine strips, usually referring to leafy greens. Roll a number of leaves up together to make a "cigar," then slice them thinly crosswise. Make sure you cut all the way through so that the final strips aren't joined to each other.

High-Altitude Cooking

Having lived at an elevation of 7,000 feet for over twenty years, I am familiar with the special set of conditions that the many people who live above 3,000 feet have to cook in. The higher the elevation, the lower the atmospheric pressure, which affects temperature, leavening, and the way foods behave.

TEMPERATURE: Each 500-foot increase in elevation means a drop of 1°F in the temperature at which water boils. If you vacation in the mountains, you may notice that your coffee never seems really hot or that foods takes longer to cook than you're used to. Hungry campers have all noticed this while watching a pot of spaghetti that boils energetically but doesn't seem to cook.

Food takes longer to cook at high altitude than it does at sea level. How long, exactly, is a matter of trial and error. You may have to boil a few eggs before you find out exactly how long it takes to cook them perfectly. In many instances, it helps to use a pressure cooker, which raises the temperature of the boiling water and steam so that the timing is almost the same as pressure cooking at sea level.

BAKING TIPS: Angel food, sponge cakes, soufflés, and other air-leavened dishes soar in their pans, while butter cakes are a little more difficult to manage at high altitudes. Local extension services can provide you with tips that apply to your area, but it's helpful to keep a record of what changes you make in your normal routines so that you can, over time, understand what works best. In the meantime, here are some practical tips:

Oven Temperature: If you live higher than 3,000 feet, raise the oven temperature 25°F. The higher oven temperature helps to set the structure of fast-rising baked goods so that they won't fall.

Moisture: At high altitudes, the air is very dry, so the flour is also dry and more absorbent. If you're baking bread, you may find that you can't incorporate all the flour called for. Adding oil or an extra egg to breads not only provides more liquid so that it can absorb more flour but also helps prevent dryness in a finished product. In cakes, increase liquid as follows:

3,000 to 5,000 feet, add 2 tablespoons liquid per cup called for.

6,000 to 7,000 feet, add 3 tablespoons liquid per cup called for.

Over 7,000 feet, add 3 to 4 tablespoons liquid per cup called for.

Leavenings and Sugar: While I adjust most ingredients more or less by feel, when it comes to leavenings, I keep the baking soda the same and reduce the baking powder and sugar as follows:

3,000 to 5,000 feet, reduce baking powder by $1/8$ teaspoon; reduce sugar by 1 tablespoon per cup called for.

5,000 feet and above, reduce baking powder by $1/4$ teaspoon; reduce sugar by 2 tablespoons per cup called for. To ensure stability in cakes, add 1 to 2 tablespoons additional flour.

When making cakes that are risen with beaten egg whites, beat the eggs a little less than you would at sea level so that the whites form only soft peaks.

Reducing yeast is optional unless you are baking large batches; then it's essential. Reducing the yeast by one-quarter to one-half the total amount results in a bread with a firmer, stronger texture. The full amount can give you a fluffy, airy bread, which may be disappointing. Yeast doughs tend to rise more quickly at higher altitudes.

OVEN TEMPERATURES

Very low	250°F or below
Low	300°F
Moderately low	325°F
Moderate	350°F
Moderately hot	375°F
Hot	400 F
Very hot	425°F or higher

Always preheat your oven for 10 to 20 minutes to allow it to come to the required temperature, unless otherwise indicated. The higher the temperature, the longer it takes to preheat the oven. If you're using a baking stone for pizza, bread, or other dishes, put it in a cold oven, and allow 25 to 30 minutes for it to heat through.

VEGAN RECIPES

(V) Throughout the book, recipes and variations that are vegan—or can easily be made so by using oil instead of butter, plant instead of dairy milk, omitting cheese, and so on—are marked with this symbol.

FOUNDATIONS OF FLAVOR

CHAPTER 2

Foundations of Flavor
Ingredients and Seasonings in the Kitchen

When we take a closer look, many of the basic ingredients we use every day in the kitchen are more complicated than they appear.

Virtually all recipes call for salt to develop flavor, while just about as many ask for a bit of pepper to warm them up, yet there's far more to salt and pepper than just white and black powders. Oils and vinegars are both essential players in anyone's kitchen, while other ingredients, such as herbs, spices, and seasonings, provide the essential underpinnings of flavor that give a dish its unique personality. Even more than vegetables themselves, it's these small, intensely flavored ingredients and how they're combined that give a culture's food its unique stamp. This is so true that certain combinations immediately signal to us the national origin of a dish—the cumin and cilantro of Mexico, for example. For the vegetarian cook especially, the importance of herbs, spices, and seasonings can't be overstated. Being familiar with our basic ingredients and foundations of flavor is a tremendous advantage for any cook. Discerning their personalities is what often makes the difference between a so-so dish and one that's really good.

Since *Vegetarian Cooking for Everyone* first came out, a host of new ingredients has become available. Almond, rice, and hemp milks are now easily found. Less so nonhomogenized milk pasteurized at low heat, but it too is becoming increasingly available. We have salts from the sea and the highest of mountains in all flavors, shapes, and hues. Smoked paprika, sprouted flours, coconut butter and oil, different kinds of sweeteners, and "new" ancient grains such as farro are among other new foods in our pantries.

Basic Ingredients

BUTTER: I generally use unsalted butter, but if you prefer salted, just be sure to taste your dishes as you cook to make sure they're not too salty, a good idea in any case. Organic butters are important since pesticides are concentrated in animal fats. My two favorites are SuperNatural by Kalona Dairy, and that made by Strauss Family Creamery. (See pages 26 through 28 for more information.)

CREAM: Descriptors of cream vary across the country. When cream is called for, I mean heavy cream that can be whipped and is preferably not ultra-pasteurized. But if it's not to be whipped, and you live where "light" cream is sold, that would work as well.

EGGS: Eggs have improved vastly since *Vegetarian Cooking for Everyone* was first published. Many more people are selling eggs from their grazing flocks at farmers' markets or they are raising them at home. A real farm (or backyard) egg is nothing like any egg from the market. The yolks are bright yellow to orange, the whites clear, and the flavor fresh and delicious. In the past, eggs were large, but with farm eggs, sizing can vary from peewee-size pullet eggs to extra large. You can judge size by eye, or by volume (see page 498). In any case, egg measurements are seldom crucial in this book.

EGG SUBSTITUTES: Eggs act as binders in foods and contribute moisture and tenderness to baked goods. A few foods mimic these qualities and can be used in their place, mainly in baking. (See page 498 for more information.)

FLOUR: Flour can be white whole wheat, spelt, quinoa, sprouted flour, all-purpose unbleached white, or a mixtures of flours. But unless otherwise specified, all-purpose unbleached white flour is what is meant by "flour." (See page 31.)

MILK: Milk can be from a cow, a goat, or made from rice, almond, soy, or hemp. Please use what you like best. I use mostly nonhomogenized cow's milk and organic, unsweetened almond milk in my kitchen. (See page 26.)

NUT OILS: These oils include those pressed from walnuts, almonds, hazelnuts, pistachios, and pine nuts. Toasted nuts produce oils with the darkest color and richest aroma. Almond oil tends to be light in both color and flavor, but walnut and hazelnut oils can be fairly robust.

OLIVE OIL: Olive oil is referred to as simply olive oil or "your best oil" to indicate extra-virgin or special high quality. (See page 29.)

PEPPER: Pepper is freshly milled, always. (See page 36.)

SALT: Salt is always fine sea salt unless it's Himalayan salt or a particular size or flavor of salt is called for. (See page 36.)

SUGAR: Sugar is described as sugar, unless some variety is specifically called for or suggested. There are many new sweeteners today, such as organic coconut sugar, stevia, agave nectar, and so forth. (See page 39.)

VEGETABLES: These are assumed to be trimmed, washed, weighed if need be, and dried if called for.

1 carrot means a medium or average one, about 4 ounces in weight and 7 inches along. I scrub, rather than peel carrots, to make best use of their nutritional offerings.

1 onion means a medium yellow or white onion, weighing 4 to 6 ounces and yielding a cup or more chopped.

1 clove garlic: unless otherwise stated, is of medium size and plump in nature. The inner cloves of softneck garlic can be extremely small and at the other extreme, the clove of hardneck garlic, now far more available, can be very large and also spicy. There are times when I find myself using only half a clove, wrapping the remainder to use the next day.

VEGETABLE OIL: Safflower, sunflower, avocado, peanut, sesame, and coconut oils are referred to simply as "oil," knowing that you may have your favorite. I do not include canola oil. It is too often a GMO product and even when organic frequently rancid or off tasting. Oil made from soybeans is also quick to turn rancid. I like to match oils with foods, using, for example, sunflower oil with vegetables from the same family. But the real reason for using these oils is that they tend to be neutral in flavor, which is sometimes preferred. (See pages 28 through 30).

Aromatics:
Herb-, Spice-, and Vegetable-Based

HERB-BASED AROMATICS: Herbs are all about aromas. They can be bright, intense, or subtle, depending on the herb. When added at the start of a dish, their flavors soften and merge with the rest of the ingredients. But they are often added again just before serving, the aromas of the herbs blossoming as they meet the heat of the dish.

Bouquet Garni: This bundle of herbs consists most commonly of parsley sprigs, a bay leaf, and a few sprigs thyme tied with string or gathered in a cheesecloth bag. (I just put them into the dish loose most of the time.) Bouquet garni is used to flavor soups, braises, stews, and many other dishes. I usually make mine rather generous—8 long, full sprigs of parsley, 4 to 6 brushy sprigs of thyme, and 2 small bay leaves—and add any other herb that's appropriate to the dish, such as a sprig of tarragon if tarragon is called for, a branch of marjoram, and so forth.

Fines Herbes: Fines herbes is a classic mixture of chopped fresh herbs, usually parsley, chervil, tarragon, and chives. Use it to season vegetable sautés and braises, beans, butter, and egg dishes of all kinds. It consists of the following herbs in more or less this proportion:

1/4 cup parsley leaves
1 tablespoon chervil leaves
2 teaspoons tarragon leaves
2 teaspoons finely sliced chives

Chop the parsley, chervil, and tarragon leaves together, then add the chives.

Chopped watercress, grated lemon zest, and minced garlic expand this herbal collection very nicely. Since chervil is seldom available, increase the tarragon to 1 tablespoon.

Gremolata: Add the grated or chopped zest of 1/2 lemon to the persillade (see below).

Persillade: Use 1 plump clove garlic to about 1/4 cup parsley leaves—or more as suits the dish or your taste for garlic. Chop them together, preferably at the last minute, then scatter over hot foods for the full effect of both ingredients. Try it with sautéed mushrooms and artichokes, fried eggplant, grilled vegetables, and warm beans. Persillade is often just described in a recipe as 1 clove garlic chopped with 3 to 4 tablespoons parsley.

SPICE-BASED AROMATICS: Spices are essentially dried herbs. Coriander is the dried spice form of cilantro, for example. Often spices boast warm flavors and they are gathered together as rubs for meats. That doesn't mean they can't work with vegetables, however. A spice rub can be excellent with tofu and tempeh, winter squash, grilled eggplant, sweet potatoes, and other plant foods. Here is one that I keep in my cupboard, ready to use when I want it, based on a rub that author Peggy Knickerbocker used in her book *Simple Soirées*. One secret to the goodness of this rub is to start with whole spices when possible and grind them in a small spice grinder.

Peggy's Spice Rub: Peggy Knickerbocker uses this spice rub for her pork ribs in *Simple Soirées*. I use my version of it on roasted squash, tofu, eggplant, sweet potato fries, and even avocados. I like having it around to add a mysterious finish to a soup that wants a little something. This makes about 1/2 cup.

3 tablespoons coriander seeds
5 whole star anise
1 tablespoon fennel seed
1 tablespoon ground ginger
1/2 teaspoon cayenne
1 teaspoon red pepper flakes
1 teaspoon ground cinnamon
1 tablespoon five-spice powder
1 teaspoon freshly milled pepper, or peppers smashed in a mortar and pestle
2 teaspoons sea salt
3 tablespoons organic brown sugar or coconut sugar

Grind the whole spices using short pulses in a spice mill (small coffee grinder). Don't let them get completely powdery—a little texture is good—then mix with the remaining ingredients.

VEGETABLE-BASED AROMATICS: In many food cultures, vegetable mixtures are used as a flavor foundation. Many stir-fries begin with a trio of aromatics—ginger, garlic, and green onions—while French, Spanish, and Italian dishes often begin with standard mixtures of aromatic vegetables that provide a flavor base for the dish that follows. Where the strong flavors of meat are absent, it's especially important to pay attention, for when care is taken at the beginning to build a good foundation, it sustains the whole dish. These foundations are used throughout this book, though not necessarily by name.

Mirepoix: The French *mirepoix* is a mixture of equal amounts of finely diced carrots, onions, and celery seasoned with bay leaf, chopped parsley, and a sprig or pinch of thyme. Cooked in oil or butter until softened, it becomes the base on which to braise other vegetables or on which to build a soup or a stew.

Sofregit: The Catalan foundation *sofregit* begins with onions or onions and leeks cooked unhurriedly until dark, glossy, and jamlike in plenty of olive oil. Peeled, chopped tomatoes, about 2 per onion, are added once the onions are a caramel brown, and then cooked until the juices evaporate. Herbs,

garlic, and peppers, if called for, are added once the onions are well softened. A rich and concentrated foundation, *sofregit* will keep, refrigerated, for 2 or more weeks. It can do service as a true convenience food, providing the first vital step at a moment's notice for all kinds of soups and vegetable stews.

Soffritto: Rosanna, my neighbor in Rome, always pointed out the three steps of the *soffritto* when she cooked. First, diced onion and parsley with—depending on the dish—carrots, celery, and garlic are cooked in olive oil until the onion is translucent and pale gold. Then the garlic is added and cooked until it too is golden. (If you add the garlic with the onion, it will be too dark by the time the onions are cooked.) Finally, the other principle vegetables are added, the heat is raised, and they're sautéed briskly for a few minutes to seal in their flavor.

Cheese

Cheese, more than many other foods, relates to place and tradition. As with wine, the characteristics of different cheeses are determined by source of milk, climate and geography, season, aging, tradition, and the cheese maker's personal style of crafting this unique food. The endlessly varied and fascinating world of cheese offers many pleasures for the palate. If you are loath to give up such an interesting and satisfying food, here are some ways to fit cheese into today's general guidelines for healthier eating.

- Don't serve rich cheeses for appetizers when people are hungry and ready to dive into food. They're too filling and they can't be savored as well then as they can later in the meal.

- Enjoy cheese as a course in itself for dessert, with fruit, or with a salad. Or use cheese as an element that enriches the flavor of a dish—the classic veiling of good parmesan on a pasta, for example.

- Always serve cheese at room temperature when its flavor is fullest. Cold cheese is missing most of its essence. Neutral-tasting breads and crackers allow the nuances of the cheese to be enjoyed rather than covered, but some specialty breads, such as walnut bread, beautifully complement particular cheeses, such as aged cheddar, mature goat cheese, or luscious triple cream.

- True gustatory pleasure is satisfying in itself, and low-fat remakes of classic dishes lack the soul of the original. When

cheese is a featured ingredient, as in pasta with Gorgonzola, use the real thing and the full amount, but place the dish more judiciously as a first course, say, rather than the main event. A fine cheese can make a dish memorable.

CHEESE ALTERNATIVES: There are now quite a few nondairy cheese substitutes on the market. They're made mainly from soy milk, along with Irish moss (seaweed), tapioca, rice, oats, oil, spices, seasonings, and other ingredients. Some use calcium caseinate, a protein derived from cow's milk, to make them stretchy and elastic, but that keeps them from being acceptable to vegans. As for taste and texture, they don't taste like cheese, and they don't melt well. However, vegans may want to use them in place of the animal milk cheeses called for.

RICOTTA: True ricotta is made from the whey remaining from other cheese-making adventures. But what we find in our stores comes to us full fat, low fat, part-skim, and nonfat. It's nothing like the ricotta you find in Italy, which is moist and as delicate as flowers. I find most of our ricotta grainy and generally slightly unpleasant, unless it's full fat or an artisanal ricotta. The latter is so special you just want to enjoy it as simply as possible. It makes a wonderful dessert or a topping for a crostini, and in lasagnes and fillings its texture isn't so problematic. You do want to make sure it's as dry as possible so it doesn't dampen the dough. Put it in a sieve lined with cheesecloth; press down on it to get rid of excess moisture.

Chiles

Many people crave the rush that comes from eating hot foods, but you don't have to be a chile head to enjoy chile. Even small amounts give an exciting warmth and tingle to the tongue. Today we have a vast vocabulary of chiles to cook with, from chipotles to cayenne to tiny but ferociously hot Thai bird peppers. Chiles have been written about extensively in the last few years, and would-be aficionados should refer to more extensive sources to learn more about chiles. Meanwhile, here are some tips on working with chiles.

The veins and seeds, which contact each other in the pod, are the hottest parts of the chile. If you don't want the optimum amount of heat, shake out the seeds and slice off the veins. If you plan to be handling a lot of chiles and you're not accustomed to it, put on a pair of rubber gloves. I never do, and I've never had a problem—or one that didn't go away quickly—but people vary in sensitivity to the volatile chile oils, so caution is always wise. At the very least, avoid touching your eyes, nose, and mouth when your fingers are covered with chile oils—whether they're gloved or not.

Before using, toast dried chiles in a pan over low heat, roast in a slow oven, or cover with boiling water to soften and then puree in a blender, depending on their intended use. Whether you use chile ground or whole, take care not to burn it by adding it to too hot a pan, for once burned it turns bitter. And stand back when you add chile to the pot or grind it, for the rising mist of volatile oils can make you cough a lot.

Ground or whole, chile eventually loses its potency, so don't buy so much that you'll have it around for years. A year is its optimum shelf life. New Mexican chile farmers tell me that they store their ground chile in the refrigerator, not the freezer, to preserve its life.

CAYENNE: Cayenne is the name of the small hot red chile ground for cayenne powder. As with all hot chiles, add it in small increments until you find the right amount.

CHIPOTLE CHILES: This smoked jalapeño chile comes packed in adobo sauce, dried, or ground. Chipotle chile combines the hot, smoky, and sweet chile essence in one ingredient and makes an excellent seasoning for soups, sauces, and salsas, but it is hot. You can temper its heat by mixing it with pureed or ground guajillo chiles. Whether in sauce or dried, if you grind it into a puree or powder first, it's easier to use in small quantities. The powder is great on fried eggs if you like your eggs "from hell." Chipotles can be found at Mexican groceries, supermarkets, and fancy food shops.

GROUND RED CHILE, NEW MEXICAN CHILE: This is simply dried finely ground New Mexican chile pods without any additions. (Chili powder is a blend of chile, spices, and powdered garlic.) Paprika and cayenne, also ground red chiles, may be used when ground red chile is called for in small amounts, but their flavors will differ from that of New Mexican red chile.

PAPRIKA: We forget that paprika is, in fact, chile. Readily available, the best is from Hungary, where it's the national seasoning. Paprika is labeled "hot" or "sweet," reflecting the basic flavor components of the pepper used. Not just something to sprinkle on deviled eggs for color, paprika is a warm and delicious seasoning to use in more generous amounts. Smoked paprika, whether sweet or hot, introduces a delicious smokiness to foods without the heat of chipotle chiles.

RED PEPPER FLAKES: These crushed dried red chiles with seeds add that edge of heat and spice to many dishes without turning them into hot food. Add a few pinches to warming oil to release their flavor. Pepper flakes should be red. If they're brownish, they're old and should be thrown out.

SMALL DRIED RED PEPPERS: There are many kinds—chile pequín, bird peppers, árbol, and so on. The general rule is, the smaller the chile, the hotter its bite. Add them whole to a dish or, for more heat, break them in two first. Remember, the seeds and veins are the hottest parts of the chile. Take them out or not, as you dare.

Citrus Fruits

Zest and Juice

The outer skin of citrus fruit is called the zest. The perfumed, volatile oils of the fruit reside in the zest rather than the juice. An inexpensive tool called a zester removes thin shreds of zest in moments. You can also remove it in strips with a vegetable peeler, then mince it with a knife, or grate the fruit on the fine holes of a Microplane. I usually pull the zest off with a zester, then chop it. I enjoy biting into a bit of orange or lemon zest, but you may prefer to use the Microplane. Just avoid taking up the white pith beneath the zest since it tends to be bitter, and be sure to use clean fruit.

The acid nip of lemon and lime juice often brings everything into balance. Bottled lemon and lime juices simply don't taste good; the added chemicals come through. Use freshly squeezed juice instead. To get the most juice out of a lemon or lime, press down on it while rolling it back and forth on the counter, then juice it. A good juicy lemon contains $1/4$ cup juice; a lime, 1 to 2 tablespoons.

Peeling and Sectioning Citrus Fruit

To neatly peel an orange or a grapefruit for salads, compotes, and desserts, first take two slices off the polar ends so that the fruit will stand. Then, using a very sharp, small knife, begin cutting in a zigzag motion down the side, from top to bottom, removing a strip of skin and the white pith that lies beneath it. You'll have to really angle your knife at the top and bottom. Continue this motion around the entire fruit until it's peeled, then pick it up in your hand and cut away any pith you missed. At this point, you can slice the fruit into rounds or sections.

To section an orange or a grapefruit, hold the peeled fruit firmly in your hand over a bowl. You'll see the edges of the membranes that separate the sections facing you; they look like white lines. Slide your knife downward, as close to the membrane as you can get, then do the same on the opposite side of the same section of fruit. When the cuts meet at the bottom, the fruit section will slide away into the bowl. Repeat this with the remaining sections. When done, squeeze the juice from what's left into the bowl.

Crostini, Croutons, and Bread Crumbs

Homemade crostini, croutons, and bread crumbs make good use of bread that might otherwise be discarded. Small croutons, either thin slices or cubes, can be floated on soups or tossed in salads. Larger ones can serve as a base for savory toppings, as in crostini and bruschetta. Fresh bread crumbs coat foods that are to be fried or add a crunchy cover to gratins. Dried bread crumbs add body and substance to a filling or a timbale. Crisped bread crumbs add textural interest to pasta, polenta, and vegetable sautés.

CROSTINI AND CROUTONS: Slice baguettes, sourdough, or country-style bread about $1/4$ inch thick. Place on a sheet pan and bake at 375°F until crisp and golden. Small croutons can be floated in a soup, larger ones broken in half, set in the bottom of a soup plate, and covered with soup. Either can be tucked into the leaves of a salad.

Garlic-Rubbed Crostini: You can, if you wish, brush the crostini with olive oil and rub them with a halved clove of garlic when they emerge from the oven.

Crisped Croutons: Remove the crust and cut the bread into small cubes. Toss with melted butter or olive oil to coat lightly, then spread on a sheet pan and toast in a moderate oven until crisp and lightly colored, 10 to 15 minutes. Or crisp them in a skillet over medium heat, stirring often so that they cook evenly. You can also toast them without the fat, if preferred.

Seasoned Croutons: While still warm, toss crisped croutons with sea salt and pepper, a little lemon juice, chopped thyme, savory, or marjoram, or spices, such as ground red chile, paprika, curry powder, or toasted cumin or fennel seeds.

BREAD CRUMBS: Japanese bread crumbs, sold at Asian markets or even your own supermarket, are crisp and white. They make a visually exciting, crunchy coating for fried foods, such as croquettes of risotto or vegetables. Other than these, I generally make my own as follows:

Fresh Bread Crumbs: Remove the crusts, tear bread into large pieces, and pulse in a food processor or blender until the crumbs are as fine as you want. One slice sandwich bread yields 1/2 cup loosely packed crumbs.

Dried Bread Crumbs: Lay bread slices on a sheet pan and set in the oven at 200°F until they're dry, crisp, and golden, 30 to 45 minutes. Let cool, then grind in a food processor until fine. They will keep for weeks in an airtight container. Two slices bread yield a scant 1/2 cup bread crumbs.

Crisped Bread Crumbs: Toss fresh bread crumbs in enough melted butter or olive oil to coat lightly, about 2 tablespoons for 1 cup crumbs. Fry in a skillet over medium heat, stirring frequently, until golden and crisp, 5 to 7 minutes, or toast in a 350°F oven until golden, about 8 to 10 minutes. Stir every few minutes so that they brown evenly.

Herb-Scented Bread Crumbs: These simple bread crumbs can add so much to pasta or vegetables. Try them tossed with spaghetti or with simply prepared asparagus, steamed potatoes, sautéed corn, and roasted squash.

To make approximately 1 3/4 cups, toss 1 1/2 cups fresh bread crumbs with enough olive oil to moisten, about 2 tablespoons, then toast in a skillet over medium-high heat until crisp and golden. Remove the crumbs to a plate. Add another tablespoon olive oil to the pan along with 1 tablespoon chopped garlic, 3 tablespoons chopped sage, rosemary, thyme, or marjoram. Sauté just until the garlic begins to color, and stir in the bread crumbs. Season to taste with salt and pepper and moisten with sherry vinegar.

PICADA: A lively seasoning of fried bread, almonds, and garlic, picada is used in Spanish dishes as a thickener and flavoring. Picada is also a good addition to pasta and plain vegetables.

To make 1/2 cup picada, toast 1/4 cup peeled almonds in a 350°F oven until they're pale gold, 8 to 10 minutes. Remove and set aside. Meanwhile, slowly fry one slice of white country-style bread in 2 tablespoons olive oil until golden on both sides. Grind the bread, almonds, and 2 large cloves garlic and pinch of salt in a food processor to make a crumbly paste.

Curry Seasonings

CURRY POWDER: Authentic Indian recipes call for combinations of spices that best complement a given dish, making each one unique rather than tasting of the same seasoning. If you're into Indian cooking, you'll undoubtedly be using Indian cookbooks and composing your spice mixtures as you go. If you're just using a curry powder to season a sauce, however, prepared curry powders are fine. Look for them at Indian markets and buy small amounts so that they don't turn stale. Penzeys Spices also has a good selection of curry blends.

CURRY PASTES: Prepared red, green, and yellow Thai and Indian curry pastes of good quality can be purchased at Asian markets and natural foods and specialty stores. A spoonful mixed into unsweetened coconut milk makes an instant sauce for tofu, noodles, rice, or a stir-fry.

GARAM MASALA: This mixture of warm spices is usually added as a seasoning at the end of an Indian dish rather than at the start. Since garam masala can be a little more difficult to find than good prepared curry powder, here is a general recipe. (For the most fragrant powder, start with whole spices and toast them.)

Put 1 tablespoon cardamom seeds, 1 tablespoon coriander seeds, 2 1/2 teaspoons cumin seeds, 1 1/4 teaspoons black peppercorns, and 1/2 teaspoon whole cloves in a small dry skillet over low heat. Sliding the pan back and forth so that they don't burn, toast them until they smell fragrant, after a few minutes. Let cool, then grind in a spice grinder until powdered. Transfer to a bowl. Grind one 3-inch cinnamon stick as fine as you can, then sift it, through a fine strainer, into the bowl. Grate in 1/2 whole nutmeg or add 3/4 teaspoon ground to the bowl.

Dairy (and Dairy Substitutes)

With regard to any form of animal dairy, I always choose organic, grass fed, and preferably nonhomogenized forms. Such dairy products are more costly, far better tasting, and I believe, better for us. But there are also milks and other forms of dairy derived from plants, which are perfect for vegans and anyone avoiding dairy.

BUTTER: Because pesticides lodge in animal fats, it's very important to use organic butter. It's expensive, it's good to eat, but it's also good not to eat it in huge amounts. As for salted or not, I generally buy unsalted. If you prefer salted, get to know its taste and adjust the amount of salt you use in the rest of a recipe. (See page 27 for more information.)

BUTTERMILK: This is a cultured product. Like kefir, it is thick and tangy and makes a refreshing drink. I nearly always use it in baking (or substitute yogurt and even kefir) because of the tenderness it imparts to a dish, and also keep it on hand for drinking, using in smoothies, or pouring over cereal. Kalona Dairy makes a buttermilk that is especially creamy and tart, giving plenty of character to cornbreads and other baked goods. Buttermilk always requires the use of baking soda along with baking powder as a leavener.

COCONUT MILK: Fragrant, naturally sweet coconut milk gives body to the sauces of Thai and Indian dishes. Most supermarkets now carry at least one brand, but Asian markets usually have many brands from all over East Asia. Avoid coconut milk that's labeled "sweetened." This is used for making mixed drinks. Like cow's milk, coconut milk separates, with the thick "cream" floating to the top. You can lift the cream off and use it to garnish a dish or shake the can so that milk and cream are blended. Light coconut milk is lacking the cream.

CRÈME FRAÎCHE: Although it doesn't perfectly duplicate the true flavor of the French version, this crème fraîche doesn't curdle when added to soups and sauces, and it's more delicately flavored than many commercial sour creams. It's a real treat when made with fresh cream that hasn't been ultra-pasteurized.

To make 1 cup crème fraîche, stir together 1 cup cream and 1 teaspoon buttermilk. Cover and set in a draft-free place for 24 hours. By then, it should be set and ready to use, but even if it's a little wobbly, it will continue to thicken in the refrigerator, where it should be stored. Crème fraîche keeps for about 2 weeks.

PLANT MILK: It's an odd way to say it, perhaps, but this refers to "milks" made from plants of all kinds—rice, almond, hemp, oat, coconut, soy. I nearly always use almond milk and coconut beverage to cook with and to add to cereal and smoothies, and enjoy them a lot. Coconut beverage milk is not as thick as the canned version and is specifically called for in some recipes. I no longer use soy, but if you do, please feel free to enjoy it in place of other dairy suggested. When these milks are transformed into yogurt, ice cream, and other foods, vegans have even more possibilities for converting recipes to be suitable.

YOGURT: When I wrote *Vegetarian Cooking for Everyone,* there was no Greek yogurt, unless you went to Greece. If you wanted a thick yogurt, or yogurt cheese, it was necessary to drain yogurt overnight in cheesecloth to get rid of the extra whey. Today that is no longer the case, given all the thick (referred to as "Greek") yogurts now available, including *labne,* often described as kefir cheese. As for other yogurts, there is an enormous choice available, from yogurt with cream floating on top, to yogurt made from nonhomogenized milk (Kalona Dairy again), to a number of organic yogurts made with different cultures.

Fats

In spite of our struggles with it, fat is one of the most important ingredients we use when it comes to making food taste good—and right. (If you're used to cooking eggs in butter, they won't taste *right* when cooked in olive oil, as any homesick traveler knows.) Fat both contributes and carries flavor. It also provides a certain voluptuous sensation in the mouth that makes us feel satisfied when we encounter it. Most of the metaphorical language associated with fat throughout history is positive; fat has been both good and, until recently, comparatively rare. Today perhaps it is far too plentiful, but we need enough fat in our diet to use fat-soluble vitamins, to make hormones, and to keep our immune systems in good order. Since no one needs an overabundance of fat, it's worth considering what kinds of fat to choose.

Because fat is simultaneously important and troublesome, it's essential that we use those fats that give us the greatest measure of satisfaction. A highly refined, tasteless oil has the same number of calories and fat grams as a rich-tasting roasted peanut oil, a fruity olive oil, or the sweetest butter. The true flavor of good oil or butter satisfies in a way that tasteless foods don't, and in smaller amounts. In every respect, good-quality fats are worth their higher cost. (For specific types of butter and oil, see Butter, opposite, and Oils, page 28.)

WHY FAT IS IMPORTANT: Fat is important in cooking for several reasons. One is it gives flavor to food. Different fats have such distinctly different characteristics that are a vital part of the character of a cuisine—the olive oil of the Mediterranean, the butter of Scandinavia, the sesame and peanut oils of Asia, the mustard oil and ghee of India. Fat is not just a lubricant; it imparts its own characteristic flavor. The step that begins so many dishes, sautéing onions and herbs in oil or butter, creates a vehicle for the disbursement of flavor throughout the dish. It doesn't take much to do this, but it does take some, more than a mere teaspoon. If you're worried about how much fat you eat, I urge you to consider what you eat over the span of a week rather than recipe by recipe. There's no reason that all the foods we eat have to be of the same composition. There are dishes that are for feasting and dishes that are lean. The secret is to find a happy balance over time and to enjoy each dish as it comes. If we can manage to listen to ourselves, we'll probably find that this is a balancing act that comes rather naturally and needn't be forced.

Butter

Butter is a big part of our culinary tradition, a taste we are used to, recognize, and like. Being an animal product and a fat has made it something of a pariah, but there are ways to use butter intelligently. You can cook with a mixture of butter and oil or simply use it where it counts most. For example, make your muffins with oil, then eat them with butter on top, where the flavor is clearly discerned and appreciated.

American butter used to be salted to preserve it, but today salt is added to give it flavor. However, many people prefer the delicacy of lightly salted or unsalted (or sweet) butter. I prefer to use unsalted or lightly salted butter and add salt to food separately, but if you haven't any on hand, you can certainly make do with salted, as I often do.

Butter contains some water, fat, and milk solids. Most butter is 80 percent butterfat, but European-style premium butters are slightly higher—82 percent. Some small or organic dairies are producing American-made premium butters. Plugrá, a brand whose name means "more fat" in relation to water, is available to the restaurant industry and can be found in better groceries around the country. These butters are so sweet and delicious that, if you're a moderate person, a little is truly satisfying. But if your love of butter is immoderate, watch out! When you melt higher-fat butter, you will see it's very clear and pure, with little separation of water and milk solids. Reduced-fat or so-called light butter is extra-watery—you can see that when you melt it. Because its fat content is so low, it should never be used in baking.

Keep the larger part of an unused pound of butter in the freezer, particularly if it's unsalted. Always wrap butter well. Like all fats, it picks up odors from other foods like a sponge. Good butter should smell sweet and pure. Organic butter is preferred, as pesticides linger in animal fats.

CLARIFIED BUTTER: Clarifying is the simple process of melting butter so that you can separate the fat from the milk solids. It's the solids that burn, so if you want to fry in butter, clarifying is necessary.

Cut the butter into chunks, put it in a small, heavy pan, and melt it over low heat. When the foam has risen to the top and the milk solids have fallen to the bottom, turn off the heat. Skim off the foam, then pour the butter carefully through a strainer lined with cheesecloth. Or decant it by eye, leaving the solids behind in the pan. One stick or 8 tablespoons butter will yield 5 to 6 tablespoons clarified. It keeps, refrigerated, almost indefinitely.

FLAVORED CLARIFIED BUTTER: Taking advantage of fat's ability to absorb flavors, add a bay leaf, thyme sprigs, crushed peppercorns or cumin seeds, red pepper flakes, or other herbs and spices to the melting butter. Strain them out before storing.

GHEE: Follow the instructions for clarified butter; once the butter has melted, lower the heat even more. Continue cooking until there's a crusty covering on top, the butter beneath is perfectly clear and deep gold, and the milk solids are light brown, 40 minutes to 1 hour. Ghee provides Indian cooking with one of its distinctive flavors. Ancient Organics makes the best (organic) ghee I know.

BROWN BUTTER: Follow instructions for ghee. Cook the butter longer still, until the milk solids are browned and the butter is brown rather than gold. The aroma should be toasty and nutty. Brown butter is delicious on many vegetables and can be used in baking.

GOAT MILK BUTTER: Not all butter is made from cow's cream. Pale but tangy-tasting goat's milk butter is preferred by those who don't digest cow dairy well, as goat butter contains no casein, the ingredient that can trigger allergies in those who are lactose-intolerant. But if you enjoy goat cheese, chances are you will appreciate the flavor of goat butter. Unfortunately, goat milk has little butterfat, which makes the butter very costly.

FLAVORED BUTTERS: See the Sauces and Condiments chapter for recipes for flavored butters and butter sauces.

COCONUT BUTTER: Coconut butter includes the solids of coconut flesh and does not become a clear oil, but a spoonful stirred in or over a dish of red lentils or rice is deliciously crumbly and sweet. I love this as a final seasoning to dishes where the tropical flavor of coconut is wanted.

Oils

Oils are described by what they're made from and how they're made. When it comes to the process, there are two main approaches, resulting in what are known as unrefined and refined oils.

UNREFINED, PARTIALLY REFINED, OR PURE OILS: These are the oils I use and recommend because of their character, intensity, and superior nutritional value. Partially refined or pure oils are made by cooking cleaned seeds or nuts at low temperatures to make the oil accessible, then pressing it out by using a screw press, or expeller. The resulting oil is rich with aroma and nutrients. Cold-pressed oil is traditionally pressed between slowly turned stones. Today even cold-pressed oils are heated, but not to the excessive temperatures refined oils are. Pure or partially refined oils may show cloudiness or deposits of natural waxes, especially when they've been refrigerated. These harmless substances are reintegrated into the oil when it's heated; they don't indicate any kind of spoilage. Your nose will tell you when oil is bad. These oils are more expensive than refined oils, but they are a far better product in every way and worth the extra cost.

REFINED OILS: This is the method used for extracting most oils today. A mash made of the seeds is treated with hexane, a solvent, to pull out the oil. To make the oil into a tasteless, odorless product, lecithin, vitamin E, minerals, and other important nutrients are removed. The oil is then bleached (which removes its carotenes), steamed to remove odors, then further clarified. In the end, refined oil is essentially just a lubricant, contributing fatty acids with no flavor, aroma, or food value. This is the bulk of the oil that's found in our supermarkets and in processed foods. In spite of its chemical treatment, it can still have unpleasant off odors.

RANCIDITY IN OIL: All fats eventually become rancid with exposure to air, and unrefined oils turn rancid more quickly than refined ones. Nut oils are the most unstable of all. When oil is off, you can tell because its odor is stale, fishy, or soapy—especially when heated. Rancid oil is unhealthy to eat and should be thrown out. When oil is good, it will smell sweet and reflect its source—olives, peanuts, walnuts, sesame seeds, and so on. Unfortunately, so many of the oil-bearing foods we eat are slightly rancid that rancidity is a taste many people have unknowingly grown accustomed to. Once you can identify it, you may be surprised at how often you encounter it.

STORAGE: The three enemies of oil are oxygen, heat, and light. To keep oils fresh, they should be kept capped, cool, and away from light. It's also a good idea to buy oils in small quantities and store them, once opened, in the refrigerator. (Olive and sesame oils, which are fairly stable, can be kept in a dark, cool cupboard.) For convenience, you might keep a small amount of the oils you use daily on the counter in a sealed jar, and refill it as needed.

Types of Oils

AVOCADO: Rich, thick with a buttery feel but not much flavor. Use it in baking, some sautéing, or with citrus and avocado salads.

CANOLA: Canola is heavy and viscous and some use it in combination with butter or olive oil, or to replace butter in baked goods, like quick breads and pancakes. I am personally not a fan, but if you are, please use it. Choose organic if you don't want to ingest GMOs. In my experience, it is often rancid, displaying off odors when heated. I have not included it in this version of *Vegetarian Cooking for Everyone*.

CITRUS OILS: Almost more like perfume than oil, use these by the droplets to add the essence of orange, lemon, and lime to flavor pastries, smoothies, and vinaigrettes. They were popular when I was first writing *Vegetarian Cooking for Everyone*, but I haven't seen—or used them—in some time.

COCONUT OIL: Unlike coconut butter, which includes the meat of the coconut, coconut oil is extracted from the kernel of mature coconuts. It is a stable oil, meaning that it's slow to turn rancid. It is deliciously redolent of coconut and can be used for sautéing (try it with sweet potatoes, onions, and greens), frying, and baking, since it behaves like butter, making it ideal for vegan pastries. Its high amount of saturated fat has, in the past, vilified coconut oil, but it's also high in the highly beneficial lauric acid, and some doctors feel it's an extremely beneficial food. Though solid and dense at room temperature, it melts to a clear oil and has the aroma of coconuts.

CORN OIL: You can occasionally find a golden unrefined corn oil that has a hint of corn in its aroma. I used to use it far more than I do today. As most corn is GMO, be sure you choose organic.

GRAPESEED OIL: This is another neutral oil to use when you don't want any pronounced flavors. It also has a moderately high smoke point, which makes it good for sautéing over high heat.

OLIVE OIL: The oil of the Mediterranean (and countries with Mediterranean climates, such as Chile), olive oil has gained much media attention for its beneficial qualities, but it's delicious oil as well. In countries where it is the principal fat, it is used in desserts as well as savory dishes.

California's olive oil industry was nascent 20 years ago and now it's quite lively, due both to large-scale industrial plantings and smaller more artisanal producers, which means it is becoming increasingly more available and affordable.

Fine estate-bottled extra-virgin olive oil, which often doesn't leave its country of origin, is referred to now as "your best oil" and is used to flavor foods just before serving. Drizzling a fine olive oil over warm asparagus, green beans, or garden tomatoes makes something simple exquisite. For sautéing, use your less expensive olive oils. By all means, avoid light, pure, and pomace oils, which are the lowest grades, made from previously crushed olives that have been treated with hexane, bleached, deodorized, then mixed with other oils to provide color and flavor. These are not true olive oil nor probably a good food to eat.

My brother, who grows olives and makes a small amount of prize-winning oil, suggests that a shopper look for these qualities when selecting olive oil:

1. It should come in a dark bottle, as light is one of the enemies of oil.

2. When poured, the oil should have color, either green (early on) or golden (later).

3. Is should have a smell and taste that is vegetable.

Extra-virgin oil should display no defects, have less than 0.8 to 0.2 acidity, depending on which organization is determining this, and should have at least one positive trait, such as fruitiness (detected in the front of the mouth), bitterness (detected in the back of the mouth), or pungency, (experienced in the throat).

Another approach with olive oil is to become familiar with the qualities of the olives and the oil they produce, whether you like a pungent Tuscan oil that makes you cough or a mild Ligurian type, or a lively Arbequina. The best way to learn is by tasting.

PEANUT OIL: The common, refined version is perfect for frying. It hasn't much character, which in this case, is what you want. Roasted peanut oil, which is saturated with the perfume of roasted peanuts, is excellent for introducing powerful flavor to stir-fries as well as in certain dressings. (Loriva, available in supermarkets and specialty stores, is the best American brand I know.)

SAFFLOWER OIL: One of the more neutral cooking oils, safflower oil is often rather plain, although a good-quality brand, like Loriva or Omega Nutrition, has a floral, nutty flavor that's very agreeable.

"SALAD" OILS: The main virtue of these mass-produced supermarket oils is that they're utterly tasteless, which is sometimes desirable for frying or to oil a pan. But I find they often have an off taste and a greasy feel. Salads are the last things they should be used for. There are other, neutral oils in this list that are far better than these dubious concoctions.

SESAME OIL: Like peanut, there is a refined, light version that is suitable for cooking; its flavor is subtle with a trace of nuttiness. A toasted sesame oil is dark and has a pronounced perfume. It's used sparingly as a seasoning, can be spooned over a stir-fry, added by the drop to miso soup, and used in certain salad dressings. Chili oil is sesame oil that has been steeped with chile to make it hot; use it in small amounts as a seasoning.

SOY OIL: I have always found soy oil it to be particularly unstable and often rancid. Personally, I never use it.

SUNFLOWER SEED OIL: I'm very fond of this oil. It has more character than other neutral oils, yet isn't overwhelming. Use it for cooking when you don't want the flavor of olive oil.

WALNUT, HAZELNUT, AND OTHER NUT OILS: Although principally for salads, you can drizzle these over hot foods that are flavor compatible, such as hazelnut oil over artichokes, toasted macadamia oil over basmati rice, and so on. You can also use them in baked goods where oil is called for. Always keep these oils refrigerated.

MISCELLANEOUS OILS: Oils can be pressed from all nuts and seeds, and some of the more unusual oils available are pumpkin seed (a delicious dark green oil), pistachio, flax oil, pine nut, and almond. I have recently read about oils pressed from different varieties of winter squash seeds, which are dark and aromatic. If you're curious, try these oils; they may have a place in your cooking vocabulary, at least as a flavoring to add to warm vegetables and grains or to use in vinaigrettes.

Edible Flowers

SOME FLAVORFUL EDIBLE FLOWERS

• Arugula	• Mint
• Borage	• Nasturtium
• Calendula	• Rose
• Chive	• Rosemary
• Daylily	• Sage
• Hyssop	• Squash and zucchini
• Lavender	• Thyme
• Marigold	• Violet

A salad with a confetti of flowers is undeniably charming, as is an herb butter laced with spicy nasturtiums or candied rose petals and violets on a cake. More than mere decoration, some flowers convey the flavor of the host plant, especially herbs. They're also serviceable; certainly many people have eaten stuffed squash blossoms, scarcely thinking of them as flowers. Though decorative, many edible flowers don't contribute much taste. My own preference is for those blossoms that contribute flavor or are an obvious part of the plant to use, such as arugula or sage that's in bloom.

Choose unsprayed garden blossoms and shake them gently to knock out any small insects. Float or swish them back and forth in a bowl of water, then shake dry. Separate those that grow in a cluster at the base, like chive blossoms. Pluck off petals of flowers like calendulas and marigolds. Unless they're small to begin with, finely slice, chop, or tear the blossoms. While pretty, a large flower or petal really isn't all that pleasant to eat.

Flour

Another ingredient that has changed in the past 17 years is flour. No longer just all-purpose unbleached white flour or whole wheat, there is now a plethora of flours to choose from. I seldom use all-purpose flour anymore, except in some desserts, and even there, I often use white whole wheat flour or spelt. I also mix flours—maybe white and spelt with a bit of sprouted flour. For brevity, baking recipes just call for flour, or all-purpose flour. But know that you can make your own mixes or choose another flour altogether.

WHITE WHOLE WHEAT FLOUR: This is a pale whole wheat flour because it's milled from white rather than red wheat. While it doesn't have the brown look of whole wheat flours we're accustomed to, it does darken when moistened and cooked. Its flavor is more delicate and its texture is lighter than regular whole wheat or whole wheat pastry flour, and more pronounced than regular all-purpose white flour.

You might want to start replacing one-third of all-purpose flour with white whole wheat and see how you like it. You can work up to adding more. I often use it as my only flour and it works fine in cookies, dense cakes, pancakes, biscuits, scones, and bars. With piecrusts, I use half white whole wheat.

WHOLE WHEAT PASTRY FLOUR: Ground from soft rather than hard wheat, whole wheat pastry flour has less protein and gluten, making it suitable for pastries. It is generally darker than the white whole wheat and has a more pronounced flavor, which might seem overwhelming if you're not accustomed to flavor in flour. You may also grow to love it. You can use it in place of white whole wheat. King Arthur's whole wheat pastry flour has many fans who use it in all their baking, and who don't mix it with white flour.

SPELT FLOUR: Milled from whole grains, spelt is a primitive form of wheat. In flour form, it can be used in all kinds of baked goods. It is more nutritious than modern wheat flour and possibly more suitable for those with sensitivities to wheat (but not those who are seriously gluten-intolerant), although it can be a little heavier than regular wheat flours. I often use spelt flour in combination with wheat flours or by itself when used in quick breads, like muffins, pancakes, and so on. Its flavor is nuttier than white flour, more like whole wheat. Because of the structure of its gluten, take care not to overmix dishes made with spelt flour, or the texture will be more crumbly than coherent.

SPROUTED WHEAT AND SPELT FLOURS (AMONG OTHERS): These have just started to appear in markets, although sprouted flours have long been used in making breads. Sprouting grains before drying and milling does several things, which make sprouted grains beneficial. Sprouting breaks down the starches so that they're easier to digest, produces vitamin C, increases the content of the B vitamins and carotene, and neutralizes enzyme inhibitors and phytic acid, which inhibits the absorption of minerals, such as calcium, magnesium, iron, copper, and zinc. Sprouted flours can be heavy and dense, so use them with that in mind, perhaps starting by mixing them with other flours until you see how they work.

FLOURS MADE FROM ANCIENT WHEATS: Einkorn, emmer, spelt, and kamut are the first wheats. Their chromosomes differ from that of modern wheat and are often enjoyed by those who can't normally eat wheat without some ill effects. More recent varieties, but still older than modern varieties, include Sonoran White, Red Fife, and Turkey Red. Bit by bit these wheats are coming back, but they are still grown in small quantities. Again, many who have difficulty with wheat find they can eat these grains. I've really enjoyed their flavor and textural qualities. Look for them at farmers' markets or online sources, such as Anson Mills and Bluebird Grain Farms.

BREAD FLOUR: Made from high-protein hard wheat, bread flour has more gluten, which contributes to the structure and rise of bread.

CAKE FLOUR: Made from soft, finely milled, low-protein, low-gluten wheat, cake flour is used when you're making a delicate cake with loft, such as the Olive Oil Cake on page 627. It's light and encourages lift but tends to clump, which is why you have to sift it. Some cake flour is chlorinated (bleached with chlorine gas) to help a cake set more quickly, which is not very appealing. But there is now a more wholesome version from King Arthur Flour available. I've also used finely milled Turkey Red and Sonoran White wheat and found both worked very well.

Herbs

Over time the word *herb* has referred to a wide range of plants, including salad greens, spice-bearing shrubs and trees, and medicinal as well as culinary plants. In today's common usage, *herb* refers mostly to plants whose uses are culinary or medicinal. The line that divides herbs and spices is a wavy one, but generally herbs are leafy and associated with savory foods, while spices are dry and hard seeds, berries, and barks and suggest an alliance with sweet and pungent foods. Sometimes a plant provides both herb and spice, as in the case of coriander: the green leaf is the herb, called cilantro; the seed is the spice, called coriander. Through travel, plain curiosity, and the arrival of new populations to our shores, the American repertoire of herbs and spices continues to grow.

Fresh Herbs or Dried?

Fresh herbs are the greatest joy to cook with. As your hands move through their leaves, the air around you fills with their scents. Their flavors are alive, their leaves and flowers varied and charming. However, dried herbs are often a necessary stand-in. Because the flavor-bearing volatile oils concentrate as the water in the leaves evaporates, dried herbs are usually considered more potent. The rule of thumb for dried herbs is to use a third of the fresh amount. I find this is true, however, only if the herbs were dried recently, so unless that's the case I generally use half. When using dried herbs, crumble some between your fingers to release the aromatic oils, then inhale to see how much aroma there is. If it's big and bold, use the conservative amount. If not, use more. When cooking with dried herbs, add them at the beginning of the process; fresh herbs, which are more volatile, are generally more effective added at the end.

Not all herbs dry successfully. Chervil, parsley, and cilantro turn flat and grassy when dried, whereas basil, sage, tarragon, and marjoram hold their flavors rather well.

Dried herbs are always preferable in their whole or cut leaf form, for powdered versions quickly lose their potency. Crushing, rubbing, pounding, or even powdering the leaves between your fingers or in a mortar is important for releasing their flavors. This is true of fresh herbs as well.

BUYING AND STORING HERBS: Fresh herbs usually come in sealed plastic containers, and depending on the herb, they'll keep well left in them and refrigerated, washed, if at all, just before using. Store dried herbs in their tightly covered jars in the cupboard and plan to replace them yearly or sooner if they've lost their punch. If you've had dried herbs for a long time, throw them out and start over. The same is true for spices and mixtures like curry powders.

A Lexicon of Herbs

BASIL: Flirting with anise and other flavor hues, basil is the main ingredient of pesto, the constant companion of tomatoes, the herb of summer. The type we use most is the Italian culinary variety, Genovese, but there are others with complex shadings of curry, cinnamon, and lemon. Opal basil has the classic aroma, but the leaves are a rich burgundy. Basil goes well with virtually all summer vegetables and even some fruits, like peaches. Keep it well wrapped in paper towels, then in a plastic bag in the vegetable bin of the refrigerator. Unless well protected, it will blacken and wilt.

BAY LEAF: Used dried or fresh should you have a bay laurel tree, this leaf is important for laying down a strong, deep aromatic base to soups and stews. Where many herbs and vegetables are sweet, bay leaves are pungent, deep, sober, authoritative. Imported bay leaves—Turkish ones are my favorite—from the *Laurus nobilis* are the leaves to use, not California bay leaves, which are fiercely aggressive. Heating a bay leaf in olive oil before sautéing flavors the oil (and scents the kitchen), as does dropping one into a pot of boiling water waiting for artichokes.

CHERVIL: A delicate, leafy green herb, favored in French cuisine and one of the fines herbs, chervil, with its flavors of parsley and anise, makes a refined addition to salads, creamy soups, leeks, and egg dishes. Parsley is often suggested as a substitute, but parsley chopped with fennel greens makes a closer flavor approximation. In the end, chervil stands uniquely alone. Because it dries poorly, fresh is the only way to use it. It's also best added at the last minute, for its subtle flavor quickly disappears when cooked.

CHIVES: These greens bring a leafy version of onion (or garlic if using garlic chives) to vegetables, salads, eggs, cheese, and soups. Snip them with scissors or slice them neatly straight across; chopping merely mangles them. Use chives fresh and add them at the end of cooking. The clusters of purple blossoms can be detached at the base and used as a garnish. Garlic chives are slightly larger, flatter, and perfumed with garlic.

CILANTRO (*RAU RAM* AND *CULANTRO*): Now firmly present in America, cilantro is an "in your face" herb, the herb that people either love or hate. While I love it, I sympathize with those who don't, because once present in a dish, it's virtually impossible to disguise. The seed form, coriander, isn't nearly as potent. If you crush and inhale the two side by side, you can detect the thread of scent that links them. In a pinch, coriander can partially replace the fresh herb, but not the other way around. Cilantro provides the warm, spicy, distinctive flavor in Asian, Mexican, and Indian cooking. *Rau ram*, also called Vietnamese coriander, is considered a cilantro mimic. It is, I believe, a better choice for those who don't like cilantro, as it is a little easier to like. You may have tasted it in Vietnamese restaurants, especially in green papaya salads, where it is featured. Culantro, another cilantro mimic, is used in Caribbean and South American cooking. It is a much stronger herb than coriander or cilantro.

DILL: Everyone knows dill and its familiar sunny perfume. The feathery green leaves and the flat seeds contribute much the same flavor. Associated with Scandinavian cooking, potatoes, beets, carrots, and yogurt sauces, dill also combines in a most interesting way with parsley, cilantro, and basil, a mix called *sabzi*, used in Afghanistan and the eastern Mediterranean.

EPAZOTE: This semiwild herb is favored in New Mexico as well as Mexico and Central and South American countries. It's frequently used with beans for both its flavor and its ability to make them more digestible. Its smell is unappealing when raw, but it softens with cooking, leaving a lingering flavor whose subtle presence makes an important difference. Epazote grows on you, and it grows easily in the garden.

LEMON BALM AND LEMON VERBENA: Soft and gentle both in the garden and in the teapot, lemon balm makes a delicate herb tea and a good addition to salads of greens and herbs. Lemon verbena is another lemon-scented herb, this one with clear, sparkly flavor. The leaves, finely sliced or chopped, make a distinctive addition to fruit and lettuce salads and an exquisite infusion for tea or ice cream.

LOVAGE: An herb that resembles giant flat-leaf parsley, lovage has a bright and bracing flavor similar to celery, only wilder—like wild celery, in fact. An approximation can be made by mixing celery leaves and flat-leaf parsley. Lovage is wonderful with potatoes, tomatoes, and corn and torn into salads, but it needs to be handled judiciously, for it's bold and assertive. A few leaves are ample for any recipe. Its hollow stems make a perfect straw for Bloody Marys or tomato juice. One plant will supply your neighborhood.

MARJORAM: Marjoram is another sweet summer herb. I use it as often as basil and frequently in its place (though about two-thirds as much) since it harmonizes with the same foods. Although often compared to its cousin oregano, marjoram is a great deal sweeter and more aromatic, without the resinous tones of oregano.

MINT: There are so many kinds, including chocolate, but I stick with the more classic culinary varieties spearmint, peppermint, and orange bergamot. Mint goes into salads and vegetable dishes more often than you might guess, and, of course, it makes a wonderful tea. Dried mint is surprisingly flavorful and can be used successfully in place of fresh.

OREGANO: Except for true Greek oregano, which is hard to find fresh, I think this is one herb that gains in flavor when it's dried. Oregano's soul mate is lemon, and the two are often juxtaposed. Mexican oregano, a different plant from the European cultivar, is stronger, more resinous and aggressive. It's very good in Mexican dishes, especially with beans. Toasting dried oregano leaves briefly in a dry pan brings out richer flavor notes.

PARSLEY: Parsley has become so ubiquitous we sometimes forget it's an herb, not a garnish. Robust and earthy, parsley has a clean bright flavor that infuses stocks, soups, and stews with unparalleled depth. Parsley can be enjoyed quite in its own right, as the primary ingredient of parsley salads. The flat-leaf varieties tend to be more flavorful than the curly and are easy to find. Dried parsley has a grassy taste and no merit. Parsley root or Hamburg parsley—the vegetable version of parsley—is very good eating when grated into salads, added to soups, or chopped into stews.

CHOPPING PARSLEY

Mud and sand often are hidden in the leaves, especially in the folds of curly parsley leaves, so a good washing is important. Vigorously swish the parsley bunch around in a large bowl of water, run your fingers through the leaves, then rinse the stems. If the water is muddy, fill the bowl with fresh water and repeat. Still keeping the bunch intact, dry it in a salad spinner. (It's impossible to sprinkle wet parsley, and wringing it dry in a towel rids it of much of its flavor and nutrients.) Grasp the dried bunch by the stems, tilt the head downward toward the cutting board, and shave off the leaves with a sharp knife. Or pluck them off by hand. (Be sure to save the stems for vegetable stocks.) Pick out the larger remaining stems, but don't worry about the rest. Using a chef's knife, start chopping. As you work, keep dragging the leaves that migrate to the edge back into the middle of the board with your knife so that all is evenly chopped. Cover chopped parsley with a damp paper towel and refrigerate until you need it. Although it's best used within a few hours, you can keep it overnight, covered with a damp towel inside a covered container in the refrigerator.

ROSEMARY: Strong, with the potential to overwhelm, rosemary is fresh in the summer, but its taste harmonizes well with winter foods, such as roasted vegetables, white beans, and split peas. In summer, its long sticklike branches can serve as skewers for vegetables. Throw some, fresh or dried, on the grill to make an appetite-enticing aromatic smoke.

SAGE: Associated with stuffings and often thought of as a wintery, musty-tasting herb—old powdered sage is indeed a musty item—in its fresh form, sage has a delicate taste with clear tones of mint. Fresh sage leaves enhance many foods that we tend to associate more with herbs like basil and marjoram, such as asparagus, corn, and peas. It also has a striking affinity for winter squash and pumpkin. Sage leaves, used alone or mixed with chamomile, make a soothing, minty tea. Pineapple sage has scarlet, pineapple-perfumed flowers and leaves that can go right into salads. Float morsels of crisp fried sage leaves in soups—especially white bean or pumpkin soups—crumble them over roasted squash and onion dishes, or insert a few into a grilled fontina sandwich. The sage family is large and eccentric, and not all of it is suitable for cooking. Be careful of wild sages, especially the artemisias—they can be bitter.

SALAD BURNET: A pretty perennial herb that you'll have to plant since stores don't carry it, salad burnet has the distinct flavor of cucumbers. Young sprigs are lovely tossed in a salad or paired with cucumbers in a sandwich.

SAVORY: So closely associated with fresh beans that it's nicknamed the bean herb, savory (both the annual summer and perennial winter varieties) is compatible with other vegetables, too. Like thyme, it lends an earthy note to vegetables that's grounding, rather than sunny and bright, the way marjoram and basil are.

SORREL: The large, soft leaves suggest none of the acidic surprise they give the tongue. Sorrel's bright, lemony tartness is perfect paired with eggs and potatoes. It wakes them right up. Sorrel leaves literally melt into a puree when heated in a pan with a little butter, making a more or less instant sauce. A cup of leaves disappears into little more than a few teaspoons, so it pays to have a few plants in the garden if you like sorrel. If you're buying them packaged for a salad, examine the leaves carefully to make sure they haven't begun to disintegrate in the dampness of the packaging.

Sorrel Puree

Use 4 cups or about 5 ounces of sorrel leaves. If the leaves are large or coarse, strip them from the stems and discard the stems. Coarsely chop the leaves. Melt 2 tablespoons butter in a skillet over medium heat. Add the leaves with a few tablespoons water and cook for 6 to 8 minutes, pushing them about with a fork to break them up. Add more water, as needed, so that they don't fry. Season with a pinch of salt and store in a covered container in the refrigerator. Makes about 1/4 cup. Use over a period of several weeks or freeze.

TARRAGON: French tarragon is full of the pungent licorice-lemon flavor that goes so well with mushrooms and potatoes, vinegars and vinaigrettes, and eggs. Tarragon is so distinctive that I find it difficult to pair with any other herb except parsley and chives. After years of romancing the new basils, lovage, and other exotics, I've recently rediscovered tarragon and found it to be a delightful addition to my repertoire.

THYME: One of the essential herbs practically around the world, thyme is included in many recipes for its mostly earthy nature. Whole sprigs can be added to soups and stews, or the leaves can be plucked off the stems, then chopped. Lemon thyme provides a little of the uplifting aroma of citrus and makes a delicious infusion to drink as tea. There are many varieties of thyme that hint of this and that perfume, but in the end basic culinary thyme is most useful in the kitchen.

Fortunately, fresh thyme from the market holds up well, but I can't imagine cooking without these aromatic, low-growing shrubs close by.

Nuts and Seeds

Nuts have long played an important part in our diet. Only recently—and mostly in the United States—have we spurned them for being too fatty, but vegetarians in particular should keep in mind that they are a good source of protein. Recent studies have revealed that they are filled with nutrients essential to a healthy diet. They have far more fiber than chips, far less saturated fat than cheese, and the same fatty acids found in fish oil. The health benefits of eating nuts should let everyone relax and enjoy these foods, not only as tasty morsels but also in their other forms—nut butters, peanut sauces, moles, tahini, coconut milk, and almond milk.

Because of their high oil content, nuts and seeds quickly turn rancid unless properly cared for. Not only is rancid oil harmful, but it just doesn't taste good. Rancidity can be detected by its off smell when cold, its fishy smell when heated, and its stale taste.

Nuts in their shells are least likely to be rancid because they are naturally protected from the oil-corrupting influences of light and air. While cracking nuts may be viewed as impractical in today's fast-paced world, it makes a pleasant fall or winter evening's activity. A bowl left on the counter provides a healthy nibble for anyone who wants to pause and crack a few.

If I can't buy nuts in their shells, I buy raw nuts still in their skins. The skins, which act as a protective coating, aren't hard to remove. I also make sure they're unroasted. Roasted nuts are more likely to have been fried than roasted and they often contain salts, MSG, and sugars. Dry-roasted nuts also may have added flavorings as well as a slow turnover.

All nuts and seeds are best stored in the refrigerator or freezer. Cold retards the spoilage of their oils so they will remain fresh longer.

TO BLANCH AND PEEL ALMONDS: Drop whole, shelled almonds into a pan of boiling water for 1 minute, then lift them out and pinch off the skins. If they don't come off easily, return them to the water for another minute and try again. Don't soak almonds longer than necessary, or they'll become waterlogged and splotchy looking.

TO PEEL HAZELNUTS: Spread nuts in a single layer on a sheet pan and bake at 300°F until the skins begin to crack, 15 to 20 minutes. Remove, wrap them in a towel for a minute, then vigorously rub them a handful at a time in the towel. This will take off all the loosened skins, but the difficult patches will remain, which can be removed with a knife or left on. If the skins are really stubborn, return them to the oven for another 5 minutes. A little skin won't hurt.

TO PEEL PISTACHIOS: The green meat of the pistachio is revealed only when the skin is removed. Cover the nuts with boiling water and let stand for 5 minutes. Drain, then rub the nuts with a towel. The loosened soft skins should slip right off. Remove more stubborn pieces with a knife. Discard any nuts that are blackened or moldy looking. To recrisp them, bake at 300°F until dry, about 15 minutes. Don't overbake them, or their colors will fade.

TO BLANCH AND ROAST WALNUTS: This simple process greatly improves the flavor of shelled walnuts that aren't freshly cracked and renders them less irritating for those who are sensitive to their skins. Bring a pan of water to a boil, add walnuts, and let them stand for 1 minute. Drain and wick up the excess moisture with a towel. Spread them out on a sheet pan, then toast in a 300°F oven until they've dried out, about 20 minutes. Remove them as soon as they're dry.

Pepper

There's nothing like the fragrance of freshly milled pepper, and that's how it should always be used. The flat, stale taste of preground pepper doesn't compare with fresh, and it's on just such a small point that the difference between something all right and something really good depends. Pepper is not only for savory dishes; it also has its place with sweets. A little pepper gives a warm vibrant note to poached fruits, mousses, and even pastries—the best-known example being pfeffernüsse. Pepper is the fruit of a vine, *Piper nigrum*. Green, black, and white pepper all come from the same plant. The difference in color is accounted for by maturity.

BLACK PEPPERCORNS: The pepper is picked green but left to dry until shriveled and black. Their flavor is stronger than either green or white peppercorns. Two of the most notable are Tellicherry and Malabar. Black pepper is complex with sweet, fruity, warm, and sometimes hot nuances.

GREEN PEPPERCORNS: Picked green, these must be eaten right away, preserved in brine, or frozen. If not, they turn black. They are intensely aromatic and so soft they can be mashed into a paste or scattered over food.

WHITE PEPPERCORNS: Picked when fully ripe and red, the berries are soaked until soft, then the outer skin is sloughed off. White pepper is what remains. It's milder than black pepper and used where the mildness—or whiteness—is desired.

Other plants are used as pepper, although they aren't true pepper:

PINK PEPPERCORNS: A well-known pepperlike berry that is not related botanically to pepper but is used along with true pepper, mainly for its color. Some people have an allergic reaction to the berries, which causes the throat to contract.

SZECHUAN PEPPER (SICHUAN OR ANISE PEPPER): Used in Chinese cooking, Szechuan pepper has become quite popular. It looks like a tiny, reddish dried flower rather than corns. It's intensely aromatic, very complex, and slightly numbing on the tongue.

Salt

Salt contributes its own flavor and brings out the flavors of the foods themselves. It enhances all foods, including sweet. It's hard to imagine caramels today without a pinch of sea salt on them. Salt is also used to draw out moisture and bitter juices from vegetables, and as a preservative in making pickles and preserving capers.

Although we think of salt as pure sodium chloride, it comes to us from the earth and the sea as a complex substance that's filled with trace minerals. It's then processed, altered, diminished, or enhanced just like other foods. In their natural states, salts have different flavors, textures, and colors, and they naturally attract moisture and clump when the air is damp. To make salt white, even grained, and pourable, it's refined with chemicals that eliminate most of the trace minerals, then fortified with more chemicals and additives. A glance at the label on a saltbox may surprise you; salt is not always so pure as we assume. Here are some common forms of salt:

IODIZED SALT: Iodine is often removed during processing of salts; when added back, we get iodized salt—important in the "goiter belt" parts of the country where there's not enough iodine in the diet.

KOSHER SALT: Kosher salt is less salty tasting than sea salt. Unlike table salt, it's ragged and rough. Chefs like it because they can grab it with their fingers and hold on to it, whereas fine salt just ebbs away.

SEA SALT: Coarse or fine grained, sea salt is more complex and saltier tasting than other salts. The complexity comes from its mineral content, which in turn reflects the composition of seawater. The most commonly available sea salt is from the Mediterranean; it comes in coarse crystals and as fine table salt. You can keep the crystals in a pepper mill and grind them directly onto your food, like pepper. Sea salt is what I've used throughout this book.

TABLE SALT: Refined and fine grained, table salt has chemical additives to keep it free flowing in all weather. ("When it rains, it pours.") Compared to other salts, its flavor is harsh and not particularly interesting.

FLAKY MALDON SEA SALT, FLEUR DE SEL: These and other fine salts are added at serving where their crunchy texture and good, salty taste will be most noticeable. Their thinness makes them suitable as a finishing salt, where as a coarse, chunky Celtic salt would be better broken up in a mortar or ground into foods through a salt grinder.

OTHER SALTS: Most countries have their own salts that are treasured for their unique flavors—pink salt from Hawaii and black Indian salt with a pronounced sulfurous odor, for example. Many can be found in natural foods and specialty stores.

SMOKED SALT: This salt, which has come onto the market since this book was first written, can be very addictive if you love smokiness in your food. It's most effective when sprinkled over a dish just before serving it, rather than at the beginning where its fragile smokiness will disappear.

TRUFFLE SALT: This fine sea salt is imbued with small pieces of truffle and is highly aromatic. The temptation is to use it on everything, but if you do, everything will taste like truffle salt. Try it with eggs, simple fresh pastas, potatoes, tender cooked beans, and celery root.

Salting to Taste and When to Salt

Salt is a matter of personal taste, so it's virtually impossible for anyone to ascertain the right amount of salt for another to use. I have suggested amounts as a place to start from, but in the end it really has to be "salt to taste." Practiced cooks know by feel how much salt to use, but even if you're new to cooking, you'll quickly develop a feel for how much is enough, especially if you really do taste as you cook. More precise measurements are given for baked goods, which are difficult to taste before they're cooked or to alter afterward.

Since salt draws out the flavors of foods, it has the best chance of doing its work if you add it at the beginning of the cooking process. When salt is added only at the end, it adds mostly a salty taste, whereas if you salt each component of a recipe, the final dish should be sufficiently seasoned, needing perhaps only a pinch to fine-tune it. When you cook this way, you'll find yourself reaching into the salt dish more often, but in the end you probably won't use any more salt than usual, and maybe even less, since the flavors of the ingredients are maximized from the beginning.

Salt and Habit: We've all had days when everything seems to need more salt and days when everything is too salty. Overall, though, the taste for salt is a matter of habit. When people have to curtail their salt use, they commonly go through a difficult adjustment where everything tastes bland. But after a while their new food begins to taste better, while the food they were used to tastes too salty. Herbs, spices, lemon juice, and vinegar help make food more palatable when salt is reduced or eliminated, just as they enhance the flavor of foods when salt is included. Often it's a bit of acid, rather than salt, that provides the final balance for a dish.

Soy Sauce

The many types of soy sauces exhibit a great range of flavor, saltiness, and depth. Dark and light soy sauces refer not only to color but also to viscosity. Dark soy sauce is thicker, leaving legs on the bottle once it is poured. Light sauce is less syrupy.

The ancient process of making soy sauce involves the fermentation of soybeans and wheat and a long maturing period in a brine solution. Shortcut chemical methods simplify the process but produce rather artificial-tasting sauces that lack the depth and character of the real thing. All soy sauce is salty, even reduced-sodium soy, but, like salt itself, soy sauce isn't used in large quantity. There's much to be learned by tasting different sauces side by side to discover their particular personalities. The following are those I use most often.

OHSAWA NAMA SOY SAUCE: Author Nancy Singleton Hachisu introduced me to this exquisite soy sauce, which she found at my co-op. This raw (nama) soy, which is aged for two years in cedar kegs, is very clean tasting, pure, and well balanced. It is now my favorite. As it is unpasteurized, it should be refrigerated.

MUSHROOM SOY: This rich, dark Chinese soy sauce is another favorite seasoning in my kitchen. I often add a little to mushroom-based dishes for its depth and color. A little goes far, as it is very full-bodied.

BLACK SOY: Another robust Chinese soy sauce, but one with an edge of sweet because it includes molasses. It's saltier than mushroom soy; good in dressings and marinades where soy is featured.

TAMARI: Well-made, aged tamari has one of the richest and most singular tastes. In small amounts, it adds unusual nuance to a sauce. Of various brands, I often choose San-J. Ohsawa also makes an organic, wheat-free tamari that is excellent.

THIN OR LIGHT: Kikkoman is but one of many thin-bodied soy sauces that's not as salty or as strong as other types of soy sauce. I mention it because it's commonly available. Use it in dishes when you want an infusion of color and mild seasoning.

Sugars and Sweeteners

There are many different kinds of sugar now available to us. For one, there are organic sugars in the same forms we're accustomed to—white, brown, and so on. They aren't as refined as your standard white cane sugar and I find that they have more interesting subtle flavors, plus cane sugar grown without pesticides, which pollute waterways and land, is preferable than the alternative. Lots of people avoid eating sugar today. I do, too, but not entirely. All sugars and sweeteners, not just high-fructose corn syrup or cane sugar, but also agave nectar, stevia, and other sweeteners have their critics, especially when it comes to artificial sweeteners. In the long run, sugar might not be such a bad choice, especially if you're not using it often. As we are accustomed to sweetness in desserts, here are a few alternative sweeteners to consider:

AGAVE NECTAR: A light or dark syrupy sweetener that's been around for a while, agave is made from blue agave plant. It's sweeter than sugar and honey, so it needs to be used "to taste." Vegans, who don't eat honey, may prefer agave. It has a lower glycemic index than sugar, but one can still eat too much. Plan to use one-third less agave than you would sugar. For sweetening liquids, like syrups or smoothies, add it to taste.

There are books on baking with agave syrup that are helpful guides for those interested.

COCONUT SUGAR: Organic and non-GMO, sugar made from the reduced juice of coconut is tawny brown, only slightly coconut flavored if at all, and more granular than moist brown sugar. Consider using it in dishes that feature other tropical fruits, brown sugar, or coconut. Replacement for cane sugar is one to one.

ERYTHRITOL (BRAND NAME ZERO, BY WHOLESOME SWEETENERS: Erythritol, an ingredient in Truvia and other non- or low-calorie sweeteners, is a naturally occurring sugar alcohol that is found in many fruits, vegetables, and even certain fermented foods. It is available in small packets to sweeten drinks. Larger packages are available to use in baking and cooking. It is not as sweet as sugar, but it's suggested that you use it in a one-to-one replacement ratio. Unlike sugar, it will not brown. Erythritol is considered very difficult to digest, so approach with caution.

MAPLE SUGAR: My favorite sweetener is this pale, brown soft sugar. The flavor of maple is present and its flavor is round and full. Maple sugar is expensive, but if you bake infrequently, it may be a good choice, especially in dishes where light brown sugar is called for. I use it in a one-to-one ratio with brown sugar or white.

MOLASSES: I'd never be without it, but I don't use it that often, for the flavor of molasses is as strong and assertive as it is dark and heavy. However, molasses, unlike most sweeteners, contributes some degree of nourishment in the form of iron, calcium, B vitamins, and chromium. Use it in recipes that call for its special flavor, or drizzle it over cornbread or corn meal in place of honey, or stir it into milk.

STEVIA: In liquid form, super-sweet stevia, derived from a plant in the sunflower family, can be added by the drop to bring up the sweetness in compotes, syrups, coffee, tea, smoothies, lemonade—any liquid. The dry form may look like sugar, but it doesn't necessarily handle the same way, which is why it's combined with other ingredients to make it more like sugar. Its use does require something of a learning curve. (See *The Stevia Cookook* by Ray Sahelian and Donna Gates to learn more.) It can have a bitter off taste. Practice makes perfect, here.

TRUVIA: A stevia-based sugar substitute. Or so it claims. That it was developed by Coca-Cola and Cargill might give you pause. And that stevia isn't listed among its ingredients might also make you wonder if it really is stevia. (It includes something derived from stevia.) Many people have reported adverse reactions to Truvia.

Tomato Products

There's no disputing the great convenience of canned toma-toes. Most of the year they're better than fresh ones, and there are many good brands on the market. I am especially fond of the organic brands, such as Eden Foods, for their good taste and texture. With a can of tomatoes, you can make a vibrant, simple sauce within minutes.

Tomato puree is sweet and very smooth. It makes an uninteresting sauce, but it can be used in an emergency to fortify one that's lackluster.

Tomato paste is the most concentrated tomato product. It's used in small amounts to bring a spot of flavor, acidity, and color to a dish or to bolster a weak sauce. Often a little dab is just enough to bring discursive elements into more harmonious play. Paste that comes in a tube is wonderfully efficient. Simply use what you want, put the cap back on, and refrigerate. It won't come back to greet you filmed with mold.

Sun-dried tomatoes—packed in oil, dry-packed, or in paste form—also can add a great deal of body to a sauce. The best ones are plump and tender, swimming in their jars of olive oil. They can be thinly slivered and added to other dishes as a seasoning, but they're meant to be used in small, not large, quantities. Dried tomatoes that aren't oil packed are leathery and concentrated. They soften as they cook, so add them at the beginning of any recipe. Tomatoes that have been sliced and dried in a dehydrator usually hold on to their colors. Break them up and add them to soups. They will swell as they hydrate and lend their flavor to the dish.

Tortilla Strips and Chips

Stale corn tortillas don't absorb as much oil as fresh ones. If yours are fresh, spread them out on the kitchen counter to dry for 30 minutes. For chips, cut them into sixths. For strips, cut them into quarters, stack them up, then slice them into skinny strips. Heat a few tablespoons of vegetable oil in a skillet over fairly high heat. When it's hot enough to quickly sizzle a piece of tortilla, add a handful and fry them just until golden and crisp. Transfer to paper towels and fry the rest.

Alternatively, brush the tortillas lightly with oil before slic-ing; spread them on a sheet pan and bake at 425°F until crisp.

Vinegar

Vinegars are important for vinaigrettes and salad dressings, but they're also used in other dishes to bring flavors that are almost "there" into sharper relief. When added to bitter greens, they have a way of softening their edge. Vinegars are essential for pickling, and a little added to vegetable stews helps keep the texture of tender vegetables from becoming mushy. Many vinegars can be used interchangeably because they're used in such small amounts, but they definitely have their own personalities.

AGED SHERRY VINEGAR: Dark, dense, and sweet but not cloying, aged sherry vinegar is far better than many of the inexpensive balsamic vinegars that are available. A little goes far. It's interesting, by the drop, with some fruits, such as poached dried figs or dead-ripe fresh ones, in a vinaigrette where apples or pears are present, and over cooked beans and dulses.

APPLE CIDER VINEGAR: With its nicely balanced, lively taste, apple cider vinegar is an interesting, mildly fruity vinegar traditionally popular in American cooking. The organic, unfiltered type has the most character.

BALSAMIC VINEGAR: Low-acid, sweet, and complex, good-quality balsamic vinegar can, by the drop, bring out the most in fruits, such as cherries, strawberries, poached quince, and others. It also complements onions, tomatoes, eggplant, and many other vegetables.

BANYULS VINEGAR: This is a slightly sweet but strong red wine vinegar made from wine aged in oak. It's especially good in vinaigrettes where walnut and hazelnut oils are used.

CHINESE BLACK VINEGAR: Made from rice, wheat, sorghum, and barley, its color is inky dark and its flavor is rich, faintly smoky, and sweet. It adds depth to wintery vegetable stews, stir-fries, or seared tofu. I sometimes use it in place of balsamic vinegar in salads or drizzled over grilled eggplant.

KALAMATA VINEGAR: From the Peloponnese, this rich, sweet, vinegar is aged in oak, which makes the flavor deeper and more distinctive.

RED WINE VINEGAR: Red wine vinegars vary in body and strength from average to high acid. Aged red wine vinegars are quite strong. A few drops enliven greens, such as spinach, chard, dandelions, and kale.

RICE WINE VINEGAR: This Japanese vinegar is mild and slightly sweet. You can use it generously because of its low acidity. It's delicious with Asian noodles, cucumbers, and in dressings where its delicacy is welcome. There are both plain and flavored rice wine vinegars. I prefer the plain, which isn't sweetened.

SHERRY VINEGAR: This delicious Spanish vinegar is superb with sweet vegetables like onions, rich dishes, or bitter greens. Sizzled with butter in a skillet, it makes a fast, big-tasting sauce for frittatas, onions, or seared radicchio.

WHITE WINE VINEGAR: This vinegar is generally milder and a little less acidic than red wine vinegar, but not always. Some white wine vinegars are aged in oak and have plenty of presence. Champagne vinegar is one of the more delicate examples, however, and a few drops will often throw the flavors of a dish into relief, the way a bit of lemon does.

SAUCES AND CONDIMENTS

CHAPTER 3

Sauces and Condiments

In the language of food, sauces are the adjectives. They embellish, enrich, and enhance other foods, raising them to greater possibilities.

Sauces moisten (mayonnaise on bread), add a bright acidic touch (tomato sauce on pasta), or enrobe and enrich (a creamy sorrel sauce or beurre blanc). Knowing how to make even a few sauces, such as a classic mayonnaise and a proper béchamel, will give your cooking finesse, allowing you to transform plain and simple foods into dishes that have more excitement and deeper dimension. Sauces are sometimes viewed as intimidating, the secret realm of chefs rather than the province of the home cook. But sauces are like anything else—some have a trick or two that can be mastered with practice, and others are utterly straightforward. And these sauces are mostly of the latter persuasion.

Sauces and condiments are quite unlike the other foods we eat. Too concentrated, too acidic, too garlicky, or too rich to eat in large amounts, they're used in small quantities to add polish to a dish. It's their intensity that brings other foods to life—the glistening flourish of a caper-filled salsa verde on steamed carrots that would otherwise be dull, the aromatic hues of an herb-infused butter that suddenly makes a baked potato unusual. A garlic-laden mayonnaise significantly transforms a bowl of chickpeas.

Condiments, pickles, and chutneys are so sharp and vinegary they're often served on the side, more like a garnish. Many condiments last for weeks or even months in the refrigerator. They're a wonderfully convenient pantry item—a spoonful of this or that sauce or condiment can magically round out a dish or a meal, giving it a unique stamp of personality. Other condiments might be comprised of just one ingredient such as smoked salt, flaky Maldon salt, or smoked paprika.

Sauces Based on Butter

Even if you're a devoted fan of all the delicious oils that grace our shelves, as I certainly am, nothing quite replaces the flavor and smell of butter. It flatters all forms of vegetables and in turn is enhanced by the numerous items it marries so well with—sage and other herbs, capers, vinegar, wine and shallots, mustard, and so forth.

You may not feel any reason to go beyond letting a pat of pure butter melt over your vegetables, but the sizzle of sage butter or a touch of beurre blanc is far more exciting. Experimenting with the flavored butters in this chapter will show you how to bring out an unsuspected wealth of possibilities in your vegetables and grains. And you can have the best of both worlds when you use the Herb-Butter and Olive Oil Sauce (see page 44)—a classic that trades in some of its buttery essence for a successful merging with fruity oil.

43

Warm Sage and Garlic Butter

This fast, sizzling sauce is particularly compatible with winter squash, ravioli, or a warm slice of baked ricotta.
Makes about ¹/₃ cup

2 tablespoons butter

2 tablespoons olive oil

1 tablespoon chopped sage or 1 teaspoon dried

2 cloves garlic, finely chopped

1 tablespoon finely chopped parsley

Sea salt and freshly milled pepper

Heat the butter and oil in a small skillet over high heat. When bubbling, add the sage and fry for about 30 seconds. Add the garlic and cook until it has perfumed the oil. Remove from the heat, stir in the parsley, and season with a pinch of salt and plenty of pepper.

Herb-Butter and Olive Oil Sauce

A sauce inspired by one of my favorite cooks, Ann Clark; try it on steamed vegetables. Makes about ¹/₂ cup

¹/₄ cup finely chopped parsley

2 tablespoons thinly sliced chives

1 tablespoon minced tarragon

1 clove garlic

¹/₄ teaspoon sea salt

2 tablespoons capers, rinsed

1 teaspoon grated lemon zest

1 shallot, minced

5 tablespoons butter, at room temperature

3 tablespoons olive oil

Fresh lemon juice

Blanch the herbs for a scant minute in a cup or so of boiling water, then drain in a fine strainer and blot dry. Pound the garlic and salt in a mortar to a paste. Beat the herbs, garlic, capers, lemon zest, shallot, and butter with a wooden spoon, then gradually mix in the olive oil. Taste and season with a pinch of salt and lemon juice. You can make the entire sauce with a mortar and pestle, if you have one that's large enough.

Beurre Blanc

Stir a spoonful of this classic French sauce into a vegetable ragout just before serving or serve with asparagus.
Makes about 1 cup

¹/₃ cup white wine vinegar or champagne vinegar

¹/₃ cup dry white wine

2 tablespoons finely diced shallot

¹/₂ teaspoon sea salt

¹/₂ pound butter, cut into small pieces

Freshly milled white pepper

Put the vinegar, wine, shallot, and salt in a small, heavy saucepan and simmer until only 3 tablespoons remain. Remove from the heat and cool until tepid. Return to very low heat and whisk in the butter piece by piece until all is incorporated. Remove from the heat and season with a little pepper. Strain (or not) and serve.

If you're making the sauce in advance or have leftover cold beurre blanc, rewarm it by setting it over low heat and whisking until warm. If the butter begins to melt and separate, it's because the heat is too high. Pull the pan off the stove and continue whisking until it has cooled and come back together. If this doesn't help, pour a little into a cold bowl and start whisking in the remaining sauce gradually. The coolness will help solidify the butter again.

Beurre Rouge: Use red wine vinegar and red wine in place of the white.

Beurre Blanc with Herbs: When the sauce is done, stir in 2 to 3 teaspoons finely cut chives, chopped basil, or tarragon.

Flavored Butters

These are all made the same way. Start with butter at room temperature, add the ingredients, and mix them together with a wooden paddle or spoon. They can be transferred to a crock or set on a sheet of wax paper, rolled into a cylinder, and frozen until firm. Once frozen, the flavored butter can be sliced into thin disks and floated on soups or used in a number of other ways, as suggested in the recipes that follow.

Herb Butter

Universally good, this butter can be tossed with virtually any vegetable, rice, or cooked dried beans. Makes $1/2$ cup

- 1/4 pound butter
- 2 tablespoons chopped thyme
- 3 tablespoons chopped marjoram
- 1 shallot, finely diced
- 1/2 teaspoon grated lemon zest
- Pinch sea salt

Saffron Butter

Saffron goes with all those Provençal vegetables—fennel, eggplant, tomato—and is also good with fresh noodles. Makes $1/2$ cup

- 2 pinches saffron threads, pulverized
- 1/4 pound butter
- 1 large shallot, finely diced
- 2 teaspoons finely chopped marjoram or basil
- 1 tablespoon finely chopped parsley
- 1/2 teaspoon grated orange or lemon zest
- Pinch cayenne
- Sea salt and freshly milled pepper

Cover the saffron with 2 teaspoons hot water and let steep until the color emerges, after a few minutes. Work it into the butter with the remaining ingredients. Add salt and pepper to taste.

Spicy Butter with Smoked Paprika

Use this complex and exotic butter with sweet potatoes or winter squash, or stir into a chickpea soup for a burst of flavor. Makes $1/2$ cup

- 1/2 bunch green onions, white parts only
- 2 cloves garlic, coarsely chopped
- 1 tablespoon sweet paprika
- 1 teaspoon smoked paprika
- 2 teaspoons ground cumin
- 1/2 teaspoon ground coriander
- 1/2 teaspoon cayenne, or more to taste
- 2 tablespoons chopped parsley
- 2 tablespoons chopped cilantro
- 1 teaspoon chopped mint
- 1/8 teaspoon sea salt
- 1/4 pound butter
- Juice of 1 lime

Pound the onions, garlic, ground spices, herbs, and sea salt in a mortar to form a slightly rough paste. (Or puree in a small food processor.) Stir this paste into the butter with the lime juice.

Blossom Butter

Streaks and flecks of color mark this delectable butter.
Makes $1/2$ cup

- $1/4$ pound butter
- 2 tablespoons finely chopped mixed herbs—opal basil, marjoram, chives, thyme
- 3 tablespoons chopped edible blossoms—sage, rosemary, borage, calendula, or nasturtium
- Sea salt and freshly milled white pepper

Nasturtium Butter: Use nasturtium blossoms along with 2 tender nasturtium leaves, finely sliced. This butter has a peppery flavor that lifts up so-so soups and is delicious in a cucumber sandwich.

Olive-Rosemary Butter

A pungent butter that's excellent with grilled vegetables or as a dynamic flavoring for a white bean or potato soup.
Makes $1/2$ cup

- $1/4$ pound butter
- $1/2$ cup finely chopped niçoise olives
- 1 tablespoon minced rosemary
- 1 teaspoon minced thyme
- $1/2$ teaspoon grated lemon zest
- Pinch sea salt

Green Chile Butter

This spicy butter goes particularly well with sweet vegetables, such as carrots, beets, sweet potatoes, and corn.
Makes $1/2$ cup

- 1 New Mexican long green chile, roasted
- Finely chopped zest of 1 lime
- $1/4$ pound butter
- 1 teaspoon lime juice, or more to taste
- 2 tablespoons chopped cilantro
- 1 green onion, including an inch of the green, thinly sliced
- A few pinches sea salt
- $1/4$ teaspoon ground coriander

Mince the chile with the lime zest, then beat into the butter and add the remaining ingredients.

Mustard Butter

Mustard-flavored butter always suits those strong members of the cabbage family, of which mustard is a member, too.
Makes $1/2$ cup

- 1 clove garlic, put through a press or pounded to a puree
- $1/4$ pound butter
- 1 tablespoon Dijon mustard or to taste
- 1 large shallot, finely diced, or 2 tablespoons minced green onion
- 2 tablespoons chopped parsley
- Sea salt and freshly milled pepper

Béchamel and Other Roux-Based Sauces

Sauces thickened with an amalgam of flour and butter, or roux, have often been scorned, mainly because they're seldom properly cooked. However, they can be quite delicious and very useful. Béchamel, or white sauce, provides the smooth layer in lasagne, the base for a soufflé, or the blanket that covers a gratin. A thin béchamel can take the place of cream in a number of situations. Any roux-based sauce can be smooth and silky if you allow it to cook for at least 25 minutes. If you use a double boiler, the sauce can cook while you do other things in the kitchen.

THE ROUX AND THE LIQUID: The roux, the mixture of flour and fat, thickens the sauce. Usually the fat is butter and the liquid is milk, but you can also make a sauce using oil and good vegetable stock or a plant milk.

PREVENTING LUMPS: If you add warm liquid to a warm roux or cold liquid to a cold roux, you won't get lumps in your sauce. Stir briskly with a whisk as you quickly add all the liquid at once. Once the sauce thickens, switch to a flat-edged wooden spoon and be sure to run it around the edges of the pan as well as the bottom as you stir so that nothing sticks and burns. If you use a double boiler, you have to stir only occasionally during the 25-minute cooking time.

FINAL SEASONINGS: Finished sauces can be flavored with vegetable purees, roasted garlic, concentrated tomato sauces, fresh herbs, curry, and grated cheeses.

Béchamel Sauce

Although it's not traditional, I always steep a little onion and some aromatics in the milk to make a better-tasting sauce. This recipe makes a sauce of medium thickness.
Makes 2 cups

---

2 cups milk
$1/4$ cup finely diced onion
Aromatics: 1 bay leaf, 3 parsley sprigs, 2 thyme sprigs
$3^1/2$ tablespoons butter
$3^1/2$ tablespoons flour
Sea salt and freshly milled white pepper
Grated nutmeg

Heat the milk with the onion and aromatics in a heavy saucepan over medium heat. Turn it off just before it boils and set aside for 15 minutes to steep.

In another saucepan, make the roux by melting the butter, adding the flour, and stirring constantly over medium heat for 2 minutes. Quickly pour the milk through a strainer into the roux and whisk until thickened. Stir until the sauce comes to a boil. Set the pan over very low heat or transfer to a double boiler. Cook for 25 to 30 minutes, stirring occasionally. Season with salt, pepper, and nutmeg to taste. If you're not ready to use the sauce right away, lay a piece of plastic wrap directly on the surface to prevent a skin from forming.

Nondairy Béchamel: Replace the butter with oil. For liquid, use plant milk, or vegetable stock, pages 174 to 177, whatever you think will best complement the dish. (V)

Herb Béchamel: To the finished sauce, add $1/3$ to $1/2$ cup chopped herbs: chervil, thyme, and tarragon, or chopped parsley mixed with other herbs of your choice.

Rich Béchamel: Add $1/2$ cup or more cream to the finished sauce.

Cheese Béchamel: When the sauce is finished, stir in $1/2$ to 1 cup grated sharp cheddar, Swiss, or Gruyère and season with a pinch of cayenne and 2 to 3 teaspoons Dijon mustard. A cheese sauce is traditional and good with cauliflower, cabbage, and broccoli.

Walnut Béchamel Sauce

Good with pasta and rice, especially when combined with greens. Pale new-crop walnuts make an ivory-colored sauce. Older, dark-colored walnuts will tint the sauce purplish pink. In both cases, the sauce darkens as it sits.
Makes about 3 cups

---

3 cups milk
$1/2$ cup finely chopped walnuts
$1/4$ cup minced leek or green onion, white part only, or shallot
2 cloves garlic, crushed or put through a press
2 bay leaves
2 tablespoons butter
2 tablespoons flour
Sea salt and freshly milled white pepper
Grated nutmeg
2 tablespoons chopped chervil, parsley, or marjoram

Bring the milk, walnuts, leek, garlic, and bay leaves to a near boil. Remove from the heat and let steep for 30 minutes. Melt the butter in another saucepan over medium heat. Stir in the flour and cook for 2 minutes, stirring frequently. Whisk in the milk mixture all at once, then bring to a boil. Reduce the heat and cook slowly for 25 minutes, stirring frequently. Season with salt, pepper, and nutmeg to taste. When done, pull out the bay leaves and stir in the herbs. If you wish your sauce to be perfectly smooth, pass it through a food mill or puree in a blender.

Mushroom Sorrel Sauce

Tart sorrel is always right with egg-based dishes such as timbales, roulades, and pudding soufflés. If I have a windfall of sorrel—say twice as much as given here—I don't make the roux but rely on the bulk of the herb to thicken the sauce.
Makes about 3 cups

---

3 tablespoons butter

3 tablespoons finely diced shallot or onion

3 cups packed sorrel leaves, large stems removed

2 cups Mushroom Stock, either homemade (page 176) or commercial

1¹/₂ tablespoons flour

1 cup crème fraîche, cream, or half-and-half

Sea salt and freshly milled pepper

Melt 1¹/₂ tablespoons of the butter in a saucepan, add the shallot, and cook over high heat, stirring frequently, until it begins to brown around the edges, after a few minutes. Add the sorrel by handfuls. When the leaves have collapsed and turned olive green, add the stock and bring to a boil. Lower the heat and simmer for 5 minutes. Cool slightly, then puree.

Melt the remaining butter in the same pan over low heat, stir in the flour, and cook for 2 minutes. Whisk the pureed sorrel into the flour, then whisk in the crème fraîche. Season with salt and pepper to taste, then cook for 25 minutes in a double boiler over very low heat, stirring frequently. Taste for salt and pepper when done.

Green Herb Sauces

These shimmering sauces are essentially top-quality olive oil made green with fresh herbs, seasoned variously with garlic, shallots, a little lemon or vinegar to perk up the flavors, and enriched with pounded nuts, capers, cheese, or hard-cooked eggs. Green herb sauces provide a verdant finishing touch for a diverse assortment of foods, from grilled vegetables to pizzas, soups, pastas, grains, cheeses, scrambled eggs, and omelets. Although they'll keep in the refrigerator for several days, their color begins to fade as soon as the acid is added. Lemon or lime juice can be added as the sauce is used, but a salsa verde really is best fresh.

Salsa Verde

Choose those herbs that best complement the dish or the meal, and an excellent fruity olive oil. Makes about 1 cup Ⓥ

---

2 shallots, finely diced

¹/₂ cup finely chopped parsley

¹/₃ cup chopped mixed herbs—tarragon, chervil, thyme, marjoram, dill

2 to 3 tablespoons capers, rinsed

Grated zest of 1 lemon

1 small clove garlic, minced

³/₄ cup olive oil

2 to 3 teaspoons champagne vinegar or fresh lemon juice

1 hard-cooked egg, optional

Sea salt and freshly milled pepper

Combine all the ingredients except the egg, salt, and pepper. Mash the egg yolk until smooth, adding a little of the sauce to thin it. Finely chop the white. Stir the yolk and the white back into the sauce, season with salt and pepper, and adjust the amount of vinegar if needed. If you're planning to serve the sauce later, wait to add the vinegar or lemon juice so that the green will remain bright.

Salsa Verde with Walnuts and Tarragon

Everything in this sauce should be very finely chopped by hand for the best texture and taste. This sauce has long been a favorite, and it's excellent with grains.

Makes about 1¹/₂ cups Ⓥ

1/2 cup walnuts, finely chopped

2 small cloves garlic, finely chopped

1 cup finely chopped parsley, about 1 large bunch

2 tablespoons finely chopped tarragon

2 tablespoons chopped rinsed capers

1 cup olive oil

1 teaspoon good-quality red wine vinegar, or to taste

Sea salt and freshly milled pepper

Combine the nuts, garlic, parsley, tarragon, and capers in a small bowl. Stir in the oil and vinegar, then season with salt and pepper to taste.

Cilantro Salsa

If you make this in a blender, the sauce will be thick, creamy, and flecked with green. If you chop everything by hand and stir it into the oil, it will be more like the traditional salsa verde, the herbs suspended in oil. Use this as a dip, in pita sandwiches, with hard–cooked eggs, or spooned over grilled vegetables. Makes about ²/₃ cup Ⓥ

1 jalapeño chile, seeded

1 large bunch cilantro, stems removed

1/2 cup mint leaves

2 cloves garlic

1/2 cup plus 2 tablespoons olive oil

Juice of lime

1/2 teaspoon ground cumin

1/2 teaspoon ground coriander

Sea salt

For a creamy sauce, coarsely chop the chile, cilantro, mint, and garlic, then puree in a food processor with ¹/₄ cup water and the oil. Add the lime juice, cumin, coriander, and salt. Taste and correct the spices.

To make the sauce by hand, very finely chop everything, then stir in ¹/₄ cup water, the oil, and the spices.

Chimichurri

The ingredients don't look that different from other green herb sauces, but somehow chimichurri stands alone and with authority. An essential element with Argentinean grilled meats, it is also excellent with grains and vegetables and can be spread over sliced toasted baguettes or drizzled over fresh cheese, like ricotta or seared halloumi.

Makes a scant ²/₃ cup Ⓥ

1 tablespoon finely diced white onion

2 cloves garlic, minced, or more if you like it garlicky

1 cup finely minced flat-leaf parsley, mostly leaves

1/4 to ³/4 cup finely minced fresh oregano

1/2 cup olive oil

1 tablespoon red wine vinegar

Grated zest and juice of 1 lime

1/4 teaspoon red pepper flakes

Sea salt

Put all the finely chopped ingredients in a bowl, then stir in the oil, vinegar, lime zest and juice, and pepper flakes. Add more oil, if needed, so that it's very moist. Add salt to taste.

Alternatively you can make this in a small food processor, but don't puree it. There should be some texture. Cover and refrigerate until ready to use.

Parsley-Caper Sauce

Sharp and lemony, this sauce brightens warm or cold vegetables, fried cheese, vegetable fritters, and grains and beans. Makes about 1¹/₂ cups Ⓥ

1/2 cup finely chopped parsley

2 tablespoons small capers, rinsed

1 shallot, finely diced

1 teaspoon grated lemon zest

1/3 cup olive oil

1 tablespoon white wine vinegar or champagne vinegar

2 teaspoons fresh lemon juice or to taste

Sea salt and freshly milled pepper

Whisk everything together, seasoning with salt and pepper to taste. Let stand for 10 minutes, then taste again and adjust the seasonings, adding more vinegar or lemon juice if needed. Serve right away.

Chermoula (Moroccan Green Sauce)

The Moroccan marinade for fish is also wonderful with vegetables, especially sweet ones like beets, carrots, and winter squash. Makes about 1³/₄ cups Ⓥ

---

4 cloves garlic, coarsely chopped

1 teaspoon sea salt

²/₃ cup finely chopped cilantro

¹/₃ cup finely chopped parsley

1¹/₂ teaspoons sweet paprika

¹/₂ teaspoon ground cumin

¹/₈ teaspoon cayenne

¹/₄ cup olive oil

Juice of 2 large lemons, or to taste

Pound the garlic with the salt in a mortar until smooth. Add the cilantro and parsley and pound a little more to bruise the leaves and release their flavor. Stir in the spices, olive oil, and lemon juice.

Pesto

Although we have taken this most popular of sauces to places where it has never gone before, pesto may still be best on pasta. The food processor makes it very easy to make pesto, but I think it's well worth making by hand. The slowed-down process of hand-grinding the leaves in a mortar lets you see the extraordinary transformation that takes place as garlic, salt, nuts, and basil are worked into a paste, all the while inhaling magnificent scents. If you have a choice at your market, use small Genovese (Italian) basil leaves. Makes about 1 cup

---

1 or 2 plump cloves garlic

¹/₂ teaspoon sea salt

3 tablespoons pine nuts

3 cups loosely packed basil leaves, stems removed, leaves washed and dried

¹/₂ cup freshly grated parmesan, preferably Parmigiano-Reggiano

2 to 3 tablespoons grated Pecorino Romano

2 tablespoons soft butter, optional

¹/₂ cup olive oil

By Hand: Smash the garlic with the salt and pine nuts to break them up, then add the basil leaves a handful at a time. (If you're impatient, you can speed things up by tearing the leaves into smaller pieces first.) Grind them, using a circular motion, until you have a fairly fine paste with very small flecks of leaves. Briefly work in the cheeses and butter, then stir in the olive oil. Taste for salt.

In a Food Processor: Use the same ingredients but in the following order: Process the garlic, salt, and pine nuts until fairly finely chopped, then add the basil and olive oil. When smooth, add the cheeses and butter and process just to combine.

Tomato-Basil Pesto

Use this red pesto to season soups, spread on grilled cheese sandwiches, or drop into a ramekin of baked eggs. Makes about ³/₄ cup

---

2 cloves garlic, coarsely chopped

¹/₂ teaspoon sea salt

1¹/₂ cups loosely packed basil leaves

¹/₃ cup olive oil

¹/₂ cup freshly grated parmesan

2 to 3 tablespoons tomato paste

Pound the garlic with the salt in a mortar until smooth. Chop the basil in a food processor and gradually add the oil to make a coarse puree. Remove and stir into the garlic with the cheese and tomato paste. Taste for salt.

Garlic Scape Pesto or Puree

This should wake up anything stodgy with its garlic essence. Pasta, yes, but it's also good spread on crostini or crackers, or spooned on hard-cooked eggs. Makes about 1 cup Ⓥ

Enough tender garlic scapes, minus their buds, to make a cup, chopped (about 10)

¹/₃ cup pine nuts or other favored nut, such as hazelnuts or almonds

¹/₂ teaspoon sea salt

¹/₂ cup olive oil

¹/₄ to ¹/₂ cup finely grated parmesan cheese, optional

Freshly milled pepper, optional

Put the scapes and nuts in a food processor with the salt and pulse until they form a rough puree. With the machine running, add the oil, then the cheese and pulse a few more times. Taste for salt and season with pepper.

Basil Puree

Since cheese is usually included on pizza, I drizzle this puree instead of pesto over the pizza when it comes out of the oven.
Makes about 3/4 cup Ⓥ

3 cloves garlic
1/2 cup olive oil
2 cups basil leaves
1/2 teaspoon sea salt

Pulverize the garlic with the oil in a blender, then add the basil by handfuls, followed by the salt. Puree until smooth. The mixture should be thin enough that you can easily spread it over the dough or drizzle it over the top.

Mayonnaise

Bottled mayonnaise is a serviceable item, but homemade mayonnaise is subtle and fine with a velvety texture, neither excessively salty nor sweet. It serves as the foundation for the many sauces that complement vegetables so well. Mayonnaise is to be enjoyed by the spoonful, not the cupful, and a little bit goes a long way.

Mayonnaise is simple to make, but if something does go wrong and your sauce breaks or disintegrates into a loose, oily mass, it can be fixed.

1. Have ingredients at room temperature. If the egg is cold from the refrigerator, rinse a bowl with hot water, dry it thoroughly, and add the yolk. Or cover the whole egg with hot water for 5 minutes before beginning.

2. Set your bowl on a damp, twisted, curled-up towel to help hold it in place.

3. Begin whisking the oil into the yolk drop by drop. Once the mayonnaise has begun to emulsify or thicken, after a third or more of the oil has been added, add the rest of the oil in a thin, steady stream.

4. The finished mayonnaise will be thick, which is fine for a sandwich, but it can be thinned to saucelike consistency by stirring in near-boiling water or additional lemon juice. Use a thinner mayonnaise as a dressing to coat or drizzle over vegetables.

5. If your mayonnaise breaks, don't despair. Instead, whisk in 1 or 2 teaspoons boiling water. If that doesn't bring it back, start over with a new yolk and use the broken sauce as the oil, whisking it in drop by drop until you have a new emulsion.

Basic Mayonnaise

Makes about 1 cup

1 large egg yolk, at room temperature
1 teaspoon Dijon mustard
Sea salt
2 to 3 teaspoons fresh lemon juice, white wine vinegar, or tarragon vinegar
3/4 cup mild olive oil
2 tablespoons fruity olive oil

By Hand: Rinse a 4-cup bowl with hot water. Dry it and set it on the counter with a towel wrapped tightly around the base to keep it stable. Add the egg yolk and whisk it vigorously back and forth until thick and sticky, then stir in the mustard, a pinch of salt, and the lemon juice. Whisk in the mild olive oil by droplets until the egg and oil have begun to thicken (when one-third to one-half the oil has been added), then whisk in the remaining mild olive oil in a thin, steady stream. Add the fruity olive oil at the end and season to taste with additional salt and a little lemon juice. To thin, whisk in lemon juice or vinegar by drops or 1 to 2 tablespoons boiling water as needed. Cover and refrigerate until ready to use.

In a Blender: Put a *whole* egg, the mustard, and a pinch of salt in the blender with ¼ cup oil and turn it on. Add the remaining oil in a steady steam until all is incorporated, then add the lemon juice. Thin with additional lemon juice or boiling water.

In a Food Processor: Use a whole egg, two yolks, or a whole egg plus a yolk. Plan to use an additional ½ cup oil and adjust the other ingredients accordingly, to taste. Start with the egg, mustard, and a pinch of salt and, with the machine running, add the oil in a steady stream until all is incorporated. Add the lemon juice and thin with additional fresh lemon juice or boiling water.

Mayonnaise with Cooked Yolks: As a precaution against the possibility of using salmonella-contaminated eggs, cooked yolks can be used in place of raw ones, though the texture will be a little coarser and heavier. Start with 2 hard-cooked or soft-cooked (3-minute) yolks, then proceed as described, either by hand or by food processor.

Chipotle Mayonnaise: For a smoky-hot mayonnaise, stir in a little pureed canned chipotle chile. Add chopped green onions, garlic, and cilantro, if desired, to taste.

Fresh Dill and Lemon Mayonnaise: Add ¼ cup chopped dill, 1 teaspoon finely grated lemon zest, and lemon juice to taste to 1 cup mayonnaise. Good with eggs and most vegetables, especially new potatoes.

Garlic Mayonnaise (Aïoli): Aïoli, a garlic-infused Provençal sauce, can be served confidently with any vegetable but especially green beans, potatoes, chickpeas, asparagus, cooked carrots, fennel, and cauliflower. It's heavenly with grilled foods, in a sandwich, or spooned into a soup or pasta. I suggest this sauce more than any other throughout this book. Coarsely chop 4 to 6 firm, unblemished cloves garlic. Put them in a mortar, add a pinch of salt, and pound until a smooth paste forms, which will happen quite quickly. (If you don't have a mortar, chop the garlic and salt together until smooth.) Stir it into the mayonnaise, add lemon juice to taste, then thin with hot water or leave it thick, depending on its intended use.

Herb Mayonnaise: Select ⅓ to ¼ cup herb leaves—basil, chervil, parsley, lovage, marjoram, chives, and tarragon, singly or in combination. If using lovage, use just 1 teaspoon, for it's very robust. Dip the leaves into boiling salted water for 5 seconds, then rinse under cold water and pat dry. Finely chop the leaves and stir into the mayonnaise. Use with potatoes, carrots, green beans, on vegetable salads and sandwiches.

Orange Mayonnaise: Stir 1 teaspoon finely grated orange zest into 1 cup mayonnaise and thin with fresh orange juice to the desired consistency. Use with asparagus, broccoli, fennel, and cauliflower.

Red Chile Mayonnaise: Stir 1 or more teaspoons ground red chile, to taste, into 1 cup mayonnaise. (Remember, the heat will increase as it sits.)

Roasted Red Pepper Mayonnaise: Roast, peel, and finely dice or puree 1 large red bell pepper. Stir it into the Garlic Mayonnaise made with just 2 cloves garlic and season with several pinches cayenne plus lemon juice to taste. Use this salmon-pink sauce to bind layers of vegetable frittatas or to serve with the Saffron Noodle Cake (page 410).

Saffron Mayonnaise: Saffron infuses mayonnaise with its yellow-orange color and intriguing flavor. Grind 2 large pinches saffron threads in a small mortar, then add 1 tablespoon boiling water. Steep for several minutes to release the color, then stir it into the mayonnaise. Serve with grilled potatoes, roasted peppers, tomatoes, fried or grilled fennel, chickpeas—in fact, with most Mediterranean vegetables and legumes

Smoky Mayonnaise: Season your mayonnaise to taste with smoked paprika.

Tarragon Mayonnaise with Capers: To 1 cup mayonnaise, stir in 2 tablespoons each chopped tarragon, snipped chives, and chopped parsley; 1 tablespoon chopped capers; and 2 tablespoons finely chopped cornichon pickle. Serve with cucumbers, as a dip for celery hearts, or with fried vegetables.

Tofu "Mayonnaise"

This ersatz mayonnaise serves as a substitute for egg-based sauces. It can be seasoned as in the variations suggested for egg-based mayonnaise but more highly to compensate for the blandness of tofu. Thinned with additional water or olive oil, it can be used as a salad dressing for vegetables.

Makes about 1 cup Ⓥ

4 ounces soft silken tofu

1/3 cup plus 2 tablespoons olive oil

2 tablespoons fresh lemon juice

2 teaspoons Dijon mustard

3 green onions, white parts only, thinly sliced

1 teaspoon grated lemon zest

Sea salt and freshly milled white pepper

Puree the tofu, 1/4 cup water, olive oil, lemon juice, and mustard in a blender or food processor until smooth. Add the onions and lemon zest and season with sea salt and pepper to taste.

Tofu Garlic "Mayonnaise": Pound 4 to 6 cloves garlic with 1/2 teaspoon salt in a mortar until it becomes a paste. Add the paste once the sauce is emulsified. Ⓥ

Tomato Sauces

Their acidity, bright color, ease of preparation, and affinity for so many dishes account for the popularity of tomato sauces. They're often just the thing to provide a needed punch of flavor or color to set off a dish. Tomato sauces are basically of two kinds—briefly cooked to preserve the fresh, bright flavor of the tomato, or long simmered with many ingredients. Whether you're making a simple basic sauce or a chunky one, fresh or canned tomatoes can be used.

USING CANNED TOMATOES: Since truly flavorful tomatoes enjoy such a short season, canned tomatoes are usually the better choice for sauces. Several brands are quite good, and the best ones aren't necessarily Italian or expensive. I like canned organic tomatoes by Eden Foods, but I also use the boxed Italian Pomì tomatoes. When choosing canned tomatoes, read the label to see what else, if anything, is with them. Cayenne, onions, and peppers may add a dimension to your sauce that you don't really want. You can choose from whole canned tomatoes, crushed tomatoes in puree, and diced tomatoes in water. If you rely on canned tomatoes, try several brands to see which one you prefer and how they differ.

USING FRESH TOMATOES: The delight of a sauce made with fresh tomatoes is its summery essence, but there's no point in using fresh fruits if they aren't perfect to start with—ripe and perfumed. The ideal tomato for sauce is one with little juice, which allows the watery juices to evaporate rapidly. Thick-fleshed, not-very-juicy Romas, San Marzanos, and other plum-shaped varieties are sauce tomatoes. You certainly can use juicier varieties, but they will require more time to cook down. Longer cooking benefits tart tomatoes or mixtures of many ingredients.

USING A FOOD MILL: A food mill is a great timesaver for making tomato sauces. Just wash, chop, and cook the tomatoes—the skins and seeds will be removed quickly by this simple mechanical device. If you want a chunky sauce, you'll have to peel, seed, and chop the tomatoes since the food mill will effectively puree them.

CORRECTING FOR LACKLUSTER FLAVOR: If your sauce seems a little weak, you can strengthen it by adding a tablespoon or two of tomato paste or puree.

ACIDITY: Since all tomatoes have some acidity, cook them in a pot that won't react, such as enamel-lined cast iron, glass, or stainless steel. Excessive acidity or tartness can be corrected with the addition of a little sugar. Yellow tomatoes can be used for sauce, but since they tend to be very low in acid and are usually quite juicy, they don't always provide the desired tartness and need more time on the stove to thicken. You may want to add a little vinegar or lemon at the end.

Fresh Tomato Sauce

This quick little sauce is one I make on a regular basis during the brief time good tomatoes are in the market. It takes about 20 minutes from start to finish, depending on the type of tomatoes used. This sauce offers simple, pure tomato flavor. It's delicious tossed with linguine. Makes about 2½ cups Ⓥ

- 3 pounds ripe tomatoes, quartered
- 3 tablespoons chopped basil, or 1 tablespoon chopped marjoram
- Sea salt and freshly milled pepper
- 2 tablespoons olive oil or butter

Put the tomatoes in a heavy pan with the basil. Cover and cook over medium-high heat. The tomatoes should yield their juices right away, but keep an eye on the pot to make sure the pan isn't dry. You don't want the tomatoes to scorch. When the tomatoes have broken down after about 10 minutes, pass them through a food mill. If you want the final sauce to be thicker, return it to the pot and cook over low heat, stirring frequently, until it's as thick as you want. Season with salt and pepper to taste and stir in the oil.

Freezing Tomato Sauce

Making sauce to freeze for the winter isn't a big production—or a time-consuming one. When tomatoes are in season, I make the Fresh Tomato Sauce using 4 to 5 pounds tomatoes or whatever is convenient. When it's cool, I ladle it into plastic freezer bags in 1- or 2-cup portions and lay the bags on the freezer floor until they harden. This makes slim packages that are easy to store upright, taking little space. When you warm the sauce, you can season it with crushed garlic or an herb that goes with the dish you're making.

Tomato Sauce Concassé

Here the finished sauce retains the texture of diced tomatoes because it's not run through a food mill.
Makes about 2 cups Ⓥ

- 2½ to 3 pounds ripe tomatoes
- 2 tablespoons olive oil or butter
- 1 small white onion, finely diced
- Sea salt and freshly milled pepper

Make an X on the bottom of each tomato with a small, sharp knife. Plunge them into a pot of boiling water until the skins roll back, 10 to 15 seconds, then peel, seed, and finely chop them. Heat the oil in a wide skillet over medium heat, add the onion, and cook until wilted, about 5 minutes. Add the chopped tomatoes and simmer, stirring occasionally, until the watery juices have cooked off, 15 to 30 minutes, depending on the tomatoes. Season with salt and pepper to taste.

Tomato Sauce with Herbs: Add 2 tablespoons chopped basil or parsley or 2 teaspoons chopped marjoram or rosemary to the onions. Ⓥ

Tomato Sauce with Pepper Flakes: Sauté the onion in olive oil with ½ teaspoon red pepper flakes, then add the tomatoes and cook as described. Ⓥ

Tomato Sauce with Cream: Stir in ¼ cup cream or crème fraîche at the end.

Cherry Tomato Sauce

Cherry and other "fruit tomatoes" often have better flavor than their larger counterparts, particularly early in the season. Try using different varieties, including the black ones and the yellow-orange Sun Golds. Makes about 1 cup (V)

1 pint cherry tomatoes, stems removed

Sea salt and freshly milled pepper

Pinch sugar

2 teaspoons olive oil or butter

1 teaspoon finely chopped herb—tarragon, basil, lovage, rosemary, or marjoram

Put the tomatoes in a saucepan or skillet with $1/3$ cup water over high heat. Cover and cook until the tomatoes begin to split, adding water in small amounts if the pan becomes dry. When most of the tomatoes have burst open, pass them through a food mill or push through a sieve to remove the skins and seeds. Season with salt, pepper, and sugar to correct the acidity if necessary. Stir in the oil and the herb.

Oven-Roasted Tomato Sauce

This is a good treatment both for tomatoes at their peak and for those that aren't quite at perfection, as roasting concentrates their flavor. The oven temperature isn't really crucial, so take advantage of an oven that's being used for something else. Makes about 2 cups (V)

$2^1/2$ pounds Roma tomatoes, halved lengthwise

1 onion, thinly sliced

4 thyme or marjoram sprigs

2 to 3 tablespoons olive oil

Sea salt and freshly milled pepper

Preheat the oven to 375°F. Put the tomatoes in a single layer in a baking pan with the onion and thyme, drizzle the oil over all, and season with salt and pepper. Bake until they're soft, shriveled, and falling apart, 45 minutes to 1 hour. Remove the thyme sprigs and puree or pass through a food mill. Taste for salt and season with pepper.

Grilled Tomato Sauce

Grilling or broiling tomatoes brings out flavor by caramelizing their sugary juices. Makes about 2 cups (V)

2 pounds ripe tomatoes

3 tablespoons olive oil

$1/2$ small onion, finely diced

Sea salt and freshly milled pepper

Pinch sugar, if needed

Rub the tomatoes lightly with oil, then grill, broil, or sear them in a heavy skillet, turning them frequently, until blistered and charred. Puree them, skin and all. Don't worry about the black flecks. Meanwhile, heat the remaining oil in a skillet over medium heat, add the onion, and sauté until translucent, about 5 minutes. Add the pureed tomatoes and cook, stirring frequently, until the sauce has thickened. Season with salt, a little pepper, and sugar to correct the acidity if needed.

Grilled Tomato Sauce with Basil Puree: Puree 1 cup packed basil leaves with 2 cloves garlic, 3 tablespoons olive oil, and water if needed. Add to the grilled tomato sauce and season with a little balsamic or red wine vinegar to taste. Use warm or at room temperature with pasta and as a sauce for grilled vegetables. (This makes a wonderful base for a vinaigrette.) Makes $2^1/2$ cups. (V)

Quick Canned Tomato Sauce

Tomatoes are in season for such a brief moment that I often end up using canned tomatoes for sauce. This one can't be surpassed for ease and is perfectly fine when made with good-quality tomatoes. Makes about 3 cups (V)

1 (28-ounce) can diced tomatoes, drained, or crushed tomatoes in puree

1/4 cup finely diced onion

1 clove garlic, peeled and smashed

2 to 4 tablespoons olive oil

Sea salt and freshly milled pepper

Combine the tomatoes, onion, garlic, and oil in a wide skillet. Simmer for 20 to 30 minutes, stirring occasionally, until the excess water is cooked off and the oil has separated. Season with salt and pepper to taste. The tomatoes will have broken down, but if you want a smooth sauce, pass it through a food mill or quickly puree it in a blender.

Variations: Use any of those suggested on page 54 for Tomato Sauce Concassé.

Red Wine Tomato Sauce

Use this as seasoning as well as a sauce. Stir a spoonful into hearty grain dishes, serve with Herb-Crusted Tofu (page 530) and Lentil and Caramelized Onion Croquettes (page 271), or toss with pasta and chickpeas for a substantial cold-weather pasta. Makes about 4 cups (V)

2 tablespoons olive oil

2 small onions, finely minced or grated

2 small bay leaves

6 thyme sprigs or 1/2 teaspoon dried

1 teaspoon dried oregano

1 teaspoon dried savory

Pinch red pepper flakes

3 large cloves garlic, minced

1 cup dry red wine

1 (28-ounce) can crushed tomatoes in puree

1/2 teaspoon sea salt

Freshly milled pepper

Heat the oil in a wide skillet. Add the onions, herbs, and pepper flakes and cook over medium heat, stirring frequently, for 15 minutes. Add the garlic during the last few minutes. Raise the heat, add the wine and 1/2 cup water, and simmer until reduced by half, 12 to 15 minutes. Add the tomatoes and salt. Simmer until the sauce has thickened, about 35 minutes. Taste for salt and season with pepper.

With Olives: This sauce is good with sturdy pasta, such as rigatoni, and grilled or fried polenta. Pit and finely chop 1/3 cup kalamata, niçoise, or oil-cured olives. Add them for the last 20 minutes of the cooking along with 1 tablespoon capers and 2 tablespoons chopped parsley. (V)

Tomato Sauce with Dried Mushrooms

Longer simmering builds a complex and mellow flavor in this sauce. Makes about 2 1/2 cups (V)

1/2 to 1 ounce dried porcini

2 tablespoons olive oil

1 small onion, finely diced

1 large clove garlic, sliced

4 thyme sprigs or 1/4 teaspoon dried

1 bay leaf

2 teaspoons chopped rosemary or 1/2 teaspoon dried

Sea salt and freshly milled pepper

1 (28-ounce) can crushed tomatoes in puree

2 tablespoons tomato paste

Balsamic or red wine vinegar

Cover the mushrooms with 1 cup warm water, let stand for 30 minutes, then squeeze dry and chop. Strain the soaking water and reserve. Warm the oil in a wide skillet with the onion, garlic, and herbs. Cook over medium-high heat for about 5 minutes, stirring frequently. Add the mushrooms and cook for 5 minutes more. Season with salt and pepper. Pour in half the mushroom-soaking liquid and cook until completely reduced, scraping the pan to work in any caramelized bits of onion. Add the tomatoes, tomato paste, and remaining mushroom liquid. Lower the heat and simmer for 30 minutes, then add 1/2 teaspoon or more vinegar to taste.

Yogurt Sauces

Smooth and creamy with a pleasant edge of tartness, yogurt-based sauces can be used as dips or cooling accompaniments to a wide range of foods: fresh or grilled vegetables—most notably cucumbers, beets, tomatoes, fennel, and carrots; falafel, grain-based dishes, chickpeas, and lentils; and as a condiment for curries and vegetable fritters.

The success of any yogurt sauce depends on the quality of the yogurt. Use plain yogurt that has not been stabilized with gums and gelatins for a sweet natural flavor with a mild tang. I recommend using whole-milk or low-fat yogurt—both taste so much better than most nonfat yogurts. If you can find goat's milk yogurt, try it mixed with cow's milk yogurt or a little sour cream. Of course, Greek yogurt is already thick and it needn't be drained.

Another crucial element is the treatment of the garlic, an essential ingredient in most of these sauces. Pounding it in a mortar with a little salt until you have a mushy paste results in something very different from garlic that's minced, whether by hand or in the food processor. And although it seems easier to reach for the garlic press, pounded garlic gains a subtle sweetness, a trade-off that's worth the small extra effort.

These sauces keep well for 4 or 5 days when refrigerated. As they stand, their flavors mellow and deepen. Vegan versions can be made using soy yogurt.

Yogurt Tahini Sauce

The tahini gives this sauce a rich, round taste that cuts the sharpness of the yogurt. Use in pita sandwiches, on grilled vegetables, and with chickpeas and other legumes. Makes 1¹/₂ cups

- 1 clove garlic
- ¹/₄ teaspoon sea salt
- 2 tablespoons tahini
- 1 cup yogurt
- 2 tablespoons fresh lemon juice and grated zest of lemon, or more to taste

Pound the garlic and ¹/₄ teaspoon salt together in a mortar to make a mushy paste. Stir in the tahini, then gradually stir in the yogurt and lemon zest. Season with lemon juice.

Yogurt Sauce with Cayenne and Dill

When my friend Clifford Wright made this sauce for me, I couldn't stop eating it. You'll see this endlessly enjoyable sauce suggested throughout the book. These many years later, it's still a favorite. Makes 1¹/₂ cups

- 1 cup yogurt
- ¹/₂ cup thick yogurt or sour cream
- 1 large clove garlic
- ¹/₂ teaspoon sea salt
- 2 teaspoons or more chopped dill
- ³/₄ teaspoon cayenne or hot paprika

Whisk the yogurts together. In a mortar, mash the garlic to a paste with the salt; measure 1 teaspoon, then add it to the yogurt with the dill and cayenne. If you have time, refrigerate for 1 hour before serving.

Yogurt Sauce with Cucumbers, Cumin, and Mint

Serve this cooling sauce with grains, vegetable fritters, and bean croquettes. Makes about 1¹/₂ cups

1 cup yogurt
¹/₂ cup thick yogurt
1 small cucumber, peeled if waxed
2 green onions, including a few inches of the greens, minced
2 tablespoons finely chopped mint
¹/₄ to ¹/₂ teaspoon ground cumin
1 tablespoon olive oil
¹/₄ teaspoon sea salt, or to taste
¹/₄ teaspoon freshly milled white pepper, or to taste

Stir all the ingredients together in a bowl and let stand at least 15 minutes for the flavors to develop. Taste, and add more salt, if needed.

Green Yogurt Sauce with Pepper Flakes and Sumac

Green with a generous amount of finely chopped herbs, this sauce pairs well with countless foods—beets, warm or chilled lentils, steamed carrots, hot or cold potatoes, braised leeks, and grains. It's worth having a mass of dill in your garden for this go-everywhere sauce. Makes about 1 cup

1 small clove garlic
¹/₄ teaspoon sea salt
³/₄ cup yogurt
¹/₄ cup sour cream
¹/₂ cup finely chopped dill, basil, and cilantro, mixed
Best olive oil
Red pepper flakes and sumac, to finish

Pound the garlic in a mortar with the salt until it has broken into a puree. Stir in the yogurt, sour cream, and dill. Taste for salt. Puree the sauce if you wish it to be a uniform pale green, or leave it flecked. Turn it into a bowl, and swirl over olive oil and sprinkle with red pepper flakes and a dash of sumac. Serve chilled.

Raita with Cucumber and Spices

This classic, cooling accompaniment to spicy or rich Indian dishes also can be used as a dip for vegetables—it makes a fragrant sauce for baked potatoes, sweet potatoes, and roasted shredded eggplant. Makes about 3 cups

1 jalapeño chile, seeded and coarsely chopped
3 cloves garlic, coarsely chopped
1 tablespoon chopped cilantro stems
1 tablespoon grated ginger
Sea salt
2 cups yogurt
1 cucumber, peeled if waxed, and grated
¹/₂ cup grated carrot
2 tablespoons ghee
1 tablespoon coriander seeds
1 tablespoon black mustard seeds
1 tablespoon cumin seeds
Juice of 1 lime, or to taste

Pound or puree the chile, garlic, cilantro, and ginger with a few pinches salt to make a fairly smooth paste, then stir it into the yogurt with the cucumber and carrot. Heat the ghee in a small pan over medium-high heat. Add the coriander, mustard, and cumin seeds and sizzle until the mustard seeds begin to turn gray, after a minute or so. Swirl this into the yogurt mixture. Add lime juice to taste, starting with ¹/₂ lime. Let stand for 1 hour or so for the flavors to develop.

Sauces Based on Nuts and Seeds

Nuts and seeds are luxurious foods because of their richness and inherent goodness, so it follows that sauces based on nuts and seeds make relatively plain foods extremely satisfying. Peanut sauces grace noodles; Middle Eastern tarator sauces based on sesame and other nuts nap all kinds of grains, legumes, and vegetables; and hazelnuts and almonds form the background of the glorious Romesco Sauce (page 62). Depending on the stability of the other ingredients, most nut-based sauces keep well for at least several days.

Tahini with Lemon and Garlic

Drizzle this silky Lebanese sauce over braised greens, chickpeas, lentils, and falafel or serve as a dip or with pita bread and sliced cucumbers. Makes about 1/2 cup (V)

1 plump clove garlic, coarsely chopped
1/4 teaspoon sea salt
1/2 cup tahini
Juice of 1 large lemon

Pound the garlic to a paste with the salt in a mortar, then stir it into the tahini. Begin stirring in about 1/2 cup water until the sauce is as thin as you want it, then add the lemon juice to taste. Taste for salt and add more if needed.

Tarator Sauce

The particular nut used in tarator (nut) sauces can vary. My favorite is made with pine nuts, which have a haunting but subtle flavor, but walnuts are also good. Excellent on grilled eggplant and other vegetables, lentils, white beans, and grains. Makes about 1 cup (V)

1/2 cup pine nuts, almonds, walnuts, or hazelnuts
1 slice sturdy white bread, crusts removed
1 clove garlic
1/4 teaspoon sea salt
2 tablespoons fresh lemon juice
Finely chopped parsley
Paprika or cayenne

Toast the pine nuts in a small skillet until golden. For other nuts, lightly roast in a moderate oven for 6 to 8 minutes.

Moisten the bread with water and set aside to soak. In a mortar, mash the garlic, salt, and nuts until smooth. Squeeze the bread and add it to the mixture with 1/2 cup water. Work by hand, in a blender, or in a food processor until the sauce is smooth and thin, adding more water if needed. Season with lemon juice and taste for salt. Tarator sauce will thicken as it sits, so you may need to thin it out again just before serving. Pour into a bowl and sprinkle with a little chopped parsley and a dash of paprika. Keeps for 2 or 3 days.

Sesame Sauce with Tofu

The tofu disappears in this sauce, but you can still enjoy its benefits. Makes about 1 cup (V)

4 ounces soft tofu
1/4 cup tahini
1 large clove garlic, coarsely chopped
Juice of 1/2 lemon, plus more to taste
1 teaspoon toasted sesame oil
Sea salt
Chopped parsley, for garnish

Puree the tofu, tahini, garlic, 2 tablespoons lemon juice, and the sesame oil in a blender or food processor, adding just enough water to thin the sauce to the desired consistency. Taste and season with salt and more lemon juice if needed. Serve in a bowl, garnished with the parsley.

Sunflower Seed Sauce

If you haven't tried sunflower butter, do—especially if you adore toasted sunflower seeds. This thin but creamy textured sauce comes together much like a peanut sauce, but with a different emphasis in flavor. You could certainly make it with peanut butter and peanut oil, or with toasted sesame butter and sesame oil. Regardless, try it with seared tofu, tempeh, black rice, rice noodles and where ever you want a silky, garlicky, seed-based sauce. Makes 1 cup Ⓥ

6 tablespoons sunflower seed butter

$^1/_4$ cup rice wine vinegar

3 tablespoons soy sauce

2 tablespoons sugar or maple syrup

$^1/_4$ cup sunflower seed oil

Pinch sea salt

1 large clove garlic, minced

3 tablespoons hot water

$^1/_2$- to 1-inch piece ginger, grated, optional

Combine all the ingredients in a blender or small food processor and puree until smooth. Taste for salt and add more if needed. Optional but good is grated ginger, which you can add to the blender if you like a stronger flavor.

Rich Sesame Sauce or Marinade

Try this scrumptious sauce over grains or grilled vegetables or as a marinade for tofu and tempeh. Makes about 1 cup

2 tablespoons Dijon mustard

3 tablespoons honey

6 tablespoons soy sauce

6 tablespoons light sesame oil

2 tablespoons toasted sesame oil

$^1/_4$ cup sesame seeds, toasted in a small pan until golden

4 to 6 cloves garlic, peeled and smashed

1 teaspoon ground ginger

$^1/_4$ teaspoon freshly milled pepper

Put all the ingredients in a blender and puree until smooth.

Variation with Peanuts: Roast or fry raw peanuts until golden and use $^1/_2$ cup light peanut oil flavored with 2 tablespoons roasted peanut oil.

Savory Cashew Cream

I've long been intrigued by cashew cream because I'm so very fond of cashews. But in fact it ends up being rather bland, although creamy of texture, because the cashews are not roasted or salted and they are soaked until they turn mushy. This results in a rather neutral cream that can be sweetened and used in place of whipped cream, or treated as a savory dip, as is done here. Spread it on toasts or crackers, add a pinch of dukkah to it, or other favored herbs or spices. If you love roasted, salted cashews, don't expect to find their briny lusciousness here. Makes 1 scant cup Ⓥ

1 cup raw, unsalted cashews

2 tablespoons olive oil

1 tablespoon finely chopped cilantro

1 clove garlic

$^1/_4$ teaspoon sea salt or smoked salt

Freshly milled pepper

Smoked paprika, optional if you use smoked salt

Cover the cashews with water and refrigerate overnight. The next day, drain, then put them in a mini-food processor with $^1/_4$ cup water, olive oil, cilantro, garlic, and salt. Pulse until smooth, light, and creamy. You may need to add another tablespoon or two of water. Taste for salt and add more if needed. Scrape into a bowl, season with pepper, and dust with the paprika.

Sweet Cashew Cream: Leave out the savory spices and add vanilla and a sweetener of your choice to make a cashew cream to serve with desserts. Ⓥ

Peanut Sauces

Rich and pungent peanut sauces greatly enhance the simplest foods, such as tofu (sim-mered, fried, or grilled), tempeh, grilled yams, Chinese noodles, brown rice, and spring rolls. These sauces will keep for several days, but the garlic flavor does grow with time.

Quick Peanut Sauce

This is truly quick and definitely good, especially with Golden Tofu (page 525) and brown rice. Makes about ¹/₂ cup ⓥ

- 3 tablespoons unsweetened peanut butter
- 1 to 2 tablespoons rice wine vinegar
- 1 tablespoon chopped cilantro
- 1 plump clove garlic, minced or put through a press
- 2 teaspoons soy sauce or to taste
- 1 teaspoon light brown sugar
- ¹/₂ teaspoon chili oil
- ¹/₄ teaspoon sea salt

Combine all the ingredients except the salt, adding 2 to 4 tablespoons warm water to make it the consistency you wish. Season with the salt, taste, and add more if needed.

Peanut-Tofu Sauce

If you're looking for more ways to eat tofu, try it here. Makes about 1 cup ⓥ

- 1 or 2 cloves garlic, minced or put through a press
- 1 tablespoon chopped shallot or green onion
- ¹/₄ cup unsweetened peanut butter
- 5 ounces soft tofu
- 1 teaspoon Lan Chi Chili Paste with soybean, or 1 serrano chile, minced
- ¹/₂ teaspoon sea salt or tamari to taste

In a food processor or blender, puree all the ingredients with enough water to loosen the mixture. Taste for salt and season as needed.

Peanut Sauce

This is a gingery but light sauce, full of flavor from the roasted peanut oil. Makes ¹/₂ cup or more, if thinned ⓥ

- 5 tablespoons Stock for Stir-Fries, page 235, or water, plus more as needed
- 2 tablespoons unsweetened peanut butter
- 1 hefty clove minced garlic, about 1¹/₂ teaspoons
- 1 teaspoon minced ginger
- 2 teaspoons brown sugar
- 1 tablespoon rice wine vinegar
- 4 teaspoons roasted peanut oil
- 1 teaspoon chili oil
- 2 teaspoons Shao-Hsing wine or sherry

Mix all the ingredients together and let stand for at least 10 minutes for the flavors to meld.

Add extra stock to thin it for dipping, if need be.

Other Sauces

Red wine, red chile, and pureed vegetables comprise sauces that flatter foods such as pasta, enchiladas or posole, egg dishes, and so forth. Certainly many other sauces fail to fit neatly into the categories already mentioned in this chapter, but there are a few stand-alone renegades that I enjoy making regularly on a seasonal basis. Here they are.

Red Chile Sauce

Also known as chile colorado, red chile sauce is mainly dried red chile and water, although different seasonings are added depending on where in the Southwest you are. Make sure you're using ground chile, not chili powder, which includes other ingredients. This smooth, brick-red sauce is served with enchiladas and burritos and used as a flavoring for posole or beans. Makes about 2¹/₂ cups Ⓥ

- 2 tablespoons oil
- 2 tablespoons finely diced onion
- 1 large clove garlic, finely chopped
- 1 teaspoon dried oregano, optional
- 2 tablespoons flour
- ¹/₂ teaspoon ground cumin, optional
- ¹/₂ cup ground red chile
- Sea salt

Heat the oil with the onion, garlic, and oregano in a heavy saucepan. Cook over medium heat until the onion begins to color a little, about 6 minutes. Add the flour and cumin and cook for at least 2 minutes, stirring constantly. The flour will brown slightly. Mix together the chile and 2¹/₂ cups warm water and pour it all at once into the roux, whisking as you do so. Keep stirring until the sauce thickens, then lower the heat and cook, stirring occasionally, for 15 minutes. Season with salt to taste. If it tastes a little harsh, just a few drops of vinegar will soften it.

Romesco Sauce

The combined essences of grilled peppers, tomatoes, chile, and roasted nuts make this Catalan sauce utterly vivid. Serve it with warm chickpeas or large white beans and/or virtually any grilled vegetable. Spread it on garlic-rubbed crostini and cover with sliced green olives and parsley for a delicious appetizer to serve with a glass of sherry. Makes about 1 cup Ⓥ

- 1 slice country-style white bread
- Olive oil, for frying
- ¹/₄ cup almonds, roasted
- ¹/₄ cup hazelnuts, roasted and peeled
- 3 cloves garlic
- 1 to 2 teaspoons ground red chile or red pepper flakes, to taste
- 4 Roma tomatoes
- 1 tablespoon parsley leaves
- Sea salt and freshly milled pepper
- 1 teaspoon sweet paprika
- 1 red bell pepper, roasted
- ¹/₄ cup sherry vinegar
- 1 cup plus 2 tablespoons olive oil

Fry the bread in a little olive oil until golden and crisp. When cool, grind the bread, nuts, garlic, and chile in a food processor. Add everything but the vinegar and oil and process until smooth. With the machine running, gradually pour in the vinegar, then the oil. Taste and make sure the sauce has plenty of piquancy and enough salt.

Fresh Horseradish Sauce

Fresh horseradish root makes the nose tingle. This sauce can be made vegan by using pureed silken tofu in place of the dairy. Serve with vegetable fritters, baked potatoes, cabbage, and beets. Makes about 1 cup Ⓥ

1 (3-inch) chunk horseradish root

1 cup thick yogurt, sour cream, or cream, whipped

2 tablespoons finely snipped chives

1 tablespoon sugar

Sea salt

White wine vinegar

Peel the horseradish, removing any green. Coarsely chop it, then partially puree in a food processor or blender with enough water to loosen the mixture. It should retain some texture—not be a puree. Drain it to get rid of the water, then combine with the yogurt, chives, sugar, a pinch of salt, and a few drops of vinegar.

Mustard-Cilantro Sauce

Because of their assertiveness, mustard-based sauces always complement broccoli and cauliflower and are good with tofu and tempeh, too. Makes about 1/2 cup

1/2 cup sour cream or thick yogurt

1/4 cup Dijon mustard

2 tablespoons fresh lime juice

2 to 3 teaspoons light brown sugar

1/4 cup finely chopped cilantro

Sea salt and freshly milled pepper

Put all the ingredients in a bowl along with 2 tablespoons water and stir until smooth. Cover and let stand for 1 hour or so for the flavors to mellow. Before serving, taste the sauce on the vegetable or tofu and make any adjustments—more tartness, more sweetness—if necessary.

Smoked Chile Salsa

This sauce is based on a bottled Mexican sauce I liked very much but which was full of dubious ingredients that none of us need to ingest. My version is based on canned chipotle chiles, which make it both hot and smoky, and is great splashed on quesadillas, in bean soups, and on eggs. One little can makes about 2 cups of hot sauce, enough to last some people forever and some a very short time. Makes 2 cups Ⓥ

1 (7-ounce) can chipotle chiles in adobo sauce

3 tablespoons tomato paste

1 tablespoon strong red wine vinegar, or balsamic vinegar

2 tablespoons brown sugar, or 4 teaspoons agave nectar

Blend the chiles and 2 cups boiling water together in a food processor or blender until smooth. Add the other ingredients and blend again. Taste and adjust the flavorings as desired. Keep in the refrigerator.

Red Pepper Sauce

Serve this silky sauce with grilled vegetables, roulades, frit-tatas, or pastas or wherever its sweet rightness is called for.
Makes about 2 ¹/₂ cups Ⓥ

- 3 large red bell peppers, roasted and peeled
- 1 tablespoon olive oil
- 1 onion, minced
- 3 tablespoons basil or 1¹/₂ teaspoons dried
- 1 tablespoon chopped marjoram or 1 teaspoon dried
- ¹/₂ teaspoon sea salt
- ¹/₂ cup dry white wine
- ¹/₄ cup tomato puree
- 1 tablespoon tomato paste
- 2 cups water or Basic Vegetable Stock (page 175) made with summer vegetables
- 2 to 3 teaspoons white wine vinegar
- 1 tablespoon butter, optional

Coarsely chop the peeled peppers. Warm the olive oil in a medium skillet with the onion and half the herbs. Add the peppers and salt and cook over medium heat until the onion is soft, about 10 minutes. Add the wine and cook until it's syrupy, then add the tomato puree, paste, and water. Simmer, covered, for 25 minutes. Puree, then pass through a food mill. Season to taste with the vinegar and stir in the butter (it rounds the flavors and gives the sauce a silky sheen). Reheat before serving and stir in the remaining herbs at the last minute.

Warm Goat Cheese Sauce

This couldn't he easier to make, and it makes a glorious finish to roasted root vegetables and summer vegetables. You have a few choices for the liquid—half-and-half, whole milk, or a flavorful vegetable stock. Makes about 1¹/₂ cups

- ³/₄ cup soft goat cheese
- 1 cup half-and-half, whole milk, or Roasted Vegetable Stock, page 177
- 1 clove garlic smashed in a mortar with ¹/₂ teaspoon sea salt
- Freshly milled white pepper
- 2 teaspoons minced rosemary, basil, or thyme

Working directly in a medium skillet, mash the cheese with the liquid and garlic until partially smooth. Just before serving, simmer it over medium heat, stirring to blend and melt the cheese. The longer you cook the sauce, the thicker it will be. (Or you can make it thinner by adding more liquid.) Taste for salt, season with pepper, stir in the herbs, and serve.

Warm Gorgonzola Sauce: Make the sauce using Gorgonzola dolcelatte in place of the goat cheese. Though you can use a stock, I think this tastes much better made with light or heavy cream, and rosemary and thyme are preferable to basil. Try this spooned over a baked potato or stirred into a simple risotto.

Condiments

These foods are hot and spicy, vinegary and acidic, or sweet. In some cases, several intense elements come together in a single bite. Like sauces, condiments enhance other foods, but their flavors tend to be so distilled or concentrated that their place in a meal is more likely to be on the side than on the top of foods. In properly sealed jars, traditional pickles and chutneys keep more or less indefinitely, but the recipes here are for quickly made, more briefly stored varieties that don't involve canning—or the large quantities that canning usually entails. Having a few condiments, pickles, or chutneys at your disposal enables you to make simple, plain foods special while easily expanding your repertoire as a cook.

Pepper Sauce

Pepper sauce—vinegar made hot by pickling hot peppers— is an essential Southern condiment, used for sprinkling over greens or wherever you want the acid nip of the vinegar combined with the bite of pickled peppers.

Makes about 1 cup Ⓥ

---

4 ounces chiles—serrano, cayenne, tabasco, or other small, straight chiles

1 cup white vinegar

Wash the peppers in cold water until clean, then drain in a colander. Drop them into a bottle that has been freshly washed in hot, soapy water and rinsed clean. It should have a narrow neck so that the vinegar can be released in drops. Bring the vinegar to a boil in a small pan, then transfer it to a measuring cup and pour it into the bottle until full. Let it sit, uncapped, until cool. The peppers will absorb some of the vinegar. Add more vinegar to fill the bottle, then cap and set aside in the cupboard. The vinegar will be ready to use in 6 weeks.

Golden Mustard Barbecue Sauce

Friends and barbecue experts Bill and Cheryl Jamison gave me this recipe with grilled or smoked vegetables especially in mind. They write that "this mustard–based sauce, common in South Carolina and Georgia, offers a tangier alternative to the sweet tomato–based barbecue sauces that have become the supermarket standard." Two to three teaspoons brown sugar can be added for those who like it sweet. Makes 2 cups Ⓥ

3/4 cup white vinegar

3/4 cup prepared yellow mustard

1/2 onion, minced

1/4 cup canned crushed tomatoes

2 teaspoons paprika

1 teaspoon smoked paprika

6 cloves garlic, minced

1 1/2 teaspoons sea salt

1/2 teaspoon cayenne

1/2 teaspoon freshly milled black pepper

Mix the ingredients, plus 1/3 cup water, in a saucepan and bring to a simmer. Reduce the heat to low and cook until the onions are tender and the mixture thickens, approximately 15 to 20 minutes. Use the sauce warm or chilled. It keeps, refrigerated, for several weeks.

Harissa

I always like to have a jar of this condiment in the refrigerator ready to use. Here are some ideas: stir it into eggs, mash it with avocado, spread it on toast, use it to season white beans and chickpeas, serve it with couscous, or use it to pick up the seasonings in a tomato- or pepper-based soup. Pounding it in a mortar provides a heady, sensual delight for the cook, but for speed and a smoother sauce you may prefer to use a food processor. Makes about 1 cup Ⓥ

6 dried red New Mexican chiles

4 guajillo chiles

3 plump cloves garlic, coarsely chopped

$1/2$ teaspoon sea salt

1 tablespoon caraway seeds

1 teaspoon coriander seeds

$1/2$ teaspoon cumin seeds

2 tablespoons olive oil, plus extra for storage

Cayenne, optional

Wipe off the chiles with a damp cloth, break off the stems, shake out as many seeds as you can, and pull out any large veins. (If you're sensitive to chiles, wear gloves—these are the hot parts.) Discard any gray or yellowed areas on the skin—they may have a moldy taste. Tear or crumble the chiles into pieces, put them in a bowl, then cover with boiling water and let stand for at least 30 minutes to soften. Drain.

In a Food Processor: Puree the chiles with the garlic, salt, spices, and oil until a smooth paste forms. (Step back! The chile can be potent.) Add a little of the chile soaking water to loosen the mixture, if needed.

By Hand: This can also be done by hand in a mortar with a heavy pestle, but plan to spend some time with it and don't expect your sauce to be perfectly smooth. The chile skins are tough. Pound the garlic to a paste with the salt and spices. Add the chile and keep pounding until you have a smooth paste. Taste for salt and stir in the oil.

Pack into a clean jar, cover the surface with oil, and refrigerate. It will keep for 3 to 4 weeks.

Roasted Pepper and Chile Paste

A much milder version of Tunisia's famous condiment harissa. Makes about $2/3$ cup Ⓥ

2 roasted red peppers

3 cloves garlic, coarsely chopped

$1/2$ teaspoon sea salt

2 tablespoons ground red New Mexican chile

1 teaspoon cumin seed

1 teaspoon coriander seed

1 teaspoon caraway seed

$1/4$ cup olive oil

3 tablespoons lemon juice

Peel and coarsely chop the peppers. Puree the garlic and salt in a food processor or pound with a mortar and pestle. Add the peppers and chile and work them into a paste. Lightly toast the whole spices in a small skillet, then grind them to a powder. Add them to the pepper mixture, then stir in the olive oil and lemon juice. Taste and balance the seasonings to your taste, if needed.

Herb Salts

These aromatic mixtures of toasted seeds and salt bring life to plain foods. The toasted seeds release their aromatic oils and saturate the salt with flavor, making the salt go further and providing a strong flavor accent without adding fat. While they don't go bad, after a week or two they begin to lose their potency.

Use herb salts as dips for crudités and as seasoning for vegetables and grains. Grind them coarsely, leaving bits of seeds, or finely. You can also put whole toasted seeds and salts in a pepper mill and grind them as you use them. Sea salt and kosher salt taste best and seem to cling best to the seeds.

Grinding Tools

The *suribachi* is the Japanese mortar and pestle. It's distinguished by ridges on its ceramic surface that catch the seeds, spices, and salt as they're being ground. This very effective, inexpensive tool can be found at Japanese markets and frequently at natural foods stores.

A mortar and pestle is always an effective tool, but if using one made of ceramic, marble, or stone, the bottom should be slightly rough to catch the ingredients so that they don't fly away.

The electric coffee or spice mill cuts rather than pounds the seeds and spices. It works best if you avoid making your herb salt too fine. Designate the mill for spices only. Coffee will pick up any residual flavors, and there always are some.

Gomashio

Gomashio, *a Japanese condiment, is delicious over rice and other grains, including hot breakfast cereals like oatmeal, corn meal, and rice cream.* Makes about 1/3 cup Ⓥ

1/3 cup white or black sesame seeds or a mixture
2 teaspoons sea salt or kosher salt

Toast the sesame seeds in a heavy skillet over medium heat until fragrant and plump, about 3 minutes. Grind them in a *suribachi* or in a small spice grinder. Leave plenty of texture; it shouldn't be a powder. Add the salt to the seeds, then set aside to cool.

Toasted Nori with Sesame Seeds

Use just as you would gomashio. *Mix it with leftover white or brown rice and form it into rice balls for a bag lunch item.* Makes about 1/2 cup Ⓥ

2 sheets nori (Japanese seaweed)
1/2 cup white sesame seeds
2 teaspoons sea salt or kosher salt
1 teaspoon red pepper flakes

Toast the nori by passing each sheet repeatedly over a hot burner until it becomes crisp and the color dulls. Put the sheets together and, using scissors, slice them into thin strips, then into small squares. Toast the seeds and salt in a dry skillet over medium heat until the seeds begin to color, then grind them just enough for the salt to adhere. Combine with the nori and pepper flakes. Cool, then store in a covered jar so that they'll stay crisp.

Indian Salt with Mixed Spices

In her classic World of the East, *Madhur Jaffrey suggests this combination in what she calls a "dry dip." It has a gutsy flavor and is indeed a good dip for vegetables.*

Makes about ¹/₂ cup ⓥ

- 3 tablespoons sesame seeds
- 2 tablespoons coriander seeds
- 1 tablespoon cumin seeds
- 2 tablespoons sea salt
- ¹/₄ teaspoon cayenne or freshly milled black pepper

Toast the seeds in a dry skillet over medium heat until fragrant. Let them cool briefly on a plate, then grind with the salt and cayenne to make a fine or coarse dipping salt.

SHICHIMI TOGARASHI

This is a Japanese seasoning mix consisting of chile, peppers, sesame, seaweed, citrus and other ingredients—seven in all. (*Shichimi* means "seven"; the *togarashi* part means "chile" or "pepper.") If you look at recipes or ingredient lists on jars, you'll find no end of variations. Like many condiments, togarashi bears the personal stamp of the maker, her preference for one ingredient over another. It can be very hot, or it can have more—or less—citrusy notes from yuzu or dried orange peel. It's delicious on all kinds of foods, from avocados to plain rice to a winter squash soup. You can find it in Asian markets or online. There are other togarashi powders too—including one that consists only of chile—so look carefully and read the labels.

Dukkah

The delicious Egyptian dry condiment of seeds, nuts and spice is eaten on bread dipped in olive oil, but so many other ways, too. Use it on roasted vegetables, like winter squash, or to give texture and flavor to a carrot puree, or with sweet potatoes. I mix it with olive oil and spoon it over the Savory Millet Grit Timbales on page 471, or toss fried chickpeas with dukkah, or season a thick cashew cream with it. Dukkah can be made with a number of ingredients, not just those given. I'm partial to sumac and dried lemon peel, but other ingredients you might include are cinnamon, caraway, turmeric, cloves, pepper flakes, and nigella seeds. Makes about 1¹/₂ cups ⓥ

- 1 cup hazelnuts, almonds, pistachios, or a mixture
- ¹/₂ cup sesame seeds
- ¹/₄ cup coriander seeds
- 2 tablespoons cumin seeds
- 1 teaspoon fennel seeds
- Several pinches dried thyme
- 1 teaspoon finely chopped dried lemon peel, optional
- ¹/₂ teaspoon sea salt
- Freshly milled pepper or ¹/₄ teaspoon red pepper flakes

Heat the oven to 350°F.

Toast the nuts until they smell fragrant, about 10 minutes. If using hazelnuts, rub them in a towel to remove any of the skins that have loosened, but not obsessively. Some skin is fine. Let them cool and turn off the oven.

Toast the sesame seeds in a dry pan set over medium heat until lightly colored and fragrant, 2 to 3 minutes. Tip them onto a plate and let them cool. Next toast the coriander, cumin, and fennel seeds until fragrant, about 2 minutes. Tip them onto the plate to cool.

Chop the nuts or pulse them in a food processor with the thyme and lemon peel, but leave a little texture rather than make a powder. Next finely chop the toasted seeds with the thyme and salt, again, leaving enough texture that they crunch. Season with several twists from the pepper mill, or the red pepper flakes.

To eat, dip bread in olive oil, then in the dukkah, or mix the dukkah with oil and spread it over bread.

Szechuan Pepper Salt

Sprinkle this Chinese condiment on raw cabbage, asparagus, or Asian pear–apples, but especially on corn and eggs, where it really shines. Makes about $^1/_3$ cup Ⓥ

2 tablespoons Szechuan peppercorns

1 teaspoon black peppercorns

$^1/_4$ cup sea salt or kosher salt

Toast the peppercorns and salt in a heavy skillet over medium heat until the peppercorns are fragrant and the salt has begun to lose its whiteness, about 4 minutes. Grind or pound in a mortar to break up the corns, then pass through a sieve to separate out the hulls. The black pepper gives spice and warmth to the perfumed Szechuan peppercorns.

Relishes

As their name implies, relishes lend a pleasing, zestful element to a plate of food. They don't last quite as long nor are they as vinegary as pickles, although they can be canned and are sometimes lightly pickled. I think of relishes as fresh and spritely condiments, whether they're raw or cooked. Some relishes are at their peak for but a few hours while others can linger for weeks and even months in the refrigerator, to be brought out at a moment's notice.

Tomato-Onion Relish

Spoon over grilled vegetables, grilled polenta, or Garlic-Rubbed Crostini (page 24). Refrigerating the onion reduces its pungency and makes it crisp and cold. Best used within the day. Makes about 1 cup Ⓥ

1 small red onion, finely and neatly diced

2 ripe tomatoes, 1 red and 1 yellow

1 tablespoon chopped parsley or basil

Several pinches red pepper flakes, or 1 serrano chile, minced, optional

Vinegar

Sea salt and freshly milled pepper

Put the onion in a bowl with cold water and a few ice cubes to cover. Refrigerate for at least 30 minutes, then drain. Meanwhile, halve, seed, and finely dice the tomatoes, reserving the inner core for another use. Combine the onion, tomatoes, parsley, and red pepper flakes in a bowl. Season to taste with a vinegar that you like—sherry, balsamic, apple cider—a pinch of salt, and pepper. Add a few tablespoons cold water for a more saucelike texture.

Corn Relish

Try this with black bean cakes or spooned over Savory Corn Waffles (page 563). Best used within the day. Makes about 2 cups Ⓥ

Kernels from 2 ears corn, about 1$^1/_2$ cups

1 Roma tomato, seeded and diced

$^1/_4$ small red or white onion, finely diced

1 or 2 serrano chiles to taste, finely chopped

Lime juice

Sea salt

1 tablespoon chopped cilantro

Blanch the corn in a small pot of boiling water for about 30 seconds; drain and shake dry. Toss the corn with the tomato, onion, and chile. Add lime juice to taste, season with salt, and stir in the cilantro. Cover and refrigerate for 30 minutes or until ready to use.

With Peppers: Add 6 tablespoons finely diced bell peppers, Corno di Toro peppers, or other sweet peppers to the salsa and stir in 1 tablespoon olive or sunflower seed oil. Ⓥ

With Black Beans: Add $1/2$ cup cooked but fairly firm black beans to the salsa, with another chile and extra lime juice to taste. Chopped basil and marjoram would both be good in this relish. (V)

Cranberry, Orange, and Tangerine Relish

Today dried cranberries are popular, but we'll probably always persist in including fresh cranberries at our Thanksgiving meal, whether jellied, ground, or made into this sweet-tart relish. Make this several days ahead of time to allow the flavors to ripen. Makes about $2^1/2$ cups (V)

4 cups cranberries, about 1 pound

1 navel orange

2 tangerines

1 cup sugar

$1/8$ teaspoon ground cloves

$1/2$ to 1 cup walnuts or pecans

Sort through the cranberries and discard any soft, squishy ones; rinse the rest. Score the orange into 4 sections, remove the peel, then slice off the thin white membrane with a knife. Halve the tangerines across the equator and remove the seeds.

Put the orange peels and tangerines in a food processor a coarsely chop them into small pieces, about as big as a dime. Add the cranberries and nuts and pulse just enough to make a coarse relish. It shouldn't be a puree. Transfer to a clean bowl, stir in the sugar and the cloves, then cover and refrigerate overnight or longer, before serving.

Pepper Relish with Anise Seeds

A great side dish or topping for crostini, this pepper mélange can also find its way into frittatas, pizzas, and pasta salads or be spooned over polenta and tofu. It keeps, refrigerated, for a week or more. Makes about 2 cups (V)

1 pound bell peppers, a variety of colors

3 large cloves garlic

$1/4$ teaspoon sea salt

3 tablespoons olive oil

1 bay leaf

1 red onion, finely diced

$1/2$ teaspoon fennel or anise seeds

1 tablespoon tomato paste

1 tablespoon red wine vinegar

Freshly milled pepper

1 tablespoon chopped basil or parsley

Seed and finely dice the peppers. Pound the garlic with the salt until mushy. Heat the oil with the bay leaf in a medium skillet over medium heat. Add the onion and fennel seeds and cook for 5 minutes, stirring occasionally. Add the garlic and peppers, lower the heat, and cook for 10 minutes. Stir in the tomato paste, add a few tablespoons water, then cover and cook until the peppers are tender, 5 minutes more. Add the vinegar, raise the heat to high, and reduce until syrupy. Taste for salt, season with pepper, and stir in the basil. Serve warm, at room temperature, or chilled.

PRESERVED LEMONS

A staple seasoning in North African cuisine, lemons preserved in salt are both a condiment and an ingredient, adding a soft, briny accent to salads and tagines that's altogether different from fresh lemon. The skin is what's used, but Kitty Morse, author of *Come with Me to the Kasbah*, uses the soft flesh as well, in vinaigrettes, soups, and other dishes. You can buy these at Middle Eastern delis, but they're not hard to make and they're a pleasure to have in the kitchen.

To make preserved lemons, first sterilize a clean jar large enough to hold the number of lemons you plan to use by submerging it in a pot of boiling water for a full minute. Carefully lift it out with a pair of tongs, allowing the water to drain out, then set it upside down on a clean towel to drain.

You'll need enough lemons to fit in the jar plus extras for juice. Rinse them under warm water, then cut four lengthwise slits in each lemon, going from near the top almost to the bottom, but don't cut all the way through the fruit. Rub sea salt or kosher salt generously into the slits, then put the lemons in the jar, packing them tightly. Add fresh lemon juice to within $1/2$ inch from the top, then cover and put in a cool dark place or the refrigerator to cure for 3 weeks. Sometimes a white film develops over the lemons—just rinse it off. Preserved lemons will keep, refrigerated, for 6 months or longer, and are vegan.

Sweet and Sour Onions with Dried Fruits

Boiling onions are much faster to prepare than the tiny pearl onions, and shallots are also delectable. Serve warm or at room temperature. This relish will keep for several weeks in the refrigerator. Makes about 2^1/$_2$ cups (V)

- 1 pound boiling onions, pearl onions, shallots, or a mixture
- 2 teaspoons butter or olive oil
- 1 tablespoon golden raisins
- 1 tablespoon dried sour cherries
- 1 tablespoon light brown sugar or honey
- 1 small rosemary sprig
- 2 tablespoons diced tomatoes, fresh or canned
- 2 tablespoons red wine vinegar
- Sea salt and freshly milled pepper

Boil the onions for 1 minute, then drain and remove the skins. Shallots needn't be parboiled. If shallots show natural divisions, pry them apart, then peel.

Heat the butter in a heavy medium skillet. Add the onions and cook over medium heat, shaking the pan every few minutes, until they're nicely browned, about 15 minutes. Add 2 cups water and the remaining ingredients except the vinegar, salt, and pepper. Cover and simmer until the onions are tender—25 minutes or more, depending on the size. Uncover, raise the heat, add the vinegar, and cook until the liquid has evaporated, leaving behind a thick glaze. Season with salt and pepper.

Sweet and Sour Quinces with Dried Fruits

A pretty, glistening condiment to serve in the winter months. The acidity and sweetness contrast well with the rich flavors and creamy textures of winter foods, such as the Winter Squash Galette (page 441). Makes about 1^1/$_2$ cups (V)

- 2 ripe yellow quinces, about 1 pound
- 1 teaspoon sea salt
- ^{1}/$_2$ cup granulated sugar
- ^{1}/$_2$ cup light brown sugar, packed
- ^{1}/$_4$ cup apple cider vinegar, preferably unfiltered
- 1 teaspoon coriander seeds
- 4 cloves
- ^{1}/$_4$ teaspoon black peppercorns
- ^{1}/$_3$ cup dried cherries or cranberries
- ^{1}/$_3$ cup dark raisins, preferably monukka
- ^{1}/$_3$ cup diced dried apricots or pears
- Balsamic or aged sherry vinegar

Cut the quinces into eighths, like apples. Peel and core each piece, then slice crosswise into small pieces slightly less than ^{1}/$_2$ inch long. Put the quinces, 2 cups water, and salt in a saucepan and boil for 5 minutes. Add the sugars, cider vinegar, and spices, then cook over low heat, covered, until the quinces turn pink, 1 to 1^1/$_2$ hours. If needed, add more water. Add the dried fruits and cook until they're soft, 12 to 15 minutes. Taste and season with ^{1}/$_2$ teaspoon or so of balsamic vinegar if more tartness and sweetness are needed. Store in a clean jar in the refrigerator for several months.

Pickled Red Onions

The easiest pickles in the world to make, these make a gorgeous garnish for sandwiches, salads, cold pastas, or just to serve on the table. The redder the onions, the pinker the pickle. Refrigerated, they keep for weeks, but as time passes they lose some of their crunch. Makes about 4 cups Ⓥ

1 pound red onions, peeled but left whole

1¹/₂ cups white wine vinegar

2 bay leaves

4 marjoram or thyme sprigs

Several small dried red chiles, optional

1 tablespoon sugar

1 teaspoon black or mixed peppercorns, bruised

Sea salt

Bring a teakettle of water to a boil. Slice the onions crosswise, ¹/₄ inch thick or thicker. Separate the rings and put them in a colander, then pour the boiling water over them. Mix the other ingredients plus ¹/₂ cups cold water and several pinches of salt in a large bowl and stir to dissolve the sugar. Add the onions, submerging them in the liquid by placing a plate on top. If there isn't enough liquid, add equal amounts of vinegar and water. The color will begin to develop in about 15 minutes. You can use the onions then or chill them first. Store in a covered jar in the refrigerator.

Pickled Carrots and Garlic with Cumin

This spunky little pickle will keep, refrigerated, for several weeks. Makes 2 cups Ⓥ

4 carrots

1 small head garlic

1 jalapeño chile, sliced into rounds, or 1 whole chile de árbol

³/₄ cup apple cider vinegar

1 teaspoon cumin seeds

¹/₂ teaspoon sugar

¹/₂ teaspoon black peppercorns

¹/₂ teaspoon sea salt

Peel the carrots and slice them diagonally or crosswise about ³/₈ inch thick. Separate the garlic cloves and peel them. Don't use any that are bruised.

Boil the carrots in salted water to cover for 3 minutes, then drain. Combine the remaining ingredients plus ³/₄ cup cold water and salt in a bowl. Stir to dissolve the salt and sugar, then add the carrots. Refrigerate overnight before serving.

Dried Fruit Chutney with Tamarind, Cilantro, and Mint

Now that I can find tamarind paste, fresh curry leaves, and very good ghee, Indian recipes have become much more appealing. This fragrant, tart chutney is excellent alongside any of the dals, with cream cheese on toast, with cucumbers. You can practically put it on ice cream. Use whatever dried fruit appeals to you—I use a mix of large raisins, small green raisins, and currants. Makes about 1 cup Ⓥ

²/₃ cup dried fruit

1 serrano chile, chopped

¹/₄ cup roughly chopped cilantro

2 tablespoons roughly chopped mint

¹/₄ cup concentrated tamarind

Pinch cayenne

¹/₂ teaspoon garam masala

¹/₂ teaspoon sea salt

Cover the dried fruit with warm water and set it aside to soak and soften while you gather the rest of the ingredients. (If the fruit is very hard, bring it, with the water, to a boil, then turn off the heat until it cools.) Pour off the soaking water and set it aside, then pulse everything in a food processor to a smooth puree. Add the soaking water, as needed, to loosen the mixture. Taste for salt.

Spicy Ginger Chutney

Ivy Amar, an Aruvedic cooking teacher in Santa Fe, made this lively chutney in one of her classes. It's absolutely good with everything—addicting, even. This is my version of Ivy's recipe. The tamarind pulp is the variable ingredient. I use a puree that you can just scoop out with a spoon, rather than soaking tamarind seeds. The puree is very dark and strong, so I've called for far less than the original recipe, but you can always add more to taste. Makes about 1 cup

- 1 (3-inch) piece ginger
- 1 tablespoon ghee
- 2 green cayenne chiles or 1 serrano chile, seeded and diced
- 1 stalk of fresh, green curry leaves (6 to 8 leaves)
- 2 to 3 teaspoons tamarind pulp, or more, to taste
- ³/₄ cup unsweetened grated coconut
- 2 tablespoons turbinado or jaggery sugar
- ¹/₂ teaspoon sea salt
- Water or yogurt for thinning
- To finish: 2 teaspoons ghee, ¹/₂ teaspoon mustard seeds, 1 stalk green curry leaves (6 to 8), 2 or 3 Thai red chile peppers, fresh cilantro leaves

Peel, then thinly slice the ginger. Heat the ghee in a small skillet and add the ginger, chiles, and curry leaves. Cook over medium–low heat, until the ginger is browned in places, turning it frequently as you do so. Turn off the heat and add the tamarind, coconut, sugar, and salt.

Grind the mixture in a small food processor until a coarse paste is formed. It will be quite dry, so add a little water to loosen the mixture some. Taste for sweetness and salt, then scrape into a bowl.

To finish, melt the ghee in a small skillet, add the mustard seeds, and cook until they begin to pop, then add the curry leaves. Pour this mixture over the chutney. Add the chiles and garnish with the fresh cilantro leaves.

Apple-Pear Chutney

Makes about 2 cups

- 3 apples
- 2 pears, preferably Anjou or Bosc
- 1 large yellow quince, if available
- 1 cup light honey
- ¹/₂ cup apple cider vinegar, preferably unfiltered
- ¹/₄ cup balsamic vinegar
- 1 (3-inch) cinnamon stick
- 5 cloves
- 10 peppercorns
- Several slices ginger, optional

Peel, core, and thinly slice the fruits. Combine the remaining ingredients in a medium saucepan and bring to a boil. Simmer each fruit in the syrup until transparent, about 15 minutes, then remove to a bowl or glass jar. The quince will take longest. When done, pour the syrup over all, cover, and refrigerate. This keeps for several months.

Apricot and Dried Fruit Chutney

Makes about 2¹/₂ cups ⓥ

- 1¹/₂ cups whole dried apricots, chopped
- ¹/₂ cup golden raisins
- ¹/₄ cup currants
- ¹/₄ cup dried cherries or cranberries
- 3¹/₂ cups apple juice or water
- ¹/₂ cup apple cider vinegar, preferably unfiltered
- 2 tablespoons julienne strips of ginger
- ¹/₂ teaspoon fennel or anise seeds
- ¹/₂ teaspoon black peppercorns
- ¹/₂ teaspoon coriander seeds
- ¹/₄ teaspoon red pepper flakes
- Pinch sea salt
- Balsamic vinegar

Put everything except the balsamic vinegar in a heavy saucepan and bring to a boil. Lower the heat and simmer until the fruit is soft but not mushy and the liquid is reduced to a syrup, about 45 minutes. Stir in ¹/₂ teaspoon or so balsamic vinegar to taste. Serve right away if desired, but the flavors will merge as it sits. Stored in the refrigerator, the finished chutney should keep for many weeks.

APPETIZERS AND FIRST COURSES

CHAPTER 4

Appetizers and First Courses
Greetings from the Cook

This collection of tasty small items assuages our hunger at day's end, when we may not be quite ready to eat or cook a meal but need a little pick-me-up or a bite to take the edge off the appetite.

Welcoming appetizers ease the wait for food and keep a clamoring family at bay. A small bite before dinner extends hospitality to guests, setting a tone of conviviality and drawing everyone into a circle of friendship and exchange. When it comes to making these intriguing morsels, there's a wealth of possibilities for the vegetarian cook. Many traditional cuisines have long featured vegetable-based appetizers knowing that meat was to follow.

Hors d'oeuvres can be as informal as a plate of Black Olives with Orange and Fennel (page 77) or a bowl of Salted Almonds (page 79). At the other extreme, your offerings can be as formal as the elaborate Silky Mushroom Pâté with a Green Onion–Walnut Topping (page 91), which clearly introduces a meal of some importance. In between is a host of items from a Spicy Eggplant Spread with Thai Basil (page 89) to small sandwiches and crostini, warm one-bite pastries, golden wedges of artichoke, and many more delicious little nibbles that are likely to dovetail with your cupboard's contents and your culinary inclinations.

Appetizers

Today appetizers needn't be numerous or complicated. People tend to want just a bite of this or that, pacing themselves so that they don't fill up before dinner. There are many items you can have on hand for such moments—a basket of crudités with a sauce for dipping, seasoned olives, or roasted nuts. Marinated vegetables or little vegetable salads also make good appetizers to serve with rounds of bread or croutons. Cheeses, if any, should come from the lighter end of the spectrum—a square of Baked Ricotta with Thyme (page 103)—saving a rich, buttery Explorateur for dessert.

Regardless of what you offer, make it easy to eat with the fingers or provide plates and forks—and offer napkins either way.

First Courses

The first course helps set the pace of a meal and extends the time spent at the table, especially important for entertaining. Often a first course is more complex than an appetizer, but it can also be as simple as a bowl of soup or a few hors d'oeuvres like olives, crudités, and a dip artfully arranged as an antipasto. Although larger than appetizers, first courses are small enough to feature those favorite foods we no longer eat in main-course quantities, such as a rich pasta or a creamy Goat Cheese Flan (page 518).

First courses can be drawn from recipes throughout the book. Many vegetable dishes—a steamed artichoke, a stuffed vegetable, or a crisply fried food are good candidates. A slice of a savory galette, a small pizza, or hand-formed ravioli make good first courses, as do soups and salads, especially composed salad plates that draw together a number of diverse elements.

Olives

There's nothing nicer than nibbling from a bowl of olives while sipping a glass of wine. Ethnic markets are where you're likely to find the widest variety of unusual olives, in bulk and at the best prices. Some olives are shipped in their brine, which continues to cure as well as to protect them. Ask for some of the brine to be included with the olives (after the olives are weighed) and store them in your refrigerator, where they'll keep for weeks. Otherwise toss them with olive oil when you get home and refrigerate to keep them longer. Olives that are old or poorly stored eventually lose their texture, becoming spongy and soft. While there are many kinds of olives and ways of curing them, here are a few of those we see most.

CERINGOLA: Whether green or black, these are enormous olives from Puglia, Italy. Their flavor is mild, and the black ones, being riper to start with, have the softer flesh. Sicilian Colossals are another substantially large olive.

CRACKED GREEN OLIVES: These firm, tart, cracked olives are produced in Morocco, Sicily, and California. Made from various varieties of unripened olives, they are tangy, sharp, and the flesh is difficult to free from the pits. They're frequently cooked in stews but can be enjoyed whole seasoned with red chile, garlic, and herbs such as rosemary, cumin, fennel seeds, and lemon. They're also good fried or simmered in tomato sauce.

GAETA: These small black Italian olives are often dry-cured in salt, which gives them a wrinkled appearance, and they have a mild, sweet flavor. They marry especially well with rosemary and provide richness to olive pastes.

KALAMATA: These large, meaty, rich-tasting purplish black olives are packed in brine. If they taste too salty, rinse them briefly. Usually imported from Greece, kalamata-style olives are also grown in California and Peru. This versatile olive can be seasoned, baked with wine and herbs, and used for olive pastes.

LUCQUES: Large (but not gigantic) and elongated, these green olives from the south of France have a mild, nutty flavor and attractive appearance.

NIÇOISE: Tiny brownish black French olives have large pits in proportion to their flesh, but they're flavorful and soft. Olive pastes made from niçoise olives are smooth and rich tasting, but it takes time to pit enough olives to make it in any quantity. Good for nibbling, they also make a bright garnish for vegetable salads and erudite plates.

NYONS: Also from France, these small olives come packed in jars, often with bits of stems and olive leaves included. They are browner and rounder than niçoise olives and have a slight bitter edge to their intense olive flavor.

OIL-CURED BLACK OLIVES: These wrinkled little olives are cured with salt, then with oil. They are usually Moroccan, but sometimes Italian, and are also produced in California. Their meaty, dense flavor goes well with paprika, garlic, and lemon. When added to stews and ragouts, they plump up grandly and impart a soft but earthy flavor to the surrounding broth or sauce.

PICHOLINE: A French green olive cured in brine, the picholine is medium size, nutty, and mild.

STUFFED GREEN OLIVES: Their tartness, paired with the sweet morsel of pimiento, almond, or garlic, makes these olives especially good for hors d'oeuvres. They're a special feature in certain vegetable salads, especially those including cauliflower, and in olive sandwiches.

Seasoned Olives

These can be stored for 2 to 3 weeks in the refrigerator, but the garlic will become stronger with time. I usually remove any garlic slices and add fresh ones when I next serve them. Before serving olives marinated in olive oil, let them come to room temperature to allow the oil to return to its liquid state.

Olives with Toasted Cumin and Paprika

Makes 1 cup Ⓥ

1¹/₂ cups kalamata, oil-cured, or cracked green olives

1 teaspoon cumin seeds

2 cloves garlic, thinly sliced

2 teaspoons paprika

Several pinches red pepper flakes

2 tablespoons olive oil

Juice of 1 lemon

Taste the olives; rinse them if they're excessively salty. Place them in a bowl. Toast the cumin seeds in a small skillet until fragrant, then bruise them with a pestle or the back of a wooden spoon to release their flavor. Add the cumin seeds and the remaining ingredients to the olives and toss. Let stand 1 hour or more before serving.

Black Olives with Orange and Fennel

The olives are the perfect garnish for salad of oranges and fennel. Makes 2 cups Ⓥ

2 cups black olives—oil-cured, niçoise, kalamata, or a mixture

6 small bay leaves

¹/₄ teaspoon fennel seeds

2 cloves garlic, thinly sliced

Zest of 1 small orange in large strips

Best olive oil, to moisten

Combine everything in a bowl. Let stand for 1 hour or more for the flavors to develop. Store in a covered container in the refrigerator for up to 2 to 3 weeks.

Mixed Olives with Rosemary and Thyme

A selection of olive varieties looks as pretty as beach stones. If using oil-cured olives, add them just before serving since they tend to stain the green ones with inky streaks. Makes 2 cups Ⓥ

2 cups mixed olives—kalamata, niçoise, Nyons, cracked green, oil-cured, etc.

6 or more thyme or lemon thyme sprigs

Several small rosemary sprigs

2 bay leaves, broken into large pieces

1 large clove garlic, thinly sliced

Olive oil, to moisten

Combine everything in a serving dish. Let stand at room temperature at least 2 hours for the flavors to develop, and then serve. Store in a covered container in the refrigerator for up to 2 weeks.

Fried Green Olives

A delicious Spanish tapa, these olives are best fried in a fruity olive oil and served hot. Serves 4 to 6

8 ounces green Spanish olives

1 egg, beaten

Flour, as needed

2 cups olive oil

Dip the olives in the egg, then toss them in a plateful of flour to coat. Heat the oil in a skillet until it begins to haze. Add the olives in batches and fry over high heat until golden. Give the pan a few shakes while they're cooking to turn the olives. Drain on paper towels and serve hot.

Olive Paste

Spread on croutons, pungent olive paste sets off all kinds of foods—fresh mozzarella, tomatoes, roasted peppers, grilled eggplant and hard-cooked eggs. Olive paste keeps more or less indefinitely in the refrigerator. Makes about 3/4 cup Ⓥ

1 cup olives, such as niçoise, kalamata, or green, pitted

1/4 cup capers, rinsed

2 small cloves garlic

2 teaspoons chopped thyme leaves or 1/2 teaspoon dried

1 to 2 tablespoons olive oil

Freshly milled pepper

Fresh lemon juice

In a food processor, make a smooth paste of the olives, capers, garlic, and thyme if using dried. Add the olive oil while the machine is running. Season with pepper and add lemon juice and thyme if using fresh.

Hot and Spicy Tapenade

One of my favorite cooks, Dan Welch, always has a lot of this spicy tapenade around his kitchen. This spread goes everywhere —even on pasta (with lots of parsley), in sandwiches, or simply spread on croutons and covered with mild goat or fresh mozzarella cheese. Makes about 2 cups Ⓥ

1/2 pound mixed olives, mostly kalamata

1/4 cup capers, rinsed

1/4 cup olive oil

2 to 3 cloves garlic, finely chopped

Grated zest and juice of 1 large lemon

1 teaspoon chopped green peppercorns, drained

1 teaspoon red pepper flakes

If the olives are excessively salty, rinse them in several changes of water. Remove the pits, then chop them by hand and mix with the remaining ingredients. Stored in the refrigerator, this will keep well for up to 2 weeks.

Baked Olives

This is a Greek way—via Sicily—to prepare olives. Just the aroma elicits sighs and exclamations. They can be served immediately, but I prefer to let them stand for several hours for the flavors to develop. Makes 2 cups Ⓥ

2 cups kalamata olives

1/2 cup dry red or white wine

3 tablespoons olive oil

3 cloves garlic, 1 sliced, 2 coarsely chopped

1 bay leaf

2 tablespoons marjoram, or 1 teaspoon dried oregano

1 tablespoon chopped parsley

Freshly milled pepper

Several pinches red pepper flakes

Preheat the oven to 375°F. Rinse the olives if salty and put them in a baking dish large enough to hold them in a single layer. Add the wine, half of the oil, the sliced garlic, and the bay leaf. Cover and bake until they're fragrant and swollen, about 45 minutes.

Meanwhile, pound the chopped garlic in a mortar with the marjoram, parsley, and a few grinds of pepper. When the olives come out of the oven, poke each one with a fork or the tip of a knife, then stir in the garlic-herb paste, the remaining oil, and the red pepper flakes.

Roasted Nuts and Salted Seeds

Roasted nuts and seeds make a perfect accompaniment to one or two simple crudités and everyone loves them.

OVEN ROASTING: Preheat the oven to 300°F. Toss the nuts or seeds with just enough oil to coat lightly—1 teaspoon should be ample for 2 cups—then spread the nuts on a sheet pan and bake until golden, from 10 to 20 minutes. At this moderate temperature, the nuts will dry out as they brown, making them crunchy once cooled. This is especially true for nuts that have been boiled first, as almonds are in order to remove their skins.

OILS: Olive oil and vegetable oils can be used in all cases, but highly aromatic oils, such as peanut, walnut, or hazelnut, emphasize the natural flavors of those particular nuts.

SEASONINGS: Use rough-edged kosher salt and flaky sea salt, which happily stick to the nuts, whereas table salt is too fine and coarse crystals of sea salt are too large. For chile, use cayenne, ground red chile, or powders you've made yourself from dried chiles, such as chipotles. Spice mixtures like garam masala and curry are also good seasonings with nuts and seeds.

STORING: If not eaten within a few days, roasted nuts can be kept in a tightly covered container in the freezer, where they'll keep for several weeks—an appetizer at the ready. To refresh them, return them to the oven for a few minutes and then cool.

Salt and Pepper Walnuts

If you're serving these as an appetizer, aim for perfect halves and save the smaller pieces for salads. Makes 1 cup Ⓥ

1 cup walnut halves or pieces
1 teaspoon walnut oil
Kosher or sea salt and freshly milled white pepper

Preheat the oven to 325°F. Bake the nuts on a sheet pan until they smell toasty, about 10 minutes. Toss with the oil, salt, and pepper to taste.

Salted Almonds

The skins can be left on or not, but blanched almonds with their pale straw-gold color are far prettier. Serve with sherry, olives, and a simple crudité. Makes 2 cups Ⓥ

2 cups whole almonds, blanched or not
1 teaspoon olive oil
1 teaspoon sea or kosher salt
1 teaspoon ground red chile or cayenne, optional

Preheat the oven to 300°F. Toss the nuts with the oil and roast on a sheet pan until light golden, about 25 minutes. Stir a few times so that they color evenly. When done, add the salt and chile and swish them around. Taste and add more salt or chile if desired.

Lacquered Almonds

This Chinese technique brings a sweet or salty flavor to nuts by simmering them in syrup or brine before drying them out. Traditionally, they're then fried, but when baked very slowly they emerge a burnished mahogany with a lustrous glaze. Makes 1 cup

1 cup whole almonds, blanched
1/4 cup honey or 2 tablespoons each honey and molasses
1/2 cup sugar
1/4 teaspoon sea salt

Simmer the almonds in boiling water to cover for 2 minutes, then drain. Bring 2 cups water and the remaining ingredients to a boil, stirring to dissolve the sugar. Add the nuts and simmer for 15 minutes.

Preheat the oven to 250°F. Drain the nuts, discarding the syrup, and spread them on a sheet pan. Put them in the oven and turn off the heat. Let dry for 2 hours, until glazed and no longer tacky. Cool completely before storing.

Roasted Chile–Peanuts

The turmeric gives the peanuts a rich golden color, but don't add too much. It can be bitter in quantity. Makes 2 cups Ⓥ

- 2 cups shelled raw peanuts
- 1 teaspoon roasted peanut oil
- 2 to 3 teaspoons ground red chile, or 1 teaspoon cayenne
- 1/2 teaspoon turmeric
- 1 teaspoon sea or kosher salt

Preheat the oven to 300°F. Toss the peanuts with the oil, spread on a sheet pan, and roast until golden, about 25 minutes. Shake the pan a few times so that they color evenly. Toss them with the chile, turmeric, and salt.

Roasted Peanuts with Chipotle Chile Powder: Chipotle chiles are smoked jalapeños, and they're hot! Toss the hot roasted peanuts with a little chipotle powder, starting with 1/4 teaspoon, and omit the cayenne and red chile. Ⓥ

Beer Nuts: These should be sour, salty, and hot. Toss the Roasted Chile–Peanuts with the juice of 1 large lime. Add enough chile to give them a nice crusty coating. Since they're moist with the lime juice, plan to eat them within the day. Ⓥ

Nut Packages

Nuts are so irresistible, it makes sense to store them in something that's a challenge to get into. Shake them with their salt and seasonings in a paper bag, twist the bag, and leave them there until ready to serve. Or wrap them in a square of twisted parchment paper. If you're giving a large cocktail party, leave the packages in strategic places around the room. Everyone loves opening presents, and the noisy rustling of the paper works as a great icebreaker.

Glazed Sunflower Seeds with Shichimi Togarashi

These soy-sauce glazed sunflower seeds are a good and inexpensive nibble and a great ingredient for salads, like the kale salad on page 138. The seven-spice Japanese powder gives the seeds a little kick, but if you don't have it, simply leave it out. It's still good. Makes 1 cup Ⓥ

- 1 cup raw, hulled sunflower seeds
- Soy sauce or tamari
- Dash shichimi togarashi (page 68), optional

Heat the sunflower seeds in a skillet, scooting them back and forth every few minutes, until golden. Turn off the heat and sprinkle soy sauce over the hot seeds. Slide the pan rapidly back and forth to coat the seeds, season with the shichimi togarashi, then turn them onto a plate to cool. You don't need a lot of soy sauce, probably about a teaspoon in all.

Sweet, Salty, and Spicy Pecans

These are immensely popular. Serve them with skewers of cucumber or honeydew melon before or after dinner. Makes 1 cup Ⓥ

- 1 cup pecan halves
- 1 teaspoon sunflower seed oil
- 1 1/2 tablespoons sugar, or more to taste
- 1/2 teaspoon kosher or flaky sea salt
- 1 teaspoon ground red chile

Preheat the oven to 300°F. Spread the pecans on a sheet pan and roast until fragrant, about 25 minutes. Stir a few times so that they color evenly. Heat the oil in a skillet over medium heat, add the nuts, and stir to coat. Sprinkle with the sugar and salt and cook, stirring continually, over medium heat, until the sugar melts and starts to caramelize and coat the nuts, about 5 minutes. Turn off the heat but keep stirring until the nuts begin to cool, then toss with the chile and turn them onto a plate to finish cooling.

Roasted Cashews with Garam Masala

You also can use a mixture of cashews, almonds, and pecans with these seasonings. The pecans are especially good since their crevices catch the seasonings. Makes 2 cups Ⓥ

2 cups raw cashew nuts
1 teaspoon oil

1 tablespoon garam masala (page 25)
1 teaspoon sugar
1 teaspoon sea salt

Preheat the oven to 300°F. Toss the nuts with the oil and roast on a sheet pan until lightly browned all over, 15 to 20 minutes. Remove and toss with the garam masala, sugar, and salt.

From the Garden: Crudités

Crudités—meaning raw, not crude—are simply cut-up vegetables offered as appetizers. Crudités can also refer to plates of small vegetable salads that are sometimes served as a first course in France. In either case, crudités are a refreshing, healthy offering. The keys to making crudités delightful are to seek out vegetables that are absolutely fresh, cut them artfully but not fussily, and gather them into easy arrangements. Using unexpected vegetables adds surprise. And just a single vegetable or two will do—you needn't gather a gardenful.

Put them in a napkin-lined basket, a silver dish, a rustic platter, or a fine china plate—whatever your fancy. If you have a garden, garnish your offering with tender pea shoots, sprigs of bean blossoms, sprays of herbs, and other garden delights.

A dish of salt flatters all vegetables and keeps things simple, but many sauces are also delicious if you care to be more elaborate. And while many vegetables are fine eaten raw, others are improved with a brief blanching in boiling salted water. Rinse under cold water, then set on a towel to dry.

ASPARAGUS: Trim the tough ends, then simmer the stalks in salted water until tender. Serve with salt, Orange Mayonnaise (page 52), Peanut Sauce (page 61), Cilantro Salsa (page 49), or Hoisin Sauce with Chili Paste and Tangerine Zest (page 522).

BEANS: Using any tender variety of bean—green, yellow, or purple—trim, blanch just until tender-firm, and rinse. Serve with salt, mayonnaise flavored with Pesto (page 50), Tarator Sauce (page 59), or Garlic Mayonnaise (page 52). Accompany with a dish of olives.

BELGIAN ENDIVE: Trim the bottom, then separate the leaves and fan them out on a platter. Cover the base of each leaf with a small bit of flavored mayonnaise, a mound of finely shredded vegetable salad, or a morsel of soft herb–flavored cheese.

CABBAGE: Slice into thick, short ribbons, pile them on a plate, and serve with salt or a seasoned herb salt. Kohlrabi, apples, and turnips would be good on this plate, too. For dipping, have a bowl of Fresh Horseradish Sauce (page 63) or Mustard–Cilantro Sauce (page 63).

CARROTS: Leave very small carrots whole and uncooked with their fresh greens still attached. Serve them with a bowl of Salsa Verde (page 48) or Indian Salt with Mixed Spices (page 68).

CAULIFLOWER AND BROCCOLI: Cut the crowns into florets; the broccoli stems can be peeled and sliced in batons. Steam just long enough to soften and take off their raw edge. Serve chilled or at room temperature with Curry Mayonnaise with Mango Chutney (page 85), Gomashio (page 67), or Mustard–Cilantro Sauce (page 63).

CELERY: The inner stalks are preferable, but the outer ones can be used if peeled. Cut them into manageable lengths, crisp in ice water, and serve them in a dish or an old-fashioned celery glass. Have a bowl of whole walnuts to crack, unsalted butter to spread in their hollows, or Green Goddess Dressing (page 169) for dipping.

CUCUMBERS: Peel unless they're organic, then cut into long spears and slice away the seeds. Use yellow lemon cucumbers, quartered lengthwise, or ridged Armenian cucumbers sliced on the diagonal. Serve with Yogurt Sauce with Cayenne and Dill (page 57), Tarator Sauce (page 59), or Toasted Nori with Sesame Seeds (page 67).

FENNEL: Slice into thin wedges or long batons and accompany with a dish of Salted Almonds (page 79) and a bowl of green olives.

JICAMA: Peel and cut into cubes or batons. Squeeze lime juice over all or serve with wedges of lime, a bowl of red pepper flakes, and crushed roasted peanuts for dipping.

PEAS: String sugar snap or snow peas, then dip into boiling water just until they brighten. Cool under running water. They're delicious just like this or dipped into Green Goddess Dressing (page 169). You can stuff them—people do—but it's rather fussy for something that's so good plain.

PEPPERS: Use all colors, cut them into sturdy strips, and remove their veins and seeds. Have a trio of sauces for dipping—Saffron Mayonnaise (page 52), Romesco Sauce (page 62), Peanut Sauce (page 61), or choose just one.

RADISHES: Multicolored Easter egg radishes, white icicles, Spanish black radishes, and daikon can all be used. Leave a few fresh leaves on the tops of small radishes and serve whole; cut larger ones into strips or paper-thin rounds. Crisp them in ice water, then drain, pile in a bowl, and serve with salt and thin slices of French bread or dark bread lightly buttered or spread with cream cheese.

TOMATOES: Slice large ones into wedges or serve clusters of currant tomatoes, whole cherry and pear tomatoes, or a glistening arrangement of all. Accompany with Herb or Garlic Mayonnaise (page 52), Cilantro Salsa (page 49), or Salsa Verde (page 48).

TURNIPS AND KOHLRABI: Cut small and tender turnips and kohlrabi into wedges or paper-thin rounds, sprinkle them with crunchy salt, and accompany with sprigs of lemon thyme, and a dish of salted seeds, or Mustard-Cilantro Sauce (page 63) for dipping.

PINZIMONIO

A bowl of fragrant green Tuscan olive oil, sea salt, and pepper—nothing could be easier to make than *pinzimonio*. It's served with a variety of vegetables but is particularly good with fennel, celery, and sweet bell peppers. Slice small fennel bulbs into wedges, celery hearts into sticks with the leaves attached, and sweet bell peppers into curved batons. Arrange the vegetables on a platter. Prepare for each person a shallow bowl of olive oil, just slightly warmed and seasoned with sea salt and freshly ground pepper; or let each person make his or her own bowl. The vegetables are dipped in the seasoned oil.

Dips, Spreads, and Salsas

The sour cream–based spreadables so many of us grew up with are replaced here by spreads and dips made with roasted vegetables, highly seasoned beans, and richly flavored vegetable purees. Spread on croutons or scooped with chips and crisps, they provide alluring predinner bites. Thick spreads can also replace butter on the table or fill a sandwich. Thinned, they become dips for chips or crudités. Salsas not only serve as dips for chips but play roles in other dishes, such as quesadillas.

Pea and Avocado Dip with Lemon Zest, Tarragon, and Chives

A bright green pea puree punctuated with the paler green chunks of creamy avocado doesn't need to be a faux guacamole, although it can with ease—just trade out the lemon for lime and go ahead with the usual seasonings for guacamole. Makes about 1 cup (V)

1 cup fresh or frozen peas
Sea salt
1 Meyer lemon
1 large avocado
2 teaspoons olive oil
1 heaping teaspoon chopped tarragon or chervil
Finely snipped chives and chive blossoms, if available, for garnish

Bring a cup or two of water to a boil. Add the peas and a pinch of salt. Cook for about 2 minutes—the water may not return to a boil but the peas should be bright green and cooked through. Tip them into a strainer, rinse with cold water, and shake dry. Pulse in a mini food processor until smooth, then scrape the puree into a bowl. Add the zest of the whole lemon to the peas along with the juice of half the lemon.

Halve the avocado, score the flesh with a knife, then scoop it into the peas. Mash with a fork to break up the avocado but leave some texture. Taste for salt and lemon, add the olive oil, and stir in the tarragon and most of the chives. Turn the puree into a serving bowl and garnish with the remaining chives and chive blossoms.

With Other Herbs: Consider basil (especially lemon basil) dill, mint, lovage, and other herbs. A garnish of salad burnet would be very pretty and make this a good dip for spears of cucumbers. Or perch the puree on top of cucumber rounds and add a sprig of burnet. (V)

With *Rau Ram* and Sesame: Season with slivers of fresh mint leaves and Vietnamese coriander (*rau ram*). Replace the olive oil with a teaspoon or less of toasted sesame oil and garnish with toasted sesame seeds. Serve on sesame crackers. (V)

With Cumin and Chile: Season with $1/2$ to 1 teaspoon ground cumin, to taste, use lime juice instead of lemon, and include half a diced jalapeño chile. Finally, stir in a tablespoon of finely chopped cilantro, or more, to taste. (V)

Roasted Red Pepper Spread

Spread this on crackers or croutons and top with grilled onions, rounds of eggplant, thinly sliced cheese, or chopped herbs. Makes about $1/2$ cup (V)

1 large red bell pepper, roasted
1 small clove garlic
1 tablespoon olive oil
A few drops red wine vinegar
Sea salt and freshly milled pepper

Puree the bell pepper, garlic, and oil in a blender or by hand in a mortar. Season to taste with the vinegar, salt, and pepper.

Avocado with Meyer Lemon, Toasted Sesame Oil, and Seven-Spice Powder

There are two ways to go here: coarsely mash the avocado to make a spread, or, if the avocado is perfect and firm, consider slicing it into wedges and seasoning it with the lemon and oil and putting it on sesame crackers. If you don't have the toga-rashi, omit it and consider adding a few red pepper flakes or freshly cracked pepper. Serves 3 or more (V)

1 ripe but firm avocado

Juice of a Meyer lemon, to taste

A few drops toasted sesame oil

Sea salt

Shichimi togarashi (page 68), to finish

Peel the avocado, and scoop it into a bowl. Season with the lemon juice to taste, then work in a few drops of the toasted sesame oil. Season with the salt and shichimi togarashi to taste. Or, slice the avocado, arrange it on a plate, then squeeze over the lemon, add a few drops oil, a few pinches of salt, and a dusting of the togarashi.

Spicy Peanut Dip

This dip makes even the most mundane crudités irresistible. If you can, get your peanut butter at a store equipped with a machine that grinds peanuts into butter while you wait. Makes about 1 cup (V)

1 cup unsweetened peanut butter

1 bunch green onions, including a few inches of the greens, coarsely chopped

1/2 cup chopped cilantro

1 or 2 serrano chiles, coarsely chopped

1 tablespoon soy sauce

Juice and zest of 2 limes

1 teaspoon turmeric

Combine all the ingredients in a food processor and blend until smooth but flecks of green still remain. Add warm water to thin the sauce if needed. Taste and adjust the soy sauce and lime, adding more of either to get the balance right.

Artichoke Pesto

A subtle spread for crostini and canapés. Fresh artichokes are plentiful in spring and again the fall. Although you can also use frozen, they do have that ascorbic acid flavor that fights with the artichoke's subtle nature. Makes about 1 cup

4 medium artichokes, trimmed and quartered (see page 295) or 1 package, frozen

3 tablespoons olive oil

3 large strips lemon zest

1 tablespoon finely diced shallot or onion

2 cloves garlic, thinly sliced

Aromatics: 1 bay leaf, 4 parsley sprigs, 2 thyme sprigs

1/2 teaspoon sea salt

1/4 cup freshly grated parmesan or dry Jack cheese

Freshly milled pepper

Thinly slice the trimmed artichokes. In a medium skillet, warm 2 tablespoons of the oil with the lemon zest. Add the shallot and garlic and cook over medium heat for about 3 minutes. Add the artichokes and aromatics, season with the salt, and add water barely to cover. Bring to a boil, then lower the heat and simmer, covered, until the artichokes are tender and a few tablespoons liquid remain, about 12 minutes.

Remove the aromatics and lemon zest. Puree the artichokes with any remaining pan juices, the cheese, and the last tablespoon of olive oil. Season with salt and pepper to taste. Store in a clean jar, covered with a layer of olive oil, in the refrigerator, where it will keep for several weeks.

Cottage Cheese with Watercress

The peppery watercress is finely minced and stirred into creamy cottage cheese. (My favorite is the nonhomogenized version made by Kalona Dairy.) This is bit unusual and it takes a matter of minutes to make. Use it as a dip with celery or fennel, or spread it over crackers. Try it spread over toasted nutty whole grain bread garnished with small halved fruit tomatoes and extra watercress leaves. Makes about 1 cup

- 1 bunch watercress
- 1 cup cottage cheese
- A few tablespoons sour cream, optional
- Sea salt to taste

If using hydroponic watercress, cut off the bulk of its long stems. Wild watercress will have much thicker stems, which also need to be cut away from the leaves. Finely chop most of the leaves, saving some for a garnish or, if you have a lot, a salad. You'll want between ¹/₂ and 1 cup.

Stir the minced watercress into the cottage cheese, along with a few spoonfuls of sour cream to taste, if the cottage cheese is not the full-fat variety. Taste and season with salt. Pepper isn't necessary because the watercress is rather peppery. Serve surrounded with the extra leaves.

With Peppercress, Land Cress, and Other Cresses: If you have access to these assertive little greens, by all means use them, but in a smaller quantity, as they tend to be quite peppery. You can always add more if you wish.

Curry Mayonnaise with Mango Chutney

This is one of the best dips I know for crudités. It's terrific with everything, but especially with hearty vegetables such as broccoli and cauliflower. If you used bottled mayonnaise, add yogurt or sour cream to even out its salty-sweet taste. Makes about 1¹/₂ cup

- ¹/₂ cup mango chutney, preferably Major Grey's
- 1 cup mayonnaise
- 4 green onions, including some of the greens, finely chopped
- 1 tablespoon curry powder
- Juice of 2 to 3 limes
- Cayenne
- ¹/₄ cup yogurt or sour cream

Chop the chutney if it's chunky and stir it into the mayonnaise along with the green onions, curry, and enough lime juice to make a tart but harmonious balance. Stir in a pinch or two or more cayenne and the yogurt. Cover and refrigerate for at least 1 hour. Taste before serving to make sure the balance is right and add a bit more lime juice if it seems too sweet.

Guacamole

Regardless of the seasonings—with or without lime, garlic, or cumin—guacamole should be a little chunky, never puree smooth. You can spread guacamole on warm tortillas with crumbly white Mexican cheese, use it in sandwiches, as a topping for nachos, and as a side for corn waffles. Makes about 2 cups, serving 6 to 8 (V)

- ¹/₃ cup finely diced white or green onions, including some of the greens
- ¹/₄ cup chopped cilantro
- 2 medium tomatoes, seeded and finely diced
- 1 or 2 serrano chiles, finely diced
- 3 large avocados, preferably Hass
- Juice of 1 or 2 limes
- ¹/₂ teaspoon sea salt

Set aside a few tablespoons of the onion, cilantro, and tomato for garnish. Grind or chop the remaining onion, cilantro, and chile with the salt to make a rough paste. Peel and mash the avocados with a fork. Add the onion mixture and tomatoes and season with lime juice and salt to taste.

If you're not serving the guacamole right away, press a piece of plastic wrap directly on the surface to keep it from browning. To serve, heap the guacamole into a bowl and garnish with the reserved onion, cilantro, and tomato.

Dips and Spreads Made with Beans

Being rather neutral, beans provide a blank canvas that can be painted with bright or subtle flavors. I generally find that bean dips are most appealing when they're warm or at room temperature. Cold, they stiffen and their full flavors are dimmed. (To warm a cold puree, add more bean broth or water until the desired consistency is reached, then reheat in a double boiler or small skillet.) Leftovers can be refrigerated for up to 4 or 5 days. Canned beans, drained and rinsed, work particularly well in purees.

Serve bean purees with tortilla chips, pita crisps, or spread over little croutons.

Black Bean and Smoked Chile Dip

Use this spicy spread for nachos, or in quesadilla, as well as for a dip. If you don't want the heat of chipotle but you do want the smoke, use smoked paprika. Makes about 2 cups Ⓥ

- 2 cups cooked black beans
- 1/2 cup water or bean broth
- 1 tablespoon oil
- 1/4 cup sliced green onion, including some of the greens
- 1 teaspoon ground coriander
- 1 teaspoon ground cumin
- 1/4 cup chopped cilantro
- 1 teaspoon pureed chipotle chile, or 1/2 teaspoon cayenne
- Juice of 2 or 3 limes
- Sea salt

Warm the beans in the water. Heat the oil in a small skillet. Add the onion and spices and cook over medium heat until tender, about 10 minutes. Stir in the cilantro and turn off the heat.

Coarsely puree the beans, onion mixture, and chile in a food processor. Taste; if you want it hotter, add more chile in small increments. Add lime juice and salt to sharpen the flavors.

Individual Nachos

Mammoth platters of chips galvanized with hot, stringy cheese are not among our culinary stars, but the same idea applied to tortilla chips one at a time has some merit. Serves 4 to 6

- Black Bean and Smoked Chile Dip (page 86) or Fried-Only-Once Refried Beans (page 284), warmed
- 4 corn tortillas, cut into sixths and baked until crisp
- Pico de Gallo (page 90) or a favorite salsa
- 1/2 cup crumbled queso fresco or feta
- Cilantro sprigs

Place a spoonful of warmed beans on the base of each chip, cover with a little salsa and crumbled cheese, then garnish with a cilantro sprig and serve.

Individual Nachos with Guacamole: Mound a spoonful of Guacamole (page 85) on the base of each chip, then add a few crumbles of feta, a dab of Tomatillo Salsa (page 90), and a cilantro sprig.

Edamame and Sesame Puree on Black Seaweed Crackers

Well, this pale green puree would be good on sesame crackers too but looks so great against the black seaweed crackers. This is one use of soybeans I like. Makes about 1 1/2 cups, enough for about 20 crackers Ⓥ

- 1 1/2 cups shelled fresh or frozen edamame beans (not in the pods)
- Sea salt
- 1/4 teaspoon minced garlic
- 1 1/2 teaspoons toasted sesame oil
- 1 teaspoon or more to taste Meyer lemon juice or yuzu juice
- 1/2 teaspoon toasted black sesame seeds—more if you're making crackers for a crowd
- 1 green onion, very thinly slivered, on the diagonal, for garnish

Bring a few cups of water to a boil. Add the edamame, a few pinches salt, and return to a simmer. Cook until they're done, about 4 minutes, then drain, but reserve at least 1 cup of the cooking water.

Put the edamame in a food processor with the garlic, 1/2 teaspoon salt, and 1 teaspoon sesame oil. Pulse to puree, adding the reserved cooking water as needed to

Appetizers and First Courses

make the mixture smooth and creamy, about ¹/₂ cup but possibly more. Add lemon juice to taste and check again for salt.

Scrape the puree into a shallow bowl and run a knife back and forth over the top. Drizzle the remaining sesame oil over the top, then scatter over the sesame seeds and the green onion. Serve at room temperature with crackers, or mound the puree on each, add a few extra black sesame seeds and garnish with slivered green onion.

PITA CRISPS

Put stale pita bread to good use by making your own pita crisps to serve with eggplant and chickpea dips. Preheat the broiler. Separate a pita bread into two circles and brush the rough inside lightly with olive oil or water. Cut into wedges, spread them on a cookie sheet, and sprinkle sesame seeds over the tops. Broil just until toasty brown, a minute or so. Serve warm or let cool. Cumin or fennel seeds, sea salt, red pepper flakes, and black pepper can be sprinkled on in place of the sesame seeds.

Spicy Chickpea Puree (Hummus)

Originally, I saw this dip as an alternative to the ever-popular hummus, but I could never keep from adding a few spoonfuls of tahini. So, hummus it is, but with an extra bit of spice. If you cook your chickpeas in a pressure cooker (and I hope you will), 1 cup dried will make 2¹/₂ cups cooked. Use them all. Cook them on high, without soaking them first, in 8 cups of water, 1 teaspoon salt for 40 minutes.
Makes about 1¹/₂ to 2 cups Ⓥ

1 plump clove garlic

¹/₂ teaspoon sea salt

1¹/₂ cups (one 15-ounce can) or more cooked chickpeas,
   ¹/₄ cup or more held back for garnish

2 heaping tablespoons tahini, or more to taste

2 tablespoons olive oil, plus extra to finish

1 teaspoon toasted ground cumin

¹/₂ teaspoon toasted, ground coriander

¹/₄ teaspoon ground fennel seeds

2 to 3 tablespoons fresh lemon juice

To finish: chopped parsley, 1 tablespoon toasted pine nuts,
   sumac, or paprika

In a mortar, mash the garlic with the salt until creamy.

Puree the cooked chickpeas until smooth with the tahini and olive oil. If you're using a blender and the mixture is too thick, add the cooking water from the beans to thin it. It will thicken up again. Season the puree with the ground spices, lemon juice, and salt to taste.

Turn into a shallow bowl or platter and use an offset spatula to make handsome swirls. Drizzle the surface with extra olive oil, then finish by adding the reserved chickpeas, a little parsley, pine nuts, sumac, and/or paprika. Serve with pita crisps or vegetables.

White Bean, Sage, and Roasted Garlic Spread

The smell of the cooking beans is so rich and savory, it's tempting to forgo the puree and just eat them as a dish in their own right. Serve as a dip for celery or fennel or spread on croutons and garnish with a sage leaf or a tiny sprig of thyme. Makes about 2 cups Ⓥ

1¹/₂ cups navy beans or cannellini, soaked and drained

5 cloves garlic

10 sage leaves

2 bay leaves

3 tablespoons olive oil

1 whole head garlic, outermost papery husk removed

1 teaspoon sea salt

Juice of 1 lemon

Freshly milled pepper

1 tablespoon chopped thyme

Boil the beans in a large pot with water to cover by 2 inches for 10 minutes. Lower the heat and add the 5 cloves garlic, sage and bay leaves, and 2 teaspoons of the oil. Simmer, covered, until the beans are tender, about 1¹/₂ hours. Remove the bay leaves and drain, reserving the broth.

Meanwhile, preheat the oven to 350°F. Rub the head of garlic with a little of the remaining oil, put it in a small baking dish, and add ¹/₃ cup water. Cover and bake until soft and lightly caramelized, about 45 minutes. Cool, then squeeze out the softened garlic. Puree the beans in a food processor with all the garlic, the remaining oil, salt, and enough bean broth to give the beans a soft, spreadable consistency. Season to taste with lemon juice and pepper. Stir in the thyme leaves and serve warm.

With Basil Puree: Omit the sage and roasted garlic and add 1 cup basil leaves and 2 cloves garlic pureed in $^1/_3$ cup olive oil. Ⓥ

With Fermented Garlic and Ghee: A few cloves of sliced black fermented garlic added to the warm beans with ghee to taste makes an unusual umami-flavored spread.

White Bean Pâté: Oil a small, deep bowl or a narrow bread pan with plastic wrap, add the puree, and smooth it down. Turn it out onto a serving dish and peel away the plastic. Smooth the top with a spatula dipped in hot water, then garnish with sage or basil leaves. Ⓥ

Farinata

This is one of my favorite winter appetizers—winter because farinata needs a very hot oven, which is not so appealing when it's hot outside. I've eaten these soft chickpea bites in Italy and, more recently, at the home of Anya Fernald, who reminded me how good farinata is—even without Italy, a wood-burning stove, and the requisite copper pan. Your cast-iron skillets will work fine. Give yourself time for the batter to rest for 2 hours. Serves 6 or more Ⓥ

---

3 cups chickpea flour
1 scant tablespoon sea salt
1 teaspoon finely chopped rosemary leaves
$^1/_2$ cup olive oil
Freshly milled pepper

Slowly whisk the chickpea flour into 4 cups warm tap water until you have a smooth batter. Let stand at room temperature for 2 hours, then skim the batter to remove any foam.

Heat the oven to 500°F.

Stir in the salt, rosemary, and half the oil. Put two 10- or 12-inch cast-iron skillets in the oven for 10 minutes. Remove them, add 2 tablespoons of the oil to each skillet, and swirl to coat the pans. Divide the batter between the skillets; it should be less than $^1/_2$ inch thick. Bake for 25 to 30 minutes, until crisp around the edges. Slide the farinata onto a board, grind pepper over the surface, then cut or tear it into wedges. Eat it while it's hot and soft with a glass of cool white wine.

Eggplant Spreads and Purees

Eggplant has a reputation for absorbing large quantities of oil, which it's quite capable of doing, but it doesn't do that here—the eggplants are roasted and the oil is used for flavoring. Serve these spreads chilled or at room temperature with flatbreads, pita crisps, crackers, or croutons or as little vegetable salads.

Eggplants in season make the sweetest spreads, with no trace of bitterness. While any eggplant can be roasted, those weighing 6 ounces or more are more efficient to handle than very small ones. The standard teardrop-shaped American eggplant or the round European varieties, such as Rosa Bianca, are good choices. After roasting, very large eggplants often exude bitter juices as they cool. Simply discard the juice.

Roasted Eggplant with Dill, Yogurt, and Walnuts

This unusual green-flecked puree is easy to make with a mortar and pestle, which gives it a pleasing, slightly irregular texture, or you can use a food processor.
Makes about $1^1/_2$ cups

---

1 large or 2 medium eggplants, about 1$^1/_4$ pounds
3 cloves garlic
$^1/_3$ cup walnuts or pine nuts
$^1/_2$ teaspoon sea salt
$^1/_2$ cup chopped dill
3 tablespoons olive oil
$^1/_3$ to $^1/_2$ cup thick yogurt
Freshly milled pepper

Make four or five short incisions in the eggplant. Thinly slice one of the garlic cloves and insert a slice in each incision. Roast the eggplant as described in Roasted Eggplant Puree (facing).

Meanwhile, toast the nuts on a small sheet pan until fragrant, watching them carefully since the oven is hot. Coarsely chop. Pound the remaining garlic with the salt in a large mortar until smooth. Add the dill and olive oil and work it into a paste. Peel the eggplant, add the flesh to the mortar, and pound just enough to make a coarse puree. Stir in the yogurt, fold in the nuts, and season with salt and pepper to taste.

Roasted Eggplant Puree

The basic roasted eggplant, as simple as it is, is absolutely delicious, especially when still a little warm. Here the eggplant is coarsely chopped, making an eggplant caviar. But if you prefer, you can shred the flesh with your fingers or puree it in a food processor until smooth.

Makes about 1 1/2 cups (V)

---

1 pound eggplant

2 tablespoons olive oil

2 cloves garlic, put through a press or pounded with salt

Sea salt and freshly milled pepper

Chopped parsley, for garnish

Preheat the oven to 425°F. Slash the eggplant in several places so it won't explode. Put it in a pan and bake until it's soft to the point of collapsing, 30 to 40 minutes. Let cool for 15 minutes or so. Discard any bitter juices that may collect. Peel off the skin, then finely chop the flesh. Stir in the olive oil and garlic, and season with salt and pepper to taste. Mound it on a plate, garnish with the parsley, and serve with crackers or pita bread.

Eggplant Jam: This produces a rich, dark spread flecked with bits of skin. From a large eggplant, remove long ribbons of the skin about 1 inch wide and 1 inch apart. Slice the eggplant into rounds a scant 1/2 inch thick, then brown them on both sides in olive oil. As the eggplant becomes tender, begin mashing it with a fork until it has a thick jam-like consistency (you may have to add water by the 1/2 cup to help it cook). At this point, you can add any of the seasonings used in the following recipes. (V)

Spicy Eggplant Spread with Thai Basil

Fragrant Thai, anise, or cinnamon basil is perfect in this sweet, spicy puree, but regular basil will also be delicious here. Makes about 2 cups (V)

---

1 pound eggplant, any variety

1 1/2 tablespoons light brown sugar

2 tablespoons rice wine vinegar

1 tablespoon mushroom or dark Chinese soy sauce

1 or 2 serrano chiles, finely minced

3 tablespoons toasted sesame or roasted peanut oil

3 cloves garlic, minced

3 tablespoons chopped basil

Sea salt

Small basil leaves, for garnish

2 tablespoons black sesame seeds, toasted in a small skillet, for garnish

Roast the eggplant as described for Roasted Eggplant Puree (opposite), allowing the skin to char in places to give the dish a smoky flavor. Remove to a colander to cool. Peel—don't worry about stubborn flecks of skin—and coarsely chop the flesh.

Mix the sugar, vinegar, soy sauce, and chiles together. Heat a wok or skillet over high heat and add the oil. When it begins to haze, add the garlic and stir-fry for 30 seconds. Add the eggplant and stir-fry for 2 minutes, then add the sauce and fry for 1 minute more. Remove from the heat and stir in the chopped basil. Taste for salt.

Mound the eggplant in a bowl and garnish with the basil leaves and sesame seeds. Or spread on croutons or crackers and garnish each individually.

Baba Ghanoush (Roasted Eggplant with Tahini)

Everyone knows this delectable spread—and for good reason. It's a summer staple in my kitchen, enjoyed at lunch with salads of sliced tomatoes and cucumbers and, as often as not, again at dinner. Makes about 1 1/2 cups (V)

---

1 large or 2 medium eggplants, about 1 1/4 pounds

3 cloves garlic, coarsely chopped

1/4 cup tahini

Juice of 1 large lemon

Sea salt

Olive oil

Chopped parsley

Roast the eggplant as described for the Roasted Eggplant Puree (opposite), but let the skin harden and char in places to give the dish a smoky flavor. Alternatively, grill it slowly over the coals until soft. Peel the eggplant, then puree it in a blender or food processor with the garlic and tahini. Season with lemon juice and salt to taste. Mound the puree in a bowl and make a depression in the top with the back of a spoon. Pour olive oil into the hollow and sprinkle with parsley.

Salsas

A lively dip for chips, salsa—really the Spanish word for sauce—also are used with quesadillas, nachos, savory corn waffles, and enchiladas, and they're wonderful stirred into scrambled eggs or a bowl of beans, or spooned over vegetable fritters. The world of salsa has expanded enormously. Here are a few basic ones that can be used with all the dishes suggested above.

Tomato-Avocado Salsa

You can emphasize the avocado or the tomato, make it mild or hot, but do use it within an hour or so.
Makes about 1¹/₂ cups (V)

---

1 avocado, peeled and diced

1 ripe firm tomato, seeded and finely chopped

2 or 3 green onions, including half of the greens, thinly sliced

1 jalapeño chile, seeded, or 1 or 2 serrano chiles, finely diced

1 clove garlic, minced

¹/₄ teaspoon sea salt

A few drops sherry vinegar or lime juice

1 tablespoon chopped cilantro

Combine the avocado, tomato, green onions, chile, and garlic in a bowl. Add the salt and vinegar to bring up the flavors. Stir in the cilantro and let the salsa stand for 20 minutes before serving for the flavors to merge.

Tomatillo Salsa

Salsas made from these green husked tomatolike fruits have a pleasantly tart bite. A little pureed chipotle chile is also very good in this salsa. Makes about 1¹/₂ cups (V)

---

8 ounces tomatillos, husked

2 serrano chiles, quartered lengthwise

¹/₂ small white onion, sliced

5 cilantro sprigs

¹/₄ teaspoon sea salt

Put the tomatillos in a saucepan with water to cover. Bring to a boil, then lower the heat and simmer until they're dull green, about 10 minutes. Drain. Puree in a blender with the chiles, onion, cilantro, and salt. Chill before serving, unless you're serving it with enchiladas—then it should be warm.

Pico de Gallo

Also known as salsa Mexicana and salsa cruda, this is what comes with the chips in Mexican restaurants. (Cruda means "raw," not "crude.") For best results, chop very finely; large chunks of tomato are hard to catch on a chip.
Makes about 2 cups (V)

---

2 large ripe tomatoes, finely diced

2 cloves garlic, finely chopped

1 or more serrano chiles, finely diced, or 1 jalapeño chile, seeded and diced

¹/₄ cup finely diced white onion

2 tablespoons chopped cilantro

¹/₄ teaspoon sea salt

Juice of 1 lime or more

Combine the tomatoes with their juices, garlic, chiles, onion, cilantro, and salt in a bowl. Add the lime juice to taste and taste for salt. If the tomatoes weren't very juicy, add 1 tablespoon water. Let stand 20 minutes or so before serving.

With Chipotle Chile: Omit the fresh chile and stir in ¹/₂ teaspoon pureed chipotle chile. Increase the amount until it's as hot as you like it. (V)

Green Chile and Mint Salsa

Use this where you want a minty bite—in eggs, quesadillas, grain-based salads, or over grilled vegetables, especially corn and onions. Makes about ³/₄ cup (V)

---

1 or 2 serrano chiles, finely diced

¹/₂ green bell pepper, finely diced

2 tablespoons finely diced white or green onion

¹/₂ cup chopped cilantro

2 to 4 tablespoons chopped mint

Juice and grated zest of 2 limes

¹/₄ teaspoon sea salt

Combine the vegetables and herbs in a bowl and toss them with the lime juice, zest, and salt. Add 2 to 3 tablespoons water, cover, and refrigerate for 30 minutes before using if time allows.

Silky Mushroom Pâté with Green Onion–Walnut Topping

Mushroom pâtés of old were tasty but chunky affairs. This silky and luxurious version, inspired by a recipe in Gourmet, is impressive, especially on a buffet table. It also keeps long enough (up to 5 days) to have on hand during the busy holiday season.

This pâté isn't difficult to make, and you'll be proud of the results. But there are a few steps to keep track of, so be sure to read the recipe over before you start. You'll need a 6- to 8-cup terrine or a narrow (10 by 4-inch) bread pan.

Serves 15 to 20

1/2 ounce dried porcini

6 tablespoons butter, plus extra for the pan

2 medium leeks, white parts only, chopped

1 large clove garlic, minced

1/2 cup walnuts

1 pound white mushrooms, thinly sliced

2 1/2 teaspoons chopped thyme, or 1 tablespoon chopped marjoram

1/4 to 1/2 pound shiitake or cremini mushrooms, thinly sliced

3 eggs

1 cup cream

1/4 cup fine dry bread crumbs

1 1/2 tablespoons fresh lemon juice

1 1/2 teaspoons sea salt

Freshly milled pepper

Cover the dried porcini with 1 1/2 cups warm water and set aside to soak. Meanwhile, butter the pan for the pâté, then line it—including the ends—with parchment or wax paper and butter again. Preheat the oven to 350°F. Now, returning to the mushrooms, lift the porcini from the water, gently squeeze them dry, then chop them. Carefully decant the liquid into a small saucepan, leaving any sediment behind, bring to a boil, and simmer until only 2 tablespoons remain.

Melt 2 tablespoons of the butter in a wide skillet. Add the leeks, garlic, and walnuts and cook over medium heat, stirring occasionally, until the leeks are tender, about 6 minutes. Season with salt and transfer to a blender.

Melt 2 tablespoons more butter in the same skillet over fairly high heat. When the butter foams, add three-quarters of the white mushrooms and a pinch of the thyme. Sauté until they begin to color, after a few minutes. Add these to the blender. Melt another 2 tablespoons butter and repeat with the remaining white mushrooms, shiitakes, and chopped porcini, plus another pinch of thyme. Set aside.

Add the eggs and cream to the blender, then puree until the mixture is completely smooth. Pour the mixture into a bowl and fold in the reserved sautéed mushrooms, remaining thyme, reduced mushroom water, bread crumbs, lemon juice, salt, and several twists of the peppermill.

Transfer the mixture to the prepared pan and cover the top tightly with aluminum foil. Set it in a baking pan and add hot water to come halfway up the sides. Bake in the center of the oven for 1 hour and 10 minutes. It should be browned on top and starting to pull away from the sides. Remove and refrigerate until completely chilled, at least 6 hours, but allow it to return to room temperature before serving.

To serve, gently pull at the paper lining to ease the pâté from the sides of the pan or run a hot knife along the edges. Set a platter over the pâté, then invert. Ease the pan off the pâté, then peel off the paper. Any rough-looking spots can be smoothed with a hot knife. Prepare the green onion–walnut topping, below, and spoon it over the top just before serving. Serve with crackers, thin toast, or fresh bread that has plenty of character.

Green Onion–Walnut Topping

1 1/2 tablespoons butter

1/3 cup walnuts, chopped

2 bunches green onion, including half of the greens, thinly sliced

4 tablespoons chopped parsley

Sea salt and freshly milled pepper

Melt the butter in a medium skillet over fairly high heat. When foamy, add the walnuts and cook, stirring frequently, until they begin to color a little, about 3 minutes. Add the onions and parsley and cook until the onions are bright green and tender, about 3 minutes. Season with salt and plenty of pepper. Spoon this mixture over the pâté just before serving.

Crostini, Canapés, Tartines

Regardless of what name they go by—crostini, canapés, tartines—small open-faced sandwiches are what many of us look to when we need an appetizer or an accompaniment to round out a soup and salad meal. They're pretty to look at, far simpler to make than individual pastries, and easy to improvise. They require so little in the way of toppings that often a tablespoon or two of a spread, a sprig of herbs, a sliced mushroom, and a dab of mayonnaise to hold everything fast is all that's needed. When friends drop by at the end of the day, I often find myself putting together a plate of canapés or tartines to have with a glass of wine. Because of their diminutive nature, small sandwiches can support an intensity and richness that might be overpowering in a large sandwich.

CANAPÉS: These old-fashioned cocktail or tea sandwiches consist of soft but not squishy bread, buttered (flavored butters shine here) or covered with a spread, and topped with fresh vegetables like cucumbers and radishes, sprigs of herbs, grated vegetable salads, and so on. Although canapés have a 1950s image, they have a contemporary feeling too since they convey freshness and flavor without being filling. Choose a soft bread—white sandwich bread, whole wheat, rye, even a pita or a specialty bread. Slice thinly, remove the crusts if they're hard, cover thinly with butter or other spread, and top. Cut them into small squares or fingers.

CROSTINI AND CROUTONS: These are the Italian and French names for little crusts, or golden rounds of toasted bread. Baguettes are perfect for crostini, although larger pieces of bread can be toasted, then cut into smaller pieces. Slice sweet or sour French bread a little less than $1/2$ inch thick and toast in a moderate (350°F) oven, turning it once, until lightly browned and crisp but still soft in the middle. Remove, then brush with olive oil. If desired, rub with a clove of garlic. If large, cut in half or into small pieces.

TARTINES: The charming French open-faced sandwiches called tartines have suddenly gained a new stature in America. San Francisco has its restaurant, Tartine, and in Santa Fe, where I live, Andrée Falls, who owns Sage Bakehouse, where she produces a small but choice selection of breads, also serves tartines with a salad or bowl of soup at lunch. She used to eat tartines in Paris at Poilâne's Bar and loved that civilized small meal. Hence, she offers tartines here.

What sets them apart from other slices of bread with toppings? First, the bread is toasted on only one side; the toppings go on on the soft side. Second, it's spread with butter and not rubbed with garlic and olive oil. And as for the bread, it's likely to be a slice of sourdough or levain bread cut into little fingers so that they're easy to pick up and eat. Andrée uses slices from a 3-pound loaf of sourdough bread. She says that the large loaf develops better flavor, just like red wine tastes better in a large glass than a smaller one. While tartine toppings more than flirt with the likes of Serrano ham, sardine paste, chicken breast, and smoked salmon, there are plenty of vegetable options too, and any of the canapés and crostini can be made into tartines.

Tartines with Asparagus Tips: Toast a piece of sourdough bread on one side. Spread Tarragon Mayonnaise with Capers (page 52) on the soft side. Lay cooked asparagus diagonally across the tartine, season with a pinch of salt and some pepper, then cut the bread into fingerlike pieces.

Radish Canapés: Radish canapés make a colorful and spicy bite, particularly when made with different colored radishes or, of course, the mild French breakfast radishes. Spread sliced baguettes with unsalted butter, then cover with thinly sliced radishes. Sprinkle with sea salt and garnish with some nice-looking radish leaves, radish sprouts, or sprouted cress.

Cucumber and Herb Canapés: Cover whole wheat or multigrain bread or toast with thick yogurt, sour cream, or tofu "mayonnaise," then sprinkle with chopped herbs, such as salad burnet, lovage, nasturtium leaves, watercress, lemon verbena, or parsley. Layer thinly sliced cucumbers on top, season with a pinch of salt or one of the herb salts on pages 67 to 69, and freshly milled white pepper. This combination also works well as a tartine. (V)

Guacamole Toasts or Tartines with Pickled Onions: Cover sourdough bread, toasted on one side only, with guacamole and top with diced Pickled Red Onions (page 72), or onion rings, cilantro sprigs, and finely diced jalapeños and a squeeze of lime juice.

Pita Triangles with Eggplant Spread and Roasted Peppers: Make pita crisps or cut fresh pita bread into triangles. Top with a spoonful of Roasted Eggplant Puree (page 89), a strip of roasted pepper, and a leaf of parsley or basil. Arrange on a plate and serve with accompanying bowl of olives and fresh celery or fennel. (V)

Frittata Sandwiches: Cut thin frittatas into pieces the same size as the bread, and place on slices of French, Italian, or American bread spread with a thin film of mayonnaise or Romesco sauce (page 62). These are good made small or large enough to make a meal.

Tartines with Mixed Tomatoes and Basil: Wait for summer's tomatoes to make this tartine. Choose different sizes, shapes, and colors and slice them in rounds. Toast a large piece of sourdough bread on one side. Spread mayonnaise over the soft side, then overlap the tomatoes, covering the bread. Season with salt and pepper. Slice them into finger shapes, intersperse small basil leaves among them, and drizzle with olive oil.

Crostini with Diced Tomatoes and Fontina Cheese: For 4 toasts, dice a large tomato and mix it with a teaspoon of minced shallot or green onion, a pinch of salt, and a little pepper. Stir in a tablespoon or two of small cubes of diced fontina or ricotta salata cheese. Add a teaspoon of olive oil and a few drops of balsamic vinegar and spoon over crostini.

Crostini with Fresh Mozzarella, Tomatoes, and Olive Paste: Bocconcini (bite-size mozzarella cheeses) and cherry tomatoes are ideal for crostini, while full-size mozzarella and tomatoes make fine tartine. Cover toasted bread with a layer of Olive Paste (page 78). Overlap layers of tomatoes and thinly sliced fresh mozzarella. Broil until the cheese is bubbling, then remove and drizzle with extra-virgin olive oil (optional) and freshly milled pepper.

Crostini with Olive Paste, Ricotta, and Marjoram: The olive paste provides the salt and intensity for this mild cheese. Spread toasted baguette or country bread with a thin layer of Olive Paste (page 78) and a thick layer of ricotta cheese. Season with freshly cracked pepper and drizzle with your best olive oil. Broil to warm the cheese, then cover with chopped marjoram or dried crumbled oregano. Serve warm.

Crostini or Tartines with White Bean, Sage, and Roasted Garlic Spread: This topping is richly flavored and aromatic. Spread warm White Bean, Sage, and Roasted Garlic Spread (page 87) over warm garlic toasts and arrange several of these on a platter. Cover with chopped parsley, Fried Sage Leaves (page 193), or finely diced pickled onions and capers. Garnish the plate with sprigs of sage leaves. (V)

Crostini or Tartines with Artichoke and Chervil: Grill or toast white sandwich bread or sweet baguette, then brush lightly with olive oil or butter and cover with the Artichoke Pesto (page 84). Garnish with chopped tarragon, chervil or chives, and a little white pepper.

Crostini with Artichoke Mayonnaise: Mix Artichoke Pesto (page 84) with homemade mayonnaise, to taste. Spread over crostini or tartines and cover with finely grated parmesan cheese. Broil just to warm, then garnish with minced parsley, tarragon, or thyme.

Crostini with Green Olives and Romesco Sauce: This lively, pretty appetizer, one of my favorites, is one to serve with a glass of sherry and a dish of toasted almonds. Spread Garlic-Rubbed Crostini (page 24) with a generous layer of Romesco Sauce (page 62), then cover with sliced green Spanish olives and sprinkle with minced parsley. (V)

Warm Goat Cheese Crostini or Tartines: Use a plain, herbed, or marinated goat cheese. Mash, then mound it on garlic-rubbed crostini or the soft side of toasted sourdough bread, drizzle over a little olive oil, then broil until the cheese begins to soften. Garnish with a pitted niçoise olive, a thin piece of roasted pepper, or finely chopped fresh herbs such as thyme, parsley, or rosemary. Serve warm.

Grilled Cheese and Green Chile "Fingers"

Of course you can eat the whole sandwich, but cut into fingers, they make a fine little appetizer. There will be none left whether you're serving two people or more. Makes 8 pieces

4 green chiles, such as Anaheim, Big Jim, or Joe Parker

1 scant cup grated medium cheddar or Monterey Jack cheese

4 slices whole wheat, rye, or your choice of bread

4 teaspoons butter

Roast the chiles on the stove, as you would bell peppers, turning them to evenly char the skins. Put them in a bowl, set a plate on top, and steam for 10 minutes or longer. Pull off the skins and scrape out the seeds, then cut the chiles into wide strips.

Place ¹/₄ cup of the cheese on one slice of bread, add the chile, then cover with another ¹/₄ cup of cheese and a second piece of bread and press down. Repeat with the rest.

Melt half the butter in a seasoned cast-iron skillet over medium heat. When bubbling, add the sandwiches. Cover the pan and cook until the bottom is crisp and golden, 3 to 4 minutes. Remove the sandwiches, melt the rest of the butter, and return the sandwiches to the pan, uncooked side down. Cook until the cheese is melted and the bread is browned and crisp. Cut diagonally into fingers, and serve.

Warm Crostini with Blue Cheese and Walnut Spread

I love these with a glass of sherry, winter squash soup, or a salad of pears and endive. The butter melts into the crisp toast; the cheese stays on top. It's heady and very aromatic. You can also make this as you would a tartine, then slice it into fingers and serve with your soup or salad. Makes 8

8 slices baguette or country bread, about 2 by 3 inches

4 ounces Roquefort, Maytag, or Danish blue cheese

3 tablespoons butter, at room temperature

1 teaspoon cognac

¹/₄ cup finely chopped walnuts

Freshly milled pepper

Finely chopped parsley, for garnish

Preheat the broiler. Toast the bread under the broiler on both sides until nicely browned on one side, a little less so on the second. Cream the cheese and butter until smooth, then work in the cognac, three-quarters of the walnuts, and season with pepper. Spread on the paler side of the toast, then broil until the cheese is bubbling. Remove, dust with the remaining nuts, and garnish with parsley. Serve warm.

Cheese Toasts

These warm, fragrant toasts are just the tease they should be—arousing but not sating the appetite. Pass them around while warm or serve them tucked among the leaves of a salad. For cheese, a good strong cheddar is fine, but so is a creamy Jack or fontina, a mild goat, Tilsit or smoked cheese—whatever's on hand at the moment.

Makes 10 to 12 little toasts

1 egg, separated, or 1 egg white only

1 teaspoon Dijon mustard

Pinch cayenne

3/4 cup grated cheese, see note

1 teaspoon minced green onion or shallot

12 slices baguette, or 3 slices sandwich bread, quartered

Sea salt and freshly milled pepper

Preheat the oven to 400°F. Combine the yolk, if using, with the mustard and cayenne, then stir in the cheese, green onion, and a little salt. Whisk the egg white until it holds soft peaks and fold it into the mixture. Spread the mixture on the bread and bake until puffed and golden, about 5 minutes. Season with salt and pepper and serve.

Chile Cheese Toasts: Use cheddar, Muenster, or Jack cheese. Spread a thin layer of pureed chipotle chile on the bread, then add the cheese mixture and bake as above. Garnish with chopped cilantro.

Feta Cheese Toasts with Marjoram and Tomato: Cream 1/2 cup feta cheese with enough milk to soften. Season with pepper and spread on the bread. Sprinkle with chopped marjoram, a slice of Roma tomato, and drizzle with olive oil. Broil until the cheese is soft.

Crostini or Tartines with Feta Cheese and Tomatoes: Cover crostini or sourdough bread toasted on one side with thinly sliced mild feta cheese. Broil until the cheese is soft and beginning to brown in places. Remove and sprinkle with chopped marjoram or basil mixed with a little fresh mint, black pepper, and olive oil. Serve with finely diced tomatoes spooned over the warm cheese.

Cheese Toasts or Tartines with Pesto: Spread Pesto (page 50) or Tomato-Basil Pesto (page 50) over the bread, then top with crumbled goat cheese or cheddar. Bake or broil until the cheese is soft and fragrant.

More Toppings for Crostini and Tartines

Egg Salad, page 112

Spicy Chickpea Puree (Hummus), page 87, with toasted pine nuts

Sliced avocado with Meyer lemon, shallot, and green herbs

Pea and Avocado Dip with Lemon Zest, Tarragon, and Chives, page 83

Grilled or caramelized onions with Gruyère cheese

Spring Rolls

Many vegetables can go inside a spring roll, and the wrapper packages usually come with recipes. Here are three very different fillings. The first is served with hot mustard, which is simply dry mustard mixed with water. The third has its own peanut dipping sauce.

Spring Rolls with Napa Cabbage and Tofu

A recipe from Eileen Yin–Fei Lo's book From the Earth: Chinese Vegetarian Cooking *was the point of departure for this filling, which makes a light and unusual salad when tossed with an orange vinaigrette.* Makes about 12 (V)

2 tablespoons dry mustard

2 slices ginger plus 1 tablespoon minced

1 tablespoon plus 3/4 teaspoon sea salt

4 cups thinly shredded napa cabbage, about 1 pound

1 bunch green onions, preferably thick ones, including 3 inches of the greens, sliced

1 cup broccoli florets, cut into small pieces

1 (10-ounce) package seasoned firm tofu, finely diced or slivered

1 tablespoon minced garlic

2 teaspoons toasted sesame oil

1 teaspoon sugar

1/2 teaspoon rice wine vinegar

12 egg roll wrappers

12 cilantro sprigs

Peanut oil, for frying

Mix the mustard with 3 tablespoons water and set aside.

Heat 8 cups water with the sliced ginger and 1 tablespoon of the salt. When it boils, add the cabbage, onions, and broccoli and cook for 1 1/2 minutes. (The water won't return to a boil.) Drain the vegetables, rinse them with cold water, then wrap them in a clean towel and squeeze several times until dry. Combine them with the tofu, minced ginger, and garlic. Sprinkle with sesame oil, sugar, vinegar, and the remaining 3/4 teaspoon salt. Toss well and taste the mixture to be sure it's seasoned sufficiently.

Lay one egg roll wrapper on the counter at a diagonal, with a corner facing you. Heap 3 tablespoons of the filling crosswise, near the base. Lay a cilantro sprig on top. Fold up the lower corner, fold in the outer corners, then wrap. Repeat, using the rest of the filling. Place the egg rolls on a plate and cover with wax paper, then with plastic, until ready to cook.

To cook, heat 1/2 inch peanut oil in a medium skillet until hot enough to quickly sizzle a corner of an egg roll. Add two egg rolls and fry until golden, about 2 minutes. Turn and fry the second side, then transfer to paper towels to drain. Continue frying the rest. Serve hot with the mustard sauce.

Spring Rolls with Shiitake Mushroom Filling

Where I live, the mung bean sprouts are often broken and limp, so I use big, fresh sunflower seed or spicy radish sprouts instead. Not a bad alternative, actually. Makes 8 to 10 (V)

1 tablespoon cornstarch

1 1/2 tablespoons soy sauce

1 1/2 tablespoons roasted peanut oil

8 to 10 fresh shiitake mushroom caps, thinly sliced

1 bunch green onions, preferably thick ones, including 3 inches of the greens, sliced diagonally

1 tablespoon minced ginger

1 large carrot, julienned, about 3/4 cup

3 cups very thinly sliced napa cabbage

1 teaspoon sea salt

8 to 10 egg roll wrappers

1 cup large mung bean or sunflower sprouts

Peanut oil, for frying

Mix the cornstarch, soy sauce, and 1/3 cup water in a small bowl and set aside.

Heat the oil in a wok or a wide skillet. When a haze appears, add the mushrooms, onions, ginger, and carrot and stir-fry for 3 minutes. Add the cabbage, sprinkle with salt, and stir-fry until bright green and starting to turn limp, about 2 minutes. Stir in the cornstarch mixture and stir-fry until the vegetables are coated and the pan is dry, up to 3 minutes. Turn off the heat. Taste for salt and transfer the vegetables to a bowl to cool.

Form the spring rolls as described in the preceding recipe. Use about 2 tablespoons filling and cover it with sprouts before rolling. Fry in hot peanut oil as described in preceding recipe. Eat while crisp and hot with or without a dipping sauce.

Vietnamese Spring Rolls

I buy these rolls for lunch whenever I visit Vancouver's bustling Granville Island Market. I make them at home for an appetizer or light lunch and serve them with a glass of Riesling. It takes a few practice tries to learn how to fold the rice paper around the filling, but your fingers will soon become nimble.

Makes 12 large or 24 small rolls, serving 6 to 12 (V)

- 2 ounces cellophane noodles
- 1 carrot
- 1 cup mung bean sprouts, blanched briefly
- 2 cups finely shredded napa cabbage
- 5 green onions, quartered lengthwise and sliced
- 1/2 cup coarsely chopped cilantro or Vietnamese coriander
- 1/3 cup coarsely chopped mint
- 1/4 cup thinly sliced Thai or Italian basil leaves
- 1/2 teaspoon sugar
- 3 cloves garlic
- Pinch sea salt
- 2 serrano chiles, thinly sliced
- Juice of 2 limes
- 12 large or 24 small round Vietnamese rice papers
- 24 butter or Boston lettuce leaves
- Peanut Dipping Sauce, recipe follows

Soak the noodles in hot water to cover until soft and pliable, about 30 minutes. Snip them into 2-inch lengths and drain. Make the sauce and set it aside.

Using a vegetable peeler, peel the carrot right down to the core, making long, thin strips. Combine them with the noodles, bean sprouts, cabbage, onions, herbs, and sugar. Smash the garlic in a mortar or food processor with a pinch of salt and chiles to make a paste, then stir in the lime juice. Toss with the vegetables.

Fill a bowl with warm water and spread a clean towel on the counter. Working with one paper at a time, slip it into the water and soak until soft and pliable, about 10 seconds, then remove and set on the towel. Mound some of the vegetable mixture at one end of the rice paper, roll it over once, fold over the sides, and roll to the end, making a neat little package. When all are done, slice the large rolls in half and stand them, cut side up, on a plate lined with lettuce leaves. Leave small rolls whole. Use the lettuce as an additional wrapper, to keep all the ingredients neatly contained. If the spring rolls aren't to be served right away, cover them with a barely damp towel and refrigerate. Serve with the sauce.

Peanut Dipping Sauce

- 2 tablespoons rice wine vinegar
- 3 tablespoons water or Vegetarian Nuoc Cham (page 528)
- 1 teaspoon chili oil
- 1 clove garlic, minced
- 3 tablespoons roasted peanuts, chopped
- 1 teaspoon sugar

Combine all the ingredients and let stand 10 minutes before using.

Other Vegetable Appetizers

More succulent than crudités simply because more has been done to them, cooked and marinated vegetables also make delicious appetizers. Many are extremely simple to make from scratch, while others can be drawn from leftovers such as Peperonata (page 363), Roasted Poblano and Sweet Pepper Strips with Onions (page 364), Caramelized Onions (page 358), or the Tunisian Pepper and Potato Stew over Couscous (page 225). You can perk up leftovers with a dash of vinegar, some grated lemon zest, or a spoonful of capers. Sometimes nothing at all is needed but a crouton or piece of bread to hold the vegetable while mopping up its savory juices.

Eggplant Rounds with Shallots and Basil

Small Asian and slender Italian eggplants fit better on a crouton if you want to serve little open-faced sandwiches. The eggplant will keep, refrigerated, for several days, but bring it to room temperature before serving.
Serves 4 to 6 Ⓥ

- 1 pound small eggplants
- Olive oil
- Sea salt and freshly milled pepper
- 2 large shallots, finely diced
- 2 cloves garlic, thinly sliced
- Balsamic, aged sherry, or Chinese black vinegar
- 15 basil leaves, torn into small pieces, plus small leaves for garnish

Preheat the broiler. Slice the eggplants into $1/2$ -inch rounds or ovals. Brush both sides with oil, set on a sheet pan, and broil on both sides until golden. Or, if you prefer, grill them. (Don't worry if the surfaces look dry; they'll soften later.) While they're still hot, make a layer on a plate, season with salt and pepper, and sprinkle with shallots, garlic, and a few drops of vinegar. Scatter the torn basil over the top, then cover with another layer of eggplant and repeat. When done, cover with plastic wrap and let stand for 15 minutes. Pile on a plate or serve on croutons and garnish with basil leaves.

Sweet and Sour Eggplant, Crumbled Feta, and Mint

The honey, vinegar, and salty cheese make an intriguing mixture of tastes on the tongue. Serves 4

- 1 pound eggplant
- Sea salt and freshly milled pepper
- $1/4$ cup olive or sunflower seed oil
- 1 red onion, finely diced
- 4 tomatoes, seeded and diced
- 3 tablespoons red wine vinegar or sherry vinegar
- 1 tablespoon honey
- 2 teaspoons chopped mint
- $1/3$ cup thinly sliced or crumbled feta or ricotta salata

Slice the eggplant into $1/2$-inch rounds, then into $1/2$-inch strips. Unless very fresh, sprinkle with salt and let stand 30 minutes or longer. Rinse and pat dry. Heat $2^1/2$ tablespoons of the oil in a wide skillet over medium heat. When a haze forms over the oil, add the eggplant and sauté, stirring frequently, until browned all over, about 12 minutes. Taste for salt and season with pepper. Heat the remaining $1^1/2$ tablespoons oil in a wide skillet, add the onion, and sauté over medium heat until beginning to color. (The amount of onion will be small for the skillet, but you'll need the surface area to quickly evaporate the vinegar in the next step.) Add the tomatoes, vinegar, and honey, raise the heat, and cook, shaking the pan frequently, until the vinegar is evaporated. Add the mint and eggplant and mix gently. Let cool, fold in the cheese, and serve.

Crispy Roasted Chickpeas with Spice and Smoke

Usually served as a snack, these crispy chickpeas can be used to garnish farinata, *hummus, or a pasta that includes chickpeas. And of course, they are great for nibbling. They need to be very dry before roasting, so don't skip that part. Often these are fried, but they really have to be deep-fried to come out crisp and crunchy. In place of frying, I prefer roasting them until they're utterly crisp. I suspect you can make quite similar dishes using cooked beans and lentils, too.* Makes 1½ cups Ⓥ

1½ cups (one 15-ounce can) cooked chickpeas

½ teaspoon toasted, ground cumin

½ teaspoon toasted, ground coriander

½ teaspoon smoked paprika

¼ teaspoon cayenne or red pepper flakes

½ teaspoon sea salt

1 tablespoon olive oil

Smoked salt, as needed

Several pinches lime zest, fresh or dried

Drain the chickpeas, give them a rinse, then turn them onto a towel. Blot up any excess moisture with the towel and let dry while you heat the oven to 375°F. Put the spices in a bowl with the sea salt and olive oil.

Line a sheet pan with parchment paper and pour over the chickpeas. Bake, giving the pan a little shake every 15 minutes or so until dark and crispy, about 45 minutes or however long is needed. They need to really dry out; if they don't, they'll be somewhat mushy and not nearly as appealing. When done, tip them into the bowl with the spices and oil and toss them to coat, then return to the oven for a few more minutes. Taste and toss with the smoked salt, as needed, and dried or fresh lime zest. Cool before eating and store in an airtight container.

Crispy Chickpeas with Dukkah: Toss the chickpeas with a tablespoon or more of Dukkah (page 68) in place of the spice mixture and salt, to taste. Ⓥ

Crispy Chickpeas with Garam Masala: In place of the given spices, put 1 tablespoon Garam Masala (page 25) in the bowl with a few pinches of salt and 2 teaspoons sunflower seed or coconut oil. Toss with this mixture plus lime juice or zest. Ⓥ

Jicama and Cucumbers with Chile and Lime

A large tuber covered with a paper tan skin, jicama has a white flesh that is crisp, juicy, and sweet. Serves 4 to 6 Ⓥ

½ small jicama, about 8 ounces

2 cucumbers

Grated zest and juice of 2 limes

1 jalapeño chile, seeded and finely diced

Sea salt

Peel the jicama and cut into bite-size cubes. Peel the cucumbers if they've been waxed; otherwise score the skins with a fork, then quarter them lengthwise and dice into cubes. If they're very mature, scrape out and discard the seeds first. Toss everything together and taste for salt and lime. Refrigerate until very cold, or serve right away on little plates with toothpicks or small forks.

Roasted Potatoes with Chile Mayonnaise

Jody Apple, a bold and fearless cook from New Mexico, serves these golden potatoes with mayonnaise made red with her homegrown chiles. Smoky ingredients are good too, such as smoked paprika, or, skipping the mayonnaise, smoked salt. Serves 4 Ⓥ

---

2 large russet potatoes, about 1 pound

Olive or other oil

Sea salt

Red Chile Mayonnaise (page 52) or mayonnaise with smoked paprika, or smoked salt

Preheat the oven to 400°F and lightly oil a baking dish.

Neatly peel the potatoes with a paring knife and cut them lengthwise into quarters or sixths if very large. Toss them with just enough oil to coat and season with salt. Bake until they're tender and covered with a golden crust, about an hour, turning them a few times so that they color evenly. Serve with the mayonnaise or, for a vegan version, with smoked salt.

Golden Artichoke Wedges

These succulent little nuggets are just the thing to offer to guests who are standing around the kitchen before dinner. Serve them with lemon wedges or a silky homemade mayonnaise for dipping. Serves 4

---

4 medium artichokes, trimmed and quartered (see page 295), or 12 baby artichokes

Juice of 1 lemon

1/2 cup flour

2 eggs

Sea salt and freshly milled pepper

1 cup olive or vegetable oil

Lemon wedges

Tarragon Mayonnaise with Capers (page 52), for dipping, optional

Slice the trimmed artichokes into wedges a little less than 1/2 inch thick, dropping them into the lemon juice mixed with water to cover as you work. When all are done, drain and pat dry. (If using the baby artichokes, trim the base and top, then slice lengthwise into thirds.)

Put the flour on a plate. Beat the eggs with a few pinches salt and a little pepper in a shallow bowl. Dip the artichokes into the egg, then toss them in the flour to coat lightly.

Heat the oil in a medium skillet until hot enough to sizzle a bread crumb. Fry a few artichokes at a time over high heat until golden, 3 to 4 minutes. Pile them on a plate, sprinkle with salt and a squeeze of lemon juice, and serve, with or without a bowl of mayonnaise for dipping.

Artichokes Leaf by Leaf: Served warm or chilled, artichokes can be a first course, or, when shared, an appetizer. And sharing a giant artichoke can certainly be an icebreaker.

Clip the leaves with scissors if they have thorns; slice off the top third and even the bottom so that it stands. Rub the cut parts with lemon, then steam over boiling water until a leaf comes easily free when tugged, about 45 minutes.

Don't just limit yourself to melted butter and plain mayonnaise. Serve with any number of sauces, allowing about 1/4 cup per person, in individual bowls. Try olive oil seasoned with salt and freshly ground pepper; one of the flavored mayonnaises, yogurt sauces, Cilantro Salsa (page 49), Salsa Verde (page 48), Herb-Butter and Olive Oil Sauce (page 44), or Green Goddess Dressing (page 169). Have an extra bowl on the table for the finished leaves.

Fennel in Lemon and White Wine

Pale fennel is lovely prepared this way, but many vegetables are good candidates for treating in this fashion, such as celery, mushrooms, carrots, pearl onions, cauliflower florets, tender turnips, and radishes. In fact, a bouqet of several pickled vegetables can be very fetching on a composed salad plate. Serves 4 to 6 Ⓥ

1 teaspoon coriander seeds

¹/₂ teaspoon peppercorns

¹/₄ teaspoon fennel seeds

2 to 3 fennel bulbs, approximately 1 pound, quartered

1 onion, thinly sliced

3 large cloves garlic, crushed

1 bay leaf

Pinch sea salt

2 teaspoons olive oil

¹/₂ cup dry white wine

Juice of 1 lemon

Gently bruise the coriander, pepper, and fennel to release their flavors. Combine everything in a noncorrosive pan with water to cover and bring to a boil. Lower the heat and simmer, covered, until the fennel is tender but still a little firm when pierced with a knife, 15 to 20 minutes, depending on the size of the pieces. Transfer the fennel to a dish. Raise the heat, reduce the cooking liquid by about one-third, then pour it over the fennel. Cover and refrigerate. Serve chilled, the pieces left whole or thinly sliced.

With Other Vegetables: Leave small carrots whole or cut larger ones into 3-inch lengths; trim celery into 3-inch lengths; leave small mushrooms and radishes whole; quarter larger mushrooms; separate cauliflower into florets and parboil for 1 minute; scrub young turnips and peel and quarter older ones; parboil and peel boiling onions. Remove individual vegetables as they become tender.

Marinated Mushrooms with Tarragon

This easy dish can be assembled up to 2 hours in advance. A great appetizer, these mushrooms are also good tossed in a spinach salad. When fresh tarragon isn't available, cumin makes an excellent alternative. Serves 3 or 4 Ⓥ

2 cloves garlic

¹/₂ teaspoon sea salt

4 to 6 green onions, including some of the greens, thinly sliced

2¹/₂ tablespoons red wine vinegar

4 teaspoons chopped tarragon, or ¹/₂ teaspoon cumin seeds

¹/₄ cup olive oil

8 ounces white mushrooms, stem ends trimmed

2 pinches red pepper flakes

Coarsely cracked pepper

Finely chop the garlic with the salt or smash it in a mortar until smooth. Combine with the onions, vinegar, and tarragon in a bowl, then whisk in the oil. (If using the cumin, toast the seeds in a small pan until they smell fragrant, then cool and grind to a powder.) Unless the mushrooms are very small, cut them into quarters, slightly angling each cut to make a more interesting shape. Pour the dressing over the mushrooms and toss with the pepper flakes. Taste for salt and season with pepper. Cover and refrigerate until ready to serve.

Cheese and Egg Appetizers

Yes, they're filling, but cheese and eggs have a place when the meal that follows is small or light. Leave the buttery triple-cream cheeses for a cheese course or dessert and offer lighter cheeses for appetizers. Remember, cold dulls the taste of most foods, especially cheeses, so make sure they're served at room temperature.

Goat Cheese Log Dusted with Herbs

Present the log whole on a small platter or use the same treatment with small rounds and logs of cheese. Serve at room temperature with bread or crackers. Serves 6 to 8

> 1/4 cup finely chopped mixed herbs—thyme or lemon thyme, parsley, marjoram, summer savory, and rosemary
> Freshly milled black pepper
> 1 (11-ounce) log or round of goat cheese
> Maldon sea salt

Toss the herbs with several grinds of pepper. Scatter this mixture on a cutting board and roll the cheese in it until well coated. Serve sliced with a sprinkling of Maldon salt.

Bocconcini with Red Pepper Flakes

These bite-size balls of fresh mozzarella can be found in Italian markets, delicatessens, and many supermarkets. They make a succulent tidbit to pop into your mouth. Allow 2 for each person

> Bocconcini
> Olive oil
> Red pepper flakes
> Coarsely milled black pepper
> Coarsely chopped parsley, plus sprigs for garnish

Drain the cheese and place in a serving dish. Drizzle the olive oil generously over it, then add a pinch or two of pepper flakes, pepper, and parsley. Gently toss everything together. Let stand for 1 hour or serve right away, garnished with long sprigs of the dark green parsley. Serve with toothpicks.

Bocconcini with Tomatoes: Toss whole red and yellow cherry, currant, or pear tomatoes with the bocconcini, torn basil leaves, and olive oil. Or thread pieces of cheese, tomatoes, and basil leaves on short skewers, drizzle with olive oil, and add freshly cracked pepper.

EGGS AS APPETIZERS

Peel hard-cooked eggs, halve them lengthwise, and set each half on a radicchio leaf. Spoon Olive Paste or Hot and Spicy Tapenade (page 78), on top of the yolk. Alternatively you can mash the yolks with the Olive Paste, then spoon it back into the whites.

Frittatas (see chapter 15 for recipes) are quite good at room temperature and can be made a few hours ahead of time. Here are three ways to serve them:

- Make them 1/2 inch thick or less, cut into small squares or diamonds, and serve on thinly sliced baguette with a dab of mayonnaise.
- Make them thicker, cut into bite-size pieces, and pile them onto a platter. Serve as a finger food or offer toothpicks.
- For an elaborate first course, make very thin frittatas (the same or different flavors) and layer them with a binding of seasoned mayonnaise. Slice into wedges and serve. For example, layer thin red pepper, zucchini, and olive frittatas with a binding of saffron mayonnaise between them.

Warm Feta Cheese with Sesame Seeds

Covered with toasted sesame seeds, this cheese makes a crunchy, succulent first course or addition to a salad. Serve with fresh bread to mop up the juices. Serves 4 to 6

8 ounces feta, in two chunks

2 tablespoons butter

2 tablespoons olive oil

2 bay leaves

Freshly milled pepper

Juice of 1 large lemon

2 teaspoons chopped marjoram

1 tablespoon toasted sesame seeds

If the feta tastes too salty, soak it in water for 20 minutes, then drain. Slice into slabs $^3/_8$ inch thick. Thicker, it won't warm through; thinner, it'll fall apart. Warm the butter and olive oil with the bay leaves in a wide skillet over medium heat until the bay releases its aroma. Add the cheese in a single layer, season with pepper, and heat until it softens and begins to bubble. Turn it over and cook the second side for 1 minute. Add the lemon juice and let it sizzle for a few seconds, then transfer the cheese to a plate. Scrape up any golden, crisp bits of cheese that have stuck to the bottom of the pan and include them, too. Sprinkle with the marjoram and sesame seeds and serve.

Fried Halloumi Cheese

Traditionally appetizers, these golden cubes of melting cheese also make a succulent garnish for rice and legumes, such as Rice with Spinach, Lemon, and Dill (page 479), effectively turning a side dish into a main course. Halloumi can be sliced into $^3/_8$-inch slabs and grilled or fried. Serves 4 to 6

8 ounces halloumi cheese

$^1/_2$ cup flour or fine semolina

$^1/_4$ cup olive oil or clarified butter

1 tablespoon chopped parsley

Freshly milled pepper

Lemon wedges

Cut the cheese into 1-inch cubes and toss them in the flour. Heat the oil in a medium skillet over medium heat until hot. Add the cheese, fry for a few seconds, then turn,

letting it brown on all sides before it melts. If the cheese sticks, scrape up the stuck parts—they're delicious—and serve them, too. Scatter the parsley on top along with pepper to taste. Serve accompanied by lemon wedges.

Baked Ricotta with Thyme

Baked ricotta with its firm texture, golden surface, and delicate milky taste is best served warm, plain, or covered with the Herb–Scented Bread Crumbs (page 25). Leftovers look uninspiring but are excellent crumbled over pasta or diced and added to soups, where they turn into tender dumplings. Serves 6 or more

1 pound ricotta

Olive oil

8 thyme sprigs, plus 1 teaspoon leaves

Freshly cracked pepper

If the ricotta is very moist, drain it in a colander lined with two layers of cheesecloth and a weight on top—a can of tomatoes will do—for 1 hour.

Preheat the oven to 375°F. Lightly oil a 2- or 3-cup shallow baking dish and evenly spread the ricotta in it. Brush the top with oil, scatter over the thyme sprigs, and season with pepper. Bake, uncovered, until the top is golden and the sides start to pull away from the dish, 45 minutes to 1 hour. If there's any milky residue, carefully pour it off. Scatter the thyme leaves over the top and let cool for 10 minutes. Cut into squares or diamonds and serve.

SANDWICHES

CHAPTER 5

Sandwiches
A Casual Meal

Sandwiches are found around the world in one form or another, but we have a special fondness for them here at home, where they seem to respond readily to all of our whims. Hot or cold, open or closed, dainty or mammoth, traditional or contemporary, sandwiches remain the informal, portable meal.

Smaller varieties—neat open-faced croutons, canapés, and crostini—can be appetizers (see chapter 4, Appetizers and First Courses) and accompaniments to soups and salads, while larger sandwiches have the heft to make a meal. For adults as well as children, sandwiches are still lunch and sometimes dinner too, so they should be nourishing as well as good to eat.

Sandwiches are casual, and that is part of their charm. Here's one area where people who otherwise want to measure compulsively will forge ahead confidently on their own. Really, making a sandwich is nothing more than putting together the tastes you like, perhaps keeping in mind to vary the textures so that your sandwiches are interesting to eat. To make assembling an interesting sandwich an easy matter,

try to keep a few basic sandwich elements on hand that are popular at your house.

Some sandwiches travel better than others. Cheese and mustard on sturdy bread is a good traveler, and a pan bagnat can sit around for hours, but chopped vegetables in a pita pocket can't go anywhere unless they go separately. Some sandwich vegetables suffer with time, tomatoes turn soggy; lettuce and sprouts wilt. Keeping some of these more fragile elements wrapped separately to be slipped into the sandwich just before eating makes a lunch sandwich more enjoyable. Otherwise, a thin coating of mayonnaise or olive paste or a layer of lettuce next to the bread helps keep a sandwich from getting soggy by lunchtime.

Building a Great Sandwich

Just four things are needed to build a sandwich—bread, a filling, a flavoring, and a garnish.

BREAD: Good bread makes the most ordinary sandwich simply delicious, while poor-quality bread disintegrates and ruins the best of fillings. Bread should be fresh, full of flavor, and strong enough to stand up to its fillings. Sandwich

breads are the traditional American-high, light loaves—heavenly when fresh. But focaccia and country breads have become new favorites, along with pita bread, tortillas, rolls, and other special breads such as olive, herb, cheese, rye, pumpernickel, and quick breads. Each bread contributes its individual personality to a sandwich—and often suggests its own fillings. A cheese bread makes an exciting cover for a tomato sandwich; fig or raisin breads are delicious with cream cheese and fresh figs; rosemary bread works well with goat cheese and braised spinach; and so on.

FILLINGS AND TOPPINGS: There are endless choices—spreads, cheeses of all kinds, grilled and fresh vegetables, salads, eggs in various forms, falafel, tofu, and tempeh. For children who want a sandwich that looks like what their friends are eating, there are meat look-alikes, such as bacon, hot dogs, and bologna made from tofu and tempeh. While I personally don't care for these ersatz foods, I do know how desperately children want to be like other kids. As a child, I usually threw away my mother's healthy sandwiches so as not to stand out from the white-bread-and-bologna crowd.

SAUCES AND CONDIMENTS: These make sandwiches succulent, moist, and intensely flavorful. It's the thin swipe of spicy mustard or flavored mayonnaise that adds the finishing touch and puts a good sandwich over the top. Beyond the usual mustard and mayonnaise, olive pastes, Romesco Sauce (page 62), Harissa (page 66), Pesto (page 50), chutneys, and other seasonings make unusual and excellent flavorings for sandwiches.

GARNISHES: A sandwich always looks better on the plate when it has a little something on the side. And it's nicer to eat that way, too, pacing your bites with nibbles of this and that. Instead of the usual chips, try grated vegetable salad, coleslaw, crisp radishes, sliced tomatoes, or a little green salad.

VEGAN SANDWICHES: Many vegetarian sandwiches include cheese as well as other ingredients. When that's the case, vegans can omit the cheese and still have a fine sandwich. And of course, vegan mayonnaise is always an option.

Simple Vegetable Sandwiches

The Vegetarian Classic—Avocado and Cheese with Sprouts: Scribbled on the blackboards of vegetarian restaurants for decades, this sandwich works because of the contrasting textures and tastes. Spread whole wheat or multigrain bread with a thin layer of mayonnaise and mustard. Add iceberg or romaine lettuce, thinly sliced Monterey Jack cheese, sliced avocado, and sliced tomato. Season with salt and pepper and a squeeze of lemon juice. Add a covering of sprouts. (Try some of the more interesting sprouts, such as leek, radish, or sunflower, but don't put too many in—just enough to make the sandwich fresh and crunchy.) Top with the second slice of bread, press down lightly, and slice.

Avocado with Green Chile and Spicy Olive Paste: One of my food pals, Dan Welch, is known for his outrageous sandwich combinations, including this one. It's hot, tangy, and messy—not for the timid or the neat. Toast a large slice of country bread or focaccia, then cover it with a generous layer of Hot and Spicy Tapenade (page 78). Next overlap slices of avocado and tomato and crumble some fresh goat cheese over the top. Slide it under the broiler and heat it just long enough to soften the cheese. Remove and sprinkle with diced jalapeño (with seeds) and finish with a dash of red wine vinegar. Serve with lots of napkins and a cold beer.

Avocado Club with Chipotle Mayonnaise: Club sandwiches always include a third piece of bread, so slice the bread thinly, or the finished sandwich will be too thick. Season several tablespoons of mayonnaise with pureed chipotle chile or smoked paprika, chopped cilantro, and lime juice to taste. Toast 3 thin pieces of bread and spread each slice with the mayonnaise. Cover one slice with a crisp lettuce leaf and 3 slices of avocado and season with salt and pepper. Add the second piece of toast, mayonnaise side up, and cover with 3 slices of Swiss cheese, sliced tomato, and another layer of lettuce. Set the third piece of toast, mayonnaise side down, over the lettuce and press down gently. To be ultratraditional, trim the crusts, then cut the sandwiches diagonally to make 4 triangles and secure each with a toothpick. Serve with pickled vegetables or a mound of finely shredded cabbage tossed with salt and lime juice.

Avocado Club with Tempeh: Barbecued Tempeh (page 532), provides some of the texture and smoke that bacon does. Add tempeh strips to the club sandwich and regular or vegan mayonnaise. (V)

Cucumber with Spicy Greens: An interesting twist on the traditional tea sandwiches. Spread white or wheat bread with mayonnaise and top with thinly sliced cucumber and sprigs of arugula, nasturtium leaves, or garden cress. Season with sea salt and white pepper, then top with a second piece of bread. If spicy greens aren't available, mix the mayonnaise with horseradish.

Cucumber with Garden Herbs: Spread white or wheat bread with herb and blossom butters (page 46), or Greek yogurt, and cover with thinly sliced cucumber. Tuck herb leaves among them: borage leaves and their sky-blue flowers, torn lovage leaves, delicate salad burnet, chives, lemon thyme leaves, or garlic chives. Use sprigs of herbs and their flowers, when available, to garnish the plate.

Cucumber and Cream Cheese with Radish Sprouts: Spread whole wheat bread or toast with a layer of cream cheese, ricotta, Boursin, or goat cheese, then top with sliced cucumber and radish sprouts. Spread a little mayonnaise on the second piece of bread or toast and cover. Slice in two and serve.

CUCUMBERS

During the summer, many varieties of cucumbers are seen at farmers' markets. All are good on sandwiches, especially when they're fresh and juicy. It's a good idea to taste a cucumber first to see if it's bitter. If it is, rubbing the two cut surfaces together until they foam seems to sweeten it. If cucumbers are unsprayed, unwaxed, and thin skinned, they needn't be peeled. And unless they're very mature, they needn't be seeded.

Cucumber with Spicy Chickpea Spread: Cucumbers make a moist and juicy foil for Spicy Chickpea Puree (page 87). For two sandwiches, toast 4 slices of white, wheat, or dark rye bread or leave it fresh. In a small bowl, combine a seeded and minced jalapeño chile, 1 tablespoon chopped cilantro, and 1 tablespoon fresh lime juice. Spread a moderate layer of the chickpea puree on two slices of the bread, cover with thinly sliced cucumbers, and spoon the sauce over all. Top with the remaining toast. Ⓥ

Grilled Portabella Mushroom Sandwich: These giant mushrooms make a succulent, meaty sandwich. For two sandwiches you'll need a large portabella mushroom.

Dislodge the stem, then slice the cap at an angle about 1/3 inch thick. Brush both sides of each slice with olive oil and season with salt and pepper. Grill, broil, or sear, on both sides until browned. Spread 2 slices of bread or toast with regular or vegan mayonnaise—Garlic Mayonnaise (page 52) is especially good—then top with sliced tomatoes, the mushrooms, and arugula, lettuce, or red mustard leaves. Add the top slices of bread, cut in two, and serve. Ⓥ

TO SWEETEN HOT ONIONS

If you love onion sandwiches, but can't get naturally sweet onions like Vidalias, slice them and put them in a bowl of water with some ice cubes. Refrigerated for 30 minutes or more, they'll become crisp and lose their pungency.

Grilled Onions on Toast with Romesco Sauce: For two people, grill 2 medium or 1 very large red onion. Toast 4 slices of country bread, spread them with Romesco Sauce (page 62), sprinkle with chopped parsley, and add the grilled onions. Season with sea salt and top with the remaining toast. Simple but superb. Ⓥ

Sweet Onions on Black Bread: The combination of sweet onion and dark bread is classic. Peel and slice sweet onions, such as Vidalias, thinly into rounds. Lightly butter 2 thin slices of dark rye or pumpernickel. Cover 1 slice with the onions, season with sea salt and pepper, add a few drops mild vinegar, and cover with the second slice of bread.

Sweet Onions on Toast: Toast 2 slices of country, multigrain, or light rye bread, then spread each slice with plain (or flavored) regular or vegan mayonnaise. Sprinkle chopped parsley or dill over the mayonnaise on 1 slice, add thinly sliced sweet onion, and top with the second slice of toast. Ⓥ

Tomato and Avocado on Toast: Although utterly simple, this sandwich manages to be crisp, succulent, and juicy all at once. Cover toasted whole wheat or multigrain bread with overlapping slices of ripe tomato, then with sliced avocado. Season with sea salt and pepper and a squeeze of lemon or a spoonful of Lemon Vinaigrette (page 164). Cover with a crisp romaine leaf and top with a second piece of toast. For additional excitement, spread the toast with Cilantro Salsa (page 49) or Harissa (page 66). Ⓥ

Tomato Sandwich with Greens and Herb Mayonnaise: Use a substantial country or whole wheat bread and spread it with Fresh Dill and Lemon Mayonnaise (page 52), Herb Mayonnaise (page 52), or vegan mayonnaise. Add sliced tomato, freshly cracked pepper, and arugula, red mustard leaves, or a handful of gourmet lettuces. Top with another slice of bread and serve. (V)

Tomato Sandwich with Olive Paste, Mozzarella, and Arugula: A lusty sandwich if the tomatoes are juicy and you're generous with the Olive Paste. Spread country or sourdough bread or garlic-rubbed toast with a layer of Olive Paste (page 78). Cover with overlapping layers of fresh mozzarella and thick-sliced tomato. Add a pinch of sea salt and plenty of arugula leaves, then top with another slice of bread and serve.

Fried Green Tomato Sandwich: I don't know why this sandwich didn't occur to me sooner. It's such a great combination of tastes and textures. For 2 sandwiches, slice 2 large green tomatoes 3/8 inch thick. Dip them into corn meal or flour seasoned with sea salt and pepper, then fry them in a thin layer of olive oil over medium-high heat on both sides until golden and tender but not mushy. Toast 2 sourdough rolls or squares of focaccia, halved horizontally, then spread with Garlic Mayonnaise (page 52) or Green Goddess Dressing (page 169). Add thinly sliced feta or fresh mozzarella, the tomatoes, and a final layer of greens, such as arugula, watercress, or a few large basil leaves. Top with the second slice of bread, then cut in half and serve.

A Beefsteak Tomato Open-Faced Sandwich: A real beefsteak tomato from the garden is so good that there is hardly a thing you have to do with it. In fact, less is more, for sure. I like them sliced and drizzled with olive oil and a pinch of sea salt just fine, but they also make a great little sandwich. Toast an English muffin or a slice of your favorite bread. Slather it with mayonnaise, then set a thick slice of tomato over that. You barely need more, not even basil, but maybe salt and pepper. Even mayonnaise from the jar will work, but homemade will be over-the-top delicious.

Cheese Sandwiches

Cheese is a natural with bread, it's versatile, and it's very satisfying. Cheese is a good source of protein, not to mention calcium and flavor. When it comes to grilled cheese sandwiches, a panini maker can be used in place of a cast-iron skillet.

Cheese, Apple, and Watercress: For this bright, fresh sandwich, spread 2 slices of nutty sandwich bread such as oat, multigrain, or whole wheat with mayonnaise. Add thinly sliced Gruyère or Jack, thinly sliced unpeeled apple, and watercress. Top with the second slice of bread, cut in half, and serve.

Smoked Mozzarella with Olive Paste and Roasted Peppers: Preheat the broiler. Toast a piece of country bread, then cover it with a layer of Olive Paste (page 78) and thin overlapping slices of smoked mozzarella. Broil just long enough to soften the cheese, then crisscross with strips of roasted peppers. Spoon a little Pesto (page 50) or Salsa Verde (page 48) over the top and shower with freshly milled pepper. Serve with a fresh, lightly dressed green salad.

Open-Faced with Blue Cheese, Pears, and Roasted Nuts: Blue cheese, pears, and roasted nuts are always right together. For cheese, try Maytag, Gorgonzola dolcelatte, Danish blue, or Cambozola; for fruit, a crisp Asian pear-apple or tender juicy Comice or Bartlett. Accompany with a salad of frizzy endive (frisée) or Belgian endive dressed with a Walnut Oil or Hazelnut Oil Vinaigrette (page 166). Lightly toast semolina or country bread, then cover with thinly sliced cheese. Sprinkle roasted walnuts or hazelnuts over the cheese and season with pepper and a little chopped chervil, tarragon, or parsley. Cover with sliced pears.

Limburger: This is a cheese that seems to be appreciated by people like my father—in other words, those of an earlier generation, though if it were better known, I think many people of my generation would like it, too. After making this sandwich for a photo shoot for *Saveur* magazine, the photographer and I sat down to feast on the props. We found this sandwich so delicious that I asked then-editor Christopher Hirsheimer for permission to use it here. Limburger is definitely a fragrant cheese, but it should be a little firm and have a good, clean scent that is appealing, not overwhelming.

Spread French bread or a white country bread with butter. Add a few butter lettuce leaves, sliced tomato, and several good slices of Limburger. Top with very thinly sliced white or red onion and roasted crushed walnuts. Top with bread and enjoy this wonderful robust combination of elements.

Classic American Grilled Cheese: Put 3 or 4 thin slices of cheese between 2 slices of sturdy white or whole wheat sandwich bread. Melt 2 or 3 teaspoons butter, ghee, or olive oil in a skillet just large enough to hold the sandwich, add the sandwich, and cook over medium-low heat until golden on the bottom. Remove, add more butter to the pan, and cook on the second side until golden and the cheese is melted. Cover the pan to hasten the cooking. Slice in half and serve. Serve this favorite with a side of pickled vegetables, Sweet and Sour Quinces with Dried Fruits (page 71) or a mound of coleslaw. In the fall, wash it down with a glass of cold apple cider.

Grilled Cheese Sandwiches

With its soft, runny cheese and crisp toast, the grilled cheese sandwich is a favorite—and for good reason. As the variations suggest, all types of breads and cheeses, not just white bread and orange cheddar, can be used. Cook grilled cheese sandwiches over moderate heat so that the cheese melts and the bread toasts at the same time. Butter is the traditional cooking fat, but olive oil works with some cheeses.

Grilled Cheddar on Rye with Onion: Use light or dark rye bread and a robust cheddar. Slice a small tomato into rounds and a small onion into thin wedges. Sauté the onion in 2 teaspoons oil in a small skillet over high heat until golden, about 7 minutes. Season with sea salt and pepper. Build the sandwich this way: bread, a thin covering of cheese, the tomato, onion, another covering of cheese, and a second slice of bread. Cook on both sides in butter or olive oil.

Grilled Fontina or Teleme with Sage Leaves: Creamy fontina, or soft rich rind Teleme, and fresh sage seem to be made for each other. Halve a square of focaccia or cut 2 slices of country bread. Cover one piece with sliced fontina or Teleme cheese. Sauté 6 fresh sage leaves in $1^1/_2$ teaspoon olive oil or butter until dark green and set them on the cheese. Cover with a few more slices of cheese and the second piece of bread. Cook on both sides in butter or olive oil. Delicious with a fennel or mushroom salad.

Grilled Cheese with Salsa: Pico de Gallo (page 90), Tomato-Avocado Salsa (page 90), Tomatillo Salsa (page 90), and Green Chile and Mint Salsa (page 90), are all good matches with grilled cheese. Layer Muenster, Monterey Jack, or mild cheddar between slices of white or wheat bread and cook in butter or oil. When done, remove the top and spoon on as much salsa as the sandwich will hold. Return the top and serve with plenty of napkins. Made with tortillas, you have a quesadilla.

Grilled Cheese with Chile and Cilantro: Thinly slice cheddar, Monterey Jack, or Muenster cheese. Spread 2 slices of bread with a layer of Harissa (page 66) or pureed chipotle chile. Top one piece with a few slices of cheese, then add fresh cilantro sprigs and sliced tomato, another slice of cheese, and the second slice of bread. Grill and serve with a side of Pickled Red Onions (page 72) or Pickled Carrots and Garlic with Cumin (page 72).

Grilled Cream Cheese: Cream cheese can be grilled, too, and it's very good this way since its delicacy sets off the flavor of the bread. Use a serious, nutty, multigrain bread; otherwise, pair it with savory condiments such as Tomato-Basil Pesto (page 50) or Salsa Verde (page 48) or with sweet ones like a tart marmalade, fruit butters, and fresh fruits. Try making grilled cream cheese sandwiches with a fruit bread. They make an unusual brunch or breakfast offering. Just spread softened cream cheese between 2 slices of bread and cook in a small amount of butter over medium heat on both sides until the cheese has softened.

Quesadillas

Quesadillas, the grilled cheese sandwich of Mexico, make a great spur-of-the-moment snack, lunch, or accompaniment to salads or soups, especially those made of beans and corn. They're also a good party food. Cheese is a part of quesadillas—it's even part of the word—but it needn't be used with a heavy hand. A light covering gives the quesadilla a satisfying taste—and helps hold everything together. Many things can go into quesadillas besides cheese, so here's a place where you can really improvise.

Basic Quesadillas

FOLDED: Start with good, fresh flour or corn tortillas. Set a heavy skillet over medium heat. When it's hot, add a tortilla. When the bottom is hot, flip it over, then cover half lightly with grated cheese—Jack, cheddar, Muenster, queso fresco, goat cheese, or Mexican Chihuahua. When the cheese is quite soft but not entirely melted, sprinkle it with chopped cilantro or add a few epazote leaves and any other fillings you might be using. Fold it in half, cook a minute or two more, then serve hot.

FLAT: Follow the directions above, but instead of folding the tortilla, spread one topping over the entire tortilla, then top with a second tortilla. Once the cheese has softened, flip the whole thing over and cook for a few minutes more. Remove and cut into wedges. Serve with Pico de Gallo (page 90) or Tomatillo Salsa (page 90). If you're feeding a crowd, start making the quesadillas when your guests arrive and keep them in a warm oven until you have enough to serve.

Some other things to put into a quesadilla are diced tomato and avocado, chopped green onions, grilled or pickled onions, chopped olives or Hot and Spicy Tapenade (page 78), scrambled or fried eggs, diced serrano or jalapeño chiles, sautéed zucchini and/or zucchini blossoms, sautéed mushrooms, and strips of roasted poblano chiles.

A Simple Avocado Quesadilla

This is a modest, almost crisp one-tortilla quesadilla, a good snack after a workout, for breakfast or the occasional breakfast or dinner. Try these with a sprouted corn tortilla and for cheese, a goat Gouda. Makes 1 quesadilla

1 sprouted organic corn tortilla
A few very thin slices of your favorite cheese
$1/2$ small avocado, sliced
Salsa (your choice)

Set the tortilla in a small pan over medium-high heat to begin warming. Flip the tortilla over and cover it with the cheese, then add the avocado. Reduce the heat to medium and cook until the cheese has begun to melt and the tortilla has started to crisp. Rather than folding it, eat it flat, with salsa, pieces cut or broken off.

Quesadilla with Smoky Black Bean Spread and Salsa

Or course you can use a ready-made pinto bean spread, but these spicy black beans are a little different. Makes 1 quesadilla

Black Bean and Smoked Chile Dip (page 86), about $1/3$ cup per tortilla
2 corn tortillas
Grated Monterey Jack, queso fresco, or goat cheese
Coarsely chopped cilantro
Pico de Gallo (page 90)
Diced serrano chile

Spread the bean dip on a tortilla and place it in a lightly oiled skillet over low heat. Scatter the cheese and cilantro over the beans and add a spoonful of salsa and diced chiles. Top with a second tortilla. Flip it over and warm the second side. When heated through, slide the quesadilla to a plate and cut into wedges.

Quesadilla with Roasted Pepper Strips (*Rajas*): The roasted pepper strips and onions on page 364 make a soft, succulent filling for quesadillas. Spread 1/2 cup or more over the bottom tortilla; add a little grated cheese or a few dabs of sour cream if you wish and chopped cilantro. Either fold it in half or cover with a second tortilla, flip the whole thing over, and cook on the second side. Cut into wedges and serve with a pile of pickled vegetables.

Whole Wheat Quesadilla with Monterey Jack and Cilantro Salsa: Set a whole wheat tortilla on a heavy, ungreased skillet over medium heat. Once the bottom has warmed, flip it over. Grate Jack cheese generously over the top. When the cheese has melted, drizzle with Cilantro Salsa (page 49), then fold the tortilla in half and serve with a small dish of sliced serrano chiles or Pico de Gallo (page 90).

Sandwich Cheeses

Beyond the familiar cheddar, Monterey Jack, and Muenster, there's a whole spectrum of cheeses to use on sandwiches.

AMERICAN FARM CHEESES: American cheese making has come a long way in recent years. Whether simple fresh goat cheeses, cheeses made in European traditional styles, or fresh, new, vibrant American cheeses, there are many excellent ones that would make anyone proud to include on a cheese tray. There are too many to list, but some of my favorites are Red Hawk and Mt. Tam from Cowgirl Creamery, Point Reyes Blue, various goat milk Camembert-style cheeses, Humboldt Fog, Cabot's Clothbound Cheddar, various goat cheeses from Haystack Mountain, Pleasant Ridge Reserve, and many others. Look in your own area for beautifully crafted cheeses.

ASIAGO: This is a lovely cow's milk cheese from Northern Italy, in the Veneto. When young, it is delicate and smooth textured, becoming more crumbly (and stronger) as it ages. I grew to like this cheese very much, even in its youthful stage, when bicycling in the Veneto, where it was served at the various *agritourismi* where we stayed, for its delicacy, softness, and subtle tang. When aged, it may remind you of parmesan.

CREAM CHEESE: Traditionally used with fruit and nut breads, it also makes a good savory filling and works in grilled cheese sandwiches. "Natural" cream cheese, free of gums and gelatins, is more delicate and spreadable than the foil-wrapped variety.

FETA: Greek, French, Bulgarian, and Israeli fetas have slightly different personalities, but overall they provide a sharp accent for less intense fillings such as a chopped vegetable salad, cucumbers, and tomatoes. Feta is best in pita or roll sandwiches, where it is less likely to fall out. Dried oregano, mint, and fresh marjoram complement feta.

FONTINA: Italian Fontina is creamy, with fruit and nut overtones. Danish and domestic versions are a blander rendition, but they're more available and less expensive. An excellent melting cheese, fontina is ideal for grilled cheese sandwiches with sage and grilled onions.

GOAT CHEESE: Whether sharp and assertive or fresh and soft, goat cheese always adds tang and character to a dish. It can be mixed with a little milk, ricotta, or cream cheese to make it even milder and more spreadable or used as is. It's very good with sourdough bread, roasted peppers, and eggplant. Rosemary, thyme, garlic, and olive oil are its natural partners. Fresh goat cheese makes an excellent grilled cheese sandwich.

GRUYÈRE: Gruyère makes the perfect grilled cheese sandwich. Thinly sliced Gruyère accompanied by mustard, fine butter, or mayonnaise on French bread is simple goodness.

HAVARTI, PLAIN OR WITH DILL: Often overlooked but easy to find, Havarti is a rather mild soft cheese with a bit of tang. Try it on dark and rye breads with cucumbers and mustard, horseradish, or sour cream.

MOZZARELLA: Delicate and delicious raw or melted, fresh mozzarella can be paired with tomatoes, olive paste, roasted peppers, and basil. Unlike the processed version, this cheese does not turn rubbery when heated but melts into slender strands.

RICOTTA: It sounds so common, but a good ricotta whether made from cow, goat, or sheep's milk, is a great find. You can spread ricotta on toast and drizzle with olive oil, fleur de sel, and fresh herbs, or you can do a sweet version with jam and butter on toast, or honey drizzled over the cheese. It needn't be on toast, either. When I have a good hand-dipped ricotta on hand, I find I use it in all sorts of ways. It's lovely with a salad of beets, spooned on hot pasta, and of course, it makes a spectacular ricotta cheesecake or lasagne.

TELEME: A soft cheese that practically flows at room temperature, Teleme is buttery but tangy. Teleme that's labeled "rice washed" or "rice rind" is the best. It makes a wonderful, runny grilled cheese sandwich.

Egg and Tofu Sandwiches

Now that eggs have been liberated from their cholesterol quarantine, maybe egg salad sandwiches will return to their rightful place on our tables. They're nutritious and sustaining and make a nice change from cheese sandwiches. They're especially good made with farm-raised eggs with bright yellow yolks. A basic egg salad can be varied in a hundred different ways—simply adding herbs and other flavorings to the mayonnaise will change its character. Tofu can even be used to make a similarly tasty sandwich spread. The versatile egg tastes good on white breads, full-flavored grains, dark ryes, and country breads. Toast the bread or not, make the sandwiches open-faced or closed. And don't forget that you can also use egg salad or tofu spread as a spread on crackers or on a salad plate.

Egg Salad

Makes 2 sandwiches

3 hard-cooked eggs (see page 499)
2 tablespoons or more mayonnaise
Sea salt and freshly milled pepper
Chopped parsley
2 teaspoons minced chives, or 1 green onion, finely chopped

Peel then mash the eggs with the mayonnaise, leaving as much or as little texture as you like. Season with salt and pepper and stir in the parsley and chives.

Other additions might include finely diced celery or green or yellow bell pepper, minced green chile, chopped watercress, diced jicama, or water chestnuts. All add crunch and color to the egg salad and expand its volume. A few drops vinegar or lemon give eggs a little sharpness if you've gone light on the mayonnaise.

Egg Salad with Herbs: Almost all herbs have an affinity for eggs. Use Herb Mayonnaise (page 52) or Tarragon Mayonnaise with Capers (page 52) or add a few tablespoons chopped fresh herbs: marjoram, dill, chervil, tarragon, and arugula are particularly pleasing to the eggs themselves. Nasturtium leaves and flowers, branches of salad burnet, flowering tips of lemon thyme, and golden cress are pretty as well as delicious.

Egg Salad with Olive Paste: Spread bread, toast, or crackers with a thin layer of Olive Paste (page 78), then mound the egg salad on top. The pungent olives really perk up the eggs.

Egg Salad with Capers and Onions: Mix the basic egg salad with 2 tablespoons finely diced onion or shallot, an equal amount of parsley, and 1 tablespoon rinsed capers. Spread on toast or crackers.

Egg Salad with Sprouts or Seedlings: Sprouts with strong flavors, like leek, radish, and mustard, mounded on top of the egg salad provide a fresh and assertive counterpoint to eggs. The same is true of garden seedlings such as arugula, leeks, radish, and green onions. Finely chop them, or leave small sprouts whole, and sprinkle them over the egg salad.

Fried Egg Sandwich: A great fast sandwich to make on the fly or when cooking has to be simple. Fry an egg any way you like—with a soft runny yolk or a firm one. Season with sea salt and pepper and tuck it between 2 slices of toast. Keep it simple or add hot sauce, a slice of cheese, or a layer of sun-dried tomato paste or spicy Harissa (page 66).

Frittata Sandwich: Frittata sandwiches make a good solid item to pack for lunch or take on a picnic. Make any thin small frittata (pages 504 to 507), sandwich it between 2 slices of bread, toast, or split focaccia covered with a little mayonnaise, and that's that.

Tempeh on Rye

Braising tempeh in its seasoning, then letting it brown in the remaining oil, improves its flavor and is more effective than marinating it. This robust sandwich is hefty and satisfying and tastes good in its own right. Makes 3 sandwiches

1 (8- or 10-ounce) package tempeh
1 large clove garlic, thinly sliced
2 tablespoons light sesame oil
1 teaspoon paprika
1/2 teaspoon dried dill
1/2 teaspoon caraway seeds
1 bay leaf
2 tablespoons apple cider vinegar
1 tablespoon soy sauce
Sea salt and freshly milled pepper
6 slices light rye bread
3 slices Swiss cheese
1 cup sauerkraut, drained and warmed
Prepared horseradish and mustard

Cut the tempeh crosswise in half, then cut each half piece into 3 very thin slabs. Steam over simmering water for at least 10 minutes. In a skillet wide enough to hold the tempeh in a single layer—though this isn't absolutely crucial—heat the garlic and oil over medium heat until the garlic begins to color. Add the tempeh pieces and turn them once to coat them with the oil, then add the paprika, dill, caraway, bay, vinegar, and soy sauce. Season with pepper to taste. Add water to cover and simmer until the water has reduced to a glaze, about 20 minutes. (If it cooks down sooner, add more water as needed—tempeh does need to cook.) Allow the tempeh to fry for several minutes in the oil that remains in the pan, turning it a few times. Taste a corner, then season with salt, if needed, and more pepper.

Preheat the broiler. Toast the bread. Lay the cheese on 3 slices of bread and broil until it begins to melt. Add the tempeh and sauerkraut. Cover the rest of the bread with horseradish and mustard, cover the sandwiches, and serve.

TLT—Tempeh, Lettuce, and Tomato: Prepare the Tempeh in a Smoky Molasses Marinade (page 533). Cover toasted bread with mayonnaise, regular or tofu-based, and add crisp lettuce, the tempeh, and thick slices of tomato. Season with sea salt and freshly milled pepper, close the sandwich, and serve. Ⓥ

Tofu Salad Spread

Tofu salad spread is surprisingly good on its own, but it is most appreciated as a replacement for egg salad. Use it in sandwiches just as you would egg salad, or as a spread for crackers. Makes enough for 3 or 4 sandwiches Ⓥ

1 pound firm tofu
1/3 cup finely diced celery
1/3 cup finely diced green bell pepper
1/3 cup finely diced carrot
2 tablespoons minced white or green onion
1 large clove garlic, put through a press
2 tablespoons chopped parsley
2 tablespoons chopped marjoram or 1 1/2 teaspoons dried
2 teaspoons chopped thyme or 1 1/2 teaspoon dried
1/8 teaspoon turmeric
2 pinches cayenne
1/2 cup mayonnaise or vegan mayonnaise
1 tablespoon capers, rinsed, or chopped sour pickles
2 to 3 teaspoons Dijon mustard
Sea salt and freshly milled pepper
Wine or apple cider vinegar

Break the tofu into large chunks and twist it in a towel to get rid of the liquid. When it's as dry as possible, put it in a bowl with the rest of the ingredients and mash them together with a fork. At first it will taste bland, but the flavors will get stronger as the spread sits. Refrigerate for 1 hour before using if time allows.

Marinated Tofu Sandwich

This has character—especially for tofu—and the marinade is also good with tempeh. Makes 3 or 4 sandwiches Ⓥ

1 block firm tofu, drained

Hot Mustard Marinade for Tofu and Tempeh (page 524 to 525)

1 tablespoon light sesame oil

Bread, toasted

Mustard

Mayonnaise or vegan mayonnaise

Lettuce and tomato

Chopped cilantro

Cut the tofu into 4 to 8 slices, place in a pie plate, and cover with the marinade. Marinate for as little as 15 minutes or as long as a few days if refrigerated. Heat a little oil in a nonstick pan, add the tofu slices, and cover the pan. Don't worry about scraping off the marinade—it makes a glaze as it cooks. Fry over medium-high heat on both sides until browned. Add more of the marinade to the pan if it seems dry. When done, set the tofu on toast, spread with mustard and mayonnaise, and cover with lettuce, tomatoes, and cilantro. Cut the sandwiches in half and serve.

Sandwiches in Rolls

Rolls also make good containers for fillings, and unlike tender pita breads, rolls are sturdy, making them good little travelers. Be sure that you use a good hard roll or one made from strong bread dough, like the Sandwich Focaccia with Rosemary (page 597) or Focaccia Sandwich Rolls (page 597).

Focaccia with Tomato, Ricotta Salata, and Salad Greens: This sandwich is inspired by a breakfast sandwich I like at Campanile in Los Angeles, but it's a great sandwich any time of day.

The tender salad greens and the seeded bread make it special. If you're not up to making bread, use a Vienna or other plain roll with strong texture. If you are, make the Focaccia with Fennel Seeds (page 597), shaping it into 3-ounce rolls. Slice the rolls in half and cover with a layer of ricotta salata or fresh mozzarella, sliced tomato, and sliced cucumber. Toss a handful of small salad greens with a pinch of sea salt, olive oil, a squeeze of lemon, and freshly milled pepper. Add to the sandwich, close the top, and serve.

Pan Bagnat

Made in a sturdy roll, this Provence-inspired sandwich should be moist with olive oil and the good juices from the vegetables. Makes 4 sandwiches Ⓥ

4 large rolls, about 6 ounces each, sourdough or any good hard roll

Olive oil

1 clove garlic

1 cup finely diced celery heart

2 ripe tomatoes, seeded and chopped

5 white mushrooms, chopped

6 marinated artichoke hearts, chopped

$^1/_2$ cup pitted niçoise olives

2 tablespoons capers, rinsed

$^1/_2$ cup cubed ricotta salata, Gruyère, or goat cheese, optional

1 tablespoon chopped parsley, marjoram, or tarragon

Sea salt and freshly milled pepper

Red wine vinegar or fresh lemon juice

Slice the rolls crosswise a third of the way down from the top. Pull out some of the bread, leaving a solid bottom. Brush the insides with oil and rub with the garlic, then mince the clove and put it in a bowl with the vegetables, olives, capers, cheese, and herb. Toss with oil to coat and season with salt and pepper. Add vinegar to taste. Fill the bottoms, add the tops, and wrap tightly. Let stand 1 hour or more.

Pan Bagnat with Saffron-Basil Vinaigrette

This filling can go into a pita sandwich, too. If so, plan to eat it right away. Makes 4 sandwiches Ⓥ

4 small tomatoes, seeded and diced

1 small cucumber, or 2 little zucchini, diced

1 small fennel bulb, or 3 small celery ribs, diced

1 large shallot, finely diced

1 large red pepper, roasted and chopped

6 marinated artichoke hearts, diced

8 kalamata olives, pitted and chopped

1/4 cup toasted pine nuts

Saffron Vinaigrette with Basil and Orange (page 166)

Sea salt and freshly milled pepper

4 (6-ounce) rolls

4 rounds of fresh mozzarella, optional

Toss the vegetables, olives, and pine nuts with enough vinaigrette to moisten well. Season with salt and pepper. Prepare the roll as described in the preceding recipe. Partially fill it with the vegetables, add a round of cheese to each, and top with more filling. Replace the top of the roll and eat right away, or let stand 1 hour before serving.

Grilled Vegetable Heroes

These succulent summer sandwiches are a bit of a production, so set aside time to make them the main event of a picnic or backyard supper. You needn't feel constrained by the suggestions made here. Other good vegetables to grill are zucchini, green onions, leeks, mushrooms, and fennel (see chapter 11, Vegetables). Makes 6 sandwiches

1 1/2 pounds eggplant small globe, Asian, or full-size Western varieties

Sea salt and freshly milled pepper

About 1/3 cup olive oil

2 large red or yellow bell peppers

2 large red onions, sliced into 1/2-inch rounds

2 sweet or sourdough baguettes, each cut into thirds

Garlic Mayonnaise (page 52)

3 ripe tomatoes, thickly sliced

Splash of red wine vinegar

Slice the eggplants into rounds a little less than 1/2 inch thick. Unless they're garden fresh, sprinkle with salt, let stand 30 minutes or longer, then pat dry. Brush the slices with oil, season with pepper, then grill or broil until browned and a little crusty on the bottom. Turn and grill on the second side for about 4 minutes. Flatten the peppers, grill until the skins separate, then steam and peel them as described on page 364. Cut the peppers into wide strips. Brush the sliced onions with oil and grill on both sides until browned. Season with salt and pepper, then turn them carefully and grill to brown the other side.

Slice the bread in half. Spread with the mayonnaise and cover the bottom layer with the vegetables, including the tomatoes. Douse lightly with vinegar and top.

Pita Sandwiches

Freshly baked pita bread—tender, pliable, and fragrant with the scent of wheat—is one of the most delicious containers for fillings, albeit a fairly fragile one. With its nourishing taste and ancient feel, pita bread is worth making at home on occasion—page 598. Otherwise, look to Middle Eastern and Mediterranean bakeries for fresh pita.

Unless it's very fresh, pita bread requires some special handling. Defrost frozen pita slowly, at room temperature or in the refrigerator. If the bread seems dry, moisten it with water, wrap in aluminum foil, and heat it briefly in the oven. Halve and carefully open the pita. Spread the sauce inside the pocket first, then fill and drizzle more sauce on top. Don't put too much filling in the sandwich, or it'll tear. And most important, assemble it just before you plan to eat. Moist fillings quickly soften the bread. Pita sandwiches will tempt you to improvise, but here are some specific combinations that I enjoy. If you are vegan, choose your pita bread carefully—some are made with honey.

Pita with Falafel, Tomatoes, Tahini, and Lemon

This classic Middle Eastern combination is one of my favorites. It's especially good when the bread and falafel are both fresh and warm. While falafel can be made by soaking and pureeing cooked chickpeas, I use a convenient mix.
Makes 1 sandwich Ⓥ

---

3 or 4 falafel patties, made from a prepared mix
1 (7-inch) pita bread
Yogurt Tahini Sauce (page 57) or Tahini with Lemon and
    Garlic (page 59)
2 ripe tomatoes, seeded and diced
Shredded lettuce
Green Chile and Mint Salsa (page 90)

Make the falafel according to the packaged instructions. Open the pita bread and spread a little sauce inside. Add the falafel, then the tomatoes and lettuce. Spoon more sauce over the top. Serve with a dish of the green chile salsa on the side.

Pita with Broiled Eggplant: Broil or grill rounds of eggplant. Tuck them into pita bread and spoon in Yogurt Sauce with Cayenne and Dill (page 57). Serve with a dish of olives or diced Preserved Lemon (page 70).

Pita with Fried Zucchini: Fry sliced zucchini in a little olive oil in a skillet over medium-high heat until golden and season with sea salt and pepper. Dice a tomato and mix it with a little chopped parsley, cilantro, and/or dill. Spread pita bread with Tarator Sauce (page 59), add the zucchini, then add the tomato-herb mixture. Top with extra sauce and serve. Ⓥ

Pita with Herb Salad and Pine Nuts: I like this best with whole wheat pita. Make Herb Salad (*Sabzi*) (page 129) and toss it with a few pine nuts or roasted walnuts. Line pita bread with Tarator Sauce (page 59) and add the salad and a few sliced tomatoes if they're in season. Spoon a little extra sauce over the top and serve. Ⓥ

Pita with Chopped Salad and Hummus: This sandwich is one of my favorite summer lunches. Don't fill it too full, or you'll have to gulp it down. Line pita bread with Spicy Chickpea Puree (Hummus) (page 87), then add a little salad of chopped cucumbers and tomatoes and drizzle with Lemon Vinaigrette (page 164), or lemon juice. Ⓥ

Supper Sandwiches

The following knife-and-fork sandwiches are fine fare for supper—lunch, too, if you eat at home, but they're definitely not the kind to carry to work. These sandwiches are warm, full of vegetables, and satisfying to eat. Similar to Italian bruschetta and, to a degree, those homey American classics such as creamed mushrooms on toast and Welsh rarebit.

The basic technique is straightforward. Start with a slice of country bread. Place it under a broiler or, if a grill is going, over the coals until browned around the edges, crisp on the outside, but still soft inside. Rub one side with the cut surface of a large garlic clove, perfuming the bread with its juice, then brush olive oil on top. I often lay a thin slice of Gruyère, parmesan, or fontina right on top of the hot bread. This small enrichment makes all the tastes resonate in a particularly satisfying way, but of course those avoiding dairy can omit it. Then add vegetables, including their juices, so that the final rendering is an exciting mingling of crisp edges with soft toast, tender cheese, and succulent, moist vegetables.

All of these have a little cheese along with the vegetables—vegans can omit or replace with an ersatz cheese.

Ricotta and Peperonata on Toast

Here's another way to use peperonata, the highly versatile summer vegetable braise, or the Sautéed Peppers on page 363. Serves 4 or more

- Peperonata (page 363) or Sautéed Peppers (page 363)
- 4 slices sourdough or country bread
- 1 clove garlic, halved
- ¹/₂ cup or more ricotta
- Thinly slivered basil leaves, to finish

If you're using peperonata that's been refrigerated, warm it up in a skillet, adding some water or a splash of white wine to thin it and make a little sauce. Toast the bread, rub with garlic, and cover with the ricotta cheese. Set on plates, spoon the peperonata over the top, and finish with the slivered basil.

Braised Spinach with Tomatoes and Sautéed Onion on Focaccia

Makes 2 large sandwiches

- Olive oil, as needed
- 2 cloves garlic, 1 sliced, 1 halved
- 1 bunch spinach, stems removed
- Sea salt and freshly milled pepper
- Several pinches red pepper flakes
- 1 small onion, thinly sliced
- 2 big squares focaccia, about 6 by 6 inches, or 4 large slices sourdough bread
- 2 small tomatoes, sliced
- 6 ¹/₂-inch rounds goat cheese
- Balsamic or red wine vinegar

Heat 1 tablespoon of oil with the sliced garlic in a medium skillet over medium-high heat until the garlic begins to color, then add the spinach and sprinkle with salt and pepper flakes. Raise the heat and sauté until wilted and tender, after a few minutes. Transfer to a colander to drain. Discard any juices left in the pan, add 2 teaspoons oil and the onion, and sauté over high heat until golden, about 5 minutes. Toast or broil the bread, then rub with the halved garlic clove.

Pile the spinach on the bottom halves of the focaccia, then top with the onion, tomato, and cheese. Drizzle with olive oil and season with pepper. Broil until the cheese begins to color in spots, about 5 minutes. Sprinkle generously with vinegar, add the tops, and press down to secure them.

Supper Sandwich with Broccoli Rabe and Olive Paste

If broccoli rabe isn't available, try this with escarole, chard, kale, or a mixture of greens. Makes 4 sandwiches

---

I hefty bunch broccoli rabe, or 2 bunches chard, trimmed

1¹/₂ tablespoons olive oil

2 cloves garlic, 1 chopped, 1 halved

A few pinches red pepper flakes

Sea salt and freshly milled pepper

4 large slices country or sourdough bread

Thinly sliced fontina or Gruyère cheese

Olive Paste (page 78)

Best olive oil, to finish

Simmer the greens in a pot of boiling salted water until nearly tender, about 5 minutes, then drain. Heat the oil in a medium to large skillet with the chopped garlic and pepper flakes. When the garlic begins to color, add the greens and simmer with 1 cup of water until completely tender. Season with salt and pepper.

Toast the bread, then rub it vigorously with the halved garlic. Lay the cheese on the hot toast, spread it with Olive Paste, then cover with the greens. Drizzle a little olive oil over the top and serve.

Mushroom and Spinach Supper Sandwich

I wouldn't hesitate to serve these to company, they're so full of flavor and so eminently satisfying. Add a soup or a salad—both if you've time—and fruit or a dessert. Makes 2 sandwiches

---

¹/₂ ounce dried porcini, about ¹/₂ cup

8 ounces large white mushrooms

2 tablespoons olive oil

2 plump cloves garlic, 1 finely chopped, 1 halved

Pinch red pepper flakes

1 bunch spinach, stems discarded, leaves coarsely chopped

1 tablespoon butter

Sea salt and freshly milled pepper

2 large slices country bread

Scant ¹/₂ cup grated fontina or Gruyère

Soak the porcini in ³/₄ cup warm water and set them aside. Slice the fresh mushrooms about ¹/₃ thick, making irregular angular cuts.

Heat the oil in a wide nonstick skillet. Add the fresh mushrooms and sauté over high heat, stirring occasionally, until browned, 5 to 7 minutes. Meanwhile, lift the dried mushrooms from their soaking water, coarsely chop them, and add them to the pan with the chopped garlic, pepper flakes, and spinach. Sauté for 1 minute, then add the soaking water and cook until the spinach is wilted and a little juice is left in the pan. Stir in the butter and season well with salt and pepper.

Toast the bread, then rub with the halved garlic and cover them with the cheese. Set them on two plates, spoon the vegetables and their juices on top, and add a grinding of black pepper.

Supper Sandwich with Grilled Eggplant and Tomato

The eggplant can be grilled well ahead of time, but have it warm rather than chilled when you make the sandwich.
Makes 4 sandwiches

4 plump Asian eggplants, strips of peel removed if desired

Olive oil

4 slices country bread

Sea salt and freshly milled pepper

1/2 cup crumbled goat cheese or feta

2 teaspoons chopped marjoram or thyme

2 ripe tomatoes, seeded and finely diced

Red wine vinegar

Cut the eggplant into diagonal slices about 3/8 inch thick. Score one side of each piece diagonally with the tip of a knife to allow the heat to penetrate quickly. Brush both sides with oil, then grill or broil on both sides until tender, 7 to 10 minutes on each side. Toast the bread. Divide the eggplant among the bread pieces, season with salt and pepper, and cover with the cheese. Broil until the cheese starts to bubble and color in places, about 7 minutes, then remove and set on individual plates. Sprinkle with the herb and spoon the tomatoes over the top. Finish with a few drops vinegar.

Other Toppings for Supper Sandwiches

Baby Artichoke and Green Onion Sauté (page 296)
Slivered Asparagus Sauté with Shallots (page 300)
Kale with Olives (page 342)
Mushrooms, Tarragon, and Cream (page 352)

Creamed Leeks on Walnut Toast

An American-style sandwich that's homey yet extravagant. Although a walnut bread is particularly good with the leeks, don't let its absence deter you. Any rustic bread, including a rye bread, will go well. Makes 2 sandwiches

4 small or 2 large leeks, trimmed and sliced into 1/4-inch rounds

1 1/2 tablespoons butter

Sea salt

1/3 cup dry white wine

1/2 cup half-and-half or créme fraîche

2 teaspoons chopped tarragon, parsley, or rosemary

1/4 cup grated parmesan, Gruyère, or crumbled goat cheese

2 slices Walnut Bread (page 594), toasted and lightly buttered

Freshly milled pepper

Wash the leeks well, but don't dry them. Melt the butter in a wide skillet, add the leeks, and toss with a little salt. Add the wine, cover, and cook over medium heat until the leeks are tender, about 20 minutes. Add the cream and herb and simmer until slightly thickened. Turn off the heat, stir in the cheese, then spoon the leeks over the toast. Add pepper and serve.

Caramelized Onions and Walnuts on Toast: Spread toasted bread with a little butter, olive oil, or softened goat cheese. Top with warm Caramelized Onions (page 358), mixed with chopped roasted walnuts and a little chopped rosemary or thyme. Serve warm. (If you don't eat cheese, know that this is also good without it. Instead, you might use a little Olive Paste (page 78) for pungency.)

Once you've made the caramelized onions, you can present them in many other ways. You can accent them with a number of pungent cheeses, layering thin slices over the hot toast or grating them on top—Gruyère, Swiss, fontina, dry Jack, and fresh or more mature goat cheeses come to mind, as do Manchego and aged Gouda. Slivers of roasted pepper or pitted niçoise olives might be combined with the onion. Sage, rosemary, and thyme all flatter, as does a burst of Italian parsley.

SALADS FOR ALL SEASONS

CHAPTER 6

Salads for All Seasons

We usually think of salads as something fresh, light, leafy and cool that precedes a main course. And green salads do just that when they're served at the beginning of a meal. They can also provide a refreshing pause at the end, however, and that's just a small example of the versatility that makes salads so appealing as well as difficult to define.

Salads may start with simple collections of tender leaves, but they can go on to become complex arrangements of varied ingredients. Composed salads, which include a number of elements on a plate, can be first courses when served small or main courses when served generously. Hearty salads based on grains, legumes, and pasta might well be presented as the main feature of a meal. And, of course, fruits, eggs, cheese, and an array of condiments also have a role to play in salads. On the very rare occasion that a person says he or she doesn't like salad, I've found that what the person really dislikes is vinegar, so perhaps it's the sharp acidic note of this single ingredient that unifies such a disparate collection of foods into "salad."

Not only do salad ingredients range widely, but so do temperatures. Cold and cool are not the only degrees for salad. Some salads use contrasting temperatures to good effect: a warm crouton or a warm dressing tossed with chilled greens tantalizes the senses, for heat brings out the fruity side of the vinegar and the full possibilities of the oil, while hot dressings temper aggressive greens like dandelions or soften other greens, like spinach.

Vinaigrettes and dressings, those richly endowed amalgamations of aromatic oils, vinegars, mustards, garlic, and herbs, are key players in the world of salads. Even with only lettuce to work with, you can make an infinite number of salads simply by changing the dressing.

Leafy Salad Greens: Lettuce, Herbs, Spinach, and Cabbages

Lettuce is one of the most lovely, pure, and beguiling foods to handle. Its delicate leaves hold a wealth of flavor, texture, coolness, and color. Exciting heirloom and new varieties of salad greens are increasingly becoming available through specialty growers and farmers' markets. Salad greens can include chicories, herbs, spinach, cabbages, and wild greens, as well as lettuce.

Here is a basic lexicon to give you the general idea of family groups and their possibilities.

BUTTERHEADS: Soft, buttery-textured leaves that form a loose and curvaceous rosette—Boston, Bibb, and butter lettuce are well-known examples; exotic varieties are etched with bronze and red. These lettuces are tender and exceptionally elegant, the perfect lettuce for a refined dinner salad.

CABBAGE: In addition to green and red Dutch cabbages, savoy and napa cabbage make excellent salads. Fine slicing or a brief wilting in boiling water make raw cabbage more appealing to many. Delicate napa cabbage is fine raw.

CHICORIES—ENDIVE, ESCAROLE, FRISÉE, DANDELION, AND RADICCHIO: These interesting greens range from slight to pronounced bitterness. They take well to fragrant nut oils, shallots, sharp vinegars, and pairings with citrus, apples and pears, walnuts and hazelnuts, and blue cheeses. They also stand up well to hot dressing, which sweetens their bitterness.

CRISPHEADS: These are the lettuces that crunch, most famous of which is iceberg. Crispheads offer texture, which Americans like as much as, and indeed confuse with, taste. Older crisphead types, from which our standard is descended, are actually quite flavorful, such as the French Reine de Glace. But iceberg is the lettuce to use when you want texture or a salad that will support a heavy dressing or when you're going camping.

GARDEN SALAD, MESCLUN, GOURMET LETTUCE MIX: These names refer to mixtures of small leaves, usually no longer than 3 inches, of lettuces and other greens such as arugula, red mustard, frisée, mâche, baby spinach, and sometimes tatsoi and mizuna. *Mesclun* is the Provençal word for fairly specific mixtures; farmers here tend to make more personal mixes, which are sold clean and ready to use. While the pound price is high, lettuce is light; if it's in good condition, there's virtually no waste of either lettuce or effort.

HERBS: Herbs provide many wonderful possibilities for salads. Arugula, sorrel, torn basil, lovage, parsley leaves, curly cress and watercress, the tender leaves of any garden herb, really—add so much. A salad composed entirely of herbs has big, exciting flavors that often need only a little lemon juice and olive oil for dressing.

LOOSELEAF LETTUCES: These are soft, open heads of loosely joined tender leaves. Red leaf and green leaf are common varieties. Red and green oakleaf lettuces have sharply indented leaves, while the frizzy, gaudy red Lollo Hossa is a new favorite. Looseleaf lettuces require lighter dressings than iceberg and romaine.

ROMAINE OR COS LETTUCES: Romaine or Cos lettuce is prized for its long, graceful leaves at the heart and its snappy texture. It also has good flavor and is the most nutritious of the lettuces, signaled by its dark green leaves. Romaine can be quite diminutive and have red or rouge-tipped leaves, but the standard variety is a good lettuce to use with a heavy dressing, such as avocado or blue cheese.

SPINACH: There are basically two types of spinach leaves: smooth and crinkled. The smooth type is preferable for salads unless the crinkled leaves are very tender little leaves with slender stems. If spinach has been in the field for a while—you can tell by its thick stems and leathery-looking leaves—it's better for cooking. Spinach is best with a robust or heated dressing.

WILD GREENS: Like herbs, wild greens can be very attractive and interesting in a salad. Some common backyard greens that I enjoy using are lamb's-quarters, miner's lettuce, amaranth, and purslane. Garden thinnings and volunteer seedlings also qualify as salad ingredients.

Care and Handling of Salad Greens

Handle salad greens gently—they bruise when roughly handled. Never open a head of lettuce by twisting it from the stem; this causes bruises and subsequent spoilage.

TRIMMING: Slice the head at its base with a sharp knife and let the leaves fall open. Discard those outside leaves that look thick and leathery—they've been exposed to the elements while protecting the rest—or use them for soup stocks. With a sure, light touch, gently tear or cut leaves that are too large to eat whole. A small, sharp knife or nimble fingers will do little harm, unlike a heavily wielded knife or aggressive tearing. With Belgian endive and escarole, the cut or torn edges discolor after an hour or so.

WASHING: It's most practical to wash greens after they've been trimmed. Plunge them into a large basin of cold water, gently swish them about with your hands, and, if very dirty, let them soak for at least 5 minutes. Lift the greens out of the water, leaving the debris behind. Take a close look, especially at the base of the leaves, to make sure they're really clean. Chicories, which are in the field for a while, are often gritty at the base, and sandy spinach frequently needs a second washing.

DRYING: Drying greens is important; if the salad isn't dry, the vinaigrette will get watered down, wasting what may be your most expensive oil. Also, if you plan to store washed greens, they won't spoil if they're well dried. If you don't have a salad spinner, dry lettuce between towels or swing it outdoors in a perforated bag. To store, roll washed and dried greens loosely in a kitchen towel, put the towel in a plastic bag, and refrigerate in the vegetable bin.

Cutting Styles

Some people are inclined to cut salad ingredients into small, evenly diced fragments; others like big uneven chunks, slices, wedges, or something in between. We naturally have our own styles. How things are cut affects the look and character of a dish but seldom affects the taste. Therefore, I've left the details of cutting sizes for salad vegetables up to your own discretion, unless, for some reason, they do make a difference.

Putting a Salad Together

AMOUNTS: Because salads are often made by eye, feel, and taste, there's no real need to measure greens. Besides, greens don't lend themselves easily to measurement—you certainly don't want to cram them into a cup. Roughly speaking, a good handful of lettuce and a few teaspoons of vinaigrette make a generous dinner salad. Many vinaigrette recipes make about $1/2$ cup because the amounts are easier to handle than minuscule measurements and the unused portion can be used over the next few days.

TOSSING: Give yourself a bowl with lots of room. I always toss my greens first with a pinch of sea salt, then add the dressing and toss until the leaves are coated evenly. Your hands are the best tool since they won't bruise the greens and you'll know by touch when you have enough dressing.

ADDING FLOWERS: If you're including edible flowers, add them after the salad is dressed so that they don't collapse or wilt under the oil. Scatter them over the finished salad, toss once more, and serve.

PRESENTATION: Most salad bowls are deep, but since salads are among the prettiest dishes we serve, you might consider a wide, shallow bowl or platter to show them off. On plates, lightly mound the leaves in a tangle so that they have a lively look. A salad that lies flat on the plate looks dispirited. Take a moment to turn a few of the prettier leaves to show their brighter sides, but quickly and without fussing.

Using Nuts and Seeds

Some salads call for roasted nuts. Use any of the nuts in chapter 4, Appetizers and First Courses, that are appropriate, such as basic roasted nuts or the Salt and Pepper Walnuts (page 79). Pine nuts, sesame seeds, and sunflower seeds can be toasted right in an ungreased skillet. Heat a small pan with the nuts in it and slide it back and forth occasionally so that the nuts brown evenly. Peanuts can be pan-fried in a little oil or roasted in the oven.

Wooden Bowl Salad

A 1913 community cookbook listed a "wooden bowl salad." It's the kind of salad that might be served before a meal or on a special plate on the side. With the wealth of new vegetables available, from Armenian cucumbers to currant tomatoes, this salad can be both exotic and familiar at the same time. Capers, artichoke hearts or roasted peppers, and olives can find a place here, too. Serves 4 to 6

Salad

1 head crisp romaine lettuce

4 tomatoes, any color or variety

8 radishes

1 cucumber, the skin left on unless waxed

3 large, firm mushrooms

2 handfuls sunflower sprouts

8 marinated artichoke hearts

3 hard-cooked eggs, quartered

12 long strips cheddar cheese, or a handful of crumbled feta

3 tablespoons snipped chives, basil, or marjoram

Sea salt and freshly milled pepper

Dressing

1 large clove garlic

1/4 teaspoon sea salt

Freshly milled pepper

1 1/2 tablespoons aged red wine vinegar

5 to 6 tablespoons olive oil

Discard any damaged outer leaves and cut the inner leaves into bite-size pieces. Pile them into a spacious salad bowl or into individual bowls. Slice the tomatoes as best suits their size. Slice the radishes into thin rounds. Slice the cucumber into rounds. Wipe the mushrooms clean and slice them thinly as well. Arrange the vegetables, eggs, and cheese decoratively over the top, scatter the herbs over all, and season with salt and pepper.

To make the dressing, mash the garlic with the salt in a mortar until it breaks down into a puree, then add pepper and the vinegar. Whisk in the oil, then taste to make sure the balance is to your liking. Adjust as needed, to taste.

Pour the dressing over the salad and toss just before serving, or let each person toss her own.

Mixed Green Salad

This simple salad is equally appropriate at the start or the close of a meal. The lettuce could be garden lettuces of mixed varieties or a single type only. Chopped herbs or tiny sprigs add unexpected bursts of flavor to a salad. Serves 4 to 6 Ⓥ

4 to 6 handfuls salad greens

1/4 teaspoon sea salt

1 teaspoon Dijon mustard

1 1/2 tablespoons white or red wine vinegar, or 1 tablespoon fresh lemon juice

5 tablespoons olive oil

Chopped herbs—chervil, small basil leaves, chives, or parsley leaves

Freshly milled pepper

Carefully sort through the greens, then trim, wash, and dry them well. In a small bowl, combine the salt, mustard, and vinegar and let stand at least 10 minutes to dissolve the salt. Whisk in the oil to make a smooth sauce or shake everything together in a jar. Taste the vinaigrette on a leaf. Add more oil if it's too tart or a little vinegar if it's too oily. Though you can make your vinaigrette ahead of time, don't actually dress the salad until you're ready to serve it—it will quickly grow limp.

Using your hands, toss the greens with the herbs and a few pinches of salt. Add 3 tablespoons dressing and toss until they're coated lightly but evenly. Taste and add more dressing, if desired. Grind a little pepper on the leaves, toss again, and serve.

SPROUTS ON SALADS

Keep an eye out for these infant plants. All sprouts are nutritious, and some are quite delicious. Long white and short pink radish sprouts are as peppery tasting as a radish. Fine, threadlike leek sprouts topped with their black seeds taste every bit like a leek, while sprouted basil tastes like basil. Sunflower sprouts, with their large fleshy leaves and white stems, look striking on a salad of dark green spinach. Sprouts from the garden, otherwise known as thinnings, or microgreens, make great additions to a salad. They don't look like much, but they're full of flavor. Beet, leek, lettuce, arugula, and carrot are just a few possibilities.

Red Lettuces with Radish Sprouts

Part of a salad's character comes from the mix of greens. Here's one based on red-leaf lettuces, such as Lollo Rossa, red romaine, red-tipped butterheads, or some slender leaves of Treviso radicchio. Pink radish sprouts add a peppery tingle to the mix. Serves 4 to 6 Ⓥ

4 good handfuls red-leaf salad greens
1 large shallot, finely diced
1¹/₂ tablespoons red wine vinegar
¹/₄ teaspoon sea salt
3 tablespoons extra-virgin olive or sunflower seed oil
1 tablespoon walnut oil
1 cup red radish sprouts

Sort through the greens, then trim, wash, and dry them well. Combine the shallot, vinegar, and salt in a bowl and let stand for 10 to 15 minutes. Whisk in the oils. Toss the greens with a few pinches salt, add the dressing, distribute the radish sprouts on top, and toss until the leaves are coated evenly.

Composed Salad of Winter Vegetables with Romesco Sauce

Romesco sauce is as good with winter vegetables as garlic mayonnaise is with summer ones. Both the sauce and the vegetables can be prepared ahead of time. Serves 4 to 6

Romesco Sauce (page 62)
1 small cauliflower, broken into florets and steamed
2 carrots, attractively cut, then steamed
3 waxy-skinned potatoes, boiled and sliced
4 small red or golden beets, steamed, peeled, and quartered, (see page 304)
3 hard-cooked eggs, quartered
12 Cerignola green olives
Chopped parsley, for garnish

Thin the sauce with enough water to give it the texture of thick cream. Arrange the cooked vegetables attractively with the eggs and olives, then spoon the sauce over or around them and garnish with the parsley.

Watercress with Slivered Endive

I love this simple yet distinctive salad with its shower of endive slivers. It's a wonderful first course for a winter meal. Follow it with a cheese or vegetable soufflé, an omelet, gratin, or even a hearty soup. Serves 4 Ⓥ

2 bunches watercress
2 Belgian endives
Lemon Vinaigrette (page 164)

Carefully sort through the greens, then trim the watercress by removing the larger stems and broken branches. Wash the watercress and endive, and spin dry. Halve the endives, remove the cores, then slice them diagonally into slender slivers. Make the vinaigrette. Taste and adjust the balance if needed. Toss the watercress with enough dressing to coat lightly, then distribute it among salad plates, piling it lightly. Toss the endive with vinaigrette to coat lightly, then scatter it over the watercress and serve.

Winter Greens with Fennel and Mushrooms

Sturdy chicories—Belgian endive, frisée, radicchio, and escarole—marry well with crisp fennel and earthy mushrooms, while a fruity olive oil ties everything together. Pears, by the way, are also stellar in this salad; use them in place of the mushrooms. Serves 4 to 6 Ⓥ

4 good handfuls mixed greens—radicchio torn into small pieces, slivered endive, tender frisée sprigs, dandelion, butter lettuce
1 fennel bulb, trimmed and very thinly sliced
6 firm white mushrooms, thinly sliced
Sea salt and freshly milled pepper
Shallot Vinaigrette (page 165)
A piece of parmesan or dry Jack cheese at room temperature, optional

Carefully sort through the greens, then trim, wash, and dry them well. Toss the greens, fennel, and mushrooms in a salad bowl with a few pinches of salt. Toss with enough vinaigrette to coat well and season with pepper. Divide among plates and shave the cheese into long shards over each serving.

Endive Leaves with Walnuts and Blue Cheese

This good salad is one I make weekly during the winter when there's a dearth of the usual salad greens but there are new walnuts in their shells. You can chop the endive, or enjoy the leaves whole, which is what I prefer. Endive is usually white ("witfloof" or "white leaf" is its other name), but a most delectable rose-colored variety can also be found.
Serves 4 to 6

Walnut Oil Vinaigrette (page 166)
4 heads of Belgian endive, either white or pink or some of each
6 freshly cracked walnuts or ¹/₃ cup walnut meats
Several ounces crumbled blue cheese—your favorite
Freshly milled pepper

First make the vinaigrette and set it aside.

Slice the base off the endive and pull off the leaves. When they no longer come easily, make another slice off the base and repeat. Keeping doing this until you get to the tiny core of leaves at the center.

When you're ready to serve, toss the endive with enough of the vinaigrette to coat, then loosely lay the leaves on a platter. Add the walnuts and crumbled cheese, a little milled pepper, and serve.

Grilled Mushroom Salad with Watercress

This impressive little salad is good for the fall and winter months. Here the mushrooms are broiled or grilled, but you also could sear them in a skillet. Serves 2 to 4 Ⓥ

1 large shallot, finely diced
¹/₄ teaspoon sea salt
1 tablespoon aged red wine vinegar
2 large portabella mushrooms, stems removed, gills scraped out
Olive oil, for the mushrooms
Freshly milled pepper
3 tablespoons walnut or olive oil
1 bunch watercress, large stems discarded, washed and dried
3 tablespoons walnuts, roasted and chopped

Put the shallot in a bowl with salt and vinegar and set aside. Meanwhile, brush the mushroom caps with olive oil and season with salt and pepper. Grill or broil for about 4 minutes on each side, then cut into wide strips. Whisk the walnut oil into the vinegar mixture and season with pepper. Toss the mushrooms with 1 tablespoon of the dressing and use the rest to dress the watercress and walnuts. Divide the greens among salad plates and arrange the mushrooms loosely among them.

Leeks in Mustard Vinaigrette

One of my favorite first courses to eat and to serve, this is inspired by my friend, cookbook author Ann Clark. Serve them as Ann does—warm, in a soup plate, with country bread to mop up the juices. Leftovers can be sliced and mounded on bread or croutons for a pass-around appetizer.
Serves 4 to 6

6 to 8 leeks, including an inch of the pale greens
Aromatics: 1 bay leaf, 5 parsley sprigs, 4 thyme sprigs
1 large carrot, thinly sliced
1 celery rib, thinly sliced
Mustard Vinaigrette (page 167)

Halve the leeks lengthwise to 1 inch above the root end. Soak them in a large bowl of water for 15 minutes, then rinse gently under running water. Put them, in a single layer, in a large skillet with the aromatics, vegetables, and water to cover. Simmer until they're tender when pierced with a knife, 20 to 25 minutes, depending on their size. Gently transfer the leeks to a platter or individual plates with some of the broth, spoon the vinaigrette generously over the top, and serve with fresh bread. Be sure to use the remaining broth for soup stock or risotto.

Tender Tatsoi with Sesame Oil Vinaigrette

Tiny spoon-shaped tatsoi leaves make an unusual salad, especially with the addition of floral Szechuan Pepper Salt and fragrant toasted sesame oil. If your tatsoi is not so small and tender, combine it with mixed salad greens and use it as an accent. Serves 4 Ⓥ

---

8 cups tender tatsoi leaves and/or salad greens

2 green onions, including some of the greens, thinly sliced

1 tablespoon thinly sliced garlic chives or regular chives

2 teaspoons rice vinegar

2 tablespoons light sesame oil

1 tablespoon toasted sesame oil

Scant 1/2 teaspoon Szechuan Pepper Salt (page 69) or sea salt

1 tablespoon toasted sesame seeds

Sort through the greens, then trim, wash, and dry them well. Toss the greens with the onions and chives. In another bowl, whisk together the vinegar, oils, and salt. Taste the dressing on a leaf and adjust the oil or vinegar if necessary. Pour over the salad, toss well, add the sesame seeds, toss again, and serve.

PURSLANE AND LAMB'S-QUARTERS

The succulent creeper purslane and the upright lamb's-quarters or wild spinach are among the first plants to emerge in freshly turned soil and are persistent residents of established gardens as well. Although usually regarded as weeds in the suburbs, in the country these plants are recognized as food. In northern New Mexico, where I live, both plants are sold in the farmers' market by traditional farmers. Purslane, almost lemony and crunchy when uncooked, is added raw to salads, sautéed, or cooked with beans. Lamb's-quarters, which are related to spinach and chard, can be included in salads when the leaves are small and tender. Larger leaves are cooked like spinach.

Aside from being unusual and delicious, purslane and lamb's-quarters are both richly endowed with antioxidant vitamins C and E, beta-carotene, and other protective substances. Purslane is a rare plant source of omega-3 fatty acids. If you have a garden, chances are you already are growing purslane and lamb's- quarters. Instead of weeding them out, try mixing them in a salad.

Sea Greens and Sesame Salad

Sea greens—or seaweeds—make a most refreshing salad. One ounce doesn't sound like a lot, but when hydrated the dried bits and pieces swell and become beautiful. You can use just one type, such as wakame or dulse, or mix sea greens together. They can be bought as dried mixed seaweed in Japanese markets. Most recipes don't call for the sesame oil, but I always include a little for the flavor it gives. Makes 6 to 8 small portions Ⓥ

---

1 ounce dried, mixed sea greens

4 teaspoons rice wine vinegar

1 tablespoon soy sauce

1 tablespoons sugar or 1 teaspoon agave nectar

1 to 2 teaspoons toasted sesame oil

2 teaspoons grated ginger, squeezed for the juice (about 1/2 teaspoon)

2 teaspoons toasted white sesame seeds

1 green onion, finely-slivered, or a few chives, snipped, for garnish, optional

Cover the dry sea greens with cold water and soak for 5 to 10 minutes, until it is the texture you like. It does get softer as it sits in the water. Drain it well and squeeze out the excess water.

Combine the vinegar, soy sauce, agave, oil, and ginger juice. Toss the sea greens with the dressing, add the sesame seeds, and toss once more. Garnish with the green onion.

Romaine Hearts with Parmesan and Lemon Vinaigrette

Romaine hearts, the crisp, pale, perfect leaves at the center of a head of romaine lettuce, are strong enough to support denser, heavier dressings. These salads make a light meal or, in smaller portions, a substantial first course. The heart constitutes only about a third of the head. Use the outer leaves in another salad or in soup stock. Serves 4 to 6

2 heads romaine lettuce

1 clove garlic

1/2 teaspoon sea salt

1 teaspoon finely grated lemon zest

2 1/2 tablespoons fresh lemon juice

1 heaping teaspoon Dijon mustard

6 tablespoons olive oil

1/2 cup freshly grated parmesan or more to taste

1/4 cup small toasted croutons

Freshly milled pepper

Slice the bottoms off the lettuce and remove most of the leaves until you get to the hearts. Wash if needed and put the hearts in a spacious, wide bowl.

Pound the garlic with the salt in a mortar until smooth. Whisk in the lemon zest and juice, the mustard, then the oil. Pour the dressing over the leaves and roll them over each other until coated. Sprinkle most of the cheese over the leaves, add the croutons, and toss again until the leaves are coated. Divide the salad among four large plates, add the remaining cheese, and finish with pepper.

Romaine Hearts with Pecans and Chive Blossoms: Omit the cheese and croutons but add 2 tablespoons snipped chives and 1/2 cup roasted pecans to the romaine. If you have chive blossoms, cut through the base of one or two clusters and scatter the blossoms on top. Ⓥ

Romaine Hearts with Blue Cheese Dressing: Toss the hearts with Blue Cheese Dressing (page 169). With sliced pears or apples and roasted walnuts, this makes a perfect fall salad.

Romaine Hearts with Feta Dressing and Tomatoes: Chop the romaine and toss with Feta Dressing with Marjoram and Mint (page 169). Slice 3 ripe tomatoes—a mixture of varieties is nice—into wedges or chunks, toss them with the greens, and finish with plenty of pepper.

Romaine Hearts with Green Goddess Dressing: Everyone will tell you that this is divine when you serve it. Make either version of Green Goddess Dressing (page 169); toss with the romaine and 1/2 cup or so small diced croutons, crisped in olive oil.

Wilted Dandelion Greens with Hard-Cooked Egg

Commercial dandelion greens, available in early spring, need the assertive tastes of garlic and good, strong vinegar to match their own aggressive nature, even though they're milder than wild ones. The hot dressing wilts them just enough to sweeten their flavor. Spinach and escarole are also good treated this way. Serves 4

1 bunch dandelion greens

2 large, thin slices sourdough bread

1 large clove garlic, halved

1/4 teaspoon sea salt

1 large shallot, finely diced

4 teaspoons sherry vinegar or aged red wine vinegar

5 tablespoons olive oil

Freshly milled pepper

2 hard-cooked eggs, quartered, for garnish

Carefully sort through the greens, then trim, wash, and dry them well. Trim and discard the long stems of the greens, then chop the remaining leaves into bite-size pieces. There should be about 6 cups. Toast the bread in the oven until crisp, then rub it with garlic and break each piece into quarters.

Pound the same clove of garlic with the salt in a mortar until smooth, then whisk in the shallot, vinegar, and oil. Heat the vinaigrette in a small skillet until it sizzles, then pour it over the dandelion greens while tossing them with tongs. Add the croutons and plenty of pepper and toss again. Serve garnished with the eggs.

With Roasted Walnuts: In place of the croutons, substitute 1/2 cup Salt and Pepper Walnuts (page 79).

With Garlic Croutons and Gruyère: Add several paper-thin slices of Gruyère to each salad. The buttery cheese, the garlicky bread, and the strong greens make a stupendous combination. Spinach is also delicious this way.

Salad with Warm Goat Cheese Croutons

The warm, near-melting goat cheese paired with greens, popularized by Alice Waters at Chez Panisse, is one of the best combinations imaginable. Use a mixture of small garden lettuces and frisée if available. Serves 6

6 ounces soft white goat cheese

3 tablespoons milk or cream

1 clove garlic, minced

2 teaspoons coarsely chopped thyme leaves, plus extra for garnish

Freshly milled pepper

6 large or 12 small baguette slices

8 to 10 cups salad greens

Pinch sea salt

Shallot Vinaigrette (page 165)

Preheat the broiler. Smooth the goat cheese with the milk, then stir in the garlic, thyme, and a little pepper. Broil the bread just until the tops are lightly colored, then spread the cheese mixture thickly over the untoasted side and set aside. Toss the salad greens with salt, then with the vinaigrette, and arrange on individual plates. Broil the croutons until the cheese begins to slump and bubble, about 3 minutes. Sprinkle on the thyme, then set the cheese toasts right on top of the greens. Grind black pepper over the top and serve.

With Figs: Include some arugula in the lettuce mix. Slice 12 ripe figs into halves or rounds and dress them separately with a little Lemon Vinaigrette (page 164), or Shallot Vinaigrette (page 165). Dress and serve the greens, placing the figs among them. Set the warm croutons on top.

Herb Salads

Salads emphasizing fresh herbs are vigorous and fill the mouth with big, robust flavors. A little goes far, and because of their intensity, they're excellent paired with milder foods or as a contrast to rich ones.

Parsley, so ubiquitous but overlooked in this capacity, makes an especially healthful—as well as good—salad. Improvising with your own garden gleanings can provide you with an ever-changing salad on the table. With so much flavor, the dressing need be only a light coating of olive oil and a squeeze of lemon.

Herb Salad (*Sabzi*)

Sabzi refers to greens or potherbs, usually a Middle Eastern combination of dill, parsley, and mint. Serve this herb salad with a warm cheese-filled turnover or falafel, or add it to a pita sandwich along with tomatoes and feta or ricotta salata. Serves 3 or 4 (V)

3 cups spinach leaves or lamb's-quarters

1 handful small arugula leaves

1/4 cup flat-leaf parsley leaves

1/4 cup cilantro leaves

1/4 cup dill sprigs

6 mint leaves, torn into small pieces

Several celery or lovage leaves, torn

2 green onions, including a few inches of the greens, thinly sliced

A few pinches sea salt

1 tablespoon olive oil or as needed

Fresh lemon juice or vinegar

Carefully sort through the greens, then wash and dry them well. Tear or cut the spinach and arugula into bite-size pieces and toss with the herbs, onions, and salt. Drizzle on enough oil to lightly coat the leaves, then squeeze on a little lemon juice and toss again.

A Salad with Garden Herbs

Serve this salad or its variation with the Rice and Ricotta Tart (page 439), roasted potatoes, or small cheese toasts. Serves 3 or 4 Ⓥ

- 2 cups lettuce leaves
- 2 cups spinach leaves
- 4 marjoram sprigs
- 2 tablespoons basil leaves
- 1/2 cup celery leaves or lovage
- 1/2 cup flat-leaf parsley leaves
- Several lemon verbena sprigs
- 1 cup small purslane sprigs
- Sea salt
- Olive oil
- Fresh lemon juice or apple cider vinegar
- Herb blossoms, if available

Sort through the leaves, then wash and dry them well. Tear or cut the lettuce and spinach into bite-size pieces. Strip the marjoram leaves from their stems. Keep the marjoram leaves whole, but tear the basil leaves unless they're the tiny piccolo fino variety, and keep the celery, parsley, and lemon verbena leaves in fairly large pieces. Toss everything with a pinch or two of salt, then with just enough oil to coat. Season with lemon juice to taste, then toss again with the herb blossoms.

Parsley Salad with Parmesan

Flat-leaf parsley has better flavor, so choose it over the curly type if possible. Include parsley salad on a composed salad plate or sprinkle it over hot pizza, grilled eggplant, a baked potato, or warm chickpeas. The heat brings out its flavor and softens the leaves. You'll need no more than 1/2 cup per person. Serves 4 to 6

- 2 1/2 cups parsley leaves
- 1 tablespoon chopped marjoram
- 1 tablespoon chopped mint
- Sea salt and freshly milled pepper
- Sherry Vinaigrette (page 166) or Lemon Vinaigrette (page 164)
- Thin shavings of parmesan or dry Jack

Pluck the parsley leaves from the stems, then wash and dry well. Toss with the herbs, a few pinches of salt and pepper to taste, then with a few tablespoons vinaigrette or enough to coat lightly. Serve covered lightly with thin shavings of cheese.

Parsley Salad with Oil and Lemon: Toss parsley leaves with 2 tablespoons olive oil and 1 1/2 to 2 teaspoons fresh lemon juice. Season with salt and freshly milled pepper. Ⓥ

Arugula Salads

Those who have come across arugula and fallen in love with it don't want an arugula accent; they (we) want an entire salad of it.

As arugula matures, the leaves get big, peppery, and hot, and those should be used sparingly. For an all-arugula salad, look for small, soft leaves with a mild but definite bite. Discard the long stems, but keep any cream-colored blossoms for a fine edible garnish. Pungent olives, hard-cooked eggs with the yolk still a little moist, grilled onions, and fresh figs with salty cheeses all form happy alliances with arugula. Vinaigrettes featuring olive oil and walnut and hazelnut oils are a good match for arugula's warm flavor, as are assertive aged red wine and sherry vinegars and lemon juice.

Impromptu Arugula Salad: Allow 1 1/2 to 2 handfuls arugula per person. Carefully sort through the leaves, then wash and dry them well. Tear any large leaves in half or thirds, put them all in a spacious bowl, and toss with a few pinches of sea salt. Drizzle on enough olive oil to coat lightly and evenly when tossed. Squeeze on a little lemon juice, then toss again and taste. Serve the leaves heaped into a high, light pile. Ⓥ

Arugula Salad with Hard-Cooked Eggs and Croutons:
For four servings, boil 2 or 3 eggs and separate the yolks and whites. Finely chop the whites and scatter them over the preceding arugula salad, then crumble or sieve the yolks over all. Add 2 large, thin Garlic-Rubbed Crostini (page 24) to each plate. Or quarter the eggs and include them among the greens and croutons.

Arugula with Tomatoes and Olive Croutons

This combination offers flavor and color contrasts—even more so if you use both red and yellow tomatoes. Serves 4 Ⓥ

2 or 3 ripe tomatoes or 1 cup cherry tomatoes
8 Garlic-Rubbed Crostini (page 24)
Olive Paste (page 78)
8 to 10 cups arugula, stems discarded, any large leaves torn
3 tablespoons Balsamic Vinaigrette (page 164)

Halve the tomatoes, remove the seeds, and cut them neatly into small pieces or simply cut the cherry tomatoes in half.

Spread the crostini with the olive paste. Toss the greens with enough vinaigrette to coat lightly. Add the tomatoes and toss again. Serve with the crostini tucked among the leaves.

Arugula with Pecorino Romano and Toasted Walnuts

An excellent salad for fall, when walnuts are new and fresh. Rich-tasting walnut oil tempers spicy late-season arugula. Serves 4

8 to 10 cups arugula, stems discarded, any large leaves torn
Sea salt
Walnut Oil Vinaigrette (page 166)
1/2 cup or more coarsely grated Pecorino Romano
1/2 cup cracked walnuts, roasted

Toss the arugula with a little salt and enough vinaigrette to coat lightly. Add the cheese and walnuts, toss again, and serve.

Spinach Salads

The best-tasting spinach salads are those made with tender small leaves, whether smooth or crinkled.

Remember to take special care to wash spinach thoroughly and make sure it's clean by tasting a few leaves. Fine sand, which is hard to see, often clings to the leaves.

Spinach and Avocado Salad with Sunflower Seeds and Sprouts

Sprouts on salad are a vegetarian cliché, but sprouted sunflower seeds, with their fleshy large leaves and stems, are far from commonplace. Serves 2 to 4 Ⓥ

6 handfuls small spinach leaves
1/3 cup sunflower seeds, toasted
2 tablespoons chopped parsley, dill, or basil

Sea salt and freshly milled pepper
1 tablespoon red wine vinegar
1 small clove garlic, minced
3 tablespoons sunflower seed or avocado oil
6 freen onions, including an inch of the greens, thinly sliced
2 handfuls sunflower sprouts
2 ripe tomatoes, seeded and chopped
1 avocado, sliced
Crumbled feta, optional

Toss the spinach with the sunflower seeds, parsley, a pinch of salt, and some pepper. Put another pinch of the salt, the vinegar, and the garlic in a small bowl; whisk in the oil and add the onions. Pour the vinaigrette over the greens and toss. Loosely arrange the greens on a large platter, then add the sprouts, tomatoes, avocado, and feta to taste.

Spinach and Tomato Salad with Basil-Walnut Dressing

Crinkly Bloomsdale spinach makes a good support for this thick, garlicky dressing. As for the tomatoes, they needn't be red. They can be yellow, orange, pink, nearly white, almost black, and green. Mix them up for a more colorful salad. Serves 4 ⓥ

1 small red onion, sliced into paper-thin rounds

4 ripe tomatoes

6 to 8 handfuls small spinach leaves, sliced into wide ribbons

8 white mushrooms, thinly sliced

1/4 cup basil leaves, torn or thinly sliced

Sea salt

Basil-Walnut Dressing

1/2 cup walnuts

2 cloves garlic

1/2 teaspoon sea salt

Scant 1/2 cup olive oil

3 tablespoons red wine vinegar or 2 tablespoons sherry vinegar

1 tablespoon chopped basil or 1 teaspoon dried

Freshly milled pepper

Cover the onion with cold water and refrigerate for 30 minutes. Meanwhile, make the dressing. Using a small food processor or a mortar and pestle, grind or pound the walnuts, garlic, and salt to a chunky paste. Gradually whisk in the oil, then add the vinegar. Stir in the basil and season with pepper. If the dressing thickens too much before serving, thin it with water to a lighter consistency.

Slice the tomatoes into eighths or large chunks and reserve 12 pieces for garnish. Put the spinach in a spacious bowl with the remaining tomatoes, the mushrooms, and the basil. Drain the onion, towel off the excess moisture, and add to the spinach. Toss with a few pinches of salt, then add the dressing and toss well. Garnish with the reserved tomato.

Wilted Spinach Salad

Tossing spinach leaves quickly in a hot oil or a heated vinaigrette brings out their flavor as well as reducing the fuzzy feel that spinach sometimes leaves in the mouth. Essentially the same salad as in The Greens Cookbook, *this is still one of my favorites, and it's a template for all wilted salads. Use spinach from a bunch rather than "baby" spinach—it's almost too tender.* Serves 4 ⓥ

1 small red onion

8 handfuls tender spinach leaves

1 clove garlic, finely chopped

4 ounces crumbled goat cheese, feta, or ricotta salata, optional

12 kalamata olives, pitted and cut into large pieces

1 tablespoon thinly sliced mint leaves

2 tablespoons sherry vinegar

Sea salt and freshly milled pepper

6 tablespoons olive oil, fragrant but not your very best

12 thin Garlic-Rubbed Crostini (page 24)

Quarter the onion and thinly slice it crosswise, then cover with ice water. Refrigerate for 30 minutes, then drain and pat dry.

Carefully sort through the leaves, then wash and dry them well. In a large bowl, toss together everything except the oil with several pinches salt. Heat the oil until almost smoking, then pour it over the salad, quickly turning the leaves with a pair of tongs as you do so. The spinach should sizzle, brighten, and soften. Taste and correct the levels of salt and vinegar. Add pepper to taste and serve, dividing the crostini evenly among the plates.

Vegetables and Fruits Dressed as Salads

Virtually all vegetables and many fruits have strong affinities with vinaigrettes and other salad dressings.

While not every fruit and vegetable has been given its own recipe, here are examples to give you a sense of what's possible. Botanically related foods usually respond well to the same kinds of seasoning: mustardy dressings work with broccoli as well as cauliflower, both brassicas; blue cheese is delicious with pears and apples, both pome fruits.

COOKED AND RAW VEGETABLES: Common sense tells you which vegetables can be dressed raw or cooked. Some, like beets and carrots, can go both ways. Vegetables are usually steamed or boiled, but there's no reason not to roast or grill them, especially if it's convenient. In fact, both roasting and grilling concentrate flavor. Roasted potatoes or grilled eggplants with a vinaigrette are simply delicious. Many leftover vegetables can be turned into salads as well.

DRESSING VEGETABLES: Vegetables are most aromatic dressed while warm, but they can be eaten warm, tepid, or chilled. If you dress green vegetables well in advance of serving them, the acid from the lemon or vinegar will gradually dull their color. Either wait to dress them or add the acidic element just before serving.

DRESSING FRUITS: Since fruits are generally eaten uncooked, it's especially important that they start out full of flavor. Salty and pungent dressings bring out the sweetness of fruit—even a little fresh lime or lemon juice or some black pepper on a piece of melon dramatically sets off its sweetness.

Warm Green Bean Salad

Little green, yellow wax, or wide Romano beans tossed warm with a vinaigrette make a stellar summer salad. If you want to mix varieties, boil each type separately so that they all are cooked perfectly. Serves 4 Ⓥ

- 1¹/₂ pounds slender green, yellow wax, or Romano beans
- 3 to 4 tablespoons olive oil, as needed
- 1 tablespoon fresh lemon juice
- Pinch sea salt
- Chopped herbs—parsley, chervil, basil, or tarragon

Tip and tail the beans. Boil the beans in plenty of salted water, uncovered; drain while they're still a little on the firm side. Shake off the excess water, then lay them on a clean kitchen towel to dry for a few minutes. Toss the beans while warm with enough oil to coat well. Then add the lemon juice to taste, salt, and herbs. Serve immediately. (If you plan to serve them later, either dress them just before serving or add the acid at the last minute.)

Warm Asparagus Salad on Arugula with Walnut Vinaigrette

A roasted walnut oil makes a fine match for arugula and the first asparagus. Serves 2 to 4

- 1 large shallot, finely diced
- 1¹/₂ tablespoons champagne vinegar or white wine vinegar
- ¹/₄ teaspoon sea salt
- 3¹/₂ tablespoons roasted walnut oil
- 1 pound asparagus, trimmed (see page 298)
- 3 or 4 handfuls arugula, stems discarded, leaves torn into small pieces
- 1 hard-cooked egg
- Toasted walnuts or Salt and Pepper Walnuts (page 79)

Combine the shallot, vinegar, and salt in a small bowl. Let stand for 10 minutes to dissolve the salt, then whisk in the oil.

Simmer the asparagus in boiling salted water until tender, 5 to 8 minutes; then drain and transfer to a clean towel.

Dress the arugula with 1 tablespoon of the vinaigrette and set it on a platter. Lay the warm asparagus directly over the leaves and spoon the remaining dressing over it. Finely chop the egg white, scatter it over the top, followed by the yolk, rubbed through a sieve. Serve at once with the walnuts tucked among the leaves.

Avocado, Jicama, and Orange Salad

Jicama is a large, roundish tuber with a papery brown skin. It looks dull, but underneath its skin the flesh is white, sweet, and crunchy. Serve this salad with enchiladas.
Serves 4 to 6 Ⓥ

8 ounces jicama

1 large or 2 small avocados

2 navel oranges

4 large radishes

About 24 small spinach leaves

Juice of 2 limes or Lime-Cumin Vinaigrette (page 165)

Sea salt

1 jalapeño chile, seeded and finely diced, or ground red chile

Handful sunflower sprouts, for garnish

Peel the jicama; thinly slice it into rounds, then slice again into narrow strips. Peel and slice the avocado. Cut the oranges either into rounds or sections. Thinly slice the radishes, then cut them into narrow strips.

Line a platter with the spinach leaves. Lightly scatter the jicama over it and intersperse with the avocado, oranges, and radishes. Squeeze lime juice or spoon the vinaigrette over all. Season with salt, sprinkle with chile, and garnish with the sunflower sprouts.

Good Vinaigrettes for Beans

Lemon Vinaigrette (page 164)
Shallot Vinaigrette (page 165)
Tomato Vinaigrette with Olives (page 168)
Walnut Oil Vinaigrette (page 166)
Creamy Herb and Shallot Dressing (page 165)

Beet Salads

I'm convinced that beets are best enjoyed in salads. The tang of a vinaigrette tames their earthy sweetness in a way that makes them easily likable.

Even after they're dressed, beets keep well for days. All varieties can be used in salads, and mixtures of red, golden, and striped Chioggias are dazzling. When mixing different colors, be sure to keep the red ones away from everything else since they stain. Beets stand up to bright acids, salty cheeses and olives, peppery greens, and pungent seeds.

Beet with Flowering Collards and Other Sprouting Brassicas

Flowering collards, kale, and choy sum have been showing up at farmers' markets more in recent years and are surprisingly good with beets. It's a good combination with the mustardy bite of the greens against the sweet and earthy beets. The larger stems are not quite tender enough to enjoy eating unless you sliver them very finely. Serves 4 Ⓥ

4 beets, golden and Chioggia together

2 teaspoons sherry vinegar

1 teaspoon Dijon or other strong mustard

¹/4 teaspoon sea salt

3 to 4 tablespoons olive oil, to taste

3 cups choy sum or sprouting collard leaves, flowers, and the smaller stems, finely slivered

2 thin green onions, including a bit of the greens, thinly slivered

Steam the beets if you haven't any on hand already cooked (see page 304), then peel them. Cut them into wedges. Make the vinaigrette, combining the vinegar, mustard, and salt, then whisking in the oil.

Toss the choy sum (including the flowers) and onions with most of the dressing and taste for salt, adding more if need be. Heap it onto plates or a platter. Slide the beets around the bowl to pick up the rest of the vinaigrette, then tuck them among the choy sum leaves.

Beet Salad with Ricotta Salata and Olives

Serves 4 to 6

1¹/₂ to 2 pounds beets, steamed and peeled (see page 304)
1 small clove garlic
¹/₄ teaspoon sea salt
2 teaspoons fresh lemon juice, or to taste
2 tablespoons olive oil
2 handfuls arugula, for garnish
4 ounces ricotta salata, thinly sliced
8 kalamata olives

Cut the beets into wedges or large dice, keeping different colors separate. Pound the garlic with the salt in a mortar until smooth, then whisk in the lemon juice and olive oil. The dressing should be a little on the tart side. Toss the beets in enough dressing to coat lightly. Arrange them on a platter and garnish with arugula. Just before serving, tuck the cheese and olives among the greens. If any dressing remains, spoon it over the cheese.

Roasted Beets with Anise Vinaigrette

The Spanish combination of anise with beets is just as right as the more familiar dill and orange. Roasting adds another layer flavor to beets, tempering their sweetness.
Serves 4 to 6 Ⓥ

1¹/₂ pounds beets
2 tablespoons olive oil, plus more for beets
Sea salt and freshly milled pepper
1 teaspoon anise seeds
1 clove garlic
2 teaspoons sherry vinegar

Preheat the oven to 375°F. Peel the beets and cut them into ¹/₂-inch dice. Toss in olive oil to coat lightly and season with salt and pepper. Spread the beets on a sheet pan—make sure they have plenty of room so they don't just steam—and bake until the juices begin to caramelize and the beets are tender but firm, about 25 minutes. Place in a bowl.

In a mortar, crush the anise seeds with the garlic and a little salt. Whisk into a bowl with the vinegar and the 2 tablespoons olive oil. Pour the vinaigrette over the beets and marinate for several hours or overnight.

Roasted Beets with Shaved Fennel: Remove the outer layer of fennel, then slice inner layers paper-thin on a mandoline. Arrange the fennel loosely around the beets and garnish with watercress sprigs or fennel greens. Ⓥ

Beets with Lemon, Cilantro, and Mint

These herbs also flatter the versatile beet. Serve with Greek yogurt or Havarti with dill and dark bread to make a salad meal. Serves 4 to 6 Ⓥ

1¹/₂ pounds beets, cooked and peeled (see page 304)
Finely grated zest of 1 lemon plus 2 tablespoons juice
2 tablespoons finely diced red onion
2 tablespoons chopped parsley
2 tablespoons chopped cilantro
1 tablespoon chopped mint, or 1 teaspoon dried mint
¹/₂ teaspoon ground coriander
¹/₄ teaspoon sea salt
Freshly milled pepper
6 tablespoons olive oil
4 handfuls salad greens, such as spinach, frisée, and/or red-leaf lettuce
¹/₄ cup oil-cured black olives

Cut the beets into quarters or sixths. Whisk together the lemon zest and juice, onion, herbs, coriander, salt, pepper to taste, and the oil in a small bowl. Taste the dressing on a beet and correct the seasonings if needed. Toss the beets with enough dressing to coat lightly. Toss the greens with the remaining dressing and arrange them on salad plates. Add the beets and olives and serve.

Cabbage Salads

Cabbage salads, coleslaw and its cousins, are an entirely agreeable way to eat this healthful and inexpensive vegetable.

Once dressed, cabbage keeps refrigerated for hours, which is one reason coleslaw is a popular picnic food. Unlike lettuce salads, leftover coleslaw makes a great bag lunch item. As a change from the smooth, heavy heads of cabbage, try using the crinkled savoy or lighter napa cabbage. Both are more tender and mild. They don't hold up for quite as long, but they do make a fairly sturdy and quite delicious salad.

Napa and Savoy Cabbage Salad with Peanut-Ginger Dressing

The dressing is warmed to bring up the aromatic quality of the oil, but the salad isn't wilted. Use a fragrant roasted peanut oil, such as Loriva. Serves 6 Ⓥ

- 1 small napa cabbage, about ³/₄ pound
- 2 medium carrots, julienned
- 1 cucumber, peeled and seeded
- 1 bunch green onions, including a few inches of the greens
- ¹/₂ small savoy cabbage, about ¹/₂ pound, thinly sliced
- 2 tablespoons finely chopped mint leaves
- 1 tablespoon finely sliced basil leaves, preferably Thai basil
- Peanut Dressing with Thai Basil (page 168)
- ¹/₂ cup roasted peanuts or Roasted Cashews with Garam Masala (page 81)

Quarter the napa cabbage, including the base, and thinly slice it crosswise. Parboil the carrots for 1 minute, then refresh under cold water. Slice the cucumber and onions into long, thin pieces and toss with the napa and savoy cabbages and the herbs. Heat the dressing in a small skillet until the aromas are released, then immediately pour it over the greens while tossing with a pair of tongs. Add the nuts, toss again, and serve.

Coleslaw with Buttermilk-Horseradish Dressing

A tangy slaw that can be made with all green or red and green ribbons of cabbage. Serves 4 to 6

- 4 cups thinly sliced green or red and green cabbage, about 1 pound
- 1 green bell pepper, finely sliced or grated
- 1 small onion, grated
- ¹/₂ teaspoon sea salt
- Buttermilk Dressing with Horseradish (page 169)
- Chopped dill, for garnish

Toss the cabbage, bell pepper, and onion in a bowl with the salt. Toss with the dressing. Cover and refrigerate for 1 hour or until needed. Taste for salt and serve garnished with the chopped dill.

Cabbage Slaw with Spicy Greens

Serves 4 to 6 Ⓥ

- 3 or 4 handfuls arugula, garden cress, watercress, or red mustard greens
- 1¹/₂ pounds green cabbage, very thinly sliced
- 1 large cucumber, peeled, seeded, and diced
- 1 small white onion, or 1 bunch green onions, including an inch or so of the greens, thinly sliced
- 3 tablespoons chopped parsley
- ¹/₂ teaspoon sea salt
- Winter Herb Vinaigrette (page 167)

Chop the greens or cut them into ribbons and put them in a bowl with the cabbage, cucumber, onion, and parsley. Toss with the salt. Add the dressing and toss again. Chill for 30 minutes or longer before serving.

January Cabbage Salad with Blue Cheese and Mustard Vinaigrette

The crinkly leaves of January cabbage, or savoy cabbage, are not as dense as storage cabbages. Thinly sliced into ribbons, they make a delicate salad. I include romaine lettuce and red butter lettuce, or whatever I have around, for a mix of textures and colors. Amounts are, of course, quite flexible. Serves 4 to 6

4 cups thinly shredded (sliced) savoy cabbage

2 cups thinly sliced romaine lettuce

2 cups thinly sliced red butter or other lettuce

1 large shallot, finely diced

2 tablespoons sherry vinegar or aged red wine vinegar

$1/2$ teaspoon sea salt

2 teaspoons smooth mustard

5 to 6 tablespoons olive oil

$1/2$ cup or more blue cheese, thinly sliced or crumbled

Toasted walnuts, optional

Combine the sliced greens in a spacious bowl and refrigerate until needed.

Make the dressing. Cover the shallot with the vinegar, add the salt, and let stand for 10 minutes. Mix in the mustard, then whisk in the oil. Taste on a piece of cabbage leaf and adjust, adding more of anything that's needed.

When ready to serve, pour the dressing over the greens and toss well with your hands. Add the blue cheese and toss once more so that it's mixed in with the greens. If the rest of your meal has been light, or if this is your meal, add some toasted walnuts as well.

Tenderizing and Sweetening Cabbage

If raw cabbage seems too tough for your taste, slice it, put it in a colander, and pour a kettle of boiling water slowly over it. Shake off the excess moisture, then blot with a dry kitchen towel. Or, slice it as thin as possible on a mandoline and don't blanch.

Warm Red Cabbage Salad with Pecans

Though included in slightly different form in The Greens Cookbook, *this recipe has held up well. It can be served as a salad or as a vegetable.* Serves 4 to 6

1 clove garlic, finely chopped

1 tablespoon sherry vinegar

3 tablespoons olive oil

1 red onion, quartered and thinly sliced

1 small red cabbage, about $1^1/4$ pounds, quartered and thinly sliced

$1/2$ teaspoon sea salt

3 ounces crumbled goat cheese or mild feta

1 red apple, quartered and thinly sliced

$1/4$ cup pitted and chopped kalamata olives

1 tablespoon chopped parsley

1 tablespoon chopped marjoram

$1/2$ cup pecans or walnuts, roasted

Freshly milled pepper

Heat the garlic, vinegar, and oil in a wide skillet, add the onion, and cook for 30 seconds.

Add the cabbage, season with the salt, and cook over high heat, tossing constantly with tongs. When the leaves begin to soften and change from red to pink, remove from the heat. Add the remaining ingredients and toss just enough to combine them, then remove from the heat. Season with plenty of pepper and serve warm.

Kale Salad with Glazed Sunflower Seeds and Hot Cider Vinaigrette

There are so many good kale salads now, and yet the idea of such a thing never even popped up when Vegetarian Cooking for Everyone *was a work in progress. Foods change. This is one of the simpler kale salads I make, tossed (and somewhat wilted) with a hot vinaigrette. You can certainly add more to it—sliced apples, crumbled feta cheese, fresh oregano, and so forth.*

Serves 2 to 4 Ⓥ

- 1 bunch Tuscan kale, enough to make 4 cups slivered, stems removed first
- 1/4 cup Glazed Sunflower Seeds with Shichimi Togarashi (page 80)
- 4 green onions, including a few inches of the greens, thinly sliced
- 1 tablespoon organic apple cider vinegar
- 1 teaspoon mustard
- 3 to 4 tablespoons olive oil
- Sea salt and freshly milled pepper

First, prepare the kale and have it ready in a shallow bowl. Glaze the sunflower seeds if you haven't done so already. Toss them, along with the onions, with the kale.

Whisk the cider, mustard, and oil together in a small skillet. Heat until bubbling, then pour it over the kale and toss immediately. Pick up some of the kale with tongs and use it to wipe out the pan. Taste and season with salt and pepper to taste.

Carrot Salads

Salads made from carrots, either cooked or raw, are simple, sturdy, and satisfying. Try using carrots of many colors for a pleasing visual effect.

Spicy Cooked Carrot Salad with Paprika, Feta, and Olives

This salad is inspired by the flavors of Tunisia's popular salad of cooked carrots. There the carrots are very finely diced, but I find larger pieces are more appealing. You might want to make this salad with white, yellow, or purple carrots as well as orange. Serves 4 to 6

- 1 pound carrots
- 1 clove garlic, minced
- 1/4 teaspoon sea salt
- 2 teaspoons hot paprika or Harissa (page 66)
- 1 tablespoon red wine vinegar or fresh lemon juice
- 3 tablespoons olive oil
- 2 tablespoons chopped parsley
- 1/2 cup crumbled or thinly sliced feta cheese
- 12 oil-cured black olives, pitted and diced

Gently simmer the carrots in salted water until tender but not soft, then drain and rinse with cold water. Slip off the skins and slice them into rounds or small pieces.

Smash the garlic with the salt, then add the paprika and vinegar, and whisk in the oil. Toss the carrots with the vinaigrette, parsley, and most of the cheese and olives. Taste for salt. Mound the carrots on a plate and garnish with the remaining cheese and olives.

Cooked Carrot Salad with Cilantro Salsa

Cooked carrots (or beets) tossed with this pungent sauce—or any salsa verde, for that matter—are delicious and beautiful together. Serves 4 to 6 Ⓥ

- 1 pound carrots, cooked
- 1/4 cup Cilantro Salsa (page 49)
- Sea salt
- Mint sprigs and oil-cured or niçoise olives, for garnish

Peel and dice the carrots, then toss with the salsa. Taste for salt. Serve chilled or at room temperature, garnished with the mint and olives.

Grated Vegetable Salads

Grated vegetables—carrots, beets, kohlrabi, celery root, and turnips—make refreshing salads that have all the virtues we want these days: they're bright and fresh, quick and easy to make, they keep well, and they require little dressing. An assortment of colorful vegetables mounded on a plate and garnished with a few shiny olives makes an ideal first course for richer winter meals, but it's right at other times of the year as well. Spooned into the curve of a small radicchio leaf or perched on the end of an endive leaf, they even can be passed around as appetizers.

Grated vegetable salads can be served as soon as they're made but also will be fine sitting for a few hours in the refrigerator until needed. Because they're so sturdy, they also make excellent picnic and brown-bag lunch fare.

WHAT TOOL TO USE: A Japanese box grater (Benriner), a French mandoline, and an American four-sided box grater are all good tools. To get nice long shreds on a box grater, roll the vegetable in your hand as you move it down the side; the greater exposed surface gives longer shreds. If you want slightly larger pieces, slice the vegetables by hand into fine julienne strips, then blanch them in boiling salted water for about 1 minute to soften. Rinse under cold water and towel-dry before dressing.

Grated Kohlrabi and Celery with Mustard Vinaigrette:
Thickly peel 12 ounces kohlrabi or turnips and cut into fine julienne strips. Thinly slice or grate 3 or 4 inner celery ribs. Toss with enough Mustard Vinaigrette (page 167) to moisten.

Cauliflower Salad with Green Olives and Capers

People always love this salad. The real secret to making it shine is to slice the cauliflower as thinly as possible. Serves 4

1 small firm head cauliflower or broccoflower, about 12 ounces

2 cups watercress or inner escarole leaves

1 hard-cooked egg

Sherry Vinaigrette (page 166)

2 green onions, including an inch of the greens, thinly sliced

1 cup diced celery heart with leaves

1 small green bell pepper, thinly sliced

1 small cucumber, peeled, seeded, and chopped

12 pimiento-stuffed Spanish green olives, halved

1 tablespoon capers, rinsed

1/2 cup parsley leaves

Slice off very thin slices of cauliflower, working your way around the head. Quarter, then thinly slice the cauliflower. Be sure to include the stalks, too, peeled and thinly sliced. Remove the large stems from the watercress and coarsely chop the rest. If you're using escarole, select the pale inner leaves and tear or cut them into small pieces.

When you make the vinaigrette, smash the hard-cooked egg yolk with the garlic and salt. Keep the dressing a little on the tart side.

Dice the egg white and toss it with the vegetables and greens, olives, capers, and parsley. Add the vinaigrette and toss again.

Celery Salad with Asian Pears, Walnuts, and Blue Cheese

This fall–winter salad is all about crisp and crunchy textures, including the sweet-crisp Asian pear. If life demands that you make this ahead of time, wait to add the pears, as they will brown. Serves 4 to 6

Walnut Viniagrette

- 1 shallot, finely diced
- 4 teaspoons apple cider or pear vinegar
- 1/4 teaspoon sea salt
- 3 tablespoons walnut oil

Salad

- 1 1/2 cups thinly sliced celery
- 2 Belgian endives
- 2 tablespoons slivered celery leaves
- 1 or 2 ripe, firm, Asian pears
- 1/2 cup walnuts, lightly toasted until fragrant
- 2 ounces blue cheese, such as Pt. Reyes Blue, thinly sliced
- Sea salt and freshly milled pepper

To make the viniagrette, cover the shallot with the vinegar, add the salt, and let stand for 5 minutes or more. Whisk in the oil and set aside.

If it seems stringy, peel the celery, then slice it thinly crosswise and put it in a roomy bowl. Halve the endives lengthwise and cut out the cores. Then slice them crosswise a scant 1/2 inch thick and add them to the celery along with the chopped leaves. Peel the pears if you wish, or leave the skins on. Quarter them, remove the cores, then cut the pears into pieces and add them to the vegetables. Add the toasted walnuts, blue cheese, and the dressing. Toss well. Taste for salt, add more if needed, and season with pepper.

Celery Root and Apple Salad with Mustard Vinaigrette

Everyone seems happy to see old-fashioned celery root salads make their winter appearance. A little goes far, and the salad can be made hours before serving. Include this on a plate of small salads for a first course or mound it at the base of an endive leaf. Serves 4 to 6

- 1/3 cup Mustard Vinaigrette (page 167)
- 1 celery root, 14 to 16 ounces
- 1 large Granny Smith apple, quartered, cored, and sliced into slivers
- Watercress sprigs, for garnish
- Truffle salt, optional

Make the vinaigrette. Thickly peel the celery root as you would an orange (see page 24), slice it into 1/8-inch-thick rounds, then stack the slices and cut them into long, thin julienne strips. Drop the celery root into a large pot of boiling salted water for 1 minute. (Don't wait for the boil to return, or it will be overcooked.) Drain, rinse with cold water, and pat dry. Toss with the apple and vinaigrette, then mound the salad on a platter and garnish with fat sprigs of watercress and season with a few pinches of truffle salt.

With Walnuts: Use walnut oil instead of olive oil in the vinaigrette and toss 1/4 cup chopped toasted walnuts with the celery root. Hazelnut oil and hazelnuts are another possibility.

Carrot Salad with Parsley and Mint

Serves 4 to 6 Ⓥ

- 1 pound carrots
- 1 tablespoon champagne vinegar, white wine vinegar, or fresh lemon juice
- 1/4 teaspoon sea salt
- 2 tablespoons olive oil
- 1 tablespoon finely chopped parsley or lovage
- 2 teaspoons finely chopped mint leaves
- Freshly milled white pepper

Scrub, then grate the carrots. Mix the vinegar with the salt, then whisk in the oil. Toss with the carrots, parsley, and mint and season with pepper to taste. Serve right away or cover and chill first.

Carrot Salad with Caper Sauce and Dill: Prepare cooked or grated carrots and toss with Parsley–Caper Sauce (page 49), replacing 2 tablespoons of the parsley with chopped dill, and/or the feathery carrot tops, finely chopped. (V)

Grated Carrot or Beet Salad with Cumin: Grate or hand–cut carrots or beets, blanch them briefly in boiling salted water, then drain and towel–dry. Dress while warm with Lime–Cumin Vinaigrette (page 165), plus 1 teaspoon orange–flower water if you like. (V)

Cucumber Salads

Subtle differences among types aside, all cucumbers more or less taste alike, and all can be used in salads. There are small yellow lemon cucumbers, scalloped Armenian cucumbers, fuzzy Italian varieties, white cucumbers, and, of course, the pricey hothouse prima donnas sealed in their plastic wrappings.

If the skins are unwaxed, you don't have to peel them unless they're very thick or prickly, and seeds need be removed only if they're very large. Cucumbers can be decoratively scored by running a fork or citrus zester down the skins, leaving white stripes in the green.

In-a-Pinch Cucumber Salad

Nothing could be simpler to prepare than these cucumbers. Although summer's cucumbers are far better than winter's waxed ones, I sometimes turn to this dish for a quick raw salad when winter greens are scarce. Serves 4 (V)

2 cucumbers, or 1 long hothouse cucumber

Sea salt and freshly milled white pepper

2 to 3 teaspoons olive oil

Champagne vinegar or fresh lemon juice

1 teaspoon fresh dill or several pinches dried dill, finely chopped watercress, or chopped parsley

Unless you're using the hothouse variety, peel the cucumbers. Cut them in half lengthwise, scoop out the seeds, leaving a nicely shaped shell with smooth sides, and thinly slice. Toss the cucumbers with a few pinches salt, pepper to taste, and enough oil to coat lightly. Add a few drops vinegar and the herb of your choice.

Cucumber and Yogurt Salad

Called tzatziki *or* cacik, *depending on where in the eastern Mediterranean it's being made, this is a hot weather dish. Thick drained yogurt makes the best version. Serve it alone or with other vegetable salads, such as roasted peppers or carrots with Lime–Cumin Vinaigrette (page 165).* Makes about 2 cups

2 small or 1 large cucumber, peeled if needed, seeded, and diced

Sea salt

2 cloves garlic

1 cup thick yogurt or labneh

2 teaspoons chopped mint

2 teaspoons chopped dill

Freshly milled white pepper

2 to 3 teaspoons white wine vinegar

1 tablespoon olive oil

In a colander, sprinkle the cucumbers lightly with salt and drain for 30 minutes.

Squeeze the cucumbers and blot with a towel. Pound the garlic with a few pinches salt in a mortar until smooth. Combine the yogurt, cucumbers, garlic, and herbs, then season with a little pepper and the vinegar. Taste for salt, drizzle the oil over the top, and serve.

Salted Cucumbers with Golden Purslane

Salt draws out the water from cucumber, rendering the chunks or slices crisp, and if refrigerated, cool. Golden purslane, an easily grown cultivar, has large, fleshy leaves that leave an obvious contrast between the two textures. Choose a cucumber with a smooth rather than prickly skin, preferably one that's organically grown so you can leave the skins on, the nutritionally valuable part. Cut the pieces large for an appetizer, smaller for a salad, and even smaller for a relish. Serves 4 or more ⓥ

Smooth cucumbers, enough to make 2 to 3 cups when diced, unpeeled

³/₄ teaspoon sea salt

Golden purslane leaves

Olive oil, for coating

Sea salt and freshly milled pepper

Chop or dice the cucumbers as large or as fine as you wish, then sprinkle with the salt. Put them in a colander set in a bowl, and refrigerate for at least 30 minutes to draw out the water. Meanwhile, pluck the purslane leaves from the stalks and give them a rinse.

When the cucumbers have sat their requisite time, give them a quick rinse, then pat them dry. Put them in a bowl with the purslane, a teaspoon or two of olive oil, and toss. Taste for salt—they may not need any. Season with pepper and serve.

Cucumbers with Green Coriander Buds, Flowering Dill, and Basil Flowers: Green coriander seeds are pungent and sweet and peppery all at once and do a great deal for the delicate cucumber. Similarly, flowering dill or the immature seeds can be used. Basil flowers, as well, are an attractive garnish. These are stages in herbs that are usually ignored, but they shouldn't be. ⓥ

Dice and salt cucumbers as in the recipe above, but instead of purslane, toss them, once drained, with the green buds of coriander and dill flowers or immature seeds. Taste for salt. Add a few splashes of white wine or rice wine vinegar for sharpness. If you're shy of green coriander, chop some cilantro and dill and toss with the cucumbers as well. Garnish with basil flowers.

Cucumber, Lovage and Farro Salad with Pine Nuts

Cucumbers are cooling but hardly substantial, so I've mixed with them with a chewy grain—in this case farro. Lovage is a natural herb to use with with cucumber. Use masses of lovage if you like its fresh taste. Other, more common leaves you can use are parsley, dill, and celery leaf—or a mixture of all three. Salad burnet and tender borage leaves are other possibilities. As for the cucumbers, use unwaxed ones and leave the skins on—that's where the vitamins are. Serves 4 or more ⓥ

---

¹/₂ cup farro (I use farro piccolo or einkorn)

Scant ¹/₂ teaspoon sea salt

Grated zest of 1 lemon plus 2 tablespoons of the juice

2 tablespoons olive oil

4 or more Persian or other small cucumbers, washed but not peeled

4 green onions, including a few inches of the greens, thinly sliced

¹/₄ to ¹/₂ cup thinly sliced lovage leaves

Freshly milled pepper

3 tablespoons pan-toasted pine nuts or sliced almonds

Cover the farro with 2 cups water. Add the salt, bring to a boil, then reduce the heat and simmer until the grain is tender but still retains a little crunch, about 30 minutes, possibly longer, depending on the size of the grain. When done, drain it well, then put it in a bowl with the lemon zest, juice, and olive oil and toss well.

While the farro is cooking, slice the cucumbers lengthwise into quarters, then crosswise into small chunks. You should have about 3 cups. Toss them with the farro, onions, and lovage. Taste for salt and season with pepper. Just before serving, toss with the pine nuts, leaving a few visible on the top.

Fennel Salads

Tender fennel bulbs make a sweet spring or fall salad, but the secret to success is to slice the fennel paper-thin on a box grater, Benriner, or mandoline. First trim off the stalks and run a vegetable peeler over the outer leaves, then slice the halves crosswise.

Garnishes for fennel salad can include thin croutons spread with olive paste, thin shavings of Parmigiano-Reggiano, pecans or walnuts, or frisée, watercress, or arugula leaves. Serve fennel salads as a first course or include them on a composed salad plate.

Fennel with Oil and Lemon: Trim the fennel, then slice it paper-thin. Toss with a few pinches sea salt, then with olive oil to coat lightly. Squeeze a little lemon juice over the top, toss, and taste. Season with white pepper and serve garnished with finely chopped fennel greens. Include a few drops of truffle oil or a sprinkle of truffle salt if you like. Ⓥ

Fennel with Tarragon Vinaigrette

Serves 4

2 small fennel bulbs, 3 to 4 ounces each
1 tablespoon crème fraîche
2 tablespoons olive oil
2 to 3 teaspoons fresh lemon juice
1½ teaspoons minced lemon zest
2 teaspoons chopped tarragon or fennel greens
1 tablespoon finely chopped parsley
Sea salt and freshly milled pepper
2 cups watercress, frisée, or mixed small salad greens

Trim the fennel bulbs, then slice paper-thin. Whisk the crème fraîche, oil, and 2 teaspoons lemon juice together; add the lemon zest, herbs, and salt and pepper to taste. Toss with the fennel. Taste and add more lemon juice if needed. Serve mounded on a plate, over or surrounded by the greens.

Shaved Fennel and Red Cabbage with Sunflower Seeds

This salad is crunchy, fresh, and raw—a substantial vegetable salad. Serves 4 to 6 Ⓥ

1 cup sunflower seeds tossed with sunflower seed oil and a few pinches of sea salt
A few spoonfuls soy sauce or tamari
Lemon Vinaigrette (page 164)
1 fennel bulb, with its greens
1 small red cabbage, a scant pound
Sea salt
A generous handful sunflower sprouts
Cilantro leaves, plucked from the stems of 1 small bunch

Toast the sunflower seeds in a wide skillet over medium heat, stirring frequently, until golden and aromatic. Add the soy sauce and stir quickly for it to evaporate and coat the seeds. Turn them onto a plate to cool. Make the vinaigrette.

Remove the tough outer "leaves" of the fennel if scarred, or peel them well with a vegetable peeler, then slice them thinly by hand or on a mandoline or equivalent. Quarter the cabbage, cut out the cores, and slice very thinly crosswise by hand. Toss the fennel and cabbage in a wide bowl with a few pinches of salt. Add the vinaigrette, then toss once more with the toasted seeds, sunflower sprouts, and cilantro.

Fennel, Pear, and Endive Salad: Plan to serve this lovely salad for fall or winter shortly after you make it, otherwise the pears will brown. Slice 1 plump Belgian endive diagonally into narrow strips. Toss it and 6 walnuts, broken into small pieces, with the fennel, sliced as in the preceding recipe. Halve and core 2 ripe but firm pears, such as Bartlett or Comice, then slice lengthwise. Toss quickly with the fennel, dress with Lemon Vinaigrette (page 164), and arrange the salad on plates. Sliced blue cheese is good here, too. Ⓥ

Roasted Pepper Salads

Sweet roasted peppers have many uses in the summer kitchen, one of which is their transformation into small, colorful salads. Like many of the little vegetable salads in this chapter, they also serve well as appetizers, toppings for crostini and crackers, or elements on a composed salad plate.

Some things that go well with roasted peppers are capers and olives, basil and marjoram, fine olive oil, balsamic vinegar, lemon juice, and cheeses, like fontina, goat cheese, and feta. Saffron, cumin, chiles, fennel, and preserved lemon match the sweetness and smokiness of grilled peppers. Roasted peppers keep for a week or so in the refrigerator, so these salads can be put together at a moment's notice if the peppers are at hand. (To roast, peel, and seed peppers, see page 364.)

Grilled Peppers with Saffron Vinaigrette: Grill and peel a selection of different-colored bell peppers, allowing $1/2$ pepper per person. Be sure to reserve any juices that collect in the bowl while they're steaming. Slice the peppers into halves or quarters, scrape out the seeds, and layer the peppers on a platter. Make Saffron Vinaigrette with Basil and Orange (page 166), adding any reserved pepper juices. Toss the peppers with vinaigrette to moisten and serve garnished with sprigs of basil and niçoise olives. (V)

Roasted Peppers with Preserved Lemon: Preserved Lemons (page 70) add a whole new dimension to peppers. For 4 roasted red or yellow bell peppers, use $1/2$ preserved lemon. Cut away and discard the inside of the lemon and dice the skin into small pieces. Peel the peppers, then cut them into strips or squares. Toss the peppers with the lemon, $1/2$ teaspoon toasted ground cumin, 1 to 2 tablespoons olive oil, and some chopped parsley. Arrange on a platter and garnish with oil-cured black olives and glossy sprigs of flat-leaf parsley. (V)

Grilled Pepper Salad with Fontina: Slice grilled and peeled yellow, red, and orange bell peppers into quarters. Put them in a bowl and toss with a few tablespoons olive oil and balsamic vinegar to taste. Arrange overlapping layers of peppers on a platter with thin strips of fontina placed between them. Garnish with finely chopped parsley.

Broccoli and Roasted Pepper Salad with Tomato Vinaigrette

Broccoli always tastes best with strong, lively accompaniments; here it's the pungent feta and the olives in the dressing that provide that punch. Green beans, cauliflower, and broccoli Romanesco are also good prepared this way.
Serves 4 to 6 (V)

2 yellow or red bell peppers, roasted (see page 364)
$1\frac{1}{2}$ pounds broccoli with the stems
Tomato Vinaigrette with Olives (page 168)
1 tablespoon chopped marjoram or parsley
Sea salt and freshly ground pepper
$1/2$ cup crumbled feta cheese, optional

Dice the peeled peppers into $1/2$-inch squares. Separate the broccoli into small florets. Thinly peel and dice the stems. Blanch both the stems and florets in boiling salted water until barely tender; drain and shake off any excess water.

In a large bowl, toss the broccoli and peppers with the vinaigrette and marjoram. Taste for salt, allowing for the feta (if using), season with pepper, and toss again with the feta. Serve warm or at room temperature.

Potato Salads

For salads, use boiling potatoes or waxy yellow-fleshed potatoes, such as fingerlings. Once cooked, both can be sliced without crumbling apart.

To cook the potatoes, first scrub them well, then put them in a pot with salted cold water to cover. Bring to a boil. Lower the heat and simmer until they're tender when pierced with a knife. When cool enough to handle fairly easily, rub off the skins. Slice the potatoes about 1/3 inch thick, then dress them. Potato salads usually are eaten at room temperature or even cold, but the flavors are sensational when they're warm.

Picnic Potato Salad with Marjoram and Pickled Onions

A straightforward potato salad that's just the kind to take on a picnic. By the time the potatoes are cooked, the onions will have turned bright pink and mellowed. Serves 10 to 12 Ⓥ

1 large dark red onion, finely diced
1/2 cup apple cider vinegar
1 teaspoon sea salt
Freshly milled pepper
1 1/2 cup olive oil
3 pounds boiling or waxy potatoes
2 tablespoons Dijon mustard
3 large cloves garlic, pounded or put through a press
3 tablespoons capers, rinsed
1 bell pepper, any color, finely diced
4 celery ribs, or 1 fennel bulb, finely diced
3 tablespoons chopped marjoram
1 tablespoon chopped thyme or lemon thyme

Put the diced onion in a strainer. Bring a kettle of water to a boil and pour it slowly over the onion. Shake the onion dry and put it in a large salad bowl. Add the vinegar, salt, several grinds of pepper, and the oil, and set aside.

Cook the potatoes, then peel and slice them. While still warm, add them to the onion along with the mustard, garlic, and capers. Toss gently with a soft rubber spatula. Add the bell pepper, celery, and herbs and toss once more. Taste for salt and grind in plenty of pepper.

Potato Salad with Green Beans and Hard-Cooked Eggs: Boil 8 ounces green beans in salted water until tender; drain and set on a towel to dry. Toss the beans with a little olive oil. Arrange the potato salad in a wide, shallow Spanish casserole or gratin dish and scatter the beans on top. Garnish with 3 or 4 hard-cooked eggs cut into quarters or halves. Tip the dish to get a little dressing and spoon it over the yolks so they don't dry out. Cover with chopped tarragon or basil and their blossoms if available. Toss just before serving, or carefully lift out so that each portion has a judicious amount of potatoes, beans, and eggs.

Warm Potato Salad with Garlic Mayonnaise

Green beans are also delicious prepared this way—and the two can be plated together. Serves 6

2 pounds boiling or waxy potatoes
1/2 cup Garlic Mayonnaise (page 52)
1 cup chopped parsley
Smoked paprika, optional

Boil, peel, and slice the potatoes. While still warm, toss them with the mayonnaise and the parsley. Serve right away with a dash of smoked paprika.

Peruvian Potatoes with Peanut Sauce and Garnishes

A Santa Fe chef whose husband is Peruvian showed me this exceptionally pretty potato salad from his native country. It sounded unlikely to me, but it's good. Serves 6

2 pounds Peruvian blue or Yellow Finn potatoes

2 ears corn, cut into 2-inch segments

Pickled Red Onions (page 72)

3 hard-cooked eggs, quartered

Kalamata or Alfonso olives

3 handfuls spicy greens, such as red mustard or arugula

Peanut Sauce

1/4 cup roasted peanut oil

1 cup skinned Spanish peanuts

1 small onion, chopped

1 clove garlic, coarsely chopped

2 jalapeño chiles, halved and seeded, or ground red chile, to taste

3/4 cup crumbled ricotta salata

1 cup milk

1/2 teaspoon turmeric

Sea salt

Boil the potatoes, then peel and slice into thick rounds. Boil the corn briefly in unsalted water and drain. To make the sauce, heat half the oil in a small skillet and fry the peanuts over medium heat, stirring frequently, until browned, 3 to 4 minutes. Put them in a blender and return the pan to the heat with the remaining oil. Add the onion and garlic and cook until soft and translucent, about 5 minutes. Add them to the blender with the rest of the ingredients and puree until smooth. Season with salt to taste. Arrange the potatoes and corn on individual plates or a large platter with the pickled onions, eggs, olives, and greens. Spoon the peanut sauce over the potatoes and serve with extra sauce on the side.

Tomato Salads

Ripe summer tomatoes make some of the best—and easiest—salads. They needn't be dressed, although tomatoes that are low in acid benefit from a squeeze of fresh lemon juice or a splash of balsamic vinegar, while more acidic tomatoes are enhanced with a thread of fruity olive oil. Spicy Indian mustard oil is also interesting. Tomatoes needn't be peeled unless their skins are tough and leathery or you want the refinement of smooth, slippery, fruitlike flesh.

Remember, tomatoes are best warm from the sun or at least at room temperature. Refrigeration deadens them, so keep them on a counter until you're ready to use them. When it comes to seasonings, many herbs and their perfumed blossoms form a natural alliance with tomatoes: dill and its yellow flowers, marjoram, chives and their purple blossoms, the various thymes, the blue star-shaped borage flowers; violet rosemary blossoms, purple sage, tarragon, and so forth. All would be excellent on this salad.

Tomato Salad of Many Colors: Today an exotic variety of tomatoes is being grown—bright green striped Zebras, tiny currant-size ones, bright yellow, matte gold, and orange as well as red. A mélange of tomatoes with basil, the classic tomato herb, is truly spectacular fare. Slice a colorful array and lay them on a platter. Add torn or thinly sliced basil leaves, using the classic Italian basil or opal basil. Drizzle with a thread of good olive oil and add a few drops of balsamic vinegar, a pinch of sea salt, and freshly milled pepper. (V)

Tomato and Sweet Onion Salad: When you can get sweet Vidalia, Walla Walla, or Maui onions as well as ripe, luscious tomatoes, this is the salad to make. Peel whole onions, then slice them into thin rounds. Slice the tomatoes into rounds as well. On a platter, overlap layers of onions and tomatoes so that both can easily be picked up at once. Serve with an ample drizzle of olive oil. (V)

Tomato and Avocado Salad: Cut 2 large tomatoes around the equator, remove the seeds, and dice them into large pieces. Toss with 1 avocado, cut in good-size chunks, and a few chopped green onions, parsley or cilantro, a pinch of sea salt, and freshly milled pepper to taste. Squeeze a little lime or lemon juice over all and serve with warm tortillas and queso fresco or feta.

Tomato and Mozzarella Salad: The simplicity and clarity of the components are what make *insalata caprese* a classic that never grows tiresome, but its success depends on top-quality ingredients. The tomatoes should have a slightly tart edge to contrast with the mildness of the cheese. Slice fresh mozzarella and tomatoes into rounds and overlap them on a plate. Drizzle olive oil over the top and season with sea salt and freshly milled pepper. Tear basil leaves over the top or tuck them in between the tomatoes and cheese.

Tomato Salad on Grilled Eggplant Rounds

This makes a stunning little salad. For an especially handsome effect, use yellow or mixed-colored tomatoes and purple basil. Look for small Italian eggplants, such as Rosa Bianca, for broiling. Serves 4 ⓥ

2 eggplants, 8 to 12 ounces each

Olive oil, for broiling

Sea salt and freshly milled pepper

3 ripe tomatoes, or 1½ cups cherry tomatoes

1 shallot, finely diced

3 tablespoons finely sliced green or opal basil leaves

1 tablespoon capers, rinsed

1 tablespoon extra-virgin olive oil

Aged red wine vinegar, for dressing

Slice the eggplants into rounds about ⅓ inch thick. Brush both sides with olive oil and grill or broil until browned and tender, 5 to 6 minutes on each side. Divide them among four plates and season with salt and pepper. While the eggplant is cooking, dice the tomatoes into nice-looking pieces or halve the cherry tomatoes and toss them with the shallot, basil, capers, a pinch of salt, and the extra-virgin oil. Add pepper and a little vinegar to taste. Spoon the tomatoes over the eggplant and serve.

Chopped Salad with Feta Dressing

For a nondairy version, use the Olive Oil Vinaigrette (page 165). This salad makes a great filling for a pita sandwich, or serve it with Lentils and Rice with Fried Onions (page 271). Makes about 2 cups ⓥ

2 green onions, including some of the greens

1 red bell pepper

1 cucumber, peeled if waxed, halved, and seeded

1 celery rib

12 cherry tomatoes, halved

¼ cup chopped parsley

10 kalamata olives, pitted and chopped

Feta Dressing with Marjoram and Mint (page 169)

1 avocado, diced

Sea salt and freshly milled pepper

Finely or coarsely chop the vegetables as you like, then toss them with the tomatoes, parsley, olives, and dressing. Add the avocado last so that it doesn't end up mushy. Taste and add salt if needed (both the feta and the olives are salty) and pepper.

Farmers' Market Salad

This is a dish I look forward to eating day after day throughout the summer when vegetables are at their peak. I use whatever the farmers' market or my garden is offering. Here's an example. Serves 1 ⓥ

1 carrot, scrubbed and finely diced

1 cucumber, peeled if waxed, seeded, and diced

2 tomatoes, chopped

1 celery rib, finely diced

4 large green olives, pitted

Small cubes of cheese, such as a goat cheddar or ricotta salata, optional

1 tablespoon toasted sunflower seeds or pine nuts

Torn leaves of basil, marjoram, lovage, or whatever herb is available

1 teaspoon olive oil or sunflower seed oil, or to taste

Sea salt and freshly milled pepper

Fresh lemon juice or red wine vinegar to taste

Gently toss everything with the oil. Season with salt and pepper and add a little lemon juice to taste.

Toasted Pita Bread with Vegetables and Herbs (*Fattoush*)

Though this salad is always delicious made with these common vegetables, consider adding the seeds of a small pomegranate, a handful of purslane sprigs or watercress, or some freshly shelled peas. Serves 3 or 4

1 small cucumber, seeded, and diced
1¼ teaspoons sea salt
2 (7-inch) pita breads
3 ripe tomatoes, chopped
1 small green pepper, diced
6 green onions, including some of the greens, finely chopped
⅓ cup chopped parsley
2 tablespoons chopped cilantro
1 tablespoon finely chopped mint
¼ cup olive oil
Juice of 1 large lemon
1 clove garlic, finely chopped
1½ teaspoons ground sumac, optional

Put the cucumber in a colander, toss with 1 teaspoon of the salt, and set aside to drain. Preheat the oven to 350°F. Open the breads and bake them on a sheet pan until crisp and light brown, about 10 minutes. Break them into bite-size pieces and set aside. Press the excess water out of the cucumbers, then rinse quickly and blot dry. Put them in a bowl with the rest of the vegetables and the herbs.

In a jar, shake together the oil, lemon juice, garlic, sumac, and the remaining ¼ teaspoon salt. Pour over the salad, then toss well. Add the bread, toss again, and serve.

Greek Salad

Many greens are far more interesting—and traditional— than the mounds of iceberg lettuce that seem to be a part of every American Greek salad. Do give them a try.
Serves 4 to 6

About 2 handfuls salad greens—watercress romaine hearts, oakleaf lettuce, escarole, purslane, and other wild greens—torn into pieces
4 ripe tomatoes, cut into wedges
1 large cucumber, halved, seeded, and sliced or diced
1 green bell pepper, thinly sliced into rings
1 small mild onion, thinly sliced
8 pepperoncini
2 tablespoons capers, rinsed
12 kalamata olives
4 ounces feta cheese, cubed or crumbled
1 teaspoon dried oregano, preferably Greek
⅓ cup coarsely chopped parsley
Sea salt and freshly milled pepper
¼ cup olive oil
1 lemon, cut into wedges

Line a platter with the greens. Arrange the tomatoes, cucumber, and green pepper on the platter. Scatter the onion rings over them and intersperse the pepperoncini, capers, and olives with the cheese. Sprinkle the oregano and parsley over the salad, then season with salt and pepper. Drizzle the oil over all and garnish with the lemon wedges.

Summer Vegetables with Garlic Mayonnaise

This can be an appetizer or an entire meal. Other vegetables that you can use here with great success are radishes, tender salad turnips, and artichoke hearts. Allow 8 to 12 ounces vegetables and 2 to 4 tablespoons mayonnaise per person

Garlic Mayonnaise (page 52)
Small new potatoes, steamed or roasted
Tender green or Romano beans, blanched
Carrots, steamed until tender, left whole if small or sliced if not
Cauliflower florets, blanched or steamed until tender
Bell peppers of different colors, cut into strips
Tomatoes, sliced or cut into wedges
Cooked chickpeas or large white beans
Hard-cooked eggs, halved or quartered
Niçoise olives

Make the Garlic Mayonnaise and set it aside to mellow. Lightly cook the vegetables as suggested. For a first course, cut them rather fine; for a main-course salad, larger pieces are more substantial. Arrange the vegetables on a platter or individual plates, then add the chickpeas, eggs, and olives. Heap the mayonnaise in a mound on the plate and serve.

Salads Featuring Fruits

Fruits as well as vegetables marry well with the savory, pungent flavors found in foods such as salty or buttery cheeses, the bitter chicories, roasted nuts, sharp vinegars, and so on— elements that make fruit into salads as opposed to desserts or compotes.

Salads with fruit elements can open or close a meal or in sufficient quantity can be the center of the meal. As with vegetables, ripe, full-flavored fruits are most fundamental to the success of these salads.

Melon and Cucumbers with Pepper and Lime

Cucumbers and melons are closely related not only botanically but also in texture and sometimes flavor, depending on the variety. Serves 4 Ⓥ

1 honeydew, cantaloupe, or other melon, chilled
3 cucumbers
2 cups watercress or arugula leaves
Lime and Fresh Mint Vinaigrette (page 167) or juice of 2 limes
Sea salt and freshly milled pepper

Scoop out the seeds, then slice the melon into narrow wedges and remove the skin.

Scrub the cucumbers or peel if the skin is thick; cut into sixths. Make a bed of greens on four plates and arrange the melon and cucumbers on top. Spoon the dressing over the top and season with a little salt and pepper.

Watermelon with Mint, Lime, and Feta

A sweet-salty-tart fruit salad that's enormously refreshing— and quite surprising. Serves 2

1 pound watermelon chunks
1 tablespoon chopped mint leaves, plus whole sprigs for garnish
¼ cup diced mild feta cheese

Juice of 1 lime
Sea salt and freshly milled pepper

Seed the melon and cut into bite-size pieces. Arrange them on plates and sprinkle with the chopped mint and feta. Season with the lime juice, a pinch of salt, and freshly milled pepper. Serve garnished with sprigs of bright green mint leaves.

Mission Figs with Walnuts and Manchego Cheese

Any variety of fig is fine as long as it's ripe and sweet, but the dense flavor of black Missions is just right with the walnuts and the slightly salty cheese. Serves 4

1 shallot, finely diced
2 teaspoons balsamic vinegar
1 teaspoon red wine vinegar
⅛ teaspoon sea salt
2 handfuls red lettuce, trimmed and torn into pieces
1 handful arugula, stems removed
3 tablespoons extra-virgin olive or walnut oil
12 ripe figs
8 walnuts in large pieces
Freshly milled pepper
Thin shavings of Manchego or dry Jack

Combine the shallot, vinegars, and salt in a bowl. Let stand while you prepare the greens, then whisk in the oil. Peel the figs only if the skins are very thick; otherwise, just wipe them with a damp cloth to remove any dust.

Slice the figs into rounds. Toss the lettuce and arugula with half the dressing and arrange on four salad plates. Add the figs and walnuts and season with pepper. Add a few thin shavings of cheese to each salad and serve.

Persian Melons with Yogurt and Coriander Dressing

Serve this salad well chilled. Bronze-leafed lettuces, like red oakleaf, set it off handsomely. If you have them, purslane sprigs and lemon verbena make interesting contributions, too, one crunchy, the other aromatic. Serves 4 to 6

2 pounds ripe Persian, honeydew, or Israeli melon, chilled

1 cup yogurt

3 green onions, thinly sliced

1/2 jalapeño chile, finely diced

Grated zest and juice of 1 lime

2 tablespoons finely chopped mint

1 tablespoon finely chopped basil

1 teaspoon minced ginger or 1/2 teaspoon dried

1/2 teaspoon ground cumin

1/2 teaspoon ground coriander

Sea salt and freshly milled white pepper

2 handfuls lettuce or mixed greens, for garnish

Halve the melons, scoop out the seeds, and slice into wedges. Slip a knife under the skin to release the fruit, then cut it into bite-size pieces.

Mix the yogurt with the rest of the ingredients except the melon and greens. Season with salt and pepper. Adjust the seasonings if needed—they should be on the strong side, the herbs and spices bright and clear. Pour the dressing over the melon and toss. Serve garnished with the greens.

Mixed Citrus Salad and Avocado

Avocados and citrus fruits grow near each other, their seasons overlap, and their textures and tastes are complementary, so it's hardly surprising that they show up together in salads—they're practically meant to. Serves 4 Ⓥ

1 lime

2 tangerines

2 navel or blood oranges

2 ruby grapefruit

2 ripe but firm avocados, preferably Hass

1 shallot, finely diced, or 2 green onions, including an inch of the greens, thinly sliced

1 tablespoon fresh lemon juice

1/8 teaspoon sea salt

1 tablespoon avocado or olive oil

1 tablespoon chopped mint

Freshly milled white pepper

1 bunch watercress, large stems removed, or the inner leaves of 1 head Boston lettuce

Grate the zest of the lime and one of the tangerines. Peel and section the fruit as described on page 24, letting the pieces fall into a bowl. Reserve 1 tablespoon of the juice and drink the rest.

Slice the avocados into the citrus. Combine the shallot with the citrus zest, reserved juice, lemon juice, and salt; whisk in the oil. Pour the dressing over the fruit, add the mint and a little pepper, and toss gently. Garnish with the watercress leaves.

Orange, Fennel, and Butter Lettuce Salad

Serve this composed salad to conclude a large or spicy meal. Celery can easily step in if fennel is not available. Serves 4 Ⓥ

3 navel or blood oranges

Orange Vinaigrette (page 166)

1 head butter lettuce

2 tablespoons chopped fennel greens

10 small mint leaves, thinly sliced

1 small fennel bulb, quartered and thinly sliced

Freshly milled pepper

12 oil-cured black olives

Peel and section the oranges (see page 24) and use the juice in the vinaigrette. Discard the outer leaves of the lettuce. Separate the remaining leaves and keep them whole or tear them into large pieces. Toss the lettuce with 2 or 3 tablespoons of the dressing and half the fennel greens and mint, then arrange the greens on plates. Toss the oranges, sliced fennel, and remaining herbs with enough dressing to coat lightly, add a little pepper, then tuck them among the lettuce and garnish with the olives. Other possible additions include toasted fennel seeds or toasted pine nuts.

Apple and Celery Salad with Gruyère

Serves 4 to 6

3 ounces Gruyère

Sea salt and freshly milled pepper

1 tablespoon tarragon vinegar

1 small shallot, finely diced

1/8 teaspoon sea salt

1 tablespoon walnut oil

1 tablespoon sour cream or mayonnaise

1 cup finely diced celery heart

2 crisp apples, unpeeled, finely diced

1/3 cup chopped walnuts or hazelnuts, roasted

2 tablespoons chopped parsley, celery leaves, or a mixture

Dice the cheese into small cubes and put them in a large bowl. Season with a little salt and plenty of pepper. Cover and let stand at room temperature for 1 hour.

Meanwhile, combine the vinegar, shallot, salt, and pepper to taste in another bowl and let stand for 15 minutes. Whisk in the oil and sour cream, then taste for salt. Add the celery, apples, and nuts to the cheese, pour on the dressing, add the parsley, and toss well.

Persimmon and Hazelnut Salad with Hazelnut Vinaigrette

Unlike the acorn-shaped Hachiyas, short, squat Fuyus can be eaten crisp or soft. They're a luscious foil for peppery watercress and striking with red lettuces and radicchio. This is an exuberant first-course salad for a festive occasion.
Serves 4 Ⓥ

1/4 cup hazelnuts, roasted

3 Fuyu persimmons, thinly sliced crosswise

3 handfuls mixed lettuces or trimmed watercress

Sea salt

3 to 4 tablespoons Hazelnut Oil Vinaigrette (page 166)

Coarsely chop the hazelnuts. Put the persimmons in a bowl with the hazelnuts and the greens, sprinkle with a few pinches of salt, and toss with enough dressing to coat lightly.

Divide among salad plates, distributing the nuts and persimmons evenly among the greens.

With Pears: Make the salad using ripe, buttery Comice or Bartlett pears and either the hazelnut dressing or Walnut Oil Vinaigrette (page 166). Ⓥ

Hearty Salads Based on Pasta, Grains, and Beans

These salads are hearty and filling enough to be served as main dishes, or they can be offered as appetizers as long as the portion sizes are on the small side so that people don't fill up right away. Whether large or small, I find that a healthy garnish of salad greens helps keep them balanced and light.

Regardless of how you serve these salads, take advantage of the fact that most of them can be made well in advance and that they keep and travel well, which makes them good choices for picnics, bag lunches, and buffets. Still, they are usually best when served as soon as they're made and dressed while warm. Any grain, bean, or pasta that holds its shape when thoroughly cooked can be turned into a salad by adding a vinaigrette, and cold leftovers can be steamed back to warmth before dressing. Because these foods are starchy and naturally bland, good strong dressings filled with herbs, mustards, and sharp vinegars are the ones to use.

COOKING GRAINS: To ensure that grains intended for salads come out separate, boil them in a generous amount of salted water until they're done, then drain. Undercook them just a bit so that they finish cooking in their own heat while absorbing the flavors of the dressing. For rice, long-grain varieties are less sticky than short-grain.

SALAD BEANS: For beans that are tender but will stay intact when tossed, soak them first, then drain and transfer to a shallow baking dish with aromatics, a teaspoon of olive oil, and boiling water to cover by an inch. Cover and bake at 325°F until tender, salting once they've begun to soften, after an hour. A slow cooker is another option. Save the remaining broth for soup.

ALTERNATIVES TO HOME-COOKED BEANS: Although certainly convenient, canned beans tend to be mushy and salty. Some brands are better than others; the organic brands seem to have the best texture, especially the chickpeas, kidney beans, and black beans. If you do use canned beans, give them a rinse first and choose brands whose cans are not lined with BPA, such as Eden Farms. Frozen baby limas and black-eyed peas strike a happy medium between canned and cooked from scratch; they taste better than the former and don't take as long as the latter.

MIXING GRAINS AND BEANS: Mixing different grains or grains with legumes makes salads with interesting colors and textures. Cook each ingredient separately unless they all cook in the same amount of time, such as brown, Wehani, and wild rice. This is where quicker-cooking legumes, like lentils, the occasional canned bean, or leftovers also can be put to good use.

USING LEFTOVERS: Leftover grains can make good material for salads, but they need to be moistened. Put them in a colander and pour a few cups of boiling water over them or steam them for 5 to 10 minutes.

USING PASTA: Dried pasta is sturdier than fresh, and its ingenious shapes can hold a flavorful dressing or the occasional pea. Salads made with Italian-style pasta taste best warm or at room temperature rather than chilled. Asian noodles, such as soba or cellophane noodles, make excellent cold salads.

FOLDING AND STIRRING: To bring all the elements together without breaking tender grains, beans, or noodles, use a wide, soft rubber spatula or your hands to gently fold all the ingredients into each other.

Wild Rice Salad with Dried Cherries and Fresh Pomegranate Seeds

Nuggets of dried cherries and shiny pomegranate seeds make this is a salad for a holiday buffet. If you haven't used native wild rice, give it a try. It cooks more quickly and has a lovely soft, complex flavor, though not the dramatic black of the cultivated rice. Unless you live in the upper Midwest, it's easiest to find native wild rice over the Internet. Serves 6 to 8 Ⓥ

1½ cups wild rice (see headnote)
½ teaspoon sea salt
4 tablespoons olive oil
1 large onion, chopped in ½-inch squares
1 cup dried cherries
½ cup balsamic vinegar, plus extra, to taste
Freshly milled pepper
6 celery ribs, finely diced
¼ cup chopped celery leaves
⅓ cup chopped parsley
1 small pomegranate, broken, the seeds removed
Red mustard leaves, radicchio, or ornamental purple kale, for garnish
½ cup toasted almond slivers

Cover the rice with cold water, swish it around and remove any bits of chaff, then drain. Bring 6 cups water to a boil in a saucepan, then add the rice and the salt. Lower the heat, then cover and cook 45 to 50 minutes or until the rice is done. (Native rice will be done in about 25 minutes.) Drain, shake off the excess water, and put the rice in a large bowl.

Warm 2 tablespoons of the oil in a wide skillet, then add the onion and cherries. Cook, stirring frequently over high heat until the onions begin to color and soften, 8 to 10 minutes. Add the vinegar, lower the heat and simmer until it has evaporated, leaving the onion glazed and the cherries plump. Season with salt and pepper, then add the onion to the rice along with the celery, herbs, pomegranate seeds, and remaining 2 tablespoons oil. Toss, then season with salt and pepper. If it doesn't seem sharp enough, add extra vinegar to bring up the acidity. Serve the salad in a spacious dish garnished with mustard leaves, and add the almonds just before serving.

With Hazelnut Oil and Hazelnuts: Cook the onions and cherries in the olive oil, as given, but use toasted hazelnut oil in the dressing and replace the almonds with roasted, chopped hazelnuts. (V)

Cool Rice and Cucumber Salad

A salad for the dog days of summer. Use white rice for its cool look and mild taste. Serves 4 to 6

- 1¹/₂ cups long-grain white rice
- 2¹/₄ teaspoons sea salt
- 2 or 3 cucumbers, seeded, and finely chopped
- ¹/₂ cup finely chopped parsley
- 3 tablespoons chopped dill
- 2 tablespoons chopped mint
- ¹/₄ cup finely sliced green onions, including some of the greens
- ¹/₄ cup champagne vinegar or white wine vinegar
- 3 tablespoons olive oil
- ¹/₂ cup yogurt
- Green oakleaf, Boston, or butter lettuce leaves, for garnish

Bring 8 cups water to a boil in a medium pan. Add the rice and 2 teaspoons of the salt and boil until tender, 12 to 15 minutes. Meanwhile, put the cucumbers in a large bowl with the herbs. In a small bowl, combine the green onions, vinegar, oil, and the remaining ¹/₄ teaspoon salt.

When the rice is done, pour it into a colander, rinse briefly, then shake off as much water as possible. Put the warm rice into the bowl with the cucumbers, add the dressing and yogurt, and toss gently with a wide rubber spatula. Taste for salt and tartness. Certain types of rice will absorb more vinegar and salt than others. Serve tepid or chilled, mounded on plates and garnished with light green lettuce leaves.

Macadamia Nut and Mixed Rice Salad

The perfume of orange, either from the orange oil (you can find it in specialty stores) or the more floral orange–flower water, along with the ginger and the warm spices in garam masala bring the flavor of macadamia nuts forward. Serves 10 (V)

Salad
- 1 cup unsalted or salted macadamia nuts
- ¹/₂ cup Wehani rice
- ¹/₂ cup wild rice
- ¹/₂ cup long-grain white rice
- ¹/₂ cup brown basmati rice
- Sea salt
- 2 green bell peppers, finely diced

Viniagrette
- 1 bunch green onions, including some of the greens, thinly sliced
- 1 clove garlic, minced
- 1 heaping tablespoon minced ginger
- 1 jalapeño chile, seeded and finely diced
- Grated zest and juice of 1 orange
- 2 tablespoons rice wine vinegar
- 2 tablespoons rice wine (mirin)
- 1 teaspoon garam masala
- 2 teaspoons orange-flower water
- Sea salt and freshly milled pepper
- ¹/₂ finely chopped parsley

Preheat the oven to 350°F. Roast the nuts on a sheet pan until golden, about 10 minutes. Keep an eye on them; they can brown suddenly. Finely chop half of the nuts and keep the rest in large pieces.

Cook each type of rice separately in salted water, then drain and toss with the peppers. Combine the ingredients to make the vinaigrette. You may need to fiddle with the seasonings, adding more of this or that to get the balance just right. It should be full of flavor but soft and balanced, not sharp. Pour the vinaigrette over the rice and toss with the finely chopped nuts. Just before serving, toss again with the remaining nuts so that they'll be nice and crisp.

Bulgur and Green Lentil Salad with Chickpeas

You'll recognize some of the qualities of tabbouleh here, but with the added textures and tastes of lentils and chickpeas. A good winter salad when there's a dearth of fresh vegetables. Makes 5 cups ⓥ

---

¹/₂ cup French green lentils, soaked for 1 hour then drained

1 bay leaf

1 teaspoon sea salt

³/₄ cup fine or medium bulgur

5 green onions, including some of the greens, thinly sliced

2 cloves garlic, finely minced

Grated zest of 2 lemons

6 to 8 tablespoons fresh lemon juice

¹/₂ cup olive oil

1 teaspoon paprika

1¹/₂ cups cooked chickpeas, rinsed if canned

2 cups finely chopped parsley

¹/₄ cup chopped mint or 2 tablespoons dried

Freshly milled pepper

Cover the drained lentils with water in a small saucepan, add the bay leaf and ¹/₂ teaspoon of the salt, and bring to a boil. Lower the heat and simmer until tender but firm, 20 to 25 minutes. Meanwhile, put the bulgur in a bowl, cover with water, and let stand until the liquid is absorbed and the grains are tender, 20 to 30 minutes.

Combine the onions, garlic, lemon zest and juice, oil, paprika, and the remaining ¹/₂ teaspoon salt in a large bowl. When the lentils are done, drain them and add them to the bowl. Press out any excess water from the bulgur. And add the bulgur to the the chickpeas, parsley, and mint. Toss gently and thoroughly, then taste for salt and season with pepper. Serve warm or cover and set aside to serve later with a fresh sprinkling of paprika.

With Vegetable Garnishes: In summer, include tomatoes, cucumbers, and peppers, all finely chopped. In winter, toss with a chopped Preserved Lemon (page 70) or rounds of steamed Jerusalem artichoke. ⓥ

With Purslane: Toss the salad with 1 or 2 handfuls purslane sprigs. ⓥ

With Walnuts and Tarragon: Replace the mint with 2 tablespoons chopped tarragon. Use half walnut oil in the dressing and add ¹/₂ cup chopped roasted walnuts to the salad. ⓥ

Couscous with Bulgur

Fine bulgur, like couscous, can also be steamed, which makes it especially light. If you mix bulgur and couscous together, you'll have something interesting—two wheats, similar but different.

Couscous or Quinoa with Pine Nuts and Dried Fruits

This sweet and tangy salad is punctuated with succulent bits of pepper and dried fruits. Serves 4 ⓥ

1¹/₃ cups raw whole wheat couscous or quinoa, or 3 cups cooked

Lime-Cumin Vinaigrette (page 165)

1 yellow bell pepper, very finely diced

6 dried apricots, finely chopped

3 tablespoons golden raisins

2 tablespoons currants

¹/₄ cup pine nuts, toasted in a small skillet

2 tablespoons chopped cilantro or slivered chives

Sea salt

Perfect whole lettuce or radicchio leaves

Cook the couscous or quinoa as described on page 495 or 472. Toss the cooked grain with ¹/₄ cup of the dressing or more to taste, add the remaining ingredients except salt and lettuce, and toss again. Taste and season with salt. Serve warm or chilled cradled in nicely formed lettuce leaves.

Quinoa Salad with Mangoes and Curry Dressing

Serves 4

- ¹/₂ teaspoon sea salt
- 1¹/₃ cups quinoa, rinsed thoroughly
- 2 large mangoes
- 1 jalapeño chile, seeded and diced
- 3 green onions, including an inch of the greens, thinly sliced
- Curry Vinaigrette (page 167)
- ¹/₃ cup whole almonds, roasted

Bring 3 cups water to a boil in a saucepan, then add the salt and the quinoa. Lower the heat, cover, and simmer until the quinoa is tender, 12 to 15 minutes. Drain.

Cut the mangoes: Stand each one upright and slice down either side of the seed, which you can't see but which runs lengthwise through the center of the fruit. Score the two pieces, then bend the skin. Cut off the squares of mango where they attach to the skin.

Toss the quinoa with the mangoes, chile, onions, and vinaigrette. Add the almonds last so that they'll stay crisp.

Tabbouleh

Tabbouleh should be so saturated with parsley that it's moist and intensly green—practically a parsley salad.
Serves 4 to 6 Ⓥ

- 1 cup fine or medium bulgur
- ¹/₂ cup fresh lemon juice
- 1 bunch green onions, including some of the greens, finely sliced
- 3 ripe tomatoes, seeded and chopped
- 3 or 4 large bunches flat-leaf parsley, finely chopped, about 4 cups
- ¹/₂ cup chopped mint
- 6 tablespoons olive oil
- ¹/₂ teaspoon sea salt
- Small Bibb or romaine lettuce leaves

Put the bulgur in a bowl, cover it with water, and let stand until the water is absorbed and the grains are soft, about 30 minutes. Press out any excess liquid, return the bulgur to the bowl, and toss with half of the lemon juice, the onions, tomatoes, parsley, and mint. Let stand again for 20 to 30 minutes for the grains to soften fully.

Meanwhile, whisk the remaining lemon juice, the oil, and the salt together. Pour the dressing over the bulgur and toss well. Check the seasoning—it should be lemony and very zesty. Mound the tabbouleh in a shallow serving bowl and surround with the lettuce leaves.

Lentil Salad with Roasted Peppers and Vegetable Garnishes

With all of its garnishes, this salad can make an entire meal. Try mixing the lentils with 1 cup cooked pasta shells, orzo, or rice—it's not only good but makes legumes more appealing to those not used to eating them. Serves 4 to 6

- 1 cup French green lentils, soaked for 1 hour then drained
- ¹/₂ teaspoon sea salt
- 2 red or yellow bell peppers, roasted, and chopped (see page 364)
- Lime-Cumin Vinaigrette (page 165)
- ¹/₂ cup chopped parsley
- 2 tablespoons chopped dill
- 1 tablespoon chopped mint
- Freshly milled pepper

Garnishes

- 2 ripe tomatoes, quartered
- ¹/₂ cup small cubes feta or goat cheese
- 2 hard-cooked eggs, quartered
- 12 kalamata olives
- 1 cucumber, cut into short spears

Cover the lentils with water in a small saucepan, add the salt, and bring to a boil. Lower the heat and simmer until tender but still a little firm, 20 to 30 minutes.

Drain the lentils and toss them while warm with the peppers, vinaigrette, parsley, dill, and mint. Taste for salt and season with pepper.

Mound the lentils on a platter and garnish with the tomatoes, cheese, eggs, olives, and cucumber. Serve warm or cold.

Lentil Salad with Golden Purslane, Cucumbers, and Walnuts

Purslane, appreciated today for its omega-3s, is a succulent weed with small leaves that creeps along the garden ground. A cultivar, called Golden Purslane, produces large leaves on upright stems. It's easy to grow, you can collect the seeds and replant them, or just let them reseed themselves.
Serves 4 to 6

1 cup black lentils, soaked for 1 hour and drained

Yogurt Sauce with Cayenne and Dill (page 57)

1/2 cup or more walnuts, toasted until fragrant

Plenty of purslane sprigs, preferably the cultivated Golden Purslane

2 Persian cucumbers, quartered lengthwise and diced

Sea salt and freshly ground pepper

Drain the lentils, cover them with fresh water, then simmer until tender but they still hold their shape, 20 to 25 minutes. When done, drain them well. You can use the liquid for an impromptu soup.

While they're cooking, make the sauce, toast the walnuts, pluck the purslane leaves, and dice the cucumbers.

Toss the warm lentils with the sauce, taste for salt and season with pepper. Scrape them into a shallow serving bowl, then strew the walnuts, purslane, and cucumber over the surface. Toss just before serving.

Green Lentils with Roasted Beets and Preserved Lemon

This salad is inspired by David Tanis, one of my longtime favorite cooks, although he says he doesn't remember it. The concentrated flavors of the beets and lemon make these lentils snap. The salad is good without the preserved lemon too, so don't be deterred if you don't have any. Serves 4 to 6 (V)

5 beets, about 1 pound

1 teaspoon olive oil

Sea salt and freshly milled pepper

1 cup French green lentils, soaked for 1 hour then drained

1 carrot, finely diced

1/2 small onion, finely diced

Aromatics: 1 bay leaf, 4 parsley sprigs, 2 thyme sprigs

1/2 teaspoon sea salt

1 Preserved Lemon (page 70) or 2 teaspoons lemon zest

Lemon Vinaigrette (page 164)

1/3 cup chopped parsley

2 tablespoons chopped mint, plus mint sprigs for garnish

Preheat the oven to 350°F. Peel 4 of the beets and cut them into small cubes. Set the last beet aside for garnish. Toss the cubed beets with the oil, season with salt and pepper, and bake on a sheet pan until tender, about 35 minutes, stirring once or twice. Meanwhile, put the lentils in a pan with water to cover, add the carrot, onion, aromatics, and 1/2 teaspoon salt, and bring to a boil. Lower the heat and simmer until tender but still a little firm, about 20 to 25 minutes. Drain well.

Cut the preserved lemon into quarters and scrape off the soft pulp. Chop the pulp finely and stir 2 teaspoons into the dressing. Finely dice the remaining skin.

Toss the lentils with the roasted beets and the vinaigrette, the preserved lemon, parsley, and mint. Peel the remaining beet and finely grate it. Put the lentils on a platter and garnish with the grated beet and sprigs of mint.

Black-Eyed Pea and Tomato Salad with Feta

Mostly we'll have to use frozen or canned peas, but this is a good salad to make if you've found some fresh black-eyed, purple hull, or crowder peas at a roadside stand. Bean salads often taste most flavorful while warm, but these succulent little beans are good chilled, too. Serves 4 to 6

1 1/2 cups black-eyed peas, fresh, frozen, or canned

2 green onions, including an inch or two of the greens, thinly sliced

1 tomato, seeded and chopped

1 tablespoon chopped parsley

1 tablespoon chopped marjoram or mint

1 teaspoon dried oregano

Lemon Vinaigrette (page 164)

2 to 3 ounces feta cheese, diced or crumbled

Sea salt and freshly milled pepper

Simmer fresh or frozen peas in salted water to cover in a saucepan until tender; it will take 35 minutes to 1 hour. Give canned peas a rinse and shake off the excess water.

Put the drained cooked peas in a bowl along with the onions, tomato, and herbs. Pour the vinaigrette over the peas and toss gently with a rubber spatula. Add the cheese, some pepper, and toss again. Taste for salt. Serve chilled or at room temperature.

Chickpea and Roasted Pepper Salad

A Spanish-inspired salad that can be enhanced by sur-rounding it with olives, hard-cooked eggs, fresh tomatoes, and sliced Manchego. Serves 4 Ⓥ

2 large red peppers, roasted (see page 364)
3 cups cooked chickpeas (2 15-ounce cans), rinsed
1/4 cup chopped parsley
2 tablespoons chopped mint
3 tablespoons capers, rinsed
1 1/4 tablespoons sherry vinegar
1/4 teaspoon sea salt
2 cloves garlic, minced
4 tablespoons olive oil
Smoked paprika, for garnish

Cut the peppers into 1/2-inch-wide strips and put them in a large bowl with the chickpeas, most of the herbs, and the capers. In a smaller bowl, whisk together the vinegar, 1/4 teaspoon salt, the garlic, and the oil. Pour it over the chickpeas and combine. Cover and refrigerate or serve right away, garnished with the remaining chopped herbs and a dusting of the paprika.

White Bean Salad with Tomato Vinaigrette and Olive Croutons

If possible, use marrow beans, cannellini, or other large white beans for their appealing plumpness. Serves 4 to 6 Ⓥ

3 cups cooked white beans, rinsed if canned
Tomato Vinaigrette (page 168)
4 green onions, including some of the greens, thinly sliced

1/4 cup small basil leaves, thinly sliced
Sea salt and freshly milled pepper
Olive Paste (page 78)
2 small crostini per serving
Frisée, escarole, or butter lettuce leaves
2 hard-cooked eggs, quartered, optional
Basil flowers if available, to finish

Put the beans in a spacious bowl or flat dish and pour on the vinaigrette. Add the onions and basil leaves and mix gently with a rubber spatula. Season with salt and pepper.

Spread the olive paste on the crostini. Place a few salad leaves on individual plates and add the beans. Add the crostini, eggs, and basil flowers.

White Bean Salad with Green Olives and Tarragon

Your beans can be cannellini, heirloom Aztecs, navy beans, flageolets, or even frozen limas. A mixture of types is unusual and makes the salad interesting to look at—and to eat. Serves 4 to 6 Ⓥ

3 cups cooked white beans, rinsed if canned
2 small celery ribs, thinly sliced, plus the leaves, finely chopped
15 Spanish green olives, pitted and sliced
2 tablespoons chopped tarragon
1 tablespoon sherry vinegar
1 clove garlic, minced
1/2 teaspoon paprika
1/4 teaspoon sea salt
4 to 5 tablespoons olive oil
Freshly milled pepper

Put the beans in a bowl with the celery, chopped leaves, olives, and tarragon and gently mix everything together. In a small bowl, combine the vinegar, garlic, paprika, and salt, then whisk in the oil. Taste and adjust the season-ings, then pour the dressing over the beans.

Add pepper and mix gently. Serve at room temperature.

Michele Anna Jordan's Spring Farro Salad

Michele is a wonderful cook, writer, and radio personality. I love this recipe of hers, which she has kindly given me permission to use. Farro is dense, so this recipe can serve a lot, especially if it's part of a buffet. Cooking times vary with this grain. Simply cook it until tender, but still a bit chewy, which could be as long as an hour or as little as 35 minutes—taste as it cooks. Serves 6 to 8

2 cups farro

3 tablespoons sea salt

Juice of 2 lemons, plus more as needed

6 green onions, white and green parts, very thinly sliced

1/2 cup mixed fresh herbs, such as parsley, marjoram, tarragon, lemon thyme and snipped chives

8 ounces Bulgarian or French feta, drained and crumbled

5 tablespoons olive oil, plus more as needed

Freshly milled pepper

Put the farro into a strainer, rinse under cool running water, and transfer to a medium saucepan. Add water to cover plus 3 inches, stir in the salt, and bring to a boil over high heat. Skim off any foam that forms on top. Reduce the heat to medium low and simmer until the farro is tender but toothsome, 35 to 45 minutes or possibly longer—you just have to taste. (Soaking farro overnight reduces the cooking time by half.) Drain, transfer to a wide shallow serving bowl, drizzle with lemon juice, and let cool for 15 minutes. Cover with a tea towel for up to 2 hours.

To finish the salad, add the green onions, herbs, and crumbled feta and toss gently. Drizzle with olive oil. Taste for acid balance, adding a bit more lemon if it is not tart enough or a bit more olive oil if it is too tart. Correct for salt and season with several generous turns of black pepper. Toss gently and serve at room temperature.

With Fava Beans: Why not incorporate spring vegetables as they come into season? Fresh favas, blanched and peeled, blanched peas, and roasted asparagus cut into 1 1/2-inch lengths are all excellent additions, as are cucumbers and diced peppers later in season. Come fall, try black-eyed peas.

Transitional Flageolet and Garden Vegetable Salad

There's a time when the garden may yield one little zucchini, a handful of beans, a few carrots, a snippet of tarragon, the first tomato, and last of the peas—in short, a little of this and a bit of that. All will find a place here beside the elegant flageolet beans. Measurements are merely suggestions; use more or less of what you have. Serves 4

2 cups cooked flageolet beans (3/4 cup dried)

1 cup whole green beans, tipped and tailed, cut into small pieces

1 small zucchini, finely diced

1 small turnip, finely diced

1 carrot, finely diced

1/2 cup freshly shucked peas or tiny cauliflower florets

1 tomato, peeled seeded and neatly cut into small pieces

Creamy Herb and Shallot Dressing, made with walnut oil (page 165)

Sea salt and freshly milled pepper

4 whole small radicchio or butter lettuce leaves

Cook, then drain the beans and set them aside in a bowl.

Boil the green beans in salted water until tender-firm, then remove to a towel to drain. Cook the zucchini, turnip, carrot, and peas in the same water just until tender-firm, then remove to the towel.

Combine the vegetables and the beans, then toss with the dressing. Taste for salt and season with pepper. Serve piled into the curved inner leaves of a head of raddichio.

Pasta Salads

In general, I find pasta salads overrated. Too many are served cold from the refrigerator, their flavors dull, their texture stodgy. But a good pasta salad can be a sensual and memorable dish.

A good example of a pasta salad is hot pasta tossed with garlic, tomatoes, olives, capers, and plenty of fresh herbs. It's the warmth that brings forth the full potential of the ingredients and the acid that makes it a salad. If you're going to make a pasta salad, try a warm one. Or turn to Asian noodle salads, which are intended to be eaten chilled.

Sesame Noodles with Asparagus Tips

Whenever people ask what they can make a lot of easily and ahead of time for a party, this is what I suggest. It's endlessly versatile–you can vary the vegetable to go with the season.
Serves 6 to 8 Ⓥ

Marinade

- 1/4 cup light sesame oil
- 1 tablespoon toasted sesame oil
- 7 tablespoons soy sauce
- 3 tablespoons Chinese black or balsamic vinegar
- 3 1/2 tablespoons dark brown sugar
- 2 teaspoons sea salt
- 2 teaspoons chili oil
- 1 tablespoon minced ginger
- 1 clove garlic, finely chopped
- 1/4 cup chopped cilantro

Noodles and Asparagus

- 2 pounds asparagus, trimmed and thinly sliced on a diagonal
- 1 (14-ounce) package thin Chinese egg noodles or rice noodles
- 10 green onions, including the firm greens, thinly sliced
- 1/4 cup sesame seeds, toasted until lightly browned

Mix the marinade ingredients together, stirring to dissolve the sugar.

Bring a large pot of water to a boil. Add salt and the asparagus. Cook until bright green and tender but still firm,

just a few minutes. Scoop the asparagus out, rinse it under cold water, and set on a towel to dry.

Pull the noodles apart with your fingers, add them to the boiling water, and give them a quick stir. Boil until tender but not overly soft, tasting them often as they cook. It should take only a few minutes. Pour the noodles into a colander and immediately rinse under cold water. Shake off the excess water.

Toss the noodles with all the marinade and most of the onions, sesame seeds, and asparagus. Mound them in a bowl or on a platter, then garnish with the remaining asparagus, onions, and sesame seeds.

Pasta Salad with Cauliflower, Capers, and Mustard Vinaigrette

A good winter salad. Serves 4 to 6

- Mustard Vinaigrette (page 167)
- 1 pound cauliflower or broccoli florets
- Sea salt
- 2 sun-dried tomatoes, very thinly sliced
- 1/2 cup chopped green onions
- 1/4 cup chopped parsley
- 8 ounces pasta shells or corkscrew pasta
- Fresh lemon juice, to finish, optional

First make the vinaigrette while you bring a large pot of water to a boil. Cook the cauliflower in the boiling, salted water until barely tender, about 2 minutes. Scoop it out with a strainer, shake off the excess water, and put it in a large bowl. Toss with the mustard vinaigrette, tomatoes, onions, and parsley. Cook the pasta in the same water, then drain. Add the pasta to the bowl with the rest of the ingredients and gently toss to combine. Serve warm, with lemon juice to sharpen the flavors, if needed.

Ravioli and Tomato Salad with Masses of Basil

This is a dish of tender mouthfuls. I have often taken this salad on a picnic; when it's finally time to eat, the flavors have mingled nicely. Serves 4 to 6

> 2 pounds ripe tomatoes
>
> 1 (6-ounce) jar artichoke hearts, drained and halved, optional
>
> 1 bunch basil, the leaves torn into pieces, about 1/2 cup
>
> 1/2 cup niçoise or Greek olives, pitted and cut into large pieces
>
> 3 tablespoons capers, rinsed
>
> 1/4 cup olive oil
>
> 1 pound cheese ravioli or tortellini
>
> Sea salt and freshly milled pepper
>
> Red wine vinegar, to finish

Bring a large pot of water to a boil for the ravioli. In another pot of boiling water, blanch the tomatoes for 15 seconds, then scoop them out. Peel, seed, and chop them into large pieces. Put the tomatoes and artichokes in a large bowl with the basil, olives, capers, and oil.

Salt the pasta water. Add the ravioli, cook until done, and drain well. Add them to the bowl and turn gently with a rubber spatula. Taste for salt, season with pepper, and sprinkle with vinegar to taste. Serve warm or tepid.

Chilled Mung Bean Noodles with Dulse and Crushed Peanuts

These cool, slippery noodles are just the thing on a hot day. They don't require cooking, and they only get better as they marinate in the refrigerator. Dulse is a delicate and delicious sea vegetable. Serves 4 (V)

> About 2 1/2 ounces mung bean noodles
>
> 2 carrots, julienned
>
> 1 cucumber, seeded and julienned
>
> 4 green onions, including a little of the greens, thinly sliced diagonally
>
> 1/4 cup rice vinegar
>
> 2 teaspoons roasted peanut oil
>
> 1 1/2 teaspoons sugar
>
> Pinch sea salt
>
> 1 tablespoon finely chopped ginger

> 1 jalapeño chile, seeded and finely diced
>
> Several red dulse "leaves," soaked in water for 5 minutes
>
> 1/4 cup chopped cilantro
>
> 1/2 cup chopped roasted peanuts

Cover the mung bean noodles with boiling water and let stand until softened, about 5 minutes. Drain and put them in a bowl with the carrots, cucumber, and onions. Whisk the vinegar, oil, sugar, and salt together, then add the ginger and chile. Pour over the noodles and toss well. Drain the dulse, coarsely chop, and add it to the noodles with the cilantro and most of the peanuts. Toss again and serve with the remaining peanuts sprinkled over the top.

Buckwheat Noodle Salad with Grilled Tofu or Tempeh and Roasted Peppers

Buckwheat noodles can be found in Asian markets and many natural foods stores. Check the package instructions—they cook more quickly than semolina pasta. Serves 4 to 6 (V)

Tofu and Marinade

> 1 package firm tofu
>
> 1/3 cup hoisin sauce
>
> 2 teaspoons toasted sesame oil
>
> 1/3 cup rice wine (mirin)
>
> 3 tablespoons soy sauce
>
> 1 1/2 tablespoons dark brown sugar
>
> 1 1/2 tablespoons tomato paste
>
> 3 cloves garlic, minced or put through a press
>
> 1 tablespoon minced ginger
>
> 2 pinches red pepper flakes

Noodles

> 2 red bell peppers, halved lengthwise and brushed with oil
>
> 1 (12-ounce) package soba noodles
>
> 1 bunch green onions, including a little of the greens, thinly sliced
>
> 2 tablespoons chopped cilantro
>
> 2 tablespoons toasted black or white sesame seeds

Cut the tofu into slabs about 3/8 inch thick and drain on paper towels. Whisk the remaining marinade ingredients together in a pie plate. Add the tofu and turn the pieces so that all are covered with the marinade. Cover and refrigerate until ready to use.

Prepare the grill or heat the broiler. Remove the tofu from the marinade, reserving the marinade. Grill or broil until browned on both sides, then slice into strips. Grill or broil the peppers until the skin blisters, then peel and slice into narrow strips. Boil the noodles in a large pot of salted water until done, according to the package instructions. Drain and rinse under cold water to stop the cooking then shake off excess water. Toss the noodles with the reserved marinade, the onions, cilantro, peppers, and tofu. Sprinkle the sesame seeds over the noodles. Toss again and serve.

Tempeh can replace the tofu. Steam it first, then slice and marinate, then sauté briefly in light sesame oil.

Vinaigrettes and Dressings

It's the dressing that completes the salad, adding a smooth coating that glides over the ingredients, bringing all the flavors and elements together. Dressings can be the simplest toss in oil and vinegar or vinaigrettes laden with mustard, shallots, olives and capers, herbs and cheeses. Some salad dressings use buttermilk and yogurt as their base and a few are sweet, especially those used with fruit, but all have an edge of tartness. No dressing is difficult or time-consuming to make. And one of the best dressings—olive oil and lemon juice or vinegar—requires only seconds. Stock your cupboard with a fine olive oil and a few vinegars, and you'll never turn to bottled dressing, with all its chemical riches, to have a salad.

Dressings are formed by bringing together oil and acid (vinegar or lemon) with or without other flavorings. Since vinegar and oil don't naturally merge, vigorous beating with a small whisk or a good shake in a covered jar is what convinces them to emulsify into a coherent sauce. As they sit, dressings and vinaigrettes will sometimes separate into these two elements, but can be quickly rejoined with a few turns of a whisk. Individual recipes may make more than you need at one time, but the leftovers will keep over several days, refrigerated or at room temperature.

Oil

What's commonly sold as salad oil is the last thing you want to put on a salad. Highly refined, bleached, deodorized, and tasteless, it only makes your salad greasy. Oil is as important an ingredient in a salad as what's dressed, so choose high-quality, delicious oils—rich, heavy nut oils, fragrant roasted sesame and peanut oils, mild sunflower oil, and even more exotic oils such as pistachio and avocado. And of course, olive oil.

HAZELNUT OIL: Hazelnut oil made from roasted nuts is amber colored, viscous, but not as robust as walnut oil. Its delicate, nutty flavor complements artichokes, wild rice, pears, and persimmons, and, of course, any dish in which hazelnuts themselves are present.

MACADAMIA NUT OIL: Even more delicate than hazelnut oil. Made from roasted macadamia nuts, it's lovely with salads featuring tropical fruits and with rice salads.

OLIVE OIL: The method of pressing olive oil has changed in the past 15 years and nearly all olive oils are extra-virgin, referring to the amount of acidity. It can be relatively inexpensive or very costly indeed, but salads provide one of the best ways to showcase the finesse of your best oil. Different olives and regions produce oils with very different characters. Tuscan oils are hot and spicy; Ligurian oils are mild and smooth. California made oils from Arbequina olives can be green tasting and lively. Use whichever style appeals to you but always use your best oil for salads.

Pomace, which is made by subjecting the waste—pits, skins, and flesh—left over from the extraction process to hexane, should be avoided at all costs. There are, alas, many dubious practices associated with European olive oils that were not known when *Vegetarian Cooking for Everyone* was first published. To learn about today's olive oils, an excellent book to read is Tom Mueller's *Extra Virginity: The Sublime and Scandalous World of Olive Oil*.

ROASTED PEANUT OIL: Light peanut oil is a good neutral-tasting oil, but the roasted version is saturated with the perfume of peanuts and should be used with that in mind. I especially like featuring roasted peanut oil in dressings that are seasoned with ginger, soy, and garlic. You can mix roasted peanut oil with lighter peanut oil or use it by itself. It makes an excellent finishing oil for stir-fries, peanut sauces, and dishes based on tofu.

SUNFLOWER SEED OIL: I'm very fond of this oil. It has more character than most of the lighter oils. Its faintly toasty, nutty flavor is definitely present, but it doesn't overwhelm. Use it in a salad where you're also including sunflower sprouts and toasted sunflower seeds.

TOASTED SESAME OIL: There's a light sesame oil that is good in cooking when you want a fairly neutral oil, and the dark, toasted version. The latter should be amber in color and have the unmistakable perfume of roasted sesame seeds. It can overwhelm, so use it in small amounts as a flavoring for vinaigrettes that coat Asian greens such as tatsoi and napa cababage.

TRUFFLE OIL: Some loathe truffle oil, whose flavor is created by chemicals rather than the infusion of truffles; others adore it and tend to overuse it. If you long for the flavor of truffles and want to use truffle oil, do so very judiciously, by the drop, added when tossing a salad. Or use the very aromatic truffle salt instead (see page 37).

WALNUT OIL: Made in France and America, walnut oil should be dark and viscous and redolent of walnuts. Use walnut oil straight or cut with olive oil or sunflower seed oil in vinaigrettes. Sherry, tarragon, and strong red wine vinegars stand up to its personality. Walnut oil seems to soften bitter greens and complement fall and winter fruits such as pears, apples, and persimmons. Always keep it refrigerated.

Acid: Vinegars and Citrus Juices

The vinegar you use contributes a great deal to the character of a salad. Vinegars range from sharp to sweet and high acid to low, depending on what they're made from and how they're made. Acidity is expressed in percent or grains; the information is usually given on the bottle. A sharp, high-acid vinegar would be 6.5 to 7.5 percent acidity; a low-acid vinegar about 4 percent. Low-acid vinegars require less oil for balance than highly acidic ones. Fresh lemon juice is more highly acidic than lime, orange, or tangerine, all of which lend good flavors to vinaigrettes. Citrus juices (and their zest) can be used alone or in combination with vinegars or even, in the case of lemon, stand on their own.

APPLE CIDER VINEGAR: This has a nicely balanced, lively taste that always seems uniquely American to me. The organic, unfiltered types are more fruity and interesting than the filtered kinds. I like this rather all-purpose inexpensive vinegar with sunflower seed and olive oils, especially on grains and legumes, such as a salad of black-eyed peas.

BALSAMIC VINEGAR: Low-acid, smooth, and complex, balsamic vinegar is excellent with fruits (sometimes improving their flavor) and for tempering the more aggressive red wine and sherry vinegars. Made from the must of white grapes, its unique flavor is gained through successive aging in open wooden barrels over many years. There are three tiers of balsamic vinegar: the first, which is aged for decades, is very costly and exquisite, used by the drop; a second tier of quality vinegar, aged 15 to 25 years, is expensive but not impossibly so; and a third tier, which is syrupy, cloying, and industrial, is neither aged nor terribly good. Because of its unique flavor and sweetness, balsamic vinegar isn't always used as the sole vinegar in a dressing, but as an accent, softening and enriching wine vinegars. Unfortunately, it has become overused, the poorest quality appearing almost everywhere and on everything. Choose the best you can afford and use it consciously. Greek vinegar from Kalamata is one you can use in place of balsamic—better quality for sure than the cheapest balsamic.

CHAMPAGNE VINEGAR: Champagne vinegar is delicate but has enough strength to support a fine olive oil. Champagne vinegar can also be used by itself, sprinkled over salad greens, by those avoiding oil in dressings. I especially like champagne vinegar with mild tender greens such as butter or Boston lettuce types, looseleaf lettuces, salad mixes comprised of tender greens, and so forth.

FRUIT VINEGARS: Fruity and mild, raspberry vinegar was all the rage some years ago. It and other fruit-enhanced vinegars can be used where you want a fruity overtone—with avocados, citrus, pears, green salads with fruit, and grains. Use fruit vinegars with discernment. They would not be so good with eggs and cheese, for example.

RED WINE VINEGAR: Frequently used for salads, red wine vinegars vary in body and strength from average to high acid. Aged red wine vinegars are excellent with heavier oils, such as nut oils, and used with dense greens, such as spinach and dark green lettuces. You can find red wine vinegars made from specific wines or blends, such as merlot or cabernet. When aged in oak, they are especially robust and delicious. Banyuls is one of my favorites.

RICE (WINE) VINEGAR: Japanese vinegar that's extra mild and sweet, it comes both plain and "seasoned." (The plain is what I have used throughout.) There are also brown rice vinegars, which are more acidic. Some, which are aged in open crocks, are as exquisite as a fine balsamic vinegar, but the lighter style is what's available here. Use rice vinegars with toasted peanut and sesame oils, especially those destined for salads including fruit, Japanese noodles, or cucumbers.

SHERRY VINEGAR: Distilled from sherry, this Spanish vinegar has an unmistakable and delicious aroma. It is very acidic and requires much more oil than the standard three-to-one ratio to balance its strength. This is a good vinegar to use with heavier nut oils, especially when used to dress bitter greens such as radicchio. Sherry vinegar made from Pedro Ximénez, a syrupy aged sherry, is more like balsamic and certainly better than the cheap stuff. I often use it where balsamic vinegar is called for.

WHITE WINE VINEGARS: Generally a little less aggressive than red wine vinegars, many white wine vinegars come flavored with a branch of tarragon, dill, or other herb— nice when the herb complements the salad. White wine vinegars allow other flavors to come through more in a dressing, such as the particular delicacy of shallots or citrus zest. They're a good choice with lighter-bodied olive oils and more neutral-tasting oils, such as sunflower.

Flavorful Additions

Beyond fine sea salt, there are lots of exciting flavorings that can go into dressings. Among them are the following:

> For sharpness: capers, olives, green peppercorns, salty cheeses
>
> For liveliness: diced shallots, green onions, snipped chives, and pickled onions
>
> For pungency: fresh garlic pounded with salt to a puree, freshly milled black pepper
>
> For nose-tingling: mustard and horseradish
>
> For richness and their ability to smooth out disparate flavors: crème fraîche, sour cream, yogurt cheese, and hard-cooked egg yolk
>
> For smoky sweetness: strained juices from roasted peppers, smoked salt
>
> For exotic fragrance: saffron, a pinch soaked in warm oil or water; truffle salt
>
> For mystery: citrus juices, including tangerine, lime, lemon, and orange, reduced, by simmering, to a concentrated sauce.
>
> For spice: ginger, cumin, paprika, and coriander; all fresh herbs
>
> For a mild acid nip: seeded and diced tomatoes

GARLIC

A subtle presence of garlic can be achieved by letting a crushed, peeled clove rest in the dressing for 10 minutes or so. For a stronger presence, finely chop a clove or pound it in a mortar with a pinch of sea salt until smooth, then whisk it into the dressing. In its roasted form, garlic is much sweeter.

Combining Oils and Vinegars

There aren't really any hard-and-fast rules, although some alliances form rather naturally. For example, heavy nut oils need the concentrated strength of an aged red wine or sherry vinegar while a more delicate oil would be overwhelmed by these assertive vinegars. It's not uncommon to mix both vinegars and oils. For example, a little balsamic vinegar tempers a sharper vinegar, whereas a little sherry vinegar adds an interesting dimension to a citrus vinaigrette or fruit vinegar. A nut oil can be mixed with a lighter oil, and the nut flavor will carry. The best approach is to experiment and taste. You may find a combination of vinegars and oils that strikes your fancy and becomes your signature dressing.

PROPORTIONS: A basic formula for combining oil and vinegar is one part acid to three parts oil. But, as you can now see, this formula can't work for all vinegar-oil combinations. Sherry vinegar, for example, is so acidic that it may need six parts oil to one, whereas wine vinegar can be mixed more like two to three parts to one. You can always start with the three-to-one formula and taste your way from there. When it comes to dressing grains and beans, a sharper dressing is usually in order.

USING ONLY OIL: Some salad combinations are so robust and peppery, such as salads of arugula, watercress, sorrel, and large amounts of herbs, that just a little oil and salt are all that's needed. The spiciness of the greens makes up for the acid, but you can include a few drops of lemon juice, too.

USING ONLY VINEGAR: You can also dress a salad with just a little salt and vinegar. Mild low-acid vinegars sharpen the flavor of greens without being overwhelming. Balsamic, rice wine vinegar, champagne vinegar, and low-acid fruit vinegars are ideal. Sprinkle a few drops over salted leaves, toss well, taste, and add more if desired.

TASTING A VINAIGRETTE: First, be sure it's well stirred so that there's a unified flavor, not a layer of vinegar on the bottom. So rather than taste it on your finger or from a spoon, taste it on a piece of whatever it will eventually go on—a leaf of lettuce or a slice of orange—then adjust the balance if needed. If the dressing is too tart, add a little more oil; if it's too oily and doesn't have enough bite, add a little more vinegar.

ADDING SEA SALT AND SHALLOTS: Unless you use a fine table variety, salt, especially coarser sea salt, takes a little while to dissolve. And shallots, which I use in many dressings, seem to taste better when they've had a chance to sit for a while in the vinegar before adding the oil. The vinegar sweetens and softens the shallots. To accommodate both, I usually let the salt and/or shallots sit for 15 minutes before whisking in the oil. If you don't do this, the world won't end, but it's an easy habit to get into and results in a better dressing.

Lemon Vinaigrette

Diced shallots, mustard, chopped herbs, and capers are all good additions to this vinaigrette, and the minced pulp from Preserved Lemons (page 70) would be good for a robust salad based on beans or greens. Makes about ¹/₂ cup Ⓥ

2 tablespoons fresh lemon juice
1 teaspoon finely chopped lemon zest
¹/₄ teaspoon sea salt
1 shallot, finely diced
5 tablespoons olive oil
Freshly milled pepper

Combine the lemon juice, zest, salt, and shallot in a small bowl. Let stand for 10 minutes, then whisk in the oil and season with a little pepper to taste. Taste and correct the balance, adding more oil if needed.

Balsamic or Fruit Vinegar Vinaigrette

A little red wine vinegar balances the sweetness of the balsamic and fruit vinegars. Especially good on salads with fruits, such as figs or citrus, with tomatoes, or with grilled onions and eggplant. Makes about ¹/₂ cup Ⓥ

4 teaspoons balsamic, raspberry, or other fruit vinegar
2 teaspoons red wine vinegar
1 shallot, finely diced
Sea salt and freshly milled pepper
5 tablespoons olive oil

Combine both vinegars and the shallot with a few pinches of salt and a little pepper in a small bowl. Let stand for 15 minutes. Whisk in the olive oil. Taste to make sure the balance is right.

Creamy Herb and Shallot Dressing

You can use this dressing with a number of foods—delicate garden lettuces, shaved fennel, white beans, and vegetables such as zucchini, asparagus, green greens, or sliced mushrooms. Makes about ¹/₂ cup

2 tablespoons tarragon vinegar or champagne vinegar

1 shallot, finely diced

¹/₄ teaspoon sea salt

¹/₄ cup olive oil or walnut oil

2 tablespoons crème fraîche or sour cream

1¹/₂ tablespoons chopped tarragon

1 tablespoon chopped parsley

1 tablespoon snipped chives

Freshly milled pepper

Combine the vinegar, shallot, and salt in a bowl and let stand for 5 to 10 minutes. Whisk in the oil and crème fraîche, then stir in the herbs and season with pepper. Taste and correct the balance of oil and vinegar if needed.

On Using Shallots

Unless they are at the peak of their season, shallots may have a bitter green sprout poking through the top of the bulb. Slice the bulb in half, then lift out the sprout with the tip of a knife. Dice the rest of the shallot finely and cleanly without randomly running your knife back and forth over the pieces. When they haven't been smashed, shallots seem to have a sweeter flavor.

Olive Oil Vinaigrette or French Dressing

This basic vinaigrette includes a little mustard to sharpen the flavors. Makes about ¹/₂ cup Ⓥ

2 tablespoons white or red wine vinegar or fresh lemon juice

1 teaspoon Dijon mustard

¹/₈ teaspoon sea salt

6 tablespoons olive oil

Freshly milled pepper

Combine the vinegar, mustard, and salt in a small bowl and let stand for 15 minutes. Then whisk in the oil, adding it in a steady stream. Season with pepper to taste. This is not a mayonnaise, so you can move boldly—it's the whisking that pulls the dressing together. (You can also put everything in a jar with a tight lid and shake until it's quickly blended.) Dip in a lettuce leaf and taste, then adjust the oil, vinegar, or mustard if needed.

Shallot Vinaigrette: The delicate onion flavor of shallots is such a worthwhile addition to vinaigrettes that you may find yourself automatically putting them in all your dressings; I certainly do! Peel and finely dice a shallot, then put it in a bowl with the vinegar and sea salt. Let it stand for at least 5 minutes or longer to sweeten the shallots. It also turns them slightly pink. Stir in mustard or any other flavorings, then whisk in the oil. Ⓥ

Lime-Cumin Vinaigrette

Cumin and lime go especially well with citrus fruits, onions, avocados, and peppers. Roasting and grinding whole spices creates higher, warmer flavors. Makes about ¹/₂ cup Ⓥ

1 clove garlic

¹/₈ teaspoon sea salt

Grated or minced zest of 2 limes

2 to 3 tablespoons fresh lime or lemon juice

2 tablespoons chopped green onion or finely diced shallot

¹/₂ jalapeño chile, seeded and minced

¹/₂ teaspoon cumin seeds

¹/₂ teaspoon coriander seeds

¹/₄ teaspoon dry mustard

¹/₃ cup olive oil

2 tablespoons chopped cilantro

Pound the garlic with the salt in a mortar until smooth (or put it through a press), then put it in a bowl with the lime zest, juice, green onion, and chile. Toast the cumin and coriander seeds in a small dry skillet until fragrant, then immediately transfer them to a plate to cool. Grind to a powder in a spice mill, then add them to the juice mixture. Whisk in the mustard and oil. Taste and adjust the balance if needed. Let the dressing stand for at least 15 minutes; add the cilantro just before using.

Walnut Oil Vinaigrette

This dressing is excellent with salads made with frisée, radicchio, escarole, and spinach, with or without their frequent companions apples, pears, nuts, and cheeses. Be sure to use an amber-colored oil that has a clear scent of walnuts. Makes about ¹/₂ cup Ⓥ

1¹/₂ tablespoons sherry vinegar or tarragon vinegar

2 shallots, finely diced

¹/₄ teaspoon sea salt

1 teaspoon Dijon mustard

6 tablespoons roasted walnut oil or a mixture of walnut and olive oils

Freshly milled pepper

Combine the vinegar, shallots, and salt in a bowl and let stand for 10 to 15 minutes. Stir in the mustard, then add the oil. Whisk well until the dressing is thick and smooth. Season with pepper. Taste and adjust the amount of vinegar or oil if needed.

Hazelnut Oil Vinaigrette: Use 2 tablespoons hazelnut oil and ¹/₄ cup olive oil in place of the walnut oil, or, if the flavor is light, use only hazelnut oil.

Sherry Vinaigrette

This assertive, garlicky vinaigrette wakes up bland beans and grains. I sometimes pound a hard-cooked egg yolk with the garlic, which smooths and binds these strong flavors. Makes about ¹/₂ cup Ⓥ

1 or 2 cloves garlic, coarsely chopped

¹/₄ teaspoon sea salt

1¹/₂ tablespoons sherry vinegar or aged red wine vinegar

1 teaspoon Dijon mustard

6 tablespoons olive oil

Freshly milled pepper

Pound the garlic with the salt in a mortar until it breaks down into a puree. Combine the garlic, vinegar, and mustard in a small bowl, then whisk in the oil and season with pepper. Taste and correct the balance.

Orange Vinaigrette

Use this citrus vinaigrette with fennel, beets, and carrots or on a citrus or avocado salad. Blood oranges make a vivid garnet-colored vinaigrette, and the orange oil or orange-flower water underscores the orange flavor. Makes about ¹/₂ cup Ⓥ

1 teaspoon finely grated or minced orange zest

¹/₄ cup fresh orange juice

2 teaspoons white wine vinegar or balsamic vinegar

¹/₈ teaspoon sea salt

3 tablespoons light olive or sunflower seed oil

1 tablespoon olive oil

2 drops orange oil, or 1 teaspoon orange-flower water, optional

Freshly milled pepper

Combine the orange zest and juice, vinegar, and ¹/₈ teaspoon sea salt in a small bowl and let stand for 10 to 15 minutes. Whisk in the olive oils and season with a little pepper. Add the orange oil, then taste for salt and adjust the vinegar and oil if needed.

Saffron Vinaigrette with Basil and Orange

For a saffron lover, this dressing will become a favorite. Use it on roasted peppers and potatoes, grilled zucchini, tomato salads, or grilled fennel. Puree it to make a more uniformly textured sauce, if desired. Makes about ¹/₂ cup Ⓥ

3 tablespoons fresh orange juice

2 teaspoons snipped chives or shallots

¹/₂ teaspoon finely grated orange zest

¹/₄ teaspoon sea salt

Freshly milled pepper

¹/₂ cup olive oil

Pinch saffron threads

2 tablespoons snipped or torn basil leaves

In a bowl, combine the orange juice, chives, orange zest, salt, and a few grinds of pepper. Warm 2 tablespoons of the oil in a small measuring cup, crumble the saffron threads into it, and let stand for a few minutes. Add this oil to the dressing and whisk in the remaining oil. Add the basil just before using. Use as is, or puree.

Lime and Fresh Mint Vinaigrette

Use with cucumbers, delicate lettuces, rice, and melon salads.
Makes about $1/2$ cup Ⓥ

- 1 teaspoon grated lime zest
- 2 tablespoons fresh lime juice
- $1/4$ teaspoon sea salt
- 5 to 6 tablespoons sunflower seed or olive oil
- 2 green onions, including an inch of the greens, thinly sliced into rounds
- 2 tablespoons chopped mint or 2 teaspoons dried, crumbled

Combine the lime zest and juice and salt, then whisk in the oil. Stir in the onions and mint. Taste and correct the seasonings for balance if needed.

Winter Herb Vinaigrette

Dried herbs and fresh parsley flavor this winter dressing. Use it with steamed or roasted winter vegetables cauliflower, celery root, turnips, carrots, leeks, and beets.
Makes about $1/2$ cup Ⓥ

- 1 clove garlic
- $1/4$ teaspoon sea salt
- $1/4$ teaspoon black peppercorns
- $1/4$ teaspoon fennel seeds
- $1/2$ teaspoon dried tarragon
- $1/2$ cup chopped parsley
- Grated zest of 1 lemon
- 1 tablespoon capers, rinsed
- 1 large shallot, finely diced, or $1/4$ cup thinly sliced green onions, including a little of the green
- $1/3$ cup olive oil
- 2 tablespoons champagne vinegar or tarragon vinegar

In a large mortar, mash the garlic with the salt, the peppercorns, fennel, tarragon, and 2 tablespoons of the parsley to make a smooth paste. Add the lemon zest, capers, shallot, oil, and remaining parsley; let stand for 30 minutes. Stir in the vinegar, taste for salt, and add more vinegar if needed for balance.

Mustard Vinaigrette

The mustard and the vigorous whisking make a very thick dressing. When applied to warm foods, it immediately thins. Use this robust dressing with warm beans (dried or fresh), grated celery root, steamed potatoes, grilled fennel, broccoli, and cauliflower. Makes about $1/2$ cup

- 2 tablespoons aged red wine vinegar, sherry vinegar, or fresh lemon juice
- 2 shallots, finely diced
- 1 clove garlic, minced
- $1/4$ teaspoon sea salt
- 1 tablespoon Dijon mustard
- 2 tablespoons crème fraîche or sour cream
- $1/3$ cup olive oil
- Freshly milled pepper
- 2 tablespoons snipped chives
- 1 tablespoon chopped parsley
- 3 tablespoons capers, rinsed

Combine the vinegar, shallots, garlic, and salt in a small bowl. Let stand for 5 to 10 minutes, then vigorously whisk in the mustard, crème fraîche, and oil until thick and smooth. Grind in a little pepper, then stir in the herbs and capers. Taste and adjust the seasonings if needed.

Curry Vinaigrette

This thick, golden dressing is delicious with beets, asparagus, broccoli, and cauliflower and with grain-based salads, especially those made of rice and quinoa. Let it stand for 15 minutes for the full flavor to flower. Makes about $1/2$ cup

- 1 clove garlic
- $1/4$ teaspoon sea salt
- 2 tablespoons yogurt, mayonnaise, or sour cream
- 2 teaspoons curry powder
- $1^1/2$ tablespoons fresh lemon juice
- 5 tablespoons light olive or sunflower seed oil
- 2 tablespoons finely chopped cilantro

Pound or mince the garlic and salt in a mortar until smooth, or put the garlic through a press. Combine the garlic and salt with the yogurt and curry in a small bowl. Stir in the lemon juice, then whisk in the oil. Let stand for 15 minutes, then stir in the cilantro. Taste for tartness and salt and adjust if needed.

Tomato Vinaigrette

The juicy tidbits of tomatoes are an unconventional addition. Use this dressing soon after making it, on green salads, especially spinach salads, or salads based on beans and grains. Makes about ¹/₂ cup Ⓥ

1 clove garlic, minced

1 shallot, finely diced

2 tablespoons red wine vinegar

2 teaspoons balsamic vinegar

¹/₄ teaspoon sea salt

Freshly milled pepper

4 to 6 tablespoons olive oil

3 Roma tomatoes, or ¹/₂ cup cherry tomatoes, neatly diced

In a small bowl, combine the garlic, shallot, both vinegars, salt, and pepper to taste. Let stand for 5 to 10 minutes, then whisk in the oil and add the tomatoes. Taste and adjust the balance if needed.

Tomato Vinaigrette with Olives: Add ¹/₄ cup halved and pitted niçoise or kalamata olives. Good with grilled vegetables, avocados, fresh goat cheese, and mozzarella. Ⓥ

Sesame Vinaigrette with Chili Oil

Use this aromatic dressing with Asian greens such as tatsoi and napa cabbage, Asian noodles, sweet potatoes, and even fruit—especially mangoes and citrus. Makes about ¹/₂ cup Ⓥ

1 clove garlic, minced

1 teaspoon minced ginger

1 shallot, finely diced

3 tablespoons rice vinegar

1 teaspoon soy sauce

1 teaspoon light brown sugar

4 tablespoons sesame oil

2 tablespoon toasted sesame oil

¹/₂ teaspoon chili oil

1 tablespoon chopped cilantro, optional

Combine the garlic, ginger, and shallot in a small bowl, cover with the vinegar, and let stand for 15 minutes. Stir in the soy sauce and sugar, then whisk in the oils. Add the cilantro. Taste and adjust the amount of soy sauce and sugar if needed.

Peanut Dressing with Thai Basil

Roasted peanut oil makes this dressing highly aromatic. Use it with napa cabbage and spinach salads, on cubes of silken tofu, or toss with Chinese egg noodles. Makes about ¹/₂ cup Ⓥ

¹/₄ cup roasted peanut oil

2¹/₂ tablespoons rice vinegar or apple cider vinegar

1 tablespoon soy sauce

1 clove garlic, finely minced

¹/₂ to 1 serrano chile, diced

2 green onions, including an inch of the greens, thinly sliced

8 mint leaves, finely chopped

2 tablespoons chopped basil, preferably Thai basil

Pinch sea salt

Combine everything in a bowl and whisk together. Taste—the soy sauce may provide enough salt; if not, add some.

Avocado Dressing

Use this thick green dressing with crisp romaine and iceberg lettuce or as a dip for crudités. It will hold well, refrigerated, for several hours. Set plastic wrap directly on the surface to keep it from browning. Makes about 1¹/₂ cups Ⓥ

¹/₄ cup fresh lime or lemon juice

1 avocado, peeled and pitted

1 clove garlic, coarsely chopped

1 jalapeño chile, seeded and diced, optional

3 green onions, including an inch of the greens, roughly chopped

¹/₄ cup chopped cilantro

¹/₂ cup plus 2 tablespoons olive, avocado, or sunflower seed oil

Sea salt

Put the lime juice, avocado, garlic, chile, onions, and cilantro in a blender and puree.

Gradually pour in the oil with the machine running. Season with salt to taste.

Variation with Tomatillos: The tartness of tomatillos slices through the richness of the avocado. Remove the husks from 4 large tomatillos, simmer them in water until they turn olive green, then puree. Chill, then stir into the dressing. Add ¹/₄ cup sour cream or yogurt if desired. Ⓥ

Blue Cheese Dressing

Spoon over hearts of romaine or serve as a dip for crudités.
Makes about $1/2$ cup

- 6 tablespoons olive oil
- 2 tablespoons sour cream or yogurt
- 5 teaspoons sherry vinegar or aged red wine vinegar
- 3 ounces blue cheese such as Maytag, crumbled
- 1 tablespoon snipped chives
- Sea salt and freshly milled pepper

Whisk all the ingredients in a bowl except the salt and pepper, leaving the cheese a little chunky or smooth as you prefer. Taste and add salt if needed—the cheese will be salty—and season with pepper.

Green Goddess Dressing

Without the anchovies, this isn't a true green goddess dressing, but it's awfully good. Use it with sturdy lettuces, such as iceberg or romaine hearts, or as a spread for sandwiches. Use it with rice and vegetables for an impromptu summer rice salad. Makes about 1 cup

- $1/2$ cup mayonnaise
- $1/2$ cup sour cream or thick yogurt
- 1 tablespoon tarragon vinegar
- $1/2$ cup chopped parsley
- 3 tablespoons snipped chives
- $1^{1}/_{2}$ tablespoons chopped tarragon
- 1 clove garlic, coarsely chopped
- $1/4$ teaspoon sea salt

Combine all the ingredients along with 2 tablespoons water in a blender or food processor and puree until smooth and pale green. Taste and add more salt if needed.

Nondairy Variation: Omit the mayonnaise and sour cream and puree one 10-ounce package of soft silken tofu with $1/2$ cup olive oil and the remaining ingredients until smooth. Ⓥ

Feta Dressing with Marjoram and Mint

Try this spunky dressing with platters of cucumbers, tomatoes, and peppers, with romaine lettuce, or spooned over warm lentils or beans. Makes about $2/3$ cup

- 2 tablespoons aged red wine vinegar
- 1 tablespoon chopped marjoram
- 2 teaspoons chopped mint
- $1/3$ cup olive oil
- $1/3$ cup crumbled feta cheese
- Sea salt and freshly milled pepper

Put the vinegar and herbs in a small bowl. Whisk in the oil, then stir in the cheese. Taste for salt—none may be needed because of the feta—and season with pepper. If you prefer a creamier dressing, mash the cheese with the oil first, then combine with the rest of the ingredients.

Buttermilk Dressing with Horseradish

Use this tangy dressing as a dip or as a topping for roasted vegetables or baked potatoes. Makes about 1 cup

- $1/2$ cup buttermilk
- $1/2$ cup yogurt, sour cream, or mayonnaise
- 1 tablespoon prepared horseradish
- $1/2$ teaspoon wasabi, optional
- 2 cloves garlic
- $1/4$ teaspoon sea salt
- $1/4$ cup chopped parsley
- Fresh lemon juice or white wine vinegar

Combine the buttermilk, yogurt, and horseradish in a bowl. Dilute the wasabi in a little water, then whisk it into the yogurt mixture. Pound the garlic with the salt until smooth, then add the parsley and pound again just to bruise the herbs. Add this to the buttermilk mixture with lemon juice to taste.

SOUPS FROM SCRATCH

CHAPTER 7

Soups from Scratch

A bowl of soup is wholesome, comforting, and often the essence of simplicity. Soups are also practical because they're relatively easy and quick to make—a good place for beginners to begin and for more practiced cooks to continue.

A forgiving food, soup happily accepts a fennel bulb where none was called for, replaces a leek with an onion, provides a home for a tasty leftover. Soup is something we can turn to again and again, and when we don't have time to cook, we're comforted by the pot that awaits us in the refrigerator, for soup always improves with time.

Soup can be a prelude to a meal, the meal itself, or even dessert. Soup can also leave home and travel to work in a thermos. A soup that comes before the main course should be light unless the dish that follows is also light. Make sure there's a contrast of color and texture between the two courses. First-course soups, often pureed and smooth, are generally more elegant than the homey, comforting soups we turn to again and again. A hearty, full-bodied soup accompanied by bread and followed with a salad makes a wholesome, nurturing meal.

A shallow soup plate frames this food perfectly. These elegant plates or small porcelain soup cups are ideal vessels for first-course soups at a sit-down dinner party. Deep bowls or cups are more informal, and their steep sides help the soup retain its warmth. A simple garnish—a swirl of crème fraîche or a spoonful of olive oil, a sprinkling of herbs—is all that's needed to bring out a soup's charm and personality, while more complex garnishes can make an ordinary soup unusual and interesting.

SERVING SIZE: For an appetizer or soup course, $3/4$ to 1 cup soup is plenty; for a main-dish serving, $1^1/2$ to 2 cups soup will do.

STORING STOCKS AND SOUPS: Always refrigerate leftover soup, then bring it to a boil to reheat. Soup often thickens as it stands, so you may have to thin a second-day soup with milk, stock, or water and add chopped herbs or other garnishes to freshen it. Except for yogurt soups and those whose charm depends on being served within moments of completion, all the stocks and soups in this book freeze well. To freeze, divide cooled soup into quantities that make sense for you—$1^1/2$ cups for a single serving, larger amounts for a family. After defrosting, all the soup needs is reheating and some fiddling—reseasoning and adding a fresh garnish—to come to perfection.

DAIRY-FREE SOUPS: Many soups don't call for butter, cream, or milk, and recipes seldom include eggs. On the other hand, adding a pat of butter, enriching a soup with milk or cream, or swirling in a spoonful of tart yogurt or pungent grated cheese at the end can provide a sharp flavor accent or meld flavors together. Soups that call for butter or small amounts of dairy can be made dairy-free by substituting a suggested oil for the butter and omitting the bit of cheese or sour cream at the end.

Stocks

Making stock isn't difficult, but it is an extra step. Most soups don't need a stock, but many will be much better with one, and a few actually do require that you make a stock. You'll find that, given even a little experience, making a stock is largely an intuitive process.

Most soup recipes taste fine made with water, but you may wish to use a stock to add body and depth of flavor. You have several options when it comes to stock. One is to use the Basic Vegetable Stock (page 175), a reliable all-purpose background stock for soups and other dishes. Another is to make a specific stock, such as a mushroom stock, that complements a particular soup. Or you might choose a commercial stock. Except for mushroom stock, I find them a little harsh and too salty, but you may not—try them and see. Take whichever approach appeals to you or that you have time for. If you make yourself familiar with the flavor-enhancing stocks in this chapter, as well as the building blocks for improvising, you'll be able to take full advantage of soup's natural flexibility.

Usually my own preference is to make a Quick Stock (page 174)—a simple, basic stock that draws on the soup's vegetable trimmings for its supportive flavor. It's effortless, yet your soups will taste deeper and fuller. Preparing it also affords the pleasure of using what might otherwise be discarded.

The following guidelines and the recipes should free you to approach stock making in a relaxed and spontaneous fashion. Stocks that are uniquely appropriate for a given type of recipe are found throughout the book.

QUICK STOCK (PAGE 174): Used for soups, this stock is made with a few basic ingredients plus trimmings of soup vegetables. It's thin but supportive.

BASIC VEGETABLE STOCK (PAGE 175): An all-purpose, all-season stock that goes practically everywhere and gives depth to dishes like risotto, when water just won't do. It can adapt to the seasons by using those vegetables that are fresh and in season where you live.

ROASTED VEGETABLE STOCK (PAGE 177): A winter stock—the vegetables are roasted first to concentrate their flavors. Hearty enough to be a broth for pasta in brodo.

MUSHROOM STOCK (PAGE 176): This is a full, deep, dark, mushroom-flavored stock, the most impressive and full-bodied of the vegetable stocks. Use it in all dishes that are mushroom based—soups, stews, risotti, pot pies, gratins, and so on.

KOMBU STOCKS (PAGES 536 TO 537): These stocks replace the traditional Japanese dashi, which includes flaked dried bonito. Kombu, like other seaweeds, has a hint of the sea in it. It's used for miso soups and Japanese noodle dishes.

STOCK FOR STIR-FRIES (PAGE 235): A stock that helps compensate for the flavor traditionally provided by chicken stock in nonvegetarian dishes.

RED STOCK (PAGE 176): A basic quick stock made with herbs and vegetables that harmonize with many Mexican dishes.

HERB AND GARLIC BROTH (PAGE 176): Essentially the Provençal garlic soup *aïgo bouïdo*. Sip this as broth or use it to float filled pasta, cubes of potato, or thin threads of noodles. It's particularly good when used in earthy and robust potato-filled casseroles.

STOCK FOR CURRIED DISHES (PAGE 175): A basic stock made with seasonings appropriate for curries and other Indian dishes.

Elements of Stock Making

When it comes to making stock, it's more useful to know how certain ingredients work with each other than to know a particular recipe. The measurement suggestions, when given, are for 8 cups of water, 6 cups finished stock.

Basic Ingredients for All Vegetable Stocks

Virtually all stocks start with these ingredients, which are the backbone ingredients for Basic Vegetable Stock (page 175).

Onions, carrots, and celery

Thyme, parsley, bay leaf

Garlic (a good place to use those hard-to-peel cloves)

Leek trimmings: roots and leaves

Sea salt

Oil for the initial sautéing of vegetables

Always-Good-to-Include Vegetables

These avoid the sweet end of the vegetable spectrum and give depth to stocks.

Chard stems and leaves; beet greens except for red ones

Fresh mushrooms; the soaking water from dried mushrooms

Green onions, in addition to or in place of onions or leeks

Potato parings, preferably organic

Celery root skins, well scrubbed

Parsley root

Jerusalem artichokes

Lettuce

Eggplant

Ingredients to Use for Their Particular Flavors

These ingredients have discernible, strong flavors and should be included in stocks that will be used in dishes that incorporate them.

Asparagus: the butt ends

Parsnips: trimmings and cores

Winter squash: the skins and seeds

Fennel: stalks and trimmings

Corn cobs

Pea pods

Cilantro or lovage

Curry spices, cumin, ginger, lemongrass, galangal, saffron

Chinese dried mushrooms

Ingredients to Use in Summer Stocks

Include any of the following seasonal vegetables and herbs in addition to the basic ingredients.

Zucchini and other squash

Tomatoes

Green beans

Eggplant

Bell peppers, especially red and yellow ones

Corn cobs

Marjoram and basil: stems or leaves

Ingredients to Use in Winter Stocks

Seek out these additions for your earthy winter vegetable stocks.

Celery root parings, well scrubbed

Parsley root

Leeks: leaves and roots

Garlic, including roasted garlic

Dried sage: 2 teaspoons per 8 cups water

Rosemary: about a 1-inch sprig

Caramelized Onions, page 358

Mushrooms, fresh and dried

Ingredients to Avoid When Making Stocks

There are very few ingredients to avoid scrupulously, and almost all are vegetables in the cabbage family.

Turnips and rutabagas

Cabbages and brussels sprouts

Broccoli and cauliflower

Red beets, unless you're making a beet soup

Tiny celery seeds, powdered herbs, ground pepper, because they can make stock bitter

Onion skins

Artichoke trimmings

Excessive amounts of greens (more than 4 cups)

Anything you wouldn't eat: no funky or spoiled vegetables

Other Ingredients That Add Depth to Stocks

Sprouted seeds, especially legumes: 1 to 2 handfuls

Lentils and mung beans: ¹/₄ cup, rinsed

Bean broth, especially from chickpeas and white beans, in place of water

Nettles, amaranth, and borage leaves: 1 or more handfuls

Miso, tamari, soy sauce: a spoonful at a time added at the end to taste

Kombu: a 6-inch piece added at the beginning

Nutritional yeast: 1 to 2 tablespoons to give a "meaty" flavor to stocks; best if cooked first with the vegetables in butter or oil; available in bulk at natural foods stores

Nuts: ¹/₂ to 1 cup, tied in cheesecloth, cooked in the soup for 20 minutes—they can be retrieved, dried in the oven, and used in cooking, such as in croquettes (thanks to Tom Ney of *Prevention* magazine for this tip)

Parmesan cheese rinds: whole chunks added to stocks that will be used for beans

Tips for Making Stocks

- A stock is not a catchall for old or spoiled vegetables, although you can use trimmings, last week's carrots, mushrooms with open caps, and so on. When in doubt, ask yourself, "Would I eat this?" If not, don't put it in the stock.

- Coarsely chop vegetables for stock into pieces about 1 inch square. The more surface area exposed, the more quickly the vegetables will yield their flavors.

- The more vegetables you use, the richer the flavor.

- Unlike meat stocks, vegetable stocks don't benefit from hours of cooking. Quick stocks take 25 to 35 minutes; basic stocks, 45 minutes to 1 hour. When the vegetables have given up their flavors, they have nothing more to offer. Once strained, the flavor of stocks can be concentrated by simmering them, uncovered, until the stock is reduced by half.

- Even after washing, some dirt may remain on vegetables like leeks and celery root. Allow the cooked stock to settle for a few minutes, then strain it carefully through a sieve into a clean container. Once cooked, don't let the stock sit with the ingredients in it—certain herbs turn bitter as they steep.

- Be cautious with unfamiliar herbs and vegetables. Some can turn grassy, like spinach, or bitter, like tiny seeds. If you're not sure about an ingredient, simmer it alone first, then taste the water to see if it's to your liking.

QUICK STOCK

Making quick stock is relaxed and improvisational, the steps intermingling with the preparation of the soup vegetables, trimmings added to the pot as you go along. Here's what I do:

- After heating a few teaspoons of oil in a large pot, I quickly peel and roughly chop an onion, a carrot, and a celery rib and add them to the pot when the oil is hot. While they're browning, I read through the soup recipe and look for vegetables that have useful trimmings. If I'm using leeks, I chop 2 cups of their inner greens and add them to the pot. If I'm using a celery root, I add the scrubbed skin. As I work, I toss in parsley, smashed garlic cloves, and bay leaves. I look for other ingredients in the recipe that might be amplified in the stock—an herb that's called for (in go extra marjoram, basil, or cilantro stems) or something from the garnish, like the green parts of green onions. Also I check the refrigerator for leftover chopped shallots, a lone mushroom, some chard stems and add them as I find them.

- During the 5 minutes it takes to do all this, I give the pot a stir or two. After 10 minutes, I add salt and water and bring it to a boil. It simmers, uncovered, while I go back to the soup. I like to give the stock about a half hour, then I strain it and add it right to the soup. Still warm, it quickly comes to a boil.

Quick Stock

Makes about 6 cups ⓥ

2 teaspoons vegetable or olive oil

1 onion, peeled and coarsely chopped

1 carrot, coarsely chopped

1 celery rib, coarsely chopped

Trimmings from the soup vegetables, rinsed

2 bay leaves

Several thyme sprigs or ¹/₂ teaspoon dried

4 or more cloves garlic, peeled and smashed

8 parsley sprigs, including the stems, or a small handful of stems

Additional herbs and spices appropriate for the soup

2 teaspoons sea salt

Heat the oil over high heat and add the onion, carrot, and celery. While they're browning, chop the vegetables and add the trimmings to the stock along with the aromatics.

Stir occasionally. After about 10 minutes, add the salt and 8 cups cold water and bring to a boil, then lower the heat and simmer, uncovered, for 25 to 35 minutes. Strain as soon as the stock is finished.

Bean Broth or Stock

The liquid that remains from cooking beans—just that alone—can work both as broth and an enriching vegetable stock. Such liquids are referred to in Italy as "crazy water" because you can get something delicious out of nothing but water, beans, aromatics, and if you wish, vegetables. Those made from white or other pale beans are most versatile, but the dark liquid that comes from black beans can also be used to good effect. (See Rice Cooked in Black Bean Broth, page 478.) You can certainly use the beans. Tying the herbs together with string will make it easier to remove them. Makes about 4 cups (V)

1 cup dried white beans, such as navy beans
2 tablespoons olive oil
1 onion, roughly chopped
1 carrot, sliced
2 celery ribs, chopped
Leek roots and pale leaves or the entire leek, if available
1 parsnip
1 heaping tablespoon tomato paste
3 plump cloves garlic
1 bushy thyme sprig or a few pinches dried
8 sage leaves
8 parsley sprigs
2 cloves
1 teaspoon sea salt

Cover the beans with boiling water for a quick soak. Heat the oil in a soup pot (or pressure cooker). Add the onion, carrot, celery, leek, parsnip, tomato paste, and the aromatics. Cook gently, stirring occasionally, until the onion is pale gold and smells enticing, 20 to 30 minutes. Add the drained beans and 10 cups fresh water. Bring to a boil and simmer, covered, for 2 hours, more if time allows (or in a pressure cooker on high for 25 minutes). Strain when done. There should be about 7 cups. Intensify by simmering the broth down to 4 cups, then taste for salt, adding more to taste if needed.

Basic Vegetable Stock

This basic stock is flavor-rich with a golden hue. Include any trimmings from the vegetables you're using that are appropriate. Take a look at "Elements of Stock Making" (page 172) to tailor this stock to the season. Makes about 6 cups (V)

1 large onion
2 large carrots
2 celery ribs, including a few leaves
1 bunch green onions, including half of the greens
1 tablespoon olive or vegetable oil
1 tablespoon nutritional yeast, optional
8 cloves garlic, peeled and smashed
8 parsley sprigs
6 thyme sprigs or 1/2 teaspoon dried
2 bay leaves
2 teaspoons sea salt

Scrub the vegetables and chop them roughly into 1-inch chunks. Heat the oil in a soup pot. Add the vegetables, yeast, garlic, and herbs and cook over high heat for 5 to 10 minutes, stirring frequently. The more color they get, the richer the flavor of the stock. Add the salt and 8 cups cold water and bring to a boil. Lower the heat and simmer, uncovered, for 30 minutes. Strain.

Dark Vegetable Stock: Brown the onion before adding the liquid or add 1 tablespoon, or more to taste, soy, tamari, or mushroom soy sauce to the finished stock. (V)

Stock for Curried Dishes: Make the basic stock, but lightly brown the vegetables in 1 to 2 tablespoons clarified butter, with 1 (3-inch) cinnamon stick, 4 cloves, 2 teaspoons coriander seeds, 1 teaspoon cumin seeds, and 1/4 teaspoon cardamom seeds.

Stock for Mexican Soups and Stews: Make the basic, summer, or winter vegetable stock using a safflower or olive oil. Sauté the base vegetables only lightly and include 1/2 bunch chopped cilantro or the stems from 1 bunch; 1/2 teaspoon dried oregano, preferably Mexican; several epazote leaves, fresh or dried; 6 cloves garlic, roasted or sautéed in their skins; and 3 tomatoes, broiled until blistered. (V)

Mushroom Stock

This stock adds so much to soups and sauces that it's worth freezing in cubes or 1-cup amounts to have on hand.
Makes about 6 cups ⓥ

1/2 to 1 ounce dried porcini, about 1/2 to 1 cup

11/2 tablespoons olive oil

1 large onion, chopped

2 carrots, diced

2 celery ribs, diced

8 ounces white mushrooms, sliced

1 cup chopped leek greens and leek roots, if available

1/4 cup chopped walnuts or almonds, optional

2 cloves garlic, roughly chopped

4 thyme sprigs or 1/4 teaspoon dried

Aromatics (page 21), including 10 sage leaves or
   1 tablespoon dried

2 teaspoons sea salt

Shake the dried mushrooms in a sieve to loosen the forest dirt, then let soak in enough warm water to cover them. Heat the oil in a soup pot. Add the onion, carrots, and celery and sauté over medium-high heat, stirring occasionally, until the onion is well browned, about 15 minutes. Scrape the bottom of the pan to loosen the juices that have collected there, then add the dried mushrooms and their soaking liquid, the remaining ingredients, and 9 cups water. Bring to a boil, then lower the heat and simmer, partially covered, for 45 minutes. Strain.

Red Stock

This stock adds great background support to Tortilla Soup (page 194) and Fideos (page 194). In addition to the listed ingredients, you can bolster the flavor by adding a handful of lentils. Makes 6 cups ⓥ

11/2 tablespoons vegetable oil

2 onions, sliced

2 celery ribs, diced

2 carrots, chopped

5 white mushrooms, sliced

1 teaspoon dried oregano

1/2 teaspoon dried thyme

2 tablespoons tomato paste

6 cloves garlic

6 outer lettuce leaves

Stems from 1 bunch cilantro, or 1 cup coarsely
   chopped cilantro

1/2 cup coarsely chopped parsley

2 teaspoons sea salt

Heat the oil in a soup pot over medium-high heat. Add the onions, celery, carrots, mushrooms, and herbs and cook, stirring occasionally, until the onions are browned, about 7 minutes. Add the tomato paste and mush it around the pan for a minute or so, then add the remaining ingredients plus 8 cups water and bring to a boil. Reduce the heat and simmer, partially covered, for 45 minutes. Strain, pressing out as much liquid as possible.

Herb and Garlic Broth

Essentially this is the Provençal aïgo bouïdo, *stepped up a bit with a little tomato to make a hearty stock. It's immensely fortifying, good for colds and hangovers, as well as an excellent medium for potato dishes and winter stews.*
Makes 4 to 6 cups ⓥ

2 heads garlic, as fresh and firm as possible

1 tablespoon olive oil

1 tablespoon tomato paste

2 bay leaves

10 peppercorns

2 cloves

6 large sage leaves or 2 teaspoons dried

6 thyme sprigs or 1/2 teaspoon dried

10 parsley sprigs

2 teaspoons sea salt

Separate the garlic cloves by pressing down on the heads. Remove most of the papery skins, then smash the cloves with the flat side of a knife to open them up.

Heat the oil in a soup pot, add the tomato paste, and fry over medium heat for about a minute. Add the garlic, remaining ingredients, and 8 cups water and bring to a boil. Lower the heat and simmer, partially covered, until the garlic cloves are soft, about 45 minutes. Strain. Press the garlic through the strainer with the back of a spoon into the broth or press it into a dish and use for another purpose.

Roasted Vegetable Stock

Roasting intensifies the flavors of all vegetables and provides an easy way of bringing added character to what is essentially a basic vegetable stock. Makes about 6 cups ⓥ

4 carrots

1 large celery rib

3 Jerusalem artichokes

1 large onion, chopped into 1-inch pieces

1 large leek, white part thinly sliced, plus 1 cup chopped inner greens

1 cup diced celery root

6 cloves garlic

2 tablespoons olive oil

2 teaspoons sea salt

¹/₄ teaspoon peppercorns

¹/₂ cup coarsely chopped parsley

Aromatics (page 21), including 4 sage leaves

1 teaspoon soy sauce or to taste

Preheat the oven to 425°F and scrub the vegetables.

Slice the carrots, celery, and Jerusalem artichokes into ¹/₄-inch slices. Put them in a bowl with the onion, the white part of the leek, the celery root, and the garlic. Toss them with the oil, then spread on a sheet pan and roast, turning them every 10 minutes, until browned, about 30 to 40 minutes.

Transfer the roasted vegetables to a soup pot and add the remaining ingredients along with 8 cups water. Bring to a boil, then reduce the heat, cover the pot, and simmer for 40 minutes. Strain, pressing out as much liquid as possible. Taste for salt. A teaspoon of soy sauce may give it a little depth and additional saltiness.

How to Make (Most) Vegetable Soups

Certain steps in soup making are encountered over and over. Often we don't know why we perform them or what they contribute to the process. Here's what they mean and why we do them—how to make a soup. For a first soup, try the basic Potato Soup (page 188). It's a simple illustration of all the steps. After, that you should have enough of a feel for the process to move confidently on to the big world of soups.

10 Basic Steps to Making Soup

1. **Warm the oil or butter.** Fat captures the perfumes of herbs and garlic (the aromatics) and carries them throughout the body of the soup. It also contributes its own flavor and gets very hot, which is important for searing and browning onions. Most recipes call for 2 tablespoons oil or a mixture of butter and oil, an ample amount for 6 to 8 cups of soup and just a teaspoon or less per serving. Even less can be used, but I encourage you to use some. Although diet books suggest using water for sautéing, water is not a substitute for fat because it doesn't contribute or carry flavor. If you must avoid fat, simply simmer the vegetables in stock or water.

2. **In a large, wide pot.** Give your vegetables a lot of room. A wide soup pot gives a generous surface area for the onions and vegetables to brown. If crowded on top of each other, they'll steam instead. The soup pot should have a heavy bottom so that the vegetables don't burn.

3. **Add the onions or leeks.** Onions, leeks, or green onions are almost always used to start a soup. They're cooked in oil or butter until they soften, often with aromatics

such as parsley, bay leaf, thyme, garlic, and sometimes diced carrots and celery. It's important not to rush this step; the longer you give it, the better your soup will be. Browning onions gives the soup body, hearty flavor, and rich color. When you want a more delicate flavor, cook the onions or leeks more gently, over lower heat and for less time. Sometimes a little water or stock is added after the first few minutes so that they stew rather than fry. In most of these recipes, we do something in between letting the onions turn golden but not brown.

4. **Cook until the ontions are soft, 10 to 20 minutes.** Onions take a while to break down, and their softening is inhibited by salt and acids such as tomatoes, wine, vinegar, and lemon juice. It's crucial that the onions be soft before tomatoes are added. If they're not, they'll remain uncooked and raw tasting and in the worst case will float to the surface of the finished soup. Softening takes at least 10 minutes, but to be safe, plan on 12 or more, especially at higher altitudes.

5. **Add the vegetables and salt and cook for a few minutes.** Since most vegetables don't keep the onions from getting soft, they're added at the beginning when we want them to brown, too. Or they're added later and cooked for just a few minutes, to warm them up before the next step. This is a good time to add salt to the soup, for it helps pull out the vegetables' flavors.

6. **Add the water or stock.** Now is the time to add the liquid to the vegetables. If you've made a quick stock, it will be warm. If you're using water, just add it cold from the tap, or heat it first on the stove.

7. **Boil, then simmer, partially covered.** The liquid needs to reach a boil, but constant boiling is too violent a motion for a good soup. Once the liquid boils, lower the heat to a simmer, which produces gentle and constant motion in the pot—hot but not destructive. The pan is covered but not all the way so that the soup doesn't escape in the form of steam, nor does it boil over; a little escaping steam keeps it all in check.

8. **Let cool, then blend or puree.** Many soups are pureed. They can be left with some texture or made silken by straining through a fine sieve. You can use a food mill, a handheld blender, a regular blender with a jar, or a food processor. Very hot soups can sputter and burn you, so it's a good idea to let them cool for 5 to 10 minutes before pureeing and to puree with care.

9. **Taste for salt, season with pepper, and add a little lemon or vinegar.** If your stock was seasoned and you salted the vegetables, you probably won't need more salt at the end, but it's always a good idea to check right before serving. If the salt seems okay but the soup still needs something, often a little lemon juice or a splash of vinegar will bring all the flavors into sudden bright relief. Add freshly milled pepper just before serving, too; a lot of pepper added at the beginning can turn bitter.

10. **Garnish and serve.** Finally, you can ladle out your soup and finish it with a garnish that will add a harmonious or contrasting flavor, color, or texture. If it's very cold or you live at a high altitude where food cools quickly, take a moment to warm the empty soup bowls either in a low oven or with hot water.

Garnishes for Soups

Garnishes make plain soups pretty, complete their seasoning, and add texture. Particular garnishes often suggest themselves, but the following suggestions are good with a great many soups and will help you improvise. Use one, two, or even three at a time.

CHOPPED FRESH HERBS: Parsley, chervil, and chives are always a good choice, but use the herbs that have gone into the soup itself, too.

COOKED GREENS: Finely chop cooked spinach, beet greens, or broccoli rabe and stir them into soup at the last minute to add vibrant flavor and color. Strong-tasting greens are especially good with bean- and potato-based soups.

CRÉME FRAÎCHE, CREAM, SOUR CREAM, YOGURT, OR WHIPPED CREAM: A spoonful of cream enriches a thin soup or accents a rich one. Crème fraîche dissolves perfectly into a soup, but sour cream and yogurt will curdle if the soup boils, so reheat it carefully. Whipped cream floats on the surface, then gradually melts and is especially pretty when mixed with chopped herbs.

CROUTONS: Small cubes of crisp bread, toasted baguette slices, or large garlic croutons add textural interest to soups, especially those with uniform textures. Narrow strips of fried or toasted tortillas also add texture as well as their warm corn flavor. Crisped bread crumbs add texture to smooth bean soups.

FRESH GREENS: Slice arugula, lettuce, spinach, or sorrel into very thin ribbons and sprinkle over the soup. These snippets wilt and turn bright green.

FRIED HERBS: Sage, parsley, celery, and lovage leaves—fried quickly in olive oil until crisp, then crumbled into the soup—are unusual and tasty.

HERB OR BLOSSOM BUTTERS: Floated or swirled into the soup, these speckled butters (pages 45 to 46) melt, and the herbs and petals spread over the surface.

OLIVE OIL: Spoon a little of your best olive oil over the surface of a soup, and the heat will bring out its full aroma. Freshly grated parmesan cheese and freshly milled pepper are usually welcome where olive oil is. This trio is particularly good with bean soups.

PASTA AND GRAINS: Cooked pasta, rice, or other grains—barley, quinoa, and large grains like spelt—give a soup body and texture. Floating dumplings or cheese and rice molds placed in the bowl before ladling the soup make a special presentation.

SAUCES: A spoonful of Pesto (page 50), Romesco Sauce (page 62), or Garlic Mayonnaise (page 52) makes a good soup sparkle and helps a soup that is a little bland.

SMOKED SALT, TRUFFLE SALT, AND SMOKED PAPRIKA: A sprinkle of these produces an intensely aromatic finish.

VEGETABLES: Lightly cooked carrot julienne strips, slivers of raw radish, and strips of greens used together can rescue a dull-looking vegetable soup or enhance one that's already striking. Stewed leeks, thinly shredded cabbage, or a few chopped tomatoes also can add greatly to a soup's presence.

VINEGAR AND LEMON: A few drops of acid often bring a soup's flavors together and make it sing. They also add dimension to soups made with little salt.

Seasonal Vegetable Soups

By following the progression of produce through the seasons, you can enjoy vegetable soups throughout the year. Vegetables at their peak of ripeness are full of natural sugars, good texture, gorgeous color, perfume, and flavor—especially important in vegetable soups, which are, after all, very simple constructions. What's in season varies widely from place to place and doesn't always correspond to what's in the supermarket. The vegetables in season where you live are likely to be the freshest, least expensive, and most rewarding to work with.

Springtime Asparagus Soup

Asparagus shouts "Spring!" Here's a good place to make a quick stock, using the trimmings from the leeks and the ends of the asparagus. Serves 4 to 6 Ⓥ

1¹/₂ pounds asparagus

1¹/₂ tablespoons olive oil or butter

1 large leek, white part plus an inch of the green, chopped

1 small onion, chopped

2 tablespoons raw white rice

6 cups Quick Stock (page 174) or water

Sea salt

Lemon juice

Freshly milled pepper

Slice the asparagus into three parts: ends, middles, and tips. Chop the middles and set the tips aside. Use the asparagus ends and leek roots and greens in the stock.

Heat the oil in a soup pot. Add the leek, onion, and rice and sauté over medium-high heat for about 8 minutes, until the onion is slightly colored. Add 1 cup of the stock and stew for 10 to 12 minutes. Add the chopped asparagus and the remaining 5 cups stock and simmer, partially covered, for 12 to 15 minutes. Cool briefly, then puree and pass through a food mill to get rid of any fibers. Taste the soup for salt, add a few drops of lemon juice to bring up the flavors, and season with pepper. Return the pot to the stove to keep it warm.

Meanwhile, drop the asparagus tips into boiling salted water and cook until tender, about 4 minutes, then add them to the finished soup.

Asparagus Soup with Herb Cream: Whip ¹/₄ cup cream until stiff and season with a pinch of salt, a little white pepper, and 2 tablespoons chopped chervil or tarragon. Set a spoonful of cream into each bowl of soup.

Asparagus Soup with Fresh Sage: Sauté 10 sage leaves with the leek, onion, and rice. If the sage is blooming, add a few of the purple flowers to garnish the soup—the essence of spring. Ⓥ

Asparagus and Pea Soup with Basil: Peas come into season when asparagus does. Boil freshly shelled peas with the asparagus tips and add them to the finished soup along with thinly sliced basil leaves. Ⓥ

Beet Soup

In spite of the inherent deep flavor of the vegetable, beet soups need a supporting stock. You can make one while preparing the ingredients for the soup. Serve hot or chilled with a dollop of sour cream. Serves 4 to 6 Ⓥ

- 6 cups Quick Stock (page 174), including ¹/₂ teaspoon dill seeds, ¹/₂ teaspoon caraway seeds, ¹/₄ cup lentils, and the beet stems, roughly chopped
- 3 large beets with their greens, about 1¹/₂ pounds, peeled and cut into ¹/₂-inch cubes
- 2 onions, or 1 onion and 1 leek, white part only, finely diced
- 2 tablespoons butter or olive oil
- 1 turnip, peeled and diced
- 1 teaspoon sea salt
- 1 teaspoon lemon juice
- Chopped dill
- Freshly milled pepper
- Sour cream or thick yogurt, optional

Begin making the stock. As you prepare the soup vegetables, add the beet skins and onion trimmings to the stock. Let it simmer while you begin the soup. Select the best beet greens, chop, and set them aside.

In a soup pot over medium heat, cook the onions in the butter until soft, about 7 minutes, stirring now and then. Add the beets, turnip, and salt and cook 5 minutes more, stirring occasionally. Strain the stock—you should have

about 6 cups—and add it to the vegetables. Simmer until the beets are tender, about 10 minutes, adding the beet greens during the last 5 minutes. Taste for salt and add the lemon juice to bring up the flavor. Serve the soup sprinkled with dill, seasoned with pepper, with a spoonful of sour cream in each bowl.

Carrot Soup with Onion Relish

If you use Pickled Red Onions (page 72) in the relish, your soup will look very festive. Serves 4 to 6 Ⓥ

- 2 tablespoons butter, olive oil, or a mixture
- 1 onion, thinly sliced
- 1 pound carrots, scrubbed and thinly sliced
- 1 bay leaf
- 2 tablespoons chopped parsley
- 3 tablespoons white rice
- 1 teaspoon sweet paprika
- 1 teaspoon ground cumin
- ¹/₂ teaspoon ground coriander
- ¹/₂ teaspoon sea salt
- Freshly milled pepper
- 7 cups water; or Basic Vegetable Stock (page 175) plus 1 cup water

Onion Relish
- ¹/₄ cup finely diced white onion or Pickled Red Onions (page 72)
- ¹/₄ serrano chile, finely chopped
- 2 tablespoons chopped cilantro
- A few leaves Thai or Italian basil
- Grated zest and juice of 2 limes

In a soup pot, melt the butter over medium heat. Add the onion, carrots, bay leaf, parsley, and rice; cook to soften the onion, stirring frequently, about 5 minutes. Add the spices, salt, and some pepper and cook 5 minutes longer. Add the water and bring to a boil, then lower the heat and simmer, partially covered, for 25 minutes.

While the soup is cooking, make the relish by mixing all the ingredients together. Remove the bay leaf from the soup. Puree 2 cups of the soup until smooth, then puree the rest, leaving a little texture and flecks of carrot. Taste for salt and serve each bowl with a spoonful of the relish.

OTHER SPICY CONDIMENTS FOR CARROT SOUPS

Harissa (page 66)

Tomatillo Salsa (page 90)

Green Chile Butter (page 46)

Pureed grilled peppers seasoned with cayenne

Chili oil—a few drops stirred into each bowl

Smoked paprika

Carrot and Red Pepper Soup

Excellent chilled as well as hot, this soup uses aromatic herbs rather than spicy seasonings—another good direction to take with carrots. Serves 4 to 6 Ⓥ

2 tablespoons butter or olive oil

1 red bell pepper, cut into 1-inch pieces

2 cups diced onion

1 pound carrots, thinly sliced

2 tablespoons white rice

1 teaspoon sea salt

Freshly milled pepper

2 tablespoons chopped parsley

3 tablespoons chopped dill or 1¹/₂ tablespoons dried

Grated zest and juice of 1 orange

6 cups water or Basic Vegetable Stock (page 175)

Finely chopped dill, chopped parsley, or Herb Butter
     (page 45), for garnish

Melt the butter in a soup pot and add the pepper, onion, carrots, rice, and salt. Cook over medium heat, covered, until the onion has softened completely, about 10 minutes, stirring several times. Add a grind of pepper, the parsley, dill, orange zest, juice, and water. Bring to a boil, then simmer, partially covered, until the rice is cooked, about 25 minutes. Cool briefly, then puree a cup or two of the soup and return it to the pot. Taste for salt, season with pepper, garnish, and serve.

Chard Soup with Sorrel or Lemon

Light-bodied but roundly flavored, this is a good soup to begin a large meal. It's quickly made and needs no stock. Chard is available year-round, sorrel mainly in the spring. If you can't get sorrel, use fresh lemon juice to give the soup its tart accent. Serves 4 to 6

2 tablespoons butter

1 onion, or 2 medium leeks, white parts only, chopped

3 small potatoes, peeled and thinly sliced

1 bunch chard, stems removed, about 10 cups leaves

2 cups sorrel leaves, stems removed, or juice of 1 large lemon

1¹/₂ teaspoons sea salt

Freshly milled pepper

¹/₃ cup crème fraîche or sour cream

¹/₂ cup cooked rice or small toasted croutons

Heat the butter in a soup pot over medium-high heat. Add the onion and potatoes and cook, stirring occasionally, until they begin to color, about 8 minutes. Add ¹/₂ cup water and scrape the bottom of the pot to release the juices that have accumulated. Add the greens and the salt. As soon as they wilt down, after 5 minutes or so, add 6¹/₂ cups water. Bring to a boil, then lower the heat and simmer, partially covered, for 12 to 15 minutes. Puree the soup, then return it to the pot. Taste for salt and season with pepper. If you didn't use sorrel, add the lemon juice. Mix the crème fraîche with some of the soup to smooth it out, then swirl it into the soup. Serve with rice or croutons in each bowl.

Chard Soup with Cilantro: Substitute a small hunch of cilantro, chopped, for the sorrel and add 1 teaspoon paprika to the onions and potatoes. The haunting flavor is hard to place at first but is a must-try for cilantro lovers.

Measuring Greens

Since bunches of chard, kale, mustard, and other greens can vary greatly—the stems long on one, short on another—to measure the leaves so that you can anticipate whether your soup will be thin or thick, gently stuff them in a 4-quart measuring cup. Don't fuss about exactitude—this needn't be more than a ballpark guess, but even that helps.

A Special Chestnut and Lentil Soup

Late autumn is the season for chestnuts and for this unusual soup. The chestnuts, which are cooked with wine and a bit of tomato, give the lentils a lively note. Serve this soup with a spoonful of your best olive oil floating over the surface and grilled bread, croutons, or crisped bread crumbs.

Fresh chestnuts need to be kept damp, which they seldom are, so they end up with shriveled, disappointing meats. It's possible to buy them in cans or vacuum packed, which probably makes sense unless you know the exceptional farmer or grocer who does keep chestnuts moist. Serves 4 to 6 Ⓥ

Chestnuts and Lentils

- 3/4 pound whole chestnuts, or 1 cup or so of the meats
- Olive oil, for coating chestnuts
- 1 cup lentils
- 1 carrot, finely diced
- 1 celery stalk, finely diced
- 1/2 small onion, diced
- 1 large clove garlic, finely chopped
- 1 bay leaf
- 5 parsley sprigs
- Pinch sea salt

To Finish the Soup

- 2 to 3 tablespoons olive oil, plus extra to finish
- 1 teaspoon chopped marjoram or 1/2 teaspoon dried
- 1/2 teaspoon crushed fennel seeds
- Several thyme sprigs
- 1/2 cup dry white wine
- 1 tablespoon tomato paste
- Sea salt and freshly milled pepper
- Chopped parsley
- Small croutons

Heat the oven to 350°F. If using fresh chestnuts, score them on their rounded sides, toss in just enough oil to coat them lightly, and bake them until the skins have opened and the meat is tender, about 20 minutes. When they're cool enough to handle, peel them and cut into small pieces.

Rinse the lentils and cover them with hot water to soak for an hour. Drain, then put them in a soup pot with 8 cups water and bring to a boil. Cook for a few minutes at a gentle boil and remove any foam that forms on the surface. Add the remaining ingredients, lower the heat, and cook slowly until the lentils are tender, about 25 minutes. When done, remove the parsley sprigs and the bay leaf.

Warm the olive oil in a pot large enough to hold the soup, then add the chestnuts and herbs. Stir frequently over medium heat for several minutes; then add the wine and tomato paste. Stir to dissolve the paste and let the wine reduce for a minute. Set the pot aside.

Puree half the lentils until they're smooth. Pour them into the pot with the chestnuts and add the remaining lentils and enough cooking liquid to thin to a good soup consistency. Heat the soup and taste for salt and season with plenty of pepper. Serve with a fine olive oil drizzled over the soup, a little fresh parsley, and the croutons.

THREE TOOLS FOR PUREEING SOUPS

The blender allows you to control how smooth your soup will be, which is an advantage, but hot soup can spurt meanly out of the jar. It's always recommended that a soup cool for 5 or 10 minutes before being blended. If you're pressed for time, fill the jar only a third full. Always turn the machine on and off in three or four short spurts before you let it run to prevent spattering. Draping a towel over the blender is another good safety precaution.

An immersion blender, or blender on a stick, brings the blender right into the soup pot. It's easy and safe but best for soups that don't require a major blending. It doesn't have the power of the traditional blender.

The food mill is an especially good choice when a soup has lots of potatoes, which can turn gummy in a blender or food processor. It's also used after blending to ensure a silky smoothness by screening out tiny fibers and seeds.

The food processor works best if you puree the solids, adding the broth as needed to loosen them. Never fill the work bowl all the way to the top and always leave the feed tube open so that steam can escape.

Sweet Corn Soup

Corn can be seasoned almost endlessly with herbs and spices. Success depends on using sweet corn, in season; frozen corn needs a supporting stock. I prefer the golden color that yellow corn gives to this soup. Serves 6 to 8 (V)

6 ears corn

1 tablespoon butter or oil

1 small onion, thinly sliced

1/2 cup grated waxy potato, such as Yellow Finn or Yukon gold

7 cups water; or Quick Stock (page 174) plus 1 cup water

1 teaspoon sea salt

Half-and-half or milk, optional

Chopped parsley, basil, lovage, tarragon, chives, or dill, to finish

Shuck the corn, remove the silk, then slice off the kernels. You should have about 4 cups. Use the flavor-filled cobs in the stock if you're making one.

In a wide soup pot, melt the butter, then add the onion, potato, and 1 cup of the water. Cover the pot and stew over medium heat until the onion is soft, about 10 minutes. Add the corn, salt, and the remaining 6 cups water and bring to a boil. Lower the heat and simmer, partially covered, for 10 minutes. Cool briefly, then puree in a blender in two batches, allowing 3 minutes for each batch. Pass through a food mill or fine strainer, then return the soup to the stove and stir in a little half-and-half to thin it if desired. Taste for salt and serve sprinkled with herbs. When reheating, stir frequently and don't boil, or the soup will curdle.

Corn Soup with Flavored Butter: Instead of herbs, float a thin slice of flavored butter in each bowl of soup. Herb or blossom butters (pages 45 to 46), are good choices. As the butter melts, the flavors and flecks of herbs and flowers are released into the soup.

Corn Soup with Poblano Chiles and Tortilla Strips: Roast, peel, and seed a poblano or other large green chile (see page 364), then cut it into thin strips. Place some in each bowl with a little crumbled feta or grated Muenster and garnish with chopped cilantro and thin, crisp ribbons of corn tortillas (see page 40).

Corn Soup with Tomatoes and Basil: Peel, seed, and dice into neat small pieces 1 red or yellow tomato. Slice several basil leaves into thin strips. Pour the soup into bowls, and garnish with the tomato, a shower of basil, and freshly milled pepper. (V)

Roasted Corn Soup: Prepare roasted or grilled corn, then remove the kernels. Or sear cut-corn kernels in a hot cast-iron skillet until lightly browned. The slightly smoky flavor goes well with additions of minced green chile, lime juice, and tortilla strips. Smoked paprika is good here, too. (V)

Other Seasonings for Corn Soups

Pureed chipotle chile mixed with sour cream

Lime juice, grated ginger, and curry powder

Pureed roasted sweet or hot peppers

Crème fraîche and chives

Cilantro Salsa (page 49)

Corn Chowder with New Potatoes, Golden Peppers, and Basil

This soup provides lots of good trimmings to use in quick stock—especially the corn cobs. Serves 4 to 6 (V)

4 cups Quick Stock (page 174) or water

1 large leek, white part plus an inch of the green, sliced into thin rounds

Kernels from 6 ears corn, about 4 cups

1 pound new potatoes, peeled and neatly diced

8 leaves green or opal basil, plucked, stems reserved

2 tablespoons plus 2 teaspoons butter or olive oil

1 large onion, finely diced

1 bay leaf

4 thyme sprigs or 1/4 teaspoon dried

1 1/2 teaspoons sea salt

1 large yellow bell pepper, diced

2 cups milk or additional stock

Freshly milled white pepper

Finely snipped chives, to finish

If you're making the stock, include 2 cups chopped leek greens, the corn cobs, potato peelings, and basil stems.

Melt 2 tablespoons butter in a soup pot and add the onion, leek, bay leaf, and thyme. Cook over low heat until the onion is soft, 10 to 12 minutes, stirring occasionally. Add the potatoes, strained stock, and salt and bring to a boil. Lower the heat and simmer, partially covered, until the potatoes are tender, about 20 minutes. While the soup is simmering, stew the pepper in the remaining butter and a few tablespoons water in a small skillet until tender, about 10 minutes.

Press some of the potatoes against the side of the pot to break them up; then add the corn and milk. Simmer until the soup is heated through and the corn is tender, about 5 minutes.

Thinly slice the basil leaves. Add the stewed peppers to the soup and serve with white pepper, basil, and chives sprinkled over each bowl.

Corn and Salsify Chowder

Corn chowder can also include salsify, or oyster plant, as it's also called. Historically, it is mentioned as an ingredient, and it is assuredly delicious, but you may have to grow it yourself. A little chopped parsley brightens this soup, but many herbs go well with corn—basil, marjoram, chives, lovage, and thyme. The Herb Butter on page 45, swirled into the hot soup, would make a splendid aromatic finish, and so does a pinch of smoked salt. Serves 4 to 6

---

5 ears of fresh sweet corn, white or yellow

2 small leeks, white part only, finely chopped, or 1 yellow onion

4 small new potatoes, scrubbed and cut into small dice, peeled or not

4 cups water or Quick Stock (page 174) made with the corncobs and leek trimmings

2 to 3 tablespoons butter

5 thyme sprigs

3 salsify roots, peeled, cut into rounds and covered with acidulated water

1 teaspoon sea salt

2¹/₂ cups milk

Freshly milled pepper

Chopped parsley, snipped chives, and/or smoked salt for garnish

Herb Butter (page 45), optional

Shuck the corn and pull off the silk. Holding an ear stem end down on the counter or in a deep bowl and using a sharp knife, slice the kernels off the corn, just the tops. Then turn your knife over and, using the dull side, press it down the length of the cob, squeezing out the rest of the corn and its milk. Repeat with the remaining ears. Wash the chopped

leeks well to get rid of any sand and grit before chopping the white shanks. Use the corncobs, leek trimmings, and potato peels if available to make a Quick Stock (page 174).

Melt the butter in a soup pot over medium heat, add the leek and thyme sprigs, and cook gently for 4 minutes. Add the potatoes, salsify, and salt, then the liquid. Bring to a boil, then lower the heat, cover, and simmer until the potatoes are tender, about 15 minutes.

Add the corn to the pot, along with the milk, bring to a boil, then lower the heat and simmer for 15 minutes. Taste for salt and season with pepper. Serve the soup garnished with the chopped herbs scattered over the top and a little smoked salt in each bowl, or with a slice of Herb Butter.

Fennel and Leek Soup with Fennel Greens

This chameleon soup accepts Pernod to emphasize the anise, orange to complement it, a little cream to enrich it, and so forth. The ingredients provide excellent material for a quick stock. Serves 4 to 6 (V)

---

2 fennel bulbs, 1 to 1¹/₄ pounds

6 cups Quick Stock (page 174) or water

2 medium leeks, white parts plus an inch of the greens, chopped

1 small potato, peeled and thinly sliced

2 tablespoons olive oil or butter

1 onion, chopped

1 teaspoon sea salt

¹/₃ cup cream, optional

Freshly milled pepper

Remove the tough outer layers of the fennel and use them in the stock, along with 1 cup or more chopped stalks, 2 cups chopped leek greens, the leek roots, and the potato skins. Chop ¹/₂ cup of the fennel greens and set them aside.

Quarter the fennel bulbs and thinly slice crosswise. Warm the oil in a soup pot and add the onion, fennel, leek, potato, salt, and 1 cup of the strained stock. Cover and stew over medium heat for 20 minutes, stirring occasionally. Add the remaining 5 cups stock and bring to a boil. Lower the heat and simmer, partially covered, until the fennel is tender, 15 to 20 minutes more. Stir in the cream and the reserved fennel greens. Taste for salt, season with pepper, and serve.

Leek and Potato Soup

This French farmhouse soup—two humble vegetables sim-mered in water—stands on its own and makes a solid base for a host of other soups. If the potatoes are organic, leave the skins on for flavor and to give the soup the rustic feel it should have. Serves 4 to 6 (V)

3 large or 6 medium leeks, white parts only, finely chopped

1¹/₂ pounds yellow-fleshed potatoes, scrubbed well

2 tablespoons butter or olive oil

1¹/₂ teaspoons sea salt

Milk or water to thin the soup, if needed

Freshly milled pepper

Set the leeks in a bowl of water to soak while you prepare the potatoes, then lift them out with a strainer, letting any sand fall to the bottom. Quarter the potatoes lengthwise and thinly slice them.

Melt the butter in a wide soup pot, add the leeks and pota-toes, and cook over low heat, covered, for 10 minutes. Add 7 cups water and the salt and bring to a boil. Lower the heat and simmer, partially covered, until the potatoes are soft to the point of falling apart, about 35 minutes. Press a few against the side of the pan to break them up and give the soup body. If needed, thin the soup with milk and heat through. Taste for salt, season with pepper, and serve.

With Cream: A little cream can replace the milk if you wish to enrich what is really quite a meager soup. If your soup is very thick because of the type of potato used, thin it with milk or water first, then add a small amount of cream at the end to give it fullness.

Creamed Leek and Potato Soup: Pass the soup through a food mill. Thin with milk or water if needed, then add ¹/₄ to ¹/₂ cup cream. Serve hot or chilled with finely chopped chives and parsley or chervil. Chilled, it becomes vichyssoise.

Celery Root or Fennel Soup: Replace at least half the potatoes with chopped celery root or fennel and cook as described. Use the fennel greens or celery leaves, finely chopped, for garnish. (V)

Potato-Sorrel Soup: Add 2 to 4 large handfuls of sorrel leaves, stems removed, to the soup along with the potatoes and leeks. Pass through a food mill or leave chunky and finish with ¹/₂ cup cream. This is a delicious, slightly tart, and very refreshing soup, hot or cold.

Watercress Soup: Remove and discard the largest stems from a bunch of watercress. Blanch the watercress briefly in salted water. Finely chop or puree it, then add to the soup along with ¹/₄ cup cream or crème fraîche.

Green Onions and Leeks

While leeks make a more delicate base for soups than onions, they're not always easy to find. Try using green onions instead—they're inexpensive, always available, and have a sweetness and unique flavor that onions, especially late winter storage onions, just can't give you.

A Creamy Leek Soup with Fresh Herbs and Cheese Croutons

Vary the garnishes to suit the season for this first-course soup. Serves 4 to 6

6 cups Quick Stock (page 174) or water

6 medium leeks, white parts plus an inch of the greens, sliced into ¹/₄-inch rounds

2 tablespoons butter

1 bay leaf

4 lemon thyme or regular thyme sprigs

1¹/₂ teaspoons sea salt

1 tablespoon flour

¹/₃ cup milk or cream

Freshly milled pepper

3 tablespoons chopped herbs: chervil, basil, dill, or tarragon or 1 tablespoon chopped rosemary or lovage

Cheese croutons, 1 for each bowl

If you're making stock, chop 3 cups of the pale green inner leaves of the leeks and include them, plus the roots.

Separate the sliced leeks into rings and soak them in a bowl of water for 5 minutes. Lift them out, letting any sand fall to the bottom. You should have about 4 cups; if not; make up the difference with green or white onions. Melt the butter in a soup pot and add the leeks, bay leaf, thyme, salt, and

1 cup of the strained stock. Cover the pan and stew over medium heat until the leeks are tender, about 10 minutes. Stir in the flour, then pour in the remaining 5 cups stock. Bring to a boil, then lower the heat and simmer, covered, for 20 minutes.

Remove the bay leaf and thyme, puree the soup, then return it to the pot. Add the milk and bring to a simmer. Taste for salt and season with pepper. Stir in the fresh herbs and serve with a crouton in each bowl.

A Creamy Mushroom Soup

This plain-looking soup masks a wealth of flavor that comes from the mushroom stock. The servings can be smaller than usual since the soup is both smooth and rich. Serves 4 to 6

> 1 pound white mushrooms
> 3 tablespoons butter or oil
> 1 cup chopped leek or onion
> 2 cloves garlic, chopped
> 4 thyme sprigs or 3 pinches dried
> 1 teaspoon sea salt
> 1 tablespoon flour
> 4 cups Mushroom Stock (page 176) or commercial
> Freshly milled pepper
> 1/2 to 1 cup cream
> Finely chopped parsley, chives, or tarragon, for garnish

Set aside a few nice-looking mushrooms for the garnish and coarsely chop the rest. Melt 2 tablespoons of the butter in a soup pot and add the leek, garlic, thyme, salt, and 1/4 cup water. Cover and stew over medium heat for 5 minutes, then raise the heat, add the chopped mushrooms, and cook for 4 to 5 minutes. Stir in the flour, add the stock, and bring to a boil. Lower the heat and simmer, partially covered, for 20 minutes. Puree the soup, return it to the pot, and stir in the cream. Season with salt and pepper. Keep warm over low heat.

Slice the reserved mushrooms. Melt the remaining 1 tablespoon butter in a small skillet, add the mushrooms, and sauté over high heat until they begin to color, 4 to 5 minutes. Season with salt and pepper. Garnish the soup with the mushrooms and the chopped herbs and serve.

Jerusalem Artichoke Soup with Thyme and Mushroom Garnish

This flecked soup is based on a one I ate in a Dublin restaurant. It had been pureed with white beans, which you can do too for added body—or not. It's good both ways, and used alone, the tubers will provide ample substance. Like most soups, this is easily made vegan. Serves 4 Ⓥ

> 2 tablespoons olive oil or butter
> 1 heaping cup diced leek or chopped onion
> 1 pound Jerusalem artichokes, well scrubbed and coarsely chopped
> 1/2 teaspoon sea salt
> Freshly milled pepper
> 2 teaspoons fresh thyme or 1/2 teaspoon dried
> 1/2 cup cooked beans, such as navy beans, optional
> 4 cups Mushroom Stock (page 176) or Bean Broth or Stock (page 175)
> 1/2 cup milk or cream, if needed

Mushroom Garnish

> 2 tablespoons olive oil or butter
> 3/4 cup diced portabella or porcini mushrooms
> Sea salt and freshly milled pepper
> Fresh thyme leaves, if available

Warm the oil in a soup pot over medium until it shimmers. Add the leeks and Jerusalem artichokes, give them a stir and season with salt, pepper, and the thyme along with the cooked beans. Cook until everything smells good and the leeks have begun to soften some, about 6 minutes, then add the stock. Bring to a boil, then simmer, partially covered, until the tubers are tender, about 25 minutes. Let cook slightly, then puree until smooth but flecked with the skins of the tubers. Add the milk if needed to thin or enrich the soup some. Taste for salt and season with pepper.

Melt the oil or butter in a medium skillet over medium-high heat. When the oil shimmers, or the butter sizzles and bubbles, add the mushrooms and immediately stir them about. Season them with a few pinches of salt and cook until they give up their moisture, then taste, add more salt if needed, and season with pepper.

Serve the soup with a spoonful of mushrooms in each, a few fresh thyme leaves, and coarsely milled black pepper.

Parsnip Soup with Ginger and Parsnip "Croutons"

I always like a parsnip soup but not its dingy color. Mixing it with of carrots gives it a warm, golden glow. The parsnip trimmings and cilantro stems from the garnish make great contributions to the stock. Serves 4 to 6 ⓥ

3 large parsnips, about 2 pounds, peeled

6 cups Basic Vegetable Stock (page 175) or water

1/2 cup chopped cilantro stems, plus sprigs for garnish

4 thin slices ginger, unpeeled

3 tablespoons butter, ghee, or oil

1 large onion, roughly chopped

3/4 pound carrots, scrubbed and thinly sliced

1 1/2 teaspoons ground coriander

1 tablespoon white rice

1/2 teaspoon sea salt

1 cup milk, cream, or almond milk to thin the soup, as needed

Freshly milled pepper

Cilantro sprigs, for garnish

Cut two of the parsnips crosswise in half, then quarter each half lengthwise. Cut away most of the cores. Reserve the other parsnip. If you're making stock, include the parsnip trimmings, cilantro stems, and 1 slice of the ginger. Brown the vegetables in a little oil before adding the water to bring out their flavors.

Heat 2 tablespoons of the butter in a soup pot over medium heat, letting it brown a little. Add the vegetables, the remaining ginger, and the coriander. Cook, stirring frequently, until the onion and carrots have begun to color here and there. Add the rice and salt and cook a few minutes more. Add the strained stock and bring to a boil. Lower the heat and simmer, partially covered, until the vegetables are very soft, about 35 minutes. Remove the ginger, then puree the soup, leaving a little texture or not, as you wish. For a very smooth soup, pass it through a food mill or sieve. Thin if necessary with the milk.

Dice the third parsnip into little cubes and cook in the remaining butter in a skillet, stirring frequently, until golden and tender, about 8 minutes. Season with salt and pepper. Serve the soup with a spoonful of the parsnips added to each bowl. Garnish with sprigs of cilantro.

Roasted Red Pepper Soup with Polenta Croquettes

A multitude of garnishes can be used to finish this soup such as Pesto (page 50) and Olive–Rosemary Butter (page 46), but the crunchy polenta croutons are unexpected and good. Serves 4

2 1/2 tablespoons olive oil

1 onion, chopped

1 small potato, peeled and thinly sliced

2 cloves garlic, sliced

1 bay leaf

1 tablespoon chopped marjoram, plus extra for garnish

1 tablespoon tomato paste

3 or 4 large red bell peppers, roasted (see page 346) and coarsely chopped

1 teaspoon sweet or smoked paprika

1 teaspoon sea salt

4 cups water or Basic Vegetable Stock (page 175)

Freshly milled pepper

Balsamic or red wine vinegar to taste

Polenta Cheddar Croquettes (page 463), for garnish

Heat the oil in a soup pot and add the onion, potato, garlic, bay leaf, and marjoram. Sauté over high heat, stirring often, until the potato and onion begin to brown, about 12 minutes. Add the tomato paste and cook for 1 minute. Add the peppers, paprika, and salt. Pour in the water and scrape the bottom of the pot. Bring to a boil, then lower the heat and simmer, partially covered, for 25 minutes.

Remove the bay leaf and blend the soup until smooth. Taste for salt, season with pepper, and add a teaspoon or so of vinegar. Serve with the croquettes on top and a sprinkling of chopped marjoram.

Potato Soup

Fast and easy, potato soup costs practically nothing if you stick with ordinary potatoes, a little more if you use fancy ones. And if you've never made soup before, this one is simple to make and will build your confidence. Improvise by including sautéed mushrooms in winter or a diced ripe tomato in the summer. Serves 4 to 6 Ⓥ

2 tablespoons olive oil or butter

2 onions, finely diced

3 small bay leaves

2 pounds Russet potatoes, peeled, or scrubbed if organic

1¹/₂ teaspoons sea salt

Freshly milled pepper

2 tablespoons chopped parsley

Heat the oil in a heavy soup pot over medium heat, add the onions and bay leaves, and cook slowly. Meanwhile, quarter each potato lengthwise, then thinly slice. Irregular pieces are fine—the smaller ones will fall apart, giving body to the soup.

Add the potatoes, raise the heat, and sauté, stirring frequently, until the onions begin to color and a glaze builds up on the bottom of the pan, about 10 minutes. Add the salt and 1 cup water. Scrape the bottom of the pot to loosen the solids. Add 8 cups water and bring to a boil. Lower the heat and simmer, partially covered, until the potatoes are soft, about 30 minutes. Remove the bay leaves, taste for salt, season with pepper, and stir in the parsley. For a soup with more body, pass 1 or 2 cups through a food mill.

Potato and Roasted Garlic Soup: Roast 2 heads of unpeeled garlic cloves (they needn't be whole heads) as described on page 340. Add them, skins and all, to the onions and potatoes. Pass the finished soup through a food mill and add a few tablespoons cream. Garnish with snipped garlic chives or a pinch of truffle salt. A stunning soup.

Potato Soup with Mustard Greens: Virtually all greens are good with potatoes, but especially assertive mustard greens. Boil 1 bunch of mustard greens, without their stems, until tender and bright green, 10 to 15 minutes, then drain and coarsely chop them. Stir them into the soup along with 2 or 3 pinches of red pepper flakes or smoked salt. Serve with thin shavings of parmesan over each bowl, if desired. Ⓥ

TIPS FOR USING POTATOES IN SOUP

- Starchy baking potatoes (Russets) fall apart when boiled, whereas boiling potatoes or waxy varieties hold their shape. Many soup recipes call for boiling potatoes, but if you include a portion of baking potatoes, they'll break down and serve as a natural thickener.

- Much flavor resides in potato skins, which is why they're often left on. But peeled potatoes give the soup a more refined appearance. You can use the skins in the stock, but use organic potatoes because you can't scrub off the chemical residues from conventionally grown ones.

- Greening in the skin and flesh naturally occurs in potatoes through exposure to light. Eating the green parts can make you nauseated, but don't throw out the whole potato—just peel as thickly as necessary to get below the green and use the rest.

- I find the quickest way to peel a potato is with a sharp paring knife rather than a peeler. Cut a slice off each end, then cradle the potato in your hand and remove the skins with five or six swift, long strokes of the knife, going from one end to the other. You'll end up with a nice-looking, quickly peeled potato. This is also true for turnips and rutabagas.

- Use a food mill to puree potato soup. A blender or food processor can turn it into a gummy mass unless used with a light touch.

Potato and Parsley Soup with Parsley Root

Easy, fast, healthful, and good. Parsley roots, also called Hamburg parsley, are often available from November through January. They make a tremendous addition to this and other vegetable soups. Serves 4 to 6 Ⓥ

1¹/₂ pounds potatoes, peeled (can be a mixture of Russet and red potatoes)

2 parsley roots if available, scrubbed

1¹/₂ tablespoons butter or olive oil

6 shallots or 1 onion, finely chopped

2 bay leaves

¹/₂ cup dry white wine

2 cups chopped parsley

1¹/₂ teaspoons sea salt

6 cups water or Basic Vegetable Stock (page 175)

1/3 cup cream or additional water

Freshly milled pepper

Quarter the potatoes lengthwise and thinly slice. Grate the parsley roots. Melt the butter in a soup pot and add the potatoes, parsley roots, shallots, and bay leaves. Cook over medium heat for 5 to 7 minutes, stirring occasionally. Raise the heat, add the wine, and let it reduce until syrupy. Add 1 1/2 cups of the parsley, the salt, and the water; bring to a boil. Lower the heat and simmer, partially covered, until the potatoes have broken apart, about 30 minutes. Stir in the cream and remaining 1/2 cup parsley and heat through. Taste for salt and season with pepper. Remove the bay leaves and serve.

Bright Green Spinach and Pea Soup

Brief cooking preserves this pale soup's vivid green. I used to always puree this soup and garnish it with edible flowers, such as yellow calendula petals. But recently I rediscovered it when I pureed about half of it and left the remaining rounds of carrots and peas intact. Serves 4 to 6 (V)

2 tablespoons olive oil, butter, or a mixture

2 bunches green onions, including half of the greens, coarsely chopped

1 small onion, quartered and thinly sliced crosswise

3 carrots, scrubbed and thinly sliced into rounds

1 celery rib, thinly sliced

10 parsley sprigs, chopped

1 teaspoon dried basil, or 1 tablespoon chopped fresh basil, if available

1 teaspoon sea salt

1 large bunch spinach, stems removed

1 cup peas, fresh or frozen

Freshly milled pepper

Lemon juice, if needed

1 teaspoon cream per bowl, for garnish, optional

Calendula petals, for garnish

Warm the oil in a soup pot, add both onions, the carrots, celery, herbs, salt, and 1/2 cup water. Cover and stew for 5 minutes, then add 5 1/2 cups water and bring to a boil. Lower the heat and simmer, uncovered, for 20 minutes. Add the spinach and peas. Poke the spinach leaves into the soup and cook until they turn bright green, 2 to 3 minutes.

Remove from the heat and blend the soup until perfectly smooth, leaving some unblended, or not, as you prefer. Taste for salt, season with pepper, and stir in enough lemon juice, starting with 1/2 teaspoon, to bring up the flavors if needed. Serve immediately with a swirl of cream in each bowl and a few petals floating on top.

Summer Squash Soups

Summer squashes are unassertive, but you can encourage their hidden strengths either by stewing them with seasonings or sautéing them over high heat until they brown a bit. Although a good basic stock provides depth, you can get away with water if your seasonings and garnishes are bright and fresh. Here's a good place to improvise with such finishing touches such as Sorrel Puree (page 34), as well as Pesto (page 50), Salsa Verde (page 48), Cilantro Salsa (page 49), herb butters (pages 45 to 46), and herb salts (pages 67 to 69)—all in chapter 3. Although I've emphasized particular varieties, summer squashes are basically interchangeable.

Summer Squash Soup with Salsa Verde

Serves 4 to 6 (V)

2 tablespoons olive oil or butter

1 1/4 pounds zucchini, crookneck, or pattypan squash

1 large onion, chopped

1 bunch green onions, including half of the greens, chopped

2 tablespoons raw white rice

1/2 cup chopped parsley

6 cups Basic Vegetable Stock (page 175), or water

1 1/2 teaspoons sea salt

Freshly milled pepper

Lemon juice

1/4 cup Salsa Verde (page 48) or Pesto (page 50), to finish

Heat the oil in a soup pot and add the vegetables, rice, and parsley. Stir to coat with the oil, then add 1/2 cup of the stock, cover, and stew for 10 minutes over medium heat. Add the remaining 5 1/2 cups stock and the salt and bring to a boil. Lower the heat and simmer, partially covered, for 25 minutes. Let cool briefly, then puree. Taste for salt, season with pepper, and add lemon juice to taste. Finish the soup by swirling in the salsa verde.

Zucchini-Cilantro Soup: A soup for cilantro lovers. Replace the parsley with 1 cup cilantro leaves. Puree the soup with a corn tortilla and finish with a squeeze of lime and a spoonful of sour cream.

Summer Squash Soup with Vegetable Garnishes: In a small skillet, briefly sauté ¹/₂ cup finely diced zucchini, the kernels from 1 ear of corn, and 4 thinly sliced green onions, including an inch of the greens, in 1 teaspoon butter or olive oil. Garnish the soup with the vegetables and finely chopped herbs. (V)

Curried Crookneck Soup: Curry is especially good with crookneck squash. If you have time, make the Stock for Curried Dishes (page 175). Sauté the onion and squash in ghee or coconut oil over medium-high heat until they've begun to color, about 10 minutes, then add 1 tablespoon curry powder and proceed as described. Thin the soup if desired with coconut, rice, or almond milk and garnish with cilantro leaves and diced jalapeño. (V)

Yellow Squash Soup with Saffron and Basil

Some might describe yellow squash as bland but others would say not. It's delicate and definitely squashy, but in this recipe, the saffron, basil, and umami boost from nutritional yeast make it something to reckon with. Serves 4 to 6 (V)

- 1 tablespoon olive oil or butter
- 1 small onion, finely diced
- 2 teaspoons nutritional yeast
- 1 pinch saffron threads
- 1 heaping tablespoon slivered basil leaves
- 4 cups plus ¹/₃ cup water, Basic Vegetable Stock (page 175) or Bean Broth or Stock (page 175)
- 1¹/₂ pounds yellow squash, quartered lengthwise and diced
- 1 teaspoon sea salt
- ¹/₂ cup cooked couscous, rice, or quinoa, to finish

Warm the oil in a soup pot. When hot, add the onion and cook over medium-low heat for 5 minutes. Stir in the yeast, saffron, and half the basil leaves, cook for another minute, then add the ¹/₃ cup water. Simmer until the water has reduced to the point of being syrupy.

Add the squash and the 4 cups water and bring to a boil. Lower the heat and simmer, uncovered, for 20 minutes. Remove and puree 2 cups of the soup, then return it to the pot. Season with the salt, and serve with a spoonful of grain and the remaining basil in each bowl.

Summer Tomato Soup

This is the sheer essence of summer and tomato. All you need are shallots, butter or olive oil, lots of ripe tomatoes, and an unattended hour. The process is very similar to making fresh tomato sauce. Serves 4 to 6 (V)

- 3 tablespoons butter or olive oil
- 1 cup diced shallots, 8 to 12
- 5 pounds ripe, red, juicy tomatoes, rinsed and cut into big pieces
- 1 teaspoon sea salt
- Freshly milled pepper

Melt the butter in a wide soup pot over low heat. Add the shallots and let them cook while you prepare the tomatoes. Add the tomatoes to the pot along with the salt and ¹/₂ cup water. Cover and cook for about 45 minutes. Give the pot a stir every now and then as you pass through the kitchen to make sure the tomatoes aren't sticking, but if you've used juicy ones, there should be plenty of liquid. Pass the tomatoes through a food mill into a clean pot. You should have about 4 cups of soup. Taste for salt and season with freshly milled pepper.

At this point, you can do several things. You can serve small bowls of the soup just as it is, or you can add a few tablespoons of cream to make gorgeous cream of tomato soup. You can swirl in a tablespoon of butter flavored with shallots and dill, pesto, or basil puree. And if you long for texture in your soup, you can add a few delicate cubed croutons crisped in a little butter. This is also exquisite chilled, served with crème fraîche or diced avocado and lime juice.

Winter Squash and Pumpkin Soups

The squashes to use for these golden soups are small hubbards, butternut, and any of the deep-orange fleshed varieties such as Honey Delight, kabocha, Marina di Chioggia. For pumpkins, use those intended for cooking rather than carving. Except for butternut, winter squashes are difficult to peel, so they're halved and baked first—this can be done well in advance. Most winter squash soups don't require a stock, but a quick stock, using the scooped-out seeds, is so easy to make and so flavorful that I generally make one.

Winter Vegetable Chowder

This is a wonderful soup—light but sustaining and full of flavor. The milk is steeped with aromatics, and the vegetables are cooked in water. The whole thing is ladled over cheese-covered toast, which falls apart and thickens the soup. (To make a dairy-free version, use plant milk, cook the vegetables in olive oil, and omit the cheese.) Serves 4 to 6 (V)

Milk

2 cups milk, preferably whole, or plant milk

3 large parsley sprigs

1/2 teaspoon dried thyme

2 bay leaves

1/2 onion, sliced

10 peppercorns, lightly crushed

5 juniper berries, lightly crushed

Soup

2 tablespoons butter or oil

2 large leeks, white parts plus an inch of the greens, chopped

4 cups chopped winter vegetables—turnips, carrots, celery or celery root, rutabagas, a little parsnip

3 boiling potatoes, about 12 ounces, peeled and diced

2 small bay leaves

2 tablespoons chopped parsley

1 1/2 teaspoons sea salt

2 tablespoons flour

Freshly milled pepper

4 to 6 large slices sourdough or country-style bread, toasted

Grated Gruyère or parmesan cheese, for toast

Chopped parsley, tarragon, or lovage, to finsh

Put everything for the milk in a saucepan, bring it to a boil, then turn off the heat. Cover and set aside while you prepare the vegetables.

Melt the butter in a soup pot over low heat. Add the vegetables, bay leaves, parsley, and the salt. Cover and cook for 10 minutes. Stir in the flour and add 5 cups water; bring to a boil. Lower the heat and simmer, partially covered, until the vegetables are tender, about 25 minutes. Pour the milk through a strainer right into the soup. Taste for salt and season with pepper. To serve, lay a piece of toast in each bowl, cover it with grated cheese, ladle the soup on top, and sprinkle with parsley.

Winter Squash Potage

This is so simple it sounds as if it might not be worth making, but it is pure squash, quickly made, and can be transformed using any of the herbs and sauces suggested on page 394. Serves 4 (V)

3 scant cups cooked winter squash, such as butternut

2 tablespons olive oil

1 large onion, cut in 1/2-inch dice (about 2 cups)

1 teaspoon sea salt

4 cups water or Quick Stock (page 174)

Freshly milled pepper

If you haven't already, bake, steam, or pressure-cook 2 pounds winter squash as described on page 395. Scrape the flesh from the skin and discard it along with seeds, unless you wish to use it to make a Quick Stock (page 174).

Warm the oil in a soup pot over medium heat. When hot, add the onion, give it a stir, then cover the pan and cook for 10 minutes, checking occasionally and giving it a stir so that it softens and turns golden, but doesn't brown or burn.

Add the squash, salt, and water. As the water comes to a boil, break up the clumps of squash with a spoon. Reduce the heat so that the soup simmers, then cook partially covered, for 25 minutes. It should be very orange, silky looking, but with some texture. Taste for salt and season with pepper, then serve.

Winter Squash Potage with Cream and Smoked Salt: Swirl 1 teaspoon of cream into each bowl and add a pinch of smoked salt or smoked paprika. These simple additions completely elevate the soup.

Winter Squash Soup with Lemongrass and Coconut Milk

Dried galangal looks like wood chips, but it imparts a delicious flavor to the stock. Butternut squash is easy to peel, so it's not prebaked. Serves 4 to 6 Ⓥ

6 cups Stock for Curried Dishes (page 175)

2½ pounds butternut squash, peeled and seeded

1 lemongrass stalk, the tender middle section minced

5 pieces galangal, or 3 slices ginger

For garnish: 2 teaspoons each finely chopped mint, basil, and cilantro

1 tablespoon roasted peanut oil

1 large onion, diced

2 jalapeño chiles, seeded and diced

1 large clove garlic, crushed

1 cup unsweetened coconut or almond milk

Sea salt

Juice of 2 limes

Include the squash skins and seeds, lemongrass trimmings, galangal, and any trimmings from the herb garnish in the stock.

Coarsely chop the squash. You should have about 4 cups. Heat the oil in a soup pot, then add the squash, onion, half the chiles, the minced lemongrass, and the garlic. Cook over medium heat for 10 minutes, stirring occasionally. Add the strained stock and bring it to a boil. Lower the heat and simmer, partially covered, until the squash is tender, about 30 minutes. Puree the soup, then return it to the stove and stir in the coconut milk. Taste for salt and add lime juice to sharpen the flavors. Serve garnished with the fresh herbs and the remaining chile.

Winter Squash Soup with Cinnamon, Cloves, and Mint

Hard-skinned squash often has dense, convoluted surfaces that are difficult to work with. Halving the squash first and baking it in the oven provides an easy way to get at the delicious meat inside. While the squash is baking, you can prepare the rest of the soup—even the rest of the meal. Cooked with the same seasonings but less liquid, this squash makes a delicious puree. Serves 4 to 6 Ⓥ

2 pounds dense winter squash such as buttercup or kabocha

Oil, for the squash

12 coriander seeds

12 peppercorns

2 cups milk (dairy or almond) or half-and-half

1 (3-inch) cinnamon stick

8 cloves

A small handful mint leaves, roughly chopped

1 jalapeño chile

2 tablespoons butter or coconut oil

1 onion, finely diced

1 teaspoon sea salt

1 teaspoon finely chopped mint, for garnish

1 teaspoon finely chopped cilantro, for garnish

Preheat the oven to 375°F. Cut the squash in half using a cleaver or a heavy chef's knife. Scoop out the seeds and brush the surfaces lightly with oil. Place them face down on a sheet pan and bake them until they're soft and tender, about 30 minutes, depending on the type of squash used. When cooked and cool enough handle, scoop out the flesh.

While the squash is baking, make an infusion with the spices, herbs, and milk. First, lightly crush the coriander seeds and peppercorns, then put them in a saucepan with the milk, cinnamon, cloves, mint leaves, and chile. Heat slowly, turning off the heat just before it comes to a boil. Set aside to steep until needed.

Melt the butter in a soup pot and add the onion. Cook over medium heat until the onions begin to soften, about 5 minutes. Add the squash and 4 cups water and season with the salt. Bring to a boil, then lower the heat and simmer about 25 minutes. Pass the soup through a food mill or puree, leaving as much texture as you like. Return the soup to the stove and add the steeped milk, pouring it through a strainer. Taste for salt and add more if needed. Gently reheat the soup, then serve garnished with the mint and cilantro.

Winter Squash Soup with Fried Sage Leaves

The technique used to make this soup can be repeated for other soups, the seasonings—be they sweet or spicy—varied to suit your tastes. Although the soup is good without it, the cheese adds a flavor note that punctuates the natural sweetness of the squash. Serves 4 to 6 Ⓥ

2¹/₂ to 3 pounds winter squash

¹/₄ cup olive oil, plus extra for the squash

6 cloves garlic, unpeeled

12 whole sage leaves, plus 2 tablespoons chopped

2 onions, finely chopped

Chopped leaves from 4 thyme sprigs or ¹/₄ teaspoon dried

¹/₄ cup chopped parsley

1¹/₂ teaspoons sea salt

8 cups water or Quick Stock (page 174) made with 10 cups water

¹/₂ cup fontina, pecorino, or ricotta salata, diced into small cubes, optional

Freshly milled pepper

Preheat the oven to 375°F. Halve the squash and scoop out the seeds. Brush the surfaces with oil, stuff the cavities with the garlic, and place the squash cut sides down on a baking sheet. Bake until tender when pressed with a finger, about 30 minutes.

Meanwhile, in a small skillet, heat the ¹/₄ cup oil until very hot, then drop in the whole sage leaves and fry until speckled and dark, about 1 minute. Set the leaves aside on a paper towel and transfer the oil to a wide soup pot. Add the onions, chopped sage, thyme, and parsley and cook over medium heat until the onions have begun to brown around the edges, 12 to 15 minutes. Scoop the squash flesh into the pot along with any juices that have accumulated in the pan. Peel the garlic and add it to the pot along with the salt and the water and bring to a boil. Lower the heat and simmer, partially covered, for 25 minutes. If the soup becomes too thick, simply add more water to thin it out. Taste for salt.

Depending on the type of squash you've used, the soup will be smooth or rough. Puree or pass it through a food mill if you want a more refined soup. Ladle it into bowls and distribute the cheese over the top.

Garnish each bowl with the fried sage leaves, add pepper, and serve.

A Cream of Tomato Soup for Winter

No one wants to eat hot soup when tomatoes are in season, but with so many people putting up tomatoes, this old standard should resurface as a respectable winter soup. Indeed, tomato bisques were cropping up in America's community cookbooks long before winter tomatoes garnered their bad reputation. Cream of tomato soup and a cheese dream sandwich was lunch in the fifties, when school kids still went home to eat. If you eat lunch at home, try it—it's still a great combination. Serves 4

2¹/₂ tablespoons butter

¹/₂ cup diced celery

¹/₂ cup diced yellow onion

Pinch ground cloves

1¹/₂ teaspoons dried basil, crushed between your fingers

2 tablespoons flour

2 (15-ounces) cans tomatoes, or 4 cups home-canned tomatoes in their juice or in sauce

Tiny pinch baking soda

2¹/₂ cups Basic Vegetable Stock (page 175) or water

1¹/₂ cups milk or light cream

Sea salt and freshly milled pepper

Tomato paste, if needed to bolster the flavor

Melt the butter in a soup pot over medium heat. Add the celery, onion, cloves, and basil. Cook, stirring occasionally, until the onion is limp, about 5 minutes. Stir in the flour, cover, and cook for a minute or so, then add the tomatoes, baking soda, and stock. Cover and simmer for 20 minutes.

Let cool briefly, then puree in a blender, in batches if necessary, until smooth. Return to the pot, add the milk or cream, and season to taste with salt and pepper. If the soup is too thick, thin it with additional milk, cream, or stock. If the tomato flavor isn't as rich as you'd like, stir in a little tomato paste to bring up the flavor. Reheat and serve piping hot with pepper ground into each bowl.

Fideos—A Mexican Dry Soup

This is too soupy to be pasta, too dry to be soup, and certainly too good to leave alone. A good supper or brunch dish—or even a side dish. Both of the suggested stocks are good. The Red Stock, however, has more body and deeper flavor. This is especially good to make when fresh vegetables are hard to come by. Serves 4 to 6

4 to 5 cups Stock for Mexican Soups and Stews (page 175) or Red Stock (page 176)

2 ancho chiles, stems and seeds removed

2 tablespoons safflower oil

8 ounces capellini, spaghettini, or skinny egg noodles, broken into 2- to 4-inch lengths

Sea salt and freshly milled pepper

1/3 cup crumbled feta cheese

1/3 to 2/3 cup grated Monterey Jack

1/2 cup sour cream or crème fraîche

1/3 cup chopped cilantro or parsley, for garnish

Make either of the stocks. Simmer with the chiles for 15 minutes, then puree in a blender until smooth, then strain again.

Heat the oil in a wide skillet over medium heat. Add the noodles and cook, stirring constantly, until browned, 3 or 4 minutes.

Add 3 1/2 cups of the stock to the skillet and bring to a boil. Simmer, stirring frequently, until most of the liquid has been absorbed and the noodles are cooked through, about 10 minutes. If they're still a little crunchy by the time the liquid is absorbed, spoon over another 1/4 cup stock and continue cooking. Meanwhile, preheat the broiler.

Season the noodles with salt and pepper and sprinkle the cheeses over the top. Broil until the cheeses have melted. Stir the sour cream with a fork to loosen it, then drizzle it over the top. Sprinkle with cilantro and serve.

Tortilla Soup

This brick-red broth with its cluster of garnishes is roundly flavorful, even without chicken stock. You do have to make a stock, but it's not a big deal—just your Basic Vegetable Stock (page 175) plus a few extra ingredients. And although fresh tomatoes are standard, this makes a warming winter soup, and I've had great results using diced canned tomatoes. Serves 4 (V)

Broth

6 cups Red Stock (page 176)

2 to 3 tablespoons safflower oil

1 1/2 onions, sliced into 1/2-inch rounds

4 large cloves garlic, unpeeled

2 jalapeño chiles

2 cups canned tomato sauce or 2 1/2 pounds fresh Roma tomatoes

1 teaspoon pureed chipotle chile, or to taste

Sea salt

Garnishes

2 pasilla chiles, stem and seeds removed

1/4 cup chopped cilantro, plus whole leaves for garnish

1 avocado, diced

Tortilla Strips (page 40) made from 8 corn tortillas

Crumbled queso fresco or feta cheese, optional

1 lime, quartered

Start making the red stock. You can prepare everything else while the stock is simmering

Preheat the broiler. Using about half of the oil, lightly oil the onions, garlic cloves, chiles, and fresh tomatoes or sauce. Put them on a sheet pan and broil 4 to 5 inches below the heat. When the onions brown, turn them over and brown the second side. Turn the chiles when they blister. Remove the garlic when browned, then peel. Turn the tomatoes several times so that the skins pucker and brown in places. Remove individual vegetables as they finish cooking. Puree everything in a blender until the sauce is as smooth as possible. (If using canned tomato sauce, puree them with the other vegetables plus an extra 1/2 cup water to thin the mixture.)

Heat the remaining oil in a wide soup pot over medium-high heat. Add the puree and cook, stirring, until it has thickened, about 5 minutes. Add the strained stock, then simmer, covered, for 25 minutes. Stir in the chipotle chile and taste for salt. At this point, strain the broth if you like a refined, thin soup. If you prefer it thicker and with a little texture, as I do, leave it as is.

To toast the chiles for the garnish, put them in a heavy skillet over medium heat. Press down on them until they're fragrant and begin to blister in places. Turn and repeat on the second side, but don't let them burn. When cool, tear or cut them into strips.

Just before serving, add the chile strips and chopped cilantro to the broth and cook for 1 minute. Ladle the broth into bowls and add the avocado, tortilla strips, and crumbled cheese. Garnish with cilantro leaves and serve with the lime wedges.

MAKING SOUPS FROM LEFTOVERS

A cup of pureed vegetables or legumes can make a little soup for one or two people. Vegetable and bean purees, cooked dried beans, plus sautéed greens, roasted peppers, grilled corn, tomato sauce, and a bit of pesto all are good examples of the kinds of leftovers to pay attention to.

A 10-Minute Soup from Vegetable Puree

Here's an example of how to turn a simple vegetable puree into a soup in about 10 minutes. Serves 1 or 2 Ⓥ

2 teaspoons olive oil or butter
2 green onions, including some of the greens, thinly sliced
1 small potato, peeled, very thinly sliced, and chopped
Sea salt and freshly milled pepper
1 cup pureed vegetable, such as broccoli
Water or milk to thin the soup, if needed

Warm the oil in a small saucepan, add the onions and potato, season with a pinch of salt, and sauté over brisk heat, stirring constantly, for 2 minutes to scar the vegetables. Add 2 cups water, scrape the pan to dislodge any tasty bits of potatoes, and bring to a boil. Lower the heat and simmer, covered, until the potato is tender, 8 to 10 minutes. Stir in the puree and add water or milk to thin if needed. Heat through, taste for salt, season with pepper, and serve.

Turnip Soup with Gruyère Croutons

Turnips are a hard sell, but they make one of the best soups I know. Take advantage of turnips with nice fresh greens the moment you see them. Their peppery bite offsets the natural sweetness of the roots. To ensure a good soup when using turnips that aren't at their peak, thickly peel them, slice them into rounds, and blanch for 1 minute in boiling salted water. Drain and rinse. This keeps them nice and sweet. Broccoli rabe or mustard greens can easily take the place of turnip greens. Serves 4 to 6

4 to 6 medium turnips, 1¹/₂ to 2 pounds, with their greens if available
3 small yellow-fleshed potatoes
2 tablespoons butter
2 leeks, white parts only, thinly sliced
1 clove garlic, minced
¹/₄ cup chopped parsley
4 thyme sprigs or ¹/₄ teaspoon dried
1¹/₂ teaspoons sea salt
6 cups water or Basic Vegetable Stock (page 175)
¹/₂ cup milk or half-and-half
Freshly milled white pepper
Cheese croutons made with Gruyère cheese, 2 per serving

Peel the turnips and potatoes, quarter, and thinly slice them. Discard the stems and any yellowed leaves from the greens. Wash the remaining leaves well.

Melt the butter in a soup pot over medium heat. Add the turnips, potatoes, leeks, garlic, parsley, and thyme. Cook for about 5 minutes, then add the salt and the water and bring to a boil. Lower the heat and simmer, partially covered, until the vegetables are tender, about 25 minutes. Puree all or just part of the soup, depending on whether you like a smooth soup or one with some texture. Stir in the milk.

While the soup is cooking, chop the greens into small pieces. There should be about 2 cups, although more is fine. Simmer them in salted water until they're tender, then drain and add them to the finished soup. Taste for salt, season with pepper, and serve with two cheese croutons in each bowl or on the side.

Soups Starring Beans and Grains

These solid citizens make especially nourishing, comforting, and filling soups—the perfect medium to persuade Americans to embrace beans and grains. Mixed with vegetables and aromatic seasonings, the plump tenderness of beans and the robust, chewy textures of grains are easily appreciated.

BEANS FROM SCRATCH: There are three advantages to cooking your own beans: by the time they're done they're surrounded with a broth that serves as the stock; you can use the exciting heirloom varieties that can't be bought canned; and home-cooked beans taste better and aren't mushy. Canned beans, of course, don't require thinking ahead, and there are times when they can nicely round out a vegetable soup. (The organic brands, such as Eden Foods, are quite good.) While beans take time to cook, the time is unattended for the most part. And with a pressure cooker, it's possible to have soup beans—and broth—in just 30 minutes.

COMBINING GRAINS AND BEANS: We usually think of bean soups in terms of a single legume, such as black bean chili or lentil soup, but older culinary cultures often mix beans or beans and grains within a single soup. Their contrasting shapes and textures make them much more interesting to eat. Having some cooked beans in the freezer and drawing on canned chickpeas and quicker-cooking lentils makes combining beans and grains easy. Since rice, bulgur, and other grains can cook right in the soup, you may have only one legume to cook separately from scratch.

USING THE PRESSURE COOKER: These recipes can easily be adapted to cooking under pressure, an advantage because a pressure cooker cooks beans and large grains in about a third of the time it takes to simmer them. There are several approaches.

One is to cook the beans, along with aromatics and a few teaspoons of oil (to prevent skins from clogging the gauge), and salt in the pressure cooker while you cut the soup vegetables. Then, when the beans are done, you add them and their broth to the vegetables.

A second approach is to sauté the vegetables in the pressure cooker pot, then add the beans and liquid and cook the whole soup under pressure. If the soup contains an element that should be fresh, like a garnish of diced tomato, add it after the soup is cooked.

An alternative approach is to cover the beans with boiling water, let them stand for an hour for a quick soak, then drain. Add them to the pressure cooker with fresh water and cook on high for 20 minutes before releasing quickly. As they may not be done, either continue cooking them at a simmer until they are, or return them to pressure for 5 minutes longer. The advantage of presoaking the beans is that they will have absorbed the liquid so that you can use less water when cooking them, which gives you more flavor.

Or, put rinsed beans into the pressure cooker without soaking them first. As they will absorb 3 cups of water per 1 cup of beans, make sure to have that much plus extra to make them soupy. Cook on high for 25 minutes, then check to see if they're done.

One word of caution: Cooking time for beans is affected by the age of the bean and the hardness of the water. Start with the given time, then release the pressure and check. If the beans are still hard, put the lid back on and return the pot to pressure—it will go up quickly—then cook for another 5 minutes and check again.

USING THE SLOW COOKER: To me, the main reason for using the slow cooker with bean soups is that you can put everything in the cooker, turn it to low, be away for the day, and come back to a finished soup. As the vegetables tend to get a little too soft, I complement the soup upon serving with a bright green parsley pesto or salsa verde. Its vivid freshness wakes up the soft and muted tones of the soup. An example of such a soup is the White Bean and Winter Squash Soup on page 198.

SOME TIPS FOR MAKING BEAN SOUPS

CLEANING: Most beans and lentils are well cleaned today, but it's a good idea to spread them out and look for (and remove) any little stones, clumps of earth, chaff, and so on. Even a tiny stone can crack a tooth.

SOAKING: When you're not using a pressure cooker, soaking beans and lentils shortens the cooking time considerably. Soak beans for 4 hours to overnight, or cover them with boiling water and soak just for 1 hour. Lentils benefit by being soaked too, but an hour is sufficient.

COOKING: After draining the beans, cover them with fresh water and bring to a boil. During the first 10 minutes a scum may form on the surface. Simply skim it off.

SALTING: People are divided about salt. Some say it makes no difference when you add it, others do. I don't usually add salt until beans have begun to soften, except in the case of lentils and peas, or when using the pressure cooker. Then I add it at the beginning.

PUREEING: To give bean soups a creamy background, puree all or just a portion of the beans and return them to the pot.

FINISHING: Croutons, extra-virgin olive oil, herb and olive purees, herb butters, and seasoned or smoked salts are all excellent ingredients for finishing bean soups. Cooked pasta adds texture and interest, as do greens of all kinds.

STORING: Beans sour more quickly than other foods, but a bean soup will keep for about 4 days in the refrigerator. To reheat, bring soup to a full boil. Give it a sniff. If it's spoiled, you'll notice the slightly sour scent of fermentation. In very hot weather, put soaking beans in the refrigerator.

ADDING GRAINS: Don't forget, wheat berries, spelt, farro, and other large grains take about 2 hours to cook on top of the stove or 30 minutes in the pressure cooker. Brown rice, Wehani, and wild rice take 35 to 45 minutes on the stove. Tiny grains, like amaranth and quinoa, cook in only 15 minutes. All should be cooked separately then added to the soup so that they don't drink up the broth. The same is true for pasta.

Pinto Bean Soup

Pinto beans are delicious plain or lavishly garnished. Plain, these are the beans to use for refried beans. Many cooks prefer using the pressure cooker to produce silky-smooth beans, others wouldn't dream of it. This choice is yours.

Serves 6 to 8 (V)

---

2 cups pinto beans, soaked for 4 hours or overnight

1 small onion, finely diced

3 cloves garlic, minced

1 teaspoon dried oregano, preferably Mexican

2 teaspoons dried or fresh epazote

Sea salt

For garnish: slivered green onions or finely diced white onion, diced jalapeño chile, chopped cilantro or mint, sour cream, Tortilla Strips (page 40)

Drain the beans, cover them with 8 cups water, and boil for 10 minutes. Add the onion, garlic, oregano, and epazote. Lower the heat and simmer, partially covered, until the beans are tender, about $1^1/_2$ hours. Season with salt and serve plain, with the broth, or with two or three of the garnishes. If using a pressure cooker, cook everything together on high for 25 minutes, then release.

Smooth Pinto Bean Soup with Chile, Pine Nuts, and Mint: Puree the cooked beans with their broth until smooth and return them to the pot. Thin, if needed, with 1 cup milk or cream and stir in chipotle chile, ground or in adobo sauce, to taste, starting with a teaspoon. Taste for salt. Serve garnished with snipped chives, chopped mint, and toasted pine nuts.

Pinto or Anasazi Bean Soup with Roasted Tomatoes and Garlic: Make the soup using pinto or Anasazi beans. Puree a portion of the beans and return them to the pot. Make the Grilled Tomato Sauce (page 55), including frying it at the end, as described. Stir this into the beans and reheat. Garnish each bowl with a dollop of sour cream or grated Muenster, if desired, and serve with tortillas. (V)

White Bean and Winter Squash Soup in the Slow Cooker with Parsley Sauce

Most all bean soups can be made this way. The vegetables are added with the beans, which means they'll get quite soft. If you want a crisper texture at the end, consider garnishing the soup with crisp, toasted bread crumbs along with the parsley sauce. Serves 6

1/2 cup navy beans or cannellini beans, rinsed

2 to 3 cups 1-inch cubes of winter squash, such as butternut

1 onion, diced

2 celery stalks, diced

1 large clove garlic, slivered

2 sage leaves

1 thyme sprig

1 tablespoon olive oil

1 teaspoon sea salt

8 cups water or a stock, made from the squash trimmings, garlic, sage, thyme, and parsley stems

Freshly milled pepper

Parsley Sauce (recipe follows)

Freshly grated parmesan cheese, to finish

Put the beans in a slow cooker with the squash, onion, celery, garlic, sage, and thyme. Add the olive oil, the salt, and the water. Cover and cook on low for 7 hours, or longer if the beans aren't done. Taste for salt and season with pepper. Add more liquid, if needed.

Make the sauce just before serving the soup. Serve the soup and add a spoonful to each bowl and additional parmesan cheese.

Parsley Sauce

1 cup roughly chopped parsley leaves

1 clove garlic

3 tablespoons olive oil, as needed

1/4 cup freshly grated parmesan cheese

Sea salt

Chop the parsley leaves with the garlic until fine. Put in a bowl or a mortar, stir in the olive oil and cheese, adding enough oil to give it the consistency of thin paste. Taste for salt and season accordingly.

Barley Soup with Caramelized Onions and Pecorino Cheese

This recipe is essentially unchanged from the original edition of this book, except that it's scaled down a bit for practicality and that it uses an organic commercial mushroom stock, which gives it a good mushroom flavor. Barley absorbs liquids to a vast degree, so don't be surprised if you find you have to thin your soup, especially any leftovers, with additional stock or water. Serves 4

2 tablespoons olive oil

1 large onion, diced into in 1/2-inch squares

1 tablespoons tomato paste

1 heaping teaspoon minced rosemary

1/2 cup diced celery root or celery

2 carrots, diced

1/2 cup barley, rinsed

4 cups commercial mushroom stock or water

Sea salt and freshly milled pepper

1/2 cup grated or shaved pecorino cheese

Warm the oil in a heavy soup pot. Add the onion, cover, and cook over low heat for 20 to 30 minutes until golden. The lid will create steam so that you don't have to stir the onions constantly, but do check them a few times as they cook.

Add the tomato paste and rosemary and cook for 1 minute more, working the paste into the onions. Add the vegetables, barley, and stock and bring to a boil. Lower the heat and simmer, partially covered, until the barley and vegetables are done, about 25 minutes. Taste for salt, season with freshly ground pepper, and serve with cheese grated over the top.

Soups from Scratch

Lentil Soups

Savored over a large part of the world, lentil soup is one of the best-liked, easiest-to-cook, and most varied of soups. The earthy flavor of lentils is complemented by Indian spices, Western herbs, cream, tomato, greens of all kinds, and anything slightly tart, such as sorrel and lemon.

German brown lentils (actually greenish) are the ones we see most commonly, and they make fine soups. But the tiny French slate-green Le Puy lentils, now available in bulk at many natural foods stores, make the prettiest soups and salads, as they don't fall apart but keep their shape. They're entirely worth the slight extra cost, and in my kitchen they are the lentil of choice. Black Beluga lentils behave similarly. Indian red split lentils turn yellow when cooked and fall into a puree, as do other split lentils, which makes them ideal for smooth lentil soups. The tiny brown Pardina lentils are especially warm and earthy flavored. And there are many kinds of lentils besides these.

It is commonly said that lentils don't need to be soaked, and that they cook in just 25 minutes. This has never been my experience. I do soak lentils, for at least an hour, possibly two, and then they cook in those promised shortened times, and I think they taste better. Even a modest soak in hot water can make a difference. However, if you live at sea level and have very soft water, you might find that soaking renders them too soft. You'll just have to give it a try and see what works best.

Lentil Minestrone

This is one of my all-time favorite soups. It's better when cooked ahead of time, but add the cooked pasta and greens just before serving so that they retain their color and texture. Serves 4 to 6 (V)

2 tablespoons olive oil, plus extra-virgin to finish

2 cups finely chopped onion

2 tablespoons tomato paste

1/4 cup chopped parsley

4 cloves garlic, chopped

3 carrots, diced

1 cup diced celery or celery root

2 teaspoons sea salt

1 cup French green lentils, sorted and soaked for 1 hour

Aromatics: 2 bay leaves, 8 parsley sprigs, 6 thyme sprigs

9 cups water or Basic Vegetable Stock (page 175)

Freshly milled pepper

Mushroom soy sauce, if needed

1 bunch greens—mustard, broccoli rabe, chard, or spinach

2 cups cooked small pasta shells, orecchiette, or other favorite shape

Thin shavings of Parmigiano-Reggiano, to finish, optional

Heat the oil in a wide soup pot with the onion. Sauté over high heat, stirring frequently, until lightly browned, about 10 minutes. Add the tomato paste, parsley, garlic, vegetables, and salt and cook 3 minutes more. Add the lentils, aromatics, and water and bring to a boil. Lower the heat and simmer, partially covered, for 30 minutes. Taste for salt and season with pepper. If it needs more depth, add mushroom soy sauce to taste, starting with 1 tablespoon. (The soup may seem bland at this point, but the flavors will come together when the soup is finished.) Remove the aromatics.

Boil the greens in salted water until they're tender and bright green, then chop them coarsely. Just before serving, add the greens and the pasta to the soup and heat through. Serve with olive oil drizzled into each bowl, a generous grind of pepper, and the cheese.

Hearty Lentil Soup

Mustard and vinegar sharpen the flavors in this familiar, hearty soup. Serves 4 to 6 (V)

2 tablespoons olive oil

2 cups finely diced onions

3 large cloves garlic

1 1/2 teaspoons sea salt

3 tablespoons tomato paste

1/3 cup finely diced celery

1/3 cup finely diced carrot

2 bay leaves

1/2 cup chopped parsley

1 1/2 cups green or brown lentils, soaked for 1 hour

1 tablespoon Dijon mustard

1 tablespoon sherry vinegar or red wine vinegar

Freshly milled pepper

Chopped celery leaves and parsley, for garnish

Heat the oil in a soup pot over high heat. Add the onion, and sauté until it begins to color around the edges, about 7 minutes. Meanwhile mince or pound the garlic in a mortar with 1 teaspoon of the salt. Work the tomato paste into the onion, then add the garlic, celery, carrot, bay leaves, and parsley and cook for 3 minutes. Add the lentils, 8 cups water, and the remaining $1/2$ teaspoon salt and bring to a boil. Lower the heat and simmer, partially covered, until the lentils are tender, 25 to 35 minutes.

Stir in the mustard and vinegar. Taste and add more of either as needed. Check the salt, season with plenty of freshly milled pepper, and serve, garnished with the chopped celery leaves and parsley. The longer the soup sits before serving, the better it will taste.

Cream of Lentil Soup with Croutons: Cook until the lentils are soft and mushy, an extra 10 minutes or so. Remove the bay leaves, puree the soup, then pass it through a food mill. Return to the stove and stir in enough milk or light cream to thin it to the right consistency. Serve garnished with chopped celery leaves and small croutons crisped in olive oil or butter.

Lentil and Celery Root Soup: Celery root lends a clean, bright note to earthy lentils. Scrub and peel a smallish root—8 ounces or so. Dice a quarter of the root into fine cubes and set them aside in a bowl with the juice of $1/2$ lemon and water to cover. Chop the rest into slightly larger pieces and add it to the soup along with the lentils. Add the reserved celery root during the last 5 minutes. The celery root will be a little crunchy, like croutons. Stir a spoonful of whisked crème fraîche into each bowl of soup and garnish with snipped chives, lovage, or chopped parsley or celery leaves.

Red Lentil Soup with Turmeric and Lime

This is one of my favorite soups and one I make often. Although the flavor is big, the soup is thin, yellow, and flecked with mustard seeds. Keep it brothy or include a mound of rice in the soup or fried pita triangles for additional body and texture. Ghee is the ideal fat for this soup because of its unique flavor, but coconut oil, for a vegan option, is also very good. Serves 6 Ⓥ

---

2 cups split red lentils, picked over and rinsed several times

2 teaspoons turmeric

3 tablespoons ghee or coconut oil

1 scant tablespoon sea salt

1 large onion, finely diced, about 2 cups

2 teaspoons ground cumin

$1^1/2$ teaspoons mustard seeds, or 1 teaspoon ground mustard

1 bunch chopped cilantro, about 1 cup

Juice of 3 limes

1 large bunch spinach leaves, chopped in small pieces

1 pita bread, separated and cut into wedges, or 1 cup freshly cooked rice

4 to 6 tablespoons yogurt, optional

Put the lentils in a soup pot with 10 cups water, the turmeric, 1 tablespoon of the ghee, and the salt. Bring to a boil, then lower the heat and simmer, covered, until the lentils are soft and falling apart, about 20 minutes. Puree for a smooth and nicer-looking soup. (An immersion blender is a great plus here.)

While the soup is cooking, cook the onion in the remaining 2 tablespoons ghee with the cumin and mustard in a medium skillet over low heat, stirring occasionally. When soft, after about 15 minutes, add the cilantro and cook for 1 minute more. Add the onion mixture to the soup, then the juice from 2 of the limes. Taste, then add more, if needed, to bring up the flavors. It should be a tad tart.

Just before serving, wilt the spinach in a few tablespoons of water with a pinch of salt. If using rice and it's warm, place a spoonful in each bowl. If using pita wedges, crisp them in olive oil or roast in the oven until brown, and use them as a garnish once the soup is served. If using rice, pack it into small ramekins and turn it out into each bowl. Ladle the soup carefully around the rice, then add the cooked spinach to each. Swirl in small spoonfuls of yogurt to each bowl.

With Coconut Milk: Use beverage coconut milk in place of water, or use $1^1/2$ cups less water and stir in a can of coconut milk once the lentils are cooked. Finish the soup with crumbles of coconut butter in each bowl. Ⓥ

With Green Onions: In place of the spinach, thinly slice green onions including a few inches of their greens in a few teaspoons ghee or coconut oil until bright green and softened, then add them to the finished soup. Ⓥ

With Forbidden Black Rice: For sheer drama and good flavor, cook black rice and use it in place of the white rice in the soup. Ⓥ

Lentil Soup with Walnut-Marjoram Cream in the Pressure Cooker

With company about to arrive, I suddenly worried that maybe there wasn't enough food, so I put this soup together and it was done as they walked in the door—in 15 minutes. The pressure cooker speeds up any lentil or bean soups, and here's how. Serves 4 (V)

Soup

2 tablespoons olive oil

1 slightly larger than medium onion, about 1 1/2 cups chopped

2 celery stalks, diced, about 1/2 cup

1 heaping teaspoon fresh thyme leaves

1 1/2 teaspoons sea salt

1 cup German green lentils, rinsed

Freshly milled pepper

Walnut-Marjoram Cream

1 plump clove garlic

Sea salt

1/2 cup walnuts

1/2 cup sour cream, cream, or Savory Cashew Cream (page 60)

2 tablespoons chopped marjoram or parsley

Heat the oil in your pressure cooker. Add the onion, celery, and thyme, give a stir, and cook over medium-high heat for 3 to 4 minutes, until the onions are golden, limp, and starting to brown in places. Add the salt, lentils, and 5 cups water, then fasten the lid and bring the pressure to high. Maintain the pressure for 15 minutes, which will yield very soft lentils, then release quickly.

Make the cream while the lentils are cooking. Pound the garlic in a mortar with a few pinches of salt until broken down, then add the walnuts and gradually break them down with sour cream and marjoram. This can also be done in a small food processor if your mortar is too small.

Puree the lentils in a blender until perfectly smooth. Taste for salt.

Serve the soup hot with a big spoonful of the sauce in each bowl and pepper ground over all. Each person can stir the sauce into their bowl of lentil soup to flavor it.

Smoky Split Pea Soup

Nothing is as comforting in cold weather as a hearty split pea soup. It needn't be thick enough to support the proverbial spoon—in fact it's much better when it's not. Smoked paprika and smoked salt provide the smoke flavor without the bacon. Serves 4 to 6 (V)

1 1/2 cups split green peas, sorted and rinsed

2 tablespoons olive oil

1 large onion, diced

2 carrots, diced

2 large cloves garlic, chopped

1/4 cup chopped parsley

1 teaspoon dried marjoram

1 teaspoon chopped rosemary

1 teaspoon paprika

Feshly milled pepper

Aromatics: 2 bay leaves, 8 parsley sprigs, 6 thyme sprigs

1 1/2 teaspoons sea salt

8 cups Basic Vegetable Stock (page 175) or water

Mushroom soy sauce, as needed

Chopped parsley, marjoram, or rosemary, to finish

1/2 cup small croutons browned in olive oil

Cover the peas with water and set aside.

Heat the oil in a soup pot over medium heat. Add the onion and carrots and sauté until the onion takes on some color, about 10 minutes. Add the garlic, parsley, herbs, paprika, and plenty of pepper and cook for another few minutes. Drain the peas and add them to the pot along with the aromatics, the salt, and stock. Stir frequently at first to keep the peas from settling to the bottom. Once the soup comes to a boil, lower the heat and simmer, partially covered, until the peas have completely broken down, 1 hour or more. Add extra water if the soup becomes too thick. Remove the aromatics.

Season to taste with the mushroom soy sauce and/or sea salt as needed. Serve with the chopped parsley and croutons in each bowl.

Split Pea Soup with Spinach or Sorrel: Spinach and sorrel add a fresh note to these dried legumes. Remove the stems from 1 small bunch spinach or 4 handfuls sorrel and cut the leaves into 1/2-inch ribbons. Roughly chop them so they won't be too long. Stir the greens into the finished soup and cook until wilted. (V)

Cream of Split Pea Soup: Both recipes that precede are good pureed. Remove the bay leaves from the finished soup and puree until smooth. Return it to the pot. If you wish, add 1 cup half-and-half, milk, or a few tablespoons cream and heat through. Serve with croutons and chopped parsley mixed with a little minced rosemary. (V)

Quinoa Chowder with Spinach, Feta, and Green Onions

Light and utterly delicious, this recipe stems from one in Chef Felipe Rojas-Lombardi's book, The Art of South American Cooking. *I was drawn to it because I simply couldn't imagine it. Now, one of my favorite dishes in any category, it makes a quick, wholesome meal.* Serves 4

³/4 cup quinoa, rinsed well in a fine sieve

1 clove garlic, finely chopped

1 jalapeño chile, seeded and finely diced

¹/2 pound boiling potatoes, peeled and cut into ¹/4-inch cubes

1 bunch green onions, including an inch of the greens, thinly sliced into rounds

3 cups finely sliced spinach leaves

¹/4 pound feta cheese, finely diced

2 tablespoons olive oil

1 teaspoon ground cumin, or to taste

1 teaspoon sea salt

¹/3 cup chopped cilantro

Freshly milled pepper

1 hard-cooked egg, chopped, for garnish

Put the quinoa and 8 cups water in a pot, bring to a boil, then lower the heat and simmer for 10 minutes. While it's cooking, dice the vegetables and cheese. Drain the quinoa, saving the liquid. Measure the liquid and add water to make 6 cups if needed. Heat the oil in a soup pot over medium heat. Add the garlic and chile. Cook for about 30 seconds, giving it a quick stir. Add the cumin, salt, and the potatoes and cook for a few minutes, stirring frequently. Don't let the garlic brown. Add the quinoa water and half the green onions and simmer until the potatoes are tender, about 15 minutes. Add the quinoa, spinach, and remaining green onions and simmer for 3 minutes more. Turn off the heat and stir in the feta and cilantro. Season the soup with pepper and garnish with the chopped egg.

A Summer Bean and Vegetable Soup with Pesto

On the first day, this niçoise minestrone is light and brothy, but a day later it's thick and substantial. If you can find fresh shelling beans, use two or three times as many in place of the dried since they don't swell. Serves 8 to 10 (V)

1 cup cannellini or other white beans, soaked for 4 hours

Aromatics: 2 bay leaves, 8 parsley sprigs, 4 sprigs of thyme

5 large cloves garlic, 2 sliced, 3 minced

3 tablespoons olive oil

3 teaspoons sea salt

3 small leeks, white parts plus an inch of the greens, chopped

2 pinches saffron threads

3 carrots, peeled and diced

3 waxy yellow boiling potatoes, chopped

2 turnips, peeled and chopped

3 zucchini, sliced into ¹/2-inch rounds or chunks

12 ounces green beans, tipped and tailed, and cut into 1-inch lengths

2 large ripe tomatoes, peeled, seeded, and diced

Freshly milled pepper

Basil Puree (page 51), to finish

Rinse the beans, put them in a pot with 12 cups water, and boil hard for 10 minutes. Add the aromatics, sliced garlic, and 1 teaspoon of the oil. Lower the heat and simmer, partially covered, for 45 minutes. Add 2 teaspoons of the salt and cook until the beans are tender, 15 to 30 minutes more. Strain the broth, measure, and add water to make 10 cups. Alternatively, cook them in a pressure cooker as described on page 265.

Warm the remaining oil in a soup pot over medium heat. Add the leeks and saffron threads and cook until the leeks look glossy and translucent and the saffron begins to release its aroma, about 10 minutes. Add the vegetables and minced garlic. Cook just to soften the vegetables, 4 to 5 minutes, then add the reserved bean broth and the remaining 1 teaspoon salt. Bring to a boil, lower the heat, and simmer until the vegetables are tender, about 30 minutes. Add the beans and taste for salt and season with pepper. Ladle the soup into bowls and stir a spoonful of basil puree into each serving.

White Bean Soup with Pasta and Rosemary Oil

Rosemary-scented oil adds an herbal essence to this soup. Make it first and set it aside to steep while you make the soup. I rather like this made with a variety of white beans so that a single bowl contains beans of different sizes.

Serves 8 to 10 Ⓥ

Rosemary Oil

- ⅓ cup olive oil
- 2 tablespoons finely chopped rosemary or 2 tablespoons dried
- 2 cloves garlic, sliced

Soup

- 2 cups cannellini, navy beans, or a mixture
- 2 tablespoons olive oil
- 1 tablespoon chopped rosemary or 2 teaspoons dried
- 1 onion, finely diced
- 2 carrots, finely diced
- 1 celery rib, finely diced
- 5 cloves garlic, sliced
- ⅓ cup chopped parsley
- 1 cup diced tomatoes, fresh or canned, with their juices
- 2 teaspoons sea salt
- 1 cup dried small pasta—shells, lumache, or other favorite shape
- Freshly milled pepper
- Thin shavings of freshly grated parmesan, to finish, optional

Slowly warm the olive oil with the rosemary and garlic until the garlic begins to color, about 3 minutes. Turn off the heat and set aside until needed.

Cover the beans with boiling water and set aside while you prepare the rest of the ingredients.

Heat the oil with the rosemary in a soup pot over medium heat. Add the onion, carrots, and celery and cook until the onion is softened and starting to color in places, about 10 minutes. Stir in the garlic and parsley and cook for a few minutes more. Drain the beans and add them to the pot along with the tomatoes and 12 cups water. Bring to a boil, lower the heat, then simmer, covered, until the beans have begun to soften, about 1 hour. Add the salt and continue cooking until the beans are completely tender, another 30 minutes or so.

Puree half the soup to give it some body—or leave it thin. (For a thicker smooth soup, puree all of it.)

Cook the pasta in boiling salted water, then drain. Strain the rosemary oil. Ladle the soup into bowls and add some pasta to each. Drizzle some of the oil over each bowl and add pepper to taste. Cover with thin shavings of parmesan.

White Bean and Pasta Soup with Sage: Sage is another fine herb with white beans. Replace the rosemary with 2 tablespoons chopped sage or 1 tablespoon dried and add ¼ teaspoon red pepper flakes. For garnish, fry 12 fresh sage leaves in ¼ cup olive oil until they darken. Serve them floating on the soup and the remaining oil drizzled over the top. Ⓥ

White Bean and Pasta Soup with Greens: Remove and discard the stems from 1 bunch of chard, spinach, mustard greens, or kale. Coarsely chop the leaves and sauté in a little olive oil with a little chopped garlic and a pinch of red pepper flakes until tender. Add a little water to the pan if it's dry and the greens aren't done. Times will vary, so taste them. Season with salt and stir them into the soup just before serving. Ⓥ

Chickpea Soup with Pine Nut and Chile Garnish

I have found several old Southwestern recipes for pine nut soups, chickpea soups, and recipes that combine them—a good idea, for pine nuts are expensive. Serves 4 (V)

- 1 tablespoon sunflower seed or olive oil
- 1 cup sliced yellow onion
- 1 small clove garlic, crushed
- 1 celery stalk, chopped
- 4 fresh sage leaves, roughly chopped
- 1/2 cup pine nuts, sunflower, or pumpkin seeds
- 1 1/2 cups freshly cooked chickpeas, or 1 (15-ounce) can, rinsed
- 4 cups broth from the chickpeas or water
- 1 1/2 teaspoons sea salt
- Chile Garnish, recipe follows
- Pine nut oil or best olive oil, to finish
- 2 tablespoons chopped fresh mint
- About 1/2 cup finely crumbled feta or queso añejo cheese, optional

Warm the oil in a soup pot. Add the onion, garlic, celery, sage, and pine nuts and cook over medium heat, stirring occasionally, until the onion is limp and the pine nuts have browned, about 10 minutes. Add the chickpeas, broth, and salt, and bring to a boil. Lower the heat, cover, and cook for 15 minutes. Let cool briefly, then puree in a blender until smooth. Return the soup to the pot.

Make the chile garnish while the soup is cooking. Serve the soup in bowls, spoon the chiles into each serving, spoon a little of the oil over the soup, then sprinkle over the mint, and cheese.

Chile Garnish

- 2 dried pasilla chiles
- 1 1/2 tablespoons olive oil
- 1 tablespoon apple cider vinegar
- 1/2 teaspoon dried oregano
- Sea salt

Snip the chiles into slivers with kitchen shears, discarding the seeds. Warm the oil in a small skillet, add the chiles, and stir for a minute or two to warm and soften. Remove from the heat and add the vinegar, 3 tablespoons water, oregano, and a little salt. Let stand for 30 minutes.

Black Bean Soup

After putting chiles in black bean soups for decades, we've forgotten how good these beans are when cooked in a more traditional American style. Although it's simple, you'll find this soup lacks no flavor. Serves 4 to 6

- 1 1/2 cups black beans, soaked
- 2 tablespoons butter or olive oil
- 1 cup finely diced onion
- 1/3 cup diced celery
- 1/3 cup diced carrot
- 1 cup diced green bell pepper
- 2 bay leaves
- 2 teaspoons chopped rosemary
- 1 teaspoon dried thyme
- 1 tablespoon tomato paste
- 2 teaspoons sea salt
- 1/2 cup Madeira
- 1/2 cup cream or milk
- Chopped parsley, for garnish

Drain the beans. Melt the butter in a soup pot, add the vegetables and herbs, and cook over medium-high heat for 5 to 7 minutes, until lightly colored. Stir in the tomato paste and cook for 1 minute more, mushing it around in the pan. Add the beans and 4 cups water and bring to a boil. Lower the heat and simmer, partially covered, for 1 hour. Add the salt and continue cooking until the beans are quite soft, another 15 to 30 minutes. Pull out the bay leaves and puree about two-thirds of the soup. Return it to the pot, add the Madeira and cream, and simmer for 5 minutes more. Serve garnished with a little chopped parsley sprinkled over each bowl.

Boston Black Bean Soup

Today we so associate black beans with the Southwest that we forget they are a relatively new addition to that pantry. Regional variations of this soup show up in community recipe books all along the Atlantic Seaboard. Serves 6

1½ cups dried black beans, picked over and soaked overnight

3 tablespoons butter or oil

1 cup finely chopped yellow onion

2 bay leaves

½ cup diced celery

2 teaspoons minced garlic

1½ teaspoons dry mustard

¼ teaspoon ground cloves

1 tablespoon sea salt

1 cup half-and half or milk

Freshly milled pepper

About 4 teaspoons fresh lemon juice

6 lemon slices, each pierced with a clove

2 tablespoons chopped parsley

1 hard-cooked egg, diced

Rinse the beans and set them aside. In a wide soup pot over medium heat, melt the butter and add the onion, bay leaves, celery, and garlic. Cook, stirring occasionally, until the onion has browned around the edges, about 5 minutes. Stir in the mustard and ground cloves, add the beans and 8 cups water, and bring to a boil. Lower the heat, cover, and cook at a gentle boil, partially covered, until the beans are soft but not quite done, about 45 minutes. Add the salt and continue to cook until the beans are fully tender, about 30 minutes more.

To cook the beans in a pressure cooker, rinse them well, put in the pot, and cover with 8 cups water and 2 teaspoons salt. Put on the lid, bring to pressure, and maintain on high for 25 minutes. Release the pressure quickly and check the beans. They should be done, or nearly so. Add the beans to the cooked onions.

Remove from the heat, let cool briefly, and, working in batches if necessary, puree the soup in a blender until smooth. Return to the pot, stir in the half-and-half, and season to taste with pepper and lemon juice. Reheat to serving temperature.

To serve, lay a clove-pierced lemon slice on each bowl of soup and scatter the parsley and diced egg over the top.

Black Bean Chili in the Slow Cooker with Smoked Paprika

I thought I'd see if I could make a version of the black bean chili from The Greens Cookbook *in the slow cooker. The texture doesn't quite hold up since the vegetables cook for so long, but it makes a delicious pot of smoky beans in about 8 hours. There will be extra liquid, which I use to make the rice cooked in bean broth on page 478.* Serves 4 to 6 ⓥ

2 cups black beans, rinsed

2½ teaspoons toasted ground cumin

1½ teaspoons dried Mexican oregano

1 teaspoon ground coriander

1 teaspoon dried epazote

2 teaspoons smoked paprika, plus extra to finish

1 large onion, diced

1 (28-ounce) can diced tomatoes, or 3 cups fresh, peeled, seeded, and diced

1½ teaspoons sea salt

1 dried red New Mexican or guajillo chile

To finish: sour cream or yogurt, optional, slivered green onions, chopped cilantro, additional smoked paprika

Put the beans in a slow cooker with 8 cups water on low. Add the spices, onion, tomatoes, and salt. Break off the stem end of the chile, knock out the seeds, and add it to the pot. Cover and cook for 8 hours.

When the beans are done, pour off (but reserve) the extra bean broth, leaving only as much as you want for the beans. Taste for salt and add additional smoked paprika if you wish.

Serve the beans with a little of the broth, garnish with a spoonful of sour cream, a scattering of slivered green onions, and chopped cilantro. Add a dash of smoked paprika to finish.

With Rice: Serve the black beans in a bowl over rice with broth. ⓥ

As a Soup: Puree most of the beans with the excess broth until smooth, and add the additional beans for texture. Use the same garnishes. ⓥ

Chilled Soups for Hot Days

Often smooth and always light, cold soups make a refreshing first course or light meal, a quick pick-me-up, and, in the case of fruit soups, a divine summer dessert. Since their flavor improves with time, they're good soups to make in quantity and have on hand during the hot days of summer and fall. A number of soups are made specifically to be eaten cold, such as yogurt soups, avocado soups, and fruit soups; but others—beet, carrot, and chard soups—can be enjoyed either way.

Avocado-Tomatillo Soup with Lime

Tart tomatillos add a spark to the creamy avocado, which is otherwise too rich and creamy to eat without immediate satiation. Serves 4 to 6 ⓥ

2 bunches green onions, including most of the greens

1 green bell pepper

2 tablespoons avocado or sunflower seed oil

12 ounces tomatillos, husked and rinsed

1 celery rib, chopped

1 scant tablespoon chopped ginger

2 tablespoons chopped parsley

2 tablespoons chopped mint

2 jalapeño chiles, seeded and diced

4 cups Basic Vegetable Stock (page 175) or water

1 teaspoon sea salt

2 large avocados

1/2 cup buttermilk, yogurt, or crumbles of coconut butter

For garnish: 2 teaspoons chopped mint and juice of 1 lime

Set aside a few onions and a quarter of the pepper, then coarsely chop the remainder. Heat the oil in a soup pot and add the tomatillos. Sauté over high heat until they color, about 5 minutes, then add the chopped vegetables, ginger, herbs, and half the chiles. Cook, stirring frequently, until the tomatillos are browned in places, about 10 minutes. Add the stock and salt and bring to a boil. Lower the heat and simmer, partially covered, until the tomatillos fall apart, 15 to 20 minutes. Let cool, then puree with the avocados and buttermilk. Chill well. Taste for salt.

Finely dice the reserved onion and pepper and mix them with the mint, lime juice, a pinch of salt, and the remaining chile. Serve a spoonful scattered over each bowl.

TIPS FOR MAKING CHILLED SOUPS

- Make a soup early in the day or the day before to allow plenty of time for flavors to mature and for the soup to get good and cold.
- Since cold dulls flavor, the seasonings need to be stronger than the same soup served warm. Always taste a cold soup just before serving to see if it needs a little lemon, salt, or a fresh herb garnish to bring up the flavor.
- To make smooth-textured soups interesting to eat, include some garnish of substance, such as finely diced vegetables and fruits or a salsa.
- Sweet fruit soups are best served as a dessert or over ice as a beverage. Their sweetness can dull the appetite for what's to follow. On the other hand, a sweet soup may be just the thing for a hot day.

Chilled Tomato Soup

This soup should be a staple in everyone's August kitchen. It requires only ripe, juicy tomatoes and time in the refrigerator (or good canned tomato juice when fresh tomatoes are lacking). So many flavors flatter tomatoes, this soup is easy to tailor to whatever else you happen to be serving—and to a multitude of garnishes. Serves 4 to 6 (V)

- 4 pounds vine-ripened tomatoes, peeled and seeded, juice reserved
- 2 teaspoons sea salt
- Sugar and/or sherry vinegar, if needed
- Olive oil or sour cream, to finish
- Freshly milled pepper
- Chopped basil or marjoram, for garnish
- 2 green onions, including a few of the greens, thinly sliced, for garnish

Finely chop the tomatoes by hand until they're very fine, almost like a puree. (You can use a blender, but it introduces so much air that the tomatoes turn frothy and pink.) Put the tomatoes in a bowl and add the reserved juice and the salt. Cover and chill well. Taste and add more salt if needed. If the tomatoes are very tart, add 1 teaspoon sugar and a few drops vinegar to balance the flavors. Taste and continue adjusting until you have it the way you like.

Ladle the soup into bowls and thread a spoonful of olive oil over the top of each. Add pepper and garnish with the basil and onions.

Chilled Tomato Soup with Avocado and Lime: Season the soup with lime juice instead of vinegar and garnish with diced avocado, chopped cilantro, and finely diced white onion. Fragrant Mexican marigolds make a stunning aromatic garnish if you have them. (V)

Chilled Tomato Soup with Little Garnishes (Gazpacho): Your guests can finish their own soup when presented with little bowls of garnishes set on a tray, as in Spain. Include white or green onion, green pepper, cucumber, hard-cooked egg, and tiny croutons crisped in olive oil. Finely dice everything and arrange in mounds or set in individual dishes.

Additional Seasonings: Try curry-flavored oil, lemon zest chopped with garlic and parsley or lovage leaves, ribbons of opal basil, cooked rice, or additional diced tomatoes. Almost all of the vinaigrettes and dressings make excellent seasonings for this hospitable soup. (V) ·

CONVERTING HOT SOUPS TO CHILLED SOUPS

Virtually all summer vegetables—eggplant, squash, peppers, onions, tomatoes, corn—are intensified when grilled. Grill them first, then cook them in water or stock and puree for rich-tasting soups, warm or chilled.

Serve cold vegetable soups with fresh garnishes that echo the ingredients—herbs, chiles, spices, and vegetables. With squash soups, sauté (rather than stew) the squash at the beginning until it's golden to bring out its flavor.

Minestrone and bean soups are not as obvious candidates as other soups, but there are times when they're traditionally served chilled, vinegar or lemon served alongside. Pureed bean and lentil soups, thoroughly cooked so that there's no trace of chalkiness, can also be served cold with spicy yogurt and other lively garnishes such as diced tomatoes, relishes, herbs, green onions, and so on.

CHILLED CARROT SOUP WITH ONION AND PICKLED CARROT RELISH: Make the Carrot Soup with Onion Relish on page 180. Puree and chill well. Make the relish using finely diced Pickled Red Onions (page 72) and/or Pickled Carrots and Garlic with Cumin (page 72). Add it to the soup just before serving and garnish with sprigs of cilantro. Serves 4 to 6. (V)

CHILLED CARROT SOUP WITH PEPPER GARNISH: Make the Carrot and Red Pepper Soup on page 181 and chill well. Very finely dice enough bell pepper—orange, yellow, purple, or green to make 1/2 cup. (The stem ends, which are often thrown away, are perfect for this.) Combine the peppers with 2 teaspoons olive oil and season with sea salt and a little pepper. Let stand for 15 minutes. Serve the soup with the peppers spooned into each bowl and garnish with thinly sliced basil leaves or a leaf of lemon verbena. Serves 4 to 6. (V)

CHILLED GRILLED RED PEPPER SOUP WITH BASIL PUREE: Make the Roasted Red Pepper Soup on page 187, grilling both the onion and the peppers first along with an extra orange or yellow pepper and adding 1/2 cup cream. Peel, seed, and dice the extra pepper. Chill the soup well. Taste for salt and add a little balsamic vinegar or sherry vinegar to sharpen the flavors. Puree a handful of basil leaves with olive oil until smooth. Stir the chopped peppers into the soup and garnish each bowl with a swirl of basil puree. Serves 4 to 6.

CHILLED LEEK AND POTATO SOUP WITH SNIPPED HERBS: Make the Leek and Potato Soup on page 185. Pass all but 2 cups through a food mill, combine with the unmilled soup, and chill well. Taste for salt and season with pepper. Assemble a collection of herbs, such as sprigs of chervil, a sprig of tarragon, a few chives, a lovage leaf, and sprigs of lemon thyme or lemon verbena. Pluck the leaves off the stems and lightly chop them. You'll need about 3 tablespoons. If there are some chive or thyme blossoms, set them aside. Whisk a few tablespoons crème fraîche until smooth, then drizzle it from a spoon over the top of the soup. Add the herbs and their blossoms and serve. Serves 4 to 6.

CHILLED CHARD SOUP WITH YOGURT: Chill the tart Chard Soup with Sorrel or Lemon (page 181) and serve with yogurt and diced cucumber in each bowl. Serves 4 to 6.

Yogurt Soups

Smooth and pleasantly tart, yogurt gets along famously with parsley, dill, and mint, chickpeas and wheat, nuts and vegetables. Yogurt soups also make excellent cool drinks or even a summer breakfast for those who like to start their day with savory foods.

The quality of the yogurt you use is crucial since it's the central ingredient. The best offerings are free of corn syrup, sugar, gums, and gelatins. Especially good are yogurts made from specific cultures, such as Bulgarian-style yogurt and divine yogurts with a layer of cream resting on top. Goat milk yogurts have a certain appeal, too.

To my taste, whole-milk or low-fat Bulgarian style makes the best soup. Its texture is loose and silky, and its flavor has just the right amount of tartness. Nonfat yogurt tends to be too sour to make good soups, though there are exceptions.

If you can't get good, natural, sweet-tasting yogurt, use buttermilk. It makes a great base for all these soups, and its taste is much more reliably balanced.

Buttermilk Soup with Barley or Farro

Just as yogurt is often stirred into soups of legumes and grains, different grains and legumes make excellent additions to yogurt or buttermilk soups. Chickpeas, lentils, wheat berries, spelt, bulgur, and couscous—even leftover tabbouleh—are all possibilities. Serves 4 to 6

1/3 cup pearl barley, or 1 cup farro

4 cups buttermilk or a mixture of buttermilk and yogurt

1/4 cup minced green onion, including some of the greens

1/3 cup chopped parsley

2 tablespoons snipped chives

1 teaspoon ground cumin

Sea salt and freshly milled white pepper

1 tablespoon crushed toasted cumin seeds

Simmer the barley in water to cover in a saucepan until soft, about 35 minutes. If you're using farro, cook as discussed on page 457.

Mix together all the ingredients except the cumin seeds. Season with a few pinches salt and pepper to taste; chill well. Serve with the crushed cumin seeds sprinkled on top.

Buttermilk Soup with Chickpeas and Herb Oil

With canned chickpeas, this soup can be assembled in minutes, then set aside to chill. Serve it with hearty whole grain bread or rolls. Serves 4 to 7

2 cloves garlic

1/2 teaspoon sea salt

4 cups buttermilk

1 large cucumber, peeled, seeded, and finely diced

1 (15-ounce) can chickpeas, rinsed well, or 1 1/2 cups cooked

1/4 cup olive oil

2 tablespoons snipped chives

1/3 cup chopped parsley

3 tablespoons chopped marjoram

Grated zest and juice of 1 lemon

Freshly milled pepper

Pound the garlic with the salt in a mortar until smooth. Combine the buttermilk, garlic, cucumber, and chickpeas in a bowl and chill well. Combine the oil, herbs, a few pinches of salt, and the lemon zest in another bowl. When cold, taste the soup for salt and season with pepper and lemon juice. Serve garnished with the olive oil.

Yogurt Soup with Herbs, Spinach, and Rice

A good stock greatly enhances this soup, but if you skip it, be extra-generous with the herbs and allow time for the flavors to marry. Serves 4 to 6

- 1 bunch green onions, including half of the greens, chopped
- 2 tablespoons olive oil
- 1 onion, chopped
- 3 cloves garlic, chopped
- 1 cup chopped parsley
- 1/3 cup chopped dill or 3 tablespoons dried
- 1 teaspoon sea salt
- 1 large bunch spinach, stems removed
- 5 cups Basic Vegetable Stock (page 175), enhanced with summer vegetables
- 1 1/2 cups yogurt, plus extra yogurt or sour cream for garnish
- Fresh lemon juice, if needed
- Freshly milled pepper
- 1 cup cooked long-grain white or brown rice
- 1 small cucumber, peeled, seeded, and finely diced

Set aside 2 tablespoons of the green onion for garnish and refrigerate.

Heat the oil in a soup pot and add the onion, garlic, and herbs. Cook over medium heat until the onion is soft, 10 to 12 minutes, stirring occasionally. Add the salt, spinach, and stock and bring to a boil. Lower the heat and simmer just enough to wilt the spinach, a few minutes. Puree, then stir in the yogurt and chill well. When cold, taste again for salt—it will probably need more, or add lemon juice to bring up the flavor. Season with pepper to taste. Serve with rice and diced cucumber in each bowl. Garnish with an additional spoonful of yogurt and the reserved green onion.

Yogurt and Cucumber Soup with Mint

Cucumber, parsley, and mint are classically delicious with yogurt. Salad burnet, with its cucumber flavor, is good, too. Serves 4 to 6

- 3 cups yogurt
- 1 1/2 cups milk or buttermilk
- 2 cloves garlic
- 1/2 teaspoon sea salt
- 2 cucumbers, peeled if waxed
- 1/4 cup chopped parsley
- 3 tablespoons chopped mint or salad burnet
- 1 tablespoon olive oil
- Freshly milled white pepper
- Few drops fresh lemon juice
- 4 to 6 mint sprigs, for garnish

Combine the yogurt and buttermilk in a bowl. Pound the garlic with the salt in a mortar until smooth. Halve the cucumbers lengthwise, scrape out the seeds, then grate them using the large holes of a grater. Stir the garlic, cucumber, herbs, and oil into the yogurt. Taste for salt and season with pepper and lemon juice. Chill well and serve garnished with mint sprigs.

Yogurt and Cucumber Soup with Green Onions and Dill: Add 4 finely sliced green onions, including most of the greens, and substitute 3 tablespoons finely chopped dill for the mint.

Yogurt Soup with Crushed Nuts and Garlic: Pound 1/2 cup shelled walnuts, pine nuts, or skinned almonds with the garlic and sea salt in a mortar until smooth, adding a little of the yogurt or milk to loosen the mixture as you work. Finely dice rather than grate the cucumber and omit the herbs. Garnish with chopped mint.

Fruit Soups

Cold, smooth, sweet soups are delicious but not everyone's idea of a meal. Try fruit soups as a beverage, poured over ice and served on a hot day. They also make an intriguing dessert and can be given texture by including a chunky fruit salsa or a scoop of fruit sorbet.

Fruit soups are among the easier soups to improvise. Start with sweet, flavorful fruit—nearly overripe fruit is often best. Puree it, season it with complementary spices, tart it a little with lemon or lime juice, and enrich it or not, with cream, yogurt, buttermilk, or the like. A pinch of sea salt brings up the flavors, as does a little vinegar or lemon juice.

The craze for salsas has demonstrated that fruit combines well with acids, chiles, and spices. Bringing some of these elements into play as garnishes for fruit soups gives them a wider role to play in the meal.

Melon Soup with Ginger-Cucumber Salsa

Wait for those juicy, dead-ripe melons to make this soup— the ones sitting on your counter attracting fruit flies are perfect. The spicy salsa adds texture and makes the soup a cooling summer appetizer. Serves 4 to 6 Ⓥ

Soup

    1 honeydew, Persian, or casaba melon, about 2¹/₂ pounds
    Grated zest and juice of 2 limes
    ¹/₂ cup yogurt, sour cream, or buttermilk, optional
    Sea salt
    Mint or basil sprigs, for garnish

Salsa

    ¹/₂ small cucumber, peeled and seeded
    Grated zest and juice of 1 lime
    1 tablespoon finely slivered Thai or regular basil
    1 tablespoon chopped mint leaves
    1 jalapeño chile, seeded and finely diced
    1 small knob of ginger, peeled and coarsely chopped
    Sea salt

Cut the melon into eighths and set one wedge aside. Seed, peel, and puree the rest. Stir in the lime zest and juice, yogurt, and a few pinches of salt. Cover and refrigerate.

Neatly and finely dice the reserved melon and the cucumber and combine with the lime zest and juice, basil, mint, and chile. Force the ginger through a garlic press and add it to the salsa. Season with a pinch of salt and chill.

Serve the soup very cold with the salsa spooned into the middle of each bowl and garnished with mint sprigs.

Watermelon and Blackberry Soup

A fruit salad in a pink "broth" of watermelon. It's a little hard to be exact with watermelon—some pieces are full of seeds, others aren't—so you may have to feel your way with amounts. Serves 4 Ⓥ

    6 cups seeded chunks of watermelon
    Fresh lemon or lime juice
    Sea salt
    2 cups blackberries
    3 tablespoons light brown sugar
    Rosewater or orange-flower water
    2 pounds watermelon, half red and half yellow
    ¹/₄ cup pomegranate seeds, if available
    4 mint sprigs, for garnish

Puree the watermelon chunks and pour the puree into a bowl. Add lemon juice to taste and a pinch of salt and refrigerate, covered. Toss the blackberries with the brown sugar and a few drops of rosewater, cover, and refrigerate for 1 hour. Seed the red and yellow melons and cut them into bite-size chunks.

When it's time to serve, flavor the melon juice with rosewater to taste, starting with 1 teaspoon. Divide the juice among chilled soup plates and add the melon pieces, then the berries. If pomegranates are in season, add about 1 tablespoon of seeds to each bowl and a squeeze of the juice as well. Garnish with the mint sprigs and serve.

Spiced Plum Soup

Here's a perfect use for those tiny plums that are too small to slice or a glut of sweet plums from a prolific tree. Unless the plums are dead ripe, you can expect an astringent edge. This makes a sublime cold drink, poured over ice into tall glasses.
Serves 4

2 pounds very ripe purple plums

2 large pieces orange zest

1 cup fresh orange juice

1 (3-inch) cinnamon stick

4 cloves

1/2 teaspoon ground cardamom

1/2 teaspoon ground coriander

1/3 to 1/2 cup mild honey

1/2 cup buttermilk

1 teaspoon orange-flower water

1 1/2 teaspoons balsamic vinegar

Fresh mint leaves, for garnish

Leave very small plums whole and cut larger ones roughly in half. Don't worry about removing the pits. Put them in a pot with the orange zest and juice, spices, and 1/3 cup honey. Bring to a boil, then lower the heat and simmer, covered, until the flesh easily falls away from the pit, about 30 minutes. Transfer the plums to a food mill set over a bowl and begin to turn it. It will grate against the pits and loosen the flesh. Pick out the pits, cinnamon stick, and cloves with your fingers as you come across them and continue to work the plums through, skins and all. Whisk the buttermilk and orange-flower water into the plum puree and chill. When the soup is cold, stir in the vinegar; taste again and correct the seasonings, adding more spice, honey, or orange-flower water if needed. Garnish with the mint leaves and serve.

Plum Soup with Wine: Use 1/2 cup orange muscat wine or Japanese plum wine in place of the orange juice and add 1 or 2 drops of orange oil, if available, to the soup.

Bicolored Plum Soup: Add the buttermilk to half the soup. Using two ladles simultaneously, pour some of each into the soup bowls. Passing a knife in a zigzag fashion through the lines where the two soups meet makes fancy-looking but easy-to-make swirls.

Winter Soup of Dried Fruit with Pearl Tapioca

A friend of Norwegian origin served this soup, then kindly shared her recipe with me. The large tapioca pearls are invisible but give it a silky quality. A great winter dish to have on hand, it keeps for weeks refrigerated. Give the pearls a head start with an overnight soak before cooking.
Serves 4 to 6 (V)

1/4 cup large tapioca pearls

1 cup dried apricots

1 cup dried pitted prunes or Mission figs

1 cup dried pears

1/2 cup golden raisins

1/2 cup dried cherries

2 (3-inch) cinnamon sticks

4 slices ginger

4 cups water or pear juice, plus extra as needed

Sour cream or drained yogurt, optional

Cover the tapioca and fruit with water and set aside to soak overnight. Drain, then put it in a soup pot with the remaining ingredients except the sour cream. Bring to a boil. Lower the heat and cook slowly, partially covered, until the tapioca pearls are clear, about 2 hours. (Some people like to see a little eye in the center, which gives them their other name, tapioca fish eyes.) Gently give a stir every so often so that nothing sticks to the bottom. If the soup becomes too thick, add water or juice as needed. Serve warm or chilled, for breakfast or dessert, plain or with a spoonful of sour cream or drained yogurt.

VEGETABLE STEWS, SAUTÉS, AND STIR-FRIES

CHAPTER 8

Vegetable Stews, Sautés, and Stir-Fries

Stew, ragout, braise, medley—all describe dishes that are composed of seasonal vegetables and their herb companions, simmered and sauced with residual juices. Cooked long enough for their flavors to mingle and marry, these dishes, along with their accompaniments, make an excellent vegetable-based main dish (or a side dish for a meat course if you're not vegetarian).

Vegetable stews are really a varied lot. Here's a cooking approach that unites such diverse dishes as a Cashew Curry (page 225), a Tunisian couscous, and a vegetable daube, to name but three. And variety is ever increased if you take into account what seasonal changes themselves suggest. If we think about putting a lid on a stew, we can go a few steps further and confer dignity on a humble dish. Puff pastry, biscuit dough, and flaky phyllo all contribute a layer of finesse to seasonal vegetable stews. While I wouldn't hesitate to serve a stew at a casual dinner party, I know that a golden covering of pastry will raise expectations and garner sighs of appreciation.

Sautés, like stews, are a mélange of vegetables. But unlike stews, they are quickly cooked dishes, but without the seasonings associated with stir-fries.

Stir-fries are also mixtures of elements, but they're better described as two-part dishes with all the cutting done at one end and all the cooking at the other. Unlike a stew, the flavors in a stir-fry are united through a brief but intense exposure to the hot sides of a wok, rendering the vegetables crisp, bright, and shiny. Stews lose some of that color and texture but gain flavor.

Stews

The word *stew* usually suggests a slow-cooked dish of robust and meaty heartiness. To me, it simply means a mélange of individual ingredients simmered together at a leisurely pace.

FOR MAKING STEWS, START WITH THE FLAVOR BASE: As with soup, sautéed onions, carrots, celery, and other aromatics provide the flavor base. It's important to the final flavor of the stews not to rush this step. Allow plenty of time for the onions to color, the sugars in the vegetables to caramelize, and the herbs to release their flavors. A good way to keep yourself from rushing is to cut your vegetables while the base is cooking. By the time you're done, it will be too.

LESS IS MORE; COOKING WITH THE SEASONS: Stews work best when they're limited to about five different vegetables in addition to the base. In choosing them, keep in mind a balance of shapes, sizes, colors, and textures as well as flavors.

Choose your vegetables from what's in season; foods that mature at the same time always taste good together: Asparagus, snow peas, and chervil in spring. Artichokes and fava beans in spring too, but artichokes and celery root in fall. Tomatoes, eggplants, and potatoes in summer. Hearty roots and tubers in winter. By seasonal, I mean the season where you live, not the season of the supermarket, which draws its goods from around the world. If you take your tips from what's grown locally and sold seasonally, it's virtually impossible to put together a poor stew.

BLANCHING: Sometimes it's preferable to cook some of the ingredients separately to preserve their fresh color and texture. Blanching one or more vegetables gives you some control over how your final dish will look since they're cooked separately, then added at the last minute. But don't be afraid to allow at least some of the vegetables to soften—that's often when they taste best. One of the best vegetable braises I've ever eaten was in a Roman restaurant one spring. Asparagus, peas, and fava beans were cooked to nearly a jamlike consistency. By American standards, the dish was impossibly overcooked, but it was over the top in terms of flavor.

With practice, you'll be able to judge how long individual vegetables take to cook when added to the stew. Start with those that take the longest cooking time and proceed on to those that take the shortest time, ensuring that everything will be cooked perfectly at the end.

WINE: Wine gives an acidic lift to the flavors and keeps the vegetables from becoming mushy. A few tablespoons of lemon juice or mild vinegar, such as champagne vinegar, can accomplish the same thing. While dry white wines are good with vegetables, I sometimes prefer a dry Riesling. Its acidity combined with its sugars doesn't fight the vegetables' natural tendency toward sweetness but harmonizes with them.

ON THE TABLE—PRESENTATION: While satisfying to eat, stews by their nature lack visual definition. This makes presentation a problem, albeit one that's easily solved. Serving stews in a pasta plate or bowl with a wide rim sets off the food to good advantage. Other elements of focus are provided by the accompaniments—golden triangles of fried polenta surrounding a mushroom stew, garlic-rubbed croutons framing braised artichokes with leeks and peas, a vegetable-chickpea tagine encircled with pellets of couscous. Stews are best served with something that absorbs their juices and provides a neutral point for the palate. Grains, couscous, polenta, croutons, toast, biscuits, and even waffles are all good candidates. You can give grains more visual definition by packing them into small molds or custard cups, turning them out onto the center of the plate or bowl, and then ladling the stew around them. Toppings of various kinds can turn stews into cobblers and pot pies.

It's also important to cut your vegetables in large, attractively shaped pieces so that the eye will be drawn to identifiable ingredients—a length of carrot, a quartered potato, a whole mushroom—rather than a confusion of small bits. When ingredients in a dish are indistinct and unrecognizable, it's difficult to elicit a receptive response, especially from children.

A fresh garnish of chopped herbs, a spoonful of salsa verde, or a diced tomato that's only warmed makes your final vegetable stew look lively and fresh.

Braised Turnips with Thyme

You can serve this ragout with buttered toast or make it into little pot pies covered with pie crust or frozen puff pastry.
Serves 4

---

1 pound turnips, preferably small
2 rutabagas, thickly peeled and diced into 1/2-inch cubes
1 to 2 tablespoons butter
1 onion, finely diced
3 small cloves garlic, halved
1 carrot, cut into medium dice
4 thyme sprigs or 1/4 teaspoon dried
1/4 teaspoon sea salt
2 teaspoons flour
2 tablespoons chopped parsley
Freshly milled pepper
1 teaspoon Dijon mustard
1/4 cup cream or crème fraîche

If you're using storage turnips, peel them thickly, cut them into sixths, and parboil in salted water for 1 minute. (Tender spring turnips can be scrubbed and left whole.) Parboil the rutabagas for 3 minutes.

Melt the butter in a Dutch oven over medium heat. Add the onion, garlic, rutabagas, carrot, and thyme. Cook for 3 to 4 minutes, then add the turnips. Season with the salt

Vegetable Stews, Sautés, and Stir-Fries

and sprinkle with the flour. Cover and cook over low heat for 4 minutes, then stir in $1^1/_2$ cups water and the parsley. Simmer, covered, until the turnips are tender, about 15 minutes. Taste for salt, season with pepper, add the mustard and cream, and simmer for 2 minutes more.

Curried Cauliflower and Peas

My friend Kathi Long raved so much about this curry that I asked her to make it for me. It's indeed exceptional—and quite easy—but you do need green mango powder, asafetida, and garam masala, all of which are available at Indian markets. Serve this over steamed rice. Serves 4 Ⓥ

$1/_4$ cup coconut oil or ghee

$1/_2$ teaspoon toasted ground cumin

$1/_2$ teaspoon asafetida

$1/_2$ cup peeled and finely diced ginger

4 teaspoons toasted ground coriander

1 teaspoon ground mild red chile, or $1/_2$ teaspoon cayenne

1 teaspoon turmeric

1 onion, thinly sliced

1 large cauliflower, cut into bite-size pieces, including the stems

$1^1/_2$ teaspoons sea salt

$1/_2$ pound sugar snap peas, strings removed

2 teaspoons ground amchoor (green mango) powder

1 teaspoon Garam Masala (page 25)

In a wide pot, heat the oil over medium–high heat. Add the cumin and asafetida and cook for 30 seconds, stirring constantly. Add the ginger, coriander, chile, and turmeric and cook for 30 seconds more. Add the onion, lower the heat, and cook until limp, stirring occasionally, about 4 minutes. Next add the cauliflower and salt. Mix everything together, then pour in $1/_2$ cup water, cover the pot, and simmer until the vegetables are tender, about 10 minutes. Add the peas and cook for a few minutes more, until they're bright green. Add the amchoor powder and garam masala, stir together, taste for salt, and serve.

Corn and Mushroom Ragout with Sage and Roasted Garlic

Make a little stock with the trimmings as you work for the final sauce. Serve with warm popovers, cornbread, or biscuits. Serves 4 Ⓥ

$1/_4$ onion, sliced

10 cloves garlic, 2 peeled, 8 unpeeled

1 teaspoon sea salt

1 large yellow bell pepper, roasted

3 cups fresh corn kernels and their scrapings, from 4 or 5 ears corn, 1 corn cob reserved

6 ounces shiitake, oyster, or white mushrooms, caps cut into large pieces, stems reserved

3 tablespoons olive oil

5 ripe but firm tomatoes

1 small onion, finely diced

8 sage leaves, finely chopped

Freshly milled pepper

1 tablespoon chopped parsley, for garnish

Simmer 3 cups water with the sliced onion, peeled garlic, and $1/_2$ teaspoon of the salt. Add any pepper trimmings, 1 corn cob, broken into pieces, and stems from the mushrooms. Simmer for 25 minutes.

Meanwhile, cut the pepper into pieces about 1 inch long and $1/_2$ inch wide, reserving the juices. Heat $1/_2$ tablespoon of the oil in a small skillet over medium heat. Add the unpeeled garlic and cook until the skins are charred and the insides are soft, about 10 minutes. Peel and mash into a paste. Sear the tomatoes in the same pan, turning them frequently, until the skin begins to split. Remove the skins, halve the tomatoes, and squeeze the juice into the stock. Chop the flesh into large pieces.

In a wide skillet, heat $1^1/_2$ tablespoons of the oil over high heat. Add the mushrooms and sauté until they begin to color, after 4 to 5 minutes. Set them aside in a bowl. Return the pan to the heat and add 1 tablespoon oil. Sauté the diced onion, garlic, corn, and all but 1 teaspoon of the sage until the corn and onion begin to color, about 5 minutes. Add the reserved mushrooms, peppers, and tomatoes. Season with the remaining $1/_2$ teaspoon salt and a little pepper.

Strain the stock right into the pan, add any reserved pepper juices, reduce the heat, cover, and simmer for 5 minutes. Serve garnished with the remaining sage and the parsley.

Placing a stew in an ovenproof dish and adding a topping makes the dish more substantial and handsome. This way it fits with ease into any occasion from family get-togethers to dinner parties to potlucks.

Biscuit Topping for Vegetable Stews

This makes enough to cover 6 to 8 cups of vegetables. Use a large gratin dish, individual ramekins, or any attractive ovenproof dish. Have the stew at room temperature before adding the top, or the heat will turn the pastry soggy.
Covers an 8 by 8-inch pan or a 12-inch gratin dish

- ²/₃ cup white whole wheat, spelt, or sprouted wheat or spelt flour
- ²/₃ cup all-purpose flour
- 1¹/₂ teaspoons baking powder
- ¹/₂ teaspoon sea salt
- 5 tablespoons cold butter, grated or chopped into small pieces
- ¹/₂ cup milk plus extra, if needed

Mix the flours in a bowl with the baking powder and salt. Cut in the butter using two knives until the texture is pebbly, then quickly and lightly stir in the milk with a fork. Mix the dough just until it comes together, then using one of your hands, knead it in the bowl, keeping the action gentle and brief—just a few turns to bring the dough together.

Preheat the oven to 375°F. Pat it out on a floured surface so that it's about ³/₈ to a scant ¹/₂ inch thick, then cut out small circles, diamonds, or squares. (If cutting out circles, use your biscuit cutter with the scraps to make half and quarter moon–shaped pieces.) Alternatively, roll out the dough to fit the baking dish, then lay it over the cool, cooked vegetables and score the top with the tip of a paring knife. Bake until the stew is hot and crust is golden, about 35 minutes.

Vegan Biscuit Topping: In place of the butter, use ¹/₃ cup solid coconut oil, and in place of the milk, use your favorite plant milk. Ⓥ

Drop Biscuit Covering: Instead of rolling out the dough, drop it by spoonfuls over the surface.

Glazed: Beaten egg, egg white, or melted butter brushed over the dough will give it a rich, burnished surface.

With Cheddar: Add ¹/₂ to 1 cup grated cheddar cheese to the dry ingredients.

With Buttermilk: Add ¹/₂ teaspoon baking soda to the dry ingredients and use buttermilk in place of regular milk.

Vegetable Pot Pies: Tender golden crust over a vegetable stew never fails to entice. Use the standard Pie Crust (page 620), Galette Dough (page 624), or the yeasted doughs (page 433), rolled very thin, or puff pastry. Make sure the vegetable stew is at room temperature. Roll out the dough, cut it to fit the dish, then brush one side of the dough with beaten egg and set it, egg side down, on the vegetables. Flute the edges as you would for a deep-dish pie. Fashion scraps into decorations—leaves, hearts, stars, geometric designs, whatever you fancy—and fasten them to the dough with a bit of egg glaze. Lacking scraps, score the top attractively with the tip of a knife, cutting into but not through the pastry. Brush with beaten egg. Bake at 425°F for 12 minutes, then lower the heat to 350°F and finish baking, about 35 minutes in all.

Phyllo Covers: Allow frozen phyllo dough to thaw in the refrigerator for 6 to 8 hours. Remove and carefully unfold it. Using the unfilled baking dish as a guide, cut out 8 pieces of phyllo pastry and cover them with plastic wrap and a barely damp towel. Rewrap the unused portion of phyllo and return it to the refrigerator.

Brush each of the cut sheets lightly with melted butter, olive oil, or a combination of the two. Stack them on top of each other as you go. You can add flavor and texture by scattering finely chopped toasted nuts between the layers. Score the top into decorative squares or diamonds with a sharp knife or designate portions by cutting completely through the dough. The finished top can be refrigerated until you're ready to use it. Preheat the oven to 375°F. Put the room-temperature cooked stew in the dish, set the phyllo lid on top, and bake until the filling is hot and the phyllo is golden, 30 to 40 minutes.

A phyllo cover would be good with Braised Artichokes with Leeks and Peas (page 219) or the Corn and Mushroom Ragout with Sage and Roasted Garlic (page 215).

Potato and Chickpea Stew with Romesco Sauce

With its deep red background and golden potatoes, this stew is still one of my favorites. It multiplies easily and improves with time. Picada, a savory bread crumb mixture, is used to thicken the broth while a bowl of Romesco Sauce (page 62) infuses it with a rich finish. Steamed spinach or chard can be added directly to the bowl—it gives the dish a fresh element—or served on the side. Serves 4 (V)

---

1 pound Yellow Finn or fingerling potatoes

3 tablespoons olive oil

1 large onion, finely diced

2 generous pinches saffron

2 large red bell peppers, finely diced

1 large yellow bell pepper, cut into 1-inch-wide strips

2 large cloves garlic, minced

1 heaping teaspoon sweet paprika

$1/4$ cup chopped parsley, plus extra for garnish

$1/4$ teaspoon red pepper flakes

$1/2$ cup medium-dry sherry

2 cups canned crushed tomatoes, plus their juices

$2^{1}/_{2}$ cups cooked chickpeas, or 2 (15-ounce) cans, rinsed

3 cups chickpea cooking broth or water

$1^{1}/_{2}$ teaspoons sea salt

Freshly milled pepper

Picada (page 25), if needed

Romesco Sauce (page 62)

If using fingerling potatoes, scrub, then halve them lengthwise. Large round potatoes can be cut into thick rounds or quartered lengthwise.

Warm the oil in a wide pot with the onion, saffron, peppers, garlic, and potatoes. Cook over medium-low heat, stirring gently every now and then until the potatoes are tender-firm, about 25 minutes. Add the paprika, parsley, and pepper flakes and cook for 3 or 4 minutes, then add the sherry and cook until the juices in the pan are thick and syrupy, about 12 minutes.

Add the tomatoes, chickpeas, and broth to cover. Season with the salt and plenty of pepper. Cover and cook over low heat until the potatoes are completely tender, about 20 minutes. If the stew is truly soupy and you plan to serve it right away, stir in $1/4$ cup picada (or more, if necessary) to thicken it. If you don't plan to serve the stew for 1 hour or more, it may not need the bread crumbs since it will

thicken as it stands. Serve in soup plates with any additional picada sprinkled over the top along with the extra parsley. Add a spoonful of the Romesco sauce to each bowl and pass the rest.

Eggplant Stew with Tomatoes, Peppers, and Green Chickpeas

This summer dish is an easy one to make. Serve it over the Saffron Noodle Cake (page 410), a rice pilaf, or with bulgur. Green chickpeas can be found fresh or frozen, but as they aren't universally available, freshly cooked or canned chickpeas can be used in their place. Serves 4 (V)

---

1 to $1/2$ pounds eggplant

6 tablespoons olive oil

1 large red onion, diced into $1/2$-inch squares

1 large yellow or red bell pepper, cut into 1-inch triangles

2 teaspoons paprika

2 plump cloves garlic, thinly sliced

2 tablespoons tomato paste

5 plum tomatoes, peeled, quartered lengthwise, and seeded

1 cup green chickpeas, or 1 (15-ounce) can chickpeas, rinsed

1 teaspoon sea salt

Freshly milled pepper

$1/4$ cup coarsely chopped parsley

Cut the eggplant lengthwise into $1/2$-inch slabs, then crosswise into $1/2$-inch sticks. Heat $1/4$ cup of the oil in a wide skillet over high heat until hazy. Add the eggplant and stir to distribute the oil. Cook, turning the pieces every few minutes, until golden, about 10 minutes.

Heat the remaining 2 tablespoons oil in a Dutch oven over medium-high heat. Add the onion, pepper, and paprika and sauté until the onion is lightly browned around the edges, 8 to 10 minutes, adding the garlic during the last few minutes. Stir in the tomato paste, fry it for a minute, then moisten with a few tablespoons water and scrape up the juices from the bottom of the pan. Add the tomatoes, eggplant, chickpeas, 1 cup water, the salt, and pepper. Lower the heat and simmer, covered, for 20 minutes, stirring once or twice. Stir in the chopped parsley and serve.

Asparagus and Artichoke Ragout

Asparagus and peas provide a sunnier aspect to this dish, while using a preponderance of artichokes gives it the soft look of a cloudy spring day. If making a stock, be sure to use the asparagus ends and mushrooms stems. Serves 4 to 6 Ⓥ

1 pound thick asparagus, tough ends trimmed

2 teaspoons sea salt

3 medium artichokes, trimmed and quartered (see page 295)

Juice of 1 lemon

3 tablespoons butter or olive oil

1/2 cup finely diced shallots, green onions, or leeks

4 sprigs thyme, leaves stripped and chopped

2 teaspoons chopped tarragon or basil

1/2 cup dry white wine

8 ounces white mushrooms, sliced about 1/4 inch thick

1 teaspoon flour

1 cup water or vegetable stock

1 cup fresh peas, from about 1 pound whole, or frozen peas

Freshly milled white pepper

Peel the asparagus stalks, then slice them diagonally, leaving the tips 2 to 3 inches long. If the tips are very thick, halve them lengthwise. Bring 4 cups water to a boil and add 1 teaspoon of the salt. Blanch the slivered stalks until bright green and tender-firm, about 2 minutes, then scoop them out and rinse with cold water. Next blanch the tips until tender-firm, about 4 minutes, then rinse and set aside. Thinly slice the quartered artichokes. Add the lemon to the water and boil until tender-firm, about 5 minutes, then drain and set aside.

Melt the butter in a 10- or 12-inch skillet or sauté pan. When foamy, add the shallots, thyme, and half the tarragon. Cook over medium heat, stirring occasionally, for 3 to 4 minutes, then add the wine and simmer until it has reduced to a syrupy consistency. Add the mushrooms and the remaining 1 teaspoon salt. Raise the heat to high, and sauté, stirring frequently, until they've given up their juices and become tender, after about 5 minutes. Add the artichokes to the pan, sprinkle the flour over the top, and carefully fold it into the vegetables. Add the water and simmer until the vegetables are heated through. (The stew can be prepared ahead of time up to this point.)

To finish the dish, add the asparagus and peas and continue cooking until they're hot. Taste for salt and season with a little pepper. Add the remaining tarragon and serve.

Artichoke, Shallot, and Fingerling Potato Ragout

Whole baby artichokes end up pleasantly plump and tender in this vegetable ragout. It's the ingredients that are special— the technique is easy. As for fingerling potatoes—choose your favorite variety and try to select ones that are about the same size. Serve this stew over a bed of braised spinach. Serves 4 Ⓥ

16 baby artichokes

1/2 lemon

8 fingerling potatoes, about 1 1/2 pounds

8 large shallots, peeled

2 tablespoons olive oil

3 cloves garlic, peeled and slivered

2 teaspoons minced rosemary, plus extra to finish

3 sprigs thyme, leaves stripped off, or 2 pinches dried

1 bay leaf

1 teaspoon sea salt

Freshly milled pepper

1/2 cup dry white wine

3 1/2 cups water or Basic Vegetable Stock (page 175)

4 teaspoons chopped parsley or tarragon, for garnish

Break the outer leaves off the artichokes until you get to the paler leaves. Don't stint here—tough leaves are stringy and unpleasant to eat. Trim the stems, slice a half inch off the top, and rub the cut parts with lemon. Boil 5 minutes in salted water, then drain. Peel the potatoes and quarter them lengthwise. Separate the shallots where natural divisions occur.

Warm the oil in a Dutch oven or sauté pan with the garlic, rosemary, thyme leaves, and bay. Add the artichokes, potatoes, and shallots and cook over a brisk heat, shaking the pan occasionally, until the potatoes start to color here and there, about 5 minutes. Season with the salt and a few twists pepper, and add the wine. Simmer 3 minutes, then lower the heat, add the water, cover the pan, and simmer 15 minutes or until the vegetables are tender when pierced with a knife. Serve with chopped rosemary and parsley or tarragon sprinkled over the top.

Braised Artichokes with Leeks and Peas

I often serve this braise with Sautéed Spinach (page 378) and long thin Garlic-Rubbed Crostini (page 24) to sop up the juices. Covered with puff pastry, this makes a lovely spring dish for a special occasion. Serves 4 to 6

4 large artichokes

2 1/2 to 3 cups Basic Vegetable Stock (page 175) or water

2 leeks, including an inch of the greens, sliced into
    1/4-inch rounds

2 fennel bulbs, cut into 1-inch wedges, joined at the root end

2 tablespoons butter or olive oil

1/4 cup diced shallot

1/2 cup white wine

1 teaspoon sea salt

12 ounces yellow-fleshed or new red potatoes,
    scrubbed and cut into quarters

1/2 cup or less crème fraîche

1 teaspoon Dijon mustard

1 cup shelled peas or fava beans

3 tablespoons chopped fennel greens or parsley

Freshly milled pepper

Trim the artichokes as described on page 295, cut into sixths, and set them aside in a bowl of acidulated water until ready to cook. If you're making a stock, be sure to include the trimmings from the leeks and fennel.

Melt the butter in a wide soup pot over medium-high heat. Add the shallot and leeks and cook, stirring frequently, without browning for 3 to 4 minutes. Add the wine, raise the heat, and simmer for 2 minutes.

Drain the artichokes and add them to the pan with the fennel and stock. Season with the salt, then press a piece of crumpled parchment or wax paper directly over the vegetables. Bring the liquid to a boil, then simmer, covered, until the artichokes are tender, about 25 minutes. Meanwhile, steam the potatoes until tender, 10 to 12 minutes.

When the artichokes and fennel are tender, remove them with a slotted spoon to a dish. Whisk enough crème fraîche and the mustard into the broth and boil briskly to make a thin sauce, 5 to 10 minutes. Add the peas and cook until tender, then return the vegetables and potatoes to the broth. Add the chopped fennel greens, season with pepper, and serve.

Artichoke, Pepper, and Chickpea Tagine with Preserved Lemons

This Moroccan-inspired tagine is richly endowed with the reds and golds of fall vegetables. Serve it spooned around a mound of steamed couscous or rice with the bright green chermoula drizzled on the top. The stew can sit while you make the couscous—time only improves it. Serves 4 (V)

Juice of 1 lemon

2 teaspoons sea salt

5 or 6 medium artichokes, trimmed and quartered

Pinch saffron threads

3 tablespoons olive oil

1 large onion, diced into 1/2-inch squares

2 large bell peppers, 1 yellow and 1 red, cut into 1/2-inch pieces

1 tablespoon Harissa (page 66)

1 (15-ounce) can chickpeas, rinsed, or 1 cup green chickpeas

12 oil-cured black olives

1 small Preserved Lemon (page 70), skin only, diced into
    small squares

2 tablespoons mixed chopped parsley and cilantro

1 cup dried couscous

Chermoula (page 50)

Bring 8 cups water to a boil, then add the lemon juice and salt. Boil the artichokes for 10 minutes, then drain and set aside. Cover the saffron with 1 tablespoon of the boiling water and set aside.

Heat the oil in a large skillet over high heat. Add the onion and peppers, sauté for 1 minute, then add the harissa. Reduce the heat to medium and cook for 5 minutes. Add the saffron and artichokes and continue cooking, turning the vegetables frequently, until they're coated with the spices and warmed through. Add the chickpeas, olives, lemon skin, herbs, and 2 cups water. Lower the heat and simmer for 15 minutes or until the artichokes are completely tender. Taste for salt.

Cook the couscous according to your favorite method. Mound it in the center of individual soup plates and spoon the vegetables around it. Drizzle the chermoula over the vegetables and serve.

Roasted Cauliflower and Tomato Curry

This recipe proves an appealing way of using cauliflower with tomatoes. What matters is that your spices are fresh and full of flavor, not old and faded. Serves 4 Ⓥ

1 cauliflower, cut into good-size florets

4 tablespoons ghee or sunflower seed oil

1 teaspoon cumin seeds

1 bay leaf

1 clove garlic, minced or pounded to a paste

2 teaspoons minced or pounded fresh ginger

1 onion, finely diced or grated

1 tablespoon ground coriander

$1/2$ teaspoon Garam Masala (page 25) or purchased

$1/2$ teaspoon turmeric

2 Thai red chiles, sliced lengthwise up to the stem, seeds removed if less heat is desired

1 (15-ounce) can diced organic tomatoes

$3/4$ teaspoon sea salt

Cilantro leaves, for garnish

Preheat the oven to 375°F. Toss the cauliflower florets with 2 tablespoons of the ghee, then turn them out onto a sheet pan and bake until they brown in places, turning them occasionally, about 20 minutes.

Melt the remaining 2 tablespoons ghee in a braising pot fitted with a lid. The heat should be medium high. When it's hot, add the cumin seeds and bay leaf, allow the seeds to sizzle, then add the garlic and ginger and stir them about the pan for about 30 seconds. Reduce the heat and add the onion. (Grated onion will be very wet and it will sputter.) Cook, stirring occasionally, until the onion has begun to color and soften, about 8 minutes.

Stir in the spices and chiles, add the tomatoes, and season with the salt. Pour in 1 cup of water, bring it to a simmer, then cover and cook over low heat for 5 minutes. Gently stir the cauliflower into the spices and tomatoes. Cover the pot again, reduce the heat to low, and cook gently until the cauliflower is done and the flavors are well blended, about 10 to 15 minutes. Taste for salt. Garnish with a small handful of cilantro leaves and serve.

Eggplant and Potatoes with Cumin, Ginger, and Yogurt

This dish of vegetables has a marvelous fragrance and pleasing textures, with the slightly firm potato and the completely softened eggplant. Both are both roasted first, leaving the cook free to prepare the rest of the meal or do something else altogether. Serve with rice and a refreshing salad of oranges and pomegranates or chilled melon with lime. Serves 4

1 large, firm eggplant (about $1^1/2$ pounds)

2 cloves garlic, thinly sliced

4 small yellow-fleshed potatoes, rubbed with oil

2 teaspoons cumin seeds

$1/4$ cup ghee or coconut oil

1 bay leaf

1 large yellow onion, diced in $1/2$-inch squares

1 tablespoon grated fresh ginger

4 medium tomatoes, or 1 (15-ounce) can, peeled, seeded, and chopped

$1/2$ cup water or juice from the tomatoes

$1/2$ teaspoon sea salt

$1/2$ cup yogurt

2 tablespoons chopped cilantro, plus cilantro leaves, for garnish

Preheat the oven to 375°F. Cut several small slits in the eggplant and stuff them with the sliced garlic. Bake the eggplant and the potatoes on a sheet pan until the eggplant has shriveled and the potatoes are soft when pierced with a knife, about 40 minutes. When cool enough to handle, peel the eggplant, then tear it into large pieces. Cut the potatoes, with their skins on, into $1/2$-inch chunks.

Roast the cumin seeds in a dry skillet until you can smell them, then turn them onto a plate. Grind half of them into a powder and set the remainder aside.

In a large, heavy pot, heat the ghee with the bay leaf. When hot, add the onion, ground cumin, and ginger. Cook, stirring frequently, until the onions are lightly colored and softened, about 12 minutes. Add the eggplant, potato, tomato, and liquid and turn gently with a rubber scraper. Season with the salt and cook over medium heat until the stew is thoroughly warmed and fully cooked. Taste for salt and add more, if needed. Stir in the yogurt and chopped cilantro, leaving marbled streaks. Garnish with the whole cumin seeds and cilantro leaves.

Corn, Tomato, and Okra Stew

Okra, known also as ladyfingers and gumbo and by many other names, is in the mallow family. Its beautiful hibiscus–like flowers, to which it's related, make it worthy as an ornamental as well as a vegetable. To be good, okra should be very small, the pods no longer than 3 inches but preferably about 2. It goes quickly from tender to tough as it increases in size. Serve over a plate of Carolina Gold rice to drink up the juices. Serves 4 or more

3 tablespoons butter, or 1½ tablespoons each butter and safflower oil

1 small yellow onion, finely diced

2 bay leaves

½ teaspoon dried thyme

½ teaspoon dried basil

½ teaspoon red pepper flakes

1 green bell pepper, seeded and finely diced

3 large ripe tomatoes, peeled, seeded, and chopped

2 cups small okra, left whole or sliced into ¼-inch rounds

Kernels from 3 ears corn

Sea salt and freshly milled pepper

Smoked paprika

Warm the butter or butter and oil in a skillet over medium heat. Add the onion, bay leaves, thyme, basil, and red pepper flakes. Sauté, stirring frequently, until the onions are limp, about 5 minutes. Add the bell pepper and cook to soften, then add the tomatoes, okra, and ½ cup water. Simmer, uncovered, for 15 minutes, then add the corn and cook until the corn is tender and heated through, 3 to 4 minutes. Season to taste with salt and pepper and a healthy dash of smoked paprika. Serve with rice.

Corn and Lima Bean Ragout

Carrot juice gives this ragout a soft glow and delicate sweet-ness. Purple basil leaves and yellow tomatoes also add con-siderable visual allure, though green basil and red tomatoes will be fine. Serve with warm biscuits split in half or over buttered toast. Serves 4 Ⓥ

1½ cups fresh or frozen lima beans

2 tablespoons diced onion

Aromatics: 1 bay leaf, 4 parsley sprigs, and 2 thyme sprigs

½ teaspoon sea salt

2 tablespoons butter or sunflower seed oil

1 bunch green onions, including 2 inches of the greens, thinly sliced

4 cups corn kernels, fresh or frozen

3 tablespoons chopped parsley

1 tablespoon chopped green or purple basil

1 tablespoon chopped thyme

½ teaspoon paprika

½ cup fresh carrot juice or bean broth

2 red or yellow tomatoes, peeled, seeded, and diced into ½-inch pieces

Freshly milled pepper

Cook the beans in a saucepan over medium heat with the onion, aromatics, the salt, and 2 cups water. When ten-der, after about 15 minutes, drain and reserve the broth. Remove the aromatics.

Melt the butter in a wide skillet or sauté pan over fairly high heat. Sauté the green onions and corn until they begin to color, about 2 minutes, then add the beans, half of the herbs, paprika, and carrot juice. Simmer for 4 minutes, then add the tomatoes and cook for 2 minutes more. Season with pepper, garnish with the remaining herbs, and serve.

Spring Vegetable Stew

Cooking the vegetables separately, then combining them, makes it possible to have everything ready in advance. Radishes and broccoli stems may be surprising, but they really give this dish an exceedingly fresh spring look.

While popovers or fresh herb noodles are good accompaniments, I sometimes add some potato gnocchi or cheese tortellini at the end for a soft, surprising mouthful. Serves 4 Ⓥ

1 tablespoon sea salt

12 baby carrots, or 2 carrots scrubbed and thinly sliced

1/2 cup snow peas

6 radishes, including 1/2 inch of the stems, halved

18 (3-inch) asparagus tips

6 green onions, including the stems, cut into 3-inch lengths

2 broccoli stems, thickly peeled and sliced diagonally

4 small turnips, or 2 rutabagas and 2 turnips, peeled and cut into sixths

3 tablespoons olive oil

4 thyme sprigs, preferably lemon thyme

1 tablespoon fresh lemon juice

1 tablespoon snipped chives

2 teaspoons finely chopped parsley

1 teaspoon chopped tarragon

Freshly milled pepper

Bring 12 cups water to a boil and add the salt. One type at a time, blanch the vegetables until barely tender, then remove to a bowl of cold water to stop the cooking. When all are blanched, reserve 1 cup of the cooking water. Drain the vegetables. (This can be done ahead of time.)

In a wide skillet, heat the oil with the thyme sprigs and reserved liquid. Add the vegetables and simmer until they're warmed through. Add the lemon juice and herbs, season with salt and pepper, and cook for 1 minute more. Serve at once.

Simple Summer Stew with Herb Butter

By choosing from all the new varieties of beans, squash, and tomatoes that appear in the market during the summer, you can create endless varieties with this single recipe.
Serves 4 Ⓥ

1 1/2 tablespoons chopped marjoram

1 1/2 tablespoons chopped basil

1 1/2 tablespoons chopped parsley

1/2 teaspoon grated lemon zest

Sea salt

1/4 cup softened butter, or olive oil

8 ounces green beans, preferably skinny ones, tipped, cut into 3-inch lengths

1 tablespoon olive oil

1 small onion, finely diced

1 clove garlic, thinly sliced

8 ounces small summer squash, diced or sliced into rounds

1 red or yellow bell pepper, cut into squares

1 large tomato, peeled, seeded, and diced

4 ears corn, shucked, about 3 cups kernels

Freshly milled pepper

In a small bowl, combine the marjoram, basil, parsley, lemon zest, a pinch of salt, and the butter. Mix thoroughly and set aside.

Bring a pot of water to a boil and add a pinch of salt. Cook the beans, uncovered, for 2 minutes and then drain.

Heat the oil in a wide pan over high heat with the onion and garlic. Sauté for 1 minute, then add 1/2 cup water, lower the heat, cover, and simmer for 5 minutes. Add the beans, squash, pepper, tomato, and corn. Season with 1/2 teaspoon sea salt, cover, and simmer over low heat for 10 minutes or until tender. Stir in the herb butter, taste for salt, and season with pepper.

Mushroom Stews

Mushroom stews are versatile, quick to make, and substantial in flavor. They serve extremely well as a main course at any time of year, for mushrooms pair well with wintry herbs, such as rosemary, as well as with the more summery mint and marjoram.

Many markets now carry portabella, cremini, shiitake, and oyster mushrooms. In specialty markets, you can even find porcini, morels, and chanterelles. All are pricey, but mushrooms are light, and a few special varieties mixed with white mushrooms make a more interesting dish. A small amount of dried wild mushrooms also adds unique, woodsy flavor notes to these dishes.

When using portabellas, I remove the gills since they are the first thing to spoil on mushrooms, plus they can turn the liquid black. Always make sure gills are dry and unbroken and have a fresh, sweet smell. A mushroom stock, whether a quick stock, the long-simmered stock, or commercial stock, adds a great deal of background flavor to these dishes.

Mushroom stews go well with soft or grilled polenta, popovers, or fresh egg noodles. Drained of their juices, they make an ideal filling for a crepe or a savory galette. Don't discard those juices; save them to use as a sauce.

Quick Mushroom Stock

Makes about 1 cup Ⓥ

- 1/4 cup or more dried porcini
- 2 teaspoons olive oil
- 1 onion, coarsely chopped
- 1 carrot, chopped
- 1 large clove garlic, sliced
- 2 mushrooms, sliced, plus any trimmings
- 2 teaspoons tomato paste
- 1 tablespoon fresh marjoram or 1 teaspoon dried
- 1/2 cup dry white or red wine
- 1 tablespoon flour
- 1/2 teaspoon sea salt
- Freshly milled pepper
- 1 teaspoon red wine vinegar

Cover the dried mushrooms with 1 1/2 cups hot water and set aside. Heat the oil in a saucepan over high heat. Add the onion, carrot, garlic, and fresh mushroom trimmings. Sauté, stirring occasionally, until well browned, about

10 minutes. Reduce the heat to medium, stir in the tomato paste, marjoram, and wine, and sprinkle on the flour. Cover the pan and cook until the wine is reduced to a syrupy glaze, about 3 minutes. Add the porcini and their soaking water, the salt, a little pepper, and the vinegar and simmer for 20 minutes. Strain. Remove the dried mushrooms and add them to the liquid. If you wish to concentrate the sauce, simmer it in an open pot until it's reduced to the desired strength.

Mushrooms with Paprika and Sour Cream

Serve over flat egg noodles, wild rice, buckwheat groats, or barley. Serves 3 or 4

- 1 1/2 tablespoons butter
- 1 1/2 tablespoons olive oil
- 1 bunch green onions, including some of the greens, chopped
- 1 pound large white mushrooms, thickly sliced or quartered
- 3/4 teaspoon sea salt
- Freshly milled pepper
- 1 teaspoon flour
- 1 tablespoon sweet Hungarian paprika
- 1 cup Mushroom Stock (page 176) or Quick Mushroom Stock (preceeding recipe)
- 1/2 cup sour cream or a mixture of sour cream and yogurt

Heat the butter and oil in a wide skillet over high heat. Add the onions and mushrooms and sauté until the mushrooms begin to color, about 6 minutes. Lower the heat and season with the salt and pepper to taste. Sprinkle the flour and paprika over the mushrooms, add the stock, and simmer, covered, for 3 to 4 minutes. Stir in the sour cream and gently heat through, but do not boil.

With Tofu: Dice a 10-ounce block of firm tofu into 1-inch cubes. Simmer in a pan of salted water for 4 minutes, then drain. Add the tofu to the mushrooms once they've colored. The tofu should color as well; move it gently in the pan with a rubber spatula so that all sides are exposed to the heat. Continue the recipe as described, adding a little more stock as needed.

Summer Mushroom Ragout

The presence of fresh tomatoes, marjoram, and mint gives this ragout a summery aspect. Serve over soft polenta, fresh egg noodles, barley, or rice. Serves 4 Ⓥ

Quick Mushroom Stock (page 223) or
    1 cup commercial stock

8 ounces oyster, shiitake, or cremini mushrooms,
    stems removed

1 pound large white mushrooms, stems trimmed

3 tablespoons olive oil

2 cloves garlic, thinly sliced

4 teaspoons chopped marjoram

2 tablespoons chopped parsley

2 large ripe tomatoes, peeled, seeded, and chopped

1/2 teaspoon sea salt

Freshly milled pepper

1 teaspoon chopped mint

Make the stock first and include the mushroom trimmings. Slice all but the oyster mushrooms about 1/3 inch thick.

Warm the oil and garlic in a wide skillet over medium heat until the garlic is fragrant and golden, about 3 minutes. Remove the garlic. Add the marjoram, parsley, and tomatoes, cook for 1 minute, then raise the heat and add the mushrooms. Season with the salt and a little pepper. Sauté until the mushrooms begin to color, about 5 minutes. Add the stock, lower the heat, and simmer until the mushrooms are tender and the stock is slightly reduced. Stir in the mint and serve.

Winter Portabella Mushroom Stew

A quick and reliable stew with big flavors and many applications. It's best if you can use mushroom stock, but not impossible without it. Serve with soft polenta, mashed potatoes, fresh Rosemary Pasta (page 401), or Wehani Rice Pilaf with Red Wine (page 482). Serves 4 Ⓥ

4 tablespoons olive oil

1 large onion, cut into 1/2-inch dice

2 teaspoons chopped rosemary

Sea salt and freshly milled pepper

2 pinches red pepper flakes

1/2 pound portabella mushrooms, gills removed,
    sliced 3/8 inch thick

1 pound large white mushrooms, thickly sliced

2 cloves garlic, minced

3 tablespoons tomato paste

1 1/2 cups Quick Mushroom Stock (page 223) or water

1 teaspoon sherry vinegar

2 tablespoons butter, optional

2 tablespoons chopped parsley or tarragon

Heat 1 tablespoon of the oil in a large skillet over medium heat. Add the onion and rosemary and cook, stirring occasionally, until lightly browned, about 12 minutes. Season with salt, pepper, and red pepper flakes and transfer to a bowl.

Return the pan to medium heat and add 1 1/2 tablespoons of the oil. When it's hot, add the portabella mushrooms and sauté until nicely browned, about 5 minutes. Add them to the onion mixture and repeat with the remaining 1 1/2 teaspoons oil and the white mushrooms. Return everything to the pan and add the garlic, tomato paste, stock, and vinegar. Simmer gently for 12 to 15 minutes, then swirl in the butter. Add the parsley, taste for salt, and season with pepper.

Tunisian Pepper and Potato Stew over Couscous

These vegetables yield a surprisingly delicious broth, part of which is used to cook the couscous. You can easily make this dish more substantial by including 1 cup of cooked dried or green chickpeas, fresh fava beans, or 6 small (4-inch) zucchini or other small summer squash. Serves 6 Ⓥ

3 large red and orange bell peppers

1 green and 1 yellow bell pepper

$^1/_3$ cup olive oil

1 large onion, cut into $^1/_2$-inch dice

1$^1/_2$ teaspoon dried spearmint

$^1/_2$ teaspoon crushed red pepper flakes

1 pound yellow-fleshed boiling potatoes, peeled and cut lengthwise in sixths

2 tablespoons tomato paste

4 cloves garlic, peeled and crushed with a knife

1$^1/_2$ teaspoons sea salt

4 tomatoes, peeled, seeded and chopped, or 1 (15-ounce) can diced

2 tablespoons butter or olive oil

1$^1/_2$ cups couscous

Harissa (page 66)

2 tablespoons chopped parsley

Slice the tops off the peppers and cut them lengthwise into strips a good inch across. Slice each piece in half if the peppers were very long, or leave them whole if no more than 3 inches long. Set aside.

In a wide deep skillet or Dutch oven, heat the oil and add the onion, mint, pepper flakes, potatoes, tomato paste, and garlic. Cook over medium heat, stirring occasionally, for 10 minutes. Add the salt and the peppers, raise the heat, and sauté the peppers, about 2 minutes, searing them well. Add the tomatoes and 3 cups water. Lower the heat and simmer, partially covered, until the potatoes are tender, about 20 minutes. When done, remove 2 cups of the liquid for the couscous.

To make the couscous, heat the reserved broth, taste, and season with salt, if needed. Melt the butter or heat the oil in a 10-inch skillet or wide pot fitted with a lid. Add the couscous and cook, stirring constantly over medium heat, about 2 minutes, without browning. Remove from the heat and pour in the reserved warm broth. It will instantly spurt up. When it subsides, shake the pan to even the contents,

cover, and set aside for 7 minutes. Fluff the grains with a fork to break, spoon another $^1/_2$ cup water over them, and cover again for 5 minutes.

Thin the harissa with a few tablespoons water or olive oil so that it's the texture of soft butter. Mound the couscous in a dish, add the parsley to the vegetables, and spoon them around the couscous. Spoon some of the harissa over the couscous and pass the rest at the table.

Cashew Curry

I am indebted to Joe Evans for this very luxurious dish. Though rich, cashew nuts are composed mainly of mono-unsaturated fat—and even small portions are filling. The cashews need 6 hours to soak, so plan ahead. Serve with basmati rice. Curry leaves are available at Indian markets. Serves 4 Ⓥ

$^1/_2$ pound whole cashew nuts

2 tablespoons coconut oil or ghee

5 shallots, thinly sliced

2 small bay leaves, or 5 curry leaves

1 (2-inch) piece lemongrass or grated zest of 1 lemon

1 tablespoon ground coriander

$^1/_2$ teaspoon turmeric

1 serrano chile, thinly sliced

2 cloves garlic, chopped

2 slices ginger

$^1/_2$ teaspoon sea salt

1 (15-ounce) can coconut milk

2 tablespoons chopped cilantro

Soak the cashews for 6 hours, changing the water several times so the nuts will whiten. Drain, then put them in a saucepan with 1$^1/_2$ cups water and simmer until tender, 12 to 15 minutes. Taste them as they cook to make sure they don't become mushy. Drain and set aside.

Heat the coconut oil in a small skillet, add the shallots, and cook over medium heat until golden, stirring occasionally, about 10 minutes. Add the bay leaves, lemongrass, coriander, turmeric, chile, garlic, ginger, and the salt. Cook until fragrant, then add the coconut milk, 1 tablespoon of the cilantro, and the cashews. Simmer over moderate heat until the sauce is thickened, stirring occasionally. Remove the bay leaves. Garnish with remaining 1 tablespoon cilantro.

Southwest Bean and Summer Vegetable Stew

Formerly known as Zuni Stew in The Greens Cookbook, *this recipe was inspired by my first trip to New Mexico. I still make it today, only I've brought some new beans into the picture, like Rio Zapes, Good Mother Stallard, and New Mexican bolitas. The pintos, originally called for, are still a good choice. Serve with cornbread or tortillas.* Serves 6 Ⓥ

Beans

1¼ cup dried beans such as Rio Zape, pinto, Anasazi, or other

1 teaspoon sea salt

1 bay leaf

1 teaspoon dried oregano

Vegetables

2 tablespoons oil

1 large onion, cut into small dice

2 cloves garlic, minced

2 tablespoons ground red chile, mild or hot, as desired

1 teaspoon toasted ground cumin

1 teaspoon toasted ground coriander seeds

Sea salt

2 ancho chiles

1 pound or 1 (15-ounce) can tomatoes, peeled, seeded, chopped, juices reserved

1 pound mixed summer squash, cut into large dice

Kernels from 4 ears corn

8 ounces plump green beans, such as Romanos, cut into 1-inch lengths

Grated Muenster or Jack cheese, optional

½ bunch cilantro, finely chopped, plus whole sprigs for garnish

Cover the beans with boiling water, soak for 1 hour, then drain and rinse. Put them in a pot with 8 cups water, the salt, bay leaf, and oregano. Bring to a boil, then cover and simmer until tender, about 1½ hours. (You can also cook them, unsoaked, in a pressure cooker until tender, but not mushy, about 25 minutes on high.) When done, drain the beans and set aside the broth for the stew.

Heat the oil in a wide soup pot, then add the onion and cook over high heat, stirring frequently, for about 5 minutes. Lower the heat, add the garlic, ground red chile, cumin, and coriander, and stir all together, adding a little bean broth so that the chile doesn't burn. Season with a few pinches of salt.

While the onions are stewing, open the ancho chile pods and remove the seeds and veins. Cut the flesh into narrow strips, then add them to the pot along with the tomatoes, summer squash, corn, and green beans. Next add the cooked beans and enough of the broth to make a thick, stewy soup. Simmer gently until the vegetables are cooked and tender, about 20 minutes. Taste for salt.

Serve with the cheese, stirred into each bowl with the minced cilantro. Garnish each bowl with whole sprigs of the herb.

Spaghetti Squash with Oyster Mushroom and Pearl Onion Ragout

With the little pearl onions and oyster mushrooms, this definitely qualifies as a company dish. Serves 4 Ⓥ

1 spaghetti squash, about 3 pounds, pierced in several places

1 pound pearl onions

2 tablespoons olive oil

1 tablespoon butter or additional oil, plus extra for the squash

1 teaspoon sugar

1 parsnip, peeled and finely diced

1 carrot, peeled and finely diced

¼ teaspoon dried thyme

1 teaspoon chopped sage leaves

Sea salt and freshly milled pepper

1 large clove garlic, minced

1 pound oyster or white mushrooms, thinly sliced

4 teaspoons tomato paste diluted with ¼ cup red wine or water

2 tablespoons mushroom soy or regular soy sauce

1 tablespoon chopped parsley, for garnish

Preheat the oven to 375°F. Set the squash in a pan and bake for 40 minutes. Turn it over and continue baking until completely tender, another 15 to 30 minutes. When done, turn off the oven and let the squash sit until needed.

Meanwhile, cut a sliver off the root ends of the onions. Boil them for 1 minute, then transfer to a bowl of cold water. Peel and cut any larger ones in half.

Heat 1 tablespoon each oil and butter, or 2 tablespoons oil, in a large skillet over medium heat. Add the onions, toss to coat, then sprinkle with sugar. Cook, giving the pan a shake now and then, until they start to color, after about 10 minutes. Add the parsnip, carrot, and herbs, season with salt and pepper, and continue cooking until the onions are nicely caramelized, about 10 minutes more.

Set the vegetables aside in a bowl, add another tablespoon of oil to the pan, then add the garlic and mushrooms. Stir quickly, season with salt and pepper, and cook until they begin to color, about 5 minutes. Add the onions back to the pan and add the diluted tomato paste and soy sauce. Cook until the mushrooms are tender, then turn off the heat. (To keep the vegetables moist and to make a little sauce, add water or mushroom stock in small increments.)

Cut the cooked squash in half lengthwise and scoop out the seeds. Pull apart the strands with a fork, toss them with butter or oil to taste, and season with salt and pepper. Pile the squash onto four individual plates, spoon the vegetables around it, garnish with parsley, and serve.

Winter Vegetable Stew with Sunchokes

An easy stew to assemble, it needs about 30 minutes to cook. Serve over Rosemary Pasta (page 401), buckwheat groats, or the Wehani Rice Pilaf with Red Wine (page 482) or under a pastry lid. If you're a tofu enthusiast, drain 8 ounces firm tofu, cut it into cubes, and then fry in olive oil until browned. Add to the stew during the last 20 minutes of cooking. Serves 4 Ⓥ

2 tablespoons olive oil

1 large onion, diced

6 cloves garlic, peeled, plus 1 clove chopped

2 bay leaves

1/4 teaspoon chopped thyme

4 large carrots, cut into 2-inch lengths

2 celery ribs, cut into 2-inch lengths

4 medium boiling potatoes, peeled and quartered

1/2 pound Jerusalem artichokes (sunchokes), scrubbed and cut into 1/2-inch pieces

1 1/2 teaspoons sea salt

Freshly milled pepper

1/8 teaspoon grated nutmeg

1 cup dry red wine

1 tablespoon tomato paste

1 tablespoon flour

2 tablespoons chopped parsley

Heat the oil in a Dutch oven over medium heat. Add the onion, 6 cloves garlic, the bay leaves, and thyme and cook, stirring occasionally, until the onion begins to brown, about 12 minutes. Add the vegetables and season with the salt, pepper, and nutmeg. Cook for 5 minutes, then raise the heat to high and add the wine. Scrape up any onion bits from the bottom, then simmer until the liquid is reduced by half. Reduce the heat to medium, add the tomato paste, sprinkle with flour, and cook, covered, for 2 minutes.

Stir in 1 cup water and cook until the liquid is again reduced by half. Reduce the heat to low, then simmer, covered, until the vegetables are tender, 20 to 25 minutes. Check the seasonings. Add the chopped parsley and garlic just before serving.

Winter Vegetable Pot Pie

Topping a stew with a puff pastry lid makes an impressive dish even if you use frozen puff pastry, which I do. The vegetable amounts given here are really suggestions. Salsify, parsley root, and other vegetables are wonderful additions if you have the good fortune to come across them. Oyster mushrooms, brussels sprouts, fennel, and Jerusalem artichokes are also good candidates for this stew. Except for the oyster mushrooms, the vegetables should be parboiled before being added to the final dish.

This stew is a little more elaborate to make than other dishes, but while the sauce is cooling, you can prepare the vegetables, and the whole dish, minus the pastry, can be put together hours or a day in advance of baking. Serves 4

1 sheet frozen puff pastry, thawed

2 cups Herb Béchamel (page 47)

1½ pounds butternut squash, peeled and cut into 1-inch dice

Flour, for dredging

2 tablespoons olive oil

2 tablespoons butter

16 shallots or boiling onions, peeled and left whole

1 small celery root

Juice of 1 lemon

3 parsnips, peeled and diced

2 kohlrabi or turnips, peeled and cut into wedges

5 medium carrots, cut into 2-inch lengths

Sea salt and freshly milled pepper

4 thyme sprigs

½ cup cream or milk

1 egg, beaten

Choose an 8-cup soufflé or gratin dish or four individual 2-cup casseroles. Roll out the pastry between ⅛ and ¼ inch thick and cut it to fit the dish. Cut out leaves or other decorative shapes from the scraps. Refrigerate the pastry until needed. Have the béchamel cooking in a double boiler while you prepare the vegetables.

Toss the squash in flour, letting the excess fall away. Heat the oil and butter in a large skillet and add the squash and shallots. Sauté over medium heat until browned and tender, 20 to 30 minutes, stirring occasionally so that they color evenly. Transfer to the baking dish.

Peel the celery root, dice it into 1-inch cubes, and put in the bowl with the juice plus water to cover. Parboil the remaining vegetables in salted water until tender but still a little firm. Drain, then parboil the celery root for 1 minute. Combine all the vegetables, season with salt and pepper, and transfer the stew to the dish. Tuck in the thyme sprigs.

Mix the béchamel and cream and pour it over the vegetables, allowing the sauce to fall between the cracks. Refrigerate if baking later, then bring to room temperature before baking.

When ready to bake, preheat the oven to 425°F. Remove the pastry from the refrigerator and lay it on top of the vegetables. Brush the top side with egg, add any decorations, and glaze them, too. Bake for 12 minutes, then lower the heat to 350°F and continue baking until the crust is golden and puffed and the sauce is bubbling, 15 to 20 minutes more. Let settle for a few minutes, then serve.

Dairy-Free Variation: Make the sauce with any vegetable stock or plant milk, using 2½ cups in all. Sauté the vegetables in olive oil. Replace the puff pastry with Yeasted Tart Dough with Olive Oil (page 433). ⓥ

Sautés

Sautés are also comprised of assorted vegetables and often include a broth or aromatic liquid but lack the convivial simmering of ragouts—they are cooked much more quickly. They are closer to stir-fries and sometimes include the ginger and soy of those dishes, but not always. These sautéed vegetables are not just side dishes, but have enough complexity to stand in as a light main dish, especially when served with rice, polenta, and other such foods.

Red Onion and Spinach Sauté in Coconut Oil

Onions alone, and greens alone, are the best sautéed in coconut oil, but together they make more of a dish and less of bite to have with something else. If you really want to round this out and make it a solo main dish, I suggest adding cooked chickpeas. If you just want to make it for yourself with half an onion and a handful of spinach, that works too.
Serves 2 to 4 Ⓥ

2 tablespoons extra-virgin coconut oil
1 large red onion, halved and sliced about ¹/₂ inch thick
Sea salt
1 bunch spinach leaves, washed and roughly chopped, stems removed
Juice of 1 lime
Coconut butter to finish

Heat the oil in a wide skillet, then add the sliced onion. Cook on high heat, tossing it about the pan, until some of the pieces get some color on them, about 5 minutes. Sprinkle with salt. They'll still be firm, but sweet. Add the spinach, sprinkle with another pinch or two of salt, then turn it into the onions until it has wilted, another 5 minutes or so. Taste for salt.

Squeeze the lime over the dish, then garnish with crumbles of coconut butter.

Green Mix Sauté with Coconut and Turmeric

"Green mix" refers to those mixes of tender, small cooking greens so often found at farmers' markets. Should the greens be larger and tougher, wilt them first before adding them to the onions. Serve with rice. Serves 4 Ⓥ

2 tablespoons coconut oil or ghee
1 onion, sliced or diced
1 tablespoon freshly grated ginger
2 plump cloves garlic, finely minced
2 teaspoons Garam Masala (page 25) or purchased
¹/₂ teaspoon turmeric
1 pound of mixed cooked greens, washed, but not dried
¹/₂ teaspoon sea salt
¹/₂ cup coconut milk
Freshly milled pepper

Heat the oil in Dutch oven. Add the onion, turn it in the oil and cook until softened, about 5 minutes, before adding the ginger, garlic, garam masala, and turmeric. Stir the spices into the onions, then add the greens. If wet, they should start steaming right away. Season with ¹/₂ teaspoon salt, add the coconut milk, cover the pan and cook until wilted and tender, from five minutes on, depending on the greens. Turn them with the onions a few times as they cook. When done, taste for salt and season with pepper. Serve over rice.

Winter Squash and Cabbage Sauté with Toasted Sesame Seeds

Savoy cabbage or an oxheart type would be my first choice, but any green cabbage is good, including napa cabbage, which takes less time to cook. This sauté, which is naturally sweet, tastes especially good with nutty-flavored short-grained brown rice. It takes about 20 minutes in all to make, so if you want to serve it with brown rice, begin the rice first. Serves 4 Ⓥ

1¹/₂ to 2 pounds butternut or delicata squash

1¹/₂ pounds green cabbage

2 tablespoons light sesame or vegetable oil

1 large onion, diced

1 teaspoon sea salt

1 tablespoon soy sauce or tamari

¹/₄ cup sesame seeds, black, white or both, toasted

1 teaspoon toasted sesame oil

Peel the squash and dice into cubes slightly less than ¹/₂ inch across. Quarter the cabbage, remove the cores, and chop into 1-inch squares.

Heat the light sesame oil in wide, heavy skillet. When hot, add the onion and squash and sauté over medium-high heat, stirring frequently, until the onion is golden and the squash has begun to brown in places, about 7 minutes. Add the cabbage, and toss with the salt. Once the cabbage is warm, add ¹/₂ cup water, cover the pan, and cook over medium heat. After 5 minutes, check the pan. If it's dry, add another ¹/₂ cup water. Continue cooking in this fashion until the squash is finally tender, after 12 to 15 minutes.

Add the soy sauce, toss well, and cook a minute longer. Add the sesame seeds, toss again with the toasted sesame oil, then serve.

With Tofu: Sauté small cubes of firm tofu in a nonstick pan with just a little sesame oil until golden. Season with salt and pepper as they cook, then glaze with a splash of soy sauce when done. If you prefer softer tofu, cut it into 1-inch cubes and steam them over the cabbage and squash as the vegetables steam. This allows the delicacy of the tofu to come forward. Ⓥ

Cauliflower, Spinach, and Potato Sauté with Coconut Milk

Though a sauté, this is an Indian-inspired dish. Serve over brown or white basmati rice. Serves 3 or 4 Ⓥ

1 small cauliflower, cut into small florets

¹/₂ pound fingerling or waxy potatoes, sliced ¹/₃ inch thick

1 bunch green onions sliced, including a few inches of the greens

¹/₂ cup chopped cilantro

¹/₂ teaspoon turmeric

2 serrano chiles, minced

3¹/₂ tablespoons peanut oil or ghee

1 large bunch spinach, stems removed

¹/₂ teaspoon sea salt

1 (15-ounce) can coconut milk

Separately boil the cauliflower and potatoes in salted water until tender, then drain. Set aside 2 tablespoons each of the onions and cilantro and puree the remaining cilantro, turmeric, chiles, and 1¹/₂ tablespoons of the peanut oil.

Heat the pan, then add 2 teaspoons of the oil and swirl it about the sides. When hot, add the remaining onions and sauté for 1 minute. Add the spinach and sauté until wilted and tender. Remove and set aside. Add another 2 teaspoons oil and fry until fragrant. Add the cauliflower and potatoes, season with the salt, and cook until heated through. Pour in the coconut milk and return the spinach to the wok. Bring to a boil and simmer for 2 minutes. Taste again for salt.

Broccoli Leaves and Onion Sauté

One of our farmers figured the smaller broccoli leaves are good to eat, too, not just the crowns. The really large outer leaves are not what we're talking about here—those leaves are thick, tough, and well worn, showing ragged edges and holes from months exposed to the elements. But smaller ones, closer to the head, about the size of a collard leaf, have more culinary possibilities. Broccoli greens are easy to cook, but they aren't timid by any means. Think of them as a less tender replacement for broccoli rabe and expect them to be assertive enough to serve with something farinaceous, like pasta, potatoes, or polenta. Serves 4 Ⓥ

12 ounces broccoli leaves, with stems

Olive oil

1 large onion, a fresh one if possible, halved and sliced in scant 1/2-inch slices

1/2 teaspoon sea salt

Red pepper flakes or freshly milled pepper

Soy sauce or vinegar, optional

Slice the stems from the base of the broccoli leaves, then cut them into 1/2-inch pieces and rinse. Cut the leaves into large pieces without removing the center stem and rinse well, but don't dry.

Heat a generous splash of oil in a 10-inch skillet. Add the onion and chopped stems and sauté over fairly high heat for 3 to 4 minutes, or until the onions are limp and have started to color. Add the leaves, turn them to bring the onions and stems to the top of the heap, season with the salt. Lower the heat and cook for 12 to 15 minutes, turning occasionally and adding a few splashes of water once or twice if the pan gets really dry.

When done to your taste—cook them even longer if you want them buttery-soft—turn off the heat and turn with a few pinches pepper flakes or season with freshly milled pepper. Taste for salt as well and add more if needed, or add a small amount of soy sauce. A dash of vinegar is always good with greens, as well.

Sauté of Cauliflower and Greens

I am indebted to Joe Evans for this dish, which marries the rich aromas of a curry with the speedy lightness of a stir-fry. The ghee is important to this dish for its flavor and high heating point. Serve with Naan (page 599) or pappadums. Serves 4

3 potatoes, peeled and cubed

4 tablespoons ghee

1 large onion, thinly sliced

1 small cauliflower, quartered and thinly sliced, including the stem

Sea salt

2 teaspoons chopped garlic

1/2 teaspoon turmeric

1 teaspoon each ground cumin and coriander

1 teaspoon mustard seeds

1 bunch spinach, stems removed

1 bunch watercress, large stems removed

1 small carrot, grated

Juice of 1 lime

Several pinches Garam Masala (page 25)

Cilantro sprigs, for garnish

Steam the potatoes until tender. Heat 2 tablespoons of the ghee in a wide sauté pan over medium-high heat. Add the onion and sauté until well browned, about 12 minutes. Remove and set aside. Melt the remaining ghee in the same pan over high heat. Add the cauliflower, season with salt, and sauté until it begins to color in places, after a few minutes. Return the onion to the pan and add the garlic, spices, and potatoes. Lower the heat and cook until everything is heated through, about 4 minutes. Add the greens, carrot, and 1/2 cup water. Cover and cook until the greens are wilted, about a minute. Season with lime juice and a few pinches garam masala, then turn onto a platter and garnish with the sprigs of cilantro.

Sautéed Cooking Greens with Pepper Sauce

Mixes of greens intended for cooking rather than for salads is something I appreciate, especially when the mix is interesting and the leaves aren't too terribly large. This is the simplest approach to cooking greens, yet it's robust and delicious, especially if the greens used are strong to start with. Choy sum and bok choy are also excellent cooked this way. Serves 4 Ⓥ

- 1 pound trimmed and washed cooking greens, a mixture or one green, such as collards
- 2 tablespoons olive oil or a more neutral-tasting oil if you prefer
- 2 cloves garlic, slivered
- 2 pinches dried red pepper flakes
- Sea salt
- Pepper Sauce (page 65) or lemon wedges

Even if your greens are already washed, it doesn't hurt to plunge them into a bowl of water and swish them around. Remove, but don't dry them.

Warm the oil in a deep pot, like a Dutch oven, with the garlic and red pepper flakes. Medium heat should be fine. Once the garlic begins to color, add the greens. Turn them about with a pair of tongs several times, season with a few pinches of salt, then cover the pot. Steam the greens in their own moisture for 10 to 15 minutes. Take a taste. They may be sufficiently cooked, depending on the type of leaves. If not, continue cooking until they're done to your liking. (I know my Southern relatives would cook these for hours, rather than minutes. It's what you're used to.) Taste for salt and add more as needed. Serve with an additional drizzle of olive oil and pepper sauce or lemon on the side.

Sautéed Brussels Sprouts with Cashews

Bharti Kirchner, an Indian-born cook, author, and world traveler, offered this unusual sauté recipe in her book Indian Inspired, *which has in turn inspired me. Finally, here's a recipe that uses those hearty sprouts made from peas, lentils, and beans to best advantage. This is delicious over brown rice.* Serves 2 Ⓥ

- 6 brussels sprouts, trimmed and sliced into 1/4-inch strips
- 6 ounces sprouted lentils, peas, adzuki, or other firm sprouts
- 1 1/2 tablespoons sesame or mustard oil
- 1/4 teaspoon cumin seeds
- 3 cloves garlic, finely chopped
- 1 bunch green onions, including 2 inches of the greens, chopped
- 1 small onion, quartered and thinly sliced
- 1/2 cup toasted cashews
- Sea salt
- Lime juice

Steam the brussels sprouts until barely tender, then rinse and set aside. Steam the sprouted beans until they're tender, 3 to 5 minutes.

Heat the oil in a wok, add the cumin seeds, and fry until they're aromatic and lightly browned. Add the garlic and, as soon as it begins to color, add the green onions and onion. Sauté until the onions are translucent, 3 to 4 minutes. Lower the heat and add the brussels sprouts, sprouted legumes, and cashews. Cook, uncovered, for 1 minute more or until heated through. Remove from the heat and season with salt and lime juice to taste.

Stir-Fries

The speed and lightness of the stir-fry have made it one of the most appealing dishes for home cooks. Many people tell me that they find the singular activity of cleaning and slicing the vegetables to be relaxing at the end of the day. I've always been more of stew person, but as I have learned about stir-frying, I have grown to appreciate its rhythm and flavors. I find it's a method that works with a variety of vegetables and non-Asian seasonings, as some of these recipes testify.

What Is Stir-Frying?

Stir-frying is, in short, a single motion made of three parts:

1. Sautéing the aromatics (chile, garlic, ginger, and green onions) in oil

2. Adding the vegetables and stock and, in some cases, steaming the tougher vegetables first

3. Thickening with cornstarch or adding other sauce ingredients

The first step infuses the oil with flavor. The second step cooks the vegetables. The third concentrates the juices and thickens the sauce.

Stir-frying developed where fuel is scarce—hence the fine slicing and the wok itself. With its thin metal walls, the wok conducts heat rapidly so that flavors are scaled in and the vegetables cook quickly. You may prefer to use a large, lightweight skillet, but the cooking motions will still be fast and energetic. You can expect to make a racket as the utensils—a large metal spatula and ladle—clang against the metal sides of the wok. One of the best ways to get a vivid sense of stir-frying is to go to a Chinese restaurant where you can watch the cooks throw themselves into it. It's exhilarating to watch.

How to Make (Most) Stir-Fries

Some stir-fries are very simple—just a single vegetable—while others have layerings of ingredients such as vegetables, tofu, condiments, noodles, and so on. Nonetheless, these basic techniques pertain to all.

1. Have all your ingredients cut, sliced, blanched when appropriate, measured, and set out in bowls within easy reach of the stove before you begin to cook.

2. Set the wok over high heat before adding the oil, then swirl or push the oil around the sides and heat until a haze forms before you begin cooking. (Author Eileen Yin-Fei Lo heats a slice of ginger in the oil and knows that when it turns light brown the oil is hot enough.)

3. Add the aromatics—green onions, ginger, garlic, red pepper flakes—and immediately begin quickly pushing and moving them around the wok. This process takes 30 seconds to 1 minute.

4. Add the vegetables and a few pinches sea salt and energetically stir them about the pan with the spatula. Keep moving the food from the center of the wok to the hot sides so it will cook quickly.

5. If called for, add stock or mushroom-soaking water, condiments, soy sauce, tofu, and so on. Also if called for, cover the wok and let everything cook until it's sufficiently tender. When the vegetables are done, make a space in the middle and add diluted cornstarch if the recipe calls for it. Once it thickens and darkens, toss to coat the vegetables.

6. Add final seasonings, such as roasted sesame or peanut oil, cilantro, toasted seeds or nuts, and so on. Taste and add more salt or soy sauce if needed.

Some Essential Ingredients

A few staples available in many Asian supermarkets will greatly enhance your stir-fries and give them an interesting range of flavors, tastes, and textures. Stir-fry enthusiasts, however, will undoubtedly go far beyond this modest list.

PEANUT OIL: Light and neutral, peanut oil has a high smoke point.

ROASTED PEANUT OIL: Richer, with the clear aroma of peanuts, used for the stir-frying or as a flavoring at the end. Two Chinese brands are Lion and Globe; Loriva is American.

TOASTED SESAME OIL: Dark color and rich, deep flavor make toasted sesame oil a potent seasoning. A few drops are added to the Stock for Stir-Fries (page 235) and to a finished stir-fry. Chili oil is chile-infused toasted sesame oil.

SOY SAUCE: A visit to an Asian market or even the Asian section of your supermarket will reveal that there's more than one kind of soy sauce. There's thin or light soy, dark soy, a deep mushroom-based soy, and the concentrated Japanese tamari. There's also sodium-reduced and lite soy sauce. When it comes to these stir-fries, thin soy sauces or regular Kikkoman are the ones to use, for they won't overwhelm the vegetables. The richer sauces, like bigger wines, go better in dishes where meat or fowl are present. However, mushroom soy and tamari do provide deep and hearty flavors. If you like them, just use half the amount called for, then add more, if needed, to taste. My favorite brand is Ohsawa Organic Naha Shoyu; it has a good, clean flavor and is unpasteurized. For tamari, San-J is full-bodied and contains no wheat.

BLACK RICE VINEGAR: A mild vinegar that is uncommonly dark and rich in color. Balsamic or apple cider vinegar can be used in its place.

WHITE RICE VINEGAR: Clear and very mild with a hint of the sweetness of rice. The Japanese version is delicate but not as interesting as some Chinese brands, such as Narcissus and Swatow.

CHINESE WINE (SHAO-HSING): A rich, mellow flavor that isn't easily duplicated by other wines, although pale dry sherry can be used in its place. Keep corked and at room temperature.

CHINESE BLACK MUSHROOMS: These can also be brown. They resemble shiitake, with the familiar mushroom shape. They need to be soaked in warm water for 20 minutes before being used. A longer soak is even better if time allows. Remove the tough stems, carefully pour off the soaking water, and use it in the stir-fry.

CLOUD EARS: These thin fungi do not have a classic mushroom shape, but they have a lovely texture that's a little crunchy and a good flavor that's on the edge of smokiness. Soak them in hot water for 25 minutes, then run your fingers over them and remove any tough knots. Tree ears are similar but larger.

TOFU AND TEMPEH: Both of these protein-dense foods easily find a home in stir-fries. As most all soybeans are genetically modified, be sure you choose organic tofu and tempeh. For more information about different kinds of tofu and tempeh, see pages 523 and 532. Use firm tofu for stir-fries, as the finer silken tofu is too soft and fragile.

CHILI PASTE WITH GARLIC OR CHILI PASTE WITH SOYBEAN (LAN CHI BRAND): These jarred pastes add immediate fire, but fire that's interesting, not just hot.

VEGETARIAN BARBECUE SAUCE: This flavorful condiment is based on mushroom powder with ginger, sesame, soybean sauce, and star anise or five-spice powder. AGV brand is the one I use. Nonvegetarian barbecue sauces are based on shrimp and fish.

HOISIN SAUCE: A red, sweet, sometimes pungent spicy sauce, hoisin can now be found in most supermarkets. If at a Chinese market, seek out Ma Ling brand.

SALTED AND FERMENTED BLACK BEANS: Black soybeans, partially fermented and preserved with salt, add a rich flavor to vegetables, especially asparagus, green beans, and broccoli. Crush them with the flat of a knife before adding them to release their flavor. The best come in a plastic bag with ginger and orange peel.

MIRIN: A sweet, low-alcohol rice wine.

Stock for Stir-Fries

You won't need much—¹/₂ cup or so—but a flavorful stock does add taste to your finished stir-fry. This stock can also serve as a base for miso soup and other Asian dishes. One recipe will give you enough stock for quite a few dishes. It will keep, refrigerated, for a week. If you don't use it that quickly, make it in half the quantity or plan to freeze what you don't use. Makes 3 to 4 cups Ⓥ

5 Chinese dried black or shiitake mushrooms
1 bunch green onions, including the greens
1 small onion or leek, finely sliced
2 large carrots, thinly sliced
1 cup mung bean sprouts
¹/₂ cup chopped cilantro stems and leaves
2 slices ginger, chopped
3 cloves garlic, chopped
1 (6-inch) piece kombu
1 tablespoon soy sauce
1 tablespoon rice wine (mirin)
1¹/₂ teaspoons sea salt
1 teaspoon dark sesame oil

Put all the ingredients except the sesame oil in a pot with 7 cups cold water. Bring to a boil and cook at a lively simmer for 40 minutes. After 20 minutes, remove the mushrooms and set them aside to use in a stir-fry or miso soup. Strain and return to the stove. Add the oil and taste for salt and soy sauce, adding more to taste if needed.

Chinese Noodle Cake

These fat cushiony cakes make an appealing accompaniment to stir-fried vegetables and a nice change from rice. The finished cakes can be held in a low oven if there's a gap in your timing. Chinese egg noodles are usually found in the Asian vegetable section of the supermarket, but spaghettini can be used in their place. Makes one 8- to 10-inch cake

¹/₂ pound thin fresh or dried Chinese egg noodles
2 teaspoons toasted sesame oil
1¹/₂ tablespoons sesame or peanut oil for frying

Gently pull the fresh noodles apart with your fingers into a large, loose heap. Boil them in a large pot of salted water until pleasantly firm, 2 to 3 minutes. Drain and rinse under cold water. Shake well, then toss with the toasted sesame oil.

Lightly film an 8- or 10-inch nonstick skillet with half the sesame oil. When it's hot, add the noodles. Then, with a spatula, neaten the sides and press down lightly on the noodles. Fry over medium heat until they're browned on the bottom, about 5 minutes. Place a plate on top, grasp the skillet, and invert the cake. Return the empty pan to the heat, add the rest of the oil, and slide the cake back in to cook the second side. Serve on a large round platter, topped with or accompanied by a stir-fry.

Vegetable Stir-Fry with Fermented Black Beans

Fermented black beans add a pungent, rich flavor to this colorful stir-fry. Serves 4 to 6 Ⓥ

Aromatics

  2 tablespoons roasted peanut oil, plus extra to finish

  2 teaspoons chopped garlic

  1 tablespoon minced ginger

  2 tablespoons chopped green onion

  2 tablespoons fermented black beans, chopped

  1 teaspoon red pepper flakes

Vegetables (select 7 to 8 cups from the following)

  Green beans, sliced diagonally

  Broccoli florets and stems, peeled and sliced, briefly parboiled

  Asparagus, sliced diagonally; briefly parboiled

  Zucchini, cut into rounds

  Snow peas, slivered or left whole

  1 cup Stock for Stir-Fries (page 235)

  1 tablespoon soy sauce

  1 tablespoon rice wine (mirin)

  2 teaspoons cornstarch mixed with 2 tablespoons stock or water

Set the wok over high heat, swirl the oil around the sides, and when hot add the garlic, ginger, green onion, black beans, and pepper flakes. Stir-fry 1 minute. Add the vegetables and stir-fry for 2 minutes. Add ½ cup of the stock, the soy sauce, and rice wine and simmer until the vegetables are tender-firm.

Remove the vegetables to a platter, add the remaining ½ cup stock to the wok, stir in the cornstarch, and simmer until the sauce is thickened. Pour it over the vegetables and drizzle a little roasted peanut oil over the top.

Stir-Fried Bok Choy with Roasted Peanuts

Bok choy is like two vegetables in one—the crisp stem, the tender leaf. Serve with rice or noodles. Serves 2 to 4 Ⓥ

  3 tablespoons raw peanuts

  2 teaspoons roasted peanut oil

  ¼ teaspoon red pepper flakes

  Sea salt

  1½ pounds bok choy

  2 tablespoons peanut oil

  1 tablespoon minced garlic

  4 teaspoons minced ginger

  2 tablespoons soy sauce

  1 teaspoon cornstarch mixed with 3 tablespoons Stock for Stir-Fries (page 235) or water

Fry the peanuts in the roasted peanut oil until they're golden. Chop with the pepper flakes and a few pinches salt and set aside.

Slice off the bok choy stems and cut them into 1-inch pieces. Leave the leaves whole. Set the wok over high heat. Add the peanut oil and roll it around the sides. When hot, add the garlic and ginger and stir-fry for 1 minute. Add the bok choy and a few pinches salt and stir-fry until wilted and glossy. Add the soy sauce and cornstarch and stir-fry for 1 or 2 minutes more or until the leaves are shiny and glazed. Add the crushed peanuts, toss, and serve.

Stir-Fried Roasted Eggplant

The eggplant is first roasted in the oven, then pulled into pieces, a process that ensures tenderness. It can be done well in advance of stir-frying, even a day before. For eggplant, my favorites are the slender Asian varieties. Serves 4 Ⓥ

1¹/₂ to 2 pounds eggplant

2 tablespoons Lan Chi Chili Bean Sauce with Garlic, or ¹/₂ teaspoon red pepper flakes

1 cup Stock for Stir-Fries (page 235)

3 tablespoons rice wine (mirin) or sherry

3 tablespoons soy sauce

1¹/₂ tablespoons black rice vinegar

¹/₄ cup tomato paste

1 tablespoon light brown sugar

1¹/₂ tablespoons roasted peanut oil

1 bunch green onions, including most of the greens, thinly sliced into rounds

1 tablespoon finely chopped ginger

1 large clove garlic, minced

2 tomatoes, seeded and diced into large pieces

Preheat the oven to 400°F. Pierce the eggplant in a few places, put it in a pan, and bake until very soft when pressed with your fingers, 35 minutes to 1 hour, depending on the size. As soon as it's cool enough to handle, pull off the skin and pull the flesh into strips about 1 inch thick. Don't worry about flecks of skin. Combine the chili sauce, stock, mirin, soy sauce, vinegar, tomato paste, and sugar in a small bowl and set aside.

Heat the wok, add the oil, and swirl it around the sides. Add half the onions, all of the ginger, and the garlic and stir-fry for 1 minute. Next add the eggplant and stir-fry for about 2 minutes. Add the tomatoes. Simmer until the eggplant is heated through, 3 to 4 minutes. Garnish with the reserved onions.

Mushrooms and Tofu in Hoisin Sauce

With its dark glossy sauce, this stir-fry is very attractive and especially good over buckwheat noodles. It can sit in the wok while you finish the accompaniments. Sprouted firm tofu would be a good choice for this dish. Serves 4 to 6 Ⓥ

8 to 12 dried Chinese black or shiitake mushrooms

1 block firm tofu, drained

2 tablespoons peanut or sesame oil

2 teaspoons chopped garlic

³/₄ pound fresh white or shiitake mushrooms, stems removed from the shiitakes, caps quartered

¹/₂ teaspoon sea salt

3 tablespoons rice vinegar

Mushroom-soaking water plus Stock for Stir-Fries (page 235) to make 2 cups

2 teaspoons toasted sesame oil

1 tablespoon soy sauce

3 tablespoons hoisin sauce

¹/₂ cup chopped tomato, fresh or canned

2 teaspoons cornstarch dissolved in 2 tablespoons water

2 green onions, including the greens, sliced diagonally, for garnish

Put the dried mushrooms in a bowl with warm water to cover and let soak for 20 minutes or until soft. Reserve the soaking water, remove the stems, and cut the caps into quarters. Cut the drained tofu into ¹/₂-inch cubes.

Heat a wok, add the oil, and swirl it around the sides. When it's hot, add the garlic. Stir-fry for 30 seconds. Add the fresh and dried mushrooms and the salt and stir-fry for 2 minutes. Add the vinegar, mushroom water plus stock, toasted sesame oil, soy sauce, hoisin sauce, and tomato. Stir everything together, then add the tofu. Lower the heat and simmer for 4 minutes. Add the dissolved cornstarch and cook until the sauce is thickened, another minute or so. Serve garnished with the onions.

Stir-Fried Broccoli, Mushrooms, and Peppers with Caramelized Tofu

The caramelized tofu provides a flavorful, chewy morsel, and the peppers add a needed spot of color. If you have no time to make the tofu, use strips of aburage, fried tofu, or commercially seasoned and pressed tofu. Serves 4 ⓥ

2¹/₂ tablespoons roasted peanut oil

2 cloves garlic, minced

1 teaspoon finely chopped ginger

8 ounces broccoli florets

6 ounces fresh shiitake or white mushrooms, stems removed from shiitakes, thickly sliced

1 tablespoon rice wine vinegar

1 tablespoon brown sugar

1 tablespoon soy sauce

¹/₂ cup water or Stock for Stir-Fries (page 235)

1 red bell pepper, cut into long narrow strips

Caramelized Golden Tofu, thinly sliced (page 526)

2 green onions, including an inch of the greens, sliced, for garnish

Add the oil to a heated wok. When hot, add the garlic and ginger and stir-fry for 1 minute. Add the broccoli and mushrooms and stir-fry for 2 minutes. Add the remaining ingredients, except the tofu and green onions, then cover and cook until the broccoli is tender, 4 to 5 minutes. Add the tofu and cook for 2 minutes more. Serve garnished with the green onions.

Vegetable Stir-Fry with Glass Noodles

Made from mung bean flour, these noodles (also called bean threads) look like a dry bundle of sticks until they're reconstituted in water. When cooked, they're clear and slippery. Serves 4 ⓥ

2 ounces mung bean noodles

6 dried Chinese black or shiitake mushrooms

1 pound vegetables, such as carrots, asparagus, broccoli, beans

3 tablespoons sesame or peanut oil

4 teaspoons chopped garlic

4 teaspoons chopped ginger

1 onion, chopped

1 head bok choy, sliced into 1-inch strips

Sea salt

2 tablespoons soy sauce

³/₄ cup mushroom-soaking water or Stock for Stir-Fries (page 235)

2 teaspoons cornstarch diluted in 3 tablespoons stock or water

1 teaspoon toasted sesame oil

Soak the noodles in warm water for 20 minutes or until soft. Drain. Cover the mushrooms with 1 cup warm water and soak for 20 minutes. Reserve the liquid, discard the stems, and slice the caps into strips. Thinly slice the vegetables.

Heat the wok, add 2 tablespoons of the oil, and swirl it around. When hot, add the garlic, ginger, onion, and mushrooms. Stir-fry for 1 minute, then add the vegetables and bok choy. Salt them lightly and stir-fry for 4 to 5 minutes or until tender-firm. Remove and set aside. Heat the remaining tablespoon oil in the wok, add the noodles, soy sauce, and mushroom water, and simmer for 2 minutes. Return the vegetables to the wok, add the diluted cornstarch, and cook until the vegetables are glazed. Toss with the dark sesame oil and serve.

Sweet and Sour Stir-Fry

This sauce is a rich red-brown and pleasantly sweet and sour. With its crunchy, crisp texture, jicama makes a good fresh replacement for water chestnuts. Serves 4 Ⓥ

Vegetables

4 carrots, roll-cut or diagonally sliced

3 large stalks broccoli, florets and stems separated, stems peeled and sliced into rounds

1 red or green bell pepper, cut into 1-inch pieces

$1/4$ pound white mushrooms, quartered

$1/2$ cup jicama, julienned

Aromatics

$1/4$ cup chopped tomatoes in sauce

2 tablespoons Chinese black or balsamic vinegar

2 tablespoons light brown sugar

$1/4$ teaspoon red pepper flakes or 1 serrano chile, minced

$1/2$ teaspoon sea salt

$3/4$ cup Stock for Stir-Fries (page 235)

2 tablespoons roasted peanut oil

1 tablespoon chopped garlic

2 teaspoons chopped ginger

1 bunch green onions, including the firm greens, chopped

2 teaspoons cornstarch

3 tablespoons chopped cilantro

Parboil the carrots and broccoli stems in salted water for 3 minutes. Rinse and set aside.

Mix the tomatoes, vinegar, sugar, pepper flakes, the salt, and $1/2$ cup of the stock in a bowl. Heat the wok, add the oil, and when it's hot, stir-fry the garlic, ginger, onions, and bell peppers for 1 minute. Add the remaining vegetables, stir-fry for 3 minutes and add the sauce. Cover and simmer for 3 minutes or until the vegetables are hot. Mix the cornstarch with the remaining $1/4$ cup stock and add to the vegetables along with the cilantro. Cook for 1 minute, then serve.

Vegetable Stir-Fry with Coconut-Basil Sauce

Somewhere between a stir-fry and a stew, this dish is very aromatic. Serve over basmati rice. Serves 3 or 4 Ⓥ

1 pound vegetables—fresh mushrooms, quartered; carrots, roll-cut; asparagus, sliced diagonally; snow peas or string beans, trimmed; jicama or water chestnuts, sliced

6 to 10 dried Chinese black or shiitake mushrooms

3 cloves garlic

2 tablespoons seeded and diced jalapeño chiles

1 stem lemongrass, minced, or $1/2$ teaspoon finely grated lemon zest

$1/2$ teaspoon finely grated lime zest

1 (15-ounce) can coconut milk

Sea salt

1 teaspoon red pepper flakes

1 tablespoon soy sauce

1 tablespoon fresh lime juice

10 large basil leaves, finely sliced

Parboil the harder vegetables (carrots, asparagus, string beans) one at a time in salted water until tender, then cool. Soak the dried mushrooms in $1/2$ cup warm water until soft. Reserve the water, discard the stems, and slice the caps in half or into strips.

In a mortar or small food processor, make a paste of the garlic, chiles, lemongrass, and zest. Heat a wok, add the coconut milk and the paste, and simmer for 1 minute. Add the vegetables and the reserved mushroom water. Season lightly with salt, then add the pepper flakes and simmer for 5 minutes. Stir in the soy sauce, lime juice, and basil leaves and simmer for 1 minute more.

GRATINS

CHAPTER 9

Gratins
Hearty Dishes for All Seasons

Gratins (and their cousins, casseroles) are enduring, unpretentious dishes that are a boon for any cook since they can be assembled ahead and baked just before serving. They are aromatic and appealing, and if you're cooking for both meat eaters and vegetarians, they offer a great solution since they can double as a side dish with meat, their traditional role, and as a vegetarian main dish, where they do quite well. Besides, everyone enjoys eating gratins, regardless of their food persuasions.

In addition to gratinéed vegetable dishes, this chapter also includes other baked dishes, such as enchiladas, tamale pie, and savory bread puddings—not gratins, exactly, but like gratins, they are versatile, warm, and comforting foods.

Despite their French origins, gratins are well-established here in America. We think of scalloped potatoes, scalloped corn as our very own, and yet they can be seen as gratins. Gratins derive their name from the word *gratter*, which means to scrape or grate, as in cheese or stale bread, to make a protective covering for what bubbles and bakes below. Gratin dishes are usually round or oval earthenware baking dishes with shallow sides that allow for a large surface area, providing plenty of the delicious crust. What matters is to use a dish that's shallow and has a large surface area, whether a French gratin dish, those low, round Spanish earthenware casseroles, or even a pie plate.

The combination of shallow baking dishes, thinly sliced vegetables, and warm liquid means that gratins need little time in the oven—a half hour or so. The important thing is to have a protective topping of bread crumbs and/or grated cheese to keep the dish moist. Besides, everyone loves those crispy bits, which provide such contrast in texture between the surface and the soft interior.

Gratin Fundamentals

Making gratins is a straightforward process once you understand the basic steps that are encountered over and over again. Below are the steps and guidelines that apply to most gratins.

BAKING: Most gratins and casseroles benefit by cooking at moderate temperature since high heat toughens proteins like cheese and eggs, which are often included. But in general, they're quite adaptable and can bake at whatever temperature is convenient. If the top of a gratin doesn't brown by the time it's done, run it under the broiler until it's golden and crisp.

THE VEGETABLES: Virtually all vegetables can be used in gratins, from leaves to roots. To save baking time, slice raw vegetables very thin, $1/8$ to $1/16$ inch.

THE TOPPINGS: These can include fresh bread crumbs, grated cheese, a custard that includes eggs and gives the dish a glossy surface, or bread moistened in milk or stock that will crisp as it keeps the vegetables beneath moist.

THE LIQUID: Some vegetables, such as summer squash, have enough moisture that no liquid need be added, but with others, a cup or more of liquid provides succulence. The liquid can be cream, milk, plant milk, a thin béchamel sauce, or a robust vegetable stock. Warm the liquid before adding it to the vegetables to shorten the baking time.

TIMING: Gratins and casseroles can be partially or entirely assembled ahead of time. If they're not to be baked for several hours or if they contain eggs, refrigerate them, then allow them to return to room temperature before baking, a half hour or so. They can also go directly from the refrigerator to the oven, but allow an extra 15 to 20 minutes baking time and cover them with foil for the first 25 minutes to help build up the heat. These dishes can linger in a warm oven without harm, if need be.

PRESENTATION: Gratins are meant to be brought to the table in their baking dishes, which is what gives them their homey, relaxed feel. Individual gratin dishes make especially handsome main course presentations since their contained shape naturally graces the dish with formality and focus.

SERVING SUGGESTIONS: I always enjoy gratins served over cooked greens or even salads. The richer the gratin, the better it goes with peppery and sharp greens, like watercress, arugula, and endive, or braised kale, chard, or other greens. When there's a sauce, a grain makes a good base to a serving of gratin, as the grains capture and absorb the juices.

LEFTOVERS: Leftovers from a gratin are a treat to take to work for lunch. Reheat them in an oven or toaster oven or brown them in a skillet. If using the latter method, add a few tablespoons water to create steam, cover the pan, and cook over medium heat for 8 to 10 minutes.

MAKING GRATINS VEGAN

Many gratins are classically creamy and rich. For vegan gratins use plant milk or vegetable stock. Heating it first with aromatics—a bay leaf, a few slices of onion, thyme, peppercorns, and a clove of garlic—adds a layer of flavor to the vegetables. A thin vegan béchamel sauce (page 47) has a creamy consistency.

Cabbage Gratin

You'll get a better reception if you call this by its French name, pain au chou. *"Cabbage loaf" simply fails to suggest how utterly delicate and delicious this country dish is.*
Serves 4

Butter and freshly grated parmesan, for the dish
$1 1/2$ pounds green or savoy cabbage, cut into 2-inch dice
$1/3$ cup flour
1 cup milk
$1/4$ cup crème fraîche or cream
2 tablespoons tomato paste
3 eggs

3 tablespoons finely chopped parsley or dill

Sea salt and freshly milled white pepper

Preheat the oven to 375°F. Butter a gratin dish and coat the sides with the cheese. Boil the cabbage, uncovered, in salted water for 5 minutes, then drain. Rinse, then press out as much water as possible. Whisk the remaining ingredients until smooth, add the cabbage, and pour the mixture into the dish. Bake until firm and lightly browned, about 50 minutes.

To Make a Loaf: Bake the cabbage in a loaf pan lined with lightly buttered parchment paper, until firm and lightly colored. Let it rest for a few minutes, then unmold and peel off the paper. The bottom, which is now the top, will be very pale, so either turn it over or cover it with minced herbs or browned bread crumbs.

With Cheese: 2 to 3 ounces Gouda, Gruyère, smoked cheddar, or Reblochon would all be delicious here.

Béchamel Sauce for Gratins

A thin béchamel sauce can be used interchangeably with cream. Don't skimp on the cooking time; it's really necessary to cook the flour thoroughly. But those 20 minutes of unattended cooking time in a double boiler frees you to prepare the vegetables. Makes 2 to 2$^{1}/_{2}$ cups (V)

2 cups milk, Basic Vegetable Stock (page 175), or plant milk

2 slices onion

Aromatics (page 21) plus 1 clove garlic, crushed

$^{1}/_{4}$ cup butter or oil

3 tablespoons flour

Sea salt and freshly milled white pepper

Grated nutmeg

$^{1}/_{2}$ cup cream, half and half, or milk, optional

In a saucepan, slowly heat the milk with the onion, aromatics, and garlic. When it reaches a boil, turn off the heat and set it aside. In another saucepan, melt the butter, stir in the flour, and cook for 1 minute. Whisk in the hot milk at once, including the aromatics. Cook until thickened, then transfer to a double boiler, cover, and cook for 20 minutes. Strain, discard the aromatics, and season with salt, pepper, and a pinch of nutmeg. Stir in the cream.

Artichoke, Celery Root, and Potato Gratin

This is one of my favorite gratins. The homey topping of soaked bread provides moisture for the dish and, eventually, a golden crust. Serve it so the crust stays on top. A somewhat elaborate but nonetheless easily made dish. Serves 4 to 6

4 tablespoons butter or olive oil

1 large onion, diced

6 medium or 4 large artichokes, trimmed and cut into quarters or eighths (see page 295)

1 large celery root, about 1 pound trimmed and thinly sliced

8 ounces Yellow Finn or Yukon gold potatoes, scrubbed and very thinly sliced

1 teaspoon sea salt

Freshly milled pepper

4 cups sturdy white bread without crusts, torn into pieces

1 cup milk

$^{1}/_{2}$ cup chopped parsley

3 cloves garlic, chopped

$^{1}/_{2}$ cup freshly grated parmesan

Preheat the oven to 375°F. Butter an 8 by 10-inch or slightly larger gratin dish. In a wide skillet, melt 2 tablespoons of the butter, add the onion, and cook over low heat, stirring occasionally. Meanwhile, blanch the artichokes in acidulated water for 10 minutes, then remove to a bowl. Using the same water, cook the celery root for 3 minutes, then the potatoes for 1 minute. Drain and add the celery root and potatoes to the pan with the onion.

Very thinly slice the cooked artichokes, add them to the onion, and stir so that all are coated. Cook until the onion is golden, then turn off the heat and season with the salt and pepper to taste.

Cover the bread with the milk and soak until it's mushy, about 5 minutes. Squeeze out the excess moisture, then toss it with the parsley, garlic, and parmesan.

Add the vegetables to the gratin dish—they shouldn't be much more than an inch deep. Cover them with the bread mixture, dot with the remaining butter or drizzle with olive oil, and bake for 35 to 40 minutes. If the top isn't brown, run it under the broiler. Let rest for a few minutes, then serve.

Kohlrabi Gratin with Blue Cheese

Poor kohlrabi gets such a bad rap. It's sometimes justified—it can be difficult to deal with if overgrown, but when kohlrabis are small—think tennis ball size—they're tender, easy to peel, and actually moist and mild. If you end up with a plethora of them in your garden or CSA box, consider this gratin. This is where that mandoline really helps, whether it's a $20 model or the $200 one. Serve this gratin with a cooked green from the same family, such as cabbage, collards, or broccoli rabe.
Serves 4 to 6

> 8 to 10 small kohlrabi, about 1¹/₂ pounds or more
> 2 tablespoons butter or oil, plus extra for the dish
> ¹/₂ onion, finely diced
> 1¹/₂ cups milk or light cream
> 1 rounded teaspoon Dijon mustard
> 1 bay leaf
> Sea salt and freshly ground pepper
> 1 to 2 ounces crumbled blue cheese
> A chunk of parmesan cheese

Heat the oven to 350°F. Butter or oil an 8 by 10-inch or larger gratin dish.

Peel the kohlrabi with a paring knife or vegetable peeler, going around them as you would an apple. When done, slice them very thinly on a mandoline and set them aside.

Warm a skillet over medium-high heat. Add the butter or oil, and when the butter foams or the oil shimmers, add the onion. Cook, stirring occasionally for several minutes until it begins to soften, then pour in the milk and add the mustard and bay leaf. Bring to a boil, then reduce the heat and simmer for 10 minutes.

Layer the kohlrabi in the gratin dish. Season each layer with salt and pepper and add a bit of the onion from the milk mixture. Continue in this fashion, ending by pouring the milk over all. Dot the blue cheese over the surface and grate the parmesan generously over all. Cover well with foil.

Bake for 40 minutes, then remove the foil and continue baking until the top is golden-brown and the kohlrabi is tender when pierced with a knife, another 10 to 15 minutes. Let the gratin rest for 5 minutes, then cut into pieces and serve.

Celery Root and Potato Gratin

A broth made from the celery root trimmings replaces half of the cream usually found in potato gratins without loss of flavor or texture. Celery root has a haunting flavor that always reminds me of truffles, which are an excellent addition should you be so lucky. (If I were using truffles, I would use all cream in the dish.) In their place, add a pinch of truffle salt before serving. Serves 4 to 6

> 1 clove garlic and butter for the dish
> 1 celery root, about 1 pound, scrubbed
> 1 pound potatoes, preferably Yellow Finn or Yukon gold
> ¹/₂ cup cream or Béchamel Sauce for Gratins (page 243)
> 2 teaspoons Dijon mustard
> ³/₄ teaspoon sea salt
> Freshly milled pepper
> 1 cup grated Gruyère
> Truffle salt

Preheat the oven to 375°F. Rub an 8-cup gratin dish with the garlic and then with butter.

Peel the celery root and put the parings in a 12-cup saucepan with 3 cups water and whatever remains of the garlic. Set a steamer over the top and bring to a boil. Quarter the root, then slice it ¹/₄ inch thick. Steam for 5 minutes and remove to a large bowl.

Peel the potatoes, slice them into thin rounds, and steam for 5 minutes or until tender, then add them to the celery root. Strain the cooking liquid, measure 1¹/₄ cups, and mix it with the cream and mustard. Pour it over the vegetables and toss well. Season with the salt and pepper to taste. Transfer the vegetables to the gratin dish, smooth them out, and cover with the cheese. Bake until bubbling and browned on top, about 30 minutes. Serve with truffle salt.

Cauliflower Gratin with Smoked Cheddar and Caraway

This is a rather old-fashioned treatment of cauliflower, but it makes a fine vegetarian main dish. I like this with a watercress salad. Its peppery flavor is just what's needed. To make this a vegan gratin, use nondairy milk, oil, and omit the cheese, but don't forget the dash of paprika. Serves 4 to 6 (V)

2 cups milk

1 bay leaf

1/2 teaspoon crushed caraway seeds

2 tablespoons grated yellow onion

1 large cauliflower, about 2 pounds

3/4 teaspoon salt, plus more to taste

Freshly milled white pepper

2 tablespoons butter

2 tablespoons all-purpose flour

1 cup grated smoked cheddar cheese

1/2 cup coarse, fresh bread crumbs, tossed with
     1 tablespoon melted butter or oil

Paprika

Lightly butter or oil an 8 by 10-inch baking dish.

Combine the milk, bay leaf, caraway, and onion in a saucepan and warm it over medium heat. When small bubbles appear around the edge of the pan, turn off the heat and set it aside to steep while you prepare the cauliflower.

Cut the cauliflower into bite-size florets, then peel and dice the stems. Steam until tender-firm, about 10 minutes. Immediately pour the cauliflower into the prepared gratin dish and season it with salt and white pepper.

Melt the butter in a saucepan over medium heat. Stir in the flour and cook, stirring, for 1 minute. Whisk in the warm milk and immediately stir until it thickens, about 30 seconds. Set over boiling water (here's where a double boiler helps) and cook over simmering water for 20 minutes. Season with 3/4 teaspoon salt and white pepper to taste. Heat the oven to 375°F.

Scatter half of the cheese over the cauliflower and wiggle it in so that it falls between the florets. Pour the sauce over the top, fish out the bay leaf, and top with the remaining cheese. Scatter the bread crumbs over the top. Bake until the cheese is melted and bubbling and the crumbs are browned, about 25 minutes. Dust with paprika and serve.

Zucchini Gratin with Basil, Olives and Pine Nuts

This is a good dish to make if those who can't eat gluten are coming to dinner, as pine nuts replace bread crumbs. If a vegan dish is desired, leave out the cheese. But if cheese is desired, make the gratin filling and more dense with a layer of sliced mozzarella, or more simply, a little grated parmesan over the surface. Serves 4 to 6 (V)

2 tablespoons olive oil

1 large red or white onion, halved and sliced thinly crosswise

1 heaping teaspoon thyme leaves

Sea salt and freshly milled pepper

1 1/2 pounds zucchini, sliced diagonally a scant 1/2 inch thick

Small handful fresh basil leaves (about 1/3 cup)

12 oil-cured olives, pitted and halved

Grated parmesan, optional

2 to 3 tablespoons pine nuts

Heat the oven to 375°F. Have ready an oval or round gratin dish.

Heat 2 teaspoons of olive oil in a wide sauté pan or skillet. When hot, add the onion and thyme leaves. Sauté over medium-high heat for several minutes, then, when the onions begin to collapse a little, cover and reduce the heat to medium. Let them cook until softened, about 12 minutes. Season with salt and pepper, then turn them into the baking dish.

Heat another 2 teaspoons oil in the pan and when hot, add the zucchini. Sauté over high heat, turning them frequently until they begin to color in places, about 7 minutes. Season with salt and pepper.

Loosely arrange half the zucchini over the onions, then add a tablespoons or so torn basil leaves and tuck in the olives. Grate some cheese over the squash, then repeat, making a second layer with the remaining squash, olives and basil.

Cover with foil and bake until the vegetables have softened, about 30 minutes. Remove the foil, add the pine nuts, drizzle with the last 2 teaspoons oil, grate over parmesan, and return to the oven for 10 minutes more. Remove the gratin from the oven and sprinkle with the remaining basil leaves, if any. The heat will make them aromatic, but also discolor them, so you may prefer to wait until the dish cools. Serve hot, warm, or tepid.

Golden Gratin of Carrots, Rutabagas, and Turnips

I can't think of any root vegetable that doesn't bake into a glorious gratin. This trio makes a cheerful yellow gratin. Serve as a side dish or a main dish. Serves 4 (V)

Béchamel Sauce for Gratins (page 243)

12 ounces rutabagas, peeled and cut into julienne strips

1 small onion, finely diced

1 tablespoon butter or oil

12 ounces turnips, peeled and julienned

8 ounces carrots, peeled and julienned

Sea salt and freshly milled pepper

1 cup fresh bread crumbs

Preheat the oven to 375°. Lightly coat an 8-cup gratin dish with butter or oil. Prepare the béchamel sauce. While the sauce is cooking, boil the rutabagas in salted water for 2 minutes and drain. Cook the onion in the butter in a small skillet over medium heat, about 8 minutes, then combine with the rest of the vegetables. Season with salt and pepper and transfer to the gratin dish. Pour the sauce over the top, cover with the bread crumbs, and bake until bubbling and golden on top, about 45 minutes.

Individual Spinach Gratins with Red Pepper Sauce

These can be served as a first course, but are filling enough to be a main dish, especially when accompanied with a red pepper or tomato sauce. Serves 4 to 6

1/2 cup grated parmesan

3 hefty bunches spinach, about 3 pounds, stems removed and leaves washed

Sea salt

1 1/2 to 2 cups Béchamel Sauce for Gratins (page 243)

1/2 cup grated Gruyère cheese

1 cup fresh bread crumbs tossed in 1 tablespoon melted butter or olive oil

Red Pepper Sauce (page 64)

Butter 4 or 6 individual gratin dishes or ramekins and coat with a few tablespoons of the parmesan cheese. Preheat the oven to 375°F.

Plunge the spinach into boiling salted water until limp. Transfer to a colander, then rinse under cool water. Press out the liquid and chop it finely. Combine the spinach, sauce, and cheeses, then transfer to the prepared dish and cover with the bread crumbs. Bake until browned on top, about 30 minutes. Serve in the ramekins with a spoonful of sauce on top, or turn them out and serve in a puddle of the sauce.

Onion Gratin

Eggs give this gratin a glossy golden top. The same filling can be baked in a crust to make a savory pie or without the eggs for those who don't eat them. Serves 4

2 tablespoons butter or olive oil

3 pounds white or yellow onions, thinly sliced

1 bay leaf

Pinch ground cloves

1/2 teaspoon dried thyme

Sea salt and freshly milled pepper

1 cup dry white wine

2 eggs

3 tablespoons flour

1 1/2 cups warm milk or Basic Vegetable Stock (page 175)

2/3 cup grated Gruyère or fontina

3/4 cup fresh bread crumbs

Preheat the oven to 375°F. Lightly butter an 8-cup gratin dish.

Warm the butter in a large skillet over medium heat. Add the onions, bay leaf, cloves, and thyme. Turn the onions over several times to coat, season with salt and pepper, then reduce the heat to low and cook, stirring occasionally, until the onions are golden and soft, 30 to 40 minutes. Add the wine, raise the heat, and cook until it has completely reduced. Remove the bay leaf.

Whisk the eggs with the flour, 1/2 teaspoon salt, and a little pepper, then stir in the warm milk. Combine with the onions and cheese and transfer to the dish. Cover with the bread crumbs and bake until set and the crumbs are browned, about 25 minutes.

Eggplant and Summer Vegetable Gratin

Simple but superb, this is a little slow to put together but not at all difficult. Don't hurry it; the slow cooking guarantees that all the flavors will be richly concentrated. Serves 4 to 6 Ⓥ

2 to 2¹/₂ pounds globe eggplant, preferably on the small side

3 tablespoons olive oil, plus more for brushing and bread crumbs

Sea salt and freshly milled pepper

2 large onions, finely diced

3 cloves garlic, chopped

1 large red bell pepper, finely diced

2 large ripe tomatoes, peeled, seeded, and chopped

10 large basil leaves, torn into small pieces

1 cup fresh bread crumbs made from sturdy white bread

¹/₄ cup freshly grated parmesan, optional

Preheat the oven to 425°F. Slice the eggplant into rounds about ¹/₂ inch thick—if it's in season, there's no need to salt them. Brush both sides of each piece with oil and bake on a sheet pan until browned and tender on both sides, about 25 minutes. Season with salt and pepper and set aside. Reduce the heat to 325°F.

Heat 3 tablespoons olive oil in a wide skillet, add the onions and garlic, and cook over medium heat until limp, about 8 minutes. Raise the heat a little, add the bell pepper and tomatoes, and continue cooking, stirring occasionally, until everything is soft and thickened to a jam, about 20 minutes. Raise the temperature at the end to reduce the juices. Add the basil and season to taste with salt and pepper.

Lightly oil a 10-cup gratin dish. Make a layer of eggplant in the bottom and spread a third of the tomato-onion mixture over it, followed by another layer of eggplant, half the remaining sauce, then the rest of the eggplant. End with the remaining sauce on top. Cover the dish and bake for 45 minutes. Toss the bread crumbs with olive oil to moisten and the grated cheese. Remove the cover, add the bread crumbs and cheese, raise the oven temperature to 375°F, and bake until the crumbs are nicely browned and crisp on top, about 25 minutes.

Polenta Gratin with Mushrooms and Tomato

A healthy and straightforward dish, good on a cold night with Braised Carrots (page 315) and a salad or cooked sautéed greens. Serves 6

Firm Polenta (page 463)

2¹/₂ tablespoons olive oil

1 large onion, finely diced

2 small bay leaves

¹/₂ teaspoon dried thyme

1 teaspoon dried marjoram or basil

12 to 16 ounces mushrooms, sliced

3 cloves garlic, chopped

¹/₂ teaspoon sea salt

¹/₂ cup dry red or white wine

2 cups tomato puree or crushed tomatoes in puree

Freshly milled pepper

1 cup grated provolone or Monterey Jack

¹/₄ cup freshly grated parmesan

Lightly oil or butter a 9 by 11-inch baking dish and have a sheet pan nearby. Preheat the oven to 400°F.

Pour half of the hot polenta—just judge it by eye—into the prepared dish and pour the remainder onto a sheet pan. Using a spatula, spread it out to roughly the size of the baking dish, then set it aside.

Heat the oil in a large skillet over medium heat. Add the onion and herbs and cook, stirring frequently, until the onion is browned around the edges, about 10 minutes. Raise the heat to high and add the mushrooms, garlic, and the salt. Sauté until the mushrooms are browned in places, about 5 minutes. Add the wine, simmer until it's completely reduced, then add the tomato puree. Simmer for 5 minutes, then taste for salt and season with pepper.

Spread half the mushrooms over the polenta in the baking dish. Cover with half the cheeses, then cover with a second layer of polenta. (For ease, cut it into smaller pieces, then place them over the tomato.) Cover with the remaining sauce and cheeses.

Bake until the casserole is bubbling and hot throughout, about 25 minutes.

Potato and Leek Gratin

Few foods elicit the rapturous sighs that a golden gratin of potatoes does. Simmering the potatoes and leeks in milk first ensures that your potatoes end up fully tender. And the leftover milk—thickened with potato starch and well flavored—makes a marvelous base for a soup. Serve with a salad and chilled Applesauce (page 607) or Quince or Pear Sauce (page 607). Serves 4 to 6

1 clove garlic and butter for the dish

3 pounds russet or Yukon gold potatoes, peeled and very thinly sliced

4 cups whole milk

1 bay leaf

3 thyme sprigs or 2 pinches dried

3 garlic cloves, thinly sliced

2 large leeks, white parts only, thinly sliced

2 teaspoons sea salt

Freshly milled white pepper

Grated nutmeg

1 to 2 cups grated Gruyère

2 tablespoons butter, cut into small pieces

Preheat the oven to 375°F. Rub a 9 by 12-inch gratin dish thoroughly with the garlic, then with butter to coat well.

Put the potatoes in a pot with the milk, herbs, sliced garlic, leeks, and 2 teaspoons salt. Slowly bring to a boil, then simmer until the potatoes are barely tender but not to the point of falling apart. Discard the bay leaf and thyme. Strain and reserve the liquid.

Make a single layer of potatoes, leeks, and garlic in the dish. Season with pepper, a little nutmeg, and cover lightly with cheese. Repeat until all the potatoes and cheese are used up, ending with a layer of cheese. Add enough of the milk to come up to the last layer of potatoes—about 1 1/2 cups—dot with the butter, then bake until a golden crust has formed on top, about an hour.

Variation with Other Cheeses: Try Italian Fontina, cheddar, Cantal, or, in half the amount, Gorgonzola dolcelatte in place of the Gruyère.

Variation with Other Vegetables: Add these vegetables to the cooked potatoes: thinly sliced, partially cooked celery root or fennel; grated parsley root; a layer of sautéed porcini, chanterelle, or white mushrooms; or trimmed, quartered artichokes, parboiled for 5 minutes, then thinly sliced.

Potato and Mushroom Gratin

Dried wild mushrooms lend their woodsy flavor to this gratin, and light cream gives it a silky texture. For a lighter, nondairy version use the Quick Mushroom Stock (page 223). Serves 4 to 6

2 cloves garlic, 1 clove finely chopped

2 tablespoons butter, plus extra for the dish and top

1 ounce dried porcini, chanterelles, or morels

Sea salt and freshly milled pepper

1 1/2 pounds waxy yellow or red potatoes, peeled and sliced 1/6 inch thick

3/4 pound white mushrooms, thinly sliced

1 cup half-and-half, Quick Mushroom Stock (page 223), or Béchamel Sauce for Gratins (page 243)

Preheat the oven to 350°F. Rub an 8-cup gratin dish with 1 clove garlic, then with butter.

Cover the dried mushrooms with 1 1/4 cups warm water, let stand for 20 minutes or longer, then run your fingers over the mushrooms to loosen any grit. Strain the liquid carefully and reserve; chop the mushrooms. Heat the butter in a medium skillet and sauté the chopped mushrooms for 3 or 4 minutes. Add the chopped garlic and season with salt and pepper.

Layer half the potatoes in the dish, season with salt and pepper, add the raw mushrooms, and cover with the dried ones. Cover with the remaining potatoes and season again. Heat the half-and-half with the mushroom liquid, then pour it over the top. Bake, uncovered, until the liquid is absorbed and the potatoes are tender and golden, about 1 1/2 hours.

New Potato Gratin with Tomatoes and Olives

Made with summer's new potatoes and garden tomatoes, this late-harvest dish is fragrant with herbs and olives. Serve warm or at room temperature, with a wedge of lemon and a spoonful of Garlic or Saffron Mayonnaise (page 52) or vegan mayonnaise. Serves 4 to 6 (V)

2 pounds fingerling or any waxy new potato, scrubbed or peeled

4 large ripe tomatoes

4 tablespoons olive oil

2 red onions, thinly sliced

$1/4$ teaspoon dried thyme

Sea salt and freshly milled pepper

$1/4$ teaspoon fennel seeds, crushed

$1/3$ cup niçoise or kalamata olives, pitted and coarsely chopped

3 cloves garlic, thinly sliced

8 thyme sprigs, preferably lemon thyme

$1/4$ lemon, thinly sliced

1 tablespoon capers, rinsed

Preheat the oven to 400°F. Oil an 8-cup gratin dish.

Slice the potatoes $3/8$ inch thick, lengthwise if they're fingerlings. Boil them in salted water for 4 minutes, then scoop them out, rinse under cold water, and set aside. Plunge the tomatoes into the same water for 10 seconds, then remove and rinse. Peel, halve, and seed. Coarsely chop half of one tomato; slice the rest crosswise.

Warm 2 tablespoons of the oil in a skillet over high heat and add the onions, dried thyme, fennel, and a little pepper. Sauté until the onions are lightly browned and wilted, about 8 minutes, then transfer them to the gratin dish.

Scatter the chopped tomato, olives, half the garlic, half the thyme sprigs, and half the lemon over the top. Cover with the potatoes, intersperse with the sliced tomatoes, and tuck in the remaining garlic, thyme, and lemon. Season with salt and pepper, scatter the capers over the top, and drizzle with the remaining 2 tablespoons oil. Cover with foil and bake for 25 minutes, then uncover and bake until the potatoes are fully tender, 20 to 30 minutes more.

Spanish Potatoes with Saffron, Almonds, and Bread Crumbs

Be sure to used skinned almonds and white rather than whole wheat bread to avoid giving this delicious dish a dingy brown appearance. Serves 4

2 pounds Yellow Finn or boiling potatoes, peeled and quartered

Sea salt and freshly milled pepper

2 pinches saffron threads

3 tablespoons olive oil

1 slice white country-style bread

$1/2$ cup blanched almonds, roughly chopped

2 large cloves garlic, unpeeled

1 teaspoon paprika

1 teaspoon chopped parsley, for garnish

Preheat the oven to 375°F. Lightly oil a gratin dish that's large enough to hold the potatoes in a single layer. Add the potatoes, season with salt and pepper, and sprinkle with the saffron.

Heat the oil in a small skillet over medium heat, tear the bread into pieces, and fry it with the almonds and garlic until golden. Remove the garlic if it gets too dark. Grind the mixture in a food processor with the paprika, adding a little boiling water to make it smooth. Season it with salt and pepper, add it to the potatoes, and pour over the remaining liquid. Cover and bake for 45 minutes, then uncover, gently stir the contents of the dish, and continue baking until the liquid has been absorbed and the potatoes are tender, about 20 to 30 minutes. Brown the top under the broiler and garnish with the parsley.

Flageolet Bean, Leek, and Artichoke Gratin

Small, pale green, and whitish beans with a delicate flavor are combined with braised artichokes and leeks, covered with soft, creamy goat cheese and a layer bread crumbs. The cheese softens and the bread crumbs crisp and brown leaving a dish with varied flavors and textures. The beans can be cooked well in advance. Serves 4 to 6 Ⓥ

1 cup dried flageolet beans or small white navy beans

1 bay leaf

1 teaspoon sea salt

2 or 3 large leeks, white parts only

2 or 3 artichokes

2 lemons

4 tablespoons olive oil

3 cloves garlic, finely chopped or pounded with a pinch of salt

1 heaping teaspoon finely chopped rosemary

1 cup bean broth or water

Freshly milled pepper

5 ounces soft goat cheese or vegan cheese, optional

2 cups fresh bread crumbs

Soak the beans overnight or do a quick soak, then drain, put them in a pot, and cover them generously with fresh water. Bring to a boil, boil vigorously for several minutes, and lower the heat. Add the bay leaf and simmer for 30 minutes. Add the salt and continue cooking until the beans are tender but still hold their shape, another 30 to 60 minutes. Keep an eye on them to make sure the beans are amply covered with water.

While the beans are cooking, prepare the vegetables: Quarter the leeks lengthwise, cut them into small dice, and rinse them well. Trim the artichokes and cut them into quarters, removing the choke with a paring knife and slicing each piece into two. Rub a little lemon on the pieces as you work so they don't discolor and put the finished pieces in water just to cover mixed with the juice from the lemon.

Warm 2 tablespoons of the olive oil in a sauté pan. Add the leeks, artichokes, garlic, and rosemary. Cook for 3 or 4 minutes, turning the pieces so that all are coated with oil. Season with salt and add the bean broth. Press a piece of parchment paper directly onto the vegetables to keep them from discoloring and cook over medium-low heat until the vegetables are tender and the liquid is reduced. (Should the liquid evaporate before the vegetables are finished cooking, add more in small amounts until they are done.) Taste and season with salt and pepper.

Heat the oven to 400°F.

When the beans are cooked, drain them, saving the cooking liquid, and mix them with the vegetables. Put them into a roomy gratin dish and add enough bean broth just to cover. Crumble the cheese over the beans. Toss the bread crumbs with the remaining 2 tablespoons olive oil to moisten; then pat them over the top. Bake until the beans are hot and the crust browned, about 25 minutes. Let settle for a few minutes before serving.

Vegetable Gratin-Soufflé

This simple but dramatic dish combines elements of a gratin and a soufflé. A host of vegetables can be used—celery root, cauliflower, winter squash, broccoli, and turnips. While Gruyère is excellent with all, there's no reason not to use another cheese—cheddar with cauliflower, for example. Serves 4

3 cups vegetables, cut into 1-inch pieces

1/2 cup fresh bread crumbs

3 tablespoons butter

1 cup milk

1/2 small onion, or 2 large shallots, finely diced

1/2 cup grated Gruyère

2 eggs, separated

Sea salt and freshly milled pepper

Pinch grated nutmeg

Preheat the oven to 375°F and lightly butter an 8 by 10-inch gratin dish. Steam or parboil the vegetables until barely tender when pierced with a knife. Drain, rinse under cold water, then finely chop them.

Lightly brown the bread crumbs in 2 tablespoons of the butter in a small saucepan, then stir in the milk. When it's hot to the touch, turn off the heat. Meanwhile, cook the onion in the remaining 1 tablespoon butter in a small skillet over medium heat until translucent, about 3 minutes. Combine the onion, vegetables, and bread crumb mixture in a bowl, then stir in the cheese and egg yolks. Season with salt, pepper, and nutmeg. Beat the whites until stiff, then fold them into the mixture. Pour into the prepared dish and bake until puffed and browned, about 25 minutes. Serve immediately.

Tamale Pie

This should feed a crowd. If you can cook your own beans, like a large runner bean or Rio Zape beans, they'll look and taste so good, plus you can use the broth for the liquid. It's the masa harina that gives tamale pie its tamale flavor—the only link this dish has to its name. Corn meal can be substituted, but it doesn't have the special flavor that masa has. Masa can be found in Mexican markets and many supermarkets. Cook it in a double boiler while you're assembling everything else to allow time for its flavor to open. Serves 6 to 8

Tamale Topping

1 1/2 cups masa harina or corn meal

1 1/2 teaspoons sea salt

1 tablespoon ground red chile

2 tablespoons vegetable oil

Filling

2 tablespoons oil

1 onion, diced

1 green or red bell pepper, seeded and diced

1 cup diced celery

2 teaspoons minced garlic

2 cups corn kernels, from 3 ears of corn

3 cups cooked beans (see headnote), or 2 (15-ounce) cans kidney or black beans

1 teaspoon dried oregano

1 teaspoon ground cumin

2 teaspoons ground red chile

1 teaspoon sea salt

1 (14-ounce) California black olives, sliced

1 cup grated cheddar cheese

Sour cream, for serving

To make the topping, place 6 cups water in a saucepan and bring just to a boil. Whisk in the masa harina and stir until a boil is reached and the mixture is uniformly thickened, after a few minutes. Add the salt, chile, and oil, then transfer to the top of a double boiler. Place it over simmering water, cover, and cook while you make the vegetable stew.

Warm the oil in a large, wide pot over high heat. When hot, add the onion, bell pepper, and celery and sauté until the onion begins to color around the edges, 5 to 7 minutes. Add the garlic, corn, beans, oregano, cumin, and chile. Season with the salt and add 1 1/2 cups water or bean broth.

Lower the heat and simmer until only a little liquid is left, about 30 minutes. Taste for salt.

Heat the oven to 375°F. Spoon half of the masa into a 12-cup baking dish and let it set for 5 minutes. Spread half of the filling over the masa layer with half the olives and half the cheese, followed by the remaining filling. Stir the remaining cheese into the masa and cover the top of the casserole. (At this point, it can be covered and refrigerated overnight or until you're ready to cook it.)

Bake uncovered, until bubbling and hot, about 1 hour. Serve with sour cream on the side.

An Over-the-Top Holiday Sweet Potato Gratin with Red Chile and Cream

There's just no way this isn't an indulgence, so it's best saved for a special occasion and enjoyed, with others, once a year. You can use any variety of sweet potato, but I'm partial to the pale-fleshed Japanese varieties, such as Hanna. They're more chestnutlike and not so sweet. Serves 8

4 pounds sweet potatoes

1 tablespoon sea salt

Ground red chile

1 cup cream or half-and-half

Smoked paprika or powdered chipotle chile

Cover the sweet potatoes with cold water, add the salt, and bring to a boil. Simmer until they are tender but still a little firm, as they will cook again in the oven. (They can be boiled a day or more ahead of time and kept refrigerated.)

Heat the oven to 350°F. Lightly butter an 8-cup gratin dish. Peel the potatoes and slice them on the diagonal or lengthwise 1/2 inch thick. Make a layer of potatoes in the dish, season with salt and a few pinches of the ground red chile. Repeat, making as many layers as you have potatoes for. Pour the cream over all, sprinkle the top with extra chile and smoked paprika, then bake until the cream is absorbed and the surface is burnished and blistered in places, about 35 minutes.

Battered and Baked Stuffed Chiles with Roasted Tomato Sauce

Proper chiles rellenos—roasted green chiles stuffed with cheese, batter dipped, and fried—are quite a production to make at home. This approach omits the frying in favor of baking. Serve these chiles with rice, black beans (see page 280), or pinto beans and the thin roasted tomato sauce that follows. Poblano chiles are often much larger (and hotter) than long green Mexican or Anaheim chiles. Serves 4

Chiles

8 poblano, or 12 New Mexican or other long green chiles

1½ cups grated Monterey Jack

1 cup crumbled fresh goat cheese (about ¼ pound)

1 bunch green onions, white part only, thinly sliced

3 tablespoons chopped cilantro

½ cup all-purpose flour

Roasted Tomato Sauce

2 pounds ripe tomatoes, preferably Romas or plum tomatoes

Approximately 3 tablespoons olive oil or more neutral oil

5 cloves garlic, unpeeled

½ teaspoon dried Mexican oregano

Sea salt

Batter

3 large eggs, separated

1 cup milk

1 tablespoon vegetable oil

1 cup all-purpose flour or white whole wheat flour

¾ teaspoon sea salt

Roast the chiles over a flame until the skins are evenly blistered but not too charred. Put them in a bowl, cover, and set aside to steam for 15 minutes, then slip off the skins. Make a lengthwise slit down the middle, leaving the stem end intact. Carefully remove and discard the seeds.

Mix the cheeses, onions, and cilantro. Loosely stuff the chiles. If they fall apart, just wrap them around the filling as best you can—the patching won't show in the end. Scatter the flour over a pie plate and carefully dredge the chiles in it so that the batter will adhere.

Butter or oil a large baking dish (or individual gratin dishes) and lay the stuffed chiles in it. Heat the oven to 400°F.

To make the sauce, toss the tomatoes with a little oil to coat them, then grill or broil until wrinkled and charred in places, about 10 minutes. Turn them several times while they're cooking to expose them to the heat source.

Toss the garlic with oil to moisten and cook in a small covered skillet over medium heat, until browned on the outside and tender when pressed, 12 to 15 minutes. Shake the pan frequently while it's cooking. Peel the garlic. Toast the oregano in a dry skillet until it begins to release its aroma, then remove to a dish.

Puree the tomatoes and garlic in a blender until smooth. Heat 2 tablespoons oil in a wide, deep skillet, and when hot, pour in the sauce and add the oregano. Fry the sauce, stirring occasionally for about 10 minutes or until it's thickened. Season with salt. Serve with the chiles.

To make the batter, whisk the egg yolks, milk, oil, flour, and salt in a bowl. When ready to bake the chiles, whip the egg whites until they form fairly stiff peaks, then fold them into the batter. Spread the batter over the chiles and bake until the top is browned and the chiles are hot, about 15 to 20 minutes. Serve with the sauce.

Turnip and Leek Gratin with Blue Cheese

I like this gratin served on a bed of curly endive or arugula dressed with a walnut vinaigrette for an interesting first course or small supper. For turnips, use small, spring salad turnips, or storage turnips. Even rutabagas can be used here. Makes 4 modest servings

1 clove garlic and butter for the dish

1 cup milk, half-and-half, or Béchamel Sauce for Gratins (page 243)

6 thyme sprigs

1 bay leaf

3 large leeks, white parts only, cut into ¼-inch rounds

Sea salt and freshly milled pepper

1½ pounds turnips, peeled and sliced into ¼-inch-thick rounds or half-rounds

2 ounces Maytag or other blue cheese, crumbled

Preheat the oven to 375°F. Rub an 8-cup gratin dish with the garlic, then with butter. Heat the half-and-half with the remains of the garlic, 2 sprigs of the thyme, and the bay leaf. When it's close to boiling, turn off the heat and set aside.

Cook the leeks in 8 cups boiling salted water for 2 minutes. Scoop them out and put them in a bowl. Add the turnips and cook for 4 minutes, then drain. Layer the vegetables in the dish, intersperse the remaining thyme sprigs among them, season lightly with salt and pepper, and add the blue cheese. Pour the half-and-half through a strainer over the top. Bake, uncovered, until the liquid is absorbed and the top is browned, about 30 minutes.

Eggplant al Forno

Back in the day, eggplant parmesan used to be the only vegetable entrée one could find on a menu. It was usually breaded and heavy, nothing like the delicate dish that can be made with eggplant in season, fresh mozzarella, and a light summer tomato sauce. Serves 4

2 medium eggplants, about 1¹/₂ pounds

Sea salt and freshly milled pepper

Olive oil

1¹/₂ to 2 cups Fresh Tomato Sauce (page 54)

8 large basil leaves, torn into pieces

4 ounces mozzarella, thinly sliced if fresh, grated otherwise

¹/₂ cup freshly grated parmesan

Preheat the oven to 375°F. Lightly oil an 8-cup gratin dish.

Slice the eggplant into rounds about ¹/₃ inch thick. Unless the eggplant is garden fresh, sprinkle it with salt and let stand for 30 minutes to an hour, then blot dry.

Preheat the broiler. Brush both sides of each round with olive oil and broil 5 to 6 inches from the heat until browned. Broil the second side until browned, then remove and season lightly with salt and pepper. Don't worry if the eggplant has a dry appearance.

Warm the tomato sauce with half the basil. Spread about a third of the sauce over the bottom of the dish, then make an overlapping layer of eggplant. Lay the mozzarella over the top, add the rest of the basil, and sprinkle with the parmesan. Add the rest of the eggplant and cover it with the remaining sauce. Bake in the middle of the oven until bubbling and hot throughout, about 30 minutes.

Butternut Squash Gratin with Onions and Sage

A fall supper for family or company. Serve with a salad of slightly bitter robust greens. Serves 4

4 tablespoons olive oil

4 cups thinly sliced onion

4 thyme sprigs

2 tablespoons chopped sage or 2 teaspoons dried

¹/₂ teaspoon sea salt

Freshly milled pepper

6 cups butternut squash, cut into ¹/₂-inch cubes

¹/₂ cup flour, optional

2 tablespoons chopped parsley

¹/₂ cup grated Gruyère or fontina

¹/₂ cup plus 2 tablespoons whole milk, heated, or Herb and Garlic Broth (page 176)

1 cup fresh bread crumbs

Preheat the oven to 350°F. Lightly oil or butter an 8-cup gratin dish.

Heat 2 tablespoons of the oil in a skillet over medium heat. Add the onion, thyme, and sage and cook, stirring frequently, until the onions are lightly caramelized, about 15 minutes. Season with the salt and pepper to taste. Spread in the gratin dish, return the skillet to medium heat, and add the remaining 2 tablespoons oil.

Toss the squash in the flour, letting the excess fall away. Add it to the pan and cook until it begins to brown in places on both sides, about 7 minutes. Add the parsley, season with salt and plenty of pepper, and cook for 1 minute more. Layer the squash over the onions, cover with the cheese, then add the milk. Cover and bake for 25 minutes, then uncover, add the bread crumbs, and bake until the top is browned and the liquid absorbed, about 25 minutes more.

Cauliflower Gratin with Tomatoes and Feta

My husband asked, "What makes this so zingy?" It's everything really, but especially the honey setting off the tart lemon, capers, and feta. This is so easy to put together you can have it ready for dinner in no time at all. Serve it with a big green salad or a Greek salad and bulgur or rice. Serves 4

2 to 3 tablespoons olive oil

1 onion, thinly sliced

2 cloves garlic, chopped

1¹/₂ teaspoons dried oregano

¹/₈ teaspoon ground cinnamon

5 fresh tomatoes, peeled, seeded, and diced, or
    1 (15-ounce) can diced tomatoes

1 teaspoon honey

1 tablespoon capers, rinsed

Sea salt and freshly milled pepper

1 large cauliflower, about 1¹/₂ pounds, broken into florets

Juice of ¹/₂ lemon

2 to 4 ounces crumbled feta

Finely chopped parsley, for garnish

Preheat the broiler and lightly oil an 8-cup gratin dish.

Heat the oil in a 10-inch skillet over medium heat. Add the onion, garlic, oregano, and cinnamon and cook until the onion is wilted, about 5 minutes. Add the tomatoes, cook for 7 minutes more, then add the honey and capers and season with salt and pepper. Slide the mixture into the dish.

Meanwhile, steam the cauliflower for 5 minutes. Set it on the sauce in the dish and season with salt and pepper. Squeeze the lemon juice over the top and add the feta. Place 5 to 6 inches under the broiler until the sauce is bubbling and the cheese is beginning to brown, about 10 minutes. Garnish with the parsley and serve. (If you are assembling the gratin ahead of time, cover and bake it at 400°F until bubbling, about 20 minutes, then brown under the broiler.)

Fresh Corn Pudding

Every community cookbook has at least one recipe for corn pudding. It was once one of America's seasonal treats and deserves to be today. It is the essence of corn, enriched with plenty of orange cheddar and finished with that ubiquitous dash of paprika. It has a kind of old-fashioned appeal that doesn't go away. Still, you could gussy it up with more contemporary flavors—cilantro, goat cheese, smoked paprika, smoked salt, and the like.

Most corn is now bred to stay sweet, even in the supermarket, which is invariably some distance from any cornfield, but do get it fresh for a truly seasonal treat. Frozen corn just won't have the moisture fresh provides. I prefer yellow corn, but white is increasingly more common. Serves 8

6 large ears of corn

1¹/₂ tablespoons butter

1 cup finely diced yellow onion or sweet onion

1 teaspoon minced garlic

1 cup evaporated milk or regular or nondairy milk

2 eggs, lightly beaten

1¹/₂ cups loosely packed mild cheddar cheese

³/₄ cup cracker crumbs or fresh bread crumbs

Sea salt and freshly ground pepper

Paprika, smoked or regular

Preheat the oven to 350°F. Lightly butter a 6-cup gratin dish.

Shuck the corn and pull off the silks. Holding an ear of corn stem end down and using a sharp knife, carefully cut off the top halves of the corn kernels, leaving behind the fibrous base, the part that gets caught in your teeth. Then turn your knife over and, using the dull side, press it down the length of the cob, squeezing out the rest of the corn and its milk. You'll end up with a mushy substance along with the kernels.

Warm the butter in a skillet over medium-high heat. Add the onions and cook just until they're limp, about 4 minutes. Add the garlic and cook for 2 to 3 minutes, without letting the onions brown. Add this to the corn and stir in the milk, eggs, 1 cup of the cheese and ¹/₂ cup of the cracker or crumbs. Season to taste with salt and pepper. Pour the mixture into the prepared dish and top with the remaining crumbs and cheese. Bake on the center rack of the oven until puffed and golden, about 45 minutes. Remove from the oven, sprinkle paprika over the top, and serve.

Navy Bean and Pasta Gratin with Basil and Ricotta

Familiar pasta combined with pesto makes this a dish to serve to reluctant bean eaters. This is an end-of-summer dish when basil and tomatoes are still plentiful. Serve with Roasted Red Pepper Soup (minus the croutons; page 187) for a first course and follow with a salad of seasonal greens and tart vinaigrette.

Serves 6

1 cup navy, cannellini, or other white beans, soaked

6 tablespoons olive oil

1/2 onion, finely chopped

1 bay leaf

6 thyme sprigs or 1/2 teaspoon dried

1/2 teaspoon sea salt

3 large cloves garlic, coarsely chopped

2 cups loosely packed basil leaves

1 cup freshly grated parmesan

Freshly milled pepper

11/2 cups dried pasta shells, wheels, or other shapes

2 large ripe tomatoes, peeled, seeded, and chopped

1 cup ricotta

1 cup bread crumbs tossed with olive oil to moisten

Parboil the beans in fresh water for 10 minutes, then drain. Heat 1 tablespoon of the oil in a soup pot over medium heat. Add the onion, bay leaf, and thyme. Cook for several minutes, then add the beans and 6 cups water. Simmer, covered, until the beans are nearly tender, about 30 minutes, adding more water if necessary to keep the beans covered. When nearly tender, season with the salt and cook for 15 minutes more or until tender. Let cool in their broth.

In a food processor, coarsely chop the garlic and basil. Scrape down the sides, then add the remaining 5 tablespoons oil and the cheese. Process until you have a coarse puree, then season with salt and pepper to taste.

Preheat the oven to 350°F. Oil an 8-cup gratin dish. Cook the pasta in salted water until more al dente than usual since it will cook further, then drain and rinse under cold water. Combine the pasta, beans, 2 cups of the bean broth, and the tomatoes in the baking dish. Slip spoonfuls of the pesto and ricotta into the beans, poking them beneath the surface. Lightly press the bread crumbs over the surface, then bake until heated through and browned, about 35 minutes.

Enchiladas

Cheese enchiladas are the perennial choice for many vegetarians, but here are three offerings that provide a welcome change. Allow two enchiladas per serving and accompany them with black, pink, or pinto beans and simple garnishes such as shredded lettuce or cabbage, jicama, sliced radishes and tomatoes, and pickled onions and carrots. These fillings are also excellent for crepes and for small stuffed vegetables.

Corn tortillas are the ones to use for enchiladas. Briefly dipping them into hot oil makes them pliable and protects them from the sauce. If you skip this step, plan to bake your enchiladas immediately. Although fried tortillas can be filled ahead of time, don't sauce or bake them until you plan to eat. Crème fraîche or sour cream drizzled over enchiladas provides a modest enrichment and tempers the heat of chiles in some cases. Both should be whisked a little first.

Mushroom Enchiladas with Epazote and Green Chile

Epazote's unique flavor is impossible to duplicate. Look for it in Latin and Mexican markets. Makes 12 enchiladas

3 tablespoons safflower oil

1 small onion, finely diced

2 teaspoons chopped garlic

1/2 teaspoon dried oregano, preferably Mexican

1 1/2 pounds mushrooms, finely diced

4 Roma tomatoes, peeled, seeded, and diced

1/2 teaspoon sea salt

3 serrano chiles, finely diced

2 teaspoons dried epazote

1/4 cup chopped cilantro

1 cup vegetable oil, for frying

12 corn tortillas

2 cups Oven-Roasted Tomato Sauce (page 55)

1/2 cup crème fraîche or sour cream

To make the filling, heat the oil in a wide skillet over high heat. Add the onion and sauté for about a minute, then add the garlic and oregano and cook for 2 minutes. Add the mushrooms and tomatoes, season with the salt, and cook, stirring occasionally, until any juices are absorbed and the mushrooms have begun to color, about 6 minutes. Add the chiles and epazote, then remove from the heat. Add the cilantro and taste again for salt.

To prepare the tortillas, cover a baking sheet with two layers of paper towels. Heat the oil in an 8- or 10-inch skillet. When hot enough to sizzle a drop of water, fry the tortillas for only 4 seconds on each side. Don't let them crisp. Lay them on the paper towels. When done, blot them again to absorb any excess oil.

To fill and sauce the enchiladas, spread 1/4 cup filling on the lower third of each tortilla, making a neat row of filling. Fold the bottom of the tortilla over it and roll. Adjust it so that the seam ends up on the bottom. Place the enchiladas in an ungreased 9 by 13- inch baking dish. Preheat the oven to 375°F. Spoon the sauce over the enchiladas, being sure to cover the ends. Bake until bubbling and heated through, about 20 minutes. Stir the crème fraîche, then drizzle it over the tops of the enchiladas.

Chayote and Corn Enchiladas

You can omit the cheese from these enchiladas, but it does help bind the vegetables and keep them on the fork, plus, it tastes so good. Try using sprouted corn tortillas here. Makes 12 enchiladas

2 small chayotes

2 zucchini

1 large red or orange bell pepper

1 white onion

3 tablespoons safflower oil

1 1/2 cups corn kernels, from 2 ears if fresh

Sea salt

1 or 2 japapeño chiles to taste, seeded and diced

2 tablespoons chopped cilantro

1/2 cup grated, then chopped Monterey Jack

1 cup vegetable oil, for frying

12 corn tortillas

2 cups Tomatillo Salsa (page 90), Oven-Roasted Tomato Sauce (page 55), or Red Chile Sauce (page 62)

1/2 cup crème fraîche or sour cream

Black beans, jicama, and lime wedges, for serving

Cut all the vegetables into 1/4-inch dice. Keep them separate. Heat the safflower oil in a wide skillet, add the onion and chayote, and cook over medium-high heat, stirring occasionally, until tender and lightly browned in places, about 5 minutes. Add the bell pepper, corn, and zucchini, cook for 2 minutes more, then remove from the heat and season with salt. Let cool a little, then add the chiles, cilantro, and cheese.

Fry and fill the tortillas as described in the preceding recipe. Preheat the oven to 375°F and spoon the salsa over the enchiladas. Bake until heated through, about 20 minutes. Serve two on each plate, drizzled with crème fraîche, with a side of black beans and finely shredded jicama with a wedge of lime.

Goat Cheese Enchiladas with Corn and Red Mole

This is a fragrant and complex sauce but not complicated to make. Tomatillo Salsa (page 90) is also very good here—its tartness sets off the cheese. You can replace a portion of the goat cheese with silken tofu (it completely disappears) if you want a less rich version. Try this filling in stuffed peppers or between two tortillas, as a quesadilla. Makes 12 enchiladas

1/4 cup golden raisins

1/4 cup pine nuts

2 tablespoons safflower oil

1 white onion, finely diced

1 teaspoon minced garlic

1 1/2 cups corn kernels

1 1/2 cups grated Jack or Muenster

2 cups soft goat cheese

1/3 cup chopped cilantro

Sea salt and freshly milled white pepper

1 cup safflower oil, for frying

12 corn tortillas

Red Chile Mole, recipe follows

1/2 cup crème fraîche or sour cream

Cover the raisins with warm water and set aside. Brown the pine nuts in a medium-dry skillet, then remove. Add the oil to the same skillet and cook the onion with the garlic over medium heat to soften, about 3 minutes, then add the corn and cook for 1 minute more. Drain the raisins and put them in a bowl with the pine nuts, onion-corn mixture, and 1 cup of the Jack, the goat cheese, and cilantro. Mix everything together well and season with salt and a little white pepper.

Fry and fill the tortillas as described on the previous page. Make the mole. When ready to bake, preheat the oven to 375°F. Sauce the enchiladas and strew the remaining cheese over the top. Bake until heated through, about 20 minutes. Serve with the crème fraîche spooned over the tops and some of the garnishes suggested on page 255—something fresh and something pickled. Extra sautéed corn is also nice added to the plate.

Red Chile Mole

Makes about 2 cups

1 1/2 teaspoons coriander seeds

1 1/4 teaspoons anise seeds

1 1/4 teaspoons cumin seeds

1 1/4 teaspoons dried Mexican oregano

2 1/2 tablespoons safflower oil

1 small onion, finely diced

1 teaspoon minced garlic

1/3 cup ground mild red chile

1 ounce Mexican chocolate, such as Ibarra, coarsely chopped

1 teaspoon sherry vinegar

Sea salt

Toast the seeds and oregano in a dry skillet, then transfer to a plate as soon as they smell fragrant. Grind in a mortar or spice grinder.

Heat the oil in an 8-cup saucepan and add the onion. Cook, stirring frequently, for about 4 minutes, or until it's brown on the edges, then add the garlic and the ground spices and cook for 1 minute more. Remove from the heat, let the pan cool for a minute, then stir the ground chile into the onions along with 1 1/2 cups water. Return to the stove and bring to a boil, stirring slowly but constantly so that the chile doesn't burn. It will thicken as it cooks, so plan to add another 1/4 cup water or more to thin it out a little.

Add the chocolate and stir until it's melted. Simmer for 10 minutes, then stir in the vinegar to bring all the flavors together. Taste and add salt, if needed.

Savory Bread Puddings

These savory bread puddings are light and hearty at the same time and, conveniently, can be set up the night before baking for breakfast or brunch or for supper. Similar to lasagna, these puddings are perfect for a crowd or for very hungry boys—and they lend themselves to improvisation. They stand not only for thrift through their use of less-than-fresh breads, but for the comfort offered by their moist, soft textures.

Many-Layered Strata

Called strata when it consists of layers of bread and vegetables baked in a custard, this dish is a bit of a chore to assemble, but people always like it. And I've streamlined it a bit, as seen in the variation. An excellent dish for a special occasion brunch or supper. Serves 6 to 8

- **Butter and smashed garlic for the pan**
- **1 (28-ounce) can crushed tomatoes, or 3 cups tomato sauce made from fresh or canned tomatoes**
- **Sea salt and freshly milled pepper**
- **2 tablespoons olive oil or a neutral oil**
- **1 pound mushrooms, thinly sliced**
- **2 bunches spinach, stems removed, leaves washed but not dried**
- **4 eggs**
- **2 1/2 cups milk**
- **5 cups cubed bread, crusts removed**
- **2 tablespoons chopped marjoram or rosemary, or 3 tablespoons slivered basil**
- **1 cup grated fontina cheese, mozzarella, or Monterey Jack**
- **1/2 cup crumbled Gorgonzola**

Lightly butter or oil a 9 by 12-inch baking dish, then rub it with a clove of crushed garlic. Make the tomato sauce if you intend to do that. Otherwise taste your canned tomatoes and season them, if needed, with salt.

Heat the oil in a wide skillet. When hot, add the mushrooms and sauté until they begin to color, about 5 minutes. Transfer them to a bowl and season with salt and pepper to taste. Return the skillet to the heat, add the spinach, and cook until wilted. Finely chop then season the spinach with and salt and pepper to taste. Beat the eggs and milk with 1/2 teaspoon salt and freshly milled pepper.

Spread 3/4 cup of tomato sauce in the baking dish. Cover with a layer of bread, followed by the spinach, half of the herbs, and half the fontina. Add a second layer of bread, cover again with tomato sauce followed by the mushrooms, the rest of the fontina, the herbs, and half the remaining tomato sauce. Add a third layer of bread and cover with the rest of the tomato sauce and the Gorgonzola. Pour the egg mixture over all. Cover and refrigerate overnight or for several hours, but allow it to come to room temperature before baking.

Heat the oven to 375°F and bake until browned and puffed, about an hour in all. Let cool 5 minutes before serving.

Strata with Tomato and Basil: Omit the mushrooms and spinach from the strata and use crushed tomatoes rather than a sauce if you want to make it really easy. Season well with salt and pepper and be sure to use all of the tomato.

Bread Pudding with Corn

In a pinch, you can make this comforting dish with frozen corn, but fresh is, of course, far tastier. This pudding is easy to improvise with, and can be set up hours in advance of baking. Serves 4 to 6

- 1 tablespoon oil or butter, plus extra for the dish
- 1 bunch green onions, including half of the greens, sliced into rounds
- 4 cups corn kernels, fresh (about 6 ears) or frozen
- 1/2 teaspoon smoked paprika or ground red chile, plus extra for the top
- 1 teaspoon sea salt
- 1/3 cup chopped parsley or cilantro
- 1/4 cup slivered or torn basil
- 4 eggs
- 2 1/2 cups milk
- 5 cups cubed bread, reserved
- 1 cup grated sharp cheddar or Monterey Jack cheese

Butter a 12-cup gratin or casserole dish.

Heat the oil or butter in a wide skillet over medium-high heat. Add the green onions, corn, and paprika and cook until the scallions have softened and the corn is heated through, about 4 minutes. Season with 1/2 teaspoon of the salt and stir in the parsley or cilantro and basil.

Whisk the eggs and milk with the remaining 1/2 teaspoon salt and pour it over the bread in a bowl. Add the corn mixture and cheese, mix it with your hands, and transfer the mixture to the prepared dish. Cover and refrigerate overnight or several hours so the bread absorbs the liquid, but let it come to room temperature before baking. Heat the oven to 375°F. Bake until puffed and browned, about 45 minutes. Add a dash of paprika or chile to the top and serve.

Variations: Toss the corn with 1/2 cup or more of chipotle salsa and include smoked mozzarella with cheddar or Jack cheese. Cook the corn with green onions and chopped roasted green chile, or mix the corn with sautéed peppers and onions. Season the corn with basil and layer with sliced tomatoes and smoked cheese. Cook diced zucchini and onions with the corn. Cover the surface with a handful of breadcrumbs.

Souffléed Bread Crumb Pudding

Here bread crumbs are used to make a light and tender pudding, so you'll want to get bite in your meal from a crisp salad. You can have this ready for the oven by the time it's preheated, and if there are only two of you, the recipe is easily cut in half. Serves 4 to 6

- 4 or 5 slices bread, such as sprouted wheat, mixed grain, or country
- 3 cups milk
- 2 cups coarsely grated aged cheddar or Gruyère
- 2 teaspoons Dijon mustard
- 1/8 teaspoon cayenne
- 4 eggs, separated
- 3/4 teaspoon sea salt
- Freshly milled pepper

Preheat the oven to 375°F and lightly butter an 8-cup baking or souffle dish.

Tear the bread into pieces, then make it into coarse crumbs in a blender or food processor. Measure 3 cups and put them in a mixing bowl. Bring the milk to a boil in a saucepan, then pour it over the bread crumbs. Stir in the cheese, mustard, cayenne, and egg yolks, then season with the salt and plenty of pepper. Beat the whites with a pinch of salt until they form firm but soft peaks. Fold them into the bread crumb mixture, pour the batter into the baking dish, and bake until puffed and browned, about 25 minutes.

BEANS PLAIN AND FANCY

CHAPTER 10

Beans Plain and Fancy

Beans, peas, and legumes, or *pulses*, as they're also called, are all seeds of leguminous plants, an extremeley large plant family that flourishes the world over. All grow in pods and are sold almost entirely in their dried forms, but when harvested green, they're called shelling beans.

One of the least adulterated foods we can buy, legumes have nourished us from the earliest times and are one of the staple foods of ancient cultures. Because they are considered a simple, humble food, however, they have been largely ignored, at least until recent years. By now, almost everyone knows that beans are vital and sustaining. They contain more protein than any other plant food—especially important for vegetarians. But they're also beneficial for everyone since they're rich in fiber and good to eat.

In addition, beans are tremendously versatile. When it comes to color and form, beans can be truly dazzling. While supermarket shelves have long confined their selection to only a few types, there is a generous wealth of varieties among the newly introduced heirloom beans that can be as small as a grain of rice or as large as a quail's egg and display a range of colorful and bizarre markings with names to match. Similarly, the vast array of lentils and peas found crammed into sacks and bins in any good Indian or other ethnic market come in every color imaginable.

The subtle virtues of their flavors are best revealed when beans are plainly cooked. But they can also be teased into fancier fare, as in the Navy Bean and Pasta Gratin with Basil and Ricotta (page 255) with its pockets of pesto and ricotta, or the delicate Flageolet Beans with Tomatoes and Green Beans (page 289). Beans appear as spreads, dips, soups, stews, gratins, salads, side dishes, and, of course, as soy foods—tofu and tempeh. While I haven't included them among the desserts, one could. I've certainly enjoyed some extraordinary Japanese sweets made from beans, and other cultures know how to sweeten beans for a meal's ending as well.

Common Variety Legumes and Some New Ones

The entire bean family is extremely diverse, and thanks to gardeners, farmers, and seed savers, a host of new beans—in the sense of unfamiliar, for these are heirlooms—have surfaced. These beans include Jacob's Cattle and Good Mother Stallard, Christmas Limas and marrow beans, Rio Zape, Black Nightfall, and many, many more. Gradually, such beans are being introduced to the marketplace via specialty stores like Rancho Gordo, farmers' markets, and seed catalogs. Seed Savers Exchange, for example, sells beans for eating as well as for planting. Heirloom beans can be quite expensive, reflecting their rarity, their appeal, and the fact that many of them involved a great deal of handwork to produce. But bean enthusiasts don't seem to mind. There are plenty of less costly beans available, too. In spite of their dramatic markings (which unfortunately fade with cooking), most beans are neutral enough that they can be used somewhat interchangeably. But when eaten side by side in a comparative tasting, you'll notice that there are differences in earthiness, sweetness, smoothness, or chalkiness of texture.

To include all the names of a seemingly infinite number of beans is still, years later, beyond the scope of this book. Should you come across some unusual dried beans not described here, just give them a try in one of these recipes, or just cook them simply to find out how they taste. After all, all beans are always delicious with nothing more than a little chopped shallot, fruity olive oil, sea salt, and freshly milled pepper.

ANASAZI BEANS: Small, purple-and-white mottled heirloom beans found in the Mesa Verde ruins in Colorado and cultivated in Colorado. Similar to pinto in flavor; slightly quicker cooking.

APPALOOSA BEANS: Small, spotted black-and-white beans; an heirloom variety, also called Dalmatian, both names being for spotted animals. Calypso is another small black-and-white heirloom bean with a creamy texture.

AZTEC BEANS: Very large white or purplish-black runner beans, apparently retrieved from Indian ruins in Aztec, New Mexico. They cook to extremely plump size and have an earthy flavor.

BLACK BEANS: Small, shiny black beans with a cream-colored interior; pronounced earthy taste with sweet tones. Used in Mexican, Carribean, and South American cooking, they have a rich, vegetal flavor. Black Valentine, an heirloom variety, is exceptionally tasty.

BOLITA BEANS (PINK BEANS): Small round pink beans; similar flavor to pinto bean, but somewhat faster cooking. They are still grown in the Southwest.

CANNELLINI BEANS: Moderately large white kidney-type beans that are very popular in Italy. Excellent for salads, soups, and purees, they have a moist, creamy interior.

CRANBERRY BEANS (BORLOTTI OR ROMAN BEANS): Popular in Italian cooking, these beans are dusty pink streaked or mottled with red strips. About 1/2 inch long, they are excellent salad beans or cooked with pasta. Sometimes available as shelling beans in the fall in Italian stores and farmers' markets. Tongues of Fire is another cranberry-type bean.

FAVA BEANS (HORSE BEAN, BROAD BEAN, FOUL, FUL, HABAS): Favas are large, flat beans that have a very distinctive, tart, pungent flavor. (Fuls are smaller.) Their skins are very hard and require a long soaking and, if possible, removal once they're cooked. Dried favas can sometimes be found without their skins, which will make your work easier unless you plan to use a food mill. Favas vary in size from 1/2 inch to almost a full inch, and in color from green, brown, or purple to yellow and splotchy. They can be found in Asian, Mediterranean, and Hispanic markets. Some people have a highly allergic reaction to fava beans, called favism, which is inherited and found among many Mediterranean peoples and some American blacks. It's important that fava beans be thoroughly cooked to prevent a reaction. Soak for 8 hours and plan to cook for up to 3 hours, although the time can vary depending on variety, age, and so on. Pressure cook 40 minutes to an hour, or slightly less if you want the finished bean to be intact.

FLAGEOLET BEANS: Known for their refined elegance, flageolets are small (3/8 inch) beans, which vary from shell white to buff to pale green. They're delicate, fine tasting, and retain their soft colors. Use in gratins; season with fines herbes, buttery sauces, or tomato.

GARBANZO BEANS (CHICKPEAS): These rough, round legumes are among the most useful. We know them as hummus, but they can go into soups, gratins with pastas, and a great many other dishes, especially if you use chickpea flour (*besan*), which is used to make farinata, socca, fritters, and many good things to eat.

GREAT NORTHERN BEANS: Larger than navy beans, Great Northerns are white beans with a more tender creamy flesh; a good bean for stews and gratins.

JACOB'S CATTLE BEANS: Old-fashioned American heirloom beans that are kidney shaped, about 1/2 inch long, cream colored with deep red splotches. A full-flavored, tannic bean, it stands up well to lots of seasoning.

LENTILS: German brown (actually green), Le Puy, Pardina, red split lentils, and Black Beluga are just some of the hundreds of lentils we see. Some are firm and hold up beautifully in a salad; others break down quickly. They are quicker cooking than beans, but like beans, cook better and faster after even a short soak.

LIMA BEANS (BUTTER BEANS): A flat, kidney-shaped bean best known for its role in succotash. Limas, both baby and regular-size ones, are starchy, have a buttery texture, and are great with butter and herbs. Often they cook more quickly than you expect, so keep an eye on them because they can quickly disintegrate. Using a pressure cooker isn't advised: they're particularly foamy and can clog the valve. If skins are removed once they're cooked, they're even nicer. Fresh and frozen Limas are pale green; they dry to white. Christmas Limas, an heirloom variety, are large and pale, mottled with purple-red splotches.

MARROW BEANS: Small, round white beans that swell to a substantial-looking nugget. If carefully cooked, they make a great salad bean; they do not taste like marrow, however, as the name suggests. They have a creamy texture and are delicious with butter, salt, pepper, and maybe an herb.

NAVY BEANS: Small white beans that hold their shape well, navy beans have good flavor and are excellent for salads, simmered dishes, or gratins. They can be used in place of flageolets.

PEAS: Split green and yellow are what we mostly see. Occasionally, one can find whole peas, which are more cube-like than bean shaped. They're best known for their roles in soups.

PINTO BEANS: The most popular beans in the Southwest, pintos are small speckled beige and pink beans. They're somewhat bland but delicious seasoned with nothing more than a little salt, plus they take well to chile and Southwestern garnishes. Used for refried beans and soups.

Giant pinto beans are a runner rather than a bush bean and are nearly an inch long. As with all runner beans, a gentle cooking is preferable to the pressure cooker.

PINQUITO BEAN: Similar to the pinto but pinker. Can be used the same way. They are closely linked to Santa Maria Barbecue. Often found in Hispanic markets.

RED NIGHTFALL AND BLACK NIGHTFALL BEANS: A newer heirloom, these pretty little beans are white and speckled on one end, as though dusted with pepper or ash. Available from ranchogordo.com.

RICE BEANS: Tiny little beans that resemble long-grain rice. Though packages claim a short 40-minute cooking without soaking, my experience with them has required much more time than that, but perhaps they were old.

RIO ZAPE: Another newcomer available from Rancho Gordo, Rio Zape beans are brown with purple markings, full and meaty tasting, and a substantial size—they are excellent.

RUNNER BEANS: Includes the Aztec, giant pinto, Madeira, black, white, and scarlet. All these beans are nearly an inch in length and swell to at least twice their size. Because of their impressive size and the difficulty and expense of obtaining them, they're probably best used in a way that they can be seen and appreciated. A slow, careful cooking befits their character. In spite their size, they often take less than an hour to cook.

SNOWCAP BEANS: Pretty 1/2-inch kidney-shaped beans that are pinkish buff on the bottom and topped with a snowy cap. Their flavor has a sharper edge than most beans; they are good with summer vegetables in soups and salads.

SOLDIER BEANS: Old New England heirlooms that show the tiny image of a soldier against a white background. A little longer than a half-inch, the pattern remains, albeit faintly, after cooking. Soldier beans are one of the original baking beans.

SOUTHERN PEAS: Includes black-eyed peas or beans, cow-peas, crowder, purple hulls, yellow-eyed peas, and many others. The flavor of these beans is mild but earthy. Beloved by Southerners, they can be bought in the shell-bean stage (fresh picked), dried, and frozen. Dried beans needn't be soaked, but I always do. They cook more quickly than other beans, so be cautious with the pressure cooker—10 minutes should be sufficient.

SOY BEANS: Soy beans are rather bland, have an exceptionally silky texture, and more protein and more fat than other beans. They're also notably difficult to digest. They are perhaps better enjoyed as tofu, miso, tempeh, and so on.

TEPARY BEANS: The native bean of the Sonoran Desert of Arizona and Mexico, these are one of the smallest beans — only about 1/4 inch round with a dented-looking surface. They come in shades from white to gray to brown. Grown without irrigation, they are extremely dessicated and can take hours to cook unless relatively fresh. They definitely require soaking, and a pressure cooker is extremely helpful. Their flavor is quite earthy and very pronounced.

Bean Basics

SELECTING BEANS: Although beans last virtually forever, with time they become increasingly dry and brittle and require excessive hours on the stove. Beans cooked within the year of their harvest are clearly best. Avoid beans that are chipped, split, and cracked—all signs of long storage.

STORING: Keep beans in a cool cupboard in an airtight container. Because they're so pretty, glass jars are perfect and they remind you of their presence.

SORTING: Legumes often come with some share of the earth—little clumps of dirt, stones, chaff, and whatnot. Spread them out on a cookie sheet, remove any foreign matter as well as discolored beans, then give them a good rinse.

SOAKING: Soaking beans reintroduces moisture, shortens their cooking time, and allows beans that are overdry or immature to float to the surface where they can be skimmed off. Soaking also removes a portion of the complex sugars that cause indigestion. Although beneficial, soaking can be skipped, especially if you're using a pressure cooker.

Overnight soak: Beans absorb three to four times their volume in water and swell to two or three times their size. "Soaking beans overnight" means covering them with water at least four times their volume for at least 4 hours, about the time it takes for most beans to absorb the maximum amount of water they can.

Quick Soak: When you don't have the time, cover sorted, rinsed beans with four times their volume of water, bring to a boil for a full minute, then turn off the heat, cover, and let stand for an hour.

DRAINING AND PARBOILING: After the beans have soaked, pour off the soaking water, cover them with fresh water, and bring to a rolling boil for 5 to 10 minutes. These steps help eliminate the sugars that cause indigestion. In the recipes that follow, it's assumed that beans have been soaked, covered with fresh water, and boiled hard unless it says otherwise.

REMOVING THE SCUM: During the initial boiling, scum frequently forms on the surface. It doesn't represent dirt but the coagulation of proteins. Skim it off before the vegetables or aromatics are added, but if you forget, don't worry—eventually it disappears.

COOKING: A perfectly cooked bean is soft and creamy inside, never hard, its skin intact, not broken. Beans can be cooked on the stove, in a pressure cooker, in the oven, or in a slow cooker. In general, soaked beans take about 1½ hours to cook, although this depends on the type of bean, its age, the altitude, and the quality of water. Old beans, high altitude, and hard water all add significant time. Size isn't necessarily an indicator. Large beans, like limas, take less time to cook than tiny rice beans.

Cooking Dried Beans

ON THE STOVE: In general, soaked beans take between 1 and 1½ hours to cook, far less time at sea level than at high altitudes.

IN THE PRESSURE COOKER: To pressure-cook beans, I generally cover my beans with boiling water, let them stand for an hour, then drain them. I then cook them with just an inch or two of water to cover in the pressure cooker on high for 20 minutes. I release the pressure quickly, then check to see if the beans are done. If not, I continue to simmer them until they are. (This method is one I use with expensive, special heirloom beans. In the case of more common pintos, I put them directly in the pressure cooker, then cook on high for 25 to 30 minutes. If they need more time, I either simmer them or return them to pressure.)

IN THE SLOW COOKER: Cooking beans is probably one of the best uses for the slow cooker for vegetarians. You can put everything in the pot, the beans unsoaked, the vegetables completely raw, and in 7 or 8 hours they're done. It's amazing. But despite the cooking being slow, it does tend to break the beans, so I wouldn't use this on the more expensive heirlooms, nor would I use the setting on high. But if you want to come home to a delicious smelling pot of pinto or black beans, to eat as pot beans or turn into a creamy soup, this is probably the best method.

A Few Additional Tips

REFRIGERATION: In hot weather, soaking beans can actually ferment if left at room temperature. The surface will be covered with fine frothy bubbles and you'll notice a yeasty, sour odor. When it's hot, soak beans in the refrigerator.

SALT: Salt draws out moisture and works against the cooking process, so add it once the beans have gained a degree of tenderness but aren't completely done, about an hour into their cooking. Do not add it to the soaking water.

ACIDS: Tomatoes, wine, vinegar, and other acidic foods inhibit the tenderizing process and for that reason shouldn't be added until after the beans are tender. Once acid is introduced, it's difficult to cook beans to full tenderness.

HARD WATER: Hard, mineral-filled water really slows the cooking time of beans. In the past, baking soda was added to soften the water and the skins of the beans. However, it also destroys nutrients and can turn the beans mushy. If you have impossibly hard water and are going to add soda, use just a pinch, or ⅛ teaspoon, per cup of beans. Soft rainwater is wonderful for cooking beans, incidentally.

Other Forms of Beans

CANNED BEANS: As convenient as they are, canned beans are seldom as good as those cooked at home. However, there are times when they can save the day. When it comes to canned beans, you'll do best with natural food brands, such as Eden Foods. They are more expensive than other brands but better tasting, often organic, and not nearly as salty.

FROZEN BEANS: Frozen peas, black-eyed peas, and lima beans cook fairly quickly, taste good, and are a good alternative to dried.

BEAN FLAKES: These are, basically, precooked beans. They're flat and flaky, like rolled oats. They cook nearly instantly to a mush. They can be added to soups or made into soups and purees.

BEAN PASTAS: The starch from bean and pea flours is used to make pasta—Chinese cellophane noodles are made from mung bean flour, for example. Some new pastas on the market are made Italian-style but from bean flours.

BEAN FLOURS: Many legumes are ground to a flour and used to make not only the pasta mentioned above but also crepes, the Provençal chickpea dish called *socca*, and fermented flatbreads. Chickpea flour is a good example.

BEANS AS DAIRY: Soybeans are eaten most in processed forms as tofu, soy milk, soy yogurt, and soy-based cheeses—forms that constitute the dairy side of the bean. (See chapter 16, Tofu, Tempeh, and Miso, page 521.)

Mixed Beans in Broth with Parsley and Parmesan

Here's a good way to use up those odds and ends of beans that tend to accumulate. They won't cook at the same rate—some always fall apart, giving more body to the dish. With a pressure cooker, this is a fast and very easy dish. I've taught this dish in classes and it never fails to surprise and delight. Serves 4 to 6

> 2 cups mixed beans
> Aromatics: 6 parsley sprigs, 3 cloves garlic, 1 bay leaf
> 2 teaspoons best olive oil, plus extra-virgin to finish
> 1¹/₂ teaspoons sea salt
> ¹/₄ cup parsley leaves chopped with 1 clove garlic
> Freshly milled pepper
> Freshly grated or shaved parmesan

Put the beans in a pressure cooker with the aromatics, oil, and 8 cups water. Bring the pressure to high and cook for 25 minutes. Release the pressure, add the salt, and if they need more cooking, return the beans to pressure for 5 minutes or simmer until tender. Remove the aromatics. Taste the beans for salt. Serve them, with a little of their broth, in soup bowls with olive oil drizzled over the top, the parsley–garlic mixture, and pepper. Grate the cheese over all or pass it separately.

Beans with Your Best Olive Oil

Often it's the simplest treatments that are best, and this way is always wonderful with virtually any type of bean. The warmth of the beans makes the aromas of the parsley, garlic, and pepper explode. Makes 2¹/₂ cups Ⓥ

> Beans with Aromatics (following recipe)
> 1 large shallot, finely diced, or 3 green onions, including a little green, thinly sliced
> 1 small clove garlic, minced
> 3 tablespoons best olive oil
> 2 tablespoons chopped parsley
> Sea salt and freshly milled pepper
> Lemon wedges

Put the warm beans in a bowl and add the shallot, garlic, olive oil, and parsley. Turn them gently with a large rubber scraper so as not to break them up. Taste and season with salt if needed and freshly milled pepper. Serve with the lemon wedges.

Variations: Toss warm beans with ¹/₃ cup Salsa Verde (page 48) or Pesto (page 50). Toss black beans with the Cilantro Salsa (page 49). Ⓥ

Beans with Aromatics

This is a very basic way of cooking virtually any bean, especially good for all varieties of white beans and chickpeas. The aromatics gently infuse the beans and their broth with their flavors yet leave them open to further embellishments. Makes about 2 ¹/₂ cups Ⓥ

> 1 cup beans, cleaned, rinsed, and soaked
> 2 bay leaves
> 1 small onion, quartered
> Several parsley sprigs
> 1 large clove garlic, sliced
> 1 teaspoon olive oil
> 1 piece kombu or pinch asafetida, optional
> 1¹/₂ teaspoons sea salt

Drain the beans, cover them with 6 cups fresh water, and bring to a boil. Boil, uncovered, for 10 minutes. Skim off any foam. Lower the heat, add the remaining ingredients except salt, cover, and simmer until the beans are partially tender, 30 minutes to an hour. Add the salt and continue cooking until tender but not mushy. Let the beans cool in their broth. Remove the aromatics with a slotted spoon and discard them. Pour off the broth and reserve it for stock. The beans can now be used wherever they're called for.

White Beans with Tarator Sauce: Cook 1 cup navy or white beans as described on page 265. Drain, then toss with $1/2$ to 1 cup Tarator Sauce (page 59), and 2 tablespoons chopped parsley. The warm beans will thin this ivory-colored nut sauce, bringing all its aromas to the fore. Accompany with grilled or sautéed artichokes or fennel. (V)

MAKING SURE THAT BEANS ARE PLEASANT TO EAT

To make beans palatable and pleasant to eat, some cooks insist on soaking, parboiling, and draining before cooking. With equal confidence, others say that beans should never be soaked because valuable nutrients are lost (although if the beans aren't digested, nutrients are also lost). Still others report that nothing you do really makes any difference, and the latest word is that soaking is simply unnecessary. The truth is that people react differently to legumes—some with great sensitivity and others with apparently none, so in the end this is something each person has to work out.

If I'm cooking for someone who is very sensitive to beans, I soak them, discard the soaking water, add fresh water, and always give them a vigorous 5- to 10-minute boil at the start. In addition, I add 1 teaspoon epazote, a pinch of asafetida, or a 6-inch piece of kelp to the pot—practices followed in bean-eating cultures to make beans digestible. However, I've also found that beans cooked in a pressure cooker with absolutely none of these precautions observed are always pleasant to eat, undoubtedly because they end up so well cooked, which may be the most important factor of all. My advice is, whatever else you do or don't do, always cook beans until they're completely tender. Firm beans may look great on the plate, but they're truly hard to eat, even for the most intrepid bean eater.

Those who are less accustomed to eating beans often find them most appealing when accompanied by vegetables, as in bean and vegetable soups, or by pasta, grains, or a mixture of elements. For that reason, beans occur in many other chapters besides this one, especially in salads and soups.

Beans with Broccoli Rabe and Garlic Croutons

Sharp greens like mustard, turnip, and broccoli rabe provide strong punctuation for white beans, plump runners, and many heirloom varieties—all beans really. Serve thin crostini on the side or make thick crostini and spoon the beans, with their greens and sauce, right over them, making a bean and green bruschetta. Serves 4 to 6 (V)

Beans with Aromatics (page 266), plus their broth
3 tablespoons best olive oil, plus extra-virgin to finish
1 onion, finely diced
1 carrot, finely diced
1 bay leaf
1 teaspoon dried oregano
1 bunch broccoli rabe
Sea salt and freshly milled pepper
2 tablespoons chopped parsley
Garlic-Rubbed Crostini (page 24)
Thin slices parmesan or dry Jack, optional

While the beans are cooking, warm the oil in a wide skillet over medium heat. Add the onion, carrot, bay leaf, and oregano, lower the heat, and cook, gently stirring every now and then until the onion is soft, about 8 minutes. Peel the tough stems of the broccoli rabe and finely chop them; chop the leaves a little more coarsely. Add both stems and leaves to the pan with the softened onions along with a cup of the bean broth. When they're wilted down, add the cooked beans and simmer, adding more broth as needed, until the greens are done, a good 15 to 20 minutes. Season with salt and pepper and add the parsley. Serve in soup plates with olive oil drizzled over the top, a few crostini tucked on the side, and paper-thin slices of cheese over all.

Beans with Juniper

This bean dish is truly simple and very satisfying. If you have a sprig of epazote, add it to the simmering beans. There are lots of tasty additions you can use to finish the dish—cilantro, mint, slivered green onions, spoonfuls of thick crema, *cheese, and so forth—but try the beans plain first. Their clean, uncluttered taste can be quite refreshing.* Serves 4 Ⓥ

2 cups dried Anasazi, bolita, or pinto beans

10 coriander seeds

8 juniper berries

1 small onion, diced

1 tablespoon sunflower seed oil

1 teaspoon ground red chile

1 teaspoon dried Mexican or Greek oregano

2 teaspoons sea salt

Sort through the beans, rinse, then cover with cold water and set aside for 4 hours or overnight. When you start cooking, drain them.

Bruise the seeds and berries in a mortar and chop the onion. Warm the oil in a wide bottomed soup pot; add the onions, coriander seeds, juniper berries, chile, and oregano. Cook over medium heat for 3 or 4 minutes, stirring occasionally. Add the drained beans to the pot along with 10 cups fresh water. Bring to a boil for 10 minutes, then lower the heat and simmer for 40 minutes. Add the salt and continue cooking until the beans are as tender as you like them—probably another 30 minutes or longer at higher altitudes. When done, taste for salt. Serve the beans in a bowl with their broth.

Pot Beans with *Crema*, Pine Nuts, and Mint

Beans have a subtle flavor that is brought out by slow, careful cooking, leaving enough broth to sip with the beans. While the pure taste of the beans and their broth alone is enjoyable, there are several condiments that go wonderfully with beans. One constellation includes the thick Mexican crema, *which can be found in Mexican markets (sour cream can be used in its place), pine nuts, green onions, and fresh mint.* Serves 4

1¹/₂ cups pinto, bolita, or pinquito beans, soaked overnight or quick-soaked

¹/₄ cup finely diced onion

1 teaspoon sea salt

¹/₂ cup or more sour cream or Mexican *crema*

¹/₄ cup pine nuts, toasted and chopped

Finely sliced chives or green onions

Several mint leaves, finely slivered

Drain the beans, put them in a soup pot with the water, and gradually bring to a boil. Skim off any foam that rises to the surface; then lower the heat, add the onion, and simmer gently for 30 minutes. Add the salt and continue cooking over low heat until the beans are soft, another 30 minutes or so.

Once the beans are cooked, put them through a food mill or puree them in a blender. Return them to the pot and stir in the sour cream, adding ¹/₂ cup or more, as you like. Taste for salt. Serve garnished with the chopped nuts, chives, and mint.

Lentils, Mung Beans, and Peas

LENTILS: Lentils can be red, green, brown, yellow, pink, and black. There are many more lentil varieties in the world than we're likely to see at home. Most common are the German lentils, actually shades of brown and green, but I much prefer the smaller dark green French lentils from Le Puy. They hold their shape better, which makes them ideal for salads. They have a wonderful deep clean flavor, and they look marvelous on the plate. French green lentils are available at specialty foods stores and natural foods stores, often in bulk. Because they taste and look so good, they're called for in most lentil recipes, but brown lentils can, of course, be used in their place. Of the more than 50 varieties of colorful Egyptian and Indian lentils, many are also available at natural foods stores and Indian and Mediterranean markets. Those that are split cook quickly and disintegrate into creamy-textured soups or purees.

Lentils are used endlessly in soups, often punctuated with greens of various kinds. They make wonderful salads and provide an interesting counterpoint when mixed with pasta or rice. Split lentils are cooked into fragrant Indian dals or mixed with rice to make a dish called *kichuri*, and Indian cookbooks are a rich source of lentil recipes. The broth that remains when lentils are drained for salads makes a homely but invigorating drink. Just heat it up and add a teaspoon of cream or milk to each cup along with some snipped chives and parsley. If there's enough to serve as soup, include some thinly sliced croutons or cooked rice. Although usually thought of as winter fare, with the right seasonal accompaniments lentils can be enjoyed year-round.

HOW TO COOK: While it's not necessary to soak whole lentils and peas, I always do—they taste better and cook in 25 minutes. They take from 25 to 60 minutes to cook unsoaked. You needn't be fearful about adding salt at the beginning of their short cooking time. In fact, this helps bring out their flavors. Like other legumes, lentils and peas need to be cleaned of debris and rinsed before cooking. French lentils especially seem to come with a good many pieces of chalky pebbles.

Basic Lentils

This is the basic method for cooking brown and green lentils. Serve them as a side dish or, keeping them slightly on the firm side, use them for lentil salads. Warm lentils are delicious served with olive oil or butter. Serves 4 to 6 (V)

---

1 1/2 cups brown or green lentils, sorted, rinsed, and soaked for 1 hour

1 onion, quartered

2 cloves garlic

2 bay leaves

1 carrot, finely diced

1 celery rib, finely diced

1 1/2 teaspoons sea salt

Freshly milled pepper

2 tablespoons olive oil, roasted walnut oil, or butter

Red wine vinegar

Chopped parsley or chervil, for garnish

Drain the lentils, then put in a soup pot, cover with 6 cups cold water, and bring to a boil. Skim off any foam that rises, then add the onion, garlic, bay leaves, carrot, celery, and salt. Lower the heat and simmer until tender but still a little firm—they shouldn't be mushy—about 25 minutes. Strain and reserve the broth for soup stock. Remove the onion, garlic, and bay leaves, taste for salt, and season with pepper. Stir in the oil and add a few drops vinegar to bring up the flavor. Garnish with parsley and serve.

Green Lentils with Wine-Glazed Vegetables

In this dish, the vegetables that are usually cooked with the lentils are cooked separately, glazed with tomato and red wine, then added to the lentils. This side dish can easily be transformed into a main dish—see the following variations. Serves 4 to 6 ⓥ

1½ cups green lentils, sorted, rinsed, and soaked for 1 hour

1½ teaspoons sea salt

1 bay leaf

1 tablespoon olive oil

1 onion, cut into ½-inch dice

1 large carrot, cut into ¼-inch dice

1 celery rib, cut into ¼-inch dice

1 clove garlic, mashed or put through a press

1 tablespoon tomato paste

⅔ cup dry red wine

2 teaspoons Dijon mustard

2 tablespoons butter or olive oil

Freshly milled pepper

2 teaspoons chopped parsley or tarragon

Put the lentils in a saucepan with 3 cups water, 1 teaspoon of the salt, and the bay leaf. Bring to a boil, then lower the heat to a lively simmer and cook until the lentils are tender but still hold a little texture, about 25 minutes.

Meanwhile, heat the oil in a medium skillet. Add the onion, carrot, and celery, season with the remaining ½ teaspoon salt, and cook over medium–high heat, stirring frequently, until the vegetables are browned, about 10 minutes. Add the garlic and tomato paste, cook for 1 minute more, and then add the wine. Bring to a boil and then lower the heat and simmer, covered, until the liquid is syrupy and the vegetables are tender, about 10 minutes. Stir in the mustard and add the cooked lentils along with their broth. Simmer until the sauce is mostly reduced, then stir in the butter and season with pepper. Serve with a flourish of freshly chopped parsley.

Lentil and Wine-Glazed Vegetables with Pastry Crust: Adding a lid of puff pastry to these lentils gives them much more focus. (This technique can be applied to most of the bean and vegetable stews in this chapter.) Divide the lentils among four ramekins or a single gratin dish. Roll defrosted puff pastry or pie dough to ⅛ inch thick, then cut it just a hair larger than the dish. Set it over the dish and cut a few decorative slashes for the steam to escape. Bake at 375°F until the pastry is puffed and golden and the lentils are heated through, about 25 minutes.

Lentils and Wine-Glazed Vegetables, Chard, and Garlic-Rubbed Crostini: Lentils and greens are a natural pairing. Just before serving, steam or sauté a large bunch chard or spinach. Pile the lentils into a flat serving dish, surround them with the greens, or stir the greens into them, and serve with thin Garlic–Rubbed Crostini (page 24). ⓥ

Green Lentils, Spinach, Hard-Cooked Eggs, and Toast

All the parts of this rustic one–dish meal can be prepared while the lentils are cooking. Serves 4 as a main dish

---

1 cup green lentils, sorted, rinsed, and soaked for 1 hour

1 teaspoon sea salt

1 tablespoon olive oil

2 to 3 tablespoons butter

2 onions, cut into ¼-inch rounds

1 bunch spinach, leaves only, cut into 1-inch strips

1 clove garlic, minced or put through a press

Freshly milled pepper

4 large thin slices toast made from country bread

2 hard-cooked eggs

Put the drained lentils and the salt in a saucepan with water to cover by 3 inches. Bring to a boil, then lower the heat and simmer until the lentils are tender, about 25 minutes. Drain, reserving the broth. Meanwhile, heat a tablespoon each olive oil and butter in a wide skillet over high heat. Add the onions and sauté until they're golden, about 10 minutes. Set them aside and add the remaining butter to the pan. Add the spinach, garlic, and a few pinches salt and cook until wilted.

Add the lentils to the pan with the spinach along with a little of the broth and an extra tad of butter if you like. Season with salt and pepper.

Make the toast and cut it into triangles. Peel and chop the eggs. Spoon the lentils into the middle of each plate. Cover with the onions and then the chopped egg. Add pepper and surround with the toasts.

Lentil and Caramelized Onion Croquettes

I think of things like lentil cakes as part of our stodgy vegetarian legacy, but they also appeared earlier in our history, when meat was far less plentiful. These croquettes date back to 1913. You could certainly include pungent additions such as roasted garlic, but I think they taste good just as they are. Serve with a simple tomato sauce or even ketchup. Makes eighteen 2 1/2-inch croquettes, serving 6 as a main course (V)

---

2 cups chopped yellow onion

2 tablespoons olive oil, butter, or a mixture

Sea salt and freshly milled pepper

1 cup lentils, sorted, rinsed, and soaked for 1 hour

1/2 cup finely diced celery

1/2 cup finely diced carrot

1 teaspoon sea salt

2 cups soft bread crumbs

1 egg or egg substitute

Vegetable oil, for frying

In a medium skillet over low heat, cook the onion in the olive oil, covered, for 20 minutes. Remove the lid and cook, stirring occasionally, until they're browned, meltingly soft, and full of aroma, about 15 minutes. Season well with salt and pepper.

Meanwhile, combine the drained lentils, celery, carrot, and salt in a saucepan. Add water to cover by 3 inches, bring to a boil, then reduce the heat and simmer until the lentils are soft, about 30 minutes. Drain, reserving the liquid for soup stock. Puree the lentils in a food processor until smooth but still retaining a little texture. Add some of the reserved broth if needed.

Mix the lentils with the onion and half of the bread crumbs. Season well with salt and pepper, then stir in the egg. Spread the mixture out on a platter or tray to cool so that it will be easier to handle. Form the mixture into 3-inch ovals or rounds 2 1/2 inches across. Spread the remaining bread crumbs on a plate and roll the croquettes in them.

Preheat the oven to 200°F. Pour the oil into a skillet to the depth of 1/4 inch and place over medium-high heat. Fry the croquettes in batches until golden brown on both sides, 5 to 8 minutes. Transfer them to paper towels to drain and put in the oven to keep warm. Finish frying the others, then serve them all together.

Lentils and Rice with Fried Onions (*Mujadarrah*)

As plain as this sounds, mujadarrah *is absolutely one of the best dishes there is. A Jordanian cook I know serves her version accompanied by a chopped vegetable salad that sparkles with parsley and lemon. Although you can cook the onions in a scant amount of oil, it's the oil that makes this otherwise humble dish so very good.* Serves 4 (V)

---

6 tablespoons olive oil

1 very large onion, sliced into rounds 1/4 inch thick

1 1/4 cups green or brown lentils, sorted, rinsed, and soaked for 1 hour

1 teaspoon sea salt

3/4 cup white or brown long-grain rice

Freshly milled pepper

Heat the oil in a large skillet over medium heat. Add the onion and cook, stirring frequently, until it's a rich, dark brown, about 12 minutes. Meanwhile, put the lentils in a saucepan with 4 cups water and the salt. Bring to a boil, then simmer for 15 minutes. Add the rice, plenty of pepper, and, if needed, additional water to cover. Cover and cook over low heat until the rice is done, about 15 minutes. Stir in half the onions, then cover and let stand off the heat for 5 minutes. Spoon the lentil-rice mixture onto plates or a platter and cover with the remaining onions.

Lentils with Pasta, Rice, and Buttery Mint Sauce

This recipe, another favorite of mine, is based on one in Claudia Roden's Mediterranean Cookery. *It's the flourish of buttery mint added at the end that makes it so special. Make this when you have leftover rice, lentils, or pasta (or all three). Otherwise it will be excessively complicated, and it should be simple.* Serves 4 to 6

1 cup farfalle or other dried pasta (2 cups cooked)

1 large onion, cut into $^1/_2$-inch cubes

2 tablespoons olive oil

8 Roma tomatoes, seeded and neatly diced

Sea salt and freshly milled pepper

2 cups cooked lentils, preferably green

1$^1/_2$ cups cooked long-grain white rice

4 to 6 tablespoons butter

3 tablespoons chopped mint leaves

Cook the pasta in plenty of salted water, then drain and rinse.

Sauté the onion in the oil in a skillet over medium heat, stirring occasionally, until well browned, 12 to 15 minutes. Add the tomatoes, season with salt and plenty of pepper, and turn off the heat. Heat the lentils, rice, and cooked pasta in a large skillet with $^1/_2$ cup water. Season well with salt and pepper, then add the tomatoes and onion and turn the heat to low. Melt the butter in a small skillet over medium-high heat. When it's sizzling, add the mint leaves and fry for 30 seconds. Grind in plenty of pepper. Pour the butter over the lentil mixture and serve immediately.

Mung Bean Dal with Cumin and Greens

Split mung beans, or moong dal, hold their shape a bit better than split red lentils, offering more bite and distinction. This is a pretty dish, the green-flecked yellow mung beans contrasting with bits of red pepper flakes and tomato. I could happily eat this any day with rice, yogurt, and the Spicy Ginger Chutney, page 73. Serves 4 to 6 Ⓥ

1 cup mung bean dal (moong dal) or split skinned mung lentils

1 teaspoon sea salt

$^1/_2$ teaspoon turmeric

1 bunch fresh spinach leaves (about $^1/_2$ pound), amaranth leaves, or a few chard leaves

3 tablespoons ghee or coconut oil

$^1/_2$ teaspoon cumin seeds

1 small onion, finely diced

1 clove garlic, minced

1 good-size tomato, peeled, seeded and diced (or $^1/_2$ cup canned)

A few pinches red pepper flakes or cayenne

1 or 2 Thai red or green cayenne chiles, split lengthwise, seeds removed

$^1/_2$ teaspoon Garam Masala (page 25) or purchased

Freshly ground pepper

Fresh lemon or lime juice, to taste

Cilantro leaves, for garnish

Rinse the mung beans and then put them in a pot with 4$^1/_2$ cups water, the salt, and turmeric. As it comes to a boil, a great deal of foam will appear. Skim it off until the foaming abates, then cover the pot and simmer until the dal is tender but not mushy, 30 to 40 minutes.

Meanwhile, wash the spinach well, then cook in a skillet with the water clinging to the leaves, turning them until wilted. Remove from the pan and finely chop. Stir it into the dal once it has cooked.

Heat the ghee in a small skillet over medium heat. Add the cumin seeds and cook until they sizzle, then add the onion and garlic. Cook, stirring frequently, until the onions are soft, about 8 minutes. Add the tomato, cover and cook for a few minutes, then add the cayenne, chiles, and garam masala. Pour in $^1/_2$ cup water, cover the pan, and cook gently for 5 minutes. Stir into the dal, taste for salt, and season with pepper and lemon juice. Serve with rice and a garnish of fresh cilantro leaves scattered over the top.

Mung Beans and Rice with Spicy Tomatoes

This mixture of mung beans and rice—kichuri—makes an excellent main dish and leftovers are delicious. When tomatoes aren't in season, replace them with steamed carrot slivers seasoned with lime juice. Serves 4 to 6 Ⓥ

3/4 cup whole green mung beans

1 cup long-grain white rice

1/4 cup chopped cilantro, plus extra for garnish

3 cloves garlic

1 tablespoon peeled and roughly chopped ginger

1 teaspoon Garam Masala (page 25)

1/2 teaspoon turmeric

1/4 teaspoon cayenne

3 tablespoons ghee or coconut oil

1 onion, finely chopped

3/4 teaspoon cumin seeds

1 1/4 teaspoons dill seeds

1 1/2 teaspoons sea salt

1 or 2 japapeño chiles to taste, seeded and finely diced

2 medium tomatoes, cut into wedges

1/2 cup yogurt, optional

In separate bowls, cover the beans and rice with water and set aside. Meanwhile, pound or puree the cilantro, garlic, ginger, and spices together.

Heat 2 tablespoons of the ghee in a 12-cup saucepan over medium heat. Add the onion, 1/2 teaspoon of the cumin seeds, and 1 teaspoon of the dill seeds. Cook until the onion starts to color, 5 to 7 minutes, then add the cilantro mixture and cook for 3 minutes more.

Drain the beans and add them to the saucepan with 4 cups water and the salt. Bring to a boil, then lower the heat and simmer, covered, for 15 minutes. Drain the rice, add it to the pot, and cook for 18 minutes more or until both the rice and beans are tender. Remove from the heat and let stand for 10 minutes.

Heat the remaining 1 tablespoon ghee in a small skillet over medium heat. Add the remaining 1/4 teaspoon cumin and 1/4 teaspoon dill along with the chiles. Cook until the seeds start to brown, then raise the heat, add the tomatoes, and sauté until they begin to soften, about 1 minute. Serve the rice and beans garnished with the tomatoes, yogurt, and a sprinkling of chopped cilantro.

Red Lentil Puree with Green Coriander Buds

Split red lentils make an excellent spread that can be crafted from scratch in about 30 minutes since they cook so quickly. You can use a food processor to puree the lentils, but they're so soft than you can make the entire dish in a mortar and pestle. (Remember this when you're in a cabin without a food processor.) Begin with the garlic and pound it to a mush before adding the lentils.

Green coriander buds are a terrific garden bonus. You can't usually buy them, but they add a green-tasting, slightly pungent—sweet touch wherever they go. If you don't have them, a likely possibility, cilantro will be just fine for a garnish, along with a pinch of sumac, paprika, or red pepper flakes. Makes about 2 cups Ⓥ

1 cup split red lentils

1/2 teaspoon sea salt

1 clove garlic, finely chopped

1 scant teaspoon turmeric

1/2 cup finely chopped cilantro, plus more for garnish if needed

Best olive oil

Juice of 1 lime or 1/2 lemon

Garnishes: green coriander seeds, if available, sumac, paprika, or red pepper flakes

Rinse the lentils several times, then put them in a small pot with 2 cups water and the salt and bring to a boil. Simmer until the lentils are squishy soft, about 15 minutes. Drain them, reserving the water, then put them in a food processor with the garlic, turmeric, cilantro, and 1 tablespoon or more olive oil, to taste. Puree until creamy and smooth. Add the lime juice, taste for salt, and scrape into a bowl.

Run a knife or spatula over the surface, raising some of the puree to form a shallow depression. Pour extra olive oil into that and garnish with the green coriander seeds (or additional cilantro) and any of the dried spices before serving. Serve cool or at room temperature. This keeps quite well, for about 5 days, refrigerated, but bring to room temperature before serving.

Red Lentil Dal with Coconut Cream

Coconut cream, the thick part that rises to the surface in a can of coconut milk, makes this dal especially good. The next recipe utilizes the milk. Makes about 2 cups Ⓥ

1 cup red lentils, rinsed

1/2 teaspoon sea salt

1 clove garlic

1/4 japapeño chile, seeded and chopped

1 tablespoon chopped cilantro stems

2 teaspoons minced ginger

Several tablespoons coconut cream or thick coconut milk

Coconut butter, to finish, optional

Combine the lentils, 3 cups water, and the salt in a saucepan. Bring to a boil, then lower the heat and simmer until they have disintegrated and turned mushy, about 20 minutes. If needed, add more water.

Meanwhile, pound or puree the garlic, chile, cilantro stems, and ginger together. Add them to the cooked lentils. Scoop the coconut cream off the top of a can of coconut milk and stir it into the lentils. Taste for salt and add more coconut cream if desired, or crumbles of coconut butter.

Red Lentil Dal with Aromatics

This dal, which is a little more elaborate than the preceding recipe, uses the coconut milk that lies under the cream. It's delicious served with basmati rice. Makes about 2 cups Ⓥ

1 cup red lentils

1 small onion, finely chopped

2 cloves garlic, sliced

1 japapeño chile, seeded and chopped

3 tablespoons coconut oil

1/2 teaspoon turmeric

1 (15-ounce) can coconut milk, minus the cream if already used

Sea salt

2 shallots, sliced

1 dried red chile, broken into pieces, or 1/4 teaspoon red pepper flakes

3 bay leaves

1 teaspoon mustard seeds

Wash the lentils in several changes of water. In a saucepan over medium-high heat, sauté the onion, garlic, and chile in 2 tablespoons of the coconut oil for 1 minute. Add the turmeric, lentils, and 3 cups water. Bring to a boil, then lower the heat and simmer, covered, until the lentils are soft, about 30 minutes. Add the coconut milk and simmer for 5 minutes more, stirring occasionally. Taste for salt and remove from the heat.

Heat the remaining 1 tablespoon coconut oil in a small skillet over high heat. Add the shallots, red chile, bay leaves, and mustard. Fry until the mustard seeds begin to turn grayish, about 1 minute. Stir this into the lentils and serve.

Black-Eyed Peas, Carolina Rice, and Smoked Paprika

Black-eyed peas can occasionally be bought fresh and fresh-frozen. They don't increase in size and they take little time to cook, so make sure the onions are softened before adding the peas. An easy recipe to make in quantity, and good served with rice, such as Carolina Gold, available from Anson Mills. Serves 4 Ⓥ

2 tablespoons safflower oil

1 large onion, diced

1 small green bell pepper, finely diced

1/2 cup diced celery

2 bay leaves

1/2 teaspoon dried thyme

1/2 teaspoon ground allspice

2 good pinches red pepper flakes

3 cups fresh or frozen black-eyed peas

1 teaspoon sea salt

4 cups water or vegetable stock

Smoked paprika

1 cup Carolina rice, white rice, or long-grained brown rice

Heat the oil in a soup pot over medium heat. Add the onion, bell pepper, celery, bay leaves, and thyme. Cook for 15 minutes, stirring occasionally, then add the allspice and red pepper flakes, the peas, the salt, and the water. Simmer for 15 minutes. Taste for salt and season with smoked paprika.

Cook the rice separately and serve it with the beans along with the broth and an extra dash of smoked paprika.

Yellow Peas, Rice, and Onion Relish (Golden *Kichuri*)

Allow several hours to soak the peas and rice before cooking.
Serves 4 to 6 Ⓥ

___

²/₃ cup yellow split peas

1²/₃ cups basmati rice

3 tablespoons ghee or coconut oil

¹/₂ teaspoon cumin seeds

¹/₄ cup chopped cilantro

¹/₂ teaspoon Garam Masala (page 25)

¹/₂ teaspoon turmeric

3 to 4 cups water or Stock for Curried Dishes (page 175)

1 teaspoon sea salt

Onion Relish

1 white onion, quartered and very thinly sliced crosswise

¹/₂ teaspoon sea salt

Juice of ¹/₂ lemon

¹/₂ teaspoon paprika

¹/₂ teaspoon cayenne

2 tablespoons chopped cilantro

Soak the peas and rice separately in enough warm water to cover amply—the peas for 3 hours and the rice for 1 hour. Drain.

Heat the ghee over medium-high heat in a heavy skillet or saucepan large enough to accommodate the rice and peas. Add the cumin and cook until fragrant, about 1 minute. Add the peas and rice and stir to coat with the ghee, then add the cilantro, garam masala, turmeric, 3 cups water, and the salt. Bring to a boil, then lower the heat and simmer, partially covered, until the peas and rice are soft and the liquid has been absorbed, 18 to 20 minutes. If necessary, add more water in ¹/₂-cup increments. Turn off the heat and let stand for 10 minutes to steam.

While the peas and rice are cooking, toss the onion with the remaining relish ingredients. Fluff the peas and rice lightly with a fork, taste for salt, and serve with the onion relish.

Swedish Brown Beans (*Bruna Bönor*)

This recipe comes from a couple who grow the traditional Swedish brown beans or peas on a small organic farm in Payson, Arizona. You can occasionally find these squarish heirloom peas at farmers' markets. With the molasses, this dish is reminiscent of our Boston baked beans. Serve them with Boston Brown Bread (page 581). Serves 4 Ⓥ

___

1¹/₂ cups Swedish brown peas or navy beans, soaked

1¹/₂ teaspoons sea salt

2 tablespoons blackstrap molasses

1 tablespoon brown sugar

¹/₄ cup apple cider vinegar

Simmer the peas in 6 cups water, covered, until they're partially tender, about an hour. Add the remaining ingredients and cook until very soft, another 30 minutes or so. When finished, the sauce should be brown and thick. If the beans are tender but the sauce is thin, raise the heat and boil, uncovered, to reduce the amount of liquid. If there isn't enough liquid, add a little water to thin it out.

Chickpeas

Also known as garbanzo beans, chickpeas are neither a true pea nor a true bean, but the chickpea is an important legume in much of the Mediterranean, India, and elsewhere in the Western hemisphere. The chickpea's culinary applications are many. It is featured in salads, soups, stews, pastas, purees, fritters, and crepes. Chickpeas are also ground into flour and used to make *farinata* (page 88), *socca*, and other flatbreads. There are Indian varieties that differ greatly in appearance from the pale, buff-colored pea we know, but all have a pleasant nutty flavor. Canned chickpeas, preferably the organic types, are convenient, but home-cooked peas provide you with their broth, a valuable ingredient for soups, stews, and stocks.

COOKING TIMES: Chickpeas can take a long time, so plan on soaking them ahead of time unless you're using a pressure cooker. (At 7,000 feet, in hard mineral water, mine can take 3 hours to cook. But in softened city water at sea level, I've cooked them in less than an hour.)

Times for cooking chickpeas in a pressure cooker are not entirely reliable because of inconsistency in the quality of the peas. But if you're cooking chickpeas for hummus, for example, when you want them very soft, plan on holding them for 40 minutes at high pressure.

CHICKPEAS IN THE PRESSURE COOKER: Bring 1 cup unsoaked chickpeas, 8 cups water, aromatics, and oil (see facing recipe) up to high pressure. Hold for 30 minutes, then quickly release. Remove the lid and check to see how done they are. They should be nearly tender. Add salt and simmer until they're fully cooked. If they are still quite firm, return them to pressure for 5 minutes more, then release quickly and check again for doneness. Repeat this as often as needed.

CHICKPEAS IN THE SLOW COOKER: This is a good method for chickpeas, for they come out beautifully. Rinse 1 cup of dried chickpeas, then put them in a slow cooker with 4 cups water, a pinch of asafetida (optional), a teaspoon of olive oil, and $1/2$ teaspoon salt. Cover and cook on low for 6 to 8 hours. You should have $2^1/2$ cups cooked chickpeas and broth to use for a stock. Finish seasoning with salt when completely cooked.

Chickpeas on the Stove

If you use chickpeas a lot, double the amount. You can freeze those that you don't use and have them ready when you are.
Makes about $2^1/2$ cups Ⓥ

1 cup dried chickpeas, cleaned and soaked

Aromatics: 1 onion, quartered; 2 parsley sprigs; 4 cloves garlic

1 tablespoon olive oil

1 (6-inch) piece kombu or a few pinches asafoetida, optional

$1^1/2$ teaspoons sea salt

Drain the chickpeas. Put them in a saucepan, cover with 8 cups fresh water, and boil for 10 minutes. Skim off any foam that collects on the surface, then lower the heat. Add the aromatics, oil, and kombu. Simmer, partially covered, until the peas are partially tender, after 45 minutes or so. Add the salt and continue cooking until they're completely tender but not mushy.

Spicy Chickpeas with Ginger

Lovers of chickpeas should look to India for inspiration, where there are many lively dishes. This one is inspired by a Bengali dish. Serve with the Yogurt Flatbread (Naan; *page 599) or basmati rice.* Serves 4 to 6 (V)

3 tablespoons ghee or coconut oil

1 large onion, finely diced

1 bay leaf

3 cloves garlic, minced

2 tablespoons grated ginger

2 teaspoons ground coriander

2 teaspoons ground cumin

1/4 teaspoon ground cardamom

1/2 teaspoon sea salt

Freshly milled pepper

2 tomatoes, peeled and diced

1 1/2 cups chickpea broth or water

3 cups cooked chickpeas, or 2 (15-ounce) cans, rinsed

Juice of 1/2 lemon

For garnish: little dishes of diced onion, minced jalapeño chile, chopped cilantro, diced tomato

Heat the ghee in a large skillet over medium heat. Add the onion and cook, stirring frequently, until well browned, 12 to 15 minutes. Lower the heat and add the bay leaf, garlic, ginger, spices, salt, pepper to taste, and the tomatoes. Cook for 5 minutes, then add the chickpea broth and chickpeas. Simmer until the liquid is reduced to a saucelike consistency. Taste for salt and season with lemon juice. Serve with the garnishes or scatter them over the chickpeas.

With Harissa: Cooked chickpeas mixed with Harissa—Tunisia's pungent red chili paste (page 66)—is a good spur-of-the-moment dish, especially if you happen to keep harissa on hand. Warm cooked chickpeas in a pan, stir in harissa to taste along with a little minced garlic and some chopped parsley, season with a little salt, and serve. (V)

Chickpeas with Garlic Mayonnaise: The warmth of the chickpeas makes this mixture enormously aromatic. Heat cooked chickpeas in a small pan, then remove and stir in Garlic Mayonnaise (page 52), to coat lightly. Taste and season with salt if needed and freshly milled pepper and toss with chopped parsley or basil. The heat of the chickpeas will thin the mayonnaise to a saucelike consistency. Serve as a warm salad or side dish.

Chickpea Soup with Condiments (*Leblebi*)

Leblebi, *a hearty Turkish breakfast dish that's sold at little stands, is enormously sustaining and a lot of fun to eat. It's one of the best examples I know of good fast food.* Serves 6 or more (V)

2 cups chickpeas, soaked

1 tablespoon olive oil, plus more to finish

2 bay leaves

1 onion, finely diced

6 cloves garlic, roughly chopped

2 teaspoons sea salt

1 1/2 teaspoons ground cumin

2 tablespoons Harissa (page 66)

Freshly milled pepper

Condiments

4 thick slices day-old country bread or pita bread, torn into pieces

6 lemon wedges

1 bunch green onions, including half the greens, sliced into rounds

Capers, rinsed

Harissa (page 66)

2 hard-cooked eggs, diced, optional

Pickled turnips, available at Middle Eastern markets

Drain the chickpeas and set them aside. Heat the oil in a soup pot with the bay leaves, add the onion, and cook over medium heat until softened, 5 to 7 minutes. Add the chickpeas and 10 cups water and bring to a boil. Simmer, covered, until the beans are soft but not completely cooked, about 1 hour. Or, cook in a pressure cooker (see page 276).

Meanwhile, pound the garlic in a mortar with 1 teaspoon of the salt, the cumin, and the harissa until smooth or use a knife to mince. Add to the chickpeas along with the remaining 1 teaspoon salt, then continue cooking until they're fully soft, 15 to 30 minutes.

Put a few pieces of bread in each bowl, ladle the chickpeas along with the broth over it, then serve with the condiments arrayed in little dishes. Dribble over a little olive oil and finish with salt and pepper.

Stewed Chickpeas, Greens, and Moroccan Spices

This stew is even better the next day. Serve it with couscous, rice, or barley. Serves 4 (V)

---

1 large bunch chard, stems removed

3 cups cooked chickpeas, or 2 (15-ounce) cans, rinsed

6 cloves garlic, coarsely chopped

1 teaspoon sea salt

2 teaspoons sweet paprika

1 teaspoon whole black peppercorns

1 1/2 teaspoons ground cumin

1 teaspoon ground coriander

1/2 teaspoon turmeric

3 tablespoons olive oil

4 tablespoons chopped cilantro

2 tablespoons chopped parsley

1 white onion, chopped

1 bell pepper, cut into 1/2-inch dice

1/4 teaspoon dried thyme

1 small dried red chile

4 tomatoes, peeled, seeded, and diced

Preserved Lemon (page 70), skin only, cut into 1/4-inch dice, optional

Steam the greens until wilted, then chop coarsely and set aside. Cover the cooked chickpeas with cold water and gently rub them between your hands to loosen the skins. Tip the bowl so that the skins flow off. Drain. (This task is optional but results in prettier chickpeas.)

Pound the garlic in a mortar with 1/2 teaspoon of the salt until smooth or mince it with a knife. Add the dried spices, 1 teaspoon of the oil to moisten the mixture, and 2 tablespoons of the cilantro and the parsley. Pound until a rough paste is formed.

Heat the remaining 2 tablespoons plus 2 teaspoons oil in a large skillet over medium-high heat. Add the onion, bell pepper, thyme, and dried chile. Cook for 7 minutes, then stir in the garlic paste, chickpeas, and 1/2 cup water or bean broth. When the onion is soft, add the tomatoes, greens, the remaining 1/2 teaspoon salt, and another 1/2 cup water. Reduce the heat to low and simmer for 5 minutes. Stir in the remaining 2 tablespoons cilantro and the lemon and serve.

Falafel with Sauce and Garnishes

Falafel, the tasty mixture of ground chickpeas, yellow peas, wheat, and herbs, is made into a thick batter, shaped, then fried. You could make falafel from scratch, but it is widely available as a mix of dry ingredients, which you moisten with water. Here's a suggestion for a lunch or dinner plate. Serves 4 (V)

Tarator Sauce (page 59) or Yogurt Tahini Sauce (page 57)

Sliced cucumbers

Sliced tomato

Olives

Feta cheese

Pita bread

Roasted peppers (see page 364) or strips of raw pepper

Falafel

1 1/2 cups falafel mix

Sunflower seed or olive oil, for frying

Sea salt

First make the sauce and prepare any garnishes you wish to use.

Stir the falafel mixture and 1 cup plus 2 tablespoons water together; then let it stand for 10 minutes. When the moisture has been absorbed, shape into 8 patties or, if thick enough, into spheres or ovals.

Heat enough oil to generously cover the bottom of a cast-iron or nonstick pan. When it is hot enough to sizzle a drop of water, add a teaspoon of the falafel mix, fry on both sides, then taste for salt. If the batter needs some, add it now. Cook the falafels on both sides until crisp and golden. Serve with the sauce and any of the garnishes you choose.

Chickpea and Spinach Stew

This makes an easy and wholesome dinner. Serve with cracked wheat, bulgur, or rice. If you don't want to bother with the mayonnaise, drizzle the finished dish with olive oil instead. Serves 4 Ⓥ

2 tablespoons olive oil

2 small onion, finely chopped

3 cloves garlic, minced

2 pinches red pepper flakes

2 teaspoon paprika

1 teaspoon fresh minced rosemary

1/4 cup chopped parsley

1 cup peeled, diced tomatoes, fresh or canned

3 cups cooked chickpeas, or 2 (15-ounce) cans, rinsed

Sea salt and freshly milled pepper

2 bunches spinach, stems removed

Garlic Mayonnaise (page 52) or fine olive oil

In a wide sauté pan, heat the oil over high heat. Add the onion, garlic, red pepper flakes, paprika, rosemary, and half the parsley. Sauté for 2 minutes, then lower the heat to medium and cook, stirring frequently, until the onion is soft, about 12 minutes. Add the tomatoes and chickpeas, season with salt and pepper, then cover and simmer for 15 minutes. Meanwhile, cook the spinach in the water clinging to its leaves until tender. Add the spinach to the chickpeas, taste for salt, and season with pepper. Serve in pasta plates, add a spoonful of mayonnaise to each, and garnish with the remaining parsley.

Chickpeas with Potatoes and Tomatoes

This Lebanese stew is good served cold, garnished with lemon wedges and black olives, as well as warm. Serves 4 Ⓥ

1/2 cup olive oil

1 large onion, chopped

3 red potatoes, peeled and diced into cubes about the size of the chickpeas

2 carrots, cut into 1/2-inch rounds

1 small dried chile

2 plump cloves garlic mashed with 1/2 teaspoon ground coriander

1 cup peeled, diced tomatoes

3 cups cooked chickpeas, or 2 (15-ounce) cans, rinsed

1 teaspoon sea salt

Freshly milled pepper

1/2 cup water or chickpea broth

1/4 cup chopped cilantro

1/2 cup chopped parsley

Heat the oil in a wide skillet over medium heat. Add the onion and cook until it's lightly colored, stirring occasionally, about 8 minutes. Add the potatoes, carrots, chile, and garlic and cook for 5 minutes more. Add the tomatoes and chickpeas, season with the salt and a few twists from the pepper mill, and add the water. Cover and simmer gently until the potatoes are tender, 15 to 20 minutes. Taste for salt and stir in the chopped fresh herbs.

Chickpeas, Pasta, and Sizzling Sage

This homey and simple supper dish is finished with fresh sage and garlic sizzled in olive oil. The same dish is excellent made with cannellini beans. Serves 4 Ⓥ

1 large onion, diced

4 tablespoons olive oil

Sea salt and freshly milled pepper

Large pinch red pepper flakes

3 cups cooked chickpeas or cannellini beans, or 2 (15-ounce) cans, rinsed

8 ounces large farfalle or other dried pasta

2 large cloves garlic, chopped

3 tablespoons chopped sage

In a wide skillet over medium heat, fry the onion in 2 tablespoons of the oil until golden, stirring frequently especially toward the end. Season with salt, plenty of pepper, and the pepper flakes. Add the chickpeas and turn the heat to low. Meanwhile, boil the pasta in salted water until al dente, then add it to the chickpeas. Heat the remaining 2 tablespoons oil in a small skillet over high heat. Add the garlic and sage and fry for 20 seconds. Immediately pour over the dish and serve.

Black Beans

Black beans are a recent favorite and much associated with the Southwest, although they're not the traditional bean there; the bolita and the pinto bean are. Perhaps part of their allure is their color, which has more glamour than the trusty beige bolita or pinto. Their texture is creamy and their flavor pleasant. Black beans cook fairly quickly, even without soaking, although soaking never hurts. Save the nutrient-rich broth to make the delicious Rice Cooked in Black Bean Broth (page 478).

Basic Black Beans

Serve these as a side dish or use them in salads, in black bean cakes, or as a filling in enchiladas and burritos. Epazote is traditionally used with Mexican black beans. It lends a distinctive flavor, which can easily become an essential part of the black bean taste. Makes 3 to 4 cups Ⓥ

1½ cups black beans, sorted and rinsed
2 teaspoons fresh or dried epazote
½ onion, finely diced
½ teaspoon dried oregano
1 teaspoon sea salt

Drain the beans, cover them with 6 cups fresh water, and boil them hard for 10 minutes, skimming off any foam that collects on the surface. Add the epazote, onion, and oregano. Lower the heat and simmer, partially covered, until the beans are partially tender, about 45 minutes. Add the salt and continue cooking until completely tender, 15 to 30 minutes more.

Black Beans, Chipotle Chile, and Tomatoes

This recipe rescues canned black beans from the blahs and does wonders for home-cooked ones. You can build this into a more substantial dish by adding the kernels from three ears of corn at the end. Serves 4 to 6 Ⓥ

1 tablespoon safflower oil
½ onion, finely diced
Basic Black Beans (preceding recipe) or 1 (28-ounce) can
1 teaspoon chipotle chile in adobo or ground chipotle chile or to taste
1 cup chopped tomatoes
4 cilantro sprigs
Sea salt
For garnish: crumbled feta cheese (optional), chopped cilantro, diced serrano or japapeño chile

Heat the oil in a roomy skillet or saucepan over fairly high heat. Add the onion and sauté for 4 to 5 minutes to soften. Add the beans, chile, tomatoes, and cilantro, lower the heat, and simmer for 15 to 30 minutes. If the beans are dry, add 1 cup or so of water. Taste for salt, then turn the beans into a dish and garnish.

Black Nightfall Beans with Red Chile Pods, Tomatoes, and Avocado

These very pretty, slender white beans are speckled with black on one end, like the rump of an Appaloosa horse. Unlike many beans, they retain their markings, even after a turn in the pressure cooker. Here they're cooked with dried red chiles, then finished served with diced tomatoes, avocado, and spoonful of yogurt or sour cream to temper the heat. Alternatively, queso fresco or feta cheeses are good to crumble over the beans, with or without any other garnish. You can also use Anasazi beans here, or black beans. Serves 4 Ⓥ

1 cup black, Black or Red Nightfall, or Anasazi beans (see headnote)

2 tablespoons safflower or light sesame oil

1 onion, diced

1 large sprig epazote

2 dried red New Mexican chile pods, stems and seeds removed

1 teaspoon dried Mexican oregano

1 teaspoon toasted, ground cumin seeds

1 teaspoon sea salt

To finish: diced tomato, sliced avocado, minced cilantro, sour cream or creamy yogurt, optional

Rinse the beans, then cover them with boiling water to soak for at least an hour.

Heat the oil in a pressure cooker. Add the onion, epazote, chile pods, and Mexican oregano. Cook over medium-high heat, stirring occasionally, for 5 minutes. Stir in the cumin, then drain the beans and add them to the pot with 4 cups water and the salt. Put on the lid, bring the pressure to high, and maintain for 20 minutes. Allow the pressure to drop slowly or do a quick release. Taste to make sure the beans are done, and if they aren't, continue simmering, covered (but not under pressure), until they are.

Dish the beans into shallow bowls and strew over the diced tomatoes, sliced avocado, and cilantro. Drizzle over sour cream or yogurt, and serve.

Smoky Black Bean Cakes

Make these cakes from the Basic Black Beans (facing page) or those seasoned with chipotle and tomatoes. If you're using the plainer beans, you might want to add several teaspoons paprika, mild red chile, or pureed chipotle for more intense flavor. Serve with your choice of salsa. Makes twelve 3-inch cakes, serving 6 Ⓥ

Basic Black Beans (opposite page) or Black Beans, Chipotle Chile, and Tomatoes (opposite page)

2 teaspoons ground cumin

1/2 cup grated smoked cheese, optional

1/2 cup chopped cilantro

Sea salt

Lime juice

Flour, for dusting

Vegetable oil, for frying

Fine corn meal, for dusting

For garnish: sour cream (optional), cilantro sprigs, salsa, smoked paprika

Drain the beans and roughly mash or puree them. Add the cumin, cheese, cilantro, and salt and lime juice to taste. Refrigerate for at least 15 minutes, then form into cakes about 1/2 inch thick and 3 inches across. Dust with flour and place on wax paper. (If they're difficult to handle, return them to the refrigerator until firm.) Heat enough oil in a heavy skillet to generously cover the bottom. Dust the cakes with corn meal, then fry over medium heat until they form a crust, about 10 to 12 minutes on each side. Keep warm in a 200°F oven until all are done. Garnish with a spoonful of sour cream and sprigs of cilantro and serve with salsa.

Pot Beans in the Slow Cooker

This method can be applied to most dried beans. There might be a slight difference in time, but they should take between 7 and 8 hours starting with dried, unsoaked beans. After about 4 hours they start to smell good, and then they just get better. They'll end up soft with plenty of broth if you wish to have pot beans or bean broth to use as a stock.

Serves 6 (V)

2 cups dried beans, such as pinto, Anasazi, or black beans

2 teaspoons dried epazote or 1 sprig fresh, if available

1 teaspoon dried oregano

2 cloves garlic, chopped

1 small onion, diced

2 teaspoons sea salt

1 (15-ounce) can organic chopped tomatoes or 1¹/₂ cup fresh

Rinse the beans then put them in the slow cooker with 8 cups water, epazote, oregano, garlic, onion, and 1 teaspoon of the salt. Set on low, cover, and cook until the beans are soft but not all the way done, about 5 to 6 hours. At that point, add the tomatoes and the remaining 1 teaspoon salt, re-cover, and continue cooking until the beans are done. Taste at 7 hours but plan to go to 8 if need be. They're now ready to use.

Bean Bowl with Greens and Rice: A nourishing bowl to sup on, this is my idea of comfort food. Make a pot of rice and sauté some greens. Both take less than 20 minutes. Heap ¹/₂ cup or more beans in a bowl, add cooked rice, and the greens. Spoon over some broth if you like a soup dish, or leave drier, as you wish. Add a little grated smoked cheese and/or a dollop of sour cream and a few slivered green onions.

Other Beans

There are a seemingly infinite number of beans that feature a range of exotic colors and patterns, shapes, and sizes. Some of them are featured in these recipes, from the red beans of the South, the pinquito and pintos of the Southwest, the meaty Rio Zapes from Mexico, the flattish limas so popular in the Midwest, and the elegant pale green flageolet and plump cannellini beans. Of course there are many more varieties not included here, but with beans, generally one can improvise.

Pinto Beans

Plain pinto beans are the usual accompaniment for New Mexican meals. There is a fondness for their unadorned flavor, but they also take well to garnishes such as green onions, grated cheese, toasted pine nuts, chile, and salsas. Anasazi beans can be cooked the same way. Serves 4 to 6 (V)

2 cups pinto beans, sorted and soaked

¹/₂ cup chopped onion

2 teaspoons dried epazote, optional

1¹/₂ teaspoons sea salt

Put the beans in a soup pot, cover them with 8 to 10 cups water, and boil hard for 10 minutes. Remove any scum, then add the onion and epazote. Lower the heat and simmer, partially covered, until they're partially tender, 30 to 45 minutes. Add the salt and continue cooking until they're soft, 15 to 30 minutes more. Serve them with a little of the broth. Some people think the beans are even better cooked in a pressure cooker. They're remarkably tender and very flavorful. Cook on high for 20 minutes if they've been soaked; 25 minutes if they haven't.

Runner Beans, Roasted Peppers, and Anise Seeds

Giant black runners, an heirloom bean, look and taste spectacular in this simple dish. Serve with chopped fresh parsley or basil and a wedge of lemon. Makes about 3 cups Ⓥ

1 cup black runner or other black beans

1 Sprig epazote

1 tablespoon olive oil

1 large onion, diced

2 tablespoons chopped basil

1/2 teaspoon anise seeds

1/2 teaspoon paprika

1/4 cup dry sherry

1/4 cup bean broth or water

1 large red pepper, roasted (see page 364) and diced

Sea salt and freshly milled pepper

Cook the beans as for Beans with Aromatics (page 266), using a sprig of epazote, if available, in place of parsley. Warm the oil in a skillet over medium heat. Add the onion, basil, and anise seeds and cook, stirring occasionally, until the onion is soft, about 10 minutes. Add the beans and stir in the paprika, sherry, broth, and roasted pepper. Simmer until the liquid is reduced to a sauce. Taste for salt and season with pepper.

Smoky-Hot Anasazi or Pinto Beans with Broth

You can also cook the giant pinto or Madeira beans this way. Serves 4 Ⓥ

1 1/2 cups Anasazi or pinto beans, soaked

1/2 chipotle chile in adobo sauce, pureed

1 teaspoon dried epazote, optional

2 tablespoons safflower oil

1 onion, finely chopped

2 cloves garlic, chopped

1 teaspoon dried oregano

1 teaspoon toasted ground cumin

1 tablespoon ground mild New Mexican chile or hot paprika

1 tablespoon flour

1 teaspoon sea salt

Drain the beans, put them in a soup pot, cover with 6 cups fresh water, and boil for 10 minutes. Remove any foam that collects, then add the chipotle and epazote. Lower the heat to a simmer. While the beans are cooking, heat the oil in a medium skillet over medium heat and cook the onion, garlic, oregano, and cumin for 4 to 5 minutes, stirring frequently. Lower the heat, add the chile and flour, and cook for a few minutes more. Stir in 1 cup water or bean broth and cook until thickened. Add this mixture to the beans.

Continue cooking the beans, partially covered, until they're tender, about an hour in all. Add the salt about halfway through. When the beans are done, taste for salt again. Serve them in bowls with their broth, accompanied by cornbread or tortillas.

Alabama Speckled Butter Beans

One of my favorite community cookbooks, Treasured Alabama Recipes, *contains such treasures as muscadine pie, molasses bread, a baked Indian pudding with ginger, fig ice cream, and speckled butter beans or Christmas limas. Fresh Christmas limas, should you have them, are divine. The dried are more likely to be found, however.* Serves 4 to 6 Ⓥ

1 1/2 cups dried Christmas lima beans, soaked overnight or quick-soaked

1 celery stalk, cut into 3 pieces

1/2 yellow onion stuck with 1 clove

1 small bay leaf

1 teaspoon butter or vegetable oil

1 teaspoon sea salt

Freshly milled pepper

Butter or fine olive oil, to finish

Drain the soaked beans, then put them in a pot with water to cover by 2 inches along with the celery, onion, bay leaf, and butter. Bring to a boil, then lower the heat and simmer, covered, until they're tender, an hour or longer. About halfway through the cooking, when they begin to soften noticeably, add the salt.

When the beans are tender, fish out the celery, onion and bay. There should be just a little broth. Taste for salt, season with pepper, and stir in butter, to taste, or thread your finest olive oil over the top.

Pinto Beans, Tomatoes, and Serrano Chiles

Pinquitos, pink beans, pintos, and Anasazis can all be used in this interpretation of the rosy-colored frijoles a la charras. With more broth, this becomes a soup. With less, the beans makes a robust filling for warm thick wheat tortillas. Serves 4 Ⓥ

2 cups pinto, pinquito, or other beans, soaked

1 small onion, halved and peeled

2 cloves garlic, 1 whole, 1 minced

2 teaspoons fresh or dried epazote, optional

1½ teaspoons sea salt

3 tablespoons safflower oil

4 tomatoes, peeled and diced

1 to 3 serrano chiles to taste, finely diced

¼ cup chopped cilantro

For garnish: cilantro sprigs, corn tortillas, crumbled queso fresco or feta, optional

Put the beans in a pot with 8 cups water and boil hard for 10 minutes. Skim off any foam, then add the onion, whole garlic, and epazote. Lower the heat and simmer for 45 minutes. Add the salt and continue cooking until the beans are soft, about 30 minutes more. Remove the onion and garlic. (Or pressure-cook unsoaked beans with the onion, garlic, epazote, and 1 teaspoon oil on high for 25 minutes.)

Heat the oil in a skillet over medium heat. Add the tomatoes and their juice, chiles, cilantro, and minced garlic. Cook briskly, pressing on the tomatoes until they break up and thicken into a sauce, about 10 minutes. Add the sauce to the beans and simmer for 15 minutes more.

Serve the beans plain or with the garnishes, if you like.

Fried-Only-Once Refried Beans

"Refried" beans are made with well-cooked beans and their broth. With a pressure cooker you can make these from start to finish in less than an hour. Serve them plain, with the usual bean garnishes, or use them as a base for nachos or as a filling for tacos and burritos. Makes about 2½ cups Ⓥ

1 cup pinto, pinquito, or pink beans, soaked

2 teaspoons fresh or dried epazote, optional

1 teaspoon sea salt

2 to 3 tablespoons safflower oil

1 small onion, finely diced

1 clove garlic, minced

For garnish: sliced green onions, cilantro, diced chiles, crumbled queso fresco or feta, optional

Put the beans in a pot, cover them with water, and boil hard for 10 minutes. Remove any scum, then add the epazote. Lower the heat and simmer, partially covered, until they're partially tender, 30 to 45 minutes. Add the salt, then continue cooking until they're very soft. Drain, reserving the broth.

Heat the oil in a nonstick or cast-iron skillet over medium heat. Add the onion and cook, stirring frequently, until it's nicely browned, 8 to 10 minutes, adding the garlic during the last few minutes. Add a third of the beans and 2 cups of the broth. Using a fork or a potato masher, mash the beans as they simmer, working them into the broth. When they're fairly smooth, add another third of the beans and continue mashing. Add more broth if the mixture gets too dry. Repeat with the rest of the beans. Taste them for salt and keep frying until they look dry on the bottom and hold together in the pan. They shouldn't be runny, but they shouldn't be a solid, dry mass either. Roll them out onto a platter, like an omelet, and add the garnishes if you choose.

Red Beans and Rice

The starchy, sweet blandness of the rice sets off the flavor of beans. Grilled sweet potato slices or golden fried delicata squash rings served alongside would give this simple food the visual definition of main dish. Serves 4 Ⓥ

1¹/₂ cups red kidney beans, picked over and soaked overnight

4 bay leaves

1¹/₂ teaspoons dried thyme

3 teaspoons dried oregano

1¹/₂ teaspoons sea salt

4 tablespoons safflower oil

5 celery stalks, diced

1 large yellow onion, diced

1 large red bell pepper, seeded and diced

3 cloves garlic, minced

¹/₂ teaspoon cayenne

¹/₂ teaspoon freshly milled black pepper, or to taste

1 cup long-grain white or brown rice

2 tablespoons chopped parsley

Drain the beans, place them in heavy saucepan, add 6 cups water, and bring to a boil. Skim off any foam, then add the bay leaves and ³/₄ teaspoon of the thyme and 1¹/₂ teaspoons of the oregano. Lower the heat and simmer, partially covered, until tender but not quite done, 50 minutes to an hour. Add 1 teaspoon of the salt once the beans have begun to soften.

Meanwhile, heat the oil in a large skillet and add the celery, onion, bell pepper, garlic, and the remaining ³/₄ teaspoon thyme and 1¹/₂ teaspoons oregano. Cook over medium-heat, stirring occasionally, until the vegetables are nicely browned, about 20 minutes. Add the cayenne and black pepper and season with salt. Combine the vegetables with the beans and continue cooking until the beans are completely tender, 15 to 30 minutes longer.

Bring 2 cups water to a boil in a small saucepan. Add ¹/₂ teaspoon salt and stir in the rice. Reduce the heat to low, cover the pan, and cook for 12 minutes. Turn off the heat and let steam for 10 minutes more. (If using brown rice, cook for 30 minutes before turning off the heat.) Fluff the grains with a fork.

Scoop the hot rice into a coffee cup or ramekin, then turn one out onto each plate. Surround it with the beans and their flavorful juices, and scatter the chopped parsley over all.

Red Beans with Greens

You'll be surprised by the amount of flavor in this dish. If you cook your own beans, by all means use the resulting broth, but I think canned beans taste fine here. Serve over plain boiled or steamed white or brown rice. Serves 4 to 6 Ⓥ

2 to 3 large bunches greens—one each from mustard, turnip, collards, broccoli rabe, and kale—stems removed and discarded

¹/₃ cup safflower oil

6 tablespoons flour

¹/₂ cup chopped parsley

1¹/₂ teaspoons dried thyme

1¹/₂ teaspoons dried oregano

1 tablespoon paprika

2 bay leaves

³/₄ teaspoon red pepper flakes

³/₄ teaspoon freshly milled pepper

2 large onions, chopped

2 bell peppers, chopped into ¹/₂-inch pieces

3 celery ribs, chopped

5 plump cloves garlic, put through a press or minced

2¹/₂ teaspoons sea salt

3 cups cooked red kidney beans, or 2 (15-ounce) cans, rinsed

Cook the greens in a large pot of boiling salted water until they're tender, about 12 minutes. Scoop them out, reserving the water. Coarsely chop and set aside.

Meanwhile, make the roux: In a wide, heavy soup pot heat the oil over medium-high heat. Whisk in the flour, reduce the heat to low, and cook, stirring constantly with a flat wooden spoon, until the roux is dark reddish brown, 10 to 15 minutes. (This red roux is what gives the dish its distinctive rich taste.) Stir in the seasonings, then add the vegetables. Cook for 5 minutes, then stir in the garlic, the salt, and 8 cups water or liquid from the greens or home-cooked beans. Continue stirring until the liquid comes to a boil, then lower the heat and simmer for 20 minutes. Add the beans and greens and cook for 15 minutes more.

At this point, start tasting. I usually find I want more salt as well as more pepper flakes or black pepper to bring up the flavors and the heat, but it may be fine as is for you.

Rio Zape Beans with Cumin and Chile

Rio Zape beans, available from Rancho Gordo, make an especially meaty, rich, pot of beans. I've mixed them with black turtle beans when I haven't had enough of the red beans, and that's a fine way to go, too.

Serve with rice, always so good with beans. Or with a little sour cream or grated cheese, either a smoky cow's milk cheese or a sharper feta or queso fresco. Serves 4 to 6 Ⓥ

1 1/2 cups Rio Zape beans

2 tablespoons olive oil or vegetable oil

1 large onion, diced

1 heaping teaspoon roasted ground cumin

1/2 teaspoons ground coriander

1/4 teaspoon ground cinnamon

Pinch powdered cloves

2 teaspoons dried red chile flakes, or 3 chiles de árbol

2 sprigs oregano, leaves only, chopped, or 1 heaping teaspoon dried

1 big bushy sprig epazote, chopped, or 1 teaspoon dried

2 cloves garlic, finely chopped

1 1/2 teaspoons sea salt

Rinse the beans, then put them in a bowl and cover them with boiling water. Let them stand for a hour while you gather your ingredients together.

Heat the oil in a pressure cooker. Add the onion, spices, chile, and herbs, give a stir, and cook over medium-high heat to sear and give flavor to the onions, about 7 minutes. Add the garlic toward the end of that time.

Drain the soaked beans, add them to the pot with 5 cups water and the salt. Fasten the lid, bring the pressure to high, and maintain it for 20 minutes. Quickly release the pressure and when it is down, undo the lid and check the beans. They may be done or close to done. Continue to simmer them until they are as soft as you like. Taste for salt and add more if needed.

White Bean and Vegetable Stew in Red Wine Sauce

Cannellini or the plump white Aztec beans make a dramatic, handsome dish, and Rio Zape beans would also be amazing. While olive oil is always splendid with beans, it's the butter that gives the dish its silky texture. Serves 4 to 6

2 cups cannellini, Great Northern, white Aztec, or Rio Zape beans, soaked

2 bay leaves

1/2 white onion, stuck with 2 cloves

6 tablespoons chopped parsley

Several thyme sprigs or 1/4 teaspoon dried

1/2 white onion, finely diced

1 celery rib, finely diced

5 carrots, 1 finely diced, 4 cut into 2-inch lengths

1 teaspoon sea salt

3 leeks, cut into 1/2-inch rounds

1 small celery root, peeled and cut into 1-inch cubes

6 tablespoons butter

3 shallots, finely diced

1 cup dry red wine

1 clove garlic, minced

Freshly milled pepper

Drain the beans, add fresh water to cover by at least 2 inches, and boil for 10 minutes. Skim off any foam, then add the bay leaves, onion, 1/4 cup of the parsley, the thyme, and the diced onion, celery, and carrot. Lower the heat and simmer, covered, for 1 hour. (Or bake the beans in a 325°F oven.) Season with the salt and remove the onion and cloves. Add the carrot sticks, leeks, and celery root plus water to cover. Cook until both the beans and vegetables are tender, about 25 minutes. Pour off the excess liquid, but reserve it.

In a medium skillet, melt 3 tablespoons of the butter with the shallots. Cook over medium heat for about 3 minutes, then add the wine and simmer until only 1/4 cup remains and the pan is nearly dry. Add this to the beans, stir in the garlic, season with pepper, and simmer gently for 5 minutes. Cut the remaining 3 tablespoons butter into small pieces, gently stir it into the beans, and simmer until the butter has emulsified with the wine and broth to make a sauce. If needed, add a few tablespoons of the reserved cooking liquid. Divide among soup plates and serve garnished with the remaining 2 tablespoons parsley.

White Bean, Escarole and Tomato Braise

Think of cannellini beans as foil for the nutty flavor of escarole. If the beans have already been cooked or you're using canned beans, this dish can be put together in just a few minutes. Serve it with a fine-flavored olive oil, plenty of pepper, and Parmigiano-Reggiano. Escarole turns a little dingy looking, but its flavor is warm, so don't let its looks bother you.

This dish provides a good illustration of how the same ingredients can be assembled in various ways. If there is leftover bean broth, you can add it and have an excellent soup. A splash of vinegar over the same dish, served tepid or slightly chilled, becomes a salad. The same beans could be put in a gratin dish, covered with bread crumbs, laced with olive oil, and baked. Food is flexible. Serves 4 or more ⓥ

1¼ cups dried cannellini beans, soaked overnight or quick-soaked, or 2 (15-ounce) cans white kidney beans

Sea salt

1 head escarole

1 tablespoon olive oil

¼ teaspoon red pepper flakes

2 large cloves garlic, finely chopped

1 large ripe tomato, halved, seeded, and chopped, or 1 cup chopped drained canned tomatoes

Best olive oil, to finish

Shavings of good parmesan cheese, or freshly grated cheese, optional

Freshly milled pepper

Drain the beans, and cover them generously with water. Bring to a boil, lower the heat, and cook gently for 30 minutes. Add salt to taste and continue cooking until the beans are tender but still hold their shape, another 30 minutes or longer, depending on the beans. Save the broth. If you're using canned beans, drain them and set the liquid aside, unless it's very salty. Wash the greens, discard the ragged outer leaves, and chop the rest into 2-inch pieces.

Heat the oil with the red pepper flakes, then add the greens with the water clinging to their leaves and garlic, and salt lightly. Cook until the greens have wilted; then add the beans and simmer until the greens are cooked and the beans are hot. Add a little of the bean broth to the pan to moisten everything and make a little sauce. Just before serving, add the chopped tomato and cook until the tomato is warmed, another few minutes. Drizzle olive oil over the top, add plenty of pepper, and a dusting of cheese, if desired.

Giant Lima Beans, Parsley, Sorrel, and Cream

Despite their size, limas are easy to overcook, so keep an eye on them. This dish can be made into a spring soup by adding the remaining broth as well as any of the starchy residue that falls to the bottom of the pot. If you can't get sorrel, use spinach along with fresh lemon juice. Serves 4

2 cups large lima beans, soaked

Aromatics: 1 bay leaf, 4 parsley sprigs, 2 thyme sprigs

1 teaspoon sea salt

1 tablespoon butter

½ cup finely diced leek or onion

1 cup chopped parsley

1 to 2 cups sorrel, stems removed and leaves chopped

¼ cup cream

Freshly milled pepper

Drain the beans, then boil them in 4 cups fresh water in a soup pot for 10 minutes. Add the aromatics, lower the heat, and simmer for 30 minutes. Add the salt and continue cooking until tender, another 15 minutes or so. Drain but reserve the broth. Run your fingers through the beans to loosen the skins, then remove them. This is a fiddly step, but it makes the beans easier to digest and gives them a silky texture.

Melt the butter in a skillet, add the leek and ¾ cup of the parsley, and cook over medium heat until the leek is soft, about 5 minutes. Add the sorrel and cook until it has wilted. Stir in 1 cup of the bean broth and simmer until most of it has evaporated. Add the beans, cream, and remaining ¼ cup parsley. Thin with additional broth if needed. Taste for salt and season with pepper.

Lima Beans, Olives, and Roasted Peppers

This dish is substantial and flavorful enough to stand on its own as a light one–dish meal. Dried limas are called for here, but you could use about 3 cups of fresh or frozen beans. If this is to be a main dish, ladle it into soup plates with some of the sauce. Or serve it chilled, as a salad, with a wedge of lemon. Serves 4 to 6 Ⓥ

1¼ cups dried lima beans, soaked overnight or quick-soaked

2 tablespoons olive oil

1 onion, finely diced

2 cloves garlic, sliced

2 carrots, peeled, quartered lengthwise, and chopped

1 celery stalk, cut into ¼-inch dice

Several celery leaves, chopped

1 bay leaf

5 tablespoons chopped parsley

2 tablespoons chopped dill

Sea salt

2 yellow bell peppers, or 1 red and 1 yellow pepper, roasted (see page 364) and cut into small squares

12 Greek olives, pits removed, cut into large pieces

Best olive oil, to finish

Drain the beans and cover them with fresh cold water. Bring them to a boil, boil rapidly for several minutes, then skim off any foam that rises to the surface. Lower the heat and cook the beans slowly until they are tender but still a little on the firm side, about an hour. Limas are tricky: they may be large, but they can cook more quickly than other beans.

When the beans are ready, warm the olive oil in a roomy skillet or sauté pan; add the onion, garlic, carrots, celery, celery leaves, bay leaf, and all but a little of the parsley and dill. Cook briskly for 1 or 2 minutes, then add the beans and enough of the cooking liquid to cover. Season with salt to taste. Simmer until the beans are tender and the liquid is mostly reduced. Stir in the peppers and the olives and cook for a few minutes. Serve the beans garnished with the remaining herbs and finish with your best oil drizzled over all.

All-Bean Chili

While there is something especially alluring about black beans, other beans can be used with great success here, such as Jacob's Cattle, pinto, or red kidney. Bean chili will keep for 4 to 5 days. To rewarm, thin it with a little water, heat it gently, and be sure to taste before serving. A splash of vinegar will wake it up if it seems dull. Serves 6 Ⓥ

2 cups black, red kidney, or other beans, sorted and soaked

2 teaspoons epazote, optional

4 teaspoons cumin seeds

2 teaspoons dried oregano, preferably Mexican

3 onions, finely diced

3 tablespoons vegetable oil

4 cloves garlic, coarsely chopped

1½ teaspoons sea salt

4 teaspoons smoked paprika

2 to 3 tablespoons ground red chile

2 cups peeled, seeded, and chopped tomato, juice reserved

1 to 2 teaspoons pureed chipotle chile

¼ cup chopped cilantro

Dash red wine or sherry vinegar

For garnish: sour cream, optional; 1 poblano or long green chile, roasted, peeled, and sliced; cilantro sprigs

Drain the beans. Put them in a soup pot, add the epazote and fresh water to cover by 4 inches, and boil for 5 to 10 minutes. Remove any surface scum. Lower the heat and simmer, partially covered. While they're cooking, toast the cumin seeds in a dry skillet over medium heat. When they turn fragrant, add the oregano, shaking the pan so that the herbs don't burn, for about 5 seconds. Turn them onto a plate to cool, then grind to a powder.

Sauté the onions in the oil in a skillet over medium heat for 7 to 8 minutes. Add the garlic, salt, the cumin mixture, paprika, and ground chile. Lower the heat and cook until the onions are soft, another 5 minutes. Add the tomatoes and juice, 1 teaspoon chipotle puree, and the cilantro. Simmer for 15 minutes, then add this mixture to the beans.

Continue cooking until the beans are completely soft, about 30 minutes altogether, making sure the water level stays at least an inch or two above them. Taste and season with more chipotle and salt, if needed, and add a dash of vinegar. Ladle the beans into bowls and garnish with a spoonful of sour cream, the chile strips, and a sprig of cilantro.

Flageolet Beans with Tomatoes and Green Beans

A dish for summer when there are slender fresh green beans to use along with the elegant dried flageolets. Although quite good cooked just with the broth, especially if the vegetables are at their peak of flavor, a touch of cream is always good with beans. Serves 4 to 6 Ⓥ

1¹/₂ cups flageolet beans, soaked

Aromatics (page 21), plus ¹/₂ onion

1 teaspoon sea salt

8 ounces slender green beans

2 tablespoons olive oil or butter

4 shallots, finely diced

¹/₂ cup dry white wine

3 ripe tomatoes, peeled, seeded, and neatly diced

2 tablespoons chopped parsley

1 tablespoon chopped marjoram, tarragon, or summer savory

Freshly milled pepper

Parboil the drained beans for 10 minutes in 6 cups fresh water. Add the aromatics, lower the heat, and simmer until partially tender, about an hour more. Add the salt and continue cooking until they're done, 15 to 30 minutes. Drain, reserving the broth. Blanch the green beans in plenty of boiling salted water until barely tender-firm, then drain and rinse with cold water.

Warm the oil in a small skillet over medium heat. Add the shallots and cook until soft, about 8 minutes. Add the wine and tomatoes, bring to a boil, and simmer until the wine is mostly cooked away.

Preheat the oven to 375°F. Lightly butter a gratin dish. Combine the flageolet beans with the green beans and half the herbs and transfer to the dish.

Season with salt and pepper to taste and add enough bean broth to moisten the beans. Cover and bake until heated through, about 25 minutes. Garnish with the remaining herbs and serve.

Crisp and Tender White Bean Croquettes with Chard

These little bites are soft on the inside and crispy on the outside. I rather like them made small—a heaping tablespoon at the most—and served garnished with watercress; but alternatively, you can make them larger, like a faux burger, and serve them with mayonnaise or the Savory Cashew Cream (page 60). Makes about 30 small croquettes

2 tablespoons olive oil, plus extra for frying

1 small onion, very finely diced

2 tablespoons chopped sage leaves

1 tablespoon chopped oregano

1 plump clove garlic, minced or pressed

2 cups finely chopped chard

1¹/₂ to 2 cups cooked white beans (such as cannellini or navy beans)

3 tablespoons grated Monterey Jack, Asiago, or parmesan cheese

¹/₄ cup finely chopped walnuts

Sea salt and freshly milled pepper

1 egg

1 cup fine bread crumbs or more, if needed (fresh or dried)

1 bunch watercress, broken into clumps and washed

Lemon wedges, for serving

Warm the oil in a skillet over medium-high heat, then add the onion, sage, and oregano and cook over medium-high heat until they start to brown a little, about 3 minutes, stirring occasionally. Add the garlic and chard and cook until the chard is wilted and mostly tender. Add the white beans and mash them with a fork as they cook to break them up. Continue cooking until the chard is fully tender, another few minutes. Remove from the heat and add the cheese and walnuts. Season well with salt and freshly milled pepper, then stir in the egg.

Heat a wide nonstick skillet with olive oil to cover generously. Put the bread crumbs in a pie plate. Scoop out rough tablespoons of the mixture, drop them in the bread crumbs, and loosely toss so that they're coated. Shape them gently with your hands into rounds or ovals, then drop them in the hot oil and fry until golden and crisp. Arrange the watercress loosely on plates and place 2 to 3 croquettes and a lemon wedge on each, or prepare a platter to pass around.

Cannellini Beans and Savoy Cabbage with Cumin

It's hard to imagine a more humble combination than beans and cabbage, but the looks and flavor are surprisingly distinctive. Use the crinkly leafed savoy cabbage if possible. It has a more delicate flavor and texture than the harder round Dutch cabbages. Serves 4 to 6 (V)

1¹/₂ cups dried cannellini (white kidney) beans, soaked overnight or quick-soaked

1 bay leaf

5 sage leaves or several pinches dried sage

3 to 4 tablespoons olive oil

1¹/₂ teaspoons sea salt

1 small head (about 1 pound) savoy cabbage

1 tablespoon cumin seeds

3 cloves garlic, peeled and sliced

Small handful parsley, chopped

Freshly milled pepper

Grated Asiago or parmesan cheese, optional

Drain the soaked beans and cover them generously with fresh cold water. Boil vigorously for 5 minutes, then skim off the foam that rises to the surface. Lower the heat and add the bay leaf, sage, and 1 tablespoon of the oil. Simmer for 30 minutes; then add 1¹/₂ teaspoons salt. Continue cooking until the beans are tender, 1 hour or more, depending on the type and age of the bean. Make sure there's enough water. There should be a few cups of broth left once the beans are cooked. (Alternatively, cook the beans and aromatics in a pressure cooker on high for 20 minutes, then release the pressure. The beans will probably require a little more cooking, which you can do gently, on the stovetop.)

Cut the cabbage into wedges about 2 inches wide, leaving most of the core so that the leaves will remain joined. When the beans are nearly tender, remove 1 cup of the water and put it in a wide skillet.

Add the cabbage wedges and cumin seeds, and salt lightly. Cook until the color begins to brighten and the leaves start to soften, about 5 to 8 minutes. Turn the cabbage over several times. The cabbage should be tender but not overcooked.

While the cabbage is cooking, heat the remaining 2 to 3 tablespoons oil in a small pan with the garlic. When the garlic is golden, remove from the heat, remove the cloves, and stir in the parsley. Combine the beans and cabbage and 1 cup of the bean broth. Pour the oil and parsley over the dish, fold gently together, and season with plenty of pepper. Grate cheese over the top if you wish.

Sprouted Beans and Seeds

Long one of the clichés of vegetarian cooking, sprouted beans and seeds have virtues that can be enjoyed by all. They're good sources of vitamins, they're easily digested, and they're a fresh, clean food that's available at all times of the year. Anyone who has nosed around food shops in London has seen those uplifting little packages of sprouted cress and mustard seeds looking like miniature green lawns. They're tempting to take home (or to a hotel room), and obviously many people do that. Happily, packaged gardens of sprouted seeds are beginning to be seen here as well.

In addition to the most common mung bean and alfalfa sprouts, some unusual varieties have begun appearing—fine delicate threads of sprouted radish, leek, and basil seeds that taste vividly of the plants they would have become; big, bold-looking sunflower sprouts that make a strong visual impression in a salad; and an array of sprouted lentils, chickpeas, and other legumes that are great in a stir-fry. Sprouted wheat berries are sometimes added to wheat bread.

WHAT TO LOOK FOR: Whenever possible, try to buy sprouts that are openly displayed in a refrigerated case, where air can circulate freely around them. Tight plastic-wrapped sprouts spoil easily, but if it's all you have to choose from, make sure they look fresh with no signs of browning or spoiling.

HOW TO STORE: Keep sprouts in a loose plastic bag perforated with a few holes so that water doesn't condense. Try to use them as soon as possible.

GROWING YOUR OWN: It's easy to make sprouts at home. Small seeds for sprouting, like radish or basil, can be found at natural foods stores, but your own cupboard is probably full of things that can be sprouted—sunflower seeds, chickpeas, whole wheat, lentils, mung beans, and arugula seeds saved from your garden. All seeds sprout, but they do have to be whole. Split peas won't sprout, nor will broken grains. Whatever you decide to sprout, be sure to use seeds that are meant for consumption. Garden seeds are often coated with fungicides, and these are not good to eat. Further, avoid tomato, eggplant, lima beans, and fava beans since their seeds can be toxic.

Soak a few tablespoons of seeds in water overnight.

The next day, pour off the soaking water, rinse them in fresh water until the water runs clear, then drain. Transfer the seeds to a large jar, such as a wide-mouthed quart or half-gallon jar. Place a piece of cheesecloth over the top and fasten it with a rubber band. Gently tip out any excess water (extra water will cause the seeds to spoil), then set the jar on its side and set it on your counter. Cover it with a cloth, leaving the screen uncovered.

Rinse and drain the sprouts two or three times a day in normal weather, more often if it's humid, so that they don't spoil. After each rinse, be sure to thoroughly drain off the excess water. Continue until the seeds have sprouted a tail two or three times as long as the seed. (In the case of mung beans and sunflower seeds, the sprouts will be two or more inches long.) Most sprouts take about 3 days to achieve their desired length—a few take longer, and some take less.

On the last day, take the cloth off and expose the sprouts to the light so that the leaves become nice and green, then store them in the refrigerator. To get the most from your efforts, try to use them as soon after they're ready as possible, when they are most nutritious.

GARDEN SPROUTS: One summer I noticed a lot of very luxurious-looking sprouts in my garden. They turned out to be sunflower seeds that had been kicked aside by the sparrows. I clipped them at the base, gave them a rinse, and used them as I would those cultivated indoors. Similarly, in spring I have a carpet of self-sown arugula and amaranth sprouts, which I either pluck or clip since they need to be thinned in any case. They add a vibrant, piquant accent to an egg salad, a bowl of cottage cheese, or a green salad. If you have a garden, be sure to check it for possibilities.

VEGETABLES

CHAPTER 11

Vegetables
The Heart of the Matter

Vegetables are at the heart of this book. Today there's a fetching plethora available in seed catalogs, from the 7,000-plus farmers' markets in the United States, and on our market shelves, but experience tells me many shoppers stay with what they're comfortable with even when they yearn to experiment.

Innumerable times at the market I've been tapped on the shoulder by someone who's dying to know what I'm going to do with that celery root or eggplant I'm holding. An unfamiliar vegetable is intimidating when you haven't a clue to its nature. I've felt that myself in Asian markets when confronted with exotic greens and warty melons; I may be curious, but I'm not inclined to buy without a guide.

This chapter is meant to be just that: a guide to vegetables—both common ones and those that are less so, or common-exotics (they may well be ordinary but are seldom cooked.)

This guide will tell you what the vegetable is and how to cook it, what special handling, if any, it requires, and the vegetable's flattering partners—the butters or oils that are most complementary, herbs and spices to use, and cheeses when appropriate, as well as condiments and other vegetables that pair well. The range of possibilities for each vegetable is presented so you can improvise with confidence. Basic recipes are given that can be made without fuss. These dishes are appealing to children, who often have plainer tastes, and those who aren't looking for complications when it comes to dinner, or those looking for simple side dishes.

Grilling Vegetables

One of the best ways to concentrate the flavors of vegetables is through grilling. As in oven roasting, the dry heat of the coals evaporates moisture, concentrates the vegetables' sugars, and deepens their flavors, but grilling also adds a smoky flavor to the vegetables. Summer vegetables, which have more moisture than winter ones, are obvious candidates for grilling. Winter vegetables, however, such as squash and sweet potatoes, are good, too.

THE TOOLS: Wood fires, charcoal, and gas grills all give good results. Wood smoke adds more flavor, but a gas grill is much easier to get going and leaves the heat outdoors in summer. (I use one year-round and grill much more often than if I were relying only on a wood fire.) Whatever type of grill you use, from a tiny hibachi to a giant gas grill, always give the rack a vigorous scrubbing when it's hot with a wire brush so that your vegetables don't stick.

A pair of spring-loaded tongs is the ideal tool for picking up and turning vegetables. Long ones allow you to stand well back from the heat and smoke. Special hinged racks allow you to grill small foods that might otherwise fall through the bars, and skewers are a convenient way to grill a number of small items at once.

THE BASIC TECHNIQUE: Make a wood or charcoal fire or preheat your gas grill for 10 to 15 minutes. A wood fire should die down until just small flames and ash-covered coals remain, which takes anywhere from 30 to 45 minutes. Precook the vegetables if necessary and slice them into slabs about 3/8 inch thick or whatever the recipe calls for. Brush both sides with oil to keep them from drying out, season with sea salt, and place them on the grill, positioning long-cooking vegetables, like eggplant, potatoes, and onions, a little farther from the hottest coals. Turn the vegetables 45 degrees halfway through their cooking time to give them those nice professional-looking grill marks and to compensate for uneven hot or cool spots.

There are many variables in grilling—the heat of the fire, how far the food is above the heat, the thickness of the vegetable, and where on the rack it sits. Perhaps more than any other form of cooking, grilling demands the cook's constant vigilance and judgment to ensure perfectly cooked vegetables.

SAUCES AND SEASONINGS FOR GRILLED VEGETABLES: Virtually all grilled vegetables are perfectly satisfying when brushed with olive oil, seasoned with salt and pepper, and garnished with chopped parsley or other herbs. But if you want something a little more elaborate, many sauces and seasonings are delicious when spread over grilled vegetables—the oft-mentioned Garlic Mayonnaise (page 52), green herb sauces, yogurt sauces, nut-based sauces, herb butters, and seasoned salts, for example. (See chapter 2, Foundations of Flavor, and chapter 3, Sauces and Condiments.) Those sauces and seasonings suggested in the following pages will naturally be excellent with the same vegetables when grilled. In addition, you can provide a grilled vegetable with more substance by spooning on a tomato and olive relish, crumbled or grated cheeses, crème fraîche, and other rich additions. The eggplant rounds on pages 331 to 332 demonstrate how this can be done.

Leftover grilled vegetables as well as those fresh off the grill are enhanced by the vinaigrettes and dressings found in chapter 6, Salads for All Seasons, such as the Saffron Vinaigrette with Basil and Orange (page 166) over grilled zucchini. They can also be finely diced, dressed, and tossed to make succulent little salads, toppings for crostini and bruschetta, or sandwich fillings. Finally, grilled vegetables can be converted to soups; grilled pepper or eggplant soup is superb!

Artichokes

To the uninitiated, artichokes, the flower buds of a large thistle, look formidable, but this unusual vegetable usually becomes a favorite once its acquaintance is made. Originally brought here by Italians, virtually all commercially grown artichokes in the United States are grown in California, but that's not the only place they grow. They're available throughout the year, but their peak seasons are in the spring—March and April—and happily again in the fall, September and October.

TYPES OF ARTICHOKES: The variety we see most is the globe artichoke, but it can assume different appearances. In the spring, the buds tend to be round and tightly closed at the top, while in the fall they're more elongated and open. The largest artichokes grow on the tip of the main stalk, where they get plenty of light and sun, while the "babies" are found at the shady base. These tiny artichokes weigh as little as a few ounces and don't have a choke. They are typically frozen and marinated but are sold fresh as well.

WHAT TO LOOK FOR: A fresh artichoke should feel heavy for its size and have heavy, smooth green leaves that squeak when you squeeze them. Scars and scratches from handling or blisters from frost don't necessarily indicate lack of freshness. In fact, artichokes that have been "kissed" with frost are often sweetest.

HOW TO STORE: Moisten the tops with water, then store in a plastic bag in the vegetable bin of the refrigerator for up to a week.

HOW TO USE: Artichokes can be steamed, fried, braised, sautéed, marinated, stuffed, grilled, and roasted. They make a succulent contribution to vegetable stews, pastas, gratins, and risotto. Cooked hearts can be pureed or added to salads. You can freeze your own by trimming them, boiling them in a *blanc* (directions follow) for 5 minutes, then letting them cool before freezing in freezer bags. Commercially frozen artichokes are best used in highly seasoned dishes.

SPECIAL HANDLING: Always use a stainless steel knife and a stainless steel or glass pot. Iron or aluminum will discolor artichokes. Never let aluminum foil come into direct contact with them for the same reason.

As you work with artichokes, rub cut areas with a lemon and put trimmed pieces in a bowl with lemon juice or vinegar mixed with water to cover—3 to 4 tablespoons juice to 4 cups water. Cooking artichokes in a *blanc*—the acidulated water mixed with 2 teaspoons each flour and olive oil—helps them keep their pale green color.

QUANTITY: Allow three or more baby artichokes or one medium artichoke per person. The hearts of jumbo artichokes are about twice as large as those of mediums. Today long stems are sometimes sold attached to the buds. They are completely edible once peeled.

Good Partners for Artichokes

Olive oil, butter, hazelnut oil, hazelnuts

Tarragon, chervil, thyme, sage, rosemary, garlic, bay, lemon, orange, capers, fennel seeds, sorrel

Goat cheese, ricotta salata, parmesan

Peas, beans, potatoes, asparagus, mushrooms, shallots

Sauces and Seasonings for Artichokes

Melted butter and olive oil

Salsa Verde (page 48)

Cilantro Salsa (page 49)

Garlic Mayonnaise (page 52)

Herb–Butter and Olive Oil Sauce (page 44)

THE FRAGRANCE OF BAY

A French friend who loves artichokes but not their cooking odor drops a bay leaf in the pot. It's a good trick any time, for the fragrance of bay perfumes the room as well.

Preparing Artichokes for Sautéing and Stuffing

FOR QUARTERS AND SLICES: Whether you're using large or baby artichokes, first snap off several layers of the tough outer leaves by pulling them downward so that they break off at the base. Stop when the inner leaves become a lighter yellowish green and look tender.

Trim the stem and slice off the top third of the artichoke. With a paring knife, smooth the rough areas around the base, removing any dark green parts. Cut the trimmed artichoke into quarters and remove the fuzzy chokes of mature artichokes with a paring knife. (Babies don't have a choke.) Leave in quarters or slice them thinly for sautéing. As you work, put the finished pieces in a bowl of acidulated water to cover.

MAKE AN ARTICHOKE CONTAINER: Steam or boil a whole artichoke (see page 296), then rinse it under cold water. Reach inside and pull out the cone of inner leaves with a twist of your fingers, then use a spoon to scrape out the choke. Trim the outer leaves if you wish. Now the artichoke can be filled with a salad, or a braise of spring peas.

HOW TO EAT AN ARTICHOKE

Almost everyone has a funny or humiliating story about his or her first confrontation with a whole artichoke. To avoid future embarrassment, here's what you do: Pull off each leaf, one by one, dip it into whatever sauce is offered, then slide the leaf between your teeth. The "meat" is at the base of the leaf; the finished leaves get tossed in a bowl in the middle of the table. Don't quit when the leaves are gone, because the best part is next. You'll see a cone of violet-tipped, thin, pale leaves in the center. Pull this off and discard it. Underneath is a fuzzy mat called the choke; slice it off with your knife. What's left is the heart—a large disk of purely edible artichoke—yours to enjoy.

Whole Steamed Artichokes

This is the easiest way to cook artichokes, though there are many other ways to enjoy them. Eating a whole artichoke is a leisurely activity and makes a convivial beginning to a meal. You can also boil artichokes, but to my taste they tend to the waterlogged. (V)

Allow 1 medium artichoke per person. If they're scarce or very costly, buy a jumbo one for several friends to share. Clip the thorns from the leaves, slice off the top third of the artichoke, and trim the stem so that it can stand upright, removing as little as possible from the base. Now give it a good rinse, pulling the leaves apart to flush them out. Rub the cut surfaces with a lemon half.

Set the artichoke upside down on a steaming rack over boiling water. Cook until a leaf comes out fairly easily when tugged, 30 to 40 minutes, depending on the size. If you plan to serve cold artichokes, drop them into a bowl of ice water to stop the cooking, then let them drain upside down on a kitchen towel in the refrigerator until ready to eat.

Grilled Artichokes

These are unusual and very good and messy to eat. Whether you're using regular or babies, trim the tops and bottoms. (V)

Cut the regular artichokes lengthwise in half, set them cut side down on the counter, and press clown on them to force the leaves open. (You can leave the babies whole or cut them as well.) Rub them generously with olive oil, pushing it into the leaves. If you like, work in chopped garlic and parsley as well. Season with salt and pepper. Set them over the coals and grill on both sides until the base is tender when pierced with a knife, 30 to 45 minutes. Arrange the artichokes on a platter, squeeze lemon juice over them, and serve with lots of napkins. Since they will be at least partially charred, there's no way to eat these neatly. Alternatively, you can grill trimmed and steamed artichoke wedges without the mess of charred leaves.

Roasted Artichokes

Roasting makes these artichokes sweet and a little crisp around the edges. Serve them as appetizers, plain, with soft goat cheese or with Garlic Mayonnaise (page 52), or spooned over a bowl of soft polenta and covered with thin shavings of parmesan. Serves 4 (V)

> 4 to 6 artichokes
> Juice of 1 large lemon
> Olive oil
> Sea salt and freshly milled pepper
> Aromatics: 4 thyme sprigs, 2 bay leaves
> 2 tablespoons dry white wine or water

Preheat the oven to 400°F. Lightly oil a gratin dish large enough to hold the artichokes in a single layer. Trim the artichokes as described on page 295 and cut them into sixths. As you work, drop them into a bowl with the lemon juice and water to cover. When all are done, drain, pat dry with a towel, and toss with enough oil to moisten well. Season with salt and pepper. Put them in the prepared dish with the aromatics and wine. Cover with wax paper, then with foil. Bake for 35 minutes, then uncover and bake until crisped around the edges and beginning to brown, about 25 minutes more.

Baby Artichoke and Green Onion Sauté

The preparation of the baby artichokes goes easily and quickly. If they're not available, use 4 to 6 medium ones, trimmed and quartered, the hearts thinly sliced. These artichokes are good on their own, tossed with spaghetti, stirred into risotto, or spooned over bruschetta. Serves 4 to 6 (V)

> 20 to 24 baby artichokes
> Juice of 2 lemons
> 2 tablespoons olive oil
> 1 bunch green onions, including an inch of the greens, thickly sliced
> 1/2 cup dry white wine
> Gremolata made with 3 tablespoons parsley leaves chopped with 1 clove garlic and 2 teaspoons lemon zest
> 1 tablespoon chopped tarragon
> Sea salt and freshly milled pepper

Trim the artichokes as described on page 295, leaving them whole. Put them in a bowl with the lemon juice and water to cover as you work. Drain, then boil them in acidulated water or a blanc (see page 295) until tender-firm, about 10 minutes, then drain again. Slice them lengthwise into halves. (This can be done ahead of time.)

Heat the oil in a large skillet over high heat. Add the artichokes and sauté until they begin to color in places, after several minutes, then add the onions and wine. When the wine boils off, add 1 cup water and half the gremolata and tarragon. Lower the heat and cook until the artichokes are fully tender, between 5 and 10 minutes, then add the rest of the gremolata and tarragon and season with salt and pepper. Tip them, with their juices, onto a serving plate.

Braised Baby Artichokes

These little whole artichokes make a wonderfully tender mouthful. If you can't find them where you live, use 5 medium artichokes, trimmed and cut into $1/2$-inch wedges. Serve as a side dish or as a course by themselves, to underscore their specialness. Serves 4 (V)

---

24 baby artichokes, trimmed
Juice of 1 large lemon
4 tablespoons olive oil
6 sage leaves, or 6 thyme sprigs
2 strips lemon zest
$1/2$ teaspoon sea salt
1 plump clove garlic, slivered
1 bay leaf
Freshly milled pepper
1 tablespoon chopped thyme or parsley, for garnish

Drop the finished artichokes into a bowl with the lemon juice and water to cover.

Warm 2 tablespoons of the oil with the sage and lemon zest in a medium sauté pan with a tight-fitting lid. Add the artichokes with $2^1/2$ cups of the lemon water, the salt, garlic, and bay leaf. Bring to a boil, then lower the heat, cover, and simmer until the artichokes are tender, 15 to 20 minutes. Scoop them into a bowl, then reduce the remaining liquid until about $1/2$ cup remains. Pour it over the artichokes and drizzle the remaining 2 tablespoons oil over the top. Garnish with a little pepper and the chopped herb.

Artichokes Stuffed with Bread Crumbs, Capers, and Herbs

Baked on a bed of onions, these artichokes are best served warm rather than piping hot. Accompany with a spoonful of Garlic Mayonnaise (page 52). Serves 4

---

4 artichokes
$1^3/4$ cups fresh bread crumbs
4 tablespoons olive oil
2 cloves garlic, minced or pounded
3 tablespoons chopped parsley
4 teaspoons chopped thyme or marjoram
$1/2$ cup freshly grated parmesan
2 tablespoons chopped green olives
2 tablespoons capers, rinsed
1 to 2 teaspoons red wine vinegar
1 Roma tomato, diced
Sea salt and freshly milled pepper
1 large onion, thinly sliced
$1/4$ cup dry white wine or water

Prepare artichoke containers as described on page 295. Toss the bread crumbs with 2 tablespoons of the oil and fry in a skillet over medium heat until crisp and golden. Combine with the garlic, parsley, 3 teaspoons of the thyme, the cheese, olives, and capers. Moisten with the vinegar, stir in the tomato, and season with salt and pepper. Pack the mixture firmly into the artichokes.

Preheat the oven to 375°F. In a skillet, sauté the onion in the remaining 2 tablespoons oil and 1 teaspoon thyme over medium heat until softened, 8 to 10 minutes. Season with salt and pepper, then transfer to a baking dish large enough to hold the artichokes comfortably. Place the artichokes on the onions and pour the wine into the dish. Cover with parchment or wax paper, then with aluminum foil. Bake until heated through, about 30 minutes, then remove the cover and brown under the broiler.

Asparagus

Asparagus signifies spring regardless of the weather. In February, asparagus comes from Mexico and California's Imperial Valley, but as the season progresses, the crop moves farther north. By mid-June, commercial crops are about finished. When asparagus appears again for the holidays, it's imported from Peru or some equally distant place. The closer to you asparagus is grown, the better it is.

TYPES OF ASPARAGUS: Asparagus comes thick and thin; green, white, and purple. The most expensive is white, a color achieved through a painstaking blanching process in the fields. Skinny stalks of wild asparagus, which can still be found, have a beguiling vegetable "gaminess." But what most of us are familiar with are either thin (pencil) asparagus or the thicker green stalks. Although the tips are the most succulent part, the whole asparagus stalk can be used.

WHAT TO LOOK FOR: Once you've found upright, firm-looking stalks, take a moment to examine the tips, particularly if the asparagus is in a bunch. The tips are the best part and the part most likely to break or spoil. They should be closed and compact, appearing neither excessively dry nor damp. The stalks should be firm and smooth, not shriveled in places. Binding asparagus with wire or rubber bands into bunches may be convenient for the grocer, but it's not good for the asparagus. The tightly bound stalks sweat, producing moisture that hastens rotting.

HOW TO STORE: As soon as you get home, remove any bands and wires from bundled asparagus. If it's not to be eaten right away, keep it loose in a plastic bag in the vegetable bin for several days. Set asparagus from the garden, a much rarer treat, in a jar of water with the tops loosely covered with a plastic bag. Be sure to enjoy it as soon as possible.

HOW TO USE: Asparagus is enjoyed hot, at room temperature, and chilled. Use it for a salad, a side dish, in soups, tarts, omelets, and soufflés. Asparagus can be steamed, boiled, roasted, stir-fried, sautéed, and even grilled. A simple presentation with the sweetest butter or best olive oil suits it just as well as more elaborate treatments.

SPECIAL HANDLING: Because asparagus is grown in fine, sandy soil, it's a good idea to soak it in a basin of water for 15 minutes before cooking to get any grit out of the tips. To trim thin asparagus, hold the stalk with one hand at the bottom and the other hand a few inches away. Bend the asparagus gently and let it snap where the tender and tough parts meet. If it doesn't snap, slide your hands upward a bit and try again. With thick asparagus, you're better off cutting it because it will break virtually anywhere on the stalk and you'll end up wasting a lot of good food. If you look, you can usually see a color change in the stalk. Cut it there, and if it seems tough or stringy, make a second cut a little higher up. Many people don't feel it's necessary to peel asparagus, but peeled stalks, especially thick ones, are far more pleasant to eat. Peel them about two-thirds of the way up with an old-fashioned swivel potato peeler.

QUANTITY: Buy as much as you can afford—people like asparagus, and most can easily eat $1/2$ pound if given the chance, especially when it's the first of the season. Allow at least 10 thin stalks and 5 or 6 thick stalks per person.

Good Partners for Asparagus

Butter, olive oil, toasted sesame and roasted peanut oils
Parmesan, fontina, eggs
Parsley, basil, fresh sage, chervil, mint, tarragon
Lemon, orange, capers, ginger, soy
Peas, leeks, green onions, artichokes, fava beans

Sauces and Seasonings for Asparagus

Green herb sauces (pages 48 to 51)
Orange, Garlic, or Herb Mayonnaise (page 52)
Beurre Blanc (page 44) or Blossom Butter (page 46)

Cooking Asparagus

There are plenty of opinions here. Special tall narrow pots are excellent, but they're not good for much else and they take up valuable kitchen space. Plunging asparagus into a big pot of boiling salted water works fine, as does simmering it in a large skillet, which is quickest and I think best. Tying the asparagus into bunches with kitchen twine keeps water from circulating freely to the stalks, but they come out with all the tips facing the same direction, which is nice for presentation. Whatever your vessel, cook asparagus anywhere from 8 to 15 minutes, depending on the thickness of the stalk. Set it on a cloth towel before dressing to wick off any extra moisture, which would dilute your sauce. If it's to be served later, rinse it under cold water first. If you plan to serve it with a vinaigrette but not right away, wait until close to serving to add the acid or it will wash out the color and give it a dull taste.

Asparagus with Sea Salt, Pepper, and Lemon: As austere as this sounds, it's perfectly delicious—especially if you can find a thin-skinned, perfumed Meyer lemon. Season cooked, drained asparagus with salt and pepper and squeeze a fresh lemon over the top just before serving. Ⓥ

Roasted Asparagus: Roasting asparagus in a hot oven gives it a robust flavor and is convenient when stove space is unavailable. Do this after the shine of the new crop has worn off a little. Preheat the oven to 425°F. Toss trimmed asparagus in olive oil to coat lightly, season with salt and pepper, and set in a shallow baking dish, no more than 2 stalks deep, with a few tablespoons water. Cover and bake 15 minutes. Uncover and continue baking until tender when pierced with a knife, 10 to 15 minutes, depending on its size. Serve on a platter or a bed of arugula greens with lemon wedges, thin shavings of parmesan, Garlic Mayonnaise (page 52), or Romesco Sauce (page 62). Ⓥ

Asparagus with Roasted Peanut Oil and Black Sesame Seeds: Dress cooked asparagus with a few teaspoons roasted peanut or toasted sesame oil and garnish with toasted black sesame seeds. Snipped garlic chives, if you have them, are a nice touch; chopped cilantro is good, too. Ⓥ

Warm Asparagus Vinaigrette: Serve warm asparagus dressed with a vinaigrette as a first-course salad or a vegetable. Shallot, Walnut Oil, Lemon, Winter Herb, and Orange Vinaigrettes (pages 164 to 167), are all good choices. Ⓥ

Asparagus Baked with Butter and Parmesan: Preheat the oven to 375°F. Simmer 2 pounds or more trimmed asparagus in a skillet until barely tender. Drain, then layer them in a wide, shallow baking dish. Brown 1/4 cup butter (page 28) and drizzle it over the asparagus, followed by a veil of freshly grated parmesan. Season with sea salt and pepper and bake until bubbling, 15 to 20 minutes. Serve hot with lemon wedges.

Skillet Asparagus

Celebrate the first asparagus of the year with your finest olive oil or sweet, pure butter and maybe a fresh spring herb, such as tarragon, chervil, or a few hothouse basil leaves. This basic cooking method is used in most of the following recipes. Serves 4 to 6 Ⓥ

---

2 to 3 pounds asparagus, trimmed
Sea salt and freshly milled pepper
3 to 6 tablespoons salted butter or olive oil
2 tablespoons finely chopped herbs

Put the asparagus in a large skillet of cold water with the tips going in the same direction. Bring to a boil, add a pinch of salt, and simmer uncovered until just tender when pierced with a knife, 8 to 10 minutes, depending on size. Don't wait for a stalk to hang limply when you pick it out of the water, for it will continue to cook. Set the asparagus on a kitchen towel to drain for a minute, then transfer to a large platter. Dot with butter or drizzle with olive oil, season with salt and pepper, and scatter over the herbs. Gently roll the stalks around to coat them, then wipe the edges of the platter and serve.

Slivered Asparagus Sauté with Shallots

A quick and easy sauté that stretches a limited supply of asparagus. Use this method with sliced artichokes, celery, mushrooms, and zucchini or a mélange of vegetables. Good garnished with thin shavings of parmesan and bread crumbs crisped in olive oil. Serves 4 Ⓥ

- 1 to 2 pounds thick asparagus, trimmed and peeled
- 2 tablespoons olive oil
- Sea salt and freshly milled pepper
- 1 large shallot, finely diced
- 1 small clove garlic, minced
- 1 teaspoon finely grated lemon zest
- 2 tablespoons finely chopped parsley
- Lemon juice

Slice the asparagus diagonally about ¼ inch thick, leaving the tips about 3 inches long. Heat the oil in a large skillet. Add the asparagus, season with a few pinches salt, and sauté over high heat until nearly tender. Add the shallot, garlic, lemon zest, and parsley; toss well and cook 1 minute more. Season with lemon juice and pepper to taste.

Grilled Asparagus: Once you've passed the point of wanting to eat those first succulent spears virtually unsullied, turn to the grill. The heat should be between medium and medium–high. Choose thick asparagus, wash them, then peel them with a vegetable peeler up to the tips. Brush or roll them in olive oil, then lay them on the grill at an angle to the grate and cook, turning or rolling the spears every so often until they are tender and grill marks have begun to show, from 5 to 10 minutes depending on the heat of the grill. (If the asparagus is already cooked, you can cook it more quickly and at a higher heat.) Remove to a platter, season with salt and pepper, and serve, warm or at room temperature. Serve just this plain, or with any of the following: shavings of parmesan or aged Gouda cheese, Salsa Verde with Walnuts and Tarragon (page 49), Chermoula (page 50), or Orange Mayonnaise (page 52). Ⓥ

Beans—Green, Yellow, and Purple

Summer's beans can be as delectable as asparagus or coarse and stringy, depending on whether they're picked young or allowed to mature past their tender prime. They come in different colors, shapes, and sizes, too. As with tomatoes, there's really nothing as good as a bean picked warm from the sun if you're a gardener.

TYPES OF BEANS: There are many, but here are a few varieties seen most commonly, especially at farmers' markets. Pole beans are varieties that are grown on poles, in contrast to bush beans. Varieties like haricots verts grow close to the ground.

Blue Lake Beans: Large, long string beans succulent if not overgrown. These are what people commonly call green beans and string beans, although other beans are green as well and today's varieties are now stringless.

Haricots Verts: Highly prized, tender, skinny French green bush beans.

Kentucky Wonder Wax Beans: An older variety of pole bean with yellow pods.

Romano Beans: Green beans with flat, pods about 4 to 6 inches long.

Royal Burgundy Beans: These deep purple beans turn green when cooked.

Yard-Long Green Beans: A very long Asian bean related to Southern peas that tastes a lot like regular green beans. Cut them into more manageable pieces and cook them the same way as other green beans or add them to stir-fries.

WHAT TO LOOK FOR: Lively, tender pods that have good color, are stiff rather than flaccid, and small rather than large.

HOW TO STORE: If you can't eat them right away, store beans in a plastic bag in the refrigerator. They'll keep for days, but cook them as soon as possible.

HOW TO USE: Cooked beans make fine salads and side dishes, and they mix well with other seasonal vegetables in soups and stews.

SPECIAL HANDLING: If the beans are really small, 3 inches or less, remove only the stem end, not the tips. Stringing is seldom necessary now that stringless varieties have been developed. Boil beans uncovered in plenty of salted water. Covering the pot turns them gray. If cooking several varieties at once, cook each type separately since their cooking times will vary. Cooked beans are best eaten right away or at least within a few hours. If dressing beans in advance, wait to add the acid until just before serving.

QUANTITY: Allow $1^1/_2$ pounds of beans for four to six servings.

Good Partners for Beans

Olive oil, walnut oil, butter, crème fraîche, toasted sesame and roasted peanut oils

Basil, parsley, dill, tarragon, summer savory, ginger

Shallots, garlic, tomatoes, olives, and capers

Sauces and Seasonings for Beans

Herb Butter (page 45)

Blossom Butter (page 46)

Tarator Sauce (page 59)

Herb Butter and Olive Oil Sauce (page 44)

Pesto (page 50)

Basil Puree (page 51)

Basic Beans

All tender bush and pole beans can be cooked this way. Dressed with a vinaigrette or yogurt-based sauce, they add a strong element to a composed salad plate. Serves 4 to 6 Ⓥ

- 1½ pounds beans, tipped and tailed
- 2 tablespoons butter or olive oil
- Sea salt and freshly milled pepper
- 2 tablespoons chopped herbs—parsley, basil, tarragon, summer savory, or dill

Cut large beans into pieces 2 to 3 inches long. Drop them by handfuls into a large pot of boiling salted water and cook at a full boil, uncovered, until they're slightly resilient to the tooth. Start tasting them after 3 or 4 minutes, although they may well take longer to cook. When they're done, drain them, shake dry, and spread on a towel. (If they'll be used later, rinse them first under cold water to stop the cooking.) Toss with butter, taste for salt, season with pepper, and toss with the herbs.

Haricots Verts with Garlic Mayonnaise: In truth, all beans taste good this way. Toss 1 pound warm beans with ½ cup Garlic Mayonnaise (page 52). Add chopped parsley and toss again. Taste for salt and season with pepper. The heat of the beans brings out the garlicky aroma of the mayonnaise and thins it to a saucelike consistency.

Green Beans with Olive Sauce: Use your more mature beans with this somewhat aggressive sauce. Toss 1 pound warm Blue Lake, Romano, or other beans with ⅓ cup Hot and Spicy Tapenade (page 78) or more to taste. Ⓥ

Green Beans and Salsa Verde with Walnuts and Tarragon: Toss warm beans with ½ cup of this salsa verde (page 49). These are most aromatic when warm. Ⓥ

Green Beans and Yogurt Sauce: Toss boiled beans that have cooled for a few minutes with Yogurt Sauce with Cayenne and Dill or Yogurt Tahini Sauce (page 57). Alternatively, drizzle the sauce over them, allowing some of the bright color of the beans to show through, then toss just before serving.

Green Beans Simmered with Tomato

The tomato disintegrates and turns into a sauce for the beans. Serves 4 to 6 Ⓥ

- 2 tablespoons olive oil
- 2 small white onions, sliced into thin rounds
- 1 clove garlic, finely chopped
- 1½ pounds green beans, tipped and cut into 2-inch lengths
- 1 large ripe tomato, peeled, seeded, and diced
- 2 teaspoons chopped parsley
- 2 teaspoons chopped summer savory, dill, or lovage
- Sea salt and freshly milled pepper

Heat the oil in a medium or large skillet, add the onions, and cook over medium heat until soft and translucent, about 4 minutes. Add the garlic, beans, tomato, and enough water just to cover. Simmer until the beans are tender, then add the herbs and simmer 1 or 2 minutes more. Timing will depend on the age and size of the bean. Season with salt and pepper to taste. Serve hot, tepid, or even chilled.

Long-Simmered Green Beans and Green Chickpeas

This version of green beans and tomatoes is cooked until the beans are soft enough to have lost their brightness. The recipe, inspired by one in Saveur, also includes canned chickpeas. I use the green ones—now available frozen and even fresh occasionally—for their brightness. Both types of chickpeas are good. A vegetarian might happily eat this over white or brown basmati rice and call it dinner. Serves 4 to 6 Ⓥ

- 2 tablespoons olive oil, plus extra for the top
- 1 onion, thinly sliced
- 2 cloves garlic, thinly sliced
- 10 ounces or 1 scant pound plump green beans, tipped and tailed
- 1 teaspoon toasted, ground cumin
- 1 tablespoon tomato paste
- 1 teaspoon paprika
- 1 can diced tomatoes, or 1½ cup fresh tomatoes, including any juices

1 teaspoon sea salt

Freshly milled pepper

1 cup frozen green chickpeas

Heat the oil in a Dutch oven or spacious sauté pan. Add the onion and garlic and cook over medium heat, stirring occasionally, until soft and golden, about 12 minutes. While the onion is cooking, tip and tail the beans. Stir the cumin, tomato paste, and paprika into the softened onion and cook for at least a minute. Next add the beans to the pan along with the tomatoes and any liquid. Season with the salt and plenty of pepper. Add 1 cup water, cover the pan, and simmer gently until the beans have softened, about an hour. Add the chickpeas once the beans have cooked long enough, re-cover the pan, and let stand for 10 to 15 minutes. Serve with extra olive oil drizzled over all.

Beets

The beet is a wonderful vegetable, but people resist it, partly because of its earthy sweetness. When beets are treated to the acidic nip of vinegar and lemon or the warmth of spices, however, many take to them with enthusiasm. Beets are available year-round but are best from summer to fall, when they're truly in season. The leaves are mild and tender like chard and spinach.

TYPES OF BEETS: In the last decade, there has been a colorful infusion of variety into the beet world, and many of the new varieties of beets can be found in farmers' and specialty markets. In addition to the basic red beet, there are two new popular varieties: Chioggia and golden beets.

The skin of the round Chioggia beet is red-orange to cherry-red, and the flesh inside is ringed with red and white bands. A very striking beet.

Richly colored golden beets are milder than most red beets and don't bleed, as red beets do. The leaves look leathery but are tender and sweet. Also, not all types of beets are round. Some varieties are quite long, which is ideal for slicing.

WHAT TO LOOK FOR: When you can, buy beets with their greens attached. If the greens are to be cooked, they should be free of stems and yellowed or wilting leaves and used as soon as possible. Since the roots store well, the absence of greens doesn't necessarily indicate inferiority, nor does size. What's important is that the roots are firm and the tail is fairly smooth.

HOW TO STORE: Beets keep well for weeks in the refrigerator in a paper or perforated plastic bag. The greens also can be stored in a plastic bag, but for only a few days at most.

HOW TO USE: Beets can be eaten raw, roasted, steamed, grilled, boiled, and baked. They are, of course, the featured vegetable in borscht, and they star in all kinds of salads. Cooked beets keep for a week in the refrigerator. The tasty greens can be used in all the ways spinach and chard are.

SPECIAL HANDLING: Regardless of how you cook them, be sure to leave the tail, skin, and at least an inch of the stems attached to keep the valuable juices locked inside. Beets are easier to peel after they're cooked, so just scrub them and cook them with their skins on. Remember, red beets bleed and tint whatever they touch. When making a salad of different-colored beets or combining them with other vegetables, keep red beets separate until the last minute.

QUANTITY: Allow 1 pound trimmed beets for three to four servings; 1 pound of greens serves two to four.

Good Partners for Beets

Olive oil, butter, mustard oil, yogurt, sour cream

All vinegars, lemon, orange, lime

Mustard, horseradish, capers, chile

Parsley, dill, tarragon, cilantro, cumin, curry

Onions, apples, endive

Sauces and Seasonings for Beets

Fresh Horseradish Sauce (page 63)
Green herb sauces (pages 48 to 51)
Yogurt Sauce with Cayenne and Dill (page 57)
Romesco Sauce (page 62)
Herb Salts (pages 67 to 69)
Shallot Vinaigrette (page 165)
Lime–Cumin Vinaigrette (page 165)

Roasted Beets: In a pan or a foil wrapper, bake scrubbed unpeeled beets at 400°F or whatever oven temperature is convenient until easily pierced with a knife. A large beet may need an hour to bake, a smaller one 25 to 35 minutes. (V)

Baked Beets: Put scrubbed unpeeled beets in a baking dish, add ¼ inch water to the dish, and cover. Bake at 375°F or whatever temperature is convenient. The steaming action speeds the cooking so that a large beet will take about 40 minutes. (V)

Steamed Beets: Set scrubbed unpeeled beets in a steaming basket, cover, and steam until tender when pierced with a knife—about 35 to 40 minutes for a large beet, 20 to 25 for smaller ones. (V)

Pressure-Cooked Beets: The pressure cooker makes it possible to have beets for supper at the last minute. Put beets in the steaming insert, bring the cooker to pressure, then maintain on high for 10 minutes for large beets, about 7 for smaller ones. Release the pressure quickly. If you find the beets aren't quite done, return the lid and bring the pressure back up. If they're very close, just steam them with the lid loosely closed until done. (V)

Beets with Butter, Sea Salt, and Pepper: A very basic vegetable dish but one of the best. Cook beets until tender when pierced with a knife. Slip off the skins when cool enough to handle. Cut them into wedges or rounds and toss with a little butter or olive oil, sea salt, and freshly milled pepper. Beets are so slick that butter just slides off them rather than becoming absorbed, so you won't need to use much. Serve with lemon wedges or a cruet of vinegar.

Vinegar-Glazed 5-to-10-Minute Beets

One reader pointed out that 10 minutes produced more succulent beets than 5, hence the title change. But the point is that once you grate or shred the beets, they cook quickly. The same method works for other root vegetables, so there's no excuse not to enjoy them often. Serves 4 to 6

4 medium beets, about 1 pound
1 tablespoon butter
½ teaspoon sea salt
Freshly milled pepper
2 tablespoons vinegar, or to taste, such as a good balsamic, aged red wine, or aged sherry vinegar
2 tablespoons chopped parsley, tarragon, dill, or other favored herb

Scrub or peel the beets then grate them into coarse shreds. Melt the butter in a skillet, add the beets, and toss them with the salt and pepper to taste. Add ¼ cup water, then cover the pan and cook over medium–high heat until the beets are mostly tender, after 5 minutes or so. Remove the lid and raise the heat to boil off any excess water. Add the vinegar, toss the beets, and cook until the vinegar has reduced to a glaze. Stir in the herbs, taste for salt, and season with pepper.

Scarlet Beets: If you don't mind the shocking color, you can stir in a tablespoon of yogurt or sour cream, always a good–tasting addition to beets.

Orange-Glazed Beets: Cook the beets in fresh orange juice with the finely grated orange zest.

With Herb Salts: Herb–scented salts (pages 67 to 69), especially those with cumin and fennel seed, make an interesting change from plain salt.

Roasted Beets, Apples, and Onions with Cider Vinegar

This is a bold dish, far greater than the sum of its parts. Any leftovers make a great little salad or item on a composed salad plate. Use any color beet or a mixture. Red beets are most common, but this would be stunning with Chioggia and golden beets together. Serves 4 (V)

---

4 beets, steamed and cut into 1/2-inch dice (see page 304)

2 cups diced Granny Smith or Arkansas Black apples, skin on

1/2 onion, diced

3/4 teaspoon sea salt

2 tablespoons apple cider vinegar

1/8 teaspoon freshly grated nutmeg

1 tablespoon brown sugar, optional

1 1/2 tablespoons butter or sunflower seed oil

Freshly milled pepper

Apple cider vinegar or horseradish, for serving

Heat the oven to 350°F. Lightly butter or oil a 4-cup casserole or gratin dish.

Toss the beets with the apples and onions, season with the salt, vinegar, and nutmeg. If you favor extra sweetness, add the sugar as well. Slide the vegetables into the baking dish and dot with the butter or drizzle with oil. Cover and bake for 1 hour. Serve right from the oven, warm, or even chilled. Season with pepper and have extra vinegar or horseradish on the table, if you like their extra bite.

Vinegared Beets Nested in Their Greens

Perfect for small garden beets about an inch across, with fresh tender tops, though you can use larger ones, cut into wedges. An assortment of red, striped, and golden beets looks irresistible. Serves 4 to 6 (V)

---

16 to 24 small beets with their greens, about 2 pounds

1 1/2 tablespoons butter or olive oil

Sea salt and freshly milled pepper

2 teaspoons good balsamic vinegar

Remove the greens, scrub the beets, and steam them until tender, 15 minutes or so if they are indeed very small. Peel and set aside. Discard any greens that don't look up to snuff and the long stems. Steam the greens until tender, about 5 minutes, then toss with half the butter and season with salt and pepper. Arrange them in a nest on a plate. In another pan, heat the beets with the remaining butter. Add the vinegar and shake the pan until it evaporates. Spoon the beets into the center of the greens and serve.

Broccoli

Broccoli is a member of the genus *Brassica*, which includes cabbages, cauliflower, and brussels sprouts, among other plants. Its clusters of buds make broccoli solid, compact, and satisfying to eat. Although available year-round, it shows up in farmers' markets from early to midsummer on, and is uncommonly good then.

TYPES OF BROCCOLI: In addition to the standard green broccoli, there are other varieties. It's not always clear what's what with broccoli; some are also called cauliflowers. We now have purple broccoli; the chartreuse broccoli Romanesco, whose configuration of spirals forms a pointed head; sprouting broccoli, which gives a longer supply of small sprouts; broccoflower, which appears to be a combination of broccoli and cauliflower; and Purple Peacock broccoli, a handsome broccoli-kale cross. As different as they look, all can be cooked and seasoned the same way.

WHAT TO LOOK FOR: Look for firm, tight heads, crisp stalks, and perky leaves if any are attached. The greens are quite delicious and can be cooked as you would cook chard or kale. Crowns that are yellowed or have loose or open florets are over the hill; they should be dark green with vibrant, tight buds.

HOW TO STORE: Refrigerate broccoli in loose or perforated plastic bags, preferably in the vegetable bin, where it will keep for several days.

HOW TO USE: Broccoli can be steamed, boiled, sautéed, stir-fried, or braised, but very young garden broccoli can be eaten raw.

SPECIAL HANDLING: If heads appear to be sandy, soak them for 15 minutes in cold water to loosen the soil, then rinse. Don't overcook broccoli or any of its relatives. When people dislike these vegetables, it's usually because of overcooking, which produces a sulfurous odor (slow braising is the exception). When cooking, steam partially covered or boil uncovered to allow the sulfur compounds to escape.

QUANTITY: Broccoli is usually sold in bunches weighing about $1\frac{1}{2}$ pounds. The crowns plus an inch or two of the stems are also sold loose. The stems are quite edible, although the trimmed broccoli yields more of everyone's favorite part, the tops. One and a half pounds will yield four very generous side dishes or six more modest ones.

Good Partners for Broccoli

Olive oil, butter, brown butter, dark sesame and roasted peanut oils
Mustard, red pepper flakes, garlic, lemon, ginger
Feta, parmesan, cheddar
Olives, capers, parsley, marjoram, curry, dill, oregano

Sauces and Seasonings for Broccoli

Tomato Vinaigrette with Olives (page 168)
Lemon Vinaigrette (page 164)
Mustard Vinaigrette (page 167)
Curry Vinaigrette (page 167)
Sesame Vinaigrette with Chili Oil (page 168)
Feta Dressing with Marjoram and Mint (page 169)
Curry Mayonnaise with Mango Chutney (page 85)

Steamed Broccoli, Lemon, and Pine Nuts

This is such a straightforward way to prepare broccoli. The pine nuts make it special indeed, and the fresh lemon zest and juice transform this too-oft disliked vegetable into something quite delicious. Serves 4 Ⓥ

$1\frac{1}{2}$ pounds broccoli
3 tablespoons olive oil or butter, or some of each
2 tablespoons pan-roasted pine nuts
Sea salt and freshly milled pepper
Grated zest and juice of half a lemon, about $1\frac{1}{2}$ tablespoons

Trim the broccoli into florets, retaining a few inches of their stems. Peel the stems and slice especially thick ones lengthwise in half so that they cook evenly. Place the broccoli in a steaming basket over boiling water, partially cover, and steam for 3 minutes. Remove the lid. Pierce a stem with the tip of a paring knife to see if it's tender. If not, cook another minute and check again. It shouldn't take more than 5 minutes for the broccoli to be utterly tender.

Meanwhile, put the oil and/or butter in a shallow bowl. Toast the pine nuts if you haven't already. When the broccoli stems are tender and the crowns are bright green, tip them into the platter, toss with the oil, season with salt, pepper, and lemon juice, and garnish with the pine nuts. Serve right away while warm, or at room temperature.

Broccoli with Mustard Butter and Capers: Toss steamed broccoli with Mustard Butter (page 46), 2 tablespoons rinsed capers, and a tablespoon or so of chopped marjoram or parsley.

Broccoli with Garlic, Red Pepper Flakes, and Parmesan: Steam or boil $1\frac{1}{2}$ pounds broccoli as described above; drain. Warm 3 tablespoons olive oil with 2 thinly sliced cloves garlic in a large skillet until the garlic begins to color. Add $\frac{1}{4}$ teaspoon pepper flakes, the broccoli, and sea salt and pepper to taste. Sauté until heated through. Turn into a dish and cover with paper-thin shavings of parmesan. The heat of the broccoli will soften the cheese and bring out its flavor.

Warm Broccoli Vinaigrette: Warm broccoli tossed with a vinaigrette is intensely fragrant, an excellent salad vegetable. Try broccoli with the vinaigrettes and sauces listed at the left. Ⓥ

Broccoli Stems: With their delicate flavor and uplifting color, broccoli stems are quite choice. Use them as a vegetable or as part of a vegetable mixture, be it a soup, salad, or stir-fry. They're exceptionally good—and pretty—with turnips and rutabagas. Peel them thickly, cutting just below the tough outer layer of skin with a paring knife. Slice them into rounds, diagonals, matchsticks, thicker batons, or small squares. Boil in salted water until tender-firm and season as you would broccoli florets.

Broccoli and Green Onion Puree

A pale green puree when a soft-textured side dish is called for. Leftovers can be turned into soup in 10 minutes or used as the base of a vegetable soufflé. Makes about 2 cups, serving 4 to 6 Ⓥ

- 1 bay leaf
- 1 teaspoon sea salt
- 1 to 1¼ pounds broccoli stems, peeled and chopped, florets separated
- 1 bunch green onions, including an inch of the greens, chopped
- 2 tablespoons butter or oil
- Freshly milled pepper
- Pinch grated nutmeg
- 2 teaspoons lemon juice
- 2 tablespoons cream or crème fraîche, optional

Bring 8 cups water to a boil with the bay leaf in a saucepan. Add the salt, then the broccoli and green onions. Cook until the stems are tender, 4 to 6 minutes. Scoop out the vegetables, discard the bay leaf, and reserve the water. Puree in a food processor, leaving a little texture. Add a little of the cooking water if needed to loosen the mixture. Stir in the butter, taste for salt, and season with a little pepper, the nutmeg, and lemon juice. The seasonings should be lively. Stir in the cream.

Variation with Sesame Oil: Unexpected but good. Omit the butter and nutmeg and season the puree with 2 teaspoons toasted sesame oil. Ⓥ

Steamed Purple Peacock Broccoli

This is such a gorgeous vegetable. I don't know why it hasn't become insanely popular, especially with chefs. With dark purple-green florets, purple stems, deeply indented leaves streaked with magenta, it's quite the handsome edible. The leaves look a lot like Red Russian kale and the plant is said to be a cross between broccoli and kale. That sounds rather newfangled, but this is also an heirloom. When I have it, I tend to cook it simply and quickly and leave it pretty much alone so that its beautiful form can be admired. This is one broccoli that is enjoyable raw, as both the florets and leaves are exceptionally tender and sweet.

It is rather expensive, but one luscious floret with leaves is an ample serving. Slice it in half right through the flower, then steam, the cut side facing down, until the stalks are tender when pierced with a knife, but not too soft. Arrange on a platter, the cut side facing up, season with sea salt, and douse with olive oil such as a spicy Koroneiki. My husband, who grew up in the South, said this was one green he didn't even want to add vinegar to, but a wedge of lemon might be included on each plate. The purple pigments will pretty much disappear, but the cooked vegetable is so dark and green you know it has to be darned good for you.

Chopped Broccoli

Something as simple as chopping the broccoli instead of leaving it large changes it completely. The smaller pieces seem to make the tastes meld in your mouth. For a heartier dish, toss more or less equal amounts of boiled diced potatoes with the chopped broccoli. Serves 4 to 6 Ⓥ

- 1 large bunch broccoli, about 1½ pounds
- 2 to 4 tablespoons olive oil or butter
- Sea salt and freshly milled pepper
- Fresh lemon juice

Chop the broccoli into small florets; peel and finely chop the stems. Put the stems in the steaming basket, add the florets, then cover and steam until just a little short of being tender. Toss with olive oil and season with salt, pepper, and lemon juice to sharpen the flavors.

Broccoli Rabe

Broccoli rabe (variously spelled *raab* and *rape*) is a tangy and spicy Italian green with succulent nubbins of florets, and more closely associated with turnips than broccoli. Anyone who has a craving for greens, especially those with an assertive tang, will be drawn to broccoli rabe. I used to peel the stems and leaves, but no longer—it just isn't necessary. A basic preparation can be enjoyed by itself, over Garlic-Rubbed Crostini (page 24), or tossed with pasta.

Broccoli Rabe with Garlic and Red Pepper Flakes

Serves 3 to 4 (V)

1 large bunch broccoli rabe, 1¹/₂ to 2 pounds
Sea salt
3 tablespoons olive oil
3 cloves garlic, sliced
Several pinches red pepper flakes
Lemon wedges or red wine vinegar, for serving

Leave the leaves and florets attached. Peel the large stalks with a paring knife only if they seem tough. Drop them into a pot of boiling salted water and cook for 5 minutes, longer if you like your greens well cooked and tender, then drain. Leave it whole or coarsely chop. Heat the oil with the garlic and pepper flakes in a large skillet over medium-high heat until the garlic just begins to color. Add the broccoli rabe and cook, turning it repeatedly so that it's coated with the oil, about 5 minutes. Taste for salt. Serve with lemon wedges or vinegar on the side.

Brussels Sprouts

Is there another vegetable that can compete for aggressiveness, lack of subtlety, and poor reputation? Poor brussels sprouts. And yet we see them more and more often, and even on their stalks. Most like cold weather, but they are grown on the mild California coast, where they don't get the freeze that makes them the tender and sweet morsels they can be. Despite all this, brussels sprouts still manage to make their yearly appearance on holiday tables. And when they're good, they're undeniably sweet, mild, and utterly delicious—a real treat.

WHAT TO LOOK FOR: Brussels sprouts look just like miniature cabbages, only instead of growing in a cluster of leaves, they cling to a large stalk topped with a crown of foliage. Whole stalks can frequently be found at farmers' markets in the fall. The sprouts should be dark green and tightly formed. Avoid those whose leaves have unfurled or have begun to yellow. And give them a sniff to make sure they don't have an off-putting odor.

HOW TO STORE: Put them in a plastic bag and refrigerate. Try to use them within a few days at most.

HOW TO USE: When brussels sprouts are at their best they need just a tad of butter or olive oil. Otherwise they demand more assertive seasonings or the tempering effect of cream- and milk-based sauces. All the things that taste good with cabbage (juniper and mustard) and cauliflower (brown butter, capers, and lemon) also go well with brussels sprouts.

SPECIAL HANDLING: Cutting an X in the bottom brings heat to their centers more quickly, but if you halve or thinly slice brussels sprouts, they better absorb their tasty sauces and dressings. You can also separate their leaves—attractive and delicious but very time-consuming. The method I prefer is to slice them into thirds or quarters. They cook quickly this way, with no unevenness in texture. Either way, soak them in cold water for 10 minutes before cooking. As with broccoli, avoid overcooking.

QUANTITY: Allow 1 pound brussels sprouts for four to six servings.

Good Partners for Brussels Sprouts

Butter, olive oil, mustard oil
Cream, béchamel, blue cheese, cheddar
Mustard, capers, garlic, lemon, vinegar
Caraway, oregano, parsley, dill, curry spices, juniper

Sauces and Seasonings for Brussels Sprouts

Cheese Béchamel made with sharp cheddar (page 47)
Parsley-Caper Sauce (page 49)
Yogurt Sauce with Cayenne and Dill (page 57)

Brussels Sprouts, Mustard Butter, and Caraway

Serves 4 to 6

1 pound brussels sprouts
4 tablespoons Mustard Butter (page 46)
1/2 teaspoon caraway or celery seeds, bruised in a mortar
Sea salt and freshly milled pepper

Bring a large pot of water to a boil. Meanwhile, trim the sprouts, pulling off any wilted leaves, and cut an X in the bottom of each or slice in halves or thirds. Salt the boiling water, add the sprouts, and cook uncovered until tender, 6 to 8 minutes. Drain and shake off the excess water. Toss with the mustard butter and caraway seeds, then season with salt and pepper to taste.

Brussels Sprouts, Walnuts, and Fennel with Red Pearl Onions

If you've been asked to bring the brussels sprouts to Thanksgiving dinner, this is the one. This gorgeous dish was inspired by a picture in Simply French *by Patricia Wells. It's an elaborate preparation for a special meal, but you can cook everything except the brussels sprouts the day before. Reheat the vegetables, blanch the sprouts, and combine them at the last minute.* Serves 8 or more at a holiday meal Ⓥ

1 cup walnut halves
1 pint red pearl onions or shallots
3 tablespoons butter or olive oil
1 teaspoon sugar
Sea salt and freshly milled pepper
1 fennel bulb, julienned, or 5 celery ribs, diced
1 cup Basic Vegetable Stock (page 175) or water
3 tablespoons chopped parsley and celery leaves, mixed
1 pound brussels sprouts, left whole if small, halved or quartered if not
2 tablespoons walnut oil
2 tablespoons chopped fennel greens and parsley, mixed

Drop the walnuts into a pan of boiling water for 1 minute, then scoop them out. Rub off what you can of their skins with a towel, then dry in a 350°F oven for 7 to 8 minutes. Scald the onions in the same pan for 1 minute, then slip off the outer skins without cutting off the root end. If using shallots, peel and separate, following their natural divisions.

Melt 1 tablespoon of the butter in an 8- or 10-inch skillet over medium heat. Add the onions, sprinkle with sugar, and season with a little salt and pepper. Cover and cook over low heat, giving the pan a shake every few minutes, until the onions are lightly browned and nearly tender, about 12 minutes. Add the fennel and continue cooking, covered, until tender, 8 to 10 minutes.

In another skillet, melt the remaining 2 tablespoons butter. Add the walnuts and cook over low heat, occasionally giving the pan a shake, until they're golden, 12 to 15 minutes. Add the stock and herbs. Simmer, covered, until the liquid is reduced to a few tablespoons of syrupy juices. Taste for salt and pepper, then combine them with the onions and fennel.

Steam or boil the brussels sprouts until tender, 6 to 8 minutes, then add them to the mixture. Add the walnut oil and fennel greens, gently stir everything together, and serve.

Slivered Brussels Sprouts with Smoked Paprika and Sharp Cheddar

Smoked paprika gives brussels sprouts their desired hit of smoke, but without the bacon. For this type of dish, I use larger sprouts and slice them into thirds or quarters. They can stand as a vegetable dish, but they're also good spooned over toast or tossed with pasta for supper. Serves 2 or 3

1 pound brussels sprouts, larger rather than smaller ones

2 teaspoons sea salt

2 tablespoons olive oil or ghee

1 large onion, cut into 1/2-inch dice or smaller

1 heaping teaspoon smoked paprika, or more, to taste

Freshly milled pepper

Grated or thinly sliced cheese such as aged cheddar, goat cheddar, Manchego, or Gouda

Slice the base of the sprouts, discard the outer leaves if they look old and tired, then slice the sprouts thinly into thirds or quarters. Bring a few quarts water to boil, add the salt, then the sprouts. Cook for 3 minutes, scoop them out, and set aside. Alternatively, steam them.

Warm the oil in a wide skillet over medium heat. Add the onion, turn to coat it in the oil, then cook slowly, stirring occasionally so that it softens and colors gradually. Once soft, after about 15 to 20 minutes, stir in the smoked paprika and season with salt and pepper to taste. Add the brussels sprouts to the pan, toss with the onions and heat through. Add the cheese just before serving.

Brussels Sprouts with Smoked Paprika on Toast: Toast a slice of country bread for each person, cover with the thinly sliced cheese, then spoon the brussels sprouts over all and season with freshly ground pepper.

Brussels Sprouts with Smoked Paprika and Pasta: Toss the brussels sprouts with short whole wheat pasta, such as penne or rigatoni, or with whole wheat spaghetti. The whole wheat easily stands up to the smoke and the sprouts.

Cabbage

Whether red or green, smooth or crinkled, cabbage is a mild, sweet vegetable, though we don't generally think of it that way. To keep it sweet and appealing, don't overcook it. And don't save cabbage for winter fare; it's delicious from June on, when the summer varieties come in.

TYPES OF CABBAGE: In addition to color and shape, what differentiates cabbages is whether they're tender, soft summer cabbages or winter varieties. Here are a few common cabbages:

Dutch head cabbages: These smooth green or purple heads are our common everyday cabbages. Some summer varieties are cone shaped, with gently furled leaves.

Savoy cabbage: Vigorously crinkled with dark green outer leaves, this is the sweetest and most dramatic-looking cabbage and the choice variety for stuffing.

Napa or Chinese cabbage: Pale and crinkled, napa cabbage is a small football-size loaf, lighter in color and weight than Dutch and savoy and milder in flavor.

WHAT TO LOOK FOR: All cabbages should have a fresh, firm appearance. Summer cabbage leaves are a bit more open than the leaves of cabbage grown for winter storage. Winter cabbage is firm and heavy, the leaves tightly laid against each other. Savoy cabbage should be wreathed in at least some of its outer leaves, though typically it's stripped clown to the heart. napa cabbage should be firm looking, the leaves compact.

HOW TO STORE: Keep cabbage in a plastic bag in your salad crisper. It will keep for weeks, but its nutritive value diminishes with time. If the outer leaves wilt, just remove them before cooking.

HOW TO USE: Cabbage is one of the easiest vegetables to prepare. There's nothing to pare, snip, or remove—just cut it and go. It's used in coleslaws and soups and is delicious braised, boiled, or steamed. Napa cabbage makes an unusual salad and a standard stir-fry ingredient. Its leaves can also be stuffed.

SPECIAL HANDLING: Long sessions in covered pots give cabbage its sulfuric odor and hence its bad reputation. Briefer cooking keeps cabbage sweet and tender. Cooking water seems to cling to it, so wick off excess moisture with a towel to avoid diluting an added sauce. Red cabbage should be cut with a stainless steel knife, or it will turn a startling blue. Being somewhat coarser than green, it takes a little longer to cook.

QUANTITY: Amounts vary, depending on the trimming needed, but a smallish cabbage, weighing about $1\frac{1}{2}$ pounds, yields 6 to 8 cups shredded or chopped cabbage and 4 to 6 cups cooked, enough for four servings.

Good Partners for Cabbage

Olive oil, butter, brown butter, mustard oil, cream, sour cream

Cheddar, Taleggio, Teleme, parmesan

Mustard, horseradish, caraway, curry spices, juniper

Dill, marjoram, sage, caraway seeds

Apples, apple cider vinegar, lemon juice

Potatoes, buckwheat, pasta

Boiled Cabbage: Nothing sounds so unappealing as boiled cabbage, but when not overcooked this is one of the nicest ways to enjoy it. Drop shredded or chopped cabbage into a large pot of boiling salted water. Cook, uncovered, until the leaves are tender, 5 to 10 minutes. Pour into a colander, shake off the water, and press a towel over the cabbage to wick off the excess moisture. Toss with butter or oil, sea salt and pepper, and any of the seasonings listed above, including a dash of apple cider vinegar to bring up the flavors. Ⓥ

Savoy Cabbage and Leek with Cream and Juniper

The sweetness and delicacy of cabbage comes to the fore in this dish. As simple as it is, it always surprises and delights. If cream isn't in the diet plan, omit it and simply braise the cabbage in a little butter or replace the cream with $\frac{1}{2}$ cup thin béchamel sauce made with dairy or nondairy milk.
Serves 4 to 6

1 small savoy cabbage, about $1\frac{1}{2}$ pounds
Sea salt and freshly milled pepper
1 leek, white part only, cut into 2-inch chunks
$1\frac{1}{2}$ tablespoons butter
10 juniper berries, bruised
$\frac{1}{4}$ cup cream

Quarter the cabbage, remove the core and any wilted leaves, and cut into wide ribbons or squares. Bring a pot of water to a boil, add a pinch of salt and the cabbage and cook 4 minutes. Drain, rinse with cool water, and press out excess moisture with your hands. Slice the white part of the leek into julienned strips and rinse well. Melt the butter, add the leeks, juniper berries, and 1 tablespoon water. Cook over medium heat until softened, 3 to 4 minutes. Add the cabbage and the cream. Taste a piece of the cabbage, and if needed, add salt. Cover the pan and cook over a low heat until the cabbage is tender, about 7 minutes. Season with plenty of pepper and serve.

With Rosemary: Replace the juniper with 1 tablespoon finely chopped rosemary.

Napa or Chinese Cabbage: This Asian cabbage cooks quickly and is even milder than European varieties. Allow $1\frac{1}{2}$ pounds or more for four servings. Chop the whole cabbage, including the firm white base, into strips of whatever width appeals to you. Heat a few tablespoons water or rice wine in a wide skillet, add the cabbage, and sprinkle with sea salt. Cook over medium-high heat, turning the leaves with tongs, until wilted. Drain, then toss with toasted sesame oil, roasted peanut oil, or butter. Garnish with chopped parsley, cilantro, or dill; snipped chives; toasted sesame seeds; or Gomashio (page 67).

Savoy Cabbage with Potatoes and Brown Butter

Take a long walk, then enjoy this rich and filling cold-weather dish. This combination of flavors is excellent on its own or with buckwheat pasta. Serves 4

8 ounces boiling or fingerling potatoes

1¹/₂ pounds savoy cabbage, cut into large squares or strips

3 tablespoons Brown Butter (page 28) or ghee

¹/₂ cup diced Taleggio or Teleme

2 tablespoons freshly grated parmesan

2 tablespoons chopped sage

Sea salt and freshly milled pepper

Peel the boiling potatoes and cut them into ¹/₂-inch chunks or scrub the fingerlings and slice diagonally about ³/₈ inch thick. Steam until tender, about 15 minutes, then transfer them to a bowl and cover to keep warm. Steam the cabbage until tender, 5 to 10 minutes. Combine the vegetables in a bowl, toss with the brown butter, cheeses, and sage, then season with salt and pepper to taste.

Red Cabbage with Apples

The combination of cabbage with apples and onion is classic. Vary it by adding boiled, whole chestnuts or toasted walnuts just before serving. Serves 4 to 6 Ⓥ

3 tablespoons sunflower seed oil

1 small onion, finely diced

1 tablespoon caraway seeds

1 medium red cabbage, about 2 pounds, quartered, cored, and finely sliced

2 Granny Smith or Pippin apples, quartered, cored, and diced

1 teaspoon sea salt

Freshly milled pepper

Apple cider vinegar

Heat the oil in a large skillet. Add the onion and caraway, give them a stir, then cook for a few minutes over medium heat until the onion is translucent. Add the cabbage and apples and season with the salt. Cover lightly and cook very slowly until the cabbage is meltingly tender, up to an hour. Taste for salt, season with pepper, and toss with vinegar to taste.

Sweet and Sour Red Cabbage

Serves 4 Ⓥ

1¹/₂ pounds red cabbage

¹/₂ teaspoon allspice berries

1¹/₂ teaspoons coriander seeds

4 cloves

1¹/₂ tablespoons oil

1 onion, finely diced

3 small bay leaves

1 tablespoon brown sugar or molasses

1 teaspoon sea salt

¹/₄ cup diced tomatoes, fresh or canned

¹/₂ cup juice from the tomatoes or water

2 tablespoons balsamic vinegar

Freshly milled pepper

Quarter the cabbage, remove the core, and slice it crosswise into ¹/₂-inch strips. Bruise the spices in a mortar or grind them in a spice mill. Heat the oil in a wide skillet with the onion, spices, and bay leaves; cook over medium heat until the onion is translucent, about 4 minutes, then add the brown sugar and cook 1 minute more. Lay the cabbage over the onion, season with the salt, and spoon the tomatoes over all. Pour in the tomato juice, then cover and cook gently until the cabbage is tender, about 15 minutes. Remove the lid and toss everything together. Add the vinegar, raise the heat, and cook until most of the liquid is evaporated, leaving a syrupy glaze. Taste for salt, season with pepper, and serve.

Steamed Cabbage with Butter and Poppy Seeds

Serves 4

1 small green cabbage, about 1¹/₂ pounds

Sea salt and freshly milled pepper

2 to 4 tablespoons butter

Poppy seeds

Remove the outer leaves, quarter the cabbage, and cut out the core. Leave the wedges whole or slice them crosswise about ¹/₂ inch thick. Steam until tender but not mushy, 5 to 10 minutes. Transfer the cabbage to a bowl, blot it quickly with a clean towel, then toss with salt, pepper, butter, and the poppy seeds.

Cabbage Wedges with Fresh Dill

One of the fastest, easiest vegetable dishes you can make.
Serves 4 to 6 Ⓥ

1¹/2 to 2 pounds green cabbage
¹/2 teaspoon sea salt
Butter or olive oil
2 tablespoons chopped dill
Freshly milled white pepper

Cut the cabbage into sixths or eighths. Pour about 1 inch water into a wide skillet, add the salt, and bring to a boil. Add the cabbage and lower the heat to a simmer. Cover and steam until bright green and tender, 8 to 10 minutes. When done, transfer to a platter, add butter to taste, sprinkle with dill, and season with white pepper.

Stuffed Cabbage

Stuffed cabbages look good on a plate and are substantial but not heavy. They're not hard to make, but they can be time-consuming in the context of preparing an entire meal. To make it easy on yourself, plan to have something done ahead of time—the sauce, the cabbage leaves, or another part of the meal. Look to leftover grain dishes, such as pilafs, for fillings—virtually all grains are good with cabbage. Crinkled savoy cabbage is preferred because of its sweetness and its stunning looks when cooked, but regular green cabbage is delicious, too. Or try napa cabbage, chard, collard greens, or any other large-leafed vegetable.

To Prepare Cabbage Leaves for Stuffing: Bring water to boil in a stockpot big enough to hold the cabbage. Cut deeply around the core at the base of the cabbage, but don't try to remove it. Immerse the entire cabbage in the boiling water for 4 to 5 minutes, then lift it out, supporting it with a strainer and guiding it with a large fork. Peel off the number of leaves you need or as many as come off easily. Return the head to the water for additional softening and repeat. Before stuffing the leaves, remove the tough white vein at the base of each leaf. You can use the rest of the cabbage in the same or another meal or as part of the filling.

Cabbage Leaves, Rice, and Green Herb Filling

The filling uses plenty of greens and herbs, looking optimistically toward spring. A low-fat, high-flavor dish. Serves 6 Ⓥ

1 savoy or green cabbage, about 1¹/2 pounds
2 tablespoons butter or olive oil
1 large leek, quartered lengthwise and chopped
1 bunch gren onions, including a few inches of the greens, chopped
1 head butter lettuce, cut into strips and chopped
1 large handful sorrel leaves, julienned, if available
¹/2 cup chopped parsley
1 teaspoon marjoram
¹/2 teaspoon thyme
1 teaspoon sea salt
1 cup cooked rice, quinoa, or farro
¹/4 cup yogurt or pureed silken tofu
Freshly milled pepper
¹/4 cup tomato juice or water
Mushroom Sorrel Sauce (page 48) or Tomato Sauce with Dried Mushrooms (page 56)

Prepare 12 of the cabbage leaves for stuffing. Preheat the oven to 375°F. Quarter the remaining cabbage, remove the core, cut it into thin strips, then chop finely.

Heat the butter in a wide skillet and add the shredded cabbage, leek, onions, lettuce, sorrel, and herbs. Season with the salt, add ¹/4 cup water, cover, and cook over medium heat until the vegetables are tender, about 15 minutes. Drain, then transfer to a bowl. Add the rice and yogurt and mix well. Season with pepper and additional salt if needed.

Divide the filling by eye into twelve portions. Set the leaves, smooth side down, on the counter. Place a portion on the base of each leaf just above the notched area, fold the ends neatly around it, and roll. Wrap each stuffed cabbage in a towel and twist firmly, forcing it into a ball. Place the balls in a single layer in a baking dish and add the tomato juice. Cover and bake for 30 minutes. Spread some sauce on each plate and place two cabbages on top.

Cabbage-Stuffed Cabbage with Blue Cheese

I love the filling cooked with cream and juniper berries, but you can also just steam the leaves and season them well with butter, salt, and pepper. Serve these light rolls on a bed of cracked wheat, farro, or Wehani Rice Pilaf with Red Wine (page 482), surrounded by a tomato sauce or Herb Béchamel (page 47). Serves 4

1 savoy or green cabbage, about 1¹/₂ pounds
Savoy Cabbage and Leek with Cream and Juniper (page 311)
8 (¹/₂-inch) cubes Gorgonzola, Roquefort, or favorite blue cheese

Blanch and separate eight cabbage leaves for stuffing as described on page 313. With the rest of the cabbage, make the Savoy Cabbage and Leek with Cream and Juniper or simply steam it, then cool. Place ¹/₂ cup cooked cabbage in the center of each leaf and set a cube of the cheese inside that. Roll up the leaf, folding in the sides as you go. Twist the roll in a towel to give it a plump, round shape. Steam until heated through, about 10 minutes, then serve.

Carrots

Carrots aren't what they used to be—or maybe they are—they weren't always orange, although that's the color we pretty much identify with carrots. Today we're seeing yellow, white, and purple carrots, especially in farmers' markets and seed catalogs. And, of course, they come in all different shapes and sizes, too. It's amusing to draw on their various shapes, colors, and sizes when making a dish of carrots. My only word of warning is not to puree the purple carrots—they turn a dreadful shade of brown.

TYPES OF CARROTS: Carrots come in a variety of shapes and sizes, from round stubby French market carrots to long pointed or cylindrical varieties, from tiny 3-inch "babies" to immense storage or "horse" carrots.

WHAT TO LOOK FOR: Nicely shaped roots, good color, firmness, and an absence of cracks—cracks usually indicate woody cores. Although not a problem for stocks or juice, cracked carrots aren't so good for eating. Attached greens assure peak freshness. Don't be put off by large size. Sometimes larger carrots have much more flavor and sweetness than smaller ones. The enormous carrots I pull from my winter garden are sweet and full of flavor. As always, taste to make sure.

HOW TO STORE: Remove the greens and keep carrots in a plastic bag in the vegetable bin of the refrigerator for up to about 2 weeks. Set aside the more tender greens to use.

HOW TO USE: Scrub, rather than peel carrots, as their vitamins lie right under the skin. It's also said that their beneficial qualities are more available when they're cooked rather than raw. Still, use them in salads if you like them, and in soups, purees, or juice. They're an ever-present element in stews, stocks, stir-fries, and many vegetable mixtures. Braising and roasting concentrate their flavor. The greens are also edible.

SPECIAL HANDLING: Scrub carrots well. Most needn't be peeled.

QUANTITY: There are four to five medium carrots in a pound, yielding about 3¹/₂ cups chopped. Allow 1 pound carrots for three to four servings.

Good Partners for Carrots

Butter, olive oil, cream, dark sesame and roasted peanut oils
Thyme, chervil, lovage, dill, cumin, ginger, mint, chile, cilantro
Mustard, honey, brown sugar, maple syrup, maple sugar
All root vegetables

Sauces and Seasonings for Carrots

Salsa Verde (page 48)

Salsa Verde with Walnuts and Tarragon (page 49)

Yogurt Sauce with Cayenne and Dill (page 57)

Green Chile Butter (page 46)

Chermoula (page 50)

Indian Salt with Mixed Spices (page 68)

Steamed Carrot Jumble

Steamed carrots may sound pretty pedestrian, but imagine the dish made with a jumble of small carrots, different colored carrots, or sliced white and purple ones. It can be anything but ordinary. Add salt, a few sprigs of a favorite herb, and a sliver of onion to the steaming water if you like.
Serves 4 Ⓥ

1¹/₂ pounds carrots, scrubbed

2 tablespoons butter or olive oil

Sea salt and freshly milled pepper

1 tablespoon minced parsley

2 teaspoons lemon thyme, regular thyme, chervil, dill, mint, or lovage

Leave small carrots whole; cut large carrots into rounds, ovals, matchsticks, or whatever shape you want. Make sure all the pieces are about the same size to ensure even cooking. Steam them, covered, over boiling water until they just yield to the tip of a knife, 5 to 12 minutes, depending on their size. Turn them into a bowl, add the butter, season with salt and pepper, and toss until the butter is melted. Add the herbs and toss again.

Boiled Carrots: Cook sliced carrots, uncovered, in plenty of boiling salted water until tender-firm, then drain and season. Start unpeeled whole carrots in cold water to cover, add salt when it boils, then cook until tender. Rinse under cool water, then slip off the skins and finish with any of the suggested sauces and seasonings (left and above). Ⓥ

Carrots with Shallots and Parsley: Heat 2 tablespoons butter or oil in a medium skillet. Add 3 tablespoons minced shallot and cook over medium heat until it begins to color, after 3 or 4 minutes. Add 1¹/₂ pounds steamed or boiled carrots, well drained, and ¹/₄ cup chopped parsley. Toss well and cook for a few minutes more. Season with pepper and serve. Simple but truly fine. Ⓥ

Braised Carrots

Braising brings out a fuller range of the carrots' flavor, concentrates their sweetness, and fringes the carrots with a golden glaze. Simple but irresistible. Serves 4 Ⓥ

1¹/₂ pounds carrots, scrubbed

2 tablespoons butter or oil

¹/₂ teaspoon sea salt

Freshly milled pepper

2 teaspoons sugar or honey, optional

3 or 4 thyme sprigs

2 tablespoons chopped parsley or chervil

Slice the carrots into rounds or ovals. Heat the butter in a wide skillet. Add the carrots, salt, a little pepper, the sugar, and thyme. Add water to come to the top of the carrots. Bring to a boil, then cover the pan and simmer until the carrots are nearly tender, 10 to 20 minutes, depending on how they were cut. Uncover the pan, raise the heat, and reduce the liquid until it's syrupy. (If you didn't have enough liquid, or it cooked away too fast, add more while the carrots are cooking.) Continue cooking the carrots until they begin to brown. Check the seasonings and toss with the parsley.

Braised Carrots with Mint, Lovage, and Cider Vinegar

The vinegar keeps the texture of the carrots firm. Add lovage if you have it—its distinctive bracing flavor makes it an exciting herb for carrots. These are good warm or cold.
Serves 4 Ⓥ

1¹/₂ pounds carrots, scrubbed

1 tablespoon olive oil

10 mint leaves, plus extra for garnish

1 tablespoon chopped lovage or celery leaves, plus extra for garnish

¹/₄ teaspoon celery seeds

¹/₂ teaspoon sea salt

2 tablespoons apple cider vinegar

Freshly milled pepper

Slice the carrots into ovals or into rounds about ¹/₃ inch thick. Warm the oil in a medium skillet with the herbs and celery seeds to bring out their fragrance, then add the carrots, the salt, the vinegar, and water to cover. Bring to a boil, then lower the heat and simmer, covered, until the carrots are tender, about 20 minutes. Remove the lid and reduce any remaining liquid so that the carrots are nicely glazed. Taste for salt, season with pepper, and garnish with the remaining chopped mint and lovage.

Carrots with Hijiki (or Arame)

Sea vegetables are among the most nutritious plants on earth, and hijiki and arame are two very likable ones, especially in this Japanese dish, which is one of my all-time favorite things to eat. I like it with A Simple Miso Soup (page 537), Golden Tofu (page 525), and brown rice, a holdover from my Zen days. Serves 2 to 4 Ⓥ

- 2 cups dried hijiki or arame
- 3 tablespoons soy sauce or tamari
- 4 teaspoons light sesame oil
- 2 tablespoons slivered ginger
- 3 carrots, scrubbed and julienned
- Sea salt
- 1 teaspoon toasted sesame oil
- Toasted sesame seeds, for garnish

Cover the hijiki with water and soak for 15 minutes. If using arame, soak for 3 minutes, then drain without parboiling. Drain, then put it in a saucepan with fresh water to cover and 2 tablespoons of the soy sauce. Bring to a boil, simmer for 15 minutes, then drain again.

Heat the oil in a wide skillet over high heat. Add the ginger and carrots and stir-fry until the carrots begin to color around the edges, about 2 minutes. Add the seaweed and cook 5 minutes more, tossing frequently. Add the remaining 1 tablespoon soy sauce and let it cook off. Taste and season with salt and/or soy sauce and the toasted sesame oil. Garnish with toasted sesame seeds.

Roasted Carrots with Garlic and Thyme

Since the garlic is roasted with the skins on, this is a good time to use all those tiny cloves that are too fiddly to peel. Leftovers are good with a squeeze of lemon. Serves 4 Ⓥ

- 1½ pounds carrots, scrubbed
- 2 tablespoons olive oil
- Sea salt and freshly milled pepper
- 10 or so tiny cloves garlic
- Several thyme sprigs
- Chopped thyme or parsley, for garnish

Preheat the oven to 400°F. Toss the carrots with the oil, then season with salt and pepper. Put them in a roomy baking dish or roasting pan with the garlic and thyme sprigs. Add 2 tablespoons water, cover tightly with aluminum foil, and bake until tender, 25 to 45 minutes. Check at least twice while they're cooking to make sure there's a little moisture in the pan and give the pan a shake while you're at it. Toward the end, remove the foil and continue roasting until the liquid is reduced and the carrots are browned. Serve garnished with chopped thyme.

Glazed Carrots with Mustard

Honeyed carrots are usually appealing to children. Parsnips, or parsnips mixed with carrots, are also delicious cooked this way—for children of any age. Serves 4 to 6 Ⓥ

- 1½ pounds carrots, scrubbed
- 1 tablespoon butter or olive oil
- 1 tablespoon honey or light brown sugar
- 2 teaspoons Dijon mustard
- Sea salt and freshly milled pepper
- Chopped parsley, to finish

Cut the carrots into 3-inch lengths; halve or quarter the thicker ends so that they'll cook evenly. Steam or boil until tender as described on page 315. In a medium skillet, melt the butter with the honey, then stir in the mustard and carrots and season with salt and plenty of pepper. Cook over medium heat until well coated and bubbling, then toss with chopped parsley and serve.

Cauliflower

A mass of snowy curds wreathed in blue-green or pale green leaves, when truly fresh, cauliflower is surprisingly fine and delicate. We think of it mainly as a winter vegetable, but cauliflower is available year-round, and tender small heads from the summer garden are exquisite. Cauliflower is handled and cooked much like its cousin, broccoli.

TYPES OF CAULIFLOWER: In addition to the familiar white cauliflower, there are lime-green and golden exotics, the crazy green spiraled variety called Romanesco, and broccoflower, which looks like a green cauliflower, and a very purple variety.

WHAT TO LOOK FOR: Firm, dense heads with tight curds and no bruises, although brown spots can be cut off. Size is not of great importance if the clusters are tight. Sometimes the surface looks fuzzy or bristly; this isn't a problem.

HOW TO STORE: Wrapped in a perforated plastic bag and refrigerated, cauliflower will keep for several days, but it loses its sweetness as it sits. Precut florets should be used within a day or two at most.

HOW TO USE: Tender, fresh cauliflower can be served raw or blanched with seasoned salts and dips. Cauliflower also finds a place in curries and stews, salads and pastas. Don't neglect the leaves and stems, which are quite good cooked alongside the florets.

SPECIAL HANDLING: Handle cauliflower gently to avoid bruising it. If serving it raw, soak the cleaned, trimmed florets in water mixed with a little lemon juice or vinegar to keep them white and tenderize them. (Skip this if using a colored cauliflower.)

QUANTITY: A medium cauliflower, weighing 1½ pounds, provides about 6 cups florets, enough to serve four to six.

Good Partners for Cauliflower

Butter, ghee, olive oil, mustard oil, coconut oil
Garlic, red pepper flakes, paprika, curry, parsley, tarragon
Cheddar, parmesan, Gruyère, blue cheese
Strong greens, saffron, green olives, capers, pine nuts

Sauces and Seasonings for Cauliflower

Salsa Verde with Walnuts and Tarragon (page 49)
Garlic Mayonnaise or Saffron Mayonnaise (page 52)
Yogurt Sauce with Cayenne and Dill (page 57)
Romesco Sauce (page 62)
Tomato sauces (pages 54 to 56)

Steamed Cauliflower

Serves 4 to 6 Ⓥ

1 cauliflower, 1½ to 2 pounds
¼ cup butter or olive oil
Sea salt and freshly milled pepper
Chopped tarragon or parsley

With a sharp paring knife, cut through the stems and pull the florets apart. Trim the ends and peel and dice the stems. Chop any leaves into small pieces. Steam everything over boiling water until the florets are tender but still a little firm when pierced with a knife, 5 to 8 minutes. (An entire head takes 15 to 20 minutes.)

Meanwhile, melt the butter in a wide skillet over medium heat. Add the cauliflower and roll it around in the butter. Cook until the butter begins to smell nutty. Season with salt, pepper, and tarragon to taste.

Broccoflower with Bread Crumbs: Brown ½ cup fresh bread crumbs in 3 tablespoons butter or olive oil in a small skillet over medium heat. Toss steamed broccoflower pieces in the bread crumbs and season with sea salt and plenty of pepper. Ⓥ

Cauliflower with Mustard Butter and Greens: Toss steamed cauliflower with 2 to 4 tablespoons Mustard Butter (page 46). Serve it on a bed of fresh arugula or cooked chard or mustard greens. A simple but handsome presentation.

Cauliflower with Curry and Toasted Cashews: In a medium skillet, heat 2 to 4 tablespoons butter or coconut oil with 1 1/2 teaspoons curry powder, the juice of 1 lime, 2 tablespoons snipped chives, and a few tablespoons chopped cilantro. Add steamed cauliflower and toss. Garnish with toasted cashews and serve with brown basmati rice for a quick and easy dinner. Ⓥ

Roasted Cauliflower with Turmeric, Spice, and Cilantro

Roasting is one of the best ways to prepare cauliflower. It can be as simple or as complex as you like when it comes to herbs, spices, and garnishes, including such goodies as roasted cashews or toasted pine nuts. Cutting the cauliflower into 1/2-inch slabs works well with a very large vegetable, but small florets are perhaps more efficient. Serves 3 or 4 Ⓥ

1 large cauliflower
1/2 teaspoon turmeric
1/2 teaspoon paprika, plus more to finish
1 teaspoon roasted, ground cumin
1 teaspoons ground coriander
1/2 teaspoon sea salt
3 tablespoons sunflower seed or coconut oil
Freshly milled pepper
Yogurt, to finish, optional
Handful cilantro leaves, for garnish

Heat the oven to 425°F. Cut the cauliflower into small florets and slice or dice the stem. Toss with the spices, salt, and the oil until well coated, then turn onto a sheet pan in a single layer and roast until tender, about 30 minutes, possibly longer depending on the size of the florets. Turn the cauliflower as it cooks so that it browns evenly.

When done, turn the cauliflower out onto a platter. Taste a piece for salt and add more if needed. Season with pepper, drizzle yogurt over all, add a final dash of paprika, and garnish with the cilantro leaves. Serve warm or at room temperature.

Cauliflower, Paprika, and Garlic Sauce

When gardener Joe Colanero sent me a package of his homegrown paprika, I was reminded how delicious pure, sweet paprika can be. After years of exploring new herbs and exotic tastes, paprika seems new again and special for its rich, warm flavor and deep color. In working with paprika, as with other ground peppers, have the oil warm but not hot when you add it; otherwise the beautiful flavor will be spoiled. Serves 4 Ⓥ

1 cauliflower, about 1 1/4 pounds
3 to 5 tablespoons olive oil
3 cloves garlic, peeled
2 tablespoons finely chopped parsley
Sea salt
1 tablespoon sweet (not hot) paprika
2 tablespoons strong red wine or sherry vinegar

Cut the cauliflower into pieces the size you'll want to serve. Steam them over boiling water until they are fairly tender but not completely cooked, about 5 minutes. Turn off the heat and cover the pan. While the cauliflower is steaming, heat the oil with the garlic in a heavy skillet over medium low heat. When the garlic has turned pale gold, turn off the heat and put the garlic cloves in a mortar. Pound the garlic with half the parsley and several pinches of salt, forming a rough paste.

Turn the cooked cauliflower onto a platter, reserving 1/4 cup of the cooking water.

Return the pan to low heat and add the paprika, vinegar, cooking water, and the garlic-parsley mixture. Stir rapidly; then pour the sauce over the cauliflower and garnish with the remaining parsley. Serve right away.

Celery

Celery used to be served at almost every meal, presented in a relish tray or celery vase. It is still enjoyed mainly raw, as a crudité and in salads, where its crispness is appreciated. But it's also ubiquitous in soups, stock, and ragouts and appears frequently in stuffings and stir-fries.

The pale leaves make a refreshing seasoning, effectively replacing or mixing with chopped parsley, and the clean taste of celery is a surprise to those who have never eaten it cooked. It's so readily available and easy to work with, I urge you to try it. Cooking softens its bossy tendency, and peeling the outer ribs makes celery more pleasant to eat, whether cooked or raw. A pound of trimmed, peeled celery ribs yields 4 to 5 cups chopped, serving four to six.

Braised Celery

Serves 4 Ⓥ

1 head celery or 2 celery hearts
Several slices leek or onion
1 carrot, thinly sliced
Aromatics (page 21), including ¹/₂ teaspoon peppercorns and a pinch celery seeds
¹/₄ teaspoon sea salt
3 tablespoons butter or olive oil
Chopped parsley and celery leaves

Remove the leafy ends of the celery and peel the large outer ribs. Wash the stalks, paying special attention to the base, then cut all the ribs into 3- to 4-inch lengths. Put the leek, carrot, aromatics, salt, 1 tablespoon of the butter, and 3 cups water in a wide skillet. Bring to a boil, add the celery, cover, and lower the heat to simmer until tender when pierced with a knife, about 30 minutes. Arrange the celery on a platter and strain the liquid into a saucepan. Boil until ¹/₂ cup remains, then whisk in the remaining 2 tablespoons butter to make a little sauce. Pour it over the celery and garnish with chopped parsley and celery leaves.

Gratinéed Celery: Put the braised celery and its sauce in a gratin dish and dust with freshly grated parmesan, cheddar, or Gruyère. Broil until the cheese melts, then serve.

Celery Root (Celeriac)

Celery root, also known as celeriac, is a gnarly, frumpy-looking root, but it has lots of character and a bracingly clean flavor—like celery, only deeper and softer. It's a marvelous vegetable, especially enjoyable during the fall and winter months, and much easier to find these days.

WHAT TO LOOK FOR: Firm, bulbous roots with good heft for the size. If they're light but large, the centers will be spongy. If they have their greens, which resemble celery ribs, so much the better—they'll be fresher.

HOW TO STORE: Stored in the refrigerator in a plastic bag, celery root will keep for several weeks.

HOW TO USE: Celery root is best known as the salad celery rémoulade, but it's wonderful in soups and purees and is especially good in gratins. Although expensive, it pairs well with other root vegetables, like potatoes, allowing you to extend it.

SPECIAL HANDLING: Scrub well, then peel a celery root just as you would an orange (see page 24). Put cut pieces in water acidulated with lemon juice or vinegar. The parings make an excellent addition to vegetable stocks.

QUANTITY: Commercially available celery roots tend to weigh about 1 pound. Plan to lose a quarter or more of the weight in trimmings. A trimmed 1-pound root will yield only about 2 cups chopped, enough for two to four modest servings—certainly enough to add ample flavor to a gratin, soup, or puree.

Good Partners for Celery Root

Butter, cream, walnut oil, sunflower seed oil

Gruyère, walnuts, hazelnuts

Parsley, thyme, mustard

Potatoes, apples, watercress, mushrooms, wild rice, truffles, truffle salt

Sauces and Seasonings for Celery Root

Mustard Vinaigrette (page 167)

Brown Butter (page 28)

Tarragon Mayonnaise with Capers (page 52)

Creamy Herb and Shallot Dressing (page 165)

Celery Root with Mustard and Chives: Peel and dice 1 pound celery root into 1¹/₂-inch cubes and boil in salted water to cover until tender, about 5 minutes. Drain, then put it in a skillet with ¹/₄ cup crème fraîche or cream mixed with 1 teaspoon Dijon mustard. Season with salt and freshly milled white pepper. Heat until the cream is hot, then sprinkle snipped chives on top. Serves 4

Celery Root and Potato Puree with Truffle Salt

Celery root and potatoes make a most delicious vegetable puree. In addition to serving it as a side dish, you can use it to blanket a vegetable ragout. Serves 4 to 6

2 pounds yellow-fleshed potatoes, peeled
1 celery root, about 1 pound, peeled
1 teaspoon sea salt
About ¹/₂ cup milk, cream, or cooking water, warmed
Freshly milled pepper
¹/₄ to ¹/₂ cup butter
Truffle salt, optional, to finish

Cut the vegetables into large pieces, keeping them separate. Put each in a saucepan, add cold water to cover and the salt, and bring to a boil. Simmer until tender, about 15 minutes for the potatoes, 10 minutes for the celery root. Drain, reserving the liquid for thinning or to use in making soup. Pass them together through a food mill or mash by hand, adding warm liquid to thin the puree as you go. Season with salt and pepper and stir in butter. Finish with a pinch of truffle salt.

Variations: Flavor the puree with Whole Roasted Garlic (page 340), or include other vegetables in the mix—turnips, parsnips, and fennel are all delicious. Coarsely chopped hazelnuts are great stirred into the puree. Instead of butter, finish the puree with walnut oil or roasted hazelnut oil. Stir in finely chopped parsley or watercress just before serving.

Braised Celery Root with Long Garlic Crostini

This can serve as a light dinner entrée or, without the crostini, as a side dish. Use the trimmings to make a flavorful quick stock. Serves 4 ⓥ

2 pounds celery root

Juice of 2 lemons

4 cups Quick Stock (page 174)

2 tablespoons butter or olive oil

1 small onion, finely diced

1 carrot, finely diced

1 celery rib, finely diced

Aromatics: 1 bay leaf, 6 parsley sprigs, 4 thyme sprigs

1/2 cup dry white wine

Sea salt and freshly milled pepper

Chopped parsley and thyme, to finish

4 large, thin Garlic-Rubbed Crostini (page 24)

Peel the celery root, quarter it, and slice crosswise 3/8 inch thick. Drop the slices into a bowl of lemon juice and water to cover and set aside. Make the stock, strain it, and return it to the stove to simmer. Preheat the oven to 375°F.

Heat the butter in a medium skillet. Add the diced vegetables and aromatics and cook over medium-low heat, stirring frequently, until softened, about 5 minutes. Add the wine and cook several minutes more, until it has reduced. Season with salt and pepper. Spread the mixture in a gratin dish and cover with the drained celery root. Add simmering stock just to cover.

Press a piece of parchment directly on the vegetables. Bake until the celery root is tender, 50 to 60 minutes. If lots of liquid is left, pour it off, boil until it's reduced to a saucelike consistency, then return it to the dish. Serve in soup plates topped with chopped parsley mixed with a little thyme and the garlic croutons.

Chard

Here's a vigorous green, leafy vegetable that's easy to cook and grow. Yet it often arrives at the market looking as if it's gone through a war zone, the leaves shredded and torn. Better to check your farmers' market for vigorous, deep green leaves in their prime. The leaves and their fleshy stalks are often treated as two different vegetables, but when the stalks are barely an inch wide, the two can be cooked as one vegetable.

TYPES OF CHARD: White ribbed and red chard are the two types most available. A third kind, perpetual spinach chard or beet, is grown more abroad than here. It has small leaves with virtually no stems and so is perfect for those who prefer only the leaves. Today we also have rainbow chard, which has brightly colored stalks.

WHAT TO LOOK FOR: Vigorous, upright, crinkled dark green leaves on smooth, succulent stalks. The leaves can be extremely large or closer to the size of spinach. Since chard grows rapidly, large leaves don't necessarily imply toughness or lack of flavor, though in general the smaller ones are sweeter and the larger ones take a little longer to cook.

HOW TO STORE: Keep chard refrigerated in a plastic bag until ready to use, preferably within a few days.

HOW TO USE: The stems are typically braised, while the leaves are used as you would spinach in soups, as braised greens, with eggs, rice, lentils, and in savory tarts. Large leaves can be stuffed. Though treated as two vegetables, there's no reason not to pair the stems and leaves on a plate. To prepare the stems, trim the tops and bottoms, then, with a paring knife, peel off the film of skin and tough fibers that covers the surface. Chard trimmings, particularly the stems, make an excellent contribution to vegetable stocks.

SPECIAL HANDLING: The red stems and veins in the ruby varieties stain, just as beets do, so take that into account when mixing them with other foods and be sure you want their rosy hints. The silver stems discolor, so cook them in acidulated water or a blanc to preserve their whiteness.

QUANTITY: Most bunches of chard weigh about a pound, but they aren't standard. Some bunches have enormous stalks; others are severely trimmed. One pound of leaves yields 12 cups, which cook down to about 3 cups, enough for three to four servings. One pound of stems, trimmed, yields about 4 cups, enough for three to four servings.

Good Partners for Chard

Olive oil, butter

Saffron, garlic, red pepper flakes, cilantro, basil

Lemon, red wine vinegar

Tomatoes, potatoes, chickpeas, pasta, eggs

Braised Chard with Cilantro

Don't be put off by the long cooking time—in the end the flavor goes far beyond what's possible with a cursory blanching. A few spoonfuls suffice for a serving, or you can use this effectively as a seasoning for rice or lentils. Serves 4 (V)

2 large bunches chard, about 2 pounds, leaves sliced into 1-inch-wide ribbons

1¹/₂ cups of the chard stems, trimmed and diced

1 onion, finely diced

¹/₂ cup chopped cilantro

¹/₃ cup olive oil

1 teaspoon paprika

1 clove garlic pounded with ¹/₂ teaspoon sea salt

Sea salt and freshly milled pepper

Place all the ingredients except the pepper in a wide, heavy pot with a few pinches salt. Add ¹/₄ cup water, cover tightly, and cook over low heat for 45 minutes. Check once or twice to make sure there's enough moisture. If anything is sticking, add a few tablespoons water. When done, taste for salt and season with pepper. The chard should be silky and very fragrant.

Chard Stems with Olive Oil

The cooking time—from 7 to 20 minutes—really depends on the tenderness of the stems, so test with the point of a knife as they cook. Serves 3 or 4 (V)

1 pound chard stems, trimmed and peeled

2 tablespoons flour

Juice of 1 lemon

2 teaspoons sea salt

Best olive oil

Chopped parsley

Freshly milled pepper

Cut the stems into 3-inch lengths. Whisk the flour into 8 cups water in a saucepan, bring to a boil, and add the lemon juice and the salt. Add the stems and boil until tender, about 10 minutes or longer, depending on their tenderness. Drain, then toss with olive oil and parsley. Taste for salt and season with pepper.

Chard Greens with Olive Oil: Slice the leaves off the stems, wash them well, then coarsely chop. Drop them into a pot of boiling salted water and cook until tender, 3 to 5 minutes or longer if older. Drain, press out the excess moisture with the back of a spoon, then toss with olive oil or butter, salt, and pepper. Or turn the cooked, drained greens into a skillet in which you've heated olive oil with a crushed clove garlic and a pinch or two of red pepper flakes. Toss to coat the leaves, season with sea salt and pepper, and serve with lemon wedges or vinegar. (V)

Chard Ribbons with Cumin and Lemon

Cilantro is a fine herb to pair with chard, along with cumin—a natural pair if there ever was one. This is for chard with heftier stems that you can remove and use in another dish (see page 322). Have this as a warm vegetable side, but it's possibly better at room temperature. Serve with rice, any color—brown, white or black—and a spoonful of yogurt, if desired. Serves 4 (V)

1¹/₂ to 2 pounds (or 20 or so) medium chard leaves, 10 to 12 cups trimmed

2 tablespoons olive oil, plus more for serving

1 small onion, finely diced

¹/₂ teaspoon or more toasted ground cumin

1 teaspoon sweet paprika

Big handful chopped cilantro

Sea salt

Juice of ¹/₂ lemon, plus more to taste

Slice the leaves off their stems, roll them up, and slice them into ribbons about an inch wide. Rinse and set aside to drain without drying.

Warm the oil in a wide skillet. Add the onion, cumin, paprika, and cilantro and cook over medium heat for about 5 minutes, stirring occasionally, until the onion has softened. Add the chard. Season with a few pinches of salt, turn with tongs, then cover the pan. Cook until tender, 15 minutes or longer, turning occasionally. Remove from the heat and taste for salt. Toss with lemon juice, adding more to taste, then pile the chard in a dish, drizzle with extra oil, and serve.

Chard Ribbons with Four Herbs—Cilantro, Dill, Parsley and Basil: Pluck the leaves from these different herbs and chop them. It needn't be too fine a chop, but you'll want a good handful in all. Add to the onion when you add the cumin and paprika. (V)

Braised Chard Stems with Saffron and Tomatoes

A fine accompaniment to the Saffron Noodle Cake (page 410), a cooked grain, or a dish to serve accompanied with Garlic-Rubbed Crostini (page 24) for the broth. Serves 3 or 4 (V)

1 pound chard stems, prepared as described on page 321, slightly undercooked, 1 cup cooking water reserved

1¹/₂ tablespoons olive oil

¹/₂ small onion, finely diced

2 teaspoons thinly sliced basil leaves, plus extra for garnish

Pinch saffron threads

Sea salt and freshly milled pepper

2 tomatoes, seeded and finely diced

2 tablespoons grated parmesan or Gruyère cheese, optional

Cook the chard stems first. (This can be done well ahead of the final baking.)

Heat the oil in a 10-inch skillet with the onion, basil, and saffron threads. Cook over medium heat, stirring occasionally, until the onions soften and the saffron begins to yield its color, about 5 minutes. Add the chard stems, season with salt and pepper, then add the reserved cooking water. Simmer, covered, until the stems are fully tender, 5 to 7 minutes. Remove the lid and allow the remaining liquid to reduce to a syrupy consistency. Add the tomatoes and cook another minute or so to warm them through. Serve with the additional basil—either small leaves or slivered ones—strewn over the stems and the grated cheese.

Chard Stems al Forno: Transfer the cooked chard stems from either of the two preceding recipes to a small gratin dish. Drizzle olive oil over the top, add a little freshly grated parmesan, and bake at 400°F until the cheese is melted and lightly browned, about 20 minutes.

Chard with Tomatoes and Asiago Cheese

You could easily serve this on toast for an informal dinner for yourself and one other. Serves 2 or more

1 large bunch chard, stems removed, leaves cut in large pieces

2 tablespoons olive oil

1 clove garlic, thinly sliced

2 tomatoes, peeled and diced (see page 388)

Several good pinches dried oregano

Grated Asiago cheese, for serving

Simmer the greens in salted water as described on page 322, then drain. Put them in a wide skillet with the oil, garlic, and tomatoes, season with the oregano, and cook over high heat until the tomatoes are heated through. Serve with cheese grated over the top.

Chard Rolls Filled with Winter Vegetables

Select nice, large leaves for stuffing. The chard stems along with root vegetables fill these plump bundles. Serves 4 Ⓥ

2 tablespoons olive oil

8 large chard leaves, stems removed and finely diced

1 onion, finely diced

3 carrots, finely diced

8 ounces potatoes, finely diced

6 to 8 cups additional finely diced vegetables, such as parsnips, parsley root, and celery root

1 plump clove garlic, minced

2 teaspoons chopped tarragon or 1/2 teaspoon dried

1/2 teaspoon sea salt

Freshly milled pepper

2 tablespoons fresh lemon juice

1 cup water or Basic Vegetable Stock (page 175)

Heat the oil in a large skillet. Add the chard stems, onion, other root vegetables, garlic, and tarragon. Season with the salt and a little pepper to taste. Cover and cook over medium heat until tender, 20 to 25 minutes. Add the lemon juice.

Plunge the chard leaves into simmering water for 4 minutes, then set on a towel to drain. Cut away the thick part at the base of each leaf. Place the leaves, smooth side down, on the counter. Place 2 heaping tablespoons of filling just above the notch of each leaf, then fold the sides over the filling and roll up the leaves. Keep the remaining filling in the skillet and set the rolls right on top of it. Add the water to the pan and cover. Simmer for 10 minutes. Serve the rolls with the extra vegetables and their juices.

Chicories (Endive, Radicchio, Escarole, and More)

While quite different in shape, size, and color, endive, radicchio, and escarole are all chicories—and as such they share a degree of bitterness that turns to nuttiness when cooked.

TYPES OF CHICORY: There are a great number of very interesting greens in this family, such as frisée or curly endive, dandelion, and other salad-type greens. All taste best in the cooler months. Here are some commonly found varieties:

Belgian Endive or Witloof: A small cone-shaped head of pale leaves. Some varieties are pink.

Radicchio: This has deep scarlet leaves, which are sometimes variegated. The variety we see most is compact, like a cabbage, but there are several long-leafed varieties, such as Treviso, seen less frequently in this country, though more today.

Escarole: A chicory that roughly resembles looseleaf lettuce, but the leaves are thick. If properly blanched in the field, the inner hearts will be creamy white.

HOW TO STORE: Keep in a plastic bag in the refrigerator as you would lettuce. It will keep for up to a week, though it's better the earlier it's used.

HOW TO USE: In addition to their uses in salad, chicories can be grilled, seared, and braised.

SPECIAL HANDLING: Chicories bruise where they've been cut, leaving a discolored area, something to consider when they're to be used in salads. Wait until close to serving time to slice or tear. Check the base of the leaves carefully for sand and dirt.

QUANTITY: Allow one Belgian endive for one or two servings; one 6- to 8-ounce head of radicchio for four servings; one head of escarole for two to four servings.

Good Partners for Chicories

Olive oil, cream, butter
Red pepper flakes, vinegar
Gruyère, parmesan, Asiago

Braised Belgian Endive: Melt 2 tablespoons butter in a 10- or 12-inch noncorrosive skillet. Halve six endives and add them, cut sides clown. Cook over medium-high heat until well browned. Turn and brown them on their second sides, then turn them back over. Add water to come about $3/4$ inch up the side of the pan. Simmer, covered, until the endives are tender when pierced with a knife, about 25 minutes. Remove the lid, raise the heat, and evaporate all but a little of the remaining liquid so that a glaze forms on the bottom. Season with sea salt and a little white pepper. Serves 6 to 12.

Braised Escarole with Onion

If you've used the tender inner leaves for salads, cook the outer ones like this. Escarole turns a little dingy looking, but its flavor is big and the parsley perks it up. Serves 4 to 6 Ⓥ

> 2 heads escarole, about 2 pounds in all
> 3 tablespoons olive oil
> 1 onion, finely chopped
> 1 plump clove garlic, minced
> Sea salt and freshly milled pepper
> Chopped parsley, to finish

Separate the escarole leaves and wash well, taking special care to go over the base of the inner leaves with your fingers where dirt often clings. Drain and coarsely chop. Heat the oil in a wide skillet. Add the onion and cook over medium heat until limp. Add the garlic and cook until it begins to color, but don't let it brown. Add the escarole with any water clinging to the leaves, salt lightly, and cook, covered, until the greens are wilted and tender, 12 to 15 minutes. Season with pepper and toss with the parsley.

Endive Sauté on Toast

A sauté of chopped Belgian endive can be prepared in less than 15 minutes, total, making it a candidate for a last minute supper of substance and panache. The lemon juice is there to keep the color lively; without it, endive can look dingy. Serves 2

3 or 4 plump white endives, about 5 ounces each

2 tablespoons butter

$1/2$ lemon

Sea salt and freshly ground white pepper

2 large slices of country bread

2 ounces thinly sliced Gruyère or fontina cheese

Minced parsley or tarragon, to finish

Quarter the endives lengthwise, then cut them into long slivers or chop them into $1/2$-inch pieces. Melt the butter in a nonstick skillet. When foamy, add the endive and cook over high heat, stirring frequently, until browned in places, about 12 minutes in all. Squeeze a little lemon over the endive while it's cooking. When tender, taste for salt and season with white pepper.

Meanwhile, toast the bread, then cover it, while hot, with the cheese. Spoon the endive over the toasts and serve with a bit of green herb over the top.

Seared Radicchio

A delicious accompaniment for soft polenta or cooked white beans, or an unusual ingredient for a risotto or hearty pasta. Escarole and Belgian endive can also be seared. Use two heads of escarole or two to four endives. The cheese isn't necessary, but it is an excellent embellishment. Serves 4 to 6 (V)

2 small firm heads radicchio, about 6 ounces each

Olive oil, for brushing

Sea salt and freshly milled pepper

1 tablespoon chopped parsley

Thin shavings of parmesan, aged Gouda, fresh mozzarella, or blue cheese, optional

Cut the radicchio into wedges about 2 inches thick at the widest point. Brush them generously with oil, season with salt and pepper, and set aside for an hour or more if time allows. Lightly film a cast-iron skillet with olive oil and set over medium-high heat. When it's very hot, add the radicchio and sear until the leaves begin to brown on the bottom, after a few minutes. Turn and cook the second side, about 5 minutes in all. Transfer to a plate and gently press the wedges to open the leaves. Season with salt and pepper, sprinkle with parsley, and cover with the shavings of cheese.

Grilled Radicchio: Though usually treated as a salad green, radicchio is particularly tasty grilled. (Escarole and Belgian endive can also be grilled.) Prepare radicchio for searing as in the preceding recipe, and grill until the color has dulled and the radicchio has softened and turned brownish, about 5 minutes on each side. Garnish with chopped parsley, thin shavings of parmesan, and olive oil or serve with Garlic Mayonnaise (page 52). Chopped grilled radicchio also makes an excellent ingredient to add to a risotto with winter squash, to white beans, or as a garnish for polenta or a hearty buckwheat pasta.

Corn

With the new supersweet varieties of corn, we no longer need to have a corn patch out back or to add milk and sugar to boiling water to get a tender, sweet ear. Today's corn is bred so that the sugars are slow to turn starchy, which means that even corn that's several days old should be tender. Nonetheless, corn that's superfresh will always be best. When you buy corn from a farmer, don't discard it if there's a worm at the tip or signs of one; just shake it off and trim the ear. Like all sweet vegetables, corn goes with all kinds of seasonings, from sweet herbs to spices to chiles.

TYPES OF CORN: There are several classes of corn that have very different uses, but for eating fresh we're interested mostly in the new sugar-enhanced and supersweet hybrids. (Some people, I among them, still prefer the older varieties with their chewy texture and "cornier" taste, such as Golden Bantam, to today's sugary ears.) Some older hybrids, like Silver Queen, are delightfully sweet but not cloying.

WHAT TO LOOK FOR: If you can, buy corn in its husks, which protect the kernels from the dry air and also tell you how fresh the corn is. Moist green husks are clearly fresher than dry old brown ones. Rather than pull down a corner of the husks, which is irritating to the farmer because it dries out the corn, run your hands over the ear to be sure the rows are plump and well-filled. Corn smut or fungus (*cuitlacoche* in Nahuatl) may be alarming to come across, but it's a delicacy with a wonderful wild-mushroom flavor. (To cook, remove it from the ear, slice or chop, then sauté in oil or butter for about 15 minutes.)

HOW TO STORE: If not being cooked right away, corn should be refrigerated in its husks, in a plastic bag. If it's still warm from the sun, cool it under water before storing.

HOW TO USE: Versatile corn is added to soups and stews, pancakes, breads, and puddings. It's delicious sautéed or creamed as well as grilled. Roasted corn kernels add a smoky flavor and chewy texture to corn salads, salsas, and soups.

SPECIAL HANDLING: None, except to use as soon as possible.

QUANTITY: An average ear of corn typically yields about $1/2$ to $3/4$ cup kernels. If the corn is really good and you're cooking it on the cob, plan to serve two or three ears per person.

Good Partners for Corn

Butter, cream, coconut oil
Cheddar, Monterey Jack, feta
Dill, basil, parsley, chile, Szechuan pepper, cumin, sage
Squash, beans, peppers, tomatoes, lime

Sauces and Seasonings for Corn

Pesto (page 50) or Salsa Verde (page 48)
Cilantro Salsa (page 49)
Harissa (page 66)
Szechuan Pepper Salt (page 69) or Indian Salt with
    Mixed Spices (page 68)
Ground chipotle chile
Green Chile Butter (page 46) or Herb or Blossom Butter
    (pages 45 and 46)
Grated cheddar
Chopped herbs, such as basil, dill, marjoram, parsley,
    cilantro, and fresh sage

Corn on the Cob (V)

Whole ears corn
Sea salt and freshly milled pepper
Butter or coconut oil

Bring a large pot of water to a boil. While it's heating, pull the husks off the corn, rub off the silk, and cut off any blemished tips. When the water comes to a boil, drop in the ears and cook for 2 minutes. (Don't salt the water—it only toughens the corn.) Pull out the ears with tongs, set them on a towel to drain briefly, then pile on a platter. Pass salt, a pepper mill, sweet butter or coconut oil, and plenty of napkins. Once the season has progressed past the stage where you want your corn pure, start putting out the Green Chile Butter (page 46), Spicy Butter with Smoked Paprika (page 45), salsas, limes, and other condiments.

CORN OFF THE COB

To get corn off the cob, hold an ear with one end resting on the counter or in a large bowl to catch the juices. Using a sharp knife and a sawing motion, slowly slice right down the ear, removing the top one-half to two-thirds of the kernels but leaving their base attached. (It's the fibrous base that gets caught in your teeth.) Then reverse your knife and, using the dull side, press it down the length of the ear to push out the rest of the corn and its milk. These are called the scrapings.

If you want corn with a finer texture, grate it on the large holes of a flat grater set over a bowl. Or draw the tip of a sharp knife through the center of each row of kernels, then slice them off as described.

1 ear of corn, sliced, yields $^1/_2$ to $^3/_4$ cup kernels
1 ear of corn, grated, yields about $^1/_3$ to $^1/_2$ cup kernels

Oven-Roasted Corn: Roast whole ears of corn with their husks and silks attached at 450°F for 15 to 20 minutes. If there are no leaves, wrap the corn in foil. When done, remove the husks. The silk will come right off the kernels. (V)

Grilled Corn: Keep the stem attached to the ears, pull back the husks, and rub off the silk. Soak for 20 minutes in cold water, then pull the husks back over the kernels, twisting them so they'll stay closed. Grill for 15 to 20 minutes, depending on the heat of the fire, turning the corn every few minutes. As the corn steams, the kernels will turn bright and glossy. Pull back the husks during the last few minutes so that the corn caramelizes just enough to intensify its flavor. Serve with butter, salt and pepper, Szechuan Pepper Salt (page 69), Indian Salt with Mixed Spices (page 68), or a squeeze of fresh lime juice. (V)

Corn Roasted in the Coals: Husk the corn, remove the silk, and wrap the ears in heavy-duty aluminum foil. Lay them right on top of the hot coals and cook for 10 minutes, turning a few times. (V)

Fresh Corn Sauté: Allow $1^1/_2$ to 2 ears per person. Slice off the kernels, then press out the scrapings. Melt a little butter or coconut oil in a skillet, add a diced shallot or a few sliced green onions, the corn, its scrapings, and 1 tablespoon water. Sauté until the corn tastes cooked, about 4 minutes. Season with sea salt and pepper. (For creamed corn, add $^1/_2$ cup cream at the end and simmer until it has thickened a bit.) (V)

USES FOR LEFTOVER CORN

Sweet nuggets of boiled, roasted, and grilled corn have great potential in the kitchen. Slice the kernels off the cobs and add them to soups and chowders, vegetable ragouts, salads and salsas, muffins and pancakes. You also can slip a few into a spoon bread or polenta.

Succotash, or *Mi'i sic quotash*

In Newington's Bicentennial Cookbook, *a contributor wrote, "Many people do not know how to make a good succotash, but all of our family has had praise on our grandmother's way of making it." Her method was to boil lima beans until done, add fresh cut corn—just the tops of the kernels—and then the scrapings. "Do not stir or boil," Mrs. Sweeton warns. "It is the scrapings that make the difference between corn and beans and succotash." Succotash can also absorb such summer vegetables as tomatoes, peppers, and squashes, becoming a great harvest stew.* Serves 4

2 cups fresh or frozen lima beans or other shelling beans
6 ears sweet corn, kernels and scrapings
2 to 4 tablespoons butter
$^1/_2$ teaspoon sea salt
Freshly milled pepper

Finely chopped parsley, to finish

Paprika, to finish

Put the beans in a saucepan, cover them with water, and simmer until tender, several minutes for frozen beans, slightly longer for fresh. Drain, reserving the cooking water.

While they're cooking, scrape the kernels off the corn and set the scrapings aside in a bowl. Add the corn kernels to cooked limas with the butter, salt, and enough of the reserved cooking water to barely cover. Simmer gently for 3 minutes, then stir in the scrapings. Turn the heat to low and cook, without stirring, until most of the liquid is cooked off, 5 to 10 minutes. Season with pepper, pour into a serving dish, and add a sprinkle of parsley and a dash of paprika.

Serve alone or over grits or with popovers.

Corn with Cumin, Chile, and Tomato

Serves 4 to 6 (V)

6 large ears corn, kernels and scrapings removed separately

1 clove garlic

1 teaspoon ground toasted cumin seeds

1/2 teaspoon sea salt

Freshly milled pepper

2 tablespoons oil or butter

1 onion, finely diced

1 long green Anaheim or New Mexican chile, roasted (see page 364) and diced

1 large ripe tomato, seeded and diced

1 tablespoon chopped parsley, cilantro, or dill

In a blender, puree 1 cup of the corn kernels with 1 cup water for 3 minutes. Strain, pushing out as much liquid as you can. Meanwhile, pound the garlic, cumin, salt, and a little pepper in a mortar until smooth.

Heat the oil in a wide skillet with the onion, pounded garlic, and chile. Sauté over medium-high heat for 4 minutes. Stir in the remaining corn kernels, scrapings, and corn milk. Lower the heat, cover the pan, and simmer for 5 minutes. Add the tomato at the end and cook until warmed through. Taste for salt, stir in the parsley, and serve.

Baked Corn with Cumin and Feta Cheese: Make the preceding dish, then transfer it to a lightly buttered gratin dish. Cover with 1/2 cup crumbled feta—it tempers the sweetness of the corn. Bake at 375°F until bubbling and hot, about 25 minutes. Brown under the broiler, then serve.

Seared Corn with Manchego and Smoked Paprika

One large ear of sweet corn per person should do, although it's easy to consume more. It's just that good, the way gooey nachos are good, only much, much better. If the corn is really fresh and juicy, you'll need two skillets (or a very wide one) in order to cook off the water and sear the kernels, but even in one pan the corn will be delicious and even caramelized in places. Serves 4

4 large ears sweet corn

2 tablespoons ghee or butter

1/2 teaspoon sea salt

1 scant teaspoon smoked paprika, hot or sweet

About 1/2 cup or more young Manchego cheese, cut into a fine dice

2 tablespoons slivered chives and/or finely chopped parsley

Shuck the corn, then slice of the kernels, taking only the top half of the kernels. Reverse your knife and press out the corn milk.

Melt the ghee in a large cast-iron skillet, or two smaller ones, then add the corn and cook over medium-high heat, stirring frequently, until colored bits appear on the pan and the liquid has begun to evaporate, about 5 minutes. Season with the salt and smoked paprika. Turn off the heat, toss with the cheese and herbs, then serve with a final flourish of the paprika.

Other Herb and Cheese Combinations for Seared Corn

Fresh mozzarella and Italian basil

Cheddar or smoked cheddar and chopped marjoram

Fresh, light goat cheese and minced dill or rosemary

Eggplant

Eggplant is the workhorse of the summer kitchen in Mediterranean and Indian cuisines. Yet it's still a difficult vegetable for many people, partly because we seldom eat it really fresh, when it's sweet and mild. But eggplant is worth demystifying, for it's highly versatile and has a dense texture and sober flavor that's particularly welcome in the vegetarian kitchen.

The season for eggplant is summer, and it truly is best then. Fresh eggplants have white or pale green flesh and no trace of the bitterness that often puts people off. Eggplants in season are far superior in flavor to storage eggplants, and you'll find them much easier to cook with since they don't require salting.

TYPES OF EGGPLANT: Americans are most familiar with the large purple–black eggplant and a few slender Asian varieties. In between, however, are a host of others, from tiny white egg-shaped fruits to plump, short purple ones, to violet, striped, magenta eggplants, pure white and red-orange eggplants. Such variety can be found at farmers' markets and Asian markets, but not so much in our supermarkets.

In terms of flavor, the lighter the hue, the more mild the eggplant—white eggplants being the most mild, followed by the pale green Thai fruits, magenta or purple and white striped varieties, then the dark purple globe eggplants. The small red-orange eggplants are bitter and intended for pickling. The long Asian eggplants, like Farmer's Long, tend to be milder than round varieties and don't require salting.

WHAT TO LOOK FOR: Regardless of variety or color, an eggplant should be smooth, firm, and taut. A glossy skin and a bright green stem indicate freshness. There should be good heft in the hand. If it's too light, the flesh may be spongy, seedy and bitter. There's no such thing as male and female eggplants, only male and female blossoms.

HOW TO STORE: A cool room (about 50°F) is best, but if you haven't such a place, you can refrigerate them. I usually wrap mine in a towel to absorb moisture, then put them in a plastic bag for extra insulation. They will keep for several days, but it's better to use them within a day. It's tempting to display eggplants in a voluptuous still life on the table, but if you do so, plan to eat them after a day of admiration. They deteriorate more rapidly than if cooled.

HOW TO USE: The versatile eggplant can be broiled, grilled (see page 331) fried, roasted, and sautéed. Use it for dips, pasta, soups, stews, casseroles, gratins, and purees. Large pieces can be rolled or layered; whole eggplants can be stuffed. Cheese often shows up with eggplant except, of course, in Asian recipes, where miso or other forms of soy are preferred.

SPECIAL HANDLING: One potential drawback with eggplant is its capacity to absorb oil. This can be overcome, however, by salting as described on page 331. It will shrivel but plump up when cooked. Salting also removes bitterness from mature, storage eggplants.

QUANTITY: Yields vary depending on the shape of the eggplant, how you plan to use it—pureed, rolled, stuffed—and whether or not you peel it. But in general, count on a pound of eggplant yielding about 4 cups chopped, serving two to four.

Good Partners for Eggplant

Olive oil, toasted sesame oil, roasted peanut oil, cream
Garlic, basil, peanuts, pine nuts, ginger, soy, cilantro, saffron
Lemon, red wine vinegar, balsamic vinegar
Parmesan, ricotta, goat cheese, Gruyère, feta, yogurt, tahini, miso, soy
Tomatoes, peppers, onions, summer squash, chickpeas, potatoes

Sauces and Seasonings for Eggplant

Yogurt Sauce with Cayenne and Dill (page 57)
Cilantro Salsa (page 49)
Chermoula (page 50)
Sauces with Nuts and Seeds (pages 59 to 60)
Peanut Sauce (page 61)
Yogurt Tahini Sauce (page 57)

SALTING EGGPLANT

Eggplant that's freshly picked, harvested before it's overly mature, and eaten within a few days is naturally sweet and doesn't need salting, nor do the slender Asian varieties. Salting can, however, leach out bitterness from eggplants that have been in storage, those that are over the hill, and when it is to be fried, since a long salting keeps it from absorbing too much oil. I know some cooks who always salt their eggplants and others who never do, reflecting perhaps their own sensitivity—or lack thereof—to eggplant.

Sprinkle eggplant slices or cubes lightly with whatever salt you normally use. Let it stand in a colander for at least 30 minutes to reduce bitterness, 1 hour or more to lessen oil absorption. Blot the juices that bead on the surface or quickly rinse the eggplant and blot it dry. When seasoning the eggplant during cooking, taste it before adding more salt to a dish.

Whole Roasted Eggplant: Roasted eggplant has a creamy pale interior, and when charred over the coals it can have a decidedly smoky flavor. Baked to the point of utter collapse, the flesh falls into a near puree that can be served as a vegetable, turned into a savory custard or soufflé, or used as the basis of any of the eggplant spreads starting on page 88. It can also be pulled into shreds, then seasoned, resulting in a coarser texture. Be sure you prick it first in a few places to allow the steam to escape so that the eggplant doesn't explode. (V)

Roasted Eggplant with Garlic: Make eight or more small incisions in a globe eggplant and wedge a sliver of garlic into each. Set on a sheet pan and roast at 400°F until tender and collapsed, 20 to 40 minutes. Remove from the oven, let rest several minutes, then slice lengthwise in half. If the shell is fairly intact, you can cut it in half and serve it seasoned with sea salt, pepper, and a spoonful of olive oil, a yogurt sauce (pages 57 to 58), or Salsa Verde (page 48). If the shells have collapsed, scoop out the flesh, then season it. One pound of eggplant yields about 1³/₄ cups roasted eggplant. (V)

Whole Eggplant Cooked on the Grill: Prick an eggplant in several places with a fork. Cook it over the coals or on a covered gas grill until it's tender to the point of collapsing, 20 to 40 minutes, depending on the size and the heat. For a smoky flavor, grill the eggplant until the skin is blackened. Transfer it to a bowl and let stand until cool enough

to handle. Split lengthwise and scoop out the flesh. Mash it until smooth or pull it into shreds. Season with olive oil, minced garlic, and chopped parsley; dark sesame or roasted peanut oil; Salsa Verde (page 48), Tarator Sauce (page 59), yogurt, and so forth. (To cook eggplant in the coals, wrap it in foil, set it on top of the coals, and cook until soft.) (V)

Sautéed Eggplant, Parsley, and Pine Nuts

Serve this eggplant as a vegetable or use it as a filling for stuffed vegetables. Leftovers make a delicious addition to pilaf or a pasta dish. Serves 4 (V)

1¹/₂ pounds eggplant, peeled
Sea salt and freshly milled pepper
¹/₂ cup olive oil
¹/₄ cup chopped parsley
1 large clove garlic
2 tablespoons toasted pine nuts

Cut the eggplant into ¹/₂-inch rounds, then into 1¹/₂-inch cubes. Sprinkle with salt and set aside for 30 minutes, then blot dry. Heat the oil in a large skillet until nearly smoking. Add the eggplant and stir immediately to coat. Lower the heat to medium and cook, stirring occasionally, until the eggplant is golden and soft, about 15 minutes. Taste, then season with salt and pepper. Chop the parsley and garlic together and toss with the eggplant along with the pine nuts.

Eggplant Rounds

Large rounds or slabs of golden eggplant, simply seasoned, can be served as a side dish, but they also serve as the foundation for other dishes, such as roll-ups and gratins. Use globe eggplant or small, plump Italian varieties. Keep all the skin on or remove it in strips to make a decorative design. Slice the eggplant into rounds or lengthwise into slabs ¹/₂ to ³/₄ inch thick, sprinkle with salt, let stand for 30 minutes, then blot dry. Brush both sides with olive oil and season with salt and pepper.

To broil: Broil the eggplant about 4 inches from the heat until browned, about 10 minutes. Turn and broil the second side.

To bake: Bake the eggplant slices on a sheet pan at 425°F until browned on the bottom, 15 to 25 minutes. Turn and bake the second side until browned.

To grill: Cut small, slender eggplants lengthwise in half. Cut larger eggplants into rounds, diagonals, or steaks about ³/₈ inch thick. Brush generously with olive oil and lay them on the grill. Leave them for 4 minutes, then turn them 45 degrees and cook another 4 minutes. Turn them over and repeat. Remove and season lightly with salt and pepper. Serve with any of the sauces suggested for eggplant (page 330), or use as a base for the more substantial dishes that follow. These make a great filling for a sandwich.

To shallow-fry: Don't brush the eggplant with oil after salting since it will be fried. Heat ¹/₂ inch light olive or vegetable oil in a heavy pan until nearly smoking. Slide in a few eggplant slices without crowding the pan and cook until both sides are nicely colored, 1 minute or so, then drain on paper towels. You can also fry in just enough oil to generously coat the bottom of the pan, but the concentrated heat of the larger amount of oil cooks the eggplant faster, and in the end it may well absorb less oil.

Eggplant Rounds with Cheese and Red Wine Tomato Sauce

This combination is substantial enough to serve as a simple main dish. Serves 4 to 6

---

2 eggplant rounds per person, grilled, broiled, or baked

³/₄ cup grated or sliced mozzarella

¹/₂ cup crumbled Gorgonzola, goat cheese, or grated fontina—or a mixture

Red Wine Tomato Sauce (page 56)

Chopped parsley or basil, for garnish

Place the cooked eggplant rounds on a sheet pan and cover with the cheeses. Bake at 375°F until the cheese melts. Serve with 2 or 3 spoonfuls of the sauce on each serving and garnish with the parsley.

Eggplant Rounds with Gremolata: First make the Gremolata, a simple mixture of chopped parsley, garlic and lemon (page 21). Prepare eggplant rounds using whatever method you prefer. As soon as they're cooked, sprinkle the gremolata over them and serve. (*V*)

Eggplant Rounds with Chermoula and Pine Nuts: All green herb sauces can be used this way, but the Moroccan marinade chermoula is especially exciting with eggplant. Prepare eggplant rounds using whatever method you prefer and arrange them on a platter. Spoon Chermoula (page 50) over the slices and let stand 1 hour or longer for the flavors to merge. Just before serving, toast pine nuts and scatter them over the top. (*V*)

Broiled or Grilled Eggplant and Tarator Sauce: Broil or grill two or three eggplant rounds per person. Generously drizzle with Tarator Sauce (page 59). Garnish with chopped parsley, toasted pine nuts or walnuts, and, if available, pomegranate seeds. Serve with a garden salad. (*V*)

Broiled or Grilled Eggplant with Goat Cheese and Salsa Verde: Cover broiled or grilled eggplant rounds with crumbled goat cheese and broil until softened. Drizzle with Salsa Verde (page 48) and garnish with neatly diced ripe tomato. A substantial appetizer or light main course.

Eggplant Rounds with Peanut Sauce: Broil or grill eggplant rounds, brushing them first with light sesame or peanut oil instead of olive oil. Serve with one of the peanut sauces (pages 61) and garnish with chopped cilantro, roasted peanuts, and a wedge of lime. (*V*)

Grilled Eggplant with Miso Sauce

A sweet and tangy miso sauce is absolutely winsome on many foods, including eggplant. You can either make eggplant rounds as described, or grill small eggplant on the grill or griddle. If you have red or green shiso leaves (easy to grow!) you can garnish the eggplant with fine slivers of them. Serves 4 or more (*V*)

---

8 Japanese eggplants, such as Little Fingers or Ichiban, about 4 inches long

Light sesame oil, for the eggplant

3 tablespoons white miso

2 tablespoons rice wine (mirin)

1 tablespoon sugar

1 teaspoon toasted sesame oil

Toasted sesame seeds, to finish

3 or more shiso leaves, thinly sliced, for garnish

Slice the eggplant lengthwise in half, leaving the calyx attached. Using the tip of a knife, make a series of shallow crisscross cuts across the surface. Brush the cut side of the eggplant with light sesame oil. Heat a grill or griddle pan and, when hot, set the eggplant on it, cut side facing down. Cook over medium-high heat until stripes appear, about 10 minutes, then turn the eggplant 45 degrees and cook another 10 minutes to make a crosshatched surface. If small, the eggplant should be tender. If not, turn it and cook it on the rounded side until it is.

While the eggplant is cooking, combine the miso, mirin, sugar, and sesame oil, and work into a smooth paste. When the eggplants are done, slather the sauce over the surface of each. Finish with the toasted sesame seeds and garnish with slivered shiso leaves.

Eggplant Roll-Ups

These fetching bundles of rolled stuffed eggplant make a good dish for entertaining. Fillings can be made from pasta, rice, or, as in the American interpretation that follows, cornbread. The three parts—eggplant, stuffing, and sauce—can all be made in advance, so the actual assembly is quite straightforward. Once assembled, they can be held up to a day before baking. Allow two or three per person for an entrée, one or two as a first course.

Eggplant Rollatini with Cornbread Stuffing

A substantial dish for fall when the weather starts to get nippy. An experienced cook can make this from scratch in about 2 hours, but I always like to have something done ahead, such as the cornbread or the sauce.
Makes 10 to 12 rolls, serving 4 to 6

2 large globe eggplants, about 3 pounds in all
Sea salt
Cornbread Stuffing, recipe follows
Red Wine Tomato Sauce (page 56)
About ¹/₃ cup olive or vegetable oil, as needed
Chopped marjoram, basil, or parsley, for garnish

Slice the eggplant lengthwise no thicker than ¹/₃ inch or they'll be difficult to roll later. Sprinkle both sides with salt and let stand an hour. Rinse and blot dry. Meanwhile, prepare the stuffing and the sauce if you haven't already.

Brush the eggplant with oil and grill, bake, fry, or broil on both sides until tender. They should be flexible, but if they're dry looking, don't worry. Just stack them on top of each other—as they finish cooking the heat will soften them.

Mound about 2 tablespoons stuffing at the widest end of each piece, roll into a cylinder, and secure with a toothpick. Place seam side down in a lightly oiled baking dish large enough to hold the eggplant rolls in a single layer. Cover the dish with aluminum foil.

When ready to eat, preheat the oven to 400°F. Bake until the eggplant rolls are heated through, about 25 minutes. Spoon a little sauce on each plate and set the rolls on top. Remove the toothpicks and garnish with the chopped herb.

Cornbread Stuffing

2 tablespoons oil
1 onion, finely chopped
1 tablespoon chopped sage or 1 teaspoon dried
¹/₂ teaspoon dried oregano
2 cups crumbled Buttermilk Skillet Cornbread (page 576)
1 egg
Sea salt and freshly milled pepper

Heat the oil in a medium skillet. Add the onion and herbs and cook over medium heat until soft and lightly browned, about 12 minutes. Mix with the cornbread and egg and season with salt and pepper to taste, then work the mixture together with your hands so that it's evenly moistened. If it seems dry, add a little water.

Eggplant Rollatini, Fresh Mozzarella, and Goat Cheese

Delicious served with rice, quinoa, or couscous and a roasted tomato or pepper sauce.
Makes 10 to 12 rolls, serving 4 to 6

1 cup grated or chopped mozzarella, preferably fresh

1 cup crumbled goat cheese

2 green onions, including a few inches of the greens, thinly sliced

2 teaspoons minced thyme or rosemary

Sea salt and freshly milled pepper

Milk, if needed

2 large globe eggplants, about 3 pounds in all, prepared as described in the preceding recipe

Red Pepper Sauce (page 64) or Oven-Roasted Tomato Sauce (page 55)

Combine the cheeses, onions, and herbs and season well with salt and pepper. If the mixture seems dry and doesn't cohere, add a little milk. Fill the eggplant slices and bake as described in the preceding recipe. Serve with the sauce of your choice.

Rollatini with Capellini

I first had these scrumptious rollatini in a Los Angeles restaurant, Tuscany, where chef Tommaso Barletta fills them with fine capellini and serves them with a fresh, light tomato sauce. Makes 12 plump rolls, serving 4 to 6

6 ounces capellini or angel hair pasta

1 cup finely diced provolone or mozzarella

3 tablespoons freshly grated parmesan

2 tablespoons chopped marjoram or basil, plus extra to finish

Sea salt and freshly milled pepper

2 large globe eggplants, about 3 pounds in all, prepared as described on page 333

2½ cups Fresh Tomato Sauce (page 54)

Boil the capellini in salted water until slightly underdone, then drain. Toss it with the cheeses and marjoram and season with salt and pepper to taste. Divide the pasta among the eggplant slices, then roll them up.

Preheat the oven to 375°F. Spread 1½ cups of the tomato sauce in a large baking dish and set the rolled eggplant, seam side down, inside. Cover with aluminum foil and bake until the sauce is bubbling and the eggplant is heated through, 25 to 30 minutes. Heat the remaining 1 cup sauce and ladle some onto each plate. Place the eggplant rolls on the sauce, dust with the extra marjoram, and serve.

Baked Eggplant with Feta and Tomatoes

Serves 4 to 6

4 oblong Asian or Italian eggplants, about 6 ounces each

4 tablespoons olive oil

Sea salt and freshly milled pepper

4 ripe tomatoes, peeled, seeded, and chopped

2 to 3 ounces feta cheese

½ teaspoon dried oregano or 2 teaspoons fresh

Preheat the oven to 375°F. Slice each eggplant lengthwise in half and score the cut sides in a crisscross pattern.

Heat 3 tablespoons of the oil in a large skillet. Add the eggplant, cut sides down, and fry over medium–high heat until golden. Fry the second sides for a few minutes, then transfer to a plate and season with salt and pepper. Wipe out the pan.

Heat the remaining 1 tablespoon fresh oil in the skillet, add the tomatoes, and cook over medium–high heat until they have broken down into a chunky sauce, 5 to 10 minutes. Season with salt and pepper to taste.

Set the eggplants, cut sides up and snugly side by side, in a baking dish. Crumble the cheese over the tops, spoon the tomato over the cheese, and sprinkle with the oregano. Cover and bake until the eggplant is tender, about 40 minutes. Uncover and bake 5 minutes more.

Fava Beans

A favorite spring shell bean with chefs, fava beans are increasingly available in Italian, Mexican, and farmers' markets. The long, fat green pods surround flat beans, further encased in a skin.

The skin needn't be removed when the bean is the size of a thumbnail, but it gets tough when the beans are larger. (To remove, blanch the beans for 1 minute in boiling water, drain, and pinch off the skins with your fingers.) If you have enough fava beans and time, cook them as a side dish. Otherwise, add them to spring vegetable stews and pasta dishes. One pound of pods yields only about $1/2$ cup of beans. They go well with olive oil, yogurt, rosemary, dill, parsley, and thyme.

Fava Beans, Cilantro, and Parsley with Rice

Fava beans always take extra time, yet their delectable flavor is present and certainly enjoyable in this rice. Sit somewhere pleasant to shell the beans and enlist help. Serves 4 to 6 Ⓥ

- 1 cup white or brown basmati rice
- 3 to 4 pounds fresh fava beans, in their pods
- $1/4$ teaspoon sea salt
- 2 tablespoons olive oil
- $1/2$ white onion, finely diced
- 1 large clove garlic, minced
- $1/2$ teaspoon ground coriander
- 2 tablespoons chopped cilantro
- 2 tablespoons chopped parsley
- Freshly milled pepper
- Lemon wedges

Cover the rice with water and set aside to soak while you shell the beans. Bring a pot of water to a boil, submerge the shucked beans for 1 minute, then drain and rinse. Remove the outer skin by pinching them loose with your thumb. If they're very small, about the size of your little fingernail, you don't have to peel them.

Drain the rice. Put it in a saucepan with 2 cups water and the salt and bring to a boil. Lower the heat, cover, and cook until the water is absorbed and the rice is tender, about 15 minutes. If it's done sooner than that and there's excess water, drain the rice, then return it to the pot to steam. Warm the oil in a sauté pan, add the onion, and cook 2 minutes over medium heat. Add the garlic, coriander, and herbs. Stew until tender, about 10 minutes. Season with salt and pepper. Gently fork the beans into the rice, then mound in a bowl and serve with the lemon wedges.

Fava Beans with Yogurt, Lemon, and Dill

Serves 4

- 4 pounds fresh fava beans in their pods
- $2^1/2$ tablespoons olive oil
- 3 green onions, including some of the greens, thinly sliced
- 1 teaspoon finely grated lemon zest
- 1 tablespoon fresh lemon juice
- Sea salt and freshly milled pepper
- 3 tablespoons finely chopped dill
- $1/3$ cup yogurt, whisked until smooth

Shell the beans and peel them if they're large. Cook them in a medium skillet over medium heat in 1 tablespoon of the olive oil until they're tender, about 10 minutes, then stir in the onions and turn off the heat. Whisk together the remaining $1^1/2$ tablespoons oil, the lemon zest, juice, and a pinch of salt. Pour it over the beans, add most of the dill, and gently mix everything together. Season with pepper. Pile the beans in a dish, drizzle the yogurt over all, and garnish with the remaining dill. Serve warm or chilled.

Fennel (Anise, Finocchio, or Florence Fennel)

Fennel is a plump, pale green bulb that appears in the spring, in summer where the weather is cool, and again in the fall, when it's most delicious. The wild fennel that grows along California roadsides produces a crown of seeds and tall stalks that are splendid for grilling, but it doesn't develop the bulbous root—that must be cultivated.

With its soft anise flavor, fennel is sweet, refreshing, and delectable. Because a bulb has a well-defined shape, fennel can assume a strong visual role on the plate, especially when cooked in halves. It can also be sliced or chopped and sautéed—a good use for the outer leaves, which often come apart from the base. And, it's delicious raw.

WHAT TO LOOK FOR: Firm, plump, compact bulbs, preferably with their stalks and some of the feathery greens, which should be lively looking. Small bulbs are preferable for salads since they're more tender, and larger ones are ideal for baking and braising. Avoid any that have begun to bolt, or plan to use them in soups.

HOW TO STORE: Keep fennel refrigerated in a plastic bag, but try to use it within 3 to 4 days. The stalks dry out more quickly than the bulbs, so if you plan to keep them longer, wrap them in a damp towel, then in a plastic bag.

HOW TO USE: Fennel always makes an interesting substitute for celery; it's delicious braised, baked, steamed, sautéed, or grilled and is a fine salad vegetable. Be sure to use the leaves for a garnish or seasoning. I've never found much use for fennel stalks (outside of using them in soup stocks or throwing dried ones in the fire for their aromatic smoke) which is a shame given that fennel is sold by the pound and always comes with lots of stalks. The part closest to the base is sometimes tender enough to add to soups and salads if thinly sliced, but taste it first to make sure it's not too stringy.

SPECIAL HANDLING: Cut off the stalks just where they emerge from the bulb. Fennel has a core, which is visible once you cut it in half. If the bulb is small, it's not necessary to remove it. If the bulb is very large, quarter it and remove the core with a paring knife if it seems tough or stringy. (Taste it to find out.) Remove scarred outer leaves by cutting a thin slice from the base of the bulb, then pulling them off. They can be used, along with the stalks, to make a quick stock, or they can be peeled, then sliced and cooked.

QUANTITY: An average bulb, trimmed, weighs 4 to 6 ounces. Two bulbs yield approximately $1^{1}/_{2}$ cups chopped or sliced, which cooks down to slightly less. Allow one whole bulb for a main-course serving of braised fennel.

Good Partners for Fennel

Olive oil, butter
Thyme, bay, parsley, fennel seeds, orange, lemon, saffron
Tomatoes, potatoes, olives, garlic, truffle salt
Parmesan, Gruyère, goat cheese, goat Gouda

Sauces and Seasonings for Fennel

Salsa Verde (page 48)
Orange Mayonnaise (page 52)
Garlic Mayonnaise (page 52)
Saffron Mayonnaise (page 52)
Tomato sauces (pages 53 to 56)
Parsley-Caper Sauce (page 49)

Steamed Fennel

This simple way of cooking fennel leaves it full of flavor.
Serves 4 Ⓥ

2 medium fennel bulbs, trimmed
1 bay leaf
Sea salt and freshly milled pepper
Olive oil, to finish
Chopped fennel greens or parsley, for garnish

Remove the tough outer leaves and rinse the bulbs. Bring an inch of water to a boil in a large saucepan with some of the fennel stalks and the bay leaf; add a steaming rack. Quarter the bulbs lengthwise and steam, covered, until tender–firm when pierced with a knife, about 20 minutes. Transfer to a plate, season with salt and pepper, thread with olive oil, and garnish with the chopped greens.

Oven-Braised Fennel with Parmesan

A handsome first course, with flavor to match. Dress this up with one of the suggested partners for a first course.
Serves 4 to 6

2 tablespoons butter or olive oil
2 or 3 fennel bulbs, trimmed and halved or quartered lengthwise
Sea salt and freshly milled pepper
1/2 cup dry white wine or water
1/3 cup freshly grated parmesan
Chopped fennel greens or parsley, to finish

Preheat the oven to 325°F. Rub a baking dish large enough to hold the fennel in a single layer with butter. Steam the fennel for 10 minutes, then arrange in the dish. Dot with butter or drizzle with olive oil, season with salt and pepper, and add the wine. Cover and bake for 20 minutes. Remove the cover, baste the fennel with its juice, then add the cheese and continue baking until the fennel is completely tender, about 10 minutes more. Serve with chopped fennel greens or parsley.

Three-Fennel Braise with Pine Nuts, Goat Cheese, and Arugula

I often serve this fennel with fettuccine or penne or by itself as a simple but very flavorful vegetable. Fennel pollen and the minced feather greens underscore its anise flavor, and the pine nuts, crumbled cheese, and pungent greens lift it from the simple to the complex. Serves 4 to 6

2 or 3 large fennel bulbs, about 10 ounces each, including the greens
2 tablespoons olive oil
1 teaspoon sea salt
1 tablespoon fresh lemon juice
Zest of 1 lemon
Freshly milled pepper
1/4 cup roasted pine nuts
A few pinches fennel pollen or truffle salt
Crumbled goat cheese or goat feta
Handful small arugula greens
Best olive oil

Peel the tough outer layers of the fennel, then quarter the bulbs and slice a scant 1/2 inch thick. There's no need to remove the core. Mince the fennel greens and set them aside.

Warm the oil in a wide skillet. When hot, add the fennel and sauté over high heat, stirring occasionally until browned in places, about 7 minutes. Season with the salt and lemon juice, then add 3/4 cup water. Reduce the heat a little and cook, covered, until the fennel is nearly soft. Remove the lid, raise the heat to a boil until the liquid has evaporated and the pan is dry. At this point continue to cook the fennel, turning it often, until browned in many places, for about 10 minutes. Toss the fennel with the lemon zest and fennel greens and season with pepper. Serve on a platter covered with the pine nuts, fennel pollen, cheese, and arugula greens. Drizzle your best olive oil over all. Toss at the table so that everything is mixed well.

Fresh Fennel Jam

Fennel is sometimes used in sweets, so its place in a jam isn't that surprising. I make this to serve right away, garnished with fennel seeds, pollen, and greens. Try it with a piece of fresh goat cheese and honey or an apple tart. Makes 1 cup Ⓥ

2 small fennel bulbs

2 to 3 tablespoons sugar or honey

Splash Pernod

Sea salt

1 teaspoon fennel seeds

Fennel pollen, optional

Minced fennel greens, to finish

Discard or peel the outer fennel layers, halve each bulb, slice thinly, then dice finely. You don't want big chunks here. Put the pieces in a heavy saucepan with the sugar, Pernod, and just a pinch of salt. Set it over low heat to start cooking.

Toast the fennel seeds in a small skillet until fragrant, then immediately turn them out onto a plate. Add most of the seeds to the diced fennel, and set the rest aside. Cook the fennel, stirring occasionally, until it is very tender, about 25 minutes. When done, turn it into a bowl and sprinkle the remaining fennel seeds over the top along with a few pinches of fennel pollen and fennel greens. If you're planning to keep the jam in the refrigerator for a while, omit the greens, and either garnish when you bring it out, or stir the reserved fennel seeds right into the jam.

Braised Fennel with Diced Vegetables

This is a most delicious treatment of fennel—a bit more complex than the preceding recipes and with correspondingly greater stature. Served with a spoonful of Saffron Mayonnaise (page 52), it makes an elegant first course or light main dish. Serves 2 to 4 Ⓥ

2 large fennel bulbs, trimmed, plus 1 tablespoon chopped fennel greens

2 tablespoons olive oil

1 carrot, finely diced

1 small onion, finely diced

1 celery rib, finely diced

Several thyme sprigs or ¼ teaspoon dried

1 bay leaf

Sea salt and freshly milled pepper

½ cup dry white wine

1 tablespoon butter or olive oil

Peel the outer layers of the fennel; if they're badly bruised, remove them. Keeping the root end intact, halve each bulb lengthwise.

Heat the oil in a large skillet, add the diced vegetables and herbs, and sauté over medium-high heat until the onion begins to color, after several minutes.

Move the vegetables to one side of the pan and add the fennel halves, cut sides clown. Spoon the vegetables over and around them, season with salt and pepper, and pour in 1 cup water. Lower the heat to medium, cover, and cook until the liquid has evaporated, 10 to 12 minutes. Give the diced vegetables a stir and add ½ cup water. Cover and cook until the fennel is tender-firm when pierced with a knife, 15 to 20 minutes. By this time it should be nicely browned on the bottom.

Remove the vegetables and the fennel to a serving dish, placing the fennel cut sides up. Return the pan to the heat, add the wine and butter, and scrape the caramelized bits from the bottom of the pan. When the wine and butter have reduced by half, add the fennel greens, taste for salt, and season with pepper. Spoon the sauce over the fennel and serve.

Grilled Fennel: Fennel is one of my favorite vegetables to grill. Trim the stalks from a fennel bulb. If the bulb is small, cut it in half lengthwise. If it's large, cut into ½-inch slices, making sure that each slice has a piece of the root attached. Steam for 10 minutes, then brush generously with olive oil and season with sea salt. Grill for 5 to 6 minutes on each side. Serve with Garlic Mayonnaise (page 52), Salsa Verde with Walnuts and Tarragon (page 49), or Mustard Vinaigrette (page 167). Ⓥ

Garlic

Good garlic heads are hard, the cloves free from bruises and sprouts. A succession of crops appears in our markets for a good portion of the year—Mexican red garlic comes in late spring, followed by California garlic (which is now in competition with China), and then there's local garlic everywhere.

White California garlic is a soft-neck variety with many cloves, including quite a few that are too small to use easily. Hard-neck garlic, especially popular in farmers' markets, has fewer but larger cloves that are often spicier, the wrappers beautifully streaked purple and red. Notice when you're using one of its cloves—some could be three times the size of the large cloves you're used to using, so you might want to use just part of it. Elephant garlic, actually a leek, also has very large, mild-tasting cloves, but they lack the feisty character of true garlic. Green garlic refers to newly formed garlic heads still attached to their greens, most likely a local specialty. Their cloves are milky and the flavor mild and delicious; it's really another vegetable altogether. Green garlic should be refrigerated, but dried heads can be kept at room temperature on the counter or in special perforated clay jars that allow air to circulate.

SPECIAL HANDLING: To open a head of garlic, set it top side down on a counter and press down on it with your palm to force the cloves apart. Regardless of how you plan to use garlic, remove the dried, knotty bit at the base, cut out any brown spots, and remove the green sprouts, which are prevalent in winter garlic.

Firm, new garlic is easy to peel with a knife. Cut off the core at the base of the clove, put the blade of your knife underneath the skin, and it should practically pop off. If your garlic is going to be chopped, minced, pounded, or thrown into a soup stock, lay the flat side of a chef's knife on the garlic and give it a whack to loosen the skin.

When cooking, try not to burn your garlic. It gets sticky and acrid and doesn't add to any dish. That's why it's often added long after onions have begun to cook, or why slices are removed from the pan when golden.

SAFETY NOTE: Garlic tastes best when it's freshly chopped; but if you want to hold it for a few hours, put it in a bowl with olive oil to cover to keep it fresh tasting and prevent oxidation. While it may be tempting to store ready-to-use chopped garlic in olive oil for days or weeks, without the presence of acid, botulism can grow in such a situation, even when it's refrigerated. It's simply not worth taking a chance. Besides, freshly chopped garlic tastes so much better. During the course of a day's cooking, however, it's fine to cover your chopped garlic with oil to keep it from drying out. But throw out any that's left over.

Fresh Garlic Puree: Pounding garlic in a mortar makes it smooth and sweet tasting, whereas the garlic press can leave a metallic off taste as well as texture. This is especially useful for flavoring a mayonnaise or any other sauce where you don't want distinct bits of garlic. It shouldn't be fried, since it will burn almost instantly.

Coarsely chop peeled garlic, then put it in a mortar with a little salt. The salt grabs at the garlic and speeds the process of breaking it down by pulling out its moisture. Pound it with the pestle until smooth, a matter of just a minute.

Roasted Garlic Puree: The puree that forms within the skins of roasted garlic can be used as a flavoring just the way fresh can, but roasted garlic has a deeper, softer flavor. To get the puree, work the softened cloves in a sieve with a rubber spatula to force it through. An average head of garlic yields only about a heaping tablespoon, but a little goes a long way.

Stewed Garlic: If you want the garlic to use as a seasoning, break apart the cloves of several heads, but don't peel them. Put them in a small saucepan, cover with water, add a tablespoon olive oil and a sprig of thyme. Bring to a boil, then cover and simmer until the cloves are tender when pressed with a finger, about 30 minutes. Pour off the liquid and pass the garlic through a food mill or sieve to strain out the pulp. Store in a jar covered with a film of olive oil, in the refrigerator.

Garlic Scapes: The curvaceous stems that grow from the hard-neck garlic bulbs are called scapes. As they draw energy from the formation of the bulb, farmers cut them off and sell them at the market. The more tender scapes can be stir-fried or sautéed, cut into pieces first for easier handling. They make a pretty zesty pesto, which can be pungent indeed (see page 50).

Whole Roasted Garlic ⓥ

Long cooking sweetens pungent garlic. Squeezed out of each clove, the soft garlic is eaten with potatoes or spread over toast. The garlic must be of the best quality—rock hard with no bruises or sprouts.

---

1 head garlic per person
Olive oil or butter

Preheat the oven to 350°F. Rub off the outer papery skins, leaving the cloves encased in the last layer. Set the heads upright in an oiled baking dish, spoon olive oil over them or place a knob of butter on each, then add a few tablespoons water to the dish. Cover tightly with foil. Bake for 45 minutes, then remove the foil and bake 30 minutes more, until the garlic is completely soft inside. Squeeze a clove open just to be sure.

Greens

Cooking greens have similar qualities yet distinctive personalities. Some are sweet and tender, others rougher and more abrasive. I believe that greens have become better known and more popular in the past 17 years—one need only think of the popularity of kale salads, and the appearance of Asian greens and new varieties of familiar leaves in our farmers' markets and even supermarkets. There is a fear that greens, like collards, will be strong tasting, but in fact, they are often mild. Perhaps they just look as if they'd be difficult.

TYPES OF GREENS: Tender, quick-cooking greens include spinach, chard, beet greens, bok choy, and other Asian greens. Collards and kale take longer to cook but are mild. More aggressive leaves in the flavor department include turnip greens, broccoli rabe, mustard, and dandelion. While individual plants differ, all greens require the same consideration from selection through storing.

WHAT TO LOOK FOR: Good greens should have a lively, bouncy look, bursting with vitality. Smaller leaves are often sweeter and more tender than large ones, but large leaves need not be avoided, for once cooked, they'll be tender, too. Yellowing, limpness, and spotting indicate age and a loss of vitality. In this state, they often have a slightly sour smell and a bitter taste.

HOW TO STORE: Cook greens as soon after picking or purchasing as possible. Until then, refrigerate them in plastic bags. Wash just before using.

HOW TO USE: Serve greens simply cooked as a side dish. They're also delicious in soups and exceedingly good combined with neutral foods, such as potatoes, pasta, and beans. Some, like chard, can be wrapped around savory fillings or themselves chopped and used as fillings for pastas and crepes. If tender enough, they can be added to salads.

SPECIAL HANDLING: Many greens are grown in fine, sandy soil. Rain splashes onto the leaves, leaving a fine but gritty deposit, so they must be washed carefully, sometimes in two or three changes of water. Trim them first, then give the leaves a rinse under the tap. Fill a sink or large bowl with plenty of water, add the greens, and gently agitate the leaves to loosen the dirt. Let them soak for a few minutes while the dirt settles to the bottom, then lift them up without stirring up the dirty water below. Repeat until they're really clean. Taste to make sure; grit will ruin the finest dish. Tough stems need to be removed in their entirety; more tender stems should be cut at the base of the leaves by slicing them off, your knife going the length of the stem.

QUANTITY: All greens diminish greatly in volume once cooked. For two generous servings, allow 1 pound greens, usually the weight of one well-filled bunch.

Good Partners for Greens

Olive oil, roasted peanut and toasted sesame oils, mustard oil, butter

Parmesan, Asiago, dry Monterey Jack

Red pepper flakes, vinegar, pepper sauce, garlic

Potatoes, legumes, pasta

A Glossary of Greens from the Cabbage Family

BOK CHOY, CHOY SUM: These mild members of the cabbage family are delectable. Bok choy has fleshy white stems and green leaves, both of which are used in stir-fries. One large bunch will make two or three servings. Choy sum, which looks like a miniature bok choy, can be treated the same way, cooked whole, or steamed and dressed with sesame oil.

COLLARDS: These are the big, round, flat-leafed greens that encircle thick stalks. They're often milder than mustard and kale but take longer to cook, 15 to 20 minutes. They don't cook down too much so that one bunch, weighing slightly less than a pound, can serve two. Include collards in soups or treat them as a vegetable. The stems are edible.

KALE: Kale is enjoyed in winter soups, especially those with potatoes and beans, as a vegetable, and as a salad. The stems are as tough as ropes unless the leaves are very small, so slice the leaves all the way off and discard the stems. The curly kale we see most commonly is fairly tough, needing 12 to 15 minutes to cook. Tuscan kale (also known as lacinato or dinosaur kale) has long, dark green frondlike leaves—it is favored for kale salad, and cooks a bit more quickly than other varieties. Red Russian kale has flat blue-green leaves

that are somewhat more tender. Even though it cooks down, kale manages to hold much of its volume. A bunch weighing about a pound yields 1 1/2 to 2 cups cooked.

MUSTARD GREENS: Light green or red, crinkled or smooth, and more tender than kale, these greens have a hot mustardy punch. Remove the stems and ribs if tough, then simmer or sauté until tender, about 10 minutes, although some cook mustard for hours. The longer it cooks, the softer its flavor becomes. Briefly cooked, it's tender but spicy. Allow a 1-pound bunch for two servings.

TURNIP GREENS: These are assertive tasting with a rough texture when raw, but many people find turnip greens delicious. Southern style demands a long cooking time, which makes them silky and deep tasting. Turnip greens are wonderful combined with their roots in soups. A bunch weighing about a pound will serve two.

WATERCRESS: Usually used for salads, when you can get it in quantity, try it sautéed or stir-fried—it's simply delicious. Remove the larger stems before cooking and allow a standard bunch for a single serving.

OTHER GREENS: Amaranth, orach, Good King Henry, and wild spinach are all tender, vitamin-rich greens. They're most likely to be found in the wild, at farmers' markets, or grown at home. They can be eaten raw, in salads, or cooked. Long stems should be removed; the remaining leaves will cook down to about half their volume.

Wilted Greens: Greens can be too voluminous to steam in a conventional pot. One way to cook them is to bring a little water—a few cups—to a boil in a large pot, like a stockpot, then add the greens, cover, and let them steam until wilted. Once they wilt down, the volume is manageable enough that you can turn them with tongs and basically steam them until tender, from 5 to 20 minutes depending on the greens. When done, or a little before, transfer them to a colander set over a bowl to drain. Press out excess moisture, then season them to taste with olive oil or butter, sea salt, and pepper. (V)

Simmered Choy Sum: These tender little vegetables cook in their entirety within minutes, look absolutely stunning, and are so delicious that you can allow one or two per person. Cut four choy sum in half lengthwise, soak them in a bowl of water for 15 minutes, then rinse carefully, giving special attention to the base. Place them in a skillet of simmering salted water and cook until bright green and tender, about 4 minutes. Remove with tongs to a platter and drizzle a tiny bit of toasted sesame oil or roasted peanut oil over all. (V)

Collard Greens, Black Rice, and Coconut Butter

Collard stems look tough at first glance, but slice them thinly and they'll be tender once cooked. The final flourish of coconut butter (or ghee) and smoked salt lifts this dark green and black dish right out of the ordinary. You can use white or brown rice you prefer it to the black. Serves 4 (V)

1 small bunch collards, 6 to 8 leaves, washed well

1 tablespoon vegetable or coconut oil

1 small onion, diced

2 healthy pinches red pepper flakes

1/4 teaspoon toasted, ground cumin

1/2 teaspoon allspice

1/2 cup black rice, rinsed and drained

1/2 teaspoon sea salt

2 tablespoons coconut butter or ghee

Smoked salt, to finish

Slice off the ragged ends of the collard stems, then slice them thinly crosswise. Roll the leaves, then slice them about 1/2 inch thick, then pass your knife over them a few times to roughly chop.

Put the vegetable oil in a pan large enough to hold the leaves and stems. When warm, add the onion, collard stems, and pepper flakes and cook over medium heat for 5 minutes. Stir in the cumin, allspice, and rice, cook everything together for about a minute, then add the collard leaves and salt. Using tongs, pick up the onion and greens and turn them over to more or less blend them, then add 1 cup water and cover the pot. Cook over low heat until the rice is done and the leaves are tender, about 25 minutes. Stir in the coconut butter or ghee, cover, and let stand for 10 minutes to steam. Serve with smoked salt.

With Coconut–Sweet Potatoes: You can give this dish more focus by using it as a base for the Coconut Pan–Roasted Sweet Potatoes on page 386. Orange–fleshed varieties give it some brightness, too. (V)

Kale with Garlicky Sesame Sauce

The sauce is robust enough to stand up to any substantial green—kale, collards, chard, broccoli leaves. You'll need at least 2 large bunches for four people, as all greens cook down considerably. I like roasted sesame paste, as the roasting gives the sauce one more layer of flavor. But plain tahini is fine as well. Serves 4 (V)

2 bunches kale, collards, or other greens

Sea salt

1 plump clove garlic

1 tablespoon tahini or roasted sesame paste

1 1/2 tablespoons olive oil

1 tablespoons yogurt, either thick or thin

Juice of 1/2 lemon

Strip the leaves from their ropy stems. Discard the stems, coarsely chop the leaves, then cook them in just a small amount of water and a few pinches salt until wilted and tender, about 5 minutes, depending on the variety of green. Take a taste to be sure they're as done as you like.

While the greens are cooking, mash the garlic with a few pinches of salt in a mortar until creamy, then work in the remaining ingredients to obtain a thick sauce.

When the greens are done, drain them, then toss while warm with the sauce. Taste and check for salt, adding more if need be. Serve warm or at room temperature.

Kale with Olives

Serves 2 to 3 (V)

1 bunch kale, green or Red Russian, stems and ribs removed

2 to 4 tablespoons olive oil

1/3 cup pitted kalamata olives, coarsely chopped

1/4 teaspoon red pepper flakes

Sea salt

1 lemon, quartered

Simmer the kale leaves, as described in the preceding recipe, until tender, about 10 minutes. Drain and press out excess moisture with the back of a spoon. Toss immediately with the oil, olives, pepper flakes, and salt to taste. Serve with the lemon wedges.

Braised Collards or Turnip Greens

This is my approximation of Southern greens. After some practice, I've settled on brown butter or ghee to give them their special taste, although it's not the traditional flavor that bacon provides. Smoked salt, however, can give that hint of smoke, especially if you're vegan. Serves 4 to 6 (V)

4 bunches collards or turnip greens, long stems and tough ribs removed

1/4 cup Brown Butter (page 28), ghee, or sesame oil

1 onion, diced

2 cloves garlic, thinly sliced

1/2 teaspoon red pepper flakes

1 teaspoon sea salt

Smoked salt, optional, for serving

Pepper Sauce (page 65), for serving

Wilt the greens (see page 341), cooking them for 10 minutes, then transfer to a bowl. Reserve 1/2 cup of the cooking water. Heat the butter with the onion, garlic, and pepper flakes in a wide skillet over medium heat, stirring occasionally, until the garlic is lightly colored and the onion is soft. Add the greens, their reserved cooking water, and the salt. Cook for 30 minutes and taste again for salt. They can use a lot. Serve with the smoked salt and sauce on the side.

Collards with Pepper Sauce: Cook two bunches collard greens, 1 1/2 to 2 pounds, as for Wilted Greens (page 341). Coarsely chop or leave in large pieces, then toss with 2 to 3 tablespoons olive oil, sea salt to taste, and a dash of Pepper Sauce (page 65). Serves 4 (V)

Collards with Peanuts: Cook the simmered collards (preceding recipe) briefly in roasted peanut oil, then toss with chopped Roasted Chile–Peanuts (page 80). (V)

Wilted Greens with Crisped Bread Crumbs

Crisped bread crumbs accomplish the same thing as bacon bits—they provide a contrast of texture and bites of intensity. Roasted chopped nuts, especially peanuts, are also good for crunch—and flavor. Serves 4 (V)

1/2 cup coarse fresh bread crumbs

1 tablespoon butter or olive oil

2 bunches greens, trimmed and washed

2 tablespoons olive, roasted peanut, or coconut oil

Sea salt and freshly milled pepper

Sauté the crumbs in the butter in a small skillet until crisp and golden. Meanwhile, wilt the greens as described on page 341, then drain. Toss with oil and season with salt and pepper. Serve with the bread crumbs sprinkled over the top.

Greens with Potatoes

This is a homey, unpretentious-looking dish but one that's full of taste and comforting. All greens are good with potatoes. Serves 4 (V)

4 yellow-fleshed potatoes, about 1 pound

Sea salt

1 to 2 pounds greens, trimmed and coarsely chopped

2 tablespoons olive oil, plus best oil for drizzling

1 large clove garlic, thinly sliced

1/2 teaspoon red pepper flakes

2 tomatoes, if in season, peeled and diced

Cover the potatoes with cold water, add salt to taste, and bring to a boil. Cook until tender, about 25 minutes. Drain, then peel and coarsely chop. Wilt the greens as described on page 341 until tender, then drain. You may need to do this in two batches. Heat the oil in the skillet with the garlic and pepper flakes. When you can smell the garlic, add the greens, potatoes, and tomatoes. Cook over medium heat, breaking up the potatoes with a fork and mashing them into the greens to make a kind of rough hash. Taste for salt and serve with olive oil drizzled over the top.

Kale with Cannellini Beans

Adding white beans to greens makes a hearty, unpretentious, and fast supper. Serve with or over Garlic–Rubbed Crostini (page 24) or topped with bread crumbs crisped in olive oil. Serves 2 to 4 Ⓥ

1¹/₂ to 2 pounds kale or mixed greens, stems and ribs removed

1 small onion, finely diced

2 to 3 tablespoons olive oil

2 plump cloves garlic, minced

Pinch red pepper flakes

2 teaspoons chopped rosemary

¹/₂ cup dry white wine

1¹/₂ cups cooked cannellini beans or 1 (15-ounce) can

Sea salt and freshly milled pepper

Freshly grated parmesan, optional

Cook the kale, as described on page 342, in salted water until tender, 7 to 10 minutes. Drain, reserving the cooking water, and chop the leaves. In a large skillet, sauté the onion in the oil with the garlic, pepper flakes, and rosemary for about 3 minutes. Add the wine and cook until it's reduced to a syrupy sauce. Add the beans, kale, and enough cooking water to keep the mixture loose. Heat through, taste for salt and season with pepper, and serve with a generous dusting of parmesan.

ACID TIP FOR GREENS

A splash of vinegar or a squeeze of lemon is often the secret element that brings a dish to life by heightening all the other flavors. This is true even with foods that are naturally strong tasting, like the more aggressive greens. That squeeze of lemon or light dousing of vinegar magically sweetens, softens, and sharpens, making everything taste better. A bit of hot chile will do the same. In fact, pepper sauce, the ubiquitous seasoning of the South, neatly combines both elements in a single jar.

Mashed Potatoes with Kale and Green Onions (Colcannon)

A variation on one of Ireland's many potato dishes, this is a perennial favorite in our house. Colcannon is usually made with cabbage, but it takes readily to kale and other greens, too. Amounts are flexible. You can use a lot more kale than a bunch of 10 leaves if you wish. Serves 4 to 6

1¹/₂ pounds russet potatoes, rinsed and peeled

Sea salt

1 or more bunches of kale, any variety

1 bunch green onions, including a few inches of the greens, thinly slivered

6 tablespoons butter, or more to taste

Freshly milled pepper

Cut the potatoes into chunks, put them in a pan with cold water to cover, add salt, and bring to a boil. Lower the heat and simmer, covered, until the potatoes are tender and starting to break apart. Drain the water into a bowl, then return the potatoes to the pan and let sit, covered, to steam for a few minutes.

While the potatoes are cooking, which takes about 25 minutes, strip the kale from its inedible stems, then steam or simmer in a small amount of water with a pinch of salt until tender, about 7 to 10 minutes. Tip the kale into a strainer, press out excess moisture, then turn it onto a cutting board and chop it finely.

Pound the potatoes with a masher, adding some of the reserved cooking liquid as needed to help break them down and render them creamy. When fairly smooth, add the onions and kale and continue to mash together to break up the kale. Taste for salt, season with pepper, and add the butter. Serve right away or keep the colcannon warm in a double boiler.

Colcannon with Parsnips: Darina Allen, in her book *Irish Traditional Cooking*, includes a variation from Dublin that mixes parsnips with the potatoes in equal amounts with the kale. The parsnips cook right along with the potatoes, cores removed first. For that matter, all root vegetables are delicious with potatoes, from celery root to Jerusalem artichokes to rutabagas.

Mixed Greens with Cumin and Paprika

Everyone seems to love greens cooked this way, warm or cold as a salad. Be sure to use at least one assertive green for character. Serves 3 or 4 (V)

12 heaping cups mixed greens—kale, broccoli rabe, chard or beet, escarole, mustard greens

4 large cloves garlic

1/2 teaspoon sea salt

1 cup chopped parsley

1 cup chopped cilantro

3 tablespoons olive oil

2 teaspoons paprika

2 teaspoons ground cumin

For garnish: oil-cured black olives, wedges of lemon, tomato

Discard any inedible parts of the greens, such as kale stems and tough ribs. Cook the leaves in a little water— the tougher ones on the bottom—until tender. Or boil each type separately in salted water, then drain. Chop into pieces about 1 inch square.

Pound the garlic with the salt in a mortar until smooth, then work in the parsley and cilantro and pound them briefly to release their flavors.

Warm the oil with the paprika and cumin in a wide skillet over medium heat until they release their fragrances. Don't let them burn. Stir in the garlic mixture, then add the greens and cook until any extra moisture has evaporated. Taste for salt. Pile into a dish and garnish with the olives, lemon, and tomato.

FIVE IDEAS FOR LEFTOVER GREENS

- Toss them with chickpeas, pasta, diced tomatoes, and freshly grated parmesan.
- Toss them with boiled, diced potatoes and mix in a little grated Gruyère. Or stir them into mashed potatoes.
- Mix finely chopped cooked greens with cooked rice, barley, quinoa, or pasta.
- Add greens to potato, lentil, and bean soups at the end of the cooking.
- Chop and combine greens with feta, ricotta salata, or Gruyère, black olives, and capers and use them to fill empanadas or spread over toast.

Jerusalem Artichokes (Sunchokes)

A true American native, the Jerusalem artichoke is neither from Jerusalem nor an artichoke. A more accurate name is sunchoke, because these tubers form beneath a sunflower. They have a sweet, nutty flavor. They're delightfully crisp, like water chestnuts, but during cooking they can quickly and unpredictably turn mushy, so they demand a watchful eye.

The knob-shaped variety is most widely available and usually comes trimmed into more or less uniform pieces. Look for firm, unblemished tubers and store them in a plastic bag in the refrigerator for up to 2 weeks. Scrub them vigorously rather than peel them. Jerusalem artichokes can be eaten raw, cooked in winter soups and stews, roasted, and sautéed. They can also be difficult to digest, so start out eating them gradually. Avoid cooking them in cast iron, which causes them to discolor. One pound is enough for four to six servings.

Roasted Jerusalem Artichokes

Serves 4 to 6 (V)

1 pound Jerusalem artichokes, sliced into ¹/₂-inch rounds or left whole
1 to 2 tablespoons sunflower seed oil
¹/₂ teaspoon sea salt
A few rosemary or thyme sprigs
Freshly milled pepper

Preheat the oven to 400°F. Toss the Jerusalem artichokes with the oil and salt. Bake them in a shallow gratin dish with the herb for 20 to 30 minutes. Pierce them with the tip of a knife—they should be mostly tender but offer some resistance. Season with pepper.

Sautéed Jerusalem Artichokes with Sunflower Seeds

Serves 4 to 6 (V)

1 pound Jerusalem artichokes, sliced into ¹/₄-inch rounds
2 tablespoons sunflower seed oil
Sea salt and freshly milled pepper

3 tablespoons toasted sunflower seeds
2 tablespoons chopped parsley
1 teaspoon chopped thyme

Sauté the Jerusalem artichokes in the oil in a large skillet over high heat until lightly browned and tender but still a bit crisp. Taste them as they cook; they can be done in 5 minutes or as long as 10. Season with salt and pepper, add the sunflower seeds, parsley, and thyme, and toss well.

Wine-Glazed Jerusalem Artichokes with Rosemary

Serves 4 (V)

1¹/₂ tablespoons olive oil
1 pound Jerusalem artichokes, sliced into rounds
1 clove garlic, finely chopped
Sea salt and freshly milled pepper
2 teaspoons chopped rosemary
¹/₂ cup dry white wine

Heat the oil in a wide skillet. Add the Jerusalem artichokes and garlic and sauté for about 1¹/₂ minutes. Season with salt and pepper, add the rosemary and wine, and continue to cook over high heat until the wine is reduced to a few tablespoons. Add 1 tablespoon water, cover, and cook for a minute more or until tender-crisp. (Although they can turn mushy in an instant, it can also take as long as 10 minutes before they're done.) Boil the excess liquid, if any, down to a glaze.

Kohlrabi

With stems branching out of purple or green globes, kohlrabi is a strange-looking vegetable. Harvested small, it's mild and sweet, like a young turnip, and altogether pleasant. It's available in summer and fall and sometimes in winter. Look for small, firm vegetables with purple or pale green skin just slightly larger than a golf ball. Keep stored in a plastic bag in the refrigerator until ready to use.

Kohlrabi can be prepared any way turnips are. It's delicious sliced into thin wedges and sprinkled with sea salt or grated into salads. The leaves are also edible and can be used in any of the preceding greens recipes. To cook, cut it in quarters, rounds, or matchsticks, then steam it. Kohlrabi goes well with butter, sour cream, dill, mustard, horseradish, and various seeds and spices. A pound will serve four.

Kohlrabi with Horseradish

Serves 4

- 4 or 5 kohlrabi, about 1 pound, peeled unless small and tender
- 2 to 4 tablespoons crème fraîche or sour cream
- Prepared horseradish in vinegar
- 2 teaspoons chopped dill
- Sea salt and freshly milled pepper

Slice the kohlrabi into julienne strips or wedges. Steam until tender, 5 to 8 minutes, then transfer to a bowl and toss with the crème fraîche, horseradish, and dill. Season with salt and pepper to taste.

Roasted Kohlrabi

This couldn't be simpler. It's fairly plain, but roasting always concentrates the flavors in vegetables, making them, somehow, just better. Kohlrabi is neutral enough that it can be finished with a variety of seeds and spices, as suggested below.
Serves 4 Ⓥ

- 4 to 6 small kohlrabi, green or purple
- Olive oil, for coating
- Sea salt and freshly milled pepper
- For garnish: smoked paprika, Malden sea salt, grated Parmesan cheese, toasted sesame seeds, toasted fennel seeds, mustard

Heat the oven to 425°F.

Peel the kohlrabi and slice it into rounds about $3/8$ inch thick. Toss them with oil to coat lightly and season with a few pinches of salt and pepper. Lay them on a baking sheet in a single layer and bake until lightly browned, 15 to 20 minutes, turning them once or twice so that they brown fairly evenly. Remove and toss with any of the suggested garnishes, then serve.

Leeks and Green Onions

Delicate-flavored leeks are becoming increasingly available. Milder and more subtle than onions, leeks are also more costly. When I say "leek or onion" in a recipe, it's mainly to spare you the expense or bother of trying to find leeks where they're unavailable. But when a dish is based on leeks, it should be made with them. Green onions, which are also tender and mild, and nearly always inexpensive, can be used in some of the ways that leeks are—especially in soups. Use their greens—they're the nutritious part.

WHAT TO LOOK FOR: The edible part of the leek is the white part (the shank) plus an inch or two of pale green. With green onions, it's the white plus whatever greens are firm and crisp. The roots and leaves of both are excellent for stocks. Some varieties of leek have a short, stubby shank while others are very long. You'll want leeks that have the largest proportion of white to green. The more tender the leek, the more suitable it is for braising or grilling. Very large leeks are better for soups and stews. When overmature, they develop a tough core at their centers, which can go into a soup stock.

HOW TO STORE: Store leeks and green onions in a plastic bag in the vegetable bin for a week. If the outer leaves turn yellowish, just strip them off; usually the rest will be edible.

HOW TO USE: Leeks can be served as salads, grilled, or featured in soups, stews, gratins, savory galettes, and tarts. When scarce, they can be stretched with green onions. Green onions are delicious stewed, grilled, and used raw as a seasoning. They make an excellent base for a soup in place of onions.

SPECIAL HANDLING: Perhaps due to new growing techniques, leeks are cleaner than in the past. But traditionally leeks do have a lot of sand and dirt lodged between their leaves. They need to be washed thoroughly but gently. Cut off the greens an inch above the white part and slice off the roots, leaving a thin piece attached so that the leaves remain joined at the base. Halve the leeks lengthwise down to an inch from the root end or all the way through. Swish them back and forth several times in a sink full of water to loosen the dirt, then soak for 15 minutes. Rinse under gently running water. Fan the leaves open so that the water can get to the base. Wash chopped leeks after cutting.

When using leeks at the start of a recipe, as a soup base for example, don't brown them as you would onions or they'll lose the delicacy that sets them apart. They don't caramelize well.

Green onions need only be trimmed of their roots and flabby greens, then rinsed.

QUANTITY: For a vegetable dish, plan on one medium leek, trimmed, per person. One pound of trimmed leeks yields four servings or about 4 cups chopped, 2 cups cooked. A bunch of green onions weighing 4 to 6 ounces, trimmed of most of its greens, yields about 1 cup chopped.

Good Partners for Leeks and Green Onions

Butter, olive oil, hazelnut oil, cream, crème fraîche
Parmesan, goat cheese, Gruyère, cheddar
Capers, wine, olives, mustard, curry spices
Thyme, parsley, chervil, tarragon, fines herbes, saffron
Potatoes, fennel, celery, eggs

Sauces and Seasonings for Leeks and Green Onions

Romesco Sauce (page 62)
Garlic Mayonnaise (page 52) or Tarragon Mayonnaise with Capers (page 52)
Green herb sauces (pages 48 to 51)
Mustard Vinaigrette (page 167)
Herb-Butter and Olive Oil Sauce (page 44)

Steamed Leeks: Allow 1 or 2 leeks per person. Halve them lengthwise, leaving the root end intact, and wash well. Steam them, cut sides down, until tender when pierced with the tip of a knife, 15 to 20 minutes, depending on their size. Remove to a platter and dress with olive oil or one of the suggested sauces. (V)

Gratinéed Leeks: You can set these leeks up in advance of baking. Steam or braise 8 to 12 small leeks, then put them in a lightly buttered baking dish. Add 1/2 cup cream, season with sea salt and white pepper, and cover with 2 tablespoons freshly grated parmesan cheese. Bake at 400°F until bubbling and browned, about 20 minutes.

Grilled Leeks: Slice trimmed leeks in half lengthwise and rinse well. Steam them, cut side down, until barely tender, then brush with olive oil and season with sea salt. Grill on both sides until light grill marks appear, turning as necessary. Serve with olive oil mixed with finely chopped parsley or chervil spooned over the leeks, Mustard Vinaigrette (page 167) or Romesco Sauce (page 62) on the side. (V)

Braised Leeks

Serve warm alone or as a side dish. Serves 4 (V)

2 teaspoons sea salt
Aromatics: 2 bay leaves, 6 parsley sprigs,
    3 thyme sprigs, 1/2 teaspoon peppercorns
2 carrots, thinly sliced
1 celery rib, sliced
4 leeks, trimmed, halved, and rinsed
Butter or olive oil, to finish
Chopped herbs—fines herbs, chives, marjoram, tarragon,
    or parsley—to finish
Freshly milled pepper

Bring 12 cups water to a simmer in a deep skillet or Dutch oven with the salt, aromatics, carrots, and celery. Slip the leeks into the pan and cook gently until tender when pierced with a knife, 15 to 25 minutes. Lift them out and arrange them, cut side up, on a platter. Glide a piece of butter over the top or drizzle with olive oil, then cover lightly with herbs and season with salt and pepper. Or serve with any of the suggested sauces and seasonings. The cooking liquid makes an excellent broth for risotto and soups.

Grilled Leeks with Parmesan and Olive Crostini

A perfect first course for an elegant light lunch. Serves 4

8 Grilled Leeks (opposite)
Thin shavings of parmesan or Gruyère
8 crostini spread with Olive Paste (page 78)
2 hard-cooked eggs, quartered
Chopped parsley or chervil, to finish
Sea salt and freshly milled pepper

Arrange two grilled leeks on individual plates, lay the cheese shavings over them, and place two small olive crostini and two egg quarters on each plate. Sprinkle parsley over all and season with salt and pepper.

Leeks Simmered in Wine

Use three or four very thin leeks per person or two larger ones, about an inch across. Serves 4 (V)

2 tablespoons butter or olive oil
8 leeks, about an inch in diameter, trimmed, halved
    lengthwise and rinsed
1/2 cup dry white wine
1/2 teaspoon sea salt
Aromatics: 2 bay leaves, 6 parsley sprigs, 3 thyme sprigs,
    1/2 teaspoon peppercorns
Freshly milled pepper
Chopped chervil, tarragon, or parsley, for garnish

In a skillet that will hold the leeks comfortably, heat the butter over medium heat. Add the leeks and cook until they begin to color a little. Add the wine and cook until it's reduced by half, then add 2 cups water, the salt, and aromatics. Simmer, partially covered, until the leeks are tender, 10 to 20 minutes. Transfer them to a platter. Continue cooking the liquid until it's the consistency of light syrup, then pour it through a strainer over the leeks. Season with salt and pepper and garnish with the chopped herb.

Mushrooms

Being a fungus rather than a true vegetable, mushrooms are different from the rest of the plants we eat. But they're highly prized for their woodsy flavor, and they're versatile, quick to prepare, and exceptionally satisfying.

TYPES OF MUSHROOMS: A mixture of cultivated mushrooms and exotics is affordable and makes standard mushroom dishes more exciting. In some places, it's possible to buy fresh wild mushrooms. Like their dried counterparts, they bring an exquisite note to any dish.

White Mushrooms: Also called *domestic, brown, cultivated, button* when small, *stuffers* when large, these are our everyday mushrooms. Buying them loose is preferable unless they look particularly fresh in their packages.

Cremini: Also called *Italian field mushrooms,* cremini are similar to white mushrooms but a little rounder and larger with tan or brown caps.

Enoki: Little clusters of pale, skinny mushrooms, these make a pretty garnish for miso and other clear soups.

King Oyster: With long, wide pale stems and small beige caps, these unusual-looking mushrooms can be found in Asian markets and occasionally at farmers' markets. If overcooked they can get tough, so it's best to cook them slowly and gently for a short time. When brushed with a marinade and seared, grilled, or roasted in the oven, they take on a rich burnished-brown glaze that makes them look gorgeous and very meaty. I cook them alone but then add them to stir-fries or to a plate of sautéed Asian greens or spinach.

Oyster: Pale, clustered mushrooms joined at the base. They have a delicate flavor and can be combined with other mushrooms or enjoyed alone. Discard the tough stems.

Portabellas: A giant with a smooth brown cap, thick stem, and black gills. Large enough to grill and stuff. Use the stems in stocks. Scoop out and discard the gills.

Shiitake: Long enjoyed as Japanese or Chinese dried mushrooms, shiitake are now available fresh. The flesh is tight and the flavor is pronounced. Discard the tough, knotty stems or use them in stocks.

WHAT TO LOOK FOR: All mushrooms should be firm, have a sweet earthy smell, and be pleasant to touch—dry and firm, never slimy. Lots of cooks prefer market mushrooms with their caps tightly closed, but the mushroom flavor actually deepens as they age and the caps open. If open, the gills should look fresh—especially in portabellas. If the gills are matted down with moisture, they're likely to have a funky smell, which can affect the taste. Give them a whiff before using. Portabellas are large enough that you can simply scrape off the gills. At the other extreme, excessive dryness doesn't mean they're spoiled, although such mushrooms aren't so attractive. Shiitakes are sometimes like this—but they revive when cooked, have more flavor, and make an excellent contribution to stocks.

HOW TO STORE: Store fresh mushrooms in a closed paper bag or in their cardboard container, the plastic replaced with a barely damp paper towel. You can keep them in a perforated plastic bag for 1 or 2 days. Much longer and they begin to turn a little slimy.

HOW TO USE: Mushrooms can be sautéed, marinated, grilled, broiled, cooked in parchment, added to stuffings, or stuffed themselves. They're wonderful cooked simply, and they provide the basis for many stews and soups. They also make fine salads and sandwiches and are a common element in stir-fries. Except for shiitake and portabella mushrooms, the stems can be cooked along with the caps.

SPECIAL HANDLING: To clean, wipe off domestic mushrooms with a damp cloth or plunge them into a basin of water, run your hands over them, and drain quickly. Portabellas should just be wiped. Enoki and oyster mushrooms don't usually need any cleaning. I slice the gills off portabellas before cooking since they bleed a dark juice into the dish.

For good color, sauté mushrooms in a roomy skillet over high heat. They quickly absorb any fat but eventually release it along with their juices, then brown.

QUANTITY: Allow 1 pound for four small servings or two main-dish servings.

Good Partners for Mushrooms

Butter, sour cream, cream, olive oil, toasted sesame oil

Garlic, parsley, lemon, rosemary, tarragon, cumin, paprika

Pine nuts, bread crumbs

Wine, sherry, Madeira

Onions, potatoes, leeks, barley, rice

Sautéed Mushrooms with Garlic and Parsley

Very simple and fast, this is one of the most basic—and best— ways to cook mushrooms. Mushrooms are delicious cooked in either butter or olive oil—or a mixture of both. Serves 4 Ⓥ

1 pound mushrooms, one or several varieties, cleaned

3 to 5 tablespoons butter, olive oil, or a mixture

Sea salt and freshly milled pepper

1/2 lemon

2 tablespoons chopped parsley

1 large clove garlic, minced

Cut the mushrooms into halves, quarters, or slices about 1/4 inch thick. Melt the butter in a wide skillet over high heat. Add the mushrooms all at once and immediately move them around the pan so they all pick up a little of the fat. Keep sautéing even though the pan appears to be dry. Once the mushrooms yield their juices and then reabsorb them, they'll begin to color nicely. When golden, season well with salt and pepper. Add a squeeze of lemon, then toss with the parsley and garlic and serve.

Roasted Mushrooms with Pine Nuts

Roasting concentrates the earthy-woodsy flavor of mushrooms. Pine nuts are always good with mushrooms, but especially when roasted. Serves 4 Ⓥ

1 pound cremini or large white mushrooms, sliced 1/3 inch thick

Sea salt and freshly milled pepper

2 to 3 tablespoons olive oil

3 tablespoons chopped parsley

2 cloves garlic

2 pinches red pepper flakes

3 tablespoons toasted pine nuts

Preheat the oven to 400°F. Put the mushrooms in a wide, shallow baking dish, season with salt and pepper, and toss with the oil. Bake until sizzling, about 25 minutes. Meanwhile, chop the parsley and garlic together. When the mushrooms are done, toss them with the parsley mixture and pepper flakes. Scatter the pine nuts over the top and serve.

INTERESTING MUSHROOM CUTS

Instead of cutting mushrooms into even halves or quarters or slicing them in parallel lines, angle your knife to make the cuts irregular. Doing this reveals the interesting shapes and markings that even the most common mushrooms have, giving them more panache on the plate.

Mushrooms, Tarragon, and Cream

A great dish to know when you need something in a hurry. Mushrooms on toast are the best with that good crunch of the toast, but there's no reason not to consider polenta, noodles, or a favorite grain as accompaniments. Serves 2 to 4

2 tablespoons butter

1 pound mushrooms, sliced at an angle, about ¹/₂ inch thick

Sea salt and freshly milled pepper

¹/₂ cup dry white wine

¹/₄ cup cream

¹/₄ cup crème fraîche or sour cream

2 tablespoons chopped parsley

1 clove garlic

2 teaspoons chopped tarragon

Heat the butter in a large skillet over high heat, add the mushrooms, and sauté until they're nicely colored. Season with salt and pepper, add the wine, lower the heat, and simmer until the wine is reduced by half. Add the cream and crème fraîche and simmer until thickened slightly. Chop the parsley, garlic, and tarragon together, add them to the mushrooms, and serve.

Mushrooms with Sherry or Maderia: In place of the wine, add ¹/₃ cup of dry sherry or Madeira. This is a little old fashioned, but good nonetheless. Use toasted pine nuts as a garnish, if you have them.

USING DRIED MUSHROOMS TO ENHANCE FLAVOR

The unique flavor of dried wild mushrooms enhances all mushroom sautés and ragouts. Use ¹/₂ ounce or even more if you have them. Cover them with warm water and set them aside to soak anywhere from 15 minutes to several hours. Drain but reserve the flavorful water. Chop the mushrooms and sauté them with fresh ones; use the liquid, carefully decanted, in place of stock or water in your dish.

Oyster Mushrooms in Parchment

Cooking in parchment conserves and concentrates the delicate flavors of these mushrooms. I have found truly gorgeous looking (and tasting) oyster mushrooms at farmers' markets. Serves 4 Ⓥ

1 pound oyster or other mushrooms

2 cloves garlic, minced

1 tablespoon finely chopped parsley

1 teaspoon chopped tarragon

2 tablespoons olive oil or butter

Juice of ¹/₂ lemon

Sea salt and freshly ground white pepper

Preheat the oven to 400°F. Separate the oyster mushrooms at the base. (If using market or other mushrooms, thinly slice them.) Toss the mushrooms with the garlic, parsley, tarragon, and olive oil, then season with the lemon juice and salt and pepper to taste.

Cut four 12-inch squares of parchment paper. Spoon a quarter of the mushrooms on the lower half of each piece of parchment. Fold the top over and twist and crease the edges together to make a half-moon shape. Place the packages on a sheet pan and bake 8 to 10 minutes. Serve, letting each diner open his or her own packet to enjoy the aroma.

Pan-Seared Portabella Mushrooms

Portabellas seared in a cast-iron skillet have the taste of grilled mushrooms. Enjoy them as a side dish, spooned over Garlic-Rubbed Crostini (page 24), in a sandwich, or on a bed of spinach. Serves 1 or 2 Ⓥ

1 large portabella mushroom, about 8 ounces, stem removed

Olive oil, for brushing

Sea salt and freshly milled pepper

Shallot Vinaigrette (page 165), sherry vinegar, or balsamic vinegar

Remove the gills, slice the cap ¹/₂ inch thick at an angle so that you'll have plenty of surface area, then brush both sides of each slice lightly with oil. Set a cast-iron skillet over high heat, film it thinly with oil, then add the mushroom slices. Sear for 4 to 5 minutes, then turn and sear the second side. Eventually they will begin to brown. Remove them to a platter and season with salt and pepper. Brush with vinaigrette or drizzle a few drops of vinegar over the top.

Grilled Portabella Mushrooms: These meaty mushroom slices are wonderful tucked into a sandwich or simply eaten by themselves. You can turn them into a substantial entrée by placing a whole cap over a mound of braised or sautéed greens. Carefully remove the stems and gills from 1 pound (two large) portabella mushrooms and wipe the caps. Chop 3 tablespoons parsley, 1 teaspoon dried oregano, and 2 cloves garlic together and stir into $1/4$ cup olive oil. Brush part of this mixture over the mushrooms, then grill until the mushrooms begin to brown and are soft to the touch, 8 to 10 minutes on each side. Slice the mushrooms on a slant to expose a wide band of flesh, then pile them on a platter, season with salt and pepper, and drizzle with the remaining parsley mixture. (V)

Grilled Baby Bella Mushrooms

These can be a side dish, served whole or sliced, or you can fill the caps with a mound of braised spinach to make a more focused main. Serves 4 to 6 (V)

6 baby bella or 4 full-size portabella mushrooms

$1/4$ cup parsley leaves

1 clove garlic

$1/4$ teaspoon sea salt

2 teaspoons fresh oregano, marjoram, or tarragon

6 tablespoons olive oil

Wipe the mushroom caps clean. Carefully dislodge the stems. If the gills are open, scrape them away with a spoon.

Finely chop the parsley with the garlic, salt, and oregano, then stir that into the olive oil. Brush $1/4$ cup of the oil over the caps and the insides of the mushrooms.

Grill over a medium-hot fire until the mushrooms have browned and are tender to the touch, about 8 to 10 minutes on each side. When done, slice the mushrooms at a slant to exposed a wide band of flesh, then pile them on a platter, season with salt and pepper, and drizzle over the remaining 2 tablespoons oil.

Pan-Grilled King Oyster Mushrooms with Toasted Sesame and Chives

These can of course be cooked over a wood fire or gas grill, too. They're good served with sautéed choy sum or seared tofu. Serves 4

2 or 3 king oyster mushrooms

1 heaping tablespoon white miso

2 tablespoons Ohsawa soy sauce

1 tablespoon rice wine vinegar

2 teaspoons sugar, or 1 teaspoon agave

Light sesame, peanut, or coconut oil

1 teaspoon toasted sesame seeds

Snipped chives, for garnish

A few pinches red pepper flakes

Slice the mushrooms lengthwise about $1/2$ inch thick or a little less.

Mix the miso with the soy sauce to form a paste, then work in the vinegar, sugar, and $1/4$ water. Brush the mushrooms on both sides with the sauce. There should be some remaining.

Heat a grill pan over medium-high heat until hot. Brush the pan with oil, then add the mushrooms. Lower the heat to medium and cook on both sides until burnished and tender, about 4 minutes in all. When they're about done, turn off the heat and add the remaining dressing. Arrange the mushrooms on a platter sprinkle with the sesame seeds, chives, and red pepper flakes, and serve.

Garnished with Shiso: If you have a bunch of deep purple shiso leaves, use them. They make a handsome garnish to a plate of these mushrooms, and so would plum-colored basil leaves.

Sautéed Mushrooms with Spinach and Pepper

This is one of those utterly simple dishes that's so easily made it should be part of everyone's repertoire. It makes a fine side dish, but mounded on an English muffin or toasted country bread, it quickly becomes an informal main dish. It's the butter that nudges it toward excellence, but you can make quite a good dish with olive oil, too. Serves 2 to 4 Ⓥ

- **4 tablespoons butter or olive oil**
- **8 ounces white mushrooms, sliced 1/4 inch thick**
- **Sea salt and freshly milled pepper**
- **1 clove garlic, slivered**
- **1 hefty bunch spinach, about a pound, stems removed, leaves washed but not dried**

Melt 2 tablespoons of the butter in a roomy skillet, add the mushrooms, and cook over high heat until they've released their juices and browned, about 6 minutes. Season with salt and plenty of pepper and set aside on a plate.

Return the pan to the heat and add the remaining 2 tablespoons butter and the garlic. When the butter is foaming, add the spinach, sprinkle with salt, and cook until tender and most of the liquid has evaporated, about 4 minutes. Return the mushrooms to the pan and toss with the spinach. Taste for salt and check to be sure everything is good and peppery.

Wild Mushrooms and Truffles

Wild mushrooms are a joy to cook with because they bring such exotic flavors to the table. They have so much character, in fact, that just a few go far, effectively flavoring eggs, soufflés, soups, and pasta. Though our fields and forests are full of these prizes, it's safest to procure those brought to local markets by knowledgeable foragers. If they're too pricey, stretch them by mixing them with more neutral white mushrooms. Should you find yourself with a bounty, however, you can use them in any of the recipes given for white varieties.

Choose wild mushrooms that are neither too dry nor too heavy with moisture—full and plump with a firm texture. Store them in the refrigerator, spread out on a tray and covered with a barely damp cloth, until ready to use.

PORCINI: *Boletus edulis*, whose Italian name is *porcini* and French name is *cèpe*, also grows in American forests and is often called a *bolete*. Looking a little like a large bun with silky grayish tan skin and dense white meat, this mushroom is truly impressive, whether fresh or dried. Instead of having gills, the bottom surface of this mushroom resembles a sponge. It should be pale and firm. Porcini enjoy an erratic season during the summer and fall months that's tied closely to the rains. Before using them, brush off any dirt and cut out any areas where bugs or needles have bored. Fresh porcini can be cut into thick slabs and grilled, sautéed, stewed, roasted—essentially cooked any way white market mushrooms are. Extras can be sliced and set on a tray to dry or dried in a dehydrator. Dried porcini are available in many groceries and specialty stores. Their price per pound is startling, but it takes just 1/2 ounce or so to add their magic to a dish.

CHANTERELLES: Mostly golden-orange in color (but there are also black ones), chanterelles can range in size from a large carpet tack to a tiger lily, which their shape resembles. Their scent is sweet and fruity, almost like apricots or spices, and their seasons are spring, late summer, and fall. They often throw off quite a lot of liquid during cooking; simply strain it off and continue cooking the mushrooms until they're done. Use the juice to flavor sauces or soups. You can dry them or freeze cooked chanterelles in their cooking liquid. They can also be purchased dried.

MORELS: Distinguished by their honeycombed surface, these comely mushrooms look like they stepped out of a fairy tale. Since they're mainly a spring mushroom, they're often paired with asparagus, fiddlehead ferns, and peas. Their flavor may remind you of very lightly smoked tea as well as the woods. They're lovely to cook whole, but cut a few open first to see if they're really clean. If not, you might want to slice them lengthwise instead and shake or pick out the forest debris. Dried morels are also available.

TRUFFLES: Nothing has quite the haunting perfume of truffles. They're extremely expensive but also one of the greatest pleasures to cook with and eat. Many traditional recipes that feature truffles are simple—truffles are sliced thinly over eggs, risotto, polenta, and other such humble foods whose simplicity sets off the splendor of the truffle to its fullest.

Italian white truffles and French black ones from Perigord are considered the best, and I would be happy with either. There are some American truffles, but they don't really compare to the European ones. A truffle for Christmas Day is better than any turkey. Store your truffle in a bowl of risotto rice and bury some eggs in it as well. The scent will penetrate both, and you can enjoy truffled eggs and risotto as well as the truffle itself. In lieu of fresh truffles, you can buy them jarred. They can be good, but they never seem to have the elusive quality of the fresh ones. Truffle salt also offers an affordable way to utilize their flavor.

Okra

A long, pointed pod with fine ridges extending the length of its body, okra's other name, lady fingers, suggests the refinement of its shape. Its African name, *gombo*, recalls okra's best-known role in the dish of the same name, gumbo. By any name, okra is slippery unless deep-fried, and rather than try to ignore this fact, perhaps it's best just to admit that's how things are. Okra has its virtues—thickening gumbos or stews and binding vegetable juices into a sauce—but crisp texture isn't one of them.

Look for green or red pods 2 to 3 inches long. This isn't just a nicety—larger okra can be as tough as ropes. Okra doesn't keep well for more than a few days. Keep it wrapped in paper or a plastic bag in the refrigerator; don't let it get wet, and use as soon as possible. Okra can be pickled, steamed, stewed, deep-fried, and even grilled. To keep its gumminess to a minimum, avoid cutting into the pods. A pound could feed a crowd, depending on how people feel about it, or as few as three or four.

Steamed Okra: The pods look stunning. Rinse 1 pound okra, leave them whole, and steam them for 4 to 6 minutes. Arrange them on a plate and serve warm with clarified butter to dip into and lemon wedges to squeeze over, or cold with Lemon Vinaigrette (page 164) or mayonnaise flavored with curry powder. Serves 4 to 8 ⓥ

Fried Okra: This remains one of the most popular ways to eat okra, probably because the crisp coating mitigates the slippery texture. Serve with a mayonnaise (page 51) or as a garnish for a summer stew of corn and beans. Slice 1 pound small okra into rounds about $1/4$ inch thick and toss with 1 cup fine corn meal or chickpea flour mixed with 1 teaspoon sea salt. Heat $1/2$ inch peanut oil in a heavy skillet until it's just short of smoking. Toss the okra in a large sieve to shake off the excess corn meal, then fry in small batches until golden. Transfer to paper towels to drain briefly, but serve hot. (You can also fry whole pods.) Serves 4 to 6 ⓥ

Grilled Okra: Grilling is one of the best things a person can do with okra. For ease of handling, skewer four or five pods onto two parallel skewers, like a ladder. Brush with vegetable oil and sprinkle with sea salt. Grill on both sides until lightly marked. Eat hot off the grill with a squeeze of lemon or a dash of Indian Salt with Mixed Spices (page 68), add it to a sauté of corn and tomatoes, or use to garnish a plate of black-eyed peas and rice. ⓥ

Onions

This is the workhorse vegetable in the kitchen, for there's hardly a dish that doesn't begin with onions. Onions, like leeks, also have their own role to play as a vegetable. Onions should not be overlooked, for they're generally very easy to prepare, inexpensive, and good to eat.

TYPES OF ONIONS: We see these basic onions in our markets throughout the year.

Boiling onions: Almost as big as golf balls, boiling onions, also called creaming onions, are perfect for cooking whole or slicing into small, compact rounds.

Cipolline: Slightly larger than boiling onions and disk shaped, these seasonal Italian summer onions are sweet and mild, perfect for roasting and braising.

Pearl onions: Actually little bulbettes, pearl onions are beautiful cooked whole in a vegetable braise but are time-consuming to peel.

Red or purple onions: Often disk shaped, sweet red onions are milder than white or yellow ones. They're excellent for pickles and for grilling.

Shallots: Small, brown-skinned bulbs with a mild onion flavor, shallots are sold mostly in packages of two or three and used for vinaigrettes. However, they are delicious braised and roasted, and if you find a good source at a farmers' market, by all means try them in quantity.

Sweet onions: Walla Walla, Maui, and Vidalia onions are extra sweet, low in sulfur, and juicy. They're available only when fresh, and they don't keep for much longer than a week. They are the very best onions to use for salads and sandwiches.

Torpedo onions: Long, oval onions with red flesh and brown papery skin, torpedo onions are also good for roasting and grilling.

White onions: Milder and not as sweet as yellow onions; preferred when you don't want to add more sweetness to a dish—and when affordable.

Yellow onions: The most ubiquitous cooking onions, yellow onions are readily available, inexpensive, and often very pungent but become sweet when cooked.

WHAT TO LOOK FOR: Onions should be firm and fresh-smelling with dry, papery skins. Avoid those that are sprouting or have a sooty appearance (wash them well if you've no choice), look greenish, or have woody-looking stems. Remove any sprouts inside. Freshly harvested onions are shiny and moist looking and haven't formed their papery skins. They're frequently mild and sweet in spite of their initial sulfur bite—a treat in the summer kitchen.

HOW TO STORE: Store onions in a cool, dry place where there's plenty of air circulating around them. This can be on your counter. Keep onions far from potatoes—they're incompatible and cause each other to spoil.

HOW TO USE: Onions can be sautéed, grilled, roasted, braised, pickled, stuffed, deep-fried, and cooked to a savory jam.

SPECIAL HANDLING: To keep from crying when you cut onions, use a very sharp knife and/or chill them in a bowl of cold water for 15 to 30 minutes before cutting. Always wrap cut onions well so that their smell doesn't permeate your butter and cheese—fats absorb odors. Save leftovers—chopped onions keep for a day or two in a sealed container, and having some on hand is always a great convenience when it's time to make dinner.

QUANTITY: An average medium yellow or white onion weighs between 4 and 6 ounces and yields approximately 1 cup sliced or chopped. Large onions can weigh up to 1 pound, smaller ones as little as 2 or 3 ounces. Onions can cook down to half—or less—of their volume, depending on how long they cook. As a vegetable, allow 1 pound of onions for three or four servings.

Good Partners for Onions

Butter, cream, olive oil
Rosemary, thyme, sage, bay, clove, cinnamon, chile
Vinegar, sugar, honey
Romesco Sauce (page 62)

Baked Whole Onions in Their Jackets: Allow one firm onion per person. Put them, unpeeled, in a baking dish, add $1/2$ inch water, and cover with aluminum foil. Bake at 375°F for 1 hour. Uncover and continue baking until tender when pierced with a knife, 15 to 30 minutes more, depending on the size. Cut them in half and serve them in their jackets or pull back the skins and slice off the root end. Season with sea salt, lots of freshly ground pepper, butter or olive oil, and finely minced parsley, thyme, or tarragon. (V)

Grilled Onions: One of my favorite ways to cook onions. I prefer fresh red or white onions from the farmers' market, but storage onions work well, too. Peel large onions, slice them into $1/2$-inch-thick rounds, and secure each slice with one or two toothpicks to keep the rings from separating. Brush both sides with olive oil and season with sea salt and pepper. Grill for 8 to 10 minutes, until they're nicely marked, then turn them carefully and cook the second side until well marked and softened. Arrange the onions on a platter. Serve with butter or olive oil and lots of freshly ground pepper, with a splash of your favorite vinegar, or sprinkle with ground chipotle chile. Romesco Sauce (page 62) makes a fine accompaniment, too. Leftovers make such good additions to salads and sandwiches that it's worth planning for extras. (V)

A QUICK VINEGAR SAUCE FOR ONIONS

Vinegar has a keen affinity for onions. Serve this sauce with baked or grilled onions or over an onion frittata. Melt 3 tablespoons butter in a small skillet over high heat. When it foams, add 2 tablespoons sherry vinegar and boil it rapidly, shaking the pan back and forth, until it's emulsified, then pour it directly over the onions. Step back when you add the vinegar—the fumes are quite powerful.

Sautéed Onions

Cooking onions over brisk heat produces one of the best anticipatory smells I know. Sautéed onions add much to simple foods, such as a grilled cheese sandwich or a plate of macaroni and cheese. Serves 2 or 3 (V)

2 tablespoons olive oil or a mixture of oil and butter
1 large onion, sliced about $1/2$ inch thick
Sea salt and freshly milled pepper

Heat the oil in a wide skillet. Add the onion and sauté, flipping often but letting them rest in the pan long enough to brown, about 5 minutes in all. Season with salt and pepper and serve right away.

Braised Cipollini, Boiling Onions, or Shallots

A handsome dish when made with a mixture of shallots, white and red boiling onions, and cipollini. Serves 4 to 6 (V)

1 pound boiling onions, cipollini, shallots, or a mixture
2 tablespoons butter or olive oil
2 small bay leaves
2 thyme sprigs
1 teaspoon sugar
$1/2$ teaspoon sea salt
Freshly milled pepper
$1/2$ cup dry white wine or vermouth

Blanch the onions in boiling water for 1 minute, then drain and remove the outer skin.

If using shallots, peel them raw and pull them apart at their natural divisions. Melt the butter in a skillet with the bay leaves and thyme and add the onions and sugar. Cook over medium heat, shaking the pan occasionally, until browned in places, 10 to 15 minutes. Season with the salt and pepper to taste and add the wine. Bring to a boil, then lower the heat, cover, and simmer until the onions are tender, 15 to 20 minutes. Check once or twice during cooking, and if the pan is dry, add a few tablespoons water. Remove the lid and reduce the remaining juices to a syrupy glaze.

Roasted Onions with Vinegar and Rosemary

Serve these easily prepared onions as a side dish, or add them, chopped, to arugula or spinach salad or spoon them over bruschetta with slivered Manchego cheese.
Serves 4 to 6 Ⓥ

4 to 5 onions, sliced into 1/2-inch rounds
2 tablespoons olive oil
2 tablespoons balsamic or aged sherry vinegar
1 tablespoon finely chopped rosemary
Sea salt and freshly milled pepper

Preheat the oven to 400°F. Toss the onions with the oil, vinegar, and rosemary. Season with salt and pepper. Put them in a baking dish with a few tablespoons water. Cover and bake for 30 minutes, then uncover and continue baking until the onions are browned around the edges and tender, about 30 minutes more. Give them a stir every 10 minutes or so toward the end.

Roasted Onions on a Bed of Herbs

A spectacular-looking dish for minimal effort—perfect for the holidays. Look for onions with crisp, papery skins.
Serves 6 Ⓥ

2 tablespoons olive oil or a mix of olive oil and butter
3 large yellow onions, halved and peeled
Sea salt and freshly milled pepper
4 sage sprigs and several thyme sprigs
1 cup dry white wine or water

Heat the oil or oil and butter in a wide skillet, then add the onions, cut sides down. Cook over medium-high heat until well browned, about 15 minutes. Check their progress occasionally—those on the outside of the pan usually take longer to cook, so partway through switch them with those in the middle. When browned, turn them over and cook on the curved side for a few minutes. Season well with salt and pepper.

Preheat the oven to 375°F. Line a 10-inch earthenware dish such as a round Spanish casserole with the herbs. Place the onions, browned side up, on the herbs and pour in the wine. Cover with aluminum foil and bake until tender when pierced with a knife, 1 hour or slightly longer. Serve warm with or without the Quick Vinegar Sauce for Onions (page 357) or Romesco Sauce (page 62).

FRIED ONION RINGS

Slice peeled yellow onions into rounds about 1/2 inch thick. Separate the rings, dip them in a bowl of milk, then in flour seasoned with sea salt and pepper. In a deep fryer, heat peanut oil to about 350°F or until it sizzles a chunk of bread to gold in about 1 minute. Add the onions a handful at a time and fry until golden, about 3 minutes. Lift them out with a strainer, drain briefly on paper towels, then sprinkle with sea salt or ground red chile. Repeat until all are done, then serve.

Caramelized Onions

This heavenly jam of caramelized onions takes about 1 1/2 hours of cooking, but most of it is unattended. I make these when I'm doing something that calls for breaks, and every 20 minutes or so I stir them. Caramelized onions are wonderful as a filling for buckwheat crepes, or tossed with pasta, walnuts, and rosemary. Makes about 3 cups Ⓥ

1/4 cup butter or oil
3 pounds onions, sliced 1/4 to 1/3 inch thick
4 thyme sprigs
1 1/4 teaspoons sea salt
1 cup dry white wine
1 tablespoon sherry vinegar
Freshly milled pepper

In a wide, deep skillet or Dutch oven, melt the butter over medium heat, letting it color a little. Add the onions and thyme, stir them about, and cover. Cook until they turn limp and reduce in volume, about 5 minutes, then turn the heat to low and toss the onions with the sea salt. Cover, cook for 20 minutes, then add the wine and cover again. Every 20 minutes or so, give them a stir. After an hour or so the onions will begin to brown. You can hear them start to sizzle. Now start stirring them more frequently so that they don't burn. When they're a rich golden brown, stir in the vinegar and turn off the heat. Taste for sea salt and season with pepper.

Parsnips

Like many root vegetables grown for animal fodder, parsnips are unjustly underestimated, for the fragrant strength of these roots is considerable. Though sweet enough to be eaten for breakfast (see page 558), their usual place is as a vegetable side dish. Parsnips are available from fall to early summer, but those dug after the first frost are always the sweetest.

WHAT TO LOOK FOR: Parsnips are a tapering, ivory-colored root; they should not be flaccid, flabby, split, or shriveled, all signs of poor care. The best parsnip I ever ate was huge, dug out from under a covering of March snow, so size isn't necessarily a deterrent to goodness. Freshness is the key; if too old or not well stored, parsnips can turn bitter. Unless they're to be chopped, choose vegetables that are more or less the same size so they'll cook evenly.

HOW TO STORE: Keep parsnips in a plastic bag in the vegetable bin. Storing at a cold temperature, close to 32°F, helps sweeten them.

HOW TO USE: Steamed, boiled, baked, roasted, or sautéed, parsnips are delicious with just butter, sea salt, and pepper. They can be stewed with other winter vegetables, added to potato puree, and made into a good soup. Parsnips are related to carrots, and they can be used in most carrot recipes to good effect. Since their flavor always dominates, use them only where you really want it.

SPECIAL HANDLING: Parsnips have a clearly demarcated core. You don't have to remove it unless it's obviously woody. Probe it with the tip of a knife to see. Peel parsnips before cooking or boil them first, then slip off the skins. Because the tops are thick and the bottoms skinny, they don't cook evenly unless cut into pieces that are more or less the same size.

QUANTITY: Allow 2 pounds parsnips for four to six servings.

Good Partners for Parsnips

Butter, brown butter, ghee, curry
Honey, maple syrup, brown sugar, mustard
Ginger, curry, parsley, thyme, tarragon, chives
Onions, apples, other root vegetables

Buttered Parsnips and Chopped Parsley

Although they're tough-looking roots, parsnips turn soft quickly—keep an eye on them. Serves 4

> 1¹/₂ to 2 pounds parsnips, peeled or scrubbed
> 2 tablespoons butter or Brown Butter (page 28)
> Sea salt and freshly milled pepper
> Chopped parsley or tarragon

Cut the parsnips into pieces of equal length, then halve or quarter the wider ends so they'll be approximately the same thickness as the rest. Steam or simmer in salted water until tender-firm, 7 to 10 minutes, checking after 5 minutes. Drain and toss with the butter, season with salt and pepper to taste, and toss with chopped parsley.

Parsnips with Bread Crumbs: Melt 1 tablespoon butter in a skillet, add ¹/₄ cup fresh bread crumbs, and fry until golden and crunchy, a few minutes. Toss them with parsnips from the preceding recipe.

Sautéed Parsnips: Slice 2 pounds peeled parsnips into ¹/₄-inch rounds. Sauté in 2 tablespoons sunflower seed oil or butter in a skillet over medium heat until tender and beginning to brown, about 6 minutes. Season with sea salt and pepper and toss with chopped parsley. Serves 4 to 6 (V)

Roasted Parsnips: Preheat the oven to 400°F. Peel 2 pounds parsnips. Leave them whole if small or cut them into batons or chunks. Toss with 2 tablespoons oil or melted butter and season with sea salt and pepper. Roast in a large gratin dish or roasting pan, uncovered, until browned and tender, 20 to 30 minutes. Give them a stir every 10 minutes so that they color evenly. Serves 4 to 6 (V)

Pureed Parsnips

You can sharpen the flavor of this puree with buttermilk, soften it with cream, or use the rich-flavored cooking water for thinning and omit the butter. Serves 6 Ⓥ

1 1/2 pounds parsnips, peeled
1/2 pound boiling potatoes, peeled
1 teaspoon sea salt
1/2 cup buttermilk, cream, or cooking water as needed
2 to 4 tablespoons butter, optional
Freshly milled pepper

Chop the parsnips and potatoes into pieces, the potatoes about half the size of the parsnips. Put them in a saucepan with cold water to cover and the salt. Bring to a boil, then lower the heat and simmer until tender. Drain, reserving the liquid. Pass the vegetables through a food mill or beat by hand into a puree. Add enough buttermilk to make the mixture smooth and easy to work. Stir in butter, taste for salt, and season with pepper.

Variation: Cook parsnips with other root vegetables, such as carrots, celery root, turnips, rutabagas, parsley root, a chopped leek or onion, then puree. Grated Swiss or Gruyère makes a good addition.

Curried Parsnips with Apples, Yogurt, and Chutney

You can make this a main dish if you serve it on a bed of braised greens or sautéed spinach. Serves 4

1 1/2 pounds parsnips, peeled and chopped into even pieces
3 tablespoons ghee or coconut oil
1 onion, thinly sliced
2 apples, cored and thinly sliced
1 teaspoon curry powder
Sea salt and freshly milled pepper
1/4 cup yogurt
1/4 cup Apricot and Dried Fruit Chutney (page 73), Apple-Pear Chutney (page 73), or a commercial mango chutney
2 tablespoons chopped cilantro

Steam the parsnips until barely tender, about 7 minutes. Melt 2 tablespoons of the ghee in a medium skillet. Add the onion, apples, and curry powder and cook over medium heat, stirring frequently, for 10 minutes. Add the parsnips, season with salt and pepper, and cook 5 minutes more with the remaining 1 tablespoon butter to help them brown. Turn off the heat, then stir in the yogurt, chutney, and cilantro, and serve.

Peas

Precious and fleeting, peas occupy a tiny window in time in late spring and early summer. The minute heat sets in, they're finished, but until then they are one of the most delectable treats in the vegetable world. Little need be done except to cook them as soon as you can. Unlike today's corn, their sugars quickly turn to starch once picked.

TYPES OF PEAS: These varieties of peas are most often found in our markets.

Pod peas: Also called English peas or shelling peas, these are the old-fashioned peas that are shucked from their pods. If they're not starchy, they can be eaten raw.

Snow peas: Eaten whole, these are the flat, pale green pods sometimes called Chinese peas. The peas themselves are barely formed; the pods are tender.

Sugar snap peas: A newer variety, these are plump-podded peas that resemble shelling peas, but the pods themselves are sweet, tender, and crisp. They're cooked and eaten whole.

Pea shoots: Found in Asian markets, these tender vines can be sautéed or stir-fried and eaten right along with the peas.

Winged peas: Also called asparagus peas, these are another vegetable altogether, but they resemble a small sugar snap pea—with wings. They should be small, no more than 1/2 inch thick. Cook them as you would peas or green beans.

WHAT TO LOOK FOR: Bright green color and a crisp, fresh look is what you want in all peas. Yellowing tells you that they've begun to turn starchy. If you can, bite into one raw to make sure it's tender. While scars may detract from a pea's visual perfection, they usually disappear when cooked.

HOW TO STORE: If you must store them, keep them in a plastic bag in the refrigerator, but try to use them as soon as you can.

HOW TO USE: Peas can be steamed, boiled, stir-fried, made into soups, and tossed shelled and uncooked into salads and pastas. They are so special and their season is so brief that they beg for simple treatments.

SPECIAL HANDLING: Strings should be removed from pods. With a paring knife, cut into the stem end, lift the string that binds the pea like a zipper, and pull down to the blossom end. Turn and pull out the second string on the other side. Very small peas needn't be strung.

QUANTITY: Allow 1 pound pod peas for 1 cup shelled, serving two or three. For edible-pod peas, 1 pound should serve four.

Good Partners for Peas

Butter, dark sesame and roasted peanut oils
Dill, chives, chervil, parsley, basil, mint, ginger, garlic
Shallots, onions, asparagus, turnips, fava beans,
    green onions

Stir-Fried Peas with Pepper Salt

I like snow peas plump and whole, but you can slice them diagonally to give the dish a more dynamic play of shapes. Serves 4 to 6 Ⓥ

2 1/2 teaspoons roasted peanut oil
1 clove garlic, chopped
1 pound snow or sugar snap peas, strung
1/2 to 1 teaspoon Szechuan Pepper Salt (page 69), to taste

Heat a wok or large skillet, then dribble in the oil. When the oil is hot, add the garlic and stir-fry for 30 seconds. Add the peas and stir-fry until they turn bright green. Turn off the heat, sprinkle with the salt, toss again, and serve.

An Assemblage of Peas

Since shelling peas and edible-pod peas cook quickly and I often find myself with some of this and a few of that, I simply cook them together. They look marvelous and taste just fine! Serves 2 to 4 Ⓥ

1 pound peas, different varieties
Sea salt and freshly milled white pepper
Butter or best olive oil
Chopped mint, basil, chives, or dill

String the snow peas and edible-pod peas; shuck any shelling peas. Bring a pot of water to a boil, add salt, and drop in the peas. Boil until they're bright green and tender, a minute or two. Drain, shake dry, then return to the empty pan, where they'll finish drying in its heat. Stir in a small piece of butter to taste, a little pepper, and whatever fresh herb appeals to you. If you have pea shoots, cook them with the peas.

Peas with Peanut Oil: Omit the butter from the preceding recipe and toss the cooked peas with a few teaspoons roasted peanut or toasted sesame oil and snipped chives. Ⓥ

Sugar Snap Peas with Green Onions and Dill

This basic dish is easy to vary: use shallots instead of green onions. A handful of peeled fava beans, pea shoots, and slivered asparagus tips added to the peas turns it into a spring vegetable sauté. Serves 4 Ⓥ

1 pound sugar snap peas, strung, or winged peas
6 green onions, including a few inches of the greens,
    finely sliced
Sea salt and freshly milled pepper
1 tablespoon butter or olive oil
2 tablespoons chopped dill or another favored herb

Put the peas in a skillet with the onions, a few pinches salt, the butter, and enough water just to cover the bottom. Cook until bright green and tender, after a minute or two—taste one to be sure. If using olive oil, add a little to the pan now. Taste for salt, season with a little pepper, and add the dill.

Peppers

One of the best parts about late summer is having a wealth of glossy, brightly hued peppers in the garden or farmers' market. Peppers are filled with juicy sweetness, have an appealing, crisp texture, and merge splendidly with all the vegetables and herbs of the season.

TYPES OF SWEET PEPPERS: The different colors reflect stage of ripeness and, in some cases, different varieties. There are many kinds of sweet peppers besides bells, including the newly introduced shishito and Padrón peppers.

Banana peppers: The sweet version of Hungarian hot peppers, about 5 inches long and pale yellow with blushes of pink, banana peppers can be used for stuffing, although they don't stand upright.

Bell peppers: Left on the plant, green peppers eventually turn red, but some varieties are selected for their red, yellow, orange, or purple pigmentation. Green and purple peppers have a more tart, or unripe, flavor than their red and yellow counterparts. Mexi-bells look like green bell peppers but are hot. Stuffers are squat, green bell peppers that easily stand upright. Peppers from the farmers' market or your garden tend to have more curves and irregular shapes than those selected for the supermarket.

Cubanelles: A variety of pepper that includes many specially named fruits, these sweet peppers are long, narrow, and oddly creased. They can be extremely sweet and are wonderful grilled and salted. Corno de Toros, or bull's horns, are curved like a horn, substantial, sweet fleshed, and gorgeous.

Italian sweet peppers: These look more like what we call a chile than a bell pepper, but they're mild, thin skinned, and sweet rather than hot. Also known as frying peppers, they're delicious sautéed or lightly grilled and salted.

Japanese frying peppers: Shishito and fushimi are glossy green, thin walled, and between 3 and 6 inches in length. In the garden, they produce prolifically. At the market, they are costly. Although green, they don't have the unripe taste of green bell peppers. They are usually sautéed until browned in spots, then salted and nibbled on with cocktails.

Padróns: These small, feisty bites are another recent addition to the pepper community, this time from Spain. They are a little plumper than shishitos, but often prepared the same way. They are usually sweet, except when you get an unpredictably hot one, which is to be expected.

Pimientos: These heart-shaped peppers come to a pointed tip and are deep red when ripe, with a rich, concentrated flavor and often very thick walls.

WHAT TO LOOK FOR: Smooth, firm flesh with no wrinkles or soft spots is your guide to a good pepper.

HOW TO STORE: If not using them right away, store peppers in a plastic bag in the refrigerator. They'll keep a week or more, but the bag can produce moisture that eventually causes peppers to spoil.

HOW TO USE: Unwaxed peppers are a treat to enjoy as a crudité or in salads. Peppers find their way into soups, spreads, salads, purees, sauces, and stews. They can also be stuffed, sautéed, or grilled.

SPECIAL HANDLING: Almost all commercial peppers are waxed. Grilling, roasting, and broiling peppers remove the wax along with the skins, gives them a faintly smoky flavor, and makes them supple. You can also wash them in a weak solution of soapy water, then rinse.

When slicing peppers, cut from the inside of the pepper rather than from the outside. A knife can bounce off the hard surface, whereas the porous cell walls inside tend to grab it—far safer, especially for inexperienced cooks or those using dull knives.

To prepare a pepper for slicing, cut into strips, slice off the top, a small piece off the bottom, then make a cut down the side. Open the pepper up, slice off the veins, scrape off the seeds, then cut it into strips, triangles, or whatever is called for. The tops can be added to stocks or diced into small pieces for salads or salsas.

QUANTITY: Peppers vary greatly in size and weight, but an average bell pepper weighs about 6 to 8 ounces and holds about 1 cup of filling. Trimmed and seeded, it will yield approximately 1½ cups thinly sliced or chopped. If roasted and peeled first, the yield will be slightly less since the softened peppers will collapse. Pimientos are obviously smaller than bells, as are shishitos, and Cubanelles have an entirely different shape and can weigh close to pound.

Good Partners for Peppers

Olive oil

Saffron, fennel, anise, basil, marjoram, garlic

Balsamic vinegar, sherry vinegar, olives, capers

Mozzarella, Fontina, goat cheese, parmesan

Tomatoes, eggplant, onions, summer squash, corn

Peperonata

In this Italian dish, the peppers are stewed with fresh tomatoes until soft, rather than seared as in the next recipe. The resulting dish is tender and juicy, but it can be used the same ways as sautéed peppers. I use it as a relish to serve with vegetable side dishes. Serves 6 or more Ⓥ

2 to 4 tablespoons olive oil

2 onions, diced

3 cloves garlic, thinly sliced

2 bay leaves

1 teaspoon chopped thyme

5 or 6 bell peppers—red, yellow, and green—diced or sliced, or Italian sweet peppers

½ teaspoon sea salt

5 ripe tomatoes, peeled, seeded, and neatly diced

Freshly milled pepper

Heat the olive oil in a wide skillet. Add the onions, garlic, bay leaves, and thyme and cook over medium-high heat, stirring frequently, until the onions are soft and lightly colored, about 10 minutes. Add the peppers, season with the salt, and raise the heat. Cook briskly until the peppers begin to soften, then add the tomatoes and reduce the heat to medium. Simmer, stirring occasionally, until the excess water from the tomato has cooked away, about 15 minutes. Taste for salt and season with pepper.

Sautéed Peppers

A dish that can be used in many ways, these will keep, refrigerated, for a week. The high heat sears the onions and peppers and gives them almost a smoky edge. If using other peppers, such as Italian sweet peppers, keep in mind that their thinner flesh will cook more quickly. Makes 3 to 4 cups Ⓥ

4 large bell peppers—red, yellow, and/or orange

2 tablespoons olive oil

1 small red onion, quartered and thinly sliced crosswise

2 cloves garlic, thinly sliced

1 tablespoon tomato paste diluted with ¼ cup water

Sea salt and freshly milled pepper

1 tablespoon balsamic vinegar, or more

1½ tablespoons chopped marjoram, or 2 tablespoons sliced basil leaves

Slice the peppers into wide or narrow strips as you prefer. Heat the oil in a wide skillet, add the onion, and sauté over high heat until translucent and beginning to color around the edges, 4 to 5 minutes. Add the garlic and peppers and continue to cook, stirring every so often, until the peppers are singed on the edges, about 10 minutes. Add the diluted tomato paste, lower the heat to medium, and continue cooking until the peppers are soft, about 10 minutes more. Season with salt and pepper to taste, add the vinegar, and raise the heat to high. Cook, stirring frequently, until the peppers are glazed, then stir in the marjoram.

USES FOR SAUTÉED PEPPERS AND PEPERONATA

Enjoy sautéed peppers warm, tepid, or even chilled. Serve them as a side dish or stir them into omelets and scrambled eggs; spoon them over grilled polenta or pasta or the Saffron Noodle Cake (page 410); toss leftovers with hot rice and parmesan or crumbled Gorgonzola. Use them to top crostini, bruschetta, and pizzas or tuck them into crepes. Include them on an antipasto plate accompanied by sliced fresh mozzarella, olives, capers, and crudités.

Roasting and Peeling Peppers and Chiles

Peppers that are best for roasting are those with thick walls and flat, smooth surfaces. They should be meaty and feel heavy in the hand. Green peppers are often too thin to roast well—but not always. Varieties vary. Try to judge by their heft if you're not sure.

Roasted and peeled peppers can be kept for a few days or so in the refrigerator. Put them in a clean jar, cover with olive oil, and cover tightly.

ON THE GRILL OR BURNER: Place whole peppers directly on a gas burner or gas or charcoal grill. If you have an electric burner, an *asador*, a small mesh grill that sits right over the element, is a great help. (It can go right over gas burners, too, and can be used for grilling other vegetables as well as warming tortillas.) Roast the peppers until the skin becomes wrinkled and loose, turning them frequently with a pair of tongs. If you want the peppers to be soft and slightly smoky, roast them until the skins are completely charred. Set the peppers in a bowl, put a plate on top, and let them steam at least 15 minutes to loosen the skins.

If you wish to grill bell peppers for eating, without peeling them, slice off the top and the tip of the pepper, open it up, and remove the veins and seeds. Brush with olive oil or Lemon Vinaigrette (page 164) and grill, skin side facing the coals, until the skins are puckery and lightly marked but not charred. Turn and grill on the second side for a few minutes, then remove and season with sea salt and pepper. Leave the peppers in large pieces or cut them into strips as desired. Skinny peppers and chiles can be brushed with oil, grilled whole until just blistered, then sprinkled with salt.

IN THE OVEN: Use this method when you want to peel the peppers without cooking them too much. Cut off the top of the pepper, then slice it in half lengthwise, remove the seeds and veins, and press down on each half to flatten. Brush the skins with oil, then set them skin side up on a sheet pan. Bake at 400°F or broil 5 to 6 inches under the heating element until the skins are wrinkled but not charred, 10 to 20 minutes. Remove and stack the peppers on top of each other to steam for 15 minutes.

PEELING PEPPERS: First, reserve any juice that has collected from the steaming peppers in the bottom of the bowl or tray. Concentrated and sweet, it makes a wonderful addition to vinaigrettes and sauces. Next, rub off the skins with your hand or a paper towel. Don't worry about getting every little fleck of skin. Although rinsing the peppers is faster, you'll wash away their good flavor, so try to be patient and do it by hand. Open the peppers and scrape out the seeds, then cut as desired.

Roasted Poblano and Sweet Pepper Strips with Onions (*Rajas*)

Rajas *are strips of roasted chile. Here they are mixed with bell peppers. They can be served as a vegetable or used in quesadillas, enchiladas, or omelets.* Makes about 1^1/$_2$ cups Ⓥ

2 poblano chiles

2 large bell peppers—1 red and 1 yellow

1 small onion, thinly sliced

1 teaspoon minced garlic

1 tablespoon oil

Sea salt

Fresh lime juice or sherry vinegar

Roast and peel the poblanos and bell peppers as described at left. Cut the chiles and peppers into strips about ^{1}/$_2$ inch wide, put them in a bowl, then strain the juices over them.

Sauté the onion and garlic in the oil in a medium skillet over medium-high heat just until the onion begins to brown around the edges, about 5 minutes. Combine with the pepper strips and season with salt. When ready to serve, add a little lime juice to sharpen the flavors. These will keep in a covered container in the refrigerator for several days.

Garden Tomato and Pepper Stew

This succulent Tunisian dish is seasoned with Harissa (page 66), which tempers the sweetness of the summer vegetables. Serve at room temperature as a side dish or warm with couscous or pasta. Use heavy, fleshy garden tomatoes if at all possible. Serves 4 to 6 (V)

2 to 3 yellow onions, diced

1 clove garlic, slivered

1/4 cup olive oil

2 pounds tomatoes, peeled, seeded, and chopped, juices reserved

4 bell peppers—red, green, and yellow—chopped into 2-inch pieces

2 teaspoons Harissa (page 66)

2 teaspoons sweet paprika

1/2 teaspoon sea salt

1 tablespoon chopped parsley or basil

Sauté the onions and garlic in the oil in a wide skillet over medium heat until softened, about 5 minutes. Add the tomatoes, peppers, harissa, paprika, and salt. Cook for several minutes, then add 1/2 cup water or juices from the tomatoes. Simmer, stirring occasionally, until the tomatoes have thickened to a sauce and the peppers are tender, about 25 minutes. Taste for salt and stir in the parsley.

Fresh Chiles

Certain parts of the country enjoy many more chiles than others, but here are four chiles that are relatively easy to find almost everywhere. If you live in the Southwest, chances are you know a lot about the chiles that are popular in the area.

Green chiles eventually ripen to red on the vine. With ripening, their flavor naturally sweetens as the sugar content rises, just as with bell peppers. The capsaicin, the source of the chiles' heat, is concentrated around the veins and seeds. If you want to minimize heat, these are the parts to remove. If you're sensitive to chiles' volatile oils, wear gloves while handling them and avoid touching your eyes, nose, and mouth. Small chiles, like japapeños and serranos, can be grilled but are most often eaten diced and raw. Larger chiles are always grilled, then peeled because their skins are quite tough and hard to digest.

JAPAPEÑO: Once consistently hot, a strain of this stubby plump short chile has been bred for mildness, so now you have to taste one to find out if it's hot. If you want heat, keep the veins and seeds; otherwise it's easy to cut the flesh away. Japapeños are plump enough to stuff, grill, fry, or pickle.

LONG GREENS: Anaheims and New Mexican are two of several chiles described as long greens. Bright green with a hint of yellow rather than dark tones, these chiles are usually, though not always, mild and good multipurpose chiles. They always taste better roasted; then they can be made into *rajas* or stuffed.

POBLANO: A luscious heart-shaped, large, dark green chile with black patches on its wide shoulders, the poblano is hot and very tasty (although sometimes you'll get one that's mild). It's often used for making *rajas*, chiles rellenos, and sauces. As with long green chiles, its flavor is improved by roasting.

SERRANO: The small—about 2 inches long—slender cylindrical chile is bright dark green. It's hot with a good chile flavor rather than a green pepper taste. Plan to use serrano chiles with their seeds because they're difficult to remove. You can use these interchangeably with japapeños, but you may find you prefer the flavor of one over the other.

Corn-Stuffed Peppers with Fresh Mozzarella Cheese

These stuffed peppers offer a sunny summer dish made fragrant with basil and laced with fresh mozzarella. For peppers choose the sweeter red or yellow bells. The filling can be used with zucchini and tomatoes as well. Serve the peppers a bed of black rice or saffron rice, surrounded with the Fresh Tomato Sauce. Makes 4 stuffed-pepper halves

2 large red or yellow bell peppers

5 large ears corn, shucked

3 tablespoons olive oil

3 tablespoons minced shallot or green onion

Sea salt and freshly milled pepper

3 tablespoons finely sliced basil leaves

1/2 cup fresh bread crumbs

1 ball whole fresh mozzarella cheese, about 4 ounces, finely diced

Fresh Tomato Sauce

2 pounds ripe tomatoes, quartered

3 basil leaves

Sea salt and freshly milled pepper

Olive oil or butter

Leave the pepper stems intact, halve them lengthwise right through the stem, then remove the seeds and veins. Bring a saucepan of water to a boil, add the peppers, and parboil 5 minutes. Drain, then rinse with cold water. Holding each ear of corn upright, slice off the tops of the kernels with a sharp knife. Reverse your knife and use the dull side of the blade to force out the bottoms of the kernels and their milk.

Heat the oil in a skillet over medium heat. Add the shallot and cook gently until wilted, stirring once or twice. Add the corn, the corn pulp and milk, raise the heat to high, and cook 3 to 4 minutes. Season to taste with salt and pepper and stir in the basil, bread crumbs, and cheese. Remove from the heat.

To make the sauce, put the tomatoes in a heavy pan, cover, and cook over high heat with the basil. After 10 minutes, when the tomatoes are soft, pass them through a food mill placed over a bowl. The sauce should be fairly thin, but if you want it thicker, return it to the pot and continue cooking over medium heat, stirring frequently, until it is

as thick as you want. Take care not to let it scorch. When done, season with salt and pepper, and stir in a few teaspoons olive oil to taste.

Heat the oven to 375°F. Oil a baking dish large enough to hold the peppers snugly. Stuff the peppers with the corn mixture, set them in the dish, and bake until heated through, about 25 minutes. Serve hot or just warm with the sauce.

Blistered Shishito, Fushimi, and Padrón Peppers

If you have a plant or two to pick from, you can cook a huge pile of these peppers and not worry about having too many. If you're paying a small fortune for them, you may want to put out only four per person. It's very easy to nibble your way through large pile of shishitos on a hot summer evening, a cool drink in hand. Serves 4 to 8 Ⓥ

1 pound shishito, fushimi, or Padrón peppers, or whatever quantity is available

Sea salt

Fresh lime or lemon juice

Film a skillet with oil. When hot, add the peppers, with their stems on, and either cook over high heat, turning them often, or over lower heat. Either way, cook them until they have softened and are well blistered in places, but not charred—you're not going to peel them. When done, season them with salt and add a squeeze of lime juice. Pile them on a plate or in a bowl and serve. One holds them by the stem and eats the whole pepper.

Should there be leftovers, remove the stems, chop them coarsely, and add them to an omelet or scrambled eggs.

Shishitos with Toasted Sesame Oil: Finish with a few drops toasted sesame oil on the shishito and fushimi peppers. Ⓥ

Potatoes

Potatoes are such a perennial favorite that some older cookbooks give them a chapter of their own. They're still delectable today, especially now that we've finally become reacquainted with some of the delicious heirloom varieties. Many of our favorite old potato recipes gain a renewed lease on life when made with some of the new varieties. We've also become acquainted with another treat—freshly dug summer potatoes. These are real new potatoes and so delicious you can enjoy them with almost nothing on them at all.

TYPES OF POTATOES: It's not always easy to figure out which potatoes to use for what. For a long time, our market choices were limited to a baker, two boilers, and a few all-purpose potatoes, so we're simply out of practice when it comes to making sense of the exciting varieties that are now surfacing. Essentially, potatoes vary in their starch content, and it's the starch that makes one type of potato more suitable for a dish than another.

Potatoes come in a startling array of shapes, sizes, and colors. Some are unique to particular regions where growing conditions are ideal—hence the Idaho or Maine potato. The more interesting heirloom potatoes have become increasingly available in farmers' markets and even grocery stores. By all means, try them if you see them.

Blue potatoes: Any blue vegetable is a novelty, but some of the new varieties of these Peruvian potatoes, such as Purple Vikings and All Blues, have a surprising amount of flavor that's a little nutty and often very sweet. Bake, roast, or steam them and use in salads.

Fingerlings: Looking roughly like large fingers, and with dense, waxy flesh, fingerlings are the best for potato salads and good in gratins and stews. They're also delicious steamed or roasted with garlic and herbs. They needn't be peeled, only scrubbed. Some excellent varieties are Rose Finn Apple, Russian Banana, Ruby Crescent, Ozettes, and La Ratte.

Goldrush, Yukon gold, Caribes: These potatoes are good bakers too, but are also good in other roles, making them basically all-purpose potatoes. Caribes have a blush in the skin and deep eyes—a very pretty potato. Yukon golds have yellow flesh but are sweeter than other potatoes.

New potatoes: Although they're often spoken of as if they were a variety, and even sold as such, all potatoes are new potatoes when they're dug, regardless of their size or type. This is when potatoes are most delicate and sweet. New potatoes are a summer vegetable. Their papery-thin skins need only be scrubbed, and the potatoes are superb steamed over water laced with herbs.

Russets: These potatoes are some of the best bakers, yielding flaky white or golden flesh. They also make excellent fries and grated potato cakes.

Yellow Finns: A pretty oval potato with buttery-looking yellow flesh. These make golden mashed potatoes, are delicious roasted and baked in gratins, but tend to fall apart in a salad.

WHAT TO LOOK FOR: Potatoes should be firm and have a sweet, earthy smell. Eyes are not a problem. Some of the tastiest varieties of potatoes have lots of deep eyes, such as Ozettes. If sprouts are starting to emerge from the eyes, simply cut them out with the tip of an old-fashioned potato peeler—that's what it's for—if they bother you. But sprouts do indicate that the potato has started to grow; its texture is diminished, gradually turning soft and spongy.

HOW TO STORE: Keep potatoes in a cool, dark place, such as a loosely closed paper bag in a cupboard, away from onions. Moisture causes them to spoil, and light turns them green. Don't refrigerate and don't plan on keeping new potatoes for more than a few weeks.

HOW TO USE: Perhaps the most versatile of vegetables, potatoes can be used in soups, stews, salads, gratins, omelets, and baked goods; they can be pureed, fried, sautéed, baked, roasted, grilled, boiled, and mashed.

SPECIAL HANDLING: If potatoes show any greening, cut it away with a knife. It will nauseate you if you eat it, but the rest of the potato can be eaten safely. If you add herbs, garlic, and other aromatics to boiling or steaming water, their flavors will be taken up by the absorbent and neutral potatoes. To absorb moisture from cooked potatoes, cover them with a clean towel. Adding warm rather than cold liquid to mashed potatoes makes them light. When adding potatoes to hot oil, make sure they're absolutely dry so the oil doesn't spatter.

QUANTITY: Peeled and sliced, 1 pound of potatoes yields about 2½ cups. Mashed, 1 pound yields a scant 2 cups. If potatoes are offered as a side dish, allow 1 pound for three or four servings; if they've been mashed, they may well serve only three since this form is so popular.

Good Partners for Potatoes

Butter, olive oil, cream, sour cream
Chervil, chives, basil, lovage, sage, rosemary, thyme
Mustard, sorrel, curry spices, saffron, pepper
Goat cheese, cheddar, Cantal, fontina, Gruyère
Tomatoes, greens, peppers, onions, garlic, leeks,
    root vegetables

Sauces and Seasonings for Potatoes

Romesco Sauce (page 62)
Garlic Mayonnaise (page 52)
Tomatillo Salsa (page 90)
Pesto (page 50)
Fresh Horseradish Sauce (page 63)
Green Goddess Dressing (page 169)
Chermoula (page 50)

Which Potatoes Are for What

Potato varieties not only differ in starch content, they also change once they're picked—growing more starchy as time passes. A chef friend of mine goes through seasonal agonies as his usually reliable Castle Rocks that he uses for french fries become less reliable for no apparent reason except time out of the ground. Potatoes can be baffling.

HIGH-STARCH POTATOES FOR BAKING AND FRYING: Starchy potatoes have dry, mealy flesh. That's what makes a baked potato fluffy and a fried one light and crisp. If you boil a baking potato, it falls apart. Potato cakes are made from raw, shredded potatoes, and are held together by the starch. Some cooks don't like the sometimes gluey quality, so they rinse it off and rely on eggs instead to hold the shreds together. These are good varieties for baking and frying:

- Burbank russets (the Idaho potato) and all other russets
- Bintje, Castle Rock

LOW-STARCH BOILING POTATOES: Potatoes that boil well hold their shape; these are the ones to use in salads, stews, and gratins—they absorb liquids, dressings, and sauces without falling apart. They're waxy fleshed, moist, and dense rather than powdery and dry. These are some familiar boiling potatoes:

- Red Bliss, Red Dale, and Norland (your supermarket boiling potatoes)
- Red Pontiac, Peruvian Purple, Purple Viking, and All Blue
- Red La Soda, Yellow Finn, and White Rose
- Rose Fir, Finn Apple, Ozette, Red Russian, Banana, and other fingerling types

ALL-PURPOSE POTATOES: The moderates fall somewhere in the middle, which makes them more or less adequate for all cooking methods. These include, to mention a few, Katahdin, Kennebec, Superior.

A TEST TO TELL: If you're not sure what kind of potato you've got, slice one with a sharp knife. If the knife is covered with a foamy substance or the potato grabs onto the knife, then it's starchy and a baker. If not, it's a boiler. So-so, it's all-purpose.

Steamed Potatoes: A perfect treatment for tender new potatoes. Bring an inch of water to a boil in a saucepan. Scrub the potatoes and set them in a steaming basket over the water.

Cover and steam until tender when pierced with a knife, 25 minutes or longer, depending on their size. Remove and toss with butter or olive oil, sea salt, and freshly milled pepper, or serve with Romesco Sauce (page 62). ⓥ

Boiled Potatoes: Put scrubbed or peeled potatoes in a saucepan, cover with cold water, and bring to a boil with a little sea salt. Then lower the heat and simmer until the potatoes are tender when pierced with a skewer or knife, 15 to 30 minutes, depending on their size. ⓥ

Broiled Potatoes: Cut steamed or boiled potatoes lengthwise in half and score the tops with the tip of a knife. Brush them with oil or butter and broil, cut side facing the heat, until bubbling and browned. Remove and garnish with garden herbs, freshly milled pepper and sea salt, or any of the sauces and seasonings suggested on page 368. ⓥ

Mashed Potatoes

An old adage says that starchier varieties make the lightest, fluffiest potatoes. In general this is true, although I've made divine mashed potatoes with spuds just one or two days from the field. The liquid that thins the potatoes can be the water they're cooked in, low-fat milk, whole milk, or cream. If you like a little tartness, try buttermilk. Leftovers are endlessly useful. Pipe them over a vegetable stew to make a shepherd's pie; form them into cakes and fry until golden on both sides; dilute them with water or stock to make a soup; or use them in bread and biscuits. Makes about 6 cups ⓥ

---

3 pounds russet or Yukon gold potatoes, scrubbed

2 teaspoons sea salt

¹/₄ to ¹/₂ cup butter or olive oil

About 1 cup milk, cream, buttermilk, or cooking water, warmed

Freshly milled pepper

Pinch grated nutmeg

Don't peel the potatoes—the peels give flavor to the cooking water. Put the potatoes in a large saucepan, cover with cold water, add the salt, and boil until tender, 15 to 30 minutes depending on size. Remove the potatoes from the water, reserving the water for soup, bread, or thinning the potatoes. Holding the potatoes in a towel, peel them, then break them into chunks and mash with an old-fashioned potato masher, a handheld mixer, a

food mill with large holes, or a ricer. (The food processor makes them gluey.) Beat in as much butter as you want to use—potatoes can absorb an infinite amount. Gradually beat in the warm liquid until the potatoes are smooth, moist, and light. Season with salt, pepper, and nutmeg. It's best to serve them right away, for they become stiff once cooled. If you must, hold them in a double boiler or a bowl set over a pan of simmering water and covered loosely with foil.

Saffron Mashed Potatoes: Crumble 2 hearty pinches saffron threads into a few tablespoons warm cooking water and steep for 5 minutes. Add it to the potatoes along with the warm liquid. ⓥ

Mashed Potatoes with Basil Puree: Serve mashed potatoes with Basil Puree (page 51) drizzled over them. Or just before serving, stir ¹/₂ cup puree into the potatoes, leaving it streaked with green. ⓥ

Mashed Potatoes with Roasted Garlic: Roast one or two large heads of garlic until tender (page 340). Squeeze out the softened garlic and stir into the potatoes. ⓥ

Mashed Potatoes with Herbs and Olive Oil: Add to the cooking water a bay leaf, a few slices onion, 6 thinly sliced cloves garlic, and several thyme sprigs. Peel and mash the potatoes, using olive oil in place of butter and thinning them with the reserved liquid. At the end, stir in 2 tablespoons chopped herbs—parsley, thyme, rosemary, or sage. ⓥ

Mashed Potatoes with Root Vegetables: Replace half the potatoes with turnips, rutabagas, parsnips, fennel, or celery root, and your mashed potatoes will have a lot more character. Peel and chop the vegetables into large pieces and cook together with the potatoes. Mash, using the cooking water, and finish with butter or olive oil. ⓥ

Baked Potatoes

A baked potato is unthinkably easy and rather comforting. No wonder many people make a meal of one. Large russets are the ones to use for the classic baked potato. Buy organic ones if you like to eat the skin. Don't wrap your potato in foil—it creates steam by holding in the moisture. You want it to escape so that the finished potato will be fluffy and dry.

Preheat the oven to 425°F. If baking more than one, choose potatoes that are approximately the same size. Scrub them and pierce them in a few places with a fork or run a large "potato" nail through the middle, which will release steam and bring heat more quickly to the center. Bake until tender, about 1 hour, depending on the size. When it's done, slice the potato along its length and once crosswise in the middle. Push the ends together to open it up. Serve with any of the sauces and seasonings suggested on page 368.

Stuffed Baked Potatoes: One of the least complicated and homiest suppers, but a step above a plain baked potato. Bake one russet potato per person. Slice the top third off the length of the potato and scoop out the inside from both pieces with a spoon, leaving the skin intact. Mash with milk, nut milk, or water, season with sea salt and pepper, and moisten with butter or olive oil; or mix with any of the sauces and seasonings on page 368. Return the filling to the potato skins and serve. (V)

Potato Skins: If you like them crisp and crunchy, snip the skins left from baked potatoes into wide strips, toss them with olive oil, season with sea salt and pepper, and bake at 425°F until crisp. (V)

Grilled Potatoes: Slice steamed or boiled potatoes in half if they're small, diagonally into pieces about 1/2 inch thick if large. Brush with olive oil and grill, turning them 45 degrees after about 7 minutes. Cook on both sides or on just one. Season with sea salt and pepper and serve with Golden Mustard Barbecue Sauce (page 65), truffle salt, or a dash of smoked paprika. (V)

Roasted Potatoes

Onions, parsnips, celery root, turnips, and artichokes are also good roasted and can be cooked right alongside the potatoes. You can use any type of potato in this dish. Serves 4 to 6 (V)

---

1 1/2 pounds potatoes, peeled and cut into chunks more or less the same size

Olive oil, for coating

1 teaspoon sea salt

Freshly milled pepper

Preheat the oven to 425°F. Toss the potatoes with enough oil to coat them lightly, the salt, and a little pepper. Bake in a shallow pan in a single layer until tender when pierced with a knife, 25 to 40 minutes, depending on the size. Stir them a few times so that they brown evenly.

Roasted Potatoes with Garlic and Herbs

This easy dish highlights the special plain goodness of potatoes. Serves 4 to 6 (V)

---

1 1/2 pounds Yellow Finn, fingerling, or regular boiling potatoes

Sea salt

1 head fresh, firm garlic, cloves separated but unpeeled

2 tablespoons olive oil

4 teaspoons chopped rosemary or sage

2 bay leaves

4 thyme sprigs

Freshly milled pepper

Scrub the potatoes well, then put them in a bowl of water with a few tablespoons salt and let stand for 15 minutes. Meanwhile, preheat the oven to 400°F and lightly oil a shallow baking dish. Drain the potatoes and pat dry with a towel. Toss them with the garlic, oil, and herbs, then season with salt and pepper. Arrange them in the prepared dish and bake, uncovered, until the potatoes are tender when pierced with a knife, 25 to 40 minutes, depending on their size. Turn them several times while they're cooking so that they brown evenly. Eat them with the softened cloves of garlic squeezed out of their paper cases.

Roasted Potatoes and Root Vegetables

To ensure even cooking and browning, use a pan large enough to hold the vegetables in a single layer. Serve showered with any of the herb salts, with Fresh Horseradish Sauce (page 63) or Romesco Sauce (page 62). Serves 4 to 6 (V)

---

2 1/2 pounds mixed root vegetables—potatoes, carrots, turnips, parsnips, beets, sweet potatoes, small onions or whole shallots

1 head garlic, separated into cloves but unpeeled

Several short rosemary sprigs, or 10 sage leaves

3 bay leaves

Olive oil, for coating

Sea salt and freshly milled pepper

Preheat the oven to 450°F. Peel the vegetables, onions, and shallots. Cut everything into pieces roughly the same size except for the parsnips, sweet potatoes, and turnips, which cook faster and can be slightly larger than the rest. Toss the vegetables, garlic, and herbs with oil to coat lightly, then season with salt and pepper. Put everything in a roomy pan. Bake, uncovered, in the top third of the oven for 20 minutes, shaking the pan once or twice. Reduce the heat to 375°F and continue baking until the vegetables are tender when pierced with a knife, 20 to 30 minutes, depending on how large they are. Remove the bay leaves. If using one of the herb salts, sprinkle it over the vegetables as soon as they come out of the oven.

Golden Pan-Fried Potatoes

Serves 4 (V)

---

1 pound boiling potatoes

2 tablespoons ghee or olive oil

Sea salt and freshly milled pepper

Peel and thinly slice the potatoes. Heat the ghee in a wide, heavy skillet such as cast iron, over high heat. Add the potatoes and fry without disturbing them until they begin to color on the bottom, about 5 minutes. Turn them over and fry on the second side until the potatoes are golden and tender, about 15 minutes in all. Season with salt and pepper and serve.

Fingerlings with Slivered Garlic

These potatoes end up moist and succulent unless you continue baking them once they're tender—they'll crisp on the bottom, and that's delicious, too. These hold their heat well in the baking dish, so you can bake them 30 minutes or so ahead of time. Serves 4 (V)

---

1 pound fingerling or other potatoes, scrubbed and halved lengthwise

6 cloves garlic, thinly sliced

3 tablespoons butter, ghee, or olive oil

Sea salt and freshly milled pepper

Preheat the oven to 400°F. Lightly butter or oil a shallow baking dish. Layer the potatoes in the dish with the garlic and small pieces of butter, ghee, or a drizzle of oil and season with salt and pepper. Make sure there's butter, ghee, or oil for the top.

Add a few tablespoons water to the dish, then cover and bake until tender, 40 to 50 minutes. Remove the foil and bake for 15 minutes longer to brown the top.

Oven-Roasted French Fries: These are irresistible. Preheat the oven to 450°F and lightly oil a sheet pan. Peel two russet potatoes, then cut them into large batons or french fries. Toss with enough oil to coat them lightly, then set them on the pan in a single layer. Bake for 10 minutes and turn them over. Bake for 20 minutes more, turning them several times so that they color on all sides. When golden and tender, sprinkle with sea salt and serve piping hot. Accompany with spicy Romesco Sauce (page 62) or mayonnaise flavored with Harissa (page 66), or dust them with cayenne. Serves 4 (V)

Potato Cakes

Many countries have their own potato cakes, all of which are made a little differently. The potatoes can be raw, boiled, or mashed; some are bound with eggs, others not. Other root vegetables sometimes join the potatoes, as do enrichments of herbs, garlic, and cheese. Virtually any kind of potato can be used, but if you use a high-starch potato—any of the russets, for example—rinse the cut potatoes in cold water to get rid of the bulk of the starch. Although some people say it's the starch that holds them together, I find that potato starch leaves an unpleasant texture. A rinse or two will leave sufficient starch to lightly bind the potatoes.

Latkes: Potato Pancakes with Eggs and Onions

Latkes are the traditional food of Hanukkah but are loved year-round. They're as good for supper as for brunch, accompanied by sour cream and chilled applesauce or set on a nest of pungent salad greens. Serves 6 to 8

> 2½ pounds russet potatoes, peeled
>
> 3 eggs, or 1 egg and 2 egg whites, beaten
>
> 1 white onion, grated or very finely chopped
>
> ¼ cup flour, toasted bread crumbs, or cracker crumbs
>
> 2 teaspoons sea salt
>
> Freshly milled pepper
>
> 3 tablespoons clarified butter, vegetable oil, or a mixture
>
> Sour cream, applesauce, chives, for serving

Peel the potatoes and coarsely grate them by hand or in a food processor. Put them in a bowl of water as you work. When ready to cook, drain the potatoes and wrap them in a towel to squeeze out the excess water. Return the potatoes to the bowl and add the eggs, onion, flour, salt, and pepper to taste.

Preheat the oven to 200°F. Film a heavy skillet with clarified butter, vegetable oil, or a mixture and set it over medium-high heat. When hot, drop in the batter by spoonfuls and cook over medium heat until browned, about 6 minutes. Repeat on the second side. Put the finished ones on a plate and keep them in the oven until all are done. Serve with sour cream and applesauce or sour cream covered with a sprinkling of snipped chives.

Straw Potato Cakes

These irresistible crisp golden cakes can be made with russets, boilers, Yukon golds, or Yellow Finns. Delicious on their own, they also make a beguiling base or accompaniment for a vegetable sauté. The Irish dish Boxty is similar. I've eaten it in Ireland with all kinds of toppings, a mound of spinach and roasted mushrooms being a favorite. Serves 4 to 6 Ⓥ

> 1½ to 2 pounds potatoes, peeled
>
> 3 to 4 tablespoons butter, ghee, or olive oil
>
> Sea salt and freshly milled pepper

Slice the potatoes into fine julienne strips by hand or on a mandoline or grate them on the large holes of a grater. If using high-starch potatoes, rinse them in cold water and towel-dry.

In a 10-inch cast-iron or nonstick skillet, heat half the butter over medium heat. When hot, add half the potatoes, making a layer about ½ inch thick. Season with salt and pepper, then cover with a second layer the same thickness. Neaten the edges, press down on the cake, and reduce the heat to low. Cook until the bottom is golden, 10 to 15 minutes. (The potatoes will become translucent as they cook.) Turn the potatoes onto a plate, add the remaining butter to the pan, and slide them back in. Cook until the second side is golden. Turn the cake onto a platter, cut into wedges, and serve.

Potato–Celery Root Cakes: Replace half the potato with peeled and finely grated celery root. Serve garnished with finely chopped celery leaves mixed with sliced green onions or chives. Grated parsley root and salsify also make excellent additions. Ⓥ

Mashed Potato Cakes

Here's where leftovers come into their own. Serve these with applesauce, Sautéed Onions (page 357), and cooked greens or with fried eggs and salsa. Makes twelve 4-inch cakes Ⓥ

2¹/₂ cups Mashed Potatoes (page 369)
1 cup dried bread crumbs or sesame seeds
Butter, ghee, or olive oil, for frying

Shape the potatoes into 12 round or oval cakes about ³/₄ inch thick. Coat them with bread crumbs and set on wax paper. Film a heavy skillet with some of the butter and set over medium heat. When hot, add the cakes and cook until golden, about 5 minutes. Turn and fry on the second side. Repeat until all are done.

Walnut and Potato Croquettes

This recipe was inspired by one I found in a 1913 cookbook. It was described as something to make when meat was scarce, but it's delicious in its own right. Go ahead and serve the croquettes with ketchup. Makes 10 to 12, serving 4 to 6

1¹/₂ tablespoons butter, ghee, or oil
¹/₂ cup grated onion
1 cup finely chopped walnuts
1 cup Mashed Potatoes (page 369)
2 cups fresh bread crumbs
1 egg
1 teaspoon sea salt
Freshly milled pepper
1 tablespoon chopped sage, rosemary, or parsley
Oil and/or butter or ghee, for frying

Melt the butter in a small skillet, add the onion, and cook over medium heat until browned, stirring frequently. In a bowl, mix the onion, walnuts, potatoes, half the bread crumbs, and the egg. Season with the salt, a little pepper, and the sage. Scoop up 2 heaping tablespoons of the mixture at a time and shape into an oval. Spread the remaining bread crumbs on a plate and roll the croquettes in them to coat evenly.

Preheat the oven to 200°F. Heat ¹/₈ inch oil in a wide skillet and place over high heat. Add as many of the croquettes as will fit comfortably, reduce the heat to medium, and cook on both sides until golden, about 10 minutes in all. Transfer them to paper towels and place in the oven while you finish frying the rest.

Comforting Potatoes Cooked in Milk

Sometimes the plainest foods are most satisfying. Soft and almost soupy, this is a dish to sup on alone or with a close friend. As good as it tastes, it's not a dish for company. Serves 4 Ⓥ

1¹/₂ pounds mixed boiling and baking potatoes
8 green onions, including a few inches of the greens, chopped
2 to 3 tablespoons butter
1 teaspoon sea salt
Milk (dairy or plant), for simmering
Freshly milled pepper
2 tablespoons chopped parsley

Peel the potatoes and cut them into ¹/₂-inch chunks. Put them in a heavy saucepan with the onions, butter, salt, and enough milk to cover. Bring to a boil, then lower the heat and simmer, covered, until the potatoes are tender and the liquid has been absorbed, about 25 minutes. Taste and season with salt and pepper. Toss with the parsley and serve.

TOPPINGS FOR POTATO CAKES

- Chopped thyme, marjoram, rosemary, or fried sage leaves
- Grated raclette, fontina, fresh mozzarella, Teleme, cheddar
- Snipped chives or sliced green onions
- Sautéed Onions (page 357) or Caramelized Onions (page 358)
- Sautéed Mushrooms with Garlic and Parsley (page 351)
- Spinach and mushrooms

Steam-Roasted Potatoes

These roasted potatoes are creamy inside, crisp on the outside. For best results, use the small golf ball–size red potatoes sold as "new" potatoes. Serves 4 to 6 Ⓥ

- 1¹/₂ pounds small red potatoes, scrubbed well
- 3 tablespoons melted butter or olive oil
- Sea salt and freshly milled pepper or one of the herb salts (pages 67 to 69)
- Chopped parsley or fines herbes, for coating

Remove a band of skin around the middle of each potato and steam until tender but shy of being done when pierced with a knife, 15 to 20 minutes. Preheat the oven to 425°F.

Put the potatoes in a baking dish and roll them around with enough butter or olive oil to coat lightly. Bake until the skin is golden brown, about 40 minutes, giving the pan a shake a couple of times so the potatoes will brown evenly. Season with salt and pepper and roll them around in the chopped parsley.

Potatoes Baked in Sea Salt

The sea salt leaves a distinct film of flavor but doesn't make the potatoes salty. Select potatoes that are the same size and on the small side and leave them whole. The salt can be reused many times and you'll want to, these are so good. Serves 4

- 2 pounds kosher or coarse sea salt
- 1¹/₂ pounds fingerling or small round potatoes, scrubbed
- Several rosemary sprigs
- Butter, for serving

Preheat the oven to 400°F. Make a base of salt about 1 inch deep in a Dutch oven or other baking dish large enough to hold the potatoes in a single layer. Set the potatoes and rosemary on the salt and add more salt to cover. Bake until the potatoes can be pierced easily with a knife, about 35 minutes. Keep the potatoes embedded in the salt until ready to serve, then scrape away the top layer and gently pull them out. Serve with butter.

Radishes

Radishes are seldom encountered as a cooked vegetable, although they're quite good this way. Once radishes get hot and spicy, I far prefer to cook them than to eat them raw, but this isn't just a fallback position for overgrown radishes. Cooking also concentrates flavors and transforms what we usually regard as a crisp vegetable into one that's practically juicy.

There are several different types of radishes—the familiar red ones, long French breakfast radishes with white tips, about the size of a finger, multicolored Easter egg radishes, Spanish black radishes, snowy icicle radishes, the gorgeous red-meat and green-meat giant radishes, and the great daikon. While all are usually eaten raw, all can be cooked, as can the leaves.

Braised Red Radishes

Serves 4

20 plump radishes, red or multicolored
1 to 2 tablespoons butter
1 shallot, diced
1 teaspoon chopped thyme or several pinches dried
Sea salt and freshly milled pepper

Trim the leaves from the radishes, leaving a bit of the green stems, and scrub them. If the leaves are tender and in good condition, wash them and set aside. Leave smaller radishes whole and halve or quarter larger ones.

Melt 2 to 3 teaspoons of the butter in a small sauté pan. Add the shallot and thyme and cook for 1 minute over medium heat. Add the radishes, a little salt and pepper, and water just to cover. Simmer until the radishes are tender, 3 to 5 minutes. Add the leaves and cook until they're wilted and tender, a minute more. Transfer the radishes to a serving dish. Reduce the liquid, adding a teaspoon or two more butter if you like, until only about 1/4 cup remains. Pour it over the radishes and serve.

Braised Black Radishes: Cooking tempers the coarser, drier flesh of these large radishes. Allow a pound for a small side dish. Trim off the leaves and the roots, then scrub the radishes well. Partially remove their black skin with a citrus zester, leaving a pattern of stripes, then slice them crosswise, about 3/8 inch thick. Put the radishes in a skillet and add water to cover and a few pinches salt. Simmer until tender, 20 minutes or possibly longer. Raise the heat to reduce any remaining water to 1/4 cup or so, then stir in a piece of butter or a few tablespoons crème fraîche, a little chopped parsley, and season with salt and pepper. Pour this over the radishes and serve. If the greens are in good shape, sauté them and serve on the side.

Pan-Roasted Radishes with Butter, Lemon, and Tarragon

When made with Easter egg radishes—red, purple, pink— it's especially pretty, the muted shades of spring coming forth as the brightness fades. But try this with other varieties as well, such as long Cincinnati reds. If the radish leaves are fresh and vibrant, leave them on for a rustic, funky look. Or—for there are no ends of options—steam them separately, then use them as a cushion for the finished radishes.

Serves 4 or more

2 bunches radishes—multicolored, red, breakfast, Cincinnati Reds, or others—fresh as possible
3 teaspoons butter, more or less
1 teaspoon light sesame or olive oil
Fresh lemon zest and juice of 1 lemon
To finish: a little finely chopped tarragon, flaky sea salt

Wash the roots and small leaves, discarding any that are yellowed or unsavory looking. Slice the radishes in half, larger ones in quarters. Melt 2 teaspoons of the butter in a 10-inch cast-iron skillet with the oil. Add the radishes and cook over medium-high heat for about 3 minutes. Give the pan and shake, add a lid, and continue cooking until they are tender and the cut surfaces are browned, about 12 minutes in all, shaking the pan occasionally to turn the vegetables. Add the remaining 1 teaspoon butter, the lemon zest, and a squeeze of lemon juice. Allow the lemon juice to reduce some and the butter to brown. Season with flaky salt and serve with the greens.

With Chard: Steam young rainbow chard leaves with their tender stems, or the radish leaves, toss with butter and lemon, and arrange on a plate. Heap the radishes over them.

With Turnips: Cook sections of scarlet or Japanese salad turnips with the radishes.

Salsify

Also known as oyster plant, salsify is an old-fashioned root vegetable that's enjoying a minor comeback thanks to some adventurous farmers and chefs. The long, thin roots are not, to my taste, particularly oysterlike, but they are subtle, nutty, and delicious.

Salsify browns the moment it's peeled, so have a bowl of water mixed with plenty of lemon juice right next to you as you work. Once it's peeled and cut, boil salsify for about 20 minutes, then dress it with butter, brown butter, or cream, or with lemon, shallots, and parsley. There's a bit of waste in the peelings, so 1 pound provides only three to four small servings.

Salsify with Shallots and Parsley

Serves 3 or 4

Juice of 2 lemons
1 pound salsify
1 tablespoon flour
2 teaspoons sea salt
1 large shallot, finely diced
2 tablespoons butter or ghee
Chopped parsley, to finish
Freshly milled pepper

Set aside ¹/₂ lemon and squeeze the juice from the rest into a bowl. Peel the roots one at a time and cut into desired lengths or julienne strips. Quickly put the finished pieces in the lemon juice and add water, as needed, to cover. Bring 8 cups water to a boil in a saucepan and add the juice of the remaining ¹/₂ lemon, the flour, and salt. Drain the salsify, add it to the pot, and boil until tender when pierced with a knife, 15 to 25 minutes. Drain again.

Cook the shallot in the butter in a medium skillet for a few minutes, then add the salsify and cook until golden, about 5 minutes more. Toss with parsley and season with salt and pepper.

Salsify and Potato Puree

It's getting to be popular again, but not so much that I can just run to town and buy salsify or its cousin, scorzanera. Fortunately it grows in my garden with gusto. Still, it never yields a lot, so I mix what I have with potatoes for this puree. If you have more salsify available, use less—or even no— potato. It's a delicate-tasting vegetable. Serves 4 to 6

Juice of 1 lemon
1 to 2 pounds salsify or scorzanera
2 teaspoons sea salt
¹/₂ pound russet potatoes
³/₄ cup milk or cooking liquid from the potatoes and/or salsify
2 tablespoons or more butter
Freshly milled white pepper
For garnish: tarragon, chives, parsley, optional

Put several cups cold water in a bowl with the lemon juice. Peel the salsify, cut it into chunks, and immediately add them to the lemon water so that they don't turn brown. When done, transfer to a pot of cold water, add 1 teaspoon of the salt and bring to a boil. Simmer until tender, about 10 minutes, then drain.

Meanwhile, peel the potatoes (or not, if they're organic), and cut them into small chunks. Put them in a separate pot, cover with cold water and add the remaining 1 teaspoon salt. Simmer until tender, about 15 minutes or more, depending on the size.

Puree both vegetables with enough hot liquid to give it a creamy texture. Stir in the butter, taste for salt, and season with white pepper. Serve plain, or garnish with a tiny bit of minced tarragon, chives, or parsley, so that you don't overwhelm the delicate flavor of the salsify.

Spinach

There's no need to push spinach disdainfully to the side of your plate. When properly cooked, spinach is utterly delicious whether eaten by itself or incorporated into other dishes. Spinach can be used interchangeably with beet greens and chard. Spinachlike plants, such as New Zealand spinach and Malabar spinach, tend to be somewhat mucilaginous.

TYPES OF SPINACH: The three basic types of spinach are the dark green, crinkled varieties, such as Bloomsdale; the pointed, smooth-leafed kind we see more frequently; and small, round tender leaves packaged for salad. The latter do not cook well, as they come out quite stemmy, more than leafy.

WHAT TO LOOK FOR: Look for whole leaves that are dark green, free of yellowed spots and bruises. (Bruises have a watery, dark appearance.) For salads, small tender leaves are choice, but larger ones will do as long as they aren't tough. You can tell by looking at the stems—if they're thick, the plant has been in the ground a while and that spinach is best for cooking.

HOW TO STORE: Stored dry in a plastic bag in the vegetable bin, spinach should keep for 3 to 4 days. Never store spinach wet.

HOW TO USE: Spinach is used in salads, as a cooked vegetable, and as a filling for pasta, crepes, cannelloni, omelets, and other foods like soufflés and savory pies. It makes delicious soup or an addition to soup, and its lustrous color sets off some of the duller-looking legumes. Discard the long stems, which are hard to eat. The crowns, which are the last 5 inches of stems joined at the root, are edible and quite good eating. Steam or blanch them.

SPECIAL HANDLING: Take special care in washing spinach. It's grown in fine sandy soil, which is invariably splashed on the leaves. It's not always visible, so test a leaf by taking a bite. After discarding the stems, sort through the leaves and discard any that are yellowed or show excessive bruising. Never cook spinach in aluminum; it ruins its color and taste.

QUANTITY: Allow one bunch of spinach, weighing a scant pound, for two servings. It takes 1 to 1½ pounds spinach leaves for 1 cup cooked, unless you're using mature Bloomsdale types, which yield about twice as much.

Good partners for Spinach

Butter, cream, olive oil, toasted sesame oil
Red pepper flakes, garlic, parsley, dill, basil, curry, nutmeg
Lentils, onions, chickpeas, mushrooms, pine nuts
Yogurt

Simple Cooked Spinach: This is the best way to cook spinach greens that will be seasoned afterward or used in another dish. Remove the stems and wash the leaves, but don't dry them. Put the leaves directly into a large skillet with the water still clinging to the leaves. Add a few pinches sea salt and cook over high heat, turning occasionally until the leaves are wilted and bright green, about 3 to 5 minutes. Turn it into a colander set over a plate to drain. Then toss with olive oil, butter, or another favored fat. (V)

Spinach with Sesame Oil and Toasted Sesame Seeds: Cook two bunches of trimmed spinach, as described above, in boiling salted water. Drain, then toss with 1 tablespoon toasted sesame oil and a few drops rice vinegar to taste. Season with sea salt and toss again with 1 tablespoon toasted sesame seeds. Serves 4 (V)

Buttered Spinach

Butter and spinach seem to be made for each other—a generous coating makes spinach unbelievably silky. But how much butter to use I leave to you. Piled on an English muffin or Garlic-Rubbed Crostini (page 24), this makes a simple supper for two. Serves 2

1 large bunch spinach, cooked until tender (page 377)

2 to 6 tablespoons butter, cut into pieces

Sea salt and freshly milled pepper

Grated nutmeg

Once the spinach is wilted, add the butter and begin picking up the spinach with tongs until the butter melts and coats the leaves. Season with salt, pepper, and a small grating of nutmeg.

Sautéed Spinach

A dish in itself, this is also another basic way to cook spinach. Serves 2 or 3 Ⓥ

2 tablespoons olive oil or butter

1 clove garlic, thinly sliced

1 large bunch spinach, stems removed, leaves washed but not dried

Sea salt and freshly milled pepper

Heat the oil in a wide skillet with the garlic. Cook over medium-high heat until the garlic turns light gold, then add the spinach, salt it lightly, and cook until bright green and limp, just a few minutes. Move the leaves around the pan, picking them up and turning them over as they cook. Season with pepper and serve.

Spinach with Croutons: If your spinach eaters are wary of its silky texture, toss buttered or sautéed spinach with small croutons sautéed in olive oil or butter until crisp or simply crisped in the oven. Ⓥ

Spinach with Mushrooms: Or call it mushrooms with spinach—it's about equal amounts of each and exquisite in either case. See the recipe on page 354. Ⓥ

Creamed Spinach with Toast

This smooth and soothing old-fashioned dish is one to enjoy once in a while. Use any leftover spinach in an omelet or scrambled eggs. Serves 2

1/3 to 1 cup cream or more

1 clove garlic, smashed

1 large bunch spinach, preferably small leaves, stems removed

2 teaspoons butter

Sea salt and freshly milled white pepper

Grated nutmeg

2 thin pieces toasted country bread, cut into triangles

Heat the cream with the garlic until fine bubbles form on the surface, then turn off the heat and set aside. Cook the spinach as described on page 377. Rinse, then squeeze out the excess water and finely chop. Melt the butter in a skillet, add the spinach, and cook until the pan is dry. Pour the cream through a strainer directly into the pan and simmer until it thickens slightly. Taste for salt and season with pepper and a few scrapings of nutmeg. Set the toast on plates and mound the spinach over them.

Spinach or Chard, Catalan-Style

Raisins and pine nuts are what make this side dish Catalan, but the same ingredients appear in the south of France and Italy—parts of the same culinary world. Serves 4 Ⓥ

2 bunches spinach, or 1 large bunch chard, stems removed, leaves blanched or steamed

2 tablespoons olive oil

1 large clove garlic, sliced

1/3 cup dark or golden raisins

1/3 cup pine nuts

Sea salt and freshly milled pepper

Coarsely chop the cooked spinach. Warm the oil with the garlic in a wide skillet over medium heat. When the garlic is golden, remove it. Add the raisins and pine nuts and cook until the pine nuts are golden and the raisins are plumped. Add the greens and cook until they're heated through. Season with salt and pepper to taste.

Sautéed Spinach with Garlic and Red Pepper

Most greens taste great cooked in this Roman style.
Serves 4 Ⓥ

2 tablespoons olive oil

2 cloves garlic, chopped

2 pinches red pepper flakes

2 bunches tender spinach, stems removed, leaves cooked (see page 377)

Sea salt

Juice of 1/2 lemon, or a few teaspoons red wine vinegar

Heat the oil with the garlic and pepper flakes in a wide skillet over medium-high heat until the garlic begins to color. Add the cooked spinach and toss to coat it with the oil. Add 1/2 cup water and cook until it's absorbed and the greens are heated through. Season with salt and a little lemon juice or vinegar.

Spinach, Beet Greens, or Chard with Green Onions, Parsley, and Dill

Serves 4 Ⓥ

2 bunches spinach, beet greens, or chard, stems removed, leaves cooked (see page 377)

2 1/2 tablespoons olive oil

2 bunches green onions, including half of the greens, sliced

3 tablespoons chopped parsley

3 tablespoons chopped dill

Sea salt and freshly milled pepper

Coarsely chop the cooked spinach. Warm the oil in a wide skillet over medium heat, then add the green onions and herbs. Cook gently until wilted and fragrant, then add the spinach and continue cooking until it's heated through. Season with salt and pepper.

Summer Squash

Summer squash are thin-skinned, tender, quick cooking, and versatile—a staple vegetable in the summer kitchen. Medium-size squash are preferable, for large ones tend to be seedy and altogether less flavorful. At the other extreme, extremely small squash can taste "green," or a little unripe. With tender young squash, the simplest preparations are sufficient. Don't be afraid to really cook summer squash—longer cooking brings out much more of its good squash flavor.

Delicata, acorn, and other varieties that we think of as winter squashes are in the same subfamily as summer squash. They arrive at the end of summer and are not great keepers, and although their skins are firmer than most summer squash, they can be eaten once the squash is cooked.

TYPES OF SUMMER SQUASH: Small to medium squash are always preferable, for large ones tend to be seedy, watery, and altogether less flavorful.

Zucchini: Long, straight, and cylindrical, zucchini are dark green, light green, variegated, or bright yellow-gold. Some varieties are ribbed.

Round zucchini: Green skin streaked with white and paler green flesh. The French variety Ronde de Nice is good up to about 6 inches in diameter. Eight Balls are better slightly smaller.

Scallop or pattypan squash: Shaped like a flying saucer with a scalloped edge running around the equator, scallop and pattypan squash are bright yellow, pale green, dark green, and garishly splashed with green and gold. After a long absence, these delectable squash are making a comeback.

Yellow crookneck or gooseneck: Named for its crook-shaped neck, this summer squash usually has large seeds but also is one of the best, with a real squash flavor. Some varieties have taken the crook out of the neck and some have a warty appearance, but all are quite tasty.

WHAT TO LOOK FOR: Freshly picked summer squash have bright, shiny skins. Look for firm, glossy-looking vegetables, small to moderate size. Avoid those that are extremely tiny or overly large.

HOW TO STORE: Store summer squash in a perforated plastic bag in the vegetable bin. This way they'll keep well for 4 to 5 days. Don't let moisture bead up on squash.

HOW TO USE: Use summer squash in stir-fries, sautés, stuffed, grilled, in frittatas, soups, pastas, timbales, and summer stews. Zucchini, always overabundant in the garden, has been known to find its way into baked goods and desserts.

SPECIAL HANDLING: Salting, an optional step, improves texture and flavor by removing excess water. Toss coarsely grated or diced squash with a small amount of salt, let it stand in a colander for 15 to 30 minutes, then rinse and squeeze dry. It's amazing how much liquid is exuded and how much more concentrated the final squash flavor is.

QUANTITY: An average zucchini, about 6 inches long, weighs between 4 and 6 ounces. Allow 1^1/$_2$ pounds for four generous servings. One pound of squash yields approximately 4 cups grated, shrinking to 2 cups if salted or about 3^1/$_2$ cups diced or sliced.

Good Partners for Summer Squash

Olive oil, butter, yogurt
Parmesan, Gruyère, goat cheese
Garlic, parsley, basil, marjoram, thyme, dill, mint, lemon
Walnuts, pine nuts
Tomatoes, corn, peppers, eggplant, chile

Sauces and Seasonings for Summer Squash

Blossom Butter (page 46)
Olive-Rosemary Butter (page 46)
Salsa Verde, Chermoula, Cilantro Salsa, or Pesto (pages 48 to 51)
Parsley-Caper Sauce (page 49)
Lemon Vinaigrette (page 164)
Yogurt Sauces (pages 57 to 58)
Fresh Tomato Sauce (page 54)
Tarator Sauce (page 59)

Steamed Squash: Slice 1^1/$_2$ pounds squash and steam until tender, 5 to 8 minutes, depending on size. When cooked, it will take on a shiny, translucent look. Toss with butter or olive oil and chopped fresh herbs and season with sea salt and pepper. Serves 4 to 6 Ⓥ

Grilled Summer Squash: Slice zucchini lengthwise into thirds or halves. Brush each side with olive oil and season with sea salt. Grill on both sides until browned, turning 45 degrees once. Arrange on a platter and brush with any of the sauces suggested for squash (above), especially Yogurt Sauce with Cayenne and Dill (page 57). Ⓥ

Crookneck Squash with Green Onions

Serves 4 to 6 Ⓥ

2 pounds small crookneck squash
2 tablespoons olive oil, butter, or a mixture
8 green onions, including some of the greens, thinly sliced
Sea salt and freshly milled pepper

Halve the squash lengthwise and slice into ^{1}/$_2$-inch-thick rounds or diagonals if larger. Heat the oil in a wide skillet, add the squash, and sauté over high heat until lightly colored around the edges, about 4 minutes. Add the onions and 2 tablespoons water, then lower the heat, cover, and cook until the squash is fully tender, 6 to 7 minutes. Season with salt and pepper to taste.

Slow-Cooked Zucchini Coins with Chopped Herbs and Crumbled Feta

A relaxed slow cooking brings out the zucchini's full squash flavor, which quick cooking eclipses. Serve these golden coins as a side dish, over hot rice, or with pasta. Serves 4 to 6

2 to 3 tablespoons olive oil or butter

1 1/2 pounds zucchini, thinly sliced

1 clove garlic, thinly sliced

Sea salt and freshly milled pepper

1/4 cup chopped mixed herbs—dill, basil, parsley, and cilantro

1/2 cup crumbled feta

Heat the oil in a wide skillet, then add the zucchini and garlic. Sprinkle lightly with salt and cook over low heat for 20 to 30 minutes, stirring every so often. The finished squash should have a light golden glaze over the surface and be caramelized in places. Taste for salt and season with pepper. Toss with the herbs and cheese and serve.

Crosshatched Zucchini: An attractive way to present tender young squash as well as small eggplants. Cut squash lengthwise in half. Using the tip of a small knife, score the cut surfaces in a crisscross pattern without cutting through the skin. Brush lightly with olive oil and season with sea salt and pepper. Heat a cast-iron skillet over medium-high heat, then brush a film of olive oil over the surface. Set the zucchini cut side down in a single layer and cook until golden. Turn, add a few tablespoons water to create a little steam, and cook on the second side until tender when pierced with a knife. Serve cut side up with a wedge of lemon, Harissa thinned with water (page 66), Tomato-Basil Pesto (page 50), or any of the sauces suggested for summer squash on the facing page. (V)

Whole Flowering Zucchini: You may come across young squash attached to their blossoms hidden in your own vines or brought to the farmers' market by an enterprising grower. Although the flowers suggest stuffing, here's another way. Allowing three or four squash per person, separate the flowers and cut them into strips. Slice the squash lengthwise into halves or thirds. Heat a little olive oil in a wide skillet, add the squash, and sauté over high heat. As soon as it begins to color and soften, add the flowers and a splash of water, and cover for 30 seconds. Season with sea salt and pepper to taste and scatter finely chopped basil over the top. Serve warm as an appetizer or as a garnish for an omelet, a vegetable custard, or a rice gratin. (V)

Zucchini and Fresh Herb Fritters

Simply delicious! Serve plain or with a yogurt sauce, Salsa Verde (page 48), or a dollop of Garlic or Chile Mayonnaise (page 52). (For a vegan version, replace the eggs with 1/2 cup pureed silken tofu.) Serves 4 (V)

Sea salt

2 pounds green or golden zucchini, coarsely grated

2 eggs, beaten

1 bunch green onions, including an inch of the greens, thinly sliced

1 cup dried bread crumbs

2 cloves garlic, finely chopped

1/2 cup chopped parsley

1 tablespoon chopped marjoram or basil

1 teaspoon chopped mint

Freshly milled pepper

Lightly salt the zucchini and set it aside in a colander to drain for 30 minutes. Meanwhile, mix the remaining ingredients together except the pepper. Quickly rinse the squash, squeeze out the excess water, then stir it into the batter. Taste for salt and season with pepper.

Film two large skillets with olive oil. When hot, drop in the batter—1/4 cup makes a fritter about 3 1/2 inches across—and cook over medium heat until golden on the bottom. Turn and cook the second side. Serve hot.

Zucchini Matchsticks with Yogurt Sauce

Each of these large, bold batons is tipped with green. Yogurt Sauce with Cayenne and Dill (page 57) is excellent here. If you shred the zucchini instead of cutting it, you get more of a "hash." It's not as pretty, but the flavors are better amalgamated, and it makes a great filling for a crepe or omelet. Serves 4

1½ pounds zucchini

1½ teaspoons sea salt

2 tablespoons olive oil

½ cup Yogurt Sauce with Cayenne and Dill (page 57)

Trim the ends of the zucchini, slice each one crosswise in half, then into long slabs about ⅓ inch thick. Angling your knife, cut the slabs into strips, also ⅓ inch wide. Toss them with the salt, set them in a colander, and let stand for 30 minutes. Rinse and pat dry. Meanwhile, prepare the sauce. Heat the olive oil in a wide skillet, add the zucchini, and sauté over high heat until lightly browned in places, about 5 minutes. (If you prefer to avoid the oil, steam the zucchini instead.) Turn into a bowl and serve the sauce spooned over the top.

Sautéed Zucchini with Garlic and Lemon

Serves 4 to 6 Ⓥ

---

2 tablespoons olive oil

2 cloves garlic, sliced

1½ pounds zucchini, thinly sliced or cut into small dice

Sea salt and freshly milled pepper

2 teaspoons finely grated lemon zest

2 tablespoons chopped herbs, such as dill, marjoram, and basil

---

Heat the oil in a wide skillet, add the garlic, and cook over medium heat until it begins to color. Raise the heat, add the zucchini, and sauté until heated through. Lower the heat and continue to cook, turning occasionally, until tender and golden around the edges, 8 to 10 minutes. Season with salt and pepper, toss with the lemon zest and herbs, and serve.

Squash and Eggplant Fans on an Onion Bed

Inspired by a recipe of Richard Olney's, fanning and stuffing the interstices of short, fat summer squash and plump eggplant gives these vegetables drama. And a mixture of squash and eggplant looks particularly nice. Measurements are relaxed and variable. Serves 4 to 8 Ⓥ

---

4 tablespoons olive oil

1 large red or yellow onion, thinly sliced

2 bell peppers, 1 red and 1 yellow, thinly sliced

1 teaspoon chopped thyme or several thyme sprigs

2 bay leaves

1 tablespoon chopped marjoram

1 cup dry white wine

½ teaspoon sea salt

Freshly milled pepper

2 short, fat zucchini, calabacitas, or Ronde de Nice

2 plump Asian or Italian eggplants, 5 to 7 inches long

4 tomatoes, halved and sliced crosswise ⅜ inch thick

12 niçoise olives, pitted

4 cloves garlic, thinly slivered

Heat 2 tablespoons of the oil in a large skillet over medium heat. Add the onion, peppers, and herbs and cook, stirring occasionally, until lightly browned, 8 to 10 minutes. Add ½ cup of the wine, simmer for 5 minutes, then season with the salt and plenty of pepper. Put the onion mixture in a baking dish large enough to hold the vegetables in a single layer.

While the onions are cooking, slice the zucchini and eggplants lengthwise in half. Placing the cut side on the counter, make two incisions starting about ½ inch below the stem end, dividing the vegetable lengthwise into three even pieces. Work the tomatoes into the spaces and stuff the empty spots with olives and slivers of garlic. (Add any leftover tomato, olives, or garlic to the onions.) Run two toothpicks through the end of each vegetable to hold everything together, then set the stuffed vegetables on the onions. Brush with the remaining 2 tablespoons oil and pour the remaining ½ cup wine over all.

Preheat the oven to 400°F. Cover the dish with foil and bake until the vegetables are tender when pierced with a knife, about 45 minutes for the squash, slightly longer for the eggplant. Serve warm or tepid with the onions and peppers.

Pan-Fried Summer Squash with Vinegar, Tomatoes, and Feta

Such a simple, straightforward dish with tang from aged sherry vinegar (or a really good balsamic), torn basil leaves, little tomatoes—and other goodies. This is the kind of dish I make regularly when zucchini is in season, usually without measuring and always improvising. Invariably, it starts out simply, just zucchini, vinegar, and basil, but I can't resist upping the panache quotient by adding, at the end, sliced small tomatoes such as Mexico Midget, Sun Gold, or currant, shards of feta cheese, and torn basil leaves. Enjoy hot or at room temperature or even cold from the fridge.
Serves 4 or more

---

1 pound summer squash, such as zucchini, pattypans, or crookneck

2 to 3 tablespoons olive oil

1 clove garlic, peeled and slivered

$^{1}/_{2}$ teaspoon sea salt

Freshly ground pepper

2 to 3 teaspoons aged sherry vinegar or aged red wine vinegar, to taste

Several basil leaves—one or two big sprigs, plus extra leaves, slivered, for garnish

Handful small tomatoes, such as yellow currants, Jaune Flamme, Sun Gold, halved or quartered

Thinly sliced feta or ricotta salata cheese

Slice the squash into rounds about $^{3}/_{8}$ inch thick or thinner.

Heat the oil with the garlic in a wide deep sauté pan, or divide between two skillets. When the garlic turns pale gold, remove it. Add the squash to the hot oil, season with the salt, and sauté over high heat, turning every few minutes, until the golden. In all, this will take about 15 minutes. Often a slice of zucchini will be beautifully colored on one side and not on the other, but you can tell it's done because it's soft and slightly translucent. If this is the case, just transfer it to a bowl. Or if you want to, remove pieces as they finish browning. When done, taste and season with more salt, if needed, and plenty of pepper. Sprinkle over the vinegar and turn the vegetables gently with a wide rubber spatula. Tear the basil into pieces and add it to the squash along with the tomatoes and the cheese.

With Eggplant: Sauté small oblong eggplants, such as Fairytales or Ichiban (sliced slightly thinner than the squash) with the squash.

With Squash Blossoms: If your squash has blossoms, shake out any bugs, sliver the blossoms, and add to the zucchini at the last minute.

With Tapenade: Add a few spoonfuls tapenade to the dish once it's done.

STUFFED SUMMER SQUASH

First boil or steam whole squash for 5 minutes to soften, then rinse under cold water. Halve zucchini lengthwise and scoop out the centers with a pointed spoon. Or slice off the top third and scoop out the flesh of the larger bottom piece. Use it, with or without the lid, as a zucchini "boat." Pattypan or scallop squash can be treated the same way. Always leave the shell at least $^{1}/_{3}$ inch thick so that it's strong enough to hold its shape. Use the flesh that's been removed in the stuffing or in a soup stock.

Broiled Zucchini Stuffed with Gruyère and Feta

This is quick, easy, and makes a nice presentation for a first course or light main dish. Serves 4

---

4 medium zucchini, about 6 ounces each

2 teaspoons butter

Sea salt and freshly milled pepper

$^{1}/_{3}$ cup feta cheese

$^{1}/_{4}$ cup cottage cheese or ricotta

$^{1}/_{4}$ cup grated Gruyère

1 egg

1 tablespoon chopped parsley

2 teaspoons chopped marjoram

1 teaspoon flour

Preheat the broiler. Lightly oil a baking dish large enough to hold the squash in a single layer. Prepare the zucchini for stuffing, halving each one and scooping out the flesh. Finely chop the flesh and cook it in the butter in a skillet, stirring frequently, until browned in places. Season with salt and combine with the remaining ingredients.

Fill the zucchini and set them side by side in the prepared baking dish. Broil about 6 inches from the heat until the filling is browned and heated through, about 20 minutes.

Zucchini with Corn and Squash Filling

The round summer squash are perfect containers for this filling. Otherwise, use zucchini. Serves 4 Ⓥ

4 Ronde de Nice or zucchini, about 6 ounces each

1 cup finely diced zucchini

2 teaspoons butter or oil

Kernels from 2 ears corn, about 1¹/₂ cups

1 cup cooked quinoa or rice

2 tablespoons grated Muenster, optional

4 green onions, including some of the greens, thinly sliced

1 jalapeño chile, seeded and minced

2 tablespoons chopped cilantro, parsley, or basil

Sea salt

Preheat the oven to 375°F. Prepare the squash for stuffing, slicing off the top third for a lid. Sauté the diced zucchini in the butter in a skillet over high heat until tender, about 4 minutes. Mix with the remaining ingredients, seasoning with salt to taste. Fill the squash, replace the tops, and set in a baking dish. Add water to come about ¹/₄ inch up the sides of the dish and cover with aluminum foil. Bake until tender when pierced with a knife, about 25 minutes.

Scallop Squash with Saffron Rice

The bright yellow Sunburst variety makes particularly pretty containers. Make sure they can stand firmly—slice a little piece off the bottom if necessary. Serve with a fresh or roasted tomato sauce. Serves 6

6 scallop or pattypan squash, 6 to 8 ounces each

Pinch saffron threads steeped in 1 tablespoon boiling water

³/₄ cup cooked long-grain white rice

3 green onions, including some of the greens, thinly sliced

3 tablespoons finely diced mozzarella, preferably fresh

3 tablespoons chopped basil leaves or Pesto (page 50)

1 teaspoon grated lemon zest

Sea salt and freshly milled pepper

Preheat the oven to 375°F. Prepare the squash for stuffing as described on page 383. Rinse, then slice off ¹/₂ inch or so from the top and set it aside. Hollow out the insides of the squash and chop the flesh. Add the saffron to the rice and add the remaining ingredients, including the chopped squash, seasoning well with salt and pepper. Fill the squash and replace the lids. Set in a baking dish, pour water into the dish to come about ¹/₄ inch up the sides of the dish, then cover with foil and bake until the squash feels tender, about 25 minutes.

Sweet Potatoes

We have long been in the habit of calling sweet potatoes "yams," although the true yam, a tropical vegetable, is not often seen outside of Latin markets. What we call "yams" at the supermarket are, in fact, sweet potatoes. Regardless of what we call them, what we mean are delectable sweet-fleshed tubers.

TYPES OF SWEET POTATOES: Sweet potatoes come with light tan, orange, and purple skins. Their flesh ranges from pale buff to dark, rich orange. In general, the darker the flesh, the sweeter and moister it is once cooked.

Beauregard: This was developed to replace the Jewel because packers don't care for the way the eyes line up in a row, like a perforation or a zipper. It has purple-rose skin and orange flesh.

Covington: A new variety that's taking over commercial production. It has a big blocky shape and more consistent size. It is orange fleshed, moist and sweet.

Garnet: This variety has deep purple skin, dark orange flesh, very sweet but with a well-balanced flavor. Garnets are nearly always available in supermarkets, and usually called yams, even though they aren't.

Hanna (also spelled Hannah): A short, stubby tuber with pointy ends, slightly darker skin, and pale yellow flesh. The chestnut flavor is especially pronounced and delicious.

Hawaiian: Long but chunky. Their skin is purple, the flesh pale, and when steamed, they are moist and nutty.

Jersey: Light-colored sweet potatoes that tend to be on the dry side. Sometimes they resemble chestnuts in flavor.

Jewel: Another sweet, super-moist orange-fleshed sweet potato with a coppery, rather than red-orange skin. It too is often called a yam, rather than sweet potato.

Kotobuki: A long, golden-skinned tuber with dry, straw-colored, nutty-tasting flesh. Delicious and reminiscent of chestnuts.

Louisiana: Sweet, moist-fleshed sweet potatoes—the standard.

WHAT TO LOOK FOR: Firm roots with pointed ends and no bruises. Although sweet potatoes look tough, they're actually easily damaged. Bruises result from even minimal rough handling. Once bruised, spoilage quickly spreads below the surface and ruins the entire vegetable.

HOW TO STORE: In spite of their sturdy appearance, sweet potatoes are not terribly good keepers, so plan to use them within a week of purchase. Your grocery is better equipped for longer storage than your home. Keep them in a cool cupboard, if you have one, or on the counter. They can be refrigerated in a perforated plastic bag, but they don't love the cold and they mustn't freeze.

HOW TO USE: Sweet potatoes are delicious simply baked or steamed and served in their jackets or in the traditional candied versions served during the holidays. They make excellent purees that can also be used in savory and sweet foods, from custards and pies to breads and waffles, and are good roasted and grilled.

SPECIAL HANDLING: Scrub well before cooking. If you want to eat the skins, look for organically grown sweet potatoes. Once peeled and sliced, put them in a bowl of water to prevent oxidation if you aren't planning to cook them for a while—lemon isn't necessary.

Sweet potatoes don't have enough starch to behave the same way regular potatoes do, so they're not really interchangeable with potatoes unless you use some of both.

QUANTITY: Sweet potatoes can weigh as little as 4 ounces or as much as 1 pound. A pound yields 3 to 4 cups chopped or about 1 1/3 cups mashed. Allow at least 4 ounces for a serving.

Good Partners for Sweet Potatoes

Butter, dark sesame and roasted peanut oil
Ginger, allspice, orange, chile, nutmeg, cinnamon
Brown sugar, molasses, maple syrup, bourbon, pecans, black walnuts

Sweet Potatoes in the Pressure Cooker: If you love a big, succulent sweet potato for dinner and don't have an hour for it to roast, try using the pressure cooker. It's a huge time saver especially when it comes to those big 12-ounce tubers.

For tubers weighing 10 to 12 ounces, put the scrubbed tubers in a steaming basket over a few cups water. Bring the pressure to high, hold for 20 minutes, then release quickly or slowly. With a quick release, the potato may be slightly firm in the center, but not uncooked.

For tubers weighing 6 to 8 ounces, bring the pressure to high, hold for 15 minutes, then release quickly.

For smaller sweet potatoes, especially the orange-fleshed varieties, 12 minutes at high pressure should do the trick.

Baked Sweet Potatoes: Nearly every time I bite into a baked sweet potato, I ask myself if anything can be more delicious. With a spinach salad, a baked sweet potato makes an easy dinner that's rich in green and yellow vegetables. Preheat the oven to 400°F. Choose sweet potatoes of similar size if cooking more than one. Scrub well and bake until very tender when pierced, 50 to 60 minutes for a 12-ounce potato. To serve, slice lengthwise, break up the flesh with a fork, and add the traditional pat of butter, coconut oil, or even a little dark sesame oil. Season with sea salt and pepper.

Steamed Sweet Potatoes: Scrub sweet potatoes and leave them whole or cut them into large pieces. Steam, covered, over boiling water until tender when pierced with a knife, 30 to 50 minutes, depending on size. Ⓥ

Grilled Sweet Potatoes: Slice steamed or boiled potatoes in half if they're small or diagonally into 1/2 inch-thick pieces if large. Brush with vegetable oil and grill, turning them 45 degrees after about 7 minutes. Cook on both sides or just one. Season with sea salt and pepper and serve with Golden Mustard Barbecue Sauce (page 65) or Peanut Sauce (page 61). Ⓥ

Boiled Sweet Potatoes: For best results, leave unpeeled potatoes whole. If cut into chunks before cooking, they tend to become waterlogged. Cover with cold water and bring to a boil. Lower the heat and simmer until tender when pierced with a knife. Peel once cooked. Slice or mash and serve with butter or coconut oil, sea salt, and pepper. (V)

Mashed Sweet Potatoes: Leaving their skins on or not as you wish, mash 2 pounds baked, boiled, or steamed sweet potatoes with 1 teaspoon grated orange or tangerine zest, the juice of an orange or tangerine, and butter to taste. Season well with sea salt and pepper and serve. Or try using any of these traditional seasonings: bits of pineapple, candied ginger, toasted pecans or black walnuts, bourbon, a few pinches nutmeg or cinnamon, allspice, and cloves. (Leftovers can be used in Sweet Potato Muffins with Candied Ginger, page 575, or waffles.) Serves 4 to 6 (V)

Mashed Sweet Potatoes with Ginger and Sesame: Boil 2 pounds whole sweet potatoes with 5 slices ginger until completely soft. Discard the ginger, peel the potatoes, and puree or pass through a food mill. Season with sea salt. Stir in 1 teaspoon ground coriander, butter, or toasted sesame oil to taste. Heap in a bowl and garnish with toasted black sesame seeds. Serves 4 to 6 (V)

Broiled Sweet Potatoes: Slice cooked but firm sweet potatoes lengthwise in half or into diagonals 1/2 inch thick, allowing one or two halves per person. Brush lightly with vegetable oil and broil until sizzling. Serve with sea salt and pepper or with a peanut sauce (page 61), Sesame Marinade (page 528), or Golden Mustard Barbecue Sauce (page 65). (V)

Candied Sweet Potatoes

These are still a holiday favorite and are even better the next day with leftover cold cranberries. Use your favorite type of sweet potato or mix all varieties in a single dish. Serves a holiday crowd (V)

3¹/₂ pounds sweet potatoes, scrubbed

1 (1-inch) knob of ginger, peeled and thinly sliced, optional

4 to 6 tablespoons butter or coconut oil

Sea salt and freshly milled pepper

¹/₃ cup maple syrup or dark brown sugar

¹/₂ cup apple juice or water

Cook the potatoes until tender but still slightly firm when pierced with a knife. Drain. When cool enough to handle, remove the skins. Cut them lengthwise into slices about 3/8 inch thick.

Preheat the oven to 375°F. Butter a large, shallow casserole and make a layer of potatoes. Scatter a few ginger slices over them, dot with butter, season with salt and pepper, and drizzle over some of the syrup. Repeat until all the potatoes are used. Dot the last layer with butter and pour in the juice. Cover with aluminum foil and bake for 1 hour. If the oven is being used for other things and is set at a lower temperature, simply bake them longer.

Coconut Pan-Roasted Sweet Potatoes

This is so simple and so good, a side dish or one you can serve with the Collard Greens, Black Rice, and Coconut Butter on page 342 or serve solo. Sweet potatoes and coconut are made for one another, whether in a dessert or this savory dish. Serves 4 to 6 (V)

2 or 3 sweet potatoes, about 2 pounds, any variety

2 tablespoons coconut oil

Sea salt

Maldon sea salt, for finishing

Scrub the sweet potatoes, then chop them into cubes a scant inch across.

Warm the oil in an 8- or 10-inch sauté pan. Add the sweet potatoes, turn them about to coat, and season with a few pinches salt. Put a lid on the pan, turn the heat to medium-low, and cook for about 20 minutes in all, giving the pan a shake every now and then to turn the potatoes. Taste a piece and if they're not yet soft, continue to cook a few minutes longer or until they are tender and browned. Serve with flaky sea salt.

Sweet Potato Puree, Black Walnuts, and Molasses

Black walnuts are the crowning touch to this puree, making this a worthy dish for the holiday table, but pecans or hickory nuts can take their place, if need be. This is a vegetable dish, but it can easily be a dessert. Just pour a little cold cream over each serving and drizzle with molasses—sort of a sweet potato sundae. Serves 6 to 8

2 pounds sweet potatoes, your favorite variety

Butter, for mashing sweet potatoes

Sea salt and freshly ground pepper

1/2 teaspoon ground ginger

2 tablespoons or less molasses

1/2 cup black walnuts pieces, lightly toasted, for garnish

Cut the sweet potatoes into large chunks. Steam them until completely soft when pierced with a knife, 15 to 20 minutes. The skins should come right off, but you can leave them on if you prefer. Mash them with a potato masher or a wooden spoon, adding as much butter as you care to, until you have a fairly smooth mixture. Season to taste with salt, pepper, and ginger, and then stir in the molasses. Pile the sweet potatoes into a serving dish garnish with the nuts.

(If you prefer to serve them later, preheat an oven to 375°F. Omit the nuts, smooth the puree into a buttered baking dish, and bake until heated through, about 25 minutes, then add the nuts.)

Tomatoes

People are passionate about tomatoes, one of the true joys of summer. Good tomatoes require conditions opposite to commercial needs—hand-picked, vine-ripened fruits grown from seeds that predict flavor rather than shipping capabilities—which is why they're so hard to come by in the supermarket. Tomatoes are well worth growing yourself, and if that's not possible, head to the farmers' market. The general rule is that tomatoes are best when they're grown locally, in season, picked when ripe, or nearly so, and not refrigerated.

TYPES OF TOMATOES: It's hard to keep up with all the exciting tomato varieties. Each year heirlooms are rediscovered and new hybrid varieties are introduced, but here are some types we're most likely to see. Curiously, many are named after other fruits.

Plum and Roma tomatoes: In some parts of the country these tomatoes are known as *Romas*, in other parts *plum tomatoes*. But by either name they are oval, 3 to 4 inches long, thick fleshed, and dry rather than juicy. Since there's little juice to cook off, they are particularly suitable for sauces and are called for in recipes where meatiness, rather than juiciness, is desired. Also called paste tomatoes.

Pear, cherry, currant, peach, and grape Tomatoes: Also called fruit tomatoes, pear-shaped and small spheres, red or yellow, these petite tomatoes are charming on a crudité plate or in a composed salad. Cherry tomatoes were once mostly one size—about the size of a cherry—but now these include the tiny currant tomatoes as well as more standard varieties. They can be made into sauces and sautéed, as well as nibbled raw.

Slicing tomatoes: Marmande is a French variety that's bright red, round, and full of the essence of tomato flavor. Early Boy and Early Girl are two standard American varieties that are also round, red, and juicy. In between are a host of unusual heirloom varieties with exotic colors, markings, and shapes—folds, creases, and pleats—that delight the eye and in no way compromise flavor.

Beefsteak: The king of tomatoes, these giant fruits—some can weigh up to 2½ pounds—are the ultimate tomato for a summer salad. The Mortgage Lifter, an heirloom variety, is an excellent example of this type.

Stuffing tomatoes: With deep cavities and thick walls, these are meant for stuffing, with no need to remove the flesh.

Yellow tomatoes: Tomatoes of yellow hue, whether pale or deep, vibrant or matte, are low in acid. Often people who don't like or can't eat red tomatoes find that they enjoy these low-acid varieties.

Green tomatoes: This usually refers to unripe tomatoes, but there are also green varieties that are ripe while they're green, such as the Green Zebra tomato and Green Grape.

WHAT TO LOOK FOR: Regardless of shape, color, or size, good aroma is the key to a good-tasting tomato. They should be firm but not rock hard. It's all right if the skin has a slightly tacky feel to it.

HOW TO STORE: Keep tomatoes at room temperature or in a cool place, but not in the refrigerator unless a glut makes it impossible to do otherwise. Cold kills everything about them that's good.

HOW TO USE: Ripe tomatoes are mostly enjoyed raw, but they make a great cooked vegetable, too. Use tomatoes for soups, salads, sauces, or juice, or sauté, stuff, or bake them. They're an important addition to stews and stir-fries, adding a bit of acid that lifts the surrounding flavors.

SPECIAL HANDLING: None, except to avoid cold. Peeling isn't necessary for raw tomatoes, except for refinement—removing the skins makes their texture silkier. Peeling is advisable when cooking for longer than a brief sauté, since the skins roll up into jagged shards. Removing the seeds is also a matter of refinement—it makes a dish look and feel nicer.

QUANTITY: One pound, or 4 medium raw tomatoes, is ample for three to four servings, two to three servings when cooked, or 1 cup peeled, seeded, and diced tomatoes.

Good Partners for Tomatoes

Butter, olive oil, cream
Parmesan, mozzarella, cheddar, goat cheese
Basil, parsley, tarragon, lovage, chives, oregano, garlic
Vinegar of all kinds
Peppers, squash, eggplant, legumes, corn, shallots

Peeling, Seeding, and Chopping Tomatoes

To peel a tomato, slash a little X at the base with a knife, then drop it into a pot of boiling water. When you see the edges of the X begin to loosen and roll back, after 10 to 20 seconds, scoop it out and drop it into a bowl of cold water to cool. Now you can easily slip off the skin. With ripe tomatoes, the skin may quickly split in other places as well. Remove the tomato as soon as that happens and plunge into cold water.

To seed the tomato, cut it in half around its equator. Hold a half in one hand and pull out the seeds with your fingers while squeezing gently. If a tomato is to be used for a sauce, coarsely chop it. If you want to add visual panache to a dish, separate the walls of the tomato from the core and use just the flat pieces. The cores can be finely diced and used in another or the same dish.

Herb-Baked Tomatoes

Serves 4 Ⓥ

4 ripe but firm slicing tomatoes
Sea salt and freshly milled pepper
Olive oil, for drizzling
2 tablespoons chopped herbs—marjoram, lovage, basil—or 1 teaspoon dried oregano

Preheat the oven to 375°F. Lightly oil a large, shallow baking dish. Cut the tomatoes around their equators and set them upright in the baking dish. Sprinkle with salt, drizzle with oil, cover with the herbs, and season with pepper. Bake until hot and beginning to color on top, about 20 minutes. Serve carefully, making sure they're not stuck to the pan.

Variation: Prepare the tomatoes as described, but reserve the herbs. Bake at 300°F until shriveled and glazed, about 2 hours, adding the herbs for the last 30 minutes. Serve them as a vegetable or perched on a thin round of mozzarella or a slice of toast. Leftovers make a rich addition to a summer soup or sauce.

Tomatoes Provençal

Parsley, garlic, and tomato are a timeless combination. Serves 4 (V)

4 medium or 8 small firm, ripe tomatoes
2 cloves garlic
1 cup parsley leaves, preferably flat-leaf
3 tablespoons chopped basil
3/4 cup bread crumbs made from day-old bread
Sea salt and freshly milled pepper
Olive oil, for drizzling

Preheat the oven to 400°F. Lightly oil a gratin dish. Cut the tomatoes in half around their equators and gently remove the seeds with your fingertips. Chop the garlic, parsley, and basil together, then mix them with the bread crumbs and season well with salt and pepper. Lightly fill the tomatoes with this mixture, set them in the gratin dish, and thread olive oil generously over their tops. Bake for 30 minutes. They'll be soft, so remove them carefully from the dish.

Moroccan Stuffed Tomatoes: I once enjoyed these at a seaside café in Morocco. Though called tomatoes Provençal on the menu, instead of parsley, the filling was rich with the flavors of mint and cilantro. Fill the tomatoes with Chermoula (page 50), cover with bread crumbs and/or grated cheese, then bake as described above. (To make this more substantial, fill the tomato with rice or couscous first and spoon the sauce over the top.)

Tomatoes Glazed with Balsamic Vinegar

This is a very easy thing to do with tomatoes—the vinegar reduces with the butter, leaving the tomatoes glistening and glazed. Serve as a side dish or with toast and chopped parsley for a quick supper. Serves 4

1 1/2 pounds ripe but firm tomatoes
2 tablespoons butter
3 tablespoons balsamic vinegar
1 plump shallot, finely diced
Sea salt and freshly milled pepper

Core the tomatoes, then cut them into wedges about 1 1/2 inches across at the widest point. In a skillet large enough to hold the tomatoes in a single layer, heat the butter until it foams. Add the tomatoes and sauté over high heat, turning them over several times, until their color begins to dull, about 3 minutes. Add the vinegar and shallot and shake the pan back and forth until the vinegar has reduced, leaving a dark, thick sauce. Season with salt and plenty of pepper.

GREEN TOMATOES

They're usually fried and they're good that way. Especially in a sandwich. But here are some other ideas. They may be green, but they're not so astringent that you'll pucker. In fact, they're quite nice raw—almost crunchy and pleasantly green, not tart.

- Slice them and use them in a sandwich for their texture and bright flavor.
- Include some green tomatoes among ripe ones in a salsa or a tomato salad.
- Have them sliced and raw with a yogurt dressing and fresh dill.
- Use them in a pasta dish such as one with broken lasagne and crumbled goat cheese.
- Pickle them whole or use them in a relish.
- Include them in a summer squash gratin.
- Have them as a salad with a blue cheese or feta cheese dressing and crisp bread crumbs.

Fried Green Tomatoes

Serve these as a first course or side dish, use them in a sandwich or pasta, or serve them as a garnish for a stew of corn and late summer vegetables. Serves 4 (V)

- 4 medium green (unripe) tomatoes
- 3/4 cup fine corn meal
- 3 to 4 tablespoons oil or ghee
- Sea salt and freshly milled pepper
- 3 tablespoons chopped basil, tarragon, or parsley, or Red Chile Mayonnaise (page 52)

Slice the tomatoes crosswise 1/3 to 1/2 inch thick. Press each piece into a plate of corn meal to coat on both sides. Heat the oil in a wide skillet over high heat until hot enough to sizzle a drop of water. Add the tomatoes, reduce the heat to medium, and fry on both sides until golden. Transfer to a plate, season with salt and pepper, and serve with the chopped herbs or mayonnaise.

Tomatoes Stuffed with Herbed Grains

Choose ripe but fairly firm tomatoes for stuffing so that they'll hold up to the oven's heat. If necessary, slice a sliver off the bottom so that they can stand. Serves 4

- 4 medium to large ripe but firm tomatoes
- 1 cup cooked rice, couscous, quinoa, or other grain
- 1/2 cup toasted pine nuts or chopped toasted almonds
- 2 cloves garlic, minced
- 3 tablespoons finely chopped parsley
- 2 tablespoons finely chopped dill or basil
- 3 tablespoons grated parmesan
- Sea salt and freshly milled pepper
- Olive oil, for brushing

Preheat the oven to 375°F. Trim the tomatoes, chop the pulp, and mix it with the rice, nuts, garlic, herbs, and cheese. Season well with salt and pepper and fill the tomatoes. Replace the tops, brush them with oil, and set closely together in a small, oiled baking dish. Bake until the filling is hot, about 25 minutes. Carefully transfer the tomatoes with a spatula to a serving plate.

Turnips and Rutabagas

Turnips and rutabagas are often treated as versions of the same vegetable. While what's good for a turnip is good for a rutabaga, rutabagas are drier fleshed and need to cook longer. If you want to interchange them, just allow extra time for the rutabagas. If both are used in the same recipe—and the creamy yellow of the rutabaga is stunning with the white turnip—parboil the rutabagas for 10 minutes to give them a head start.

TYPES OF TURNIPS AND RUTABAGAS: For many people, the only turnips ever seen are large storage turnips, scarred from handling, their greens long discarded, their flesh sometimes bitter. Rutabagas are even worse off, with their heavy coatings of preservative wax. But both turnips and rutabagas have their shining moments. Turnips in their youth, small and firm with shiny white skin and fresh tender greens, are nothing short of exquisite. Rutabagas are rarely sold with their greens, but if you can find them freshly pulled in the fall, they too are an excellent vegetable. Both can be found in their prime at farmers' markets. However, storage turnips and rutabagas shouldn't be overlooked, for they can be a valuable addition to the winter kitchen and their limitations are manageable.

WHAT TO LOOK FOR: In spring and summer, look for small, fresh salad turnips with smooth creamy skins. Greens are a bonus. Avoid giant rutabagas or vegetables that are shriveled or cracked. Look for golden turnips in late summer.

HOW TO STORE: Stored in a plastic bag in the refrigerator, storage turnips and rutabagas will keep for several weeks; fresh turnips keep a few days.

HOW TO USE: Serve fresh turnips raw, with sea salt, as a crudité. Turnips and rutabagas can be included in winter vegetable stews and soups, steamed, pureed, cut into julienne strips and combined with other vegetables, or roasted.

SPECIAL HANDLING: Tender garden turnips needn't be peeled unless you wish to. To sweeten older turnips, thickly peel and slice them, then cook them in boiling salted water for 1 minute. Drain and rinse with cold water. Rutabagas should be thickly peeled.

QUANTITY: One pound, or 4 to 6 small to average turnips or rutabagas, yields 3 to 4 cups chopped, enough for four to six servings.

Good Partners for Turnips and Rutabagas

Butter, cream
Gruyère, blue cheese
Thyme, savory, tarragon, rosemary
Watercress, roasted garlic, leeks, other root vegetables

Roasted Turnips or Rutabagas

A good dish for colder weather, these are especially tasty with crumbs of blue cheese scattered over the top. Serves 4 to 6 (V)

1¹/2 pounds turnips or rutabagas, peeled and quartered
Safflower or sunflower seed oil, for coating
Sea salt and freshly milled pepper
3 small bay leaves
2 rosemary sprigs, or 6 thyme sprigs

Preheat the oven to 375°F. Lightly oil a shallow roasting pan or baking dish. Boil the turnips in salted water for 3 minutes and drain. Wick off the extra moisture with a towel. If using rutabagas, parboil them for 15 minutes or until barely tender. Toss with enough oil to coat them lightly, then season with salt and pepper. Transfer them to the dish with the herbs and bake, uncovered, until tender when pierced with a knife and browned, 25 to 30 minutes.

Buttered Turnips and Rutabagas with Mixed Herbs

This recipe, inspired by British writer Jane Grigson, has long been a favorite of mine. Serves 4 to 6 Ⓥ

1½ pounds turnips and/or rutabagas, peeled
2 tablespoons sunflower seed oil or butter
1 tablespoon chopped parsley
2 teaspoons chopped tarragon or thyme
2 tablespoons snipped chives
1 clove garlic, minced
Sea salt and freshly milled pepper
½ cup fresh bread crumbs browned in 1 tablespoon
    butter or oil

Dice the turnips and rutabagas into ½-inch cubes. Boil them separately in salted water until they're tender-firm, about 12 minutes for the turnips and 20 minutes for the rutabagas. Drain. Heat the oil in a wide skillet. When foamy, add the vegetables and sauté over medium-high heat, stirring frequently, until golden. Toss with the herbs and garlic, taste for salt, and season with pepper. Remove to a serving dish and scatter the crisped bread crumbs over the top.

Julienned Turnips or Rutabagas with Savory

Serves 4 to 6 Ⓥ

1½ to 2 pounds turnips or rutabagas, peeled and julienned
Sea salt and freshly milled pepper
2 tablespoons olive oil, or 1 tablespoon each oil and butter
1 teaspoon finely minced winter savory or ½ teaspoon dried
1 tablespoon chopped parsley

Sprinkle the turnips lightly with salt and set aside in a colander for 30 minutes. Squeeze out the excess moisture.

Warm the oil in a skillet over medium heat. Add the turnips and savory. Cook gently, stirring occasionally, until tender, 12 to 15 minutes. Add the parsley, taste for salt, season with pepper, and toss again before serving.

(If you wish to make this dish with rutabagas, don't salt them, but add them directly to the pan with the oil. Once they're warmed through, add ½ cup water, cover, and cook for 10 minutes. Uncover and continue cooking until tender and browned in places.)

Rutabaga Fries: Peel and slice rutabagas into long batons or french fries. Soak them in water for 30 minutes, then drain and towel-dry. Toss with vegetable oil to coat lightly and a few pinches sea salt. Spread them on a sheet pan and bake at 400°F, turning occasionally, until golden and tender, 30 to 40 minutes. When done, toss them with a little finely minced rosemary, sea salt or smoked salt, and freshly milled pepper.

Turnip or Rutabaga Puree with Leeks

Rutabagas tint the puree butter yellow, and the potato helps make the texture creamy. Serves 4 to 6

---

1 small russet potato, peeled
2 pounds turnips and/or rutabagas, thickly peeled
2 medium leeks, white parts only, chopped
1 clove garlic, thinly sliced
½ teaspoon sea salt
2 tablespoons or more cream, buttermilk, milk, or
    reserved broth
2 tablespoons butter
2 teaspoons chopped thyme
Freshly milled pepper

Chop the potato and turnips the same size. If using rutabagas, chop them about half the size of the potato. Put the vegetables, leeks, and garlic in a pot with cold water just to cover, add the salt, and simmer, partially covered, until tender, 15 to 20 minutes. Drain, reserving the liquid.

Mash the vegetables with a fork for a rough-textured puree or pass them through a food mill. Add the cream or reserved broth to thin the puree. Stir in the butter and thyme and season with salt and pepper to taste.

Variations: Stir 1 cup grated Gruyère cheese into the puree. Or simmer the vegetables in milk instead of water. Add a tablespoon Whole Roasted Garlic (page 340) and a teaspoon finely chopped rosemary to the puree. Or enrich the puree with a little crème fraîche and stir in 1 cup watercress sprigs that have been blanched briefly in boiling water, then finely chopped.

Early Japanese Turnips with Their Greens and Lemon Thyme

The little white Japanese turnips come to the farmers' market in early summer. This 10-minute braise doesn't involve much other than cooking the roots and their greens. The turnips magically sweeten, the leaves temper the sweetness with their peppery tenderness, and the thyme holds everything together in its fragrant, earthy grasp. Serves 4

1 bunch of small white Japanese turnips, at least 8 turnips
4 teaspoons butter
2 teaspoon olive oil
2 sprigs lemon or regular thyme
³/₈ teaspoon sea salt
Splash white wine
Freshly milled pepper

Cut the leaves from the turnips, leaving about ¹/₂ inch of the stems. Slice the turnips in halves or quarters, as you like, so that they're all more or less the same size. Wash them in a bowl of water, taking special care where the stems join the bulbs.

Melt 2 teaspoons of the butter in a small pan with the olive oil. Add ¹/₃ cup water and the turnips. Season them with the salt, bring the water to a boil, then cover the pan and cook on low heat for 5 minutes.

While the turnips are cooking, slice the greens into strips about ¹/₄ inch wide, then wash them in fresh water. Add them to the pan once the 5 minutes have passed and cook 3 minutes. Add the remaining 2 teaspoons butter, the thyme, and the wine and continue cooking, covered, until the liquid has turned to a glaze and the greens and turnips are tender, 2 minutes. Of course the time will depend on the size of your turnips, so judge accordingly by taking a taste. But know that the greens do not take more than 4 or 5 minutes. Season with more salt, if needed, and add just a little freshly milled pepper. Remove the thyme and serve.

Winter Squash and Pumpkins

Winter squash is the name given to those cucurbits that develop tough skins, which allow them to be stored and kept over the winter. Once limited to a few varieties, there is now a plethora of these squashes, including some stunningly rich-tasting ones. While they differ in size, shape, color, and density, nearly all winter squash have a sweet yellow or orange flesh. With the exception of pumpkins grown specifically for eating, squash always makes a better vegetable than pumpkin.

TYPES OF SQUASH: The names and types of squash are ever changing, but these are reliably available:

Acorn squash: This is one winter squash most Americans know—acorn shaped with smooth skin that's dark green, orange, or a splashy mixture of the two. The flavor can be a little bland, which may be one reason it's often sweetened.

Banana squash: This is the squash you used to find cut into slabs and wrapped in plastic at the market. Whole, it's much too huge for most people to lift, carry, store, or cook. But once cut, it's an easy squash to work with. The skin is light pinkish tan, the flesh yellow, and the flavor rather mild. Sibley, an heirloom relative, is beginning to make an appearance.

Buttercup squash: Honey Delight, Black Forest, Red Kuri, and the Japanese kabocha are squat and round and usually dark green except for the Kuri, which is red-orange. All these squash have dense, sweet flesh. You'll be asked if you added sugar to your soups. Although the shape suggests fillings of broth and cream, these are not particularly good for that purpose since the flesh readily absorbs liquids.

Butternut squash: This buff-skinned squash has a long, straight solid neck and a round bottom that contains the seeds. Not only does it have exceptionally good flavor, but butternut squash is easy to peel, which makes it ideal for gratins and other dishes. An excellent all-purpose winter squash. Rogosa Violina is a large heirloom variety.

Delicata Squash: Yellow, orange, or cream-colored with dark green strips, oblong and usually slender, these delicious squash are generally small, weighing about a pound, though toward the end of the season, they can get fairly large. Their shape makes them good shallow containers, and their skins are easy to peel. A similar squash—upright and lighter in color—is Sweet Dumpling. The skins are edible once cooked. Both are closely related to zucchini.

Hubbard squash: Orange, blue-skinned, or slate-colored, large, ungainly, and sometimes covered with "warts," this old-fashioned squash is nonetheless one of the best for eating. Fortunately, new varieties, such as Queensland Blue, are small enough for the home cook to handle.

Mini squash and pumpkins: Sweet Dumplings, Jack-be-Littles, and other tiny varieties can be stuffed, baked, or steamed. One squash is perfect for one person, especially a child who will love having his or her own baby pumpkin. They're cute, convenient, and quite good to eat, too.

Spaghetti squash: Oval and yellow-skinned with pale yellow flesh, this squash is so coarse that its cooked flesh can be pulled into long strands resembling spaghetti. It's somewhat bland but good treated just as spaghetti, with sauces. Chilled cooked squash can be tossed with a vinaigrette and served as a winter salad.

Turban squash: With their high striped "hats," these look very exotic but are not nearly as pleasant to eat as to look at. Better for decorations and doorstops.

WHAT TO LOOK FOR: Winter squash and pumpkins should be firm and hefty for their size. The heavier they are, the denser and moister the flesh. There may be rough patches on the skin, but the only real problem is soft, spongy spots; avoid them if you can or cut them out if you can't. Choose squash that still have their stems.

HOW TO STORE: Keep whole squash in a cool, dry place that has plenty of ventilation—a back porch would be ideal. If you like to keep them out where they can be seen, try to use them within a month or two, before they dry out. Cut squash can be wrapped and refrigerated for up to a few days.

HOW TO USE: Winter squash are easy to bake, roast, or steam. They can be made into purees and soups and used in pies, breads, and cakes. Slices and chunks can be fried, sautéed, or baked in gratins and simmered in stews. The skins and seeds are effective in soup stocks.

SPECIAL HANDLING: Cutting large squash can be difficult. A heavy knife or cleaver and a rubber mallet are useful tools. Whack the knife into the squash, then bear down or tap it with the mallet to open the squash. Cut next to the stem rather than through it—it'll be easier on your knife. Or bake squash whole until they begin to soften, then cut them. Spaghetti squash needs to be punctured in several places before baking, or it will explode in the oven. Some nonchalant cooks I know drop large squash on the floor to break them open—advisable only when all else fails.

QUANTITY: Allowing for the seeds and skins, a 1-pound squash, halved and baked, is adequate for two or more servings, and 1 pound of peeled, seeded squash yields approximately 2 cups pureed. Whole weights and trimmed weights will vary from one squash variety to another, so it's difficult to give absolute quantities. However, those who love squash will wish for large portions, and leftover cooked squash is always easy to reheat.

Good Partners for Winter Squash and Pumpkins

Olive oil, butter, brown butter, sunflower seed oil

Fontina, Gruyère, Pecorino Romano, parmesan

Sage, rosemary, garlic, red pepper flakes, chile, cumin, coriander

Brown sugar, coconut milk, ginger, lime, lemongrass, curry

Onions, radicchio, apple, quince

Sauces and Seasonings for Winter Squash

Green Chile Butter (page 46)

Chermoula (page 50)

Quick Vinegar Sauce for Onions (page 357)

Harissa (page 66)

Persillade and Gremolata (page 21)

Warm Sage and Garlic Butter (page 44)

Salsa Verde (page 48)

Baked Winter Squash: A practical approach to preparing squash for any number of uses. Cut a squash in half, then scoop out the seeds and fibers. Brush the cut surfaces with a thin film of oil and set the squash, cut side down, on a sheet pan. Bake at 375°F or whatever oven temperature is convenient, until the squash looks wrinkled, soft, and about to collapse, usually about 30 minutes. The cut side should be richly glazed. Place upright on a serving plate, season with sea salt and pepper, a tad of butter, and serve. Or scoop out the flesh, mash it with butter or oil, and return it to the shell. You can also use this squash to make a puree, soup, or pie filling. Ⓥ

Sometimes young squash exudes a clear, sweet liquid. If you let it sit for about 15 minutes, the liquid will become reabsorbed into the flesh as it cools.

Baked Whole Squash: If a squash is too tough to cut into pieces or too large to handle easily, pierce it a few times with a knife and bake it whole at 350°F or so until it feels soft when pressed, 30 minutes or longer, depending on size. Remove, then halve and scrape out the seeds. Return it to the oven and continue cooking until it's done. Or cook until completely soft, then halve and seed.

Steamed Squash: Cut winter squash into halves, quarters, or wedges, scrape out the seeds, and place in a steamer basket over boiling water. Steam, covered, until tender, 30 to 40 minutes, depending on size. Season with butter or oil, sea salt, and pepper or scrape out the flesh and use for other dishes. Ⓥ

Squash in the Pressure Cooker: Here's a way to cook squash simply and quickly without having to remove their skins—or seeds—first. Cut your squash into big chunks, as big as your hand or larger, fit them in the pressure cooker, add water, and bring the pressure to high. Hold it for 15 minutes, then release quickly. Now you can easily scrape the flesh from the skins and discard the skins. Two pounds of squash yields between 2 and 3 cups of cooked flesh. Ⓥ

Grilled Winter Squash or Pumpkin: This is for those who like to grill in all seasons. If you plan to leave the skins on, you can use any variety of winter squash. If peeling them is important, stick to butternut or delicata squash. Cut squash into slices a scant 1/2 inch thick, remove fibers and seeds, and steam until barely tender. Combine 2 minced cloves garlic with 1 teaspoon each chopped rosemary and thyme and 1/3 cup olive oil. Brush it over the squash and season with sea salt and pepper. Grill on both sides until marked and tender, then serve with a dash of apple cider vinegar or a spicier condiment such as Harissa (page 66). Ⓥ

Winter Squash Puree: Easy, versatile, and useful, this can fill ravioli, turn into a soup, or be added to muffins, breads, biscuits, and waffles. Halve, seed, and bake 3 pounds squash until tender. Scrape the flesh away from the skin, then beat until smooth by hand with a large wooden spoon. This should be easy unless the squash is stringy, in which case use a food processor or food mill. Stir in butter or oil to taste and season with sea salt and pepper. Makes about 2 cups.

To enrich the puree, grate Gruyère, fontina, or Emmentaler into it. Crumble fried sage leaves on top. Add mascarpone and freshly grated nutmeg to taste. Flavor with extra-virgin or dark sesame oil, smoked paprika, or mix in Sautéed Onions (page 357). Ⓥ

Roasted Winter Squash or Pumpkin: Use a squash that's easy to peel, such as butternut or banana. Preheat the oven to 400°F. Peel and seed 2 1/2 to 3 pounds squash and cut into 2-inch cubes. Toss it with olive or vegetable oil to coat lightly and season with sea salt and pepper. Spread the squash in a large baking dish or sheet pan. Roast for 15 minutes, turn the pieces, and roast for 15 minutes more. Turn again and bake until the squash is completely tender, 10 to 15 minutes longer. Ⓥ

Steam-Baked Acorn Squash: Preheat the oven to 375°F. Cut an acorn squash in half from stem to tip and remove the seeds. Brush with oil and place cut side down in a baking dish. Add 1/2 inch water and bake until soft, about 30 minutes. By this time, the water will have evaporated and the bottom will have begun to color. Serve with butter or oil, sea salt, and pepper, or sweeten with a spoonful of maple syrup, honey, or brown sugar and a dash of cinnamon, nutmeg, or allspice. Ⓥ

Baked Delicata Squash: Delicata is one of the easiest squashes to handle and one of the quickest to cook. Preheat the oven to 350°F. Allow one 8- to 12-ounce squash per person. Place a large knife on one of the green grooves that run down the surface of the squash, bear down, and cut the squash in half lengthwise. Scrape out the seeds, brush the cut surface with olive oil, season with sea salt and pepper, and set, cut side up, in a baking dish. Add about 1/3 inch water, cover with aluminum foil, and bake until tender, 25 to 35 minutes. Ⓥ

Provençal Winter Squash Gratin

A long, slow baking intensifies the already deep flavor of the squash. In his book Simple French Food, *Richard Olney suggests cutting the squash into tiny cubes. For special meals, I make it his way—it's marvelous looking with the crusty cubes of squash tinged brown on the edges. But for every day, I cut the squash into larger pieces.* Serves 4 to 6 (V)

2 to 2 1/2 pounds butternut squash

5 cloves garlic, finely chopped

1/2 cup chopped parsley

Sea salt and freshly milled pepper

3 tablespoons flour

Olive oil, for drizzling

Preheat the oven to 325°F and oil a shallow earthenware baking dish. Peel the squash and cut it into even-size cubes, from 1/2 inch to 1 inch. Toss it with the garlic, parsley, salt, and pepper. Add the flour and toss again until the pieces are coated lightly, letting the excess fall to the bottom. Pile the squash into the dish and drizzle oil generously over the top. Bake, uncovered, until the squash is browned and tender when pierced with a knife, about 2 hours. When served, the individual pieces will collapse into a puree.

Delicata Squash Rings

These take just 10 to 12 minutes to cook and when finished are glazed with a rich caramel coating from the natural sugars in the squash. Serve these as a side dish or add them as an attractive garnish to winter vegetable stews.
Serves 2 to 4 (V)

2 delicata squash, 12 to 16 ounces each

1 1/2 tablespoons olive or vegetable oil

Sea salt and freshly milled pepper

Chopped parsley and Gremolata (page 21), for garnish, or any of the suggested sauces and seasonings on page 394

Slice off the ends of the squash and scoop out the seeds with a teaspoon. Cut the squash into rings about 1/3 inch thick. Heat the oil in a wide skillet, add the squash, and fry over medium heat until richly colored on the bottom, about 6 minutes. Turn and cook on the second side until tender. Transfer to a serving plate, season with salt and pepper, and garnish with parsley. Remember, you can eat the skins.

Roasted Red Kuri Squash Wedges with Spice Rub and Pistachio

Winter squash wedges are rubbed with spice, then baked until tender and fragrant. If you have some spice rub already made (and even if you don't), this can be prepared by the time the oven is hot. Red Kuri is readily available, but it's not as sweet as some of the other varieties we eat, so the sugar and salt do help bring its savory flavors to the fore. Serves 6 (V)

1 (3-pound) winter squash, such as Red Kuri

2 tablespoons Peggy's Spice Rub (page 21)

1/3 cup pistachio nuts, finely chopped

Coconut oil (melted) or light sesame oil, as needed

Heat the oven to 400°F. Line a sheet pan with parchment paper.

Knock the stem off the squash, then slice it in half through the stem end. Scoop out the seeds, then slice each half into wedges about 2 inches across at the widest, or less if you can manage it.

Mix the spice rub and pistachio nuts with the coconut oil, then rub it over just one surface of each piece. Lay the squash, unrubbed surface facing down, on the sheet pan. Bake in the center of the oven until the squash is tender, 20 to 30 minutes, depending on the thickness. Carefully set the pieces on a platter and serve.

Butternut Squash Coins

Butternut squash is the easiest and prettiest of the squashes to use because of is long, smooth neck. Serve these squash coins with Sautéed Onions (page 357), drizzled with Chermoula (page 50) or Salsa Verde (page 48), or with plenty of freshly milled pepper and a few drops of apple cider vinegar or balsamic vinegar. Serves 4 to 6 ⓥ

1 large butternut squash, about 3 pounds
4 to 6 tablespoons olive oil or sunflower seed oil
Sea salt and freshly milled pepper

Slice the neck from the squash where it joins the bulb. Peel it with a vegetable peeler or a knife, using long, even strokes. Reserve the bottom for another use. Slice the neck crosswise about 1/4 inch thick. Preheat the oven to 200°F. (The bulb can be steamed another time.)

Heat 2 tablespoons of the oil in a wide skillet over medium-high heat. Add a single layer of squash and fry until golden and flecked with brown, about 10 minutes. Turn and fry the second side. Remove to paper towels to drain and keep warm in the oven. Repeat with the rest, adding oil as needed. Season with salt and pepper. Serve drizzled with vinegar, smothered with Sautéed Onions (page 357), or with one of the suggested sauces on page 394.

Spaghetti Squash with Gruyère Cheese

A simple and very satisfying combination of flavors. Be sure to puncture the squash in at least a few places, or it will explode in the oven and make a truly amazing mess—I know this from experience. Even when properly cooked, the strands of squash will be a little crunchy. Serves 4

1 spaghetti squash, about 3 pounds, punctured
1 cup grated Gruyère
1/4 cup parsley chopped with 1 clove garlic
2 to 4 tablespoons butter
Sea salt and freshly milled pepper

Preheat the oven to 375°F. Bake the squash until the flesh is yielding and soft, an hour or more. Slice the squash in half and scrape out the seeds. Now drag a fork through the flesh, pulling the strands apart. Toss them with the cheese, parsley–garlic mixture, and butter. Season with salt and pepper and serve. Very nice with smoked salt.

Spaghetti Squash with Tomato Sauce: Tomato sauces of all kinds are good with spaghetti squash. Toss the strands lightly with olive oil, salt, and freshly milled pepper, then pile them on a platter. Make a nest in the middle for 1 to 2 cups tomato sauce. Toss, then serve. Pass parmesan cheese at the table, if desired. ⓥ

Spaghetti Squash with Mushroom Ragout: Serve spaghetti squash with any of the mushroom ragouts or with Sautéed Mushrooms with Garlic and Parsley (page 351). Season the squash with butter or olive oil, sea salt, and pepper, then mound it on a platter and surround with the mushrooms. Toss before serving. ⓥ

PASTA, DUMPLINGS, AND NOODLES

CHAPTER 12

Pasta, Dumplings, and Noodles

In the 1980s and even into the '90s, pasta was considered an ideal food, perfect for any busy person who wanted to eat simply, quickly, and well at home. After all, a plethora of dishes can be made from a pound of noodles and a few vegetables, often in the amount of time it takes to boil water and cook the pasta.

Certainly one of the beauties of pasta is that it pairs endlessly well with vegetables, adapting with ease to the nuances of the changing seasons. Pasta is equally good with summer's ripe tomatoes, spring's asparagus, or the pungent greens of fall and winter. Cheese-enriched dishes and baked pastas are befitting for the colder months, while pastas paired with shelling beans are stellar in the fall or in winter when dried or canned beans will do quite well in their stead. For people who want to eat more vegetables, pasta may well be one of the best ways to go.

But what used to be a standby has now been shunted to the same little corner crowded with other foods we used to eat with abandon—butter, bread, cheese, cream. Why? Pasta is carbs. Pasta makes us fat. Pasta is a refined food. Most pasta contains wheat. It's not a food we should be eating at all, say many. Like bread and butter, pasta has become more of treat and less than the answer to the what's-for-dinner question.

But pasta has changed in some good ways, too. It's not all made of unrefined white flour or the better durum flour. Much is now organic. Many are whole wheat. And newly available are those made of ancient grains such as spelt and einkorn. (They look formidably dark but cook up very nicely, indeed.) Buckwheat noodles (soba and *pizzocher*) have been around forever and there are, of course, all those Asian noodles based on different starches than wheat altogether, such as rice, mung bean, and yam. The increasing bounty of Asian noodles takes us into entirely new realms of possibility. There are gluten-free pastas, like corn spaghetti, which are not always stellar in terms of texture, but for those who are seriously intolerant, a godsend, I would imagine. Quinoa flour also gets transformed into pasta nowadays.

All in all, pasta still remains an excellent hook for drawing plenty of vegetables to the plate. I can't think of a vegetable pasta isn't good with, except maybe avocados and sweet potatoes, and I'm sure there are exceptions. You can smother pastas with vegetables and some of us find them the best thing about a plate of spaghetti. In fact, I sometimes insert some cooked pasta shapes or ravioli into vegetable ragouts just to add some different texture, so we can have vegetables with pasta as well as pasta with vegetables. Of course there are also those times when an upset tummy wants nothing more than some soothing plain egg noodles.

Pasta dishes that are to be baked can be set up hours ahead of time so that they're ready to heat when you're ready to eat. More elaborate pastas, such as ravioli, cannelloni, and layered lasagne are dishes worthy of a special occasion. Dumplings, a close relative, are tender morsels that rank among the most comforting foods we know.

VEGAN PASTAS: I find that a bit of cheese at the end always makes pasta dishes come alive. But often that's the only dairy involved in a pasta recipe, so you can simply leave it out. Almost all the pasta recipes are vegan if you do that. There are some exceptions where the flavor of butter and other cheeses are what makes the dish. Usually the cheese used appears in the recipe title in such cases.

SERVING SIZES: Four ounces of pasta, fresh or dried, is more than adequate for a main course serving. In truth, I find that 3 ounces is ample, and that 2 ounces is even a better amount. If you're serving pasta for a first course or making a very rich pasta, which you'll eat in smaller quantity, then 1 to 2 ounces should be plenty. Of course, serving sizes relate to what else you're having in the meal—how much and how rich it is—and who's eating, how big and how young they are.

Making Fresh Pasta

It's easy to get the hang of making pasta, and it's always amazing to see the noodles that accumulate from your rather minimal efforts. For equipment, all you need is a relatively inexpensive hand-cranked pasta machine. For ingredients, use all-purpose flour, good-quality eggs, olive oil, and sea salt. Throughout the book, I've used large eggs, but for pasta, extra large seem to provide just the right amount of moisture. If your climate is very dry, you may need to use a little extra liquid—beaten egg, olive oil, milk, or water. Although a wet dough is easy to knead, it's harder to handle later on because it will stick to itself when you roll it out. Make it soft enough to knead with ease, but try not to make it overly moist. A dry dough will smooth out as you pass it through the pasta machine.

Egg Pasta

Makes about 1 pound

- 2 cups flour
- 2 extra large eggs
- 2 teaspoons olive oil or water, if needed
- 1/4 teaspoon sea salt

By Hand: Put the flour on a clean counter, shape it into a mound, and make a well in the center. Put the eggs, oil, and salt in the center, break them up with a fork, then gradually begin pulling in the flour from the sides. Bring in as much flour as you can and still have a smooth mass of dough that doesn't stick to your hands.

When you can't add any more flour, pass the flour remaining on the counter through a strainer, returning it to the counter; discard the lumps. Knead the dough, picking up as much of the flour on the counter as it will hold, until it's silky and moist but not sticky, 3 to 4 minutes. Slip the dough into a plastic bag and set it aside to rest for 10 to 15 before rolling it out. If your dough is dry and difficult to knead, this resting period will help soften it.

In the Mixer: You'll need a heavy-duty mixer with a paddle attachment. Mix the flour and salt in the bowl. Beat the eggs and oil together with a fork in a cup. With the mixer on low, add the eggs and oil and mix until the flour is absorbed. It will look rather lumpy. Grasp it with your hand, form it into a ball, and knead until smooth and pliant. Cover and let rest for 10 to 15 minutes.

In the Food Processor: Combine the flour and salt in a food processor and turn on the motor. Add the oil, then the eggs. Work until little pealike particles are formed, then turn the dough out, gather it together, and knead until smooth. Cover and let rest for 10 to 15 minutes.

Rolling Out the Dough

The pasta machine is essentially foolproof and will work the dough to smoothness even if your own kneading techniques are weak.

Flatten the dough out with your hands to make a piece of the width that will fit your machine. (If you're increasing the recipe to make 1½ pounds, divide the dough into two pieces.) Set the machine at the widest setting (the lowest number) and feed the dough through once. Now fold the dough into thirds, press down on any excessively thick parts, and run it through again with the open edges going through first. Repeat this process until the dough is smooth, four or five times.

Go to the next notch on the machine and run the dough all the way through without folding it. (With this and every pass through the machine, lightly dust the dough with flour or semolina.) Turn the gear to the next notch and pass the dough through once. Continue through the next-to-the-last setting. The dough should be very thin. If it isn't (machines differ), go on to the last setting.

To make the increasingly long piece of dough easier to handle, you can cut it into smaller lengths at any point and roll each one separately, but it's surprisingly resilient and will tolerate being flipped back and forth over the machine. The dough can now be cut into noodles.

EGG PASTA AMOUNTS

- 1 cup flour + 1 extra large egg yields 8 ounces or enough for 2 large and 4 medium portions
- 2 cups flour + 2 extra-large eggs yields 1 pound pasta or enough for 4 large or 6 medium portions, or a lasagne recipe
- 3 cups flour + 3 extra large eggs yields 1½ pounds pasta or enough for a lasagne recipe for 6 large or 8 medium portions

Cutting the Noodles

You may want to use your machine's cutting attachment, but cutting by hand leaves a rougher edge—better for catching the sauce.

Fold a piece of dough roughly 15 inches long into thirds, then cut firmly across the folds into the width you want your pasta to be. Toss the strands in a little flour or semolina to separate them and keep them from sticking. You can cook the pasta right away or set it aside on a floured surface covered with a cotton towel for up to several hours, or to cook the next day.

FLAVORED PASTAS

The following amounts are for 1 pound of pasta, using the Egg Pasta recipe on page 400.

SAFFRON PASTA: Crumble 3 pinches saffron threads and steep them in 2 tablespoons hot water until the water cools. Add it to the flour when you add the eggs.

RED PEPPER PASTA: Add 1 tablespoon ground red chile, red pepper flakes, or paprika to the flour.

BLACK PEPPER PASTA: Add 2 tablespoons coarsely milled pepper to the flour.

SPINACH PASTA: Wash and dry 2 cups lightly packed spinach leaves, then puree them with the eggs. Use this as the liquid for the pasta. You may need to add a little extra flour to the dough, which will be emerald green.

ROSEMARY PASTA: Add 3 tablespoons minced fresh rosemary to the dough.

GREEN HERB PASTA: Roughly chop ¼ cup assorted fresh herbs, such as thyme, marjoram, parsley, basil, arugula, and/or sage. Blanch them for 10 seconds in boiling water, squeeze dry, then finely chop. Add them, with the eggs, to the flour. Emphasize a single herb or make a mixture.

Seven Steps to Cooking Pasta

1. **Bring a large pot of water to a rolling boil.** Whether the noodles are fresh or dried, long or short, using a large pot of water gives them lots of room to swim around so they don't stick to each other. The volume also helps maintain the rolling boil that keeps the pasta aloft and in motion. For 1 pound, use 6 quarts of water. If you're parboiling vegetables, use the same water and cook the vegetables first.

2. **Add salt, then the pasta.** Add plenty of sea salt—at least a teaspoon for every 4 cups water. Add it just before you add the pasta since salty water is slower to boil and the salt can develop an odd taste after a short time. It isn't necessary to add oil to the water.

3. **Boil until the pasta is al dente.** Part of the charm of dried pasta is its texture. It needs to have a little bite, to be firm to the tooth, which is what *al dente* means. Cooking time is always relative to the size of the pot, the vigor of the boil, and your altitude. Instead of relying on the clock, taste the pasta as it cooks, until it is tender but retains a pleasant firmness. There shouldn't be a chalky core at the center of the pasta, which indicates rawness. The moment between rawness and perfection is brief, so be on your toes. Pasta with holes in it may cook more quickly than you anticipate since it cooks from both the inside and the outside. Pasta made from grains other than wheat also cooks differently, so consult the instructions before starting, but rely on your taste. Fresh egg pasta cooks in just a few minutes and doesn't achieve the same degree of toothiness as dried.

4. **Drain the pasta.** You can drain pasta into a colander, scoop it out with a strainer, or lift it out with a pair of tongs (just hold the tongs upright so the scalding water doesn't flow down your arm). If your sink is filled when the crucial moment comes, a strainer will be very useful. A large flat Chinese strainer works well, as does the special oval Italian scoop that you can slide in right next to the edge of the pot. If it's important that the pasta be dry so as not to dilute the sauce, use a colander.

5. **Put the pasta directly into the sauce, letting some of the cooking water drip into the pan.** Often I let some of the water drip into the pasta vegetables—it seems to add just the right amount of moisture to thin the sauce and keep the noodles from sticking. There is no need to rinse pasta unless you need to stop the cooking at once, as for baked pasta dishes that will be finished later. In this case, toss the cooked, cooled noodles with a little olive oil to prevent them from sticking.

6. **Serve in heated pasta plates.** Pasta cools quickly, and as it loses its heat, it becomes increasingly less wonderful. So just before serving pasta, ladle some of the boiling water into the serving bowl or pasta plates to warm them or have the dishes warming in a low oven. Bowls designed specifically for pasta and soup plates are the perfect shape and size.

7. **Pass a piece of cheese with the grater.** While you might add a little cheese to the pasta when you toss it, you don't want to add so much that the noodles cling together. Instead, have a chunk of hard grating cheese on a plate with a small grater and pass it around the table. Freshly grated cheese is always preferable to pregrated—it has better flavor.

Spaghetti with Artichokes

Artichokes have one season in the spring and a second in the fall. A spring dish might be seasoned with fresh tarragon, a fall dish with rosemary and toasted walnuts or with bread crumbs crisped in olive oil. Serves 4 to 6 Ⓥ

---

4 to 6 medium artichokes, trimmed and quartered

Juice of 2 large lemons

1/3 cup olive oil

1 large onion, finely diced

4 cloves garlic, chopped

2 small bay leaves

3 tablespoons chopped tarragon (spring) or rosemary (fall)

1/2 cup dry white wine

1/2 teaspoon sea salt

1 pound spaghetti

Freshly milled pepper

Freshly grated parmesan, plus a chunk of parmesan for the table, optional

---

Thinly slice the artichoke quarters and put them in a bowl with the lemon juice and water to cover. Start heating a large pot of water for the pasta.

Heat 3 tablespoons of the oil in a wide skillet with the onion. Drain and add the artichokes. Sauté over high heat, stirring frequently, until they're well colored, about 7 minutes. Lower the heat and add the garlic, bay leaves, half the tarragon, and the wine. Simmer, scraping the pan, until the wine is reduced. Add 1 cup water and the salt and cook until the artichokes are tender, about 10 minutes. Taste for salt.

Cook the spaghetti in boiling salted water until al dente. Scoop it out and add it to the artichokes with the remaining oil and tarragon. Season with salt and freshly milled pepper and toss well. Serve the pasta lightly covered with grated cheese, then pass the cheese and grater at the table.

Einkorn or Brown Rice Spaghetti with Arugula, Walnuts, and Ricotta Salata

Pastas made with einkorn flour or brown rice (Jovial makes both) are dark looking and robust tasting. They're also heartier than those made with refined wheat flour, thus a good match for spicy late arugula and toasted walnuts. A good fall dish. In place of arugula, try this with seared ribbons of radicchio or escarole. Serves 4

12 ounces einkorn spaghetti

Sea salt and freshly ground pepper

1/4 cup olive oil, plus 1 tablespoon fine olive or walnut oil, to finish

Several pinches red pepper flakes

6 to 8 cups or large handfuls arugula, long, large stems removed

1/2 cup walnuts, lightly toasted, or Salt and Pepper Walnuts (page 79)

1 tablespoon chopped parsley or rosemary

Ricotta salata, thinly sliced

Cook the pasta in salted boiling water until al dente. While it's cooking, heat the oil in a wide skillet, add the pepper flakes and the arugula. Cook to wilt the arugula, then season it with salt and a little pepper.

When the spaghetti is done, lift it out with tongs into a bowl, then scrape in the contents from the skillet and toss well. Taste for salt and season with pepper. Add the walnuts, walnut oil and herb, and toss well. Cover with the shaved ricotta salata and serve.

Linguine with Asparagus, Lemon, and Spring Herbs

A minimal but true pasta primavera. Should they come your way, stew a handful of peas or fava beans with the green onions as well. This dish can be made with butter or olive oil or a mixture. Serves 4 to 6 Ⓥ

4 tablespoons olive oil or butter, or 2 tablespoons of each

1 large bunch green onions, including half of the greens, thinly sliced

2 1/2 teaspoons grated lemon zest

1 tablespoon finely chopped thyme, sage, or tarragon

Sea salt and freshly milled pepper

2 pounds asparagus, tough ends removed

1 pound linguine

4 tablespoons pine nuts, toasted in a small skillet

3 tablespoons chopped parsley, chervil, or tarragon

2 tablespoons snipped chives, plus blossoms if available, for garnish

Freshly grated parmesan, optional

While water is heating for the pasta, heat half the oil in a wide skillet over low heat. Add the green onions, lemon zest, thyme, and a few pinches salt and cook slowly, stirring occasionally.

Meanwhile, slice 3-inch tips off the asparagus, then slice the remaining stalks diagonally or make a roll cut. When the water boils, salt it, add the asparagus, and cook until partially tender, 3 to 4 minutes. Scoop it out and add it to the onions. Cook the pasta, then add it to the pan with some of the water clinging to the strands. Raise the heat and stir in the remaining 2 tablespoons oil, the pine nuts, herbs, pepper to taste, and a few tablespoons cheese. Divide among pasta plates, grate a little cheese over each portion, and garnish with the chive blossoms.

Butterflies with Chickpeas

Nothing could be quicker to make than this dish, and since it's quite likely you already have chickpeas and pasta and good olive oil on hand, it makes a great last-minute supper.
Serves 2 to 4 Ⓥ

3 tablespoons olive oil

1 plump clove garlic, minced

3 tablespoons chopped parsley

1/4 teaspoon red pepper flakes

1 1/2 cups cooked chickpeas, rinsed if canned

8 ounces farfalle or orecchiette

Sea salt and freshly milled pepper

3 tablespoons mixed freshly grated parmesan and Pecorino Romano, optional

1/2 cup bread crumbs crisped in olive oil or toasted in the oven

Warm half the oil in a large skillet with the garlic, parsley, and pepper flakes. Add the chickpeas and 1/2 cup water and simmer gently over medium heat. Meanwhile, cook the pasta in plenty of salted boiling water until al dente. Drain and add it to the chickpeas. Toss, taste for salt, season with pepper to taste, and add the remaining oil. Serve covered with a sprinkling of the cheeses and the toasted bread crumbs.

Lumache with Broccoli and Capers

A fast little pasta for busy nights—although there's nothing second rate about this dish, with its succulent hits of broccoli nestled inside pasta. Serves 4 to 6 Ⓥ

2 cloves garlic, peeled

1/2 teaspoon sea salt

1/3 cup olive oil

1/2 teaspoon red pepper flakes

1/4 cup capers, rinsed

1 1/2 pounds broccoli

1 pound lumache, conchiglie, or gnocchi

Freshly milled pepper

Freshly grated parmesan, optional

Mince or mash the garlic with the salt until smooth, then put it in a large bowl with the oil, pepper flakes, and capers. Thickly peel the broccoli stems. Cut both the crowns and stems into small bite-size pieces.

Bring plenty of water to a boil for the pasta. When it boils, add salt and broccoli and cook, uncovered, until tender, 4 to 5 minutes. Scoop it out, shake off the water, add it to the bowl, and toss with the oil mixture. Cover. Cook the pasta until al dente, then drain and add it to the broccoli. Toss well, season with plenty of pepper, and toss with the cheese.

With Broccoflower or Romanesco: Use either or both of these vegetables in place of or along with the broccoli. Also good with these vegetables are diced roasted red peppers, Salsa Verde (page 48), pitted black olives, fresh marjoram, or a few pinches dried oregano.

Whole Wheat or Einkorn Spaghetti with Handfuls of Sage

If you have even one mature sage plant, you can make this dish without making a dent in its crown of leaves, which is good because you will want a good handful or two of leaves. They're fried in olive oil, which flavors the oil at the same time. Bread crumbs add texture, a bit of cheese another dimension. Serves 4 Ⓥ

1/4 cup olive oil

1 clove garlic, slivered

At least 10 sage leaves per person

8 ounces whole wheat, einkorn, or spelt spaghetti

A few pinches red pepper flakes

1/2 cup dry toasted bread crumbs

Freshly grated good parmesan, optional

Sea salt and freshly ground pepper

Heat the oil with the garlic until fragrant and the garlic has colored. Discard the garlic. Add the sage leaves to the oil and cook, turning frequently, over medium-high heat until they've darkened and take on a pebbly appearance. Remove the pan from the heat. Cook the pasta in generously salted boiling water until done. Strain it and transfer it to a warm bowl. Pour the oil with the sage leaves over the pasta, setting aside a few for garnish. Toss the pasta with the red pepper flakes, then with the bread crumbs. Grate the cheese over the top, season with salt and pepper, and serve.

Pasta with Broccoli Rabe and Tomatoes: Add 2 or 3 tomatoes, seeded and diced, to the greens toward the end of their cooking, then add the pasta and season as described. Toast a few tablespoons pine nuts in a small skillet until golden, then scatter them over the top. Serve with or without the lemon.

Fusilli with Broccoflower, Olives, and Herbs

I like cauliflower accompanied by strong, clean tastes like those provided by olives and herbs. Broccoflower, used here, looks and tastes a lot like cauliflower and you can use them together or interchangeably. Serves 4 to 6 Ⓥ

1 large head broccoflower, cauliflower, or a mixture
1 bunch green onions, including most of the greens, thinly sliced
1 bunch parsley, stems removed, leaves finely chopped
2 tablespoons finely chopped tarragon
1/2 cup pitted and chopped Spanish green olives
1/3 cup olive oil
1 pound fusilli, rotelle, or other sturdy pasta
Sea salt and freshly milled pepper
Coarsely grated ricotta salata, optional

Bring a large pot of water to a boil. Cut the broccoflower into small florets, then peel and dice the stems. Salt the water, add the broccoflower, and boil until partially tender, 3 to 5 minutes. Scoop the broccoflower into a large bowl and add the green onions, herbs, olives, and oil. Cover to keep warm. Cook the pasta in the salted boiling water, then drain, add it to the bowl, and toss well. Taste for salt and season with pepper. Add the cheese, toss again, and serve.

Einkorn Spaghetti with Garlic, Parsley, and Bread Crumbs

A dish for all seasons that's made from pantry staples. The ubiquitous Roman trio—garlic, olive oil, and red pepper flakes—seasons this simplest of pastas. Serves 4 to 6 Ⓥ

12 ounces einkorn spaghetti
1/3 cup olive oil
4 cloves garlic, chopped
1/2 teaspoon red pepper flakes

1/2 cup chopped flat-leaf parsley
1/2 cup mixed freshly grated parmesan and Pecorino Romano, optional
Sea salt and freshly milled pepper
1/2 cup fresh bread crumbs crisped in 1 tablespoon olive oil

Cook the spaghetti in plenty of salted boiling water. Meanwhile, warm the oil with the garlic and pepper flakes in a wide skillet over medium heat. As soon as the garlic starts to color, remove the pan from the heat.

Drain the spaghetti, shaking off the excess water, and put it in a warmed pasta bowl. Pour the oil mixture over the top and toss with the parsley and cheese. Taste for salt, season with pepper, and serve with the bread crumbs scattered on top.

Orecchiette with Broccoli Rabe

Orecchiette, the little ear-shaped pasta, is traditionally combined with robust broccoli rabe. I make this often when broccoli rabe is available, and when it's not, I find the Chopped Broccoli (page 307) is delicious here, too. Serves 3 or 4 Ⓥ

1 bunch broccoli rabe, about 1 1/2 pounds
12 ounces orecchiette
1/4 cup olive oil, plus best oil to finish
3 cloves garlic, thinly sliced
1/2 teaspoon red pepper flakes
Sea salt
Freshly grated parmesan, optional
Lemon wedges

While the pasta water is heating, trim the rugged stems of the broccoli rabe, then add the whole bunch to the boiling water. Boil for 5 minutes, then remove it with a strainer and coarsely chop. Start cooking the pasta in boiling salted water.

Meanwhile, warm the oil with the garlic and pepper flakes in a wide skillet over medium heat until fragrant. Add the broccoli rabe and cook gently, occasionally adding a little pasta water to the pan so it doesn't dry out. Drain the pasta, add it directly into the greens, and toss with a spoonful of the olive oil, salt to taste, and a little grated parmesan. Toss well and serve with an additional dusting of cheese and a wedge of lemon on each plate.

Whole Wheat Spaghettini with Cauliflower, Butter, and Pepper

The simplicity of this dish is deceiving. It's very good—full of warm, lively flavors. Serves 4 to 6

Sea salt and freshly milled pepper

1 cauliflower, cut into tiny florets, stems peeled and chopped

$1/4$ cup butter

$1/2$ cup finely chopped parsley

1 teaspoon coarse mustard

$1/4$ teaspoon red pepper flakes

1 pound whole wheat spaghettini, orecchiette, or small conchiglie

$1/2$ cup freshly grated parmesan, Pecorino Romano, or a mixture

$1/2$ cup fresh bread crumbs, toasted until golden and crisp

Bring a large pot of salted water to a rolling boil. Add the cauliflower, and cook for 3 minutes. Scoop the cauliflower into a large pasta bowl and add the butter, parsley, mustard, and pepper flakes. Add the pasta to the salted boiling water and set the bowl over the pot to keep it warm, leaving a crack so the water doesn't boil over, while the pasta cooks. Drain the pasta when it's done and add it to the cauliflower. Grind a generous amount of pepper over all, then toss with the cheeses and crumbs.

Summer Spaghetti with Corn and Tomatoes

Those with severe allergies to wheat can try this nontraditional summer pasta and take advantage of the parallel flavors. Don't expect corn-flour or quinoa pasta to have the same texture as wheat, though. Serves 3 or 4

12 ounces corn or quinoa spaghetti

2 tablespoons butter

1 bunch green onions, including half of the greens, chopped

2 cups corn kernels, from 3 ears corn

1 bell pepper, any color, finely diced

1 jalapeño chile, seeded and diced

3 tomatoes, halved, seeded, and diced

$1/2$ cup chopped cilantro

$1/2$ teaspoon sea salt

Freshly milled pepper

2 ounces queso fresco or feta

1 lime, quartered

Cook the pasta in plenty of salted boiling water until al dente. Meanwhile, heat the butter in a large skillet and add the green onions, corn, bell pepper, and chile. Sauté over high heat for 3 minutes, then add the tomatoes, most of the cilantro, and a ladle of the pasta water. Season with the salt and a little pepper and turn the heat to low. Drain the pasta, shaking off the excess water. Add it to the vegetables and toss well. Divide among pasta plates, crumble the cheese over the top, and add the remaining cilantro. Serve with a wedge of lime.

Summer Pasta with Garden Vegetables and Tarragon

The vegetables are what's in the summer garden—if not your garden exactly, then perhaps at your local farmers' market. The measurements, as well as the vegetables, are suggestions. All things in season together taste good together, so it's hard to go astray.

This is surprisingly pleasing at room temperature with a dash of good balsamic or wine vinegar. Serves 3 or 4 Ⓥ

3 ripe garden tomatoes

3 slender carrots, scrubbed and thinly sliced in rounds

4 small summer squash, thinly sliced or cubed

$1/2$ cup shucked pod peas or a handful sugar snap peas

1 small red onion, quartered and thinly sliced crosswise

2 cloves garlic, minced

1 yellow or red bell pepper, quartered and thinly sliced crosswise

2 tablespoons chopped tarragon

3 tablespoons olive oil

Sea salt and freshly milled pepper

12 ounces penne or fusilli or other favorite pasta shape

Bring a large pot of water to a boil. Blanch the tomatoes for 10 seconds, then peel, seed, and neatly dice them. Put them in a large bowl. Blanch the carrots and summer squash for 2 minutes and the peas for 1 minute. As they finish cooking, scoop them out with a strainer, shake off the excess water, and add them to the tomatoes along with the onion, garlic, bell pepper, tarragon, and oil. Add salt to the water and cook the pasta until al dente. Scoop it out, add it to the vegetables, and toss well. Taste for salt, season with pepper, and serve.

Fresh Linguine with Tomato Sauce

When made with fresh pasta, this simple dish is divine. Good food is often the simplest, but relies on fine ingredients. A fresh summer tomato sauce is really a treat. Serves 4 Ⓥ

2 cloves garlic

1/3 cup olive oil

2 cups Fresh Tomato Sauce (page 54)

2 tablespoons chopped basil

2 tablespoons chopped parsley

Sea salt and freshly milled pepper

12 ounces fresh linguine

Red pepper flakes, for serving

Start heating a large pot of water for the pasta. Meanwhile, whack the garlic with the flat side of a knife and remove the skins. Warm the oil in a large skillet over medium heat, add the garlic, and cook gently until the cloves are golden. Remove them and discard. Add the tomato sauce and herbs and simmer gently over medium heat, stirring occasionally. Season with a few pinches salt. If the sauce looks a little dry, add a ladle of the pasta water. Cook the pasta in the boiling water until al dente, drain, and put it in a serving bowl. Add the sauce and toss well. Season with pepper to taste and pass red pepper flakes at the table.

Spaghetti with Tomatoes, Olives, and Capers

This summer spaghetti has lots of spirit with its summer tomatoes, olives, capers, and herbs. It's almost a warm pasta salad. Serves 4 to 6 Ⓥ

1/3 cup olive oil

3 large cloves garlic, 2 sliced and 1 chopped

1 pound Roma tomatoes, peeled, seeded, and chopped; 1 pint cherry tomatoes, quartered; or 1 (15-ounce) can tomatoes, chopped

24 kalamata olives, pitted and coarsely chopped

1/4 cup capers, rinsed

1/2 teaspoon red pepper flakes

3 tablespoons chopped marjoram

Sea salt and freshly milled pepper

1 pound spaghetti or spaghettini

1/2 cup chopped parsley

Heat the oil with the garlic slices in a wide skillet over medium heat. When the garlic is golden, remove and discard it. Add the chopped garlic, tomatoes, olives, capers, pepper flakes, and marjoram. Simmer briskly for 10 minutes and season with salt and pepper. Cook the spaghetti in plenty of boiling salted water, drain, and add it to the sauce along with the parsley. Toss well and serve.

With Roasted Peppers: Add a red and yellow bell pepper, roasted (see page 364), or 1 cup jarred roasted peppers, peeled, seeded, and chopped, to the skillet with the tomatoes. Ⓥ

Fettuccine and Sautéed Peppers with Parsley

Colorful and uncomplicated, and the peppers echo the shape of the fettuccine. Do consider the variation as well. Serves 4 to 6 Ⓥ

4 large bell peppers—red, yellow, and orange or all one color

1/4 cup olive oil

Sea salt and freshly milled pepper

1 pound fettuccine

2/3 cup chopped parsley

Freshly grated parmesan, optional

Start heating a large pot of water for the pasta. Meanwhile, cut the peppers into strips about as wide as the fettuccine. Heat the oil in a large skillet over high heat, then add the peppers; give a stir, let them sit for a few minutes, and stir again. Continue cooking in this fashion for about 10 minutes. The peppers should caramelize here and there along the edges, soften, and yield their juices but not lose their skins. They'll smell very sweet. Season with salt and pepper, add a ladle of the pasta water, and turn the heat to low.

Add salt to the boiling water and cook the pasta until al dente. Scoop it out and add it to the peppers, allowing some of the water to drip into the pan. Raise the heat and toss the pasta and peppers with the parsley. Distribute the pasta among the plates, then go back to the pan for the peppers that have fallen aside. Grate a little cheese over the top and serve.

With Saffron or Garlic Mayonnaise: Toss 1 pound rigatoni or other sturdy dried pasta shape with 1/2 cup Saffron or Garlic Mayonnaise (page 52), then add the peppers. This makes a very luscious dish of pasta.

Penne with Tomatoes, Olives, Lemon, and Basil

The tomatoes cook by the heat of the pasta, which leaves them fresh but fully aromatic. Peeling them is optional, but it makes their texture silky. Serves 2 to 4 (V)

1 1/2 pounds ripe tomatoes, 1 or more varieties, large and small

3 tablespoons finely diced shallot or onion

Handful torn basil leaves

1 tablespoon chopped parsley

20 niçoise olives, pitted and chopped

Grated zest of 1 lemon

2 cloves garlic, minced

2 pinches red pepper flakes

3 tablespoons olive oil

Sea salt and freshly milled pepper

8 ounces penne, conchiglie, or rigatoni

Bring a large pot of water to a boil for the pasta. Plunge in the tomatoes for 10 seconds, then peel, halve, gently squeeze out the seeds, and chop into 1/2-inch pieces. Combine the tomatoes in a large bowl with the shallot, basil, parsley, olives, lemon zest, garlic, pepper flakes, and oil. (This sauce can sit for an hour before being used.) Add salt to the boiling water and cook the pasta until al dente. Drain and add it to the tomatoes. Toss gently with a wide rubber scraper. Divide among pasta plates, season with salt and pepper, and serve.

Perciatelli with Roasted Tomatoes, Saffron, and Garlic

Perciatelli—spaghetti with a hole down the middle—is ideal for high altitudes since it cooks from both the inside and the outside, taking less time as a result. Serves 4 to 6 (V)

3 pounds Roma or other paste tomatoes, halved lengthwise

1/3 cup olive oil

1 large slice white sourdough or country bread

4 plump cloves garlic, coarsely chopped

1/2 teaspoon sea salt

3 pinches saffron threads

1 pound perciatelli or spaghetti

Freshly milled pepper

1/3 cup coarsely chopped parsley, to finish

Preheat the broiler. Set the tomatoes cut side down in a baking dish in a single layer. Brush them with some of the oil and broil about 6 inches from the heat until the skins begin to char, about 5 minutes. Turn them over with a spatula and broil the second side until browned in places. Don't worry if they start to fall apart.

Brush both sides of the bread with oil and broil until golden on both sides. Break it into large pieces and pulse in a food processor with 1 clove garlic to make fine crumbs. Pound the remaining 3 cloves garlic in a mortar (a large one if you have one) with the salt and the saffron until smooth. Stir in a tablespoon hot water and the remaining oil, then add the tomatoes one by one and pound to make a sauce with a slightly rough texture. (This last step can also be done in a food processor.)

Cook the pasta in plenty of boiling salted water until al dente. Drain, then put it in a warm serving bowl. Toss with most of the sauce, then divide among pasta plates. Spoon the remaining sauce over each portion and finish with the bread crumbs, pepper, and parsley.

Broken Lasagne, Fried Green Tomatoes, and Parsley

Strong, curly-edged pieces of lasagne stand up well to fried green tomatoes. Though this one is not a traditional recipe, there are a number of traditional lasagne dishes that are tossed rather than layered. Lasagne doesn't always need to be a laborious effort. Serves 4 to 6 (V)

2 pounds green tomatoes, sliced 1/3 inch thick

1/2 cup fine corn meal

Sea salt and freshly milled pepper

Vegetable oil, for frying

1/4 cup olive oil

4 cloves garlic, finely chopped

1 heaping cup coarsely chopped parsley

1 pound lasagne noodles, broken into large pieces

Parmesan, dry Jack, or aged Asiago, optional

Coat the tomatoes with corn meal seasoned with salt and pepper. Heat about 1/8 inch vegetable oil in a skillet. When hot, add the tomatoes and fry over medium heat until browned but not soft, about 30 minutes on each side. Transfer to paper towels to drain.

Put the olive oil, garlic, and parsley in a wide pasta bowl. Cook the lasagne in plenty of boiling salted water until al dente, then drain it, add it to the bowl, and toss. Season with plenty of pepper. Divide among heated plates, cover with the tomatoes, add more pepper, and grate the cheese lightly over all.

Linguine or Lumache with Onions, Peas, and Basil

New onions from the summer garden and fresh peas make a delicate dish for late spring or early summer. Butter and olive oil are both good with peas—although I prefer the butter here. The linguine is delicate and filling for the tender peas, but lumache will actually catch the peas. Serves 2 to 4 (V)

3 tablespoons butter or olive oil

1 red onion, quartered and thinly sliced crosswise

1¹/₂ pounds fresh peas, shucked, or 2 cups frozen

Sea salt and freshly milled white pepper

8 ounces fresh or dried linguine

¹/₄ cup small basil leaves, plucked into pieces

3 tablespoons freshly grated parmesan, optional

Start heating a large pot of water for the pasta. Meanwhile, melt 1 tablespoon of the butter in a wide skillet. Add the onion and a few spoonfuls water and stew over low heat until the onions are soft, 8 to 10 minutes. Add the peas and cook until they're bright green and tender, a minute or two. Season with salt and a little pepper.

Cook the pasta in the boiling salted water, then scoop it out and add it to the peas, allowing a little water to fall into the pan. Add the basil and remaining 2 tablespoons butter, then toss with a large fork and spoon. Distribute the pasta among heated plates, then go back for the peas that have stayed behind and spoon them over the pasta. Add a dusting of parmesan to each plate.

Rosemary Pappardelle with Roasted Winter Vegetable and Red Wine Ragout

You can cook the vegetables for this hearty pasta a day or two in advance since they don't suffer with time, but plan to thin the sauce with mushroom stock or water. The root vegetables should be cut slightly smaller than the other vegetables. Serves 4 to 6 (V)

¹/₂ ounce dried porcini, about ¹/₂ cup

1 large onion, chopped into ¹/₂-inch pieces

1 large red bell pepper, chopped into ¹/₂-inch pieces

¹/₂ pound mushrooms, chopped into ¹/₂-inch pieces

4 cups root vegetables cut into small dice—carrots, celery root, turnips, parsnips

2 cloves garlic, chopped

2 tablespoons olive oil

1 teaspoon sea salt

1 tablespoon tomato paste

Aromatics: 8 sprigs parsley, 4 sprigs thyme, 1 bay leaf, 1 (3-inch) sprig rosemary

1¹/₂ tablespoons flour

2 cups dry red wine

1 pound Rosemary Pasta (page 401) or dried wide pasta

3 tablespoons butter or olive oil

Chopped rosemary or parsley, to finish

Preheat the oven to 450°F. Cover the dried mushrooms with 1 cup warm water and set aside for 20 minutes, then drain. Reserve the liquid and chop the mushrooms.

Toss all the onions, peppers, fresh mushrooms, root vegetables, and garlic with the oil and salt. Roast them on a sheet pan until browned in places, about 25 minutes. Transfer the vegetables to a wide skillet set over medium heat. Add the chopped mushrooms, tomato paste, and aromatics. Stir in the flour, then add the wine and reserved mushroom water. Simmer, partially covered, for 30 minutes. Season with salt and pepper. Remove the aromatics just before serving.

Meanwhile, make the pasta, roll it out, and cut it into ¹/₂-inch-wide strips, or pappardelle. Cook the pasta in plenty of boiling salted water until done, then drain. Toss the pasta with the butter and half the vegetables in a wide pasta bowl. Divide it among individual plates and spoon the remaining vegetables over the top along with the rosemary.

Saffron Noodle Cake

This versatile and attractive dish goes well with spring and summer vegetables. The eggs bind the cake and give it more substance, but vegans can omit them. You can make Saffron Pasta (page 401) or buy dried saffron linguine. If you use the latter, omit the saffron from the recipe.

Accompany with crumbled goat cheese; Garlic Mayonnaise (page 52) and roasted peppers; or serve with garlicky braised greens and any spring or summer vegetable ragout. Serves 3 or 4 (V)

- 2 tablespoons olive oil
- 2 pinches saffron threads
- 8 ounces saffron pasta, linguine, or spaghettini
- 2 eggs, beaten
- $1/2$ cup freshly grated parmesan or Asiago, optional
- 1 bunch green onions, including an inch of the greens, finely sliced
- $1/2$ cup finely chopped parsley
- $1/3$ cup finely chopped basil or marjoram
- Sea salt and freshly milled pepper
- 2 tablespoons butter, olive oil, or a mixture of butter and oil

Warm the oil in a small metal measuring cup, add the saffron, and set aside. Cook the pasta in plenty of boiling salted water until al dente, then drain. Rinse under cold water and shake dry. Combine it with the saffron oil, eggs, cheese, green onions, and herbs and mix well—your hands will be the best tool. Season with salt and plenty of pepper.

Heat half the butter in an 8- or 10-inch nonstick skillet. Add the pasta, pat it down, and even the edges. Cook over medium heat until golden on the bottom, about 5 minutes. Turn the cake out onto a plate, add the remaining butter to the pan, slide the cake back in, and cook until the second side is crisp and golden. Cut into wedges and serve.

Saffron Noodle Cake with Cheese: Add just half the noodles to the skillet, then cover with a layer of fresh mozzarella, provolone, or fontina, leaving a $1/2$-inch margin around the edge. Cover with the rest of the noodles and finish cooking. When you slice the cake, there will he a thin, succulent layer of cheese in the center.

Saffron Noodle Cake with Pepper Filling: Spread 2 cups Peperonata (page 363) over the bottom layer of noodles, then cover with the remainder. (V)

Portabella Mushrooms with Pappardelle

Even if you make the pasta yourself, this is an easy but impressive, bold dish. The pasta can be made several hours in advance, or you can use dried pasta. Serves 2 to 4

- 8 ounces fresh Egg Pasta (page 400), cut into $1/2$-inch-wide noodles, or 8 ounces dried pappardelle
- 2 portabella mushrooms, about 1 pound
- 2 tablespoons olive oil
- 1 small onion, finely diced
- Sea salt and freshly milled pepper
- 2 cloves garlic, finely chopped
- 1 tablespoon tomato paste
- $1/2$ cup dry white or red wine
- $1/3$ to $1/2$ cup cream to taste, optional
- $1/4$ cup chopped parsley
- 2 teaspoons minced rosemary or marjoram
- 2 tablespoons toasted bread crumbs
- Freshly grated or shaved parmesan, to finish

Make the pasta first and set it aside. Meanwhile, remove the stems and scrape the gills from the portabellas and slice the caps into $1/2$-inch strips. Cut the larger pieces in half.

Heat the oil in a large skillet, add the onion, and cook over medium heat until lightly colored. Raise the heat, add the mushrooms, and sauté until they begin to brown, about 4 to 5 minutes. Season with salt and pepper and add half the garlic. Mix the tomato paste and wine and add it to the mushrooms. Lower the heat and cook for 5 minutes more. If the pan dries, add a little pasta water.

Add the cooked pasta to the mushrooms along with the cream, herbs, and remaining garlic. Toss, correct the seasonings, and divide among warm serving plates. Scatter the bread crumbs and a very light dusting of freshly grated cheese over each serving.

Spaghettini with Salsa Verde

Green and pungent with flecks of parsley, tart capers, and garlic, the sauce can be made ahead of time. Serves 4 to 6 (V)

1 cup Salsa Verde (page 48), at room temperature
1 pound spaghettini or long fusilli
Freshly grated parmesan, optional

Put the salsa verde in a pasta bowl. Cook the pasta in plenty of boiling salted water until al dente, then drain and shake off the water. Add it to the bowl and toss well. If using, grate a little parmesan over the top or pass around separately.

With Zucchini: Dice 8 ounces tender green zucchini into small cubes and boil in the pasta water until tender, about 4 minutes. Scoop it out, shake off the water, and add to the bowl with the salsa verde. Cook the pasta and toss it with the sauce and zucchini. (V)

Pasta and Cheese

Cheese is an irresistible partner for pasta. When the heat of the pasta meets the crumbles and shards of cheese, there's an explosion of fragrance that's truly sensational. Cheeses are an immensely enjoyable food, and they can support a good wine. Cheese is especially appealing in cold weather—appropriate for winter festivities and celebrations. Don't try to make these pastas with less of anything to save calories and fat—just enjoy them fully on special occasions—or in smaller portions.

Fettuccine, Parmigiano-Reggiano, and Butter

Every mouthful of this classic pasta is a treasure. Though simple, it relies on care each step of the way, starting with the ingredients—the best butter you can get, golden Parmigiano-Reggiano, and fresh egg pasta. Makes 4 to 6 small servings

8 ounces Parmigiano-Reggiano, in chunks, at room temperature
1/4 pound butter, in small pieces, at room temperature
1 pound Egg Pasta (page 400), cut as fettuccine
Freshly milled pepper

Allow time to grate the cheese finely by hand. Have the wine opened, the table set, and the plates warmed before you begin. Also have a large shallow bowl at hand since you'll need plenty of room to toss the cooked pasta. (This applies to all pasta dishes, but here you especially don't want to waste the perfection of your ingredients.)

Put half the butter in the bottom of the bowl. Cook the pasta in plenty of salted boiling water until done, drain it in a colander, and add to the bowl. Add about 1/2 cup cheese and begin lifting the strands of pasta with a fork and spoon, working quickly and letting the strands fall back into the bowl. Continue until the butter is melted and the strands are coated.

Add the rest of the butter and another 1/2 cup cheese and repeat until the strands of pasta are coated with the sauce formed by the melting butter mingling with the cheese. Scatter the rest of the cheese over the top and serve. Pass a pepper mill at the table.

Macaroni and Potatoes Smothered with Onions and Gruyère

A dish to come home to after a day of skiing or some other vigorous outdoor activity. Serve with a crisp salad and fresh pears or a chilled winter fruit compote. Serves 4 or more

3 tablespoons clarified butter, or 1 1/2 tablespoon each butter and vegetable oil, mixed
2 large onions, thinly sliced into half-rounds
4 small potatoes, peeled and cut into 1/2-inch chunks
1 pound macaroni
1 cup grated Gruyère
1/4 cup chopped parsley
Sea salt and freshly milled pepper

Start by heating a large pot of water for the pasta. Meanwhile, melt the butter in a wide skillet. Add the onions and cook over medium heat, stirring occasionally, until nicely browned, about 20 minutes. Salt the boiling water, add the potatoes, and boil until tender, about 8 minutes. Scoop them out and put them in a warmed pasta bowl. Add the pasta to the boiling water and cook until al dente. Drain and add to the potatoes. Toss with the cheese and parsley and season with salt and plenty of pepper. Serve smothered with the onions.

Fettuccine with Gorgonzola

This favorite pasta can support a full-bodied red wine and is so uncomplicated that it can make a classy spur-of-the-moment or company meal. Make sure your cheese is pale and creamy, with no off odors. Serves 4

 1 clove garlic, thinly sliced

 8 ounces Gorgonzola dolcelatte, broken into chunks

 2 tablespoons butter

 1/4 cup cream or milk

 12 ounces fresh fettuccine

 Sea salt and freshly milled pepper

Start heating a large pot of water for the pasta. Meanwhile, set a large bowl with the garlic, cheese, butter, and cream over the pot. As the water heats, the butter and cheese will soften. Don't worry about lumps of cheese—the heat of the pasta will smooth everything out. When the water comes to a boil, remove the bowl and salt the water. Add the pasta and cook the pasta until done. Drain, add it to the cheese, and toss everything with a fork and spoon until the pasta is coated with the sauce. Taste for salt, season with pepper, and serve on warmed pasta plates.

With Goat Cheese: Replace the Gorgonzola with 8 ounces fresh goat cheese. Cook as described but toss with chopped thyme or rosemary.

Baked Pastas

Baked pasta dishes usually consist of a number of elements—the pasta, vegetable, cheese, and plenty of sauce to keep everything moist. Some preparations are very straightforward, others far less so. Lasagne made from scratch can be quite involved, but a tossed lasagne gratin is not. The advantage of all of them is that they can be put together long before they're baked. They're wonderful to come home to when you've been out all day, and they're great dishes for gatherings when you don't want to be in the kitchen.

Angel Hair Pasta and Cheese Soufflé

The finest of pasta strands, angel hair is used to make these airy pasta gratins. Bake this gratin in a standard soufflé dish, individual gratin dishes, or a single large one. Serves 4

 Béchamel Sauce (page 47), using 2 1/2 cups milk, 5 tablespoons butter, salt and pepper, 1/8 teaspoon grated nutmeg

 3 eggs, separated

 1/2 cup grated Gruyère

 1/2 cup freshly grated parmesan

 8 ounces angel hair pasta

Begin making the béchamel sauce. While it's cooking, heat the oven to 450°F. Butter an 8-cup soufflé dish, gratin dish, or four individual dishes. Whisk a little of the sauce into the egg yolks to warm them, then whisk in the rest along with the Gruyère and all but 2 tablespoons of the parmesan.

Cook the pasta in plenty of boiling salted water until barely al dente, then drain and rinse under cold water. Combine the pasta with the sauce in a roomy bowl. Whisk the egg whites until they hold stiff peaks, then fold them into the pasta. Scrape everything into the prepared dish and sprinkle the remaining parmesan over the top. Bake until puffed and golden brown, about 25 minutes.

Pasta and Mushroom Soufflé: Sauté 8 ounces chopped mushrooms in 1 1/2 tablespoons olive oil over high heat until they release their juices and begin to brown, about 5 minutes. Season with salt, pepper, and 2 teaspoons finely chopped marjoram or rosemary. Stir this mixture into the béchamel sauce and proceed as described above. You can replace a portion or all of the milk with homemade Mushroom Stock (page 176) or commercial mushroom stock.

Pasta and Spinach Soufflé: Remove the stems from 1 large bunch spinach, wash well, and cook in the water clinging to its leaves until wilted and tender. Chop finely, add to the béchamel sauce, and proceed as described.

Ziti with Sharp Cheddar and Mushrooms

Ziti, a tubular pasta, comes in both long strands and short tubes. The long coils are a lot of fun to work with. Macaroni or mostaccioli can also be used. Serves 6

3 tablespoons butter, olive oil, or a mixture of oil and butter

1 celery rib, finely chopped

8 ounces mushrooms, chopped

2 leeks, white parts only, quartered lengthwise and sliced

1 teaspoon dried marjoram

$^1/_4$ cup flour

3 cups milk, warmed

1 teaspoon sea salt

Freshly milled pepper

$^1/_8$ teaspoon grated nutmeg

1 heaping tablespoon mustard

1 pound ziti, macaroni, or mostaccioli

$1^1/_2$ cups grated sharp cheddar

1 cup fresh bread crumbs

Warm the butter in a saucepan. Add the celery, mushrooms, leeks, and marjoram and cook over medium heat for about 5 minutes. Stir in the flour and cook for 1 minute, then quickly whisk in the milk. Simmer for 15 minutes, stirring occasionally. Season the sauce with the salt, pepper to taste, nutmeg, and mustard.

Preheat the oven to 350°F and lightly butter or oil a 12-cup baking dish. Cook the ziti in plenty of salted boiling water until barely done. Drain it in a colander, then rinse under cold water. Combine the pasta with the sauce and cheese, then pour it into the baking dish and cover with the bread crumbs. Bake until bubbling and browned on top, 25 to 30 minutes.

BAKING PASTA IN A MOLD

To give baked pasta dishes a more finished look, brush the bottom and sides of an 10-inch springform pan generously with butter or oil, then coat with fine dried bread crumbs or ground almonds. Place the pan on a cookie sheet. Add 2 beaten eggs to the pasta to ensure that its form will hold, then add the pasta to the mold. Bake at 350°F for 25 minutes until hot. To serve, transfer the pan to a large plate, gently loosen the sides, and remove. Slice into wedges.

Penne with Eggplant and Mozzarella

The tomato sauce here is quite straightforward, but if you have a little extra time or wish to make this without the cheese, prepare the more robust Red Wine Tomato Sauce (page 56) and include the olives as suggested in the variation. You'll need 3 to 4 cups sauce. Serves 4 to 6

$1^1/_2$ to 2 pounds eggplant

Sea salt and freshly milled pepper

5 tablespoons olive oil

1 onion, finely diced

$^1/_2$ teaspoon dried thyme

$^1/_4$ teaspoon red pepper flakes

3 cloves garlic, minced

1 (28-ounce) can crushed tomatoes

$^1/_4$ cup chopped basil or marjoram

1 pound penne or macaroni, cooked until al dente and rinsed under cold water

1 cup grated mozzarella

1 cup grated Gruyère

Slice the eggplant into rounds or ovals $^1/_2$ inch thick, then into $^1/_2$-inch-wide strips about 2 inches long. Lightly salt it and set aside while you make the sauce.

Warm $1^1/_2$ tablespoons of the oil in a medium skillet, add the onion, thyme, and pepper flakes, and cook over medium heat until the onion has softened, about 10 minutes. Add the garlic and cook for a few minutes more. Add the tomatoes and simmer for 30 minutes. Season with salt and pepper.

Preheat the oven to 375°F. Oil a 12-cup baking dish. Pat the eggplant dry. Heat the remaining $3^1/_2$ tablespoons oil in a large skillet, add the eggplant, and cook over medium heat until golden and tender, stirring occasionally, about 20 minutes. Season with pepper and toss with the herb. Mix the eggplant with the tomato sauce, pasta, and cheeses in the baking dish, then cover with aluminum foil and bake for 35 minutes or until heated through.

Noodle Kugel

Ann Katzen's kugel and its reputation among Santa Fe friends long preceded our meeting. Slightly sweet, kugels are often served as if they were savory, though you can certainly serve this as dessert. I like this one with chilled Applesauce (page 607) or Quince Sauce (page 607) and a simple watercress salad. Serves 6 to 8

1 pound wide egg noodles

2 cups cottage cheese

2 cups sour cream

4 eggs, lightly beaten

1/2 cup sugar

1/2 cup golden raisins

1 cup grated tart apple, or 1/2 cup diced apricot

Topping

1 cup fresh bread crumbs

1 teaspoon each ground cinnamon and coriander

1 teaspoon light brown sugar

6 tablespoons butter, melted

Butter a 12-cup baking dish and preheat the oven to 350°F. Cook the noodles in boiling salted water just until they're done, then drain and rinse to stop the cooking. Combine the remaining ingredients in a bowl, stir in the noodles, then turn them into the baking dish. Mix the topping ingredients, then cover the surface with the topping and bake until the top is browned, 45 to 55 minutes. Let it rest for 10 minutes, then turn onto a platter and serve.

Lasagne

Lasagne is not just a casserole to serve to a crowd but an elaborate and very special dish. While lasagne can be relatively simple—some dishes are tossed rather than layered, such as the Tossed Spinach Lasagne and Goat Cheese Gratin (page 415)—making a lasagne dish is always a bit of work and expense whether you're using dried pasta or fresh, layering it or not. The filling needn't be thick—lasagne is still a pasta dish, after all. Although six layers of pasta are deep and dramatic, I usually use just four, especially if I'm using dried pasta.

Dried, instant, and fresh are the three choices for pasta. Dried pasta tends to be thick. I strongly favor De Cecco, because its wider, shorter sheets are much easier to work with than the more common long, skinny ones. I usually use 10 to 12 ounces for a four-layer lasagne, a pound for six layers, using an 8 1/2 by 11-inch baking dish. Instant or no-boil pasta, a recent product, doesn't require precooking, ends up more like fresh lasagne, and greatly simplifies this complicated dish. (If you parboil it for 1 minute before layering, it's even better.)

FRESH EGG PASTA FOR LASAGNE: Make a 1 1/2-pound batch of Egg Pasta (page 400) using 3 cups flour, 3 extra-large eggs, 1 tablespoon olive oil or water if needed, and 1/2 teaspoon salt. This may make more than you need, but you can dry the leftover dough and use it another time.

Roll the dough through to the last setting on your pasta machine. Cut the sheets into lengths that equal the length or width of your pan. Let the strips rest on lightly floured towels while you continue preparing the dish. They can stand for up to 2 hours before being cooked.

To cook the pasta, bring a large pot of water to a boil and add salt. Have a large bowl of cold water next to the stove. Add a few strips of pasta to the pot at a time, cook for 1 minute, then scoop them out and immediately transfer to the cold water. As you assemble the dish, remove the pieces you need and let them dry briefly on a clean towel. (If using dried pasta, follow the package instructions.)

AHEAD OF TIME: Lasagne can be completely formed, then allowed to rest for a few hours in the refrigerator before baking. It can also be frozen at this point. But according to Clifford Wright, who has made more lasagne than anyone I know because he's the author of *Lasagne* (Little, Brown, 1995), lasagne is even better upon rebaking. Cover well with foil, keeping it tented over the center. Bake the lasagne just short of the final browning, then let it cool to room temperature, refrigerate it, or even freeze it. Allow time to let it return to room temperature, then cover with foil and bake at 325°F for 45 minutes or until the center is hot.

Eggplant Lasagne with Garlic Béchamel

This lasagne is packed with summer's sweet eggplant. I accompany the squares of lasagne with Oven-Roasted Tomato Sauce (page 55), or a sauté of cherry tomatoes. It can use both the color and the acid bite. Serves 4 to 6

3 pounds eggplant, sliced lengthwise about 1/3 inch thick

Sea salt and freshly milled pepper

Olive oil, for brushing

1 pound instant lasagne or Egg Pasta dough (page 400), cut for lasagne

2 fresh mozzarella balls, about 8 ounces

1/2 cup freshly grated parmesan

6 basil leaves, torn into pieces

Garlic Béchamel

2 1/2 cups milk

3 cloves garlic, smashed with the flat side of a knife, then peeled

1/4 cup butter

1/4 cup flour

1/2 cup half-and-half

Sea salt and freshly milled white pepper

Salt the eggplant unless it's garden fresh, then set it aside for 30 minutes. Preheat the oven to 425°F. Blot the eggplant dry and brush both sides with the oil. Set the slices on sheet pans and bake until browned on the bottom, 15 to 20 minutes. Turn the slices over and bake until the second side is browned, another 15 to 20 minutes or less. The eggplant will look rather dry but will become moist as it sits. Season with salt and pepper. Make the béchamel.

Slowly heat the milk with the garlic in a saucepan. When it comes to a boil, cover the pan, turn off the heat, and set aside to steep for 15 minutes. Melt the butter in another saucepan over medium heat, stir in the flour, and cook for 2 minutes. Pour in the milk all at once through a strainer and stir until the sauce is thickened. Cook over very low heat or in a double boiler over simmering water for 20 minutes, stirring occasionally. Pour in the half-and-half and season with salt and white pepper to taste.

Lightly butter an 8 by 10-inch baking dish. Spread 1/2 cup béchamel over the bottom. Add a layer of pasta and cover with 1/3 cup béchamel. Lay down one-third of the eggplant,

cover with one-third of the mozzarella, 2 tablespoons parmesan, and 2 of the basil leaves, torn into small pieces. Repeat with two more layers. Top with a final layer of pasta and cover it with the remaining béchamel and parmesan. Cover with foil. Heat the oven to 400°F . Bake for 25 to 30 minutes or until heated through. Remove the foil and bake for 10 to 15 minutes more. Let stand before serving for the dish to settle.

Tossed Spinach Lasagne and Goat Cheese Gratin

Homemade noodles make this dish light and extraordinary. Tossing them with the sauce is not just for speed—it also results in charmingly irregular lasagne, with small mountains of pasta that rise above the rest, turning crisp and golden. Serves 6

1 pound fresh Spinach Pasta (page 401)

2 cups Herb Béchamel (page 47)

1/2 cup cream or milk

8 ounces goat cheese, crumbled

1 tablespoon chopped thyme

Freshly milled pepper

1/2 cup freshly grated parmesan or aged goat cheese

2 tablespoons cold butter, thinly shaved

Make the pasta dough and, while it's resting, make the béchamel. Add the cream and goat cheese to the sauce. Don't worry about lumps of cheese—they're wonderful to bite into.

Preheat the oven to 375°F. Lightly butter a 12-cup gratin dish. Roll the dough through to the thinnest setting on your pasta machine, then cut it into strips about 8 inches long and 2 inches wide. Boil them for 1 minute in plenty of salted water, transfer the strips to cold water, then drain. Toss the pasta with the sauce, thyme, pepper, and all but 2 tablespoons of the parmesan. Pile it in the gratin dish and covered with the remaining cheese and shaved butter. Bake until bubbling and browned here and there on top, 30 to 40 minutes.

Mushroom Lasagne

You can have this fragrant mushroom lasagne ready for baking in less than an hour if you use instant lasagne. I make only four layers of mushrooms with dried lasagne; with fresh, which is thinner, I prefer to make six. Instead of using milk in the béchamel sauce, use mushroom stock to underscore to woodsy flavor. Serves 4 to 6

- 1/2 to 1 ounce dried porcini or morels
- Béchamel Sauce (page 47), using 2 1/2 cups milk or mushroom stock, 4 1/2 tablespoons butter, 4 1/2 tablespoons flour, sea salt and white pepper, 1/8 teaspoon grated nutmeg
- 1 pound portabella mushrooms, stems and gills removed, caps thinly sliced
- 1/4 cup olive oil
- 4 tablespoons butter
- 1 pound white mushrooms, thinly sliced
- 1/3 cup chopped parsley
- 3 large cloves garlic, finely chopped
- Sea salt and freshly milled pepper
- 1 pound instant lasagne, dried lasagne, or Egg Pasta (page 400), cut for lasagne
- 3/4 cup freshly grated parmesan

Cover the porcini with 1 cup warm water and set aside to soak. Make the béchamel sauce. Cook it in a double boiler over simmering water or over low heat along with the stems from the portabella mushrooms. After 30 minutes, remove the stems. Strain the porcini and add the liquid to the sauce.

Coarsely chop the porcini. Heat half the oil and butter in a wide skillet over high heat. Add half the white mushrooms and sauté until they begin to color around the edges and soften, about 5 minutes. Toss them with half the parsley and garlic, season with salt and pepper, and remove them to a bowl. Repeat with the remaining oil, butter, mushrooms, including the porcini the parsley, and garlic. Add any juices that collect to the sauce.

If using fresh pasta, prepare it as described on page 400. If using dried pasta, parboil it as directed on the box. Instant lasagne can be dipped in boiling water for 1 minute.

Butter a 9 by 12-inch baking dish. Cover with a layer of pasta, then with 1/2 cup béchamel sauce, one-fourth of the filling, and 2 tablespoons grated cheese. Repeat this layering until you have four layers of filling. Spread the final layer of pasta with the remaining sauce and cheese.

When ready to eat, preheat the oven to 400°F. Cover the lasagne with foil and bake for 20 to 30 minutes or until heated through. Remove the foil and continue baking until browned in spots on top, 10 to 15 minutes more.

Lasagne-Mushroom Gratin: In this variation, the same ingredients are tossed together rather than layered. I love the visual effect of the jumbled noodles. Prepare the mushrooms and sauce as described. Cook lasagna noodles, then toss everything, except one-fourth of the cheese, together. Bake at 425°F in a large buttered gratin dish—a large earthenware Spanish casserole is especially attractive—covered with the remaining cheese, until bubbling and browned on top.

Lasagne with Eggplant and Chard

Over the years, I've discovered that when eggplant and chard are combined, they produce an unsuspected depth of flavor. Lasagne expert Clifford Wright inspired the use of this duo in lasagne. This filling is excellent in cannelloni and crepes, too. Serves 6 to 8

- 1 1/2 pounds Egg Pasta (page 400), or 1 box dried or instant
- 1 cup Fresh Tomato Sauce (page 54) or Quick Canned Tomato Sauce (page 56)
- 1 1/2 pounds eggplant, sliced crosswise 1/4 inch thick
- 2 tablespoons olive oil, plus extra for the eggplant
- 2 tablespoons butter
- 1/2 onion, finely diced
- 3 cloves garlic, finely chopped
- 1 bunch green chard, about 1 1/2 pounds, stems removed
- 1 teaspoon sea salt
- 1/2 cup dry white wine
- 1 cup ricotta
- 1 egg
- 3/4 cup grated Pecorino Romano
- 8 ounces fresh mozzarella, thinly sliced
- Freshly milled pepper

Prepare the pasta dough, if using fresh, and tomato sauce. Roll and cut the dough, set it aside on towels to dry while you prepare the vegetables, then parboil as described on page 414. Unless it's garden fresh, salt the eggplant, let stand 30 minutes, then blot dry.

Preheat the oven to 400°F. Brush both sides of the eggplant lightly with oil. Place the slices on a sheet pan and bake, turning once, until browned on both sides, about 30 minutes in all. Chop coarsely.

Heat the oil and butter in a large skillet. Add the onion and garlic and cook over medium heat for about 3 minutes, stirring frequently. Add the chard, sprinkle with the salt, and cook until wilted, about 5 minutes. Add the wine, cover, and cook until the chard is tender and the pan is dry, about 10 minutes. Turn the mixture out onto a cutting board and finely chop. In a bowl, mix together the ricotta, $1/3$ cup water, and the egg, then stir in the chard. Taste and season with salt and freshly ground pepper.

Oil a 9 by 12-inch baking dish. Spread $1/3$ cup tomato sauce over the bottom and cover with a layer of pasta. Scatter a quarter of the grated cheese over the top and add a quarter of the eggplant, ricotta mixture, and mozzarella. Follow with another layer of pasta and repeat for three more layers. End with a layer of pasta and the remaining sauce. Cover with foil, tenting it above the surface.

Preheat the oven to 400°F. Bake 20 to 30 minutes or until heated through. Remove the foil and bake for 5 to 10 minutes more.

Ravioli

As grateful as we are for frozen ravioli, it's the fresh, supple dough and unusual fillings that make the homemade versions so beguiling. Handmade pastas are eminently suitable for special occasions, and the process is fairly straightforward for those with reasonable pasta-making skills.

MAKING FILLED PASTAS: To make these dishes go smoothly, here are a few things to keep in mind. Cheese fillings are easy to make, and since vegetable fillings should be cool, they can be made hours in advance. If you have a shop that sells fresh sheets of thin pasta, you can bypass making your own.

Wonton wrappers also come in handy for making ravioli. Use these paper-thin squares, found in the produce section of your supermarket usually near the Asian vegetables, as you would fresh pasta. Egg roll wrappers can be used for cannelloni, and so can crepes.

The sauces, which are generally simple, can be made ahead of time unless they're the last-minute type, in which case they're usually quite fast and better made *à la minute*. And once formed, the pasta can be held for several hours before being cooked, providing another window of time.

As always, take a moment to study the recipe before you start and look for lag times, such as the half hour it takes to bake a squash for winter squash ravioli, that you can use for another part of the dish, the meal, or something else altogether.

Tips for Making Small Filled Pastas

Well liked because of their curious shapes and succulent fillings, these stuffed pastas make a very special first or main course. You can float them in a roasted vegetable broth or wild mushroom stock, and although untraditional, I find that a few crescent-shaped agnolotti or cheese-filled ravioli slipped into a vegetable stew add an unexpected and luscious bite. Making the pasta, filling, and sauce takes 2 hours at the most for complicated fillings; an hour or less for a simpler one.

AMOUNTS: A $1^1/2$-pound recipe of egg pasta (using 3 cups flour, 3 extra-large eggs, 1 tablespoon olive oil, and $1/2$ teaspoon salt) makes enough for 36 to 48 filled pastas or four to six servings. (This depends in part on whether you roll your pasta to the last or next-to-the-last setting as well as on the size and shape.) Each ravioli takes a mounded teaspoon of filling, so you'll need $1^1/2$ to 2 cups filling.

TO FORM RAVIOLI: Dust the counter lightly with flour. Divide the dough into two or three pieces so that it's easy to handle and roll out one piece at a time, using a pasta machine. It should be thin, but not so thin that it tears easily. Cut the final long strip into smaller lengths so that it's easy to handle. Cover the strips with plastic wrap to keep them supple until you can shape them. Work quickly so that the pasta dough doesn't dry out.

There are many ways to form and shape stuffed pastas. For square ravioli, crease a strip of dough lengthwise, then dot it with evenly placed mounds of filling as each recipe suggests. Alternatively, crease a length of dough crosswise, lay out a double row of filling on one half, then bring the second half over the top. You can also place one narrow strip on top of a second strip, dotted with the filling. Some people find that using ravioli forms saves them time. I am not one of them.

Always dampen the dough before sealing it tightly. I find a finger does the job best; a pastry brush can also be used, but watch that it doesn't leave too much moisture. Pinch the edges to form a seal. If you're not cooking them within a short time, cover them loosely with a piece of wax paper and then a towel. You can refrigerate them, but preferably no more than an hour or two; otherwise the moisture from the filling will cause the dough to soften on the bottom.

TO COOK RAVIOLI: Using a wide Chinese strainer, lower all the ravioli at once into a pot of gently boiling salted water. If the ravioli have air pockets in them—a not-uncommon occurrence—they'll float to the top, but that doesn't indicate that they're done. Check by tasting a bit of the edge after about 4 minutes. They need 4 to 5 minutes to cook—possibly longer if your dough is on the thick side. When done, lift them out with the strainer rather than dumping them into a colander.

Unlike other pasta, ravioli, which are more fragile, don't need to be in a large quantity of boiling water. Instead they can be cooked in a wide soup pot in salted water that's only gently boiling so that they don't break apart. Gentleness is key.

MAKING RAVIOLI AHEAD OF TIME: Ravioli can be placed on wax paper and refrigerated, uncovered, for a few hours before cooking. Because their fillings are moist and the dough is fragile, they won't keep much longer than that. They can be frozen, however: Spread them on a cookie sheet and freeze until they're hardened, then transfer them to freezer bags.

A NOTE ABOUT RICOTTA: True ricotta is made from the whey remaining from other cheese-making adventures. But what we find in our stores is not that, as it comes in full-fat, low-fat, part-skim, and nonfat. It's nothing like the ricotta you find in Italy, in its baskets, dripping wet and delicate as flowers. I find most of our ricotta grainy and generally unpleasant, unless it's full-fat or some artisanal-made ricotta, which is so special you just want to enjoy it as simply as possible. However, in lasagne and fillings, its texture isn't so problematic. You do want to make sure it's as dry as possible so it doesn't dampen the dough. Put it in a sieve lined with cheesecloth; press down on it to get rid of excess moisture.

Butternut Squash Ravioli with Toasted Pecans and Sage

This is one of my favorite winter pasta dishes, but you might consider it a model for other vegetable-filled ravioli. Sweet potato can be substituted for the squash, or you can go in an entirely different direction, using a potato and winter vegetable puree, or pureed peas, asparagus, or cauliflower.
Serves 4 to 6

1 butternut squash, about 2 pounds
Vegetable oil, for the squash
2 tablespoons butter
Sea salt and freshly milled pepper
1/2 cup freshly grated parmesan
1/2 cup dried bread crumbs
1 1/2 pounds Egg Pasta (page 400)

Brown Butter with Pecans and Sage
4 to 6 tablespoons butter
1 clove garlic, thinly sliced
2 tablespoons chopped sage leaves
2 tablespoons chopped parsley
2 teaspoons chopped thyme
1/3 cup pecans, toasted and coarsely chopped
Freshly grated parmesan, for serving

Preheat the oven to 375°F. Slice the squash in two, remove the seeds, and brush the cut surfaces with oil. Bake cut side down on a sheet pan until soft, 30 to 40 minutes. Scoop out the flesh and measure 2 cups. Beat it with the butter until smooth and season well with salt and pepper. (If the squash seems watery, dry it out by stirring it in a skillet over high heat to get rid of extra moisture.) Add the cheese and bread crumbs and mix well.

Roll out the dough and form into 2-inch ravioli, circles, or crescents as described on page 417. In a skillet large enough to hold the finished pasta, melt the butter with the sliced garlic, sage, 1 tablespoon of the parsley, and the thyme and cook over medium heat until the butter is lightly browned and has a nutty aroma. Cook the ravioli in the gently boiling salted water for 4 or 5 minutes, then drain. Add the pecans to the skillet with the remaining parsley, then add the ravioli to the sauce. Cook for 30 seconds, then serve dusted with parmesan.

Spinach Tortellini with Walnuts, Parsley, and Pecorino

This nut sauce is a quick enhancement for store-bought or homemade pastas alike. The shape of this pasta catches the nuts and shards of cheese in its fold, but you can make a simpler square ravioli if you prefer. Serves 4 to 6

1¹/₂ pounds Egg Pasta (page 400)

¹/₂ onion, finely diced

1 clove garlic, minced

1 tablespoon olive oil

1 tablespoon butter

1 large bunch spinach, about 1 pound, stems removed, leaves roughly chopped

¹/₂ teaspoon sea salt

1 cup ricotta, drained

1 egg

Freshly milled pepper

¹/₈ teaspoon grated nutmeg

Walnut Sauce

¹/₂ cup walnuts, roasted and finely chopped

2 tablespoons pine nuts, toasted in a small skillet and finely chopped

1 clove garlic, minced

¹/₂ cup chopped parsley

2 tablespoons butter

3 tablespoons olive oil

¹/₄ cup grated Pecorino Romano or parmesan, plus extra to finish

Sea salt and freshly milled pepper

Make the pasta dough and set it aside to rest.

Cook the onion and garlic in the oil and butter in a skillet over medium heat until the onion has softened, about 6 minutes. Add the spinach, season with the salt, and cook until tender. Raise the heat to evaporate the remaining juices, then remove and finely chop. Mix with the ricotta and egg and season with the salt, pepper, and nutmeg. If the filling seems wet, drain it in a strainer set over a bowl.

Roll out the dough and cut it into 2-inch squares or circles. Place a dab of filling—about ¹/₂ teaspoon—in the center of a square. Fold the square corner to corner, forming a triangle. One side should fall just a little short of the other. Press the edges together. Pick up the triangle and hold it with the long side facing the counter. Wrap the two lower corners around your finger, lapping one over the other, and press to secure them. Repeat with the rest.

Start heating water for the pasta. Meanwhile, in a large bowl combine the nuts, garlic, parsley, butter, olive oil, cheese, a pinch salt, and pepper to taste. Cook the tortellini in the gently boiling salted water for 4 or 5 minutes, then drain and add them to the walnut sauce. Gently mix them into it to melt the butter, then serve lightly dusted with additional cheese.

Gorgonzola Ravioli with Tomato Sauce

While I suffered through a bowl of enormous unpeeled fava beans in Italy, I had to admit that my husband's choice of Gorgonzola ravioli was far more appealing. Serves 4 to 6

1¹/₂ pounds Egg Pasta (page 400)

Fresh Tomato Sauce (page 54)

1 cup ricotta

1 cup crumbled Gorgonzola

¹/₄ cup freshly grated parmesan, plus extra to finish

1 egg

Sea salt and freshly milled pepper

¹/₈ teaspoon grated nutmeg

1 tablespoon finely chopped parsley or mixed rosemary and parsley, for garnish

Make the pasta dough and tomato sauce and set aside. Beat the cheeses and egg together until smooth, then season with salt, pepper, and nutmeg.

Roll out the pasta dough and form the ravioli as described on page 417). To cook, lower the ravioli into a pot of gently boiling salted water and cook for 4 or 5 minutes. Warm the sauce and pour about ¹/₂ cup into each warmed pasta bowl or plate. Scoop out the ravioli and shake off the water. Set them on top of the sauce, then spoon a little extra sauce over the top. Grate a veil of parmesan over the top and garnish with the parsley.

With Tomato-Cream Sauce: A few tablespoons of cream will smooth and enrich the sauce. Add it once the sauce is finished and cook to heat it through. Add the cooked ravioli to the sauce, swirl them about, then serve.

Eggplant Agnolotti with Tomato Sauce

If you have a mortar that's large enough, use it for the eggplant. It goes just as quickly as a food processor and leaves a little texture. The eggplant mixture—minus the eggs—makes an excellent spread for crostini. Serves 4 to 6

1 pound eggplant, peeled and thinly sliced

Olive oil, for brushing

1/3 cup walnuts

1 cup ricotta

1/2 cup grated Pecorino Romano, plus extra to finish

2 eggs, beaten

2 tablespoons chopped basil

2 tablespoons chopped parsley

4 teaspoons chopped mint

Sea salt and freshly milled pepper

1 1/2 pounds Egg Pasta (page 400) or Saffron Pasta (page 401)

Fresh Tomato Sauce (page 54)

1/4 cup roughly chopped or torn basil leaves

Heat the oven to 400°F. Brush both sides of the eggplant slices with oil, set on a sheet pan, and bake until browned on the bottom, about 15 minutes. Turn and brown the other side, about 15 minutes more. Pound the walnuts in a mortar or grind in a food processor, then work in the eggplant until fairly smooth. Remove the mixture to a bowl and add the cheeses, eggs, and herbs. Season to taste with salt and pepper. Set aside to cool.

Meanwhile, make the pasta dough. While it's resting, make the tomato sauce. To form the agnolotti, roll out the pasta dough and cut out 3-inch circles with a fluted biscuit cutter. Place the filling on one half of a circle. Brush the edges with water, fold in half, and press together. With your fingers, gently bend the half-circle to form a crescent. Cook them in gently boiling salted water for 4 or 5 minutes. Scoop them onto a platter, interspersed with the sauce, basil, and additional grated cheese.

Cannelloni

Cannelloni are squares of pasta rolled around a filling, blanketed with a protective layer of sauce, and baked. Traditional fillings tend to be based on ricotta cheese or on greens—the same fillings used for ravioli. Like ravioli, cannelloni are traditionally served as a first course, but here they're featured as the main event, garnished with vegetables that harmonize with the filling.

PASTA FOR CANNELLONI: Egg pasta made with 1 cup flour, 1 extra-large egg, 1 teaspoon olive oil, and a pinch of salt makes enough pasta for 12 cannelloni, which serves four generously or six modestly. Roll the dough to the thinnest setting on the pasta machine and cut the strips into 12 pieces 5 inches long. Parboil two or three squares at a time until they rise to the surface. Transfer them to a bowl of cold water to stop the cooking, then lay them on a clean kitchen towel to dry for about 10 minutes before filling.

FORMING THE CANNELLONI: Spoon or pipe 2 tablespoons filling through a pastry tube along one of the long edges of a pasta square, going almost to the end. Loosely roll the pasta to form a tube, like a cigar. Place the stuffed pastas in a lightly buttered baking dish so that they're just touching but aren't crowded. Keeping the flap side facing up makes them easier to remove. Make only a single layer of cannelloni and cover with béchamel sauce.

MAKING CANNELLONI AHEAD OF TIME: Cannelloni can be formed a day ahead of baking, covered with plastic wrap, and refrigerated. They can also be frozen, but it seems a shame to go to so much effort for frozen food. Either way, allow the cannelloni to come to room temperature before baking.

USING CREPES: Crepes (page 584) can be used in place of pasta sheets in making cannelloni. They are remarkably tender.

Cannelloni with Greens and Sautéed Artichokes

These greens have plenty of character. They also make a good filling for empanadas. Serves 4 to 6

8 ounces Egg Pasta (page 400)

Béchamel Sauce (page 47), made with 1¹/₂ cups milk, 3 tablespoons butter, 3¹/₂ tablespoons flour, sea salt and freshly milled white pepper, ¹/₈ teaspoon grated nutmeg

1¹/₂ pounds mixed greens, such as chard, kale, watercress, beets, spinach, arugula, stems removed

3 tablespoons chopped parsley

3 tablespoons chopped basil

2 tablespoons chopped marjoram

2 cloves garlic, finely chopped

1 cup ricotta

1 egg

¹/₄ cup fresh bread crumbs

Sea salt, freshly milled pepper, and grated nutmeg

Sautéed Artichokes

3 medium artichokes, trimmed and quartered

Juice of 1 large lemon

2 tablespoons olive oil

Sea salt and freshly milled pepper

2 tablespoons parsley chopped with 1 small clove garlic

Make the pasta and set it aside to rest. Make the béchamel sauce. While it's cooking, steam the greens with a few cups of salted water until tender, about 5 minutes. Drain, rinse under cold water, then squeeze out the excess moisture and finely chop them. Mix the greens with the herbs, garlic, ricotta, egg, and bread crumbs. Season to taste with salt, pepper, and a few pinches grated nutmeg.

Preheat the oven to 375°F. Shape and fill 12 cannelloni as described on page 420. Arrange them in a lightly buttered gratin dish and cover with the béchamel sauce. Bake until lightly browned on top and heated through, about 30 minutes.

Meanwhile, dice the artichoke hearts into ¹/₂-inch pieces. As you work, toss the pieces with lemon juice. Heat the oil in a wide skillet. Drain the artichokes, add them to the oil, and sauté over high heat until golden and tender, about 7 minutes. Season with salt and pepper and toss with the parsley-garlic mixture. Serve the cannelloni with the artichokes spooned around them and over the top.

Cannelloni with Ricotta, Pesto, and Sautéed Tomatoes

Serves 4 to 6

8 ounces Egg Pasta (page 400)

Béchamel Sauce (page 47), made with 1¹/₂ cups milk, 3 tablespoons butter, 3¹/₂ tablespoons flour, sea salt, and freshly milled white pepper

1¹/₂ cups ricotta

¹/₂ cup freshly grated parmesan, plus extra for serving

¹/₄ cup Pesto (page 50) or Basil Puree (page 51)

1 egg

Sea salt and freshly milled pepper

Sautéed Tomatoes

2 large ripe tomatoes, peeled and seeded

1 tablespoon butter or olive oil

Sea salt and freshly milled pepper

1 teaspoon balsamic vinegar

Make the pasta dough and set it aside to rest. Make the béchamel sauce. Combine the ricotta, parmesan, pesto, and egg. Season with salt and pepper. If you wish a more pronounced basil flavor, add a little more of the pesto or basil puree to pick it up.

Roll out the pasta and form 12 cannelloni as described on page 420. Lay them in a buttered gratin dish, cover with the sauce, and grate a little extra parmesan over the top. Preheat the oven to 375°F and bake until hot, about 30 minutes. Meanwhile, neatly dice the tomatoes, discarding the core. Heat the butter in a medium skillet over high heat. When foamy, add the tomatoes and quickly sauté them just long enough to warm them through. Season with salt and pepper, add the vinegar, and swirl the pan over the heat for a few seconds. Serve the tomatoes scattered around each portion of cannelloni.

Green Cannelloni with Ricotta and Roasted Peppers

A particularly attractive white, green, and red pasta dish. Serves 4 to 6

8 ounces Spinach Pasta (page 401)

Béchamel Sauce (page 47), made with 1½ cups milk, 3 tablespoons butter, 3½ tablespoons flour, sea salt and freshly milled white pepper, and ⅛ teaspoon nutmeg

2 large red bell peppers, roasted (see page 364)

Sea salt and freshly milled pepper

1 tablespoon thinly sliced basil leaves

Olive oil, for the peppers

1 cup ricotta

1 cup freshly grated parmesan

1 egg

2 tablespoons chopped parsley

Make the pasta dough and set it aside to rest. Meanwhile, make the béchamel sauce. While it's cooking, finely dice the peppers and toss them with salt and pepper, the basil, and enough olive oil to moisten. Set aside.

Beat the cheeses with the egg and parsley and season with ½ teaspoon sea salt and a few twists of the peppermill. Shape and fill 12 cannelloni as described on page 420. Lay them in a lightly buttered baking dish, then spoon the béchamel sauce over them. Preheat the oven to 375°F. Bake the cannelloni for 25 minutes. Let stand for a few minutes, then serve, garnished with the roasted peppers.

Green Cannelloni with Sautéed Mushrooms: Sautéed mushrooms are another vegetable that flatters these cannelloni. Thinly slice a pound of mushrooms, then sauté them in butter and olive oil. Add a little chopped garlic and parsley once they're cooked, then spoon them around the cannelloni.

Saffron Cannelloni with Chard Filling and Chard Stem Garnish

Here the chard stems, so often thrown away, are finely diced and used to garnish the cannelloni. Serves 4 to 6

8 ounces Saffron Pasta (page 401)

Béchamel Sauce (page 47), made with 1½ cups milk, 3 tablespoons butter, 3½ tablespoons flour, sea salt, and freshly milled white pepper

2 large bunches chard, stems removed but reserved

1½ tablespoons olive oil

1 white onion, finely diced

¼ cup finely chopped parsley

1 cup ricotta

½ cup freshly grated parmesan

2 tablespoons mascarpone or crème fraîche

1 teaspoon grated lemon zest

⅛ teaspoon grated nutmeg

1 teaspoon sea salt

Freshly milled pepper

Fresh lemon juice

Butter or best olive oil, for the chard stems

Make the pasta dough and set it aside to rest while you make the béchamel sauce. Cook the chard leaves in boiling salted water until tender, about 5 minutes. Drain, rinse under cold water, then press out the excess moisture and finely chop. Put the chard in a bowl.

Heat the oil in a small skillet over medium heat. Add the onion and parsley and cook until the onion is translucent, about 5 minutes. Add the onion to the chard and mix with the ricotta, half of the parmesan, the mascarpone, lemon zest, and nutmeg. Season with ½ teaspoon of the salt or more to taste and a little pepper.

Shape and fill 12 cannelloni as described on page 420. Preheat the oven to 375°F. Arrange them in a buttered gratin dish and cover with the béchamel sauce and remaining cheese. Bake until browned and bubbling, 25 to 30 minutes. Meanwhile, trim the chard stems, then go over them lightly with a vegetable peeler. Dice them into small cubes—you'll need about a cup—then put them in a pan with water to cover, a tablespoon lemon juice, and the remaining ½ teaspoon salt. Simmer until tender, about 7 minutes, then drain. Toss them with a little butter or olive oil and season with pepper. Serve the cannelloni with the chard stems scattered around them.

Dumplings

I think of dumplings as tender little mouthfuls that are ultimately soothing, the way soft and starchy foods should be. We don't make dumplings much anymore, but they're so good they deserve a fresh look. You can make them out of nothing fancier than your cupboard items, like flour and semolina, milk, and perhaps eggs.

Potato Gnocchi

Gnocchi is one of those foods that can be heavenly or ghastly. The art is in getting the feel of the dough. Practice before making them for company and follow these tips: use baking potatoes and bake rather than boil them; pass them through a ricer or a food mill so they'll stay light and fluffy; and don't heat or mash them. There are two stages at which the gnocchi can rest before baking. Makes about 100 little dumplings, serving 4 to 6 as a main course, 8 as an appetizer

2 large russet potatoes, about 2 pounds

1¹/4 cups flour, or more if needed

1 teaspoon sea salt

3 tablespoons cold butter

¹/2 cup freshly grated parmesan

Freshly milled pepper

Preheat the oven to 400°F. Pierce the potatoes and bake until tender when a knife is inserted, 45 minutes to an hour, depending on the size. Peel them while they're hot and pass them through a food mill or ricer, letting them fall into a large bowl. They should be light and fluffy. Cool for 15 minutes, then sprinkle with the flour and salt. Using your hands, gently work until you have a smooth, soft dough. If it seems sticky, add a few tablespoons more flour, but don't knead or overwork it.

Take a quarter of the dough and roll it into a long rope about ¹/2 inch thick. Cut it diagonally into pieces about ³/4 inch long. You can either roll them into little balls or press one side against the tines of a fork. Set them in a single layer on a baking sheet lightly dusted with flour or lined with parchment paper. Repeat with the remaining dough, then cover with a towel and refrigerate for a few hours if you aren't ready to cook them.

To cook, bring a wide casserole or skillet of water to a boil and butter a large gratin dish. Add salt to the water, then lower the heat to a simmer. Add a batch of 10 or 15 gnocchi and cook gently until they rise to the top. Count 10 seconds, then lift them out with a strainer and remove them to the dish. Finish cooking the rest. (This can be done ahead of time.) When you're ready to eat, preheat the oven to 400°F. Shave the cold butter over the top and cover with a thick veil of cheese. Bake until bubbling and the cheese is beginning to brown in places, about 25 minutes. Add fresh pepper and serve.

With Tomato Sauce: Instead of baking the gnocchi, use two pans, simmer them all at once, then gently lift them out of the water into a serving bowl. Pour on melted butter and add the cheese or serve them with a light Fresh Tomato Sauce (page 54). A few gnocchi make a tender addition to a spring vegetable stew.

Semolina Coins

Everyone is happy to eat these little dumplings. The batter can be made and cut hours before they're baked. Accompany with a light tomato sauce, kale or other skillet greens, Sautéed Peppers (page 363), or an Herb-Baked Tomato (page 388). Serves 4

- 3¹/2 cups milk
- 2 pinches saffron threads, optional
- 1 teaspoon sea salt
- 1 cup plus 2 tablespoons semolina
- 1/4 cup butter
- 3 eggs, or 2 whole eggs and 2 egg yolks
- 1/2 cup grated Gruyère
- 1/2 cup freshly grated parmesan
- 1/8 teaspoon grated nutmeg
- 2 tablespoons melted butter

Lightly butter a sheet pan and an 8- to 12-cup gratin dish.

Heat the milk in a spacious saucepan, crumble in the saffron, and add the salt. When it's almost boiling, whisk in the semolina, adding it in a fine, steady stream. Stir constantly as the milk comes to a boil, then cook until stiff enough to support a spoon, about 3 minutes. Remove from the heat. Beat in the butter and then the eggs, one at a time. Then stir in the Gruyère, half the parmesan, and the nutmeg. Pour the mixture onto the sheet pan and spread it out to a thickness of 1/3 inch. It will cover about half the pan. Let stand until set, about 2 hours or overnight. Cover with plastic wrap if longer than 2 hours.

Preheat the oven to 375°F. Using a juice glass or wine glass, cut out 2-inch circles of the firm semolina, pick them up with a spatula, and overlap them in the baking dish. (Mine never look very even at this point, but they end up just fine.) Reserve the scraps. With the scraps, you can form oval dumplings by scooping it up in one teaspoon and shaping it with a second, then baking them in a gratin dish. Or pack the scraps into buttered ramekins and bake them later, then turn them onto a plate with a little tomato sauce, sautéed mushrooms, or surrounded by a vegetable stew. Drizzle the melted butter and scatter over the rest of the parmesan.

Bake until hot, bubbling, and beginning to color on top, 20 to 25 minutes. Run them under the broiler at the end until the top is golden.

Saffron Dumplings

These little dumplings, based on a classic cream puff batter, can be added to vegetable stew or broiled. Serve with Sautéed Spinach (page 378) and Tomatoes Glazed with Balsamic Vinegar (page 389). Serves 3 or 4

- 1 cup milk
- 2 pinches saffron threads
- 3 tablespoons butter
- 3 tablespoons minced herbs—parsley with chives, marjoram, or basil
- 1³/4 teaspoon sea salt
- Freshly milled pepper
- 1 cup flour
- 4 eggs
- 3 tablespoons melted butter
- Grated parmesan, to finish

Preheat your broiler and lightly butter a large gratin dish.

Heat the milk with the saffron threads, butter, herbs, 3/4 teaspoon of the salt and a little pepper. When boiling and the butter has melted, stir in flour all at once, then remove the pan from the heat and beat it vigorously with a wooden spoon to make a smooth paste. Return the pan to a low heat and continue beating until the paste leaves a film on the bottom of the pan. Turn off the heat, and beat in the eggs, one at a time, until smooth and completely incorporated. (In a mixer, use a paddle attachment.)

Bring a wide, deep skillet of water to a simmer and add the remaining teaspoon salt. Drop the batter by tablespoons (smaller, if they're for soup), into the water and cook for 6 minutes. Turn and cook on the second side for 6 minutes more. (Don't let the water boil—the dumplings will fall apart.) When done, remove them to the prepared dish. Drizzle the melted butter over the top, dust with cheese, and broil until golden and sizzling.

Asian Noodles

Like Italians, Asians are enthusiastic noodle eaters. Unlike Italian noodles, however, Asian noodles are made from all kinds of flour, not only the wheat that is prevalent in China but also yam, potato, rice, and other starches. Their shapes and textures range from clear and silky mung bean threads to green tea and buckwheat soba to thick, plump rice noodles. There are probably hundreds of different Asian noodles, a number of which are available at Asian groceries, natural food stores, and even supermarkets.

One of the frustrations of Asian noodle dishes for many strict vegetarians is the ubiquitous presence of fish sauce, oyster sauce, and dried bonito. If you use these products, more flavors are available to you. In the following recipes, these popular seasonings have been replaced by others that leave the finished dish just as flavorful.

Cooking Asian Noodles

Asian noodles are cooked differently from Italian pasta. First, the water isn't salted, and second, the noodles are cooked until tender, not al dente. In the case of Japanese soba, somen, and udon, the water foams and rises when the water returns to a boil, then cold water is added to make it subside. After this happens three or four times, the noodles are usually done—taste them to be sure. Depending on thickness, they cook in 5 to 7 minutes. Rice noodles and mung bean noodles are soaked to tenderness rather than cooked.

Asian noodles are often drained, rinsed well to wash off the starch, then added to the dish and reheated, unlike Italian pastas, which are best added directly from the cooking pot to the sauce.

CELLOPHANE OR BEAN-THREAD NOODLES: Made from mung bean starch, these wrinkled nests of silvery, thin noodles become clear and soft once soaked. Soak dried noodles in a bowl of warm water for about 15 minutes if they are to be cooked further, 30 minutes if not. Snip the strands to shorter lengths with scissors. If the dried noodles are thrown into hot oil, they'll instantly puff up into white, crunchy strands resembling shredded Styrofoam. They make a dramatic bed—or garnish—for stir-fries.

CHINESE EGG NOODLES OR MEIN: Sold both fresh and dry, these noodles most resemble Western pasta—in fact, linguine and fettuccine are often suggested as substitutes for thin and wide mein, but their flavor is unique. The fresh noodles come tightly packed and wrapped in plastic. Before cooking, you'll need to pull all the strands apart, fluffing them as you go. When loosened, a small package becomes quite a large pile. Dried egg noodles look something like bedsprings. They're cooked in unsalted boiling water. When they begin to soften, start pulling the strands apart with a pair of chopsticks.

RICE NOODLES OR RICE VERMICELLI OR RICE STICKS: These are the noodles used for pad thai and other dishes from Southeast Asia and southern China. Sold dried outside of large Asian communities, rice sticks are whitish, either wavy or straight, and about as long as a chopstick. Rather than cooked, thin noodles or rice sticks are soaked in warm water for 10 to 15 minutes until soft, then added to soup or stir-fried. Wider flat rice noodles are covered with boiling water and then allowed to soften. Like mung bean noodles, rice sticks can be thrown into hot oil, which turns them crisp and light within moments. When fresh, rice noodles are called fun.

SHIRITAKI (YAM) NOODLES: Also called Konjac noodles. Although their appearance in supermarkets is recent, shiritaki are a traditional Japanese noodle made from yam starch. They have almost no flavor, are somewhat rubbery, translucent, gelatinous, and have few calories and virtually no carbohydrates, which is largely what people like about them. (A new type is made with tofu so it has some caloric value, but also resembles wheat pasta more closely.) When packed in liquid, they can have an off odor, which is corrected by drying the noodles in a pan over high heat until they squeak, after a minute or two, after which they can go into a soup or a broth.

SOBA OR BUCKWHEAT NOODLES: These Japanese noodles are very refined, their taste both delicate and earthy. Some of the fancier varieties are quite elegant and very expensive. Soba is served cold during the sultry Japanese summers or hot in winter. You also can use soba to replace the Italian buckwheat pasta, *pizzoccheri*, which is hard to find here.

UDON AND SOMEN: These Japanese noodles are made from wheat flour and come packaged in little 8-inch-long bundles. They are usually served in broth with accompanying garnishes. Some varieties are extremely fine. Those about the thickness of a toothpick are served chilled with cucumbers. Others are large, some smooth and machine made, others rougher looking. I especially like the latter, for they have a very handmade look when cooked.

Rice Noodles in Curry Sauce with Tempeh

A café I like for lunch serves their stir-fries and noodle dishes with an optional side of tempeh, which I always order. It's very simply done as a side rather than something that's incorporated, and utterly optional if tempeh isn't your thing. Serves 4 (V)

---

8 ounces dried rice noodles, about 1/4 inch wide or thinner, if you prefer

Sea salt

1 tablespoon peanut oil

2 plump cloves garlic, minced

1 teaspoon minced ginger

2 large shallots, thinly sliced into rounds

1 (15-ounce) can coconut milk

1 teaspoon or more red Thai curry paste

2 tablespoons soy sauce

1/2 cup roasted, salted peanuts or cashews

2 green onions, thinly sliced into rounds

Thai basil leaves and cilantro sprigs, to finish

Fried Tempeh (page 533)

Cover the noodles with cold water and set aside to soften, 20 to 30 minutes, while you prepare the sauce and the tempeh. Bring a pot of water to a boil for the noodles, add salt, and then the noodles. Cook until warmed through and tender, 2 to 4 minutes. Drain and set aside.

Heat the oil in a wok or skillet. Add the garlic, ginger, and shallots and stir-fry over high heat until softened, about a minute. Add the coconut milk, curry paste, and soy sauce. Stir to break up the paste, then lower the heat and simmer until everything is well-blended and hot. Add the noodles and simmer until they're warmed through.

To serve, turn them onto a platter or individual plates, garnish with the nuts, green onions, basil, and cilantro, and arrange triangles of tempeh around the edge.

Burmese Noodles

A friend with a passion for Asian food created this vegetarian version of one of his favorite dishes for me. The fresh noodles soak up the sauce and all its rich flavors. Serves 2 (V)

Curry Paste

1/2 onion, chopped

2 large cloves garlic

2 (1/4-inch rounds) fresh ginger

1 teaspoon paprika

1/2 teaspoon turmeric

1/2 teaspoon sea salt

2 red bird chiles, sliced in rounds

Noodles and Vegetables

5 dried shiitake or Chinese black mushrooms

8 ounces fresh Chinese egg noodles or rice noodles

1/3 cup chopped roasted peanuts

2 tablespoons roasted peanut oil

1 large tomato, seeded and cut into 1/2-inch pieces

1/2 can coconut milk, the cream reserved

1 handful snow peas, trimmed

2 green onions, including most of the greens, cut into 1-inch pieces

2 tablespoons soy sauce

Cilantro or *rau ram*, basil, and mint leaves, for garnish

Using a mortar and pestle or a food processor, work all the curry paste ingredients into a rough paste and set aside.

Soak the mushrooms in warm water in a small bowl for 15 minutes or longer; drain, reserving the liquid. Discard the stems and slice the caps into strips. Pull the noodles apart with your fingers. Prepare the peanuts.

Heat the oil in a wok over high heat, add the curry paste, and move it around the pan for 30 seconds. Lower the heat to medium and cook for 12 to 15 minutes, stirring frequently and adding small amounts of water from time to time to keep it from sticking. When it begins to release some of the oil, add the tomato, raise the heat, and add the mushroom liquid and coconut milk. Simmer for a minute, then add the mushrooms, snow peas, green onions, and soy sauce; turn off the heat.

Cook the noodles in plenty of boiling water until tender, about 4 minutes for fresh noodles. Scoop them out, shake off the excess water, and add them to the wok. Lift several times to coat thoroughly with the sauce. Pile the noodles onto platter and garnish with the reserved coconut cream, the peanuts, and the herbs.

Soba with Hijiki and Stir-Fried Vegetables

Hijiki, a delicious black sea vegetable, garnishes this robust cold-weather buckwheat pasta. Serves 3 or 4 Ⓥ

1/4 cup dried hijiki, soaked for 30 minutes and drained

3 1/2 tablespoons soy sauce

2 teaspoons sugar

6 ounces soba

1 1/2 tablespoons peanut oil

1 bunch green onions, whites thinly sliced into rounds and greens sliced diagonally

4 teaspoons chopped fresh ginger

1 large clove garlic, chopped

2 carrots, cut into julienne strips

5 large mushrooms, thinly sliced

1/2 teaspoon sea salt

1 tablespoon rice wine (mirin)

4 cups napa cabbage leaves sliced into 1/2-inch ribbons

2 teaspoons toasted sesame oil

2 tablespoons sesame seeds, toasted in a small skillet

Chili oil, to finish

Put the hijiki in a saucepan with 2 tablespoons of the soy sauce, the sugar, and water to cover. Simmer for 15 minutes or until soft, then drain, reserving the liquid.

Cook the soba in plenty of boiling water until tender, 5 to 7 minutes. When the water foams up, add a cup of cold water to bring it down and repeat if necessary. Drain and rinse well under running water.

Place the peanut oil in a wok and heat until hot but short of smoking. Add the white parts of the green onions, the ginger, and garlic and stir-fry over high heat for 45 seconds. Add the carrots and mushrooms and stir-fry for 1 minute, then add the salt, the remaining 1 1/2 tablespoons soy sauce, and the mirin. Toss, then cover the pan and cook for 1 minute. Add the soba, cabbage, and most of the hijiki and toss until the noodles are heated through. Turn off the heat and toss once more with toasted sesame oil and sesame seeds. Remove to a platter and garnish with the remaining hijiki, the onion greens, and drops of chili oil to taste.

Somen in Broth with Soft Tofu and Spinach

A light, brothy noodle dish—so simple and clean. A small cluster of enoki mushrooms would make an aesthetically appealing garnish here—or use one or two white mushrooms, thinly sliced. Serves 2 Ⓥ

3 cups Stock for Stir-Fries (page 235) or Kombu Stock with Dried Mushrooms (page 536)

Few drops soy sauce, preferably mushroom soy

1 tablespoon rice wine (mirin)

2 ounces somen

1/2 package silken or soft tofu, drained and finely diced

2 mushrooms, thinly sliced

12 spinach leaves, cut into wide ribbons

1/2 teaspoon toasted sesame oil

2 green onions, thinly sliced

2 teaspoons toasted sesame seeds

Chili oil, optional, to finish

Make the stock and taste it. You may need to build the flavor by adding a little soy sauce and mirin to taste.

Cook the somen in plenty of boiling water until tender, 3 to 5 minutes, adding cold water when it begins to foam to the top of the pot. Drain and rinse thoroughly under cold water. Shake dry.

Add the tofu, mushrooms, spinach, and sesame oil to the stock and simmer gently for about 3 minutes. Add the somen and simmer until it's heated through. Divide between two bowls and garnish with the green onions and sesame seeds. Add a few drops chili oil if you like the heat.

Chinese Dumplings with Shredded Cabbage, Mushrooms, and Leeks

These dumplings are surprisingly easy to make. Steaming produces a more flavorful dumpling, but they can also be fried, as for potstickers. Serve with one of the Asian dipping sauces (page 522). Makes approximately 20 dumplings Ⓥ

1 pound napa cabbage

Sea salt

1/4 cup dried black Chinese mushrooms

1/4 cup dried tree ear mushrooms

6 fresh mushrooms, finely chopped

2 tablespoons chopped leek or green onion

1 teaspoon minced garlic

1 teaspoon minced ginger

1 teaspoon rice wine vinegar

Szechuan Pepper Salt (page 69) or sea salt and freshly milled white pepper

24 wonton wrappers

Slice the cabbage leaves into strips 1/2 inch wide and the base about 1/8 inch wide. Measure 4 cups into a colander. Sprinkle lightly with salt, toss, and set aside for an hour. Squeeze out the excess moisture. It shouldn't be necessary to rinse it, but taste to make sure. Meanwhile, cover the dried mushrooms generously with boiling water and let soak for 15 minutes. Squeeze dry, remove the stems, and slice the caps into thin strips. Reserve the soaking liquid.

Combine the cabbage, dried and fresh mushrooms, leek, garlic, ginger, and vinegar. Add Szechuan pepper salt to taste and more vinegar if needed to bring up the flavors. Put a spoonful of the filling in the middle of a wonton wrapper, paint the edges with water, and fold the opposite corners together. Use as much filling as you can and still be able to close the dumpling. Make two or three pleats on each side, then set the dumpling down firmly to make a solid, flat bottom. Repeat with the remaining filling and wrappers. Cover with a barely damp towel until ready to cook.

To steam the dumplings, lightly oil the surface of the steamer, set the dumplings on top, and bring the water to a boil. Cover and steam for 7 minutes.

To fry the dumplings, coat a 12-inch cast-iron skillet generously with peanut oil, add the dumplings, and fry over medium-high heat until golden on the bottom. Add enough of the reserved mushroom soaking liquid, plus water if needed, to come about one-third up the side of the dumplings—stand back—and cover until the hissing subsides. Boil briskly until the liquid is reduced and the potstickers begin to fry again. Now is when they stick to the pot. Turn off the heat and gently loosen them with a thin metal spatula.

Soba in Broth with Spinach, Purple Dulse, and Silken Tofu

A very light, fresh, and pretty noodle dish. Purple-colored dulse, a kind of seaweed, is gorgeous in the bowl. You can also use wakame, a similar but slightly more substantial sea green. Take a few dried clumps of either and soak them briefly in cool water. The leaves will open up. Separate them if joined at the base. Serves 4 Ⓥ

Kombu Stock with Dried Mushrooms (page 536)

6 ounces soba

2 clumps dulse or wakame

1 slender carrot, very thinly sliced on the diagonal

1 package silken or soft tofu, cut into small dice

2 cups small spinach leaves, stems removed

2 green onions, diagonally sliced, for garnish

16 cilantro leaves, for garnish

Chili oil, to finish

Make the kombu stock and strain it carefully. Remove the stems from the mushrooms and thinly slice the caps. Cook the noodles in plenty of boiling water until tender but slightly undercooked since they will be reheated later. Rinse under cold water. Cover the dulse with cool water and run your fingers over it to loosen any tiny seashells or sand. Pull the leaves apart with your fingers.

Bring the stock to a boil in a saucepan. Add the mushrooms and carrot and simmer for 1 minute. Add the noodles and tofu and simmer very gently until both are heated through, after several minutes. Finally add the spinach and cook until it's wilted. Divide the noodles among heated bowls, then ladle the broth and vegetables over them. Drain the dulse and add it to the bowls as well. Garnish with the green onions and cilantro and serve with a few drops chili oil in each bowl.

Udon with Stir-Fry and Five-Spice Tofu

An exceptionally flavorful plate of noodles. The tofu, available at natural foods stores, is baked and flavored with five-spice powder. It's perfectly seasoned for this dish. Serves 2 to 4 Ⓥ

Sauce

- ¹/₃ cup Stock for Stir-Fries (page 235) or water
- 3 tablespoons hoisin sauce
- 1¹/₂ tablespoons soy sauce
- 1¹/₂ tablespoons tomato paste
- 2 cloves garlic, minced
- 2 jalapeño chiles, seeded and finely chopped
- 1 tablespoon grated lemon zest or minced lemongrass

Noodles and Vegetables

- 1 (7- or 8-ounce) package udon
- 2 tablespoons roasted peanut oil
- ¹/₂ package five-spice tofu, thinly sliced
- 2 medium leeks, white parts only, julienned
- 1 red bell pepper, or ¹/₂ each red and green, thinly sliced into long strips
- 4 mushrooms, thinly sliced
- Sea salt and freshly milled pepper
- Coarsely chopped cilantro, for garnish

Mix all the sauce ingredients together and set aside.

Cook the noodles in plenty of boiling water until tender, 5 to 7 minutes. When the water foams up, add a cup cold water to make the foam subside and repeat if needed. Drain and rinse when done.

Heat the wok with the oil until hot but not smoking. Add the tofu and stir-fry over high heat until it's sizzling, about 1 minute. Remove and set aside. In the same oil, stir-fry the leeks and bell pepper for 1 minute. Add the mushrooms and cook for 1 minute more, then season with a few pinches salt. Return the tofu to the wok and add the sauce. Cook for 30 seconds and turn off the heat.

Drain the udon, shake it dry, and put it on a platter with the vegetables and tofu over the top. Season with pepper and garnish with the cilantro.

Glass Noodles with Spinach

In The Modern Art of Chinese Cooking, *Barbara Tropp sings the praises of this dish. She calls for a rich chicken stock, but I use vegetable stock in its place. Keep this dish in mind when spinach is tender and young.* Serves 3 to 4 Ⓥ

- 2 bunches young spinach
- 2 ounces bean-thread or cellophane noodles
- 1 cup Basic Vegetable Stock (page 175)
- 1¹/₂ tablespoons sesame oil
- ¹/₂ teaspoon sea salt
- ¹/₂ teaspoon sugar
- 2 teaspoons toasted sesame oil

Bring a medium pot of water to a boil. Meanwhile, separate the clumps of spinach, remove the leaves, and trim the root ends to about 1¹/₂ inches in length. These are called the crowns. Wash both leaves and crowns in plenty of cold water. Flush out the roots under running water. Add salt to the water and blanch the crowns until the colors glow, then scoop them out. Blanch the leaves until wilted and bright green. Drain and rinse along with the crowns under cold water. Gently press out the excess liquid.

Soak the noodles in hot water until softened, about 3 minutes, then drain. Simmer the noodles in the stock until tender and silky, 3 to 5 minutes. They will have absorbed most of the stock.

Warm a wok, then add the sesame oil and heat until almost smoking. Add the spinach leaves and crowns and stir-fry for 30 seconds. Add ¹/₂ teaspoon salt and the sugar and continue to stir-fry until the leaves are hot. Add the noodles and toasted sesame oil, stir a few more times, taste for salt, and serve.

SAVORY TARTS, PIES, GALETTES, TURNOVERS, AND PIZZAS

CHAPTER 13

Savory Tarts, Pies, Galettes, Turnovers, and Pizzas

Everyone likes a pie. Tarts, flans, galettes, turnovers, and pizzas—all the ways crusts and fillings are combined—have universal appeal. If you're wondering what to serve a guest whose eating disposition runs away from vegetarian dishes, try one of these recipes. Pies are trusty and familiar, and always welcome on the table.

There's quite a range of possibilities when it comes to pairing crusts with fillings. Some savory tarts are silky smooth—such as the Tender Tomato Tart (page 435), a tart of garden vegetables, or the resounding Roasted Eggplant and Tomato Tart (page 434). Their flaky crusts provide an important textural contrast to the smooth filling, but you could easily bake these in ramekins without a crust and provide texture elsewhere, with a leaner crouton, toasted nuts, or a crisp vegetable. Other tarts are naturally full of texture, and some use vegetables as a crust in place of pastry.

Some of these pies are affectionately called galettes, rustic fabrications of dough folded over vegetable fillings. They're rather flat and informal and can be big or sized for a single serving. I used to make them only as desserts, until one day I figured out that they were just as good with savory fillings. Tender, golden yeasted doughs—essentially glorified pizza doughs—come into play here as well as standard pie dough.

Pizza is another kind of pie, a very familiar one that everyone enjoys. Easy to improvise, pizzas are not merely the realm of sophisticated adults but the kind of food that children can happily get involved in without taxing their parents too much. Calzones and their close relations, empanadas, are essentially folded pizzas or turnovers, a casual food with enormous appeal. They can be filled with rustic mixtures of greens and olives as well as cheeses.

Because there are always two parts to these dishes—a crust and a filling—they can be a little time-consuming. I wouldn't suggest making them on the spur of the moment for a weekday dinner unless you're comfortable in the kitchen and a speedy cook. Being familiar with pastry certainly helps move things along, too. Doughs and their fillings, however, can often be made ahead of time, and all that's left to do at the last minute is to assemble and bake your pie.

Tips for Savory Pies

THE DOUGH: The flakiest crusts are made with butter, but you can use an oil-based pastry or one of the less rich yeasted doughs. (Pie dough recipes are in the dessert chapter; yeasted doughs in this chapter.) Since dough takes only a few minutes to make, make it first, then let it rest while you gather the filling ingredients.

PREBAKING TART AND PIE SHELLS: Prebaking tart shells or pie crusts without a filling (that is, blind) long enough for the crust to set creates a finished pastry whose crust is thoroughly cooked and crisp. The easiest way I've found to do this is to first put the formed tart or pie shell in the freezer until it hardens, at least 15 minutes. Once the oven is preheated to 400°F, I put the shell on a sheet pan (so I won't have to handle it later—crusts on tart shells are fragile), add foil and pie weights, and bake until the foil comes easily away from the dough, about 15 minutes. I lift out the weights and return the tart to the oven until set and pale gold, another 10 to 15 minutes. Check once or twice while baking and if any bubbles have formed, deflate them with the tip of the paring knife. If you've saved a scrap of the dough, you can use it to patch any holes as soon as the shell comes out of the oven. Just gently rub a piece of the soft dough into any holes. To remove the rim from a filled, finished tart, see page 622.

SERVING: These savory tarts and pies are best served warm from the oven, but some of them keep surprisingly well. Many are good at room temperature, and some are sturdy enough to take on a picnic or withstand the rigors of the buffet table. When it comes to leftovers, the crust may lose its crispness, but they're easily reheated and very nearly as good.

TRANSFORMING TARTS AND GALETTES INTO SAVORY FLANS

If making a crust involves too much time, too many calories, or anything else that's problematic, you can omit it altogether, and change the dish from a tart to a timbale or a flan. To make up for the lost texture of the crust, grace the top of the dish with fresh bread crumbs crisped in olive oil or butter, or toasted nuts.

To bake a savory timbale or flan, select a glass or ceramic loaf pan, gratin dish, or four to six ramekins. Butter them well. Add two or three beaten eggs to the vegetable mixture if it doesn't have any binder and increase the seasonings by half. Pour the mixture into the buttered dish. Set the flan in a larger dish and add warm water to come halfway up the sides. Bake at 375°F until well set, and the top is beginning to brown, for 20 to 35 minutes, depending on the size or the dish. When a toothpick comes out clean, the flan is done.

Yeasted Pastry Tarts and Pies

Yeast-risen doughs require less fat than standard short crusts do because the yeast provides the tenderness and elasticity. The yeast also gives them good flavor. Angelic to handle, these doughs make gorgeous pies, tarts, and galettes, with golden sculpted surfaces. The only caveat is to roll them very thin. If you don't, your crust will end up bready. There will be more dough than you need, but you can always use the extra dough to make a few breadsticks or rolls. For information on flour choices, see page 31.

Yeasted Tart Dough with Olive Oil

The egg contributes to the strength and suppleness of the dough. If you don't eat eggs, leave it out and replace with oil and water, as specified below. Makes one 9-, 10-, or 11-inch tart, pie, or galette, or 6 to 8 individual shells ⓥ

- 2 teaspoons active dry yeast
- 1/2 teaspoon sugar
- 3 tablespoons olive oil
- 1 egg, lightly beaten, or 3 tablespoons water plus 1 tablespoon oil
- 3/8 teaspoon sea salt
- 13/4 cups flour, as needed

Dissolve the yeast and sugar in 1/2 cup warm water in a medium bowl and let stand until bubbly, about 10 minutes. Add the oil, egg, and salt, then stir in the flour. When the dough is too stiff to work with a spoon, turn it onto the counter and knead until smooth and elastic, about 4 minutes. Add more flour if necessary to keep it from sticking. Set the dough in an oiled bowl, turn it over to coat, cover with a towel, and let rise until doubled in bulk, 45 minutes to an hour. Turn the dough out. Roll it into a thin circle and use it to line a tart or pie pan or to make a free-form galette. (For individual tarts, divide it into six pieces, shape into balls, and let rest under a towel for 15 minutes before rolling them out.)

Yeasted Tart Dough with Butter

Slightly sticky and needing a good beating when the butter is added, it's best made using a mixer with a paddle attachment. Work in as much flour as you can before kneading. Makes one 9- to 11-inch tart, pie, or galette shell

- 2 teaspoons active dry yeast
- 1/2 teaspoon sugar
- 1/2 cup warm milk or water
- 1 egg, at room temperature
- 1/4 teaspoon sea salt
- Approximately 2 cups flour
- 1/4 cup butter at room temperature

Dissolve the yeast and sugar in the milk in a mixing bowl and let stand until bubbly, about 10 minutes. Stir in the egg and salt, then begin adding the flour 1/2 cup at a time. After you've added a cup, beat in the butter, then continue adding flour until the dough pulls away from the edge of the bowl. Turn it out onto a counter and knead until shiny and smooth, after a few minutes.

Transfer the dough to a lightly buttered bowl, cover with a towel, and let rise until doubled in bulk, 45 minutes to an hour. Turn the dough out and roll it into a 13- to 14- inch circle. Use it to line a large tart or pie pan or to make a free-form galette. (Or divide the dough into six smaller pieces for individual pastries. Shape into balls, then let them rest under a towel for 15 minutes before rolling them out.)

Yeasted Pastry for a Double-Crusted Tart: Increase the milk or water from the dough recipe to 1 cup, the butter to 6 tablespoons, and the flour to 3 cups or more, as needed.

Savory Tarts and Pies

Fresh Herb Tart with Goat Cheese

This quivering, herb-flecked tart is one of the true glories of the summer garden. I have been making it since Geraldene Holt arrived from England with the gift of her beautiful book, Recipes from a French Herb Garden. *My American garden is a good herb provider as well. Serve this tart warm or at room temperature surrounded by sliced tomatoes and crisp new lettuces.* Makes one 9-inch tart

Tart Pastry (page 621)
1 small clove garlic, smashed with a knife
2 whole eggs
2 egg yolks, or another whole egg
1/2 cup half-and-half
2 ounces fresh goat cheese, crumbled
1/2 cup finely chopped herb leaves—a mixture including flat-leaf parsley, chervil, tarragon or marjoram, lemon thyme, sorrel
1/2 teaspoon sea salt
Freshly milled white pepper

Make the tart dough, roll it out, and line a 9-inch tart pan. Freeze it for at least 15 minutes, then set on a sheet pan and bake it in a 400°F oven until lightly browned, 20 to 25 minutes. Remove and reduce the temperature to 350°F.

Spear the garlic with a fork and use it to beat the eggs, egg yolks, half-and-half, and goat cheese together. Let it steep in the custard while you chop the herbs, then remove it. Pour the custard through a sieve into a bowl, then add the herbs and season with the salt and a little white pepper. Pour the custard into the shell and bake until set and golden, about 30 minutes. Let cool to tepid or room temperature, then remove from the rim and place on a platter.

Roasted Eggplant and Tomato Tart

The somewhat dull color of this tart makes it hard to imagine the fullness of its flavor. Some sprigs of opal basil help set it off to best advantage. The eggplant and tomatoes can be roasted well in advance of baking. Makes one 9-inch tart

Tart Pastry (page 621)
1 pound eggplant, any variety
3 Roma or plum tomatoes
2 eggs
1 cup half-and-half
1/2 teaspoon sea salt
Freshly milled pepper
1/8 teaspoon grated nutmeg
1 tablespoon finely chopped basil, for garnish
Several basil sprigs, preferably opal basil, for garnish

Make the tart dough, then roll it out and line a 9-inch tart pan. Set in the freezer to harden.

Puncture the eggplant in several places, then roast on a sheet pan in a 375°F oven until it's completely soft and collapsed, 30 to 40 minutes. Broil or grill the tomatoes until lightly charred. When cool enough to handle, remove the eggplant skins and puree the flesh with the whole tomatoes. Beat the eggs in a bowl, then stir in the eggplant puree and half-and-half. Season with the salt, a little pepper, the nutmeg, and garnish with the chopped basil.

Preheat the oven to 400°F. Remove the tart shell from the freezer, set it on a sheet pan, and bake until lightly colored, about 25 minutes. Remove. Lower the temperature to 375°F. Add the filling to the shell and bake until set and a knife comes out clean, 25 to 30 minutes. Let rest for 10 minutes, then remove the rim, set the tart on a platter, and serve, garnished with sprigs of opal basil.

Tender Tomato Tart

A luscious, tender tart made with summer's sweetest vegeta-bles. In this case, you might prefer to start the vegetables first since they need an hour on the stove. Something crunchy and acidic enhances this tart, like a salad of chopped vegetables dressed with olive oil and a dash of vinegar or lemon.
Makes one 9-inch tart

2 tablespoons olive oil

2 small celery ribs

1 carrot, finely diced

1¹/₂ pounds ripe tomatoes, coarsely chopped

1 onion, finely diced

1 clove garlic, minced

2 tablespoons chopped parsley

5 large basil leaves

Tart Pastry (page 621) or Olive Oil Pie Crust (page 620)

¹/₂ teaspoon sea salt

Freshly milled pepper

3 eggs, well beaten

Warm the oil in a heavy pot, add the vegetables and herbs, and stew, covered, over low heat for 1 hour. Occasionally give the pot a stir to make sure nothing is sticking, add-ing a few tablespoons water if the pot seems dry. Pass the vegetables through a food mill or puree. While they're cooking, prepare the pastry, line a 9-inch tart pan, and prebake as described on page 432 until lightly colored.

Heat oven to 400°F. Season the puree with the salt and a little pepper. Stir in the eggs and taste for salt. Pour the filling into the shell and bake until it appears set and a cake tester comes out clean, 25 to 35 minutes. Let cool for 10 minutes before serving.

Tomato and Red Pepper Tart

With crisscrossed strips of peppers and olives, this is still one of my favorite late summer dishes. There's not a speck of cheese, egg, or cream—it's just a jam of sweet seasonal veg-etables. The filling is also stellar in small turnovers or baked in a galette. Serve with a green salad, followed by a cheese plate. Makes one 10-inch tart Ⓥ

Yeasted Tart Dough with Olive Oil (page 433)

2 red onions, finely diced

3 tablespoons olive oil, plus extra for the crust

1¹/₂ pounds ripe paste tomatoes

3 large red bell peppers

3 large cloves garlic, minced

¹/₈ teaspoon saffron threads

¹/₄ teaspoon anise seeds

¹/₂ teaspoon sea salt

Freshly milled pepper

2 tablespoons chopped basil

16 niçoise or 8 small kalamata olives, halved and pitted

Make the dough and set it aside to rise. Cook the onions in the oil over medium heat until soft, about 12 minutes, stir-ring occasionally. While they're cooking, peel, seed, and finely chop the tomatoes. Roast the peppers (see page 364). Set aside two-thirds of one pepper and finely chop the rest. Add the garlic, tomatoes, and diced peppers to the onions, crumble the saffron and anise seeds into the mixture, and season with the salt and a little pepper. Cook for 30 min-utes, stirring occasionally, especially toward the end. The mixture should be quite thick. Taste for salt and stir in the basil leaves.

Heat the oven to 400°F. Roll out the dough and drape it over a 10-inch tart pan. There will be plenty of overhang. Trim it and crimp the dough around the rim. Add the filling. Cut the reserved pepper into narrow strips and use them to make a lattice design over the top. Place the olives in the spaces formed by the peppers. Bake for 35 minutes. Remove and brush the rim of the crust with olive oil. Unmold the tart onto a platter and serve.

Green Herb Tart (*Torta d'Erbe*)

This large golden pie filled with greens and herbs—chard, sorrel, arugula, anise hyssop leaves, beet greens, and so forth—truly celebrates spring. This looks impressive and holds well. Rest assured, the double crust is easy to make and form. Makes one 11-inch tart, serving 8 to 12

Yeasted Pastry for a Double-Crust Tart (page 433)

2 bunches chard, or chard and beet greens to make 12 to 16 cups chopped leaves

3 tablespoons butter or a mixture of butter and olive oil

1 teaspoon sea salt

2 bunches green onions, including half the greens, finely chopped

2 to 3 ounces sorrel leaves, 1 to 1 1/2 cups, if available

1/2 cup chopped parsley

1 cup chopped arugula

2 tablespoons chopped basil or anise hyssop

Freshly milled pepper

1 cup ricotta

2 eggs, lightly beaten

1/2 cup milk

1/2 cup grated Gruyère

2 tablespoons freshly grated parmesan

1/8 teaspoon grated nutmeg

Make the dough and set it aside to rise.

Meanwhile, chop the chard into bite-size pieces and wash. (It will look like a huge amount, but it cooks down.) Melt 2 tablespoons of the butter in a large skillet over medium heat. Add the chard with the water clinging to its leaves, or as much as will fit, sprinkle with the salt, and cook, turning it as it wilts, until it has cooked down and is tender. Should the pan become dry, add a few tablespoons water, as needed.

Heat the remaining 1 tablespoon butter in a medium skillet. Add the green onions, sorrel, parsley, arugula, and basil, and cook over medium heat until tender, about 5 minutes. Add them to the cooked chard and taste for salt and season with pepper.

Beat the ricotta, all but 2 tablespoons of the beaten eggs, and milk until smooth, then stir in the cheeses and greens. Taste for salt and season with pepper and the nutmeg.

When the dough has doubled in bulk, preheat the oven to 375°F. Divide the dough into two pieces. Roll one piece

out no thicker than 1/8 inch and drape it over an 11-inch tart pan with a removable rim, or a shallow pie plate. Ease the dough into the edges of the pan without stretching and trim the edge so that it's a little larger than the pan. Add the filling. Roll out the second piece of dough and cut out a circle the same size as the surface of the tart. Place it right on the filling, then fold the longer piece of dough over it. Crimp the edges. Using the tip of a paring knife, score the top of the tart in a crisscross design without cutting through the dough. Brush it with the reserved egg.

Bake for 35 minutes or until the top crust is well browned. Carefully remove the rim, then return the tart to the oven for 10 minutes more to brown and crisp the edges. Let cool for 10 minutes, then transfer to a platter. Serve warm or tepid.

With Dill and Feta: Add 1/2 cup chopped dill and replace the Gruyère with feta. Don't add salt to the cheese mixture, as feta is quite salty.

Eggplant Torta

This is definitely a dish to make when presentation counts. It's not particularly difficult, but it does involve at least an hour to make and assemble the parts. The torta holds its heat well and needn't be served piping hot. In fact, it's excellent at room temperature. Serves 6 to 8

3 1/2 pounds eggplant, sliced lengthwise 1/4 inch thick

3 tablespoons olive oil

Sea salt and freshly milled pepper

1 large bunch chard, stems discarded

1 onion, finely diced

2 pinches saffron threads

2 large cloves garlic, minced or put through a press

1/2 teaspoon sea salt

1/4 cup chopped basil

1/3 cup grated Gruyère

3/4 cup fresh goat cheese, about 3 ounces

3 tablespoons freshly grated parmesan

3 eggs, beaten with 1 tablespoon water

Fresh Tomato Sauce (page 54) or Warm Goat Cheese Sauce (page 64), for serving

Preheat the oven to 400°F. Unless it's garden fresh, salt the eggplant, let stand 30 minutes, then blot dry. Brush both sides of the eggplant with oil, lay them on a sheet pan, and bake until the bottom is browned, after about 12 minutes. Turn and bake to brown the second side, about 10 minutes. Remove and season with salt and pepper.

Meanwhile, finely chop the chard. Heat 3 tablespoons oil in a wide skillet over medium heat, add the onion, and sprinkle on the saffron. Cook slowly, stirring occasionally, until the onion is quite soft, about 12 minutes, then stir in the garlic and chard with the water clinging to its leaves. Sprinkle over the salt and cook slowly, stirring occasionally with tongs, until the chard is fully tender, about 15 minutes. If the pan seems dry at any point, add water about $1/3$ cup at a time. When tender, stir in the basil, taste for salt, and season with plenty of pepper.

To form the torta, brush a 9-inch springform pan with oil or butter. Arrange five or six slices of eggplant around the edge, overlapping them as you go. They need to come at least 2 inches up the side. Next make overlapping layers of the eggplant to cover the bottom of the pan. Trim the eggplant slices, if needed, to make them fit, and use any odd pieces to fill in the gaps. The eggplant may be higher in the center than at the rim.

Sprinkle the eggplant with half of the Gruyère, then make a layer with half of the chard. Cover the chard with half the goat cheese and a tablespoon of parmesan. Use half of the remaining eggplant to make a layer—the trimmings are fine—and cover with the rest of the Gruyère, followed by the remaining chard and goat cheese. Sprinkle with a tablespoon of parmesan.

Now slowly pour the beaten eggs over the torta, letting them seep into the vegetables. Make a final layer of eggplant, arranging the slices attractively since this is the side that will be seen. Cover with the remaining 1 tablespoon parmesan and bake until the custard is set, 35 to 40 minutes. Let cool for 10 or 15 minutes, then run a knife around the edge and carefully dislodge the springform. Set the torta on a serving plate if you plan to serve it whole. Or slice it into wedges and surround with the sauce.

Tomato Tartlets with Rosemary

These little free-form tarts are full of Provençal flavors. Use tomatoes in season, mixing varieties and colors. Serve them warm from the oven or at room temperature. These are durable enough to take on a picnic.

Makes 6 individual tarts (V)

Galette Dough (page 624), Yeasted Tart Dough with Olive Oil (page 433), or Yeasted Tart Dough with Butter (page 433)

2 tablespoons finely chopped rosemary

Approximately 1 pound tomatoes, thinly sliced

18 niçoise olives, pitted and halved

Olive oil, for drizzling

Sea salt and freshly milled pepper

2 tablespoons finely grated parmesan, optional

Heat the oven to 425°F. Divide the dough into six equal pieces and roll each piece into a circle about $1/8$ inch thick. Sprinkle $1/2$ teaspoon rosemary over each circle and gently roll it into the dough. Overlap five or six slices of tomato on each round, leaving a 1-inch border around the edge. Tuck in the olives, sprinkle more rosemary on top, drizzle with oil, and season with salt and pepper. Fold the edges of the dough over the tomatoes, creasing every inch or so. Cup your hands around the tarts and press together to make a firm little package. Brush the tops lightly with olive oil.

Bake until the crust is golden, 20 to 25 minutes. Add the cheese during the last 5 minutes. Serve hot, warm, or at room temperature. To reheat, place in a hot oven for about 8 minutes.

Chard Tart with Saffron and Fennel Seeds

With saffron, fennel seeds, and pine nuts, this dish of greens boasts some complex flavors. And with this crust, it's also durable enough to travel. Serves 4 to 6.

Olive Oil Pie Crust (page 620)

12 to 14 cups roughly chopped chard or beet greens

2 tablespoons olive oil

$1/2$ onion, diced (about 1 cup)

1 pinch saffron threads

1 scant teaspoon lightly roasted fennel seeds

Sea salt and freshly milled pepper

2 eggs, beaten

$1/3$ cup grated Gruyère or ricotta

2 tablespoons pine nuts, optional

Make the dough and form a 9-inch tart shell or use it to line a pie plate. Freeze until hard while you preheat the oven to 400°F. Bake, on a sheet pan, until lightly browned, about 25 minutes.

To make the filling, rinse the greens well, but don't dry them. And don't be afraid to have a bit of chard stem included—it gives texture to the tart. Heat a wide, deep pan and add the greens, cover, and allow them to cook down in the steam created by the wet leaves. (Beet greens will take a little less time to cook than chard.) When they're collapsed and are mostly tender, a matter of 5 minutes or so, slide the leaves into a colander and let drain and cool.

Meanwhile, heat a wide skillet and add the olive oil. Add the onion and the saffron threads and fennel seeds, and cook over medium heat, stirring occasionally, for about 2 minutes. Cover the pan and continue cooking while you return to the chard. Squeeze or press out as much of the liquid as you easily can (this is good to drink), then chop the cooked leaves fairly finely. Add them to the onion mixture and turn them about. Season with salt and plenty of pepper and cook a few minutes more. Remove from the heat.

Heat the oven to 350°F.

Quickly stir the beaten eggs into the greens and add the Gruyère, if using. If using ricotta, add it by the teaspoon and gently mix it in. Pour the mixture into the prebaked crust, cover with the pine nuts, and bake until the filling is set, about 30 minutes. Let cool and serve warm or at room temperature.

Ricotta Tart with Saffron and Herbs

An aromatic and pretty golden tart. The bran in the crust makes a nice nutty foil for the mild cheese. Serves 4 to 8

Pie Crust with Bran (page 620) or Olive Oil Pie Crust (page 620)

2 pinches saffron threads

2 tablespoons butter

1 large shallot, finely diced

$1/4$ cup white wine

2 cups ricotta

2 eggs

$1/4$ cup freshly grated parmesan or dry Jack

2 tablespoons chopped parsley

1 tablespoon chopped marjoram

$1/2$ teaspoon sea salt

Freshly milled white pepper

Fit the pie crust into a 9-inch tart pan. Freeze until hard while you preheat the oven to 400°F. Bake, on a sheet pan, until lightly browned, about 25 minutes. Remove and lower the temperature to 350°F. Cover the saffron threads with a tablespoon boiling water and set aside.

Melt the butter in a small skillet over medium-high heat. Add the shallot and cook, stirring frequently, for about 2 minutes. Add the wine and simmer until it's reduced. Beat the ricotta and eggs in a mixer or food processor until smooth, then, by hand, stir in the diluted saffron, cheese, shallot, and herbs. Season with the salt and a little white pepper. Transfer to the tart shell and bake until set on top and golden, about 25 minutes.

Rice and Ricotta Tart

This sturdy, reheatable tart can easily be varied with the addition of different cheese and even types of rice. Heavier rices, like wild rice, will tend to fall to the bottom, however.
Serves 4 to 6

Pie Crust with Bran (page 620) or Yeasted Tart Dough with Butter (page 433)

1/2 cup medium- or long-grain rice

3/4 teaspoon sea salt

1 cup ricotta

2 eggs

1 cup milk

1/8 teaspoon grated nutmeg

1/2 cup freshly grated parmesan

Fit the dough into a 9-inch tart pan or shallow pie pan. Freeze until firm. Preheat the oven to 400°F and bake the frozen crust until lightly colored and set, about 25 minutes. Remove and lower the temperature to 350°F.

Boil the rice in 3 cups water with 1/2 teaspoon of the salt. When cooked but still just a bit firm, pour it through a sieve, reserving the water. Beat the ricotta with the eggs and milk until smooth, then add the remaining 1/4 teaspoon salt, the nutmeg, the parmesan, and the rice. Pour the filling into the shell and bake until golden and set, about 40 minutes.

(The rice water is viscous and naturally sweet. It makes a soothing and delicious chilled drink, plain or flavored with a drop of almond extract or almond syrup. It's a boon to someone who's been suffering an upset stomach or sore throat.)

Savory Cottage Cheese and Herb Pie

I like a cottage cheese pie for dessert, but also this savory one that's laced with fresh herbs and green onions. Serve small pieces for a first course or larger ones for dinner with thick-cut tomatoes alongside. For the pie dough, use one made with oil or with coconut oil and a mix of spelt and all-purpose flour.
Serves 4 to 6

One partially prebaked 9-inch pie crust (see headnote)

2 cups cottage cheese

2 tablespoons flour

1/4 cup thinly sliced green onions (about 1 bunch)

2 heaping tablespoons chopped parsley and marjoram, mixed

3 eggs

1 tablespoon Dijon mustard

1 cup whole milk or half-and-half

1/2 teaspoon sea salt

Freshly milled white pepper

1/4 cup grated Parmesan cheese

Heat the oven to 350°F and place the partially baked pie shell on a sheet pan.

Mix the cottage cheese and flour together, then add the remaining ingredients and mix well. Pour the filling into the shell, and bake on the center rack of the oven until the filling is set and browning, about an hour or just slightly longer. Remove the pie from the oven and let it rest for at least 10 minutes before serving, or until it ceases to bubble and settles into a firm filling.

Savory Vegetable Galettes

These savory flat pies occupy a place somewhere between pizzas and tarts. Their free-form crusts are entirely forgiving—ragged edges and lopsided circles are part of their charm—but they can be made perfectly round with evenly trimmed edges for those who prefer symmetry.

Thin slices of galette can be served as an appetizers or first course, while larger portions make an excellent vegetable entrée. Galettes can also be made into individual pastries that take center stage with authority. Less fragile than their larger siblings, individual galettes can be made a few hours ahead of time and reheated in a hot oven.

ACCOMPANIMENTS: Individual pastries can be surrounded by braised greens or a complementary vegetable finely cut so that it encircles the pastry. I particularly like galettes set on a bed of salad, such as watercress or frisée, dressed with a shallot-rich vinaigrette. The salad offers a fresh contrast to the galette, while the heat of the pastry brings out the flavor of the shallots.

QUANTITY: A recipe for galette dough makes one 10-inch or six individual galettes. One large pie serves 8 to 10 as a first course, or 4 to 6 as a main course. A recipe for yeasted dough makes enough for two fairly open tarts or one enclosed tart.

MAKING GALETTES: First make the filling and allow it to cool to room temperature. This can be done ahead of time. Make the dough of your choice. Roll it into a circle about 14 inches across and ¼ inch thick, leaving the edges rough or trimming them. Place the dough on a cookie sheet or the back of a jelly roll pan so that when done it can be slid easily onto a serving plate.

Spread the filling over the dough, leaving a 1½- to 3-inch border around the edge. The wider the border, the more the filling will be covered. Slide your hand under the edge of the dough and bring it up over the filling, going all the way around the galette, overlapping the folds. You can make neat, sharply defined pleats or soft, irregular folds. Yeasted dough lends itself much more to soft, rounded edges than galette dough. Brush the galette dough with melted butter or an egg wash to give it sheen and color, then bake right away.

For individual galettes, divide the dough into six equal pieces and shape them into disks. Roll into circles between 6 and 8 inches across, add the filling, and gently pleat all the way around. Or roll the dough into a square and fold the edges over the filling like a four-sided envelope.

MAKING AHEAD OF TIME: Doughs for galettes can be rolled out in advance and refrigerated—useful if you're planning on making several at once for a party or holiday meal. Fillings can also be made a day or two ahead. Plan ahead and at the last minute you need only combine the shell and the filling and bake them. While galettes are always best freshly baked, leftovers can be reheated. Set pieces directly on a pizza stone or cookie sheet and warm them in a hot oven.

Cabbage and Mushroom Galette with Horseradish Sauce

A tender yeasted tart dough is good with this winter filling. Serve with wild rice or buckwheat groats and julienne strips of kohlrabi, steamed and tossed with chopped tarragon or dill. Serves 4 to 6

- Yeasted Tart Dough with Butter (page 433) or Galette Dough (page 624)
- 2 tablespoons butter
- 1 large onion, finely diced
- 4 ounces fresh shiitake mushrooms, stems discarded, caps thinly sliced
- 1 teaspoon chopped thyme or ¹/₂ teaspoon dried
- 1 teaspoon chopped tarragon or ¹/₂ teaspoon dried
- 1 tablespoon chopped dill or 1 teaspoon dried
- 6 cups thinly sliced cabbage, preferably savoy, or 4 cups cabbage plus 2 cups other greens, such as beet, chard, or kale
- 1 teaspoon sea salt
- ¹/₄ cup chopped parsley
- 1 hard-cooked egg, chopped
- ¹/₄ cup sour cream or yogurt
- 1 teaspoon tarragon vinegar
- Freshly milled pepper
- 2 tablespoons melted butter
- Fresh Horseradish Sauce (page 63), for serving

Make the dough and set aside to rise or chill while you make the filling.

Heat the butter in a large skillet over medium heat. Add the onion, mushrooms, and herbs and cook until softened, about 10 minutes. Add the cabbage, the salt, and ¹/₂ cup water. Cover and cook slowly until the cabbage is tender, 15 to 20 minutes, turning it occasionally. Add more liquid. When tender, uncover and raise the heat to evaporate any excess moisture. The mixture should be fairly dry. Stir in the parsley, egg, and sour cream. Season with vinegar and taste for salt and pepper.

Preheat the oven to 400°F. Roll the dough into a large, thin circle and set it on the back of a sheet pan, or a cookie sheet. The edges will hang over the sides. Add the filling, making a mound 7 to 8 inches across, then fold the edges over and brush with the melted butter. Pour any extra butter into the vegetables. Bake until browned, 25 to 30 minutes. Carefully slide it onto a serving plate. Serve with the horseradish sauce on the side.

Winter Squash Galette

This is one of my favorite holiday dishes. The cheese and sweet squash make an intriguing combination, and a yeasted dough is particularly good here. Consider serving this with the Watercress with Slivered Endive (page 125). Serves 6

- Yeasted Tart Dough with Olive Oil (page 433), Yeasted Tart Dough with Butter (page 433), or Galette Dough (page 624)
- 2¹/₂ pounds winter squash, such as butternut
- 1 tablespoon olive oil, plus extra for the squash
- 1 small head garlic, cloves separated but not peeled
- 1 onion, finely diced
- 12 fresh sage leaves, chopped, or 2 teaspoons dried
- ¹/₂ cup freshly grated Pecorino Romano or parmesan
- Sea salt and freshly milled pepper
- 1 egg, beaten

Make the dough. Preheat the oven to 375°F. Cut the squash in half, scrape out the seeds, and brush the cut surface with oil. Stuff the garlic into the cavities and place the squash cut side down on a sheet pan. Bake until the flesh is tender, about 40 minutes. Scoop out the squash and squeeze the garlic cloves. Mash them together with a fork until fairly smooth, leaving some texture.

Warm 1 tablespoon oil in a skillet over medium heat. Add the onion and sage and cook until the onion is soft and beginning to color, about 12 minutes. Add it to the squash along with the grated cheese and season with salt and pepper to taste.

Roll out the dough into a 14-inch circle and spread the filling over it, leaving a border of 2 inches or more. Pleat the dough over the filling, then brush the edges with beaten egg. Bake until the crust is golden, about 25 minutes.

Mushroom Galette

This is a dish I'd choose for a special occasion. It's a production, requiring a mushroom stock for the sauce, a filling, and a crust. But all the parts can be made in advance of the final baking. Serves 6

Galette Dough (page 624) or Yeasted Tart Dough with Olive Oil (page 433)

2 cups Quick Mushroom Stock (page 223) or commercial stock

2 to 3 teaspoons Dijon mustard

Aged red wine vinegar or sherry vinegar, for the stock

4 tablespoons olive oil

1 large onion, cut into ½-inch dice

2 teaspoons minced rosemary

½ teaspoon sea salt

Freshly milled pepper

2 pinches red pepper flakes

½ pound portabella or shiitake mushrooms

1 pound large white mushrooms

2 cloves garlic, minced

3 tablespoons tomato paste

1 tablespoon butter

2 tablespoons chopped parsley

2 tablespoons melted butter or beaten egg for the glaze, optional

Make the dough.

Season the stock with a few teaspoons mustard and just enough vinegar to sharpen the flavors. Set it aside.

Heat 1 tablespoon of the oil in a large skillet. Add the onion and rosemary and cook over medium heat until the onion is lightly browned, about 12 minutes. Season with the salt, a little pepper, and the red pepper flakes. Remove to a bowl.

Heat 1½ tablespoons of the oil in the same skillet over high heat. Add half the mushrooms and sauté until browned, then season with salt and pepper. Remove to the bowl with the onions, then repeat with the remaining mushrooms. Return everything to the pan, add the garlic and tomato paste diluted with a few spoonfuls of the stock, and a teaspoon of the vinegar. Add the remaining stock, bring to a boil, then stir in the butter and the parsley. Cook for 5 minutes, then drain, reserving the juices.

Preheat the oven to 400°F. Roll out the dough for one large or six individual galettes, then add the mushrooms. Loosely fold the dough over the filling and brush it with melted butter or egg. Bake until the crust is browned, about 25 minutes. Heat any reserved juices and spoon them into the mushrooms.

Onion Galette with Mustard Cream

A slightly slimmer version of the creamier quiche of years past. The sweetness of the onions needs the pungent, salty accent of the cheese and herbs. Serves 4 to 6

Galette Dough (page 624) or Yeasted Tart Dough with Butter (page 433)

3 tablespoons butter

6 cups thinly sliced yellow onion

1 tablespoon chopped thyme or rosemary

½ cup dry white wine

Sea salt and freshly milled pepper

2 eggs, beaten

1 tablespoon Dijon mustard mixed with ¼ cup cream

½ cup fresh bread crumbs

¼ cup grated Pecorino Romano or parmesan

Make the dough and set it aside.

Melt the butter in a large skillet over medium heat. Add the onion and thyme and cook, stirring occasionally, until they soften and turn golden, about 15 minutes. Add the wine, cook until it has reduced, then season with salt and pepper.

In a bowl, combine all but 2 tablespoons of the egg with the mustard and cream. Stir in the onion, bread crumbs, and cheese.

Preheat the oven to 400°F. Roll the dough into a 14-inch circle. Put the onion on the dough, leaving a 2- to 3-inch edge. Fold the dough over the onion and brush with the reserved egg. Bake until shiny and golden, about 25 minutes.

Leek and Goat Cheese Galette

This galette takes plenty of leeks to make it plump, so if they're hard to come by, use a mixture of leeks and green onions. Served on a salad of peppery watercress, it makes one of my favorite spring dinners. If you don't want to use cream, leave it out rather than replacing it with milk. Serves 6

6 large leeks, including an inch of the green

3 tablespoons butter

1 teaspoon chopped thyme

$1/2$ cup dry white wine

$1/2$ cup cream or crème fraîche

Sea salt and freshly milled pepper

1 egg, beaten

3 tablespoons chopped parsley, or 1 tablespoon chopped tarragon

Galette Dough (page 624)

$1/2$ to 1 cup soft goat cheese, about 4 ounces

Thinly slice and wash the leeks. You should have about 6 cups.

Melt the butter in a medium skillet. Add the leeks, thyme, and $1/2$ cup water. Stew over medium heat, stirring frequently, until the leeks are tender, about 12 minutes. Add the wine and continue cooking until it's reduced, then add the cream and cook until it just coats the leeks and little liquid remains. Season with salt and plenty of pepper. Let cool 10 minutes, then stir in all but 1 tablespoon of the beaten egg, and 2 tablespoons of the parsley.

Preheat the oven to 400°F. Roll out the dough for one large or six individual galettes. Spread the leek mixture on top, leaving a 2-inch border around the edge. Crumble the cheese over the top then fold the dough over the filling. Brush with the reserved egg and bake until the crust is browned, 25 to 30 minutes. Remove, scatter the remaining parsley over the top, and serve.

Turnovers

Folded filled pastries appear the world over, known in their various tongues and guises as turnovers, calzones, Cornish pasties, empanadas, and so forth. They make a portable meal, easy to carry away and eat elsewhere, whether across the room at a cocktail party or to a grassy riverbank.

Virtually any savory filling you like can be tucked into the folds of pastry just as long it's not too moist. Certainly most of the fillings used for the galettes and vegetable tarts will work well. After all, it's not a far cry from a galette to an empanada—it's even the same dough, with the folds extended and sealed so that the filling is entirely contained.

Making Turnovers

DOUGHS: For turnovers, you can use Galette Dough (page 624), Pie Crust (page 620), and the yeasted doughs (page 433), including Pizza Dough (page 447). One recipe Galette Dough yields twelve 3-inch turnovers, each one holding $1^{1}/_{2}$ to 2 tablespoons filling. Twelve ounces pizza or other yeasted dough, one recipe, yields twelve to sixteen pieces.

SHAPING THE TURNOVERS: Divide the dough into the number of pastries you want to make and roll each one separately into circles about $1/8$ inch thick. (With stretchy yeast dough, you can roll out the entire amount, then cut out 3-inch circles with a biscuit cutter.) Set the circles on a sheet pan, cover, and refrigerate until you're ready to fill them. Let them warm up for 5 minutes to soften.

Place $1^{1}/_{2}$ to 2 tablespoons filling on the lower half of each circle, then fold the top half down to form a crescent. Too much filling makes it difficult to seal the pastry, as experience will quickly show. If you're having trouble getting floury dough to stick to itself, paint the edge with water or beaten egg, then use your fingers to press them together. Working your way around the edge, fold the dough into little pleats or press the edges with the tines of a fork to seal them. Brush the turnovers with beaten egg, dust them with poppy or sesame seeds if you like, and bake at 375°F until they're golden and glossy, about 25 minutes. They can be served hot, warm, or at room temperature.

MAKING AHEAD OF TIME: Turnovers can be prebaked, then returned to the oven to rewarm for 5 to 10 minutes. If well wrapped, they can be frozen for a month or so, either cooked or uncooked.

OTHER FILLINGS FOR TURNOVERS

Turnovers are easy to improvise using a number of recipes that appear elsewhere in the book. The following galette fillings given are particularly easy to adapt.

- Blue Cheese and Walnut Spread (page 94): use for small pastries only
- Goat cheese mixed with ricotta and rosemary
- Winter squash puree with caramelized onions
- Sautéed Mushrooms with Garlic and Parsley (page 351)
- Sautéed Peppers (page 363) mixed with shredded mozzarella or goat cheese
- Mixed Greens with Cumin and Paprika (page 345)

Feta Cheese and Herb Turnovers

Serve the small ones for appetizers. Large ones, set hot on a plate of Herb Salad (page 129), make a nice little dinner entrée. Makes 12 small or 4 to 6 large turnovers

Galette Dough (page 624)

1/4 pound feta

1/4 pound farmer's cheese

3 green onions, including an inch or two of the greens, thinly sliced

1 tablespoon chopped dill

1 tablespoon chopped marjoram

2 large lemon thyme or regular thyme sprigs, leaves only

Freshly milled pepper

1 egg yolk, beaten with 1 tablespoon milk

Sesame or poppy seeds

Divide the dough into four, six, or twelve pieces and roll each into a ball. Dust the counter lightly with flour and roll each ball into a circle about 1/8 inch thick.

Work the cheeses, green onions, herbs, and pepper to taste together—the mixture needn't cohere. Divide the filling among the pieces of dough, fold the edges over, then crimp them with your thumbs, making small pleats around the edge, or seal with a fork.

Preheat the oven to 375°F. Brush the pastries with the beaten egg, sprinkle with sesame seeds, and bake for about 25 minutes, until browned all over. Let cool for 5 or 10 minutes before serving.

Mushroom Turnovers

Makes 6 to 12 turnovers

Yeasted Tart Dough with Olive Oil (page 433), Yeasted Tart Dough with Butter (page 433), or Galette Dough (page 624)

12 ounces mushrooms

2 tablespoons olive oil

1/4 cup finely diced onion

1 clove garlic, minced

1 tablespoon chopped tarragon or dill

2 tablespoons chopped parsley

1 1/2 tablespoons tomato paste

Sea salt and freshly milled pepper

2/3 cup toasted bread crumbs

1 egg, beaten, optional

1/2 cup sour cream, optional

Divide the dough into the number of turnovers you'll be making and roll each into a ball. Dust the counter lightly with flour and roll each ball into a circle about 1/8 inch thick. Preheat the oven to 375°F.

Finely chop half the mushrooms and thinly slice the rest. In 8-inch-wide sauté pan, heat half the oil over high heat. Add the onion and finely chopped mushrooms and sauté until the mushrooms release their juices, about 5 minutes. Toss in the garlic and cook until the mixture is dry. Stir in the herbs and tomato paste, season with salt and pepper, and remove to a bowl.

Using the same skillet, heat the remaining oil. Sauté the sliced mushrooms over high heat until browned, after a few minutes. Add these to the bowl and mix with the bread crumbs, all but a tablespoon of the egg, and the sour cream. Season with salt and pepper to taste. Let cool, then fill the turnovers, fold and seal the edges, and brush the tops with the reserved egg mixed with 1 tablespoon water. Bake until nicely browned, about 15 minutes.

Empanadas with Greens and Olives

A robust little pastry based on greens, olives, and a paprika-flavored dough. Makes 12 pastries Ⓥ

Galette Dough (page 624), Yeasted Tart Dough with Butter (page 433), or Yeasted Tart Dough with Olive Oil (page 433)

2 teaspoons sweet paprika

10 cups mixed greens, such as beet greens, chard, spinach, kale

2 tablespoons olive oil

1 small onion, finely diced

2 cloves garlic, chopped

2 bay leaves

1/4 cup chopped parsley

1/4 teaspoon red pepper flakes

1/2 cup pitted olives, such as kalamata

1/2 cup grated provolone, optional

1 beaten egg, optional

Sea salt and freshly milled pepper

Make the dough, adding the paprika to the flour. Divide it into 12 pieces and roll each into a 3- to 4-inch circle. Set on a sheet pan and refrigerate. Preheat the oven to 375°F.

Wash the greens, but don't dry them. Heat the oil in a wide skillet over fairly high heat. Sauté the onion with the garlic, bay leaves, parsley, and pepper flakes until the onion begins to color a little, about 4 minutes. Add the greens and cook until they're tender, 8 to 12 minutes, turning them with tongs as they cook. If there's a lot of moisture when they're done, press it out with the back of a spoon. Finely chop the greens, then mix them with the olives, cheese, and half of the egg. Season to taste with salt and pepper.

Place 1 1/2 tablespoons filling on the lower half of each dough circle, then fold the pastry over and seal the edges. Brush with the remaining egg. Bake for 20 minutes or until nicely browned. Serve warm or at room temperature.

Escarole Calzone

Escarole, a large lettucelike chicory, has a pleasant bitter edge that is tempered here with walnuts and cheeses. These calzones are large enough to make a meal. Makes 4 calzones

Pizza Dough (page 447)

1/2 cup walnuts

Sea salt and freshly milled pepper

2 bunches escarole, separated at the base

2 tablespoons olive oil, plus extra for brushing

4 cloves garlic, chopped

1/2 teaspoon red pepper flakes

1/2 cup pitted kalamata or niçoise olives

2 tablespoons capers, rinsed

3/4 cup grated mozzarella

14 cup grated fontina

2 tablespoons freshly grated parmesan

1 to 2 teaspoons balsamic vinegar

Make the pizza dough and set it aside to rise. Preheat the oven to 350°F. Roast the walnuts on a sheet pan for 5 minutes, then season them with salt and pepper. Finely chop. Turn the oven up to 450°F. If you have a baking stone, heat it at the same time.

Discard any escarole leaves that are yellowed. Wash, then coarsely chop them. Heat the oil in a wide skillet over medium-high heat with the garlic and pepper flakes. When the garlic is fragrant, add the escarole and sauté, turning it frequently with tongs until tender, about 7 minutes. (It may work best to do this in two batches.) Transfer to a colander and press out as much liquid as possible. Combine with the remaining ingredients, seasoning to taste with vinegar and plenty of pepper.

Divide the dough into six pieces. Use two to make into rolls or breadsticks. Roll the rest into four thin 6 1/2-inch circles and set them on a floured pizza peel or the back of a sheet pan; see page 447. Let them rest for 15 minutes. Place the filling over half of each circle, leaving a 1-inch border. Brush the edge with water, fold the top down, then crimp the edges. Slide the calzone onto the baking stone and bake until browned on top, 15 to 20 minutes. Brush with olive oil to make them shine.

Calzone with Mozzarella and Goat Cheese Filling

Chez Panisse's famous calzone with goat cheese and pro-sciutto is the departure for this scrumptious all-out cheesy pastry. Makes 6 calzones

Pizza Dough (page 447)

2 cups grated mozzarella, about 8 ounces

1 cup crumbled goat cheese, about 4 ounces

2 tablespoons parsley chopped with 2 cloves garlic

$1/4$ cup finely sliced green onions, including some greens

Sea salt and freshly milled pepper

Olive oil, for brushing

Finely grated parmesan, to finish

Make the pizza dough and divide it into six pieces. Shape them into balls, then roll into thin circles about $6^1/2$ inches across. Let them rest on the counter, dusted with flour, while you make the filling. Preheat the oven to 450°F. Combine the cheeses, parsely-garlic mixture, and green onions, seasoning with salt and pepper to taste.

Mound 3 heaping tablespoons filling on the bottom half of each circle. Paint the edges with water, then fold the top down, press the dough together, and crimp the edges. Bake until browned on top, 15 to 20 minutes. Brush the top with olive oil, sprinkle with parmesan, and serve.

Pizza Pie Variation: Instead of the crescent shape, roll out two circles the same size and place the filling over one, leaving a $1/2$-inch border. Place the second round on top and crimp the edges together. Bake until browned, then brush with olive oil. These can be made in individual portions or as a single large pie, cut into wedges.

Pizza

While making pizza isn't as fast as ordering it on the phone, what arrives in a box doesn't compare to what comes out of your oven. Pizza appeals to everyone, especially kids, and pizza making is a pleasantly chaotic activity that enjoys the special excitement of anticipation. Pizza is the kind of food that draws everyone to the kitchen. Everyone can take part. While the cook is busy baking, family and friends can be put to work pitting olives, slicing mushrooms, grating cheese, arranging the toppings. Or they can just relax. (I met my husband over an olive-pitting pizza session, so you never know what might come out of it!) Unlike boxed pizzas, homemade pizzas always bear a personal stamp. Spare and elegant, loaded with chiles, rough and tumble or whatever—if you enjoy informality plus made-to-order cooking with drama and flair, then pizzas are probably for you.

Some pizzas have thick, bready crusts, others are crisp crusted and thin, and some are folded to make the calzones that precede. Most of the pizzas described here are the thin-crusted variety. If you prefer a breadier pizza, use half again as much dough, roll it about $1/2$ inch thick, and allow an additional 10 to 15 minutes for baking.

SPECIAL EQUIPMENT: Two pieces of equipment help make excellent pizzas and hearth breads: a pizza stone and a peel—a large, flat paddle made of wood or metal. A stone provides intense bottom heat that burns off moisture, giving the crust a firm, crisp texture. The peel allows you to slide the pizza directly onto the stone, but you can use the back side of a baking sheet almost as easily.

THE DOUGH: Pizza dough is essentially a bread dough enriched with olive oil. It's easy and straightforward to make and can be ready to use in about an hour. Leftover dough can be frozen, but it needs more time to thaw than it takes to make it fresh. You can always bake extra into rolls or a little focaccia.

THE TOPPINGS: Be generous with the toppings, but don't forget that a heavily laden piece of dough is difficult to slide into the oven. Cheese smells irresistible and tastes wonderful, but a light hand keeps it from overwhelming the other ingredients. Good pizza cheeses are fresh mozzarella, fontina, Gorgonzola, and goat cheese, with freshly grated parmesan, dry Jack, or pecorino providing a sharper accent. Regular mozzarella and soy-based cheeses are improved if moistened with fruity olive oil, seasoned with pepper, and allowed to stand 15 minutes before being used. Herbs really come into their glory on pizzas. Tossed on the pie as it comes out of the oven, their volatile oils leap to life. Olives, capers, and a good pinch of red pepper flakes provide pungent, sharp accents.

Cheese can be grated, vegetables sliced and sautéed, garlic and herbs chopped while the dough is rising.

THE OVEN: Oven temperature is most important to the success of your pizza. It takes a hot oven to make a crisp, brown crust without drying out the top. Preheat your oven to 500°F, allowing 30 minutes rather than the usual 10. Adjust your rack to the center or top third of the oven. If you're using a pizza stone, make sure it's already in the oven when you turn it on since it takes 30 minutes to heat up fully.

USING A PEEL: To use a peel, first dust it with semolina, flour, or fine corn meal—coarse polenta is too gritty. Place the dough on the peel and work up the edges a bit to make a rim. Jerk the peel back and forth to make sure the dough is loose. If it isn't, take it off and dust it again. When you're satisfied that the dough can slide easily, add the toppings, open the oven door, and tip the peel at the back edge of the baking stone. Give it a jerk as you pull the peel away, easing the pizza onto the stone. When the pizza is done, slide the peel back under it and take it out of the oven. Or, if you've another pizza on the peel, just lift it out with a spatula.

VEGAN PIZZAS: You don't have to use vegan cheese unless you want to. Many pizzas are naturally good without cheese, such as simple tomato–herb toppings, caramelized onions, sautéed artichokes with olive oil and salt, grilled eggplant with tomatoes and olives, or onion and tomato with capers and lemon zest. And use the Basil Puree (page 51) instead of pesto.

Pizza Dough

There's nothing complicated about pizza dough. It's simply a bread dough that includes some olive oil, like the focaccia dough on page 596. If you're new to yeast doughs, take a look at pages 585 to 588 first to learn about what makes them work, or you can just plunge ahead. Makes enough dough for eight 6-inch pizzas, four 10-inch pizzas, or two 12- to 14-inch pizzas (V)

---

2 teaspoons active dry yeast

2 tablespoons olive oil

1 1/2 teaspoons sea salt

1/2 to 1 cup whole wheat flour or rye flour

3 to 3 1/2 cups flour

Pour 1/2 cup warm water into a mixing bowl, stir in the yeast, and set aside until foamy, about 10 minutes. Add 1 cup warm water, olive oil, and salt, then beat in the whole wheat or rye flour, as much as you want to use followed by enough white flour to form a shaggy dough. Turn it out onto the counter and knead until smooth, adding more flour as needed to keep it from sticking. For a crisp, light crust, pizza dough should be on the moist side, which means it will be slightly tacky.

Put the dough into an oiled bowl, turn it once to coat, then cover with a towel and set aside to rise until doubled in size, 40 to 60 minutes. Turn the dough onto the counter and divide into the number of pizzas you want. Shape each piece into a ball, set on a lightly floured counter, cover with a towel, and let rise for another 20 to 30 minutes.

Shaping the Dough: Taking one ball at a time, flatten it into a disk, pushing it outward with your palm. Working from the middle, push the dough out with your fingers until it's about 1/4 inch thick and fairly even, thickening slightly at the edge. Or roll the dough into a circle, then push up the sides to make a slight rim. Dust the peel or pan with semolina, fine corn meal, or flour, set the dough on top, cover with a towel, and let it rest for 10 or 15 minutes before you add the toppings.

Tomato Sauce for Pizza

I now prefer this sauce to the denser cooked sauce I used to use on pizza. It really does not need to be any more compli-cated than this. The dough needn't be saturated with tomato; a few tablespoons are sufficient for an 8- to 10-inch round pizza. **Makes about 1¹/₂ cups** Ⓥ

1 (15-ounce) can tomatoes or about 1¹/₂ pounds fresh
1 tablespoon olive oil
Pinch of sea salt

Choose the best tomatoes you know, whether they're San Marzanos or your regular, organic diced tomatoes. Put them in a blender and give them two short pulses to break them up, leaving a chunky puree. Remove, stir in the olive oil and salt, and there you are.

If using fresh tomatoes, choose only ripe, red plum toma-toes in season, ones that are full of fragrance and flavor. Slice them lengthwise, pull out the seeds with your fingers, then dice them. Pulse quickly in the blender (or food pro-cessor) to break them up into a somewhat chunky puree, then add the olive oil and salt.

OTHER SAUCES FOR PIZZA

Pesto (page 50)
Basil Puree (page 51)
Salsa Verde (page 48)
Garlic Scape Pesto (page 50)
Smoked Chile Salsa (page 63)
Red Pepper Sauce (page 64)
Hot and Spicy Tapenade (page 78)

PIZZA TIPS

- Pizzas need not be only round. Another style is to press the dough into sheet pans and bake big rectangles. This is often done in Rome and you buy a square for a pronto kind of meal.

- It's easy to make several kinds of pizza at one sitting. For example, choose two of the simpler pizzas and one or two of the heartier, more involved toppings, keeping in mind an interesting balance of flavors, particularly in the cheese department. Sautéed mushrooms, caramel-ized onions, and other toppings can be prepared well ahead of time.

- If using a pizza stone, you can make only one large pizza at a time. But while it's in the oven, you can roll out the dough for the next, set it on the peel, and let it rest while you assemble the toppings. It all flows together.

- I find that many cheeses are fine baked for the entire time, which is, after all, very short. Other cheeses, such as goat cheese or parmesan, are better added during the last 1 or 2 minutes, just enough to warm them up and bring out their flavors.

- These recipes are for 8- to 10-inch pizzas, which use 8 ounces or a quarter of the dough. Of course you can make smaller—or larger—pizzas, adjusting the toppings accordingly.

- A long-rising dough made with just a bit of yeast makes an especially good pizza crust. Jim Lahey is the mas-ter of this dough and his pizzas are light and superb. Fortunately he has written *My Pizza*, an excellent guide.

Pizza Margherita

This classic Italian pizza combines the timeless good flavors of tomato, mozzarella, and basil. Makes one 10-inch pizza

1/4 recipe Pizza Dough (page 447)
3/4 cup Tomato Sauce for Pizza (page 448)
4 ounces fresh mozzarella, thinly sliced
Best olive oil, for drizzling
8 fresh basil leaves, torn into small pieces

Preheat the oven to 500°F.

Roll or stretch out the dough to make a 10-inch circle, place it on a floured peel or pizza pan, and let it rest for 10 minutes. Spread the tomato sauce over the dough, leaving a 1/2-inch border around the edge. Lay the mozzarella over the sauce and drizzle a little oil over all. Bake on a pizza stone or in the pan until the crust is browned, 7 minutes, then remove and brush the crust with a little oil and scatter the torn basil leaves over the top.

Pizza with Grilled Eggplant, Tomato, and Basil Puree

Makes one 10-inch pizza Ⓥ

3 small oblong eggplants, sliced into rounds 1/3 inch thick
Olive oil, for brushing
Sea salt and freshly milled pepper
1/4 recipe Pizza Dough (page 447)
1/4 cup Basil Puree (page 51)
2 Roma or plum tomatoes, sliced into 1/4-inch rounds
2 tablespoons freshly grated parmesan, optional

Brush each side of the eggplant with oil and broil or grill on both sides until nicely colored and tender. Season with salt and pepper.

Preheat the oven to 500°F.

Shape the dough into a 10-inch circle, set it on a floured peel or pizza pan, and let rest for 10 minutes. Brush a little of the basil puree over the bottom, leaving a 1/2-inch border, then cover with overlapping slices of the eggplant and tomatoes. Bake for 6 minutes, then add the cheese and return to the oven for 2 minutes more. Drizzle with the remaining puree and season with pepper.

Pizza with Tomato, Mozzarella, and Olives

The success of a simple pizza, like this one, depends on the quality of your oil and herbs—which should be fruity and fragrant, respectively. Makes one 10-inch pizza

1/4 recipe Pizza Dough (page 447)
3/4 cup Tomato Sauce for Pizza (page 448)
3 to 4 ounces mozzarella, cut into small dice
12 gaeta, niçoise, or kalamata olives, pitted and quartered
1 tablespoon chopped marjoram
Freshly milled pepper
Best olive oil, for drizzling

Preheat the oven to 500°F.

Roll or stretch out the dough into a 10-inch circle, place it on a floured peel or pizza pan, and let rest for 10 minutes. Spread on the tomato sauce, leaving a 1/2-inch border around the edge. Scatter the cheese and olives over the sauce, then add half the marjoram and a little pepper. Drizzle a little oil over all. Bake on a stone or in the pan until the pizza is bubbling, about 10 minutes, then remove and add the remaining marjoram.

Pizza with Tomato and Gorgonzola

This pizza contains the combined delights of tomato, rosemary, and Gorgonzola. Use the Gorgonzola dolcelatte or, if you can't find it, Cambazola or Saga blue. Makes one 10-inch pizza

1/4 recipe Pizza Dough (page 447)
1/3 cup Tomato Sauce for Pizza (page 448)
3 ounces Gorgonzola, crumbled
2 tablespoons freshly grated parmesan
1 teaspoon finely chopped rosemary
Sea salt and freshly milled pepper

Preheat the oven to 500°F.

Roll or stretch the dough into a 10-inch circle, set it on a floured peel or pizza pan, and let rest for 10 minutes. Cover it with the tomato sauce, then the Gorgonzola. Bake on a stone or in the pan until the cheese is melted and bubbling and the crust is browned, about 7 minutes. Add the parmesan and rosemary and bake for 2 minutes more. Remove and season with a little salt and pepper.

Pizza with Eggplant and Oregano

Makes one 10-inch pizza Ⓥ

- 3 tablespoons olive oil
- 8 to 12 ounces eggplant, cut into ¹/₂-inch dice
- ¹/₄ recipe Pizza Dough (page 447)
- 2 tablespoons parsley chopped with 1 clove garlic
- Sea salt and freshly milled pepper
- ¹/₂ teaspoon dried oregano
- 4 ounces mozzarella, preferably fresh, cut into small dice, optional

Preheat the oven to 500°F.

Heat the olive oil in a wide skillet over medium-high heat. Add the eggplant and sauté, stirring every few minutes, until golden and tender, about 15 minutes. Meanwhile, roll or stretch the dough into a 10-inch circle, set it on a floured peel or pizza pan, and let it rest for 10 minutes.

Remove the skillet from the heat, add the parsley-garlic mixture, and season with salt, plenty of pepper, and the oregano. Toss the eggplant with the cheese.

Cover the dough with the eggplant and cheese and bake on a stone or in the pan for 7 to 8 minutes or until the crust is browned.

Pizza with Sautéed Artichoke Heart

Prepare the artichoke before you make the pizza.
Makes one 10-inch pizza

- 1 large artichoke, trimmed, the heart thinly sliced
- 3 tablespoons olive oil
- Juice of ¹/₂ lemon
- Sea salt and freshly milled pepper or red pepper flakes
- ¹/₄ recipe Pizza Dough (page 447)
- 2 tablespoons tomato paste
- ¹/₃ cup grated fontina
- 2 teaspoons capers, rinsed
- 2 tablespoons freshly grated parmesan
- 2 teaspoons chopped parsley

Preheat the oven to 500°F

In a medium skillet over high heat, sauté the artichoke heart in 2 tablespoons of the olive oil until tender and

browned, 10 to 12 minutes. Squeeze lemon juice over the artichokes and season with salt and pepper.

Roll or stretch the dough into a 10-inch circle, set it on a floured peel or pizza pan, and let it rest for 10 minutes. Dilute the tomato paste with the remaining 1 tablespoon oil and spread it over the dough. Lay the artichokes on top, then add the cheese and capers. Bake for 6 minutes, add the parmesan, and bake for 2 minutes more. Remove, scatter the parsley over the top, and season with pepper.

Potato and Roasted Pepper Pizza

People are usually surprised by the idea of putting potatoes on pizza, but it is done in Italy and is especially good made with summer's moist and tender new potatoes.
Makes one 10-inch pizza

- ¹/₄ recipe Pizza Dough (page 447)
- 1 red or yellow bell pepper, roasted (see page 364)
- 4 teaspoons olive oil
- Sea salt and freshly milled pepper
- 6 ounces new fingerling or other potatoes, scrubbed
- 1 clove garlic, minced
- 2 teaspoons chopped thyme
- 2 ounces smoked mozzarella or provolone, grated
- 2 teaspoons capers, rinsed
- 15 niçoise olives, pitted and chopped
- Red pepper flakes

Preheat the oven to 500°F.

Roll or stretch the dough into a 10-inch circle, set it on a floured peel or pizza pan, and let it rest for 10 minutes.

Finely dice the bell pepper, moisten it with a teaspoon of the oil, and season it with salt and pepper. Thinly slice the potatoes. Heat the remaining 1 tablespoon olive oil in a wide skillet over medium heat. Add the potatoes and a few tablespoons water, cover, and cook until tender, about 5 minutes. Season with salt, pepper, the garlic, and the thyme. Toss the potatoes with the cheese, bell peppers, capers, and olives.

Cover the dough with the potato mixture and bake for 7 minutes. Remove and add a few good pinches of red pepper flakes.

Pizza with Mozzarella, Olives, and Salsa Verde

Makes one 10-inch pizza

1/4 recipe Pizza Dough (page 447)

3 ounces mozzarella, cut into small dice

3 Roma or plum tomatoes, seeded and diced

15 niçoise or 10 kalamata olives, pitted and coarsely chopped

Freshly milled pepper

1 teaspoon olive oil

2 tablespoons freshly grated parmesan

2 tablespoons Salsa Verde (page 48)

Preheat the oven to 500°F.

Roll the dough into a 10-inch circle, set it on a floured peel or pizza pan, and let it rest for 10 minutes. Combine the cheese, tomatoes, and olives and season with a little pepper and the olive oil. Spread this over the dough and bake on a stone or in the pan for 6 minutes. Add the parmesan and bake for 2 minutes more. Remove and drizzle with the salsa verde.

White Pizza with Sage

Use delicate fresh mozzarella accented with a young pecorino or a good parmesan. Makes one 10-inch pizza

1/4 recipe Pizza Dough (page 447)

Best olive oil, for topping

4 ounces fresh mozzarella, very thinly sliced or cubed

2 tablespoons freshly grated pecorino or parmesan

8 fresh sage leaves

Freshly milled pepper or red pepper flakes

Preheat the oven to 500°F.

Roll or stretch the dough into a 10-inch circle, set it on a floured peel or pizza pan, and let rest for 10 minutes. Brush a little oil over the dough, then cover with the mozzarella. Drizzle a little more oil over the top and bake on a stone or in the pan until bubbling, about 7 minutes. Add the grated cheese and sage, return to the oven for 2 minutes more. Season with some pepper over the top.

Black and White Pizza: Cover the dough with a thin layer of Olive Paste (page 78) instead of the olive oil. Thyme, marjoram, or dried oregano as well as sage are also good herbs to use.

Tomato Pizza with Olives and Oregano

A very simple pizza, indeed, but don't be fooled. Other herbs could go here, too—basil, rosemary, and marjoram (a bit more flowery than oregano) are especially good.
Makes one 10-inch pizza Ⓥ

1/4 recipe Pizza Dough (page 447)

3 to 4 tablespoons Tomato Sauce for Pizza (page 448)

24 pitted black olives

8 oregano leaves

Have the pizza dough and the sauce made.

Heat the oven to 500°F with a stone, if using, or large sheet pan.

Stretch the ball of pizza dough to make an 8- to 10-inch round. Don't worry about it's being uneven. Set it on a peel dusted with corn meal, then spoon over the tomato sauce and scatter the olives on top. Drizzle a little extra olive oil over all and slide it onto the stone or waiting sheet pan. Bake until bubbling and brown, about 10 minutes. Remove and scatter the oregano leaves over the pizza, then slice and serve.

Tomato Pizza with Gorgonzola: Use twice as much dough and make this into a large pan pizza, or keep your pizzas roundish. To the pizza above, drop mounds of Gorgonzola onto the tomato-covered dough and bake. When done, grate a little parmesan over the surface, add the leaves or not, and serve.

Mushroom Pizza with Tomato and Smoked Cheese

I like to use big fleshy mushrooms, like portabellas or, with luck, porcini. Makes one 10-inch pizza

- ¹/₄ recipe Pizza Dough (page 447)
- 2 tablespoons olive oil
- 6 ounces mushrooms, thinly sliced
- Sea salt and freshly milled pepper
- ¹/₃ cup Tomato Sauce for Pizza (page 448)
- 1 tomato, seeded and diced
- 2 to 3 ounces smoked mozzarella or provolone, coarsely grated
- 2 tablespoons freshly grated parmesan
- 2 tablespoons parsley chopped with 1 clove garlic
- Red pepper flakes, for topping

Preheat the oven to 500°F.

Roll the dough into a 10-inch circle, set on a floured peel or pizza pan, and let rest for 10 minutes. Heat the oil in a wide skillet over high heat. Sauté the mushrooms until browned, about 5 minutes. Season well with salt and pepper.

Spread the tomato sauce over the dough. Add the diced tomato, then the mushrooms. Bake for 5 minutes, add the cheeses, and bake for 3 minutes more. Remove and scatter the parsley-garlic mixture and pepper flakes over the top.

Zucchini Pizza with Cherry Tomatoes and Goat Cheese

Use any mix of small, sweet tomatoes—cherry, currant, and pear. Makes one 10-inch pizza

- ¹/₄ recipe Pizza Dough (page 447)
- 3 small to medium zucchini, thinly sliced into rounds
- 1 tablespoon olive oil, plus best olive oil for the top
- Sea salt and freshly milled pepper
- Approximately 4 ounces cherry tomatoes
- 1 clove garlic, finely chopped
- 4 basil leaves, torn into small pieces or very thinly sliced
- 2 ounces mozzarella, thinly sliced or diced
- 2 ounces goat cheese or feta, crumbled

Preheat the oven to 500°F.

Roll or stretch the dough into a 10-inch circle, set it on a floured peel or pizza pan, and let it rest for 10 minutes.

Sauté the zucchini in the oil in a skillet over medium heat until tender and beginning to color, about 4 minutes. Season with salt and pepper. Slice the tomatoes into halves or quarters and toss them with the garlic, a little olive oil, some pepper, and half the basil.

Distribute the mozzarella and zucchini over the dough, then add the tomatoes. Bake on a stone or in the pan for 5 minutes, then add the goat cheese and bake for 3 minutes more. Remove, drizzle with a little olive oil, and sprinkle on the rest of the basil leaves.

Zucchini Pizza with Salsa Verde

Use any of the green herb sauces that appeal to you here— Cilantro Salsa (page 49), Chimmichuri (page 49), and so on. I like one that is chunky with capers and lemon zest. The choice is yours. You can also make this with yellow squash. Makes 1 pan or 2 round pizzas Ⓥ

- ¹/₂ recipe Pizza Dough (page 447)
- 2 small zucchini, about 8 to 10 ounces
- 1 teaspoon olive oil, plus more for dough
- Sea salt and freshly milled pepper
- 3 to 4 tablespoons Salsa Verde (page 48)

Have the pizza dough ready. Heat the oven to 500°F.

Slice the zucchini on a mandoline so that they are very thin and even. Toss them with olive oil. Shape the dough, either pressing it onto an oiled sheet pan or forming two rounds (see page 447). Spread a little oil on the dough, add the squash, season with salt and pepper, and bake until the crust is browned and the squash are also browned in places, 12 to 15 minutes. Take the pizza from the oven and dab the sauce over it here and there. Cut and serve.

Zucchini Pizza with Salsa Verde and Mozzarella: Cover the dough sparsely with 2 to 4 ounces shredded fresh mozzarella cheese, then cover with the zucchini. Grate a little parmesan over the pizza as soon as it comes out of the oven. Or, omit the mozzarella and finish with just a veil of freshly grated cheese.

Roasted Pepper Pizza

Roast the peppers and have them ready before you assemble this pizza. A mixture of colors—red, yellow, and orange—is gorgeous. I often throw in a diced jalapeño as well for its snappy presence. The cheese can be left out, and you'll still have a moist and richly flavorful pizza.
Makes one 10-inch pizza ⓥ

1/4 recipe Pizza Dough (page 447)

1 1/2 cups roasted bell peppers (see page 364), cut into thin strips

1 jalapeño chile, seeded and finely diced

8 oil-cured black olives, pitted and torn into small pieces

Sea salt and freshly milled pepper

1 scant cup shredded or thinly sliced mozzarella, optional

1 tablespoon best olive oil or Basil Puree (page 51)

Preheat the oven to 500°F.

Roll or stretch the dough into a 10-inch circle, set it on a floured peel or pizza pan, and let it rest for 10 minutes.

Toss the peppers, chile, and olives together and season with salt and pepper. Lay the cheese over the dough, leaving a 1/2-inch border, then cover with the peppers. Bake for 7 minutes, then remove and drizzle with the oil.

Pizza with Other Peppers: Use the Peperonata (page 363) or Sautéed Peppers (page 363) mixed with 2 teaspoons rinsed capers. Bake as described, using cheese or not as you prefer. Serve garnished with a flourish of chopped parsley or basil. Or cover a pizza with Roasted Poblano and Sweet Pepper Strips and Onions (*Rajas*) (page 364) and garnish with Cilantro Salsa (page 49) or chopped cilantro. ⓥ

Red Onion Pizza with Rosemary

Onions are sweet, so they need the grounding savory note of rosemary. Oregano leaves and thyme also do the trick if rosemary isn't available. Makes 1 pan or 2 round pizzas ⓥ

1/2 recipe Pizza Dough (page 447)

2 large red onions, scant 2 pounds

2 tablespoons olive oil

1/2 teaspoon sea salt

Freshly milled pepper

2 teaspoons minced fresh rosemary

1/2 teaspoon red wine vinegar

Make the pizza dough if you haven't already. Halve the onions, peel them, then slice them about 1/2 inch thick.

Warm the olive oil over medium-high heat in a wide pan large enough to hold all the onions. When hot, add the onions, turn them with a pair of tongs to coat them with the oil, then reduce the heat to low, cover the pan, and let the onions cook until softened and somewhat caramelized, about 30 minutes. Turn them once or twice while they're cooking. The lid will create the moisture needed so that they don't burn. When done, season them with the salt, pepper, then the rosemary and vinegar.

Heat the oven to 500°F. Press the dough onto an oiled sheet pan, pushing it out nearly to the sides. There won't be quite enough dough to completely cover the pan, but make sure you don't leave the edges too large or they'll be bready. Uneven thickness is fine.

Distribute the onions over the dough, going as far as you can to the edges, then bake until the crust is browned and the onions are glossy and fragrant, about 12 to 15 minutes. Cut the pizza into big square or rectangles.

Red Onion Pizza with Cheese: Grate good parmesan generously over the top when the pizza comes out of the oven. Its sharpness will balance the onions' sweetness. Other good cheeses with onion pizza are Gruyère and blue cheeses.

GRAINS

CHAPTER 14

Grains
Seeds of Life

Grain is at the center of nearly every civilization, so much so that cultures are defined by their grains more than any other food. Consider the rice and millet of Asia, the corn of the Americas, the amaranth of the Aztecs and quinoa of the Incas, the oats of the Scots, the farro and durum wheat of Italy, and so forth.

Although Americans are big consumers of grain, especially wheat, we don't consume most of it directly, for most of our grains are fed to animals, used in industry, or made into alcohol. And of late, grain has gotten a bad rap as being unhealthy for humans, if not actually unfit. Modern wheat, America's principal grain, is now problematic for many who range from having mild allergies to it to full-blown celiac disease, and many have ceased the to eat it in any form at all. Despite problems with wheat, there are plenty of people who appreciate the flavors and textures of whole grains, and for those, grain has regained a status that was once lost. Others, who cannot eat wheat, appreciate the variety of other grains available. Quinoa, amaranth, spelt, kamut, and buckwheat can show up on the table as easily as wheat has in the past. Such grains have also found their way into breads and other baked goods as increasingly more people find themselves challenged by modern wheat. Ancient and older forms of wheat are slowly becoming known, from einkorn and emmer to Turkey Red, Red Fife, Sonoran White, and others. These older wheats are sometimes tolerated by those with allergies to modern wheat. (Often these have to be bought online or at farmers' markets.) When it comes to rice, there are all kinds of varieties available—scented grains like jasmine and pecan rice, black rice, red rice, native wild rice, and Carolina Gold rice. Short-grained brown rice is now being grown organically in Northern California. Couscous, essentially a pasta, has become commonplace, and risotto has made significant headway into our kitchens (often assuming a major role in vegetarian kitchens), as has paella.

Except for the occasional bow, we have yet to center our meals around grain the way many Asian cultures make everything else on the plate relate to a bowl of rice. But given grain's immense diversity and the possibility of appearing in any course of any meal, in our own way, we end up eating it throughout the day.

The Parts of a Grain

Starting from the outside of the kernel, grains are made up of a protective fibrous hull called the bran, then the starchy endosperm, and, at the heart, the germ. In the refining process, we lose the bran, which contains most of the minerals, fiber, and much of the riboflavin inherent in grains. The oil-rich germ, which can quickly turn rancid, is frequently removed as well. What we end up eating is the starchy middle, which has the most carbohydrate and the fewest vitamins and minerals. Although lost nutrients are added to refined grains through enrichments, whole grains retain more fiber and trace minerals, which is why they're considered nutritionally superior. In the health food industry, for example, whole wheat flour, wheat germ, and bran have always been featured in baked goods, flours, and cereals because of the contributions they make to our health and diet.

Knowing Your Grits from Your Groats

WHOLE GRAINS (GROATS): These grains do not undergo processing or refining and contain their bran, germ, and endosperm. They also take the longest to cook—except buckwheat (kasha), the tiny quinoa, amaranth, and teff—which are very small and not actually true grains (as they aren't true grasses). While nutritionally beneficial, whole groats—whether oats, wheat, barley, or spelt—tend to be the least appealing form of grain, especially if served alone. They're chewy, so they work much better when they're combined with other foods—used in casseroles, soups, croquettes, salads, and other dishes. Farro is, perhaps, the exception, as it is such a new and stylish grain, but it is a whole grain.

POLISHED GRAINS: The tough husk, along with some or all of the bran, is removed from these grains, which include wheat berries, brown rice, and pearl barley. Polished grains cook more quickly than those with the husks still intact, but they still take a good 40 minutes or longer.

GRITS, MEAL, AND CRACKED GRAINS: When, during the milling process, grains are further broken down in size, they become grits. Examples include hominy or corn grits, cracked wheat, and steel-cut oats. Some are derived from whole grains; others are more refined. Their textures are toothy and substantial, but less dense than groats.

FLAKES: When sliced groats or cracked grains are steamed and rolled, they become flakes. Rolled oats, or oatmeal, is one flake we all know, but rolled barley, wheat, rye, and spelt are others. Flakes cook quickly and are light, fluffy, and easy to digest. They are good as a savory side dish, not just as a morning cereal.

FLOUR: With further milling, grain becomes flour. When the bran and germ are left in grain, it's whole grain flour, whether wheat, corn, quinoa, and so on. Depending on the type of wheat and the milling process, whole wheat flour can be flaky with large bits of bran, grainy and dense, or soft and fine, almost like white flour. In fact, a newer flour on the market is called white whole wheat, a lighter-colored wheat that is still darker than refined white flour, but absolutely fine in all kinds of recipes. Whole wheat pastry flour is the finest of the various whole wheat flours. I almost never use white flour—desserts, where I would use them, have become a rarity—but if I do, I choose organic, unbleached (and unbromated) flour. For baking breads, artisan loaves and pizzas, King Arthur Sir Lancelot's Unbleached Hi-Gluten flour is ideal. Lower protein flours have less gluten and are what are used for pastry. (For more information on flour, see page 31.)

SPROUTED GRAINS/FLOUR: Relatively new are breads, corn tortillas, and other baked goods made from sprouted flour. Even sprouted whole wheat and spelt flours are now available in natural groceries. What are they? Grain that has been sprouted is said to have three major benefits: food enzymes are activated, vitamin content is increased, and phytic acid, a nonnutrient, is neutralized. In addition, flours made from sprouted grains are lower on the glycemic index, have fewer carbohydrates, have more protein, are more easily digested, and also have less gluten. (For that reason, gluten is sometimes added back into bread recipes that call for sprouted flour so that they rise in a way we're accustomed to.) There are those who feel the breads made from sprouted grains don't offer as great a benefit as others would have, but certainly both whole wheat and sprouted grain flours are a far better choice than all-purpose white flour.

How to Select, Store, and Cook Grains

SELECTING: Organically grown stone-ground grains and flours can be found in many supermarkets and most natural foods stores, in packages and in bulk. Buy 1-pound bags of grains you use only occasionally and replace them more frequently. When buying grains and their flours from bins, make sure they have a nice, fresh smell and have not turned rancid.

STORING: Because the germ of whole grains contains oil, they deteriorate more quickly than refined ones. To keep them fresh, store grains in tightly covered glass jars in a cool place. Three to four months is a reasonable period for keeping whole or cracked grains. Oil-rich flours and meals, such as stone-ground corn meal made from whole corn that has not been degerminated, should be kept in the refrigerator or freezer, as should sprouted flours.

SOAKING: Like beans, large grains and short-grain brown rice cook more quickly and are more easily digested if soaked before cooking. Although this is not entirely necessary, soaking them in cool water anywhere from an hour to overnight does help to soften them. Basmati rice is soaked to plump and lengthen the grains.

COOKING: An 8-cup saucepan with a tight-fitting lid is ample for cooking 1 to 2 cups of raw grains. A nonstick surface makes it easier to clean the pans, but if grain does stick to the pan, a short soak should be sufficient to loosen it.

After the grains have cooked, let them stand for 5 to 10 minutes to continue absorbing moisture. To produce fluffy, separate grains, put a clean towel under the lid once they've finished cooking, then let stand. The towel, rather than the grain, will absorb the steam.

USING A PRESSURE COOKER: A pressure cooker is a great timesaver with long-cooking grains such as brown rice, spelt, kamut, wheat berries, and other whole groats. Cook them without soaking at high pressure for one-third the time suggested for regular cooking. If they're not done, return to pressure and continue cooking for another 5 to 10 minutes. Smaller grains are usually quick cooking and, in my opinion, too delicate for the pressure cooker.

SALTING: Salt doesn't seem to be as necessary to bring out the flavor of grains as it is for other foods. You'll find you can use it in small amounts—$1/4$ to $1/2$ teaspoon for 1 cup uncooked grain. When cooking large, whole grains, add salt during the last 30 minutes just as you do with beans.

USING A SLOW COOKER: As with beans and soups, a slow cooker is most useful if it allows you to really eliminate prep time and be away from what's cooking, whether in bed or at work. A slow cook, then, is especially useful for cooking big, solid groats (whole grains) like wheat berries, farro, oats, and so forth. Some also use it for steel-cut oats, but I find that in my slow cooker they take only 3 hours, which isn't quite long enough to useful. The various recipes for cooking polenta in a slow cooker make it so much more complicated than simply making it as described on pages 463 and 465, that I can't imagine it's worth the effort. Plus it doesn't come out as well as simply stirred or simmered polenta. As with other foods, you have to figure out the limits and benefits of your slow cooker. There are many models and styles and they all differ from one another. But in general, the bigger, chewier, and more whole the grains, the better they'll do.

COOKING LARGE WHOLE GRAINS IN THE PRESSURE COOKER

Large grains like kamut and spelt take almost an hour to cook unless you use a pressure cooker, which reduces the time to about 20 minutes and makes it far more likely that you might actually give these sturdy grains a try. A cup of dry grain yields about 2 cups (or slightly more) cooked. Regardless of the amount of grain you're using, give it a rinse, then put it in a pressure cooker with four times as much water and a pinch of salt. Fasten the lid, bring the pressure up, then leave it on high for 18 to 20 minutes. Quickly release the pressure, then remove the lid. Take a taste. The grains will probably be a little chewy but split open and done. If you wish them to be softer, return the lid to the pot, return to pressure, and cook another 5 minutes or so.

Making Grains Attractive and Appealing

Many people resist the earthy brown tones and hearty, chewy textures of grains. Grains, by themselves, just don't have the sensual appeal of glossy peppers or a bunch of fragrant herbs, plus they're more often than not piled on a plate in plain, ungainly portions. So to make the most of grains' considerable virtues, consider the following approaches.

1. When you plan a grain dish, make sure there's plenty of color and contrast on the plate, not all brown foods. Peppers, asparagus, greens, carrots, and zucchini are just a few colorful vegetables to consider.

2. Accompany grains with lively garnishes. Sautéed tomatoes, braised greens, yogurt, chopped fresh herbs, salsas, and toasted nuts are delicious as well as attractive.

3. Gradually add grains to your menu. Mixing cooked brown and white rice together makes a dish that's lighter and more familiar than all brown rice. Or start with grits, rice, and polenta, which are soft, comforting, and easy to like. Add a cup of leftover cooked grains to your favorite muffin or pancake recipe.

4. I've found that by themselves the large kernels of oats, wheat, kamut, and spelt are the most difficult grains for people to warm up to; they're just too dense. However, they are enjoyable when added to soups—a cup or so of cooked grain to a pot—where their chewy texture provides a welcome contrast to softer elements. Kamut, spelt, tiny amaranth, and quinoa are also available as flours, which can easily be added to breads, muffins, and other baked goods.

Barley

Until recently, barley was used mostly in soup, especially the classic mushroom–barley soup or Scotch broth. Today we also enjoy it cooked like risotto as well. Barley is usually polished, or pearled, as it's commonly called. It's bland but pleasantly textured and toothsome—easy to serve in place of rice and a nice change. Barley grits make a good breakfast cereal. Malted barley is a sweetener that can be used in place of sugar or honey in bread baking.

Barley with Butter or Roasted Nut Oil

Serve simply cooked, soft, chewy barley with a winter vegetable stew or a mushroom ragout. The additions for kasha—browned onions, pasta, and leeks with rosemary oil—are also good with barley. Makes about 3¹/₂ cups Ⓥ

3 cups water, Basic Vegetable Stock (page 175), or Mushroom Stock (page 176)

¹/₄ teaspoon sea salt

1 cup pearl barley, rinsed

Butter or walnut or hazelnut oil, for serving

Freshly milled pepper

Bring the water to a boil in an 8-cup saucepan. Add the salt and stir in the barley. Lower the heat, cover the pan, and simmer until tender, 25 to 30 minutes. Let stand for 5 minutes before serving. Serve tossed with a little butter and pepper or season with one of the delicious roasted nut oils.

Green Barley and Kale Gratin

Not a dowdy dish at all—the kale turns the barley bright green. Bake it in a gratin dish or individual ramekins.
Serves 4 to 6

²/₃ cup pearl barley, rinsed

¹/₂ teaspoon sea salt

1 large bunch kale, about 1¹/₄ pounds, stems entirely removed

2 tablespoons butter

3 tablespoons flour

1¹/₂ cups milk or Basic Vegetable Stock (page 175)

¹/₄ teaspoon allspice

¹/₈ teaspoon grated nutmeg

Freshly milled pepper

¹/₂ cup grated Gruyère or provolone

In a saucepan, add the barley to 4 cups boiling water with the salt and simmer, uncovered until tender, about 30 minutes. Drain. While it's cooking, cook the kale in a skillet of boiling salted water until tender, 6 to 10 minutes. Drain, then puree with ¹/₄ cup of the cooking water until smooth.

Preheat the oven to 375°F. Melt the butter in a small saucepan, whisk in the flour, then add the milk. Cook, stirring constantly over medium heat, until thick. Season with allspice, nutmeg, salt, and pepper. Combine all the ingredients, check the seasonings, then transfer to a lightly buttered baking dish or ramekins.

Bake until lightly browned on top, about 30 minutes. If you've used ramekins, run a knife around the edges, then unmold them by giving them a sharp rap on the counter. Present them browned side up.

Barley-Mushroom Pilaf with Sautéed Mushrooms

A hearty side dish or a good filling for stuffed cabbage. This recipe makes enough for 12 cabbage rolls. Serves 4 to 6 Ⓥ

1/2 ounce dried porcini, about 1/2 cup

1 pound white mushrooms

5 tablespoons olive oil or a mixture of oil and butter

Sea salt and freshly milled pepper

2 cloves garlic, chopped

1/2 cup dry white or red wine

1 onion, finely chopped

1 cup pearl barley, rinsed

1/2 teaspoon sea salt

1/4 cup chopped parsley mixed with a little tarragon or rosemary

Cover the dried mushrooms with 3 cups warm water. Set aside to soften for at least 15 minutes, then remove and finely chop. Reserve the liquid and add enough water to make 3 cups, if necessary. Meanwhile, chop half the fresh mushrooms and slice the rest.

Heat 2 tablespoons of the oil in a wide skillet over high heat. Add the chopped fresh mushrooms and cook, stirring frequently, until well colored, about 5 minutes. Season with salt and pepper, then add the dried mushrooms, garlic, and wine. Reduce the heat to medium and cook until the wine is absorbed and the pan is nearly dry, about 2 minutes.

In a 12-cup saucepan, heat 1 tablespoon of the oil. Add the onion and cook over medium heat until limp, 5 minutes. Add the barley, stir in the cooked mushrooms, reserved mushroom liquid, and the salt. Bring to a boil. Lower the heat and simmer, covered, until tender, 35 to 40 minutes.

Meanwhile, sauté the sliced mushrooms in the remaining 1 tablespoon oil over high heat until golden, about 5 minutes. Season with salt and pepper. Loosen the cooked barley with a fork, toss it with the herbs, and pile it into a serving dish. Garnish with the sautéed mushrooms.

Barley "Risotto" with Sautéed Mushrooms and Truffle Salt

Because barley is such a thirsty grain, it can easily drink up all the broth in a soup. When that happened to me I thought, why not treat it as a risotto? Here's a robust, creamy grain dish to eat in small portions at the start of a winter's meal. It's very easy and very satisfying. Serves 3 or 4 Ⓥ

Barley Soup with Caramelized Onions (page 198)

2 tablespoons olive oil

4 baby bella mushrooms, sliced about 3/8 inch thick

Sea salt and freshly milled pepper

1/2 cup cream or plant milk

Finely chopped parsley, to finish

Truffle salt, to finish

Make the soup as suggested (you won't need the cheese). While it's simmering, prepare the mushrooms. Heat the oil in a skillet and when hot add the mushrooms, sprinkle with salt, and sauté over fairly high heat until seared and golden brown. Remove from the heat. When the soup vegetables are tender, turn up the heat and cook, stirring, until the broth has cooked away, leaving a risotto-like dish. Stir in the cream and half the mushrooms and cook to heat through. Season with pepper.

Serve in four bowls with the remaining mushrooms on top, a little parsley in each, and a pinch of truffle salt.

Savory Barley Flakes

Ready in 10 minutes, barley flakes are light and easy to digest. With a bit of butter or oil and a shower of pepper, they're simply delicious—a great change from rice. Serves 4 Ⓥ

2 cups barley flakes

1/2 teaspoon sea salt

Butter or roasted nut oil

Freshly milled pepper

Toast the flakes in a dry skillet over medium heat, stirring frequently, until they smell good. Bring 2 cups water to a boil in a saucepan. Add the salt, then the flakes. Cover the pot, lower the heat, and cook for 5 minutes. Turn off the heat and let stand for 5 minutes more. Fluff with a fork, add butter to taste, and season with pepper.

Buckwheat (Kasha)

Buckwheat isn't a true grain; however, we treat it as if it were a grain. We know buckwheat groats as kasha and buckwheat flour as the special element in buckwheat pancakes or blini and in Japanese soba noodles. Buckwheat groats are sold both roasted (as used in the following recipes) and unroasted. Unroasted buckwheat groats are pale and bland, but when roasted, they become dark and their earthy flavor blossoms. Buckwheat is light and quick cooking. An egg—or just the white—stirred into the kernels before adding the liquid keeps the texture light and fluffy. If you omit the egg coating, the grains remain separate, falling off your fork rather than clinging together, but it does make these dishes suitable for vegans.

Kasha (Toasted Buckwheat Groats)

Serve this fluffy grain with roasted root vegetables, steamed kohlrabi, or braised cabbage. It makes a good filling for stuffed cabbage, too. Serves 4

2 cups water or Basic Vegetable Stock (page 175)

1 egg or 2 egg whites

1 cup toasted buckwheat groats

1 tablespoon butter or nut oil

1/2 teaspoon sea salt

Freshly milled pepper

Bring the water to a boil in a 12-cup saucepan. Beat the egg in a bowl with a fork, then stir in the groats. Heat a wide skillet over medium heat, add the groats, and cook, stirring constantly until the grains are dry and separate, about 3 minutes. Add them to the water with the butter and salt. Lower the heat and simmer, covered, until all the liquid is absorbed, 7 to 12 minutes—some brands cook more quickly than others. Let stand for 5 minutes, then lightly fluff with a fork and season with pepper before serving.

Kasha with Fried Onions: Sauté 3 cups sliced onion in 2 tablespoons clarified butter or oil in a skillet until well browned, 12 to 15 minutes. Season with salt and pepper and serve strewn over the kasha along with chopped parsley for color.

Kasha Varnishkes (Kasha with Bow Ties): When I tested this recipe, I realized how long it had been since I last had this Eastern European classic and what I had been missing. Time your cooking so that the noodles and onions are done when the kasha is—they take about the same time to cook.

Boil 1 cup of bow tie noodles or farfalle pasta in salted water until done, then drain them. Sauté 1 large onion, chopped, in 2 tablespoons butter or oil in a skillet over medium heat until lightly browned, about 12 minutes. Season well with salt and pepper. When the kasha is done, toss it with the noodles and onions and serve.

Kasha with Toasted Walnuts and Green Onions: This simple garnish gives textural variation and a fresh element to either the Kasha or Kasha Varnishkes. Melt 1 or 2 tablespoons butter or sunflower seed oil in a medium skillet. Add 1 cup chopped walnuts, 1 bunch sliced green onions, including half the greens, and cook over medium heat until everything smells toasty and the nuts have begun to color, about 5 minutes. Season well with salt and pepper, then add thyme and parsley. Gently stir this mixture into the finished kasha.

Corn

Corn is America's native grain, and there's a great deal to be said about it—its history and lore, its enormous prevalence in the food industry, and our romance and fascination with it. While there are many types and forms of corn, we eat most of it unknowingly in processed foods where it appears as a sweetener, a starch, and an oil. Of course, we also enjoy it as a fresh vegetable, in addition to corn meal, polenta, grits, hominy or posole, and popcorn. And corn is also milled into flour. Note that unless certified organic, corn is probably genetically modified.

While I'm quite certain that we lead the world in the number and variety of corn recipes, it's fallen to Italy to make that unsavory-sounding dish, corn meal mush, a star in the culinary sky.

CORN MEAL: Corn meal can be white, yellow, blue, or yellow flecked with red. The color comes from the corn itself. But regardless of color, the most nutritious corn meal still contains the germ. Because it's rich with oils, whole grain corn meal should be refrigerated. If you're mail ordering stone-ground corn meal, buy extra and keep it in the freezer. (Anson Mills has absolutely sublime grains, including corn, available, but look for freshly milled whole corn meals in your farmers' markets, too.) Degerminated corn meal, found boxed in the baking section of your market, needn't be refrigerated. It usually announces itself as "degerminated" on the label so you know what you're getting, which is less in terms of nutrition and taste.

Corn meal can be very fine, almost like flour, or coarse and gritty. It seems to vary from brand to brand. I use corn meal that has a little texture but isn't floury in dishes like the Spoon Bread on page 578, sometimes for polenta, and certainly for hot cereal or in pastries.

Polenta

Polenta is essentially grits or coarse corn meal. In fact, one company labels its yellow and white corn grits parenthetically as polenta. The Italian name certainly teases the imagination more than our corn meal mush does. But wherever corn is eaten, corn meal mush exists. And regardless of what it's called, it's makes a practical and highly versatile dish. Polenta can even put in an appearance for dessert when served with a spoonful of mascarpone and drizzled with molasses in recollection of our own worthy Indian pudding, or garnished with sour cream, warm honey, and poppy seeds.

American corn meal cereal isn't usually cooked longer than 20 minutes, but when it comes to polenta, tradition calls for 45 or more. Averse as we are to giving time to simple tasks, it's the time spent cooking that brings out the full corn flavor and softens the pebbly grits. I don't mind the stirring if I'm not rushed. I find it provides a quiet time to think about things that need thinking, or I can prop up a book and read. But even Marcella Hazan doesn't say you have to stir constantly for an hour. She suggests one minute of stirring every ten minutes, which means you don't have to be a slave to the pot, but that it does get stirred.

I find 35 minutes makes good-tasting polenta. Longer makes a better, softer polenta. Using a double boiler eliminates the need for constant stirring, as does using the oven or slow cooker for polenta, but that can take 45 minutes or even longer. If you plan to serve soft polenta, use 6 parts water to 1 part polenta; for firm polenta, 4 parts water to 1 part polenta is better. However, these ratios have to be taken with a grain of salt, for you may find yourself adding more water just to make the polenta easier to stir. But in general, for polenta that you intend to harden then grill, use less water than for polenta that you wish to pour.

If you use stone-ground whole corn meal from Anson Mills, or other good mills, or even grind it yourself, you will be rewarded with an exceptional bowl of polenta. If you're limiting your consumption of carbs (and even if you're not), starchy foods like polenta might as well be a real treat.

Soft Polenta

If the polenta erupts into volcanic spurts at any point, wrap a napkin around your stirring hand and charge ahead. This is the polenta to make if you wish to let it harden for another use. Serves 6 Ⓥ

2 teaspoons sea salt

2 cups coarse stone-ground corn meal or a mixture of coarse and fine corn meal

2 to 6 tablespoons butter or equivalent

Bring 8 cups water to a boil in a heavy saucepan. Add the salt followed by the corn meal. Whisk it in a steady stream, stirring constantly to avoid making lumps. (You can also use 2 cups of the water to make a slurry with the meal, then whisk it in all at once to the cold water, then heat it.) Lower the heat and cook, stirring more or less constantly at first, about 10 minutes, or until the polenta takes hold, then cook for another 45 minutes, stirring for 1 minute every 10 minutes. If the polenta seizes up into a hard mass, add boiling water in small increments while it cooks, to smooth it out. When done, taste for salt, then turn off the heat and stir in as much butter as you wish, to taste. Serve soft polenta immediately, or hold it in a double boiler until ready to serve.

Firm Polenta: When cooled, polenta firms up quickly. It can then can be sliced and broiled, grilled, fried, or baked into casseroles and gratins. Make the recipe above using 6 cups water to make a stiffer, drier polenta. As soon as it's done, pour it onto a clean counter, sheet pan, a large baking dish, loaf pan, or two pie plates. Using a spatula or knife dipped in cold water, immediately spread the polenta out to a thickness of $^3/_8$ inch or so. Let it cool until firm, then cut it into desired shapes. Covered with plastic, firm polenta will hold for 1 or 2 days in the refrigerator.

Polenta Croquettes with Tomato Sauce

Serve these croquettes with a Fresh Tomato Sauce (page 54) in summer or a more robust one in winter, such as the Red Wine Tomato Sauce (page 56). Makes 10 or more

Firm Polenta (preceding recipe)

2 eggs, beaten with 1/4 cup milk

Sea salt and freshly milled pepper

1 cup fresh bread crumbs

Olive oil, for frying

2 cups Fresh Tomato Sauce (page 54)

Chopped parsley, for garnish

Cut firm polenta into 3-inch circles, squares, or other shapes. Beat the eggs and milk with a few pinches salt and a little pepper. Dip the polenta into the egg mixture, then coat it with the bread crumbs. Heat oil about $^3/_8$ inch deep in a medium skillet over medium-high heat until hot enough to quickly sizzle a bread crumb. Fry the croquettes until crisp and pale gold on both sides, turning them once. Transfer them briefly to paper towels, then arrange them on a platter or individual plates. Top each croquette with the tomato sauce and garnish with parsley.

Polenta Cheddar Croquettes: Stir 1 to $1^1/_2$ cups grated sharp cheddar, 6 thinly sliced green onions, including some of the greens, 3 tablespoons chopped parsley, and a few pinches red pepper flakes into cooked firm polenta. Let cool, then make into croquettes, as above. Serve with a dab of Olive-Rosemary Butter (page 46), a spoonful of the Corn Relish (page 69), or the Tomato-Onion Relish (page 69).

Soft Polenta with Gorgonzola and Bread Crumbs

A luxurious treatment of a humble food, this makes an utterly delicious, informal, easy meal with an additional vegetable or two. Serves 6

Cooked polenta, any method
1 cup milk
1 cup freshly grated parmesan
6 to 8 ounces Gorgonzola
3/4 cup bread crumbs crisped in butter
1/4 cup chopped parsley
Freshly milled pepper

When the polenta is done, stir in the milk and parmesan. Pour it into individual serving bowls, crumble the Gorgonzola over the top, and garnish with the bread crumbs and parsley. Pepper liberally and serve.

Grilled or Broiled Polenta: This makes a substantial accompaniment to vegetable ragouts and sautés, or it can be simply served with a tomato sauce and crumbled Gorgonzola or goat cheese.

Cut firm polenta into squares, diamonds, rectangles, or other shapes. Brush both sides lightly with olive oil. Make sure your grill is very clean so that the polenta won't stick. Grill until lightly marked, then turn and grill the second side. Or broil the polenta on both sides until browned in places.

Golden Polenta Cakes: Cut firm polenta into desired shapes, then coat each piece with bread crumbs, semolina, or fine corn meal. Fry in olive oil or clarified butter on both sides until golden. Sprinkle lightly with salt and serve.

Polenta Cakes with Parsley Salad: For an appetizer or first course, make the golden polenta cakes and top with a small mound of Parsley Salad with Parmesan (page 130).

Crisp Polenta Sticks and Flaky Croutons: A tasty, hot appetizer to serve with salt, herb salt, smoked paprika, or sauce, such as Red Chile Mayonnaise (page 52) or Romesco Sauce (page 62). Slice firm polenta into pieces about 3 inches long and 3/8 inch wide. Heat an inch or so of peanut or olive oil in a cast-iron or nonstick skillet until it's hot enough to sizzle a crumb of polenta. Add several sticks at a time to the pan and fry until crisp. They won't brown much, and they'll probably clump together, but don't worry. Transfer them to paper towels to drain for a moment, then pry them apart. Salt lightly and serve. To make a crisp crouton for a soup, cut firm polenta into cubes and fry in the same way.

Polenta Gratin with Tomato, Fontina, and Rosemary

The fragrance of the rosemary and cheese in this layered gratin is irresistible. The tomato sauce can be of the simplest kind, and the dish can be assembled ahead of time and then baked when needed. Serves 4

Firm Polenta (page 463)
1 to 1 1/2 cups grated fontina
2 tablespoons butter
1 1/2 cups Fresh Tomato Sauce (page 54)
1 tablespoon finely chopped rosemary
Sea salt and freshly milled pepper
1/2 cup Gorgonzola
Chopped parsley, for garnish

Make the polenta. During the last few minutes of cooking, stir in half the fontina and the butter, then spread it, about 3/8 inch thick, on a clean counter or sheet pan to harden. Slice into rectangles or rounds—the exact size doesn't matter. This can be done hours in advance.

Heat the tomato sauce with half of the rosemary. Taste and season with salt, if needed, and a little pepper.

Preheat the oven to 400°F. Spread 3/4 cup of the tomato sauce in a 12-cup gratin dish, then overlap the pieces of polenta with the remaining fontina. Spoon the remaining sauce carefully in bands over the polenta, leaving the edges exposed. Crumble the Gorgonzola over the top and sprinkle with the rest of the rosemary.

Bake, uncovered, for about 30 minutes or until the gratin is hot and bubbly. Garnish with parsley, season with a little pepper, and serve.

Polenta with Fontina and Parmesan

The flavor of corn is remarkably well suited to cheese. The choice of cheese can be deliberate or simply be a way to use scraps of good cheeses. Gorgonzola, fontina, and parmesan are traditional Italian enrichments, while cheddar gives a much more American taste. Smoked cheeses provide a heartiness that contributes a great deal to a vegetarian meal. Eight cups cooked polenta can easily absorb between 1 and 2 cups cheese.
Serves 6

Cooked polenta, any method
1 to 2 cups grated fontina
$^1/_2$ cup freshly grated parmesan, plus extra for garnish
Butter
Freshly milled pepper

Make the polenta. When it's done, turn off the heat, stir in the cheeses, and add butter to taste. Season with pepper and serve with an additional sprinkle of grated parmesan.

Polenta with Browned Onions and Thyme: The addition of onion gives a larger range of flavor and texture to polenta. While the polenta is cooking, heat 2 tablespoons butter or olive oil in a medium skillet. Stirring occasionally, cook 1 large, finely diced onion with $2^1/_2$ teaspoons chopped thyme (or rosemary) until soft, about 15 minutes. Season with salt and pepper. Stir it into the polenta during the last 10 minutes or so that the polenta is cooking. When done, turn off the heat and stir in 1 cup grated parmesan. Taste for salt and season with pepper.

Polenta Dumplings with Warm Sage and Garlic Butter

This simple polenta dish is very attractive baked in individual gratin dishes. If they're not available, though, individual portions can be served from a larger dish.
Makes 6 appetizer servings

$^1/_2$ recipe Firm Polenta (page 463)
$^1/_2$ cup grated parmesan
Warm Sage and Garlic Butter (page 44), for drizzling
Freshly milled pepper

Cut the cooled, firm polenta into $2^1/_2$-inch rounds. Butter individual gratin dishes or a single large one. Overlap the rounds of polenta, allowing 3 to 4 per serving. Sprinkle with the parmesan, drizzle with the sage butter, then broil about 6 inches from the heat until the cheese is bubbling and the polenta is hot, 3 to 5 minutes. Remove from the oven, season with pepper, and serve. Alternatively pour soft polenta into individual dishes and finish as described.

Double Boiler Method for Soft Polenta

This technique produces good soft polenta without requiring constant attention. It does, however, take longer since it doesn't cook directly over the heat. Serves 6 Ⓥ

$1^1/_2$ teaspoons sea salt or to taste
2 cups coarse corn meal, preferably stone ground
2 to 6 tablespoons butter or equivalent

Bring a few inches water to a boil in the lower half of a double boiler, then lower the heat. Bring 8 cups water to a boil in the top part of the double boiler directly over the heat, then add the salt and corn meal as for traditional polenta. Cook, stirring constantly, until the consistency is even, then place the pan over the simmering water and cover. Cook for $1^1/_2$ hours. If you're in the kitchen, give it a stir every now and then, but it will come out all right if left unattended. Taste for salt, turn off the heat, and stir in butter. To hold, lower the heat so that the water barely simmers and let stand until ready to use.

Polenta Cooked in Milk: For a richer, creamier polenta, replace half or all of the water with milk.

Spoon Bread with Fresh Corn Kernels

You can serve a comforting, practical spoon bread as a savory or sweet dish, depending on whether you serve it with a spoonful of salsa or a spoonful of molasses. Buttermilk gives this puddinglike dish a cheesy tang, and if you use a good, stone ground corn meal, you'll have a classic dish that's indeed special. Serves 4

1 cup white or yellow stone-ground corn meal

2 teaspoons baking powder

1/2 teaspoon sea salt

Freshly milled white pepper

2 to 4 tablespoons butter

4 eggs

1 cup buttermilk or regular milk

2 cups corn kernels, fresh, from 3 ears of corn

Preheat the oven to 375°F. Butter an 8-cup soufflé or gratin dish.

Stir the corn meal and baking powder together with the salt and a little pepper, then stir in 1 1/2 cups boiling water and the butter. In a second bowl, whisk the eggs with the buttermilk, then stir them into the corn meal. Stir in the fresh corn. Pour the batter into the prepared dish and bake until puffed and golden on top, 45 minutes if using a soufflé dish, about 30 minutes if using a shallow gratin dish.

Corn and Hominy Grits

White or yellow, corn grits are prepared and served much the way polenta is—warm with butter, enriched with cheese, allowed to cool, then fried, and so forth. True hominy grits are milled from corn that has been soaked with lime to soften the skins, a treatment that gives them an unusual flavor. Old-fashioned stone-ground grits are the best-tasting grits by far. They take about 40 minutes to cook as opposed to fast-cooking yet bland instant grits, but they can cook in a double boiler without much attention from you.

IMPROVISING GRAIN PUDDINGS

Millet, barley, grits, rice, quinoa—virtually all cooked grains will set into a pudding when eggs and milk are added, as in the grits pudding or the souffléed variation. Cooked this way, they emerge light and tender and comforting, the way a pudding should be.

Grits

This is about as complicated as some people like them. This recipe is written for stone-ground grits. Serves 4 Ⓥ

4 cups water, or 2 cups each water and milk

1 cup stone-ground grits

1/2 to 1 teaspoon sea salt

Butter, optional

Freshly milled pepper

Bring the water to a boil in the top of a double boiler, then stir in the grits and add the salt. Cook, stirring constantly until the grits thicken, about 5 minutes, then set them over simmering water. Cover and cook until they're tender, about an hour. If you're not using a double boiler, cook the grits over very low heat, stirring frequently, for at least 35 to 40 minutes. (The longer they cook, the better grits taste. If they get too thick, just add water to thin them.) You can nurse them along for hours! Stir in as much butter as you like and season with pepper.

Breakfast Grits: Skip the pepper and add a spoonful of sorghum, molasses, or maple syrup to each bowl along with cold milk.

Cheese Grits: Add 1 cup grated cheddar into the hot grits and add a few shakes of Tabasco or other favorite hot sauce.

Fried Grits

Serve these golden croquettes with greens and fried eggs, with salsa and beans, or alongside a summer vegetable stew.
Makes sixteen 2-inch croquettes

Cheese Grits (preceding recipe)
1 egg beaten with 1 tablespoon water or milk
About 2 cups fresh bread crumbs
Vegetable oil, for frying

Pour the cooked grits into an 8-inch square pan or whatever is convenient and let cool until firm, 30 minutes or so. Cut into 16 fingers, squares, or triangles. Dip them into the beaten egg, then roll them in the bread crumbs. (They can be refrigerated at this point, but allow them to return to room temperature before frying.)

Heat ¹/₄ inch of oil in a cast-iron skillet until it's hot enough to sizzle a drop of water. Add the grits and fry in a single layer on both sides until golden brown. Keep the finished ones warm in the oven until all are done, then serve.

Hominy Grits Pudding

This pudding holds well in the oven and is one of those dishes you can enjoy for breakfast, lunch, or a casual supper. If you add whole, plump hominy kernels, they'll give your teeth something to bite into. Serves 4

¹/₄ cup butter
Cheese Grits (page 466)
1 cup milk
2 eggs, beaten
¹/₄ teaspoon cayenne, or 1 teaspoon paprika
Freshly milled pepper
1 (15-ounce) can white or golden hominy, rinsed, optional

Preheat the oven to 350°F and lightly butter an 8-cup casserole or soufflé dish. Stir the butter into the grits. Cool for 5 minutes, then stir in the milk and eggs and season with cayenne and pepper. Add the hominy. Pour into the casserole and bake until the pudding is firm and a knife inserted in the center comes out clean, about 45 minutes. Serve with honey or strawberry jam for breakfast or accompanied with a tomato-onion salad for supper.

Souffléd Grits Pudding: In the preceding dish, use 4 eggs, separated. Whip the whites until they hold firm peaks, then fold them into the grits. Pour into the dish, set it in a pan, and add boiling water to come partially up the sides. Bake until risen and firm, 40 to 50 minutes.

Pecan-Covered Grits

Originally from the Bronxville Women's Club, these crispy bites consist of plain grits, shaped into balls or other shpaes, then coated in egg, dusted in pecans, and fried. They're crisp and golden brown on the outside; the insides are soft. You could pour maple syrup or sorghum on them; you could serve them with greens, or you might embellish the grits by lacing them with sliced green onions and a cup of grated cheddar cheese. Makes 16 golf ball–size spheres, or 32 large marble–size ones. Serves 4 to 6

Grits (page 466)
1 egg
1¹/₂ cups finely chopped pecans
Sea salt and freshly milled pepper
¹/₂ cup vegetable oil

Cook the grits, then pour them into a pan and set aside. When cool, dip your hands into cold water, pick up some of the grits, and roll them into balls, large like golf balls or small like marbles, as you like. Set them on waxed paper as you work.

Beat the egg in a pie plate. In a second pie plate season the pecans with a few pinches salt and a few grindings of pepper (unless you're serving these with syrup). With one hand, dip each ball into the egg, then drop it into the crumbs. With the other hand, roll it around so that it is coated.

In a wide skillet, heat the oil over medium-high heat. When hot enough to sizzle a bread crumb, fry the balls until they're golden all over, turning them as they cook. You'll need to do this in 2 batches, or use two pans. Set them briefly on paper towels to drain, then transfer to a plate and serve hot.

Hominy and Posole

Hominy and posole are whole kernels of corn that have been treated with lime or the ashes of certain plants. The alkali solutions loosen the skins, which are scrubbed off and washed away; then the corn is either frozen or dried. The rich and unique flavor of posole (it's called pozole in Mexico) is the same as that in tamales or in corn tortillas, both of which are made from flour ground from lime-treated corn. Canned hominy, the Southern version, is precooked, but in a pinch it can take the place of posole. Posole is very popular in New Mexico, where it's available in white, yellow, blue, and even red varieties.

Dried Posole, Avocado, and Lime in the Slow Cooker

Dried posole takes hours to cook and lots of tending to the water level. But with the slow cooker it gently plumps then softens while you sleep or work. Rather than making it into a more elaborate dish, I simply season it with smoked paprika and serve it with sliced avocados and lime. A nontraditional but simple and good supper. Serves 4 to 6 (V)

2 cups dried posole—blue, red, or white

1 onion, diced

2 scant teaspoons dried oregano, preferably Mexican

1 teaspoon sea salt

2 teaspoons or more smoked hot or sweet paprika

1 or 2 avocados, sliced

Quartered limes, for serving

Sour cream, optional

Wash the posole well in a bowl of water, swishing it around so that small bits rise to the surface. Pour out the water along with any dust and chaff, then put the clean corn into a slow cooker with 8 cups water, the onion, oregano, and the salt. Put on low and cook until the kernels have flowered (opened) and the corn is soft but not mushy. Mine is edible after 7 hours, but better if it cooks for 8. Check the liquid after a few hours to make sure there's some covering the corn for a little broth.

When cooked, season with more salt. Stir in the smoked paprika, to taste, and if you want more heat, add some cayenne or hot ground chili powder. Serve with the avocado sliced into each bowl, a squeeze of lime, and a spoonful of sour cream. Of course, you can add any number of other garnishes as well—slivered green onions, fresh oregano, tortilla crisps, slivered cabbage, grated cheese, and so forth.

FROZEN POSOLE

Frozen posole can be found in bags in the meat cases of many supermarkets in the Southwest. It cooks much more quickly than dried posole and doesn't require soaking. If using frozen posole, use 2 pounds or 4 cups posole and 14 cups water. It should be done in about an hour.

Posole with Red Chile Pods

Although simmered only with onion, oregano, and dried red chiles, this rustic dish bursts with flavor. It's the kind of dish I like to have on hand to heat up at a moment's notice for a quick meal. Serves 4 to 6 (V)

2¹/₂ cups dried posole

¹/₂ onion, diced

2 large cloves garlic, peeled and smashed

3 dried red New Mexican chile pods or guajillo chiles

1 teaspoon dried oregano, preferably Mexican

2 teaspoons sea salt

Freshly milled pepper

Garnishes: finely shredded cabbage, thin tortilla strips (page 40), diced avocado, lime wedges, chopped cilantro, diced white onion, toasted dried oregano, crumbled queso fresco or feta, optional

Cover dried posole with boiling water and let stand for at least an hour or overnight. Drain the posole and combine 4 quarts water with all the ingredients, except the salt, pepper, and garnishes, in a soup pot. Bring to a boil, then lower the heat and simmer, covered, until the posole is tender and many of the kernels have opened up or flowered, like popcorn, about 2 hours. (This flowering gives it another name—popcorn soup.) Time can vary a great deal from brand to brand—it could be done in 1¹/₂ hours or take as long as 3. Season with the salt about halfway through, then season with salt and pepper to taste when finished.

Ladle the posole into bowls with some of the broth. Pile a lofty nest of shredded cabbage or tortilla strips over each bowl of posole, then spoon the remaining garnishes around the sides. Or arrange the garnishes on a platter and let your guests help themselves.

Posole with Red Chile Sauce: Once the posole is tender, stir in Red Chile Sauce (page 62) to taste, starting with ¹/₂ cup. Serve with any of the suggested garnishes, including grated Jack or crumbled goat cheese, if desired. Ⓥ

USING SORREL LEAVES

Mexican culinary maestra Diana Kennedy recommends using sorrel instead of the lime for tartness. I've done this whenever I've had sorrel, and it is delicious. Use 15 to 20 leaves with the stems removed instead of the lettuce and omit the limes in the garnish.

Masa Cakes with Black Beans

Masa harina, made from lime-treated corn, is what gives these cakes their distinctive flavor. It can be found in Mexican markets and in many supermarkets. Made small, these cakes can be served as an appetizer; larger, a main dish. Masa cakes are filling, so accompany them with something light and fresh, such as julienned jicama with lime juice and salt.
Serves 4 to 6

1 pound russet potatoes, peeled and chopped
1 to 1¹/₂ cups grated then chopped queso fresco or Muenster
2 cups masa harina
1 teaspoon baking powder
1 teaspoon sea salt
Vegetable oil, for frying
1 cup cooked black beans, canned or homemade (page 280)
¹/₃ cup sour cream or Greek yogurt
Pico de Gallo (page 90)

Boil the potatoes until tender, then break them up with a fork. Mash the potatoes with the cheese until smooth, then stir in the masa, baking powder, and the salt. Mix together with just enough water to make a dough that's soft, like a cookie dough. Divide it into the number of cakes you want. Pat each one into a circle about ¹/₂ inch thick, forming a depression in the center for the beans. (This can be done ahead of time; the cakes covered and refrigerated. Allow them to come to room temperature before frying.)

Heat ¹/₈ inch oil in a heavy skillet over fairly high heat. Add as many cakes as will fit in a single layer and reduce the heat a little. Cook until nicely browned on both sides. When done, transfer to paper towels to drain. Serve hot with a spoonful of warm beans in the depression, a dab of sour cream, and the Pico de Gallo.

Millet

A round golden grain that resembles couscous, millet remains the primary grain in much of Asia and parts of Africa. Americans know it mostly as birdseed, yet it deserves a place at our tables for its light, pleasant taste. Millet is a rich source of B vitamins and magnesium, surpassing even brown rice and whole wheat.

Millet can be a bit quirky to cook. It doesn't cook into even, separate grains. Some grains will be soft, like mashed potatoes, while others are still crunchy. I find the textural variations to be part of millet's appeal, but if you don't, try millet grits.

Toasted Millet

Makes about 3 cups (V)

1 cup millet
1/2 teaspoon sea salt
Freshly milled pepper
Butter or olive oil

Give the millet a quick rinse to wash off any dust, then drain, shaking off as much moisture as possible. Toast it in a large skillet over medium heat until the grains are dry, separate, and smell good. Bring 3 cups water to a boil in an 8- or 12-cup saucepan, add the salt, then stir in the millet.

Lower the heat and simmer, covered, for 30 minutes or longer, if needed. Turn the millet into a bowl, season with pepper, and stir in butter or oil to taste.

Millet with Pan-Roasted Corn and Tomatillo Salsa

You might serve this with a big colorful array of grilled summer vegetables or use it to stuff peppers or as a filling for stuffed chard leaves. Serves 4 to 6 (V)

1 1/2 tablespoons oil
1 large onion, chopped
1/2 teaspoon ground cumin
3 cloves garlic, finely chopped
1 cup millet, rinsed
1 teaspoon sea salt
3 cups corn kernels, fresh or frozen
3 Anaheim or New Mexican green chiles, roasted
1/4 cup chopped cilantro
Tomatillo Salsa (page 90), for serving
Sour cream, optional, for serving

Heat the oil in a wide soup pot over medium heat. Add the onion and cumin and sauté, stirring frequently, until softened, about 5 minutes. Add the garlic and cook for 1 minute more. Stir in the millet, salt, and 2 3/4 cups water. Cover and simmer for 25 minutes, then let stand for 10 minutes. Remove the millet to a large bowl and fluff with a fork.

While the millet is cooking, sear the corn in a dry cast-iron skillet over high heat, stirring constantly until the kernels take on a parched smell. Peel, then chop chiles. Toss the millet, chile, corn, and cilantro together. Serve with the salsa and sour cream on the side.

Savory Millet Grit Timbales

It seems like such a small matter to cut whole grains that into even smaller pieces, but with millet it makes a big difference: it cooks evenly instead of leaving you with mushy and crunchy grains in the same batch and is somehow more delicious.

These grits are close to polenta in texture, and you could serve them in place of polenta cakes, but the flavor differs. Use timbale molds or small 1/2-cup capacity ramekins if you wish to give these grits form. Serve with a mushroom ragout, or with seared peppers plus a dollop of the Yogurt Sauce with Cayenne and Dill (page 57) or Romesco Sauce (page 62). Makes 6 timbales

Ghee, butter, or oil, for the ramekins and for frying

1 scant teaspoon sea salt

1 cup millet grits

1 teaspoon smoked paprika, plus extra to finish

1/2 cup grated cheddar or Manchego cheese

2 tablespoons butter or ghee

Freshly milled pepper

Rub 6 ramekins or timbale molds with ghee and set them aside.

Bring 3 cups water to a boil, add the salt, then whisk in the millet grits. Cook, stirring, until they "catch," that is begin to thicken, then continue to cook, stirring often, until quite thick, 15 to 20 minutes more. Stir in the paprika, cheese, and butter. Taste for salt and season with pepper.

Divide the grits among the prepared dishes, then cover them with waxed paper and set aside to cool. As they cool, they will pull away from the sides. To serve, heat a wide skillet. Add a tablespoon of butter or ghee. When hot, give the ramekins a rap on your cutting board, then turn each onto your hands. Slide them into the pan, then cook on medium heat until golden and crusty, about 8 minutes. Carefully turn them over to cook the second side. When done, dust with additional smoked paprika and serve.

Millet and Chickpea Pilaf with Saffron and Tomatoes

I always enjoy millet most when it's mixed with foods of contrasting texture, such as chickpeas. Serve this with lots of garlicky braised chard or spinach. Leftovers are delicious browned in olive oil. Serves 4 to 6 (V)

2 1/2 tablespoons olive oil

1 cup millet, rinsed

1/2 onion, finely diced

1/2 teaspoon dried basil

Pinch saffron threads

1 1/2 cups cooked or 1 (15-ounce) can chickpeas, rinsed

1 1/2 cups diced tomatoes, fresh or canned

1 teaspoon sweet paprika

1 teaspoon sea salt

2 1/2 cups boiling water or a mixture of water and tomato juice

Freshly milled pepper

2 tablespoons finely chopped parsley

3 tablespoons grated parmesan or Gruyère, optional

Heat 1 1/2 tablespoons of the oil in a heavy 10-inch skillet, add the millet, and cook over medium heat until the grains begin to color, 4 to 5 minutes. Scrape the millet into a bowl, return the pan to the heat, and add the remaining 1 tablespoon oil along with the onion, basil, and saffron. Cook over medium-high heat until the onion begins to color, 5 to 7 minutes.

Reduce the heat to low and add the millet, chickpeas, tomatoes, and paprika. Season with salt and add the boiling water. Cover and cook until the liquid is absorbed and the millet is done, about 35 minutes. If it's still a little raw, add 1/4 cup water and continue cooking. Gently break up the grains with a fork. Taste for salt, season with pepper, then stir in the parsley and cheese.

Quinoa

Once the staple food of the Incan civilization, quinoa has twice been introduced to the United States, and it has finally caught on. Pronounced *keen-wa*, these tiny grains are generally met with enthusiasm. Quinoa is light, pleasant tasting without textural idiosyncrasies—and it cooks in 15 minutes. Often called a superfood, quinoa is a good source of plant protein and iron, potassium, magnesium, and lysine. It is not a true grain but the seed of a plant in the Amaranth family.

You can find both the grain and flour forms of quinoa just about anywhere now. Quinoa's many uses have been well described by one of its main champions, Rebecca Wood, whose book, *Quinoa: The Supergrain*, contains hundreds of recipes.

Quinoa is naturally covered with a protective coating called saponin. In the fields, bitter saponin protects the seed from birds and insects. Although much of it is removed before you buy it, always give quinoa a thorough rinsing in a fine sieve under cold water to ensure that it's sweet, not bitter or soapy tasting.

One especially unusual feature of quinoa is that when cooking, a tiny opaque spiral appears, encircling the grain and curling into its center. Expect to see this and know that everything is as it should be.

When I first wrote *Vegetarian Cooking for Everyone* there was only beige quinoa available, and it was hard to find. Today, red and black varieties are easily found in addition to beige, and some of it is American grown.

Quinoa

Serve this as a side dish, put it under a stir-fry in place of rice, or use it as a filling for stuffed vegetables or as a crunchy addition to muffins, pancakes, and breads.

Makes about 3 cups (V)

1 cup quinoa

2 cups water or Basic Vegetable Stock (page 175)

¹/4 teaspoon sea salt

1 tablespoon butter or sunflower seed oil

Freshly milled pepper

Rinse the quinoa several times in a bowl of cold water to remove the saponin, draining it each time in a fine sieve. Bring the water to a boil in a small saucepan, then add the salt and quinoa. Lower the heat, cover the pan, and simmer until the liquid is absorbed and the spiral of the germ is visible, 12 to 15 minutes. Let stand for 5 minutes. Toss with butter or oil and season with pepper.

If cooking black or red quinoa, allow an additional 10 minutes, or more.

Spicy Quinoa and Potato Croquettes

Cheese adds substance and flavor, but it can be omitted or replaced with soy-based cheese or even mashed tofu. Serve these croquettes with salsa, sour cream, and finely shredded salted cabbage or Jicama and Cucumbers with Chile and Lime (page 99). Serves 4

1 large russet potato, about 10 ounces

1 cup cooked quinoa

1 small onion, finely diced

2 tablespoons sunflower seed oil, plus more for cooking croquettes

2 teaspoons paprika

1 teaspoon ground coriander

1 teaspoon ground cumin

1/2 teaspoon dried oregano

2 cloves garlic, minced

1/4 cup chopped parsley and/or cilantro

1 egg

1/3 cup cottage cheese, grated Jack, or mashed tofu

Sea salt

1 cup fresh or dried bread crumbs

Boil or steam the potato until tender, then mash it with a fork and mix it with the quinoa. Sauté the onion in the oil in a small skillet over medium heat for 2 minutes, then add the spices and oregano. Cook over medium heat, stirring frequently, until the onion is soft, about 8 minutes, then add the garlic and cook for 1 minute more. Add this to the potato-quinoa mixture along with the parsley, egg, cheese, and salt to taste.

Work the mixture together, then divide it into four large or eight smaller portions and shape them into ovals. Press each croquette gently into the bread crumbs. Generously film a nonstick skillet with oil and set over medium heat. When hot, add the croquettes and cook on both sides until nicely browned.

Quinoa Timbales with Currants and Pine Nuts

Timbales refer to those little drum-shaped metal molds found in good cookware stores. If you don't have them, ramekins, custard cups, or teacups will do. Pressing quinoa and other grains into a mold, then turning them out, gives them visual appeal and a starring role on the plate. Surround them with black beans, braised greens, peas, or your chosen accompaniment. Serves 4 to 6 Ⓥ

3/4 cup quinoa, thoroughly rinsed

1/4 teaspoon sea salt

1 tablespoon olive or sunflower seed oil

1 red onion, finely diced

3/4 teaspoon ground cumin

1/4 teaspoon ground cinnamon

1/4 teaspoon ground ginger

1/4 teaspoon ground coriander

1/8 teaspoon turmeric

Freshly milled pepper

1/4 cup chopped cilantro or parsley

1/4 cup currants

3 tablespoons pine nuts or almonds, toasted and chopped

1 teaspoon grated orange or lemon zest

Cook the quinoa in 1 1/2 cups water with the salt as described on page 472. Meanwhile, warm the oil in a small skillet. Add the onion, spices, and several grinds of pepper, and cook gently until softened, about 10 minutes. Season with salt.

Drain the quinoa when it's done and toss it with the onion mixture along with the cilantro, currants, pine nuts, and orange zest. Pack servings of the mixture into timbale molds, cups, or ramekins, then immediately turn them out onto individual plates.

Curried Quinoa with Peas and Cashews

Carrot juice gives this one-dish meal a vibrant color and flavor. Serves 4 Ⓥ

2 tablespoons oil or butter

1 onion, ¹/₄ finely diced, ³/₄ coarsely chopped

1 cup quinoa, thoroughly rinsed

2 teaspoons curry powder

³/₄ teaspoon sea salt

2 zucchini, diced into small cubes

1 cup carrot juice

1 cup peas

¹/₄ cup thinly sliced green onions, including a little of the greens

¹/₂ cup cashews, roasted and coarsely chopped

Freshly milled pepper

2 tablespoons chopped cilantro, for garnish

Heat 1 tablespoon of the oil in a small soup pot, add the finely diced onion, and cook over medium heat for about 3 minutes. Stir in the quinoa, ¹/₂ teaspoon of the curry powder, and ¹/₄ teaspoon of the salt and cook for 2 minutes. Add 2 cups boiling water, then lower the heat. Cover and cook for 15 minutes.

Meanwhile, heat the remaining 1 tablespoon oil in a 10-inch skillet. Add the chopped onion, zucchini, and remaining 1¹/₂ teaspoons curry powder. Cook, stirring frequently, over medium heat for 5 minutes. Add ¹/₂ cup water, the carrot juice, and the remaining ¹/₂ teaspoon salt. Cover and simmer for 5 minutes, then add the peas and green onions and cook for a few minutes more. Stir the vegetables and cashews into the quinoa. Taste for salt and season with pepper. Serve in soup plates, garnished with cilantro.

Red Quinoa and Fresh Corn with Green Onions and Feta

Serve as a side dish or use as a filling for chard leaves, tomatoes, or zucchini. Serves 4

3 plump ears of corn

2 cups Quick Stock (page 174) or water

1 cup red quinoa, thoroughly rinsed

¹/₂ teaspoon sea salt

1 tablespoon butter or safflower oil

¹/₂ cup thinly sliced green onions, including some of the greens

Freshly milled pepper

¹/₃ cup crumbled feta or grated cheddar, for garnish

Shuck the corn, slice off the kernels, and set them aside. Reverse your knife and scrape the cobs to get the milk. Bring the stock to a boil in a saucepan; add the quinoa, corn scrapings, and salt. Lower the heat, cover, and simmer for 15 minutes. Turn off the heat and let stand for 5 minutes. Melt the butter in a small skillet, add the green onions and corn kernels, and cook over medium-high heat until the green onions are bright green, about 3 minutes. Toss them with the quinoa. Season with pepper and serve, garnished with the crumbled cheese.

TWO TINY GRAINS: AMARANTH AND TEFF

Just as quinoa was the mother grain of the Incas, amaranth was the principal food of the Aztecs, and teff dates back more than 3,000 years to ancient Egypt. These grains are now being cultivated in the Western mountain states. Their nutritional qualities far surpass those of wheat, rice, and corn. One of the easiest ways to use these grains is in baked goods, for both are made into flour.

AMARANTH: As with quinoa, these tiny seeds are not true grains, that is members of the grass family, but we treat them as if they were. Containing more of the essential amino acids than almost any other plant food, amaranth is second only to quinoa in iron and is a strong provider of calcium. It requires neither soaking nor a lengthy turn on the stove. Its texture is pleasantly crunchy and its flavor both sweet and peppery, with molasses-like tones. When cooked, it has a slightly gelatinous quality. In fact, amaranth can be used to thicken soups. It makes a delicious breakfast cereal and in flour form can be added to baked goods. The grains can also be sprouted or popped in a dry skillet to make miniature "popcorn."

TEFF: A true grain, teff is remarkably minuscule—according to the box, 150 grains of teff weigh as much as a single grain of wheat. Teff is high in calcium and protein, but its minute size makes it a little difficult to enjoy as a side dish of any substantial proportions. In grain form, it is best used as a breakfast cereal or mixed with other grains. As a flour, combine it with wheat or use it to make the Ethiopian flatbread injera.

Rice

Rice is the most consumed grain, in its natural grain form, in the United States. We usually treat it as a side dish, but for much of the world rice is the center of the plate, garnished with vegetables and small amounts of meat or fish. In its whole form, rice is a good source of B vitamins, which are the most difficult to obtain in a plant-based diet. Otherwise, rice is not particularly nutritious unless it's combined with beans, greens, and other vitamin-rich foods. Rice is, however, easily digested, free of gluten, and versatile.

The shape of the grain, which is related to its starch content, affects how rice cooks: long-grain rice, which has the lowest amount of starch, emerges separate and fluffy; medium-grain rice is moister, tenderer, and somewhat chewier than long-grain varieties; and short-grain rice, which is nearly round, either clumps together or remains separate but bound with its own smooth, starchy sauce, depending on how it's cooked.

Rice, especially white rice, is the chameleon grain, easily taking on any flavor you care to introduce. Try adding a slice of frozen herb butter or other flavored butter to a pot of hot rice or a teaspoon of toasted sesame oil, roasted peanut, or roasted walnut oil to impart flavor. A few teaspoons grated lemon zest or grated ginger and a tablespoon of soy sauce take it in another direction altogether. Saffron, bay leaves, fresh herbs, spinach, or a few tablespoons salsa verde, pesto, or salsa added to cooked rice make it very aromatic and flecked with green. Use your imagination and look out for choice, highly seasoned leftovers in your refrigerator.

How Rice Is Processed

Rice is classified according to how it's milled and processed, both of which affect cooking time and nutritional value.

BROWN RICE has only its husk removed during the milling process. Because the bran stays intact, it's richer in fiber, trace minerals, and those all-important B vitamins. Brown rice takes the longest time to cook, 30 to 40 minutes.

WHITE RICE has the husk, bran, and most of the germ removed during milling, which reduces the amount of fiber and vitamins. Its flavor is mild, its texture soft, and the cooking time is shorter by half.

ENRICHED RICE compensates for what's lost in the milling of white rice by having nutrients added back to the rice in the form of a coating. In the end, it may be more nutrient rich than brown rice, but it lacks fiber. Enriched rice shouldn't be rinsed.

CONVERTED OR PARBOILED RICE has been steamed under pressure before milling to force some of the nutrients into the endosperm to preserve them. Converted rice is also enriched. When cooked, the texture is fluffy and somewhat peculiar. The same is true of instant rice, which is precooked, dehydrated, then cooked again, which means all of the rice's flavor is gone, along with its texture.

How to Cook Rice

Rice needn't be rinsed unless it looks dusty and needs picking over for pebbles, which is rare nowadays. Enriched, converted, or instant rice should never be rinsed. Soaking basmati rice for 30 minutes produces delicate, elongated grains. In general, brown rice, especially short-grain, takes about twice as long to cook as white rice. As with beans, the cooking time can be reduced if the grain is soaked first or is cooked in a pressure cooker.

BOILED RICE: Add rice to a pot of (unmeasured) boiling salted water and cook like pasta until done, which means tasting frequently after 12 to 15 minutes. Cooking rice this way is called free boiling, and this method is used for rice salads. Although the rice won't stick, water-soluble vitamins and enrichments are lost, and the unique texture of starchy Italian and Spanish rice is completely destroyed by this method.

STEAMED RICE: Add rice to measured boiling salted water—twice the amount of water to white rice and two and a half times for brown. Butter and seasonings can be included as well. Cover the pan and cook for 15 to 20 minutes for white rice, 35 to 45 for brown.

PILAF STYLE: Sauté rice in oil or butter with seasonings, stirring the rice to make sure all the grains are coated. Add the water and follow the directions for steamed rice. When done, cover the pan with a towel and a lid, then let stand for 5 to 10 minutes. The towel will absorb the steam and keep the grains separate.

RICE COOKER METHOD: An electric rice cooker, a staple in many Asian homes and restaurants, provides an extremely reliable way to cook perfect rice. The rice stays warm for hours. Originally intended for Asian white rice, it can be adapted to other grains as well, although it may take a few attempts to figure out the exact times and amounts.

ARSENIC IN RICE

Today rice is not the soothing, nourishing food we once thought, due to the arsenic that has been found lurking in this grain in higher than acceptable amounts. Arsenic is a chemical element found in our water, soil, and air, so it's to be expected that it would appear in foods as well. Arsenic occurs naturally from volcanic eruptions and other disturbances in the earth's crust, but some of our human activities also add arsenic to the environment, such as burning coal, oil, gasoline, mining, and the use of arsenic compounds in pesticides. Data collection and its analysis of rice and rice products is still going on. Rice is not just rice, but is present in many gluten-free foods, rice crackers, rice cereals, and, of course, rice milk. Many have suggested reducing the amount eaten while others take a stronger stance and suggest avoiding rice altogether. The Environmental Working Group suggests washing rice thoroughly and cooking brown rice as we cook pasta, that is in plenty of boiling water, as well as reducing the amount of rice eaten.

Rice Varieties

Increasingly more varieties of rice are being exported to and grown in the United States. Ethnic markets carry exotic varieties, such as the glutinous sweet rices or golden Egyptian rice. Most natural foods stores and many supermarkets are well stocked with a number of varieties, especially fragrant ones like jasmine and basmati rice.

BLACK RICE: Also known as purple rice and forbidden rice, black rice actually includes a range of rice types—such as glutinous and black jasmine rice. The type I am able to buy easily in my co-op and other stores is neither of these, but a somewhat long-grained rice referred to as Chinese forbidden rice. It can be bought in packages and in bulk. When you rinse it, the water turns purple. When cooked, the rice is black. It's nutty, clean tasting, and delicious. I use it in many ways over a period of days—as a simple grain, mixed with collards and other vegetables, with coconut milk or coconut oil, and in rice puddings.

BROWN RICE: The brownness is actually a result of the milling process, not the variety. Before polishing, all rice is brown. Mottled, flecked, long-grain or short-grain, this is the most wholesome form of rice. Its well-pronounced flavor is nutty and its texture chewy. Brown rice is better known in America than in rice-eating cultures, where white rice is preferred.

CAROLINA GOLD RICE: This long-grain white rice has been grown in South Carolina since the eighteenth century. A treasured and delicious rice, you can get it from Anson Mills.

FRAGRANT RICES: These have subtle floral or nutty nuances. Basmati rice from Pakistan, India, and the Middle East has a very long grain and is soaked to extend its length. In India, basmati is considered a luxury rice. Basmati is now grown in Arkansas and Texas, under the trade name Texmati. Another basmati hybrid is pecan rice, whose flavor suggests pecans. Jasmine rice from Thailand is more floral, with a smooth, silky texture. Popcorn rice is another aromatic variety.

ITALIAN AND SPANISH RICE: Arborio is the best known of the short-grain rice varieties from Northern Italy, but Carnaroli and Vialone Nano are also popular. Valencia rice is the Spanish equivalent. Very round and starchy, these are the rices used for risotto and paella. When they are cooked in these dishes, the starch is released but a firm core remains, which gives the rice an exciting combination of textures. Such rice should never be rinsed or boiled and drained, or its creamy starch will be wasted.

SWEET (OR GLUTINOUS) RICE: Another short, round grain with a high starch content, this Asian rice is sticky and sweet. It is used to make mochi, rice that is pounded into a glutinous mass, then formed into dumplings, sweet puddings, and restorative soups called congee. Its unique flavor and texture distinguish it from other varieties.

WEHANI: A hybrid grown in California, Wehani is a long-grain, mahogany-hued rice with a very rich, nutty, and slightly floral flavor. It's grown by Lundberg Family Farms, rice growers in Northern California, who also grow a superior short-grain organic brown rice.

WILD RICE: Neither a true rice nor always wild, this long black grass is native to North America and was once a staple food of native North Americans. Chewy and very earthy tasting, wild rice has more B vitamins and proteins than true rice. It's a labor-intensive crop to harvest—in some places it's still hand-gathered. When cooked, it expands greatly, which helps offset its high price. The native rice is not as black as the cultivated rice and it cooks in half the time.

EXTRA RICE IS NICE

Leftover rice can be made into fried rice, added to soups for a toothsome garnish, cooked with eggs, and added to breads, pancakes, muffins, and other baked goods. If the rice is short-grain and a little sticky, simmer it in water or milk, top with cinnamon and raisins, and enjoy as a breakfast cereal. If the grains are separate, toss them with a vinaigrette and bits of vegetables, herbs, cheese, and other odds and ends. Cooked Wehani, brown, or wild rice can be frozen and thawed as needed.

White Rice

A general all-purpose method that showcases the flavor nuance of each variety. Long-grain rice, whose grains come out separate and distinct, is ideal for salads. Medium and short grains are starchier and tend to stick together. Makes about 2¹/₂ cups (V)

1/4 to 1/2 teaspoon sea salt
1 tablespoon butter or oil
1 cup white rice

Bring 1³/₄ to 2 cups water to a boil in a saucepan, add the salt and butter, then stir in the rice. (Use the larger amount of water for softer rice or if cooking at higher altitudes.) Lower the heat, cover the pot, and cook without looking, for 15 to 20 minutes. Carefully fluff the grains with a fork.

Checking Rice for Doneness. Altitude, hardness of water, whether the rice has been soaked or not at all affect the cooking time of rice. If the water has been absorbed but the rice isn't as tender as you'd like, sprinkle 1 to 2 tablespoons water over the top, cover, and return to the heat for 5 minutes more. Repeat if necessary. If the rice is done but there is a little extra water, wait for a few minutes—it will be absorbed. If there's a lot of extra water, drain it.

White Basmati Rice

Use this rice with Indian dishes. Rinsing and soaking the grains before cooking allows the rice to lengthen, yielding exceptionally fine long grains. Makes about 3 cups (V)

1 cup white basmati rice
1/4 teaspoon sea salt

Wash the rice in a bowl of cold water, gently swishing it back and forth with your fingers. Let the rice settle to the bottom, then pour off the water to remove any bits of bran as well as excess starch so that the grains will be separate and springy when cooked. Repeat until the water runs almost clear, then drain. Cover the rice with a few cups water and let stand for 30 minutes. Drain, reserving 1³/₄ cups. Combine the rice and reserved water in an 8-cup pot, add the salt, and bring it to a boil. Reduce the heat to low, cover, and cook until the water is absorbed and the rice is tender, about 15 minutes. Let rest for 5 minutes, then fluff with a fork.

Brown Basmati Rice

More perfumed than regular short-grain brown rice. Makes about 3 cups (V)

1 cup brown basmati rice
1/4 teaspoon sea salt

Rinse and soak the rice, as for white basmati rice, but measure out 2 cups plus 2 tablespoons of the soaking water. Cook, as described, with the salt for 30 to 40 minutes. Taste a grain. If it isn't quite done but the water has been absorbed, sprinkle with 2 tablespoons water and cook for 5 to 10 minutes more. Let stand for 5 minutes, then fluff with a fork and serve.

Basic Brown Rice

Enhance brown rice with butter, salt, and pepper as well as sesame salt (gomashio) or other herb salts and soy sauce. Makes about 2½ cups Ⓥ

1 cup short-grain brown rice
½ teaspoon sea salt

Rinse the rice in a bowl of water and drain. (If time allows, first soak it for an hour or overnight in water to cover.) Bring 2 cups plus 2 tablespoons water to a boil in a saucepan and add the rice and salt. Lower the heat, cover tightly, and cook over low heat without disturbing the lid for 40 to 50 minutes. Taste for salt after the rice is cooked, and season as needed.

Brown Rice or Wehani Rice in the Pressure Cooker

The pressure cooker works for short- or long-grain brown rice, brown basmati, and Wehani rice. They can even be cooked together. The pressure cooker method produces slightly stickier rice than other methods. Makes about 2¼ cups Ⓥ

1 cup long- or short-grain brown rice
2 cups water or Basic Vegetable Stock (page 175)
1 tablespoon vegetable oil or butter
A few pinches sea salt

Combine the rice, water, oil, and salt in a pressure cooker. Bring the pressure to high, then lower the heat to maintain it. Cook for 20 minutes, then turn off the heat and quick-release for long-grain rice. For short-grain rice, allow the pressure to drop slowly on its own.

Seasoned Brown Rice: Those who are new to brown rice may like it better when cooked with seasonings. Add ½ teaspoon dried marjoram and a pinch of thyme to the pot along with 2 tablespoons diced onion and a little butter or olive oil. Cook as for basic brown rice or in the pressure cooker. Ⓥ

Sesame Rice: Cook the rice with 2 teaspoons toasted sesame oil and serve with Gomashio (page 67). Ⓥ

Lacquered Rice: Add 1 tablespoon tamari or soy sauce to the pot. The tamari will turn the rice a deep, lacquered hue and impart a rich taste, especially when the rice is cooked in the pressure cooker. Ⓥ

Calico Rice: Here's a way to introduce the heartier brown rices to your family or extend expensive wild rice. Cook long-cooking rice—brown rice, Wehani, and wild rice—together. Separately cook white rice, then combine them. Toss with butter or oil and season with salt and pepper. (Keep this in mind for when you have leftover brown or wild rice.) Ⓥ

Rice Cooked in Black Bean Broth

The nutritious broth that remains from cooking black beans makes a flavorful, rich broth for cooking rice. Although motivated by common sense not to waste this delicious broth, I was delighted to find that using the broth this way is also a Mexican tradition. Of course, rice can be cooked in any of the leftover liquid from cooking beans. Serves 4 Ⓥ

2 tablespoons safflower oil
½ white onion, finely diced
1¼ cups white or brown rice, rinsed well
2 cloves garlic, finely chopped
⅛ teaspoon anise seeds
2 cups broth from cooked black beans or broth plus water
1 cup peeled, diced tomatoes, fresh or canned
½ teaspoon sea salt
Garnishes: queso fresco, diced jalapeño chiles, chopped cilantro, slivered green onions, chopped tomatoes, and/or sour cream

Heat the oil in a 12-cup saucepan. Add the onion and sauté over medium-high heat for 4 to 5 minutes. Add the rice, garlic, and anise and stir to coat the rice. Cook until it's light gold, 3 to 4 minutes, then add the broth, tomatoes, and salt and bring to a boil. Cover and cook over low heat until the rice is done, 15 to 18 minutes for white rice and 35 to 40 minutes for brown rice. Turn into a dish and serve with any or all of the garnishes.

Green Rice with Roasted Chiles

Delicious on its own or as a filling for summer vegetables, such as tomatoes, peppers, and squash. Add a little crumbled queso fresco or feta to the top and bake. Serves 3 or 4 (V)

2 cups Stock for Mexican Soups and Stews (page 175) or water

1 celery rib, finely chopped

1/2 white onion, chopped

1 clove garlic, chopped

1/2 cup parsley leaves, large stems removed

5 tablespoons coarsely chopped cilantro

Sea salt

1 tablespoon oil

1 cup white rice

3 Anaheim or New Mexican green chiles, roasted

5 mint leaves, chopped

Simmer the stock with the celery, onion, garlic, parsley, and 2 tablespoons of the cilantro until the celery is tender, about 5 minutes. Puree and return it to the pan. Season to taste with salt.

Heat the oil in an 8-cup saucepan over medium heat. Add the rice and cook, stirring constantly, for several minutes, until clear and pale gold. Add the warm stock and bring to a boil. Cover and cook over low heat for 15 minutes. Let stand for 5 to 10 minutes. Meanwhile, peel, seed, and chop the chiles. Add them to the pan along with the remaining cilantro and the mint and gently fluff them into the rice with a fork.

Variation with Peas: Add 1 cup fresh or frozen peas while the rice is standing. The heat of the rice should cook them. (V)

Red Rice: Cook white rice in the Red Stock (page 176), according to the recipe on page 477. (V)

Rice with Spinach, Lemon, and Dill

Cooking the spinach with the rice adds character, but don't expect its color to be bright green. Serves 4 (V)

2 tablespoons olive oil, butter, or a mixture

1 cup finely chopped green onions, including an inch or two of the greens

1 cup long-grain white or brown rice

1 large bunch spinach leaves, finely chopped

2 tablespoons chopped dill or 2 teaspoons dried

Grated zest and juice of 1 lemon

1/2 teaspoon sea salt

Freshly milled pepper

Warm the oil in a saucepan over medium heat. Add the green onions and cook, stirring frequently, until wilted, 3 to 4 minutes. Add the rice, spinach, dill, lemon zest, and salt; cook until the spinach has wilted. If you're using white rice, add 1 3/4 cups water; for brown rice, add 2 1/4 cups. Bring to a boil, then lower the heat, cover, and cook until the liquid is absorbed, 15 to 18 minutes for white rice, 30 to 40 minutes for brown. Add the lemon juice and gently loosen the grains with a fork. Cover and let stand for 5 minutes. Season with pepper and serve.

Truly Wild Wild Rice

Native wild rice is grayish and greenish—not as dramatic as cultivated, but quicker cooking and more interesting to eat. It cooks in about 20 minutes. Even if you're going to make a salad with it, start by cooking your rice this way. If you have excess liquid at the end, don't discard it. Take a sip. It is extraordinarily hearty and delicious. Native Wild Rice can be found online and in some Minnesota farmers' markets. Makes 3 cups (V)

1 cup native wild rice (*manoomin*)

1/2 teaspoon sea salt

Rinse the rice 3 or 4 times in water until any dust is washed away.

Put it in the pot with 3 cups water and the salt, bring to a boil, then lower the heat and simmer gently, the pot covered, for 20 minutes. At this point it should be done. Take a taste. If there's extra liquid, pour it through a strainer into a bowl, then return the rice to the pot, cover, and let stand for a few minutes. You can now use it for a salad, in pancakes or muffins, or toss it with butter, salt, and pepper for a sensational dish.

Cultivated Wild Rice

Cultivated wild rice is savored for its long black grains and earthy flavor. It can be served alone, combined with other varieties of rice, or used in stuffings, salads, and as an exotic addition to pancakes and waffles, breads, and even soups.
Makes about 3 cups (V)

1 cup wild rice

1/2 teaspoon sea salt

Freshly milled pepper

1 tablespoon butter or roasted hazelnut oil

Cover the rice with cold water, remove any bits of chaff or other odd particles that float to the surface, and drain. Bring 4 cups water to a boil in a saucepan and add the rice and salt. Lower the heat, cover, and cook until the rice is done, 45 to 50 minutes. Take a taste—it should have a little bite, and many of the grains will have blossomed or split. If there's any extra water, simply pour it off. Return the cover and let the rice stand for 5 to 10 minutes. Fluff the grains with a fork. Taste for salt, season with pepper, and stir in the butter.

Wild Rice with Walnut and Green Onion Sauté

I prefer cultivated wild rice mixed with other grains or seasoned with something fresh and highly aromatic, like this green onion sauté. Serves 4 to 6 (V)

1 tablespoon olive oil or butter

1/2 cup coarsely chopped walnuts

2 bunches green onions, including half the greens, sliced in 1/4-inch rounds

2 tablespoons thinly sliced tarragon

Sea salt and freshly milled pepper

Grated zest of 1 lemon

3 cups cooked wild rice, either cultivated or native

1 tablespoon roasted walnut oil

Heat the oil in a medium skillet over high heat. Add the walnuts and cook for a minute or so, then add the onions and tarragon. Season with salt and pepper and sauté until the onions are bright green and soft, after a few minutes. Stir in the lemon zest, then toss the mixture with the rice. Drizzle with the walnut oil and toss again.

Wild Rice–Stuffed Cabbages with Sweet and Sour Tomato Sauce

Like the pepper, cabbages have long served as sturdy, economical vessels for stuffing. In place of meat, wild rice is mixed with toasted hazelnuts, and the whole is baked in a tomato sauce that is softly sweet and sour. Savoy cabbage is the variety to use for stuffed cabbage, if possible, for it's beautiful crinkled leaf and more delicate flavor.
Serves 4 to 6 (V)

Cabbage

1 large head green cabbage, preferably savoy

1/2 teaspoon salt

1 cup wild rice

2 tablespoons hazelnut oil or sunflower seed oil

1/2 cup finely diced yellow onion

1/2 cup finely diced celery

1/4 teaspoon celery seeds

1 clove garlic, minced

3/4 cup toasted hazelnuts

1/4 cup chopped parsley

2 teaspoons minced thyme leaves or 1/2 teaspoon thyme

1 bunch green onions, including half of the greens, thinly sliced

Freshly milled pepper

Butter or hazelnut oil, to finish

Sweet and Sour Tomato Sauce

2 tablespoons olive oil

1/2 cup finely chopped yellow onion

1 teaspoon minced garlic

1 bay leaf

1 teaspoon dried oregano

1/2 cup white wine or water

1 (28-ounce) can organic crushed tomatoes

2 teaspoons sugar

1/2 teaspoon salt

Freshly milled pepper

1 teaspoon red wine vinegar, or to taste

To remove the leaves from the cabbage without tearing them, bring a large pot filled three-fourths with water to a boil. Cut the core out of the base, then submerge the whole head in boiling water for about 1 minute. Remove the cabbage from the pot and place it on a work surface. Carefully peel off as many leaves as will come off easily. Repeat as many times as necessary to secure 12 perfect leaves. When done, cut the core out of the base of each leaf and set the leaves, seam side up, on a towel or cutting board. Use the rest of the cabbage for the accompaniment.

To cook the rice, bring 3 cups water to a boil and add the salt. Add the rice, then simmer until tender. Cultivated wild rice will take about 40 minutes; native rice about half that long. When done, drain and set aside. (Reserve the liquid for soup stock or to drink.)

Meanwhile, make the sauce: Warm the olive oil in a skillet over medium heat. Add the onion, garlic, bay leaf, and oregano and cook, stirring occasionally, until the onion is soft, about 10 minutes. Add the wine and let the onions simmer, covered, over low heat 7 to 10 minutes longer. Add the tomatoes to the onion, along with the sugar, salt, and pepper to taste. Simmer for 20 minutes, then add the vinegar. Taste and make sure the sauce is sweet or tart enough to your liking. Set aside.

Continuing with the cabbage, warm the hazelnut oil in a skillet over medium heat. Add the onion, celery and celery seeds, and cook, stirring occasionally, until the onion is limp, about 5 minutes. Add the garlic, toasted hazelnuts, parsley, thyme and green onions. Season with salt and pepper.

Preheat the oven to 375°F. Place approximately 1/4 cup of the filling at the base of each leaf, just above where the stem was cut out. Fold the sides over, then the top, to make a neat package. Ladle enough sauce over a baking dish to cover it generously, then place the cabbage rolls in it, seam side down. Cover and bake until bubbling and hot, about 35 minutes.

Reheat the remaining sauce. Finely shred the rest of cabbage, then place it on a steamer rack over boiling water, cover, and steam until tender, about 8 minutes. Transfer to a bowl and toss with salt and pepper, to taste, and a little butter. Place a mound of the cabbage on each plate and nestle the stuffed cabbage leaves in the center with the extra sauce.

Rice Pilafs

The preliminary sautéing with onions sets pilaf apart from risotto and other rice dishes. Using long-grain rice, whether white or brown, ensures that the finished dish is light, the grains separate, though you can certainly make a decent pilaf with medium-grain rice. The rice is first cooked in a little butter or olive oil, then finished in simmering water or stock. An 8- to 12-cup heavy, ovenproof pot or saucepan with a tight-fitting lid is best for pilafs. You'll find that improvisation when making pilafs is tempting—and entirely appropriate.

Basic Rice Pilaf

Serves 4 (V)

---

2 tablespoons butter, olive oil, or a mixture

1 small onion, finely diced

1 1/4 cups long-grain white or brown rice, rinsed well

2 cups simmering water or stock for white rice, 2 1/2 cups for brown

1 small bay leaf

1/2 teaspoon sea salt

Freshly milled pepper

Heat the butter with the onion in an 8- to 12-cup saucepan and cook over medium heat until the onion is translucent, about 3 minutes. Add the rice, stir to coat, and cook for 2 minutes. Add the water, bay leaf, salt, and a little pepper. Cover, lower the heat as much as you can, and cook until the rice is done—about 20 minutes for white rice, 40 for brown. (If cooking brown rice and the pan seems dry but the rice isn't done, dribble 2 to 4 tablespoons water over the surface, return the lid, and cook for 10 minutes more.) When the rice is done, put a towel under the lid, turn off the heat, and let it stand for 5 to 10 minutes to finish steaming. Gently break the grains apart with a fork, discard the bay leaf, and serve.

Baked Rice Pilaf: Preheat the oven to 375°F. After adding the water or stock, transfer the covered pot to the oven and bake for 30 minutes for white rice, 45 minutes for brown, or until the liquid is absorbed. (V)

Rice Pilaf with Mushrooms: Add 1 cup chopped mushrooms to the onion and cook for 4 to 5 minutes before adding the rice. To emphasize the flavor, use Mushroom Stock (page 176), the dried mushroom soaking water, or commercial mushroom stock. Garnish with fresh parsley or tarragon. Ⓥ

Curried Rice Pilaf with Opal Basil

This is especially good made with basmati rice. Plum-colored opal basil leaves dramatically set off the tan-colored rice, but use green basil if opal isn't available. Serves 4 to 6

- Basic Rice Pilaf (page 481)
- 1 tablespoon ghee
- 2 teaspoons curry powder
- 1/3 cup golden raisins
- 1/4 cup chopped mixed parsley and cilantro
- 2 tablespoons thinly sliced basil
- 1/4 cup slivered almonds or pine nuts, toasted

Cook the onion for the Basic Rice Pilaf using the ghee, curry powder, and raisins. Add the rice, then proceed as described. When done, add the herbs and toasted almonds and separate the grains with a fork.

Rice Pilaf with Saffron and Spice

With this method, the rice sits unattended for 40 minutes, but even if you use that time to prepare the rest of the meal, the rice will still be quite warm at serving time. This pilaf is fragrant with whole spices. Serves 4 Ⓥ

- 2 tablespoons olive oil or ghee
- 1/2 small onion, finely diced
- 1/2 teaspoon ground cardamom
- 2 pinches saffron threads
- 1 (3-inch) cinnamon stick
- 5 whole cloves
- 1 1/2 cups basmati rice, well rinsed then soaked for 30 minutes and drained
- 1/2 teaspoon sea salt
- 1 tablespoon finely chopped parsley

Warm the oil in an 8- or 12-cup saucepan. Add the onion and spices and cook over low heat, stirring frequently, for about 3 minutes. Add the rice and stir to coat, then add 3 cups water and the salt. Increase the heat to medium and simmer, uncovered, until the liquid is absorbed and holes have appeared over the surface. Turn off the heat, put a clean towel over the pot, and cover with a tight lid. Set on the back of the stove for 40 minutes. When ready to serve, gently fluff the rice with a fork and scatter the parsley on top.

Wehani Rice Pilaf with Red Wine

Wehani is a dense grain—consider stirring in another cooked grain at the end, such as long-grain brown or white rice, barley, amaranth, or quinoa to lighten it. Serves 4 Ⓥ

- 1 1/2 cups Wehani rice
- 1 1/2 tablespoons oil or butter
- 1/2 cup finely diced onion
- 1 bay leaf
- 1/2 teaspoon dried marjoram
- 1/4 teaspoon dried thyme
- 1/3 cup dry red wine
- 1/2 teaspoon sea salt
- Freshly milled pepper

Rinse the rice, then cover it with 5 1/4 cups boiling water and let stand for 15 minutes.

Heat the oil in a heavy 8- or 12-cup saucepan. Add the onion and herbs and cook over medium heat until the onion is translucent, about 8 minutes. Add the wine, raise the heat, and cook until reduced to a syrupy consistency. Add the rice with its soaking liquid and salt and bring to a boil. Lower the heat, cover, and cook for 45 to 50 minutes. (If you're using a pressure cooker, bring to pressure and cook for 15 minutes, then let the pressure fall rather than using the quick release.) Separate the grains with a fork, season with pepper, and serve.

Rice or Quinoa Stuffing with Pine Nuts and Currants

Here's a filling for small eggplant, peppers, and stuffing tomatoes, but this is also good as an accompaniment to grilled eggplants or pepper strips and other vegetables, such as sautéed artichokes. Quinoa and long-grain rice will produce light, separate grains, while short-grain rice will be stickier and hold together. You may prefer one or the other, but both will work as a filling for summer vegetables. Makes about 2 cups ⓥ

1 cup brown basmati rice or quinoa (any color)

¹/₄ cup currants

2 tablespoons green or golden raisins

¹/₃ cup pine nuts, toasted in a dry pan

2 to 3 tablespoons olive oil

1 onion, finely chopped

¹/₂ teaspoon sea salt

¹/₃ cup finely chopped parsley

Sumac, optional, for serving

Rinse the rice or quinoa well and set it aside. Cover the currants and raisins with warm water to soak until softened and plump, about 15 minutes. Drain them and squeeze out the excess water. Toast the pine nuts.

Warm the oil in a sauté pan large enough to hold the rice plus 2 cups water. Add the onion and cook over medium-high heat, stirring occasionally until softened and golden, about 10 minutes. Add the currants and the rice, give them a stir, and cook to warm through, then add 2 cups water and the salt. Bring to a boil, then reduce the heat to low, cover the pan, and cook until the rice is done, about 30 minutes (15 minutes for the quinoa.) Turn off the heat and let it stand, covered, for 10 minutes, then toss the grains with a fork and add the parsley and pine nuts. Serve with a dash of sumac over the surface.

Rice and Chickpea Pilaf with Pine Nuts and Currants

Serve this light pilaf with grilled or braised vegetables or use as a filling for eggplant, zucchini, stuffed cabbage, or grape leaves. Serves 4 ⓥ

1 large onion, grated or minced

3 tablespoons olive oil

¹/₂ cup toasted pine nuts

1 teaspoon allspice

1 cup white or brown rice

¹/₃ cup currants

¹/₄ cup chopped parsley

3 tablespoons chopped mint leaves

3 tablespoons chopped dill or 1 tablespoon dried

¹/₂ teaspoon sea salt

Freshly milled pepper

Juice of 1 lemon

1 (15-ounce) can chickpeas, drained and rinsed, or 1¹/₂ cups cooked

Put the onion in a wide saucepan with the oil, pine nuts, and allspice. Cook over medium heat until the onion is soft, 6 to 8 minutes. Add the rice, currants, and herbs and cook for a few minutes more. Season with the salt and a little pepper, then add the water—2 cups for white rice, 2¹/₄ cups for brown—and the lemon juice. Bring to a boil. Cover the pan, reduce the heat to low, and cook until the liquid is absorbed and the rice is tender, 18 to 20 minutes for white, 40 minutes or longer for brown. Toss gently with the chickpeas, cover, and let stand for 10 minutes for the chickpeas to heat through.

Variation with Lentils: In place of all or a portion of the chickpeas, use cooked lentils, preferably the French green ones from Le Puy. ⓥ

Rice Gratins

Instead of serving rice and a vegetable, combining the two and binding them with a light béchamel sauce makes a more substantial main dish. Like vegetable gratins, rice gratins can be made ahead of time and baked later. They can even be made from leftover rice. These gratins are easy to multiply and to improvise using vegetables and grains other than those suggested or by adding a covering of bread crumbs for contrasting texture. Leftovers can be cut into squares and heated in an oven or in a skillet. Allow 25 to 35 minutes for baking, depending on whether or not the ingredients are warm or chilled from the refrigerator. Those who don't eat dairy can use oil in place of butter and nondairy milk or stock.

Rice and Spinach Gratin

Serve warm with a sauce of tomatoes or peppers, or cold with Saffron Mayonnaise (page 52) or Salsa Verde (page 48).
Serves 4 (V)

Béchamel for Rice Gratins (opposite)

2 bunches spinach leaves

2 tablespoons olive oil or butter

$1/2$ cup finely chopped green onions, including an inch or two of the greens

2 small cloves garlic, minced

2 tablespoons chopped parsley

2 tablespoons chopped dill

2 tablespoons chopped marjoram

Sea salt and freshly milled pepper

1 cup white or brown rice, cooked

1 cup ricotta or cottage cheese, optional

Preheat the oven to 400°F and lightly butter or oil a baking dish. Make the béchamel sauce. Cook the spinach in a wide skillet in the water clinging to its leaves until limp, just a few minutes. Rinse it quickly, then squeeze out the water and finely chop.

In a wide skillet, cook the spinach in the oil with the green onions, garlic, and chopped herbs for about 3 minutes. Season with salt and pepper to taste. Combine the rice with the spinach, sauce, and ricotta. Turn into the dish and bake until puffed and lightly browned, about 25 minutes.

Béchamel for Rice Gratins

Makes about $1^1/_2$ cups (V)

$1/4$ cup minced shallot or onion

3 tablespoons butter or oil

2 tablespoons flour

$1^1/_2$ cups milk, scalded (can be nondairy milk)

$1/2$ teaspoon sea salt

Freshly milled white pepper

$1/2$ teaspoon grated nutmeg

Cook the shallot in the butter in a small saucepan over low heat for 3 minutes. Stir in the flour and cook for 2 minutes more. Whisk in the hot milk all at once, then cook for 20 minutes, stirring frequently, or for 30 minutes in the top of a double boiler. Season with the salt, a little white pepper, and the nutmeg.

Wild Rice and Celery Root Gratin

You can make a very good version of this gratin without dairy by using Mushroom Stock (page 176) in the béchamel sauce and omitting the cheese. In place of the cheese, add $1/2$ cup toasted ground walnuts or almonds. Serves 4 to 6 (V)

Béchamel for Rice Gratins (above)

1 tablespoon butter

1 small celery root, peeled and grated

Juice of 1 lemon

1 clove garlic, minced

2 tablespoons chopped parsley, plus extra for garnish

Sea salt and freshly milled pepper

3 cups wild rice or Calico Rice (page 478), cooked

$1/2$ cup grated Gruyère

$1/4$ cup freshly grated parmesan

Preheat the oven to 400°F. Lightly butter or oil a baking dish and make the béchamel. Melt the butter in a medium skillet over medium heat. Add the celery root with the lemon juice, garlic, and parsley and cook until tender, about 5 to 7 minutes. Season with salt and pepper to taste. Combine the wild rice, celery root, and sauce and stir in the cheeses. Turn into the dish and bake until firm, about 25 minutes. Sprinkle with chopped parsley and serve.

Rice and Summer Squash Gratin

Here's a summer variation of the preceding recipe. Serves 4

- 1 cup white rice, cooked
- Béchamel for Rice Gratins (page 484)
- 1 tablespoon olive oil
- 1 pound zucchini, coarsely grated
- 1 clove garlic, minced
- 1 tablespoon chopped marjoram, or 2 tablespoons chopped basil
- Sea salt and freshly milled pepper
- 1/4 cup freshly grated parmesan
- 1/2 cup grated mozzarella
- Red Pepper Sauce (page 64) or Fresh Tomato Sauce (page 54), for serving

Preheat the oven to 400°F. Lightly butter or oil an 8- to 12-cup gratin dish. Cook the rice and make the béchamel sauce. Heat the oil in a wide skillet. Add the zucchini and sauté, stirring frequently, over high heat until dry and beginning to color in places, about 12 to 15 minutes. Toward the end, add the garlic and marjoram and season with salt and pepper. Combine the rice, zucchini mixture, cheeses, and béchamel sauce. Turn into the dish and bake until firm and golden, about 25 minutes. Serve with either sauce.

Rice and Winter Squash Gratin

Serves 4

- Béchamel for Rice Gratins (page 484)
- 1 cup long-grain brown or white rice, cooked
- 1 tablespoon butter or olive oil
- 1 tablespoon chopped sage or 2 teaspoons crumbled dried
- 2 to 3 cups coarsely grated butternut or other winter squash
- 1/2 teaspoon sea salt
- 2 cloves garlic, chopped
- 1/4 cup chopped parsley
- 1/2 cup grated Gruyère or fontina
- Freshly milled pepper

Preheat the oven to 400°F. Lightly butter a 6- to 8-cup gratin dish or 4 individual ramekins. Make the sauce and cook the rice, unless you're using leftovers. Heat the butter with the sage in a wide skillet over medium-high heat. Add the squash and salt and sauté until the squash begins to brown in places, about 8 minutes. Toward the end, stir in the garlic and parsley. Combine the rice, sauce, squash, and cheese. Taste for salt and season with pepper. Turn into the dish and bake until hot and beginning to form a crust on top, 25 to 35 minutes.

Rice and Eggs: Wholesome Fast Food

Made from ingredients anyone's likely to have on hand, this combination makes a fast, nourishing dish that is homey and comforting. The heat of the rice cooks the egg—and any hot grain or noodle would do the same. One cup cooked rice to one egg is a reasonable proportion. Embellishments include a little grated cheese, a spoonful of pesto, a handful of chopped herbs, toasted nuts, cooked greens or artichokes, roasted peppers, sautéed mushrooms, or peas.

Brown Rice and Eggs with Pungent Greens and Walnuts

Serves 4 to 6

- 1 1/2 cups brown rice
- 2 bunches mustard greens, stems removed
- 1 large clove garlic, minced or pressed
- 2 tablespoons olive oil
- Sea salt
- 1 or 2 eggs
- 1/2 cup toasted chopped walnuts or Salt and Pepper Walnuts (page 79)
- Grated Pecorino Romano, for serving

Boil the rice in salted water until tender, 30 to 50 minutes, depending on whether it's long- or short-grain. Meanwhile, cook the greens in 8 cups salted boiling water until tender, 5 to 7 minutes. Drain, then press out the liquid and coarsely chop them. Toss the greens with the garlic and oil and season with salt to taste. When the rice is done, drain it, then return it to the pot and rapidly stir in the eggs until well coated. Add the greens and walnuts and toss again. Serve with a light covering of grated cheese.

Basic Rice and Eggs

Serves 4 to 6

1½ cups rice
1 or 2 eggs
Sea salt and freshly milled pepper
2 tablespoons butter
½ to 1 cup grated provolone

Boil or steam the rice as described on pages 475–476. Beat the eggs until light and frothy, with a few pinches salt and plenty of pepper. When the rice is done, drain it and shake off the water if boiled and return it to the pot. Rapidly stir in the beaten egg, butter, and cheese. If you work quickly, the egg should cook evenly and be invisible except for its shine.

Rice and Eggs with Pesto, Pine Nuts, and Tomatoes

This summer dish is good hot or tepid. Use pesto or any other favorite herb sauce, such as the Cilantro Salsa (page 49) or Salsa Verde with Walnuts and Tarragon (page 49), in which case omit the pine nuts from the recipe. Serves 4

Basic Rice and Eggs (opposite), without cheese
⅓ cup Pesto (page 50) or Basil Puree (page 51)
2 tablespoons pine nuts, toasted until golden
¼ cup finely diced feta or freshly grated parmesan
Sea salt
1 ripe tomato, seeded and diced

Make the rice and eggs as described, then add the pesto, pine nuts, and cheese. Taste for salt. Serve with the tomatoes scattered over the top.

Risotto

Like pasta, these creamy grains of rice serve as a backdrop for an array of vegetable seasonings. While perhaps most comforting in colder weather, risotto can move gracefully through the seasons, especially where summers are cool. Spring starts with a risotto of asparagus and saffron, then moves on to summer with tiny cubes of tender squash. Fall follows with a robust wild mushroom and red wine risotto, and winter is the season for a scarlet beet risotto or a luxurious risotto gratin.

The most important ingredient in risotto is the rice itself, which must be a short, plump, starchy grain. Italian Arborio and Carnaroli rice can be found easily today, where once it was only found in gourmet markets. The way the rice is cooked enables the starch to form a velvety sauce, yielding a marvelous combination of silky and chewy textures—at once comforting and titillating.

How to Make Risotto

This method applies to virtually all risotto dishes. Once you've grasped these basics, you'll see how quickly improvisations suggest themselves.

1. **Have your stock simmering on the stove.** For one recipe, you'll need 5½ to 6½ cups stock. Use a well-made stock that's full of flavor and seasoned with salt. The Basic Vegetable Stock (page 175), fortified with extra vegetables plus generous trimmings from the risotto vegetables, will do fine. Season it with salt and have it simmering on the stove when you begin.

2. **Melt the butter in a wide pot.** In risotto, butter is a seasoning as well as a cooking medium, although it is possible to use oil. You need a wide pot so that the broth can cook sufficiently quickly. A narrow, tall pot just won't work; a wide skillet is a better choice.

3. **Add the onion and cook until softened.** As with a soup, onion helps create a flavor base. It should take just 3 to 4 minutes over medium heat to soften; it needn't brown.

4. **Add the rice to the pot.** Stir it around for a minute or so to thoroughly coat the grains with the butter. (And never rinse the rice, or you'll lose the starch that's essential to the dish.)

5. **Add the wine and stir until it's absorbed.** Wine gives risotto an acid note that lifts up the flavors. If you cook two risottos, one with and one without wine, you can readily taste the difference. If you don't want to use wine, bring up the flavors at the end with just a little lemon juice.

6. **Begin adding the simmering stock.** When you add the stock, the heat should be high enough to maintain a lively bubble. There are two ways to incorporate it into the rice. The most traditional way is to add it in $1/2$-cup increments. With constant stirring and the right heat, each increment should take about 2 minutes to be absorbed. The other way is to start by adding 2 cups of the stock and letting it simmer, stirring only occasionally, until it's absorbed by the rice. The remainder of the stock is then added in $1/2$-cup increments until the risotto is done, stirring continually. While less traditional, this method gives you a little grace period at the beginning of the cooking if something else comes up, and it makes perfectly good risotto. You can also use a pressure cooker, but I think that one of the nice things about making risotto is actually standing there, stirring, and seeing it come, as if by magic, together.

7. **Add the final broth, vegetables, and seasonings.** The timing of the last two additions is a fiddly stage that requires tasting and adjusting to make sure the grain is cooked and the sauce is right. The risotto should be pourable but not thin. The vegetables, cheese, cream, and herbs are added during the last few minutes. Once they've gone in, turn off the heat and stir more energetically to combine them. Taste for salt and, if adding lemon, do so now. Serve right away in heated soup plates.

ALTITUDE: At altitudes higher than 5,000 feet, you'll need to increase your cooking time by 5 to 15 minutes to make up for the lower temperature of the boiling stock. This also means that you'll need an extra cup or so of stock.

TIMING: Risotto is best when you make the dish from start to finish without a pause. Before you begin, have the table set, soup plates warmed, and everyone ready to eat. However, most restaurants have a trick that you can use at home. You will need an extra cup of stock.

A RESTAURANT TRICK: Cook the risotto up to the last two additions of stock, then spread it out on a sheet pan and refrigerate immediately to stop the cooking. When you're ready to resume, return it to the pan and add the extra cup of stock to loosen the grains. Finish the risotto as you would normally, making the last two additions plus the vegetables and seasonings.

Vegans can make many of these risotto recipes if they simply omit the cheese and cream, and use oil in place of butter.

Artichoke Risotto

Make this at the peak of artichoke season—during April and again in September. If you aren't able to get mascarpone, use crème fraîche in its place. Serves 4 Ⓥ

4 large artichokes, trimmed, quartered, and thinly sliced (page 295)

2 tablespoons olive oil

Sea salt and freshly milled pepper

$5^{1}/_{2}$ to $6^{1}/_{2}$ cups Basic Vegetable Stock (page 175)

2 tablespoons butter

$1/2$ cup finely diced onion

1 clove garlic, minced

$1^{1}/_{2}$ cups Arborio or Carnaroli rice

$1/2$ cup dry white wine

$1/2$ cup mascarpone, crème fraîche, or cream

$3/4$ cup freshly grated parmesan

$1/2$ cup finely chopped parsley, chervil, or tarragon

Prepare the artichokes, then drain and pat them dry. Heat the oil in a wide skillet. Add the artichokes and sauté over medium–high heat until golden and tender, 10 to 12 minutes. Season with salt and pepper and set half of them aside. Chop the remainder. (This can be done ahead of time.)

Have the stock simmering on the stove. Melt the butter in a wide soup pot. Add the onion and cook over medium heat until softened, about 4 minutes, adding the chopped artichokes and the garlic halfway through. Add the rice and cook and stir for 1 minute. Pour in the wine and simmer until it has been absorbed.

Add 2 cups stock, cover, and cook at a lively simmer until it's absorbed. Begin adding the stock in $^1/_2$-cup increments, stirring constantly until each addition is absorbed before adding the next. When the rice tastes done, stir in the mascarpone, $^1/_2$ cup of the parmesan, and all but 2 tablespoons of the parsley. Taste and season with salt and pepper. Warm the remaining artichokes in their pan during the last few minutes of cooking, then spoon them over the rice and serve garnished with the remaining parmesan and parsley.

Dried Wild Mushroom Risotto

The mushroom stock combined with the red wine makes a risotto with flavor to match its mahogany color. A good choice for a company meal. In lieu of making your own stock, a commercial mushroom stock is not a bad choice. Serves 4

$^1/_2$ ounce or more dried porcini

$5^1/_2$ cups Mushroom Stock (page 176) or commercial mushroom stock

2 tablespoons butter, plus extra to finish

3 plump shallots, finely diced

$1^1/_2$ cups Arborio or Carnaroli rice

$^1/_2$ cup dry red wine

3 tablespoons chopped parsley or a mixture of parsley and rosemary

$^1/_2$ cup freshly grated parmesan

Sea salt and freshly milled pepper

Soak the dried mushrooms in 1 cup warm water for 30 minutes, then lift them out and strain the liquid. Add it to the stock and bring to a simmer. Finely chop the mushrooms.

Heat the butter in a wide soup pot, add the shallots, and cook over medium heat until translucent and soft, 3 to 5 minutes. Add the rice and cook, stirring frequently, for 1 minute. Add the mushrooms and wine and simmer until the wine is absorbed, stirring a few times, then add 2 cups stock, cover, and cook at a lively simmer until it's

absorbed. Begin adding the stock in $^1/_2$-cup increments, stirring constantly until each addition is absorbed before adding the next. When the rice is cooked, stir in the parsley, cheese, and an additional tablespoon or two of butter. Taste for salt and season with pepper.

Beet Risotto with Greens

If you're wary of beets—I ordered my first beet risotto with great doubts—be assured that this risotto has not only an incredible jewel-like color but also a delicious, deep taste, tempered by the greens, lemon, and parmesan. Serves 4

$5^1/_2$ to $6^1/_2$ cups Basic Vegetable Stock (page 175), including beet or chard stems

3 tablespoons butter or a mixture of butter and olive oil

$^1/_2$ cup finely diced onion

$1^1/_2$ cups Arborio or Carnaroli rice

$^1/_2$ cup dry white wine

2 tablespoons chopped parsley

2 tablespoons chopped basil or 1 tablespoon dried

2 or 3 medium beets, peeled and grated, about 2 cups

2 to 3 cups greens—beet, chard, kale, or spinach—stems removed, finely chopped

Sea salt and freshly milled pepper

Grated zest and juice of 1 lemon

$^1/_2$ cup freshly grated parmesan

Have the stock simmering on the stove. Heat the butter in a wide pot, add the onion, and cook over medium heat for 3 minutes, stirring frequently. Add the rice, stir to coat it well, and cook for 1 minute. Add the wine and simmer until it's absorbed, then stir in half the parsley, the basil, grated beets, and the beet greens, chard, or kale. Add 2 cups stock, cover, and cook at a lively simmer until the stock is absorbed. Begin adding the remaining stock in $^1/_2$-cup increments, stirring constantly until each addition is absorbed before adding the next. When you have 1 cup left, add the spinach, if using. Taste for salt, season with pepper, then stir in the lemon zest and juice to taste. Serve dusted with the cheese and the remaining parsley.

Fresh Mushroom Risotto

Mushroom Stock supplies this risotto with a huge amount of flavor. You can have it ready ahead of time. Serves 4

Mushrooms

2 tablespoons butter

1 tablespoon olive oil

1/2 cup finely diced white onion or shallot

12 to 16 ounces white or portabella mushrooms, thinly sliced

1 large clove garlic, finely chopped

Sea salt and freshly milled pepper

1/2 lemon

Rice

5 1/2 to 6 1/2 cups Mushroom Stock (page 176) or commercial stock

2 tablespoons butter

1/3 cup finely diced onion or shallot

1 1/2 cups Arborio or Carnaroli rice

1/2 cup dry white wine or Marsala

1/3 to 1/2 cup cream

Salt and freshly milled pepper

1/2 cup freshly grated parmesan

1/4 cup chopped parsley

Heat the butter and oil in a wide skillet, add the white onion, and cook over medium heat for about 5 minutes, stirring frequently. Add the mushrooms, raise the heat, and sauté until browned around the edges, about 5 minutes. Add the garlic, season with salt and pepper, and squeeze the lemon juice over all. Turn off the heat and set aside.

Have the stock at a simmer. Melt the butter in a wide pot. Add the onion and cook over medium heat to soften, 3 to 4 minutes. Add the rice, stir to coat, and cook for 1 minute. Add the wine and simmer until it's completely absorbed. Add 2 cups stock, cover, and cook at a lively simmer until it's absorbed. Begin adding the stock in 1/2-cup increments, stirring constantly until each addition is absorbed before adding the next one. About halfway through, add the mushrooms. After the last addition, add the cream and stir with more vigor. Taste for salt and season with pepper. Stir in the parmesan and parsley and serve.

Risotto with Green Onions, Lemon, and Basil

Scallions, lemon zest, a few hothouse basil leaves—these simple ingredients taste bright and springy, making this a dish to turn to when the weather is drab. Be sure to use the green onion roots and extra greens in the stock. Serves 4

4 bunches green onions, including a few inches of the greens

3 tablespoons butter

Sea salt and freshly milled pepper

5 1/2 to 6 1/2 cups Basic Vegetable Stock (page 175)

1/3 cup finely diced shallot or white onion

1 1/2 cups Arborio or Carnaroli rice

1/2 cup dry white wine

1/2 cup cream or crème fraîche

1 cup finely chopped parsley

4 thinly slivered basil leaves

2 teaspoons finely grated lemon zest

1 1/3 cup freshly grated parmesan

Trim and thinly slice the green onions. Cook them in 1 tablespoon of the butter until softened, 3 to 4 minutes, then season with salt and pepper and set aside.

Have the stock simmering on the stove. Melt the remaining butter in a wide pot. Add the shallot and cook over medium heat for 3 to 4 minutes, stirring frequently. Add the rice, stir to coat the grains, and cook for 1 minute. Add the wine and simmer until it's absorbed. Add 2 cups stock, cover, and cook at a lively simmer until it's absorbed. Begin adding the rest in 1/2-cup increments, stirring constantly until each addition is absorbed before adding the next. When the rice is nearly finished cooking, stir in the green onions and cream and cook for 1 minute. Add the parsley, basil, and lemon zest. Taste for salt, season with pepper, and serve with a dusting of cheese.

Vivid Parsley and Pea Risotto

These ingredients are so simple, yet the overall effect is stunningly green and fresh tasting. The parsley sauce can be made a day ahead. Serves 4 ⓥ

2 large bunches parsley, preferably flat-leaf

1/4 teaspoon sea salt

4 to 5 lovage leaves

Freshly milled white pepper

4 1/2 or 5 cups Basic Vegetable Stock (page 175) or water

2 tablespoons butter

1/2 cup diced onion or leek

1 1/2 cups Arborio or Carnaroli rice

1/2 cup dry white wine

1 1/2 cups fresh or frozen peas

1/2 cup cream, optional

1/2 cup freshly grated parmesan

Pea shoots, for garnish

With a sharp knife, shave off most of the parsley leaves. Using your fingers, break off the larger stems and use them in the vegetable stock. Measure 3 cups leaves, well packed but not crammed.

Bring 1 1/2 cups water to a boil. Add the salt, parsley, and lovage. Boil for 1 minute. Turn off the heat, let stand for 5 minutes, then puree in a blender at high speed until smooth. Taste for salt and season with white pepper.

Have the stock simmering on the stove. If the parsley sauce has been refrigerated, bring it to a boil, then turn off the heat.

Melt the butter in a wide pot. Add the onion and cook over medium heat until softened, 3 to 4 minutes. Add the rice and cook, stirring frequently for 1 minute, then pour in the wine and simmer until it's absorbed. Add 2 cups stock, cover, and simmer, stirring occasionally until it's absorbed. Begin adding the remaining stock in 1/2-cup increments, stirring constantly until each addition is absorbed before adding the next. When all has been absorbed and the rice is very nearly clone, add the parsley sauce. Raise the heat and cook briskly while stirring until the rice is done and most of the sauce has been absorbed. Add the peas and cream. Taste for salt and season with pepper. Turn off the heat and stir in half the cheese. Serve dusted with the remaining cheese and garnish with pea shoots.

Risotto with Garden Peas, Basil, and Saffron

The last of the peas and the first of the tomatoes are captured in this early summer risotto. This is one of the nicest ways to feature garden peas. Use a few handfuls of the pods in the vegetable stock. Serves 4 ⓥ

2 pounds fresh pod peas or 2 cups frozen

6 cups Basic Vegetable Stock (page 175)

2 tablespoons butter

1/2 cup finely chopped shallot or onion

2 pinches saffron threads, ground in a mortar

1 1/2 cups Arborio or Carnaroli rice

1/2 cup dry white wine

1/2 cup mascarpone or crème fraîche, optional

1/2 cup freshly grated parmesan, plus extra to finish

3 tomatoes, peeled, seeded, and diced

8 large basil leaves, thinly sliced

Sea salt and freshly milled pepper

Snipped chives, to finish

Shuck the peas if using fresh ones. Have the stock simmering on the stove.

Melt the butter in a wide pot. Add the shallot and saffron and cook over low heat, stirring occasionally, until the shallot has softened and the saffron has released its color, about 3 minutes. Stir in the rice and cook for 1 minute. Raise the heat, add the wine, and cook until it's absorbed. Add 2 cups stock, cover, and cook at a lively simmer until it's absorbed. Begin adding the stock in 1/2-cup increments, stirring constantly until each addition is absorbed before adding the next. When the rice is nearly done and only two more additions remain, stir in the peas. Add the last of the stock, then stir in the mascarpone, parmesan, tomatoes, and basil. Taste for salt, season with pepper, and serve with extra cheese and chives strewn over the top.

Sizzling Risotto Gratin

This glorious and utterly luxurious recipe hails from the Val d' Aosta, a region near the Italian Alps that's famous for its creamy Fontina. Unlike most, this risotto is cooked in advance and then finished in the oven. It makes a stunning winter supper, preceded by an array of grated vegetable salads. I considered removing this recipe from the new edition of this book, but two young women I met insisted I leave it, saying it was their favorite dish. Serves 4 to 6 (V)

3¹/₂ cups Basic Vegetable Stock (page 175)

¹/₄ cup butter

1 small red onion, finely diced

1³/₄ cups Arborio or Carnaroli rice

1 cup dry white wine

8 ounces Italian Fontina, cut into tiny cubes, about 2 cups

1 cup cream

Few pinches freshly grated nutmeg

Have the stock simmering on the stove. Butter an 8-cup gratin dish.

Melt the butter in a wide pot. Add the onion and cook over medium heat until soft and translucent, about 3 minutes. Add the rice, raise the heat a little, and cook, stirring constantly, for about 3 minutes. Add the wine, raise the heat to high, and simmer until it's completely absorbed. Add half the stock, adjust the heat so that the liquid is simmering briskly, and cook, stirring occasionally until it is mostly absorbed, about 12 minutes. Add the remaining stock in ¹/₂-cup increments, stirring constantly, until each addition is absorbed before adding the next.

Remove the rice from the heat and stir in the cheese, cream, and nutmeg. Taste and adjust the seasonings if needed, then pour the rice into the gratin dish. Cover with plastic wrap and leave at room temperature until you're ready to serve.

Preheat the oven to 450°F and set the oven rack in the top third of the oven. Bake the risotto until it's sizzling and golden, about 15 minutes. If it's not browning, turn on the broiler for a final minute so that the surface is a rich gold. Serve immediately.

Risotto Croquettes

Croquettes made with leftover risotto are so good that you might actually start out with them in mind rather than hope for leftovers. They make a charming vegetarian main dish set on a plate surrounded with salad greens, a sauce, or a simple vegetable accompaniment. Serves 4 to 6

2 eggs

¹/₂ cup milk

Sea salt and freshly milled pepper

3 cups fresh bread crumbs

Risotto, any of the preceding recipes, chilled

Clarified butter or light olive oil, for frying

Beat the eggs with the milk in a pie plate and season with salt and pepper. Put the bread crumbs in another pie plate. Scoop the risotto up with a spoon and form it into a flattened oval about 3 inches long. (Or simply divide the rice into the number of portions you need.) Using one hand, slide the croquettes into the egg, then scoop them out and put them in the dish with the bread crumbs. Using the other hand, roll them around so that they're covered, then transfer to a large plate.

If you're not planning to cook them right away, cover with wax paper and refrigerate, but allow them to come to room temperature before cooking. Fry them in clarified butter until crisp and golden. Serve hot.

Risotto-Stuffed Vegetables: If you'd rather avoid breading and frying, use leftover risotto to fill stuffed peppers, tomatoes, eggplants, cabbage, or chard leaves. Mound the filling, but don't pack it, then bake at 375°F until heated through, about 25 minutes.

Wheat: New and Ancient Forms

Wheat is one of the principal cereals consumed throughout the world. Most of it is eaten in its milled form in bread and pasta, but is also enjoyed as cracked wheat and bulgur, wheat flakes, wheat berries, semolina, and couscous (which is actually a pasta).

There are many varieties and strains of wheat, including some of the truly ancient forms that have become known in recent years, namely einkorn, emmer, spelt, and kamut. These grains are of special interest to those who are challenged by the higher gluten content of modern wheat. They can be eaten as a grain or in milled form where they are included in pasta and sold as flour. Farro is chic, popular, and expensive. It is now more readily available in stores, and is easily bought online from such places as Bluebird Grain Farms and Anson Mills.

The ancient strains are the antecedents to our modern hybrids. Spelt and kamut are of special interest to those who have wheat intolerances, for they contain a more digestible form of gluten. Yet in terms of flavor and texture, they behave enough like wheat to make them a successful alternative ingredient in some processed foods, such as pasta. Similarly, older varieties (but not ancient ones) like Turkey Red, Sonoran White, and Red Fife are making a comeback and are better tolerated than modern wheats by those with gluten sensitivities.

Whole Spelt and Kamut: These very large, dense grains are best added to soups, mixed with other grains, or used in grain-based salads. Both benefit from an overnight soaking or quick soak. They take 1 to 2 hours to cook, 40 minutes in a pressure cooker, or overnight in a slow cooker. As with dried beans, add salt toward the end of cooking. Ⓥ

1 cup spelt yields about 2¼ cups cooked
1 cup kamut yields about 2¾ cups cooked

Rolled and Flaked Spelt: In this form, spelt is easy and fast to cook, perhaps more accessible than the same grain in its longer-cooking whole form. Cover 1 cup flaked spelt with 2 cups boiling water, cover, and allow to stand for 10 minutes or until the liquid is absorbed. Season with a pinch of salt, freshly milled pepper, and a little butter, olive oil, or nut oil. Also see Savory Barley Flakes (page 460) for another use for spelt. Ⓥ

Wheat Berries

Frozen cooked wheat berries are a convenient item to have on hand, so cook enough to have some left over. If you have time to soak wheat berries overnight, they'll cook more quickly and be easier to digest. A quick soak is also helpful.
Makes about 4 cups Ⓥ

1 cup wheat berries, soaked overnight and drained
¹⁄₂ teaspoon sea salt

On the Stove: Put the wheat berries in a pot with plenty of water to cover by a few inches. Bring to a boil, then lower the heat, cover the pot, and simmer until they're tender, 1 to 2 hours. Add the salt once they've started to soften.

In the Pressure Cooker: Combine unsoaked wheat berries, 8 cups water, and the salt. Bring to pressure and cook for 30 minutes. Let the pressure drop slowly or release, then check for doneness. If they're still a little hard, cover the pot and simmer until they're soft.

Peeled Wheat Kernels

These skinned grains of wheat cook more quickly and tenderly than wheat berries, but finding them might be difficult. I buy mine at a Middle Eastern market, where they're sold as golden peeled wheat. Makes about 3 cups (V)

---

1 cup peeled wheat, soaked overnight and drained

1/2 teaspoon sea salt

Put the wheat in a saucepan with water to cover by several inches and bring to a boil. Lower the heat, cover the pan, and simmer until the grain is tender, 30 to 40 minutes. Add the salt after 15 minutes. If it cooks for the longer amount of time, it will become glutinous, like barley, making a soothing morning cereal, pudding, or addition to baked goods. Cooked slightly less, it remains distinct and can be added to soups and other grain dishes.

Wheat Berries with Chickpeas, Lentils, and Tarragon

Here's where those frozen wheat berries can come in handy. If you use canned chickpeas, you can make this dish in about 25 minutes. Serves 4 to 6 (V)

---

1 1/2 tablespoons olive oil

1 onion, diced

1 green bell pepper, finely chopped

1 tablespoon chopped tarragon

3/4 cup French green lentils, sorted and soaked for 1 hour, if possible

1/2 teaspoon sea salt

2 cups cooked wheat berries or peeled wheat

1 1/2 cups cooked chickpeas, rinsed if canned

Freshly milled pepper

Additional olive oil or roasted walnut oil, to finish

Heat the oil in a small soup pot. Add the onion, bell pepper, and tarragon and cook over medium heat, stirring frequently, until the onion begins to color, about 7 minutes. Add the lentils, 5 cups water, and salt and bring to a boil. Lower the heat and simmer, covered, until nearly tender, about 20 minutes. Add the wheat berries and chickpeas; continue cooking until they're warmed through and the lentils are tender, about 5 minutes. Drain (reserve the liquid for stock) and pour the grains into a serving dish. Taste for salt, season with pepper, and drizzle generously with olive or walnut oil.

Variations: A splash of fresh lemon juice, chopped parsley, and additional fresh tarragon transform this dish into a salad. Any left over can be tossed with pasta, such as farfalle, along with fresh herbs and toasted chopped walnuts. (V)

Bulgur

Spelled many ways and often mistaken for cracked wheat, bulgur is wheat that has been steamed whole, then dried and cracked into grits. The steaming precooks the grain, making bulgur very quick to prepare, a boon for today's busy cooks.

Bulgur comes in three sizes. Very fine bulgur is used for tabbouleh, and the coarsest size is used for pilafs. The medium size can go in either direction. Bulgur needs only to be soaked to become tender, but it can also be cooked. Middle Eastern markets as well as natural foods stores are good sources for bulgur.

Light but roundly flavored, bulgur is excellent on its own or mixed with rice, chickpeas, and lentils in salads, soups, or side dishes.

Cooked Bulgur

Anyone looking for a quick grain to prepare need look no further. Serves 4 (V)

---

1 cup bulgur, any size

Sea salt and freshly milled pepper

1 tablespoon butter, olive oil, or roasted walnut oil

Garnishes: chopped parsley, dill or tarragon; toasted pine nuts or walnuts; currants, dried cherries, or pomegranate seeds, optional

---

Rinse the bulgur to remove any dust. Put it in a bowl with a few pinches salt and pour on 2 1/2 cups boiling water. Cover and let stand for 15 minutes for fine bulgur, 25 minutes for medium. If there's any excess water, pour the bulgur into a strainer. Toss with butter. Taste for salt, season with pepper, and toss with any of the garnishes.

Bulgur Pilaf with Pine Nuts and Currants

Not only a quick-cooking side dish, this pilaf also makes an excellent filling for cabbage, chard, and grape leaves.
Makes 4 cups (V)

1 to 2 tablespoons olive oil
1 small onion, very finely diced
1 clove garlic, minced
1 tablespoon chopped dill or 1 teaspoon dried
1/2 teaspoon ground allspice
1 cup buigur, rinsed
1/4 teaspoon sea salt
1/3 cup currants, dried cranberries, or dried cherries
1/3 cup toasted pine nuts

Heat the oil in an 8-inch skillet or a 12-cup saucepan over medium heat. Add the onion, garlic, dill, and allspice and cook, stirring frequently, until the onion is translucent, 3 to 4 minutes. Add the bulgur and salt and cook for 1 minute more. Pour in 1 1/4 cups water, bring it to a boil, then lower the heat and cook, covered, for 10 minutes. Stir in the currants, remove from the heat, cover, and let stand for 5 minutes more. Fluff with a fork, add the pine nuts, and fluff again.

Cracked Wheat

Cracked wheat resembles bulgur, but the whole kernels have not been steamed previously, so it needs to be cooked. Cracked wheat comes in two sizes—medium and coarse. Medium is what we usually see. Cracked wheat doesn't take long to cook, and like bulgur, it's very good mixed with legumes, especially chickpeas and lentils, as well as with pasta and rice.

Cracked Wheat

The flavor of this grain may remind you of Wheatena or Bear Mush cereal. You can cook this right in a deep skillet. If you don't have one with 2-inch sides, add the toasted wheat to the water in a saucepan. Serves 4 to 6 (V)

1 cup cracked wheat
1/2 teaspoon sea salt

1 tablespoon butter or olive oil
2 tablespoons chopped parsley
Freshly milled pepper

Toast the wheat in a dry skillet with 2-inch sides over medium heat. Stir constantly, until it gives off a warm, nutty aroma, after a few minutes. Stir in 2 1/2 cups boiling water and salt. Lower the heat and simmer, covered, until the grain is tender, about 15 minutes. Set a cloth under the lid and let stand for 5 to 10 minutes. With a fork, fluff in the butter, adding more to taste if you like, then lightly stir in the parsley, and season with pepper.

Cracked Wheat Pilaf with Tomato and Cinnamon

Serve this pilaf with a yogurt sauce and accompany with grilled eggplant, golden zucchini coins, or a vegetable stew, especially one based on eggplant and chickpeas.
Serves 4 to 6 (V)

2 tablespoons olive oil or butter
1 onion, finely diced
1 cup cracked wheat
1/4 teaspoon ground cinnamon
1/2 teaspoon sea salt
1 cup finely diced tomatoes, juice reserved
1/4 cup chopped parsley
Freshly milled pepper

Heat the oil in a heavy saucepan over medium heat. Add the onion and cook, stirring frequently, until it begins to color, about 10 minutes. Add the cracked wheat, cinnamon, and salt and stir to coat the grains. Stir in the tomatoes and the reserved juice plus enough water to make 2 1/2 cups, and bring to a boil. Lower the heat, cover the pot, and simmer until the liquid is absorbed and the wheat is tender, about 15 minutes. Remove from the heat and let stand for 5 minutes. With a fork, lightly stir in the parsley. Taste for salt and season with pepper.

Variation: After the cracked wheat is cooked, toss in 1 to 2 cups cooked chickpeas, lentils, pasta, or green peas. Cover the pan and let stand for 10 minutes. Season with chopped tarragon or dill mixed with or in place of the parsley. (V)

Couscous

Although we treat it as a grain, couscous is actually a small, granular pasta made of semolina. Traditionally, couscous is steamed, which renders it wonderfully light and delicate and nothing like the instant kind most people know. The pilaf method—toasting the grains in oil before adding liquid—also produces couscous with distinctly separate grains; not as light as steamed, but a clear improvement over the box method.

Couscous comes in different sizes: very fine, medium, and large. The extra-fine grains are seldom seen outside of Middle Eastern markets, but the medium is easy to find in boxes or bulk bins, as is the large "Israeli couscous." Couscous sold in bulk seems to be fresher than the packaged, which I've found to be stale. Whole wheat and light-colored couscous cook in the same amount of time and are equally light.

Incidentally, other grains and even pasta can be steamed. Steamed bulgur makes the most delicate tabbouleh, and combining it with couscous makes a more interesting salad than if just one grain is used. Small grains and bulgur cook in about the same time as couscous, and the method is the same.

In *Couscous and Other Good Food from Morocco*, Paula Wolfert describes how to steam couscous, and I more or less follow her method. I admit that I was intimidated before I actually did it. But once you see how it works, you can do it without giving it a second thought.

Couscous by the Pilaf Method

This method is easy to do and the grains come out nice and separate. Makes about 4 cups (V)

- 3 cups water or vegetable broth
- 1 to 2 tablespoons butter, ghee, or olive oil
- 1 cup fine or medium couscous
- 1/2 teaspoon sea salt

Bring the water to a boil. Meanwhile, melt the butter in a 10-inch skillet over medium heat. Add the couscous, stir to coat the grains, and cook for 1 to 2 minutes. The grains will color slightly. Remove from the heat, add the salt, and pour in 2 cups of the water. It will instantly bubble up. When it subsides, shake the pan to even the contents, cover, and set aside for 7 minutes to steam. Fluff the grains with a fork, pour in the last cup of the boiling water, cover, and let stand for 5 minutes. Remove the lid and fluff the couscous before serving.

Israeli Couscous in Mushroom Broth

Those pearls known as Israeli couscous are in fact wheat pasta, as is the smaller couscous. They cook quickly in water, but when mushroom broth is the liquid, they become infused with its flavor, something like a risotto. With a bit of onion and 8 ounces of mushrooms losing luster in the refrigerator I made a quick stock that did the job quite nicely. Of course you can make Mushroom Stock (page 176) or use a commercial one, too. Serves 4

- 2 cups mushroom stock (see headnote)
- 1 1/2 cups Israeli couscous
- Sea salt
- Freshly ground pepper
- Butter to taste
- Freshly grated parmesan, optional

Bring the mushroom stock to a boil in a small saucepan. Add the couscous, return the stock to a boil, then simmer until the liquid is absorbed and the couscous is done, about 10 minutes. Taste for salt—the stock may have been seasoned sufficiently—and grind in plenty of pepper. Stir in butter and grate the cheese over all.

With Mushroom Ragout: Cook the couscous in water and serve it with any of the mushroom ragouts. Or cook in the mushroom stock, then garnish with sautéed mushrooms, tarragon, and finely sliced green onions.

EGGS AND CHEESE

CHAPTER 15

Eggs and Cheese

Eggs are often described as the perfect food. They provide solid nourishment at modest cost in a form that can be used simply and quickly. Parents would do a great service to their offspring by teaching them how to scramble an egg or make an omelet.

Surely no home-cooked food is faster to make than a plate of eggs, nothing is more comforting than a custard, and only eggs can create the magical loft of a soufflé or put a glossy glaze on a bread or pastry. Simply put, eggs do things in the kitchen that other foods just can't do.

We tend to forget that eggs aren't just for breakfast. Sometimes it takes visiting another country to see their potential. In Spain, there's the ubiquitous tortilla, or potato frittata, available everywhere from bars to museum cafeterias from morning until night. In Italy, you can add a slice of frittata to your antipasto plate or slurp a warm froth of zabaglione. Occasionally here at home, one can still find a basket of hard-cooked eggs on a bar or deli counter for quick sustenance. In short, eggs are perfectly suitable for any hour of the day. If you can't or don't eat eggs, but you remember them fondly, turn to egg substitutes or scrambled tofu or ricotta to fill a similar role, especially for breakfast.

While cheese is a very different food altogether, it too is a ready source of solid nourishment. Eggs and cheese flatter one another on such a regular basis that it makes sense for them to reside in the same chapter. A cheese soufflé represents the perfect marriage of eggs and cheese with the eggs providing height, lightness, and strength and the cheese contributing its unique flavor. But these two foods meet in other dishes too—in omelets, flans, custards, savory puddings, timbales, and so forth.

Egg Basics

Since the first edition of *Vegetarian Cooking for Everyone*, our experience with eggs has improved. More and more, people have become familiar with the taste of truly fresh eggs from pastured chickens via their farmers' market or even their own backyard flocks. The popularity of raising chickens for their eccentric friendships as well as theyir good-tasting eggs has risen to heights I couldn't have imagined 15 years ago. It is finally possible to enjoy eggs that do not come from questionable industrial practices.

Hens' eggs come in colors from white and brown to pale green and blue, depending on the breed of the chicken. Nutritionally, however, they're the same, as are fertile and nonfertile eggs. When cracked, a fresh egg looks perky, the yolk and white are bound closely together. As eggs age, they flatten out, and older ones are better for baking than for scrambling, frying, or boiling since their flavor is no longer at its best. Floating an egg in a bowl of water is one way to tell if an egg is fresh: old eggs float; fresh ones sink.

The color of the yolks reflects what chickens have been eating. Chickens I've known that peck at this kernel of corn and that fresh green plant, bug, or blossom as they wander over the yard have eggs with bright, yellow-orange yolks. A friend of mine in New Mexico feeds chile scraps to her hens, and their yolks are a near-alarming shade of orange. The flecks of blood that sometimes appear on the yolk aren't harmful; they indicate that the egg has been fertilized, but you can lift them out with the edge of a shell for aesthetic reasons.

ORGANIC EGGS: While organically raised food is always preferable to use, it's especially important when sound methods are applied to laying hens. Eggs that come from chickens that aren't crammed into small cages, then given boosters of hormones to encourage laying and antibiotics to compensate for the disease crowding fosters, are simply better—for the chickens and for us. They look lively and healthy, the yolks are yellow, they taste better, the chickens who laid them are healthier, and you don't add additional hormones and antibiotics to your own body. Organic feed is expensive and not easy to come by for those who raise chickens, which means their eggs are more expensive. But the taste is worth it, plus they have more omega-3s and I never worry about salmonella when I use them. I find, as do others, they are completely worth the extra cost. The first time you pay five dollars for a dozen eggs might be hard, but soon you realize there's no going back.

CARE AND HANDLING: It's best to store eggs in the refrigerator, preferably in their insulated cartons, at 45°F or less. Eggs are porous and absorb the flavors of nearby foods, so keep them away from onions and other strong flavors. To avoid any possibility of salmonella, discard cracked eggs and handle eggs with clean hands.

Extra egg whites and yolks can be refrigerated for several days. Cover yolks with a little water so that they don't form a skin, then cover with a lid. Egg whites need just a lidded container, whether refrigerated or frozen.

SIZES: Size is determined by weight. A large egg weighs 2 ounces. Five large eggs (or four extra-large or six medium or seven small) equal 1 cup. The yolk is a third of the egg's volume. Large eggs are what I usually buy and are used in the recipes in this book, except for pasta. There I use extra-large eggs. Often a carton from a farmer will have a variety of sizes.

TO SEPARATE THE YOLK FROM THE WHITE: Sharply crack an egg on the edge of a glass or metal bowl, then pry open the shell and let the whites fall into the bowl as you pass the yolk back and forth from shell to shell. The cautionary cry not to have even a speck of yolk in the whites is, in my experience, somewhat exaggerated. Most often, whites will whip up fine even with a speck of yolk present. But as a precautionary measure, break each white into a cup, then add it to the rest. That way, if a lot of yolk gets into one white, you can discard the offending egg without losing the entire batch.

EGG WHITES: Egg whites don't have the richness or flavor of yolks, but they contribute protein and structure to a dish.

Beaten whites expand and trap air, adding volume, lightness, and loft to cakes, soufflés, puffed omelets, and other foods. To reach their maximum volume, they should be at room temperature: cover cold eggs with hot tap water for about 5 minutes to bring them to room temperature, then separate them. Or separate cold eggs, then take the bowl with the whites and swirl it about 4 inches over a burner. Test them frequently with your finger and stop as soon as they feel warm.

When beating whites, avoid using plastic bowls and make sure that all utensils are clean and free of grease, for that's what prevents whites from expanding. Use a whisk, hand mixer, or heavy-duty mixer with a balloon whisk. Begin electric mixers on low speed until the eggs are foamy, then raise the speed to high.

Most recipes will direct you to whisk whites into either soft or firm peaks. Soft peaks droop a little when a clump is taken up on the end of a whisk or a spoon, whereas stiff whites stand straight out. Their look should be glossy and uniform, not dry. When dry, the whites clump and are difficult to fold without overworking and losing loft. I find it's better to err on the side of slightly underbeating whites than overbeating them so that the eggs can be folded in quickly without loss of volume.

EGG YOLKS: Yolks contribute moisture, tenderness, richness, and color—if they themselves have color—to food. One of their other functions is to thicken sauces, such as a béchamel sauce when it becomes the base for a soufflé. To keep egg yolks from curdling in hot liquid, they must first be tempered: whisk the yolks together in a small bowl and gradually add 1/2 cup or so of the hot liquid until the mixture is warm, then return the mixture to the pot.

EGG SUBSTITUTES: Eggs act as binders in foods and contribute moisture and tenderness. A few foods mimic these qualities and can be used in their place. For one egg, substitute:

- 1/2 cup mashed banana, applesauce, or pureed prune in muffins, quick breads, and pancakes, for moisture
- 2 tablespoons cornstarch or arrowroot added to the dry ingredients or dissolved in a few tablespoons water
- Commercial egg replacer
- Crumbled firm tofu or ricotta for scrambled eggs
- 1 tablespoon ground flaxseed mixed with 3 tablespoons water can work as a binder in baked goods to build structure—it will not foam enough to replace beaten egg whites, though.

A NOTE ABOUT SALMONELLA: The bacterium *Salmonella enteridis* can cause illness and, in very extreme cases, death. While a bout with salmonella is bound to be unpleasant, even avian scientists are divided about what to recommend. Outbreaks always cause alarm, but data suggest that it's out of proportion to the actual probability of contracting salmonella poisoning. Outbreaks are also usually traced to mishandling of eggs in institutional settings, where practices are used that home cooks don't usually encounter, such as pooling raw eggs and holding cooked ones. How we respond in our own kitchens is, I believe, a personal matter. I feel confident in the eggs I buy, which are from small free-range flocks raised locally without added hormones and antibiotics. But if I didn't have this option, lived in a part of the country where outbreaks of salmonella poisoning are numerous, or cooked for an elderly or ill person, I might well take the precautions suggested by the American Egg Board: avoid using raw eggs and cook eggs adequately.

Cooking induces pasteurization, which takes place at 140°F if held for 3½ minutes, killing harmful bacteria. Instant-read thermometers (dip them in boiling water first to make them most effective) are best for checking temperatures, but also just cook your eggs until the whites are set and the yolk has begun to thicken.

Eggs: Boiled, Poached, Fried, Scrambled, Steamed, and Baked

To end up with tender eggs rather than rubbery ones, keep the cooking temperature moderate. Heat makes proteins hard, and egg whites are pure protein. The exception is the omelet, which goes into a hot pan of sizzling butter, but it's cooked so quickly that the eggs remain tender.

Boiled Eggs: People tend to boil an egg as they were taught at home. Some prick the end of the egg with a pin so that pressure doesn't build up and crack the shell. Some start eggs in cold water; others lower them into a pot that's already simmering. It really doesn't matter as long as you don't overcook them—that's what makes them dry and hard and surrounds the yolks with a green ring.

The times given are for large eggs cooked at sea level. Above 5,000 feet, water boils at increasingly lower temperatures, so cooking times will be longer. In spite of altitude conversion formulas, I've found that some experimentation is necessary to figure out exact time for high-altitude eggs.

Incidentally, peeling hard-cooked eggs that are very fresh can be a nightmare—the shell breaks into pieces, sticks to the membrane, and when you finally get a piece to come off, a good chunk of the white comes off as well. In the end, the peeled egg looks pockmarked. If you don't mind eating the egg right out of the shell, this isn't a problem. But if you need perfectly peeled eggs, older eggs are preferable.

Soft-Boiled Eggs: The white solidifies but is tender; the yolk is warm and runny. Bring a small saucepan of enough water to cover the egg to a gentle boil, just above a simmer. Set the egg on a spoon, lower it into the pot, and cook for 3 to 3½ minutes. If you're cooking several eggs at once, lower them into the water in a basket so that they'll all begin cooking at the same time.

Medium-Boiled Eggs: These aren't quite as loose as the soft-boiled variety; the egg white is firmer, the yolk soft but not so runny, and the whole thing is actually peelable. Bring water to a gentle boil, lower the egg into the pan, turn off the heat, add a lid, and let stand for 5 minutes.

Hard-Boiled (Hard-Cooked) Eggs: These are the eggs to eat warm with a pinch of salt and pepper, to use for egg salads or composed salad plates. When cut in half, the yolk should have a dime-size moist dot in the center. The boiling time is minimal so that the cooked egg will be tender and moist rather than hard and dry.

Put eggs in a pot with cold water to cover. Bring them to a gentle boil and boil for 1 minute. Turn off the heat, cover, and let stand for 6 minutes. (At 7,000 to 8,000 feet, I find it takes 8 to 10 minutes.) If you're not eating them right away, plunge them into cold water to stop the cooking. Leftover eggs can be refrigerated.

Poached Eggs: Those little oval-shaped poaching tins on legs are reliable, but what you get isn't a true poached egg. A real poached egg swims freely in a swirling water bath. A little vinegar added to the cooking liquid aids in setting the whites, especially when the eggs are very fresh.

Cover an egg with hot water to bring it to room temperature. Put 2 to 3 inches water in a small skillet, bring it to a boil, and add $1/2$ teaspoon vinegar and a few pinches salt. Lower the heat to a simmer. Break the egg on a plate. Stir the water in a circular direction, then slip the egg into the whirlpool. The swirling motion keeps the whites from floating away like rags. Baste the yolks by spooning the water over them until they turn opaque and are set, about 3 minutes or longer for a firmer yolk. Remove the egg with a slotted spoon and set on a slice of waiting toast.

Fried Eggs: Melt a few teaspoons butter in a small nonstick skillet. When it's foaming, break one or two eggs into the pan and set the heat to medium. Cook until the whites are set and the yolks are partially set, about 3 minutes. Serve them sunny side up or give the pan a shake to loosen the eggs and turn them over. Fry on the second side briefly or until the yolk is as firm as you like.

Steam-Fried Eggs, Sunny Side Up: Fry an egg as described, but when the white is set, add a few tablespoons of water, cover the pan, and cook over medium heat until the yolk loses its shine, about 2 minutes.

Steam-Fried Eggs with Chipotle Chile and Grated Cheese: These are breakfast eggs with strength! Make steam-fried eggs, but before adding the water, sprinkle them liberally with grated Jack or cheddar and ground chipotle chile or cayenne. The cheese melts, the chile runs into it, and it's very good. If you don't want the heat of chipotle, use smoked paprika.

Scrambled Eggs

Properly made, scrambled eggs are soft and tender curds. They're wonderful piled on a crisp English muffin or a slice of toasted country bread, accompanied by a mound of spinach or a baked tomato. They're also generously receptive to additions of fresh herbs, cheeses, asparagus tips, or sautéed diced mushrooms—as long as they're in small pieces. Allow two large eggs per person. Serves 2

4 or 5 eggs

2 tablespoons water or milk

Sea salt and freshly milled pepper

1 tablespoon or more butter

Briskly beat the eggs in a bowl with the water and a few pinches salt and pepper. Melt the butter in an omelet pan or a small nonstick skillet. When it's sizzling, lower the heat to low, add the eggs, and slowly begin to stir with a flat-bottomed wooden spoon. Drag the spoon over the bottom of the pan, pulling the cooked egg up with it. As soon as the eggs are as dry or as wet as you like them—or even a moment before—remove them to a warm plate. Scrambled eggs continue to cook from their own heat.

Scrambled Eggs with Fines Herbes: Add 2 teaspoons each chopped chives, parsley, tarragon, and chervil to the eggs before cooking.

Scrambled Eggs with Cheese: Have ready $1/4$ to $1/2$ cup grated cheese near the stove, then add it after the eggs are in the pan. All kinds of cheeses go well with eggs—strong cheddar, mild Jack, cottage cheese, goat cheese, fontina, Gruyère, and smoked cheeses.

Deluxe Scrambled Eggs: Scramble the eggs with cheese and snipped chives or other favored herb, then stir in a few tablespoons small croutons.

Scrambled Eggs with Vegetables: In a tablespoon of butter, sauté 2 to 3 tablespoons diced cooked artichoke hearts, mushrooms, or small cooked asparagus tips. Add mushrooms or asparagus to the eggs once they're in the pan: artichokes should be added at the very end so that they don't discolor the eggs.

Scrambled Eggs with Harissa: If you like your morning eggs with some spice, try these. Beat 2 to 3 teaspoons Harissa (page 66) into the eggs and cook them in a combination of olive oil and butter. Garnish with a few pinches chopped parsley.

Baked or Shirred Eggs

A reliable, easy method for beginners or those who get the willies when it comes to cooking eggs for more than one or two. And that's what this recipe is for, for it doesn't make sense to take the time or trouble to heat up an oven for just a single serving. Use a shallow ovenproof dish that can be brought to the table, so that the eggs nestle next to each other.
Serves 6

---

12 eggs, or 2 eggs per person
Sea salt and freshly milled pepper

Preheat the oven to 400°F. Butter an 8 by 12-inch or equivalent gratin dish. Carefully break the eggs into it, placing them next to each other, then season with salt and pepper. Bake, covered or open, until the yolks are nearly set, anywhere from 6 to 10 minutes. The exact time depends on how quickly the dish conducts the heat, so check them after five minutes. The eggs will continue cooking when removed from the oven.

Baked Eggs with Herbs: Add a sprinkling of chopped parsley, chervil, tarragon, or basil to the eggs as soon as they come out of the oven.

Baked Eggs with Cheese and Bread Crumbs: Loosely cover the bottom of the dish with grated cheese, crack the eggs on top, and cover with additional cheese mixed with several tablespoons fresh bread crumbs and chopped herbs, if desired. Season and bake as described.

Chile Baked Eggs: Spread a little Harissa (page 66) in the bottom of the baking dish along with butter or olive oil. Instead of black pepper, sprinkle ground red chile or paprika over the eggs, then bake as described. Smoked paprika is another good possibility here.

Baked Eggs on Peperonata: Brush the baking dish with olive oil. Heat Peperonata—stewed peppers and tomatoes (page 363)—in a saucepan, then spread it thinly or thickly in the dish. Make small depressions, break the eggs into them, then bake as described.

Baked Eggs with Feta, Tomato, and Marjoram: Butter or oil the dish and add the eggs. Crumble a few tablespoons of feta over the top followed by a scattering of finely diced tomatoes. Season with pepper (the feta will be salty enough that you don't need to add more salt). Bake as described, then remove, and sprinkle freshly chopped marjoram over the top.

Other Ingredients To Use with Baked Eggs

Caramelized Onions (page 358)
Sautéed Mushrooms with Garlic and Parsley (page 351)
Sautéed leeks
Sautéed Spinach (page 378)
Creamed Spinach (page 378)
Cooked summer squash
Gruyére
Toasted bread crumbs

Steamed Eggs

Those little poaching contraptions don't really poach eggs, but they do steam them, leaving a very pure, clean-tasting egg if you don't add anything else, though you can do that. Similarly, you can butter a ramekin or heavy china cup, break in an egg, then steam it, covered, until set and cooked as much as you like. It will take about 4 minutes for the whites to set, leaving the yolks moist and creamy, so have your toast ready.

Steamed Eggs on Toast with Herbs and Vinegar: Finely chop some fresh parsley, chervil, lovage, majoram, or whatever your favorite herb happens to be. Steam the eggs and have your toast ready. When the eggs are done, tip them out onto the toast and mash them gently onto it. Add the herbs, flaky sea salt, freshly milled pepper, and a few drops excellent vinegar, such as Banyuls, sherry vinegar, or a zesty white wine vinegar. Don't use balsamic—it's too sweet.

Omelets

An omelet makes a fine meal, regardless of the hour. From start to finish, an omelet takes just minutes to make. Since they're best when made with just two or three eggs—the heat of the butter and depth of the eggs being easiest to control in small amounts—it's easy to make several omelets in a row when feeding a group. Large omelets aren't impossible to make, but they lose in finesse. Read the instructions first for "A Simple Omelet" if you're not familiar with the technique, because there won't be time to study once you begin.

There are different styles of omelet making. A French omelet is made by simultaneously scrambling the eggs and jerking the pan until the eggs, barely set, can be rolled onto a plate. Another style, so charmingly executed to a Joplin rag in the Japanese movie *Tampopo*, consists of rolling the eggs once they've set by hitting the handle and jerking the pan so that they're thrown to the far edge of the pan. When the whites are separated, beaten, then folded into the yolks, you have the makings of a puffy souffléd omelet.

A Simple Omelet

Serves 1 or 2

2 or 3 eggs
Sea salt and freshly milled pepper
1 tablespoon butter

Using a fork or whisk, beat the eggs in a small bowl with a few pinches salt and pepper just to blend, about 20 strokes. It shouldn't be a uniform mixture. Melt the butter over high heat in an 8-inch omelet pan or nonstick skillet, rotating the pan so that butter coats the bottom and the sides. Allow the butter to sizzle and the foam to subside, then add the beaten eggs and let them sit for 2 to 3 seconds. With a fork—or rubber spatula if using a nonstick pan—begin to draw the lightly cooked egg toward the center of the pan. As you do so, tilt the pan so that uncooked beaten eggs flow into the bare part of the pan. Continue working your way around the pan, pulling the cooked egg in and tilting the pan. When there's just a little moist egg puddled on top, add your filling, if using one, then tilt the pan away from you. Give a few raps on the handle and the far edge should

fall back on itself, then turn the pan over the plate so that the folded omelet falls out. It should be golden on the outside, soft and moist inside.

Omelet Fillings: Except for herbs, which are beaten right into the eggs, add omelet fillings just before you fold the eggs and turn them onto a plate. Fillings can be sautéed vegetables, small croutons, and/or cheese. In Japan, they often put rice in omelets and serve them with ketchup—it sounds awful but tastes good, at least there, when eaten in context. Here's a place for improvisation—as a glance at any diner breakfast menu will show you. Avoid overstuffing omelets with too many ingredients, too much bulk, or too-wet fillings.

Cheese Omelet: Sprinkle a few tablespoons crumbled or grated cheese over the eggs—Gruyère, Emmentaler, cheddar, goat, feta, whatever your pleasure.

Herb Omelet: Whisk a tablespoon of finely chopped herbs into the eggs—fines herbes, marjoram, flat-leaf parsley, or an exotic combination of parsley, dill, cilantro, and green onions. The Sorrel Puree (page 34) is practically meant for eggs.

Omelet with Tiny Croutons: Lightly brown several tablespoons small fresh bread cubes in a tad of butter or teaspoon olive oil and add them to the omelet just before folding it. They provide a wonderful contrast to the smooth eggs. I sometimes add a little Gruyère as well.

Mushroom Omelet: Sauté 3/4 cup sliced mushrooms in butter or olive oil and season with a little minced garlic and chopped parsley or marjoram. Spread them over the eggs before folding or serve them on the side.

Vegetable Omelet: Add ¹/₂ cup steamed or blanched vegetables, seasoned and tossed in a little butter. Try asparagus tips, braised spinach, sautéed onions, broccoli florets, sautéed artichokes, grilled peppers, and so forth.

Omelet with Truffle Salt: Sprinkle truffle salt over a plain omelet.

Stuffed Green Chile Omelet

A rough-and-ready plate of eggs in which roasted green chiles are stuffed loosely with cheese and cooked within the omelet. Serves 1 or 2

2 large green chiles—Anaheim, New Mexican, poblano—roasted (see page 364)

¹/₄ cup or more grated cheddar, Jack, goat cheese, or Muenster

2 tablespoons chopped cilantro

2 tablespoons sliced green onions

3 eggs

Pinch sea salt

2 teaspoons butter or oil

Slip the skins off the chiles, cut a slit in the middle of each one, and carefully pull out the seeds. Mix the cheese, cilantro, and green onions together and loosely stuff the chiles. Whisk the eggs with the salt and stir in any leftover cheese mixture.

Preheat the broiler. Heat the butter in a 10-inch skillet and set the chiles in it slit side up. Cook over high heat for a few minutes, then pour in the eggs. Go around the edge of the pan several times with a fork, pulling the cooked egg in toward the center and mounding it around the chiles. When no more of the egg is fluid, slide the pan 6 inches under the broiler and leave until golden and barely set. Serve the omelet with warm tortillas, black beans or plain pinto beans, and a side of salsa.

Egg White Omelet with Spinach and Herbs

Personally, I can never bring myself to discard those beautiful yolks, but a bit of butter helps richen the flavor of the whites, as does the inclusion of herbs and greens. Serves 1

2 cups cleaned spinach, washed but not dried

Sea salt and freshly milled pepper

1 tablespoon butter

3 egg whites, beaten with ¹/₂ teaspoon chopped marjoram or chives

In a small nonstick skillet or omelet pan cook the spinach just until it's wilted. Season with salt and pepper, toss with half the butter, then move it to a plate. Wipe out the pan, add the second bit of butter, and once it melts and foams, pour in the whites. Tilt the pan to spread them out, then cook over medium heat until they're set. Season with a pinch of salt and freshly milled pepper, arrange the spinach over a third of the eggs, then gently prod the eggs over it to make a rolled omelet.

More Additions: Anything you can put in a regular omelet can be added to one made only of egg whites. Avocado gives it some of the rich, soft feel that yolks have. A sprinkling of ground red chile make a strong accent; diced sautéed zucchini, sautéed peppers and onions, fresh chopped herbs, smoked paprika or smoked salt, cheese—all add flavor and texture.

Frittatas

Frittata is the Italian—and most common—name for a flat, opened-faced omelet, but similar egg dishes are found in many other Mediterranean countries: Spain's *tortilla*, Tunisia's *tagine*, Persian *kuku*, Provence's *trouchia*. These thick, sturdy omelets are saturated with vegetables, herbs, and other substantial additions. Extremely versatile, they can be enjoyed warm or at room temperature, and they can also be made thin, stacked on top of each other, and bound with a layer of mayonnaise. Cut them into small squares and serve as appetizers, slice them into wedges and place on a composed salad plate, take them on picnics, serve them for brunch, and so forth.

HOW TO COOK A FRITTATA: Whisk the eggs just to break them up, add salt, pepper, herbs, garlic, and cheese if called for, then stir in the prepared vegetables. Heat butter, olive oil, or a combination in a nonstick skillet. Its size determines the thickness of the frittata. The thicker the frittata, the more slowly you need to cook it so that it will cook through without burning. For six eggs, an 8- to 10-inch skillet should be fine. Once the fat is hot, tilt the pan to coat it, then add the eggs and lower the heat. Allow the eggs to sit for a minute, then give the pan a gentle shake to make sure they aren't sticking. If they are, loosen them carefully with a thin rubber spatula. Cook the eggs over low to medium heat until they're set and the top is nearly dry, about 10 minutes.

FINISHING IN THE PAN: Place a large plate over the skillet, secure both plate and skillet with your hands, and invert the entire thing. Add a little more butter or oil to the pan, slide the eggs back in, and finish cooking, just 2 to 3 minutes. When done, invert onto a serving plate.

FINISHING UNDER THE BROILER: Once the eggs are nearly set, put the frittata under the broiler 4 to 6 inches from the heat, to brown and finish cooking, a matter of just a few minutes. Remove, then invert the frittata onto a serving plate.

Zucchini Frittata with Marjoram

This frittata can serve as the blueprint for the recipes that follow, except that you don't have to salt other vegetables. (Grating and salting the squash draws out its moisture, which keeps the eggs from becoming watery.) Zucchini is so amenable to variations that you can enjoy different versions of this frittata all summer long. Serves 4 to 6

1¼ pounds zucchini, coarsely grated

1 teaspoon sea salt

3 tablespoons olive oil or butter

6 eggs

Freshly milled pepper

1 large clove garlic, crushed or minced

1 tablespoon chopped marjoram

⅓ cup freshly grated parmesan or dry Jack cheese

Toss the zucchini with the salt and set it aside in a colander for 20 to 30 minutes. Rinse briefly, then squeeze dry.

Warm half the oil in a wide skillet over medium-high heat. Add the zucchini and cook, stirring frequently, until it's dry and flecked with gold in a few places, about 6 minutes. Transfer the zucchini to a bowl and wipe out the pan.

Preheat the broiler. Beat the eggs with a few pinches of salt and some pepper, then stir in the garlic, zucchini, marjoram, and cheese. Add the remaining oil to the pan and, when it's hot, add the eggs. Lower the heat, cook for a minute or so, then give the pan a few jerks to make sure the eggs are loose on the bottom. If they're sticking, loosen them carefully with a thin rubber spatula. Cook over medium-low heat until the eggs are set and the top is nearly dry, about 10 minutes. Put the frittata 4 to 6 inches under the broiler to finish cooking the top.

Zucchini Frittata with Basil: Basil is another wonderful herb with squash. Add a few tablespoons chopped basil leaves to the eggs in place of the marjoram—or stir in a few tablespoons Pesto (page 50) and omit the cheese.

Zucchini Frittata with Ricotta: Add 1/2 to 1 cup ricotta cheese to the eggs.

Zucchini Frittata with Salsa Verde: In place of the chopped fresh herbs, stir 1/4 cup Salsa Verde or any of its variations (pages 48 to 49) into the eggs.

Zucchini Frittata with Walnuts or Pine Nuts: Once the top of the frittata is nearly set, cover it lightly with toasted walnuts or pine nuts.

Zucchini Frittata with Squash Blossoms: Slice a dozen squash blossoms into ribbons and add them to the zucchini at the end of its cooking.

Tunisian Eggs with Grilled Peppers and Harissa

These eggs, streaked red with spicy harissa, really get the day started or keep it going! Serves 4 to 6

4 bell peppers—2 red, 1 green, and 1 yellow, roasted (see page 364) and peeled
1 clove garlic, minced
Sea salt
6 eggs
2 to 3 teaspoons Harissa (page 66)
2 tablespoons chopped parsley
1 tablespoon olive oil

Cut the peeled bell peppers into 1/4-inch strips and dice them finely. Mix them with the garlic and a pinch of salt. Beat the eggs with a few pinches salt, then stir in the harissa, parsley, and bell peppers. Heat the oil in a 10-inch nonstick skillet. When hot, pour in the eggs, lower the heat, and cook until set, 8 to 10 minutes. Invert onto a plate, return the eggs to the pan, and finish cooking the second side, about 3 minutes.

Onion Frittata with Vinegar and Walnuts

It's easy to overlook an onion omelet, but it makes your house smell so inviting, especially when the sizzling sherry vinegar and butter are added at the end. Remember, sharp knives and cold onions don't cause tears. Serves 4 to 6

1 1/2 pounds onions, peeled and quartered
1 1/2 tablespoons olive oil
2 tablespoons sherry vinegar
3/4 teaspoon sea salt
Freshly milled pepper
1/8 teaspoon ground cloves
6 eggs
2 tablespoons chopped parsley
2 tablespoons butter
1/2 cup walnuts, roasted

Slice the onions crosswise about 1/4 inch wide. Warm the olive oil in a 10-inch skillet, add the onions, and cook over medium heat, stirring occasionally, until they're golden and soft, about 30 minutes. Add half the vinegar, let it reduce, then season well with the salt, pepper to taste, and the cloves. Preheat the broiler.

Whisk the eggs, season them with a few pinches salt, then add the onions and parsley. Melt a tablespoon of the butter in a 10-inch skillet until it's sizzling, then add the eggs and lower the heat. Cook until the eggs are set and nicely browned on the bottom, 8 to 10 minutes, then scatter the walnuts on top. Slide the pan 4 to 6 inches under the broiler to finish cooking the top, but take care not to burn the walnuts.

Loosen the frittata and tilt it onto a serving platter. Return the pan to the stove and raise the heat. Add the remaining 1 tablespoon butter and, when it begins to foam, add the remaining vinegar. Slide the pan back and forth to combine the two, then pour it over the eggs.

Spaghettini and Parsley Frittata

A great way to use leftover pasta. Finish as described here or melt 2 tablespoons butter in a small skillet, add as much white wine vinegar, and swirl it over the heat until the sauce emulsifies. Pour over the omelet and serve. Serves 4 to 6

6 to 8 eggs

1 heaping cup chopped parsley

2¹/₂ tablespoons chopped marjoram

2 cloves garlic mashed with ¹/₄ teaspoon sea salt

¹/₂ teaspoon finely grated lemon zest

¹/₂ cup freshly grated parmesan

Sea salt and freshly milled pepper

4 ounces dried spaghettini or linguine (2 to 3 cups cooked)

2 tablespoons butter or olive oil, plus oil to finish

Beat the eggs with a fork, then stir in all but a tablespoon of the herbs, the garlic, lemon zest, and cheese. Season with salt and pepper and let stand while you cook the pasta. When the pasta is done, drain, then rinse with cold water to cool; you should have 2 to 3 cups. Shake off the excess and add it to the eggs.

Preheat the broiler. Heat the butter in a large nonstick skillet until foamy, then pour in the egg mixture. Lower the heat, gently shake the pan back and forth a few times to distribute the pasta, then cook until the eggs are firm, 8 to 10 minutes. Place 4 to 6 inches under the broiler until the top is browned. Loosen the frittata with a rubber spatula and slide it onto a serving dish. Mix the reserved tablespoon of herbs with a little olive oil and brush this mixture over the top right before serving.

Chard and Onion Omelet (*Trouchia*)

These Provençal eggs, laced with softened onions and chard, never fail to elicit sighs of appreciation. I'm forever grateful to Nathalie Waag for making trouchia *when she came to visit—it has since become a favorite—and still is. The trick to its success is to cook everything slowly so that the flavors really deepen and sweeten.* Serves 4 to 6

3 tablespoons olive oil

1 large red or white onion, quartered and thinly sliced crosswise

1 bunch chard, leaves only, chopped

Sea salt and freshly milled pepper

1 clove garlic

6 to 8 eggs, lightly beaten

2 tablespoons chopped parsley

2 tablespoons chopped basil

2 teaspoons chopped thyme

1 cup grated Gruyère

2 tablespoons freshly grated parmesan

Heat 2 tablespoons of the oil in a 10-inch skillet, add the onion, and cook over low heat, stirring occasionally, until completely soft but not colored, about 15 minutes. Add the chard and continue cooking, stirring occasionally, until all the moisture has cooked off and the chard is tender, about 15 minutes. Season well with salt and pepper.

Meanwhile, mash the garlic in a mortar with a few pinches of salt (or chop them finely together), then stir it into the eggs along with the herbs. Combine the chard mixture with the eggs and stir in the Gruyère and half the parmesan.

Preheat the broiler. Heat the remaining 1 tablespoon oil in the skillet and, when it's hot, add the eggs. Give a stir and keep the heat at medium-high for about a minute, then turn it to low. Cook until the eggs are set but still a little moist on top, 10 to 15 minutes. Add the remaining parmesan and broil 4 to 6 inches from the heat, until browned.

Serve *trouchia* in the pan or slide it onto a serving dish and cut it into wedges. The gratinéed top and the golden bottom are equally presentable.

Spanish Potato and Onion Frittata (*Tortilla Español*)

This cushionlike golden omelet is present in Spanish bars everywhere, providing a nourishing boost for flagging energy from morning through night. The generous amount of olive oil gives the potatoes a velvety, tender texture. The finished dish should be completely moist and golden, not the least bit dry. Serves 6 to 8

Scant 8 tablespoons fruity olive oil, Spanish if you have it

2 pounds white or red potatoes, peeled and very thinly sliced

1 large onion, thinly sliced or diced

Sea salt and freshly milled pepper

6 to 8 eggs, beaten

Warm 5 tablespoons of the oil in a very wide nonstick or cast-iron skillet. Add the potatoes and cook over medium heat, stirring frequently, until they're cooked through and golden, about 20 minutes. When done, the potatoes will have lost their opaque white centers. Separate any slices that stick together so that they'll cook evenly. When done, transfer the potatoes to a bowl with a slotted spoon. If there's no oil remaining in the pan, add another table-spoon and sauté the onions until they're lightly browned. Add them to the potatoes and season well with salt and pepper. Pour in the beaten eggs.

Wipe out the pan with a towel, then return it to the stove and add the remaining 2 tablespoons oil. Pour in the egg mixture, smooth down any potatoes that stick up, and cook over low heat until golden on the bottom, about 10 min-utes. Invert the omelet onto a plate, slide it back into the pan, and cook until set, a few minutes.

Potato Frittata with Rosemary: Add 2 teaspoons minced rosemary to the potatoes while they're frying.

Potato Frittata with Smoked Cheese: Add ¹/₂ cup grated smoked cheese—mozzarella, Gouda, cheddar. This makes a good dish for fall or winter, served with sautéed apples or applesauce flavored with quince.

Frittata with Tomatoes and Feta

Use tomatoes that aren't too juicy—meaty plum or Roma are best here. If fresh marjoram isn't available, use dried oregano in its place—a scant teaspoon in the eggs and extra on top. Serves 4 to 6

6 eggs

Sea salt and freshly milled pepper

1 bunch green onions, including an inch of the greens, finely sliced

1 clove garlic, minced

¹/₄ cup chopped parsley

1 tablespoon chopped marjoram, plus extra for garnish

1 tablespoon each butter and olive oil, or a mixture

4 Roma tomatoes, halved, seeded, and diced

2 ounces feta, thinly sliced

Beat the eggs with a few pinches salt, then add the green onions, garlic, and herbs. Preheat the broiler.

Heat the butter and oil in an 8- or 10-inch skillet until foaming. Pour in the eggs, lower the heat, and distribute the tomatoes and feta evenly over the top. Cook until the eggs are set, then slide the pan 4 to 6 inches under the broiler and brown the top. Instead of inverting the omelet, slide it onto a large platter, keeping the top side up. Garnish with the additional marjoram and serve.

Soufflés

Few dishes are as dramatic as a soufflé. The whole dish swells like an enormous inhalation, then—within moments of serving—collapses. In spite of such drama, soufflés are not at all difficult to make. You simply make a stiff béchamel, beat in egg yolks, add cheese and/ or other fillings, and finally fold in billowy whisked egg whites. Vegetable soufflés incorporate a cup or so of pureed vegetable into the base. They don't rise quite as high but are still impressive. A pudding soufflé is the same dish baked in a water bath, which tempers the rise but also slows the fall, giving the cook some leeway for serving as well as the further advantage of reheating. Roulades are soufflés baked flat in sheet pans (jelly roll pans), then rolled around a filling and sliced or, if you prefer, cut into strips, stacked, and served like a soft, savory Napoleon.

Goat Cheese Soufflé with Thyme

Of all soufflés, this is still my favorite. The enticing aroma of goat cheese is very seductive and the little pockets of melted cheese are treasures to find. Although a classic soufflé dish forms a high, puffed crown, I often bake this, and other souf- flés, in a large shallow gratin dish instead. It still looks mar- velous, bakes more quickly, and ensures there's plenty of crust for everyone. Serves 4

> Butter, plus 2 tablespoons freshly grated parmesan, for the dish
>
> 1¼ cups milk
>
> Aromatics: 1 bay leaf, several thyme sprigs, 2 thin onion slices
>
> 3 tablespoons butter
>
> 3 tablespoons flour
>
> ¼ teaspoon sea salt
>
> Freshly milled pepper
>
> Pinch cayenne
>
> 4 egg yolks
>
> 1 cup (about 4 ounces) crumbled goat cheese, preferably a Bucheron or other strong-flavored cheese
>
> 6 egg whites
>
> Several plump thyme sprigs, leaves only

Preheat the oven to 400°F. Butter a 6-cup soufflé dish or an 8-cup gratin dish and coat it with the parmesan. Heat the milk with the aromatics until it boils. Set it aside to steep for 15 minutes, then strain.

Melt the butter in a saucepan. When foamy, stir in the flour and cook over low heat for several minutes. Whisk in the milk all at once and stir vigorously for a minute or so as it thickens, then add the salt, a few twists of pepper, and the cayenne. Remove from heat. Beat in the egg yolks one at a time until well blended, then stir in the cheese. Don't worry about getting it smooth.

Beat the egg whites with a pinch of salt until they form firm peaks, then stir a quarter of them into the base to lighten the mixture. Fold in the rest, transfer to the prepared dish, then put in the center of the oven and lower the heat to 375°F. Bake for 30 minutes or until golden and just a bit wobbly in the center. Remove, scatter the thyme over the top, and serve immediately.

Gruyère Soufflé: This is every bit as enticing as a goat cheese soufflé. Omit the aromatics and add a pinch of nutmeg to the base along with the cayenne. In place of goat cheese, stir in 1 cup coarsely grated Gruyère.

Eggs and Cheese

Vegetable Soufflés

While spinach and eggs form a classic alliance, other vegetables make handsome additions to a soufflé base too. They should be cooked, seasoned, and finely chopped or pureed before being folded into the base along with the egg yolks. Add the cheese, whisk in the whites, and bake in a 6-cup soufflé dish, individual ramekins, or a gratin dish as described.

Asparagus Soufflé: Fold ³/₄ cup finely chopped asparagus tips into the base. For the cheese, use fontina or Gruyère.

Broccoli Soufflé: Stir 2 teaspoons Dijon mustard into the béchamel base, then fold in 1 cup finely chopped cooked and seasoned broccoli. For cheese, use ¹/₂ cup grated sharp cheddar.

Shallot Soufflé: When making the base for the Goat Cheese Soufflé (facing page), cook a diced shallot (or 3 sliced green onions, including just a little of the green) in the butter for a few minutes before adding the flour.

Spinach Soufflé: Cook a large bunch of spinach leaves with the water clinging to them until tender, then finely chop and season with salt, pepper, and a pinch of nutmeg. For cheese, stay with the goat cheese or use fontina, Gruyère, or cheddar. You can use other greens as well—chard and tender kale come to mind.

Winter Squash Soufflé: Fold in 1 to 2 cups pureed baked winter squash (or sweet potatoes) into the base and for cheese use fontina or Gruyère. Crumble fried sage leaves over the top as soon as it comes out of the oven.

Double Spinach Soufflé

A spinach soufflé is a fine supper dish. Serves 4

---

¹/₃ cup freshly grated parmesan cheese or fine dried bread crumbs

2 bunches spinach, about 2 pounds, the stems removed

5 tablespoons butter

Sea salt and freshly milled white pepper

Freshly grated nutmeg

¹/₄ cup all-purpose flour

1 cup milk, heated

4 eggs, separated

¹/₂ cup grated Gruyére

Heat the oven to 375°F. Butter a 6-cup soufflé dish or shallow gratin dish. Coat the sides with the cheese.

Go through the spinach leaves and throw out any that are bruised or yellowed. Wash them well in 2 or more changes of water until free of grit, then put them in a large pot with the water clinging to the leaves. Cook over medium heat until wilted, turning them with a pair of tongs to help them cook evenly. Drain in a sieve or colander, pressing out any extra moisture. Chop finely, toss with 1 tablespoon of the butter, and season well with salt, white pepper, and a grating of nutmeg. Set aside.

To make the soufflé batter, melt the remaining ¹/₄ cup butter in a saucepan over medium heat, stir in the flour, and cook, stirring frequently, for 2 minutes. Whisk in the hot milk all at once and cook, stirring, until the sauce has thickened and is smooth, about 5 minutes. Season with ¹/₂ teaspoon salt, white pepper to taste, and a few scrapings of nutmeg. Place the yolks in a bowl and whisk in ¹/₂ cup of the hot sauce to warm them, then return them to the rest of the sauce and stir in the cheese. When the cheese has melted, stir in 1 cup of the spinach.

By hand or with a mixer, beat the egg whites until stiff, but not dry. Stir a quarter of them into the soufflé base, then fold in the remainder, just until no white streaks show. Cover the prepared dish with the remaining spinach, then pour the soufflé batter on top.

Bake on rack set in the middle of the oven until risen, golden, and mostly firm except for the middle, which may be slightly wobbly, 25 to 30 minutes. Serve right away.

Giant Cheddar Soufflé

This grand-looking soufflé is baked in a round Spanish terra-cotta casserole—13 to 14 inches across and a little over 2 inches high—or an equivalent-size ovenproof dish. You can make the base ahead of time, guide a small pat of butter over the surface, set a piece of plastic directly on top, and hold until needed. Before using, rewarm the base in the top of a double boiler set over simmering water. Serves 6 to 8

Butter, plus 2 tablespoons freshly grated parmesan, for the dish

5 tablespoons butter

6 tablespoons flour

2 cups warm milk

6 egg yolks

1³/₄ cups grated aged cheddar

³/₄ teaspoon sea salt

1 teaspoon paprika or ground red chile

10 egg whites

Preheat the oven to 400°F. Butter a 12-cup gratin dish and dust the sides with parmesan.

Melt the butter in a saucepan, whisk in the flour, and cook over low heat for several minutes. Whisk in the warm milk all at once, lower the heat, and cook for 1 minute, stirring. Remove from the heat and beat in the yolks two at a time. Stir in the cheese. Season with the salt and paprika.

Beat the whites with a pinch of salt until they hold firm peaks. Fold them into the yolk mixture, then pour into the casserole. Put in the center of the oven and lower the heat to 375°F. Bake until the soufflé has risen and is golden brown all over the top, about 30 minutes. A slight quivering in the middle and firmness around the edges mean that the center will be loose enough to provide a creamy sauce. If you prefer a firmer center, bake 5 minutes longer. In either case, serve it as soon as it's ready.

Corn Pudding Soufflé

This pudding forms a soufflé's crown but is slower to fall. In lieu of the Cilantro Salsa, try serving this with a spoonful of Pesto (page 50), Salsa Verde (page 48), or other sauce of your choosing. For a summer dinner, serve the pudding accompanied with Tomatoes Glazed with Balsamic Vinegar (page 389), grilled zucchini, and a side of black beans. Serves 4

2 cups corn kernels, preferably fresh, from about 3 ears

1 cup milk

3 tablespoons butter

2 tablespoons finely diced shallot or green onion

3 tablespoons flour

¹/₂ cup crumbled goat cheese, cheddar, or feta

¹/₂ teaspoon sea salt

Freshly milled white pepper

3 eggs, separated

Cilantro Salsa (page 49)

Preheat the oven to 375°F. Butter a 6-cup soufflé dish. Puree 1¹/₂ cups of the corn with the milk for a full 3 minutes, then pour it into a fine sieve and press out the liquid with a soft rubber scraper. Set aside.

Melt the butter in a saucepan, add the shallot, and cook over heat for 1 minute. Stir in the flour, then whisk in the corn-milk and cook over medium heat, stirring constantly, for 5 minutes. Remove, stir in the remaining corn, the cheese, salt, and a little white pepper. Warm the yolks with ¹/₂ cup of the mixture, then return them to the pan, stirring briskly.

Beat the whites until they hold firm peaks, then fold them into the base. Pour the batter into the dish and set in a baking pan with boiling water to come halfway up the side. Bake until a golden puffy crown has emerged and the pudding is sturdy, about an hour. Serve warm with the salsa.

Rolled and Stacked Soufflés

Everyone will wonder how you did it, but you don't have to say how easy it is to make a rolled soufflé, or roulade. All you do is bake your soufflé on a four-sided sheet pan or jelly roll pan, then add a filling and roll it up. These versatile roulades can be served hot or cold; they can be made hours in advance of serving; they're an ideal dish for a brunch and sturdy enough to be carried to a picnic. If you're preparing a roulade to be served later, securely wrap it in plastic wrap and refrigerate until ready to use. Remove 20 minutes or so before reheating, brush it with milk or cream, cover lightly with a folded piece of foil, and bake for 25 to 30 minutes at 400°F.

Roulades don't always have to be rolled into large logs. You can divide the base in two and make smaller, more delicate rolls that, when sliced, are an ideal size for an appetizer or as an element on a composed salad plate. You can also cut the base into same-size long rectangles once it's covered with its filling and then stack the roulade pieces on top of each other, which is a very attractive way to present this dish.

SERVING SUGGESTIONS: For appetizers, cut the soufflé base in half lengthwise, roll each of the pieces to make very small roulades, and serve them, thinly sliced, as pass-arounds or set on a piece of rye or sourdough bread. Slice full-size roulades 1/2 to 1 inch wide, arrange two pieces on a plate at a jaunty angle to each other, then surround them with salad greens tossed with Shallot Vinaigrette (page 165). Spoon a little of the vinaigrette onto the roulade.

Roulade Base

Makes enough for a roulade serving 6 to 12

1/4 cup butter

5 tablespoons flour

1 1/2 cups warm milk

Sea salt and freshly milled white pepper

Pinch cayenne

5 eggs, separated and at room temperature

1/2 cup freshly grated parmesan or Gruyère

Preheat the oven to 400°F. Dab the corners of a 10 by 15-inch sheet pan or jelly roll pan with a little butter, then line with wax paper or parchment, including the sides. Lightly butter, then flour the paper or mist with cooking spray.

Melt the butter in a saucepan, stir in the flour, and cook for 1 minute. Whisk in the warm milk, then turn the heat to low and cook, stirring constantly, for 3 to 4 minutes more. Season with salt, a few twists of white pepper, and the cayenne. Whisk 1/2 cup of the base into the yolks, then whisk the yolks back into the base and stir in the cheese.

Beat the egg whites with a pinch salt until they form smooth, firm peaks, then fold them into the base. Spread the batter evenly over the sheet pan, reaching into the corners—an offset spatula is ideal here. Bake in the middle of the oven until the top is lightly browned, puffed, and starting to crack in places, about 15 minutes. Don't underbake it, but don't let it get dry either. Let cool in the pan for 10 minutes, then slide the soufflé off the pan on its paper and flip it over onto a counter lined with wax paper. Peel off the paper.

Spread the filling over the top and roll tightly toward or away from you, whichever feels most natural. When you come to the end, roll the paper tightly around the roulade, slide it onto your outstretched arm to support it, and set it in the refrigerator. Reheat if required. To serve, slice it into 1-inch rounds. Or form the soufflé as suggested, using small rolls or stacked.

Roulade with Roasted Peppers and Tomato Sauce

Use just red peppers or a mixture of colors. Accompany with an arugula salad. Serves 6 to 12

Roulade Base (preceding recipe)

About 1 cup Saffron Mayonnaise (page 52)

3 large red and/or yellow peppers, roasted (see page 364) and finely diced

Fresh Tomato Sauce (page 54)

Red wine or balsamic vinegar, for the sauce

Spread the roulade base with a layer of saffron mayonnaise, cover with the peppers, then roll or layer as described in the preceding recipe. Chill the tomato sauce and season with a few drops of vinegar to brighten the flavor. Serve the roulade chilled or at room temperature with the sauce pooled on the plate.

Roulade with Greek Yogurt and Fresh Herb Filling

I like this roulade surrounded with watercress or tender red mustard greens, tossed with a finely diced tomato and Shallot Vinaigrette (page 165). Serves 6 to 12

$^1/_2$ cup cream cheese or soft fresh goat cheese

3 tablespoons mayonnaise

1 cup Greek yogurt

Sea salt and freshly milled pepper

Roulade Base (page 511)

4 green onions, including a little of the green, finely sliced, or 3 shallots, diced

$^1/_2$ cup chopped parsley

$^1/_4$ cup chopped dill

$^1/_4$ cup chopped basil

2 tablespoons chopped cilantro

Grated zest of 1 large lemon

1 teaspoon olive oil

Beat the cream cheese with the mayonnaise until smooth, then stir in the yogurt. Taste for salt, season with pepper, then spread over the roulade. Mix the green onions, herbs, and lemon zest together in a bowl, add a pinch of salt, and toss with a teaspoon of olive oil. Sprinkle them evenly over the yogurt mixture, then roll tightly or stack.

Roulade with Tomatoes, Ricotta, and Basil

Serves 6 to 12

6 firm but ripe tomatoes, seeded and finely diced

$^1/_2$ teaspoon sea salt

1 cup ricotta

$^1/_2$ cup mayonnaise or sour cream

4 green onions, including some of the greens, thinly sliced

$^1/_2$ cup chopped parsley

10 large basil leaves, sliced into thin ribbons

Freshly milled pepper

Roulade Base (page 511)

A few handfuls spinach, optional

Mustard Vinaigrette (page 167), optional

Sprinkle the tomatoes with the salt and let them stand in a colander to drain for 20 minutes. Beat the ricotta until smooth with mayonnaise to thin it, stir in the green onions and herbs, and season with salt and pepper. Spread evenly over the roulade, cover with the tomatoes, and roll. Serve right away or chilled, surrounded with very finely sliced spinach leaves tossed with Mustard Vinaigrette.

Roulade with Chipotle and Cilantro: Season the ricotta mixture with 2 to 3 teaspoons pureed chipotle chile in adobo sauce. Instead of the basil, use $^1/_4$ cup chopped cilantro leaves.

Roulade with Ricotta, Cucumbers, and Dill: In place of tomatoes, salt 2 large peeled, seeded, and diced cucumbers for 30 minutes, then squeeze dry before scattering them over the base. Serve with a salad of butter lettuce and mint or nasturtium leaves.

Cheese and Other Dairy Products

Along with eggs, beans, and grains, dairy foods are the cornerstones of virtually all traditional cuisines—Asian cuisines being the main exception. As with eggs, many dairy foods are shunned because of their fat and now the use of growth hormones and pesticide residues, but to many, dairy foods are still an integral part of our food culture. Dairy foods still have an important place in our diet as a source of not only calcium and protein but also pleasure. Cheeses are divine examples of human culture as well as bacterial cultures, and there's nothing like the aroma of good butter or the feel in your mouth of softly whipped cream or the velvety tang of crème fraîche, or tart, refreshing yogurt and kefir. I believe that if you like a food, moderation and balance are still the best guidelines for its use.

Despite the many good things about dairy, it has its critics. Cow milk versus goat milk, the latter being possibly easier to digest. Cows treated with rGBH or not. Milk produced by cows on grass or those on grain. We thought low-fat was the best not so many years ago, but now we're not so sure. A number of dairy products are fat reduced and fat-free. But reduced-fat butter is watery and cannot be used in baking, and the flavor and texture of cheese and sour cream diminish when fat is reduced or eliminated.

Raw milk is still strongly preferred by many, but also illegal in many states. It's probably easier to buy heroin than raw milk. A new product we're now seeing is nonhomogenized dairy, which has its fans. I count myself as one; nonhomogenized dairy is delicious. With nonhomogenized cottage cheese, for example, cream rises to the top and is stirred in, and the same is true of yogurt. This is the milk the way it used to be, with the cream on top. When the cream was skimmed off, skim milk remained. A shake of the bottle distributes the cream throughout, but not to the degree that homogenized milk is broken down to make a uniform substance. Some people believe that the forcefully broken-down globules of cream in homogenized milk has harmful side effects. Others say not. But the taste of nonhomogenized milk and milk products is truly special. More and more dairies are producing milk this way, among them Kalona, Straus, Organic Valley's "grass milk," and others.

ALTERNATIVES TO DAIRY: There are now quite a few alternatives to cow's milk beyond soy—hemp, almond, rice, and coconut are commonly available as well. Some are sweetened, others are not, and not all are organic, so read the labels. For cooking, I use organic, unsweetened almond milk and coconut milk more frequently than cow's milk, but when using the latter, I choose nonhomogenized dairy.

BOVINE GROWTH HORMONE: Bovine growth hormone, referred to as rBGH or rBST, is injected into dairy cows to increase their milk production. Among its side effects are increased occurrences of udder infections in the cows and a subsequent need for more antibiotics. Many small dairies do not use the growth hormone and they are now allowed to print on their cartons that the milk comes from cows not treated with rBST. Due to pressure from consumers, some natural foods stores post information about their milk, or have information available upon request. However, if you buy national brands of milk, cheese, and butter, it's likely that it will come from cows treated with growth hormones. You may find out which companies are GMO- and rBGH- free at nongmoshoppingguide.com. Large manufacturers draw from milk pools whose dairies have in part, if not all, used the hormone. The growth hormone is not used in Europe, and you'll usually find that your small, local dairies do not use it. I have noticed more labeling than when *Vegetarian Cooking for Everyone* first came out, both labels that read "milk treated with rGBH" as well as "rGBH free." Hopefully GMOs and rGBH products will be labeled as well one day.

Some Favorite Cheeses

There are many wonderful cheeses in the world, and fortunately, there are some excellent cheese books that go into great detail about what is available here and overseas. But here are those that I tend to turn to over and over again, partly because they are what's most readily available where I live and because I like them. Of course, when opportunity arises through travel, I enjoy trying cheeses that are hard to find in the American Southwest.

AMERICAN FARM CHEESE: American cheese making has come a long way in recent years. Whether simple fresh goat cheeses, cheeses made in European traditional styles, or fresh, new, vibrant American cheeses, there are many excellent ones that would make anyone proud to include on a cheese tray. There are too many to list, but some of my favorites are Red Hawk and Mt. Tam from Cowgirl Creamery, Point Reyes Blue, various goat milk Camembert-style cheeses. Humboldt Fog, Cabot's Clothbound Cheddar, various goat cheeses from Haystack Mountain, Pleasant Ridge Reserve, and many others. These happen to be cheeses that are easier to find than others, but look in your own area for beautifully crafted cheeses.

ASIAGO: This is a lovely cow's milk cheese from Northern Italy, in the Veneto. When young, it is delicate and smooth textured, becoming more crumbly (and stronger) as it ages. I grew to like this cheese very much, even in its youthful stage, when bicycling in the Veneto, where it was served at the various *agritourismi* where we stayed, for its delicacy, softness, and subtle tang. When aged, it may remind you of parmesan.

BLUE CHEESE: Roquefort, Maytag, Gorgonzola, Saga, and Stilton, among others, have strong though differing characters. The French Roquefort and American Maytag are robust and crumbly, the former a little salty, both excellent eating cheeses. Gorgonzola seems to be everybody's favorite blue these days. The dolcelatte, or sweet milk type, is the creamy one. It should be an ivory color with no pink or beige tones and no puddling in its wrapper. It's a superb cheese for eating and cooking, but getting a piece in prime condition can be difficult. Always try to taste it first and buy it cut from the wheel rather than wrapped. The other Gorgonzola is more crumbly and less creamy—heartier and more robust. There is now an excellent Gorgonzola of this type made in Wisconsin (Bel Gioso), but most American-made Gorgonzolas don't have the intrigue and nuance of the Italian ones. Saga is a rather mild, creamy-textured blue, a

dessert cheese to enjoy with pears. There's also the magnificent Stilton, with its crumbly texture and big bold flavor, a great cheese for hearty red wines, sherry, and port. The Bleu D'Auvergne also pairs well with red wines of strong character.

BURRATA: I found my first burrata in a cheese shop in Rome. From Puglia, it was wrapped in blades of green grass. I couldn't resist such a package. Once the grass is removed, cut into its mozzarella skin, and inside is a most delicious cream that flows out over the cheese. This cheese is now being made in small quantities in the United States. Eat it fresh and simply; it is creamy perfection as is.

CHEDDAR: Americans as well as the English are good makers of cheddar cheeses. (*Cheddaring* refers to the process of cutting and stacking the curds.) Dense in texture, cheddars range from mild to tangy and sharp. They become more complex and deep with age. (I recently enjoyed a 10-year-old Wisconsin cheddar that was absolutely superb!) Cheddars can be white—Vermont's Grafton Village Cheddar, for example—or yellowed with annatto seed as in Wisconsin cheddars. Cheddar is always good with eggs, in baked dishes of all kinds, in sandwiches, and also with fruits and nuts. To me, the cheddar is always a distinctly American taste, but often a good goat or Gruyère can be used where cheddar is called for with excellent results. I always find cheddars a good match for crisp, fall apples or hard cider and freshly cracked walnuts, pecans, or, best, hickory nuts. Cheddar is also good paired with rye breads and berry jams. A slice goes nicely with grape as well as apple pie.

COTTAGE CHEESE: So common as to be practically forgotten except as an ingredient, cottage cheese is still a wonderful fresh-style cheese, creamy but with tang and texture. Try it with olive oil and pepper, pureed with watercress (page 85), or mixed with yogurt and topped with fruit.

FETA: Greek, French, Bulgarian, and Israeli versions have slightly different personalities, depending on, among other things, the type of milk used. But overall, feta provides a sharp accent to everything from eggs and vegetable salads to vegetable gratins. A slice of feta drizzled with a few drops olive oil and cracked pepper makes a fine bite to enjoy with a glass of wine, and you can enjoy it in sandwiches, too. When baked, feta softens and becomes more perfumed. Dried oregano, mint, and fresh marjoram are particularly complementary with feta. If yours is very salty, a few brief soakings in cold water helps reduce the saltiness.

FONTINA: True Italian Fontina is superb. It's wonderfully creamy, and its flavor is almost fruity with nutty overtones. True Fontina Val d'Aosta has the image of a jagged mountain in a circle stamped on top. Danish and domestic versions are rather bland, but, like Italian Fontina, they melt well, which is one of this cheese's virtues. They're far more available and less expensive than true Italian Fontina, but try the real thing if you have a chance. Fontella and fontinella are fontina-like cheeses, also produced in Northern Italy.

GOAT CHEESE: Most American goat cheese is fresh, tangy, and very mild. But there are other forms that are more interesting, from aged goat cheeses to more robust cheeses made in the French style, especially Bucheron. Whether sharp and assertive or fresh and delicate, goat cheese always adds character to a dish. It pairs uncommonly well with levain breads, roasted peppers, and eggplant, while rosemary, thyme, garlic, and olive oil are its natural seasonings. Fresh goat cheese makes an excellent grilled cheese sandwich and a heavenly soufflé. But don't leave it just to the savory realm. The slight tang of mild fresh goat cheese is interesting with fruit and nut breads, dates, pears, and other sweet partners. When it comes to more interesting styles such as the banon, crouin, or pyramide, I enjoy those made by Capriole, Coach Farm, and Laura Chenel.

GRANA PADANO: From Lombardy, Grana Padano is similar to parmesan in style but is often used when young, so it ends up with a creamier texture and a somewhat less salty flavor than older Parmigiano-Reggiano. As it ages, it gains a crumbly texture and more character.

GRUYÈRE: Gruyère has a classic goodness that draws me back to it year after year. It's dense and rich, at first grainy but quick to soften on the tongue. It has a nutty, buttery quality that makes it a natural to serve with pears, apples, and quince preserves. It's wonderful in omelets and soufflés, gratins and soups. It makes a superb grilled cheese sandwich and is excellent in other sandwiches as well or on brushetta. Try it thinly sliced and accompanied by fine butter on French bread or walnut bread.

MANCHEGO: This Spanish sheep milk's cheese was not around 15 years ago, but today it is and it's a well-liked, handsome, buttery cheese. It has such a distinctive and delicious flavor that I'd be loathe to use it in cooking. It's really a cheese to enjoy on its own with a glass of sherry, with fruit (try fresh or dried figs) and nuts (almonds and walnuts). It must be aged at least 60 days. This young Manchego is pale and tangy, with grassy notes. Manchego Viejo, which has been aged at least a year, is more golden, crumbly, and has sweet notes flitting about.

MEXICAN CHEESES: These are becoming increasingly easy to find. Here are some you're likely to find and use:

Queso Blanco: A fresh white cheese, somewhat similar to the Indian panir. Mild but a bit salty and tangy, its texture is somewhat spongy. When cooked, it softens but doesn't melt.

Queso Fresco: This popular fresh cheese is more crumbly then queso blanco. In fact, it is used as a sharp accent, crumbled over salads, tacos, refried beans, fideos, and other dishes. A mild feta can be used in its place.

Asadero and Queso Chihuahua: Both are good melting cheeses, the ones used in quesadillas. Monterey Jack and Muenster can successfully take their place, however.

Cotija: A hard grating cheese to use with fideos, chilaquiles, and enchiladas. Parmesan or Asiago can be used in its place.

MONTEREY JACK AND DRY JACK: This is a true American cheese. The anonymous mass-produced Jacks are not particularly remarkable, but Vella's Bear Flag Jack from California and Viviani's Sonoma Jack are really delightful, smooth, soft white cheeses with tiny eyes, delicacy, and mild acidity or tang. Dry Jack is aged for up to 10 months. Its crumb and intensity will make you think of parmesan. It's excellent for grating or eating.

MOZZARELLA: Delicate and milky, fresh mozzarella is classically paired with tomatoes and is also excellent with olive paste, roasted peppers, or simply a good fruity olive oil, cracked pepper, and fresh herbs. Unlike the processed version, fresh mozzarella does not turn rubbery when heated but melts into tender strands. It's glorious in a lasagne or gratin but also enjoyable as a delicate dessert cheese.

PARMESAN: We are finally enjoying a love affair with the real thing—Parmigiano-Reggiano, the cheese that many connoisseurs have described as the world's greatest cheese. This grainy, straw-colored cheese comes to us through years of tradition and adherence to numerous restrictions that must be observed if it's to be given the name, which is, by the way, stamped on the rind. The flavor of this cheese is big and complex. A little goes far, but it must be treated well. Cut off what you need, let it come to room temperature, and grate it as you use it. Don't buy it grated; its flavor will have dissipated. Wrap well what you haven't used, and please don't waste this treasure by using it to improve the flavor of an inferior food, like low-fat mayonnaise. Just enjoy it for its own sake. Many may not realize that parmesan is an excellent eating cheese. Try it shaved or slivered over a salad or with pears and a dessert wine. When you buy parmesan, whether Reggiano or another type, avoid hard dry pieces with a great deal of rind. The rind isn't edible, but it does add flavor to a bean soup or minestrone—just throw a piece in the pot.

PECORINO: Pecorino cheeses are made from sheep's milk, and Pecorino Romano is a classic example that's easy to find here. Most pecorinos share two characteristics—pronounced sharpness and sheepiness that may or may not be to your liking. Pecorino from Umbria is one exception; it is mild and sweet, an excellent eating cheese. Pecorino Romano is used mostly as a grating cheese and often in company with parmesan. I find it particularly pleasing with roasted walnuts and arugula, especially if it's grated into shards and allowed to come to room temperature.

RICOTTA: More versatile than you might think, ricotta doesn't only go into lasagne and ravioli but also makes a delicate filling for a sandwich or a crepe. It can go in a sweet direction too if you drizzle it with honey or rum, dust it with cocoa, or combine it with richer cheeses to make a coeur à la crème. It can also be scrambled and baked. Ricotta should be sweet, delicate, and smooth, not at all grainy. Whole-milk ricotta tends to have a better texture. Otherwise, quality varies depending on where you are in the country. It's generally much better on the East Coast than in the Southwest and West until you find an Italian neighborhood. When I have a good hand-dipped ricotta on hand, I find I use it in all sorts of ways—not only those mentioned. It's lovely with a salad of beets or one of blood oranges, spooned on hot pasta, and of course, it makes a spectacular ricotta cheesecake or lasagne.

RICOTTA SALATA: This is a salted then pressed ricotta. It is smooth and dense and can be shaved or crumbled over pasta, over grilled eggplant, over salads, vegetables of all kinds, and cooked beans. Traditionally, it's made of sheep's milk. Ricotta salata is dry to almost chalky, a bit salty, and pure white, as it is not an aged cheese.

TELEME: Another true American cheese, Teleme is both buttery and tangy, practically flowing when it's at room temperature. Look for the words *rice washed* or *rice rind* on the label. (The less expensive Teleme that doesn't say *rice washed* on the label just doesn't have the magic.) Teleme makes a particularly wonderful grilled cheese sandwich, and it's a fine cheese to serve with French bread.

Skillet Cheese

A very fast bite that makes a substantial snack or a light meal when accompanied by warm pita bread and sliced tomatoes. Be ready to serve the cheese immediately; it neither waits nor reheats. Serves 1

Olive oil, for frying
1 ($^1/_2$-inch) slice scamorza, provolone, or halloumi
Freshly milled pepper

Warm a serving plate. If you're serving accompaniments, have them ready. Film a small skillet with olive oil. Set over medium heat. When the oil is hot, add the cheese and cook until it begins to soften and the bottom is golden. Turn it over and cook on the second side until soft but not melted. Remove to a plate and shower with freshly milled black pepper.

Ricotta and Spinach Fritters

These little fritters are just delicious and so easy to put together. Serve them for lunch with a platter of tomatoes or as a first course at dinner. You can certainly include herbs here if you like. Makes eight $2^1/_2$-inch fritters

---

1 bunch spinach, leaves only
1 cup ricotta
2 eggs
$^1/_2$ teaspoon sea salt
Freshly milled white pepper
$^1/_8$ teaspoon grated nutmeg
$^1/_4$ cup flour
$^1/_2$ cup grated Gruyère
2 tablespoons freshly grated parmesan
Butter or olive oil, for frying

Wilt the spinach in a skillet over medium-high heat in the water clinging to its leaves. When tender, after 4 to 5 minutes, remove, squeeze out any water, chop finely, then combine with the rest of the ingredients except butter.

Lightly film a skillet with butter. When hot, drop the batter by spoonfuls and fry slowly, over medium heat, until browned on the bottom, about 5 minutes. Turn and cook on the second side. Arrange on a platter and serve warm.

Cottage Cheese with Olive Oil and Black Pepper: This is one of the fastest dishes ever—plus it's delicious. If you can find it (I fear it's hardly ever made anymore, at least in the Southwest), use large-curd cottage cheese, preferably made from unhomogenized organic milk. Put some on a plate, season it with some freshly milled sea salt and coarse black pepper, then drizzle a little olive oil over the top. No need to embellish further, although you can do so by sprinkling on some snipped chives, a favorite herb, or chopped watercress or arugula. Enjoy this with a whole grain bread or cracker, some crisp celery, and a few olives or purely by itself.

Baked Cheese on Toast with Wine

Add a salad and a piece of fruit, and you'll dine quickly and well. Serves 2 to 4

- 2 cups grated Gruyère or Emmentaler
- 2 eggs, lightly beaten
- 1/2 cup dry white wine
- 4 slices country bread or wheat bread
- 2 tablespoons butter
- Dash cayenne

Preheat the oven to 400°F. Mix the cheese, eggs, and half the wine and spread the mixture over the bread. Melt the butter in a heavy skillet large enough to hold all four slices. Swirl in the remaining wine, then settle the bread into the pan. Add cayenne. Bake until the cheese melts, 12 to 15 minutes.

Savory Custards and Timbales

These dishes are generally quick to assemble and require 30 minutes or so for baking—a useful window of time for making a salad and setting the table. They're excellent for a brunch, a Sunday supper, and other low-key food events, but they also make a refined first course at the beginning of a more elaborate dinner. Custards in their various forms are smooth, subtle, and soothing, good when you need warmth and nourishment but aren't in the mood for a culinary challenge.

Using a water bath, or bain-marie, is important with all custards to ensure tenderness. To make a water bath, place a dish that's larger than your baking dish in a preheated oven, then add hot to near-boiling water to come at least halfway up the sides of the filled baking dish. The water modulates the heat so that the custard cooks evenly and smoothly. A pair of spring-loaded tongs is useful for removing small ramekins easily from the water bath.

To unmold individual ramekins, let them stand for 5 minutes, then run a knife around the edge and turn them out onto a wide spatula, like a pancake turner. Turn them over once more so that the golden surface is upright and place them on individual serving plates.

To reheat custards and timbales, brush them with milk or cream, cover them with foil, and bake at 375°F for 15 to 25 minutes. The milk moistens the tops and allows them to swell, becoming fresh and tender again. Cream works even better.

Savory Cheese Custards

Accompany these tender custards with toast and a tossed green salad with plenty of chopped vegetables. Serves 4

- 3 eggs
- 1 1/2 cups milk
- 3/4 teaspoon sea salt
- Freshly milled white pepper
- 1/2 cup grated fontina
- 1/3 cup freshly grated parmesan
- 2 pinches cayenne
- 2 teaspoons snipped chives

Preheat oven to 350°F. Lightly butter four 1-cup ramekins or custard cups. Beat the eggs with the milk, the salt, and a little white pepper. Strain into a bowl, then stir in the remaining ingredients, except the chives. Pour into the ramekins and sprinkle the chives over each one. Bake them in a water bath until golden on top and set, except for a dime-size quivery center, about 20 minutes. Remove, let stand 5 minutes and then serve.

Cheddar Custards: Replace the fontina with a sharp, aged cheddar or Gouda and dust the unbaked custards with paprika.

Winter Squash Flans with Greens and Red Wine–Shallot Sauce

This dish is one I often suggest to people looking for a worthy Thanksgiving entree or a formal dish. Have the squash cooked ahead of time, and both the flans and sauce will hold or can be reheated. I would start with a soup or a salad, then the flans, and for dessert, a selection of blue cheeses with walnuts and pears. Serves 6

Squash Flans

> 2 cups pureed cooked winter squash
>
> 1/4 teaspoon ground cumin
>
> 1/4 teaspoon ground cinnamon
>
> 2 eggs
>
> 1 teaspoon sea salt
>
> 1/3 cup cream or milk

Sauce

> 6 tablespoons butter
>
> 6 plump shallots, sliced
>
> 5 juniper berries, slightly crushed
>
> 1/2 teaspoon peppercorns, crushed
>
> 1 1/2 cups Merlot, Zinfandel, or other red wine
>
> Few drops balsamic vinegar

Greens

> 1 tablespoon butter
>
> 1 tablespoon olive oil
>
> 8 cups chopped greens—chard, kale, or spinach—washed and chopped
>
> Sea salt

Preheat the oven to 375°F. Lightly butter six 1-cup ramekins.

Combine the flan ingredients, divide them among the ramekins, and set in a baking pan. Pour boiling water halfway up the sides of the ramekins and bake until the custards are set and pulling away from the sides a bit, 30 to 40 minutes. Remove them from the oven, let rest for 5 minutes, then slide a knife around the edges. If you're not serving right away, leave them in the pan with the water and a piece of foil over the top to keep them warm. They'll hold their heat for about 30 minutes.

Meanwhile, make the sauce. Melt half the butter in a medium skillet and add the shallots and spices. Cook over medium heat until the shallots are golden, about 6 to

8 minutes, then add the wine. Simmer until it's reduced by about half, then whisk in the remaining butter and the vinegar.

To make the greens, heat the butter and oil in a wide skillet, add the greens, and sauté over high heat until wilted and tender, 4 to 6 minutes. Season with salt. If the sauce is cold, warm it, while whisking, over low heat.

Turn the warm custards out onto individual plates. Place the greens around the custards, then spoon the sauce over and around the greens.

Goat Cheese Flan

For years, one of my favorite foods was a warm goat cheese tart, but now I find I prefer the silky custard baked in a ramekin, turned out and served with a salad (watercress, for example), instead of in a buttery crust. Yes, you can use milk, but the cream gives these flans an ethereal silken texture. If you wish, use a 9- or 10-inch tart pan lined with Tart Pastry (page 621) and partially baked. Makes six 1/2-cup flans

> 8 ounces goat cheese, preferably Bucheron or other strong goat cheese, or a mixture of fresh goat cheese and a few tablespoons grated aged goat cheese
>
> 3 eggs
>
> 1 cup cream or half-and-half
>
> 1 cup crème fraîche
>
> 1/4 teaspoon sea salt
>
> Freshly milled white pepper
>
> 1 teaspoon chopped thyme

Preheat the oven to 350°F. Generously butter six 1/2-cup ramekins.

Cream the goat cheese with the eggs, then stir in the cream and crème fraîche. Pour this mixture through a strainer, then stir in the salt, a few twists white pepper, and the thyme. Divide the custard among the ramekins, place them in a dish, and add near-boiling water to come halfway up the sides. Bake until the custards are well set except for a small circle in the center, about 20 to 25 minutes. Remove and let stand for 10 minutes. Serve them in the ramekins or carefully run a knife around the edge and turn them out onto individual plates. Surround with a salad if this your main dish, or Roasted Potatoes and Root Vegetables (page 371).

Vegetable Custard

Those who partake of chawan-mushi in Japanese restaurants won't find the notion of a savory custard strange. This is a comforting, easy supper dish that can be put together with leftover cooked vegetables in about a minute. Serves 4 to 6

1¹/₂ cups milk

3 whole eggs, or 4 egg whites

Sea salt and freshly milled white pepper

Pinch grated nutmeg

2 cups chopped cooked vegetables, such as spinach or chard, broccoli, cauliflower, shredded zucchini, or corn

¹/₂ cup grated cheese, such as cheddar, Gouda, or Swiss

2 tablespoons freshly grated parmesan

Preheat the oven to 350°F. Lightly butter a 4-cup soufflé dish or six 1-cup ramekins.

Whisk the milk and eggs until smooth, then add the rest of the ingredients. Pour the batter into the prepared dish and set it in a pan with near-boiling water to come halfway up the sides. Bake until the custard is set and a knife inserted comes out clean, 40 to 50 minutes for a single large custard, 25 minutes for individual ones. Let cool for 5 minutes before serving.

Corn Custard with Szechuan Pepper Salt

Szechuan pepper adds an intriguing twist to a traditional Shaker dish, but if you don't have it, simply use white pepper, which also has a floral quality. Serves 4

3 eggs

2 tablespoons flour

1 cup milk or light cream

¹/₂ teaspoon sea salt

3 cups fresh corn kernels, from about 5 ears corn

4 green onions, thinly sliced

2 tablespoons chives, sliced into rounds

Szechuan Pepper Salt (page 69)

Preheat the oven to 325°F. Lightly butter a 6-cup casserole or four 1-cup ramekins.

Whisk together the eggs, flour, milk, and salt, then stir in corn, green onions, and chives. Pour the batter into the prepared dish, set it in a pan, and add enough boiling water to come at least halfway up the sides. Cover loosely with aluminum foil and bake until firm when shaken gently or until a knife inserted in the center comes out clean, about 1¹/₂ hours, or an hour for individual custards. Remove the foil during the last 20 minutes of cooking. Serve warm with the pepper salt sprinkled over the top.

Zucchini Timbales with Red Pepper Sauce

Make the pepper sauce while the timbales are cooking—or, if you prefer, use one of the fresh tomato sauces or the Sorrel Puree (page 34). Serves 6

1¹/₂ pounds zucchini, coarsely grated

1 teaspoon sea salt

2 tablespoons olive oil

1 small onion, finely diced

2 cloves garlic, minced

3 tablespoons chopped parsley

1 tablespoon chopped marjoram

1 teaspoon chopped mint

Freshly milled pepper

3 eggs

1 cup milk, preferably whole

¹/₃ cup freshly grated parmesan

Red Pepper Sauce (page 64)

Extra parlsey, marjoram, and mint, for garnish

Preheat the oven to 350°F. Lightly butter six 1-cup ramekins. Toss the zucchini with the salt, set it in a colander for 30 minutes, then squeeze out the excess moisture.

Warm the olive oil in a skillet and add the onion. Cook over medium heat for 2 minutes, then add the zucchini and continue cooking, stirring frequently, until the moisture has cooked away, about 20 minutes. Add the garlic and herbs and season with salt and pepper to taste. Beat the eggs and milk, then stir in the zucchini mixture and the cheese. Divide among the ramekins, set in a pan, and add hot water to come at least an inch up the sides. Bake until the custards are set and lightly browned on top, about 45 minutes. Let cool for 5 minutes, then run a spatula around the edge and turn them out onto your hand, then onto serving plates. Serve with the sauce and garnish with a generous smattering of herbs.

TOFU, TEMPEH, AND MISO

CHAPTER 16

Tofu, Tempeh, and Miso

Soy was the big hope in the 1970s, '80s, and into the '90s, for its protein, lack of cholesterol, its ability to imitate meat in many forms, and its possible health benefits.

Then suddenly it was under suspicion, and it still is. Tofu, which is difficult to digest, should be thought of as a food you eat in small quantities, while fermented soy products, like miso and tempeh, are now preferred. (You can explore this subject in detail at the whfoods.com site, under *soy*, and in many articles and books.)

As the "cow of Asia," the soybean provides many forms of nourishing high-protein foods, just as cattle do. In Asia, soybeans are enjoyed not as beans per se, but in forms that are more easily assimilated. When ground with water, cooked, then strained, soybeans yield a milky liquid called soy milk. With the addition of coagulants and heat, soy milk can be turned into tofu, which itself comes in many forms from silken custards to firm to extra-firm blocks. The quest for dairy substitutes has spawned an industry that has succeeded in converting soy milk into yogurt, sour cream, ice cream, and cheese. Tempeh, a high-protein, fermented Indonesian soy food with a dense, meaty quality, can be used to make simulated strips of bacon and other such foods, or prepared far more simply. Fermentation of soybeans also creates miso, a flavorful paste that forms the base of many soups, and the more familiar seasoning, soy sauce. Natto is another fermented soybean product, but a hard sell with its gooey strands. All in all, the soybean has a huge sphere of culinary influence in Asia, which has been explored and pushed to new horizons in America. Anyone who wants a reliable nonmeat protein source will be naturally interested in the many forms the soybean can take.

But many soy products, including tofu and soy milk, have taken a bad rap, and not always unjustifiably. The highly processed TVP (textured vegetable protein), a sawdustlike by-product used as a filler in meat dishes, sits on the bottom of my list of wholesome and delicious foods. "Natural" soy products are frequently treated with the solvent hexane, a neurotoxin. Soy oil and soy flour are, in my experience, too often rancid, but both are prevalent in the supermarket as the base of "vegetable" oils and baked goods. Soy milk and tofu are not without problems either. Their wholesomeness depends a lot on the company who produces them, the sources of their soybeans, whether they're organic or not (and GMO when they're not) and who certifies them when they're from China. Eden Foods gets high marks from critics for its integrity and taste. SILK, a product of Dean Foods, gets low marks for being a highly processed sweetened food whose parent company has refused to give the source of its beans. In addition, while soy milk might be a beneficial food for those who are seriously lactose-intolerant, it doesn't necessarily benefit everyone. Some people have a difficult time digesting soy milk and other soy products. And other plant milks that are easier on the body are now readily available.

And finally, 90 percent of the soy crop in this country is genetically modified and treated with pesticides, leaving only a small amount to be certified organic and thus, hopefully, GMO free. I, for one, am not as enthusiastic about soy as I once was. I still like and appreciate the density of tofu, but it's certainly not an everyday food. (Fortunately I do like miso and, to a lesser degree, tempeh.) I don't use soy milk anymore. I actually think that almond milk or nonhomogenized organic cow's milk is a better choice.

The soy foods that are considered to be most beneficial are those that are fermented (miso, tempeh, and natto).

Soybeans are especially rich in phytates, enzyme inhibitors and goitrogens, and other nonnutrients. Phytates are especially problematic in soy. With other legumes, soaking is sufficient to reduce their effect, but not so with soybeans. It takes fermentation to significantly reduce the amount of phytates and render soy a beneficial food. Tofu is not fermented, but it's not a highly processed food either (especially if you make your own) and is considered fine to eat on occasion (especially if supplemented with sea vegetables). However, all the highly derived and manufactured soy products, from soy yogurt to hot dogs to ice cream, including the beans themselves, are not considered worth eating. A critical read of soy will be very different from, say, the site for SILK, which declares all the possible problems with soy to be merely myths. I leave that to you, but do suggest that you become more familiar with miso and tempeh and natto, if you can. These are the beneficial forms of soy.

Asian Dipping Sauces

Use these versatile sauces with potstickers and dumplings, as a marinade or sauce for tofu and tempeh, and with grilled vegetables, especially eggplant.

Hoisin Sauce with Chili Paste and Tangerine Zest

A dark, luscious, aromatic sauce. Makes about $1/2$ cup

3 tablespoons dark soy sauce

2 tablespoons dark sesame oil

1 tablespoon hoisin sauce

2 teaspoons Lan Chi Chili Paste with Garlic

1 tablespoon sugar

2 teaspoons finely chopped tangerine or orange zest

1 tablespoon minced ginger

2 tablespoons chopped cilantro

Stir all the ingredients together in a bowl. Taste and adjust the seasonings if necessary.

Peanut Soy Sauce with Ginger and Green Onions

Heating the oil brings out the flavors of the ginger and green onion. Makes about $1/4$ cup

2 tablespoons soy sauce

1 teaspoon minced ginger

1 tablespoon chopped green onion, white part only

1 tablespoon roasted peanut oil

Combine the soy sauce, ginger, and grenn onion in a small bowl. Heat the oil in a small skillet over medium heat until hot but not smoking, then whisk it into the soy sauce mixture.

Sesame Soy Sauce

A very simple sauce for tofu and blanched vegetables. Makes about $1/4$ cup

2 tablespoons soy sauce

1 tablespoon roasted sesame oil

1 tablespoon finely chopped green onion

Stir all the ingredients together.

Rice Wine Vinegar with Garlic

This sweet vinegar is good with dumplings and spring rolls. Makes about $1/2$ cup

$1/2$ cup rice wine vinegar

1 small clove garlic, slivered

Combine the vinegar and garlic and let stand for at least 15 minutes before using.

Tofu

A source of protein and satisfying to eat for that reason, tofu can replace meat and to some extent dairy and eggs. Serious enthusiasts use it to replace everything from ricotta to ground beef. Personally, I find it annoying to see bland tofu masquerading as pungent feta cheese, but in some instances, such as in the Sesame Sauce with Tofu (page 59), its presence goes completely unnoticed. Certainly tofu is a willing partner for all kinds of seasonings and versatile enough to show up at every stage of the meal. Those who find highly processed meat analogues disquieting or those who are new to tofu may enjoy it most in stir-fries or other Asian dishes that don't try to present tofu as something other than what it is. Thai, Japanese, and Chinese food is already "foreign," and tofu is just part of what makes it exotic.

Tofu is made when soy milk is heated and coagulants are added. It solidifies into curds, which are pressed to make blocks of tofu. Depending on the coagulant and the method, tofu can be very firm or it can have the creamy texture of a flan. The process of making tofu is similar to making cheese and, like your homemade cheeses, homemade tofu is far more subtle and delicious than store-bought. If you want to give making tofu a try, see Nancy Singleton Haschisu's book, *Japanese Farm Food*, or Andrea Nguyen's book, *Asian Tofu*. Both give instructions for making your own.

TYPES OF TOFU: In addition to these commonly seen forms of tofu, there are countless more esoteric forms to be found in Chinese and Japanese markets—tofu skins, freeze-dried tofu, fermented tofu, and so forth. Tofu used to be a food that was made in small shops and eaten the same day. Today the tofu business is huge, and mass-produced blocks of tofu come with use-by dates that are weeks from purchase, a far cry from the 24-hour window of the past. If you ever have a chance to taste really fresh tofu, you'll see that its nothing like what we find in our supermarkets. As for tofu that's sealed in cartons that don't need refrigeration, use it if you like. Even with its limitations, I prefer tofu that comes packed in water, which keeps the tofu from spoiling. The weights vary from about 12 to 19 ounces, depending on the brand and the density of the tofu. All tofu should be used within a few days after opening. Unused pieces need to be covered with water. I find it easier to use leftover tofu than to store it in water.

Extra-Firm Tofu: Dense and somewhat coarse looking, this tough, meaty tofu can withstand long marinating, frying, and grilling. This is the kind of tofu to use on brochettes or to freeze.

Firm Tofu: This tofu is also pressed to make it firm, but it's not as dense as extra-firm tofu. When cooked in a braise, its texture becomes soft and pleasing, yet it's strong enough to be sautéed or fried.

Soft Tofu: The smoothest texture whether raw or cooked, soft tofu is my favorite. I use it in braised or stir-fried vegetables, but in the latter case, I don't move it around the pan, as it will break.

Silken Tofu: This aptly named tofu is silky smooth, fragile, and tender. It's best for miso soups, in tofu salads, for pureeing, for mock mayonnaise, egg substitutes, and so forth. But it can be baked, braised, or broiled if handled carefully. It most commonly comes in sealed boxes that keep indefinitely at room temperature, but I often find it in Asian markets packed in water.

Marinated Baked Tofu: Made from firm tofu, these slabs are very firm indeed, deep brown, and seasoned with five-spice powder, peanut and sesame seeds, barbecue sauce, and so forth. All have a chewy texture and their flavor is improved if they're sautéed first in a little peanut or sesame oil. They make a meaty addition to stir-fries and Asian pasta dishes, like dumplings and spring rolls.

Frozen Tofu: Japanese freeze-dried tofu is finely textured, resembling a dried sponge. When thrown into a marinade or broth it immediately drinks up the liquid and expands. Its flavor is more pronounced than fresh tofu and the spongy texture doesn't diminish, so it's not necessarily an easy food to fall in love with. However, it's not hard to freeze your own. Use extra-firm tofu, drained and cut in 1-inch slabs. Put it in a plastic bag and freeze. To use, let it thaw, then squeeze out the moisture. Its network of holes draws seasonings and marinades into it and its toughness allows for a meaty texture. Just crumble it up and treat it the way a recipe featuring ground meat would ask, only plan to increase the seasonings. Frozen tofu shouldn't be fried (it absorbs too much oil) or used in any of the pureed forms (it's too tough).

Sprouted Bean Tofu: New on the market, this is tofu made from soybeans that have been sprouted first, making the tofu more easy to digest.

Tofu Made From Organic Black Soybeans: Another new product, the package claims that it offers more nutrition than tofu made with other soybeans. It's flecked with brownish-black bits and tastes and behaves like other tofu.

Draining

Getting rid of the water in tofu makes room for a marinade to penetrate or allows the tofu to be fried without sputtering. A big fuss is often made about this step. However, effective draining can be as quick as a cursory blotting. Unless you're deep-frying, this step shouldn't deter you from cooking tofu.

Just put a few paper towels on a cutting board, cut the tofu into slabs, and place them on the towels. Usually I simply blot the top surface with more towels. If I'm planning to fry it, I cover the tofu with a towel, put a weight like a can of tomatoes on it, and tilt the board toward the sink to drain for 15 minutes or so. Sturdy firm tofu can take this handling; silken tofu, which is more fragile, should be treated the first way.

Firming and Precooking

Many recipes call for shallow- or deep-frying tofu in oil to give it a chewy texture and an attractive color. Once fried, it can be marinated and then broiled, used in stir-fries, or added to stews. Another way to firm up tofu is to drop cubes into a pot of simmering water for about 5 minutes. In both cases, heat makes the proteins firm so that cubes of tofu won't fall apart when cooked further.

SAUCES FOR TOFU AND TEMPEH

- Sesame Sauce with Tofu (page 59)
- Rich Sesame Sauce or Marinade (page 60)
- Quick Peanut Sauce (page 61)
- Peanut Sauce (page 61)
- Asian Dipping Sauces (page 522)

Marinating Tofu and Tempeh

Both tofu and tempeh benefit by a turn in a marinade before being cooked. Tempeh absorbs much better than tofu, becoming flavor saturated in about 20 minutes. With tofu, only the outside is really affected by the marinade. Tempeh should be steamed for 15 to 20 minutes, then put in a shallow dish, like a pie plate, with the marinade. For tofu, drain it well, or its moisture will dilute the marinade. Slice and cover with the marinade. Tofu can rest, refrigerated, for several days in its marinade.

Amounts: All recipes make enough for a 1-pound block of Chinese-style tofu, two 10-ounce packages of silken tofu, or two 8-ounce pieces of tempeh.

Hot Mustard Marinade for Tofu and Tempeh

Hot, spicy, and a little sweet. The molasses makes a rich caramel glaze, especially on tempeh. Makes about $^3/_4$ cup Ⓥ

2 teaspoons minced garlic

2 teaspoons grated onion

3 tablespoons hot mustard

$^1/_2$ teaspoon cayenne

3 tablespoons roasted peanut oil

3 tablespoons balsamic vinegar or Chinese black rice vinegar

1¹/₂ tablespoons unsulfured molasses

Combine the ingredients, then brush over sliced, drained tofu or steamed tempeh. Both can be sautéed, broiled, or baked, and the marinade used as a sauce.

Sesame-Ginger Marinade for Tofu and Tempeh

Use this as a marinade for firm or soft tofu.
Makes about ¹/₂ cup Ⓥ

2 large cloves garlic, minced or put through a press

4 teaspoons finely chopped ginger

¹/₂ teaspoon red pepper flakes

1 tablespoon toasted sesame oil

2 tablespoons sesame oil

4 teaspoons brown sugar

3 tablespoons soy sauce

Combine the ingredients in a bowl, then pour over drained, sliced tofu or steamed tempeh. Gently push the pieces around so that all are covered. Refrigerate until ready to use. Grill or broil, using the extra marinade as a sauce.

Hoisin Marinade for Tofu and Tempeh

Hoisin sauce can be found at most supermarkets and Asian groceries. Use the marinated tofu with Chinese noodles or in stir-fries. Makes about ³/₄ cup Ⓥ

¹/₄ cup hoisin sauce

¹/₄ cup rice wine (mirin)

2¹/₂ tablespoons soy sauce

1¹/₂ tablespoons brown sugar

1¹/₂ tablespoons ketchup

3 cloves garlic, finely minced or pounded until smooth

Combine the ingredients in a small bowl. Spread over tofu or steamed tempeh and marinate for several hours or overnight.

Thai Coconut Marinade and Sauce for Tofu and Tempeh

Makes about ³/₄ cup Ⓥ

1 tablespoon finely chopped ginger

5 cloves garlic

¹/₂ cup chopped cilantro

¹/₂ cup canned coconut milk

1¹/₂ tablespoons soy sauce or 1 tablespoon mushroom soy

2 tablespoons roasted peanut oil

2 tablespoons brown sugar

1 to 2 teaspoons Thai green curry paste, or 2 serrano chiles, chopped

2 shallots, or 1 bunch green onions, including an inch of the greens, finely diced

Puree or pound everything but the shallots into a paste. Add the shallots. Brush half over steamed tempeh or drained tofu. Marinate for 20 minutes for tempeh, an hour or more for tofu. Grill or broil and serve the remaining marinade as a sauce.

Golden Tofu

Golden, meaty, and chewy, this is one of the easiest ways to prepare tofu. Use it in stir-fries, serve it with salt, soy sauce, or one of the sauces suggested for tofu. Serves 2 to 4 Ⓥ

1 (1-pound) package firm tofu, cut into slabs about ³/₄ inch thick

2 tablespoons peanut oil

Sea salt

Drain, then blot the tofu with paper towels. Cut it into ³/₄-inch cubes. Heat the oil in a medium nonstick skillet over fairly high heat. Add the tofu and fry until golden. It takes several minutes to color, so let it cook undisturbed while you do something else, then come back and turn the pieces. While they should color, don't let them get dry and hard. Drain briefly on paper towels, then slide onto a heated serving dish and salt lightly. You can also fry tofu without oil, as it has plenty of its own, enough to render the pieces golden.

Golden Tofu with Quick Peanut Sauce: Always a popular dish in Thai restaurants, this is unthinkably easy to make, including the sauce. Fry the tofu as described on page 525. If it's for an appetizer, cut it into cubes; if it's your main dish, cut it into slabs. While it's cooking, make the Quick Peanut Sauce on page 61. Serve the tofu with the sauce spooned over the top and garnish, if you wish, with thinly sliced green onions, cilantro sprigs, or toasted sesame seeds. Ⓥ

Gently Simmered Tofu: If you wish to cook tofu with no oil, simply cut it into cubes without bothering to drain it, then lower it into a pot of lightly salted simmering water or the Stock for Stir-Fries (page 235). Simmer gently for 5 minutes. Remove with a slotted spoon, drain briefly on paper towels, then serve, warm or chilled with Gomashio (page 67), Toasted Nori with Sesame Seeds (page 67), or tamari. Or arrange the tofu in individual dishes and serve with any of the following sauces spooned over the top: Hoisin Sauce with Chili Paste and Tangerine Zest (page 522), Peanut Soy Sauce with Ginger and Green Onions (page 522), or Rice Wine Vinegar with Garlic (page 522). Ⓥ

Caramelized Golden Tofu

This process transforms the Golden Tofu into richly lacquered pieces that are delicious in stir-fries and Chinese noodles. Cut it into triangles about 1/2 inch thick and serve with slivered green onions and toasted sesame seeds.
Makes about 1¹/₂ cups Ⓥ

Golden Tofu (page 525)
2 tablespoons soy sauce
3¹/₂ tablespoons light brown sugar

While the tofu is cooking, mix the soy sauce and sugar in a small bowl. Heat a wok or heavy skillet, add a tablespoon of the oil used to fry the tofu or fresh peanut oil, and swirl it around the wok. When hot, add the soy mixture, reduce the heat to medium, and add the tofu. Toss well, then simmer for 2 minutes. Add 5 tablespoons water and cook until the sauce coats the tofu with a syrupy glaze. Turn off the heat. Let the tofu cool in the syrup for 10 minutes, then transfer to a serving dish.

Spicy Stir-Fried Tofu with Coconut Rice

This dish consists of two parts, fragrant coconut rice and spicy tofu. Serves 6 Ⓥ

Rice

1³/₄ cups basmati rice
4 teaspoons roasted peanut or coconut oil
1 small onion, finely diced
1 tablespoon minced ginger
1 clove garlic, minced
1/4 teaspoon turmeric
1/2 teaspoon sea salt
1 (15-ounce) can coconut milk
3 leaves kaffir lime leaves, or 1/2 teaspoon lime zest

Tofu

1 package firm or extra-firm tofu
1 tablespoon ground coriander
1 tablespoon ground cumin
1/2 teaspoon paprika
1/4 teaspoon cayenne
1 teaspoon sea salt
2 teaspoons sugar
2 tablespoons peanut oil
4 green onions, including half of the greens, coarsely chopped
2 tablespoons fresh lime juice
1/2 cup cilantro, chopped, for garnish

Gently wash the rice in a bowl, soak for 30 minutes, then drain. Warm the oil in a 12-cup saucepan with the onion, ginger, garlic, and turmeric. Cook over medium-low heat for 8 minutes, then add the rice and salt. Stir to coat the grains, then add the coconut milk, 2 cups water, and the lime leaves. Bring to a boil, turn the heat to low, cover, and cook until the rice is done, 15 to 18 minutes, stirring twice during cooking. Turn off the heat and set it aside while you prepare the tofu. It will look a little wet at first, but the liquid will be absorbed by the time you're ready.

Drain the tofu, then cut it into 1/2-inch cubes. Combine the spices, salt, and sugar in a bowl, add the tofu, and toss gently with a rubber spatula. Heat the oil in a wok or skillet, add the tofu, and stir-fry until crispy and golden, about 5 to 7 minutes. Add the green onions and cook just until they're wilted, then add the lime juice. Serve the tofu on the rice, garnished with the cilantro.

Thai Tofu and Winter Squash Stew

Squash simmered in a spicy coconut milk broth is anything but dull, and it's very easy to make. Frying the tofu, as in the recipe for Golden Tofu (page 525) in roasted peanut oil until golden and crisp adds both flavor and texture. Serve over basmati or jasmine rice. Serves 3 or 4 (V)

- 2 or 3 medium leeks, white parts only, about 6 ounces
- 2 tablespoons roasted peanut oil, plus extra for the tofu, if frying, and peanuts
- 2 cloves garlic, finely chopped
- 2 serrano chiles, minced
- 1 tablespoon finely chopped ginger
- 1 tablespoon curry powder
- 1 teaspoon light brown sugar
- 3 tablespoons mushroom soy sauce
- 1 (15-ounce) can unsweetened coconut milk
- 1 1/2 pounds butternut squash, peeled and diced into 1/2-inch cubes
- 1 teaspoon sea salt
- 1 package firm tofu, cut into 1/2-inch cubes
- Juice of 1 lime
- 1/3 cup raw peanuts
- 1/4 cup chopped cilantro

Halve the leeks lengthwise, then cut them crosswise into 1/4-inch pieces. Wash well in a bowl of water, then drain.

Heat the oil in a wide soup pot. Add the leeks and cook over fairly high heat, stirring frequently, until partially softened, about 3 minutes. Add the garlic, most of the chiles, and the ginger, cook 1 minute more, then add the curry, sugar, and soy sauce. Reduce the heat to medium, scrape the pan, and cook for a few minutes more. Add 3 cups water, the coconut milk, squash, and the salt. Bring to a boil, then lower the heat and simmer, covered, for 15 minutes. Add the tofu, fried or not, to the stew once the squash is almost tender, then simmer until it's done. Taste for salt and add the lime juice.

Meanwhile, brown the peanuts in a few drops of peanut oil in a small skillet over medium heat, then coarsely chop. Serve the stew over rice with the cilantro, peanuts, and remaining chile scattered over the top.

Tofu with Braised Peppers, Mushrooms, and Olives

Here tofu is smothered extravagantly with a stew of summer vegetables and herbs. Serves 4 (V)

Tofu and Vegetables

- 1 package firm tofu, well drained
- 2 tablespoons olive oil
- 2 onions, thinly sliced
- 1 teaspoon chopped thyme or 1/2 teaspoon dried
- 1 tablespoon chopped marjoram or basil
- 1/4 cup chopped parsley
- 3 bell peppers—red, yellow, and orange—thinly sliced
- 1 cup thinly sliced mushrooms
- 1 clove garlic, minced
- Sea salt and freshly milled pepper
- 1/2 cup dry white wine
- 20 niçoise olives, halved and pitted
- 1/4 cup freshly grated parmesan

Sauce

- 2 tablespoons olive oil
- 2 tablespoons sherry vinegar or red wine vinegar
- 1 tablespoon tomato paste
- 1 teaspoon Dijon mustard
- 2 cloves garlic, minced
- Freshly milled pepper
- 1/2 teaspoon tamari or soy sauce

Preheat the oven to 375°F. Cut the drained tofu into triangles or slabs about 1 1/2 inches wide. Set them in an ungreased pie plate and bake until they're slightly firm and liquids are released, about 20 minutes. Pour off the excess liquid if any remains.

Heat the oil in a wide skillet, add the onions, and sauté over high heat for 2 minutes. Add the herbs, bell peppers, mushrooms, and garlic, sauté for 2 minutes more, then lower the heat to medium and cook until the onions have softened, stirring occasionally, about 6 minutes. Season with salt and pepper. Add the wine and olives and simmer until the vegetables are coated with a syrupy sauce, about 8 minutes. Spread them in a lightly oiled casserole or gratin dish and wiggle the tofu into the vegetables.

Whisk the ingredients for the sauce together, then pour it over the vegetables and tofu. Bake, covered, until heated through, about 25 minutes. Serve with grated parmesan.

Sesame Tofu

Serve this tofu over brown rice for a very easy weekday meal. If you haven't marinated the tofu ahead of time, you can still make the dish, and the strength of the sauce will carry it. The marinade also makes an excellent sauce for grilled eggplant and Chinese noodles. Serves 3 or 4 Ⓥ

- 1 package firm tofu, drained and pressed
- Sesame Marinade, recipe follows
- 1 tablespoon toasted sesame oil
- 1 tablespoon toasted sesame seeds, for garnish
- Chopped cilantro, for garnish

Cut the tofu into slabs and blot well with paper towels. For silken tofu, blot the whole squares, then slice, making a total of eight slabs. Make the marinade and pour half into a pie plate. Add the drained tofu, then the rest of the marinade. Cover and let stand for an hour or as long as you have time for.

When ready to cook, pour off the marinade and set it aside. Heat a nonstick skillet with the oil, add the tofu, and fry until firm and browned, about 5 minutes on each side. Add the marinade to the pan and cook until bubbling and hot. Serve the tofu and the sauce over brown rice and garnish with sesame seeds and chopped cilantro.

Sesame Marinade Ⓥ

- 2 tablespoons sesame oil
- 1 tablespoon toasted sesame oil
- 1/4 cup soy sauce
- 5 teaspoons balsamic or rice wine vinegar
- 1 1/2 tablespoons sugar
- 1/2 teaspoon red pepper flakes or chili oil
- 2 tablespoons finely chopped green onion
- 1 1/2 tablespoons chopped cilantro

Combine the ingredients in a bowl and stir until the sugar is dissolved. Taste and adjust for sweetness if needed. Depending on the type of soy sauce you've used, you may need to add more sugar for balance.

Golden Fried Tofu with Tomatoes

A vegetarian version of nuoc cham, the ubiquitous fish sauce, follows. Make it first so that it has time to mellow. Serves 2 Ⓥ

- 1 package firm tofu, drained
- 1 cup peanut oil, for frying
- 4 shallots, thinly sliced
- 4 cloves garlic, thinly sliced
- 1 1/4 pounds ripe tomatoes, seeded and diced into 1/2 -inch pieces
- Vegetarian Nuoc Cham, recipe follows
- 1 tablespoon light brown sugar
- 1/2 cup Stock for Stir-Fries (page 235)
- 1 teaspoon rice wine vinegar
- 2 green onions, including the greens, sliced diagonally, for garnish
- 2 tablespoons cilantro leaves, for garnish

Drain the tofu, then cut it into cubes about 3/4 inch across. Heat the oil in a wok or skillet. When hot enough to sizzle a drop of water, fry the tofu in two batches until golden and firm, about 7 minutes. Carefully pour off the oil and save it to use again.

Return the wok to the heat and add 1 tablespoon peanut oil. When hot, add the shallots, stir-fry for 30 seconds, then add the garlic and stir-fry for 1 minute more. Add the tomatoes, 2 tablespoons of the sauce, and the sugar. Stir-fry for 1 minute, then lower the heat and simmer, covered, for 15 minutes. Pour in the stock, add the tofu, and cook until the tofu is heated through, about 5 minutes. Season to taste with the rice wine vinegar and additional sauce. Transfer to a bowl, garnish with the green onions and cilantro, and serve.

Vegetarian Nuoc Cham

Makes about 1/2 cup Ⓥ

- 2 cloves garlic, minced
- 1 or 2 serrano chiles, minced
- 2 tablespoons light brown sugar
- 2 tablespoons fresh lime juice
- 1/4 cup rice wine vinegar
- 1/4 cup mushroom soy sauce

Stir everything together in a small bowl.

Sweet and Sour Tofu

This approach works for tempeh as well as for tofu (see variation). Serve over rice or noodles—or rice noodles.
Serves 4 (V)

Golden Tofu (page 525)
1 bunch green onions, including the firm greens
1/4 cup diced canned tomatoes, in sauce
2 tablespoons Chinese black vinegar or balsamic vinegar
2 tablespoons light brown sugar
1 serrano chiles, minced
1/2 teaspoon sea salt
1 1/2 tablespoons organic cornstarch dissolved in 1/2 cup water
1 tablespoon roasted peanut oil
1 tablespoon chopped garlic
2 teaspoons chopped ginger
3/4 cup Stock for Stir-Fries (page 235) or water

Prepare the tofu. Slice two of the green onions diagonally, set them aside, and chop the rest into 1/2-inch pieces. Combine the tomatoes, vinegar, sugar, chiles, and salt in a bowl. Mix the cornstarch and water in a small dish.

Heat a wok, add the roasted peanut oil, and swirl it around the sides. As soon as the oil shimmers, add the garlic, ginger, and remaining green onions and stir-fry for 1 minute. Add the sauce ingredients and the stock, simmer about 4 minutes, then add the tofu, chopped green onions, and diluted cornstarch. Cook until the sauce is thickened and the tofu is heated through, several minutes more. Garnish with the reserved green onions and serve.

With Tempeh: If using tempeh, slice it into strips, triangles, or small cubes and steam the pieces for 10 minutes over simmering water. Heat a wide skillet and add 3 tablespoons peanut oil. When hot, add the tempeh, a sprinkle of salt, and cook over medium heat, stirring occasionally, until brown and the edges are crisp. Add the tempeh to the wok when you'd add the tofu, above. (V)

Pan-Seared Tofu with Orange, Tamari, and Ginger Marinade

Serve these tofu triangles with a simple steamed or sautéed vegetable, such as broccoli or bok choy, with rice, or with a favorite stir-fry. Serves 4 (V)

---

1 block firm or extra-firm tofu, well drained
Grated zest and juice of 1 large orange (about 1/3 cup)
1 tablespoon tamari
2 teaspoons grated ginger
2 teaspoons coconut sugar or brown sugar
1 tablespoon toasted sesame, roasted peanut, or coconut oil

Drain the tofu first so it doesn't dilute the marinade. While it's draining, stir the orange juice and zest, tamari, ginger, sugar, and oil together. Slice the tofu crosswise into six slabs, then cut each slab diagonally in two. Put the tofu in a pie plate and cover with the marinade. Cover and marinate for an hour or up to overnight, sloshing the marinade over the top of the tofu from time to time.

To cook, warm a nonstick skillet with a little sesame or peanut oil. When hot, add the tofu and cook over medium-high heat until browned. Turn and cook the second side. When browned, add the marinade to the pan and let it sizzle over the tofu to glaze it.

Tofu in Curry-Coconut Sauce

Fast and resoundingly flavorful, this Vietnamese dish traditionally calls for frying the tofu until it's firm and golden—a process that adds texture and luster, but you can simmer it instead. Serves 2 or 3 Ⓥ

1 tablespoon roasted peanut oil

1 small onion, thinly sliced

1 small green or red pepper, thinly sliced

2 Thai chiles

1 to 2 teaspoons Thai curry paste or curry powder

1/2 cup canned coconut milk

1/2 cup Stock for Stir-Fries (page 235) or water

1/2 teaspoon sea salt

Golden Tofu (page 525) or Gently Simmered Tofu (page 526)

1/2 cup cilantro or *rau ram* leaves, coarsely chopped, for garnish

3 tablespoons roasted chopped peanuts, for garnish

Heat a wok, add the peanut oil, and, when it's hot, add the onion, pepper, and chiles and stir-fry for 1 minute. Stir in the curry paste, then add the coconut milk, stock, salt, and the tofu. Simmer for 2 minutes more or until the tofu is heated through. Serve over rice or noodles, garnished with the cilantro and peanuts.

Herb-Crusted Tofu

A savory coating of bread crumbs, herbs, and grated cheese gives this tofu an especially pleasing texture. Serves 2 to 4

1 package firm or extra-firm tofu

1 cup fine bread crumbs, fresh or dried

1/2 cup freshly grated parmesan, aged Asiago, or other hard cheese

1 tablespoon chopped parsley

1 teaspoon dried basil or marjoram

1/2 teaspoon dried thyme

1/2 teaspoon dried savory

1 egg, beaten with 2 tablespoons milk

Olive oil, for frying

Slice the tofu into slabs about 1/3 inch thick and set them on paper towels to drain. Meanwhile, combine the bread crumbs, cheese, and herbs in a flat dish. Dip each piece of tofu into the egg mixture, then the bread crumbs.

Film a skillet with the oil. When hot, add the tofu and fry over medium heat on both sides until golden, 10 to 12 minutes in all.

Marinated Grilled Tofu with Hoisin Sauce

Ken Hom is the inspiration for this blend of flavors. Use the firm tofu if you intend to grill it and give the tofu plenty of time to sit in the marinade. A day or two isn't too long, but if a half hour is all you have, don't be deterred. Accompany with a salad of finely ribboned spinach or napa cabbage dressed with Sesame Vinaigrette with Chili Oil (page 168). Serves 2 to 4 Ⓥ

1 package firm or extra-firm tofu

1/3 cup hoisin sauce

2 teaspoons lemon thyme or regular thyme, chopped

1 teaspoon marjoram, chopped, or 2 pinches dried

1/4 cup dry sherry

2 tablespoons olive oil

1 large clove garlic, crushed

1/2 teaspoon freshly milled pepper

1 tablespoon toasted black or white sesame seeds

2 green onions, including the greens, sliced into rounds

Cut the tofu into rectangles or triangles 1/2 inch thick. Set on paper towels to drain. Combine the hoisin sauce with the herbs, sherry, olive oil, garlic, and pepper. Place the drained tofu in a baking dish and score the tops, making diagonal cuts about halfway through each piece. Brush the marinade generously over the tofu, cover, and refrigerate until ready to cook.

To broil, place the tofu 4 or 5 inches under the heat and broil until the top is bubbling and the tofu is heated through, 7 to 10 minutes. For grilling, brush both sides with the marinade and grill on both sides, about 15 minutes in all. Serve with the sesame seeds and green onions over the top.

Malaysian-Inspired Tofu Curry

This dish is very simple to make and full of sweet and spicy flavors. Tamarind, which provides tartness, is available at many natural foods stores and Indian groceries. Serve this curry over Chinese egg noodles, linguine, or rice. This is also a good recipe made with tempeh. Serves 3 or 4 Ⓥ

- 1 package firm tofu
- 2 (15-ounce) cans unsweetened coconut milk, or 1 can coconut milk mixed with 1 cup water
- 2 teaspoons light brown sugar
- 1/2 teaspoon sea salt
- 1 tablespoon ground coriander
- 2 teaspoons curry powder
- 1/2 teaspoon turmeric
- 1/4 teaspoon cayenne
- 1 teaspoon tamarind paste
- 2 large cloves garlic, minced
- 1 tablespoon finely chopped ginger
- 4 Roma tomatoes, seeded and diced
- 4 green onions, including the firm greens, chopped
- Juice of 1 lime
- Cilantro, chopped, for garnish

Drain, then dice the tofu into 1/2-inch cubes. Combine the coconut milk, sugar, salt, spices, tamarind paste, garlic, and ginger in a medium skillet. Boil for 1 minute, then add the tofu. Lower the heat and simmer for 10 minutes. Add the tomatoes and green onions and simmer for approximately 10 minutes more. Add the lime juice and taste for salt. (I sometimes find a little mushroom soy sauce makes a good addition.) Serve garnished with chopped cilantro.

Tofu and Steamed Cabbage with Rice and Peanut Sauce

This dish is light and quick if the peanut sauce is already prepared. Serves 2 Ⓥ

- 1 cup brown basmati rice
- 1 pound savoy or napa cabbage, quartered and cored
- Sea salt
- 1 package soft or firm tofu, cut into 1/2-inch dice
- 3 tablespoons chopped cilantro, for garnish
- Quick Peanut Sauce (page 61)
- 1 tablespoon roasted peanuts, for garnish

If using basmati rice, first soak it for 30 minutes, then drain and cook (see page 477). Cut the cabbage into 1/4-inch ribbons. If using napa cabbage, thinly slice the base as well. Set a steaming basket in a saucepan over boiling water. Lay the cabbage over the bottom, sprinkle lightly with salt, then set the tofu on top. Cover and steam until the cabbage is bright green and tender, 8 to 10 minutes. Carefully remove and arrange over the cooked rice. Garnish with the cilantro, drizzle with peanut sauce, and garnish with peanuts.

Variation with Golden Tofu: If you want a little more punch to this dish, fry the tofu as described on page 525, then season with salt or Gomashio (page 67). Serve on top of the cabbage. Ⓥ

Tempeh

A high-protein Indonesian food, tempeh is made from cooked soybeans that are inoculated with a spore, then fermented. It looks like a firm, flat cake that's mottled with small brown and gray spots. It might look a bit weird, as if the cake of soybeans were covered in mold, but that's how it should be. Fermentation turns tempeh into the kind of soy food that is best for us to eat. The process breaks down the phytates that make soy a difficult food to digest. In addition, tempeh's protein is about equal to that of meat. It's a good source of vitamin B and has plenty of fiber. Four ounces is quite a generous portion because of its density. Two ounces would be plenty. As with tofu, should you ever undertake making your tempeh from scratch, you may find it is actually quite delicate and delicious.

While tempeh readily accepts seasonings, it also has a pronounced taste of its own. Its texture is chewy; its flavor nutty, but it can be faintly bitter unless thoroughly cooked. To get ahead of the bitterness problem, I suggest that you make a habit of taking 10 minutes to steam your tempeh first, then go ahead and marinate it, or not. The steaming tempers tempeh and softens it, making it more receptive to the flavors of a marinade or sauce.

Its ability to absorb flavors and its texture makes tempeh quite versatile. At any stage, tempeh can be cut into strips, wedges, and chunks, or crumbled. Many vegetarians like tempeh's ability to pass for hamburger or bacon, while others find this use unnecessary. Traditionally, tempeh isn't used as a mock meat, but as a food with its own properties and flavors.

TYPES OF TEMPEH: Tempeh, though based on soy beans, now comes made with rice, millet, sesame, peanuts, and quinoa; some is even flavored with Italian herbs. The traditional all-soy tempeh holds its shape best and, to my taste, has the best flavor. Added seasonings tend to get lost; you can more effectively add your own. Tempeh can be found frozen in your market. Once defrosted, it's best used within 5 days. Once cooked, it will keep several days in the refrigerator. I have made my own with inoculants, and, as with tofu, I found it absolutely delicious in a way that mass-produced tempeh isn't. It's not that hard to do, but then, you have to do it.

STEAMED TEMPEH: Steaming is a simple way of precooking tempeh that removes bitterness without adding any additional flavors. Once steamed, the tempeh can be fried, crumbled, or added to a marinade. Cut tempeh into desired shapes or leave whole, then steam over boiling water, covered, for 10 minutes.

SIMMERING IN HOT MARINADE: You can precook tempeh directly in a marinade instead of steaming. Simmer it slowly for 15 to 20 minutes in any thin marinade, such as the Sesame-Ginger Marinade (page 525).

Barbecued Tempeh

Serves 2 to 4 (V)

- 1 (8- or 10-ounce) package tempeh, cut into strips ¹/₂ inch thick
- 1 cup Golden Mustard Barbecue Sauce (page 65) or favorite commercial sauce

Steam or simmer the tempeh in broth for 10 minutes, then put it in a dish and cover with barbecue sauce. Turn it over so both sides are coated, then cover and refrigerate until ready to eat or overnight. Grill or broil for about 5 minutes on each side.

Tempeh Simmered in Broth

After cooking tempeh in a very mild, thin broth, it can be fur-ther seasoned. If there's a particular flavor you're planning to use later with the tempeh, such as oregano or ginger, tailor the broth to your needs by adding a pinch or slice. Serves 2 Ⓥ

1 (8- or 10-ounce) package tempeh

1 cup water

2 cloves garlic, crushed through a press

A few onion slices

2 bay leaves

¹/4 cup soy sauce

Optional additions: smoked chile, red pepper flakes, thyme sprigs, sliced ginger, rosemary, dried mushrooms, tomato paste, and so forth

Quarter the tempeh or cut it into the shape you'll be using later. Put everything in a skillet just large enough to hold the tempeh, bring it to a boil, then cover and simmer slowly until the broth has been absorbed, about 15 minutes. Turn it over once during the cooking.

Tempeh Triangles

Braised in tamari with a little ginger, these triangles end up golden, but without an excessive amount of oil, and tempeh can drink up unlimited amounts of oil. I use these triangles to garnish a stir-fry or noodles dishes. Lisa Mase taught me this method, based on her years living in Indonesia. Serves 2 to 4 Ⓥ

1 (8- or 10-ounce) package tempeh

A few teaspoons toasted sesame or roasted peanut oil

1 teaspoon grated ginger

A few teaspoons tamari

Slice the tempeh lengthwise in two (making it half as thick, essentially), then cut each piece into triangles. Steam over simmering water for at least 10 minutes, then remove.

Put the tempeh in a wide shallow saucepan and add water to cover along with the oil, ginger, and the tamari, to taste. Simmer, uncovered, for ten minutes, then turn the tempeh over and continue cooking. After another 10 minutes the water will have boiled away, leaving the tempeh to color and "fry" in the remaining oil.

Fried Tempeh

Fried tempeh makes a good snack with a little sea salt and plenty of pepper sprinkled over the top and is excellent served with peanut sauce. Serves 2 to 4 Ⓥ

1 (8- or 10-ounce) package tempeh, steamed for 10 minutes

³/4 cup peanut or sesame oil

Sea salt and freshly milled pepper

Cut the steamed tempeh into triangles, thin slices, nuggets, or whatever shape works for your dish. Heat the oil in an 8-inch skillet until it sizzles a bread crumb, then add the tempeh a few pieces at a time. When golden, transfer to a paper towel to drain. Season with salt and pepper.

Tempeh in a Smoky Molasses Marinade

This tempeh has a delicious smoky-sweet flavor that's remi-niscent of bacon. Makes 18 to 20 strips Ⓥ

1 (8- or 10-ounce) package tempeh

Broth ingredients, from Tempeh Simmered in Broth (facing)

4 thin slices ginger

1 whole clove

¹/4 teaspoon pureed chipotle chile or ¹/2 teaspoon smoked paprika

2 tablespoons molasses

1¹/2 teaspoons tomato paste

1 tablespoon sesame oil

Slice the tempeh crosswise into ¹/4-inch strips. Combine the remaining ingredients in a small skillet, bring them to a boil, and add the tempeh. Simmer slowly, covered, for 15 minutes, remove the lid, and continue cooking until all the liquid has been absorbed. At this point, the tempeh will begin to fry in the oil. Cook until it's glazed and browned, about 5 minutes.

With Maple Syrup: Replace the molasses with maple syrup for a sweet but softer flavor. Ⓥ

Tempeh in Spicy Coconut Sauce with Spinach

Possibly my favorite tempeh dish. Try this over black rice—delicious. You can also make this dish with tofu, and even both tempeh and tofu, which gives a nice contrast of textures.
Serves 4 (V)

1 (8- or 10-ounce) package tempeh

3 tablespoons peanut oil

Sea salt

1 tablespoon tamarind paste thinned in ¼ cup water

⅓ cup finely sliced cilantro stems and ⅓ cup leaves

1 small white onion, diced

1 heaping teaspoon chopped ginger

2 tablespoons minced lemongrass, from the middle stalk

1 teaspoon chopped, peeled turmeric or ½ teaspoon dried

1 teaspoon ground coriander

½ teaspoon ground cumin

1 (15-ounce) can coconut milk, plus water to make 2 cups

2 Thai red chiles

A few handfuls spinach leaves

Cut the tempeh crosswise into six pieces. Cut each one in half lengthwise, then into cubes.

Steam it over boiling water for 10 minutes. Heat 2 tablespoons of the oil in a skillet. When hot, add the tempeh, toss immediately to distribute the oil, then cook over medium heat until golden in places, about 5 minutes. If the pan seems too dry, add the last tablespoon of oil. When done, turn off the heat and season with salt.

Puree the tamarind and water with the cilantro stems, onion, ginger, lemongrass, and spices.

Heat a wide skillet or sauté pan. Add the puree plus the coconut milk and the Thai chiles. Mix everything together, then simmer, covered, for 15 minutes to get rid of the raw taste of the onion. Add the tempeh cubes and simmer until they're heated through, then add the spinach leaves. Turn them over in the pan and, as soon as they're wilted, turn off the heat.

Serve over rice with the cilantro leaves over all.

With Tofu: I like the contrast of the chewy tempeh and soft tofu in this dish, but I also include the latter because my husband doesn't care for tempeh but loves tofu. You can, of course, make it with just one or the other. I use a half package of firm tofu, drained, cut into cubes, then fried in a little peanut oil over medium-high heat, flipping the cubes occasionally, until golden, about 5 minutes. Season with salt. Add them to the coconut sauce when you would add the tempeh. (V)

Tempeh with Braised Peppers, Mushrooms, and Olives

This is good with tofu (page 527) and also good with tempeh, which is a little chewier. Make the same recipe as given, but with tempeh, as described. Serves 4 (V)

1 (8- or 10-ounce) package tempeh

3 tablespoons olive oil

Recipe for Tofu with Braised Peppers, Mushrooms, and Olives (page 527), minus the tofu

Parmesan cheese, optional, for serving

Preheat the oven to 375°F. Cut the tempeh into slabs, cubes, or triangles and steam for 10 minutes. When done, heat the oil in a skillet, add the tempeh, and fry over medium-high heat until crisp around the edges and golden.

Prepare the vegetables as described on page 527, adding the tempeh where you'd normally add the tofu. Make the sauce recipe and pour it over the vegetables. Cover and bake until heated through, about 25 minutes. Serve with parmesan cheese grated over the top.

Marinated and Fried Tempeh, Indonesian Style

Both marinating and frying are used in this traditional dish. Serves 2 to 4 Ⓥ

1 (8- or 10-ounce) package tempeh

1¹/₂ teaspoons tamarind paste

¹/₂ onion, thinly sliced

3 slices ginger

1 teaspoon ground coriander

1 bay leaf

¹/₈ teaspoon red pepper flakes

1 teaspoon brown sugar

2 pieces galangal or fresh ginger, optional

³/₄ cup peanut oil

Cut the tempeh into slices about ¹/₂-inch thick or a little less. Combine 1¹/₂ cups water with the remaining ingredients except the oil and bring to a boil. Add the tempeh, then lower the heat and simmer, covered, for 30 minutes or until all the liquid is absorbed. Heat the oil in a medium skillet. When hot enough to sizzle a bread crumb, add the tempeh and fry in batches over high heat until golden and crisp, 3 to 5 minutes. Drain briefly on paper towels, then serve with salt, a chutney, one of the peanut sauces, or Golden Mustard Barbecue Sauce (page 65).

Baked Tempeh or Tofu with Mustard-Honey Marinade

The marinade can also serve as a sauce to accompany rice or noodles. Serves 4 Ⓥ

2 (8- or 10-ounce) packages tempeh, or 1 (1-pound) package firm tofu

3 tablespoons mild honey or sorghum

1 tablespoon molasses

1 tablespoon peanut oil

1 teaspoon soy sauce

3¹/₂ tablespoons mustard

2 teaspoons curry powder

Salt and freshly milled pepper

If using tempeh, cut it into ¹/₂-inch slabs and steam for 10 minutes. If using tofu, cut it into cubes or slabs and set on paper towels to drain while you mix the remaining ingredients for the marinade in a bowl. Place the tempeh or tofu in a pie plate and brush the marinade over it. Let stand for at least 20 minutes or as long as overnight. Preheat the oven to 400°F. Bake until sizzling and hot, about 20 minutes, basting midway through the cooking. Serve with any extra marinade on the side.

Miso

Along with tempeh, miso is another fermented food that is highlighted as a beneficial form of soy. Unlike chewy, dense tempeh, miso is more of a condiment, which means it gets used in smaller quantities. It's hard to imagine dipping into a tub of miso the way you might a jar of peanut butter, but it can become a seasoning to turn to on a regular basis. As a student at Tassajara Zen Mountain Center in the early 1970s, I ate quite a few miso and peanut butter sandwiches, but it is perhaps better known (and appreciated) in miso soups. If you frequent Japanese restaurants, you've certainly begun many a meal with a bowl of cloudy broth with tiny cubes of tofu, floating ribbons of seaweed, and a few choice vegetables. Light yet sustaining, miso soup is inexpensive, essentially instant, and noncaloric, and can be enjoyed at a meal (including breakfast) or as a pick-me-up. The making of miso soup is a valued part of daily life in Japan. It is usually made with dashi, a fish stock, but there are some vegetarian alternatives.

Salty miso is made from fermented soybeans, but often those beans are combined with some sort of grain, which influence the color and taste of a particular miso. Barley, rice, buckwheat, millet—even hemp—are just some of the grains and seeds used. They contribute to making misos that can be light and sweet, dark and robust, savory, salty, and so forth. The mixtures might ferment for less than a week or as long as several years. Because miso is living food, it should be kept refrigerated, and in soups, it should not be boiled.

There are many kinds of miso, but among the best known are the dark and earthy red miso (*akamiso*). When used with care, it can increase the umami quotient in a dish without its tasting like miso. White miso (*shiromiso*) is creamy colored, like pale honey, and sweet. It has more barley in relation to soybeans, and is also the most popular miso made in Japan. It is especially popular here as *dengaku*, dishes in which the miso is spread over fish and vegetables to be broiled. Keep in mind that boiling changes miso's flavor and destroys some of its nutritional value. Miso can also be used as a dip, a marinade, in sauces and elsewhere, and of course, in miso soup. Miso soup should be eaten at once.

Simple Kombu Stock

Kombu, a type of kelp, is filled with trace minerals. It comes in long sheets or strips, but only a small piece is used at a time. Makes about 4 cups Ⓥ

1 (4- to 6-inch) strip dried kombu
Dash soy sauce

Place 4½ cups water and the kombu in a pot. Cover and simmer for 20 minutes, then add a little soy sauce for flavor.

Kombu Stock with Dried Mushrooms

It's hard to get the particular flavor that dried bonito gives to a Japanese stock, but this stock does add greatly to miso soups. You may have to fiddle with the balance, adjusting the saltiness of the soy with the sweetness of the mirin since soy sauces vary. Refrigerated, this will keep for a week. Makes 6 cups Ⓥ

6 dried Chinese black or shiitake mushrooms
1 bunch green onions, including most of their greens, chopped
1 carrot, thinly sliced

1 (4- to 6-inch) strip dried kombu

2 to 4 tablespoons soy sauce

2 teaspoons dark sesame oil

2 tablespoons rice wine (mirin)

Sea salt and sugar, if needed

Shake the mushrooms in a strainer to loosen any dirt, then put them in a pot along with 7 cups cold water and the rest of the ingredients except the salt and sugar. Bring to a boil, then lower the heat and simmer, covered, for 20 minutes. Taste and add a pinch of salt and/or sugar to bring up the flavors. Adjust the balance of soy sauce to mirin if needed. Strain the stock but retrieve the mushrooms to use in a soup.

A Simple Miso Soup

You'll find through experience how much miso is right for you. Usually 2 to 3 teaspoons is plenty for a cup, but it depends on the type of miso. This simplest of miso soups makes an instant pick-me-up. Serves 1 (V)

2 to 3 teaspoons white or red miso, to taste

1 cup boiling water or one of the kombu stocks (page 536)

A few drops dark sesame oil or chili oil

Sliced mushroom or slivered gren onion, optional, for garnish

Put the miso in a cup, add a few tablespoons of the water, and work it into the miso, diluting it to a thick cream. Add the rest of the water, then pour the soup into a bowl or mug. Add a few drops sesame oil, garnishes—or none—and sip.

White Miso Soup with Aburage and Seven-Spice Powder

Aburage, a commercial deep-fried tofu, is puffy, golden, and sliced in thin strips. Shichimi togarashi is a pungent, spicy powder of seven spices that truly enlivens this soup in a different way. Serves 2 (V)

1 piece aburage (deep-fried tofu)

Handful mung bean sprouts

2 cups Simple Kombu Stock (page 536)

3 tablespoons white miso or white miso mixed with red miso

1 green onion, with the firm greens, thinly sliced

Shichimi togarashi or few drops toasted sesame oil

Slice the aburage very thinly into strips. Bring a few cups water to a boil and pour half of it over the aburage. Pour the rest over the beans sprouts.

Heat the stock. Use some of it to dilute the miso. Once the stock boils, add the aburage and simmer for 1 minute. Turn off the heat and add the miso, sprouts, and thinly sliced green onions. Serve with a peppering of togarashi or a few drops sesame oil.

Miso-Tofu Soup with Wakame

Wakame is a leafy sea vegetable that is easy to find in Japanese markets and natural foods stores. Dulse, a red seaweed, needs no presoaking and can be used with or in place of wakame. Serves 4 (V)

8 leaves dried wakame "leaves" or dulse sprigs

4 cups Kombu Stock (page 536) or water

3 tablespoons red or barley miso or a mixture of red with a lighter miso

1 cup finely diced soft or silken tofu

3 green onions, thinly sliced

A few drops chili oil or dark sesame oil

Soak the wakame in lukewarm water until soft, about 15 minutes. Feel for any tough parts and cut them away—there's usually a kind of core. Tear the rest into smaller pieces or slice into thin ribbons. Bring the stock to a boil.

Dilute the miso with 1 cup of the stock. Add the wakame and tofu to the remaining stock and simmer until the tofu has risen to the surface, 4 to 5 minutes. Stir the diluted miso back into the pot and bring nearly to a boil. Add the green onions and chili oil and serve.

MORE GARNISHES FOR MISO SOUPS

The simplest garnishes—a drop of dark toasted sesame oil, the wavy fronds of sea greens, the translucent rings of a green onion—lend beauty, flavor, and nuance to miso soups. Hard vegetables should be precooked briefly in boiling salted water so that they're tender and bright when added to the soup.

- Asparagus, diagonally sliced and blanched
- Napa cabbage, thinly sliced
- Chinese chives or regular chives, thinly slivered
- Mustard greens
- Spinach leaves, whole if small or thinly sliced if large
- Sweet potatoes, peeled, cubed, and steamed
- Fresh mushrooms, thinly sliced
- Dried shiitake mushrooms, retrieved from the kombu stock, caps thinly sliced
- Snow peas, whole or julienned, shucked pod peas
- Mung bean sprouts, blanched
- Carrot, thinly sliced on a diagonal, cut into fine matchsticks, or finely diced
- Small daikon, thinly sliced, and tender young leaves
- Fried tofu (aburage), thinly sliced and rinsed with boiling water
- Shichimi togarashi (seven-spice powder with chile)

A Miso Dip or Dressing for Vegetables

Elizabeth Andoh is the inspiration for this recipe, as she is for many other miso dishes (and Japanese dishes in general). Her book Kansha *is a treasure. She uses this sauce with bitter melon but suggests it can be used with vegetables, and so it can. Try it with steamed broccoli nubbins and their stems, asparagus spears, and even firm avocado, but as a dressing rather than a dip. While she suggests using lemon juice, I like the gentleness of Meyer lemon or even yuzu fruit, when I can find it.* Makes 1/2 cup Ⓥ

6 tablespoons white miso

2 teaspoons white sugar

2 tablespoons of fresh lemon, Meyer lemon, or yuzu juice (to taste)

1/2 teaspoon lemon zest

2 tablespoons rice wine vinegar

Toasted sesame seeds, to finish

Using a small saucepan, mix the miso with the sugar and lemon juice. Cook over low heat while stirring until the sugar is dissolved and the mixture is bubbly, about a minute. Let it cool, then stir in the lemon zest and vinegar. Taste to make sure the mixture has enough lemon—if using Meyer lemon, you might want to add a little more juice. Also make sure it's thin enough for dipping, and if not, stir in warm water until it is.

Mound in a bowl, garnish with the sesame seeds, and serve with vegetables, such as those mentioned above.

Roasted Squash with Miso-Tahini Sauce

The wedges of squash come out burnished and caramelized; the salty miso sauce is the seasoning. Serves 4 (V)

1 small winter squash, such as **Carnival**

Light sesame oil, for brushing

2 tablespoons white miso

2 teaspoons red miso

1/4 cup tahini

1 teaspoon toasted sesame oil

1 teaspoons rice wine (mirin)

2 tablespoons lemon juice

1 teaspoon toasted sesame seeds, for garnish

Heat the oven to 400°F.

Cut the squash into wedges about 2 inches across at the widest part. Brush them with oil, lay them on a sheet pan lined with parchment paper, then roast until burnished, about 20 minutes. Turn the squash over to cook on the second side, another 10 to 15 minutes, until tender when pierced with a knife.

While the squash is baking, make the sauce. Combine the misos, tahini, sesame oil, mirin, and lemon juice in a bowl and mix together. Thin with water, as needed, then taste and adjust the seasonings, adding more mirin if you think it needs it, a little more sesame oil, and so on. Spoon the sauce over the squash and garnish with the toasted sesame seeds.

Griddled Small Eggplant with Sweet Miso Sauce

This is one of those universal sauces that's perfect with eggplant, very good with roasted winter squash, over brown rice, seared or griddled tofu, or tempeh. For eggplant, you'll want to use the small Japanese varieties. They are easy to grill or griddle, and make a handsome presentation. Sugar is usually called for in this kind of sauce, but the mirin may well be sweet enough. Serves 4 to 6 (V)

6 or more small eggplant, about 4 inches long

Sesame oil

3 tablespoons white miso

2 tablespoons rice wine (mirin)

2 tablespoons sake

Sugar, if needed

2 slivered slender green onions, for garnish

Toasted black sesame seeds, for garnish

Cut the eggplant in half lengthwise. Score the surfaces in a crisscross pattern with the tip of a knife, then brush with the sesame oil. Heat a griddle or grill pan, add the eggplant, cut side facing down, over medium high heat until colored on the bottom, 7 to 10 minutes. Turn the pieces 45 degrees and cook another 5 minutes or so. (The timing could be more or less, depending on the size of the vegetable and the amount of heat. They should cook slowly enough that they collapse and soften as they brown.)

Combine the miso, mirin, sake, and sugar if needed. Thin with a few tablespoons water, then cook over medium heat until the sauce thickens some, just a few minutes.

When the eggplant has finished cooking, arrange it cut-side up on platter, spoon the sauce down the middle of each piece, then garnish with the green onions and black sesame seeds. Serve hot, warm, or at room temperature.

BREAKFAST ANYTIME

CHAPTER 17

Breakfast Any Time

If you want to see diversity in a population, just think about the American breakfast for a moment. Yes, there's an underlying belief that this is not the meal to skip because it's a good breakfast that gives you a what you need for a day of clear thinking. But when it comes to eating breakfast, whole family units cease to cohere. Each member heads off in a different direction. Some eat on the run; others insist on a real meal; some—perhaps many or most—just skip it and grab something later. And there are those who far prefer savory breakfasts, even leftover soups and vegetables, to the usual bowl of cereal or toast.

Breakfast is a sensitive meal. Not everyone is ready to face food in the morning. My husband has learned not to ask if he can fix me anything, although sometimes it turns out that I'm frying an egg for myself only moments after he's made an omelet. No one's offended. When it comes to breakfast, we go our own ways, occasionally colliding and sitting down together. I suspect a lot of families are like this.

Largely it's our hectic morning schedules that make breakfast such a hit-and-miss affair. Yet for many, breakfast is an important meal, especially for children, who seriously need food to start the day. (In my state, more than half the kids get their breakfast at school rather than at home.) But the opportunity for sharing doesn't come until the weekend, and even then, not always. But often that's when breakfast turns into that strange hybrid called brunch, a meal that includes not only breakfast foods but dishes you might well serve for dinner or dessert. In fact, recipes that are suitable for brunch are scattered throughout the book.

Conversely, many of the foods we associate with the morning hour are great for dinner. How many of us have turned to a bowl of cereal when we've come home late at night, hungry but tired? Who doesn't enjoy an omelet for lunch or pancakes and fried eggs for supper? There's a calming, easy feeling about eating breakfast for dinner, as if it doesn't really count somehow. It's backward and fun, like taking a holiday or leaving work early.

Certainly eggs are one of our traditional breakfast foods, but they're such a quick and easy food to cook for other meals that they have their own chapter. Look to chapter 15, Eggs and Cheese (pages 497 to 519) for most egg recipes, including those breakfast basics like scrambled and fried. Breakfast breads, like corn bread and coffee cakes, are in the next chapter (page 571).

One of the obstacles to eating wholesome breakfasts is time, of course. But a little planning and some ingenious uses of some common household items may help make eating breakfast possible again, and enjoyable. And, as is often said, breakfast is not the meal to skip; it carries us into and sometimes throughout the day.

Breakfast Fruits

For a weekday meal, breakfast fruit, if it exists at all, probably consists of a banana or an apple grabbed on the run. Certainly when time allows, breakfast fruits can be prepared somewhat more elaborately, but a good piece of fruit needs little fiddling. Tropical resorts, for example, do little more for their breakfast fruit than to thinly slice and then skillfully fan a papaya or pineapple and accompany it with wedges of lime. Compotes are certainly attractive for brunches or breakfasts when one has more time for cooking, but once made, they keep for many days in the refrigerator, to be drawn from throughout the week. Virtually all of the simple fruit desserts and compotes are just as good for breakfast or for more elaborate brunches.

APPLESAUCE: A perennial favorite, cold or warm, applesauce is a soothing breakfast fruit to enjoy alone, with cottage cheese, yogurt, and a dash of nutmeg or cinnamon. Applesauce couldn't be easier to make (page 607).

SAUTÉED APPLES OR PEARS: Both a simple dessert and a morning fruit, these can be made in moments and are delicious by themselves or served over oatmeal.

BERRIES: Sprinkle berries lightly with brown sugar and serve them with sour cream or yogurt, or simply have them available to add to the cereal bowl.

GRAPEFRUIT: Grapefruit is a winter fruit, and the old-fashioned way of preparing it is still good today. Cut it in half across the equator, then, using a grapefruit knife, cut along each section. Serve like this or sprinkle with brown sugar and place under the broiler until the sugar is melted or, skip the sugar and broiling altogether.

MANGOES: Make a "porcupine mango." Slice a mango lengthwise about one-third of the way in. You'll have 2 pieces plus the center, which contains the seed. (This piece is for you.) Score the flesh of the 2 remaining pieces in a crisscross fashion, cutting down to the skin but not through it. Pull the ends toward you, forcing the center out to reveal little cubes of mango ready to eat. Serve with wedges of lime or lime juice squeezed over the fruit. Or peel then slice the mangoes into a bowl of blackberries, raspberries, or Rhubarb, Strawberry, and Mango Compote (page 614).

MELONS: An unchallenging breakfast fruit in every respect. Rather than serving entire half melons, slice a melon into whatever size wedge seems appropriate, then scoop out the seeds. Slide a knife just between the fruit and the rind to loosen it, then slice the melon crosswise into bite-size pieces. If it's a very wide piece, slice it lengthwise down the center as well. Serve with a wedge of lemon or lime or salt and pepper. Or, slice the melon into very thin slices and fan them on a platter. Serve plain or intersperse berries and lime or lemon wedges.

PAPAYA: Slice a papaya in half and remove the seeds. Squeeze lime juice over the fruit or serve with lime wedges. The seeds are crunchy and quite edible. Try rinsing a few and using them to garnish the fruit. Or fill the papaya center with raspberries and squeeze passion fruit over them.

DRIED FRUITS AND NUTS

A plateful of dried fruits—figs, dates, prunes, apples, pears—and nuts, cracked or in their shells, couldn't be easier to assemble for breakfast or to take to work.

Poached Prunes with Lemon

Poached dried fruits are good at any meal in my opinion. Serve them plain or with yogurt, a spoonful of mascarpone, or even cream. Serves 4 to 6 Ⓥ

- 1 lemon or small orange
- 1 (12-ounce) package prunes
- 1 (3-inch) cinnamon stick

Remove several long bands of zest from the lemon, then slice them into thin strips. Combine everything in a saucepan and add water to cover. Bring to a boil, then lower the heat and simmer gently until the prunes are tender and plump, about 25 minutes. Serve warm or cold with their juices.

Poached Gingered Apricots: In place of prunes, cook dried apricots as described, adding several slices of fresh ginger to the pot and omitting the cinnamon. Ⓥ

Stewed Rhubarb

Cold stewed rhubarb with yogurt makes bracing breakfast fruit. Serves 4 to 6 Ⓥ

- 1¹/₂ pounds rhubarb
- ¹/₂ cup sugar or ¹/₃ cup honey or other sweetener
- 3 whole cloves
- Grated zest and juice of 1 orange or 2 tangerines

Chop the rhubarb into 1-inch pieces and put in a heavy pan with the sugar, cloves, zest, and juice. Cook over low heat until the rhubarb has broken down, about 10 minutes. Taste and sweeten if needed.

Variations: Add whole or halved strawberries, sections of blood orange or tangerine, sliced kumquat, or sliced mango to the fruit once it's cooked. Season the compote with a few drops of orange-flower water, to taste.

Winter Breakfast Compote

Fruit syrups, such as passion fruit—available in specialty stores—add exotic flavors as well as a little extra sweetness to this breakfast compote. Serves 4 to 6 Ⓥ

- 2 grapefruits, 1 white and 1 red
- 2 navel oranges
- 2 large tangerines
- 2 small red bananas, or 1 yellow banana
- 2 kiwifruit
- ¹/₂ cup pomegranate seeds, optional
- ¹/₂ cup passion fruit, pomegranate syrup to taste, or ¹/₄ cup warmed orange honey
- ¹/₂ cup unsweetened shredded coconut

Peel and section the citrus fruits and place them in a serving dish. Squeeze the pulp over them. Slice the bananas diagonally, peel and slice the kiwifruit, and tuck them among the citrus sections; cover with the pomegranate seeds. Drizzle the syrup over the fruit and chill until ready to serve. Toast the coconut in a dry pan until lightly browned, then transfer to a plate to cool. Serve the compote with the coconut dusted over the top.

Beverages for Breakfast and Brunch and Sparkling Coolers

Aside from coffee, tea, and juice, there are a number of delicious drinks to enjoy for breakfast and brunch—or even later in the day when the addition of club soda or mineral water turns them into sparkling coolers.

While beverages are usually accompaniments to food, they also make a soothing breakfast. A smoothie, whether based on vegetables or fruit, for example, can make a good start to the day. If you're looking for ways to eat more protein, all kinds of powders can be found to add to your smoothie. If you don't care for dairy, rice milk, coconut milk, and almond milk as well as hemp and other plant milks can be used. On the other hand, yogurt and buttermilk make pleasantly tart additions to creamy smoothies. Almost any fruit can be used, not only fresh ripe fruits but also unsweetened frozen berries, peaches, and cherries and cooked dried fruits such as prunes and apricots. For flavorings, vanilla is always good—I practically pour it in—but so are almond extract and orange–flower water. Spices, like cinnamon, nutmeg, and cardamom, are both delicious and beneficial to eat. And you can also include such additions as flaxseeds and oil, chia seeds, walnuts and almonds, and fresh herbs, such as mint. Here are some ideas to get you started.

Honeydew and Lime Juice with Mint

Dead–ripe melons make superlative drinks. Lime and mint are classic with melon, but try ginger, lemon verbena, or lemon balm as well. Serves 4 Ⓥ

1/2 large ripe green or pink honeydew melon
Juice of 2 to 4 large limes
1/2 cup mint leaves
Club soda or sparkling mineral water, optional

Puree the honeydew in a blender with the lime juice and mint leaves. Chill or serve right away, over ice with a dash of club soda.

Real Almond Milk

This almond milk, which is nothing like its commercial counterpart, makes a very restoring and refreshing drink. Serve it chilled and plain or mix with mineral water to make a cooler. Makes about 3 cups Ⓥ

1/2 cup blanched and peeled almonds
6 tablespoons sugar or light honey
A few drops almond extract
1 tablespoon orange-flower water or to taste

Put 3 cups cold water in a blender, turn it to high speed, and gradually add the almonds.

Blend until well pulverized—about 5 minutes—then strain through cheesecloth into a saucepan. Stir in the sugar, bring to a boil, and simmer for 2 minutes. Turn off the heat and let cool. Stir in the almond extract and orange–flower water and refrigerate until well chilled. To serve, mix in a glass with ice. If the mixture is too thick, add a little water or mineral water.

Variation: Omit the orange–flower water and flavor the milk with 1/4 teaspoon or more ground cardamom or nutmeg or with 1/2 to 1 teaspoon ground cinnamon and the finely grated zest of a lemon. Ⓥ

Banana-Pineapple Frappé

For more tropical flavor, add the pulp of one or two passion fruits or passion fruit syrup. Serves 2 to 3 (V)

2 ripe bananas

1 tablespoon honey, or 1 teaspoon agave nectar

2 tablespoons buttermilk, yogurt, or coconut milk beverage

1 cup fresh pineapple or pineapple juice

Pineapple sage or mint sprigs, for garnish

Puree the bananas in a blender with the honey, buttermilk, and pineapple. Pour over ice and garnish with sprigs of pineapple sage if available.

Nectarine-Mango Frappé

Serves 2 to 3

2 nectarines or peaches

1 large mango

1¹/₂ cups kefir or buttermilk

A few drops vanilla

6 ice cubes

Fresh lemon or lime juice

Peel and slice the fruit, then puree in a blender or food processor with the kefir, vanilla, and ice until smooth. Add the lemon or lime juice to taste and serve.

White Grape Juice with Orange and Basil

This fragrant drink is a gentle eye-opener in the morning or, come evening, a sparkling cooler. Serves 4 (V)

4 cups white grape juice

1 large orange, thinly sliced

10 sprigs lemon basil or lemon verbena, plus extra for garnish

Sparkling mineral water, optional

Combine the juice, orange, and herbs in a pitcher and steep for several hours or overnight in the refrigerator. Strain and serve chilled, with a few ice cubes and a fresh sprig of basil in each glass. For fizz, add mineral water to each glass to taste.

Pear Smoothie

Serves 1 to 2

1 cup pear juice

1 ripe pear

2 drops almond extract

1 cup yogurt, buttermilk, or kefir

¹/₄ teaspoon ground cardamom

Puree everything in a blender until smooth, then pour over ice.

Banana Smoothie

Serves 1 (V)

1 ripe banana

³/₄ cup dairy or plant milk, or more as needed

¹/₄ cup yogurt or buttermilk, optional

1 teaspoon sugar or honey

¹/₂ teaspoon vanilla

¹/₄ teaspoon cinnamon

Puree the banana, milk, yogurt, and sugar in a blender, then add enough vanilla and cinnamon to give it a good flavor.

Mango-Orange Cooler

A luscious orange beverage to remember when mangoes are plentiful. A little tamarind sharpens the sweet mango. Serves 4 (V)

2 ripe mangoes, weighing about 1 pound each

2 cups orange juice

¹/₂ teaspoon or more tamarind, to taste

8 ice cubes

Juice of 2 to 3 limes

Sparkling water, optional

Mint sprigs or lime wedges, for serving

Peel the mangoes and cut as much of the flesh off the pits as possible. Add the orange juice and tamarind and ice and puree until smooth. Add lime juice to taste. Pour into a pitcher over ice cubes and let the foam settle a few moments, then thin with sparkling water and serve with a sprig of mint.

Pineapple–Coconut Milk Drink

If you're ending a day of leisure with this drink, add a splash of rum. Serves 2 to 4 Ⓥ

---

2 cups chopped fresh or canned pineapple

1 cups coconut milk beverage (not canned)

1 banana

1 teaspoon orange-flower water

Blend all the ingredients plus $1/2$ cup water together and pour over ice.

Protein Drink

Of course you can add a serving of protein powder to any smoothie, or start with this recipe and then improvise. Makes 1 large serving Ⓥ

---

1 cup dairy or plant milk

$1/4$ cup yogurt, optional

2 tablespoons vegan protein powder

$1/2$ cup fresh or frozen fruit—berries, peach, mango, banana

$1/4$ teaspoon cinnamon

1 teaspoon vanilla

Combine everything in a blender and puree until frothy and smooth.

Kale Smoothie with Lemon and Ginger

Makes 1 Ⓥ

---

1 cup coconut water or water

$1/2$ lemon, seeded and thinly sliced

1 (1-inch) piece of ginger, thinly sliced

2 handfuls kale, spinach, or other greens

A few ice cubes, optional

Put the coconut water in a blender with the lemon and ginger and puree until smooth. Add the greens and continue to blend until creamy smooth. If the mixture is too thick, thin it with additional water. Add the ice to make the smoothie cold, if you wish.

Green Smoothie with Chia Seeds, Orange, and Lemon

Makes 1 Ⓥ

---

1 heaping tablespoon chia seeds

1 cup unsweetened coconut water or water

2 oranges, peels removed, the flesh coarsely chopped

$1/2$ lemon or lime, seeded and thinly sliced

Protein powder, as directed

3 handfuls kale, spinach, or other greens, torn and washed

Put the chia seeds in the blender jar with the coconut water and set aside to soak while you remove the peels from the oranges, slice the lemon, and wash the greens. Turn on the blender, add the fruit and protein powder, and blend until smooth, then gradually add the greens and continue blending until completely pulverized and smooth.

My Morning Smoothie

This is my morning smoothie, a much appreciated and enjoyed meal on mornings when I go early to the gym. I sometimes use vegan powders, other times whey, but always $1/2$ cup or more frozen raspberries and a dash of vanilla. Makes 1 Ⓥ

---

1 cup rice milk or coconut milk

1 or 2 scoops vegan protein powder, as suggested

1 heaping tablespoon sprouted, ground flax meal

About $1/2$ cup frozen raspberries

Good dash of cinnamon

Splash of vanilla

Small pinch of maia powder or turmeric

Put everything in a blender and puree until the berries are broken up and everything is well blended. Pour into a glass, then rinse the blender jar with a little water and add it to the glass. Give a stir and you're set.

Shrubs and Switchels

A shrub is a syrup, often based on fruit, sharpened with vinegar (it's sometimes called drinking vinegar), then stirred into sparkling water to make the most refreshing hot weather drink imaginable. Shrubs date back to colonial times but are new again to us and deservedly popular, both in cocktails as well as nonalcoholic drinks. A few people I know of have been very experimental with their shrubs, using vegetables, all kinds of fruits from rhubarb to pomegranates to pears, and botanicals, suggesting that one can really get very experimental here. Like shrubs, switchels are also old-fashioned vinegar-based drinks that are ultimately refreshing, once used by farmers during the haying season to quench their thirst. Switchels are more immediately available to drink, as they don't need but a few hours or overnight to sit and steep.

Ginger–Honey Switchel

A farmer friend sent me this recipe for a version she likes, and I like it, too. If you can't get fresh ginger to grate, use dried powdered ginger, starting with half the quantity given for fresh. You can always add more. Serves 4

- 1/2 cup organic apple cider vinegar
- 2 heaping tablespoons honey
- 1 scant tablespoon grated ginger
- Slice of lime, for garnish
- Club soda or sparkling mineral water, optional

Combine all the ingredients with 2 cups water in a clean jar, then cover and refrigerate overnight or for several hours. Before serving, shake the jar and taste the mixture. If it isn't sweet enough, add more honey or other sweetener. Strain, then pour over a glass of ice and garnish with a thin slice of lime. This can be mixed with soda water if you wish to have the bubbles.

Berry Shrub

As with any fermented or preserved food, cleanliness is all-important, so start with clean hands and make sure all your jars and utensils are super-clean. Makes 4 cups of syrup Ⓥ

- 2 cups berries—raspberries, blackberries, black raspberries, fragrant strawberries
- 2 cups organic apple cider vinegar
- 1 1/2 cups sugar
- Club soda or sparkling mineral water, for serving
- Sprigs of fresh mint or lemon verbena, for serving

Begin by washing a 1-quart jar and its lid in hot soapy water, then rinse. Drop both the jar and lids into a pan of boiling water and keep them there for 7 to 8 minutes. Remove and set upright, then add the berries.

Heat the vinegar to near-boiling, then pour it over the fruit, leaving a little headspace to allow for expansion. Wipe well and cover tightly. Set aside in a cool, dark cupboard or the refrigerator for up to a month. You can use it after a day or two, but as it sits the flavor develops and becomes stronger. When it's as strong as you like, strain it.

Put the sugar in a clean saucepan then add the strained vinegar. Bring to a boil and stir to dissolve the sugar. You can tell when it's thoroughly dissolved by rubbing a drop between your fingers: there will be no graininess.

While the syrup is cooking, resterilize the jar. When the syrup is done, pour it into the jar, seal, and refrigerate.

To make a glass of shrub, stir a tablespoon (or more, to taste) into a glass of cold sparkling water. Add ice, a sprig of mint or lemon verbena, and serve.

Breakfast Cereal

Certainly one of our national food embarrassments is packaged cereal. The sheer volume of it, coupled with the high cost and its quantities of added sugar, must surely discourage any well-meaning shopper trying to put something wholesome on the breakfast table. But among the junky offerings, there are many delicious cereals of reasonable quality. Natural foods stores abound in good grains, many of which are sold more cheaply in bulk, but most supermarkets have a section where you can buy excellent "health food" cereals. The old American favorites like Wheatena, farina, and Roman Meal are entirely wheat-based and problematic for those sensitive to wheat. But there are other grains—oatmeal, steel-cut oats, couscous, puffed buckwheat, and grits made not just from corn but also barley, millet, and brown rice. In short, there are plenty of good choices and those cereals sold in bulk are quite reasonable.

If you or your family have known only sugar-coated flakes, pops, and loops, try introducing real cereal at home. An array of garnishes from toasted nuts to dried fruits and sweeteners will make them especially appealing to young eaters whose TV-tailored taste leads them right to those cereals you would probably prefer to avoid.

MAKING HOT CEREALS: The smaller the grain, the more quickly it cooks. Chewy groats can take as long as 2 hours, stone-ground grits 45 minutes, whereas fine cream of wheat cooks in minutes. If you're in a hurry, use the smaller-size grains or flakes, such as rolled oats. Or if you prefer groats and grits, you might utilize a slow cooker.

Depending on whether the grain is coarse, fine, or flaked, the ratio of water to cereal differs. Packaged cereals have their own cooking instructions, but all cereal is very easy to make and it's made the same way: just stir the cereal into boiling, lightly salted water, usually 1 part cereal to 3 parts water, then cook over medium-low heat, stirring occasionally, until it has thickened and tastes cooked. If the finished cereal is too thick for your liking, simply stir in more liquid. If it's too thin, you can even whisk in additional cereal as long as you give it time to cook through. Some people like lumps, or knots, but if you prefer to avoid them, be sure to add the cereal gradually to the water, whisking while you do so. (Lumps are most likely to appear in fine cereals, which thicken quickly.) However, the flavor of cooked cereals emerges more fully if you can give them extra time on the stove. Not only will the cereal taste better, it will be more digestible too.

Water is the usual cooking medium for cereal, but milk and juice are other possibilities—oatmeal cooked in apple juice or Cream of Wheat cooked in milk, for example. A little butter or sweetener can be stirred in at the end, or not. While Americans prefer sweetened cereals, savory toppings, such as sesame-salt (*gomashio*) or grated cheese are also good.

Multigrain cereals are popular today. You can make your own just by cooking your cereal odds and ends together. Leftover rice, wheat berries, quinoa, and other grains also make interesting additions to cooked cereals. Add them once the cereal has thickened.

Tips for Cooking Breakfast Cereals

TOASTING CEREALS: All grains and flakes can be given a flavor boost by toasting. Put cereal in a dry skillet set over medium heat and stir frequently until it begins to smell toasty and takes on a little color. Remove to a plate as soon as it's toasted so it doesn't burn. Cook the grains as you normally would.

USING A DOUBLE BOILER: A double boiler cooks cereal perfectly without your attention, so you can shower and dress, make lunches, or tend to other things while it's cooking. Corn meal, noninstant oats, multigrain cereals, and steel-cut oats are good cereals for this method, although any cereal can be cooked this way. Cook the cereal in the top part of the double boiler directly over the heat just until it begins to thicken, then set it over simmering water, cover, and cook for 20 minutes (30 to 40 for steel-cut oats).

USING A SLOW COOKER: The slow cooker is ideal for grits and long-cooking grains like steel-cut oats. Combine the ingredients the night before, set the cooker on low, and awake to the aroma of hot cereal. But a word of caution—get to know your own slow cooker. Mine cooks steel-cut oats in only 3 hours, for example. If your cooker doesn't have an automatic turn off, you won't appreciate getting up in the middle of the night to turn it off.

USING A THERMOS: This method is suitable for most every cereal. Fill a wide-mouth thermos with hot water and set it aside. Meanwhile, cook cereal in boiling water just until it has begun to thicken. Drain the thermos, add the cereal, screw on the lid, and leave it until morning. If you have no time to eat before leaving, you can take it with you.

Breakfast Porridge

Fine meals, like Cream of Rice and Cream of Wheat, semolina, and fine corn meal, absorb less water and cook more quickly than grits. Such cereals are ideal for those with queasy tummies—soft and soothing. Makes about 3 cups (V)

1/4 teaspoon sea salt
1 cup cereal

Bring 3 cups water to a boil, add the salt, and gradually whisk in the cereal. Lower the heat and cook over low heat, stirring frequently, until thickened, 10 to 20 minutes. Cover the pan and let stand 5 to 10 minutes more.

TOPPINGS FOR COOKED CEREALS

- Brown sugar, maple syrup, molasses, sorghum, or honey
- Milk, including soy, rice, and almond milk, or other plant milks, and buttermilk
- Fruit juices, especially apple and pear
- Butter, yogurt, or sour cream, especially when combined with molasses
- Ghee, as little as 1/2 teaspoon per bowl
- Grated cheddar, especially on grits
- Toasted nuts and seeds
- Ground flaxseeds or flaxseed oil
- Raisins, currants, chopped dates, or chopped dried apricots
- Stewed prunes, especially in Cream of Wheat, rice, and couscous
- Sautéed apples, especially on steel-cut oats and toasted barley flakes
- Spice, especially cinnamon, nutmeg, and cardamom
- Almond butter, peanut butter, or sunflower butter

Hot Cereal with Sesame Salt: Gomashio (page 67), toasted sesame seeds ground with salt, is a popular Japanese condiment that's eaten with rice and all sorts of other foods. It really is quite delicious and is just the thing for those who don't care for sweetened cereals and for those who prefer to skip the milk. If you like its nutty flavor, you'll find that gomashio tastes wonderful on all grains, including those we eat for breakfast.

Quick-Cooking Oats and Other Rolled (or Flaked) Grains

Because of their flattened appearance, rolled grains are also called flakes. Other grains can be cooked just as oatmeal is, although they end up with varying textures.
Makes about 3 cups Ⓥ

1/4 teaspoon sea salt
1 1/4 cups rolled grains

Bring 3 cups water to a boil, add the salt, then stir in the grain. Lower the heat and simmer until the cereal is thickened, about 5 minutes. Cover and let stand for 5 minutes before serving.

Maple-Nut Cereal

The combination of maple syrup and toasted nuts is always welcome on wheat-based and mixed-grain cereals.
Makes about 4 cups Ⓥ

Pinch sea salt
1 cup cracked wheat or multigrain cereal
1/2 teaspoon ground cinnamon
1/2 cup toasted pecans or walnuts
Maple syrup, to finish
Dairy or plant milk, for serving

Bring 3 cups water to a boil, add the salt, and stir in the cereal and cinnamon. Stir for a few minutes, then lower the heat, cover the pan, and cook until thick, about 7 minutes. Pour into bowls, serve with the toasted nuts on top, and rim the edge with maple syrup. Serve with a pitcher of milk.

Corn Meal with Vanilla and Molasses

It's the splash of vanilla that makes this cereal so good. Corn meal needs to be a little gritty to avoid lumps. If what you have looks more like corn flour, mix it into half the water before heating. Stir this slurry into the remaining water when it boils and simmer until done. Makes about 4 cups Ⓥ

---

1 cup fine white or yellow corn meal, preferably stone-ground
Sea salt
2 teaspoons vanilla
Butter or coconut oil
Unsulfured molasses, for serving

Gradually whisk the corn meal into 4 cups boiling water. Add a few pinches salt, lower the heat, and cook until thickened. Stir frequently, especially at the beginning. Fine corn meal will be done in 4 to 5 minutes, coarse grits in 30 to 40 minutes. When done, stir in the vanilla and butter to taste. Serve with molasses.

Fried Corn Meal Mush: Today we call this polenta, but many of us who enjoyed this as children know it as mush. My father always made extra corn meal for breakfast, then poured the leftovers into a loaf pan to cool for the next day.

Cut cooled, cooked corn meal cereal into 1/2-inch slices and fry it in a little coconut oil or butter. You can give it a little more substance by dipping it first into beaten egg, then into corn meal, then frying until golden and crisp. Serve with molasses, honey, or jam. Oatmeal is also good prepared this way.

Steel-Cut Oats

These hearty oats, also called Scotch or Irish oats, take longer to cook than most cereals and are ideal candidates for the slow cooker and the double boiler. Leftovers make such a wonderful chewy addition to pancakes, muffins, and breads, or they can be thinned with water and reheated for cereal. Makes about 4¹/₂ cups Ⓥ

1/2 teaspoon sea salt
1³/4 cups steel-cut oats

Bring 5 cups water to a boil, add the salt, then gradually stir in the oats. Return to a boil until the mixture thickens, after a few minutes, then transfer them to the top of a double boiler and cook, covered, over simmering water until tender but still a little chewy, about 35 minutes. Or combine the ingredients and add them to a slow cooker and cook overnight over low heat. The next morning, spoon out the cereal.

Another suggestion, from *The Breakfast Book* by Marion Cunningham, is to simmer the oats in the top of a double boiler for 5 minutes the night before, cover the pot, turn off the heat, and go to bed. Next morning, just reheat them over simmering water.

Breakfast Grits

These have a reassuring, simple appeal that's more interesting than Cream of Wheat yet not overly challenging. Enjoy grits with a spoonful of molasses and butter or with cheddar and a dash of tabasco sauce. Makes about 4 cups Ⓥ

1/2 teaspoon sea salt
1 cup stone-ground corn grits

Bring 4 cups water to a boil, add the salt, and whisk in the grits. Stir for the first minute or so, then lower the heat and cook for 35 to 40 minutes, giving an occasional stir. Or cook them in a slow cooker or double boiler as described on page 549. If you like texture in your cereal, add whole hominy, drained and rinsed, to breakfast grits.

Breakfast Couscous with Honey and Dates

This breakfast pudding is quite easy to elaborate on. Prunes are always good with wheat, while a teaspoon of orange zest or orange-flower water lends fragrance. You could cook the couscous in water and pour almond milk over the top and serve with toasted slivered almonds. Serves 4

1 cup milk
Sea salt
1 cup fine or regular couscous
8 dates, pitted and chopped
Butter, cinnamon, and honey, for serving

Combine 2 cups water and the milk in a saucepan with a pinch of salt and bring to a boil. Stir in the couscous and add the dates. Cook for about 30 seconds, then turn off the heat, cover the pan, and let stand until the liquid is absorbed, 10 to 15 minutes. Serve with a pat of butter and a dash of cinnamon and drizzle with honey.

Breakfast Quinoa with Raisins and Walnuts

For those who don't want wheat or other gluten-filled grains, try having quinoa for breakfast. It won't get soft and mushy, but it's very easy to eat. I make a few cups and keep them in the refrigerator to have over the course of 5 days or so. Makes 4 cups or more Ⓥ

1 cup beige quinoa
1/4 teaspoon sea salt
1/2 cup raisins—your choice
Chopped walnuts or pecans, for serving
1 teaspoon of ghee or butter per serving, optional
Dairy or plant milk, optional

Rinse the quinoa well then put it in a pot with 2 cups water and the salt. Bring to a boil, then simmer, partially covered, until the quinoa is cooked but still offers a little bite, about 15 minutes. Taste for salt and add more if you like. Stir in the raisins. Serve warm with walnuts and ghee, as a grain, or with milk.

Wild Rice Cereal with Currants

A mixture of wild and white rice cooked with dried fruit makes an unusual and hearty morning cereal. The currants may make it sweet enough, but if not, add a sprinkling of brown sugar. Serve with milk, or not, as you wish. Serves 4 Ⓥ

1/3 cup wild rice, preferably native wild rice, if possible

1/3 cup short–grain white rice

2 tablespoons dried currants

1/4 teaspoon salt

Rinse both rices well and put them in a saucepan with the rest of the ingredients and 4 cups water. Bring to a boil, then cover partially and simmer until the wild rice is tender, about 40 minutes. This will make a fairly dry rice, one without much extra liquid. If you prefer it to be wetter, just add more water or even milk while it's cooking.

Amaranth with Cooked Rice or Quinoa

With cooking, amaranth turns slightly gelatinous, which isn't to everyone's liking, particularly first thing in the morning. However, adding a handful of cooked rice, leftover steel-cut oats, quinoa—any cooked grain you have on hand—gives it the texture it needs. Makes about 1¹/₂ cups Ⓥ

1/2 cup amaranth, preferably golden

1/2 cup cooked rice, quinoa, or other grain

Pinch sea salt

Combine the ingredients and 1¹/₂ cups water in a small saucepan, bring to a boil, then reduce the heat to a simmer. Cover and cook over low heat until the water is absorbed, about 15 minutes. Add additional water or milk if you feel it needs thinning.

Creamy Rice Cereal

Rice with milk is one of the most soothing, comforting foods I know. It can consist of just a bowl of dinner rice with milk poured over it or this luxurious version, in which rice is cooked slowly in milk. When done, it is thick and creamy, like a rice pudding, and naturally sweet from the sugars in the milk. Serve it with additional milk, a pat of butter, and a sprinkling of brown sugar if desired. Serves 4 Ⓥ

1 cup short–grain white rice

Sea salt

1/4 teaspoon ground cinnamon

A few gratings of nutmeg

3 cups dairy or plant milk, such as coconut, almond, or rice

Bring the rice and 1 cup water to a boil in a saucepan. Simmer until the water is absorbed, then add another 1 cup water, a pinch of salt, the spices, and the milk. Bring to a boil, then lower the heat and simmer, stirring occasionally, until the milk is absorbed, about 45 minutes. Serve right away.

If left to cool, the rice will become completely firm. To reheat it, just thin it with a cup or so of water and reheat it in a pan. Eventually it will break apart and become creamy and smooth.

Sweet Rice Breakfast Soup

Short-grain rice turns soft and creamy—soothing when you're recovering from the flu or a cold. Use the Japanese sweet rice, either white and brown, Arborio, or other short-grain rice. Makes about 3 cups

- 1/2 cup short-grain white or brown rice
- 3 cups water or almond milk
- 1/2 teaspoon sea salt
- 1 short cinnamon stick
- Butter, brown sugar, and cold milk, for serving

Put the rice, water, salt, and cinnamon stick in a pot, bring to a boil, then simmer slowly until the mixture is creamy and thick, 20 minutes for white rice and about an hour for brown. Remove the cinnamon stick and serve with a tad of butter, brown sugar, and cold milk.

Savory Rice Soup

A rice soup makes a savory and invigorating start to the day. You can make it even more so by adding diced serrano chiles or chili oil. Makes about 3 cups

- Sweet Rice Breakfast Soup (preceding recipe), without the cinnamon
- 1 sheet nori
- Soy sauce or tamari, for the rice
- 1 or 2 green onions, thinly sliced
- Chopped cilantro
- Toasted sesame seeds or Gomashio (page 67)

While the rice is cooking, toast a sheet of nori by passing it back and forth through a flame or over an electric burner. After several passes, it will become crisp. Season the cooked rice with a little soy sauce to taste. Stir in the onions, then crumble the toasted nori over the top and top with the onion, cilantro, and toasted sesame seeds.

Cooked Amaranth

The tiny seeds cluster and float on the surface at first, but eventually they absorb the water. Amaranth turns slightly gelatinous. Makes about 1 1/2 cups Ⓥ

- 1/2 cup amaranth
- Sea salt

Combine 1 1/2 cups water, the amaranth, and a pinch of salt in a small saucepan, bring to a boil, and then reduce the heat to a simmer. Cover and cook over low heat for 25 minutes or until the water is absorbed, about 15 minutes.

Variation with Mixed Tiny Grains: Mix teff, amaranth, and quinoa, the latter thoroughly rinsed, and cook as described. Ⓥ

Cold Cereals

When you look at the sugared cereals on our supermarket shelves, it's hard to believe that cold cereals began as an invention of health food enthusiasts. However, there are always alternatives to the mainstream offerings, many of which are easily within reach. Here are a few alternatives for homemade cold cereals that you might also enjoy.

Scots Crowdie: This is something I thought I made up on my own, but it turns out that it's actually a Scottish dish. Simply cover uncooked rolled oats with thick, cold buttermilk and add a spoonful of honey, berries, or a sliced banana if you wish. If you don't like buttermilk, try it with yogurt.

Granola

Another early health food that has gone mainstream and is no longer so healthy. Use this version if you're trying to wean kids away from sugary cereals or as a topping for yogurt and fruit. Makes about 8 cups Ⓥ

6 cups flaked or rolled grains
1 cup chopped nuts
1 cup wheat germ
1 teaspoon grated nutmeg
1 tablespoon ground cinnamon
Sea salt
1/2 cup safflower or coconut oil
3/4 cup honey, golden syrup, or maple syrup
1 cup raisins

Preheat the oven to 300°F. Toss the grains, nuts, germ, spices, and salt together, then add the oil and sweetener and toss again to coat them thoroughly. Spread the mixture on two sheet pans and bake until golden, turning every 10 minutes so that it browns evenly. When done, after about 30 minutes, add the raisins and let cool. As the granola cools, it will lose its stickiness and become crunchy. Store in a tightly covered jar.

Leaner Granola: Omit the oil and toast everything as suggested. Keep the sweetener or reduce it. It does give the cereal a nice crunch and is perhaps a better idea than simply passing the sugar bowl. Ⓥ

Granola with Vanilla and Fruit Juice

Another way to make granola is to use juice instead of oil. Makes about 6 cups Ⓥ

4 cups rolled flakes—oat, wheat, spelt, barley
1 cup quinoa, rinsed well
2 teaspoons ground cinnamon
1 teaspoon grated nutmeg
1/2 cup sliced or slivered almonds
1 teaspoon vanilla
1 cup pear or apple juice
1/2 cup honey or maple syrup
1/2 cup raisins or dried cherries

Preheat the oven to 300°F. Mix the flakes, quinoa, spices, and almonds together, then add the vanilla, juice, and honey. Toss well to moisten evenly, then toast on a sheet pan until browned, about 30 minutes, stirring a few times. Add the dried fruit once the cereal is cooked.

ADDITIONS TO GRANOLA

Except for adding dried fruit after the granola is baked so that it won't turn rock hard, there are no hard-and-fast rules about ingredients. All of these can be added.

- Oat, wheat, spelt, barley, or rye flakes
- Cashews, walnuts, pecans, almonds, or other nuts
- Sesame seeds, sunflower seeds, popped amaranth, or toasted quinoa
- Flaked coconut, banana chips, or chopped dates
- Dried cranberries, cherries, apples, or other fruit
- Wheat, rice or oat bran, or wheat germ
- Vanilla or almond extract
- Cinnamon, nutmeg, cardamom, or mace

Savory Breakfast Foods

Generally, this category would refer to eggs, but there are other savory foods people eat for breakfast. A summer spent in Japan revealed breakfast of grilled fish over rice with broth that was absolutely invigorating. During my years as a Zen student, our breakfasts were often savory—sesame soybeans, miso soups, cereal with *gomashio* rather than sugar, and they too were satisfying. In New Mexico, it's the breakfast burrito that's standard fare, whether you make it yourself, pick it up at a takeout counter, or eat it in a restaurant. And, of course, there are enchiladas topped with a fried egg, a great breakfast if you're planning to farm all day. Menudo is available at Mexican cafés on Saturday mornings. Many people find that soup makes a good start to the day, not just Saturday's menudo, and fried egg sandwiches are good any time of day. Who's to argue? Here are a few recipes with a definite Southwestern inclination; other egg recipes are found on pages 499 to 512.

Breakfast Eggs in Tortillas

Serves 2

- 2 large whole wheat tortillas
- 4 eggs, beaten with 1 tablespoon water
- Sea salt
- 2 tablespoons butter
- 1/2 cup grated Monterey Jack cheese
- 2 teaspoons diced jalapeño chile
- 2 green onions, including half the greens, chopped
- Chopped cilantro to taste

Place the tortillas, one on top of the other, in an ungreased skillet over low heat. As the bottom one warms, flip them over to warm the second one. Reverse the tortillas and repeat for the other sides.

Meanwhile, season the eggs with a few pinches of salt. Heat the butter in a nonstick skillet over medium heat until it sizzles. Add the eggs and scramble them. When they're nearly done, turn off the heat and stir in the cheese, chile, green onions, and cilantro. Scoop the eggs into the warm tortillas, fold them over, and serve alone or with a favorite salsa.

With Tofu: If you don't eat eggs, fill the burritos with Scrambled Tofu (page 556), adding cheese if you eat it. Since tofu is on the dry side, plan to add some salsa to the burrito as well. Ⓥ

With Scrambled Ricotta: You can also fill your burrito with the Scrambled Ricotta (page 556). Just add plenty of diced chiles, green onions, and cilantro.

Migas

Migas, a Tex-Mex dish, are eggs scrambled with tortilla crisps, preferably homemade ones, making a hearty, rustic plate of eggs. I never pass up the chance to enjoy them when I'm in Texas. Serves 2

2 or 3 corn tortillas or a few handfuls broken tortilla chips, plus extra tortillas for serving

1 tablespoon oil or butter

2 green onions, including the greens, chopped

1 jalapeño chile, finely diced

4 eggs, beaten with 1 tablespoon water

2 plum or Roma tomatoes, chopped

1/2 cup grated Monterey Jack or cheddar

Chopped cilantro to taste

Sea salt

Salsa or Pico de Gallo (page 90)

Cut the tortillas into strips or triangles and bake or fry them until crisp (page 40). Break them into bite-size pieces. Heat the oil in a nonstick skillet. Add the green onions and chile and sauté until the green onions are limp. Pour in the beaten eggs and start stirring them. Just before they're finished cooking, add the chips, tomatoes, cheese, and cilantro. Finish cooking, then season with salt to taste. Serve with warm tortillas and salsa on the side.

Variations: There's nothing hard-and-fast about migas except the presence of the tortilla chips. You can fry a little onion and bell pepper to start, use a tomato-based salsa in place of the fresh tomato, double the cheese or leave it out. Unless I have a great salsa on hand, I nearly always end up adding a good dusting of hot and smoky chipotle chile powder.

Scrambled Ricotta Cheese with Salsa

I never even thought of doing this until I saw a recipe in Diana Kennedy's The Art of Mexican Cooking. *Scrambled ricotta makes a great filling for tortillas.* Serves 2

2 tablespoons safflower oil

1/4 cup finely diced onion

2 serrano chiles, minced

1 1/2 cups ricotta

A few tablespoons crumbled feta or cheddar

Sea salt

1/2 cup Pico de Gallo (page 90) or commercial salsa

Heat the oil in an 8-inch skillet over medium heat. Add the onion and chiles and cook for a minute or so without letting them brown. Add the ricotta and feta, taste, then season with salt. Raise the heat to medium and cook, occasionally moving the cheese about the pan, until it becomes firm and the bottom has begun to color, about 5 minutes. Turn out and serve with the salsa.

Variations: Leave out the chiles and add 3 tablespoons chopped herbs such as those used in the Scrambled Tofu with Herbs (page 557).

Scrambled Tofu

Whatever gets added to scrambled eggs can go into tofu. Turmeric gives tofu a yellow egglike hue, but use it with restraint—it is bitter in quantity. Roll up in a warm tortilla or serve with toast. Serves 2 (V)

1 tablespoon oil

3 tablespoons thinly sliced green onion or onion

1 package soft tofu, drained

1/4 teaspoon turmeric

Sea salt and freshly milled pepper

Heat the oil in a small skillet, add the green onion, and sauté over medium heat until soft, 2 or 3 minutes. Crumble in the tofu, add the turmeric, season well with salt and pepper, and cook over high heat, stirring frequently, until the curds have firmed up and are heated through.

Variations: Try adding ground cumin, cilantro, roasted green chile, diced jalapeños, or salsa.

Scrambled Tofu with Herbs

Serves 4

- 1 tablespoon olive or safflower oil
- 2 teaspoons butter or additional oil
- 1 package soft tofu, drained
- 2 tablespoons chopped parsley
- 2 tablespoons chopped tarragon, basil, or marjoram
- 2 tablespoons finely sliced green onion
- 1/2 cup grated cheddar, Muenster, goat cheese, or feta, optional
- Sea salt and freshly milled pepper
- Dash paprika

Heat the oil and butter and, when hot, crumble the tofu into the pan. Cook over high heat, stirring frequently, until it begins to look firm, after several minutes. Add the herbs, onion, and cheese, taste and season with salt, then season with pepper. Serve with a dash of paprika over the top.

Scrambled Tofu with Salsa

Serve in corn or wheat tortillas. Serves 4

- 1 1/2 tablespoons oil
- 3 tablespoons diced onion or green onion
- 1 serrano chile, diced
- 1/2 teaspoon ground cumin
- 1/4 teaspoon dried oregano
- 1 package soft tofu, drained
- 3 tablespoons chopped cilantro
- Sea salt
- 1/2 cup grated cheddar, optional
- Warm tortillas, corn or wheat, for serving
- Salsa of your choosing, for serving

Heat the oil in a skillet, add the onion, and sauté over high heat for 1 or 2 minutes to sear it. Add the chiles, cumin, and oregano and cook for 1 or 2 minutes more. Crumble in the tofu and cook, stirring frequently, until it's firm and hot. Stir in the cilantro, season with salt, remove from the heat, and add the cheese. Serve with warm tortillas and plenty of salsa.

Scrambled Eggs and Corn in Tortillas

Wrapped in a hot tortilla with some grated cheese, given a few hard splashes of Smoked Chile Salsa (page 63), these eggs make a fast small breakfast or lunch. I often let the tortillas get a little crisp on the bottom, then spoon the eggs over the top and eat them like a tostada. Both ways are good. Serves 1

- 2 to 3 teaspoons butter, safflower oil, or sunflower seed oil
- 2 green onions, including some of the firm green parts, chopped
- 5 cilantro sprigs, chopped
- Kernels from 1 ear corn, raw or cooked,
- 2 eggs, lightly beaten
- Sea salt
- 2 small corn tortillas
- Grated Monterey Jack or Muenster, or thinly sliced goat Gouda, for serving
- Smoked Chile Salsa (page 63), for serving

Melt the butter in an 8-inch pan and add the green onions, cilantro, and corn. Cook for a few minutes, or until the corn is tender. Leave it in the pan.

Beat the eggs with a spoonful of water and a few pinches of salt, then pour them into the pan, and scramble them gently with a fork. Simultaneously, be warming the tortillas in a dry cast-iron or nonstick pan.

Transfer the tortillas to a plate and ladle the eggs over them. Sprinkle the cheese and salsa over the eggs.

With Other Chiles: In lieu of salsa, mince half of a seeded jalapeño chile and stir it into the eggs. Or, if you have left-over seared shishito peppers, pull off the stems and cook them with the eggs.

Hash Brown Potatoes

Some versions of this American breakfast staple start with raw potatoes, others with boiled grated ones. I always think they taste better when the potato has been precooked—something you can do the night before. If you start with raw grated potato, allow a little extra time for it to cook all the way through and brown. Serves 4 to 6 (V)

1¹⁄₂ pounds russet potatoes
¹⁄₄ cup finely diced onion, optional
3 tablespoons ghee, olive oil, or vegetable oil
Sea salt and freshly milled pepper

Cover the potatoes with cold water, boil until nearly tender, then drain. When cool, remove the skins and grate coarsely. Mix with the onion.

Heat the ghee in a cast-iron skillet. When hot enough to sputter a drop of water, add the potatoes. Season them with salt and plenty of pepper, lower the heat, and fry until golden on the bottom, about 5 minutes. While they cook, press them lightly with a spatula and give the pan a shake once or twice to make sure they're not sticking. Turn them over and fry on the second side. Or, if you don't want them in a cake form, just stir them around the pan every few minutes, letting them stand between stirrings, until browned all over.

Hash Browns with Green Chile and Cheese: Add 3 to 4 tablespoons roasted green chile, jalapeño, poblano, or Anaheim and several chopped green onions to the cooking potatoes. Once the potatoes are lightly browned, stir in a few tablespoons chopped cilantro and ¹⁄₂ cup grated Jack, cheddar, Muenster, or even large-curd cottage cheese.

Hash Browns with Melted Cheese and Smoked Paprika: Finish the potatoes by grating a little Monterey Jack or Teleme cheese over the top and dust generously with smoked paprika. Serve alongside your eggs, or scramble an egg, put it on top, and wrap the whole thing in a large tortilla for a sensational breakfast burrito.

With Smoked Salt or Paprika: Season the potatoes with either of these condiments just before serving. (V)

Eliot's Breakfast Parsnips

Master organic gardener Eliot Coleman made these parsnips for me one cold spring Vermont morning with monster-sized roots dug from the under the snow-covered ground. They were the best parsnips I've ever tasted. Serves 4

3 tablespoons butter or ghee
1 pound parsnips, as fresh and plump as possible, peeled and sliced into thin rounds
Sea salt
¹⁄₂ cup toasted chopped walnuts or pecans
Warm maple syrup

Melt the butter in a heavy skillet over medium heat. Don't let it get too hot. Add the parsnips and a pinch of salt. Cook, stirring frequently, until golden all over from their caramelizing sugars, 7 to 10 minutes. Serve covered with the nuts and maple syrup.

Pancakes, Griddle Cakes, and Hot Cakes

Pancakes, griddle cakes, and hot cakes—they're the same thing, really—are a hallowed Sunday morning tradition for many families. The assembly is the same as for quick breads: combine dry ingredients in one bowl, the wet ingredients in another, then mix them together with a few strokes of fork or spoon. Don't overwork the gluten by mixing too hard—any lumps always seem to take care of themselves. If the batter is too thick, gently stir in additional milk or water. For extra-light, fluffy pancakes beat the egg whites separately, then fold them into the batter.

I make pancakes at least once a week and while I almost never use a recipe, I usually use a mixture of flours—white whole wheat, regular whole wheat, spelt flour, corn flour, oat, quinoa, buckwheat—you name it. (Not that many all at once, of course!) I also add other foods such as cooked quinoa or leftover rice. What I've happily learned is that lightness has nothing to do with the flour, but the flours have a lot to do with goodness. I make what someone might call "healthy" pancakes, but they are tender, light, and because of the flours, more delicious than those made with just white flour.

For fat, I use safflower oil in the batter plus a tablespoon melted ghee for its flavor. Milk might be dairy or plant milk of some kind. I never use sugar because I don't like the taste of sweetened grains. Instead, maple syrup, honey, or jam can cover the cakes.

Cook pancakes in a heavy skillet or on a griddle heated gradually over medium-high heat. When hot, add the batter, then reduce the heat to medium so that the cakes will be cooked by the time they brown. Bubbles should cover the surface before you flip. If you cook your cakes in a little butter or oil, they'll come out crisper on the outside. Cooking them in a dry pan yields more uniform-looking cakes.

DOING WITHOUT BUTTERMILK

What's nice about buttermilk is that it gives pancakes tenderness and tang. When you don't have any, add a tablespoon vinegar to a cup of milk and let it stand for 10 minutes. It will curdle slightly. If you prefer to use regular milk, just omit the baking soda from the recipe.

Improvised Pancakes

This is pretty much how I make pancakes without a recipe, but being improvised, it changes each time. Still, the basic formula works. I love buttermilk but have been known to use yogurt, kefir, and when none of those are around, almond milk. If you want thinner pancakes, simply thin the batter with additional liquid. Makes sixteen 5-inch pancakes

Wet Ingredients

- **2 eggs**
- **1 cup buttermilk, milk, yogurt, or kefir**
- **1 teaspoon vanilla**
- **¹/4 cup safflower oil**
- **1 tablespoon ghee or melted butter**

Dry Ingredients

- **³/4 cup wheat flour, such as white whole wheat**
- **¹/4 cup corn flour**
- **¹/2 cup spelt flour**
- **2 teaspoons baking powder**
- **1 teaspoon baking soda (omit if you're not using fermented milk)**
- **¹/4 teaspoon sea salt**
- **Miscellaneous additional ingredients (see page 561)**

Mix all the wet ingredients together in a bowl, except the ghee. Melt the ghee in the pan you're going to cook the pancakes in, then pour the excess into the wet ingredients.

Mix the dry ingredients together in a second bowl. Make a well in the middle, add the wet ingredients, and stir everything together with a fork, combining well but not obsessively. If the batter seems too thick (I make these for a person who prefers thinner cakes), thin it with additional liquid. Add any other ingredients you might wish to use.

Heat the skillet (cast-iron is great) and when hot, add the batter. About $1/4$ cup batter will make a 4- to 5-inch cake, but you can certainly make them tiny silver dollar size, or larger. Cook over medium heat until holes appear over the surface and bottom is browned, then turn, just once, and without patting the cakes down. The second side will cook more quickly. Serve the cakes on a warm plate with any of the suggested accompaniments (see page 561).

Buttermilk Pancakes

The classic American pancake is light, white, and tender. Serve them with fruit, syrup, or yogurt or vary them with the addition of fruit, nuts, and different flours. Makes fourteen 4-inch cakes

---

1$1/2$ cups all-purpose flour or whole wheat pastry flour

1 to 3 tablespoons sugar

1 teaspoon baking soda

2 teaspoons baking powder

$1/2$ teaspoon sea salt

$1/4$ teaspoon grated nutmeg

2 eggs

3 tablespoons melted butter or oil

1$1/2$ cups buttermilk

1 teaspoon vanilla

Mix the dry ingredients in one bowl. In a second bowl, beat the eggs and add the butter, buttermilk, and vanilla. Pour the wet ingredients into the dry and stir just enough to combine.

For each pancake, drop $1/4$ cup batter onto a nonstick griddle or skillet set over medium-high heat. Cook, without disturbing, until fine bubbles appear over the surface after a few minutes. Flip them over and cook until browned on the second side, about 1 minute. Refrain from patting them or turning them a second time—both actions will make the pancakes lose their lightness.

When done, remove to a platter and serve right away or keep warm in a low (200°F) oven until all are finished.

Whole Wheat Pancakes: Use whole wheat flour, 1 cup whole wheat flour mixed with $1/2$ cup wheat bran, or white whole wheat flour.

Mixed-Grain Pancakes: These are light and ethereal with a nice play of textures and flavors. Use $1/2$ cup flour, $1/2$ cup cooked grain such as rice or quinoa, $1/4$ cup corn meal, and $1/4$ cup rye or buckwheat flour, or improvise a mixture of your own. Other grains to consider are semolina, mixed-grain cereals, oats and other baked grains, and toasted millet or amaranth for crunchiness.

Banana-Nut Pancakes: Add 2 thinly sliced bananas and $1/2$ cup lightly toasted chopped pecans or walnuts to the batter.

Apple or Pear Pancakes: Thinly slice 1 or 2 apples or pears and stir them into the batter. Flavor the batter with $1/4$ teaspoon ground cardamom or $1/2$ teaspoon ground cinnamon or grated nutmeg. Serve with Applesauce or its variations (page 607).

Quince Cakes: Grate a ripe, fragrant quince and add it to the batter.

Berry Pancakes: Berries always make a wonderful addition to griddle cakes. Use $1/2$ to 1 cup berries and either fold them into the batter or distribute them over the top of the cakes while the first side is cooking. Serve with maple syrup and yogurt or sour cream or dust with powdered sugar and drizzle with fresh lemon juice.

Rice Pancakes: For a chewy, substantial accent, fold $1/2$ to 1 cup cooked wild rice, brown rice, or white rice into the batter.

Corn Cakes: Replace $1/2$ cup of the flour with corn meal and stir 1 cup corn kernels into the batter. If using fresh corn, be sure to include the corn milk and scrapings, too. Delicious with honey or molasses.

Quinoa Cakes: For a feathery-light cake with delectable texture and taste, fold in $1/2$ to 1$1/2$ cups cooked quinoa or as much as the batter will hold. The tiny grains will pop in your mouth.

Suggested Accompaniments for Pancakes and Waffles

Maple syrup warmed with butter (or not)

Molasses butter (page 562)

Warm honey and sour cream

Apple syrup made from reduced apple juice

Sorghum

Applesauce or quince sauce (page 607) and yogurt

Mixed berry compote

Cooked dried fruits, alone or in a compote

Some Additional Ingredients for Pancakes and Waffles

Grated apple or quince

Grated pear

Sliced bananas

Leftover cooked grains, such as wild rice

Cooked quinoa

Chopped nuts

Coconut, toasted

Toasted millet or amaranth seeds

Cottage Cheese and Nutmeg Pancakes

These are wonderful! They tend to stick a little, so plan to add some oil or butter to the pan each time. Serve with sour cream and strawberry jam or a compote of dried cherries and golden raisins. Makes twelve 4–inch pancakes

2 eggs, separated

1/2 cup buttermilk

1 cup cottage cheese

1/4 cup butter, melted

1 teaspoon vanilla

1/2 teaspoon grated nutmeg

1 tablespoon sugar

1/4 teaspoon sea salt

1/2 teaspoon baking soda

1 cup spelt or white whole wheat flour

Whisk the yolks and buttermilk together in a bowl. Stir in the cottage cheese, butter, and vanilla. Add the dry ingredients and whisk them together in a few swift strokes. Beat the egg whites until they form soft peaks, then fold them into the batter.

For each pancake, drop 1/4 cup batter onto an oiled or buttered griddle or large skillet set over medium heat. Cook until the surface is thoroughly laced with bubbles, about 4 minutes, then turn once and cook briefly on the second side. These generally take a little longer to cook than other cakes, and sometimes the cottage cheese sticks, so don't be surprised if that happens.

Wild Rice and Ricotta Pancakes

Not too sweet and very light, these small cakes have the chewy texture and nutty taste of wild rice. Brown basmati or other brown rice would also have plenty of character and be delicious treated the same way. Serve these fritters with honey or syrup, a squeeze of lemon juice, a dollop of sour cream, or whatever you fancy. These cakes are very moist. Makes eight 3–inch pancakes

1 cup ricotta cheese

3 eggs, separated

1/2 teaspoon salt

1 to 2 tablespoons sugar

1/4 cup melted butter

1 tablespoon grated lemon zest

1/4 cup white whole wheat flour or spelt flour

1 1/2 cups cooked wild rice

Beat the ricotta with the egg yolks, salt, and sugar until smooth, then stir in the melted butter, lemon zest, and flour. Beat the egg whites until they hold soft peaks; then fold them into the batter. Gently fold in the rice.

Heat a griddle or large skillet, then lower the heat. Drop the batter into small cakes and smooth them out with the back of the spoon to make circles. Cook until browned on the bottom, then flip and cook the other side.

Oatmeal Pancakes

These don't have the usual cakelike crumb that most cakes do, but they taste wonderful. Use coarse-textured rolled oats for the best texture and serve with applesauce or sautéed apples and creamy yogurt. Makes fourteen 4-inch pancakes

    1¹/₂ cups rolled oats

    2 cups buttermilk

    2 eggs

    1 teaspoon vanilla

    2 tablespoons brown sugar or maple syrup

    ¹/₄ cup oil

    ¹/₂ teaspoon sea salt

    ¹/₂ cup flour

    ¹/₄ teaspoon grated nutmeg

    ¹/₂ teaspoon baking soda

Stir the oats and buttermilk together and let stand for 20 minutes. Beat the eggs with the vanilla, sugar, and oil, then stir in the soaked oats. Combine the dry ingredients and add them to the oat mixture as well. For each pancake, drop ¹/₄ cup batter onto a heated griddle or skillet and cook over a medium-low heat until the tops are covered with holes. Turn the cakes over and cook the second side. Because of the moisture in this batter, the cakes need to cook slowly, but turn them only once.

Oatmeal-Buttermilk Pancakes with Fruit: Gently stir a cup of blackberries, raspberries, or mulberries into the batter, then cook as described. Or serve oatmeal pancakes with a mound of blackberries sweetened with brown sugar and a dollop of yogurt.

Oatmeal-Buttermilk Pancakes with Steel-Cut Oats: Soak steel-cut oats overnight in the buttermilk so that they soften. Next morning, add the rest of the ingredients as given.

Buckwheat Flapjacks with Molasses Butter

Buttermilk, buckwheat, and molasses are naturals together. A sprinkle of turbinado sugar on top provides crackle and crunch. Buckwheat is very absorbent, so don't be surprised if you have to add extra liquid. Makes fourteen 4-inch pancakes

    ³/₄ cup buckwheat flour

    ³/₄ cup all-purpose flour

    1 teaspoon baking powder

    ¹/₂ teaspoon baking soda

    ¹/₂ teaspoon sea salt

    ¹/₄ cup unsulfured molasses

    2 eggs

    ¹/₄ cup vegetable oil

    1³/₄ cups buttermilk

    Molasses Butter, recipe follows, for serving

    Turbinado sugar, for sprinkling

Whisk the dry ingredients together in a large bowl. In a second bowl, combine the molasses, eggs, oil, and buttermilk. Pour the wet ingredients into the dry and stir together briskly to combine.

Make the molasses butter while the batter rests. For each pancake, drop ¹/₄ cup batter onto a lightly greased nonstick skillet or griddle. Cook over medium heat until covered with bubbles, then flip once and cook about ¹/₂ minute more. Serve with the molasses butter and a sprinkling of raw sugar.

Molasses Butter

    ¹/₃ cup unslfured molasses

    2 tablespoons butter

    ¹/₃ to ¹/₂ cup crème fraîche

Heat the molasses and butter in a pan until the butter is melted. Remove from heat and whisk in the crème fraîche until smooth.

Waffles

Modern waffle irons are a breeze to use with their nonstick coatings and reliable thermostats. This is one time I'm delighted to have the guesswork removed—the old kinds offered quite a challenge unless well seasoned. Most pancake batters work for waffles, though you may want to thin the batter with extra milk and add an extra 2 tablespoons oil or melted butter. The extra butter helps give waffles their crisp exterior. For very light waffles, separate the whites, beat them until they hold soft peaks, and fold them into the batter. Waffles needn't be just for breakfast—they can include corn or grated cheese, or they can be served alongside a vegetable ragout or bean stew. They can make a dessert, too, embellished with fresh or poached dried fruits, dessert sauces, and yogurt or whipped cream.

Basic Waffles

Makes 8 waffles

- **3 eggs, beaten**
- **1¹/₂ cups milk or buttermilk**
- **¹/₄ cup safflower oil or butter, melted**
- **1 teaspoon vanilla extract**
- **2 cups flour—including a portion of white whole wheat**
- **1 teaspoon baking powder**
- **¹/₂ teaspoon baking soda**
- **¹/₄ teaspoon salt**

In a bowl, mix the wet ingredients together. In another bowl, stir together the dry ingredients. Pour the wet ingredients into the dry and combine them with a fork. The batter should be on the thin side or your waffles will be too cakey. Test a spoonful in the iron to be sure and add more milk if it's too thick. Cook according to your waffle iron's instructions.

Multigrain Waffles: For the flour, use 1 cup all-purpose or whole wheat pastry flour and ¹/₄ cup each wheat or oat bran, corn meal, rye, and soy or quinoa flour. Sometimes I add just a tablespoon or two of odds and ends, including cereal mixes, such as seven-grain, in place of one of the other flours.

Pecan Waffles: Stir 1 cup finely chopped pecans (or other nuts) into the batter or sprinkle the nuts over the batter as soon as it's poured into the waffle iron.

Rice Waffles: Stir 1 cup cooked, drained wild rice, basmati, or brown rice into the batter to give your waffles chewiness and character. Cooked quinoa and millet are also good additions.

Savory Corn Waffles

Try corn waffles for a Sunday night supper or brunch served with chile butter, salsa, or Pepper Relish with Anise Seeds (page 70) and crumbled feta. Makes 10 to 12 waffles

- **1¹/₂ cups whole wheat pastry flour**
- **1¹/₄ cups fine corn meal or corn flour**
- **2 teaspoons baking powder**
- **¹/₂ teaspoon baking soda, if using buttermilk**
- **1 teaspoon sea salt**
- **3 eggs, separated**
- **2¹/₂ cups buttermilk or milk**
- **6 tablespoons safflower oil or butter, melted**
- **Kernels from 2 ears of corn**

Combine the dry ingredients in one bowl. In a second bowl, whisk together the egg yolks, milk, and oil. In a third bowl, whisk the whites until they hold soft peaks. Make a well in the dry ingredients, pour in the wet ingredients and stir to combine, then fold in the whites along with the corn kernels. Cook according to your waffle iron's instructions, then serve with an array of condiments (see note).

Yeasted Waffles and Pancakes

Raising pancakes and waffles with yeast is an old American tradition that predates the invention of baking powder. The overnight proofing develops the flavor of the flours, and the yeast ensures lightness even for heavier grains. The batter keeps well, covered and refrigerated, for several days. This batter is ideal for Belgian waffles.
Makes 10 to 12 small or 3 Belgian waffles

2¹/₄ teaspoons (1 envelope) active dry yeast

2 tablespoons plus 1 teaspoon sugar

2 cups lukewarm milk

¹/₂ teaspoon salt

1¹/₂ cups unbleached all-purpose flour

1 cup white whole wheat, quinoa, spelt, or other flour

5 tablespoons safflower oil or butter, melted

2 eggs, beaten

¹/₂ teaspoon baking soda

In a small bowl, sprinkle the yeast into ¹/₄ cup warm water and stir in the 1teaspoon sugar. Let stand until foamy, about 10 minutes. Put the warm milk and salt in a large bowl, then add the yeast mixture and whisk in the flours. Cover and refrigerate overnight if the weather is warm or leave out on the counter if it's cool. Next morning, add the 2 tablespoons sugar, the oil, eggs, and baking soda. Cook according to your waffle iron's instructions or on a pre-heated griddle.

French Toast

While French toast provides a way to use slightly stale bread, you can certainly use fresh bread. Serve French toast with powdered sugar, warm maple syrup, applesauce, berries—whatever for toppings you like on pancakes. Serves 2

2 eggs

1 tablespoon sugar

¹/₂ teaspoon orange-flower water, optional

1¹/₂ teaspoons vanilla extract

¹/₂ teaspoon ground cinnamon

1 cup milk

4 slices bread

Whisk the eggs with the sugar, orange-flower water, vanilla, and cinnamon, then stir in the milk. Pour the batter into a pie plate and put in two pieces of the bread. Let stand for 3 minutes, then turn them over and let stand again to absorb the batter. Really stale bread will take longer. Press on them with your fingers to see if they're still dry. Melt a little butter in a large nonstick skillet.

When it's bubbling, pick up the bread and put it in the skillet. Cook both sides until nicely browned. Repeat with the remaining bread and batter.

Breakfast Breads

Coffee cakes and fruit- and nut-studded breads are part of weekend or special holiday breakfasts, as are simpler fare, like muffins and biscuits. Those recipes that depend on yeasted dough or are served at other meals—cinnamon rolls, muffins, and biscuits, for example—can be found in the bread chapter. Croissants, Danish pastries, and brioche fortunately can be found in bakeries. Here are some quick breads that are eminently suitable for breakfast and brunch, quick and easy to prepare. More breads can be found in the next chapter.

Applesauce Spice Bread

Serve this tender loaf plain or drizzled with a powdered sugar glaze. A narrow bread pan (4 by 10 inches), makes an especially fine-looking bread. Makes one 4 by 10-inch loaf

- ¹/₂ cup butter, at room temperature
- ¹/₂ cup sugar
- ³/₄ cup light brown sugar, packed
- 2 eggs, at room temperature
- 1 cup applesauce mixed with 1¹/₂ teaspoons baking soda
- 2 cups white whole wheat or whole wheat pastry flour
- ¹/₂ teaspoon sea salt
- 2 teaspoons ground cardamom or cinnamon
- ¹/₂ teaspoon grated nutmeg
- ¹/₂ teaspoon ground ginger
- ¹/₄ teaspoon ground cloves

Preheat the oven to 375°F. Lightly butter a bread pan. Line it with wax paper or parchment paper, then butter and flour it. (A spray hasn't worked well for me in this recipe.)

Cream the butter with the two sugars in a mixing bowl until light and fluffy. Add the eggs one at a time, scraping down the sides in between additions, then stir in the applesauce mixture. Stir the dry ingredients together in a bowl, then add them to the butter mixture and stir just enough to combine well.

Turn into the pan and bake in the top third of the oven until firm and a cake tester comes out clean, about 50 minutes. Let cool in the pan for 5 minutes, then carefully turn out onto a rack to finish cooling.

Oat and Brown Sugar Coffee Cake

Tender, with good oat flavor, this is an old American coffee cake that one doesn't see much anymore. Serves 6 to 8

- 1 cup rolled oats, preferably noninstant
- ¹/₂ cup butter
- 1 cup light brown sugar, packed
- 2 eggs, at room temperature
- 1¹/₂ teaspoons vanilla
- 1 teaspoon ground cinnamon
- 1 teaspoon baking powder
- ¹/₂ teaspoon baking soda
- ¹/₂ teaspoon sea salt
- 1¹/₂ cups flour
- 1 cup Pecan Streusel (page 574)

Preheat the oven to 375°F. Spray or butter and flour a 9 by 12-inch baking dish.

Pour 1¹/₂ cups boiling water over the oats and set them aside. Cream the butter and sugar until light and fluffy, then add the eggs one at a time. Scrape down the bowl and continue beating until the mixture is smooth, then add the vanilla, cinnamon, and oats. Combine the dry ingredients and stir them in with a rubber scraper or wooden spoon. Pour into the prepared baking dish, cover with streusel, and bake until a skewer comes out clean—about 35 minutes.

Sweet Corn Coffee Cake with Berries

This moist coffee cake is studded with berries and dusted with powdered sugar. Try making this with heritage corn meals, such as Red Floriani, which you can sometimes find at farmers' markets. Makes one 8-inch round cake

1¹/₃ cups flour

³/₄ cup corn meal or corn flour, any color

¹/₂ cup plus 2 tablespoons sugar, or ¹/₄ cup agave nectar

1 teaspoon baking soda

2 teaspoons baking powder

¹/₂ teaspoon sea salt

1 cup buttermilk

Grated zest of 1 lemon

2 teaspoons vanilla extract

2 eggs

¹/₃ cup melted butter or safflower oil

1 to 2 cups raspberries, blackberries, or blueberries

Powdered sugar, for dusting

Preheat the oven to 375°F. Butter and flour or spray an 8-inch springform cake pan or an 8-inch square pan.

Whisk the dry ingredients together in a bowl. In a second bowl, combine the wet ingredients. Quickly stir them together, then scrape into the pan. Scatter the berries over the top and bake in the center of the oven until the cake is browned and beginning to pull away from the sides of the pan, about 45 minutes. Remove the rim if you've used a springform pan, transfer the cake to a serving plate, and dust with powdered sugar. Serve warm.

Cranberry-Nut Bread

For this delicious breakfast bread or tea cake, you can start with fresh cranberries, as described here, or use 1 cup cooked cranberries. Makes 1 loaf or 18 muffins

2 cups raw cranberries, preferably organic

¹/₂ cup sugar

Grated zest of 1 orange plus 1 tablespoon orange juice

6 tablespoons butter, softened

³/₄ cup light brown sugar, packed

2 eggs, at room temperature

1 cup buttermilk

2¹/₂ cups all-purpose or whole wheat pastry flour

¹/₈ teaspoon ground cloves

1 teaspoon baking soda

1¹/₂ teaspoons baking powder

¹/₂ teaspoon sea salt

1 cup pecans or walnuts, finely chopped

Preheat the oven to 375°F. Spray or butter and flour a bread pan or 18 muffin cups.

Put the cranberries in a saucepan with the sugar, orange zest, and juice. Cook over high heat, stirring frequently, until most of the berries burst and the sugar is dissolved, 4 to 5 minutes.

Cream the butter and sugar in a mixing bowl until light and fluffy, then add the eggs one at a time and beat until smooth. Add the buttermilk. Combine the dry ingredients except the nuts and stir half into the batter. Add the cranberries, then the remaining flour mixture, and fold in the nuts. Spoon the batter into the pan and bake in the center of the oven until well browned on top and a toothpick comes out clean, about 1 hour and 10 minutes. Turn out onto a rack to cool.

Currant Buns

I like these little yeasted buns toasted for breakfast any time of year, but a teaspoon of vanilla and freshly grated nutmeg added to the hot milk turns them into hot cross buns. For a more wholesome and rustic bun, use whole wheat flour.
Makes twenty to twenty-four 2-inch buns

1^1/$_3$ cups milk

^{1}/$_4$ cup butter, cut into small pieces

^{1}/$_2$ teaspoon sea salt

2 tablespoons honey or sugar

2^1/$_4$ teaspoons (1 envelope) dry yeast

1 egg, beaten, 2 tablespoons reserved for the glaze

1 cup currants or raisins, plumped in warm water if very dry

^{1}/$_2$ cup untoasted wheat germ

4 to 5 cups all-purpose flour, white whole wheat, or a mixture of flours

Fine sugar, for sprinkling, optional

Warm the milk with the butter, salt, and honey in a small saucepan, just long enough to melt the butter. Avoid overheating the milk. If it gets very hot, you'll have to wait until it is just warm before adding the yeast. Pour the milk into a large mixing bowl and scrape out any sugar that hasn't dissolved, and add it to the bowl.

Sprinkle the yeast over ^{1}/$_4$ cup warm water in a bowl. As soon as it's foamy, stir it into the milk mixture along with the beaten egg. Add the currants and the wheat germ, then begin beating in the flour. As soon as the dough clears the bowl, turn it out and knead until smooth, adding extra flour as needed. Turn it into a lightly buttered or oiled bowl and turn once to coat the top. Cover and set aside to rise until doubled, about 1^1/$_2$ hours.

Turn out the dough and roll it into a circle about ^{3}/$_8$ inch thick. Cut with a biscuit or cookie cutter into rounds and set them on a sheet pan to rise for 30 minutes. (Knead the scraps quickly back together and roll them out; cut as before.) Heat the oven to 375°F. Brush the tops with the reserved egg and sprinkle them with fine sugar.

Bake until golden brown, about 20 minutes.

Breakfast Bread Pudding

Here's a recipe to make use of that extra loaf of raisin bread or holiday panettone. It's soft and luxurious, a good dish for a holiday breakfast or brunch, and you can set it up the night before. Serves 6 or more

3 tablespoons butter, melted

1 pound raisin bread or panettone, sliced, crusts removed, unless they're very soft

^{1}/$_2$ cup maple syrup

3 large eggs

2^1/$_2$ cups milk

1 teaspoon vanilla

1 teaspoon ground cinnamon

Yogurt, for serving

Brush some of the melted butter over a 10-cup gratin dish. Cut the loaf diagonally in two, then into slices. Make a layer in the dish, breaking the bread to fill any gaps. Drizzle over half the syrup. Make a second layer of bread and cover with the remaining syrup.

Beat the eggs with the milk, vanilla, and cinnamon. Pour it over the bread. Brush the surface with the remaining butter, then cover and let stand for at least an hour or longer in the refrigerator. Remove a half hour before baking.

Heat the oven to 350°F. Bake until the pudding has set and the top is browned, about 50 minutes. Serve warm with yogurt.

With Cheese: In the Southwest, bread puddings, even when sweet, often include cheese. It jars the senses with its salty sharpness against the sweet in just the right way. Grate 3 or 4 ounces of cheddar cheese. Cover the first layer of bread with half the cheese and use the rest to cover the second layer. Or, serve the pudding with a slice of cheese, cheddar or goat.

Babka with Dried Cherry–Almond Filling

This is my grandmother's and mother's recipe for a silken dough that makes the most luxurious, tender sweet rolls. You can make this dough the day before you plan to bake it, then give it 2 hours to return to room temperature. An electric mixer with a paddle attachment is a great help in mixing this soft, sticky dough. The cherry–almond filling is one of many wonderful fillings you can use. A classic poppy seed filling is another. There are also fillings based on prunes and raisins, or you can treat the dough as for cinnamon rolls.

Makes 1 large bread, serving 10

2 1/4 teaspoons (1 envelope) active dry yeast

1/2 cup warm milk

1/3 cup plus 1 teaspoon sugar, plus extra for the top

1/2 cup butter, preferably unsalted, at room temperature

1/2 teaspoon salt

2 eggs, at room temperature

1/2 cup sour cream

3 to 3 1/2 cups all-purpose flour

Egg Glaze (page 588)

Cherry-Almond Filling

1 cup dried cherries or a mixture of cherries and golden raisins

1 1/4 cups whole or slivered almonds, toasted

1/2 cup butter, preferably unsalted, at room temperature

1/2 cup packed light brown sugar

1/2 teaspoon vanilla

1/4 teaspoon almond extract

1 egg, at room temperature

Stir the yeast, milk, and 1 teaspoon of the sugar together in a small bowl and set aside until foamy, about 10 minutes. Meanwhile, in a mixing bowl, beat the butter with the remaining 1/3 cup sugar and the salt until creamy. Add the eggs one at a time, followed by the sour cream and yeast. Add the flour by the cup until it clears the sides of the bowl, then turn it out and knead until the dough feels silky and smooth. Transfer to a buttered bowl, place a piece of plastic wrap directly over the surface, and set aside to rise until doubled in bulk. Or refrigerate overnight.

Make the filling. Cover the dried fruit, if hard, with hot water until softened, 10 to 15 minutes. Drain, squeeze dry, and set aside. Grind the almonds finely. Cream the butter with the sugar until smooth, then add the vanilla, almond extract, egg, and ground almonds. Set aside.

Punch down the dough, then roll it into a rectangle approximately 1 by 2 feet. (If you've refrigerated it, leave it at room temperature for about 2 hours before rolling. It will still feel a little cold.) Cover with the almond filling, leaving a 1 1/2-inch border all the way around, then scatter the cherries on top. Roll it up tightly and transfer to a lightly buttered cookie sheet. Form it into a crescent, with the ends pointing toward the center, or slice crosswise to make individual rolls. Set aside, covered with a towel until doubled in bulk, about an hour.

During the last 15 minutes, preheat the oven to 375°F. Brush the bread with the glaze, sprinkle generously with sugar, then bake in the center of the oven until golden brown and cooked through, about 1 hour. If it gets too dark while baking, cover it loosely with foil. Let cool on a rack, but serve warm.

Ann's Cheese Stollen (A Quick Bread)

Ample and impressive with its fine aroma and delicate, rich crumb, this is a wonderful bread to have in your repertoire. If you use candied fruits that you've prepared yourself, it will be even better. (Candied grapefruit is especially good.) It can easily be mixed and baked the morning you plan to serve it, and leftover bread makes delicious toast. Serves 6 to 8

1/2 cup butter, at room temperature

1/2 cup sugar

1 tablespoon grated lemon zest

1 teaspoon grated orange zest

1 teaspoon almond extract

1 large egg, at room temperature

2 egg yolks, at room temperature

1 cup ricotta cheese

1 cup plain yogurt or cottage cheese

1/2 cup golden raisins

1/2 cup black raisins

3/4 cup chopped candied grapefruit peels, or a mixture of different citrus peels

1/3 cup pine nuts, walnuts, or almonds

1/4 cup peeled and roughly chopped unsalted pistachio nuts

3 cups unbleached white flour

2 teaspoons baking powder

1/2 teaspoon baking soda

1/2 teaspoon salt

Powdered sugar, for dusting, or powdered sugar mixed with lemon juice, optional, for icing

Preheat the oven to 350°F. Butter and flour a large bread pan. By hand or in a mixer, cream the butter with the sugar until it is light and fluffy. Add the zest, almond extract, and the egg and egg yolks, one at a time. When well mixed, add the ricotta cheese and the yogurt and continue mixing until well incorporated.

Combine the fruits and nuts in a bowl. In another bowl, sift together the flour, baking powder, baking soda, and salt. With the mixer running, add half the fruits, then gradually add half the flour mixture. When it is mixed in, add the rest of the fruit; then, again gradually, add the remaining flour mixture. Continue mixing until everything is well combined, but don't overwork. The batter will be quite dense. If you're mixing by hand, you might prefer to flour a counter, turn out the dough, and knead it as if it were a yeast dough.

Turn the dough into the prepared pan or baking sheet and bake for 1 hour and 15 minutes.

Although it may look done sooner, it's a moist dough with the addition of the cheeses and needs the full baking time to be actually cooked. Dust the stollen with powdered sugar or drizzle a simple icing of powdered sugar mixed with lemon juice over the top.

Orange and Dried Fruit Coffee Cake

This is a favorite recipe for an old-fashioned dessert. I have modified it by omitting the sugar glaze and some of the sugar in the cake and including a wider variety of fruits. Makes one 9 by 13-inch cake

1/2 cup butter

Grated zest and juice of 1 large orange

3/4 cup light brown sugar, packed

2 eggs, at room temperature

1/2 teaspoon salt

1 teaspoon baking powder

1 teaspoon baking soda

2 1/4 cups flour

3/4 cup buttermilk

1 cup dried cherries, cranberries, chopped dates, or chopped prunes

1/2 to 1 cup chopped pecans or walnuts

Preheat the oven to 350°F. Butter and flour a 9 by 13-inch baking pan or a kugelhopf pan.

Cream the butter with the orange zest and sugar until light and fluffy. Add the eggs, one at a time, and beat until smooth, then stir in the juice and the salt, baking powder, and soda. Alternately add the flour and buttermilk, in thirds, beating just until smooth, then fold in the dried fruits and the nuts. Bake until lightly browned and firm to the touch and a skewer comes out clean, about 45 minutes.

BREADS BY HAND

CHAPTER 18

Breads by Hand

Nothing conveys the feeling of home and hearth like the smell of baking bread or the warmth of a basket of biscuits being passed around the table.

In fact, the sight and smell of homemade bread have always evoked a sense that all is well and that, I'm convinced, was behind the popularity of bread machines or Jim Lahey's now-famous no-knead bread. Good bread is not as difficult to find for sale today as it once was, but still we make our own so we can wake up or come home to the reassuring smell of bread baking.

Many people think that their lives are too busy to include baking bread, but, conveniently, breads fall into two categories—quick breads, which depend on fast-working baking powder and baking soda, and yeast breads, which often need several hours or more to rise before baking. These different leavenings and ways of using them give us a number of options for baking strategies that make sense for our lives. For example, most quick breads (muffins, cornbread, biscuits) can be assembled by the time the oven is heated, and that, indeed, is quick. If you have 25 minutes to an hour or so for baking, you can fit them in. Yeasted risen pancakes and waffles take longer to ready, but they can be started the night before, plus they gain in flavor as they spend the night rising. Yeasted breads, like sandwich breads, spread their several stages over a number of hours, but it's easy to accommodate them to our schedules. On the other hand, some yeasted breads can be baked without pausing for kneading or a second rise, which makes them far quicker to make than conventionally thought. Small batches of dough rise more quickly than large ones, and flatbreads, like pita, naan, and focaccia can be ready for the oven within an hour. So regardless of whether they're quick or long rising, we can find some type of baked good that works with our lives.

Quick Breads

Since they rely on baking powder, baking soda, and often eggs to gain their rise, muffins, scones, biscuits, and tea cakes can be made from start to finish in an hour or less. Even a novice can assemble these batters and doughs in the time it takes the oven to preheat. While many quick breads are breakfast favorites, most are equally enjoyable at other meals as well. Freshly made biscuits and cornbread turn an otherwise ordinary meal into a special one. Before you start, take a look at "flour" on page 31.

FLOUR: All-purpose unbleached white flour makes the light, high baked goods that are the trademark of American baking. Today white whole wheat pastry flour, which behaves just like white flour without making breads stodgy or heavy, is also available. Graham flour—whole wheat flour with flakes of bran—also makes a fairly light but more wholesome bread. Other flours—rye, barley, corn, amaranth, quinoa, spelt, and buckwheat—contribute flavor, texture, and nutrition, but they need to be blended with wheat flour, which contains gluten, the stretchy substance that allows doughs to rise.

To measure flour, spoon it into a dry cup measure, one that's calibrated to the top, then sweep off the excess with a knife. Don't pack the flour down.

SWEETENERS: Sweeteners include sugar, maple sugar, honey, molasses, agave, barley malt syrup, Sucanat, and sorghum. Grains have their own inherent sweetness, so I find that just a small amount of sweetening, if any, is sufficient. Others, however, may prefer to go to the higher end of the range offered in recipes.

EGGS: Eggs bind, tenderize, and enrich quick breads while helping them rise. Those who wish to can replace the yolks with extra whites. You can also leave them out entirely, but your breads will be more crumbly and dry. To maintain moisture, you can replace eggs with fruit purees and pureed silken tofu volume for volume, about 3 tablespoons per large egg. Or use a mixture of 1 tablespoon ground flaxseed and 3 tablespoons water. For more, see page 498.

FAT: Oils can be used successfully in many quick breads, but where you want a more cakelike product, use butter and cream it with the sugar to incorporate air. I like to use enough fat to keep my baked goods moist and tender. With less, I've noticed that people just add more butter at the table.

LIQUIDS: I'm an ardent fan of buttermilk because of its tangy note and the tenderness it produces in baked goods. Dried buttermilk, found in the baking section of supermarkets, can be added to the flour mixture in place of fresh, and natural yogurts (without added gums) can also replace buttermilk. Fermented milk products such as buttermilk and yogurt always require baking soda for leavening. If you're using regular milk, omit the soda and add an extra $1/2$ teaspoon baking powder. Other liquids that can be used in quick breads are fruit juices and plant milks.

If you don't have buttermilk on hand, add 1 tablespoon distilled vinegar or lemon juice to 1 cup warm cow's milk or plant milk, stir until it curdles, then let stand 5 minutes before using. Chemically, it will behave like buttermilk, requiring soda for the best rise.

Mixing and Baking Quick Breads

Have the ingredients at room temperature so that the batter will begin its rise as soon as it enters the oven. The only exception to this rule are biscuits or any bread where cold solid fat is worked into the flour. To bring eggs to room temperature, cover them with hot tap water and they will lose their chill after a few minutes.

Whisk together the dry ingredients before adding the wets so that they're well blended and there are no lumps of baking soda or powder. And don't forget to mix well from the bottom of the bowl up.

Quick bread batters are more resilient than we're led to believe, but avoid overmixing them. Light handling makes a lighter product. If you feel a batter has been overworked, let it stand for 10 to 15 minutes before baking to allow it to relax. Double-acting baking powder starts its second rising action when it enters the oven, so resting won't keep the bread from rising.

BAKING: Quick breads generally bake at around 375°F and should be baked in the center or top third of the oven. When baking several pans at once, leave a few inches between them so that air can circulate and an even temperature can be maintained. Turn them once during baking so that they'll brown evenly. Test bread for doneness by inserting a long straw or thin skewer in the middle; it should come out dry and clean.

BAKING STONES: A pizza stone, also called a baking stone, is wonderful not only for getting a good crust on a pizza but for many breads as well. Since I always leave my stone in the oven, I've come to explore its possibilities. Biscuits, scones, and soda breads can be baked directly on the hot stone if you like a crisp bottom crust, or you can bake them on a sheet pan on top of the stone.

COOLING AND STORING: Quick breads are tempting to eat warm, but they slice more easily when cool. Always let loaves and muffins cool in their pans for 5 to 10 minutes before turning them out on a rack to finish cooling. Baked goods that contain fruit and vegetable purees keep well for days, wrapped and at room temperature. Breads that have gone a little stale can be moistened with water, put in a paper bag, and reheated at 375°F. All quick breads are great toasted. Having muffins and breads on hand in the freezer can be a boon to a busy cook. To freeze baked goods, wrap cooled breads in a layer of plastic wrap followed by foil.

Muffins can just go right into a zippered plastic bag. Let them thaw at room temperature or in the refrigerator before unwrapping. To reheat, wrap them loosely in foil and put in a 350°F oven for 15 to 20 minutes.

Muffins

Muffins may be our favorite quick bread. They're easy and versatile, and they make a tidy little bread that freezes well. Streusel, the crunchy, sweet toppings on page 574, makes them Sunday morning special. Not all muffins are sweet, though—look to the cheese and corn-rye muffins as savory accompaniments for soups or a savory breakfast.

Basic Buttermilk Muffins

A plain, moist muffin that you can add to or embellish with ease. Makes 12 muffins

2¹/₂ cups all-purpose or whole wheat pastry flour

2 teaspoons baking powder

1 teaspoon baking soda

¹/₂ teaspoon sea salt

¹/₂ to ³/₄ cup packed light brown sugar

2 eggs, lightly beaten

¹/₂ cups buttermilk

¹/₃ cup safflower oil or butter, melted

1¹/₂ teaspoons vanilla extract

Preheat the oven to 375°F. Spray, oil, or butter muffin tins. Mix the dry ingredients in one bowl and the wets in a second bowl, then combine them with a few swift strokes. Using a rubber spatula, stir the batter up from the bottom

of the bowl to make sure that there aren't any pockets of flour. Don't beat the batter and don't worry about a slightly uneven appearance. Spoon or scoop the batter into the tins, going nearly to the top for a nicely rounded muffin. Bake in the upper third of the oven until browned and well risen, about 25 minutes. Turn out the muffins and serve.

High-Protein Flour Muffins: Replace up to 1¹/₄ cups flour with quinoa or amaranth flour, sprouted spelt, or other flours.

Spice Muffins: Add 2 teaspoons ground cinnamon, 1 teaspoon grated nutmeg or ¹/₂ teaspoon ground cardamom, ¹/₈ teaspoon ground clove, and 1 teaspoon powdered ginger to the dry ingredients.

Fresh Fruit Muffins: Add 1 cup of any of the following fruits to the batter: raspberries, blackberries, blueberries, tossed with a tablespoon of flour; apples or pears, finely diced; cranberries or finely diced rhubarb, tossed with 1 teaspoon orange zest; or grated quince. Be sure to mix it thoroughly from the bottom.

Dried Apricot and Ginger Muffins: Dice 1 cup dried apricots into raisin-size pieces and put them in a bowl with boiling water to cover. Let stand for 10 minutes or until soft, then drain. Add ¹/₂ teaspoons ground ginger to the dry ingredients and ¹/₂ cup diced candied ginger. Combine the wet and dry ingredients, then stir in the apricots. Add ¹/₂ cup chopped nuts or a streusel topping for a fancy muffin.

Date-Nut Muffins: Add 1 cup chopped pitted dates and 1 cup chopped pecans or walnuts to the batter. Cover the muffins with Pecan or Orange Streusel topping (see page 574).

Streusel Toppings for Muffins and Coffee Cakes

Sprinkle these mixtures over muffins, coffee cakes, or baked fruits before baking for a sweet, crunchy topping. Leftovers freeze well, and it's always nice to have some ready to use. Use cold butter and mix the ingredients together in a small bowl with your fingers or in a food processor until crumbly. Sprinkle over the batter, pressing lightly into it, just before they go into the oven.

AMOUNTS: These recipes make enough for a dozen muffins. Double the recipe to cover a coffee cake.

Basic Streusel

1/4 cup packed light brown sugar

1/2 cup flour, or 1/4 cup flour plus 1/4 cup rolled oats

1/2 teaspoon grated nutmeg or ground cinnamon

1/4 cup cold butter or coconut oil

Orange Streusel

1 1/2 tablespoons finely grated orange zest

1/3 cup packed light brown sugar

1/2 teaspoon ground cinnamon or 1/4 teaspoon ground cardamom

1/4 cup butter or coconut oil

1/2 cup flour

Pecan Streusel

1/2 cup packed brown sugar

2 teaspoons flour

1/2 teaspoon ground cinnamon

1/4 teaspoon grated nutmeg

3 tablespoons butter or coconut oil

2/3 cup chopped pecans

Banana-Oat Muffins

A tender muffin for banana bread lovers.
Makes 9 plump muffins

2 large ripe bananas, mashed

3/4 cup buttermilk

1/3 cup packed light brown sugar

1 whole egg, or 2 egg whites, at room temperature

2 tablespoons safflower oil or melted butter

1 cup rolled oats

1 1/2 cups all-purpose or whole-wheat pastry flour

1 teaspoon grated nutmeg

1 1/2 teaspoons baking soda

Preheat the oven to 375°F. Spray or oil muffin tins.

In one bowl, mix the bananas with the buttermilk, sugar, egg, and oil, then add the oats. In another bowl, combine the flour, nutmeg, and baking soda. Pour the wet ingredients into the dry and quickly stir them together. Fill the muffin tins two-thirds full. (Put a little water in the empty cups.) Bake until golden brown and springy when pressed lightly with a finger, about 25 minutes. Run a knife around the edge of each muffin and remove.

Corn-Rye Muffins

Multigrained and filling, these are good, hearty lunch muffins. Makes 10 muffins

3/4 cup whole wheat pastry flour

1/2 cup rye flour

1/4 cup amaranth flour

1/2 cup stone-ground corn meal

2 teaspoons baking powder

2 to 4 tablespoons unsulfured molasses

1/2 teaspoon sea salt

2 eggs, or 1 whole egg and 2 egg whites

1 cup milk, dairy or plant milk

1/3 cup safflower oil

Preheat the oven to 375°F and spray or oil muffin tins. Mix the dry ingredients in one bowl, the wet ingredients in another, then combine them and stir together quickly. Fill muffin cups about two-thirds full and bake until risen and lightly browned, about 25 minutes.

Breads by Hand

Sweet Potato Muffins with Candied Ginger

Chunks of candied ginger make these particularly good. If you don't have ginger readily at hand, replace it with chopped dates, raisins, or fresh pineapple. Serve these with Brie or other mild cheese, butter, or cream cheese.

Makes 10 to 12 muffins

- 1/3 cup chopped candied ginger or chopped pineapple, dates, or raisins
- 1/4 cup butter, melted, or safflower oil
- 1/3 cup unsulfured molasses
- 1 cup mashed cooked sweet potato or winter squash
- 2 eggs, at room temperature
- 1/2 cup buttermilk
- 1/2 cup packed light brown sugar
- 1 3/4 cups flour
- 1 teaspoon baking powder
- 1 teaspoon baking soda
- 1/4 teaspoon sea salt
- 1 teaspoon ground cinnamon

Preheat the oven to 375°F. Oil or spray muffin tins. Mix the ginger and wet ingredients in a bowl until smooth; mix the dry ingredients in a second bowl. Combine the two, mixing gently until well blended. Spoon the batter into the muffin tins and bake on the middle rack until lightly browned, 25 minutes.

Cheese Muffins

Serve these savory muffins with summer soups made of corn, tomato, or roasted peppers or with the All-Bean Chili (page 288). Makes 10 muffins

- 1 1/4 cups spelt or white whole wheat flour
- 1/2 cup stone-ground corn meal
- 2 1/2 teaspoons baking powder
- 1/2 teaspoon sea salt
- 2 eggs, at room temperature
- 1 cup milk, dairy or plant milk
- 2 tablespoons safflower oil
- 1 1/2 tablespoons honey
- 1 to 2 cups grated cheddar

Preheat the oven to 400°F. Oil or spray muffin tins. Combine the dry ingredients in one bowl and the eggs, milk, oil, and honey in another. Pour the wet ingredients into the dry, stir them quickly together, then stir in the cheese. Fill the muffin cups about three-quarters full, then bake until the muffins are browned and springy, about 25 minutes.

Cheese Muffins with Herbs: Add 2 tablespoons chopped dill and 1 teaspoon toasted ground cumin seeds or caraway seeds to the batter.

Cheese-Corn Muffins: Add 1 cup uncooked corn kernels to the batter with the cheese. If you like it hot, include 1/2 cup chopped roasted green chiles.

Quinoa Muffins

These are crunchy and so good! If you have no leftover quinoa, remember that you can cook fresh in practically the time it takes to preheat the oven. This has been a favorite in cooking classes. Makes 9 to 12 muffins

- 1 cup cooked quinoa or 1/2 cup raw
- 1 cup whole wheat pastry flour
- 1 cup quinoa flour
- 1/4 teaspoon sea salt
- 1 teaspoon baking soda
- 1/2 cup packed light brown sugar
- 1 egg, at room temperature
- 1/4 cup butter, melted, or safflower oil
- 1 1/4 cups buttermilk or yogurt
- 1 teaspoon vanilla extract

Preheat the oven to 375°F. Spray or oil muffin tins.

If cooking quinoa, rinse it well, put it in a small saucepan with 1 cup water, and bring to a boil. Simmer, covered, until the water is absorbed, about 15 minutes, then drain.

Meanwhile, combine the flours, salt, soda, and sugar in a mixing bowl. Beat the egg with the butter, buttermilk, and vanilla. Stir the wet ingredients into the dry, add the quinoa, and mix with a spatula, scraping up from the bottom so that the flour is mixed in thoroughly. Scoop the batter into the muffin cups and bake until firm and light brown on top, 25 to 30 minutes.

Molasses-Buttermilk Bread

Dark, crumbly, and moist with the tangy flavor of butter-milk, this is a close cousin of Boston brown bread. Serve with whipped cream cheese, fresh ricotta, or a mild cheese, such as St. Andre or Explorateur.

Makes one 4 by 8-inch loaf or 10 muffins

1/2 cup rye or amaranth flour

1/3 cup fine stone-ground corn meal

1 cup all-purpose or whole wheat pastry flour

1/2 teaspoon baking soda

1 teaspoon baking powder

3/4 teaspoon sea salt

1 cup buttermilk

3 tablespoons safflower oil or butter, melted

1/2 cup unsulfured molasses

2 whole eggs, or 3 egg whites, at room temperature

3/4 cup raisins, chopped dates, or currants

Preheat the oven to 350°F and spray or butter and flour a bread pan. Combine the dry ingredients in a mixing bowl; whisk the wet ingredients together in a second bowl. Pour the wet ingredients into the dry and stir quickly to combine. Stir in the raisins. Transfer to the prepared pan and bake for 45 minutes or until a cake tester comes out clean. Let cool for at least 15 minutes in the pan before turning out onto a rack or serving.

Cornbreads

This American favorite can be whipped together by the time the oven is heated. Cornbreads are most accommodating. You can use white, yellow, or blue corn meal; buttermilk or sweet milk; butter or corn oil, which enhances the flavor of corn. Stone-ground corn meal, whatever the color, will make the best-tasting breads.

Buttermilk Skillet Cornbread

A big, tender golden cake baked in a cast-iron skillet, this is traditionally made only with stone-ground corn meal, which means it's also gluten free. Serves 6

---

3 tablespoons butter

1 3/4 cup stone-ground white or yellow corn meal

1 teaspoon baking powder

1/2 teaspoon baking soda

1/2 teaspoon sea salt

2 eggs, beaten

2 tablespoons sugar or honey, optional

1 1/2 cups buttermilk

Preheat the oven to 375°F. Put the butter in a 10-inch cast-iron skillet and place in the oven while you get everything else together. Sift the dry ingredients in one bowl and mix the eggs, sugar, and buttermilk in another. Remove the pan from the oven, brush the butter over the sides, then pour the rest into the wet ingredients. Combine the wet and dry ingredients, and stir long enough to make a smooth batter. Pour the batter into the hot pan and bake until lightly browned and springy to the touch, 25 to 30 minutes.

Marion's Custard Cornbread: A first-rate Sunday morning or supper bread. Pour a cup of cream over the batter just as the bread goes into the oven, but don't stir it. It will settle into the bread while baking, leaving a custardy layer on top. Delicious drizzled with molasses, honey, or blackberry jam.

Cornbread or Muffins with Fresh Corn Kernels

This is sweetened only by the presence of sweet corn kernels. Your corn can be raw, or you can use leftover corn on the cob, the kernels removed. For corn meal, see if you can find one of the more delicious and unusual ones, most likely at a farmers' market, such as Calais flint corn or Floriani red, blue corn, or Iroquois white.

Makes one 8 to 9-inch round cornbread or 12 muffins

- 1¼ cups corn flour
- 1¼ cups all-purpose flour
- 1½ teaspoons baking powder
- ½ teaspoon baking powder
- ½ teaspoon salt
- 1 cup yogurt or buttermilk
- ⅓ cup milk
- 2 large eggs
- ¼ cup corn or sesame oil
- Kernels from 3 ears corn

Preheat the oven to 400°F. Butter or oil a 9-inch cast iron skillet, a cake pan, or 12 muffin cups.

Combine the dry ingredients in a bowl and blend them with a whisk.

Combine the wet ingredients in another bowl and whisk together. Pour the wet ingredients into the dry ingredients, then stir just until everything is combined. Add the corn kernels and fold them into the batter. Scrape the batter into the prepared pan or muffin tins, then bake until firm and golden on top and a cake tester comes out clean— about 20 minutes for muffins, 30 minutes for a cake. Serve warm with butter and honey or molasses, if desired.

Northern Cornbread

This cornbread uses sweet milk rather than buttermilk, resulting in a more cakelike crumb than the recipe on page 576. The sweetener is up to you.

Makes one 8-inch square pan or 10-inch skillet

- 2 tablespoons butter
- 1 cup stone-ground corn meal
- 1 cup all-purpose or whole wheat pastry flour
- ½ teaspoon sea salt
- 2 teaspoons baking powder
- 2 eggs
- ¼ cup safflower oil or butter, melted
- 2 to 4 tablespoons honey, optional
- 1⅓ cups milk, dairy or plant

Preheat the oven to 425°F. Put the butter in an 8-inch square baking pan and set in the oven while it's heating. Meanwhile, stir the dry ingredients together and make a well in the center of the bowl. In another bowl, whisk together the wet ingredients. As soon as the oven is hot, remove the pan and brush the butter around the edges. Pour any excess into the wet ingredients. Quickly mix the wet and dry ingredients together, then pour the batter into the pan and bake in the middle of the oven until golden brown on top and beginning to pull away from the edges, about 25 minutes. Serve hot right from the pan.

Green Chile and Cheese Cornbread: Add ½ cup grated Jack or cheddar and ¼ cup or more diced roasted green chiles to the batter.

Vanilla Cornbread: Vanilla sets off the sweetness of corn and is good when you want a slightly sweeter breakfast bread. Add 1 teaspoon vanilla extract to the wet ingredients and use the larger amount of honey.

Corn-Husk Muffins: For a popular Southwestern effect, moisten 10 dried corn husks, the kind used for tamales, in hot water. Place one in the bottom of each muffin cup. Secure them with a dab of the batter and leave one end sticking up several inches. Bake at 375°F for 20 to 25 minutes.

Muffins with Corn Kernels: Stir 1 cup fresh or frozen corn kernels into the batter for a little extra crunch.

Spoon Bread

A cross between cornbread and a pudding, practical spoon bread uses ordinary ingredients, is easy to make, and is comforting and nourishing. Serve it any time of day, with butter and molasses, or with savory accompaniments. Serves 4

3/4 cup fine stone-ground white or yellow corn meal

2 teaspoons baking powder

3/4 teaspoon sea salt

Freshly milled white pepper to taste, if savory

1/4 cup butter, cut into chunks

4 eggs, beaten

3/4 cup milk

Preheat the oven to 375°F. Lightly butter an 8-cup soufflé or other baking dish. Stir the corn meal, baking powder, salt and white pepper, together, then add the butter and pour 1 1/2 cups boiling water over all. Stir to break up any lumps, then let stand until the butter is melted. Add the eggs and milk, pour into the baking dish, and bake until puffed, golden, and set, 45 to 50 minutes. Serve hot.

Cheese and Chile Spoon Bread: Stir 1/3 to 1/2 cup chopped roasted green chiles into the batter and scatter 1/2 cup finely grated Muenster or Jack over the top before baking.

Spoon Bread with Condiments: Mentioned in Huntley Dent's classic work *The Feast of Santa Fe*, this is a great way to enjoy spoon bread for brunch or supper. Arrange a variety of condiments in little bowls: salsas, Red Chile Sauce (page 62), chopped cilantro and chopped green onion, diced jalapeño chile or chopped roasted green chile, grated Jack or Muenster or crumbled goat cheese. Serve the bread with a large spoon to make a neat mound, then let each person scatter condiments over the top.

Biscuits and Scones

Basic biscuits are easy and fast to make—the oven won't even be hot by the time you're ready to pop them in. If you're reheating soup for dinner, biscuits will make it special. Here are a few things to know about making good biscuits:

- The less the dough is worked, the more tender the biscuits will be. Knead the dough just until it comes together in a smooth ball—about a dozen kneadings. Gently rework the scraps and use them, too.
- Placing biscuits close together makes them rise higher and the steam coming off them keeps them from drying out. Placed an inch apart or more, they'll be crustier. Biscuits baked directly on a heated pizza stone have an especially good crust.
- If you don't have a biscuit cutter, a drinking glass, wineglass, shot glass—a glass of any kind will do. Biscuit dough can also be cut with a knife into diamonds or squares.
- Enjoy them while they're still warm from the oven. Biscuits aren't meant to be kept around, but leftovers are good toasted.
- Since biscuits don't require eggs, they can be made vegan by using coconut oil in place of butter and plant milk mixed with vinegar in place of buttermilk (see page 559).

Buttermilk Biscuits

Buttermilk biscuits are exceptionally tender with a slightly tangy edge. Makes 12 to 16 biscuits

---

2 cups all-purpose or whole wheat pastry flour or white whole wheat

2 teaspoons baking powder

1/2 teaspoon baking soda

1/2 teaspoon sea salt

6 tablespoons butter

1 cup buttermilk

Preheat the oven to 450°F. If you have a baking stone, heat the oven for an extra 10 minutes. Otherwise, lightly grease a sheet pan and set it aside.

Combine the dry ingredients in a bowl and cut in the butter with your fingers or two knives until the mixture looks like coarse meal. Pour in the buttermilk and stir it with a fork until the dry ingredients are evenly moistened. Lightly flour the counter, turn out the dough, and pat it into a circle about ³/₄ inch thick. Cut into rounds or another shape. Reassemble the scraps and cut them out as well. Bake the biscuits directly on the hot baking stone or on the sheet pan until light brown, 15 to 20 minutes.

Baking Powder Biscuits: Instead of buttermilk, use regular milk and omit the baking soda.

Biscuits Made with Oil: In place of butter and shortening, use the same amount of oil. Stir the oil into the milk, then add this mixture to the dry ingredients. Stir just until the dough leaves the sides of the bowl and don't worry about its lumpy appearance. Flour the counter, knead briefly or simply pat it into a circle, then cut out the biscuits and bake.

Dropped Biscuits: Increase the liquid in Buttermilk Biscuits (page 578) or Baking Powder Biscuits (above) to 1¹/₃ cups. Instead of rolling it out, drop the dough by spoonfuls onto the sheet pan. They will be rough and cobbled looking rather than smooth, but just as good.

Seeded Cheese Biscuits: To the dry ingredients for Buttermilk Biscuits (page 578) or Baking Powder Biscuits (above), add 1 cup coarsely grated, then chopped, cheese, such as sharp cheddar or Gruyère. Roll them out, brush the tops of the biscuits with beaten egg, and sprinkle generously with poppy or sesame seeds before baking.

Whole Wheat Biscuits: A coarse-milled flour filled with bran, such as graham flour, makes a light but very substantial biscuit—one that will hold you all morning. Replace white flour with graham flour or 1¹/₂ cups whole wheat flour mixed with ¹/₂ cup wheat bran.

Yeasted Potato Biscuits

Unlike the Angel Biscuits (page 580), these exceptional biscuits do require rising time, so they're not for last-minute baking. The potato combined with the yeast makes them feather light and tender, with a delectable fragrance.

Makes ten 2-inch biscuits

2¹/₄ teaspoons (1 envelope) active dry yeast

¹/₂ cup buttermilk or regular milk

2 tablespoons butter, cut into small pieces

1 tablespoon sugar

¹/₂ cup warmed mashed potatoes, about 1 medium potato

1 teaspoon sea salt

2¹/₂ cups all-purpose bread flour, or a mix of white and whole wheat

Beaten egg, milk, or cream, for glazing

Stir the yeast into ¹/₄ cup warm water in a small bowl and set it aside. Slowly warm the buttermilk with the butter and sugar in a small pan. (Buttermilk may curdle, but it will smooth out in the end.) When the butter has melted, pour the liquid into a bowl and beat in the potatoes, salt, ¹/₄ cup of the flour, and the proofed yeast. Cover and let stand until light and foamy, about 30 minutes.

Stir in the remaining 2¹/₄ cups flour until no more can be added easily, then knead the dough until smooth and elastic. Cover and let rise until doubled in bulk, 45 minutes to an hour. Turn it out, then roll into a circle about ¹/₈ inch thick and cut into 2-inch rounds. Place on a lightly greased sheet pan, cover, and let rise again until nearly doubled, 45 minutes to an hour.

Preheat the oven to 400°F. Brush the biscuits with the beaten egg and bake until the biscuits are golden, about 20 minutes.

Angel Biscuits

Three kinds of leavening raise these heavenly biscuits. Although they contain yeast, they aren't kneaded and they require only as much time as it takes to preheat the oven. Make them small and serve them with a spot of good jam, a thin slice of Gruyère cheese. Originally, I made these with all-purpose flour, which certainly contributes to their lightness, but today I use a mix of all-purpose with white whole wheat, spelt, or sprouted flour.

Makes about fifty 1-inch or twenty-four 2-inch biscuits

2¼ teaspoons (1 envelope) active dry yeast

2 teaspoons sugar

4 cups all-purpose flour or a mixture of flours

2 teaspoons baking powder

1 teaspoon baking soda

1½ teaspoons sea salt

1 cup butter

1½ cups buttermilk

1 egg, beaten

Stir the yeast into ¼ cup warm water with 1 teaspoon of the sugar in a small bowl and set aside to proof. Meanwhile, mix the remaining 1 teaspoon sugar with the flour, baking powder, baking soda, and salt in a mixing bowl, then cut in the butter with your fingers or two knives until coarse crumbs are formed. Stir in the yeast mixture and the buttermilk and bring it together with a fork.

Turn the dough out onto a counter and knead lightly until smooth, then roll it out about ³⁄₈ inch thick. Cut out the biscuits any size you like. I like using a cordial or sherry glass so that they're small—one or two bites—good for a cocktail biscuit or brunch where there's lots of other food. Transfer them to a lightly buttered sheet pan, brush with beaten egg, and let rise for 15 minutes while you preheat the oven to 375°F. Bake until the biscuits are browned, about 20 minutes.

Oat Scones

Scones, closely related to biscuits, are usually enriched with an egg, frequently sweeter, and sometimes richer. Serve these tender oat scones with bitter marmalade, strong honey, or apple butter and Tangy Whipped Cream (page 644). For variety, try rye, barley, or other flakes in place of the oats.

Makes 8 scones

1 cup rolled oats, plus extra for the counter

1½ cups all-purpose, white whole wheat, or whole wheat pastry flour

3 tablespoons brown sugar

2 teaspoons baking powder

½ teaspoon sea salt

7 tablespoons cold butter, cut into small pieces

1 egg

½ cup plus 2 tablespoons milk or cream

½ teaspoon vanilla extract

Preheat the oven to 425°F. If you have a baking stone, heat it for an extra 10 minutes.

Mix the dry ingredients together, then cut in the butter with your fingers or two knives until coarse crumbs are formed. Beat the egg with the milk and vanilla and stir it into the dough. Mix just enough to moisten the dry ingredients evenly. Scatter some oats on the counter and turn the dough out on top of them. Pat into a circle about ½ inch thick, then cut into eight wedges and place each piece on the hot baking stone, if using, or on a sheet pan. Bake until nicely browned, 15 to 18 minutes. Serve warm.

Ginger Cream Scones

When I was pastry chef at Café Escalera in Santa Fe, I used to make these for early-morning customers who wanted just a little something with their coffee. It's the cream that makes them melt in your mouth like nothing else does. Ginger scones make an exceptional base for strawberry, peach, or dried winter fruit compote shortcake. Makes 12 scones

- ¹/₂ to 1 cup candied ginger, chopped to the size of a raisin
- 2 cups unbleached flour
- 2 teaspoons baking powder
- 1 tablespoon sugar, plus extra for the top
- ¹/₂ teaspoon sea salt
- ¹/₄ cup cold butter, cut into small pieces
- 2 eggs
- ¹/₂ cup plus 1 tablespoon cream or a mixture of milk and cream
- ¹/₂ teaspoon vanilla extract

Preheat the oven to 425°F. If you have a baking stone, heat it for an extra 10 minutes. Or lightly butter a sheet pan.

Toss the ginger with a tablespoon of the flour. Mix the remaining flour with the baking powder, sugar, and sea salt, then cut in the butter with your fingers or two knives until the mixture resembles meal. Combine the eggs, the ¹/₂ cup cream, and the vanilla, then stir it into the flour mixture along with the ginger. Turn the dough onto a floured board and lightly knead 8 to 10 times. Pat or roll the dough into a circle about ¹/₄ inch thick, then brush the top with the remaining 1 tablespoon cream and sprinkle with sugar. Cut into twelve wedges or into small circles and bake directly on the stone or on the sheet pan until golden, about 15 minutes. Serve warm.

Some Other Flavorings for Scones: The following are always good additions whether you're making the hearty oat or cream scones: 1 heaping teaspoon grated orange or lemon zest; ¹/₃ cup currants, dried cherries, berries, or raisins, plumped in warm water and then squeezed dry; ¹/₃ cup chopped dates; ¹/₂ cup chopped pecans, walnuts, or roasted hazelnuts; caramelized pecans or walnuts; grated nutmeg or ground cinnamon.

Boston Brown Bread

This healthful brown bread was once made all over New England, but it's commonly called Boston brown bread. It was our Sunday night supper, along with baked beans when we still lived in New England. Boston brown bread can still be bought in cans, but it's not at all hard to make. The steaming is what gives the bread its characteristic texture, which is resilient and spongelike. The bread takes about a minute to assemble, but the steaming an hour or so of your unattended time. Cream cheese is the classic and delicious pairing. Other ingredients that sometimes appear in the batter are orange zest, walnuts, and allspice. For cans, use a 28-ounce tomato can or two smaller ones. Makes 1 loaf

- ¹/₂ cup whole wheat flour
- ¹/₂ cup rye flour
- ¹/₂ cup corn meal
- ¹/₂ teaspoon baking soda
- ¹/₂ teaspoon salt
- ¹/₂ cup molasses
- 1¹/₂ cups buttermilk
- ¹/₂ cup dark raisins

Combine the flours, corn meal, baking soda, and salt in a bowl and make a well in the center. Pour the molasses and buttermilk into the well and then stir everything together. Add the raisins.

Butter a 1-pound coffee can or 4-cup pudding mold and its lid. Pour in the batter and cover with the lid or, if using the can, with heavy aluminum foil secured with a piece of string. Set in a deep pot on a rack or the lid of a canning jar to keep it from direct contact with the bottom of the pot, and add boiling water to a few inches up the sides of the mold. Adjust the heat so that the water burbles at a slow boil, then cover and cook for 45 minutes or until a cake tester comes out clean and the bread has pulled away from the sides of the can. It shouldn't be necessary to replenish the water if the pot has a good, heavy lid. When done, remove the foil. Let rest for at least 30 minutes, then ease the bread out of the can or mold. Serve warm or at room temperature.

With Amaranth: It's not traditional, but amaranth flour is very good in this bread, replacing the rye flour in part or altogether.

Irish Soda Bread with Bran and Oats

There are many kinds of Irish soda bread, but this one, filled with honest ingredients—flaky bran and rolled oats—is one of my favorites. If you have a baking stone, bake the bread right on it, but allow 25 minutes for it to preheat. This bread is very good with cheeses of all kinds—from aged cheddar to St. Andre or mild goat cheese—and strong, bitter marmalade.

Serves 6

- 1 cup all-purpose flour
- 1 cup whole wheat flour
- 1/2 cup wheat bran
- 1/2 cup rolled oats
- 1 1/2 teaspoons baking soda
- 1/2 teaspoon sea salt
- 5 tablespoons cold butter
- 1 1/4 cups buttermilk
- 2 tablespoons molasses or honey

Preheat the oven to 400°F. If you have a baking stone, heat it for an extra 10 minutes. Otherwise lightly butter or oil a sheet pan.

Mix the dry ingredients in a bowl, then cut in the butter with two knives (or use a food processor) until it's crumbly and fine. Stir in the buttermilk and molasses, bringing everything into a ball, then turn the dough onto a floured counter and knead until smooth but still soft, no more than a minute. Shape into a disk 7 or 8 inches across, then slash an X in the center. Set directly on the hot baking stone or on the pan and bake until browned, about 35 minutes. Though it's very tempting to eat the bread piping hot, it tastes better if it can cool on a rack for at least 30 minutes.

Graham, Rye, and Spelt Cracker Breads

These gritty crunchy crackers were inspired by a photograph in Saveur *of a stunning flatbread with a hole in the middle—that and a supply of flours from Anson Mills, including graham flour and some Italian rye. Beautiful flours.*

You can make these into small, 3-inch rounds, which I've done, but in the end, but it's the larger, plate-size crackers that are most fetching. Setting stack of these crackers out for others to break off, or lining a long table with them and setting out some fresh ricotta cheese or quark is far more exciting than putting out RyKrisp.

Graham flour is slightly coarser than whole wheat because of the way it's milled, but if whole wheat is what you have, fine. I like one that's flecked with bran.

Makes 4 or 5 cracker breads

- 1 cup milk
- 1 tablespoon honey or barely malt syrup
- 2 1/4 teaspoons (1 envelope) active dry yeast
- 1 1/2 cups graham flour
- 2/3 cup rye flour
- 1/3 cup spelt flour or white whole wheat flour
- 1 scant teaspoon salt
- Fennel seeds, to taste, for topping
- Flaked salt, for finishing

Warm the milk. It shouldn't be hot, only warm, about 115°F. Pour it into a large bowl and stir in the honey and yeast. Let it stand while you mix the flours and salt together.

When foamy, after 5 to 10 minutes, stir in the flours to make a shaggy dough. (If you can't incorporate all the flour, leave any extra in the bowl to use later when you roll it out. This may happen where the air is very dry.)

Knead the dough together briefly until smooth but a little damp and tacky. The *Saveur* recipe didn't say to do this, but I rub a bowl with ghee then put the dough in and smear what's on my fingers over the top. Cover and leave it for an hour to rise. For a cover, a plastic shower cap from a hotel is perfect.

Heat the oven to 425°F. Turn out the dough, divide it into four or five pieces, and roll into rough circles, about 1/8 inch thick, which is to say, quite thin. They can be ragged around the edges. Sprinkle fennel seeds and just a pinch of flaked salt over the surface and roll them into the dough. Even if you're not going to dry it on a pole, the reason for the hole in the middle, you can cut out a circle using a glass or a biscuit cutter. Dock the dough with the tines of a fork, then place each circle on one or two sheet pans, lined with parchment paper. Run cool water over your hand, then sprinkle it over each bread.

Bake until the bread is browned around the edges, a bit in the center, and crisp, 8 to 10 minutes. Turn it over and bake the second side for 3 to 4 minutes more. Let cool, then stack the breads on a plate.

Seed Crackers

Certainly there are many good crackers on the market, but none will look or taste like these. The dough takes about 2 minutes to make in a food processor plus 15 minutes to rest, and, once rolled and cut, 10 minutes to bake. Use half the dough at a time and freeze the rest if you need just a few dozen crackers. Makes about 50 crackers

- 1 cup all-purpose or whole wheat pastry flour
- 1/2 teaspoon sea salt, plus extra for sprinkling
- 2 tablespoons butter
- 1 teaspoon mustard
- 1 heaping cup cheddar, grated
- 1/3 cup freshly grated parmesan
- 2 eggs
- 2 tablespoons seeds, such as caraway, cumin, sesame, poppy, fennel, and black mustard seeds
- Red pepper flakes, optional

Mix the flour and sea salt in a bowl, then work in the butter with your fingers until small crumbs are formed. Add the mustard, cheeses, and eggs and work the dough lightly so that it forms a coherent mass. Wrap in plastic, press into a disk, and let rest for 15 minutes in the refrigerator.

Preheat the oven to 375°F. Divide the dough into two pieces. Lightly flour your work surface and roll each piece into a rectangle about 10 by 14 inches. Scatter the extra sea salt, seeds, and pepper flakes over the top and lightly press them into the dough with the rolling pin. (Make a mixture of seeds or visually divide the dough into strips and use just one kind of seed on each strip.) Cut into squares, diamonds, or strips, transfer to a sheet pan, and bake until golden brown and slightly puffed, 8 to 10 minutes. Serve within the day or store in an airtight container until needed. Reheat frozen crackers for about 5 minutes in a 350° oven to freshen them.

Emily's Oat Cakes

I love my friend Emily's oat cakes. They have such a sturdy goodness to them and are good with cheese and jam. Makes about sixteen 2¹/₄-inch oat cakes

- 2 cups rolled oats (not instant)
- 1/4 teaspoon baking soda
- Scant 1/2 teaspoon sea salt
- 2 tablespoons butter, cut into chunks

Preheat the oven to 350°F.

Put half the oats in the blender or spice grinder, whizz them into a flour, then put them in a bowl with the remaining oats, baking soda, and salt.

Simmer 1/3 cup water with the butter. When the butter melts, pour it into dry ingredients and stir everything together. Knead briefly by hand, then roll out as thin as possible. Cut into circles and transfer, with a spatula, to a sheet pan.

Bake 30 minutes, or until lightly browned. Let cool. Serve with cheese and/or jam.

Crepes

Although not as popular as they once were, crepes are always well received. They can make simple foods special, can be adapted in various ways, and are not difficult to make!

Here are a few things to know about making crepes:

1. After being mixed, the batter needs to rest so that the gluten can relax and absorb the flour, ensuring that the crepes will be supple and tender when cooked. Although you'll be able to use the batter within 30 minutes, it's better if it can rest for 2 hours, or overnight.

2. Start heating the pan over a fairly high heat, then reduce the temperature to medium once the pan is hot. If the pan gets too hot, just wave it back and forth in the air several times to cool it down.

3. If the batter is the right consistency, it will coat the pan quickly and evenly. If it's too thick, it will be sluggish. Thin a too-thick batter by gently stirring in additional milk or water until it's the right consistency. The first crepe usually never turns out, so just throw it out and go onto the second, which will probably be fine. You don't need to oil the pan each time, only the first time.

Crepe Batter

Makes eighteen to twenty 6-inch crepes

2 eggs
1 cup milk, dairy or plant
$1/2$ cup water
$1/2$ teaspoon sea salt
1 cup all-purpose flour
3 tablespoons melted butter or oil

Combine all the ingredients in a blender or food processor and blend until smooth, about 5 seconds. Scrape down the sides, then blend 5 seconds more. Cover and set aside in the refrigerator to rest.

Heat a crepe pan (a 7- to 10-inch lightweight skillet with sloping sides) then brush it with a little oil or butter as soon as it's hot. When it sizzles, pour in a little more than 2 tablespoons batter (for a 7-inch pan) and immediately swirl it around the pan. Cook until golden on the bottom, about 1 minute. Slide a knife under an edge to loosen the crepe, grab it with your fingers, and flip it over. The second side need only cook until it's set, about 30 seconds.

Set the finished crepe on a plate, then continue making the rest. If you stack the finished crepes on top of each other, they'll hold their heat quite well until all are done.

Variations to the Batter: For half the flour, substitute with other more interesting flours, such as buckwheat, corn flour, masa, quinoa, rye, and so forth. Or add 2 pinches saffron threads diluted in 1 tablespoon hot water to the batter, or $1/4$ cup chopped herbs—parsley, basil, thyme, marjoram, rosemary are some good ones.

CREPE SHAPES

Crepes can be rolled, folded into quarters, folded into packages, quartered then rolled into cones, or filled then rolled and sliced. Always place your filling on the second (paler) side so that when finished, the golden side is exposed. Filled crepes can be brushed with butter and heated in a 350°F oven for 12 to 15 minutes or browned in a skillet.

How to Use Crepes

Filling needn't be more than a little cheese grated over top and freshly peppered, or, for dessert, a squeeze of lemon juice and a dusting of sugar. More elaborate preparations, of course, are to be considered too. Some savory fillings can be formed from many of the simpler recipes in the book, such as the following:

- Sautéed Spinach (page 378) with ricotta cheese and a spoonful of pesto
- Sautéed Mushrooms with Garlic and Parsley (page 351)
- Mushrooms, Tarragon, and Cream (page 352)
- Skillet Asparagus (page 299) with warm sage and garlic butter

- Roasted Asparagus (page 299) and fontina cheese
- Corn and Mushroom Ragout with Sage and Roasted Garlic (page 215)
- Simple Summer Stew with Herb Butter or Oil (page 222)
- Chopped Broccoli (page 307)
- Sautéed Zucchini with Garlic and Lemon (page 382)
- Corn and Lima Bean Ragout (page 221)

Breads Made with Yeast

Bread baking is a life-renewing experience. For many, the very act of baking—bringing dry granules of yeast and flour into living dough, working it under your hands, and inhaling its good smells while it bakes—is its own reward. But many people also bake because of the quality and kinds of bread they can make at home. While good bread is getting much easier to find, good bakeries don't yet exist in every community. To have breads based on whole grains and interesting flours and leavenings, many still have to make them at home.

In addition to our traditional American breads, we are now baking a host of new favorites—flatbreads and coarse, chewy country breads based on slow-developing wild yeasts. There's no shortage of information for the aspiring home baker on how to make these challenging new—or, rather, ancient—breads, for many good bakers have written extensively about their craft. This chapter is a sampler of both basic and new breads that fit our needs and wants today and isn't meant to cover the entire vast territory of bread baking.

While many have found the bread machine an answer to the problems of time and scheduling, bread machines have their own recipe requirements and formulations. The recipes in this chapter are the conventional, hands-on variety and shouldn't be used in bread machines.

Yeasted Bread Basics

Bread baking is not difficult, but it helps to understand how the ingredients you'll be using function. If you're new to bread baking, take a look at this section before you start.

YEAST: Yeast is a living organism that gives bread life, loft, and character. Because it's alive, its allure is very powerful. Beginners are often afraid of killing the yeast, but it's actually easy to make it thrive and difficult to kill. Usually, the first attempt is successful, but if it isn't, remember that all you've lost is some water, yeast, and a little flour.

Yeast comes in two forms: compressed cakes and dried granules. Cake yeast, which used to be common, is now rather hard to find. More common and convenient is dry yeast. It can be found in the baking section of your supermarket in small foil packets, but it's far cheaper and more convenient to buy it in bulk at a natural foods store and measure it out as needed.

In general, a $1/4$-ounce package, which contains about $2^1/4$ teaspoons yeast, will raise 6 cups flour mixed with 2 cups liquid. At high altitudes, where breads tend to rise too high and too fast, you might use 2 teaspoons instead. Using less yeast also means the dough develops more flavor during its extended rise, as has been proven by the success of the No-Knead Bread (see page 595), which uses only $1/4$ teaspoon yeast.

GETTING YEAST GROWING: Yeast comes alive in a warm environment. Its life usually begins when it's dissolved in warm water that's pleasant to the touch, between 100 and 115°F on a thermometer, or baby bottle temperature. If you're just starting out, take the temperature of the water the first time so you can see what it is; sprinkle it on your inner wrist to see how it feels, then use the skin test thereafter. You'll get the feel of it quickly.

PROOFING: Yeast wasn't always as reliable as it is today, so it had to be proved (or proofed) to make sure it would work. That's what we're doing when we stir it into a small amount of warm water, sometimes with a pinch of sugar. If it's alive, it will begin to foam in 5 to 10 minutes. Today's commercial yeast is virtually fail-safe, and new fast-rising yeasts are added directly to the flour. If using fast-rising or instant yeasts, read the instructions—they often call for smaller amounts.

SUGAR AND SEA SALT: Sugar in any form (malt syrups, honey, molasses, and so on) feeds the yeast and speeds its growth. Whole grains contain natural sugars that also provide food for the yeast. Sea salt keeps the yeast from growing too fast or too much, and, of course, it gives flavor to bread.

FLOUR: The type of flour you use determines how a bread looks, tastes, and handles. Gluten, a protein found in wheat, has elasticity that allows the dough to rise by trapping the released gases from the yeast. Gluten is developed by kneading and beating. Flour milled from hard winter wheat, called bread flour, has more gluten than pastry flour, which is made from soft wheat. All-purpose flour, made from a blend of wheats, has enough gluten to give bread its rise but not so much that it can't also be used for quick breads and pastries. Some flours like rye, corn, and quinoa have virtually no gluten, so they need to be blended with a portion of wheat flour—at least half—to work in these recipes.

Usually 3 cups flour, or about a pound, requires 1 cup liquid. Some special flours, like buckwheat, require more liquid, and flour in dry climates will also need more liquid. This is why the last bit of flour is held back, to be kneaded in as required.

In addition to wheat, interesting textural and flavor additions are gained by adding bran, wheat berries, cracked wheat, cooked rice, oats, flakes, bulgur, and corn meal. Mashed potatoes, nuts, dried fruits, olives, cheese, and herbs are other additions that find their way into specialty breads. See page 31 for more about flour.

LIQUID: Water is usually the liquid in yeasted breads. Milk (including buttermilk) is used when you want softer dough with a fine crumb. Other liquids you can use for bread are the whey that separates from yogurt when you're making yogurt cheese, the water left from boiling potatoes, and beer. Eggs are added to the liquid for richer breads.

FAT: Most breads do not depend on fat for structure. However, it does contribute flavor and tenderness and also helps keep breads moist, which is important in dry climates.

If fat isn't called for and you wish to include some, add 2 to 4 tablespoons when you add the proofed yeast to the water (for a recipe calling for 5 to 6 cups flour). If leaving out fat where it's called for, be sure to replace its volume with water or milk.

A NOTE ABOUT WHOLE WHEAT FLOUR

Whole wheat flours differ from one another according to how they're milled. Most are fine and powdery, just like white flour. In fact, there is a white whole wheat flour, although most are brown. However, I am particularly fond of a coarser type with visible flecks of bran. Its roughness makes a lighter, less dense product but one with character. A small mill in New Mexico (Valencia) produces just such a flour, but, of course, it's not available nationwide. You can achieve a similar effect by using graham flour, which is usually coarser than regular whole wheat, or by replacing up to a quarter of the flour with wheat bran. Keep your eye out for small mills in your area that aren't nationally known—you may find just the flour you like.

BAKING EQUIPMENT: Not a great deal of equipment is needed for bread baking. Most of what's needed are kitchen fixtures—a small bowl or teacup for proofing yeast, a large bowl, and a large bowl for mixing the dough, preferably heavy ceramic or pottery, which holds its warmth, although stainless and glass are also fine. Aside from measuring spoons and cups, you'll want a wooden spoon for mixing doughs and a dough scraper—a metal 4 by 6-inch dull blade with a handle—for scraping dough up off the counter or for assisting in working wet, sticky doughs.

A kitchen scale is useful for weighing rolls and loaves so they'll be equal in size, although you'll do well using your eyes. Sheet pans and a baking stone are used for baking rolls and free-form breads. For standard loaves, you'll want two bread pans, $8\frac{1}{2}$ by $4\frac{1}{2}$ inches or, my favorite, 4 by 10 inches (available at good kitchen stores). A spray bottle is handy for introducing moisture to the oven to develop the crust, and a pastry brush is for brushing on glazes.

A stand mixer with paddle attachment certainly isn't necessary for making bread, but it's very nice to use if you have one. My KitchenAid is my best-loved kitchen luxury.

Ten Basic Steps to Making Yeasted Breads

Most recipes for yeasted breads follow these steps. Variations are always given in the particular recipes where they occur.

1. **Proof the yeast in ¹/₄ cup warm water.** This step proves to you that the yeast is active and ready to work. Stir the yeast into warm tap water and let it stand until it's covered with foamy bubbles, which takes about 10 minutes. If nothing happens in 15 minutes, throw it out and start over.

2. **Combine the liquids and salt, then begin working in the flour.** Using either a wooden spoon or an electric mixer with a paddle attachment, work in as much flour and other dry ingredients such as whole grains and milk powders. Beat vigorously until you have a shaggy, heavy dough that pulls away from the sides of the mixing bowl.

3. **Turn the dough onto a counter and knead until smooth.** Kneading is the heart of bread baking. The steady, rhythmic motion of folding, pressing, and turning develops the strands of gluten and determines the fineness of the crumb. Since kneading involves pushing, try to work at a height where you can comfortably lean into it, using your whole body, not just your arms.

   Dust your counter or breadboard lightly with flour, then turn out the dough, scraping everything out of the bowl. The dough will be rough and sticky. Have the flour you haven't used in a mound on the counter and a metal dough scraper for moving wet doughs and scraping it off your fingers. Dust some flour over the top, then gather the dough into a mass and bring the far portion of it toward you, folding it over. Press on it with both hands, where the folded part meets the bulk of the dough, and push it away from you. Push at the rate the dough will accept the pressure—don't try to force it into any particular speed. When you've pushed it out, give the dough a quarter turn, then repeat. As you knead, brush in small amounts of flour if it feels damp and sticky. Usually 5 to 8 minutes is enough time. Don't worry about working in all the flour. Just work in enough so that by the time you've finished kneading, the dough is smooth and elastic but still a bit tacky rather than dry.

4. **Put the dough into an oiled bowl, turning once to coat the top.** Use a deep bowl with room for the dough to double in size. Oil (or butter) prevents the dough from sticking to the bowl and keeps the dough from drying out and forming a crust. Always prepare your bowl as you're setting up since it's awkward to stop in midstream.

5. **Cover with a damp towel.** Covering with a damp cotton kitchen towel or a piece of plastic wrap stretched over the bowl keeps a crust from forming over the surface; a shower cap is perfect. You can also use a thin plastic produce bag—just lay it directly on the dough, pressing it over the sides so that when the dough expands it will remain protected from the drying effects of the air.

6. **Set in a warm place to rise until doubled in bulk.** A warm spot can be near the stove, in an oven with the pilot light or light bulb on, or on top of a hot water heater. In cold weather, I've even put dough in my car, a highly effective incubator, to rise. It usually takes about an hour and a little more for the dough to rise until it's twice its size. Doughs containing eggs and lots of butter are more sluggish. "Double in bulk" gives you a visual suggestion. A properly risen dough should be very soft and hold a depression when poked with a finger. Don't use a place that's too warm, or the yeast will grow too fast. It's better to take more time at a cooler temperature than to rush the dough. A cool, slow rise develops different layers of flavors in bread. In fact, many European breads are made with less yeast to ensure a slow rise. Dough can remain overnight, even for days, in the refrigerator, but you need to allow at least a few hours for it to come to room temperature before completing its rise.

7. **Push the dough down.** This step deflates the dough and strengthens it. Push your fist into the dough in several places to knock the air out of it, then turn it out onto a lightly floured counter. At this point, if you're too busy to shape the dough, just return it to the bowl, cover, and let rise again. It will double again but in about half the time.

8. **Shape the dough and let it rise a second time.** You can now shape the dough into loaves (or rolls or buns) and put them into their pans or on the back of a peel if baking on a stone. Once shaped, cover again and let it rise. This rise will take less time than the first, but it's important not to rush it, especially with breads made with heavy flours. If you press the side of round bread gently with your fingers, it should be very soft and tender, like a relaxed calf or arm muscle. Breads in loaf

pans should have risen to the top of the pan, swelling noticeably in the center. Preheat the oven during the last 15 minutes of this rise.

9. **Score the breads.** Slashing the tops of the breads before they go into the oven allows steam to escape. With loaf breads, this isn't always necessary, but if you don't score free-form breads, they'll make their own vents by tearing at the base. The designs for scoring are often deliberate, not merely decorations, although they are indeed attractive. At this point, you can brush the surface with a glaze to give your dough a burnished surface and provide a surface for seeds to adhere to.

10. **Bake until browned and pulling away from the sides of the pan.** Bake bread in the middle of a preheated oven. Breads gain their full rise right away—called oven spring—then they brown. Most loaf breads take between 45 and 55 minutes to bake through. If the tops get too brown, lay a piece of foil loosely over them. When done, the bread will have shrunk a little from the sides of the pans, and when you turn them out, the sides should be firm and brown. If they're pale looking, return the breads to the oven without their pans for 5 to 10 minutes more. One test for doneness is to tap the loaves on the bottom and listen for a hollow sound rather than a dull thud, but unless you bake a lot, it's not always easy to tell one sound from the other. Although it's tempting to eat bread hot from the oven, it slices better if you let it cool on a rack for at least an hour, preferably longer.

Trouble Spots

Making yeasted breads is generally a trouble-free activity, but there are a few things that just might go wrong, some of which are easy to correct.

THE DOUGH WON'T RISE: Chances are your yeast was too old. (If using foil packets, check their expiration date.) But if you proofed it first in warm water to make sure it was alive, it could be that your general atmosphere plus the added liquid was too cold. If that's the case, turn on the oven for 10 minutes, turn off the heat, then put the dough in. Its warmth should get it going. If it still doesn't rise, and the yeast proofed, your liquid might have been too hot. This is the one time you just have to give up and start over.

OVERPROOFING: If you let your dough rise too long, it will begin to get puckery looking on top and eventually will collapse. Just punch it down and let it rise again. If you bake it without doing this, the bread will have a flabby, rippled appearance on top.

THE DOUGH IS READY, BUT YOU'RE NOT: Bread dough is very forgiving if something comes up and you can't attend to your risen dough—just punch it down to press out the air and let it rise again. If you need more time than the 20 minutes or so that its rise will take, or you can't get to it until much later, put a piece of plastic wrap over the top and stick it in the refrigerator. Since it takes a while for the mass of dough to cool, it may still obtain its rise rather quickly. Just punch it down again. Eventually, it will cool and settle down. Allow an hour or more for it to return to room temperature before resuming.

YOU'VE SHAPED YOUR BREADS AND THEN CHANGED YOUR MIND: You want three breads instead of two, or one looks funny, or you suspect a bread is too big for the pan. Re-portion the dough, give it 15 minutes or so to relax, then reshape it as you wish.

Glazes for Breads, Pies, and Other Pastries

Glazes give a glossy coat and finished appearance to baked goods, not only breads but also scones, pies, biscuits, and galettes. They also make a surface amenable to making seeds stick. When glazing yeasted breads, reserve a little so that once the breads have expanded, about 15 minutes into the baking, you can brush the newly exposed areas as well. When glazing sweet pastries, adding a few teaspoons sugar to the glaze increases the luster and shine of the finished product.

Egg Glaze

1 egg yolk, or 1 whole egg

1 tablespoon water, milk, or cream

1 teaspoon sugar for sweet breads

Whisk everything together until smooth.

Egg Yolks: The yolk makes a glaze that's far more lustrous, giving the bread a richly burnished look. Use with egg breads and white breads, including the basic sandwich loaf.

Egg Whites: Use 1 egg white instead of a whole egg, and salt instead of sugar for savory breads.

Melted Butter: Melted butter also gives a lustrous dark appearance and good texture to crusts. For two loaves, melt 3 tablespoons butter and spread it over the breads just before baking. Reserve a little and add it once the oven spring has taken place.

Classic Sandwich Bread

High, fine-grained, and white, this is our basic white sandwich bread. You can use the same dough for dinner rolls, bread sticks, and cinnamon buns. Makes 2 loaves

> 2¼ teaspoons (1 envelope) active dry yeast
> ½ teaspoon sugar
> 1 cup warm milk
> 1 tablespoon honey
> ¼ cup sunflower seed oil
> 2½ teaspoons sea salt
> 2 cups all-purpose flour
> 3 to 4 cups bread flour
> Egg Glaze (page 588)

In a small bowl, stir ½ cup warm water and the yeast together, add the sugar, and set aside until foamy, about 10 minutes. In a larger bowl, combine the milk, 1 cup warm water, the honey, oil, and sea salt, then stir in the proofed yeast. Using a wooden spoon or the paddle attachment of an electric mixer, work in the flour a cup at a time until you have a shaggy, heavy dough that leaves the sides of the bowl. Turn it out onto a lightly floured counter and gradually knead in the remaining flour until the dough is smooth and resilient, about 5 minutes. Put it in a deep oiled bowl, turning it so that the top is oiled, too. Cover with a damp towel and set in a warm place to rise until doubled in bulk, an hour or longer.

Deflate the dough by pressing down on it, then divide it into two equal pieces, shape into balls, cover, and let rest for 10 minutes. Meanwhile, oil two bread pans. Flatten the dough into two rectangles the length of the pan. Roll it up tightly, pinch the seams together to seal the ends, and place in the pans, seam side down. Cover again and let rise until the dough is just above the edge of the pan, about 3 to 5 minutes. Preheat the oven to 375°F. Leave the dough as is or score the top with three diagonal slashes. Brush with the egg glaze and bake until browned and pulling away from the sides, 40 to 45 minutes. If the tops get too dark, cover loosely with foil. Turn the bread out, tap the bottom to make sure it has a hollow sound, not a thud, then set on a rack to cool.

Buttermilk Sandwich Bread: Heat buttermilk instead of regular milk—it will separate but will smooth out in the end. Or add ½ cup dried buttermilk to the dry ingredients.

Seeded Sandwich Bread: Brush the shaped loaves with a beaten egg, then coat with poppy or sesame seeds. Be particularly generous around the edges so that the seeds will roll down the newly exposed dough as it bakes.

Dill Bread: Add 2 tablespoons dried dill weed and 1 tablespoon dill seed to the dry ingredients. Glaze with egg and sprinkle with dill seeds.

Cheddar Bread: Knead 2 cups coarsely grated sharp cheddar in with the flour. It has a tantalizing aroma, especially when added to buttermilk bread.

Using Specialty Flours: While we're fond of white breads, they lack the fiber that whole grains have. Nonetheless, it's possible to improve them by including other flours that can't be used alone because they lack gluten. Quinoa, amaranth, spelt, and kamut are all high-protein flours. Use them in place of the all-purpose white flour. If you have access to some heritage wheat flours, such as Red Fife or Turkey Red, include a portion as well. Expect to gain less rise than if you were to use all wheat.

Whole Wheat Sandwich Bread

Even made with 100 percent whole wheat flour, this bread is fine and light, perfect for sandwiches. The gluten flour helps develop the lightness, as does taking the time to make a sponge, a two-step approach to making whole grain breads. (If you don't have time to make a sponge, follow the basic directions given in the preceding Classic Sandwich Bread recipe, using half or all whole wheat flour.) Makes 2 loaves

Sponge

2¹/₄ teaspoons (1 envelope) active dry yeast

¹/₄ cup unsulfured molasses or honey

²/₃ cup nonfat dry milk or dried buttermilk

¹/₂ cup gluten flour

2 cups whole wheat flour

Bread

¹/₃ cup sunflower seed oil

2¹/₂ teaspoons sea salt

3¹/₂ cups whole wheat flour

Stir 2¹/₄ cups warm water, the yeast, molasses, dry milk, gluten flour, and the 2 cups whole wheat flour until smooth. Scrape down the sides of the bowl, cover with a damp cloth, and set aside in a warm place for an hour until it's foamy on top and doubled in volume.

Gently stir down the sponge, then add the oil, sea salt, and 1 cup of the flour and beat until smooth. Begin adding the remaining flour by ¹/₂-cup increments until you have a shaggy, heavy dough. Turn it out onto a lightly floured counter and knead in as much flour as the dough will take, adding it a few tablespoons at a time. Knead until the dough is smooth but still a little tacky, 3 to 5 minutes.

Place the dough in an oiled bowl, turn it to coat the top, then cover and set in a warm place to rise until doubled in bulk, about 1¹/₂ hours or possibly longer. Deflate the dough, then divide it in two, shape into loaves, and place them seam side down in two greased 4¹/₂ by 8¹/₂-inch bread pans. (If you like a rustic look, roll the loaves into wheat bran or wheat flakes before putting them in the pans.) Cover again and set aside until the dough has risen to the edge of the pans, about 45 minutes. During the last 15 minutes, preheat the oven to 375°F. Bake in the center of the oven until browned, 45 to 50 minutes. Let cool completely before slicing.

Cracked Wheat–Honey Bread

This ratio of whole wheat to white flour makes a moderately high sandwich bread, while the cracked wheat gives it textural strength. I actually prefer bulgur to cracked wheat since it's precooked and not as hard. Makes 2 loaves

1 teaspoon sugar

2¹/₄ teaspoons (1 envelope) active dry yeast

1¹/₄ cups milk or buttermilk

¹/₄ cup unsulfured molasses or honey

3 tablespoons vegetable oil

2 teaspoons sea salt

1 cup fine or medium bulgur or cracked wheat

2 cups whole-wheat flour

2 to 3 cups bread flour or all-purpose white flour

Combine ¹/₄ cup warm water with the sugar and yeast in a small bowl and set aside until foamy, about 10 minutes. Prepare two 8¹/₂ by 4¹/₂-inch bread pans and oil a bowl for the dough.

In a mixing bowl, combine 1¹/₂ cups hot water and the milk, then stir in the molasses, oil, and salt. Add the yeast and bulgur, then begin beating in the flour, adding as much as you can until the dough leaves the sides of the bowl. Turn onto a lightly floured counter and knead until smooth, about 5 minutes, adding flour a little at a time. Put it in an oiled bowl, turn once to coat the top, then cover and set aside to rise until doubled in bulk, about 1¹/₄ hours.

Push the dough down, then turn it out and divide it in two. Form two loaves and set them in oiled or sprayed 4¹/₂ by 8¹/₂-inch bread pans. Cover again and let rise until the dough has risen to the top of the pan, about 40 minutes. Preheat the oven to 375°F. Bake for 45 minutes or until well browned.

Potato Bread

*Mashed potatoes make bread moist, tender, and exception-
ally flavorful. This makes delicious toast and fine dinner rolls
as well as bread. If you don't have mashed potatoes on hand,
simply boil a peeled, sliced baking potato in plenty of water
until soft enough to mash.* Makes 2 loaves

2¹/₄ teaspoons (1 envelope) active dry yeast

¹/₂ teaspoon sugar

1¹/₂ cups buttermilk

3 tablespoons butter, softened

2 teaspoons sea salt

1 cup mashed potatoes

4 cups bread flour

3 cups all-purpose flour

Egg Glaze (page 588)

Poppy seeds or sesame seeds, for topping

Stir the yeast and sugar into ¹/₄ cup warm water in a small
bowl and let stand until foamy, 10 minutes. Meanwhile
butter or spray two 8¹/₂ by 4¹/₂-inch bread pans and oil a
bowl for the dough.

In a mixing bowl, combine the buttermilk, 1¹/₂ cups hot
water, the butter, sea salt, and potatoes. Stir in the yeast,
then beat in the flour by cupfuls, starting with the bread
flour, until it leaves the side of the bowl. Turn the dough
out onto the counter and knead until smooth, working
in as much flour as the dough will hold and still be a little
tacky. Transfer the dough to an oiled bowl, turn it to coat the
top, then cover and set aside until doubled in bulk, about
1¹/₄ hours.

Push the dough down, shape into two loaves, and set it
in two greased 4¹/₂ by 8¹/₂-inch pans. Cover and let rise
again until doubled in bulk, about 45 minutes. Preheat
the oven to 375°F. Brush the egg glaze over the top, cover
with poppy seeds, and bake until nicely browned, about
45 minutes.

Oat Bread

*A loaf with a rustic-looking crust covered with oats and
bran.* Makes 1 loaf Ⓥ

¹/₂ teaspoon sugar

2¹/₄ teaspoons (1 envelope) active dry yeast

1 cup warm water or milk

¹/₄ cup honey or 2 tablespoons agave nectar

2 tablespoons butter, softened, or sunflower seed oil

1¹/₂ teaspoons sea salt

1 cup whole wheat flour

1 cup rolled oats

1 cup oat or wheat bran

2 to 3 cups bread flour or all-purpose flour

Additional oats and bran, for the top

Combine ¹/₄ cup warm water, the sugar, and the yeast in
a small bowl and set aside until foamy, about 10 minutes.
Meanwhile, butter or spray a 9 by 5-inch loaf pan and oil
a bowl for the dough.

In a mixing bowl, stir together 1 cup warm water, the honey,
butter, and sea salt. Stir in the yeast, then add the whole
wheat flour, oats, and bran. Beat in the bread flour until the
dough pulls away from the bowl. Turn it out onto a lightly
floured counter and knead for 5 minutes, adding as much
of the remaining flour as it will hold and still be a little
tacky. Put the dough in the oiled bowl, turn it once, then
cover and set aside until doubled in bulk, about an hour.

Push down the dough, then shape it into a loaf. Roll it into
a mixture of bran and oats to coat the top, then set it in a
5 by 9-inch loaf pan. Cover and let rise until again doubled, about 35 minutes. Preheat the oven to 375°F during
the last 15 minutes. Bake for 45 minutes or until the bread
pulls slightly away from the sides of the pan.

Light Rye Bread

A mild, moist, light-colored bread. Without caraway seeds, it won't seem like rye bread to those who always associate the two. Makes 1 loaf

Sponge

2¼ teaspoons (1 envelope) active dry yeast

1½ tablespoons unsulfured molasses

1¼ cups whole wheat or bread flour

¼ cup nonfat dry milk or dried buttermilk

Bread

2 tablespoons sunflower seed oil

2 teaspoons sea salt

1½ cups rye flour

¾ to 1 cup bread flour or all-purpose flour

Egg White Glaze (page 589)

Mix together everything for the sponge in a bowl with 1½ cups warm water, then cover and let rise for 2 hours. It should be foamy.

Stir down the sponge, then add the oil, salt, and rye flour. Beat in the bread flour until the dough is shaggy and pulls away from the side, then turn it out onto a lightly floured counter and knead in the remainder. You can expect it to be a little stickier to handle than all wheat flour doughs.

Transfer to an oiled bowl, cover, and set in a warm place until doubled in bulk, about 1 hour. Push the dough down, then shape into an oval loaf about 10 inches long. Scatter corn meal over a baking pan or peel if you're using a baking stone. Place the bread on it, cover, then let rise until doubled in bulk, about 40 minutes. Preheat the oven to 375°F during the last 15 minutes. Make three diagonal slashes across the top and brush with the glaze. Bake for 45 to 50 minutes or until browned.

Seeded Rye: Knead 1 tablespoon caraway or fennel seeds into the dough. Shape into a 5 by 9-inch loaf or free-form oblong loaf, brush with an egg glaze, sprinkle with additional seeds, and make several diagonal slashes in the top.

Multigrain Bread with Sunflower Seeds

Multigrain mixes containing flaxseeds and a variety of cracked grains work well in this bread. Extra sunflower seeds make this delicious loaf even better. Makes 2 loaves

Sponge

1 cup uncooked multigrain cereal

1 cup buttermilk or regular milk

2¼ teaspoons (1 envelope) active dry yeast

2 tablespoons honey or malt syrup

1 cup whole wheat flour

Bread

2½ teaspoons sea salt

2 tablespoons sunflower seed oil, plus extra for glazing

¾ cup sunflower seeds

4 cups whole wheat, all-purpose, or bread flour

Combine everything for the sponge in a mixing bowl with 1½ cups warm water, cover loosely, and set aside for an hour to soften the grains and proof the yeast.

Stir down the sponge, then stir in the sea salt, oil, and sunflower seeds. Begin beating in the flour until the dough is too heavy to stir, then turn out the dough and knead in the rest by hand until the dough is smooth and supple but still a little tacky. Turn the dough into an oiled bowl, cover well with plastic wrap, and set aside until doubled in bulk, about 1½ hours.

Push down the dough, divide it into two pieces, and shape into loaves. Place in two sprayed or buttered and floured 4½ by 8½-inch bread pans and let rise until doubled again, about 45 minutes. During the last 15 minutes, preheat the oven to 375°F. Slash the bread and brush it with the extra sunflower seed oil. Bake in the center of the oven until the loaves are golden brown and well risen and firm, about 45 minutes.

Amaranth–Corn Meal Bread

This bread features two grains of the New World—amaranth and corn meal. Whole amaranth is very nutritious and very tiny. You can use it whole or pop it first, as you would popcorn, in a dry skillet. Makes 1 loaf

Sponge

- 2¹/₄ teaspoons (1 envelope) active dry yeast
- 1¹/₂ tablespoons honey
- 1¹/₂ cups bread flour
- 2 tablespoons nonfat dry milk
- Egg Glaze (page 588)

Bread

- 2 tablespoons sunflower seed oil
- 1¹/₂ teaspoons sea salt
- ¹/₂ cup whole amaranth
- ¹/₂ cup amaranth flour
- ³/₄ cup stone-ground corn meal, plus extra for the top
- 1 cup whole wheat flour
- 1 cup bread flour

Stir together everything for the sponge in a mixing bowl with 1¹/₂ cups warm water until smooth, then cover and let rise for 1 hour.

Stir the oil and sea salt into the sponge, then begin beating in the remaining ingredients except the glaze. When the dough is shaggy, turn it out onto a counter and knead until smooth and elastic, 6 to 8 minutes. (Because of the amaranth, the gluten needs to be worked a little more than usual.) Cover and let rise until doubled in bulk, about 1 hour, then deflate and shape the dough into a loaf. Place in an oiled or sprayed 4¹/₂ by 8¹/₂-inch bread pan and let rise until doubled again, about 30 minutes. Preheat the oven to 375°F during the last 15 minutes. Slash the top with a knife, making three diagonal cuts, then brush the bread with the glaze and dust the top with corn meal. Bake until browned and pulling slightly away from the pan, about 45 minutes.

Peppered Cheese Bread

A good party bread—it looks so festive and pretty with its shiny golden crust. Made with white flour, the bread is tender and soft; with whole wheat it's more robust and hearty—or you can use a mixture. Makes 1 round loaf

- 1¹/₃ cups warm milk or water
- 2¹/₄ teaspoons (1 envelope) active dry yeast
- 1¹/₂ teaspoons sea salt
- 2 teaspoons coarsely ground black pepper
- 1 teaspoon red pepper flakes
- 1 egg, well beaten
- 3 cups all-purpose flour or a mixture of whole wheat and white
- 1 cup grated or finely diced cheddar

Put the milk in a large bowl and stir in the yeast. Let stand until foamy, about 10 minutes, then whisk in the sea salt, pepper, pepper flakes, all but 1 tablespoon of the beaten egg, and 1 cup of the flour. When smooth, start adding the remaining flour. When the dough gets too heavy for the spoon, turn it out and knead until smooth.

Flatten the dough with your hands and scatter half the cheese over it. Knead it into the dough, then repeat with the rest of the cheese. Place the dough in a lightly oiled bowl, turn once, then cover and set aside until doubled in bulk, 45 minutes to an hour.

Push the dough down, then turn it out onto the counter. Shape it into a tight ball. Cover and set aside until doubled in bulk, about 45 minutes, preheating the oven to 375°F during the last 15 minutes. Slash a large X in the top, then brush it with remaining beaten egg. Bake for 45 minutes, then turn onto a rack to cool.

Walnut Bread

Dense with wheat and walnuts, this crusty free-form bread derives its excellent flavor from roasted walnut oil as well as from the nuts. This is a wonderful bread to serve with soft cheese of all kinds—fontina, Taleggio, St. Andre, a home-made ricotta or ricotta-goat mixture, or cream cheese. A coarse whole wheat flour containing lots of bran is the best choice. If yours is fine, add a cup of wheat bran and decrease the whole wheat flour by 1 cup. Makes 2 or 3 round loaves

2¼ teaspoons (1 envelope) active dry yeast

¼ cup roasted walnut oil

1 tablespoon honey or malt syrup

½ cup nonfat dry milk

2 teaspoons sea salt

1 cup wheat bran, if whole wheat flour is smooth

3 to 4 cups whole wheat flour

About 2 cups all-purpose flour

1½ cups chopped walnuts, preferably blanched and roasted

Melted butter, for the top

Stir the yeast into ¼ cup warm water in a small bowl and set it aside while you gather your ingredients.

Put 2¼ cups warm water in a mixing bowl and stir in the oil, honey, dry milk, and sea salt. Add the bran and whole wheat flour. Beat well until the batter is smooth. Add enough all-purpose flour to make a heavy dough that pulls away from the sides of the bowl, then add the walnuts. Turn the dough out onto a counter and knead until smooth, adding more all-purpose flour as needed to keep it from sticking. Put the dough in an oiled bowl, turn it once, cover with plastic wrap, and set aside to rise until doubled, about 1½ hours.

Turn the dough out and cut it into two or three pieces. Shape each piece into a tight ball, cupping your hands around the dough to give it a plump, round shape. Place each ball on an oiled baking sheet, cover, and set aside until doubled in bulk, about 45 minutes. During the last 15 minutes, preheat the oven to 375°F.

Slash the breads, making three or four parallel cuts across the loaves, then brush with melted butter. Bake until a rich brown crust is formed and the bread is done, about 40 minutes.

Challah

When I was in high school, our neighbor used to bake this every Friday for Sabbath. The smells that wafted over the fence were so enticing they pulled me right into her kitchen. She showed me what to do, then I made this bread every weekend for a year. Leftovers make great French toast and bread puddings, both sweet and savory. Makes 2 large braids

2¼ teaspoons (1 envelope) active dry yeast

3 tablespoons sugar

3 eggs, beaten, 2 tablespoons reserved

¼ cup sunflower seed oil

2½ teaspoons sea salt

6 to 7 cups all-purpose flour

Poppy seeds, for the top

Mix the yeast with ¼ cup of the warm water and a tea-spoon of the sugar in a small bowl. Set aside until foamy, about 10 minutes, then stir it into 2 cups warm water in a mixing bowl along with the rest of the sugar, the eggs, oil, and sea salt. Add the flour a cup at a time, stirring to make a smooth batter. When it becomes heavy, turn it onto the counter and knead in the rest of the flour until the dough is satiny smooth, about 8 minutes. Set it in an oiled bowl, turn once, then cover. Set aside until doubled in bulk about an hour. Push down the dough, divide it in half, then divide each half into three equal pieces.

To shape the bread, roll each piece of dough into a rope 10 to 12 inches long. Cross the strands over each other in the middle, then begin braiding the strands, moving toward you. When you finish one end, turn the bread and braid the other end. Tuck in the ends to make them look smooth and finished. (You may find it easier to join the ropes at one end and then braid.)

Place the braids on an oiled sheet pan. Cover them with a damp towel and set aside until doubled, about 45 minutes. Preheat the oven to 375°F during the last 15 minutes. Beat the reserved egg with a tablespoon of water, then brush most of it over the breads and sprinkle with poppy seeds. Once the bread has risen, brush the remaining egg wash into newly exposed areas. Bake until the bread is bur-nished gold, about 45 minutes, then cool on a rack.

No-Knead Bread and Variations

When Penni Wisner and I taught an intensive cooking class at the spa Rancho la Puerta, she offered to show our students how to make Jim Lahey's famous no-knead bread if they wanted, and they all did. It was my first experience with it, too, and I could see why people were so nuts about this wonderful bread, and I'm thrilled that Penni graciously offered this version of Jim Lahey's recipe for inclusion in Vegetarian Cooking for Everyone. *She uses weights rather than volume, and so do I—a scale makes everything easier and more accurate. "But," Penni adds, "since the recipe does not need to be so precise, and different flours (in different climates, I might add) have different absorption qualities, volume works as well. I use a 5-ounce (142-gram) cup for both whole wheat and bread flour, and I know whole wheat is slightly heavier, but it's just one less thing to remember. So the total flour would be 4 cups."*

In any case, bread is something one always makes by eye and by feel, so don't ignore this recipe if you don't have a scale. It's worth making! Makes 1 loaf

---

- 425 grams (3 cups) organic, unbleached bread flour, plus more for dusting work surfaces
- 142 grams (1 cup) organic whole wheat flour
- 2 teaspoons kosher salt
- 1/4 teaspoon instant yeast
- About 1/2 cup corn meal

Place a 12-cup bowl on a scale and measure in the bread flour, whole wheat flour, salt, and yeast. Mix with a wooden spoon and make a well in the center.

Zero out the scale and add 411 grams (1³/4 cups) water to the bowl. Mix with the spoon until evenly blended, then finish mixing with a bowl scraper: clean the inside edges of the bowl and fold any loose bits of flour into the dough. Drizzle in more water as needed to incorporate all the flour into a soft, fairly wet dough. It will be pretty shaggy, nothing like your usual bread dough.

Cover with a shower cap or plastic wrap and set aside to rest 15 to 30 minutes, then, with the bowl scraper, work your way around the bowl, folding the dough over onto itself and working in any bits of ragged dough. Re-cover. Ideally, repeat twice more if you can.

Let the dough rise at room temperature until it's very bubbly, 18 to 24 hours.

Heavily flour a work surface. Scrape the dough out onto the work surface. Flour the top of the dough, and then fold the dough over on itself like an envelope: right to center, left to center, top to center, bottom to center. Repeat. Flip the dough seam side down, cover with the bowl, and let rest 15 minutes.

Dust a clean kitchen towel very lightly with flour and more heavily with corn meal. Gently shape the dough into a ball and place, seam side down, on the prepared cloth. Top with more polenta, cover with another kitchen towel, and place the whole thing into a large plastic bag. Let proof at room temperature about 60 minutes.

Meanwhile, preheat the oven to 500°F. Put your baking stones, if you have them, and a heavy, covered Dutch oven (cast-iron is great for this) in the oven to preheat as well. Make sure the oven is blasting hot.

When the dough is ready, take the hot Dutch oven out and turn the dough into the hot pot so that the dough is now seam side up. Give the pot a good shake to center the dough. Re-cover the pot, place in the oven, and lower the heat to 425°F. Bake 30 minutes. Uncover the pot and bake until dark brown, another 30 minutes. Remove and cool on a rack.

With Fennel Seed: Add 1¹/2 tablespoons fennel seed to the dry ingredients.

Meyer Lemon–Rosemary: Follow the mixing method in the main recipe, adding the zest of 1 or 2 large lemons, and a generous tablespoon finely chopped rosemary to the water. Ferment the dough as usual. Prepare the kitchen towel for the final proofing as usual, and then lightly sprinkle the cloth with gray salt or Maldon salt. Put the dough on the cloth, seam side down, and continue as above. Bake at 450°F.

With Semolina: Follow the formula in the main recipe, substituting semolina flour for the whole wheat flour. Stir 45 grams (about 1/3 cup) toasted sesame seeds into the dry ingredients before you add the water.

Buckwheat-Raisin Bread

Buckwheat flour bakes quite nicely into breads as long as it's mixed with wheat to provide gluten. This is a dark loaf, warmed with cinnamon and studded with fruit. Serve with cream cheese and apple butter or use it to make a breakfast grilled cheese sandwich and serve with sautéed apples or applesauce. Makes 1 loaf

---

Sponge

    2¹/₄ teaspoons (1 envelope) active dry yeast

    1¹/₃ cups bread flour

    ¹/₂ cup dried buttermilk or nonfat dry milk

    3 tablespoons unsulfured molasses or honey

Bread

    2 tablespoons oil or butter, melted

    1³/₄ teaspoons sea salt

    1¹/₂ cups dark raisins, large monukkas if possible

    2 teaspoons cinnamon

    1 cup chopped walnuts

    1 cup buckwheat flour

    1 to 1¹/₄ cups bread flour or all-purpose flour

    Egg Glaze (page 588)

Mix everything for the sponge in a bowl with 1¹/₄ cups warm water until smooth, then cover and set in a warm place for 1 hour.

Stir down the sponge, then add the oil, sea salt, raisins, cinnamon, and nuts. Stir in the buckwheat, then work in the bread flour until you can't add any more. Turn the dough onto a counter and knead until smooth and resilient, about 6 minutes. Put in an oiled bowl, turn once, cover, and let rise until doubled, 1 to 1¹/₂ hours.

Push the dough down and form it into a loaf. Place in a buttered or sprayed 4¹/₂ by 8¹/₂-inch bread pan, cover, and let rise until doubled again, about 40 minutes. Preheat the oven to 375°F during the last 15 minutes. Brush the bread with the glaze or dust with buckwheat flour. Bake until browned and pulling away from the sides of the pan, about 45 minutes.

Focaccia

Focaccia has found a secure footing in America and whole books are devoted to this famous Italian flatbread. This recipe makes one plump little focaccia, enough to serve six at dinner, or eight as an appetizer. Offering fresh bread at a meal is a nice touch, and this one can be ready to bake in a scant hour. Serves 6 to 8 Ⓥ

---

    2 teaspoons active dry yeast

    ¹/₂ teaspoon sugar

    1 teaspoon sea salt

    2 tablespoons fruity olive oil, plus extra for the top

    2¹/₂ to 3 cups all-purpose flour or a mixture of whole wheat and white

    Corn meal, if using a stone

    1¹/₂ teaspoons coarse sea salt

Dissolve the yeast and sugar in ¹/₄ cup warm water in a small bowl and set aside until bubbly, about 10 minutes. Meanwhile, oil a bowl for the dough.

In a mixing bowl, combine 1 cup warm water with the proofed yeast, then add the sea salt, oil, and as much flour as the dough will hold. Turn it out onto a floured surface and knead until smooth, working in enough flour to make it easy to handle, about 5 minutes. Place in the oiled bowl, turn once, and cover with a damp cloth. Set in a warm place to rise until doubled in bulk, about 45 minutes to an hour.

Turn out the dough and roll it into circle or oval about ¹/₂ inch thick. Leave it whole or slash it decoratively in several places, then pull on the dough to open the cuts. Place on the back of a sheet pan or a wooden peel dusted with corn meal, brush with olive oil, and sprinkle with coarse sea salt. Cover and let rise again, about 30 minutes.

Meanwhile, heat the oven to 400°F with a baking stone if you have one. Bake the bread in the middle of the oven until the bread is browned, about 30 minutes. To develop a crisp crust, spray the bread with water two or three times during the first 10 minutes in the oven.

Focaccia with Fennel Seeds: Crush 1 teaspoon fennel seeds in a mortar or with the dull side of a knife just to bruise them and knead them into the dough. When it's time to roll out the dough, sprinkle whole fennel seeds over the top, then roll them in with a rolling pin. (V)

Herb Focaccia: Mince 2 tablespoons fresh rosemary or sage leaves. Knead half into the dough and sprinkle the remainder on top, along with the sea salt, just before baking. If using sage leaves, set aside some whole ones for garnish and add them when the bread comes out of the oven. (V)

Focaccia with Caramelized Onions: Thinly slice 1 large onion and cook it in 2 tablespoons olive oil over medium heat until soft and golden, about 20 minutes. Stir more frequently as the pan begins to dry. Season with sea salt and pepper. Spread the onions over the risen focaccia and sprinkle with dried oregano or chopped rosemary. (Pitted gaeta or niçoise olives are good too: their salty tang sets off the sweetness of the onions. Walnuts are also good with onions and olives.) (V)

Focaccia with Blue Cheese and Walnuts: After the rolled dough has risen, press your fingertips over the top to make indentations. Crumble Gorgonzola over the top and bake. Take the bread out after 25 minutes, add a sprinkling of chopped walnuts, and return it to the oven for 5 minutes more. Serve with pepper cracked over the top and a scattering of chopped parsley.

Focaccia Sandwich Rolls: Divide the dough into four to six pieces and knead each piece into a round. Press or roll it out into a disk a scant 1/2 inch thick. If the dough doesn't want to be worked, let it rest for 5 or 10 minutes, then go back to it. Cover and let rise, then bake at 400°F until the rolls are well browned, about 30 minutes. Spray them with water when they go into the oven and once or twice more during the baking. Remove from the oven and brush with oil. (V)

Sandwich Focaccia with Rosemary

This focaccia is thick enough to slice in half for sandwiches, or it can be served as bread, cut into squares or rectangles. Add any of the toppings used for focaccia—sautéed onions, fennel seeds, crumbled Gorgonzola. Makes one 10 by 15-inch bread (V)

2 1/4 teaspoons (1 envelope) active dry yeast
1 teaspoon sugar
3 tablespoons fruity olive oil, plus extra for the top
1 1/2 teaspoons sea salt
1 to 2 tablespoons finely minced rosemary
1 cup whole wheat flour
5 cups all-purpose or bread flour

Stir the yeast into 2 cups warm water with the sugar in a mixing bowl and set aside until foamy, about 10 minutes. Meanwhile, oil a bowl for the dough.

In a larger mixing bowl, stir the water with the yeast, add in the olive oil, salt, rosemary, and whole wheat flour. Gradually add the remaining flour until it's too heavy to work, then turn out the dough and knead until smooth. Place it in the oiled bowl, turn it once, then cover and let rise until doubled in bulk, about 1 1/4 hours.

Lightly dust a counter with flour. Lightly oil a sheet pan and dust it with fine corn meal. Roll out the dough to more or less fit the pan. Press it so that the thickness is more or less even. Cover and let rise for another hour or until tender to the touch. Preheat the oven to 400°F during the last 15 minutes. Dimple the dough by poking it with your fingertips, then brush it generously with olive oil. Bake in the bottom third of the oven until nicely browned, about 30 minutes.

Pita Bread

Homemade pita bread is fragrant and tender—just as enchanting as any other homemade bread. It's also relatively quick (for a yeasted bread) and very enjoyable to make. Pita bread should puff, but if it doesn't, it's still delicious and can be used as a wrapper or a dipping bread. A table of appetizers becomes truly special when warm, fresh pitas are added. Using bread flour helps to give your bread loft.

Makes ten 8-inch breads Ⓥ

2¼ teaspoons (1 envelope) active dry yeast

1 teaspoon honey or barley malt syrup

1¾ teaspoons sea salt

2 tablespoons olive oil

1½ cups whole wheat flour, preferably coarsely ground with flakes of bran, or 1 cup whole wheat flour mixed with ½ cup wheat bran

2 cups bread flour

Put 1½ cups warm water in a mixing bowl, stir in the yeast and honey, and set aside until foamy, about 10 minutes. Meanwhile, oil a bowl for the dough.

Stir in the salt and olive oil, then beat in the whole wheat flour and bran until smooth. Add the remaining flour in small increments until the dough is too heavy to stir. Turn it onto a counter and knead until you have a smooth, supple dough, after a few minutes, adding more flour as required. Put it in the oiled bowl, turn to coat, then cover and set aside until doubled in bulk, 50 minutes to an hour.

Punch the dough down and divide into ten pieces for 8-inch breads. Roll each piece into a ball, then cover them with a damp towel. If baking in the oven, preheat it now with a baking stone or sheet pans in it to 475°F. Let the dough relax while the oven heats, about 15 minutes, then roll each piece into a circle a little less than ¼ inch thick. Don't stack the rolled breads.

In the Oven: Pitas will almost always balloon when baked in the oven, but they won't have the pretty mottled appearance they get when cooked on a griddle. Drop the rounds of dough directly onto the stone or heated pans and bake for 3 minutes. They should be completely puffed. Remove them from the oven and cover with a towel to help them deflate.

On the Stove: Cooked this way, my pitas don't swell in a very predictable fashion. However, they end up beautifully mottled and are pliable enough to wrap around a filling. Heat a cast-iron skillet or griddle over high heat. When hot, turn the heat to medium, then brush a little oil over the surface. Set a circle of dough in the middle. Let it sit for 30 seconds, then turn it over. Slowly, the bread should begin to puff. You can encourage its puffing by gently pressing the bubbles to spread the hot air outward. Once the bread has swollen, after a minute or two, turn it over to brown the top side another minute or so. Put the finished breads under a towel or in a plastic bag to keep them soft.

Barley-Sesame Flatbreads

Tibetan barley bread, a dense sustaining loaf, used to be a favorite of residents of Tassajara Zen Mountain Center in the late 1960s. This version, baked in the style of an Afghani flatbread, is still substantial but a little less dense, and the entire surface is coated with golden, crunchy sesame seeds. Enjoy these warm from the pan and serve them, cut into wedges, with yogurt cheese, olives, and Herb Salad (page 129).

Makes 18 to 20 small breads

2¼ teaspoons (1 envelope) active dry yeast

1 cup barley flour

2 tablespoons barley malt syrup or honey

2 tablespoons toasted sesame oil

2 teaspoons sea salt

½ cup nonfat dry milk or dried buttermilk

¾ cup whole wheat flour

¼ cup wheat bran

2 cups bread flour

½ cup sesame seeds

Olive or sesame oil, for frying

Sprinkle the yeast into ¼ cup warm water in a small bowl and set aside until bubbly. Meanwhile, toast the barley flour in a dry skillet over medium heat, stirring occasionally until it has a good smell and has turned from white to light brown.

In a mixing bowl, combine 1½ cups warm water with the malt syrup, oil, salt, and yeast. Stir in the dry milk, then begin adding the flours and bran in the order given. When the dough becomes too heavy to mix, turn it out and knead until smooth. Place it in an oiled bowl, turn once to coat the top, then cover with a damp towel and set in a warm place to rise until doubled in bulk, about 1½ hours.

Push the dough down and divide it into eighteen 2-ounce pieces. Roll them into balls, then cover them with a towel and let rest for 15 minutes. Press the balls into disks, scatter sesame seeds on the counter, and roll out each piece of dough to make a circle about ¼ inch thick. Turn them once, scatter sesame seeds on the second side, and press them in with your hands. Cover with a towel and let rise for 20 to 30 minutes.

Film a cast-iron skillet or griddle with the oil. When the pan is hot, add as many breads as will fit and reduce the heat to medium-low. Cook slowly so that the breads have time to cook through as they brown, 5 to 7 minutes on each side. Serve warm.

Yogurt Flatbread (*Naan*)

Naan are flatbreads that are found, in varying forms, throughout Central Asia. This particular recipe, taught to me by Joe Evans, is made with yogurt, which makes the breads tender and slightly sour. Serve these breads warm with a vegetable stew or dipped into a spicy yogurt sauce or a salsa of green chiles and cilantro.
Makes 8 to 10 small breads

2¼ teaspoons (1 envelope) active dry yeast
¾ cup plain yogurt, preferably whole milk
¼ cup ghee or clarified butter
1½ teaspoons sea salt
1 cup whole wheat flour
¼ cup wheat bran
3 cups all-purpose or bread flour

Sprinkle the yeast over ¼ cup warm water in a small bowl and set aside until foamy, about 10 minutes. Meanwhile, combine ¾ cup hot water, the yogurt, ghee, and salt in a bowl, then stir in the yeast, whole wheat flour, and bran. Work in enough all-purpose flour to form a heavy dough, then turn it out and knead, adding more flour if needed, until smooth but slightly tacky. Put the dough in an oiled bowl, turn it to coat the top, then cover and put in a warm place until doubled in bulk, about 1 hour.

Preheat the oven to 450°F with a pizza stone or a sheet pan. Turn out the dough onto a lightly floured counter and divide into eight or ten pieces. Roll them into balls, cover with a towel, and let rest for 10 minutes.

Here are two options for shaping the dough:

1. Pat the dough into a circle using your fingertips to dimple it all over. Then gently pull it in opposite directions to make a dimpled oblong. The texture will be uneven, providing crisp and bready parts. Place right on the baking stone or hot sheet pan and bake until browned on top, 12 to 15 minutes. (This is based on the traditional "snowshoe" *naan*, a much larger bread.)

2. Pat or roll the dough into a circle about ¼ inch thick. Make five short knife cuts, radiating from the center like a sand dollar, then transfer to the baking stone and bake until browned. (This idea comes from Naomi Duguid, author of *Flatbreads & Flavors*). You can also make plain rounds, like pita breads, but this cut bread is very pretty.

When the breads are done, stack them on top of each other and serve, warm if possible. I sometimes brush a little softened butter over them and sprinkle them very lightly with freshly milled sea salt.

Stuffed Flatbreads

Indian restaurants always have a variety of irresistible stuffed flatbreads. Here the dough is rolled over a stuffing of seasoned minced onion—moist and very tasty. Makes 8

Yogurt Flatbread, preceding recipe
1 cup finely minced onion
2 cloves garlic, minced
½ teaspoon sea salt
½ teaspoon ground cumin
¼ teaspoon cayenne
⅓ cup chopped cilantro

Make the dough. Mix the remaining ingredients together. Roll the dough into 8 circles and spread 2 tablespoons filling over half of each one. Fold the dough over the filling and gently roll or pat it out again, forming a thin cake, then bake.

Dinner Rolls

Dinner rolls were once seen much more frequently on the American table than they are today. I don't think we serve or eat bread as much as we used to, and when we do, it's apt to be a sliced loaf rather than a roll. Still, a tender roll served warm is such a nice refinement, it's a pleasure to revive this tradition on occasion. Beautifully shaped, well-glazed rolls always give the impression that they were made especially for you. But the real joy is for the baker, for rolls are a delight to shape and bake.

Refrigerator rolls were once a busy cook's way of having fresh rolls on the table every night with little effort. A bowl of bread dough would sit at the ready in the refrigerator for 4 or 5 days. The cook would lop off a piece as needed, form it into rolls, and let them rise while dinner preparation was under way. As the dough aged, it would acquire a little sourness and, with it, character.

Today we're mildly amazed if we get dinner on the table every night, and fresh rolls are certainly far above anyone's expectations. However, if the desire seizes you at any time, know that rolls can be made from any bread dough. A batch of dough made with 3 cups flour will make:

- 1 loaf of bread
- Ten to twelve 2-ounce dinner rolls
- Four to six 4-ounce sandwich-size rolls

To make rolls from any bread dough, make the bread through its first rise, then push it down. Divide the dough into pieces the size you wish. You can make very tiny 1-ounce rolls, more typical dinner-size 2-ounce rolls, or even something as large as a miniature bread.

If the dough is too springy to work and doesn't want to cooperate, let it rest for 15 minutes, then try shaping it again. Set the shaped doughs on a lightly greased sheet pan seam side down, cover with a towel, and let them rise until doubled, 30 to 45 minutes. (At this point, you can decoratively slash round or oval rolls.) For a burnished look, brush the rolls with one of the egg glazes on page 588, or with melted butter. Now is the time to scatter any seeds over the top since they'll stick to the glaze.

Bake rolls in a preheated 375°F oven until risen and golden, 15 to 25 minutes, depending on their size.

ROUNDS: To shape dough into rounds, cup your hand tightly over a piece, then move your hand rapidly around in a circle, keeping it close in at the base and pressing downward as you move. These actions will force it into a sphere. Once risen, slash a cross in the top, make two or three parallel cuts with a sharp knife, or make two snips of the scissors to provide air vents. A single sphere makes a pretty little bread, but you can also make three marble-size rounds and stick them together, either on a sheet pan or in a buttered muffin tin to make a classic cloverleaf roll.

OVALS: Using your hands, shape a loosely formed round into an oval torpedo-like shape. Make three scissor snips down the top or slash the rolls diagonally with a razor blade or sharp knife.

TWISTS AND KNOTS: Roll each piece of dough into a rope about 1/2 inch thick and, if using a standard 2-ounce piece, about 8 inches long. Try tying it into a knot, tucking the ends underneath for a complicated-looking roll. Or bend it in the middle, then twist the two ends like a rope. Or coil the dough around itself to make a snail shape or simply have fun creating shapes that catch your fancy. No slashing is necessary with twists and knots; seeds look wonderful.

MAKING REFRIGERATOR ROLLS: After shaping rolls, cover them with lightly buttered or oiled plastic wrap and refrigerate them for up to a few hours or overnight. Remove from the refrigerator an hour or even as little as 30 minutes before baking if they haven't been chilled for more than a few hours.

More traditionally, make the dough but don't shape it. After it has been kneaded, instead of letting it rise, place it in a well-oiled or buttered spacious bowl, turned so that the top is coated. Put the bowl in a plastic bag or cover it securely with plastic wrap and refrigerate. If you happen to notice that the dough has risen, just punch it down and return it to the refrigerator.

To use, remove as much dough as you need—a scale will give you a good idea if you don't feel confident judging by eye—and shape it into rolls. Since the dough will be very cold after a long stay in the refrigerator, allow at least 2 to 3 hours for it to warm up and begin to rise.

Yeasted Corn-Rye Buttermilk Rolls

Because of the low-gluten flours and their limited, rising powers, I prefer this fine-crumbed dough for rolls, although you can bake it into a bread—just don't expect it to rise as high as others. Slightly rough stone-ground flours make the tastiest rolls. Makes ten 3-inch rolls

———————

2^1/$_4$ teaspoons (1 envelope) active dry yeast

2^1/$_4$ cups warm water, whey, or potato water

^{1}/$_4$ cup corn oil, preferably unrefined

^{1}/$_4$ cup molasses

2^1/$_2$ teaspoons sea salt

^{1}/$_2$ cup dried buttermilk or nonfat dry milk

1 cup whole wheat flour

1 cup rye flour

1 cup fine stone-ground corn meal

3 cups all-purpose or bread flour

Wheat bran, for coating

Stir the yeast into ^{1}/$_4$ cup of the warm water in a small bowl and set aside until foamy. Meanwhile, oil a bowl for the dough.

Put the remaining 2 cups warm water in a mixing bowl and add the oil, molasses, salt, and yeast. Whisk in the dry milk, then beat in the whole wheat flour, rye flour, and corn meal until smooth.

Begin adding the all-purpose flour ^{1}/$_2$ cup at a time. When you can't work in any more, turn it out onto a counter and knead until smooth and springy, about 3 minutes. The dough should be a little tacky. Set it in an oiled bowl, turn it once, cover, and set aside to rise until doubled in bulk, 1^1/$_2$ to 2 hours.

Divide into equal pieces, depending on the size roll you want, and shape each piece into a ball. Roll them in the wheat bran, then set them on a baking sheet and slash to make a cross. Cover with a towel and set aside until doubled in size and soft to the touch, 40 minutes to an hour. During the last 15 minutes, preheat the oven to 375°F. Bake the rolls for 25 minutes, until browned.

Little Lemon Biscuits

When I saw a picture of these little yeasted cakes in The Flavors of France *by Jean Conil and Fay Franklin, I couldn't wait to try them. They're tender, golden, and fragrant—completely divine. Cornstarch makes them feather-light, but a day later they'll be inedibly dry. You can, however, roll and cut them out, and refrigerate them the night before.*
Makes twelve 2-inch to twenty 1-inch biscuits

———————

2^1/$_4$ teaspoons (1 envelope) active dry yeast

3 tablespoons sugar or honey, plus extra sugar for the tops

^{1}/$_2$ cup crème fraîche, yogurt, or buttermilk

6 tablespoons melted butter

Finely grated zest of 1 lemon

^{1}/$_4$ cup cornstarch

^{3}/$_8$ teaspoon sea salt

2^1/$_4$ to 2^1/$_2$ cups all-purpose flour

In a mixing bowl, scatter the yeast over ^{1}/$_4$ cup warm water and stir in a teaspoon of the sugar. When it has proofed, after 10 to 15 minutes, stir in the remaining sugar, crème fraîche, ^{1}/$_4$ cup of the melted butter, and the lemon zest. When smooth, add the cornstarch and salt, then begin beating in the flour. When the dough is too heavy to mix with a spoon, turn it out and knead in the remaining flour. The dough should be smooth and shiny and still a little tacky. Turn it into a buttered bowl, cover the top, and set aside to rise until doubled in bulk. Although the amount of dough is small, because of the crème fraîche and butter, it will take at least an hour to rise.

Turn the dough onto a lightly floured counter and roll it out about ^{3}/$_8$ inch thick. Cut out the cakes with a small biscuit cutter or a glass so that they measure 1 to 2 inches across. Reroll the scraps and cut them out, too. Arrange the biscuits on a sheet pan about an inch or more apart. Remelt the remaining 2 tablespoons butter, brush the tops, and sprinkle with fine sugar. Let them rise until doubled in bulk while you preheat the oven to 375°F. Bake them until they're deep gold, high, and crisp. Remove and serve warm.

Cardamom Holiday Bread

The sweetened dough is studded with raisins, rich and tender with butter and eggs. The woven surface is varnished golden, covered with pine nuts or little squares of sugar. It's just the thing to have on Christmas morning. Leftover bread makes superlative bread puddings and French toast, so it's worth keeping that in mind and making the full amount. This is a lovely dough to knead by hand. It's soft and silky to the touch with fragrant whispers of cardamom coming toward you with every push.

Makes three 1-pound loaves or two braided wreaths

1½ cups milk

½ cup butter, soft

1½ teaspoons freshly ground cardamom

½ cup sugar

1 teaspoon salt

Grated zest of 1 lemon

2¼ teaspoons (1 envelope) active dry yeast

1 cup golden raisins

3 eggs, at room temperature

6 cups or more white whole wheat flour, or a mixture of white whole wheat and spelt with all-purpose flour

¼ cup pine nuts or slivered almonds

Crystal sugar, if available, or turbinado sugar, for the top

Warm the milk with the butter, cardamom, sugar, salt, and lemon zest. Stir occasionally until the butter is melted and the sugar is dissolved. When the milk has cooled to lukewarm, stir in the yeast and let the mixture stand for 10 minutes or until the yeast is foamy.

While the milk is cooling, cover the raisins with warm water, let them stand until the yeast is finished proofing, and then pour off the water and gently squeeze out any excess.

Lightly beat the eggs together with a fork, set aside a few spoonfuls for the glaze, and add the remainder to the milk and yeast mixture along with the raisins. Next, begin adding the flour, whisking it in to make a smooth batter until it becomes too thick; then change to a wooden spoon and continue adding flour until it is again too thick, at which point you can turn the dough out onto a floured surface and begin kneading. Work in more flour as is necessary to keep it from sticking.

Knead for at least 7 minutes, until the dough is smooth and shiny; then set it aside in a bowl that has been lightly filmed with butter or a flavorless oil. Rub a little of the butter or oil over the top; then cover with a damp towel or plastic wrap and set it aside in a warm place to rise until doubled in bulk. When the dough has risen, turn it out onto the counter.

To make braids, divide the dough for each bread into three equal pieces; then roll each piece into a long rope, about ½ inch thick. Braid the ropes tightly together, crossing them first in the middle and then working out from both ends. Leave the braid long and straight, bend it to make a circle, or curve it gently into a horseshoe shape, drawing the ends up toward the middle together, like a pretzel. Set the breads on a cookie sheet.

To make loaves, butter three bread pans. Divide the dough into three pieces and press each piece into a rectangle roughly the length of the pan. Roll it up, pinch the seam together, and place the dough seam side down in the pan.

Brush the reserved beaten egg over the surface, press in the pine nuts, and sprinkle the surface with the crystal sugar. Loosely cover the breads and set them aside again to rise until about doubled in bulk, about 45 minutes.

While the breads are rising, preheat the oven to 350°F. Just before putting them in the oven, look at the breads and see if the dough has expanded so that some areas are now unglazed and unsugared. Brush some more egg glaze on these areas and cover them with a sprinkling of sugar and more pine nuts. Bake the breads until they are a deep golden brown on top, about 40 minutes. Allow them to cool on cooling racks.

Rosemary Holiday Bread

The rosemary in this holiday bread suggests pine or angelica more than it does savory flavors. Bake this pretty bread in a large Bundt pan, a 9-inch springform, or two brioche pans. This bread makes delicious toast. Serve for breakfast or later in the day with a glass of dessert wine, sherry, or coffee. This is still one of my favorite breads, and I make it every year for the holidays. Makes 1 large holiday bread or 2 loaves

1 cup milk, preferably whole

5 tablespoons butter, cut into small chunks

1/4 cup honey

2 teaspoons finely chopped rosemary

Finely chopped zest of 1 large lemon

2 eggs, beaten

2 1/4 teaspoons (1 envelope) active dry yeast

3/4 teaspoon sea salt

1 cup toasted pine nuts or chopped walnuts

1 cup golden raisins

4 cups all-purpose flour

Egg Glaze (page 588) or melted butter

2 tablespoons crystal sugar or granulated sugar

In a small saucepan, warm the milk over medium heat with the butter, honey, rosemary, and lemon zest. Stir to help the butter melt, then pour into a mixing bowl and set it aside until the milk has cooled to lukewarm. Beat in the eggs.

Meanwhile, sprinkle the yeast over 1/4 cup warm water and let stand until foamy, 10 to 15 minutes. Stir it into the milk mixture and add the salt, nuts, and raisins. Vigorously beat in the flour 1 cup at a time until it clears the sides of the bowl. Turn it out onto a counter and knead for several minutes until smooth. Place in a buttered bowl, cover, and set aside to rise until doubled in bulk, 1 to 1 1/2 hours. Meanwhile, generously butter a baking pan (or pans), going all the way up the sides. Punch down the dough once it has risen, form it into a ball, and place in the pan(s). Let it rise again until very soft to the touch and doubled in bulk, another hour. During the last 15 minutes, preheat the oven to 350°F. Brush the bread with the glaze and sprinkle with sugar. Bake until golden and high, about 45 minutes. Gently release the bread from the pan and let cool on a rack.

Cinnamon Rolls

These classic morning rolls can be made with the basic dough for Classic Sandwich Bread (page 589) or the silky rich Babka dough (page 568). If using the bread dough, cut the recipe in half or make the full amount and use half for bread. The mixture of butter, sugar, and syrup make is what makes these buns sticky. You can omit it if you wish and have very good plain cinnamon rolls. Makes 16 to 20 rolls

Classic Sandwich Bread (page 589) or Babka (page 568)

1 tablespoon ground cinnamon

1/2 cup packed brown sugar

1/2 cup chopped pecans or walnuts

1/2 cup raisins or currants

2 tablespoons melted butter

While the dough is rising, mix the cinnamon, brown sugar, nuts, and raisins in a small bowl.

Push the dough down. If using the bread dough, divide it in half and use one half to make a loaf of bread. Roll the remainder (or the babka dough) into a 12 by 16-inch rectangle. Brush it with the melted butter, sprinkle the sugar mixture over the surface, and tightly roll up lengthwise. Slice into rounds about 1 inch wide and set them in a butter-coated pan, cut side facing up. Don't hesitate to cram them together. Let rise for 30 minutes.

Preheat the oven to 375°F. Bake the rolls in the center of the oven until well risen and browned, about 30 minutes. Invert them onto a serving plate—the sugar will have caramelized and coated the rolls. You can also serve them baked side up if you prefer.

Sticky Buns: Beat 6 tablespoons butter with 1/4 cup dark brown sugar and 1 1/2 tablespoons dark corn syrup until smooth, then spread it in a 9-inch pie plate or baking dish. Set the rolled buns, cut sides facing up, on this mixture. Let rise for 30 minutes, then bake. Turn them out onto a serving plate while they're still warm, before the syrup cools and hardens.

DESESERTS

CHAPTER 19

Desserts
Ending on a Sweet Note

I love making desserts—so much that I have worked on more than one occasion as a pastry chef and written a book on desserts called *Seasonal Fruit Desserts.*

Indeed, I am most attracted to desserts based on fruit rather than elaborate pastries and towering confections, for I enjoy the same qualities in fruits that I do in vegetables—their aromas, their vivid or subtle flavors, their sensuality, and their seasonality, which marks our own passage through the year. I also enjoy the interplay that fruits enjoy with one another and with those foods that accompany them, spices and nuts, wines and liquors.

If we were able to count on a good tasting parade of local fruits throughout the year, we would be able to enjoy, without effort, the most simple and healthful of desserts. Unfortunately, the hardest part about assembling a worthy fruit dessert is finding the fruit. I suspect that because we generally lack the fruit that delivers breathtaking pleasure, we have become a nation that's excessively fond of pastry. But as with vegetables, good fruit can be found if you keep a watchful eye out for what grows where you live and eat within the season.

Many desserts break the very rules that people strive to live by. The desire to have our cake and eat it too has spawned an industry that produces desserts and sweets based on ersatz fats and sugars, foods that only distantly mirror the real thing. When it comes to desserts, I don't have them often. In fact, cakes and such are a rare treat. But I like real ones when I do have them—cakes made with butter,

flaky pie crusts, whipped cream on the side, fine cheeses. The desserts I've chosen to include are honest indulgences to be savored and enjoyed, leaving cravings and longings satisfied instead of merely teased.

In addition to the desserts found in this chapter, there are some delectable yeasted buns and holiday breads (in the bread chapter) that can double as desserts, especially when paired with soft cheeses or fruit compotes.

A word about sweeteners. As with other basic ingredients, the choices have widened during the past 15 years and today there are many sweeteners to choose from, from organic cane sugar to coconut sugar, from stevia to Truvia, agave nectars, syrups of various kinds, honey (not an option for vegans, of course), and others. For a description of different sweeteners, see page 39.

Vegan Desserts: Vegans end up having the most healthful desserts—all those that are based on fresh fruits, fruit compotes, fruit ices, and sorbets. As for the pastries, most of my desserts do include butter and eggs, though not all. Butter can replaced with a coconut oil, other oils, and vegetable shortening. There are lots of new books on vegan desserts, so you needn't do without, but I am not naturally inclined to make them well.

Fruit: The Perfect Dessert

Without a doubt, the healthiest dessert is a fine piece of fruit. Sadly, fruits suffer even more than vegetables at the hands of growers, shippers, and rough-handed stockboys. Modern agriculture isn't beneficial to fruit the way hands-on, careful cultivation is. If fruit were as good as it could be or as it looks, we wouldn't need a bit of convincing to eat it. So try to search out fruit that's grown near where you live—you may be rewarded with flavor that's far beyond your expectations. Once you've sat down to a really fine nectarine, a tree-ripened fig, or a crisp fall apple, you can easily understand why serving fruit at the end of the meal has long been the European tradition.

SERVING FRESH FRUIT: A bowl or basket of fruit arranges itself beautifully regardless of what we do to it. It matters not whether it's a silver bowl of heirloom apples lined with golden fall leaves; a baroque assembly of grapes, persimmons, muskmelons, and nuts; or just a plate of sliced watermelon. Just select the best fruit you can and let everyone choose a piece. Provide fruit knives and small plates for pits and peels. Peeling, coring, and slicing, then eating bite by bite, slows us down, allowing us to really taste the fruit.

Since cold deadens flavors, fruit is most aromatic and fragrant when it's at room temperature—with certain exceptions. A chilled orange or melon, both of which are exceptionally sweet, can be wildly refreshing. And a crisp fall apple picked off the tree is also good cold. But stone fruits—peaches, apricots, plums, cherries, and nectarines—tropical fruits, and berries are always better at room temperature.

Spur-of-the-Moment Fruit Desserts

Often a little cooking or a few added ingredients make fruit seem more like a proper dessert for those who aren't entirely happy just reaching for an apple or a date and a walnut. They also bring out flavors in fruits that are less than stellar.

Sautéed Apple Rings with Raisins and Pine Nuts

You can also make this with firm, ripe pears. They'll give up more juices than apples do, making a nice little sauce for a scoop of ice cream. Serves 4 (V)

- 4 apples, cored and peeled
- 1 tablespoon butter or oil
- 1 tablespoon sugar
- 1/4 cup apple juice or water
- 1/4 cup golden raisins or currants
- 1/4 cup toasted pine nuts or almonds
- 3 tablespoons applejack, apple brandy, or membrillo (a quince liqueur)

Slice the apples into rounds about 3/8 inch thick. Heat the butter in a large skillet, add the apples, and toss with the sugar. Cook over high heat, flipping the apples in the pan every 30 seconds or so, until they have begun to caramelize, about 12 minutes. Poke one with a knife; if they're not tender, add the juice to create a little steam. When tender, add the raisins and pine nuts, cook for another few minutes, then add the applejack and cook until it has evaporated. Serve warm with ice cream or yogurt.

Applesauce

Applesauce can begin as a soothing breakfast fruit and end as a dessert, tucked inside a buckwheat crepe or made into the glorious dessert.

The pressure cooker in tandem with the food mill elimi-nates the need to peel and core the apples. You can have applesauce in 15 minutes. Fresh fall apples are especially great, but don't overlook those older ones whose texture is no longer good for eating out of hand. Apples with red skins tint the sauce pink. Makes about 4 cups Ⓥ

3 pounds apples, quartered

Honey or sugar

Fresh lemon juice

$1/2$ teaspoon ground cinnamon, cardamom, or allspice, or a pinch ground cloves, optional

If you're using a food mill, put the apples in a pot, add $1/3$ cup water, cover securely, and cook until the apples are completely tender, about 20 minutes. Or put them in a pressure cooker with $1/2$ cup water, bring the pressure to high, and cook for 15 minutes. Release the pressure or let it fall by itself. Pass the cooked fruit through the food mill into a clean pot. Taste and sweeten with honey if the sauce is tart or add the lemon juice if the apples are too sweet. Add the spices. Simmer for 5 minutes, then cool. If you're not using a food mill, peel and core the apples first, then cook until they're broken clown into a sauce.

Quince or Pear Sauce: Quinces and pears give applesauce an elusive perfume, and quinces turn it rosy pink. Add 2 quinces to the apples. If cooking in a pressure cooker, cut the quinces into sixths. If not, thinly slice them, chop, then stew them with the apples. Or add 3 or 4 ripe pears to the apples and cook, seasoning with cardamom or nut-meg. There's no reason not to combine all three fruits in a single sauce. In fact, it's a delectable combination that makes a common food rather exotic. Ⓥ

Applesauce Bread Crumb Pudding

This warm Danish–American dessert appears fairly regu-larly in community cookbooks. A quince- or pear-flavored applesauce is much more haunting, but apple is delicious, too. Bake this ahead of time, then hold it in a low oven during dinner. Serves 8

4 cups applesauce (preceding recipe)

$1/2$ teaspoon freshly ground cardamom

5 tablespoons butter, plus extra to finish

$2^1/2$ cups fresh bread crumbs made from sturdy white sandwich bread

$2/3$ cup quince, raspberry, or lingonberry preserves

1 cup whipping cream

Honey

Ground cardamom

Preheat the oven to 325°F. Butter a 6-cup soufflé mold or glass baking dish.

Season the applesauce with the cardamom. Melt the butter in a medium skillet over medium heat. Stir in the crumbs. They'll lump up, but keep stirring until they're golden brown, at which point they'll separate again. Put a quarter of the bread crumbs in the dish, add a third of the sauce, and dot with a third of the preserves. Repeat twice more, ending with a layer of crumbs. Bake for 25 minutes.

Whip the cream and sweeten it with just a little honey to taste and a pinch of cardamom. Serve the dessert warm and pass the whipped cream in a bowl.

Medjool Dates with Mascarpone

This combination is exquisite. Serve in winter when dates are in season and at their best—moist and soft. Include a few walnuts or toasted pecans alongside or on top for their contrasting texture. Allow 2 or 3 dates per person

Large, moist Medjool dates

Mascarpone or cream cheese

Walnuts or toasted pecans, optional

Slit the dates in half lengthwise and remove their seeds. Spread, spoon, or squeeze about a teaspoon of the mascarpone into each date half. Serve the dates on a plate with the nuts, resting in paper cases if you like. Or simply put out a plate of dates and a bowl of cheese and let everyone make their own.

Caramelized Figs with Orange-Flower Water

An intense and fragrant dessert. Serves 4

12 to 16 mission or other fresh figs, sliced lengthwise

1/2 cup sugar, or 1/4 cup agave nectar

3 tablespoons cream or crème fraîche

1 to 2 teaspoons orange-flower water to taste

Dip each fig into the sugar on a plate, heavily coating the cut surface. Heat a cast-iron skillet and add the figs, cut sides down. Cook over medium-high heat until the sugar begins to melt and caramelize, turning an amber color. Turn them over and cook for a minute more, then transfer them to a serving dish. Turn off the heat and immediately whisk the cream into the pan, stirring to dissolve the sugar. This should take less than a minute. Add the orange-flower water, pour the sauce over the figs, and serve.

Broiled Figs

Serve these with Frozen Honey Mousse (page 636), a spoonful of mascarpone, or over a mound of ricotta cheese. Serves 2 Ⓥ

4 plump, ripe fresh figs, any variety

1 teaspoon sugar

Preheat the broiler. Slice the figs in half lengthwise, lay them on a sheet pan, and sprinkle with the sugar. Set them about 4 inches under the heat until they begin to brown, 2 to 3 minutes. Serve them warm with any of the suggested accompaniments.

Nectarine Gratin with Almond Frangipane

All kinds of fruits are marvelous baked under this almond custard, especially those in the rose family—peaches, plums, berries, nectarines, and apricots. Pears are my favorite for late fall; plums, cherries, and apricots for early summer, while nectarines, peaches, and plums follow. Serves 4 to 6

About 2 pounds nectarines (white, if possible), rinsed and sliced 1/2 inch thick

2 tablespoons maple or other sugar

6 tablespoons unsalted butter, at room temperature

2 eggs

1 cup confectioners' sugar, plus extra for dusting

1 cup finely ground almonds

2 tablespoons flour

1 tablespoon kirsch

1/8 teaspoon almond extract

Heat the oven to 350°F. Lightly butter a shallow, oval baking dish. Gently toss the nectarines with the sugar, then spread them into the baking dish.

Beat the butter in the bowl of a mixer fitted with the paddle until smooth. Add the eggs, one at a time, again beating until smooth, then add the confectioners' sugar, almonds, flour, kirsch, and almond extract and mix until well blended. Smooth the batter over the nectarines.

Bake in the center of the oven until firm and golden brown, 25 to 25 minutes. Remove to a rack to cool somewhat, then dust with confectioners' sugar. Serve warm or at room temperature.

Sautéed Nectarines

Serve with a spoonful of cold cream poured over each, Tangy Whipped Cream (page 644), or ice cream. Serves 4

4 ripe but firm nectarines

2 teaspoons butter

1 tablespoon light brown sugar or maple syrup or maple sugar

1 tablespoon maraschino liqueur or kirsch

Wash the fruit but leave the skins on. Cut them into quarters or sixths and discard the stones. Melt the butter in a skillet over medium heat. Add the sugar, then the nectarines. Cook for about 4 minutes, carefully turning the fruit a few times, then add a few tablespoons water and let the fruit simmer. When the skins look as if they're going to slip off, add the liqueur and cook for 30 seconds more. Serve warm with the juices.

Braised Apricots with Greek Yogurt, Pomegranate Seeds, and Pine Nuts

You could assemble little apricot "sandwiches" for each person, but I like it better when people can fiddle with the ingredients at the table in a leisurely fashion, mounding a spoonful of yogurt on each apricot, nibbling on the pomegranate seeds here and pine nuts there. Serves 6

1 cup Greek yogurt

18 to 24 Oven-Braised Apricots, recipe follows, or other fruits

1/4 cup pomegranate seeds

2 tablespoons toasted pine nuts

Mound or scoop the yogurt on four plates and arrange the apricots around them. Scatter the pomegranate seeds around the plate along with the pine nuts and serve.

Oven-Braised Apricots

These plump, fragrant pillows of vanilla-scented apricots can be offered as sweetmeats at the end of a meal. You might put a few on a plate with toasted almonds and a piece of dark chocolate for a more or less instant winter dessert, or serve them with ice cream or yogurt. Because the fruit is so concentrated, you don't need more than a few per person. Makes about $1^1/_4$ cup

1 cup dried apricots, preferably Blenheims

1/2 vanilla bean, halved lengthwise

2 tablespoons honey

2 tablespoons sweet wine, such as Essencia or Beaumes de Venise

Cover the apricots with warm water and let them soak while the oven heats to 350°F. Then, drain them and put them in a shallow baking dish, one that will accommodate them in a single layer with the vanilla bean. Pour in 1 cup water, drizzle the honey over the fruit, then bake, uncovered, until the water has cooked away and the apricots are tender and plump, about 50 minutes.

Add the wine and return to dish to the oven for 10 minutes, by which time the apricots should be glazed. Squeeze or scrape the vanilla seeds out of the pods and gently mix them into the apricots. Taste. They are likely to be both sweet and tart. If the apricots are very tart, sprinkle over a little sugar or some additional honey.

Oven Braised Red Plums and Pluots: In place of, or along with the apricots, make this dessert with dried red plums or pluots, definitely farmers' market finds. They are sometimes a bit more leathery than other fruits and may take a little extra time soaking or in the oven.

Sautéed Bananas with Dates, Blood Orange Juice, and Passion Fruit

As ordinary as bananas are, they still make a good, quick dessert when you have few other options—and, for that matter, even when you do. And they may not always be as common as they are today. The Cavendish, "a mutant clone that hasn't had sex in a thousand years," as one writer describes it, is in danger of succumbing to the fungus that felled its predecessor, the Gros Michel, in the 1960s. Made at the last minute and quickly, this dessert features caramelized sections of bananas and dates swimming in a sauce of blood orange juice dotted with pellets of passion fruit seeds. Serves 4 (V)

3 or 4 medium bananas, ripe, but still firm

1 tablespoon coconut oil or butter

1½ tablespoons coconut sugar

3 Medjool or Deglet Noor dates, pitted and quartered

Juice of 2 blood orange or Cara Caras, about ½ cup

1 passion fruit, halved

Peel the bananas and cut them in half lengthwise, then crosswise to make four quarters.

Choose a large skillet that will hold all the fruit in a single layer, or use two skillets. Melt the butter in the pan(s), sprinkle over the sugar, then add the bananas, cut sides down. Intersperse the dates among them and cook over medium-high heat without moving the bananas for about 1½ minutes so that they have a chance to brown. Then carefully turn them over so that they color on the second side and cook for 1 or 2 minutes more at the most. Arrange them on plates or a platter with the dates.

Add the orange juice to the pan, raise the heat to high, and cook for a minute, letting it bubble up as you scrape in the bits of caramelized sugar. Pour the sauce over the bananas and spoon the passion fruit over all. Accompany with unsweetened yogurt, if desired, or serve the bananas with a tropical fruit sorbet for a different kind of banana split. In lieu of passion fruit, garnish the bananas with toasted and chopped macadamia nuts or pistachio nuts.

Tropical Fruits with Passion Fruit

It's the passion fruit that makes this really special. You can use all kinds of fruits in different combinations as long as you have at least one of these wrinkled purple-skinned fruits on hand. A half of passion fruit for each serving would be ideal, but know that if they're very expensive, even one will lend its perfumed effect. And if there are none? Well, make it anyway and just leave it out. Serves 6 (V)

2 mangoes, peeled and neatly sliced or diced

2 kiwifruits, peeled and sliced

2 oranges (any kind), peeled and sectioned

½ small pineapple, peeled, cored, and cut into small, neat pieces, not too thick

Finger bananas, peeled and halved lengthwise

Lychees, either fresh and peeled and seeded, or canned

Finely grated zest and juice of 2 blood oranges

1 to 3 passion fruits

Agave nectar, to taste

Arrange the fruit on individual serving plates or in shallow bowls. Mix the zest and juice of the blood orange with agave nectar until dissolved, then spoon it over the fruit. Halve the passion fruit and spoon the yellow pulp over each plate, including the seeds, which have a delectable crunch that shouldn't be missed.

If it's more convenient, put all the fruit in a glass bowl, add a little agave nectar or liquid from canned lychee, then let stand in the refrigerator for the flavors to meld, for an hour or more.

Caramelized Pineapple

This is one of my favorite last-minute fruit desserts. Serve it warm from the pan with Frozen Honey Mousse (page 636), whipped crème fraiche, vanilla ice cream, or over tapioca or rice puddings. Coconut sugar maintains the tropical theme here. Serves 6 to 8 Ⓥ

1 large ripe pineapple
About 2 teaspoons butter or coconut oil
About 3 tablespoons coconut sugar
3 tablespoons maraschino liqueur, kirsch, or rum, optional
Squeeze of lime juice, optional

Slice the skin off the pineapple and remove the eyes with the tip of a potato peeler. Cut it into rounds or half-rounds about 1/2 inch thick. Carefully remove the core from each piece.

Melt the butter in a wide skillet, sprinkle some of the sugar evenly over it in a thin layer, and add the pineapple. Cook over high heat until the sugar has caramelized and the bottom side is richly glazed, 4 to 5 minutes. Sprinkle the tops with sugar, turn the pineapple over, and cook until the second side is caramelized, another 4 to 5 minutes. Remove it from the pan and serve. Or add the liqueur and a squeeze of lime juice to the pan, scrape the bottom, reduce until syrupy, and pour the sauce over the pineapple.

Oranges with Pomegranate Seeds

Pomegranates appear in the late fall, around Thanksgiving, and are generally still available when oranges come into season. Inside their leathery-looking skins are ruby seeds and a sweet-tart juice. Serves 4 Ⓥ

6 oranges—navels, Cara Cara, or blood oranges
1 lemon
1 pomegranate
10 mint leaves, plus extra for garnish
1/3 cup sugar or honey
1 (2-inch) cinnamon stick
5 whole cloves

Using a zester, remove long strands of the zest from one of the oranges and the lemon. Plunge the zest into boiling water for 10 seconds, then drain and set aside. Peel the oranges, slice them into 1/4-inch rounds, and put them in a dessert bowl. Slowly and carefully cut a pomegranate in half, peel back the skin, and remove the seeds from half of it. Add the seeds to the oranges with the mint. Juice the remaining half by placing it in a bowl in the sink and leaning down hard on it to force out the juices.

Put 1 cup water, the sugar, spices, and zest in a saucepan and bring to a boil. Stir to dissolve the sugar and simmer for a few minutes. Remove from the heat and add the pomegranate juice. Pour the syrup, with the spices, over the oranges and refrigerate. Serve chilled, garnished with fresh mint leaves.

Yogurt with Wine-Simmered Dried Fruits

Once cooked, these fruits can be kept for weeks in the refrigerator, becoming a staple for last-minute winter desserts. (Try it on a rice pudding or cooked quinoa.) For yogurt, use the fat level you prefer as long as it's thick. A few tablespoons served from an oval ice cream scoop will be both plenty and attractive. Serves 6

1/3 cup prunes, cut into halves and quarters
1/3 cup large mixed raisins, including golden raisins
3 tablespoons dried sweet or sour cherries
1/4 cup dried figs, chopped into small pieces
1 cup port, Amarone, or Zinfandel
1 tablespoon honey
1 cup thick yogurt, such as Greek or Labneh

Put the fruit in a small saucepan or shallow skillet. Add the port, cook over low heat for 20 minutes, then stir in the honey. Chill well.

Scoop the yogurt onto a small dessert plate and spoon the fruit, with its sauce, over and around it.

Compotes and Poached Fruits

Mixtures of fruits sweetened and suspended in syrups, compotes are one of the best ways of presenting both perfect fruits and those that don't have quite the flavor or sweetness to stand on their own. Compotes provide us with desserts that avoid added crusts, fillings, and creams. Just a spoonful of crème fraîche or whipped cream sets off the fruit beautifully. Most compotes are best chilled, accompanied, if at all, with a simple cookie or a thin slice of cake. Leftovers are wonderful for breakfast or brunch.

Many compotes leave a residue of tinted fruit-flavored syrup. It keeps more or less indefinitely, refrigerated, and can be used to sweeten iced tea, mixed with club soda or champagne, or spooned around a scoop of vanilla ice cream or yogurt.

Apricot and Berry Compote for Early Summer

Luscious is the word that describes this bowl of fruit. If fresh apricots aren't available, you can use canned ones or 1 cup dried, simmered in the water and sugar for 25 minutes or until they're tender. Look for exceptional varieties of apricots, such as Blenheim. Serves 6 Ⓥ

---

8 or more apricots, ripe but still firm, about 1¹/₂ pounds

¹/₂ cup sugar

1 cup raspberries

1 cup blackberries or boysenberries

¹/₂ vanilla bean, split lengthwise

Cut the apricots into halves or quarters. Bring the sugar and 2 cups water to a boil in an 8-cup saucepan. Add the apricots, lower the heat, and simmer just until they're tender and the skin is getting loose, 3 to 4 minutes. With a slotted spoon, transfer them to a serving bowl and add the berries. Boil the syrup for 3 or 4 minutes to reduce it, then remove from the heat. Scrape the seeds from the vanilla bean into it, pour it over the fruit, then chill. Serve the compote in individual bowls or use it to accompany vanilla or apricot ice cream or a slice of sponge cake.

Mango and Berry Compote: Mangoes are often ripe at the same time apricots and berries are. Peel one or two, cut them into small chunks, and add them to the compote. Pitted cherries are another seasonal addition that look and taste wonderful here. Ⓥ

Winter Citrus Compote in Tangerine Syrup

This cheerful-looking compote makes a perfect end to a winter meal or beginning to a festive brunch. You can use every conceivable variety of citrus fruit or just a few kinds. Following are some suggestions—improvise with what you have. Some special fruits to keep your eye out for are small pink Texas grapefruit, blood oranges, Honeybells, Satsumas, and kumquats. Serves 6 Ⓥ

---

³/₄ cup fresh tangerine juice or a mixture of tangerine and orange juices

3 tablespoons sugar

6 large kumquats, sliced into rounds

2 tablespoons zest removed from any of the citrus below

1 teaspoon orange-flower water

3 small pink grapefruit

3 navel oranges

3 blood oranges

3 tangelos, Honeybells, or other citrus

Mint sprigs, for garnish

Bring the juice and sugar to a boil in a small saucepan. Add the kumquats and zest, then lower the heat and simmer for 10 minutes. Stir in the orange-flower water and set aside.

Peel the grapefruit, oranges, and tangelos as described on page 24. If the grapefruits are small ones, slice them into rounds; otherwise section them. Slice the remaining fruits into rounds about ¹/₃ inch wide. Place the fruit and juices in a serving bowl or deep platter. Pour the syrup with the kumquats and zest over the fruit and chill until ready to serve. Serve garnished with sprigs of mint.

With Other Tropical Fruits: Other fruits happily complement citrus and add to the luster of this dish. Add thinly sliced small star fruits or kiwifruit, or drizzle the contents, seeds and all, of one or two passion fruits over the compote.

Peach and White Nectarine Compote with Beaumes de Venise and Raspberries

This compote uses a generous amount of dessert wine. Muscat Beaumes de Venise is one of my favorites, but you could also use the Quady's Essensia Orange Muscat. In all you'll want 1½ pounds stone fruit or a little more. Serves 4 to 6 Ⓥ

3/4 cup Beaumes de Venise or Essensia Orange Muscat wine

2 tablespoons sugar or light, floral honey

2 ripe freestone peaches

2 white nectarines

1 cup raspberries (1 small carton)

Bring the wine and sugar to a gentle boil with ¼ cup water. While it's heating, bring 4 cups water to a boil, add the peaches for 5 to 10 seconds each, then plunge them in cold water to cool. Peel off the skins.

Slice the peaches and nectarines lengthwise about ½ inch thick at the center or wider. Add them to the syrup and simmer for just 1 to 2 minutes. Tip both the fruit and the syrup into a compote dish and add the berries. Refrigerate and serve chilled, as is or garnished with a sprig of fresh mint leaves, lemon verbena, or lavender.

Pear Compote with Beaumes de Venise: Use pears in place of the peaches, peeling them first or not, as you wish. The raspberries, if in season, go well with pears, but if it's past their prime, use the pears by themselves.

Pears (and Other Fruits) Poached in Vanilla Syrup

Use this light syrup with peaches, apricots, nectarines, and other fruits. Although this is a lot of sugar, there will be left-over syrup. Serves 4 to 6 Ⓥ

1½ cups sugar

Several 2-inch pieces lemon zest, removed with a vegetable peeler

1/2 vanilla bean, halved lengthwise

4 to 6 ripe but firm pears, such as Winter Nelis, Bartletts, Bosc, or Anjou

Bring 4 cups water to a boil with the sugar, lemon zest, and vanilla bean. Stir to dissolve the sugar, then lower the heat to a simmer.

Neatly peel the pears in long even strokes, then cut them in half. Remove the cores and stem ends with a pear corer. As you work, add them directly to the simmering syrup. Cook gently until they begin to look translucent around the edges, anywhere from 20 to 40 minutes, depending on the type of pear. Remove them with a slotted spoon to a bowl.

Scrape the seeds of the vanilla bean into the syrup and pour the syrup over the pears, along with the vanilla bean. (Later you can dry it and use it to flavor sugar.) Cover and refrigerate until needed.

Pears with Star Anise: In place of or along with the vanilla bean, you can flavor the syrup with 3 star anise, 4 whole cloves, a 3-inch cinnamon stick, or several pieces of thinly sliced ginger. Ⓥ

Dried Fruit and Honey Compote

Serve these fruits for dessert with warm cookies or for breakfast with the Ginger Cream Scones (page 581). Serves 4 to 6

1½ cups dried apricots

1/2 cup dried pears

1/4 cup dried cherries

1/4 cup currants

Zest of 1 lemon

4 kumquats, sliced into rounds

3 tablespoons honey or agave nectar

1 cup fresh orange juice

2 tablespoons butter

Cover the apricots, pears, and cherries with warm water and set aside to steep for 4 hours or overnight. The next morning, pour off the soaking water and put them in a baking dish with the currants, lemon zest, and kumquats. Mix the honey with the orange juice, pour over the fruits, and dot the top with butter.

Preheat the oven to 375°F. Cover and bake for 20 minutes, then remove the cover and continue baking for 15 minutes. Serve warm or at room temperature.

Fall Compote with Pears, Persimmons, and Figs

For persimmons, use the small squat Fuyus rather than the acorn-shaped Hachiya. They can be eaten when crisp whereas the Hachiyas make your mouth pucker unless they're very soft. Serves 4 to 6 (V)

Pears Poached in Riesling (page 615)

1/4 cup golden raisins

Zest of 1 lemon, removed with a zester

2 Fuyu persimmons

6 fresh figs, halved

1/2 pint raspberries

24 muscat grapes

Pour the syrup off the pears, put it in a small pot, and simmer with the raisins and lemon zest until the raisins are plumped. Pour it back over the pears and refrigerate until cool.

Arrange the pears in a large bowl or in individual soup plates. Serve two halves per person or slice the halves into strips, leaving them joined at the top and fan them into the dish. Thinly slice the persimmons crosswise and divide them among the dishes along with the figs, raspberries, and grapes. Spoon the raisins, lemon zest, and juice over each and serve.

Rhubarb, Strawberry, and Mango Compote

Not an elegant compote—the rhubarb loses its shape and turns mushy—but it's thick and red with plenty of juice and chunks of yellow mango. Serve it, chilled, with a slice of the Yeasted Sugar Cake (page 627) or Little Lemon Biscuits (page 601) and a dollop of whipped cream. This is also a good breakfast compote. Serves 6 (V)

1 1/2 pounds rhubarb, cut into 1/2-inch lengths

1 cup sugar

1/8 teaspoon ground cloves

Grated zest and juice of 1 large orange

1 pint strawberries, sliced in half or left whole if small

1 mango, peeled and cut into small pieces

Toss the rhubarb with the sugar, cloves, and orange zest and juice, then put it in a wide skillet or pot. Cook over medium heat, stirring occasionally. As soon as the rhubarb is tender—some pieces will have fallen apart while others are still whole—transfer it to a bowl and stir in the strawberries and mango. Toss gently, then cover and chill. As it cools, its red juices will be released.

Rhubarb Compote with Citrus: Add sections of 2 blood oranges to the chilled compote. Or cook the rhubarb with 6 kumquats, sliced into thin rounds, seeds removed. (V)

Rhubarb Compote with Star Anise: Make the compote as given, with 2 pieces of star anise in addition to the cloves. (V)

Winter Compote with Poached Pears and Dried Fruits

A stunning jewel-like compote, especially with large multi-colored raisins. The pears, as well as the rest of the fruits, can be poached many days in advance—and, in fact, they're better that way. Serves 6 to 8

Poached Pears in Riesling (page 615)

1/4 cup large mixed or golden raisins

1/4 cup dried cherries

Zest of 1 orange, removed with a zester or finely slivered

8 dried prunes or apricots, soaked in warm water for 15 minutes

1/2 cup whipping cream

1 tablespoon sugar

1/2 teaspoon ground cinnamon

Pour 1 cup of the syrup from the pears into a saucepan and add the raisins, cherries, zest, and prunes. (Leave enough liquid to cover the pears or lay a piece of plastic wrap directly on them to keep them from browning.) Simmer, covered, until the fruits are soft, 10 to 20 minutes. Chill. Whip the cream with the sugar and cinnamon until soft peaks are formed.

Arrange the pears in a large bowl or individual serving plates. Add the dried fruits and zest along with their syrup. Add a spoonful of the cream to each plate and serve with Cardamom Cookies (page 642) or the Yeasted Sugar Cake (page 627).

Pears Poached in Riesling

Serves 6 Ⓥ

3 cups Riesling

1 cup water or fresh orange juice

1 large piece orange zest, removed with a vegetable peeler

1/4 cup sugar

6 ripe firm pears, such as Winter Nelis, Bartletts, or small Bosc

1 tablespoon honey or light agave nectar

Combine the wine, water, orange zest, and sugar in a 12-cup saucepan and gradually bring to a boil. Meanwhile, peel the pears. If small, leave them whole; if larger, halve them lengthwise and remove the core and stem with a pear corer. Simmer until the pears are translucent around the edges, 20 to 40 minutes. Transfer the pears to a bowl. Add the honey to the wine and simmer until amber colored and syrupy. Pour over the syrup, lay a piece of plastic wrap directly over the pears to keep them from browning, and refrigerate. Serve the pears with their syrup, accompanied by Frozen Honey Mousse (page 636), a spoonful of mascarpone, or softly whipped cream.

Pears in Red Wine: For 4 to 6 pears, simmer 2 cups red wine—a light Côtes du Rhône or Zinfandel—with 2 cups water, 1 1/2 cups sugar, 3 cloves, a strip of orange or lemon zest, and 1/4 vanilla bean. Peel and core the pears and cook as described.

Dried Mission Figs in Red Wine with Anise

These poached figs with their hint of anise make a good accompaniment to rice pudding, or you can serve them alone, accompanied by something creamy and cold—whipped crème fraîche would be good. Prunes are also delicious cooked this way, with or without the anise. Serves 4 to 6

12 ounces dried Mission figs

1 1/2 cups red wine, such as Merlot or Cabernet

1/2 cup water

1/2 cup honey

3 large strips lemon zest

4 whole cloves

1/2 teaspoon anise seeds

Cut the knotty stems off the figs. If the figs are very hard, cover them with warm water and let stand until they're soft, 30 minutes to an hour, then drain. Put them in a saucepan with the remaining ingredients. Bring to a boil, then simmer, partially covered, until the figs are tender, about 30 minutes. Remove the figs to a dish with a slotted spoon, then simmer the liquid until it's syrupy, after several minutes. Pour the syrup back over the figs and chill before serving.

Dried Fruit Gratin with Pistachio-Walnut Topping

The scent of the vanilla permeates this assemblage of fruits, and the nut-crumb topping provides a fine crunch. It's the perfect dessert when just a bite of something sweet is wanted. Serve it with a mound of thick, creamy yogurt or a spoonful of mascarpone. Serves 4 to 6

1/2 vanilla bean, split lengthwise

1 cup dried apricots

1 cup pitted dried prunes

1/2 cup dried cherries or cranberries

3 tablespoons sugar

1/4 cup mixed nuts—peeled pistachios, walnuts, hazelnuts

1 tablespoon butter

Cover the dried fruits with warm water and set them aside until they've plumped up, about 20 to 30 minutes. Drain.

Preheat the oven to 350°F. Lightly butter or oil a shallow baking dish and set the vanilla bean on the bottom.

Arrange the fruit loosely in the dish. Mix 3/4 cup hot water with 2 tablespoons of the sugar, pour it over the fruit, cover the dish with foil, and bake for 25 minutes. Chop the nuts with the remaining 1 tablespoon sugar and mix with the butter. Uncover the fruit, sprinkle the topping over it, and return to the oven until the nuts are lightly browned, about 10 to 15 minutes more.

Prunes Stuffed with Walnuts, Chocolate, and Orange Zest

People are always surprised by the combination of prunes with chocolate, but the two have a natural affinity for each other. Orange also goes beautifully with both, and the three together make a very tasty bite. These confections can be assembled in moments from ingredients you might already have on hand. Allow 2 or 3 prunes per person

Large pitted prunes, preferably organic
Good chocolate, strong and dark, cut into chunks
Walnuts, pieces and quarters are fine
Fine strands of orange zest
Superfine sugar, optional

If the prunes aren't pitted, steam them over hot water until they are soft; then remove the pits.

Let them cool, then insert a nugget of chocolate and a piece or two of walnut into each prune. Gently stuff a few strands of orange zest inside, leaving some showing or not, as you like. Sprinkle superfine sugar over the prunes if you want to give them a frosted look. Put them in paper cases to make them especially festive.

Tangerine Dreams: Use tangerine peel or thin slices of kumquats in place of the orange. Though similar, their flavors will seem vaguely mysterious when mixed with the prunes and chocolate.

With Hazelnuts: Make a mixture of chopped toasted hazelnuts, grated chocolate, and fine lemon zest. Stuff it into the prunes and roll the prunes in fine sugar.

Dried Figs with Almonds and Anise Seeds: Use either dried dark Mission figs or the lighter Calimyrnas. Set out as many almonds as you have dried figs. Cover them with boiling water for a minute or as long as it takes to loosen the skins; then drain the almonds and slip off the skins. Toast the almonds in a moderate oven, until they turn golden. They'll crisp as they cool. Cut a slit in a dried fig, insert a roasted almond and a few dried anise seeds. Cover tightly with the flesh of the fig and serve in paper cases.

Fruit Crisps

Crisps are among our best-loved desserts. They're so easy to put together, and the crumb topping gives them the succulence of pie without the trouble of making a crust. Everyone knows apple crisp, but peaches, apricots, plums, cherries, berries, pears, rhubarb, cranberries, plus combinations of fruits also make prime crisps. Improvisation is easy here. If crisps are popular in your house, make the crisp topping in large amounts and store it in the freezer until you're ready to bake. Crisps bake best in a 2-inch-high baking dish or gratin dish. Set your crisp on a cookie sheet to catch any drips.

Crisp Topping

Makes enough for one 8 by 10-inch crisp

6 tablespoons butter, cut into 1/2-inch chunks, or margarine
3/4 cup light or dark brown sugar, packed
2/3 cup flour
1/2 cup rolled oats or chopped nuts
1/4 teaspoon sea salt
1/2 teaspoon grated nutmeg
1 teaspoon ground cinnamon or cardamom

Using your fingers or the paddle attachment of a mixer, work the butter with the rest of the ingredients so that each piece is coated and you have a coarse, crumbly mixture. Use it to cover a shallow gratin dish of sliced fruit.

Vegan Crisp Topping: In place of butter, use 6 tablespoons coconut oil or sunflower seed oil, alone or mixed with a rich-flavored nut oil, such as walnut or hazelnut. ⓥ

Rhubarb-Apple Crisp

You need the apples for texture, but they also temper the natural tartness of the rhubarb. Serves 4 to 6 ⓥ

Crisp Topping (preceding recipe)
1 1/2 pounds apples, peeled and cored
2 pounds rhubarb, diced into 1-inch pieces
1 1/4 cups sugar
1/4 cup flour
1 teaspoon ground cinnamon
Pinch ground cloves

Preheat the oven to 375°F. Make the topping and set it aside. Dice the apples, then put them in a bowl and toss with the remaining ingredients. Arrange the fruit in an 8-cup gratin dish and cover with the topping. Set the dish on a sheet pan to catch any drips and bake until the juices from the fruit are bubbling and the topping is brown, about 1 hour and 10 minutes.

Blueberry Crisp: Toss 6 cups or more blueberries with ¼ cup light brown sugar and 1 teaspoon finely grated lemon or lime zest. Ⓥ

Plum Crisp: Toss 3 pounds plums, quartered, with ¼ cup sugar, 1 teaspoon grated orange zest, and a pinch ground cloves. Ⓥ

Nectarine and Raspberry Crisp: Use scant 3 pounds nectarines, peeled and sliced ½ inch thick, tossed with 2 tablespoons sugar and a pint or more raspberries. Ⓥ

Pear Crisp: Here, 2½ pounds peeled, cored, and sliced ripe but firm pears, about ½ inch thick, are tossed with ½ teaspoon grated nutmeg or ground cardamom and covered with an almond crisp topping. Pears are also good mixed with blackberries, raspberries, and apples. Ⓥ

Apple Crisp: Toss 2½ pounds peeled, cored, and thinly sliced apples with 1 teaspoon ground cinnamon, 1 teaspoon grated lemon zest, 1 tablespoon fresh lemon juice, and 2 tablespoons sugar. When using older, soft, organic apples, you can leave the stems on. Ⓥ

Apricot and Cherry Crisp with Almond Topping

If pressed to choose, this crisp might be my favorite. These juicy fruits are also good baked under the Cobbler Topping (page 618). Apricots are frequently uneven in their ripening— the part facing the sun can be as soft as jam, the opposite side still quite firm. This is not a problem. Use the entire fruit. Serves 4 to 6 Ⓥ

Crisp Topping (page 616), made with chopped almonds instead of rolled oats

2½ pounds ripe apricots

1 pound cherries, dark red Bing or sour pie cherries

2 tablespoons sugar

1½ tablespoons minute tapioca

⅛ teaspoon almond extract

Preheat the oven to 375°F. Lightly butter or oil a 10-cup gratin dish. Make the topping.

Pit the apricots and cut them into quarters. Pit the cherries and slice them in two or leave whole. Toss both fruits with the sugar, tapioca, and almond extract. Lay the fruit in the prepared dish and cover with the topping. Set the dish on a baking pan to catch the juices and bake until the top is browned and the juices have thickened around the edge, about 45 minutes. Serve warm with vanilla or honey ice cream.

Peach, Raspberry, and Blackberry Crisp

The combination of peaches and berries is superb. Serve it with the classic accompaniment—vanilla ice cream. Peaches vary in juiciness, and this amount of flour is right for ripe, juicy fruits. If your peaches aren't juicy, reduce the flour by a tablespoon. Serves 4 to 6

Crisp Topping (page 616)

2 pounds ripe peaches

1 cup blackberries

1 cup raspberries

½ cup sugar

3 tablespoons flour

Preheat the oven to 375°F. Butter an 8- to 10-cup baking dish. Make the topping and set aside. To peel the peaches, drop them into a pot of boiling water for 10 seconds, then transfer them to a bowl of cold water. Their skins should slip right off.

Slice the peaches into a large bowl, in wedges ½ inch thick at the center. Add the berries, sugar, and flour and toss gently. Transfer the fruit to the baking dish and cover with the topping. Set it on a baking sheet to catch the juices and bake until the top is well browned and the peaches are tender when pierced with a knife, about 45 minutes.

Fruit Cobblers

Warm fruit cobblers are another classic American dessert. They're especially good made with juicy fruits since the dough on top draws up the juices just as a dumpling does. Cobblers are easy to make for a crowd. They hold their heat well, so they can be baked just before or during dinner and still be warm enough to melt a scoop of ice cream when it's time for dessert.

The basic recipe for fruit cobbler serves four generously or six modestly. It uses 6 to 8 cups fruit, sweetened and seasoned when appropriate with lemon or spice and covered with a biscuit dough. Dropping the dough by small spoonfuls gives the finished dish a cobbled appearance; hence its name. A shallow gratin dish or pie plate gives plenty of crust in proportion to fruit. I prefer a tender, tangy buttermilk biscuit dough, but if your preference is for sweet milk or cream biscuits, use the appropriate liquid and omit the baking soda.

Cobbler Topping

Makes one 8 by 10-inch cobbler

1½ cups white whole wheat flour or a mix of spelt and all-purpose flours

⅓ cup sugar

1 teaspoon baking powder

½ teaspoon baking soda

½ teaspoon sea salt

6 tablespoons cold butter, cut into small pieces

½ cup buttermilk

½ teaspoon vanilla

Mix the dry ingredients together, then cut in the butter using your fingers or two knives until it forms coarse crumbs. Stir in the buttermilk and vanilla with a fork until dough clings together when grabbed with your hand. If too dry, add a little more buttermilk until all the flour is moist enough to cohere. Spoon the dough over the fruit using a small spoon to give the surface a cobbled appearance. For a smoother look, you can roll the dough and cut out biscuits or simply lay the whole sheet of dough over the fruit.

Stone Fruit Cobbler

Stone fruits are those tree fruits that have a stone or a pit. They are always good together, so don't hesitate to improvise. And include a few cherries if they're in season. Serves 4 to 6

---

6 to 8 cups sliced peeled ripe peaches, plums, apricots, or nectarines

½ cup light brown sugar, plus extra for the top, optional

1 teaspoon ground cinnamon, or ½ teaspoon ground nutmeg or cardamom

¼ cup flour

Grated zest of 1 lemon

1 tablespoon fresh lemon juice

Cobbler Topping, preceding recipe

1 egg, beaten, or 1 tablespoon cream or milk, optional

Preheat the oven to 375°F. Lightly butter an 8 by 10-inch baking dish.

Toss the fruit with the sugar, spice, flour, zest, and juice. Put the fruit in the dish, then cover it with the topping. Brush the top with the beaten egg and sprinkle it with sugar for a shiny, sparkly crust. Bake until the fruit is cooked and bubbling around the edges, about 25 minutes. Let the cobbler sit for a while before serving, but serve it warm with cream, yogurt, or ice cream.

Blueberry Cobbler: Toss 6 cups blueberries with ¼ cup flour, ⅓ cup packed brown sugar, 1 tablespoon molasses, the grated zest of 1 lemon, and 1 tablespoon fresh lemon juice.

Spiced Peach Cobbler: Toss sliced peeled peaches with ¼ cup white or packed light brown sugar, ⅛ teaspoon each ground ginger, cloves, and nutmeg, 1 teaspoon ground cinnamon, and 2 tablespoons flour.

Good Fruit Combinations for Cobblers: Try blueberries with peaches; peaches, nectarines, and plums; apricots and cherries; rhubarb and apples; or cranberries and apples.

Tarts and Galettes

There's nothing like a piece of warm pie for dessert or the same pie reheated for breakfast. American pies are deep and hearty, while tarts tend to be less so. Galettes are free-form pies that have a rustic appearance. But regardless of what you call your pie, you have to start with the pastry.

ABOUT THE PASTRY: I made my first pie when I was 13, and I can vividly recall my frustration as the crust split, tore, and crumbled. I was in tears—it was to be a peach pie for my mother, and it was a mess. I didn't really grasp how to make pie dough until, many years later, I found myself baking a lot of pies in a row for a benefit. After a dozen pies, I began to get it! Pie dough is one of those things where the wisdom of your hands must be allowed to develop. Words, in the end, are really no replacement for experience. Nonetheless, my advice is to use a light but firm hand as you work. You don't want to be rough with your dough, but don't be too timid either. You have to take charge and be respectful at once.

INGREDIENTS: Fat provides flavor and flakiness. A mixture of butter and shortening provides for both, but because I don't use hydrogenated oil, I tend to use all butter in my crusts. Oil can be used, but it is more difficult to make a tender crust with it. When it comes to flour, you want an all-purpose flour with only a moderate amount of gluten so that the dough doesn't become too stretchy. I use a portion of white whole wheat flour, or spelt flour mixed with all-purpose flour (about 1/3 to 1/2).

The more fat in proportion to flour, the easier the dough is to handle. The leaner the dough, the greater the likelihood of its being difficult to work. That's why classic pie dough takes more practice to make well than short tart doughs.

In the case of pie and galette doughs, the butter and water are cold. This helps to create a flaky texture when the dough bakes. Cutting in the butter so that a mealy texture remains—described as coarse crumbs or like corn meal—also helps ensure lightness and flakiness. Classic tart dough, which has much more butter in proportion to flour, can be made with the butter at room temperature, and it's almost impossible to overwork it. Egg yolks also help bind a crust and make it tender, as well as enrich its flavor. If you're nervous about making dough, add an egg yolk along with the butter, and you'll be fine.

Always use just as much water as you need to bring your dough together and no more. Add it gradually and handle the dough lightly. Although using a lot of water makes the dough easy to roll out, when baked it will be tough and shrunken. (If you live where the air is extremely dry, you can expect to use extra water. Don't worry about it—in this instance it will be fine.)

ROLLING THE DOUGH: Once your dough comes together into a ball, gently press it into a disk. It will be easier to roll this way. When it comes to rolling out dough, there's no reason to refrigerate it first unless it's a hot day and the butter or shortening has become squishy. In this case, slip it into a plastic bag and refrigerate for 15 minutes.

Place your disk of dough on a lightly floured work surface or a special cloth made for pie dough. Roll the dough from the center, going in the four cardinal directions, then in between. In the end, the dough should be large enough to fit the pan easily if it's intended for one (galettes don't require pans), and it should be about 1/8 inch thick.

The easiest way to move the dough is to fold it into quarters, pick the whole thing up, and set it down with its point at the center of the pan. Then you simply unfold it. Always ease the dough into the pan rather than stretch it since the dough will shrink when it bakes. Trim the edges before or after filling the shell, then crimp them, using your thumb and forefingers or a fork. For a galette, you can leave the edges ragged or trimmed.

Pie Crust

Makes one 9-inch pie shell

- 1¹/₂ cups flour—1 cup all-purpose flour plus ¹/₂ cup whole wheat or spelt pastry flour
- ¹/₂ teaspoon sea salt
- ¹/₂ cup cold butter
- 3 to 5 tablespoons ice water, as needed

Mix the flour and salt in a bowl, then cut in the butter, using your fingers or two knives, until it resembles coarse meal. Lightly stir in the water a tablespoon at a time until you can bring the dough together in a ball. If crumbs remain on the bottom, add a few drops of water so that you can pull them together as well. Shape the dough into a disk and roll it out into a circle ¹/₈ inch thick. If the dough is so warm that it's sticky, refrigerate it for 15 minutes, then roll it out.

Pie Crust with Bran

The nutty flavor of bran is always particularly good with custard or ricotta fillings, whether sweet or savory.
Makes one 9-inch pie shell or 10-inch tart shell (V)

- 1¹/₄ cup flour
- ¹/₄ cup wheat bran
- ¹/₄ teaspoon sea salt
- ¹/₂ cup butter, cut into small pieces, or ¹/₄ cup oil
- 3 to 5 tablespoons ice water, as needed

Combine the flour, bran, and salt in a bowl, using your fingers or two knives, then cut in the butter, until the mixture resembles coarse meal. Lightly work in enough water for the dough to cohere when brought together with the hands. Gently flatten the dough into a disk. Slip it into a plastic bag and let rest for 15 minutes in the refrigerator if the dough feels too soft or overworked; otherwise, immediately roll it out into a circle ¹/₈ inch thick.

Olive Oil Pie Crust

I have had absolutely wonderful tender crusts made with oil by someone else, but I think it takes a lot of practice to succeed. Fortunately, even if yours is less than tender, it will still taste good. Makes one 9-inch pie shell (V)

- 1¹/₂ cups flour
- ¹/₂ teaspoon sea salt
- ¹/₂ cup olive oil
- 2 tablespoons milk, soy milk, or water

Mix the flour and salt together in one bowl, the oil and the milk in another. Gently stir the liquids into the flour until the dough comes together. Shape the dough into a flat disk, then roll it out between two sheets of wax paper, ¹/₈ inch thick. Peel off the top sheet of paper, invert the dough into a pie pan, and carefully remove the second sheet. If any tears occur—and they probably will—simply press the dough back together.

Pie Crust with Coconut Oil and Spelt Flour

Coconut oil (preferably solid, which it won't be in hot weather, so refrigerate it) is another answer to making a vegan pie crust without resorting to margarine. Its flavor is subtle and with the spelt flour it's nutty and warm. I like this dough to line a pie pan, but have used it in a tart pan as well.
For one 9-inch pie or tart (V)

- ³/₄ cup spelt flour
- ³/₄ cup all-purpose or white whole wheat flour
- ¹/₂ teaspoon salt
- 8 tablespoons coconut oil (solid rather than melted, see headnote)
- 3 to 5 tablespoons ice water, as needed

Mix the flours with the salt. Add the coconut oil and pulse or work it in with your fingers, as you would butter, until you have a coarse crumbly mixture that adheres when you squeeze a handful. Next toss in the water with a fork just until the dough comes together. Using just a few strokes, knead the dough to bring it together, then press it into a disk, slide it into a plastic bag, and refrigerate until it is firm or until you're ready to use it.

Using a clean board or a pastry cloth, either dusted with flour, roll the dough out into a thin circle. Roll it onto the rolling pin, then unroll it into your pie pan. Crimp the edges or treat them as you would a butter or lard-based tart dough.

Tart Pastry

A tender dough for lining those French tart pans with a removable bottom. Because the dough is so short, it's virtually impossible to overwork it. If you intend to use this for a savory tart instead of a sweet one, leave out the sugar and the vanilla. Makes one 9-inch tart

- 1 cup plus 2 tablespoons all-purpose flour
- $1/4$ teaspoon salt
- 1 tablespoon sugar
- $1/2$ cup butter, cut in small pieces and at room temperature
- $1/2$ teaspoon vanilla mixed with 2 tablespoons water

Stir the flour, salt, and sugar together, then work in the butter with your fingers or a mixer until it makes fine crumbs. Don't let it become completely smooth, though. Stir in only enough of the vanilla-water mixture to pull the dough together. Since the butter is at room temperature, it may not take much. Shape the dough into a disk, slide it in a plastic bag, and refrigerate for 15 minutes or longer. (This dough can be frozen to use later, too.)

Roll the dough out into a 10-inch circle, then set it in the pan. Using the heel of your palm, press the dough up the side. If some pieces are too long, pinch them off and add them to areas that are too short. The sides should be about $1/4$ inch thick, rise $1/4$ inch above the rim, and be slightly thinner at the base of the pan. This way when the dough begins to slump during the baking, this shallow space will be evenly filled instead of being thick and under-baked. Carefully set the tart shell in the freezer to harden.

Heat the oven 400°F. Place the frozen shell on a sheet pan, line it with foil, and fill it with beans or pie weights. Bake for 15 minutes or until you can easily and carefully peel the foil off the dough without the dough sticking to it. Return the empty shell to the oven to bake until lightly browned. Check several times for swells, and prick any large bubbles with the tip of a knife. Now the tart is ready to fill.

Alsatian Tart Dough

This batter bakes into a tender, almost cakelike crust with a rich, eggy flavor. Not only does it go particularly well with fruits, but it's very easy to make, and great for anyone who's intimidated by pie crust. Makes one 11-inch tart

- $1/2$ cup unsalted butter
- $1/2$ cups sugar
- $1/8$ teaspoon sea salt
- 3 eggs, at room temperature
- $1/2$ teaspoon vanilla extract
- 2 teaspoons grated orange zest
- 1 cup flour

Cream the butter, sugar, and salt until light and fluffy, then add the eggs one at a time and beat until smooth after each addition. Add the vanilla and orange zest, then stir in the flour. Using a spatula, smooth the batter into the tart pan, pushing it up against the edges to make a slight rim. Fill and bake.

Nut Crust

A rich, crunchy crust—the ideal lining for a smooth-textured tart such as the Brown Sugar–Yogurt Tart (page 622). Makes one 9-inch tart or pie shell (V)

- $1/2$ cup almonds, pecans, or walnuts
- $3/4$ cup white or whole wheat pastry flour
- $1/4$ teaspoon sea salt
- 3 tablespoons maple or coconut sugar
- 5 tablespoons butter, cut into small pieces, or coconut oil
- $1/2$ teaspoon vanilla mixed with 2 tablespoons water

Preheat the oven to 350°F. Toast the nuts on a sheet pan until they smell good, about 8 minutes. Cool, then chop half the nuts finely and the other half coarsely. Toss all the nuts, flour, salt, and sugar in a bowl, then cut in the butter using your fingers or two knives. Add the vanilla-water mixture bit by bit. Use your hands to bring the dough together into a ball.

Press the dough into a tart shell or pie pan, building it evenly up the sides. Freeze until firm before filling and baking.

Tip for Handling Tart Shells

I always bake tarts on a sheet pan. That way it's easy to remove them from the oven without accidentally damaging the edges or loosening the bottom.

To remove the rim from a finished tart, first make sure the crook of your arm is covered if the tart is still hot. Carefully move one hand under the pan, then, with the other hand, ease the rim down your arm and let it rest there. Tilt the far edge of the tart toward the serving plate, then lower the pan nearly all the way down. Before slipping your hand out, rest the pan on the tip of a knife, then let it down onto the plate. This way you won't crumble the pastry.

Blueberry Custard Tart

Huckleberries and blueberries from the wild are especially choice in this tart. If you're picking them yourself, remember it takes only 2 cups of fruit—really not that much. Makes one 9-inch tart

Tart Pastry (page 621)
1 pint blueberries or huckleberries
1 tablespoon flour
3 tablespoons unsulfured molasses
1 teaspoon finely grated lemon zest
1 egg
$2/3$ cup sour cream or crème fraîche
$1/2$ teaspoon vanilla
$1/8$ teaspoon grated nutmeg

Line a 9-inch tart pan with the tart pastry and freeze it until it's hard. Preheat the oven to 400°F. Set the frozen shell on a sheet pan and bake until lightly browned, about 25 minutes.

Sort through the berries and remove any stems or badly bruised fruits. Toss them with the flour, molasses, and lemon zest and arrange them loosely over the bottom of the tart shell. Mix the remaining ingredients together and pour over the berries. Bake until the custard is browned and puffed, about 35 minutes. Let cool before serving.

Brown Sugar–Yogurt Tart

Serve the tart still slightly warm, plain or accompanied by sweetened blackberries. Makes one 9-inch tart

Nut Crust (page 621)
$1 1/4$ cups creamy yogurt, preferably whole milk
2 eggs
3 tablespoons butter, melted
$1 1/2$ teaspoons vanilla extract
$2/3$ cup dark brown sugar, packed
2 tablespoons flour

Make the crust and line a 9-inch tart pan or shallow pie pan. Refrigerate until firm while you preheat the oven to 350°F. Whisk together the yogurt, eggs, butter, vanilla, and sugar, then stir in the flour. Set the shell on a sheet pan, pour in the batter, and bake until set and browned, 30 to 35 minutes. Serve warm.

Nutmeg Pie

A delicate cottage cheese pie that blossoms with spice. Perfect for a brunch or a modest dessert, accompanied by sweetened berries in summer or a spoonful of the Spiced Dried Fruits in Wine Syrup (page 647) in winter. Makes one 9-inch pie

Nut Crust (page 621) or Pie Crust with Bran (page 620)
2 cups cottage cheese
$1/2$ cup sour cream or crème fraîche
3 eggs
1 teaspoon freshly grated nutmeg
$1/8$ teaspoon sea salt
$1/3$ cup light honey, sugar, or maple sugar

Line a 9-inch pie or tart pan with the dough and freeze until hardened. Preheat the oven to 425°F. Set the frozen shell on a sheet pan and bake until the crust is set and lightly colored, about 25 minutes. Remove and lower the oven temperature to 350°F.

Whisk the remaining ingredients together until smooth. Pour the filling into the shell and bake in the center of the oven until puffed, barely firm, and starting to color in places, 30 to 40 minutes. Serve warm or at room temperature.

Cinnamon Tart: Substitute 1 teaspoon freshly ground cinnamon for the nutmeg. This tart makes a soothing ending to meals that are heavily flavored with chile and spice.

Pecan Coffee Tart

This recipe makes a large, shallow tart with just a single layer of pecans, each one placed with the curved side facing up. It is a handsome and somewhat lighter variation on the traditional holiday pecan pie. Make it in a 9-inch tart pan with a removable rim, and serve it on a large, handsome platter. Makes one 9-inch tart, serving 10

Tart Pastry (page 621)

8 peppercorns

4 whole cloves

1 (2-inch) cinnamon stick

³/4 cup dark brown sugar and 2 tablespoons molasses

¹/2 cup corn syrup

¹/2 cup brewed espresso or other strong coffee

6 tablespoons unsalted butter

1 large egg

2 large egg yolks

3 tablespoons half-and-half or cream

Pinch sea salt

¹/2 teaspoon vanilla extract

1 tablespoon unbleached all-purpose flour

2 cups pecan halves

Begin by making the tart shell. Keep it in the refrigerator until ready to fill. Bruise the peppercorns and cloves, crushing them a little with a pestle; then combine them with the cinnamon, sugar, molasses, syrup, and coffee in a saucepan. Bring to a boil, then simmer to dissolve the sugar. Strain, then stir in the butter.

Beat the egg and egg yolks together, warm them with some of the sugar mixture, and then stir them back into the mixture. Add the rest of the ingredients except the pecans.

Preheat the oven to 325°F. Roast the pecans on a cookie sheet until they begin to smell toasty, about 5 minutes.

Set them on the prebaked tart shell, placing them so that the rounded sides are all facing up for an especially pretty tart. Carefully pour the syrup around the nuts and bake the tart for 35 minutes or until set.

Prune Tart in Almond Custard

No one believes prunes (now called dried plums) can make an exquisite pastry until they eat this tart. I wouldn't hesitate a moment to serve this for an important winter meal. It's best when still a little warm. Serves 8 to 10

Tart Pastry (page 621)

12 ounces pitted prunes, cut into quarters

1 cup crème fraîche

1 egg

1 tablespoon orange-flower water

¹/4 cup sugar

1 cup finely ground almonds or walnuts

3 tablespoons Armagnac or brandy

Powdered sugar, for dusting

Make the pastry, line a 9-inch tart pan, and prebake in a 400°F oven as described on page 621.

Simmer the prunes in water until tender, about 25 minutes. Drain them well, then arrange them on the tart shell. Whisk together ¹/2 cup of the crème fraîche, the egg, orange-flower water, sugar, and ground nuts. Pour this custard over the prunes. Bake until the custard is set, puffed, and golden, about 35 minutes. Remove it from the oven and immediately spoon the Armagnac over the top. Take the rim of the pan and set the tart on a platter. Loosen the remaining crème fraîche with a fork. Dust the edge of the tart with powdered sugar and serve with a spoonful of crème fraîche on the side of each piece.

Prune Galette: You can also make this tart into a galette. After folding the pastry over the prunes, slowly pour the custard into the galette. You may not be able to use all of it. Brush the dough with melted butter, sprinkle with sugar, and bake at 425°F until browned, about 30 minutes. Spoon the Armagnac into the fruit while hot, then allow the galette to cool before serving.

Fruit Galettes

For these rustic open-faced pies, the dough is rolled out in a free-form fashion, left untrimmed, the edges loosely draped over the fruit. They don't require crimping, weaving, or other manipulations of the dough. You can use all kinds of fruit—apricots, nectarines, grapes, cherries, and plums. If the fruit promises to be juicy, scatter 1/2 cup or more toasted bread crumbs or crushed amaretti under them to absorb the juice. Form your galette on a cookie sheet or on the back side of a jelly roll pan so that you can slide it off onto a serving plate once it's done. If you prefer, you can make galettes using one of the less rich Yeasted Tart Doughs on page 433.

Galette Dough

As with other doughs, you can use a mixture of 1 cup flour mixed with whole wheat pastry, spelt, or sprouted wheat flour. Makes one large galette or twelve 3-inch turnovers

> 2 cups pastry flour
>
> 1/2 teaspoon sea salt
>
> 1 tablespoon sugar
>
> 3/4 cup cold, unsalted butter, cut into small pieces
>
> 1/3 to 1/2 cup ice water, as needed

Mix the flour, salt, and sugar together in a bowl. Cut in the butter by hand or using a mixer with a paddle attachment, leaving some pea-size chunks. Sprinkle the ice water over the top by the tablespoon and toss it with the flour mixture until you can bring the dough together into a ball. Press it into a disk and refrigerate for 15 minutes if the butter feels soft.

To form a galette, roll it out on a lightly floured counter into a 14-inch irregular circle about 1/8 inch thick. Fold it into quarters and transfer it to the back of a sheet pan or a cookie sheet without sides. Unfold it. It will be larger than the pan.

Add the fruit according to the recipe, leaving a border 2 to 4 inches wide. Fold the edges of the dough over the fruit, overlapping them as you go. Depending on how much of an edge you have left, the galette will be partially or completely covered, almost like a two-crust pie. Brush the top with melted butter—it will take about a tablespoon—or an egg beaten with a little milk or cream. Sprinkle it heavily with sugar—using about 2 tablespoons—then bake according to the recipe instructions.

Fresh Fig and Honey Galette

The figs must be sweet and nearly overripe with thin, splitting skins. Serve with goat cheese, or Frozen Honey Mousse (page 636). Serves 6

> Galette Dough (preceding recipe) or Yeasted Tart Dough with Butter (page 433)
>
> 3 to 4 tablespoons butter, as needed
>
> 1/2 cup fresh white bread crumbs, if using galette dough
>
> 12 to 16 large ripe purple figs, stems removed
>
> 2 tablespoons honey
>
> 1/8 teaspoon ground cloves
>
> 1/4 teaspoon ground anise
>
> 1 tablespoon sugar

Preheat the oven to 400°F. Roll the dough into a large circle and drape it on a flat cookie sheet pan or over the back of a sheet pan.

If you're using the galette dough, melt 1 tablespoon of the butter in a small skillet, add the bread crumbs, and cook over low heat until they're golden and crisp. Scatter them in the center of the dough, making an 8-inch circle.

Cut the figs in half and lay them over the bread crumbs, cut side up. Heat the honey with 1 tablespoon of the butter and the spices in a small pan, then drizzle it over the figs. Fold the edge of the dough over the top. Melt the remaining tablespoon of butter in the same pan, brush it over the dough, and sprinkle with the sugar. Bake until the crust is nicely browned, 35 to 40 minutes.

Apricot Galette

Fragrant ripe apricots make the most luscious fruit desserts. If you can't get fresh ripe fruit but you long for this tart, you can approximate it by using dried apricots, poached to tenderness. Because fresh apricots can yield quite a lot of juice, I scatter dry crumbs over the dough to absorb the juices and protect the crust. Serves 6 to 8

Galette Dough (page 624)
1/3 cup crushed amaretti, biscotti, or dry bread crumbs
12 large ripe apricots, sliced in half
2 tablespoons butter, melted
2 tablespoons sugar, or more to taste
Crème fraîche or ice cream, for serving

Preheat the oven to 425°F. Roll the dough into a 14-inch circle and drape it over the back of a sheet pan. Leaving a border of 2 inches or so, cover the center of the dough with the crumbs. Arrange the apricots over the crumbs, cut side down, making a single layer or overlapping them if they're very large or if you have extra fruit. Fold the edges of the dough over the fruit, overlapping it to make wide pleats. Brush the dough with butter and drizzle any remaining butter over the fruit. Sprinkle both the crust and apricots generously with sugar. Bake for 15 minutes, then reduce the heat to 375°F and continue baking until the fruit is tender and the crust is browned, 20 to 25 minutes more. Remove and let cool to lukewarm before serving. Slice into wedges and serve with crème fraîche, a scoop of honey ice cream, or vanilla ice cream.

Apple Galette with Pine Nuts and Candied Lemon

A homey dessert for brunch or supper. The technique of mounding diced apples in the center to form a soft base comes from Lindsey Shere, my pastry mentor. For apples, try Gala, Jonathan, McIntosh, or Granny Smith. Serves 6 to 8

Candied Lemon Slices, recipe follows
Galette Dough (page 624)
1 1/2 to 2 pounds apples, peeled, cored, and halved
1/3 cup currants, golden raisins, or Monukka raisins
2 tablespoons sweet sherry or Calvados
1/4 cup toasted pine nuts
1/4 cup sugar
1/2 teaspoon ground cinnamon
2 tablespoons butter, melted
Tangy Whipped Cream (page 644), to serve, optional

First, make the candied lemon slices. Make the dough, roll it into a large circle 1/8 inch thick, and set it on the back of a sheet pan or on a cookie sheet without sides. Preheat the oven to 400°F.

Thinly slice half of the apples crosswise and toss them with the currants, sherry, pine nuts, 4 teaspoons of the sugar, and the cinnamon. Finely chop the remaining apples, then toss them with 4 teaspoons sugar. Mound them in the center of the dough, forming a 7-inch circle, and arrange the sliced apples over the top. Add the juice from the bowl. Cut about half the lemon slices in half and tuck them among the apples.

Fold the edges of the dough over the fruit, pleating it as you go, partially covering the apples. Brush with the melted butter and sprinkle with the remaining sugar. Pour any extra butter over the apples. Bake until the crust is richly glazed and the apples are tender, about 45 minutes. Serve warm with Tangy Whipped Cream.

Candied Lemon Slices: Bring a cup of water and a cup of sugar to a boil in a small heavy saucepan. Add 2 thinly sliced lemons and simmer, covered, for 25 minutes. Let cool, then transfer to a covered container. They will keep for at least a month, refrigerated.

Cakes

There are occasions when a great cake makes a celebratory statement that other desserts, as good as they might be, just don't do. I'm very fond of elaborate cakes, especially when they're made by someone else, but my home repertoire relies largely on cakes that, while varied in texture and feature, are far simpler to make than the multilayered marvels of the professional. They are cakes that fill a number of our needs when it comes to pastry. The poppyseed cake, which is especially enjoyable during the cooler months, stays moist for days and feeds many. At the opposite end of the spectrum, the yeast-risen sugar cake might make its ethereal appearance at the table in the company of fresh fruits, clouds of cream, and a glass of sparkling wine. The olive oil cake introduces a mysterious new flavor and the fine texture of the chiffon cake, while polenta appears as the featured ingredient in a moist pound cake that can be enjoyed year around. That favorite American confection, the upside-down cake, takes on a host of new appearances with the fragrant almond batter supporting a variety of seasonal fruits. And of course there are some chocolate confections. See pages 31 and 39 for more on about flour and sugar.

Poppyseed Cake

No mere sprinkling of seeds here—this cake is dense with poppyseeds that have been allowed to swell in hot milk. You can let them steep for several hours and the cake will be better for it, but if you decide to make this at the last minute, just start them soaking first thing, then drain off any milk that didn't get absorbed before adding the poppyseeds to the batter. Serve this cake dusted with confectioners' sugar and accompanied with whipped cream and sliced strawberries—or just plain. Makes one 9-inch cake, serving 10 to 12

1 cup poppyseeds stirred into ¹/₂ cup hot milk

2 cups all-purpose or cake flour

1 teaspoon baking powder

1 teaspoon baking soda

³/₈ teaspoon sea salt

3 eggs, separated

¹/₂ cup butter

1 cup sugar

2 teaspoons vanilla extract

1 cup sour cream or buttermilk

Set the poppyseeds aside to soak in the milk until needed. Preheat the oven to 375°F. Lightly butter and flour (or spray) a 9-inch springform pan. Mix the flour, baking powder, baking soda, and salt together and set them aside.

In a bowl, beat the egg whites until they form firm but moist peaks and scrape into a large bowl. In another bowl beat the butter with the sugar until light and fluffy. Add the vanilla, then beat in the yolks one at a time until smooth. Scrape down the bowl, then stir in the sour cream and drained poppy seeds. Add the dry ingredients in thirds. (If using a mixer, this can be done on low speed.) Scrape up the batter from the bottom of the bowl to make sure it's well mixed, then stir in a quarter of the beaten egg whites before folding in the rest. Smooth the batter into the pan, then bake until golden, firm, and beginning to pull away from the sides of the pan, about 50 minutes. Remove from the oven, set the cake on a rack, and gently remove the rim so that the cake can cool.

Olive Oil Cake

When baked, olive oil has a rich and somewhat mysterious flavor. This cake is high and handsome, much like a chiffon cake. In fact, call this a chiffon cake—people often balk at the idea, but not the taste, of an olive oil cake. Serve this delicate confection with a dessert wine or sherry and accompany with sliced nectarines, pears, berries, and whipped cream flavored with apricot preserves. The cake flour is necessary for lightness. King Arthur makes a wholesome cake flour that works.

Makes a tall 10-inch cake, serving 10 to 12

4 eggs, separated, plus 1 egg white, at room temperature

1 cup sugar

1 teaspoon vanilla extract

1 tablespoon orange-flower water

Finely grated zest of 1 large orange and 1 lemon

1/2 teaspoon sea salt

1/2 cup plus 2 tablespoons olive oil

1 1/3 cups orange juice

2 1/2 cups sifted cake flour

2 teaspoons baking powder

Confectioners' sugar, for dusting

Preheat the oven to 375°F. Oil or butter and flour a 10-inch springform or Bundt pan.

Beat the egg whites until they form soft peaks, then gradually add 1/3 cup of the sugar and continue beating until firm peaks are formed. Scrape them into a large bowl and set aside. In the same mixing bowl—don't bother to rinse it—beat the yolks with the remaining sugar until thick and light colored. Lower the speed, add the vanilla, orange-flower water, zest, and salt, then gradually pour in the oil. The batter will be thick, like mayonnaise. Slowly add the orange juice, then whisk in the flour and baking powder. Reach thoroughly around the bottom of the bowl to make sure everything is well mixed. Fold in the egg whites. Scrape the batter into the prepared pan.

Bake in the center of the oven for 25 minutes. Reduce the temperature to 325°F and bake for 40 minutes more or until a cake tester comes out clean and the cake has begun to pull away from the sides. (It's better to err on the side of overbaking than underbaking this cake.) Let cool in the pan for 10 minutes. Remove the rim or invert, if using a Bundt pan, onto a cooling rack. When cool, gently transfer the cake to a cake plate and dust with confectioners' sugar.

Yeasted Sugar Cake

Covered with a cracked sugar crust, this cake is fragrant with butter—yet it uses far less than most cakes. And although it's made with yeast, the rising time is brief. I love this cake at any time of day, with raspberries, with fruit compotes of all kinds, and in place of shortcake with strawberries and cream.

Serves 10 to 12

Cake

2 1/4 teaspoons (1 envelope) active dry yeast

4 tablespoons sugar

2 cups all-purpose flour

1/2 teaspoon sea salt

1/2 cup warm milk

2 eggs, at room temperature

1/4 cup butter, at room temperature

Topping

2 tablespoons butter, at room temperature

1/4 cup light brown or white sugar

Stir the yeast and 1 teaspoon of the sugar into 1/2 cup warm water in a small bowl and let stand until foamy, about 10 minutes. Combine the flour, remaining sugar, and salt in a mixing bowl. Add the yeast, milk, and eggs and beat until smooth. Add the butter and beat vigorously until the batter is silky. Scrape down the sides, then cover and let rise until doubled in bulk, about 45 minutes.

Lightly butter a 9-inch tart pan or cake pan. Stir down the dough, turn it onto a lightly floured counter, and gently shape it into a disk. Set it in the pan and flatten it with your hands. Rub the softened butter all over the top, then cover with the sugar, using all of it. Let rise for 30 minutes. During the last 15 minutes, preheat the oven to 400°F.

Bake the cake in the center of the oven until well risen and the sugar has begun to melt and brown, about 25 minutes. The surface should be covered with cracks. When done, let it cool briefly, then unmold and serve, still a little warm, with fruit and softly whipped cream.

Variations: Add 1 teaspoon finely grated lemon zest to the batter along with 1/2 teaspoon vanilla extract or 1/2 teaspoon crushed anise seeds. A half cup of finely ground almonds and a drop of almond extract are also good additions.

Polenta Pound Cake

This is a cake I made when I was cooking at Café Escalera in Santa Fe. It's a great year-round cake, as it goes with any and all seasonal fruits. Look for freshly-ground unusual corn meal like Iroquois White, Royal Calais, or Red Floriani for a cake with extra distinction. For a big round cake, double the recipe. Makes 1 loaf cake, serving 8 to 10

1/2 cup butter, preferably unsalted

1 cup sugar

Finely grated zest of 1 lemon

3 eggs, at room temperature

1 teaspoon vanilla extract

1/2 teaspoon almond extract

1/2 cup sour cream or yogurt

1/2 cup plus 2 tablespoons fine corn meal

1 cup flour

1/2 teaspoon baking powder

1/4 teaspoon sea salt

1/2 cup pine nuts

Confectioners' sugar, for dusting

Preheat the oven to 350°F. Brush a 4 by 10-inch or 5 by 8-inch loaf pan with butter and dust it with flour.

Cream the butter, sugar, and lemon zest until light and fluffy, about 3 minutes. Add the eggs one at a time, then the vanilla and almond extracts and sour cream. Stir in the corn meal followed by the flour, baking powder, and sea salt.

Spoon the batter into the pan, smooth the top, then give the pan a sharp rap to remove any air pockets. Scatter pine nuts over the top and gently press them into the batter. Bake in the center of the oven until the top is firm to the touch and golden brown or a cake tester comes out clean, about an hour. Let cool for 10 minutes, then turn out onto a rack. Serve dusted with confectioners' sugar.

Semolina Cream Cake

You'll be waiting impatiently for your oven to heat when you make this cake, as the batter comes together almost instantly. The crumb is velvety and tender. Because the flavors of this cake are simple, it can be a showcase for the sweetener you use. Light brown sugar gives the cake more character than white sugar, as do coconut and turbinado sugars. It also goes with all kinds of fruit. Serves 8

1/2 cup all-purpose flour

3/4 cup cake flour, preferably King Arthur's

1/2 cup semolina

1 1/2 teaspoons baking powder

1/4 teaspoon salt

2 large eggs, at room temperature

1 cup whipping cream

3/4 cup sugar (see note)

1 teaspoon vanilla extract

1/2 teaspoon almond extract

1/3 cup pine nuts or slivered almonds, for the top

Butter and flour an 8-inch springform pan or loaf pan. If using the latter, line the bottom and ends with parchment paper, and butter and flour the sides. Heat the oven to 350°F.

Whisk the flours, baking powder and salt in a large bowl and make a well in the middle.

Beat the eggs until foamy, about 3 minutes in an electric mixer, then add the cream, all but a tablespoon of the sugar, and the vanilla and almond extracts. Beat until you have what looks like soft whipped cream. Pour it into the center of the flour mixture, then fold it in until just combined and free of lumps. Scrape the batter into the pan and even it out.

Scatter the nuts or other toppings over the top surface along with the remaining 1 tablespoon of sugar. Bake until a cake tester comes out clean, 50 to 60 minutes. Let cool for 15 minutes, then remove the rim or turn out of the pan and remove the paper. Let cool before slicing.

Cardamom Cream Cakes: Flavor the batter with 1 teaspoon ground cardamom. Cover the surface with sliced almonds or pine nuts.

With Nutmeg: Freshly grate a generous teaspoon of nutmeg and fold it into the batter.

With Anise Seeds: Add 1 teaspoon anise seeds to the batter.

A Moist Orange-Currant-Walnut Cake

This cake is based on an old family recipe. I remember watching my mother put the orange through a meat grinder clamped to the table. Happily, a food processor works quite well in its place. The syrup, perfumed with orange-flower water, is poured over the finished cake to ensure that it stays moist for days. Makes one 9-inch round cake, serving 8 to 10

Cake

- 1 cup dried currants
- 1 navel orange, preferably organic since you'll be using the skin
- 3/4 cup shelled walnuts
- 1/2 cup butter
- 3/4 cup sugar
- 1/2 teaspoon vanilla extract
- 3 eggs
- 2 1/2 cups all-purpose flour or a mixture of flours
- 2 teaspoons baking powder
- 1 teaspoon baking soda
- 1/2 teaspoon salt
- 1 cup buttermilk

Syrup

- 2 tablespoons butter
- 2 tablespoons orange-blossom honey
- 2 tablespoons organic light brown or white sugar
- 2 teaspoons grated orange zest
- 1 teaspoon orange-flower water

Preheat the oven to 325°F. Line a 9-inch round baking pan with parchment or wax paper and butter and flour the sides. Cover the currants with warm water and set them aside to soak until they are plumped and soft, about 10 minutes, but longer if they are as hard as pebbles. Once they have softened, squeeze out the water and set aside a quarter of them.

Wash the orange, cut it roughly into chunks, and put it in a food processor with the walnuts and three-quarters of the currants. Pulse until you have a paste that is flecked with currants and small pieces of nuts. There should be a little texture.

Cream the butter with the sugar until it is light and airy, then stir in the vanilla. Add the eggs one at a time and beat until smooth. Sift the flour with the baking powder, soda, and salt; then gradually stir it into the butter mixture, a third at a time, alternating with the buttermilk. Stir in the orange-currant-walnut paste and the reserved currants. Turn the batter into the pan and rap the pan a few times on the counter to settle the batter. Bake the cake in the center of the oven until the top is browned and springs back to the touch, about 50 minutes.

Remove the cake from the oven and set it on a rack, still in the pan, to cool while you make the syrup. To make the syrup, melt the butter in a small saucepan with the honey, sugar, and orange zest. Cook for several minutes over medium-high heat until the sugar is dissolved; then stir in the orange-flower water.

When the syrup is done, turn the cake out of the pan and brush half the syrup over the bottom, letting it soak in as you do so. Then turn the cake onto the serving platter you're going to use, top side up, and paint the remaining syrup over the surface and a little around the sides to make them shine.

Pear-Almond Upside-Down Cake

When I first wrote this recipe, almond meal wasn't readily available. Now you can buy it, ready to go. But for a fine, feathery texture, grind almonds them in a hand-cranked grinder rather than a food processor. Serve with softly whipped cream flavored with a little almond extract or orange zest or with a scoop of honey ice cream. Serves 6 to 8

Pears

3 tablespoons butter

³/₄ cup light brown sugar, packed

2 large Comice or Bartlett pears

Almond Cake

¹/₂ cup unsalted butter, at room temperature

³/₄ cup granulated sugar

1 teaspoon vanilla extract

¹/₄ teaspoon almond extract

3 eggs, at room temperature

²/₃ cup blanched almonds, finely ground

1 cup flour

1 teaspoon baking powder

¹/₄ teaspoon sea salt

Preheat the oven to 375°F. Heat the butter with the brown sugar in a 10-inch cast-iron skillet over medium heat until the sugar is melted and smooth, then remove the pan from the heat. Peel, halve, and core the pears. Set one of the halves aside and cut the other three lengthwise into slices about ¹/₄ inch thick, angling your knife around the pears so that all the slices are the same thickness. Overlap the slices in the sugared pan, going around the outside. Slice the remaining half pear crosswise and fan it into the center.

For the cake, cream the butter and sugar until light and fluffy, then add the vanilla and almond extract. Beat in the eggs one at a time until smooth. Stir in the nuts, followed by the remaining dry ingredients. Spoon the batter over the fruit and smooth it out with an offset spatula.

Bake in the center of the oven until the cake is golden and springy when pressed with a fingertip, 35 to 40 minutes. Let cool in the pan for a few minutes, then set a cake plate on top of the pan, grasp both the plate and the pan tightly, and turn it over. Carefully ease the pan off the cake. If any fruits have stuck to the pan, simply pry them off and return them to the cake.

Peach Upside-Down Cake: Peel and halve 5 freestone peaches. Place them cut side facing up on the sugared surface as described. Fill the spaces in between with ¹/₃ cup chopped pecans and cover with the almond batter in the preceding recipe. Bake as directed and serve warm with whipped cream or Buttery Bourbon Sauce (page 645).

Apple Upside-Down Cake: Peel and core 3 apples, then halve them lengthwise. Slice them crosswise about ¹/₄ inch thick. Overlap the apples around the outer edge of the sugared pan, then, reversing directions, fill in the center. Cover with the almond batter and bake as described. Serve with Caramel Nut Sauce (page 645).

Tangerine Pudding Cake with Raspberry Coulis

Usually a pudding cake is made with lemon, but here the zest and juice of ultra-sweet tangerines assume the citrus role. The exact variety isn't crucial—I've used Pixie tangerines, which peak in mid-April, Satsumas, which arrive in November, and those that fall in between—Honeybell, Page, Dancy, and so forth. A pudding cake requires a water bath, so be sure you have a large enough baking dish to hold your custard cups, or a single 4-cup gratin dish. Serves 4 to 6

Pudding

3 eggs, separated

¹/₂ cup plus 2 tablespoons organic sugar

¹/₈ teaspoon salt

3 tablespoons unsalted butter, at room temperature

2 teaspoons finely grated tangerine zest

1 cup milk or light cream

¹/₃ cup tangerine juice (from 2 to 4 tangerines, depending on their size)

3 tablespoons all-purpose flour

Softly whipped cream, for serving

Raspberry Coulis

3 tablespoons sugar or sugar substitute, or more, to taste

1 package (3 cups) frozen organic, unsweetened raspberries

3 tablespoons orange Muscat wine or other sweet wine, optional

1 teaspoon fresh lemon or tangerine juice, or more, to taste

Heat the oven to 350°F. Lightly butter four custard cups or six smaller ramekins. Put up a kettle of water to boil for the water bath.

Whisk the egg whites with the salt on medium speed until foamy. Increase the speed and gradually add 2 tablespoons of the sugar and continue beating until the whites are thick and glossy. Scrape them into a large bowl. Rinse out the mixing bowl, wipe it dry, and return it to the mixer. Beat the butter with the remaining ½ cup sugar and tangerine zest until light and fluffy. Add the egg yolks one at a time. When well mixed, gradually pour in the milk and juice, then whisk in the flour.

Pour the batter over the whites and fold them together. Distribute among the custard cups, then put the cups in a larger baking pan and add boiling water to come halfway up the sides of the cups. Bake until the tops have risen, are golden, and spring back when pressed with a finger, about 30 minutes.

Meanwhile, make the Raspberry Coulis. Bring ⅔ cup water to a boil with the sugar, give it a stir, and simmer until the sugar is dissolved. Add the raspberries, simmer for 1 minute then turn off the heat and let the fruit stand in the syrup for 5 minutes. Force the juice through the sieve with a pestle or a rubber scraper. Stir in the wine and the lemon juice, then chill.

Remove the puddings from the water bath. Serve slightly warm or at room temperature, the sauce drizzled over the puddings and with a small cloud of whipped cream.

Chocolate Terrine

This isn't a cake in the usual sense, but it is served in slices. This luscious dessert goes far, and it's simple to make. It needs no baking but requires 6 hours to firm up, and it's great for a large group. If you can't get or make ladyfingers, use crisp, thin European butter biscuits. Serves 12 or more

8 ounces bittersweet or semisweet chocolate

¼ cup freshly brewed espresso or strong coffee

1 cup unsalted butter, cut into small pieces

2 eggs, separated

2 tablespoons sugar

1 cup ladyfingers or Petite Beurre brand cookies, broken into ½-inch pieces

1 cup chopped toasted almonds

2 tablespoons brandy

Crème Chantilly (page 645), for serving

Lightly oil a 4 by 10-inch bread pan, an 8-cup bowl, or another container that will look attractive when unmolded.

Melt the chocolate and espresso in the top of a double boiler with half the butter, stirring occasionally. Remove from the heat and beat in the remaining butter followed by the egg yolks.

Beat the whites until they hold soft peaks, then add the sugar and continue beating until they're glossy and firm. Fold them into the chocolate, then stir in the ladyfingers, almonds, and liquor. Transfer the mixture to the prepared pan. Refrigerate until firm, about 6 hours or overnight.

To unmold, carefully hold the dessert in a large bowl of very hot water until the edges are melted. Invert it onto a platter and give the pan a sharp tap. If it doesn't come out right away, wrap the pan in a steaming hot towel for a few minutes and try again. Serve sliced into thin wedges, accompanied by Crème Chantilly.

Variations: Substitute hazelnuts and Frangelico liqueur for the almonds and brandy; crushed amaretti for the ladyfingers and Amaretto for the brandy. If you like the contrast of fruit with chocolate, include ½ cup dried cherries, raisins, or chopped prunes, macerated first in brandy to cover for 20 minutes. Or accompany the terrine with fresh raspberries. Orange is always good with chocolate, too. Include 2 teaspoons finely grated orange zest or ½ cup chopped candied orange peel and use Grand Marnier instead of brandy.

An Airy Chocolate Cake with Ground Nuts

This is an airy but somehow fudgy chocolate cake that sinks in the middle leaving the perfect spot for a mound of whipped cream. It uses ground nuts in place of flour. The cake seems so light when you eat it you can't imagine it has calories, but it does, alas. Makes one 8-inch cake

5 ounces semisweet chocolate

$1/2$ cup butter

$1/4$ cup brewed espresso or strong coffee

4 large eggs, at room temperature

$1/8$ teaspoon sea salt

$2/3$ cup sugar

$1/4$ teaspoon almond extract

$1/2$ teaspoon vanilla extract

1 cup packed ground walnuts, pecans, or almonds

Crème Chantilly (page 645), for serving

Preheat the oven to 350°F. Butter and flour an 8-inch springform pan or dust it with ground nuts.

Break the chocolate and butter into small pieces and put them in a heavy saucepan or double boiler with the coffee. Heat slowly until the butter and chocolate have melted. Stir occasionally, but make sure the mixture stays just warm and doesn't get too hot. While the chocolate is melting, beat the eggs, salt, and sugar with an electric mixer on high speed until thick, foamy, and pale yellow, 5 to 7 minutes. Add the almond and vanilla extracts, then gradually and slowly add the melted chocolate. Fold in the ground nuts.

Pour the batter into the prepared pan and bake it in the center of the oven until the cake is firm at the edges and springs back when touched in the center, about 40 minutes. Remove from the oven and allow to cool in the pan. The cake will fall. When ready to serve, loosen the edges with a knife, then set the cake on a cake plate. Make the whipped cream, and just before serving, pile it in the center of the cake. A dramatic confection for a birthday.

Chocolate-Chestnut Loaf with Hazelnuts and Whipped Cream

This winter confection is made from chestnut puree, which can be found easily in supermarkets. (I would suggest using fresh chestnuts if their quality weren't so unreliable. Chestnuts need to be kept cool and damp or they shrivel up, an expensive and time-consuming disappointment, to be sure.) Except for the hazelnuts, this loaf is dense and smooth, but not overly sweet or rich. It can be put together easily, and days before you plan to serve it. You can make it festive with decorative piped whipped cream, or leave it more austere, embellished with only a few hazelnuts. Serves 10

$3/4$ cup unsalted butter, sliced into pieces

6 ounces dark chocolate, chopped into small chunks (about $11/2$ cups)

1-pound can of sweetened chestnut puree

$1/4$ cup Frangelico (hazelnut liqueur) or dark rum

1 cup toasted hazelnuts, chopped into large pieces, plus 12 perfect hazelnuts for decoration

1 small bottle or can chestnuts in syrup

1 cup heavy cream, softly whipped and sweetened

Line a loaf pan with parchment paper or plastic wrap.

Put the butter in a bowl and lay the chocolate on top. Set the bowl over, but not touching, simmering water, to melt both the butter and chocolate. When melted, give them a stir to combine. Pour the chocolate–butter mixture into the chestnut puree and the Frangelico. Stir until the mixture is smooth and shiny, then stir in the chopped hazelnuts. Scrape the mixture into the prepared pan, smooth the surface, then cover the top with additional paper and refrigerate until firm and set, at least 3 hours, but better if left overnight.

To serve, remove the paper from the top surface and turn the loaf onto a serving platter. Peel away the paper. Decorate the top with the reserved hazelnuts and whole chestnuts in syrup, allowing the syrup to drip over the sides (or use it to sweeten the cream.) Cut into slices and serve with whipped cream.

Winter Jewel Upside-Down Cake with Pomegranate Compote

This jewel-like cake is served with sweetened pomegranate seeds and softly whipped orange-flavored cream. The dried fruits are unexpected and beautiful.

Makes one 10-inch cake

Fruit

- 3 tablespoons butter
- 1 cup light brown sugar
- 2/3 cup dried apricots
- 1/3 cup dried prunes
- 2 tablespoons each dark raisins, golden raisins, and dried cranberries

Batter

- 1 cup cake flour
- 1 cup all-purpose flour
- 1 teaspoon baking powder
- 1 teaspoon baking soda
- 3/8 teaspoon sea salt
- 1/2 cup butter
- 1 cup sugar
- 1 1/2 teaspoons vanilla extract
- 1/8 teaspoon almond extract
- 2 eggs, at room temperature
- 1 cup buttermilk

Compote

- Seeds of 1 pomegranate
- 1 tablespoon sugar
- 1 teaspoon orange-flower water
- Whipped cream flavored with 2 teaspoons grated orange zest, for serving

Melt the butter in a 10-inch cast-iron pan over medium heat. Stir in the sugar, cook until it's dissolved, then remove the pan from the heat.

Cut some of the apricots into quarters and leave the rest whole. Put all the dried fruits in a saucepan, add water to cover, and simmer until softened, about 15 minutes. Drain, gently squeezing out the moisture. Arrange them over the bottom of the pan.

Preheat the oven to 375°F. Mix the dry ingredients for the cake batter together. Cream the butter with the sugar until light and fluffy. Add the vanilla and almond extracts, then beat in the eggs one at a time until smooth. Scrape down the bowl, stir again to blend in any bits of butter, then stir in the buttermilk. Add the dry ingredients in thirds to the butter mixture. (If using a mixer, this can be done on low speed.) Scrape up the batter from the bottom of the bowl to make sure it's well mixed. Smooth the batter over the fruit.

Bake in the center of the oven until springy to the touch and beginning to pull away from the pan, about 35 minutes. Let cool for a few minutes, then invert onto a cake plate. While the cake is baking, sprinkle the pomegranate seeds with a tablespoon sugar and the orange-flower water. Refrigerate. Sweeten the whipped cream to taste, and add the orange zest. Serve the cake warm with the chilled pomegranate seeds and whipped cream.

Puddings

Puddings can be made of most anything and served warm or chilled, but they're universally tender and soft, which makes them at once comforting and homey, always well received by children and adults alike.

Pear Pudding with Almond Topping

This dessert merges the French clafouti with the crunchy surface of a crisp. Since this pudding is best warm from the oven, have the batter and fruit ready, then combine them at the last minute and bake while everyone's eating. If you like Amaretto, sprinkle a few tablespoons over the top as soon as it comes out of the oven. Serves 6

3 eggs
¹/₃ cup sugar, or ¹/₄ cup honey
1¹/₂ teaspoons vanilla extract
¹/₄ teaspoon almond extract
¹/₈ teaspoon sea salt
¹/₄ teaspoon grated nutmeg or ground cardamom
1¹/₂ cups milk
¹/₃ cup flour
4 firm but ripe pears, such as Cornice or Bartlett
¹/₂ cup crumbled amaretti or Crisp Topping (page 616), made with almonds
Cream, optional, for serving

Preheat the oven to 375°F. Generously butter an 8-cup gratin dish or pie plate. Combine the eggs, sugar, extracts, salt, nutmeg, milk, and flour in a blender and puree until smooth. Scrape down the sides and blend for a few seconds more. Set aside until ready to use.

Peel, halve, and core the pears, then slice them thinly into the baking dish. Pour the batter over the top, add the crushed amaretti, and bake in the center of the oven until puffed and golden, about 50 minutes. Serve warm, accompanied by a pitcher of cream.

Stovetop Rice Pudding

Many know rice pudding as a warm, slow-baked comfort food, but it can also be a cool, refreshing dessert. Although medium-grain rice is traditional, you can also use the fat, starchy risotto rice or even long-grain rice, though it won't be so starchy. Almond and rice milk make fragrant substitutes for milk. Serves 4 to 6 Ⓥ

1 cup medium- or short-grain rice
1 (3-inch) cinnamon stick or vanilla bean, halved lengthwise
1 tablespoon grated orange zest
¹/₄ teaspoon sea salt
3 cups milk, dairy or almond
¹/₃ to ¹/₂ cup sugar or honey to taste
Ground cinnamon

In a small saucepan, simmer the rice in 2¹/₂ cups water with the cinnamon stick, orange zest, and salt until the liquid is absorbed, 15 to 20 minutes. Add the milk and stir in the sugar, starting with the smaller amount. Bring to a boil, then lower the heat and simmer, stirring frequently, until thickened but still a little soupy, about 30 minutes. Taste for sweetness and add more sugar or honey if desired. (I sometimes add a tablespoon of strong chestnut honey for flavor as well as sweetness.) Serve warm or chilled with a dash of cinnamon on top. Accompany with a spoonful of the Spiced Dried Fruits in Wine Syrup (page 647), or other wine-poached fruits such as pears, figs, and prunes.

Rice Pudding with Anise: Use lemon instead of orange zest, and add 1 heaping teaspoon anise seeds, lightly crushed between your fingers, to the milk. Serve warm or chilled, with the Dried Misson Figs in Red Wine with Anise (page 615). Ⓥ

Rice Pudding with Sherry: Add ¹/₂ cup cream sherry to the pudding during the last 10 minutes. Ⓥ

Rice Pudding with Meringue: A satiny meringue lightens the pudding and gives it a more glamorous feel. Whisk 3 egg whites, at room temperature, until they form soft peaks, then gradually add ⅓ cup sugar. Continue beating until the peaks are firm and glossy, then fold them into the warm rice pudding. Leave plenty of airy, sweet pockets and streaks.

Cream Cheese Pudding Soufflé

Plan the rest of your meal so that there aren't too many last-minute details to attend to. You can have the base ready to go, then beat the whites and complete the dish. Serve plain, with berries or with any fresh fruit sauce. I like the Warm Cherry Sauce (page 647). If you prefer to have this in a single dish, scoop two large spoonfuls onto each plate, garnish with fruit, and dust the top with confectioners' sugar. Serves 4

- 4 egg whites, at room temperature
- 5 tablespoons confectioners' sugar, plus extra for the top
- 8 ounces cream cheese
- 2 to 4 egg yolks
- 1 teaspoon vanilla extract
- 1 teaspoon orange-flower water
- 2 teaspoons finely grated orange zest
- 1 cup sugared blackberries, sliced blood oranges, Warm Cherry Sauce (page 647) or fresh fruit sauces (pages 646 to 647)

Preheat the oven to 400°F. Butter four 1-cup ramekins and dust them with sugar.

Whip the whites until they hold soft peaks. Add 2 tablespoons of the sugar and continue beating until the peaks are stiff but not dry. Transfer them to a large bowl. Put the cream cheese in the same mixing bowl (no need to wash it) and beat until smooth. Add the yolks one at a time, followed by the remaining ingredients except the fruit. Stir a quarter of the whites into the mixture to lighten it, then fold in the rest.

Divide among the ramekins and set them in a baking pan. Add hot water to come halfway up the sides and bake until golden, about 25 minutes. There should be a little cap, and the souffles should be set.

Serve each souffle in its dish or slide a knife around the edge, then turn each out onto your hand, reverse it, and put it on a plate. Dust with confectioners' sugar and serve plain or with the suggested accompaniments.

Coconut and Black Rice Pudding with Tropical Fruit

This pudding starts out lavender, then looks like chocolate, but ends up black. This is true even when part of the rice is a short-grained sweet rice, which I add for its creamy starch. Serves 6 Ⓥ

- ¾ cup black rice
- ⅓ cup short-grain white rice (Japanese sweet rice or risotto rice)
- 1 (15-ounce) can coconut milk (light or with the cream)
- ½ teaspoon sea salt
- ¼ cup coconut sugar or brown sugar, or more to taste
- 1 teaspoon vanilla extract
- 1 tablespoon coconut oil
- 1 or 2 limes
- 2 cups diced fruit, such as mangoes, banana, pineapple, kiwifruit, and passion fruit

Rinse the two rices, then put them in a pot with 2 cups water and the coconut milk. Bring to a boil, then reduce the heat so that the rice just simmers. Cover and cook for 25 minutes.

Remove the lid, raise the heat a little and add the salt, sugar, and vanilla. Cook, while stirring, until creamy, about 10 minutes, then add the coconut oil and turn off the heat. Taste for salt and sugar. Pour into a dish and let cool to room temperature.

Squeeze the limes over the diced fruits and gently toss. Let stand for the flavors to marry.

Serve the rice with the fruit spooned over it. You could gild the lily by adding a spoonful of coconut cream, especially if you used full-fat coconut milk to start with, and/or toasted shreds of coconut. I also pour coconut beverage over the pudding. It's not as intense as canned coconut milk, but provides that extra moisture and is somehow thick and creamy.

Vanilla Custard

In its simplest form, mother's custard, as this used to be called, is made by the formula 1 cup milk to 1 egg, a table-spoon or so of sugar, and a splash of vanilla. Additional yolks make it richer and more tender, and cream instead of milk does the same. Serves 4 to 6

---

2 cups milk or any combination of milk and cream or half-and-half

1/2 vanilla bean, or 1 teaspoon vanilla extract

1/4 cup sugar or stevia

2 whole eggs

1 egg yolk, optional

Grated nutmeg or ground cinnamon

Heat the milk with the vanilla bean and sugar in a small saucepan over low heat without letting it boil. Meanwhile, preheat the oven to 325°F. Have ready a single baking dish or four to six custard cups. Stir the milk several times to make sure the sugar is dissolved.

Beat the eggs and egg yolk in a 4-cup measuring cup, then gradually whisk in the hot milk. Scrape the seeds from the vanilla bean into the custard. If using vanilla extract, stir it in. Pour the custard through a strainer into the dish. Set in a baking pan and grate a little nutmeg over the top. Add warm water to come at least an inch up the sides, then bake until the custard is set and a knife inserted comes out clean, about 35 minutes for small custards, 45 to 50 minutes for a single custard. Chill. Serve plain or accompanied by fruit, especially berries, poached dried fruits, or a citrus compote.

Frozen Honey Mousse

A cold and creamy accompaniment that seems perfect with all fruits, but especially the Caramelized Pineapple (page 611) and anything made with figs. You can serve the mousse in individual ramekins garnished with fruit, and you can also serve it soft instead of frozen. Serves 8

---

1 cup whipping cream

3 egg yolks

1/2 cup strongly flavored honey

Finely grated zest of 1 tangerine or 1/2 orange

1/4 cup peeled pistachios, coarsely chopped

1 tablespoon orange-flower water

Whip the cream until it holds soft but firm peaks. Scrape it into another bowl and refrigerate. Without rinsing the mixing bowl, beat the yolks and honey until they thicken and turn pale, 8 to 10 minutes at high speed. Add the zest, pistachios, and orange-flower water, then fold in the cream and whisk at low speed until everything is well combined. Freeze in individual ramekins or a single container. It will take about 3 hours for the mousse to set, although you can serve it at any time. Before serving, allow it to stand at room temperature for 5 to 10 minutes to soften to the right consistency.

Cream Cheese Mousse with Blackberries and Rose Geranium Leaves

I love this kind of dessert with the aromatic leaves leaving their perfumed imprint on the cheese. There shouldn't be too much cheese—just enough to fill a small mold or a single larger one. Makes 10 to 12 servings

---

Cream Cheese Mousse (page 637)

1 teaspoon rose water, or more, to taste

A rose geranium for each mold, plus extra for garnish

2 pints blackberries

Maple sugar or light brown sugar for the berries, as needed

Cream, about a teaspoon per serving

Vanilla sugar, for serving

Make the cheese mixture and stir in rose water to taste. Lay the rose geranium leaves on the bottom of the mold or molds lined with cheesecloth; then pour in the cream cheese mixture and fold the cloth over the top. Let stand overnight, then unmold onto a platter. Remove the leaves or let them remain, as you wish.

An hour or so before serving, toss the blackberries with sugar to taste, starting with a teaspoon. To serve, scatter them around the cheese and garnish with additional geranium leaves. Pour a little cream over the top and sprinkle with vanilla sugar.

Cream Cheese Mousse

When molded in heart-shaped molds, this becomes coeur à la crème. Serve this mousselike cheese, one of the simplest and most flexible of desserts, with fresh berries, fruit purees, poached fruit, Caramelized Pineapple (page 611), or alongside a piece of warm prune tart. Since this consists of little more than cream and cheese, use the finest ingredients possible. Make it a day before serving so that it can firm up.
Serves 6 to 8

> ³/₄ cup crème fraîche or whipping cream
>
> 8 ounces cream cheese or neufchâtel
>
> 2 tablespoons honey, or ¹/₄ cup confectioners' sugar
>
> Extra cream and vanilla sugar, for serving, if desired

Line a small colander, basket, or perforated heart-shaped molds with a double layer of damp cheesecloth. There should be enough cloth to hang over the rim by several inches.

Whip the crème fraîche until stiff and scrape it into a bowl. Add the cream cheese and honey to the mixing bowl (no need to rinse it out) and beat until light. Stir a quarter of the whipped crème fraîche into the cream cheese and beat until smooth, then fold in the remaining crème fraîche. Scrape the mixture into the colander and fold the ends of the cheesecloth over the top. Set the colander in a bowl and refrigerate for 24 hours. Check several times and pour off any liquid that has drained to the bottom of the bowl.

To serve the cheese whole, unfold the cloth, turn the cheese onto a serving plate, and peel off the cheesecloth. Or simply lift out a portion with a soupspoon, then place it on each dessert plate. Serve, if you wish, with a little cream poured over the top and a sprinkle of vanilla sugar. This is also good along with fruit or a fruit sauce.

Variation with Goat Cheese: Mild, fresh goat cheeses give another kind of tang to this cheese. Follow the same procedure, but use cream instead of crème fraîche and 6 ounces each cream cheese and goat cheese.

Ices

Ices, be they granitas, sorbets, or sherbets, fill the role of a light and sweet ending to a meal. Fruit ices are not difficult to improvise, as the following formula illustrates, but the secret to making these simple desserts memorable rests, not surprisingly, on the quality of the fruit. Since fruit ices consist only of fruit, except for some sugar, the fruit really has to taste good to start with.

Serve ices on plates, in ice cream dishes, or tucked into champagne flutes or wineglasses. (Champagne or Prosecco drizzled over a flute full of ice is wonderfully festive.) A sprig of mint or other flattering herb, such as lemon verbena, rose geranium leaves and their flowers, or lemon verbena sprigs, makes a pretty garnish, as do extra fruit, candied citrus peels, and, of course, cookies.

A General Formula for Making Fruit Ices and Sorbets

I learned this years ago from Lindsey Shere, who was Chez Panisse's esteemed pastry chef, and it has stood me in good stead ever since. With it in hand, you can improvise with whatever fruits you have. Just be sure to taste your final puree before freezing to adjust the amount of acidity if needed, since fruits vary in sweetness. Sometimes a squeeze of lemon balances everything nicely. This proportion provides enough sugar to make a smooth-textured sorbet if eaten within the first day. After that, it will get chalkier and more crumbly, the trade-off for using less sugar.

1. Juice or puree your fruits. Some fruits yield more flavor—and pulp—if cooked first, such as apricots and plums: just put them in a pan with a little water and cook until they've fallen off their pits. Skins, pits, and small seeds can be removed by passing them through a food mill.

2. Measure the amount of fruit puree, then divide by 4 to determine how much sugar to use. If you have 4 cups of puree, you'll need 1 cup of sugar.

3. Put the sugar in a small saucepan and add just enough puree to moisten it, about $1/2$ cup. (There's no need to heat the entire amount; besides, color is lost when it's heated.) Heat, stirring frequently, until clear. When you rub a drop between your fingers, it should feel perfectly smooth. If it feels grainy, cook for a few minutes more, then test again.

4. Combine the syrup with the remaining puree and add your flavorings—citrus zest, a few drops of liquor, or a bit of fresh lemon or lime juice.

5. Freeze according to the directions for your ice cream maker.

Strawberry Ice

This sounds so ordinary, but it's so good when it's homemade. You can set aside some of the sweetened strawberry puree to drizzle over the finished ice if desired.
Makes about 4 cups Ⓥ

---

4 cups ripe red strawberries, rinsed
1 cup sugar
Few drops kirsch
Mint or other herb, for garnish
4 to 6 perfect small berries, for garnish

Hull the berries, pulling out the core using the tip of a vegetable peeler, then puree them in a blender or food processor. Measure the puree, divide by four, and measure out that much sugar. It will probably be about $7/8$ cup sugar. Put the sugar in a saucepan, add $1/3$ cup of the puree or water, and heat, stirring until the sugar is dissolved and the mixture doesn't feel grainy when rubbed between your fingers. Combine the syrup with the rest of the puree and chill. Stir in the kirsch and set aside $1/2$ cup, if desired, to spoon over the finished sorbet.

Freeze according to your ice cream maker's instructions. Serve with the reserved sauce drizzled over the top. Garnish with sprigs of mint or another sweet herb and a perfect fresh berry.

Pink Grapefruit Sorbet

One of the most refreshing endings to a filling winter's meal I can imagine. If you're inclined to make candied citrus peels, be sure to serve a few alongside. Serves 6 Ⓥ

---

1 tablespoon finely grated grapefruit zest
3 cups grapefruit juice, from 3 or 4 ruby grapefruits
Juice of 1 lemon
$3/4$ cup sugar

Put the zest in a bowl and add the grapefruit and lemon juice. If there are seeds in the juice, pour it through a coarse sieve so that the small bits of pulp will still go through. Put the sugar in a saucepan, add $1/2$ cup juice, and simmer until the sugar is completely dissolved. Add the syrup back to the juice and chill. Freeze according to the instructions of your ice cream maker.

Grapefruit Coupe with Champagne: Serve the sorbet in champagne flutes, then pour champagne over the top. Serve with candied grapefruit peels. Ⓥ

Grapefruit Sorbet with Lime and Tequila: Serve the sorbet with a splash of tequila and a wedge of lime on the glass. Ⓥ

Grapefruit-Campari Slush: The Campari underscores the rosy color of the grapefruit. Add ¹/₂ cup to the chilled sorbet mixture, then freeze. The alcohol will make this a little slushier than usual. Garnish with a flourish of mint. Ⓥ

Cardamom Ice Cream

This light and fragrant ice is best served the day it's made, or it tends to turn crumbly. My favorite accompaniment is a plate of crispy Phyllo Cigars (page 644). Makes about 4 cups

3 cups whole milk

1 cup cream

Zest of 1 lemon, removed with a zester

2 or 3 large strips orange zest

1 cup sugar, or ²/₃ cup sugar plus 3 tablespoons honey

3 (3-inch) cinnamon sticks

1 teaspoon hulled cardamom seeds, coarsely crushed

4 whole cloves

1 teaspoon each finely grated orange and lemon zest

¹/₄ cup peeled pistachios, chopped

Put the milk, cream, citrus zest strips, sugar, and spices in a saucepan and very slowly bring to a boil. Turn off the heat and let stand for an hour or longer for the flavors to develop. Strain. Stir in the finely grated zest and pistachios. If still warm, cool in the refrigerator or over ice. Freeze in an ice cream maker according to the manufacturer's directions.

Cinnamon-Lemon Ice Milk with Espresso (*Blanco y Negro*)

This turned out to be the favorite dessert at Café Escalera— aside from anything chocolate, that is. Espresso poured over champagne flutes of delicate ice milk topped with a cloud of whipped cream makes a magnificent little ice cream float. Blanco y Negro neatly fills the gap when good fresh fruits aren't available, but it's really excellent at any time of year. A Little Nut Cookie (page 642) on the side is the perfect accompaniment. Makes about 4 cups

3 cups milk, preferably whole

1 cup cream

Zest of 2 lemons, removed with a zester

4 (3-inch) cinnamon sticks

³/₄ cup sugar

Pinch sea salt

3 egg whites

Garnishes: warm or chilled espresso, whipped cream, toasted slivered almonds

Very slowly heat the milk and cream with the lemon zest, cinnamon sticks, ¹/₂ cup of the sugar, and the salt. When nearly boiling, turn off the heat and let it steep until cool to allow the flavors of the lemon and cinnamon to be absorbed thoroughly.

Beat the whites until soft peaks form. Add the remaining ¹/₄ cup sugar and continue beating until they're glossy but still soft. Strain the milk into a bowl and fold in the whites. Freeze according to your ice cream maker's instructions. (I prefer to make this only a few hours before serving so that it doesn't have a chance to become stone hard.)

To serve, pour a little espresso into the bottom of a champagne flute, add a few spoonfuls of the ice milk, then pour in more espresso. It will fall down the glass and cover the ice. Top with a spoonful of sweetened whipped cream, add a few toasted almonds, and serve.

Wild Blackberry Sherbet

Blackberries seem to grow by country roadsides everywhere. Irrigated only by chance rains, the fruits are often small, but their flavor is concentrated and full, which is why some water is used in making the syrup. It's worth the scratches to make this at least once a season. Being partial to the combination of blackberries with roses (members of the same botanical family), I serve this either with a confetti of rose petals or a pouring custard flavored with the fragrant leaves of the rose geranium. Makes about 4 cups Ⓥ

---

6 cups blackberries

²/₃ to 1 cup sugar

Pinch of sea salt

Freshly squeezed lemon juice

Mash the berries into a coarse puree using a potato masher (a blender or food processor breaks up the seeds too much); then work the puree through a sieve or fine meshed food mill, forcing out as much juice as possible. You should have approximately 3 cups. Taste the puree; if it is quite tart, use the larger amount of sugar in the next step.

Combine the sugar and ²/₃ cup water in a saucepan and bring to a boil. Stir; as soon as the sugar is completely dissolved, remove it from the heat. The sugar is dissolved when you can rub a drop of syrup between your thumb and finger and it doesn't feel gritty. Transfer the syrup to a bowl and cool over ice or in the refrigerator.

When cool, combine the syrup and the puree and add a pinch of salt and lemon juice to taste. Freeze it in an ice cream maker according to the manufacturer's instructions; then pack it into a covered container and store it in the freezer. Let soften a bit before serving.

Lemon-Rose Sherbet

The lemon–rose combination comes from an old collection of American recipes. Traditionally the crushed petals of old-fashioned fragrant roses would supply the rose flavoring, but I find rose geranium leaves sometimes easier to come by. Rose water can also be used, lacking either of the plants. Both the sweet Meyer lemons and the more acidic Eurekas make excellent sherbets. Meyers are sweetly perfumed, while the Eureka, which is what we usually find in supermarkets, has a sharp, clean scent and flavor. Serve this sherbet alone or with plump blackberries, wild strawberries, and a candied rose petal finely chopped and sprinkled on top. Makes approximately 6 cups

---

6 rose geranium leaves or 2 teaspoons rose water, or to taste

2 cups cream

Grated zest of 3 lemons

1 cup freshly squeezed lemon juice

1 cup sugar, or more to taste

Pinch sea salt

Very small pinch ground cloves

2 cups whole milk

Rose geranium flowers or fresh or candied rose petals for garnish

Bruise the rose geranium leaves lightly with your fingers; then put them in a saucepan with the cream. Slowly bring to a boil, then remove from the heat and set aside to cool and steep.

Combine the grated zest, lemon juice, sugar, salt, and cloves in a bowl and stir to combine. Pour the steeped cream through a strainer into this mixture, add the milk, and stir to dissolve the sugar. The milk will curdle, but once frozen, the ice will be smooth. If you're using rose water, stir it into the mixture. Taste the mixture and add more sugar or rose water if needed.

Freeze in an ice cream maker according to the manufacturer's instructions. Be sure to scrape the lemon zest off the dasher and fold it into the sherbet. Pack it into a container, cover tightly, and freeze.

Let soften some before serving. Garnish the sherbet with rose geranium flowers or fine slivers of fresh or candied rose petals.

Lemon Verbena Sherbet

Lemon verbena gives another citrus dimension to this old-fashioned dessert. If you don't have the herb, though, omit it and you'll still have a classic milk sherbet. Serve with Warm Cherry Sauce (page 647) spooned over the top.
Makes 3 cups, serving 4 to 6 (V)

2 cups milk—whole, dairy, or almond milk

2 cups lemon verbena leaves, rinsed

1/2 cup plus 2 tablespoons sugar

Pinch sea salt

1/2 cup fresh lemon juice

Lemon verbena leaves, for garnish

Put the milk, lemon verbena, sugar, and salt in a saucepan and slowly bring to a boil. Turn off the heat and let stand for an hour, stirring occasionally to dissolve the sugar. Strain, then stir in the lemon juice. The mixture will curdle, but it doesn't matter—it smooths out when frozen. Freeze in an ice cream maker according to the manufacturer's instructions. Serve garnished with fresh verbena leaves or violets if you have them.

Fig and Kefir Ice with Lemon Thyme

Increase the figs if you can—more are better, especially if you're a fig lover. The kefir gives a little lift of tartness to the ice. Thick yogurt is good here, too. Makes about 1 pint

12 to 20 or so large, ripe, figs, any variety as long as their flavor is full and intense

1 1/2 cups plain kefir

1/3 cup honey, preferably orange or thyme honey, or more, to taste

1 tablespoon orange-flower water

Pinch salt

Lemon thyme sprigs, to finish, optional

Remove the stems from the figs, rinse them, then puree them in a food processor with their skins on. Combine the figs with the kefir, honey, orange-flower water, and a tiny pinch of salt. Freeze according to the directions on your ice cream maker. Serve with garnished with the thyme sprigs.

Other garnishes: Toasted pine nuts, chopped pistachio nuts, toasted slivered almonds

Variations: Try this with buttermilk, crème fraîche, or goat milk yogurt.

Mango Sherbet

Mango makes a sherbet with intense color and flavor. It's wonderful alone and even better served with blackberries, raspberries, or sliced mangoes splashed with tequila or rum.
Serves 4 (V)

2 ripe mangoes, 8 to 10 ounces each

1/2 cup light brown sugar, packed

1/2 cup buttermilk, yogurt, or water

Juice of 2 limes

Pinch sea salt

Peel the mangoes, cut the flesh into a bowl, then squeeze the pits to get off as much flesh and juice as possible. Puree the mango. Heat the sugar with 1/2 cup of the puree until smooth to the touch. Combine it with the remaining puree, buttermilk, lime juice, and salt. Freeze according to the manufacturer's instructions. Let soften before serving.

Cookies on the Side

Crisp, crumbly, and buttery, cookies are often just the thing to complete the simpler desserts like sliced fruit or compotes, ices and ice creams, fresh cheeses, or custard. They needn't be big or elaborate—just a rich little bite to bring a meal nicely to its conclusion. Of course, cookies are also great to enjoy with cup of tea or coffee at midday or to find tucked into a bag lunch. If you make a batch for dinner but don't want the extras tempting you, just put them in an airtight container and freeze them for another time.

A Little Nut Cookie

This is the easiest cookie in the world to make. You can drop the dough, roll it out between your hands, or roll it into a log and freeze it to slice and have later. You can also vary it. Roasted nut oil underscores the flavor of the nuts.
Makes three dozen 2-inch cookies

1/2 cup butter

1 tablespoon roasted nut oil—walnut, hazelnut, or macadamia—optional

3/4 cup light brown sugar, packed, or a mixture of white and brown sugar

1 egg

1 teaspoon vanilla

1/4 teaspoon sea salt

1 1/4 cups all-purpose flour

1 cup finely chopped nuts—walnuts, hazelnuts, macadamia nuts, or pecans

Confectioners' sugar, for dusting

Preheat the oven to 375°F. If you're using the nut oil, take away a tablespoon of the butter. Cream the butter, oil, and sugar until smooth and light. Beat in the egg, then add the vanilla and salt. With the mixer on low, stir in the flour, then stir in the nuts.

Drop the dough by teaspoons onto cookie sheets, about 2 inches apart. Or, for a more evenly shaped cookie, roll the dough between your palms. Bake until lightly browned on top and slightly browner on the bottom, 8 to 10 minutes. Let cool on a rack, then dust with confectioners' sugar.

Spice Nut Cookies: Add 1/2 teaspoon ground cinnamon or grated nutmeg when you add the flour.

Almond Cookies: Finely grind 1 cup lightly toasted almonds, peeled or not. Reduce the vanilla to 1/2 teaspoon and add 1/4 teaspoon almond extract.

Chocolate Nut Cookies: Coarsely chop 1 to 2 ounces bittersweet chocolate and stir it into the batter.

Cardamom Cookies

Cardamom is a perfect spice for pears and is lovely with all fruits. Commercial ground cardamom is quite good if it's fresh. Makes three dozen 2-inch cookies

1/2 cup unsalted butter

1/2 cup confectioners' sugar, plus extra for dusting

2 tablespoons sugar

1 egg yolk

1 teaspoon ground cardamom

3/8 teaspoon sea salt

1 1/4 cups white whole wheat flour

Cream the butter and sugars until light and fluffy, then beat in the egg yolk. Stir in the cardamom, salt, and flour. Divide the dough in two, roughly shape each piece into a log about 1 inch thick, then roll in plastic wrap or wax paper. Pull each log through your thumb and first finger to make it even and, if you prefer, longer and narrower. Refrigerate until firm or freeze until ready to use.

Preheat the oven to 375°F. Cut the dough into 1/4-inch rounds or diagonals and set them on cookie sheets at least 1 inch apart. Bake until pale golden on top and lightly browned around the edges, 8 to 10 minutes. Cool. Serve plain or dusted with confectioners' sugar.

Hachiya Persimmon Bars with Meyer Lemon Glaze

These bars are tender and not too sweet, with the gentle bite of a Meyer lemon and the warmth of spice. With walnuts and raisins studding the persimmon-laced batter, this is a very Northern Californian dessert. Makes one large (10 by 14-inch) pan, about 32 bars

1 cup raisins or chopped dates

2 dead-ripe Hachiya persimmons (the large, acorn shaped ones)

1³/4 cups white whole wheat flour or all-purpose flour

1 teaspoons ground cinnamon

1 teaspoon freshly grated nutmeg

1/8 teaspoons ground cloves

1 teaspoon baking soda

1/4 teaspoons sea salt

Juice of 1 Meyer lemon

1 egg

1 scant cup brown or white organic sugar or coconut sugar

1/2 cup melted butter, coconut oil, or sunflower seed oil

1 cup chopped walnuts

1 cup confectioners' sugar

Heat the oven to 350°F. Butter (or oil) and flour a 10 by 14-inch pan or other large baking dish. If the raisins are hard, cover them with warm water and set aside to soften while you gather your ingredients. As for the persimmons, cut them open and scoop out the pulp, which should be utterly soft and jamlike. You'll need about 1 cup of the pulp.

Put the flour and spices in a bowl and mix them together with a whisk.

In another larger bowl, beat the pulp until it is smooth, then stir in the baking soda. It will change texture when you add the soda, but that's as it should be. Next add the salt, 1¹/2 teaspoons lemon juice, the egg, and sugar, then pour in the melted butter or oil and stir all together.

Add the flour and spices into the wet ingredients. Drain the raisins if they were soaking and add them, along with nuts, to the batter. Spread the batter into the prepared pan and bake until risen, firm, lightly browned on top about 25 minutes. Remove and let cool in the pan.

Mix the remaining lemon juice and confectioners' sugar together so that it's the texture of thick cream. When the bars are cool, dribble the glaze from the end of a fork over the surface, then cut into pieces.

Finnish Biscotti (Rusks)

The Finnish version of biscotti, rusks, are also "twice-baked" cookies, good for dunking into coffee or wine and good keepers unless they get scarfed up, which is possible. Try these with different kinds of nuts—almonds, walnuts, hazelnuts and pine nuts—or a mixture of your favorite nuts. Makes about fifty 3-inch cookies

1/2 cup butter, at room temperature

1/2 cup sugar

1/2 cup light brown sugar

2 eggs, at room temperature

1 teaspoon vanilla extract

1/2 cup sour cream

3 cups all-purpose flour or a blend of flours, such as spelt

1/2 teaspoon sea salt

1/2 teaspoon baking soda

1 cup white whole wheat flour

1/2 cup finely chopped almonds or walnuts

1/4 cup roughly chopped almonds or walnuts

Preheat the oven to 325°F. Beat the butter until soft; then gradually add the sugars and beat until light. Add the eggs one at a time; then add the vanilla and sour cream and beat until the mixture is smooth.

Sift the all-purpose flour, salt, and baking soda together, then work it into the butter and egg mixture a little at a time along with the white whole wheat flour and the nuts. When it becomes too stiff to work with a spoon, stop and use your hand to mix in the remaining flour.

Roll the dough into logs about 1 inch across, lay them on a cookie sheet, and bake them in the middle of the oven until they are golden all over, about 40 minutes. Remove them from the oven and lower the temperature to 300°F. Slice the cooked logs diagonally about 1/2 inch thick or slightly less for a more delicate cookie. Place the slices, cut side down, on the cookie sheet and return them to the oven. Bake until browned on both sides, about 15 minutes or so. Transfer them to a rack to cool. Store the rusks in a covered tin, or stash a supply in the freezer.

Phyllo Cigars

They can be formed ahead of time, but the filling hardens as it cools, so they're best baked close to serving.
Makes 24 to 30 cookies (V)

- 1/2 pound frozen phyllo pastry
- 2 cups blanched almonds
- 3/4 cup sugar
- 1/4 teaspoon ground cardamom
- 2 tablespoons orange-flower water
- 1/4 cup butter or coconut oil, melted

Put frozen phyllo pastry in the refrigerator the night before you make these, allowing it to thaw gradually.

Preheat the oven to 400°F. Grind the almonds in a hand-cranked grinder so that you end up with a light powder or finely chop them in a food processor. Toss with the sugar, cardamom, and enough orange-flower water to dampen the mixture slightly.

Unroll the phyllo and cut it crosswise into strips 5 to 7 inches wide. Stack the strips in a pile and cover with a barely damp towel. Place a piece of pastry on the table, heap 2 teaspoons almond mixture at one end, then fold over the outer edges and roll it up. Brush the surface with butter. Bake on ungreased cookie sheets until golden brown, about 12 minutes.

Jam Bars or Tart

Everyone needs a dessert to fall back on in a pinch, and this is one. If you make the dough in a tart pan, you can cut it into wedges and serve it as a tart. Otherwise, cut it into small squares. Serves 10

- 1/2 cup butter
- 1/2 cup confectioners' sugar
- 1/2 cup packed light brown or white sugar
- 1 teaspoon vanilla extract
- 1 egg
- 1/2 teaspoon baking powder
- 1/2 teaspoon ground cinnamon
- 1 1/2 cups white whole wheat flour
- 1/4 teaspoon sea salt
- 1 1/2 to 2 cups preserves, such as fig, raspberry, or marmalade
- 3/4 cup chopped walnuts, pecans, or rolled oats

Preheat the oven to 350°F. Cream the butter with the sugars until light and fluffy. Add the vanilla and egg, beat until smooth, then add the dry ingredients except the nuts.

Set aside approximately 3/4 cup of the dough and press the rest evenly into an 8 by 10-inch baking pan, or a 9-inch tart pan with a removable bottom, or a 9-inch pie plate. Spread the preserves over the top. Mix the reserved dough with the nuts and crumble it over the top. Bake until lightly browned on top, about 40 minutes. Let cool, then serve.

Whipped Cream and Other Dessert Sauces

Simple desserts are made special by the simple enhancement of softly whipped cream and sauces based on old favorites such as caramel, chocolate, bourbon, and fruit. All are easy to make, and they can do a great deal to upgrade a pint of ice cream or an unfrosted cake. In some cases, they can go right over pancakes and waffles, too.

Tangy Whipped Cream

Crème fraîche or sour cream gives a tart and silky dimension to whipped cream. Makes enough for 4 to 6 servings

- 1/2 cup whipping cream
- 1/2 cup crème fraîche or sour cream

- 1 tablespoon light brown sugar or confectioners' sugar or to taste
- 1 teaspoon vanilla extract or other flavoring, such as a few drops almond extract, orange-flower water, liqueur, jam, or pureed fruit

Combine the creams in a bowl and whisk until soft and billowy. Stir in the sugar and your chosen flavoring.

Crème Chantilly (Softly Whipped Cream)

This is such a ubiquitous garnish, yet all too often it ends up stiff instead of mounding into soft drifts. Just take care not to overbeat the cream. If you do, stir in some extra to soften it. Makes enough for 4 to 6 servings

- 1/2 cup whipping cream
- 2 to 3 teaspoons confectioners' sugar to taste, or slightly less granulated sugar
- 1/2 teaspoon vanilla extract or other flavoring, such as a few drops almond extract, orange-flower water, liqueur, jam, or pureed fruit

With a whisk or a mixer, beat the cream until it forms soft, billowy peaks. Add the sugar and any flavorings that go with your dish. If you're not ready to use the cream, cover it well and refrigerate. If the cream has returned to liquid on the bottom, give it a few turns with the whisk.

Cinnamon Cream: Stir in 1/2 teaspoon or more ground cinnamon.

Ginger Cream: Stir in 1/4 to 1/2 teaspoon ground ginger and a few tablespoons finely diced candied ginger.

Blueberry Sauce

This makes a striking purple sauce. I always find that lime does wonders for blueberries, as does ginger and even a touch of molasses. Makes about 1 2/3 cups Ⓥ

- 3 cups blueberries, stems removed
- 2 teaspoons molasses
- 1/3 to 1/2 cup sugar
- 1 teaspoon ground cinnamon or ginger, or 1/2 teaspoon grated nutmeg
- Juice of 1 lime to taste

Rinse the berries and put them in a saucepan with the water clinging to them. Add the molasses and sugar, starting with the lesser amount, and the spice. Bring to a boil, stirring occasionally. The berries should burst and fall apart. Taste, add the rest of the sugar if needed, and stir in the lime juice. At this point, you can serve the sauce as it is, warm and textured with fruit, or you can force it through a strainer to make it smooth and serve it warm or chilled.

Caramel Nut Sauce

A classic nut-studded caramel sauce to spoon over ice cream. Makes about 2 cups

- 1/2 cup pecans or walnuts
- 1 cup light brown sugar, packed
- 1/2 cup light or dark corn syrup
- 1 cup cream
- Pinch sea salt
- 1/2 teaspoon vanilla

Preheat the oven to 350°F. Toast the nuts for 5 minutes, then coarsely chop them. Combine the sugar and corn syrup in a saucepan with the cream. Cook over medium heat, stirring frequently, until the mixture is smooth. Add the salt and cook until it has thickened a little more, about 5 minutes. Stir in the vanilla and nuts.

Buttery Bourbon Sauce

A boozy enhancement for peaches and/or ice cream, topped with toasted pecans. Makes about 1 cup

- 1 cup light brown sugar, packed
- 1/2 cup unsalted butter
- 1/2 cup cream or half-and-half
- 2 tablespoons bourbon, such as Maker's Mark

Put the sugar, butter, and cream in a saucepan and stir to dissolve the sugar. Cook over medium heat until smooth and hot, then stir in the bourbon.

Mango Puree

Spoon this vivid sauce over fresh fruit or blend it with buttermilk or yogurt for smoothies. Makes about 1 1/2 cups Ⓥ

- 2 large ripe mangoes
- 1/2 cup fresh lime juice or orange juice
- Freshly grated nutmeg

Peel the mangoes and slice off as much flesh from the seed as possible. Puree it with the lime juice. Add a little freshly grated nutmeg to taste.

Apricot Sauce

Try this sauce with crepes, pancakes, and French toast as well as with ice cream. Makes about 1¹/₂ cups Ⓥ

1 cup dried apricots, roughly chopped
¹/₂ vanilla bean, split lengthwise
2 to 4 tablespoons sugar or honey
A few drops fresh lemon juice

In a saucepan, bring the apricots, 2¹/₂ cups water, and the vanilla bean to a boil. Lower the heat and simmer until the fruit is soft. Scrape the seeds out of the vanilla bean with a knife. Puree the apricots and return them to the heat. Add sugar or honey to taste and cook until there's no granulation. Add a few drops of lemon juice.

Maple Rum-Raisin Sauce

A great choice for ice cream—not just vanilla, but coffee too. Makes about 1¹/₂ cups

¹/₂ cup raisins
3 tablespoons dark or light rum
1 cup maple syrup
¹/₄ cup maple sugar or brown sugar, packed
Grated nutmeg
2 tablespoons butter

Cover the raisins with the rum and set aside to soften for 15 minutes. Heat the syrup and sugar in a saucepan with a tablespoon of water. Add the raisins and the rum and season with a little nutmeg. Simmer for 2 minutes and whisk in the butter.

Yogurt Topping with Orange Zest

Somewhat leaner than the Tangy Whipped Cream (page 644). Makes 1 cup

1 cup Greek yogurt
Honey or maple syrup to taste
1 teaspoon orange or lemon zest
¹/₂ teaspoon freshly grated nutmeg or ground cinnamon

Combine everything in a bowl.

Chocolate Sauce

This sauce is thin, rich, and very chocolaty. The better the chocolate, the better the sauce. Makes about 1¹/₂ cups

8 ounces bittersweet chocolate, coarsely chopped
¹/₄ cup water or freshly brewed strong coffee
¹/₂ cup cream
2 tablespoons unsalted butter
1 teaspoon vanilla
2 teaspoons brandy, Grand Marnier, or Chartreuse

In a heavy saucepan set over low heat, combine the chocolate, water, and cream, stirring frequently, until the chocolate is melted. Remove from the heat and stir in the butter, vanilla, and brandy. Cool slightly, then drizzle over ice cream or fruits.

Raspberry or Strawberry Sauce

This carmine-colored sauce is wonderful with peaches, sliced pears, and figs. Makes about 1¹/₃ cups Ⓥ

¹/₄ to ¹/₂ cup sugar to taste
2 cups fresh or frozen raspberries, strawberries, or a mixture
1 teaspoon kirsch or framboise or to taste

Boil ¹/₄ cup water and the sugar, using the larger amount if the berries are tart, in a small saucepan until no graininess remains when you rub a drop between your fingers. Set aside to cool. Crush or puree the berries, then press them through a fine sieve with a soft rubber scraper until all the juice is forced out and only the seeds remain. Stir in the cooled syrup, then add kirsch to taste. If the berries were lackluster, you might use framboise to bolster the raspberry flavor.

Blackberry Sauce: Try this sauce not only on ice cream but drizzled over chunks of cold watermelon as well. Substitute blackberries, fresh or frozen, for the raspberries and 3 tablespoons light brown sugar for the granulated. If the berries were very sweet, add a few drops lemon juice to the sauce to sharpen their flavors. Stir in Grand Marnier, Cointreau, or orange flower water to taste. Ⓥ

Blackberry Sauce for Yogurt and Ice Creams

Enjoy this dark, fruity sauce over coffee ice cream or thick yogurt. The sauce is slightly thickened with arrowroot, but if you wish it thinner, leave it out.

Makes about 1 cup

---

2 cups blackberries (or other berries, such as marionberries)

3 to 4 tablespoons sugar, to taste

1 tablespoon arrowroot, or 2 teaspoons organic cornstarch dissolved in 2 tablespoons water

1 teaspoon Cointreau, or more, to taste

Mash the berries with a potato masher to break them up or puree the berries in a food processor, but don't attempt to break up the seeds, which are bitter. Instead, pour the smashed or partially pureed berries into a sieve and force through as much juice as you possibly can using a rubber spatula. Transfer the juice to a small saucepan and heat with the sugar, stirring to dissolve. Stir in the diluted arrowroot. When the juice is clear and lightly thickened, add the Cointreau. Taste and add more, if desired. Chill and use as a sauce.

Warm Cherry Sauce

Warm cherries, swimming in their juices, can grace a slice of cake, go over ice cream or rice puddings, and flatter almost anything chocolate. Makes about 2 cups (V)

---

1 pound ripe, dark red cherries, pitted

4 tablespoons sugar or as needed

1 tablespoon kirsch or to taste

A few drops lemon juice or balsamic vinegar

Put a single layer of the cherries in a large sauté pan over high heat. Sprinkle 2 tablespoons sugar over them and cook, shaking the pan back and forth, until the sugar melts and the cherries begin to release their juices, after just a few minutes. Transfer to a bowl and repeat with the rest. When done, stir in the kirsch and a few drops lemon juice.

Spiced Dried Fruits in Wine Syrup

During the winter, this is a very handy item to have on hand to garnish a simple cake, embellish poached pears, or spoon over custard. It will keep, refrigerated for up to 2 months.

Makes 3 cups (V)

Syrup

2 cups Muscat or Riesling

1¹/₂ cups sugar

¹/₂ vanilla bean

1 (3-inch) cinnamon stick

Zest of 1 orange or lemon, removed with a zester

Fruit

¹/₂ cup dried apricots, cut into small pieces

¹/₂ cup whole dried apricots

1 cup pitted prunes

1 cup mixed raisins: monukka, muscat, or golden

¹/₂ cup currants

¹/₄ cup dried cherries or cranberries

Bring 2 cups water, the wine, and the sugar to a boil in a saucepan with the spices and citrus zest. When the sugar has dissolved, add the fruits. Reduce the heat and simmer, partially covered, until the fruits are tender and the sauce syrupy, about 30 minutes. Let cool, then transfer to a container with a tight-fitting lid. Store in the refrigerator.

Cheese

Instead of sweets, cheese is favored by many at the close of a meal. I find that this is the best time to savor these unique, often hand-crafted foods. Since hunger has already been sated, one can really taste for enjoyment, slowly enjoying the range of flavors and textures that fine cheeses offer.

There are different ways to approach serving cheese. You can simply choose one that you like, make a random assortment from whatever looks good, or select a number of cheeses made in the same style such as blue cheeses, or with the same kind of milk, such as goat's milk. A grouping of goat cheeses might include a goat blue, a goat cheddar, a tangy fresh cheese as well as an aged one.

Very delicate cheeses, such as a ricotta or other fresh cheese, can be served with honey or sweetened dried fruits or combined with other cheeses, to make a coeur à la crème and served with a handful of ripe berries. There are the sensational triple creams, like St. Andre, which are lovely to eat with freshly cracked walnuts, pears, or fresh cherries. Aged cheeses, such as a golden wedge of Parmigiano-Reggiano, Gouda, or an aged Asiago, shouldn't be overlooked as dessert cheeses; aged cheeses often exhibit great character as eating cheeses—they aren't just for grating.

Regardless of the cheese you choose, what's most important is to serve cheese at room temperature—with the exception of ricotta and yogurt cheeses. A cold cheese is deadened. It needs to warm up for its flavor to emerge and bloom. In winter, this can take several hours, so arrange your cheese tray ahead of time. Fine cheese is rare and expensive, and it's a great waste to eat it cold.

CHOOSING CHEESES: Although each cheese has its own particulars to consider, you always want a cheese that's not only interesting but has a fresh, clean, appetizing smell. Avoid cheeses that have an ammoniated or other off-putting odor. Sniff cheese, ask to taste it, and try to have a piece cut for you from a wheel rather than settle for one that has been cut, wrapped, and allowed to stand until liquids separate from the cheese. When it comes to knowing about particular cheeses, it's a good idea to consult a good guide, such as Vivienne Marquis and Patricia Haskells's *The Cheese Book* or Steven Jenkins's *Cheese Primer*. Food magazines are frequently a good resource for information on small dairies producing excellent farmhouse cheeses and how to get them.

MAKING YOUR OWN: There are a number of fresh-style cheeses that are not at all difficult to make. If you enjoy things like making bread and sprouting seeds, you may find it very exciting to make your own cream cheese, mascarpone, ricotta, panir, and other simple cheeses. Something as simple as cream cheese becomes exquisite when homemade, especially if you have access to milk from a local dairy. Contact the New England Cheese Making Supply Company (cheesemaking.com). The company carries equipment, cultures, and advice that really works.

Some Cheese Combinations

Try fresh cream cheese, ricotta, or yogurt cheese drizzled with honey and served with Whole Wheat Biscuits to Eat with Cheese (page 649), dried fruits, and a glass of dessert wine. Or serve a small mound of ricotta with the Spiced Dried Fruits in Wine Syrup (page 647).

Cream Cheese Mousse or coeur à la crème is classically served with a little cream poured over the top, a sprinkling of vanilla sugar, and a handful of tender, sweet berries. Fresh goat cheese, ricotta, and mascarpone are delicious served with ripe figs and new crop walnuts.

Stilton and English blues are wonderful with apples, especially when the apples are at the peak of their season. Cox Orange Pippin, Golden Russet, Mutsu, and Braeburn are some favorites. Buttery Cornice or Bartlett pears are also fine with blue cheeses. Try Gorgonzola dolcelatte with pears, apples, or apple-pears. This cheese is especially interesting when thinly sliced, drizzled with warm honey, and served with lightly roasted almonds. Cabrales—a marvelously fortifying Spanish blue cheese that is at last beginning to appear in our markets—is wonderful with toasted Walnut Bread (page 594) or freshly cracked walnuts and sherry. (Before the meal, serve it with a drier sherry or a full-bodied Spanish red wine.)

Aged cheddars are also cheeses to serve with crisp fall apples or apple-pears, hard cider, and a handful of cracked walnuts or, even better, buttery hickory nuts. Wisconsin produces some excellent aged cheddars as well as an aged Gruyère, a yellow Muenster made from Guernsey milk, and other fine cheeses.

With cream cheese, Manchego, or ricotta salata, try a slice of pink, jellied quince paste or a slice of fruit bread, such as the Applesauce Spice Bread (page 565). Mascarpone, yogurt cheese, ricotta, or a mild goat cheese, are excellent with moist fresh dates.

Try double and triple cream cheeses with cherries and a glass of kirsch, with Walnut Bread (page 594) or a date nut bread.

Manouri Cheese with Warm Thyme Honey and Sea Salt

Manouri is a Greek cheese with a wonderfully odd texture that is both chalky and truffle-like. It is made from whey (though enriched with cream) and like feta, it doesn't have a rind. But unlike feta it is not a salty cheese. It has a creamy, uniform texture, yet it is not a buttery cheese. It is mild, but hardly insipid, and one of my favorite cheeses both for its texture and its taste. One of many possibilities for serving cheese at the end of a meal.

Manouri cheese

Thyme honey

Maldon sea salt

Roasted pine nuts

A slice of pear

Manouri usually comes in rounds or wedges cut from a larger piece. Set your cheese on individual plates. Allow it to come to room temperature, then drizzle warm honey over the surface. Serve with a sprinkle of salt, toasted pine nuts, and a luscious slice of ripe pear.

Whole Wheat Biscuits to Eat with Cheese

Not too sweet, these biscuits are a good accompaniment for all kinds of cheese, from triple cream to blue to Fresh Cream Cheese made with goat cheese.

Makes about sixty 2-inch biscuits

1 cup all-purpose flour

1¼ cups whole wheat flour

½ cup wheat bran

1 teaspoon baking powder

½ teaspoon baking soda

½ teaspoon sea salt

¼ cup light brown sugar, packed, optional

½ cup cold unsalted butter, cut into small pieces

1 egg, beaten with ½ cup buttermilk or water

Preheat the oven to 375°F. Combine the dry ingredients together in a mixing bowl. Add the butter and mix with a paddle attachment or rub between your fingers until it resembles coarse meal. Stir in the egg mixture until distributed evenly. Squeeze a handful of dough; if it clings, the dough is ready. If it's too crumbly, add more buttermilk—by drops until it coheres. Shape into a disk and let rest for 10 minutes.

Roll the dough out on a lightly floured surface ⅛ inch thick for a thin, crisp wafer or ¼ inch thick for a thicker, more crumbly one. Cut out the cookies with a biscuit cutter or a glass 2 inches across. Prick the tops in several places with a fork, then set them on an ungreased cookie sheet and bake until lightly browned, 12 to 15 minutes.

Resources

CHEESE MAKING

New England Cheesemaking Supply: www.cheesemaking.com

BEANS

Rancho Gordo New World Specialty Food (heirloom beans, dried corn, chiles, amaranth, and quinoa): www.ranchogordo.com

San Xavier Cooperative Farm: www.sanxaviercoop.org

Seed Savers Exchange (heirloom beans for eating and planting): www.seedsavers.org

The Spanish Table (Pardina lentils and large white beans): www.spanishtable.com

DAIRY

Kalona Supernatural (delicious, organic, low-heat pasteurized, nonhomogenized products): www.kalonasupernatural.com

Redwood Hill Farm and Creamery (goat milk yogurt available nationwide): www.redwoodhill.com

Straus Family Creamery (100% organic and non-GMO): www.strausfamilycreamery.com

DATES

Flying Disc Ranch (some unusual varieties and exceptional Medjools): www.flyingdiscranch.com

GHEE

Ancient Organics (organic ghee made from Straus Family Creamery butter): www.ancientorganics.com

GRAINS, GRITS, AND FLOURS

Anson Mills (wide variety of unusual grains and flours): www.ansonmills.com

Bluebird Grain Farms (emmer wheat, farro, and flours milled to order): www.bluebirdgrainfarms.com

Bob's Red Mill (great selection of grains and baking ingredients): www.bobsredmill.com

Cayuga Pure Organics (organic farro, freekeh, oat groats, and stone-ground corn and flours): www.cporganics.com

Falls Mill (stone ground grains and grits): www.fallsmill.com

Heritage Grain Conservancy (seed grains, einkorn, and heritage wheats): www.growseed.org

Jovial Foods (einkorn pasta, flours, and other products): www.jovialfoods.com

Lentz Spelt Farms (farro, spelt, and spelt products): www.lentzspelt.com

Spence Farm (Iroquois White corn meal): www.thespencefarm.com

Sunrise Flour Mill (Turkey Red flour and berries): www.sunriseflourmill.com

RICE

Koda Farms (best known for Kokuho Rose, an heirloom brown rice): www.kodafarms.com

Massa Organics (organic brown rice): www.massaorganics.com

Moose Lake Wild Rice (native wild rice): www.mooselakewildrice.com

White Earth Land Recovery Project (native wild rice): www.nativeharvest.com

SEASONED SALT

Allstar Organics (smoked and seasoned salts): www.allstarorganics.com

SWEETENERS

Heavenly Organics (organic, fair trade organic honey, condensed milk, and sugar): www.heavenlyorganics.com

Wholesome Sweeteners (a variety of organic, fair trade sugars, honey, and agave): www.wholesomesweeteners.com

Index